T0215734

Lecture Notes in Computer Science 9386

Commenced Publication in 1973
Founding and Former Series Editors:
Gerhard Goos, Juris Hartmanis, and Jan van Leeuwen

More information about this series at http://www.springer.com/series/7412

Sebastiano Battiato · Jacques Blanc-Talon
Giovanni Gallo · Wilfried Philips
Dan Popescu · Paul Scheunders (Eds.)

Advanced Concepts for Intelligent Vision Systems

16th International Conference, ACIVS 2015
Catania, Italy, October 26–29, 2015
Proceedings

 Springer

Editors

Sebastiano Battiato
Dipartimento di Matematica e Informatica
Università di Catania
Catania
Italy

Jacques Blanc-Talon
DGA Paris
France

Giovanni Gallo
Dipartimento di Matematica e Informatica
Università di Catania
Catania
Italy

Wilfried Philips
Telecommunications and Information
    processing (TELIN)
Ghent University
Gent
Belgium

Dan Popescu
CSIRO
Canberra, ACT
Australia

Paul Scheunders
Vision Lab.
University of Antwerp
Antwerpen
Belgium

ISSN 0302-9743   ISSN 1611-3349 (electronic)
Lecture Notes in Computer Science
ISBN 978-3-319-25902-4   ISBN 978-3-319-25903-1 (eBook)
DOI 10.1007/978-3-319-25903-1

Library of Congress Control Number: 2015952064

LNCS Sublibrary: SL6 – Image Processing, Computer Vision, Pattern Recognition, and Graphics

Springer Cham Heidelberg New York Dordrecht London

Springer International Publishing AG Switzerland is part of Springer Science+Business Media
(www.springer.com)

Preface

These proceedings gather the selected papers of the Advanced Concepts for Intelligent Vision Systems (ACIVS) conference which was held in Catania, Italy, during October 26–29, 2015.

This event was the 16th ACIVS. After the first event in Germany in 1999, ACIVS has become a larger and independent scientific conference. However, the seminal distinctive governance rules have been maintained:

- To update the conference scope on a yearly basis. While keeping a technical backbone (the classic low-level image processing techniques), we have introduced topics of interest such as – chronologically – image and video compression, 3D, surveillance, etc., in order to fit the conference scope to our scientific community's needs. In addition, speakers usually give invited talks on hot issues.
- To remain a single-track conference in order to promote scientific exchanges within the audience.
- To grant oral presentations a duration of 25 minutes and published papers a length of 12 pages, which is significantly different from most other conferences.

The second and third items generate a complex management of the conference; in particular, the number of time slots is rather small. Although the selection between the two presentation formats is primarily determined by the need to compose a well-balanced program, papers presented during plenary and poster sessions enjoy the same importance and publication format.

The first item is strengthened by the notoriety of ACIVS, which has been growing over the years: official 2015 Springer records show a cumulated number of downloads on January 1, of more than 325,000.

ACIVS 2015 started with a special session on the topic of large-scale video processing and embedded intelligence highlighted by invited talks from Michael Tchagaspanian (CEA, France) and Alessandro Capra (STMicroelectronics, Italy). The goal of this special session was to facilitate discussion of the state of the art and future challenges in the booming research area of computer vision and video processing for interconnected camera systems. The session provided an opportunity for liaison between academic and industrial research and development in this field demonstrated by several successful cross-national projects and collaborations whose representatives were among the session participants.

The regular sessions also included a couple of invited talks by Prof. Raimondo Schettini (University of Milano Bicocca) and Prof. Gabriela Csurka (Xerox Research Centre Europe). We would like to thank all of them for enhancing the technical program with their presentations.

ACIVS 2015 attracted submissions from many different countries, mostly from Europe, but also from the rest of the world: Algeria, Australia, Austria, Brazil, Belgium, Canada, China, Cyprus, Czech Republic, Denmark, Ecuador, France, Finland,

Germany, Hungary, India, Israel, Italy, Korea, Mexico, The Netherlands, Poland, Romania, Russia, Switzerland, Taiwan, Tunisia, Turkey, the Ukraine, United Arab Emirates, the UK, and the USA.

From 129 submissions, 35 were selected for oral presentation and 41 as posters. The paper submission and review procedure was carried out electronically and a minimum of three reviewers were assigned to each paper. A large and energetic Program Committee (87 people), helped by additional referees (about 150 people in total), as listed on the following pages, completed the long and demanding reviewing process. We would like to thank all of them for their timely and high-quality reviews, achieved in quite a short time and just before the summer holidays.

Also, we would like to thank our sponsors (in alphabetical order) Antwerp University, University of Catania, CSIRO (Commonwealth Scientific and Industrial Research Organization), Ghent University, and GIRPR (Gruppo Italiano Ricercatori in Pattern Recognition) for their valuable support.

Finally, we would like to thank all the participants who trusted in our ability to organize this conference for the 16th time. We hope they attended a different and stimulating scientific event and that they enjoyed the atmosphere of the ACIVS social events in the city of Catania.

As explained, a conference like ACIVS would not be feasible without the concerted effort of many people and the support of various institutions. We are indebted to the local organizers for having smoothed all the harsh practical details of an event venue, and we hope to welcome them in the near future.

July 2015

Sebastiano Battiato
Jacques Blanc-Talon
Giovanni Gallo
Wilfried Philips
Dan Popescu
Paul Scheunders

About the Volume Editors

Sebastiano Battiato received his degree in computer science (summa cum laude) in 1995 from the University of Catania and his PhD in computer science and applied mathematics from the University of Naples in 1999. From 1999 to 2003 he was the leader of the "Imaging" team at STMicroelectronics in Catania. He joined the Department of Mathematics and Computer Science at the University of Catania as assistant professor in 2004 and became associate professor in the same department in 2011. His research interests include image enhancement and processing, image coding, camera imaging technology, and multimedia forensics. He has edited six books and co-authored more than 180 papers in international journals, conference proceedings, and book chapters. He is a co-inventor of about 20 international patents, reviewer for several international journals, and he has been regularly a member of numerous international conference committees. Prof. Battiato has participated in many international and national research projects. He has chaired several international events (VAAM 2014, 2015; VISAPP 2012, 2013, 2014, 2015; ICIAP 2011; ACM MiFor 2010, 2011; SPIE EI Digital Photography 2011, 2012, 2013, etc.); he served as associate editor for IEEE TCSVT (2008–2011) and for SPIE *Journal of Electronic Imaging*. Prof. Battiato has been guest editor of several special issues on various topics related to imaging applications for the following journals: *EURASIP Journal on Image and Video Processing* (2010), *IEEE Multimedia Magazine* (2012), and *Pattern Recognition Letters* (2015). He is the recipient of the 2011 Best Associate Editor Award of the *IEEE Transactions on Circuits and Systems for Video Technology*. He is director (and co-founder) of the International Computer Vision Summer School (ICVSS), Sicily, Italy. Prof. Battiato is a senior member of the IEEE.

Jacques Blanc-Talon received his PhD degree from Paris XI (Orsay) University in 1991. After a postdoc at CSIRO in Australia, he joined the Ministry of Defence in France. He worked as Scientific Manager, Head of the "Information Engineering and Robotics" scientific domain at the DGA/MRIS and is currently with the Integrated Navigation Systems department. He was the French delegate of several NATO Groups and of the Horizon 2020 Security Research Programme Committee. J. Blanc-Talon has conducted the review of around 400 PhD and postdoc grant applications, has participated in 80 defence juries and has supervised some 40 PhD students. He has published about 90 scientific papers and was the editor or co-editor of 12 books and special journals issues. He served as associate editor for IOS ICAE from 2000 to 2006, and IEEE TIP from 2005 to 2008; he is a reviewer for IEEE PAMI and TIP, IEE *Electronics Letters*, *SIAM Journal on Applied Mathematics,* and *IAPR Pattern Recognition*. He has been involved in the organization of more than 90 international conferences. J. Blanc-Talon was promoted to "Chevalier de l'ordre des Palmes Académiques" in 2010, and IEEE Senior Member in 2015. He is currently the IEEE Chapter Chair for the French Signal Processing Chapter.

Wilfried Philips received a diploma in electrical engineering (1989, summa cum laude) and a PhD degree in applied sciences (1993, summa cum laude), both from

Ghent University, Belgium. He is currently a senior full professor at the Department of Telecommunications and Information Processing of Ghent University, where he heads the research group "Image Processing and Interpretation," which currently consists of about 35 researchers. The current interests of the group are in real-time video improvement, image analysis, multi-camera computer vision and big data analysis, for a variety of applications; these include remote sensing, analysis of the behavior of people, visual odometry, and traffic scene analysis. W. Philips is co-author of over 750 papers in scientific conference and journal papers. He is also on the editorial board of the *Journal of Ambient Intelligence and Smart Environments* (JAISE).

W. Philips is a senior member of IEEE. Recently, he also became a founding partner of the company Senso2Me, which currently focuses on Internet of Things solutions for elderly care. He is also the promoter of Ghent University's Innovation Centre for Intelligent Information Processing — iKnow, which aims to market Ghent University's research through partnerships with companies, licensing agreements, and the creation of spin-offs.

Dan Popescu completed his undergraduate and postgraduate studies at the Polytechnical Institute of Bucharest, Romania, between 1975 and 1980, graduating with an MEngSc degree (honors) in Computer Science. In 1977 he won the national mathematical competition for engineering students, and represented Romania at the 6th Balkan Mathematics Olympiad, in Belgrade (Serbia), where he won the first prize. From 1980 until 1990 he worked in a joint research team from industry and academia, firstly as an engineer with the Factory for Computer Peripherals (1980–1984), and then as a research engineer and adjunct professor in the Electronics and Telecommunications Department of the Polythechnical Institute of Bucharest (1984–1990). During this period he developed both system and application software for a new graphical personal computer. He provided technical assistance and took part in the installation of the system in Sofia, Dresden, and Magdeburg. In 1991, he briefly worked for a software development company in Dusseldorf, Germany. During 1992–1996 he completed his PhD studies at Sydney University, in the department of Electrical Engineering. Since April 1996, he has been a research scientist with CSIRO, initially with the Division of Information Technology, and currently with the ICT Centre. He worked on several projects focusing on the themes of imaging and vision, with applications to remote sensing, image coding and acquisition, and virtual reality and haptic interaction, applied to the simulation of medical procedures. His interests include image and signal processing, pattern recognition, coding theory, modeling and simulation. He likes to combine his natural mathematical skills and his engineering background to solve real-world problems.

Paul Scheunders received a BS degree and a PhD degree in physics, with work in the field of statistical mechanics, from the University of Antwerp, Belgium, in 1983 and 1990, respectively. In 1991, he became a research associate with the Vision Lab, Department of Physics, University of Antwerp, where he is currently a professor. His current research interest includes remote sensing and hyper-spectral image processing. He has published over 150 papers in international journals and proceedings in the field of image processing, pattern recognition, and remote sensing. Paul Scheunders is associate editor of the *IEEE Transactions in Geoscience and Remote Sensing*, and has served as program committee member in numerous international conferences on remote sensing. He is senior member of the IEEE Geoscience and Remote Sensing Society.

Organization

Acivs 2015 was organized by the University of Catania, Italy.

Steering Committee

Sebastiano Battiato	University of Catania, Italy
Jacques Blanc-Talon	DGA, France
Giovanni Gallo	University of Catania, Italy
Wilfried Philips	Ghent University/iMinds, Belgium
Dan Popescu	CSIRO, Australia
Paul Scheunders	University of Antwerp, Belgium

Organizing Committee

Giovanni Maria Farinella	Università degli Studi di Catania, Italy
Francesco Pappalardo	University of Catania, Italy
Giovanni Puglisi	University of Cagliari, Italy
Filippo Stanco	Università degli Studi di Catania, Italy

Program Committee

Alin Achim	University of Bristol, UK
Sos Agaian	The University of Texas, USA
Yiannis Andreopoulos	University College London, UK
Marc Antonini	Nice Sophia Antipolis University, France
Edoardo Ardizzone	University of Palermo, Italy
Marie Babel	Inria-IRISA, France
Atilla Baskurt	INSA, France
Kathrin Berkner	Ricoh Innovations, USA
Thomas Blumensath	University of Southampton, UK
Miroslaw Bober	University of Surrey, UK
Philippe Bolon	Université de Savoie, France
Egor Bondarev	Technische Universiteit Eindhoven, The Netherlands
Don Bone	Wirriga Pty Ltd., Australia
Salah Bourennane	Ecole Centrale de Marseille, France
Catarina Brites	Instituto Superior Técnico, Portugal
Arcangelo Bruna	STMicroelectronics, Italy
Dan Dumitru Burdescu	University of Craiova, Romania
Giuseppe Cattaneo	University of Salerno, Italy
Andrea Cavallaro	Queen Mary University of London, UK
Emre Celebi	Louisiana State University in Shreveport, USA
Jocelyn Chanussot	Grenoble Institute of Technology, France
Pamela Cosman	University of California at San Diego, USA

Carlo Sansone	University of Naples, Italy
Riccardo Scateni	University of Cagliari, Italy
Raimondo Schettini	University of Milano Bicocca, Italy
Ivan Selesnick	NYU Polytechnic School of Engineering, USA
Véronique Serfaty	DGA, France
Mubarak Shah	University of Central Florida, USA
Andrzej Sluzek	Khalifa University, United Arab Emirates
Concetto Spampinato	University of Catania, Italy
Changming Sun	CSIRO, Australia
Hugues Talbot	ESIEE, France
Domenico Tegolo	University of Palermo, Italy
Alain Trémeau	Université de Saint-Etienne, France
Frédéric Truchetet	Burgundy University, France
Sotirios Tsaftaris	IMT Lucca, Italy
Stefano Tubaro	Politecnico di Milano, Italy
Marc Van Droogenbroeck	University of Liège, Belgium
Peter Veelaert	Ghent University/iMinds, Belgium
Nicole Vincent	Paris Descartes University, France
Domenico Vitulano	IAC CNR, Italy
Gerald Zauner	Fachhochschule Oberösterreich, Austria
Pavel Zemcik	Brno University of Technology, Czech Republic
Djemel Ziou	Sherbrooke University, Canada

Additional Reviewers

Alin Achim	University of Bristol, UK
Jan Aelterman	Ghent University, Belgium
Sos Agaian	The University of Texas, USA
Hamid Aghajan	Stanford University, USA
Edoardo Ardizzone	University of Palermo, Italy
Marie Babel	Inria-IRISA, France
Kathrin Berkner	Ricoh Innovations, USA
Jacques Blanc-Talon	DGA, France
Philippe Bolon	Université de Savoie, France
Egor Bondarev	Technische Universiteit Eindhoven, The Netherlands
Don Bone	Wirriga Pty Ltd., Australia
Salah Bourennane	Ecole Centrale de Marseille, France
Catarina Brites	Instituto Superior Técnico, Portugal
Arcangelo Bruna	STMicroelectronics, Italy
Dan Dumitru Burdescu	University of Craiova, Romania
Sema Candemir	National Institutes of Health, USA
Alessandro Capra	STMicroelectronics, Italy
Giuseppe Cattaneo	University of Salerno, Italy
Emre Celebi	Louisiana State University in Shreveport, USA
Amani Chaker	University of Nice Sophia Antipolis, France
Jocelyn Chanussot	Grenoble Institute of Technology, France

Pamela Cosman	University of California at San Diego, USA
Luis Gerardo de la Fraga	CINVESTAV, Mexico
Jonas De Vylder	Ghent University, Belgium
Eric Debreuve	Nice Sophia Antipolis University, France
Cosimo Distante	CNR INO - Lecce, Italy
Qing-Li Dong	University of Shanghai for Science and Technology, China
Frédéric Dufaux	ENST, France
Andreas Fischer	University of Fribourg, Switzerland
Don Fraser	Australian Defence Force Academy, Australia
Jérôme Gilles	San Diego State University, USA
Georgy Gimel'farb	The University of Auckland, New Zealand
Bart Goossens	Ghent University/iMinds, Belgium
Lewis Griffin	University College, UK
Christine Guillemot	Inria, France
Ugur Halici	Middle East Technical University, Turkey
Jari Hannuksela	University of Oulu, Finland
Martin Hell	Lund University, Sweden
Adam Herout	Brno University of Technology, Czech Republic
Daniel Herrera	University of Oulu, Finland
Mark Holden	Kyoto University, Japan
Dimitris Iakovidis	Technological Educational Institute of Lamia, Greece
Francisco Imai	Canon Inc., USA
Vedran Jelaca	Ghent University, Belgium
Ljubomir Jovanov	Ghent University/iMinds, Belgium
Arto Kaarna	Lappeenranta University of Technology, Finland
Dang Khoa Nguyen	Orange-Labs, France
Ron Kimmel	Technion, Israel
Richard Kleihorst	Senso2Me and Ghent University, Belgium
Asli Kumcu	University of Ghent, Belgium
Patrick Lambert	Polytech' Savoie, France
Ivan Laptev	Inria, France
Maylor Leung	Nanyang Technological University, Singapore
Wenzhi Liao	Gent University, Belgium
Liang Lin	Sun Yat-Sen University, China, China
Hiep Luong	Ghent University, Belgium
Vishal M. Patel	University of Maryland, USA
Xavier Maldague	Université Laval, Canada
Antoine Manzanera	ENSTA ParisTech, France
David Marshall	Cardiff University, UK
Gonzalo Pajares Martinsanz	Universidad Complutense, Spain
Javier Mateos	University of Granada, Spain
Jean Meunier	Université de Montréal, Canada
Amar Mitiche	INRS, Canada
Jean-Michel Morel	ENS, France
Adrian Munteanu	Vrije Universiteit Brussel, Belgium

Contents

Motion and Tracking

Security, Forensics and Biometrics

Depth and 3D

Image Quality Improvement and Assessment

Classification and Recognition

Multidimensional Signal Processing

Multimedia Compression. Retrieval and Navigation

Low-Level Image Processing

BNRFBE Method for Blur Estimation in Document Images

Van Cuong Kieu(✉), Florence Cloppet, and Nicole Vincent

LIPADE: Laboratoire d'Informatique Paris Descartes,
Paris Descartes University, Paris, France
{van-cuong.kieu,florence.cloppet,nicole.vincent}@parisdescartes.fr

Abstract. The efficiency of document image processing techniques depends on image quality that is impaired by many sources of degradation. These sources can be in document itself or arise from the acquisition process. In this paper, we are concerned with blur degradation without any prior knowledge on the blur origin. We propose to evaluate the blur parameter at local level on predefined zones without relying on any blur model. This parameter is linked to a fuzzy statistical analysis of the textual part of the document extracted in the initial image. The proposed measure is evaluated on DIQA database where the correlation between blur degree and OCR accuracy is computed. The results show that our blur estimation can help to predict OCR accuracy.

1 Introduction

Whereas ten years ago, in the perspective of retroconversion, paper documents were transformed in digital documents by means of scanner or fixed camera acquisition in specific environment to obtain high quality images. The popularization and the improvement of camera quality on mobile devices have changed the way of image acquisition. Photos with a large number of pixels are possible with such devices. Many applications developed on mobile devices use this opportunity, for example in case of QR codes [4]. However, the un-manageable acquisition context may yield some high incidence on the quality of the captured document image (*e.g.* Fig.1). We can identify several origins for document degradation. Some are linked to the document itself such as ink bleed-through, wrinkled and stained parchment. Others are linked to the image acquisition. For instance, wrapped paper or non-plan support yield to perspective distortion in document images. The environment illumination, camera/document movement may be potential causes of low-contrast and/or blur images.

Among the most annoying degradation that can be caused by such conditions we are studying blur that is one of the most significant degradation with respect to OCR quality. It can be caused by the movement of the camera or by the lack of manual support. In this paper, we are measuring document image quality with respect to blur. Many OCR softs are quite sensitive to this degradation and some databases, as DIQA database for example, have even been created to test the ability of commercial software [10] toward blur degree.

© Springer International Publishing Switzerland 2015
S. Battiato et al. (Eds.): ACIVS 2015, LNCS 9386, pp. 3–14, 2015.
DOI: 10.1007/978-3-319-25903-1_1

In Section 2 the notion of blur is analyzed and the related works are investigated. Section 3 is devoted to the principle of the method we are proposing to define a blur index. In Section 4, we present the results and compare with state-of-the-art results. In the last section, we conclude and give some perspectives of the work.

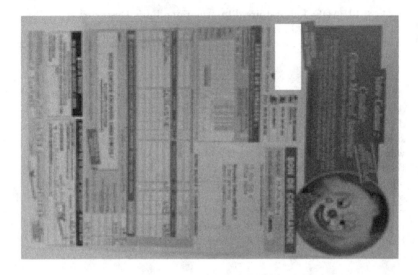

Fig. 1. A complex color document captured by smart phone

2 Blur Analysis

Several studies have addressed the document degradation causes. The most recent one was presented in 2013 in ICDAR conference in [20]. It turns out that the aim of quality assessment is mostly related to OCR accuracy prediction. Of course this is possible when textual parts are already segmented. Nevertheless, in real life document management the quality has to be measured for a whole document.

Among the most common degradation causes, blur takes an important part. In the company we are collaborating with, one third of captured images from 200 real documents were blurred. Thus, before processing the document images, the degradation, in our case, blur, has to be detected. Then, several solutions appear; either it is possible to automatically improve document image quality, or to reacquire the document if the improvement is not enough efficient.

To estimate blur, many assumptions are often made. In particular, the blur is supposed to be equal all over the image. This hypothesis does not hold in many cases. Indeed, blur can come from different origins. Among them, we can mention the motion or the defocusing of the camera. The last origin is due to the inefficiency of camera depth field. These origins are all possible when mobile acquisition of documents is considered. The paper document can be hold in hand, the camera can be moved at different levels, and the document plan can be not horizontal or parallel to the camera lens. As a result, blur can vary according to the different parts of the document. Furthermore, in the context of mobile acquisition, the captured image contains not only the document but also some background that has no significance for document analysis.

In natural image quality assessment, many methods have been developed to estimate blur and even to remove it. Most of the methods make the assumption that the blur is homogeneous all over the image and are looking for models that are most often adapted to one type of blur but not to all. In [3], the problem of defocusing and linear motion blur is addressed and limited to the horizontal direction whereas in [6] only blur due to motion is processed. The second method needs a GPU implementation because of the complexity of the method that is common in these kind of approaches. In [16] an iterative approach is presented to define a right kernel for minimizing an energy function. Unfortunately, a learning process is needed. In [18] a simpler filter method is proposed, it enables to enforce the perceptual vision without any blur model but needs some parameter evaluation depending on the application.

In document image quality assessment, a recent survey can be read in [20]. The use of models is emphasized. Indeed, document image quality assessment is different from blur estimation but several studies are mentioned. In [8] a measure of sharpness is defined as the standard deviation associated with the pixel grey levels of text and background issued from a clustering of grey levels in a three-cluster process. The other method in [9] uses a median filtering considered separately in the horizontal and vertical directions. The results are finally combined to define a sharpness index. In [12] gradient along contours of characters is used. In [19] unsupervised features are learned in order to predict OCR accuracy. In [15] some features issued from [13] are computed on the DIQA database to evaluate document image quality. Taking advantage of the image content, in [17], bar code images are deblurred, based on ridgelet transform to estimate the blur degree.

Most of the processes developed in document quality assessment make the assumption that images contain only the document. With mobile acquisition, this assumption does not hold anymore. For instance, a document can occupy less than half of the image. Thus, we assume that the document has a rectangular shape on any background as the following definition.

$$I = F \cup B \ and \ D = R(F) \tag{1}$$

Where F is the zone of interest, B is the background, D is the document to be extracted from image I, and R is an operator that transforms the argument in a rectangular shape. The blur estimation must only consider the D part.

In this paper, we are considering color document images with a main part being printed/handwritten characters or graphic elements as shown in Fig.1. Thus, the proposed method may be unsuitable for general images. We assume that the document part (F) and its rectangular shape are ready for blur estimation in the next section.

3   Blur Measuring

Blur is a difficult property to estimate, as its causes may be various according to the location in the image. Therefore, no global model can be used nor a mixture of several models. Since blur is high relevant to transitional region between edge (text edge in our case) and background (*e.g.* Fig. 2), edge based approaches are considered [1,2,5,11]. Considering this direction, we chose to build a new local method in the neighborhood of each pixel, and more precisely around transitional pixels. Therefore, blur is estimated by considering grey level of pixels such as the method in [8]. Our proposed method named BNRFBE (Block No Reference Fuzzy Blur Estimation) uses Fuzzy-C-Mean clustering to calculate the membership degrees of each pixel belonging to text or non-text classes. The transitional region contains pixels having membership value in $]0,1[$ whereas text and non-text regions contain pixels having membership value 0 and 1, respectively.

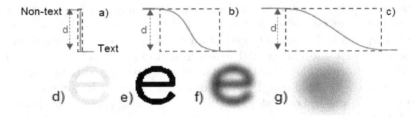

Fig. 2. Transition region (red rectangles) between text (edge) and non-text (background) regions is high relevant to blur : non-blur images d) and e) with contrast different show the transition region in a). They show the difference between blur and contrast ; image f) shows an example of b); image g) shows an example of c).

3.1   Principle of the Measurement

To measure blur in a grey level image, we assume that two classes are present and then a fuzzy clustering of the pixels according to their grey level can be performed. For example, a fuzzy c-mean can be used with two clusters: Text (C_1) and Background (C_2). This enables to associate with each pixel x of the image, a couple of membership values, $^t(\mu_1(x), \mu_2(x))$, where $\mu_2(x)=1-\mu_1(x)$, to respectively the text part and the background. From a crisp point of view, the pixel may belong to the text or the background parts according to the position of the membership value with respect to 0.5. If one $\mu_1(x)$ value is greater than 0.5 but rather near to 0.5, some ambiguity appears and the pixel tends to belong to the text but with a high uncertainty that is perceived as a blur pixel in the image and thus considered as blur. The blur measure is linked to the fuzziness rate of the two parts deduced from the clustering. It can also be considered as the compactness of each cluster C_1 and C_2. In this study, we have chosen the second approach.

Let c_1 and c_2 be the gravity centers of the membership values of the two clusters C_1 (where $\mu_1(x)$ is greater than 0.5) and C_2 (where $\mu_1(x)$ is less than 0.5).

$$c_1 = \frac{1}{n_1} \sum_{x \in C_1} \mu_1(x) \ \ and \ \ c_2 = \frac{1}{n_2} \sum_{x \in C_2} \mu_2(x) \tag{2}$$

Where n_1 and n_2 are the respective numbers of pixels in the clusters. Then we define a blur parameter by formula:

$$bl = \frac{1}{n_1} \sqrt{\sum_{x \in C_1} (\mu_1(x) - c_1)^2} + \frac{1}{n_2} \sqrt{\sum_{x \in C_2} (\mu_2(x) - c_2)^2} \tag{3}$$

In case of a non-blurred document, only two colors are present in the image and the membership values are only 1 and 0 (see Fig. 2-d and e), then the **bl** parameter value will be equal to 0. Otherwise, the more the image is blurred, the higher blur value will be. As $(\mu_i - c_i)$ is less than 0.5,   **bl** index values belong to the interval [0, 1]. In this way, we do not measure a contrast that could be improved by histogram normalization, but the dispersion of the color levels present in the image.

3.2   Text Blur Measurement

In blur document image estimation for mobile devices, the computation time is important. The fuzzy clustering processing time depends on the number of pixels in the image. Thus, we limit the process to pixels in the neighborhood of a contour part, where blur can appear. Besides, the process will be applied on patches covering the image. On a non-uniform background patch that does not contain text part, the results would not be significant according to our problem. The clustering process is only performed on the pixels near the characters contours or may be drawings or logos.

As blur is heterogeneously distributed, we work in an independent way on square patches that make a partition of the document image. Preliminary experiments have shown that a patch size of 100 pixels wide, yields to a good compromise between quality of results and time processing. Indeed, it reduces approximately 42% of time computing for a DIQA 1840x3264 image when patch size decreases from 200 to 100. A contour detection step is introduced in order to limit the fuzzy clustering on a text zone. It has to be noticed that on a color and complex documents as the one illustrated on Fig.1, we have information neither on the color of the text part nor on the number of colors contained in the document image. In order to decrease the complexity, we first transform the color image in a grey level image, and then apply a binarisation transform to the image. Of course many binarisation methods exist, but we have privileged simple approaches regarding time processing constraints of our application.

In the case of a homogeneous background without text, several background pixels are considered as text. To prevent this, the Nick method is applied [7]. It is well known to improve the binarisation in case of white pages or with a low contrast. The method uses a threshold computed using formula:

$$Threshold = m + k\sqrt{\frac{\sum p_i^2 - m^2}{NP}} \qquad (4)$$

Where k varies between 0.1 and -0.2 according to the application, m is the mean grey level, p_i is the grey level of pixel i and NP is the total number of pixels in the processed image. This binarisation step is used as a text detector. If the image contains only one-class pixels, it is assumed to contain only a homogeneous background. We decide to qualify this image as a good quality image, even if the background is blurred because our goal is not to measure the quality of the background. From this step, we assume that text has been extracted.

$$I = B \cup T \qquad (5)$$

Where B denotes the background and T denotes the text extracted from binarized image.

In order to decrease processing time, we define a working zone $Z_\lambda(I)$ in the neighborhood of the text before **bl** parameter computation. The working zone $Z_\lambda(I)$ is obtained as a dilation of T.

$$Z_\lambda(I) = D_{S_k}(T) \ with \ \begin{cases} S_i = \{x \ : \ d(x,0) < i\} \\ k = min\{A(D_{S_i}) > \lambda \times A(T)\} \end{cases} \qquad (6)$$

When λ is equal to 2, then Z_λ (I) will be simply noted Z(I).

Finally the computation of **bl** parameter is applied to Z(I) pixels. Indeed, the results of the measurement are only interesting in these parts of the document. In Fig. 3 the flowchart of the BNRFBE method is presented.

Fig. 3. Flowchart of the BNRFBE method

4   Experiments

To evaluate our blur estimation, we have carried out several experiments on:

- simulated blur images by Gaussian filter and motion blur model.
- one image on which the definition of Z is varying in order to show the robustness of the method toward the diminution of the processed zone.

- real images comprising complex layout as the one shown in Fig. 1, which have been tagged thanks to human perception. In particular, this enables to match the human scale perception with the **bl** parameter.
- images where the content is mastered so that some OCR can be performed. Indeed, the actual capacities of the OCR do not enable to use them as objective tools to measure the quality of a complex document. To assess the significance of the **bl** parameter with respect to blur degree, we have used DIQA database published in [10].

4.1 Simulated Blur

The first experiment aims at proving that the **bl** parameter is increasing from zero upward when blur is increasing. We used a Gaussian filter (with its size varying from 1 to 79) to simulate out-of-focus blur images and a motion blur model (with its length varying from 1 to 39, its angle = 5) to generate motion blurred images. Then, we estimated the blur parameter **bl** on such images. Fig. 4-(b), (c), and (d) illustrate three blurred images by applying a Gaussian filter on the binary image (a) (without blur).

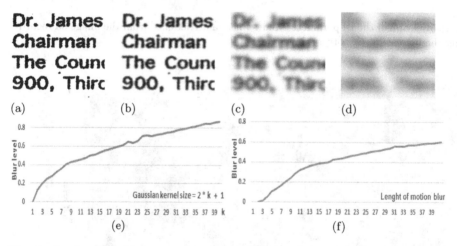

Fig. 4. Graph of the **bl** parameter values for images deduced from the out-of-focus and motion blur images. Such blurred images are simulated by Gaussian kernel size = 2 × K + 1 and by a motion blur model with the length = K and the angle = 5. For example, the initial image I in (a) and blurred images with size of Gaussian kernel respectively 7 (b), 27 (c) and 79 (d).

Fig.4-e and f show that the **bl** value increases progressively when the filter size increases, especially, the value of 0.75 corresponds to a very high blur level. The estimated blur is correlative with the increase of filter size.

4.2 Influence of Working Zone Z

We have repeated the first experiment but with the increasing of the size of working zone $Z_\lambda(I)$ to evaluate its influence on **bl** values. Fig. 5 shows three curve lines of **bl** with $Z = 1, 2$ and 3 corresponding to $\lambda = 2, 4$, and 6, respectively. The three curve lines show the same tendency for **bl**, illustrated by a homogeneous behavior in the different experimental conditions. Since the influence of λ on the estimated blur level is small, we fix $\lambda = 2$ in order to reduce processing time.

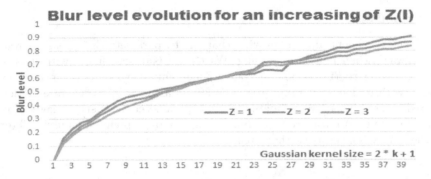

Fig. 5. Graph of the **bl** parameter values for images deduced from the image 3a regarding the increasing size of working zone $Z_\lambda(I)$.

Fig. 6. The estimated local blur of the document image in Fig. 1 : the blur level is high on the left and bottom parts of the document image.

4.3 Real Images

We have applied the BNRFBE method on images of a private database. The result is shown in Fig. 6 for the document presented in Fig. 1. We have seen that most often only some parts of the document are blurred. The blur property of the document is not uniform at all. The blur is strong on the left and bottom parts of the document. A LUT (from blue color, the lowest level of blur to red color, the highest level of blur) is considered to illustrate the blur property of each patch in the document image.

4.4 DIQA Database

In this experiment, we evaluate our blur measurement approach in a quantitative way. As it is a well-known fact, the quality of OCR is sensible to blurred characters, we have used the method introduced in [10] to evaluate our **bl** parameter. In order to assess its meaning, we are testing its correlation with the efficiency of a commercial OCR on the same documents. The DIQA database described in [10] considers 175 document images and comprises 25 sets; each set are images of a single document. Its acquisition context differs for varying blur level in such images.

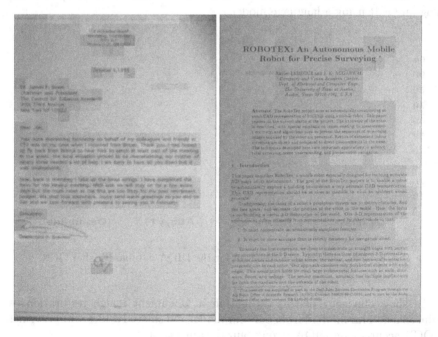

Fig. 7. Measurement of blur in DIQA documents : (a) image "set1/2012-04-16_17-43-50_544.jpg" (strong and homogeneous blur), (b) image "set11/2012-04-19_18-26-18_334.jpg" (medium and heterogeneous blur).

On Fig. 7, blur estimation on DIQA document images are visualized, each patch **bl** parameter value is set according to the LUT presented in Fig. 6. The estimated blur is correlative with human perception. For each image, we have computed the mean value $\overline{Bl}$ of the **bl** parameter values calculated on each patch of an image. This value $\overline{Bl}$ is considered as the blur level of the whole image. Besides, we have applied OCR of Adobe-Reader 8 to compute the character accuracy as defined in [14]. We also re-use OCR results from [10] to evaluate the correlation between $\overline{Bl}$ and character accuracy on each set by Spearman Rank Order Correlation Coefficient (SROCC) and also by Pearson Linear Correlation Coefficient. Finally the results are given as in [10] by the 25th, 50th and 75th percentiles.

To show the high correlation between blur level and OCR, we used an OCR without language model such as Adobe 8 and Tesseract. Indeed, three quartiles of SROCC index with Adobe 8 are 89%, 100% and 100% with 13/25 exact ranking sets. When using finereader10 (86, 94.3, 100) we outperform the results from [10] but do not rely on any training. Fig. 8 illustrates the Pearsons correlation of our blur estimation with four OCR (two with language models and two without). Fig. 8 indicates the three quartiles in the rectangle, the two outside bars are min and max. The result shows the blur estimation is significantly correlated with the two left OCR that do not use a language model. Thus, our previous assumption is confirmed. Nevertheless comparison is difficult as [10] gives results using an OCR using a language model.

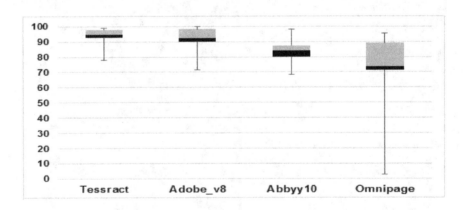

Fig. 8. Pearson linear correlation for the DIQA database with 4 OCR.

To show efficiency of this estimation in document image restoration, we deduced a de-blur method from our blur model and showed a 16.1% improvement in OCR accuracy on DIQA strong blur document.

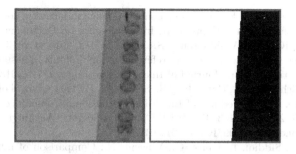

Fig. 9. Initial image I in (a) and binarised version in (b).

5 Conclusion

We presented a no-reference method BNRFBE for estimating locally blur degree of document images captured by mobile phone. This method considers each text patch of document image to extract a working zone in order to limit computation time. The pixels in the zone are classified into two classes based on fuzzy c-means approach. The fuzziness rate of each pixel in the two classes is then employed to measure the blur level. The visual results show that the estimated blur is fitted with human blur perception. The quantitative evaluation is made comparing **bl** index with OCR accuracy. We calculated SROCC for 25 sets of the database DIQA with the estimated blur. This experiment shows that our blur estimation method can rank and select images with best OCR accuracy. In addition, the measured Pearson's correlation scores for 25 sets show that our method outperforms unsupervised and supervised approaches. Next step is to use the present computation in order to improve the quality of the document and in particular the OCR accuracy. Nevertheless we can mention the limit of the method in case of color images when the binarisation step is not focusing on the text but on other graphic elements in the document (as illustrated in Fig. 9). Therefore we have also to concentrate on text extraction in the complex document images.

References

1. Caviedes, J., Gurbuz, S.: No-reference sharpness metric based on local edge kurtosis. In: Proceedings of the 2002 International Conference on Image Processing, vol. 3, pp. III-53–III-56 (2002)
2. Chung, Y.C., Wang, J.M., Bailey, R., Chen, S.W., Chang, S.L.: A non-parametric blur measure based on edge analysis for image processing applications. In: 2004 IEEE Conference on Cybernetics and Intelligent Systems, vol. 1, pp. 356–360, December 2004
3. Couzinie, F., Sun, J., Alamari, K., Ponce, J.: Learning to estimate and remove non-uniform image blur. In: Conference on Computer Vision and Pattern Recognition, Portland, USA, pp. 1075–1082, June 2013

4. Cutter, M., Manduchi, R.: Real time camera phone guidance for compliant, document image acquisition without sight. In: Conference on Document Analysis and Recognition, ICDAR, Washington, USA, pp. 408–412, August 2013

5. De, K., Masilamani, V.: A new no-reference image quality measure for blurred images in spatial domain. Journal of Image and Graphics **1**(1) (2013)

6. Hirsch, M., Schuler, C.J., Harmeling, S., Scholkopf, B.: Fast removal of non-uniform camera shake. In: Proceedings of the 2011 International Conference on Computer Vision, ICCV 2011, pp. 463–470. IEEE Computer Society, Washington, DC (2011). http://dx.doi.org/10.1109/ICCV.2011.6126276

7. Khurshid, K., Siddiqi, I., Faure, C., Vincent, N.: Comparison of niblack inspired binarization methods for ancient documents. In: Proceedings of the Document Recognition and Retrieval XVI, DRR 2009, San Jose, CA, USA, pp. 463–470 (2009)

8. Kumar, D., Ramakrishnan, A.G.: Quad: Quality assessment of documents. In: Proceedings of the 2011 Camera-Based Document Analysis and Recognition, CBDAR 2011, Beijing, China, pp. 463–470 (2011)

9. Kumar, J., Chen, F., Doermann, D.: Sharpness estimation for document and scene images. In: 2012 21st International Conference on Pattern Recognition (ICPR), Tsukuba, Japan, November 2012

10. Kumar, J., Ye, P., Doermann, D.: A dataset for quality assessment of camera captured document images. In: Proceedings of the 2013 Camera-Based Document Analysis and Recognition, CBDAR 2013, Washington, DC, USA, pp. 113–125 (2013)

11. Marziliano, P., Dufaux, F., Winkler, S., Ebrahimi, T.: A no-reference perceptual blur metric. In: Proceedings of the 2002 International Conference on Image Processing, vol. 3, pp. III-57–III-60 (2002)

12. Peng, X., Cao, H., Subramanian, K., Prasad, R., Natarajan, P.: Automated image quality assessment for camera-captured ocr. In: 2011 18th IEEE International Conference on Image Processing (ICIP), Brussels, pp. 2621–2624, September 2011

13. Pertuz, S., Puig, D., Garcia, M.A.: Analysis of focus measure operators for shape-from-focus. Pattern Recogn. **46**(5), 1415–1432 (2013)

14. Rice, S.V., Kanai, J., Nartker, T.A.: The fifth annual test of ocr accuracy. Tech. rep. (1996)

15. Rusinol, M., Chazalon, J., Ogier, J.M.: Normalisation et validation d'images de documents captures en mobilité. In: CIFED 2014, Nancy, France, pp. 109–124, September 2014

16. Sun, L., Cho, S., Wang, J., Hays, J.: Edge-based blur kernel estimation using patch priors. In: 2013 IEEE International Conference on Computational Photography (ICCP), Cambridge, MA, pp. 1–8, April 2013

17. Tiwari, S., Shukla, V.P., Biradar, S.R., Singh, A.K.: Blind restoration of motion blurred barcode images using ridgelet transform and radial basis function neural network, pp. 63–80, April 2014

18. Tomasi, C., Manduchi, R.: Bilateral filtering for gray and color images. In: Sixth International Conference on Computer Vision, Bombay, Inde, pp. 839–846, January 1998

19. Ye, P., Doermann, D.: Learning features for predicting ocr accuracy. In: 2012 21st International Conference on Pattern Recognition (ICPR), Tsukuba, Japan, pp. 3204–3207, November 2012

20. Ye, P., Doermann, D.: Document image quality assessment: A brief survey. In: 2013 12th International Conference on Document Analysis and Recognition (ICDAR), Washington, USA, pp. 723–727, August 2013

Edge Width Estimation for Defocus Map from a Single Image

Andrey Nasonov, Alexandra Nasonova, and Andrey Krylov$^{(\boxtimes)}$

Laboratory of Mathematical Methods of Image Processing, Faculty of Computational Mathematics and Cybernetics, Lomonosov Moscow State University, Moscow, Russia
kryl@cs.msu.ru

Abstract. The paper presents a new edge width estimation method based on Gaussian edge model and unsharp mask analysis. The proposed method is accurate and robust to noise. Its effectiveness is demonstrated by its application for the problem of defocus map estimation from a single image. Sparse defocus map is constructed using edge detection algorithm followed by the proposed edge width estimation algorithm. Then full defocus map is obtained by propagating the blur amount at edge locations to the entire image. Experimental results show the effectiveness of the proposed method in providing a reliable estimation of the defocus map.

Keywords: Edge width · Image blur · Defocus map · Edge model

1 Introduction

There are two general approaches for defocus estimation: methods that require multiple images [5,15] and methods that use only one image [1,4]. The former use a set of images captured with multiple camera focus settings. This approach has limited application due to the occlusion problem and requirements of a scene to be static. The latter split the problem into two steps: construction of a sparse defocus map via blur level estimation at edge locations and obtaining the full defocus map using a propagation method.

Elder and Zucker [4] find the locations and the blur amount of edges according to the first- and second-order derivatives of the input image, they only get a sparse defocus map. Bae and Durand [1] extend this work to get a full defocus map from the sparse map by a defocus interpolation method.

In [16] authors propose a blur estimation method based on the Gaussian gradient ratio, and show that it is robust to noise, inaccurate edge location and interference from neighboring edges. In [14] the image blur estimation method is based on the observation that defocusing can significantly affect the spectrum amplitude at the object edge locations in an image. Both these methods use matting Laplacian [8] for defocus map interpolation. These methods are the state-of-the-art methods. References to other methods can be found in these papers.

© Springer International Publishing Switzerland 2015
S. Battiato et al. (Eds.): ACIVS 2015, LNCS 9386, pp. 15–22, 2015.
DOI: 10.1007/978-3-319-25903-1_2

General purpose blur estimation methods can also be used for sparse defocus map construction problem. The method [6] is based on the assumption that the blur of the image is close to Gaussian. The image is divided into blocks, and the blur kernel is supposed to be uniform inside the block. The estimation of the blurriness of the block is based on the maximum of difference ratio between an original image and its two re-blurred versions. Block-based approach provides good blur estimation for highly textured areas but it shows inadequate results for blocks not containing edges, for example, flat areas.

There are some simple and fast methods for blur estimation at edge locations [9–11], but generally they are not adequate for noisy images. A lot of methods use Gaussian filter as blurring approximation. In [2,4] authors propose methods of multi-scale edge detection, where the scale of detection for each edge can roughly approximate blur level. In [13] neural networks are used. In [7] edge neighborhood is expanded in radial-symmetric functions with the method of principal components as a classifier of blur level.

In this work we present a novel approach for edge width estimation suggested in [12] which is accurate and is robust to noise. Then we demonstrate the effectiveness of the proposed method for the problem of obtaining the defocus map from a single image.

2   Edge Width

2.1   Gaussian Edge Model

We propose modeling an edge as a convolution of the ideal step edge function with a Gaussian filter (see Fig. 1):

$$E_\sigma(x) = [H * G_\sigma](x),$$

where $*$ denotes convolution.

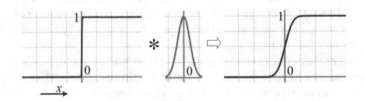

Fig. 1. Edge model

In our model we use the following definitions of the Gaussian filter and ideal step edge function

$$G_\sigma(x) = \frac{1}{\sqrt{2\pi}\sigma}e^{-\frac{x^2}{2\sigma^2}}, \qquad H(x) = \begin{cases} 1, & x \geq 0, \\ 0, & x < 0. \end{cases}$$

It should be noted that $H(kx) = H(x) \; \forall k > 0$, which leads to the following property for the model edge:

$$E_\sigma(x) = E_{\sigma'}(\frac{\sigma'}{\sigma}x) \qquad \forall \sigma > 0, \sigma' > 0. \tag{1}$$

2.2 Estimation of Edge Width

For the estimation of edge width we use the unsharp masking approach.

Let $U_{\sigma,\alpha}[E_{\sigma_0}](x)$ be the result of unsharp masking applied to the edge $E_{\sigma_0}(x)$:

$$U_{\sigma,\alpha}[E_{\sigma_0}](x) = (1+\alpha)E_{\sigma_0}(x) - \alpha E_{\sigma_0} * G_\sigma =$$
$$= (1+\alpha)E_{\sigma_0}(x) - \alpha E_{\sqrt{\sigma_0^2+\sigma^2}}(x). \tag{2}$$

Using (1) and supposing $\sigma = \sigma_0 = \sigma_1$, (2) holds

$$U_{\sigma_1,\alpha}[E_{\sigma_1}](x) = (1+\alpha)E_{\sigma_1}(x) - \alpha E_{\sqrt{2}\sigma_1}(x) =$$
$$= (1+\alpha)E_{\sigma_1}(x) - \alpha E_{\sqrt{2}\sigma_2}(\frac{\sqrt{2}\sigma_2}{\sqrt{2}\sigma_1}x) = U_{\sigma_2,\alpha}[E_{\sigma_2}](\frac{\sigma_2}{\sigma_1}x). \tag{3}$$

The unsharp masking approach (2), due to (3), holds that for a fixed value of parameter α the intensity values of corresponding extrema of $U_{\sigma,\alpha}[E_\sigma](x)$ are the same for all $\sigma > 0$ (note that here unsharp masking uses the same σ as the model edge):

$$U^*(\alpha) = \max_x U_{\sigma,\alpha}[E_\sigma](x),$$
$$U_*(\alpha) = \min_x U_{\sigma,\alpha}[E_\sigma](x) = 1 - U^*(\alpha)$$

Thus, taking into account the monotonicity of $U_{\sigma,\alpha}[E_\sigma](x)$ as a function of σ due to (3) and the properties of Gaussian functions:

$$\sigma < \sigma_0 : \max_x U_{\sigma,\alpha}[E_{\sigma_0}](x) < U^*(\alpha),$$
$$\min_x U_{\sigma,\alpha}[E_{\sigma_0}](x) > U_*(\alpha),$$
$$\sigma > \sigma_0 : \max_x U_{\sigma,\alpha}[E_{\sigma_0}](x) > U^*(\alpha),$$
$$\min_x U_{\sigma,\alpha}[E_{\sigma_0}](x) < U_*(\alpha). \tag{4}$$

2.3 The Edge Width Estimation Algorithm

The edge width estimation algorithm takes the following form:

1. Given values: α, $U^*(\alpha)$, 1-dimensional edge profile $E_{\sigma_0}(x)$.
2. for $\sigma = \sigma_{min}$ to $\sigma_{max} : \sigma_{step}$

       compute $U_{\sigma,\alpha}[E_{\sigma_0}](x)$,
       find local maxima x_{max} of $U_{\sigma,\alpha}[E_{\sigma_0}](x)$,
       if $U_{\sigma,\alpha}[E_{\sigma_0}](x_{max}) \geq U^*(\alpha)$
          result $= \sigma$,
          stop cycle.
  3. Output: result.

We use $\alpha = 4$, $U^*(4) \approx 1.24$, $\sigma_{min} = 0.5$ (the smallest possible value for the edge blur due to the digitization of the image), $\sigma_{max} = 10$, the value of σ_{step} is fixed to 0.1 as this is an acceptable accuracy for the task.

3   Defocus Blur Estimation

3.1   Sparse Defocus Map

The previous section deals with isolated edge profiles with values from 0 to 1. In practice real image edge profiles are rarely isolated, and all of them have different amplitude.

For sparse blur map, we have to obtain edge map using an edge detector (we use Canny edge detector [3]). For each edge pixel we construct an edge profile along the gradient direction at this pixel using an interpolation method (we use bilinear interpolation). Then the values of edge profile are scaled into interval from 0 to 1 and the algorithm from section 2.3 is used.

Also, for non-isolated edge profiles we isolate the central edge: we find the nearest local maximum to the right from the center and the nearest local minimum to the left, and duplicate those values (see Fig. 2).

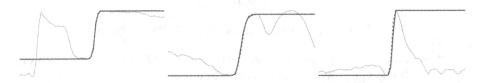

Fig. 2. Edge profile examples and the result of the proposed edge width estimation method. The blue thin line is the original profile, the red thick line is an isolated edge, the green puncture line is a model edge with found edge width.

3.2   Full Defocus Map

Using sparse defocus map at edge locations, the full defocus map is recovered by an edge-aware interpolation method [8]. We use the MatLab software provided by Zhuo and Sim [16] and substitute their sparse defocus map with ours.

4   Results and Discussion

We demonstrate the effectiveness of the proposed method by comparing our full defocus maps with results provided by [14] and [16]. The proposed edge width estimation method works well on images with a relatively low amount of noise, which is usually the case with defocused images. For noisy images some preliminary blurring can be applied.

In Fig. 3 it can be seen that the proposed method makes the background more homogenous than [16]. In Fig. 4 the proposed method correctly processes the grass area and results in more gradual depth change. In Fig. 5, the proposed method and methods [14,16] show results with almost the same quality.

a. Input image   b. Edge map for the proposed algorithm

b. Edge width estimation   c. Proposed edge width estimation
by Zhuo and Sim [16]

Fig. 3. Full defocus map for bird image. Blue and purple areas are sharp regions, yellow are white areas are blurry regions.

a. Input image   b. Zhuo and Sim [16]   c. Proposed edge width

Fig. 4. Full defocus map for pumpkin image

a. Input image   b. Zhuo and Sim [16]

c. Tang et al. [14]   d. Proposed edge width

Fig. 5. Full defocus map for flower image

4.1   Possible Improvement

Fig. 6 is the challenging problem for existing defocus map estimation algorithms because they construct sparse defocus map only using edge pixels. We suggest adding ridges and textures to the sparse defocus map as a possible improvement.

Ridges are linear image structures that also contain important information about image blur. Edge detection algorithms usually detect borders of only some ridges. Ignoring ridges results in missing thin lines from a defocus map. For example, the method [14] does not include stems into the foreground in Fig. 6.

Textured areas contain multiple edges that are hard to analyze with edge detection algorithms. Special algorithms for blur estimation in textured areas may improve the accuracy of blur estimation in these areas. Both the proposed method and the method [16] falsely include the image bottom into the foreground due to lack of edges provided by the edge detection algorithm in Fig. 6.

a. Input image

b. Zhuo and Sim [16]

c. Tang et al. [14]

d. Proposed method

Fig. 6. Full defocus map for second flower image

5   Conclusion

In this paper, we have presented new edge width estimation method and its application for the problem of obtaining full defocus map from a single image.

The proposed edge width estimation is accurate, robust to noise and edge interference, and it can be used to generate accurate sparse defocus map. Possible ways to improve the defocus map are discussed.

The work was supported by Russian Science Foundation grant 14-11-00308.

References

1. Bae, S., Durand, F.: Defocus magnification. Computer Graphics Forum **26**(3), 571–579 (2007)
2. Basu, M.: Gaussian-based edge-detection methods - a survey. IEEE Transactions on Systems, Man and Cybernetics, Part C **32**, 252–260 (2002)
3. Canny, J.: A computational approach to edge detection. IEEE Trans. Pattern Analysis and Machine Intelligence **8**, 679–698 (1986)
4. Elder, J.H., Zucker, S.W.: Local scale control for edge detection and blur estimation. IEEE Transactions on Pattern Analysis and Machine Intelligence **20**(7), 699–716 (1998)
5. Favaro, P., Soatto, S.: A geometric approach to shape from defocus. IEEE Transactions on Pattern Analysis and Machine Intelligence **27**(3), 406–417 (2005)
6. Hu, H., de Haan, G.: Low cost robust blur estimator. In: IEEE International Conference on Image Processing, pp. 617–620 (2006)
7. Hua, Z., Wei, Z., Yaowu, C.: A no-reference perceptual blur metric by using ols-rbf network. In: Pacific-Asia Workshop on Computational Intelligence and Industrial Application, PACIIA 2008, vol. 1, pp. 1007–1011 (2008)
8. Levin, A., Lischinski, D., Weiss, Y.: A closed-form solution to natural image matting. IEEE Transactions on Pattern Analysis and Machine Intelligence **30**(2), 228–242 (2008)
9. Marziliano, P., Dufaux, F., Winkler, S., Ebrahimi, T.: A no-reference perceptual blur metric. Proceedings of the International Conference on Image Processing **3**, 57–60 (2002)
10. Marziliano, P., Dufaux, F., Winkler, S., Ebrahimi, T.: Perceptual blur and ringing metrics: Application to JPEG2000. Signal Processing: Image Communications **3**(2), 163–172 (2004)
11. Narvekar, N.D., Karam, L.J.: A no-reference perceptural image sharpness metric based on a cumulative probability of blur detection. In: International Workshop on Quality of Multimedia Experience, QoMEx 2009 (2009)
12. Nasonova, A.A., Krylov, A.S.: Determination of image edge width by unsharp masking. Computational Mathematics and Modeling **25**(1), 72–78 (2014)
13. Suzuki, K., Horiba, I., Sugie, N.: Neural edge enhancer for supervised edge enhancement from noisy images. IEEE Transactions on Pattern Analysis and Machine Intelligence **25**, 1582–1596 (2003)
14. Tang, C., Hou, C., Song, Z.: Defocus map estimation from a single image via spectrum contrast. Optics letters **38**(10), 1706–1708 (2013)
15. Zhou, C., Cossairt, O., Nayar, S.: Depth from diffusion. In: 2010 IEEE Conference on Computer Vision and Pattern Recognition (CVPR), pp. 1110–1117. IEEE (2010)
16. Zhuo, S., Sim, T.: Defocus map estimation from a single image. Pattern Recognition **44**(9), 1852–1858 (2011)

RSD-DOG: A New Image Descriptor Based on Second Order Derivatives

Darshan Venkatrayappa[(✉)], Philippe Montesinos, Daniel Diep, and Baptiste Magnier

LGI2P - Ecole des Mines d'Ales, Nimes, France
{darshan.venkatrayappa,philippe.montesinos,daniel.diep,
baptiste.magnier}@mines-ales.fr

Abstract. This paper introduces the new and powerful image patch descriptor based on second order image statistics/derivatives. Here, the image patch is treated as a 3D surface with intensity being the 3rd dimension. The considered 3D surface has a rich set of second order features/statistics such as ridges, valleys, cliffs and so on, that can be easily captured by using the difference of rotating semi Gaussian filters. The originality of this method is based on successfully combining the response of the directional filters with that of the Difference of Gaussian (DOG) approach. The obtained descriptor shows a good discriminative power when dealing with the variations in illumination, scale, rotation, blur, viewpoint and compression. The experiments on image matching, demonstrates the advantage of the obtained descriptor when compared to its first order counterparts such as SIFT, DAISY, GLOH, GIST and LIDRIC.

Keywords: Rotating filter · Difference of Gaussian · Second order image derivatives · Anisotropic half Gaussian kernel · Image matching

1 Introduction

Local image feature extraction has evolved into one of the hot research topics in the field of computer vision. Extracting features that exhibit high repeatability and distinctiveness against variations in viewpoint, rotation, blur, compression, etc., is the basic requirement for many vision applications such as image matching, image retrieval, object detection, visual tracking and so on. For this purpose, a number of feature detectors [4] and descriptors [2] have been proposed. In the computer vision literature, features related to first order image statistics such as segments, edges, image gradients and corners have been used in abundance for image matching and object detection. Whereas, features related to second order statistics such as cliff, ridges, summits, valleys and so on have been sparsely used for the image matching and object recognition purpose. The scope of the work lies in the use of second order statistics for the task of image matching.

© Springer International Publishing Switzerland 2015
S. Battiato et al. (Eds.): ACIVS 2015, LNCS 9386, pp. 23–34, 2015.
DOI: 10.1007/978-3-319-25903-1_3

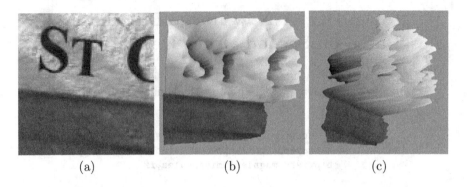

(a)   (b)   (c)

Fig. 1. (a) Image representation in 2D. (b) and (c) The same image being represented in 3D, with intensity being the third dimension. Both (b) and (c) when viewed from different angles, exhibits a set of second order statistics such as ridges, valleys, summits, edges etc.

1.1   Related Work

In one dimension, the first order gradient extracted at a point gives the slope of the curve at the given point. In case of an image, the first order gradient at a pixel measures the slope of the luminance profile at that pixel. Several local image descriptors such as SIFT [1], GLOH [2], DAISY [3], and LBP [5] are based on first order gradient information of the image. And amongst all, SIFT is one of the most widely used local image descriptor. It is constructed by capturing the gradient information at every pixel around an interest point. Extensions of SIFT such as PCA-SIFT [8], F-SIFT [10], MI-SIFT [9] are an improved version of the original SHIFT descriptor, by introducing the new invariance properties while using the same first order gradients as their bases. While GLOH [2] improves on the robustness and distinctiveness of the SIFT descriptor by using radial binning strategy, Fan et al. [11] pool the first order image gradients based on their intensity orders in multiple support regions. By doing so, they achieve rotation invariance without actually calculating the reference orientation. DAISY, combines both SIFT and GLOH binning strategy for fast and dense matching.

Ojala et al. [5] came up with local descriptor made of first order binary patterns (LBP) for texture classification. Center-Symmetric LBP (CS-LBP) [6] and orthogonal color LBP (OC-LBP) [7] provides a compact representation of the LBP descriptor while keeping the same discriminative power. Zambanini et al. [15] propose LIDRIC descriptor, based on multi-scale and multi-oriented even Gabor filters. The descriptor is constructed in such a way that typical effects of illumination variations like changes of edge polarity or spatially varying brightness changes at each pixel are taken into account for illumination insensitivity. LIDRIC has a dimension of 768. Oliva et al. [14] employ Gabor filters to the greyscale input image at four different angles and at four spatial scales to obtain the GIST descriptor. The descriptor has a dimension of 512 and is more global. Authors of [12] propose a new descriptor called RSD-HoG. It is based on the orientation of the edges. The edge orientations are extracted by using a rotating half Gaussian kernel. The descriptor is constructed in a novel way, by embedding the response of the rotating half Gaussian kernel in a Histogram of oriented Gradient (HoG) framework.

On the other hand, in one dimension second order derivative at a point measures the local curvature at that point i.e. how much the curve bends at that point. The authors of [16] use an oriented second derivative filter of Gaussians to capture isotropic as well as anisotropic characteristics of surface by the use of single scale for descriptor generation. Fischer et al. [17] proposed a new image descriptor based on second order statistics for image classification and object detection. Their descriptor extracts the direction and magnitude of the curvature and embeds these information in the HOG framework. But, one of the disadvantage of this descriptor is the dimension. Eigenstetter et al. [13] have proposed an object representation framework based on curvature self-similarity. This method goes beyond the popular approximation of objects using straight lines. However, like most of the descriptors using second order statistics, this approach also exhibits a very high dimensionality.

As shown in Fig. 1, An image represented by a two dimensional function can be considered as a surface in a 3D space. Such a surface in 3D, consists of features such as ridges, valleys, summits or basins. The geometric properties of these features can be accurately characterized by local curvatures of differential geometry through second order statistics. The motivation behind this work is to extract these 2nd order image statistics and represent them as a compact image descriptor for image matching. The main contribution of this work is:

1. The idea was to consider the 2D image patch as 3D surface made of ridges, valleys, summits, etc and to extract these second order statistics by using a local directional maximization or minimization of the response of difference of two rotating half smoothing filters.
2. These directions correspond to the orientation of ridges, valleys or a junction of ridges/valleys. The orientations at which these second order statistics occur, are binned to form a local image descriptor RSD-DOG of dimension/length 256. By construction, the dimension of the descriptor is almost 3 to 4 times less when compared to other descriptors based on second order statistics.
3. This descriptor is evaluated for invariance to blur, rotation, compression, scale and viewpoint changes. Additionally, by construction, the descriptor shows enormous robustness to variations in illumination. To highlight this property, we rigorously evaluate the descriptor on dataset consisting of images with linear and non-linear illumination changes.

The remainder of the paper is organized as follows. In the section 2, we present a directional filter made of anisotropic smoothing half Gaussian kernels. In section 3, we present our robust method for extracting the ridge/valley directions using difference of half directional Gaussian filters. Section 4 is devoted to descriptor construction process and section 5, discusses about experiments and results. Finally, section 6 concludes this paper with the future work.

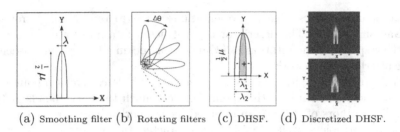

(a) Smoothing filter (b) Rotating filters   (c) DHSF.   (d) Discretized DHSF.

Fig. 2. A smoothing rotating filter and Difference of Half smoothing Filters (DHSF). For (d) top: $\mu = 10$ and $\lambda = 1$. For (d) bottom: $\mu = 10$ and $\lambda = 1.5$.

2   Directional Filter

In our method, we use a directional filter made of anisotropic smoothing half Gaussian kernels. For every pixel in the image patch, we spin this directional filter to obtain a Rotating Signal Descriptor (RSD), which is a function of a rotation angle θ and the underlying signal. As shown in [18] and [19], smoothing with rotating filters means that the image patch is smoothed with a bank of rotated anisotropic Gaussian kernels:

$$G_{(\mu,\lambda)}(x,y,\theta) = C.H\left(R_\theta\begin{pmatrix}x\\y\end{pmatrix}\right)e^{-\left(x\;y\right)R_\theta^{-1}\left(\begin{smallmatrix}\frac{1}{2\,\mu^2} & 0\\ 0 & \frac{1}{2\lambda^2}\end{smallmatrix}\right)R_\theta\begin{pmatrix}x\\y\end{pmatrix}} \tag{1}$$

where C is a normalization coefficient, R_θ a rotation matrix of angle θ, x and y are pixel coordinates and μ and λ are the standard-deviations of the Gaussian filter. As we require only the causal part of the filter (illustrated on figure 2(a)), we simply "cut" the smoothing kernel at the middle, and this operation corresponds to the Heaviside function H [18]. By convolving the image patch with these rotated kernels (see figure 2(b)), we obtain a stack of directional smoothed image patches $I_\theta = I * G_{(\mu,\lambda)}(\theta)$.

To reduce the computational complexity, in the first step we rotate the image at some discrete orientations from 0 to 360 degrees (of $\Delta\theta = 1, 2, 5,$ or 10 degrees, depending on the angular precision required and the smoothing parameters) before applying non rotated smoothing filters. As the image is rotated instead of the filters, the filtering implementation can use efficient recursive approximation of the Gaussian filter. As presented in [18], the implementation of the method is clear and direct. In the second step, we apply an inverse rotation of the smoothed image and obtain a bank of $360/\Delta\theta$ images.

3   Ridge and Valley Detection Using Difference of Gaussian Filters

3.1   Difference of Half Smoothing Filters (DHSF)

At every pixel in the image patch, we are required to estimate a smoothed second order derivative of the image along a curve crossing these pixels. In one dimension,

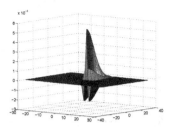 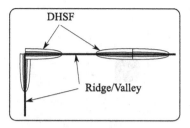

(a) A DHSF in 3 dimension   (b) DHSF in the ridge/valley directions

Fig. 3. DHSF filter descriptions.

the second order derivative of a signal can be easily estimated using a Difference Of Gaussian (DOG)operator [1]. In our method, as in [21], we directly apply two half Gaussian filters with two different λ and the same μ to obtain the directional derivatives. An example for the two discretized filters is shown in Fig. 2(d). Later, we compute the difference of the response of these two filters to obtain the desired smoothed second order derivative information in the ridge/valley directions (illustrated in Fig. 3(b)). We refer to this half Gaussian filter combination as the difference of half smoothing filters (DHSF). An illustration of DHSF is presented in Fig. 3(a) and Fig. 2(c).

3.2 Estimating the Direction of Second Order Statistics Such as Ridges and Valleys

By convolving the image patch with the DHSF (by the technique of rotating the images, as explained above), for each pixel in the image patch we obtain a pixel signal which captures a directional second order information around the pixel. The idea is to extract the directions at which these second order statistics such as ridges and valleys occur and to construct a descriptor from this information. Let us consider $D(x, y, \theta)$ to be the pixel signal obtained at pixel P located at (x, y). $D(x, y, \theta)$ is a function of the direction θ such that:

$$D(x, y, \theta) = G_{(\mu, \lambda_1)}(x, y, \theta) - G_{(\mu, \lambda_2)}(x, y, \theta) \tag{2}$$

μ, λ_1 and λ_2 correspond to the standard-deviations of the Gaussians. At each pixel in the image patch, we are interested in the response of the DHSF at θ_{M_1}, θ_{M_2}, θ_{m_1} and θ_{m_2}. Where, θ_{M_1} and θ_{M_2} are the directions at which the local maxima of the function D occurs. $D(x, y, \theta_{M_1})$ and $D(x, y, \theta_{M_2})$ are the response of DHSF at θ_{M_1} and θ_{M_2}. θ_{m_1} and θ_{m_2} are the directions at which the local minima of the function D occurs. $D(x, y, \theta_{m_1})$ and $D(x, y, \theta_{m_2})$ are the response of DHSF at θ_{m_1} and θ_{m_2}.

Some examples of the signal $D(x, y, \theta)$ obtained by spinning the DHSF around the selected key-points extracted from the synthetic image are shown in Fig. 4. On a typical valley (point 1 in Fig. 4), the pixel signal at the minimum of a valley consists of at least two negative sharp peaks. For ridges (point

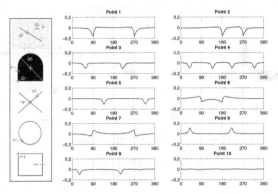

Fig. 4. Points selection on a synthetic image. Examples of functions $D(x, y, \theta)$ on the points selected on synthetic image using $\mu = 10, \lambda_1 = 1, \lambda_2 = 1.5$. *The x-axis corresponds to the value of θ (in degrees) and the y-axis to $D(x, y, \theta)$.*

7 in Fig. 4), the pixel signal at the maximum of a ridge contains at least two positive peaks. These sharp peaks correspond to the two directions of the curve (an entering and leaving path). In case of a junction, the number of peaks corresponds to the number of crest lines (ridges/valleys) in the junction (point 4 in Fig. 4). We obtain the same information for the bent lines (illustrated in point 2 on Fig. 4). Finally, due to the strong smoothing (parameter μ), D is close to 0 in the presence of noise without any crest line nor edge (illustrated in point 10 in Fig. 4). This illustrates the robustness of this method in the presence of noise.

4   Descriptor Construction

The descriptor construction process as shown in Fig. 5, in the initial stage, as in [4], for each detected key-point we follow the standard procedure to obtain the rotation and affine normalized gray level image patch. This normalization procedure is followed in the construction of all the descriptors (SIFT, DAISY, GLOH) used in our experiments. We consider this image patch as a 3D surface, with intensity being the 3rd dimension. As in Fig. 5, for each pixel in the image patch, we spin the DHSF and obtain a stack of DOG patches. From this stack of DOG patches, for each pixel we extract the signal $D(x, y, \theta)$ (for simplicity and proper viewing, in Fig. 5 signal is not shown and a stack of image patch is

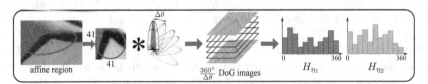

Fig. 5. Methodology involved in the construction of RSD-DOG descriptor.

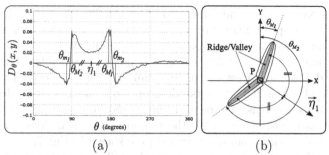

(a)   (b)

Fig. 6. (a) η_1 computation from θ_{M_1} and θ_{M_2}. (b) η_1 corresponds to the direction perpendicular to the ridge/valley at the level of a pixel P.

shown). From each signal we extract the four angles θ_{M_1}, θ_{M_2}, θ_{m_1}, θ_{m_2} and their corresponding responses $||D(x, y, \theta_{M_1})||$, $||D(x, y, \theta_{M_2})||$, $||D(x, y, \theta_{m_1})||$ and $||D(x, y, \theta_{m_2})||$. Once these informations are obtained, for each pixel P, we estimate the average angles η_1 and η_2 and there respective average magnitudes δ_1 and δ_2 by:

$$\begin{cases} \eta_1(x, y) = (\theta_{M_1} + \theta_{M_2})/2 \\ \eta_2(x, y) = (\theta_{m_1} + \theta_{m_2})/2 \\ \delta_1 = (||D(x, y, \theta_{M_1})|| + ||D(x, y, \theta_{M_2})||)/2 \\ \delta_2 = (||D(x, y, \theta_{m_1})|| + ||D(x, y, \theta_{m_2})||)/2 \end{cases}$$

The angle η_1 is weighed by δ_1 and η_2 by δ_2 and binned as in Eq. 3. Later, H_{η_1} and H_{η_2} are concatenated to form the final 256 length/dimension RSD-DOG descriptor.

$$\begin{cases} H_{\eta_1} = \{\eta_{1_{bin1}}, \eta_{1_{bin2}}, \eta_{1_{bin3}}, \eta_{1_{bin4}} \cdots\cdots \eta_{1_{bin128}}\} \\ H_{\eta_2} = \{\eta_{2_{bin1}}, \eta_{2_{bin2}}, \eta_{2_{bin3}}, \eta_{2_{bin4}} \cdots\cdots \eta_{2_{bin128}}\} \end{cases} \quad (3)$$

5   Experiments and Results

5.1   Dataset and Evaluation

Matlab platform is used for the experiments. Harris affine key points [4] were used for image patch extraction as well as the key points obtained from other detectors can also be used for extracting these image patches. We evaluate and compare the performance of our descriptor as against the state of the art descriptors on the standard dataset, using the standard protocol provided by the Oxford group. The binaries and dataset are publicly available on-line[1].

The dataset used in our experiments has different geometric and photometric transformations, such as, change of scale and image rotation (boat), viewpoint change (graf), image blur (bike), JPEG compression (compression) and illumination change (Leuven). For each type of the image transformation, there is

---

[1] http://www.robots.ox.ac.uk/~vgg/research/affine/

a set of six images with established ground truth homographies. In-order to study in detail the performance of our descriptor for changes in illumination, we also evaluated our descriptors on four image pairs, with complex illumination changes and the data set for the same is publicly available[2]. The complex illumination dataset has 4 set of images, namely 'desktop', 'corridor', 'square' and 'square root'. The first two sets, 'desktop' and 'corridor' have drastic illumination changes, whereas 'square' and 'square root' datasets are obtained by a square and square root operation on the second image of the 'desktop' set [22]. Some of the image pairs from both datasets are shown in Fig. 7.

The evaluation criterion used as proposed by [2], is based on the number of correspondences, correct matches and false matches between two images. Here, we test the descriptors using similarity threshold based matching, since this technique is better suited for representing the distribution of the descriptor in its feature space[2]. Due to the space limitation, we restrain from going into the details of this method. A detailed description of this method can be found in [2]. The results are presented using the recall vs 1-precision curves. As in Eq.4, recall is defined as the total number of correctly matched affine regions over the number of corresponding affine regions between two images of the same scene. From Eq.5, 1-precision is represented by the number of false matches relative to the total number of matches. In all our experiments, Euclidean distance is used as the distance measure.

$$\text{recall} = \frac{\text{Total No of correct matches}}{\text{No of correspondences}} \qquad (4)$$

$$\text{1-precision} = \frac{\text{No of false matches}}{\text{No of correct matches} + \text{No of false matches}} \qquad (5)$$

Our descriptor depends on 5 different parameters: $\Delta\theta$, $No-of-bins$, μ, λ_1 and λ_2. The rotation step $\Delta\theta$ is fixed to $10°$. Increasing the rotation step results in loss of information. As in [1] the image patch is divided into 16 blocks. All blocks are of the size 10x10 (Since we are using a patch of size 41x41, the blocks in the extreme right and bottom have 11x11 size). As in [1], the number of bins ($No-of-bins$) is fixed to 8 per block, resulting in a $8 * 16 = 128$ bins for 16 blocks. Increasing the number of bins results in same performance as in previous case, but it increases the dimensionality of the descriptor. Filter height μ is fixed to 6. As in [1], for DHSF the ratio between successive scales is fixed to $\sqrt{2}$. So, filter widths λ_1 and λ_2 are fixed to 2 and $2\sqrt{2}$ respectively. In our experiments, we obtain state of art results by using just two scales. Height ($\mu = 6$) and Width ($\lambda_1 = 2$, $\lambda_2 = 2\sqrt{2}$) parameters are chosen to have a ratio sharpness length that is suitable for robust second order feature detection [18], which generally gives good results in most cases. This ratio is compatible with the angle filtering step.

5.2   Descriptor Performance

In our experiments, we have used two variations of our descriptor (1) RSD-DOG (2-SCALES) with height $\mu = 6$ and width $\lambda = 2, 2\sqrt{2}$ respectively. This has

---

[2] http://zhwang.me/publication/liop/

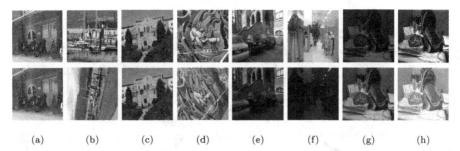

(a)   (b)   (c)   (d)   (e)   (f)   (g)   (h)

Fig. 7. A few examples of image pairs used in our evaluations. Images in the first column (a) has variations in blur (BIKE), second column (b) has changes in rotation (BOAT), third column (c) has compression changes, fourth column (d) has changes in view-point (GRAFF). Images in the fifth, sixth and seventh column have variations in illumination((e) LUEVEN, (f) CORRIDOR, (g) DESKTOP, (h) SQUARE-ROOT).

a dimension of 256. (2) RSD-DOG (3-SCALES) with height $\mu = 6$ and width $\lambda = 2, 2\sqrt{2}, 4$ respectively. Here, in step one, we smooth the image patch with $\mu = 6$, $\lambda_1 = 2$ and $\lambda_2 = 2\sqrt{2}$ to obtain a 256 length descriptor. In the second step, we smooth the image patch with $\mu = 6$, $\lambda_1 = 2\sqrt{2}$ and $\lambda_2 = 4$ and obtain another 256 length descriptor. Lastly, we concatenate the two parts to form a 512 size RSD-DOG(3-SCALES) descriptor.

The performance of these two variants of RSD-DOG is compared with the performance of SIFT, GLOH, DAISY, GIST and LIDRIC descriptors. For SIFT and GLOH, the descriptors are extracted from the binaries provided by Oxford group. For DAISY descriptor, the patches are extracted from the code provided by [3]. The matlab code for GIST and LIDRIC descriptors were obtained from [4] and [5] respectively.

For changes in rotation, viewpoint, blur and compression both variants of the RSD-DOG shows better performance than the other 5 descriptors. The precision vs (1-recall) plots in the first 4 rows of the Fig. 8 illustrates the superiority of our descriptor. Image pair graf(1-5) is a complex image pair. As a result, performance of all the descriptors deteriorates. It should be noted that, in most of the cases, RSD-DOG (3-SCALES) performs similar to or slightly better than that of RSD-DOG (2-SCALES). So, increasing the number of scales increases the complexity and descriptor dimension with very little gain in performance. For variations in illumination, in all cases, both the variants of RSD-DOG performs consistently better than all the other descriptors. When it comes to 'square' and 'square root' images SIFT, DAISY, LIDRIC and GIST descriptors exhibit poor performance and GLOH descriptor fails miserably. The graphs in the last 4 rows of Fig. 8, illustrate the superior nature of our descriptor for complex illumination changes.

---

[3] http://cvlab.epfl.ch/software/daisy

[4] http://people.csail.mit.edu/torralba/code/spatialenvelope/

[5] http://www.caa.tuwien.ac.at/cvl/project/ilac/

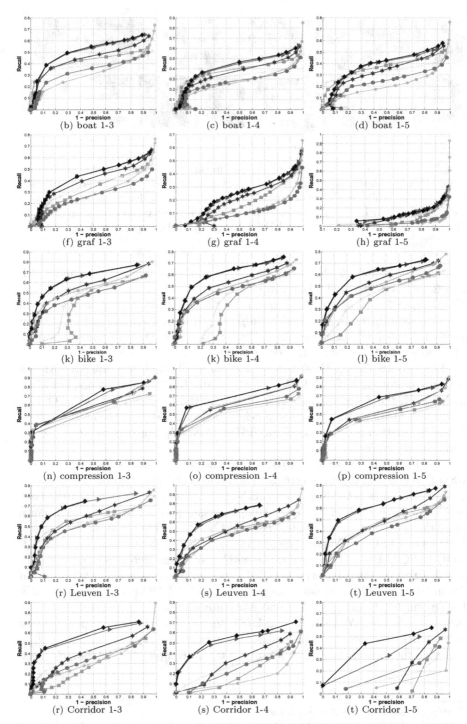

Fig. 8. Recall vs 1-Precision curves for SIFT, GLOH, DAISY, GIST, LIRDC and RSD-DOG. Similarity matching is used for evaluation.

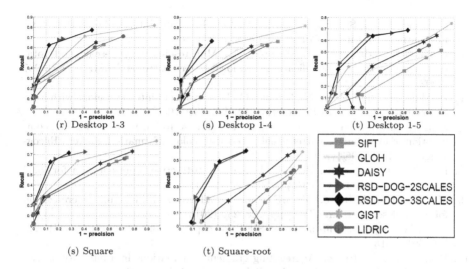

(r) Desktop 1-3   (s) Desktop 1-4   (t) Desktop 1-5

(s) Square   (t) Square-root

Fig. 8. (*Continued*)

6   Conclusion

The paper proposes a novel image patch descriptor based on second order statistics such as ridges, valleys, basins and so on. The originality of our method lies in combining the response of directional filter with that of the Difference of Gaussian (DOG) approach. One of the advantage of the proposed descriptor is the dimension/length. Our descriptor has a dimension of 256, which is almost 2 to 4 times less than other descriptors based on second order statistics. The experiments on complex illumination dataset illustrates the robustness of our descriptor to complex illumination changes. On the standard dataset provided by the Oxford group our descriptor outperforms SIFT, GLOH, DAISY, GIST and LIDRIC. In the future, we would like to use our descriptors for applications related to object detection, classification and image retrial. Additionally, we would like to learn the parameters by introducing a learning stage. The speed of the descriptor generation can be boosted by parallel programming.

Acknowledgments. The work is funded by L'institut Mediterraneen des Metiers de la Longevite (I2ML).

References

1. Lowe, D.G.: Distinctive Image Features from Scale-Invariant Keypoints. International Journal of Computer Vision (IJCV) **60**, 91–110 (2004)
2. Mikolajczyk, K., Schmid, C.: A Performance Evaluation of Local Descriptors. IEEE Trans. Pattern Anal. Mach. Intell, 1615–1630 (2005)
3. Tola, E., Lepetit, V., Fua, P.: DAISY: An Efficient Dense Descriptor Applied to Wide Baseline Stereo. TPAMI **32**, 815–830 (2010)

4. Mikolajczyk, K., Schmid, C.: Scale & Affine Invariant Interest Point Detectors. International Journal of Computer Vision (IJCV) **60**, 63–86 (2004)
5. Ojala, T., Pietikainen, M., Maenpaa, T.: Multiresolution gray-scale and rotation invariant texture classification with local binary patterns. PAMI **24**, 971–987 (2002)
6. Heikkila, M., Pietikainen, M., Schmid, C.: Description of interest regions with local binary patterns. Pattern Recognition **42**, 425–436 (2009)
7. Zhu, C., Bichot, C.-E., Chen, L.: Image region description using orthogonal combination of local binary patterns enhanced with color information. Pattern Recognition **46**, 1949–1963 (2013)
8. Ke, Y., Sukthankar, R.: PCA-SIFT: a more distinctive representation for local image descriptors. In: CVPR, pp. 506–513 (2004)
9. Ma, R., Chen, J., Su, Z.: MI-SIFT: mirror and inversion invariant generalization for SIFT descriptor. In: CIVR, pp. 228–235 (2010)
10. Zhao, W., Ngo, C.: Flip-invariant SIFT for copy and object detection. TIP **22**, 980–991 (2013)
11. Fan, B., Wu, F., Hu, Z.: Aggregating gradient distributions into intensity orders: a novel local image descriptor. In: CVPR, pp. 2377–2384 (2011)
12. Venkatrayappa, D., Montesinos, P., Diep, D., Magnier, B.: RSD-HoG: a new image descriptor. In: Paulsen, R.R., Pedersen, K.S. (eds.) SCIA 2015. LNCS, vol. 9127, pp. 400–409. Springer, Heidelberg (2015)
13. Eigenstetter, A., Ommer, B.: Visual recognition using embedded feature selection for curvature self-similarity. In: NIPS (2012)
14. Oliva, A., Torralba, A.: Modeling the Shape of the Scene: A Holistic Representation of the Spatial Envelope. IJCV **42**, 145–175 (2001)
15. Zambanini, S., Kampel, M.: A local image descriptor robust to illumination changes. In: Kämäräinen, J.-K., Koskela, M. (eds.) SCIA 2013. LNCS, vol. 7944, pp. 11–21. Springer, Heidelberg (2013)
16. Osadchy, M., Jacobs, D., Lindenbaum, M.: Surface dependent representations for illumination insensitive image comparison. PAMI **29**, 98–111 (2007)
17. Fischer, P., Brox, T.: Image descriptors based on curvature histograms. In: Jiang, X., Hornegger, J., Koch, R. (eds.) GCPR 2014. LNCS, vol. 8753, pp. 239–249. Springer, Heidelberg (2014)
18. Montesinos, P., Magnier, B.: A new perceptual edge detector in color images. In: Advanced Concepts for Intelligent Vision Systems (2010)
19. Magnier, B., Montesinos, P., Diep, D.: Texture removal by pixel classification using a rotating filter. In: ICASS (2011)
20. Armande, N., Montesinos, P., Monga, O.: Thin nets extraction using a multi-scale approach. In: Scale-Space Theory in Computer Vision, pp. 361–36 (1997)
21. Magnier, B., Montesinos, P., Diep, D.: Ridges and valleys detection in images using difference of rotating half smoothing filters. In: Blanc-Talon, J., Kleihorst, R., Philips, W., Popescu, D., Scheunders, P. (eds.) ACIVS 2011. LNCS, vol. 6915, pp. 261–272. Springer, Heidelberg (2011)
22. Wang, Z., Fan, B., Wu, F.: Local intensity order pattern for feature description. In: ICCV, pp. 603–610 (2011)

Ringing Artifact Suppression Using Sparse Representation

Alexey V. Umnov, Andrey S. Krylov$^{(\boxtimes)}$, and Andrey V. Nasonov

Laboratory of Mathematical Methods of Image Processing, Faculty of Computational Mathematics and Cybernetics, Lomonosov Moscow State University, Moscow, Russia
kryl@cs.msu.ru

Abstract. The article refers to the problem of ringing artifact suppression. The ringing effect is caused by high-frequency information corruption or loss, it appears as waves or oscillations near strong edges. We propose a novel method for ringing artifact suppression after Fourier cut-off filtering. It can be also used for image deringing in the case of image resampling and other applications where the frequency loss can be estimated. The method is based on the joint sparse coding approach. The proposed method preserves more small image details than the state-of-the-art algorithms based on total variation minimization, and outperforms them in terms of image quality metrics.

Keywords: Ringing artifact · Ringing suppression · Sparse coding

1 Introduction

Gibbs phenomenon also known as ringing effect appears as waves or oscillations near strong edges. An example of ringing effect is shown in Fig. 1. The source of the ringing effect is high-frequency information corruption or loss [9]. It can be the result of many image processing algorithms and applications that change the high-frequency information, i.e. image and video compression, deblurring, resampling, denoising, and in analog video [16].

There are many papers that consider the problem of ringing effect detection and suppression in JPEG and JPEG2000 images [7,11]. On the other hand there are only few works that pose the problem of general ringing detection and suppression [13,17,23,24]. Suppression algorithms are based on the connection of ringing effect with total variation [9], and total variation minimization proposed for image enhancement in [21]. However these methods do not distinguish between ringing oscillations and small image details, thus these details are usually corrupted.

In this work we present a novel method for ringing suppression after Fourier cut-off filtering. It can be also used for image deringing in the case of image resampling and other applications where the frequency loss can be estimated. The method is based on sparse representation approach, widely used in many image processing tasks [3], including image quality enhancement problems.

© Springer International Publishing Switzerland 2015
S. Battiato et al. (Eds.): ACIVS 2015, LNCS 9386, pp. 35–45, 2015.
DOI: 10.1007/978-3-319-25903-1_4

The proposed method is based on the joint sparse coding method, which was previously used for image deblurring and image super-resolution [25]. The joint sparse coding method is described in detail in subsection 2.2.

Fig. 1. Example of the ringing effect: reference image (left) and image with ringing effect (right).

2   Ringing Suppression

2.1   Problem Formulation

Consider the ringing effect produced by high frequency cut-off filter R_d which removes all the frequencies in the Fourier domain outside the circular mask with radius $\omega_d = \frac{1}{2d}$ centered at zero frequency point:

$$R_d(\boldsymbol{I}) = \mathcal{F}^{-1}(\mathcal{F}(\boldsymbol{I}) \cdot \boldsymbol{l_d}),$$

where $\mathcal{F}$ and $\mathcal{F}^{-1}$ are Fourier transform and inverse Fourier transform respectively, $\boldsymbol{l_d}$ is the mask

$$\boldsymbol{l_d}(\omega_x, \omega_y) = \begin{cases} 1, \text{ if } & \sqrt{\omega_x^2 + \omega_y^2} \leq \omega_d, \\ 0, \text{ if } & \sqrt{\omega_x^2 + \omega_y^2} > \omega_d. \end{cases}$$

This filter produce ringing effect with oscillation width equal to d.

Let us denote the original image as $\boldsymbol{y_s}$ and the image with ringing effect as $\boldsymbol{y_r}$. Then

$$\boldsymbol{y_r} = R_d(\boldsymbol{y_s}).$$

Given $\boldsymbol{y_r}$, the problem of ringing suppression is to find $\hat{\boldsymbol{y}}_s$ so that $\hat{\boldsymbol{y}}_s \approx \boldsymbol{y_s}$. The problem is ill-posed, as the solution is not unique.

2.2   Joint Sparse Coding

In order to solve the problem of ringing suppression we use the joint sparse coding approach introduced by Yang et al. [25]. We assume that the original image can be sparsely represented in some dictionary D_s with sparsity α:

$$y_s = D_s x, \quad \|x\|_0 \leq \alpha.$$

We also assume that it is possible to recover the original sparse codes from the image with ringing effect. Therefore the image with the ringing effect can be sparsely represented in some dictionary D_r with the same codes:

$$y_r = D_r x.$$

If dictionaries D_s and D_r, and α are known, the ringing suppression procedure is done as follows. Given the image with the ringing effect y_r, the sparse representation problem with dictionary D_r is solved:

$$\hat{x} = \arg\min_x \|y_r - D_r x\|_2, \quad \text{s.t.} \quad \|x\|_0 \leq \alpha.$$

The vector $\hat{x}$ is the estimation of the sparse representation of the both y_s and y_r with the dictionaries D_s and D_r respectively. Thus it can be used to get the original image estimation:

$$\hat{y}_s = D_s \hat{x}.$$

However in the general case the dictionaries are not known so it is necessary to estimate them using dictionary learning procedure. This can be done using the training set of images with the ringing effect and the corresponding original images.

Denote Y_s as the matrix with original images as columns and Y_r as the matrix with the corresponding images with ringing effect as columns. Then the dictionary learning problem can be formulated as follows:

$$\min_{D_s, D_r, X} \|Y_s - D_s X\|_F^2 + \|Y_r - D_r X\|_F^2, \quad \text{s.t.} \quad \|X\|_{0,\inf} \leq \alpha,$$

where the $\|\cdot\|_{0,\inf}$ norm for the matrix X with columns $x_1, \ldots, x_n$ is defined as follows:

$$\|X\|_{0,\inf} = \max_{i=1,\ldots,n} \|x_i\|_0.$$

So the $\|X\|_{0,\inf} \leq \alpha$ condition effectively means that all representations are α-sparse.

Denoting

$$Y = \begin{bmatrix} Y_s \\ Y_r \end{bmatrix}$$

and

$$D = \begin{bmatrix} D_s \\ D_r \end{bmatrix},$$

the problem can be rewritten as

$$\min_{D,X} \|Y - DX\|_F^2, \quad \text{s.t.} \quad \|X\|_{0,\inf} \leq \alpha.$$

This problem can be solved using any sparse dictionary learning algorithm. In our work we use the K-SVD algorithm [1] for dictionary learning and OMP algorithm [10] for sparse coding.

2.3   Ringing Suppression Method

The proposed method requires a set of images for learning. We split all images into overlapping 6×6 blocks and process each block separately. The images from the learning set are used to create a set of corresponding original blocks and blocks with ringing effect. Then the joint dictionary learning procedure is applied to this set of samples.

The ringing suppression method uses learned joint dictionaries to get sparse codes of the blocks with ringing artifact and then to get the original block estimation from these codes. The resulting full image is composed from the estimated blocks by averaging the values in the overlapping areas.

In order to improve the ringing suppression performance we add several modifications to the joint sparse coding approach.

Regularization. In our preliminary experiments we have found that the method performs better when different sparsity parameter is used in learning and testing phase ($\alpha_{learn} = 10$ and $\alpha_{test} = 2$). We suppose that it is caused by the fact that the blocks with ringing effect are less informative than the ringing free blocks. Thus in the testing phase (when the method builds the representation only from the block with ringing) stronger regularization makes the method more stable.

Extending Dictionary by Rotations. Edges play the most important role in the ringing suppression problem because ringing effect is the most noticeable near strong edges. We have also discovered that some blocks with edges are not represented well enough in the testing phase due to absence of edges with approximately the same direction in the training set. In order to improve the performance for these blocks we extend the dictionaries by their rotated versions after the learning process. Denote the Rot_a as the operator that rotates all atoms in the dictionary by $a°$, then the extended dictionaries are built as follows (here D_s^{base}, D_r^{base} are the dictionaries obtained in the dictionary learning phase):

$$D_s = \left[D_s^{base}; Rot_{90}(D_s^{base}); Rot_{180}(D_s^{base}); Rot_{270}(D_s^{base})\right]$$

$$D_r = \left[D_r^{base}; Rot_{90}(D_r^{base}); Rot_{180}(D_r^{base}); Rot_{270}(D_r^{base})\right]$$

We use only these three rotations ($90°$, $180°$, $270°$) because they can be applied to the square images without introducing interpolation errors.

Postprocessing. The joint sparse coding approach provides good results in most parts of the image, but the total variation minimization approach [17] works better for edges. The total variation deringing method is formulated as the minimization problem

$$I_R = \arg\min_{I} \|I - I_0\|_2^2 + \lambda TV(I), \tag{1}$$

where I_0 is the given image with ringing effect, λ is the regularization parameter that controls the strength of ringing suppression, $TV(I)$ is the total variation of the image I:

$$TV(I) = \sum_{x,y} |\nabla I(x,y)|.$$

In order to improve the performance of the proposed method we merge the results of the joint sparse coding deringing and the results of the total variation minimization deringing. Denote the image obtained by joint sparse coding deringing as $I_{sc}(x,y)$, the image obtained by total variation minimization as $I_{tv}(x,y)$ and the distance from the nearest edge as $\rho(x,y)$ (see below). Then the final image is constructed as follows:

$$I(x,y) = \begin{cases} I_{tv}(x,y), \text{ if } \rho(x,y) \le 3; \\ I_{sc}(x,y), \text{ else.} \end{cases}$$

Thus the values on the edges are taken from the total variation minimization deringing method, and other values are taken from the joint sparse coding deringing method.

The set of edge pixels is constructed by Canny edge detection algorithm [2]. Then edge masking is applied to remove ringing oscillations and textures from the edge pixel set. We use edge masking approach from [14,15] and take only the edge pixels that match the condition

$$g(x_0, y_0) > \max_{x,y} g(x,y)\phi((x - x_0)^2 + (y - y_0)^2),$$

where $g(x,y)$ is the gradient modulus at pixel (x,y), $\phi(d^2) = \frac{1}{2}\exp\left(-\frac{d^2}{2\sigma^2}\right)$, σ is the parameter of Canny edge detection algorithm. We use $\sigma = 2$. The distance to the nearest edge is then calculated using eucludean distance transform [4].

3   Evaluation

We test our method using images from the MMIP Ringing Database [12]. This database uses the reference images from TID [20] and LIVE [22] databases and contains images with modeled ringing effect produced by different image processing methods. A subset of images containing strong edges is taken for the evaluation of the proposed algorithm.

For dictionary learning, we use 5 images (avion, bikes, boats, house, lighthouse) with ideal ringing effect produced by cut-off filter. Dictionaries are learned individually for each ringing parameter d.

The performance of the proposed algorithm is analyzed using images with ringing effect produced by cut-off filter and resampling algorithms. A weak white noise is also added to the test images in order to model the real ringing effect. We compare the proposed method with the method based on total variation minimization (1) with parameter λ maximizing the target metric. SSIM metric is used for measuring the performance of ringing suppression algorithms.

The comparison of the proposed method with total variation deringing is shown in Fig. 2 and Fig. 3. Both the proposed method and the method based on the total variation minimization suppress almost all ringing effect. Unlike the total variation minimization method, the proposed method preserves most of the small details. The proposed method is also able to reduce aliasing effect and make the edges smoother.

Numerical results for images with ringing effect produced by cut-off filter with $d = 2$ and $d = 2.5$ are shown in Table 1 and Table 2 respectively. The results of ringing suppression after resampling with a factor of 2 using regularization-based algorithm [8] are shown in Table 3. We base on the fact that for the problem of image resampling the ringing parameter d equals to the scale factor [14].

For the images 'barbara' and 'clown' from Table 3, the proposed method does not show satisfactory results in the areas containing a lot of parallel lines due to texture corruption during downsampling process.

Table 1. Results of the ringing suppression ($d = 2$) after high frequency cut-off, SSIM. Best value in each row is highlighted. The overall average value is given in the last row.

Image name	Ringing	TV-based	Proposed
cameraman	0.8924	0.9162	**0.9180**
caps	0.9319	0.9541	**0.9560**
house2	0.9282	0.9490	**0.9512**
peppers	0.9297	0.9482	**0.9509**
plane	0.9301	0.9491	**0.9497**
barbara	0.8223	0.8307	**0.8318**
clown	0.9223	0.9360	**0.9369**
lena	0.9400	0.9555	**0.9581**
lighthouse2	0.9030	0.9182	**0.9186**
mandarin	0.9260	0.9435	**0.9447**
monarch	0.9504	0.9748	**0.9753**
paintedhouse	0.8884	0.8988	**0.8998**
parrots	0.9491	0.9725	**0.9735**
Average	0.9164	0.9343	**0.9357**

The proposed algorithm takes d as the input parameter and assumes that the input image contains ringing effect. Application of the proposed method to images without ringing effect results in edge and texture smoothing, and the edge width [18] of sharp edges becomes equal to d.

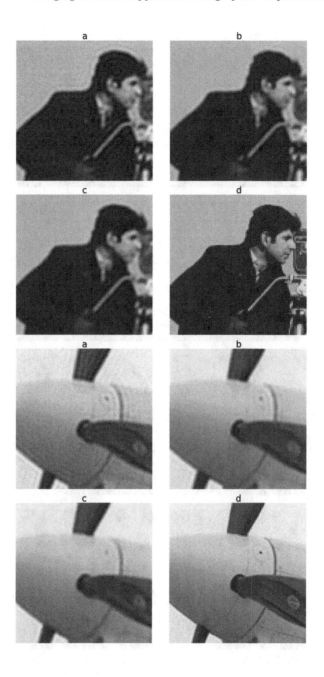

Fig. 2. Ringing suppression examples ($d = 2$) near edges for cameraman and plane images with ringing effect modeled by cut-off filter. a) Image with ringing, b) ringing suppression using total variation minimization, c) ringing suppression using the proposed method, d) reference image.

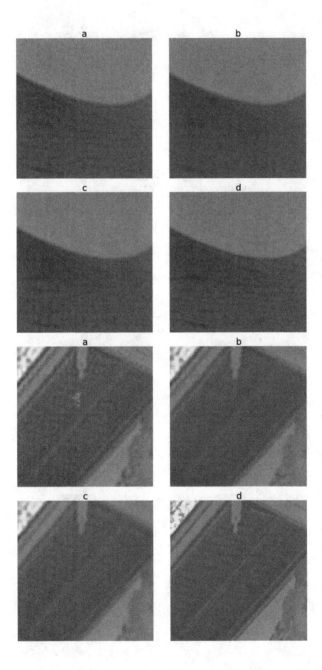

Fig. 3. Ringing suppression examples ($d = 2$) in areas with small details for caps and paintedhouse images. a) Image with ringing, b) ringing suppression using total variation minimization, c) ringing suppression using the proposed method, d) reference image.

Table 2. Results of the ringing suppression ($d = 2.5$) after high frequency cut-off, SSIM. Best value in each row is highlighted. The overall average value is given in the last row.

Image name	Ringing	TV-based	Proposed
cameraman	0.8600	0.8863	**0.9009**
caps	0.9148	0.9403	**0.9489**
house2	0.9144	0.9384	**0.9453**
peppers	0.9178	0.9394	**0.9460**
plane	0.9104	0.9316	**0.9395**
barbara	0.7987	0.8097	**0.8202**
clown	0.8975	0.9129	**0.9198**
lena	0.9239	0.9423	**0.9509**
lighthouse2	0.8684	0.8857	**0.8990**
mandarin	0.8918	0.9118	**0.9225**
monarch	0.9362	0.9621	**0.9662**
paintedhouse	0.8462	0.8584	**0.8739**
parrots	0.9378	0.9632	**0.9677**
Average	0.8937	0.9140	**0.9231**

Table 3. Results of the ringing suppression after resampling ($d = 2$), SSIM. Best value in each row is highlighted. The overall average value is given in the last row.

Image name	Ringing	TV-based	Proposed
cameraman	0.9200	0.9162	**0.9276**
caps	0.9591	0.9541	**0.9626**
house2	0.9489	0.9490	**0.9555**
peppers	0.9499	0.9482	**0.9527**
plane	0.9510	0.9491	**0.9580**
barbara	**0.8587**	0.8307	0.8533
clown	0.9294	**0.9360**	0.9298
lena	0.9576	0.9555	**0.9594**
lighthouse2	0.9218	0.9182	**0.9305**
mandarin	0.9478	0.9435	**0.9550**
monarch	0.9739	0.9747	**0.9748**
paintedhouse	0.9087	0.8988	**0.9185**
parrots	0.9761	0.9725	**0.9773**
Average	0.9387	0.9343	**0.9427**

4 Conclusion

A novel ringing suppression method has been presented. Its advantages are fine detail preserving including textures, almost all ringing oscillations removal and aliased edge smoothing. The open problems are automatic choosing the parameter d and testing on images with different sources of ringing artifacts.

Acknowledgments. The SciPy [6], Matplotlib [5] and Scikit-learn [19] Python libraries were used in this work.

The work was supported by the Russian Science Foundation grant no. 14-11-00308.

References

1. Aharon, M., Elad, M., Bruckstein, A.: K-SVD: An algorithm for designing over-complete dictionaries for sparse representation. IEEE Transactions on Signal Processing **54**(11), 4311–4322 (2006)
2. Canny, J.: A computational approach to edge detection. IEEE Trans. PAMI **8**, 679–714 (1986)
3. Elad, M., Figueiredo, M.A., Ma, Y.: On the role of sparse and redundant representations in image processing. Proceedings of the IEEE **98**(6), 972–982 (2010)
4. Fabbri, R., Costa, L.D.F., Torelli, J.C., Bruno, O.M.: 2D Euclidean distance transforms: a comparative survey. ACM Computing Surveys **40**(1), 2:1–2:44 (2008)
5. Hunter, J.D.: Matplotlib: A 2D graphics environment. Computing in Science & Engineering **9**(3), 90–95 (2007)
6. Jones, E., Oliphant, T., Peterson, P., et al.: SciPy: open source scientific tools for Python (2001). http://www.scipy.org/ (online accessed April 30, 2015)
7. Liu, H., Klomp, N., Heynderickx, I.: A perceptually relevant approach to ringing region detection. IEEE Transactions on Image Processing **19**(6), 1414–1426 (2010)
8. Lukin, A., Krylov, A., Nasonov, A.: Image interpolation by super-resolution. In: 16th International Conference Graphicon 2006, pp. 239–242. Novosibirsk Akademgorodok, Russia, July 2006
9. Mallat, S.: A Wavelet Tour of Signal Processing. Academic Press (1999)
10. Mallat, S.G., Zhang, Z.: Matching pursuits with time-frequency dictionaries. IEEE Transactions on Signal Processing **41**(12), 3397–3415 (1993)
11. Marziliano, P., Dufaux, F., Winkler, S., Ebrahimi, T.: Perceptual blur and ringing metrics: application to JPEG2000. Signal Processing: Image Communication **19**, 163–172 (2004)
12. MMIP Lab: MMIP Ringing Database (2015). http://imaging.cs.msu.ru/en/research/ringing/database
13. Mosleh, A., Langlois, J.M.P., Green, P.: Image deconvolution ringing artifact detection and removal via psf frequency analysis. In: Fleet, D., Pajdla, T., Schiele, B., Tuytelaars, T. (eds.) ECCV 2014, Part IV. LNCS, vol. 8692, pp. 247–262. Springer, Heidelberg (2014)
14. Nasonov, A.V., Krylov, A.S.: Finding areas of typical artifacts of image enhancement methods. Pattern Recognition and Image Analysis **21**(2), 316–318 (2011)
15. Nasonov, A.V., Krylov, A.S.: Image enhancement quality metrics. In: 21th International Conference on Computer Graphics GraphiCon 2011, pp. 128–131 (2011)
16. Nasonov, A.V., Krylov, A.S.: Edge quality metrics for image enhancement. Pattern Recognition and Image Analysis **22**(1), 346–353 (2012)
17. Nasonov, A.V., Krylov, A.S.: Adaptive image deringing. In: Proceedings of GraphiCon 2009, pp. 151–154 (2009)
18. Nasonova, A.A., Krylov, A.S.: Determination of image edge width by unsharp masking. Computational Mathematics and Modeling **25**(1), 72–78 (2014)
19. Pedregosa, F., Varoquaux, G., Gramfort, A., Michel, V., Thirion, B., Grisel, O., Blondel, M., Prettenhofer, P., Weiss, R., Dubourg, V., Vanderplas, J., Passos, A., Cournapeau, D., Brucher, M., Perrot, M., Duchesnay, E.: Scikit-learn: Machine learning in Python. Journal of Machine Learning Research **12**, 2825–2830 (2011)

20. Ponomarenko, N., Lukin, V., Zelensky, A., Egiazarian, K., Carli, M., Battisti, F.: TID2008-a database for evaluation of full-reference visual quality assessment metrics. Advances of Modern Radioelectronics **10**(4), 30–45 (2009)
21. Rudin, L., Osher, S., Fatemi, E.: Nonlinear total variation based noise removal algorithms. Physica D **60**, 259–268 (1992)
22. Sheikh, H.R., Wang, Z., Cormack, L., Bovik, A.C.: Live image quality assessment database rel. 2 (2005)
23. Sitdikov, I.T., Krylov, A.S.: Variational image deringing using varying regularization parameter. Pattern Recognition and Image Analysis **25**(1), 96–100 (2015)
24. Umnov, A.V., Nasonov, A.V., Krylov, A.S., Yong, D.: Sparse method for ringing artifact detection. In: 2014 12th International Conference on Signal Processing (ICSP), pp. 662–667. IEEE (2014)
25. Yang, J., Wright, J., Huang, T.S., Ma, Y.: Image super-resolution via sparse representation. IEEE Transactions on Image Processing **19**(11), 2861–2873 (2010)

Patch-Based Mathematical Morphology for Image Processing, Segmentation and Classification

Olivier Lézoray[(⊠)]

Normandie University, UNICAEN, ENSICAEN, GREYC UMR CNRS 6072,
Caen, France
olivier.lezoray@unicaen.fr

Abstract. In this paper, a new formulation of patch-based adaptive mathematical morphology is addressed. In contrast to classical approaches, the shape of structuring elements is not modified but adaptivity is directly integrated into the definition of a patch-based complete lattice. The manifold of patches is learned with a nonlinear bijective mapping, interpreted in the form of a learned rank transformation together with an ordering of vectors. This ordering of patches relies on three steps: dictionary learning, manifold learning and out of sample extension. The performance of the approach is illustrated with innovative examples of patch-based image processing, segmentation and texture classification.

1 Introduction

Mathematical Morphology (MM) is a powerful framework for nonlinear processing of images. Morphological operators are usually defined by using the concept of Structuring Elements (SEs), small subsets used to explore images. The output of a morphological filtering operation is then obtained by the interaction between the image and a given SE. This idea has been extended to grey scale images using the concept of complete lattices (orderings between the elements to be processed) and MM relies on the application of lattice theory to spatial structures in images. In classical MM, SEs remain the same for all points in the image domain, i.e., one single SE is used to process the whole image by translating it to every point in the image. Adaptive MM refers to morphological filtering techniques that adjust SEs to the local context of the image. With the need of more efficient morphological image processing operators, there has been recently much interest in the development of adaptive mathematical morphology (see [8] for a recent survey). Roughly, two types of adaptive MM can be considered [8,14,17]: i) location-adaptive MM: the shape of the structuring element depends on the location x in the image, ii) input-adaptive MM: the shape of the structuring element depends on local features extracted at the location x. In the same time, image processing using local patches has become very popular and was shown to be highly effective [6]. The processing proceeds by operating on the image patches and exploiting their similarities, making the processing

© Springer International Publishing Switzerland 2015
S. Battiato et al. (Eds.): ACIVS 2015, LNCS 9386, pp. 46–57, 2015.
DOI: 10.1007/978-3-319-25903-1_5

much more adaptive to the image. Patches being simply feature vectors locally describing a pixel at a given location in the image, some authors have considered the use of patches within adaptive morphological operators.

Ta *et al.* [20–22] were the first to propose the use of patches for MM processing. They have proposed a framework for adapting continuous MM on discrete graph structures and the adaptivity is input-adaptive at two levels: the shape of the SE is expressed by the graph topology that depends on a patch nearest neighbor graph, and the PDE morphological process is also adaptive by incorporating weights into it. Other works have followed and considered the algebraic formulation of MM. In [19], Salembier has introduced flat MM with adaptive SE obtained from a patch nearest neighbor graph (this is a special case of [20–22]) and non-flat MM with patch similarities incorporated into the SE. Then, Velasco-Forero and Angulo [25] have recast the works of Salembier in the general framework of adaptive MM and presented their necessary properties to be considered as algebraic MM operators. Recently, in [26] Yang and Li have considered a new type of adaptive SE based on amoeba SE combining local geodesic distance and non-local patch distance for spatially variant morphological filters.

In this paper we consider a radically different approach for patch-based adaptive MM. Indeed, in these patch-adaptive MM approaches the shape of the SE is classically modified to account for patch similarities. Since MM is based on complete lattices, we can instead integrate the adaptivity directly into the definition of the complete lattice and therefore define an ordering relationship between patches. To deal with this difficult objective, we build upon our previous work [13] that constructs complete lattices in vector spaces as a rank transform learned through a nonlinear mapping. In the next section we show how complete lattice construction by learning the patch manifold can be performed. Then we show the benefit of our approach for patch-based morphological image processing, segmentation and texture classification.

2   Patch Complete Lattice Learning

2.1   Complete Lattice from Patches

An image is represented by the mapping $f : \Omega \subset \mathbb{Z}^l \to \mathcal{T} \subset \mathbb{R}^n$ where l is the image dimension, n the number of channels, and $\mathcal{T}$ is a non-empty set of the image multivariate vectors. To each pixel $x_i \in \Omega$ of an image is associated a vector $\mathbf{v}_i = f(x_i)$. We denote as $\mathcal{P}$ the vector space of patches of width w associated to pixels of f, which is represented as the mapping: $F_w : \Omega \subset \mathbb{Z}^l \to \mathcal{P} \subset \mathbb{R}^{nw^2}$. One has $\mathbf{p}_i^w = F_w(x_i) = \left(f(x_i + t), \forall t \in [-w/2, w/2]^2\right)^T$. Performing MM operations for functions on patch vector spaces therefore requires the definition of a complete lattice $(\mathcal{P}, \leq)$ [18] which means that we have to be able to compare patches to order them. Comparing color vectors to define color complete lattice being already difficult [3], one easily see that defining a complete lattice for patches' vectors is much more challenging (a classical lexicographic ordering [2] being obviously of no interest). One way to define an ordering relation between vectors of a set $\mathcal{T}$ is to use the framework of h-orderings [10]. This corresponds to defining a surjective transform h from $\mathcal{T}$ to $\mathcal{L}$ where $\mathcal{L}$ is a complete lattice equipped with the conditional total ordering [10]. We refer to $\leq_h$ as the h-ordering given by:

$$h : \mathcal{T} \to \mathcal{L} \text{ and } \mathbf{v} \to h(\mathbf{v}), \forall (\mathbf{v}_i, \mathbf{v}_j) \in \mathcal{T} \times \mathcal{T}, \quad \mathbf{v}_i \leq_h \mathbf{v}_j \Leftrightarrow h(\mathbf{v}_i) \leq h(\mathbf{v}_j) . \quad (1)$$

Then, $\mathcal{T}$ is no longer required to be a complete lattice, since the ordering of $\mathcal{T}$ can be induced upon $\mathcal{L}$ by means of h [3]. When h is bijective, this corresponds to defining a space filling curve [7] or equivalently a rank transform [12]. We propose to adapt the h-ordering framework to our problem of complete lattice construction from patches for morphological image processing. Since a unique patch $\mathbf{p}_i^w \in \mathcal{P}$ is associated to a given vector $\mathbf{v}_i \in \mathcal{T}$ (and vice-versa), a complete lattice $(\mathcal{T}, \leq_h^w)$ can be directly deduced from a complete lattice of patches $(\mathcal{P}, \leq_h^w)$: $\mathbf{v}_i \leq_h^w \mathbf{v}_j \Leftrightarrow \mathbf{p}_i^w \leq_h^w \mathbf{p}_j^w$. This means that vectors of $\mathcal{T}$ can be ordered using a patch comparison and we obtain a patch adaptive complete lattice definition for all the vectors of the image. We denote by $\mathbf{p}^w(\mathbf{v}_i)$ the patch of width w associated to a vector $\mathbf{v}_i$. We obtain the following patch-based complete lattice $(\mathcal{T}, \leq_h^w)$ definition:

$$h^w : \mathcal{T} \to \mathcal{L} \text{ and } \mathbf{v} \to h(\mathbf{p}^w(\mathbf{v}))$$

$$\forall (\mathbf{p}^w(\mathbf{v}_i), \mathbf{p}^w(\mathbf{v}_j)) \in \mathcal{P} \times \mathcal{P} \text{ associated to } (\mathbf{v}_i, \mathbf{v}_j) \in \mathcal{T} \times \mathcal{T}$$

$$\mathbf{v}_i \leq_h \mathbf{v}_j \Leftrightarrow h^w(\mathbf{p}^w(\mathbf{v}_i)) \leq h^w(\mathbf{p}^w(\mathbf{v}_j)) . \quad (2)$$

The question is now on how to construct the mapping h^w to compare patches. It is obvious that h^w cannot be linear [16] since a distortion of the space topology is inevitable. As a consequence, we choose to focus our developments on learning the patch manifold to construct h^w to compare patches.

2.2   Complete Lattice Learning

We show how to construct a h^w-ordering for patches extracted from an image. This is an adaptation of our previous works [13] and we summarize its principle in the sequel, the whole approach being detailed in the form of an algorithm in Algorithm 1. The approach consists in learning the manifold of patches with a non linear mapping from a given image and to define the patch h^w-ordering from this projection. To learn the manifold of patches, we use Laplacian EigenMaps (LE), a technique for non-linear dimensionality reduction [11]. Computationally, performing LE on the whole space of patches is not tractable in reasonable time, so we use a four-step strategy that enables us to construct efficiently a h^w-ordering. Given an image $f : \Omega \to \mathcal{T} \subset \mathbb{R}^n$ that provides a set $\mathcal{T}$ of m vectors in $\mathbb{R}^n$, a sampling (both regular and random) is performed on the set $\mathcal{P}$ of all m patches of f to obtain a smaller $\mathcal{P}'$ (but representative) set of m' patches. From $\mathcal{P}'$, a dictionary $\mathcal{D} = \{\mathbf{x}_1', \cdots, \mathbf{x}_p'\}$ of p vectors is build by Vector Quantization [9]. Manifold learning by Laplacian EigenMaps is performed on this dictionary. One starts by computing a similarity matrix $\mathbf{K}_\mathcal{D}$ that contains the pairwise similarities $K_\mathcal{D}(i, j)$ between all the dictionary vectors $\mathbf{x}_i'$. To have a parameter-free algorithm, σ is set to the maximum distance between input vectors. The normalized Laplacian matrix $\mathbf{L} = \mathbf{I} - \mathbf{D}_{\mathcal{D}}^{-\frac{1}{2}} \mathbf{K}_{\mathcal{D}} \mathbf{D}_{\mathcal{D}}^{-\frac{1}{2}}$ is then computed. Laplacian Eigenmaps Manifold Learning consists in searching for a new representation $\mathbf{Y}$ obtained by minimizing $\frac{1}{2} \sum_{ij} \|\mathbf{y}_i - \mathbf{y}_j\|_2 K_{\mathcal{D}}(i,j) = Tr(\mathbf{Y}^T \mathbf{L} \mathbf{Y})$ under the constraint $\mathbf{Y}^T \mathbf{D} \mathbf{Y} = \mathbf{I}$. This cost function encourages nearby sample vectors to be mapped to nearby outputs. The solution is obtained [5] by finding the eigenvectors $\mathbf{\Phi}_{\mathcal{D}}$ of $\mathbf{L}$. This obtained projection operator corresponds to constructing a $h_{\mathcal{D}}$-ordering from the data of the dictionary $\mathcal{D}$ and a new representation $h_{\mathcal{D}}^w(\mathbf{x}'_i)$ is obtained for each element $\mathbf{x}'_i$ of the dictionary:

$$h_{\mathcal{D}}^w : \mathbf{x}'_i \rightarrow (\phi_{\mathcal{D}}^1(\mathbf{x}'_i), \cdots, \phi_{\mathcal{D}}^p(\mathbf{x}'_i))^T \in \mathbb{R}^p \ . \tag{3}$$

Such a strategy of modeling the manifold from a patch dictionary was also explored in [16]. This correspond to the construction of the complete lattice $(\mathcal{D}, \leq_{h_{\mathcal{D}}^w})$ with a $h_{\mathcal{D}}^w$-ordering, and this ordering is only valid for the set of patches of the dictionary. Since we need the complete lattice $(\mathcal{P}, \leq_h^w)$, the reduced dictionary lattice is extended to all the patches of the initial lattice $\mathcal{P}$ by Nyström extrapolation [23] of $h_{\mathcal{D}}^w$ on $\mathcal{P}$, and the complete lattice $(\mathcal{P}, \leq_h^w)$ is obtained as $h^w : \mathbf{p}^w(\mathbf{v}_i) \rightarrow (\phi^1(\mathbf{p}^w(\mathbf{v}_i)), \cdots, \phi^p(\mathbf{p}^w(\mathbf{v}_i)))^T \in \mathbb{R}^p$. From this complete lattice on patches, is deduced the patch-based complete lattice $(\mathcal{T}, \leq_h^w)$ on the initial vectors of f.

2.3   Patch-Based MM Operators

Given the patch-based complete lattice $(\mathcal{T}, \leq_h^w)$, we sort all vectors of f according to $\leq_h^w$ (the conditional total ordering on $h^w(\mathbf{x})$) and obtain a sorted image f_h^w. This sorted image $f_h^w : [1, m] \rightarrow \mathbb{R}^n$ defines the ordering of the vectors of f. This corresponds to a view of the learned complete lattice $(\mathcal{T}, \leq_h^w)$. From this ordering, we can deduce the rank of a vector on the complete lattice $\mathcal{L}$ defined as $r : \mathbb{R}^p \rightarrow [1, m]$, and construct a rank image as

$$f_r : \Omega \rightarrow [1, m], \text{ with } f_r(x_i) = (r \circ h^w \circ f)(x_i), \forall x_i \in \Omega \ . \tag{4}$$

In addition, we have also the definition of the inverse

$$(h^w)^{-1}(x_i) = (f_h^w \circ r)(x_i), \forall x_i \in \Omega \tag{5}$$

which is unique. With these elements, the original image f is now represented by the rank image f_r and the ordering of the pixels' vectors f_h^w. The original image f is recovered exactly since $f(x_i) = (f_h^w \circ f_r)(x_i), \forall x_i \in \Omega$. This shows that each pixel x_i vector is recovered by getting its corresponding vector in the Look-Up-Table f_h^w with the index $f_r(x_i)$. Given a specific morphological processing g, the corresponding processed multivariate image is obtained by

$$g(f(x_i)) = (f_h^w \circ g \circ f_r)(x_i), \forall x_i \in \Omega \ . \tag{6}$$

Algorithm 1. Learning the Patch-based h^w-ordering

Inputs:

Image $f : \Omega \subset \mathbb{Z}^l \to \mathcal{T} \subset \mathbb{R}^n$

Set $\mathcal{T}$ of m input multivariate vectors $\mathbf{v}_i$ of f

Set $\mathcal{P}$ of m patches $\mathbf{p}^w(\mathbf{v}_i)$ extracted from f

Step 1: Patch Sampling

Construct from $\mathcal{P}$, by sampling, a new set $\mathcal{P}' = \{\mathbf{x}_1, \dots, \mathbf{x}_{m'}\} \subset \mathcal{P}$ of m' patches

Step 2: Patch Dictionary Construction

Build from $\mathcal{P}'$, by VQ, a patch dictionary $\mathcal{D} = \{\mathbf{x}'_1, \dots, \mathbf{x}'_p\}$ with $p \ll m'$

Step 3: Patch Manifold Learning on the dictionary

Compute the similarity matrix $\mathbf{K}_\mathcal{D}$ between vectors $\mathbf{x}'_i \in \mathcal{D}$ with

$$K_\mathcal{D}(i,j) = k(\mathbf{x}'_i, \mathbf{x}'_j) = \exp\left(-\frac{\|\mathbf{x}'_i - \mathbf{x}'_j\|_2^2}{\sigma^2}\right) \text{ with } \sigma = \max_{(\mathbf{x}'_i, \mathbf{x}'_j) \in \mathcal{D}} \|\mathbf{x}'_i - \mathbf{x}'_j\|_2^2$$

Compute the degree diagonal matrix $\mathbf{D}_\mathcal{D}$ of $\mathbf{K}_\mathcal{D}$

Compute the eigen-decomposition of the normalized Laplacian

$\mathbf{L} = \mathbf{I} - \mathbf{D}_\mathcal{D}^{-\frac{1}{2}} \mathbf{K}_\mathcal{D} \mathbf{D}_\mathcal{D}^{-\frac{1}{2}}$ as $\mathbf{L} = \mathbf{\Phi}_\mathcal{D} \mathbf{\Pi}_\mathcal{D} \mathbf{\Phi}_\mathcal{D}^T$

with eigenvectors $\mathbf{\Phi}_\mathcal{D} = [\mathbf{\Phi}_\mathcal{D}^1, \cdots, \mathbf{\Phi}_\mathcal{D}^p]$ and eigenvalues $\mathbf{\Pi}_\mathcal{D} = \text{diag}[\lambda_1, \cdots, \lambda_p]$

Step 4: Extrapolation of the projection $\mathbf{\Phi}_\mathcal{D}$ to all the patches of $\mathcal{P}$

Compute similarity matrices $\mathbf{K}_\mathcal{P}$ on $\mathcal{P}$ and $\mathbf{K}_{\mathcal{D}\mathcal{P}}$ between sets $\mathcal{D}$ and $\mathcal{P}$

Compute the degree diagonal matrix $\mathbf{D}_{\mathcal{D}\mathcal{P}}$ of $\mathbf{K}_{\mathcal{D}\mathcal{P}}$

Extrapolate eigenvectors obtained from $\mathcal{D}$ to $\mathcal{P}$ with

$$\mathbf{\Phi} = \mathbf{D}_{\mathcal{D}\mathcal{P}}^{-\frac{1}{2}} \mathbf{K}_{\mathcal{D}\mathcal{P}}^T \mathbf{D}_\mathcal{D}^{-\frac{1}{2}} \mathbf{\Phi}_\mathcal{D} (\text{diag}[\mathbb{1}] - \mathbf{\Pi}_\mathcal{D})^{-1}$$

Output:

The projection $h_w : \mathcal{T} \subset \mathbb{R}^n \to \mathcal{L} \subset \mathbb{R}^p$ is given by $\mathbf{\Phi}$ and defines the h^w-ordering.

We can now formulate the corresponding h^w-erosion $\epsilon_{h^w,B}$ and h^w-dilation $\delta_{h^w,B}$ of an image f at pixel $x_i \in \Omega$ by the structuring element $B \subset \Omega$ as:

$$\epsilon_{h^w,B}(f)(x_i) = \{f_h^w(\wedge f_r(p_j)), p_j \in B(x)\} = \{f_h^w(\epsilon_B(f_r)(x_i))\} \tag{7}$$

and

$$\delta_{h^w,B}(f)(x_i) = \{f_h^w(\vee f_r(p_j)), p_j \in B(x)\} = \{f_h^w(\delta_B(f_r)(x_i))\} \tag{8}$$

with ϵ_B and δ_B the classical erosion and dilation on scalar images. This shows that the MM operators operate on the ranks f_r, and the image is reconstructed through the sorted vectors f_h^w that represent the learned lattice. It is easy to see that these operators inherit the standard algebraic properties of morphological operators since they fit into the theory of h-adjunctions [24]. From these basic operators, we can obtain many morphological filters such as the h^w-openings and h^w-closings:

$$\gamma_{h^w,B}(f) = \delta_{h^w,B}(\epsilon_{h^w,B}(f)) = f_h^w(\delta_B(\epsilon_B(f_r))) \tag{9}$$

$$\phi_{h^w,B}(f) = \epsilon_{h^w,B}(\delta_{h^w,B}(f)) = f_h^w(\epsilon_B(\delta_B(f_r))) \tag{10}$$

3   Applications

To illustrate the benefit of the approach, we provide several examples of its use for morphological image processing, image segmentation and texture classification.

In all the experiments, the number of elements of the dictionary $\mathcal{D}$ depends on the number m' of vectors sampled from the original image and it is automatically fixed to $p = 2^k$ with k the largest integer value such that $2^k \leq \sqrt{m'}/8$. When colors are considered instead of patches (in this case $w = 1$), no sampling is performed and $m' = m$.

3.1 Color Image Processing

To illustrate our approach, we consider a color image $f : \Omega \to \mathcal{T} \subset \mathbb{R}^3$. The complete lattice is learned from the image and we obtain both rank $f_r : \Omega \to [1, m]$ and ordering $f_h^w : [1, m] \to \mathbb{R}^3$. Then, we compute the following morphological operators: h^w-erosion $\epsilon_{h^w, B}$, h^w-dilation $\delta_{h^w, B}$, h^w-opening $\gamma_{h^w, B}$, h^w-closing $\phi_{h^w, B}(f)$, h^w-morphological gradient $\nabla_{h^w, B}(f) = \delta_B(f_r) - \epsilon_B(f_r)$, and h^w-white top hat. To see the effect of using a patch lattice instead of of color lattice, we learn the lattice either directly from color vectors ($w = 1$) or color 3×3 patches ($w = 3$). Figure 1 presents the results. Second line shows the dictionary $\mathcal{D}$ and the extrapolated manifold eigenvectors Φ (shown on the three first axis). Third line presents the induced learned lattice illustrated by the rank and the ordering. As it can be seen, with the learned color lattice, we recover the classical aspects of MM operators: erosion contracts structures of color far from first color (black) of the complete lattice. Dilation provides the dual effect and extends structures of color close to last color (white) of the complete lattice. If we now compare the results between a color and a patch lattice, with a patch-based ordering, the simplification effect is less strong and texture is much better preserved and sharper results are obtained. Meanwhile the patch-based morphological processing still exhibits the dual effect between both opening and closing filters. Finally, patch-based gradient and white top hat provide much contrasted results than color ones. Figure 2 presents results of an opening by reconstruction with the classical lexicographic ordering and our proposed learned complete lattice from color and patches. The patch-based processing shows again much better results: the images have been strongly simplified but the color and texture are much coherent and better preserved than with the other lattices.

3.2 Color Image Segmentation

To further show the interest of a patch-based processing, we consider its application for image segmentation. Figure 3 presents such results. From the original image, morphological gradients are computed with the classical lexicographic ordering and our proposed approach from color and patches of different sizes. One can see (first row of Figure 3) on the patch based gradient images that, in areas of similar textures no high gradient values are found whereas in the color based gradients, high gradient values are found at strong color variations. In addition, the patch-based gradients become smoother as the patch size grows, assessing the capture of larger texture cues. Then, region seeds are superimposed interactively (second row of Figure 3). Using the gradients and the seeds, a marker controlled watershed is computed on the considered gradients (last row

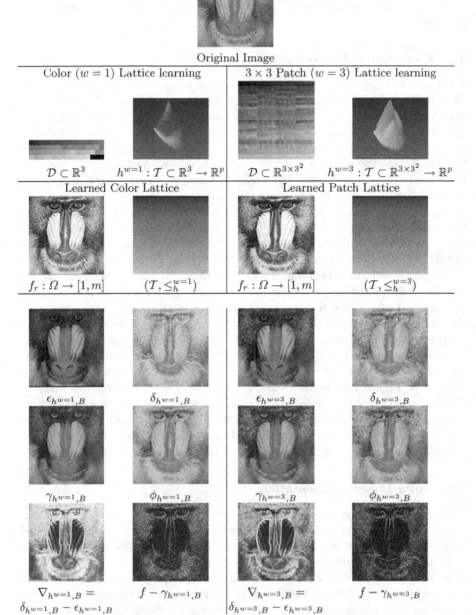

Fig. 1. Morphological processing of color images with a learned complete lattice from colors ($h^{w=1}$) or 3×3 patches ($h^{w=3}$). The structuring element is a circle of radius 5.

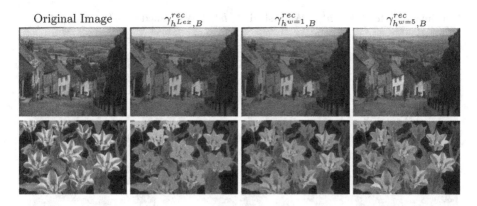

Fig. 2. Opening by reconstruction of color images by lexicographic color lattice (h^{Lex}) or learned complete lattice from color ($h^{w=1}$) and 5×5 patches ($h^{w=5}$). The marker image is obtained from an erosion in the same lattice with a square structuring element of side 11 pixels.

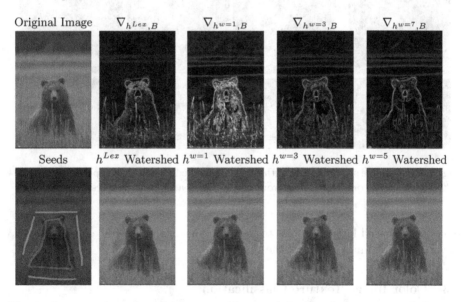

Fig. 3. Segmentation of a color image with a seeded watershed on a morphological gradient computed from lexicographic color lattice (h^{Lex}) or learned complete lattice from color ($h^{w=1}$), 3×3 patches ($h^{w=3}$), and 7×7 patches ($h^{w=7}$).

of Figure 3). The interest of a patch based processing appears then evident since it enables to obtain a smoother and more precise segmentation.

Figure 4 presents three additional MM segmentation from seeds. Only large patches are now considered as they exhibited good results in Figure 3. The results of the learned color lattice are slightly better than with lexicographic ordering,

Color image with seeds h^{Lex} Watershed $h^{w=1}$ Watershed $h^{w=7}$ Watershed

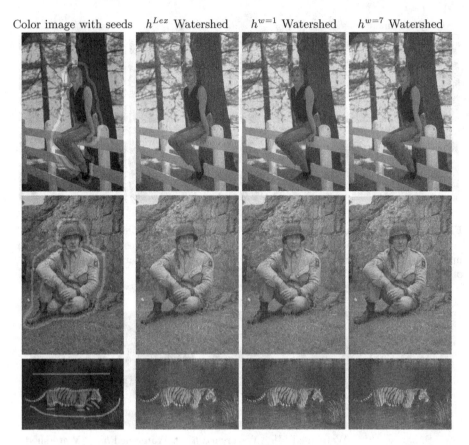

Fig. 4. Color image segmentation with a seed watershed from lexicographic color lattice (h^{Lex}) or learned complete lattice from color ($h^{w=1}$) and 7×7 patches ($h^{w=7}$).

but a patch based lattice enables to better delineate the objects' contours, even in very difficult images such as the tiger one.

3.3 Color Image Texture Classification

For color image texture classification, we consider the color textures of Outex13 [15]. This set contains 68 textures where every image has been divided into 20 non-overlapping sub-images each of size 128×128, thus providing a total of 1360 images, which have been evenly divided as training and test sets. We employ the morphological covariance as a texture descriptor [1]. Morphological covariance K' of an image f is defined as the volume Vol of the image (i.e., the sum of pixel values), eroded by a pair of points $P_{2,v}$ separated by a vector v (the SE is composed of only two pixels): $K'(f, P_{2,v}) = Vol(\epsilon_{P_{2,v}}(f))$. In practice K' is computed for varying length of v and the normalized version K is used for measurements: $K(f) = Vol(\epsilon_{P_{2,v}}(f))/Vol(f)$. The covariance based feature

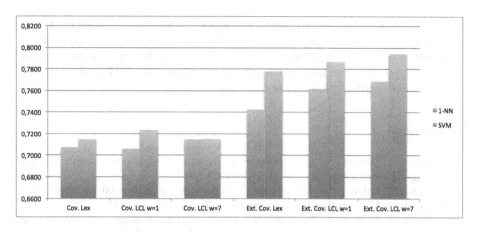

Fig. 5. Comparison between 1-Nearest Neighbor and SVM texture classification with Morphological covariances (Cov.) and extended covariances (Ext. Cov.) with lexicographic color lattice h^{Lex} or Learned Complete Lattice (LCL) from color ($h^{w=1}$) and 7×7 patches ($h^{w=7}$).

vector that describes a color image texture is computed using four directions $(0°, 45°, 90°, 135°)$ with distances ranging from 1 to 49 pixels in steps of size two. So, 25 values are available for the 4 directions on the 3 color channel making a vector of 300 values to describe an image. We also consider the extended MM covariance formulation of [4] that consider the concatenated results of three types of SEs (2 points, a cross, a square) within a 3×3 square, providing a vector of 900 values. With the obtained feature set, we considered two classifiers: a 1-nearest neighbor and a SVM. Figure 5 presents the classification accuracies. For classical covariance that uses SEs of only 2 points, the results are relatively close but better results are obtained with a learned complete lattice from colors. In this case there is no strong benefit in the use of patches. However, for the extended morphological covariance that uses more complex SEs, a significant gain appears: the learned complete lattice of colors is now much better than the classical lexicographic lattice and the patch-based learned lattice performs the best. The gain of using patches for MM texture classification appears now evident and confirms that the use of higher level cues than simple color in a MM texture feature extraction enables to obtain better features, and consequently better classification (whatever the considered classifier).

4   Conclusion

This paper has detailed an approach towards the construction of patch-based adaptive MM operators. The complete lattice of patches if learned by manifold learning from images and induces a patch-based learned complete lattice of the initial vectors of the image. To be efficient a three step strategy based on dictionary learning, manifold learning and out of sample extension has been devised. Patch-based adaptivity has been highlighted for morphological processing as an efficient way to preserve fine and repetitive structures for MM processing but also for image segmentation and texture classification.

References

1. Aptoula, E., Lefèvre, S.: A comparative study on multivariate mathematical morphology. Pattern Recognit. **40**(11), 2914–2929 (2007)
2. Aptoula, E., Lefèvre, S.: On lexicographical ordering in multivariate mathematical morphology. Pattern Recognition Letters **29**(2), 109–118 (2008)
3. Aptoula, E., Lefèvre, S.: Multivariate mathematical morphology applied to colour image analysis. In: Collet, C., Chanussot, J., Chehdi, K. (eds.) Multivariate Image Processing: Methods and Applications, pp. 303–337. ISTE - John Wiley (2009)
4. Aptoula, E.: Extending morphological covariance. Pattern Recognition **45**(12), 4524–4535 (2012)
5. Belkin, M., Niyogi, P.: Laplacian eigenmaps for dimensionality reduction and data representation. Neural Comput. **15**(6), 1373–1396 (2003)
6. Buades, A., Coll, B., Morel, J.M.: Image denoising methods. A new nonlocal principle. SIAM Review **52**(1), 113–147 (2010)
7. Chanussot, J., Lambert, P.: Bit mixing paradigm for multivalued morphological filters. In: International Conference on Image Processing and Its Applications, vol. 2, pp. 804–808 (1997)
8. Ćurić, V., Landström, A., Thurley, M.J., Hendriks, C.L.L.: Adaptive mathematical morphology - a survey of the field. Pattern Recognition Letters **47**, 18–28 (2014)
9. Gersho, A., Gray, R.: Vector Quantization and Signal Compression. Kluwer Academic (1991)
10. Goutsias, J., Heijmans, H., Sivakumar, K.: Morphological operators for image sequences. Computer Vision and Image Understanding **62**(3), 326–346 (1995)
11. Lee, J.A., Verleysen, M.: Nonlinear Dimensionality Reduction. Springer (2007)
12. Lezoray, O., Charrier, C., Elmoataz, A.: Rank transformation and manifold learning for multivariate mathematical morphology. In: EUSIPCO (European Signal Processing Conference), pp. 35–39 (2009)
13. Lézoray, O., Elmoataz, A.: Nonlocal and multivariate mathematical morphology. In: International Conference on Image Processing (IEEE), pp. 129–132 (2012)
14. Maragos, P., Vachier, C.: Overview of adaptive morphology: trends and perspectives. In: 2009 16th IEEE International Conference on Image Processing (ICIP), pp. 2241–2244, November 2009
15. Ojala, T., Maenpaa, T., Pietikainen, M., Viertola, J., Kyllonen, J., Huovinen, S.: Outex - new framework for empirical evaluation of texture analysis algorithms. In: 2002 Proceedings of the 16th International Conference on Pattern Recognition, vol. 1, pp. 701–706 (2002)
16. Peyré, G.: Manifold models for signals and images. Computer Vision and Image Understanding **113**(2), 249–260 (2009)
17. Roerdink, J.: Adaptivity and group invariance in mathematical morphology. In: 2009 16th IEEE International Conference on Image Processing (ICIP), pp. 2253–2256, November 2009

18. Ronse, C.: Why mathematical morphology needs complete lattices. Signal Processing **21**(2), 129–154 (1990)
19. Salembier, P.: Study on nonlocal morphological operators. In: International Conference on Image Processing (IEEE), pp. 2269–2272 (2009)
20. Ta, V.T., Elmoataz, A., Lezoray, O.: Nonlocal morphological levelings by partial difference equations over weighted graphs. In: CD Proceedings of the ICPR (International Conference on Pattern Recognition) (2008)
21. Ta, V.-T., Elmoataz, A., Lézoray, O.: Partial difference equations over graphs: morphological processing of arbitrary discrete data. In: Forsyth, D., Torr, P., Zisserman, A. (eds.) ECCV 2008, Part III. LNCS, vol. 5304, pp. 668–680. Springer, Heidelberg (2008)
22. Ta, V., Elmoataz, A., Lézoray, O.: Nonlocal PDES-based morphology on weighted graphs for image and data processing. IEEE Transactions on Image Processing **20**(6), 1504–1516 (2011)
23. Talwalkar, A., Kumar, S., Mohri, M., Rowley, H.A.: Large-scale SVD and manifold learning. Journal of Machine Learning Research **14**(1), 3129–3152 (2013)
24. Velasco-Forero, S., Angulo, J.: Mathematical morphology for vector images using statistical depth. In: Soille, P., Pesaresi, M., Ouzounis, G.K. (eds.) ISMM 2011. LNCS, vol. 6671, pp. 355–366. Springer, Heidelberg (2011)
25. Velasco-Forero, S., Angulo, J.: On nonlocal mathematical morphology. In: Hendriks, C.L.L., Borgefors, G., Strand, R. (eds.) ISMM 2013. LNCS, vol. 7883, pp. 219–230. Springer, Heidelberg (2013)
26. Yang, S., Li, J.X.: Spatial-variant morphological filters with nonlocal-patch-distance-based amoeba kernel for image denoising. Image Analysis and Stereology **34**(1), 63–72 (2015)

Time Ordering Shuffling for Improving Background Subtraction

Benjamin Laugraud$^{(\boxtimes)}$, Philippe Latour, and Marc Van Droogenbroeck

INTELSIG Laboratory, Department of Electrical Engineering and Computer Science,
University of Liège, Liège, Belgium
{blaugraud,philippe.latour,m.vandroogenbroeck}@ulg.ac.be

Abstract. By construction, a video is a series of ordered frames, whose order is defined at the time of the acquisition process. Background subtraction methods then take this input video and produce a series of segmentation maps expressed in terms of foreground objects and scene background. To our knowledge, this natural ordering of frames has never been questioned or challenged.

In this paper, we propose to challenge, in a prospective view, the natural ordering of video frames in the context of background subtraction, and examine alternative time orderings. The idea consists in changing the order before background subtraction is applied, by means of shuffling strategies, and re-ordering the segmentation maps afterwards. For this purpose, we propose several shuffling strategies and show that, for some background subtraction methods, results are preserved or even improved. The practical advantage of time shuffling is that it can been applied to any existing background subtraction seamlessly.

Keywords: Background subtraction · Motion analysis · Change detection · Time ordering shuffling · Updating strategy

1 Introduction

Background subtraction is an essential task in many video applications (such as video-surveillance), that consists in discriminating between moving objects and the background of the scene. While this operation seems obvious, it is very difficult to accommodate to the large variety of scenes and to deal with dynamical effects such as sudden lighting changes, dynamic backgrounds, shadows, etc. Therefore, many techniques have been proposed and reviewed for background subtraction (see for example Brutzer *et al.* [1], Bouwmans [2,3], or Jodoin *et al.* [4]).

Background subtraction involves a background model and several steps: initialization, segmentation, and updating. During the initialization, the algorithm builds a background model. We are not focusing on initialization in this paper. Therefore, we assume that the learning sequence is long enough to build a model of the background. After initialization, we perform a segmentation, that produces the binary foreground/background segmentation map, and update the background model. The quality of the final segmentation maps is usually expressed

© Springer International Publishing Switzerland 2015
S. Battiato et al. (Eds.): ACIVS 2015, LNCS 9386, pp. 58–69, 2015.
DOI: 10.1007/978-3-319-25903-1_6

in terms of False (F) or True (T) Negatives (N) or Positives (P), or with global measures such as the F_1 score [5], defined as:

$$F_1 = \frac{TP}{TP + \dfrac{FN + FP}{2}}.$$ (1)

It is assumed that only an appropriate background model, which is dynamic by essence, can lead to a good performance. This implies an efficient adaptation of the model over time, which is the purpose of the updating step.

Updating the background model is challenging because, among others, there is a trade-off between the adaptability to fast changes and the required inertia to avoid the rapid inclusion of abandoned objects into the background. Consequently, the updating mechanism, which is intrinsically related to the segmentation step, is an essential part of any background subtraction process.

The goal of this paper is to question the impact of changing the time ordering of frames for the segmentation and updating phases; the flowchart of our method is given in Figure 1.

This paper is organized as follows. Section 2 describes several strategies for changing the natural time ordering. These strategies are evaluated on a selection of sequences that are part of the Change Detection 2014 dataset [6] (denoted CDnet 2014 hereafter), and results are reported in Section 3. Finally, Section 4 concludes this paper.

2   Time Shuffling Strategies

The natural order (which is the chronological one) is the most common order, although it might happen that some events are easier to interpret by running a video sequence backwards. In the field of background subtraction, some authors have recently tried to build background models that are less sensitive to the chronological order. For instance, while Wang and Suter have proposed a non parametric model that is updated by forgetting the oldest samples first [7], Barnich and Van Droogenbroeck rely on a random selection of samples to be replaced [8]; in this case, a video sequence is not seen as an *ordered list* of frames anymore, but rather as a *collection* of frames [9].

In the following, we first introduce the shuffling principle and then elaborate on a random policy and on deterministic shuffling strategies.

2.1   Principle

The time shuffling principle is the following. Let I be the ordered set of time indices of an N-frames long video sequence; I is then equal to $\{1, 2, \ldots, N\}$, and the video V comprises the ordered frame sequence $F_1 F_2 \ldots F_N$. The purpose of time shuffling consists to apply a *shuffling strategy* first, in order to obtain a new video whose frames are re-ordered. For example, after time shuffling, we have $F_{13} F_2 F_N \ldots F_1$. This new video sequence is used as an input for a

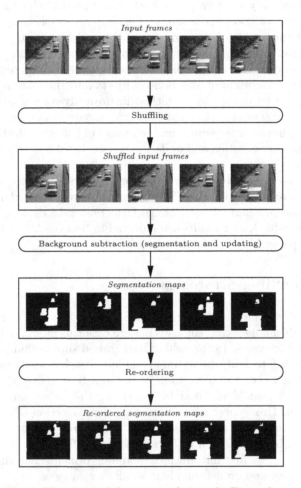

Fig. 1. Flowchart of the proposed time shuffling scheme.

background subtraction algorithm. This results in a video sequence made of the corresponding segmentation maps $S_{13}S_2S_N \ldots S_1$. Finally, we recover the original order for the frames to obtain the output sequence $S_1S_2 \ldots S_N$. The whole process is illustrated in Figure 1.

2.2   Random Time Shuffling Strategy

In practice, we take for granted that the natural, chronological, time order is the most appropriate for dealing with videos. However, this has never been extensively checked. The opposite conception to the chronological time ordering is the absence of any order, that is, an entirely random ordering.

There are two reasons which justify the fact that we are interested in testing a random frame order. The first reason is that, since it can be seen as the opposite strategy to the forwards (chronological) ordering, we hope to span a large set of possible strategies and derive some insights on the importance of any kind of ordering. The second reason is that it is very difficult to imagine, at this stage of knowledge, a particular deterministic ordering. More precisely, if we introduce two of them in the next section, we remain unsure about the relevance of other non chronological deterministic strategies.

2.3   Deterministic Time Shuffling Strategies

A more conservative approach consists in avoiding a random ordering. New strategies, that are deterministic, can be based on the content, on the time difference, or on both. In this paper, we examine two strategies based on the difference δ between any pair of frames. Let F_1 and F_2 be two frames, we compute the difference as follows:

$$\delta\left(F_1, F_2\right) = \sum_{p \in h \times w} |F_1(p) - F_2(p)|, \tag{2}$$

where p is a pixel location taken in the frame of size $h \times w$.

Once we have computed all the differences, we choose an order that minimizes or maximizes the differences between successive images. The first strategy, named $\delta_{\min}$, is designed to minimize the amount of energy accumulated by δ. The underlying justification for proposing this strategy is that some algorithms are designed to accommodate to small variations in the image content and that most algorithms have troubles for dealing with large changes.

The reason for the strategy that maximizes the differences (strategy named $\delta_{\max}$ hereafter) is different. We want to evaluate if background subtraction techniques are performing better if they learn large changes as soon as possible, instead of learning them progressively. This would result in a model capable to embrace large changes earlier during the sequence, and a smooth adaptation to small changes later in the sequence.

Note that all the strategies are equally applicable to any type of background subtraction technique, because we do not change the techniques themselves.

Despite that, the choice of a strategy directly impacts on the performance of the updating scheme, as the methods are not all equally designed to deal with small or large changes.

2.4   Implementation of the Deterministic Strategies

Ideally, to implement our proposed deterministic strategies, we should look for the global optimum by finding the index order that minimizes or maximizes the cumulative difference energy. However, this exhaustive search is intractable. Thus, despite that, from a theoretical perspective, it is sub-optimal to proceed step by step (in other words, to find the new frame index at each step), an iterative algorithm has been implemented using this method to carry out the experiments of this paper.

Let Ω_i and Φ_i be two ordered sets of indices built after the ith iteration (starting from 1), whose elements correspond to the remaining frames to shuffle and to the frames that have been shuffled, respectively. Considering the two initial sets $\Omega_0 = I$ and $\Phi_0 = \emptyset$, the operations performed during the ith iteration of the developed iterative algorithm are the following:

1. Select the element $k_i \in \Omega_{i-1}$ which minimizes or maximizes the cumulative difference energy according to the chosen strategy. Note that the selection of k_1 is discussed in Section 3.1.
2. Construct the set $\Omega_i = \Omega_{i-1} \setminus \{k_i\}$.
3. Construct the set $\Phi_i = \Phi_{i-1} \cup \{k_i\}$.

It should be noted that, applied on a N-frames long video sequence, the algorithm terminates after N iterations. In such a case, considering that $P(I)$ is a permutation of I, we have that $\Omega_N = \emptyset$, and $\Phi_N = P(I)$ which is the set of indices for the shuffled images.

In the example of Section 2.1, at the first iteration, once the frame indexed by 13 is selected, the sets $\Omega_1 = \{1, \ldots, 12, 14, \ldots, N\}$ and $\Phi_1 = \{13\}$ are built in such a way that this frame is removed from the set of the next candidates to select, and then included into the set of the shuffled frames.

3   Experiments and Results

This section discusses preliminary results obtained for different shuffling strategies. First, we present how we deal with the initialization, then we discuss the chosen dataset, and finally we present our results.

3.1   Initialization

It is common acceptance that a background subtraction technique must initialize its model and that the first frames of a video sequence are used to build the model. Here, we have the choice to preserve the initial order for the initialization frames or to shuffle them. We decided to preserve the order during the initialization step. By doing so, our experiments highlight the behavior of background subtraction techniques during the dynamic updating process only, without requiring any specific assumption about the initialization mechanism. As a consequence, we arbitrarily decided that the algorithm presented in Section 2.4 selects the first shuffled frame (k_1) according to the differences δ between the last initialization frame and the frames indexed by the elements of Ω_0.

3.2 Dataset

In our experiments, we have used the CDnet 2014 dataset [6]. It is composed of 53 video sequences whose resolution varies from 320×240 to 720×576 pixels and duration from 600 to 7999 frames. The video sequences are provided with a ground truth annotated at the pixel level and they are divided among 11 categories to focus on specific challenges: Bad Weather, Baseline, Camera Jitter, Dynamic Background, Intermittent Object Motion, Low Framerate, Night Videos, PTZ, Shadow, Thermal, and Turbulence.

This dataset has several major advantages. First, as it is accompanied by ground truth segmentation maps, it is possible to perform an accurate evaluation [10] of our results. Second, since it contains many video sequences that cover a large variety of application scenarios, it offers the possibility to determine in which context the time ordering shuffling is relevant. And, last but not least, as it contains long sequences, it is more meaningful for the evaluation of time shuffling strategies than a dataset with very short sequences.

It should be noted that all the sequences of the CDnet 2014 dataset have been used, except for the ones from the PTZ category (where one model might fall short for dealing with the scenes), and the Low Framerate category (where motion between consecutive frames might be too large to understand the behavior of our shuffling strategies).

3.3 Background Subtraction Algorithms

In this paper, we consider six background subtraction algorithms, all of them operating at the pixel level, to challenge the relevance of time shuffling strategies. The simplest one, the exponential filter (denoted "Exp. Filter"), applies a temporal exponential filter on the observed value and thresholds the result. We have also used two mixture of Gaussians techniques, dedicated to the segmentation of scenes with dynamic backgrounds: the technique by Stauffer and Grimson [11] ("MoG G."), and the one by Zivkovic, which adapts the number of Gaussians over time [12] ("MoG Z."). We also consider the VuMeter algorithm, proposed by Goyat et al. [13], which is a non parametric method that estimates the background with a probability mass function. In this technique, the estimation is derived from the temporal histogram of the observed values.

The ViBe algorithm [8], proposed by Barnich and Van Droogenbroeck, is an alternative non parametric method which compares an observed value to a set of past samples using an Euclidean distance. Note that in order to update its model, ViBe combines a spatial propagation mechanism with a random sampling policy.

To our knowledge, ViBe is the first technique to consider a non chronological policy for updating the model. Therefore, it is also a good candidate for testing shuffling strategies.

The last method we have considered is an approach based on self organization through artificial neural networks, the so-called SOBS algorithm, as proposed by Maddalena and Petrosino [14], whose idea is inspired from biologically problem-solving methods. It should be noted that the implementations of these algorithms are provided by the BGSLibrary [15] or by the authors.

3.4   Results and Interpretation

Obviously, shuffling frames if a scene cut or illumination change occurs is irrelevant because background models before and after such an event are different. Therefore, we only use video sequences that do not contain this type of events; sequences of the CDnet 2014 dataset comply with this assumption.

Likewise, one may wonder on the practical feasibility of a shuffling mechanism that would shuffle frames from the whole sequence. While we agree that, in practice, one should work with slices of the video sequence (by 100 frames for example), we perform experiments on the whole sequence because it helps to understand the impact of re-ordering frames prior to segmentation; by doing this on parts of the video sequence, we might not be able to evaluate the impact correctly. In addition, it should be noted that this problem of causality is nonexistent for off-line video processing.

Table 1. F_1 scores for the forwards (fw) ordering and the random shuffling of frames (rd). While we believe that averaging F_1 scores is questionable, we still provide the mean values for the whole dataset in the last row, for convenience.

		Technique and strategy										
		\multicolumn{2}{}{Exp. Filter}		MoG G.		MoG Z.		VuMeter		ViBe		SOBS
		fw	rd	fw	rd	fw	rd	fw	rd	fw	rd	fw	rd
Category	Bad Weather	0.35	0.28	0.69	0.68	0.74	0.74	0.49	0.74	0.62	0.66	0.63	0.62
	Baseline	0.37	0.34	0.66	0.65	0.79	0.77	0.52	0.57	0.78	0.80	0.77	0.71
	Camera Jitter	0.23	0.22	0.45	0.47	0.51	0.51	0.49	0.52	0.54	0.54	0.44	0.44
	Dyn. Background	0.09	0.09	0.26	0.27	0.42	0.41	0.44	0.57	0.47	0.47	0.17	0.17
	Intermittent Obj.	0.29	0.31	0.43	0.49	0.46	0.49	0.20	0.31	0.41	0.46	0.51	0.51
	Night Videos	0.26	0.20	0.38	0.36	0.37	0.36	0.30	0.28	0.39	0.38	0.35	0.35
	Shadow	0.40	0.28	0.69	0.63	0.71	0.69	0.46	0.56	0.73	0.71	0.65	0.60
	Thermal	0.48	0.61	0.52	0.67	0.63	0.63	0.29	0.49	0.52	0.60	0.76	0.74
	Turbulence	0.07	0.07	0.30	0.25	0.53	0.52	0.54	0.53	0.67	0.57	0.17	0.17
	Dataset	0.28	0.27	0.49	0.50	0.57	0.57	0.41	0.51	0.57	0.58	0.50	0.48

In Table 1, we present the F_1 scores for the set of background subtraction algorithms described in the Section 3.3. It is difficult to draw definitive conclusions from these experiments. In most cases, there are no big differences, despite that the random shuffling strategy is completely opposite to the chronological ordering. Only for the SOBS algorithm did we notice a significant performance decrease. We believe that this might be due to the small number of templates used in this technique and its inability to deal with a wide variety of background templates, such as that encountered when shuffling the video frames. Likewise, the exponential filter has a very limited memory capability. Therefore, it is counter-productive for it to try to estimate the model with shuffled frames.

In a second series of experiments, we compare the three new ordering strategies (random, δ_{min}, and δ_{max}) and the chronological ordering (forwards) for a subset of categories only (it was impossible to check all our ideas, because there are too many possible deterministic strategies). Results for these experiments are given in Table 2 for the Baseline category (which gathers the most "standard" type of sequences), in Table 3 for the Camera Jitter category (which gathers sequences captured with unstable cameras), in Table 4 for the Dynamic Background category (which gathers outdoor sequences with moving backgrounds), and in Table 5 for the Intermittent Object Motion category (which gathers sequences with foreground objects that remains stationary for some time). With all the cautiousness required by our prospective experiments, we can formulate the following observations:

1. The δ_{max} strategy is usually not the best one. This means that algorithms for background subtraction are intrinsically mainly designed to handle small changes instead of large ones. This is not really surprising, but these experiments seem to confirm that intuition.
2. We observed that the δ_{min} strategy tends to mimic the forwards ordering, except when large changes occur in the image. Since computing δ_{min} is time consuming, it appears that the forwards ordering is more adequate. However, one should observe that δ_{min} always improves the segmentation of the sequences belonging to the Camera Jitter category (Table 3). This is coherent with the fact that background subtraction techniques are better in adapting to small changes.
3. The forwards strategy is never a clear winner for the video sequences of the Camera Jitter category (Table 3) and at least one of shuffling strategies improves the performance with respect to that of the natural ordering. This could be explained by the fact that shuffling the frames might reduce the amount of differences, due to camera motion, between consecutive frames (this is, again, coherent with our observation for the δ_{min} strategy). Figure 2 illustrates the improvement obtained by the use of a shuffling strategy on a sequence of the Camera Jitter category.

4. Except for the SOBS algorithm, the forwards strategy is never the best for the video sequences of the Intermittent Object Motion category (Table 5). Our feeling is that, because random and δ_{max} strategies will interlace frames with and without stationary objects, they slow down the inclusion of those objects into the background (which is considered as being the right approach by the designers of the CDnet dataset).

5. For most methods, the random strategy outperforms the natural ordering in the Thermal category (Table 1). Figure 3 illustrates the improvement obtained by the use of a shuffling strategy on a sequence of this category.

6. For the VuMeter algorithm, in all cases, at least one shuffling strategy increases the score of the chronological ordering.

7. For the baseline category, there is no clear winning strategy. It is interesting to note that ViBe, which natively incorporates a random updating policy, performs best for the random shuffling strategy. This suggests that the sequences have backgrounds with a lot of inertia, so that the modification of the time order has no large impact on the performances.

8. It is worth considering alternative time orderings as the forwards strategy is not always the best strategy. This raises questions about the dynamic behavior of background subtraction techniques in general.

Fig. 2. Segmentation of frame numbered 820 of the *boulevard* sequence (Camera Jitter category) by the MoG G. algorithm using the forwards (left-hand side image) and δ_{max} (middle image) shuffling strategies. The last column shows the ground truth.

Fig. 3. Segmentation of frame numbered 2018 of the *corridor* sequence (Thermal category) by the VuMeter algorithm using the forwards (left-hand side image) and random (middle image) shuffling strategies. The last column shows the ground truth.

Table 2. F_1 scores for different shuffling strategies applied on the Baseline category.

		Strategy			
		forwards	random	δ_{min}	δ_{max}
Technique	Exp. Filter	**0.374**	0.342	**0.374**	0.349
	MoG G.	**0.658**	0.657	**0.658**	0.653
	MoG Z.	**0.794**	0.778	0.791	0.782
	VuMeter	0.523	**0.572**	0.525	0.489
	ViBe	0.777	**0.801**	0.778	0.790
	SOBS	**0.771**	0.710	0.760	0.755

Table 3. F_1 scores for different shuffling strategies applied on the Camera Jitter category.

		Strategy			
		forwards	random	δ_{min}	δ_{max}
Technique	Exp. Filter	0.228	0.222	**0.265**	0.237
	MoG G.	0.452	0.469	0.504	**0.505**
	MoG Z.	0.505	0.505	**0.515**	0.498
	VuMeter	0.486	**0.519**	0.503	0.498
	ViBe	0.542	0.539	**0.558**	0.537
	SOBS	0.437	0.437	0.439	**0.443**

Table 4. F_1 scores for different shuffling strategies applied on the Dynamic Background category.

		Strategy			
		forwards	random	δ_{min}	δ_{max}
Technique	Exp. Filter	**0.094**	0.091	**0.094**	0.090
	MoG G.	0.258	**0.270**	0.258	0.260
	MoG Z.	**0.420**	0.410	**0.420**	0.410
	VuMeter	0.441	**0.572**	0.441	0.417
	ViBe	0.472	**0.473**	0.471	0.463
	SOBS	**0.169**	0.166	**0.169**	0.167

Table 5. F_1 scores for different shuffling strategies applied on the Intermittent Object Motion category.

		Strategy			
		forwards	random	δ_{min}	δ_{max}
Technique	Exp. Filter	0.287	**0.306**	0.284	0.302
	MoG G.	0.426	**0.483**	0.414	0.454
	MoG Z.	0.461	**0.490**	0.462	0.461
	VuMeter	0.197	**0.309**	0.200	0.204
	ViBe	0.408	**0.460**	0.408	0.431
	SOBS	**0.514**	0.508	**0.514**	0.508

4   Conclusions

In this prospective paper, we examine how changing the time ordering of video frames impacts on the the task of background subtraction. This questions the notion of chronological order and introduces a new view on the problem. For that purpose, we have developed several shuffling strategies for re-ordering the frames and have evaluated them for different algorithms on the CDnet 2014 dataset. This highlights whether techniques are or not dependent with respect to the frame order, but it also shows that a principle applicable to any background subtraction technique can affect the performance. Our results remain difficult to interpret, because they illustrate that the updating process of some algorithms is sensitive to the time ordering of the frames, while other techniques are less sensitive to it. In addition, we observe that the chronological ordering is rarely the best one for background subtraction, and that for some categories of video sequences, at least one shuffling strategy systematically improves the F_1 score. While this is a question to be challenged in future work, it also points out that the general understanding of background subtraction updating mechanisms has to be refined.

References

1. Brutzer, S., Höferlin, B., Heidemann, G.: Evaluation of background subtraction techniques for video surveillance. In: IEEE International Conference on Computer Vision and Pattern Recognition (CVPR), pp. 1937–1944 (2011)
2. Bouwmans, T.: Recent advanced statistical background modeling for foreground detection - A systematic survey. Recent Patents on Computer Science **4**(3), 147–176 (2011)
3. Bouwmans, T.: Traditional and recent approaches in background modeling for foreground detection: an overview. Computer Science Review **11**(12), 31–66 (2014)
4. Jodoin, P.-M., Piérard, S., Wang, Y., Van Droogenbroeck, M.: Overview and benchmarking of motion detection methods. In: Bouwmans, T., Porikli, F., Hoferlin, B., Vacavant, A. (eds.) Background Modeling and Foreground Detection for Video Surveillance, chap. 24. Chapman and Hall/CRC (2014)
5. Baumann, A., Boltz, M., Ebling, J., Koenig, M., Loos, H., Merkel, M., Niem, W., Warzelhan, J., Yu, J.: A review and comparison of measures for automatic video surveillance systems. EURASIP Journal on Image and Video Processingm, 30 (2008)
6. Wang, Y., Jodoin, P.-M., Porikli, F., Konrad, J., Benezeth, Y., Ishwar, P.: CDnet 2014: an expanded change detection benchmark dataset. In: IEEE International Conference on Computer Vision and Pattern Recognition Workshops (CVPRW), pp. 393–400 (2014)
7. Wang, H., Suter, D.: A consensus-based method for tracking: Modelling background scenario and foreground appearance. Pattern Recognition **40**(3), 1091–1105 (2007)
8. Barnich, O., Van Droogenbroeck, M.: ViBe: A universal background subtraction algorithm for video sequences. IEEE Transactions on Image Processing **20**(6), 1709–1724 (2011)

9. Van Droogenbroeck, M., Barnich, O.: Visual background extractor. World Intellectual Property Organization, WO 2009/007198, 36 pages (2009)
10. Goyette, N., Jodoin, P.-M., Porikli, F., Konrad, J., Ishwar, P.: A novel video dataset for change detection benchmarking. IEEE Transactions on Image Processing **23**(11), 4663–4679 (2014)
11. Stauffer, C., Grimson, E.: Adaptive background mixture models for real-time tracking. In: IEEE International Conference on Computer Vision and Pattern Recognition(CVPR), vol. 2, pp. 246–252 (1999)
12. Zivkovic, Z.: Improved adaptive Gaussian mixture model for background subtraction. In: IEEE International Conference on Pattern Recognition (ICPR), vol. 2, pp. 28–31 (2004)
13. Goyat, Y., Chateau, T., Malaterre, L., Trassoudaine, L.: Vehicle trajectories evaluation by static video sensors. In: IEEE Intelligent Transportation Systems Conference (ITSC), pp. 864–869 (2006)
14. Maddalena, L., Petrosino, A.: A self-organizing approach to background subtraction for visual surveillance applications. IEEE Transactions on Image Processing **17**(7), 1168–1177 (2008)
15. Sobral, A.: BGSLibrary: an OpenCV C++ background subtraction library. In: Workshop de Visao Computacional (WVC) (2013)

Fast and Low Power Consumption Outliers Removal for Motion Vector Estimation

Giuseppe Spampinato[1], Arcangelo Bruna[1], Giovanni Maria Farinella[2], Sebastiano Battiato[2(✉)], and Giovanni Puglisi[3]

[1] STMicroelectronics, Advanced System Technology, Catania, Italy
{giuseppe.spampinato,arcangelo.bruna}@st.com
[2] Dipartimento di Matematica e Informatica, Università degli Studi di Catania, Catania, Italy
{gfarinella,battiato}@dmi.unict.it
[3] Dipartimento di Matematica e Informatica, Università degli Studi di Cagliari, Cagliari, Italy
puglisi@unica.it

Abstract. When in a pipeline a robust global motion estimation is needed, RANSAC algorithm is the usual choice. Unfortunately, since RANSAC is an iterative method based on random analysis, it is not suitable for real-time processing. This paper presents an outlier removal algorithm, which reaches a robust estimation (at least equal to RANSAC) with really low power consumption and can be employed for embedded time implementation.

Keywords: Motion estimation · Outlier removal · Optical flow · Motion retrieval · Real time

1 Introduction

One of the problems in computer vision is to design, given a set of observed data, a mathematical model able to describe the global transformation between images or frames of a video. Fields of application are: visual search, image registration, optical flow, shape alignment [1], digital video stabilization [2,3,4] and so on, which need a robust estimator to retrieve the global motion vector between two images making use of local motion estimator. The local motion estimator is usually based on matching of portions of the image content in one image with portions in the second image. The techniques aiming to solve this problem are known as "regression systems". Unfortunately, lots of methods used in statistics are not reliable for computer vision since the dataset are usually affected by noise. Such noise is produced by problems in the estimation phase. As example, in the global motion estimator, the local estimator could be deceived by regular pattern or also by the noise in the images or by the fact that the zone under consideration is homogeneous. In order to have a good estimator, unreliable matching pairs must be discarded, facing with false matching or with deceiving matching (e.g. related to moving objects in the scene). In general, the data correctly transformed according to the transformation model are called "inliers", while the

© Springer International Publishing Switzerland 2015
S. Battiato et al. (Eds.): ACIVS 2015, LNCS 9386, pp. 70–80, 2015.
DOI: 10.1007/978-3-319-25903-1_7

others are called "outliers". There are also algorithms aimed to provide reliable results with outliers. They are called "robust regression" in statistics or, as known in computer vision, "outliers removal" algorithms.

Several algorithms have been proposed in literature concerning the motion estimation from dense or sparse keypoint matching. Among them the LSE (Least Square Error) is one of the most used, but it is unreliable to outliers. Other authors use non liner digital filters [5,6,7], which are quite effective in removing outliers in off-line data analysis, but not suitable for real time processing. *RANSAC* [8] is the most commonly used method for robust transformation estimation problems in computer vision, due to its ability to cope with outliers. There have been a number of recent efforts aimed at increasing the efficiency of the basic *RANSAC* algorithm. Some of these strategies aim to optimize the process of model verification [9,10,11]; while others seek to modify the sampling process in order to preferentially generate more useful hypotheses [12,13,14]. Even if these techniques are promising, still none of them are directly applicable in real-time processing. Only some authors went in the direction of formulating *RANSAC* for real-time applications. In particular, Nister [15] describes the so called preemptive *RANSAC*, where a limited number of hypotheses are evaluated in parallel, to find the best solution from the limited set of hypotheses. This algorithm facilitates real-time implementation, but in some conditions it can evaluate more hypotheses than standard *RANSAC* (so becoming slower) and in some cases it cannot find the optimal solution since it does not evaluate enough hypotheses. Moreover, the limited set of hypotheses considered implies that a prior estimate of inlier ratio is available, but often this is not possible.

However, since *RANSAC* is so widely used in computer vision, we will use it as reference algorithm. Even if it is quite reliable to outliers and to noise, we do not investigate more on it, since it is a non-deterministic algorithm (the results are not replicable) and the estimation is reasonable only with a certain probability (based on number of iterations). In this paper, we propose a fast and accurate (at least as *RANSAC*) motion vector estimator, which works with low computational resources. The proposed outlier removal algorithm is partially based on the concepts of voting approach, deterministic algorithm described in [16]. This algorithm has in input the matched pairs $\{(x_s, y_s),(x_r, y_r)\}$ between two images and gives as output, apart a rough estimation of the transformation parameters, the inliers vector V_a, obtained pruning the matching pairs with the elimination of the outliers according to such estimation. The alignment is performed by employing a similarity transformation of keypoint pairs corresponding to matched entries. Despite the proposed approach is a deterministic and iterative method, it is computationally expensive, because it takes into consideration all possible rotations [-180 .. 180] and translation $[min_{Txy} .. max_{Txy}]$.

The rest of the document is organized as follows: *Section 2* describes the proposed method; *Section 3* presents the experimental results; *Section 4* reports the comparison between the proposed approach and *RANSAC* in terms of computational complexity; finally, *Section 5* concludes the paper with final remarks.

2   Proposed Method

The schema of the proposed system is shown in Fig. 1. The system is composed by three main blocks:

- *Pre-processing*: the set of matching pairs M are processed to obtain a rough estimation of translation $(T_{x'}, T_{y'})$ [17];
- *Advanced Voting*: considering the rough $(T_{x'}, T_{y'})$, a filtering threshold t_a and a rotation range $\alpha_{range} = [-\alpha_{range}, \alpha_{range}]$, this step removes the outliers from M, obtaining the new set of matching pairs M'' [16];
- *Motion Model Estimation*: to obtain from M'', the final motion estimation parameters of $(T_x, T_y, \alpha, \sigma)$, related to traslation, rotation and scale, are obtained with an improved low-cost version of *Ordinary Least Square (OLS)*.

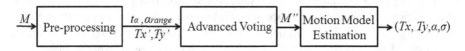

Fig. 1. Schema of the proposed solution.

2.1   Pre-processing

In the proposed pipeline, the aim of the *Pre-processing* block is to obtain a *Global Motion Vector (GMV)*, that is a rough estimation of translation $(T_{x'}, T_{y'})$. This step is an improvement of the approach proposed in [17]. It is important to note that while [17] is a complete algorithm by itself, the proposed *Pre-processing* is just a block of the proposed system to have a rough estimation of translational parameters. The schema of the *Pre-processing* block is shown in Fig. 2. We have three main sub-blocks:

- *Histogram construction*: it constructs the 2D histogram of the local *Motion Vectors (MVs)*. The value of $H(x,y)$ is incremented by one each time the local $MV(x,y)$ is encountered. Of course, the local $MV(x,y)$ is obtained as $(x_r - x_s, y_r - y_s)$.
- *Detect peak*: it is composed by two parts:
  - Local maximum identification: it marks in a *3x3* neighbourhood of H the local maximum MV (to speed up the following sub-step).
  - *Varying Low Pass Filter (LPF)*: the peak value using the raw data is sensitive to noise. To solve the problem, a *TxZ Low Pass Filter (LPF)* is applied to H before the peak detection. It is applied only on marked MVs. The value of T and Z will vary depending on image dimensions and maximum allowed rotation (eventually also on maximum allowed scaling). A simple LPF used is $[1 \ldots 1]$ T times in horizontal and $[1 \ldots 1]$ Z times in vertical. It is different than [17], which uses a fixed simple 5x5 LPF to be applied to all MVs of H.
- *Determination of GMV*: A selective maximum of the filtered bins in H is considered as *GMV*. It is applied only on marked MVs. In particular for each marked MV, it is taken the current MV. If its hits are at least *MAX_TIMES_PRE* times

higher than previous maximum *MV* hits or if its hits are at least *MIN_TIMES_PRE* times higher than previous maximum *MV* hits and it is nearest to (0,0). This step is useful for the robustness of the *Pre-processing block.*

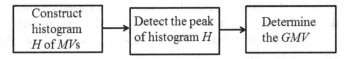

Fig. 2. Schema of the *Pre-processing* block.

2.2   Advanced Voting

The aim of the *Advanced Voting* block is to remove the outliers from *M*, previously estimated set of matching pairs, to obtain the new set of matching pairs *M''*. This step is an improvement of the approach presented in [16]. The schema of the *Advanced Voting* block is shown in Fig. 3. This block is composed by the following modules:

- *Rotation filtering*: it eliminates outliers by taking into account dominant orientations differences, coming from the used descriptor (e.g. *SIFT* [18]). This module follows the formulation described in [16].Differently than in [16], in our pipeline the activation of this module for filtering is optional. For instance, in our experimental results reported in Section 3, we use *FAST* detector [19] and *BRIEF* descriptor [20], so no dominant orientation is available and used for estimation;
- *Matching Matrix MM construction*: it constructs the 3D *Votes* array, that is the voting space related to x and y translation and rotation angle θ. Since in our experiments the proposed pipeline is applied on video sequences, we can assume as rotation range [-5° ... 5°], instead of generic [-180° ... 180°] indicated in [16]. This allows to speed up the computation and it allows the usage of lower computational resources. Moreover, since the *Pre-processing* block (see *Section 2.1*) gives a rough estimation of translation $(T_{x'}, T_{y'})$, we do not consider the whole translations range [-32 ... 32] for *VGA* and [-64 ... 64] for *720p* (as indicated in [16]), but for robustness and speeding we just consider values around the previously estimated $(T_{x'}, T_{y'})$, that is translations range $[T_{x'}-8... T_{x'}+8]$ for *VGA* and $[T_{x'}-16 ... T_{x'}+16]$ for *720p* (the same is done for $T_{y'}$). Finally, to further have a speed up, a pyramidal approach can be used for rotation range. For example it can be executed in two steps estimation. Instead of having a final estimation in a range of [-5° ... 5°] with the step of 0.5°, we use a rough rotation estimation *roughθ* in a first step ([-5° ... 5°] with the step of 2°) and a refinement in a second step ([*roughθ* - 1° ... *roughθ* +1°] with the step of 0.5°);
- *Find MM maximum*: it is composed by four sub-blocks:
  - *Find first N maximum in MM*: in our experimental results (see *Section 3*) we use $N=2$, to not increase too much the computational cost;
  - *Scale computation*: for each matching pairs $((x_s,y_s),(x_r,y_r))$ and for each of the N maximum, calculate σ_1 and σ_2 as indicated in formula (3) and (4);

- *Consider elements near scale median*: it retains only scales in the range [*median-SCALE_RANGE ... median+SCALE_RANGE*] (for video just retain scales in the range [1-*SCALE_RANGE ... 1+SCALE_RANGE*]);
- *Take selective maximum*: it takes the current maximum, if its retained scales are at least *MAX_TIMES* times higher than previous maximum retained scales or if its retained scales are at least *MIN_TIMES* times higher than previous maximum retained scales and it is nearest to (0,0). This step is made for the robustness of the *Advanced Voting* block.

The transformation is expressed as $(x_r, y_r) = f(x_s, y_s)$. For roto-translation transformation $(T_x, T_y, \alpha, \sigma)$, the formula is expressed as following:

$$x_r = x_s \sigma \cos \alpha - y_s \sigma \sin \alpha + T_x \tag{1}$$

$$y_r = x_s \sigma \sin \alpha + y_s \sigma \cos \alpha + T_y \tag{2}$$

The model assumes that a point (x_s, y_s) in the source image I_s is transformed in a point (x_r, y_r) in the image I_r with a combination of rotation (α), scaling (σ) and translation (T_x, T_y). In the sub-block *Calculate related elements scale*, the scale values σ_1 and σ_2 are obtained from equations (1) and (2), as follows:

$$\sigma_1 = \frac{x_r - T_x}{x_s \cos \alpha - y_s \sin \alpha} \tag{3}$$

$$\sigma_2 = \frac{y_r - T_y}{x_s \sin \alpha + y_s \cos \alpha} \tag{4}$$

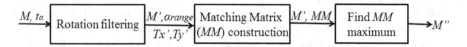

Fig. 3. Block based schema of *Advanced Voting* block.

2.3   Motion Estimation Model

The proposed model is aimed to describe inter-frame motion using four different parameters (rigid estimation), namely the two traslational shifts, one rotation angle and a scale factor. It considers the transformation of a point (x_i, y_i) in frame I_n with respect to a point (x_f, y_f) in frame I_{n+1} as following:

$$\begin{cases} x_f = x_i \sigma \cos \alpha - y_i \sigma \sin \alpha + T_x \\ y_f = x_i \sigma \sin \alpha + y_i \sigma \cos \alpha + T_y \end{cases} \tag{5}$$

where σ is the scale parameter, α the rotation angle, T_x and T_y respectively X-axis and Y-axis shifts. Considering N motion vectors and $P=4$ parameters, we obtain the following over-constrained linear system:

$$Cf = \begin{pmatrix} x_{f1} \\ \vdots \\ x_{fN} \\ y_{f1} \\ \vdots \\ y_{fN} \end{pmatrix} = A \times Par = \begin{pmatrix} x_{i1} & -y_{i1} & 1 & 0 \\ \vdots & \vdots & \vdots & \vdots \\ x_{iN} & -y_{iN} & 1 & 0 \\ y_{i1} & x_{i1} & 0 & 1 \\ \vdots & \vdots & \vdots & \vdots \\ y_{iN} & x_{iN} & 0 & 1 \end{pmatrix} \times \begin{pmatrix} a \\ b \\ c \\ d \end{pmatrix} \tag{6}$$

where $a=\sigma cos\alpha$, $b=\sigma sin\alpha$, $c=T_x$ and $d=T_y$. Cf is vector of $Nx1$ dimension, A is a matrix with dimension NxP and Par is a $1xP$ vector. Vectors computation may be affected by noise so it is useful to apply an *Ordinary Least Squares* method on a set of redundant equations to obtain the parameters vector, as:

$$Par = (A'\times A)^{-1} \cdot A'\times Cf \tag{7}$$

The parameters σ, α, T_x, T_y can be easily derived from Par vector components in the following way:

$$\begin{cases} \sigma = \sqrt{a^2 + b^2} \\ \alpha = \tan^{-1}(b/a) \\ T_x = c \\ T_y = d \end{cases} \tag{8}$$

Ordinary Least Squares method performs well when outliers have been eliminated from the total set of features, as in this case, thanks to the application of the previous *Advanced Voting* block. Since we are interested in an optimized method to solve (7), we can obtain parameters from (8), using the following simplified formula:

$$\begin{bmatrix} a \\ b \\ c \\ d \end{bmatrix} = [A'*A]^{-1} * A'*Cf = \frac{1}{D*N - Sxi^2 - Syi^2} \begin{bmatrix} N & 0 & -Sxi & -Syi \\ 0 & N & Syi & -Sxi \\ -Sxi & Syi & D & 0 \\ -Syi & -Sxi & 0 & D \end{bmatrix} \begin{bmatrix} S2 \\ S3 \\ Sxf \\ Syf \end{bmatrix} \tag{9}$$

$$\begin{bmatrix} a \\ b \\ c \\ d \end{bmatrix} = \frac{1}{D*N - Sxi^2 - Syi^2} \begin{bmatrix} N*S2 - Sxi*Sxf - Syi*Syf \\ N*S3 + Syi*Sxf - Sxi*Syf \\ -Sxi*S2 + Syi*S3 + D*Sxf \\ -Syi*S2 - Sxi*S3 + D*Syf \end{bmatrix} \tag{10}$$

where:

$$D = Xi'^*Xi + Yi'^*Yi = \sum_{k=1}^{N} xi_k^2 + \sum_{k=1}^{N} yi_k^2$$

$$Sxi = Xi'^*ones(N,1) = ones(N,1)'^*Xi = \sum_{k=1}^{N} xi_k$$

$$Syi = Yi'^*ones(N,1) = ones(N,1)'^*Yi = \sum_{k=1}^{N} yi_k \qquad (11)$$

$$S2 = Xi'^*Xf + Yi'Yf = \sum_{k=1}^{N} xi_k * xf_k + \sum_{k=1}^{N} yi_k * yf_k$$

$$S3 = -Yi'^*Xf + Xi'Yf = -\sum_{k=1}^{N} yi_k * xf_k + \sum_{k=1}^{N} xi_k * yf_k$$

$$Sxf = ones(N,1)'^*Xf = \sum_{k=1}^{N} xf_k$$

$$Syf = ones(N,1)'^*Yf = \sum_{k=1}^{N} yf_k$$

3   Experimental Results

The application considered in this paper is the Video Stabilization. We consider *FAST* detector [19] and *BRIEF* descriptor [20] to perform the point matching. Lots of testing have been executed on the proposed and state of art solutions for measure both subjective quality (to demonstrate the robustness of the method) and operations count (to demonstrate the lightness of the method). Testing have been executed on different image sizes (from *CIF* to *720p*) and in different critical conditions such as: artificial motion, noise, shearing, slow panning, regular pattern, motion blur, moving objects, autofocus, fixed (no movement), scene change, illumination change, low light. The algorithm used to do the testing is the one indicated in [21], using as "outlier removal" the proposed and the state of art solutions for comparison. We noted that the proposed algorithm reaches at least the *RANSAC* performances also in critical conditions (artificial motion and regular pattern).

To visually access the results of the proposed approach, let's consider some frames of the "Artificial Motion" sequence. Fig. 4 shows five frames of this input sequence; Fig. 5 shows the same frames elaborated using as "outlier removal" the *RANSAC* algorithm; while Fig. 6 shows the same frames elaborated with the proposed system. It is important to note that the proposed system tends to stabilize very well the input frames, maintaining original frames behavior, without introducing false slight translation or rotation. Results are similar compared to *RANSAC*.

Another example is reported in Fig. 7, Fig.8 and Fig. 9, where frames of the "Regular Pattern" sequence are considered. Fig. 7 shows five frames of this input sequence; Fig. 8 shows the same frames elaborated using as "outlier removal" the *RANSAC* algorithm; while Fig. 9 shows the same frames elaborated with the proposed system. It is important to note that also in this difficult situation, the proposed system tends to stabilize very well the input frames, while *RANSAC* suffers more losing the white spot on the window.

At the following link are available the input video and the video stabilization results obtained with *RANSAC* and with our method on the two sequences in Fig. 4 and Fig. 7: http://iplab.dmi.unict.it/acivs2015.

Fig. 4. Five subsequent frames of input "Artificial Motion" sequence.

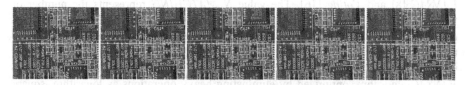

Fig. 5. Same frames of Fig. 4 elaborated with *RANSAC* algorithm.

Fig. 6. Same frames of Fig. 4 elaborated with the proposed system.

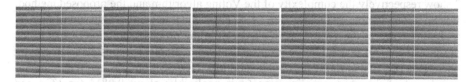

Fig. 7. Five subsequent frames of input "Regular Pattern" sequence.

Fig. 8. Same frames of Fig. 7 elaborated with *RANSAC* algorithm.

Fig. 9. Same frames of Fig. 7 elaborated with the proposed system.

4   Computational Cost Comparison

To properly highlight the peculiarity in terms of computational complexity of the proposed solution, we compared it with respect to prior state of the art algorithms: *RANSAC* [8] and *Voting* [16]. The value *N_MATCHING* represents the number of fixed input matching obtained with *FAST* detector [19] and *BRIEF* descriptor [20] optical flow and it is different according to sequence dimension: up to *VGA* is 800; up to *720p* is 1400.

Table 1 summarizes the complexity, in terms of operations count, related to *RANSAC* algorithm, optimized by eliminating heavy operations as logarithm, square root etc. From elaborations made on a large set of sequences, the *N_TRIALS*, representing the number of trials needed to the execution of *RANSAC*, can be limited to *N_TRIALS_MAX* (1000) to obtain good results, while the *N_TRIALS_MEAN* are the mean of *N_TRIALS* executed by *RANSAC*, distinguished by sequence dimensions. At the end, the complexity is expressed in both cases: the worst case (that is considering *N_TRIALS_MAX*) and the average case (that is considering *N_TRIALS_MEAN*). It is important to note that, for complexity comparison, usually only the worst case is considered. We included also the average case to demonstrate that the proposed solution have got lower complexity also considering the *RANSAC* mean case. Table 2 and 3 show respectively the complexity of the Voting algorithm and the proposed method. It is important to note that while *THETA_STEP* is equal in the two algorithms, there is a big difference in the *TRASL_STEP*, reduced in the proposed solution thanks to the pre-processing. Of course, in the proposed solution complexity considers some extra operations due to *Find MM maximum* sub-block (see Section 2.2) and the computational cost of the pre-processing step (it is negligible: about 0.08M for *VGA* and 0.28M for *720p*).

The prosed solution is about ten times speeder than *RANSAC* (averaging *VGA* and *720p* cases) and more than three times speeder than *Voting*. Also considering *RANSAC* in the average case, the proposed solution is almost one time and half speeder.

Table 1. Operation count of *RANSAC* algorithm.

RANSAC	N_MATCHING	N_TRIALS	COMPLEXITY
VGA	800	1000 (*MAX*)	27.20M
720p	1400	1000 (*MAX*)	47.66M
VGA	800	100 (*MEAN*)	2.72M
720p	1400	200 (*MEAN*)	9.52M

Table 2. Operation count of *Voting* algorithm.

VOTING	N_MATCHING	THETA_STEP	TRASL_STEP	COMPLEXITY
VGA	800	20 [-5..5] step 0.5	32 [-32..32] step 2	6.40M
720p	1400	20 [-5..5] step 0.5	64 [-64..64] step 2	21.95M

Table 3. Operation count of the proposed solution.

PROPOSED	N_MATCHIN G	THETA_STEP	TRASL_STEP	COMPLEXIT Y
VGA	800	20 [-5..5] step 0.5	8 $[Tx'-8..Tx'+8]$ step 2	2.08M
720p	1400	20 [-5..5] step 0.5	16 $[Tx'-16..Tx'+16]$ step 2	6.47M

5   Conclusion

The proposed method has been experimentally tested on a representative dataset of scenes obtaining effective results in terms of estimation accuracy (results are similar to *RANSAC*). A very reliable and low-cost robust regression system has been developed with the following characteristics:

- Robust to outliers also in critical conditions;
- Fixed cycles count (not iterative method);
- Very low computational count;
- Results are replicable (deterministic method).

In particular, the proposed pipeline reaches at least the *RANSAC* performances also in particular critical conditions (artificial motion and regular pattern) and it is about ten times speeder than *RANSAC* (averaging *VGA* and *720p* cases) and more than three times speeder than *Voting*.

References

1. Battiato, S., Farinella, G.M., Giudice, O., Puglisi, G.: Aligning Shapes for Symbol Classification and Retrieval Multimedia Tools and Applications. Springer (2015)
2. Bosco, A., Bruna, A., Battiato, S., Bella G., Puglisi, G.: Digital Video Stabilization through Curve Warping Techniques. IEEE Transactions on Consumer Electronics (2008)
3. Battiato, S., Bruna, A., Puglisi, G.: A Robust Block Based Image/Video Registration Approach for Mobile Imaging Devices. IEEE Transactions on Multimedia (2010)
4. Puglisi, G., Battiato, S.: A Robust Image Alignment Algorithm for Video Stabilization Purposes. IEEE Transactions on Circuits and Systems for Video Technology (2011)
5. Astola, J., Kuosmanen, P.: Fundamentals of Nonlinear Digital Filtering. CRC Press. Boca Raton, New York (1997)
6. Ling, L., Yin, R., Wang, X.: Nonlinear filters for reducing spiky noise: 2-dimensions. In: Proceedings of the IEEE International Conference on Acoustic Speech and Signal Processing (1984)

7. Pearson, R.: Data cleaning for dynamic modeling and control. In: European Control Conference (1999)
8. Fischler, M.A., Bolles, R.C.: Random Sample Consensus: A Paradigm for Model Fitting with Applications to Image Analysis and Automated Cartography. Communications of the ACM **24** (1981)
9. Matas, J., Chum, O.: Randomized RANSAC with Td, d test. Image and Vision Computing (2004)
10. Capel, D.: An effective bail-out test for RANSAC consensus scoring. In: Proceedings of British Machine Vision Conference (2005)
11. Matas, J., Chum, O.: Randomized RANSAC with sequential probability ratio test. In: Proceedings of ICCV (2005)
12. Chum, O., Matas, J., Kittler, J.: Locally optimized RANSAC. In: Michaelis, B., Krell, G. (eds.) DAGM 2003. LNCS, vol. 2781, pp. 236–243. Springer, Heidelberg (2003)
13. Tordoff, B., Murray, D.W.: Guided sampling and consensus for motion estimation. In: Heyden, A., Sparr, G., Nielsen, M., Johansen, P. (eds.) ECCV 2002, Part I. LNCS, vol. 2350, pp. 82–96. Springer, Heidelberg (2002)
14. Chum, O., Matas, J.: Matching with PROSAC - progressive sample consensus. In: Proceedings of CVPR (2005)
15. Nister, D.: Preemptive RANSAC for live structure and motion estimation. In: Proceedings of ICCV (2003)
16. Battiato, S., Farinella, G.M., Messina, E., Puglisi, G.: A Robust Forensic Hash Component for Image Alignment. International Conference on Image Analysis and Processing (2011)
17. Chen, H.H., Liang, C., Peng, Y., Chang, H.: Integration of Digital Stabilizer With Video Codec for Digital Video Cameras. IEEE Transaction Circuits System Video Technology (2007)
18. Lowe, D.G.: Distinctive image features from scale-invariant keypoints. International Journal of Computer Vision (2004)
19. Rosten, E., Drummond, T.: Machine learning for high-speed corner detection. In: Leonardis, A., Bischof, H., Pinz, A. (eds.) ECCV 2006. LNCS, vol. 3951, pp. 430–443. Springer, Heidelberg (2006)
20. Calonder, M., Lepetit, V., Ozuysal, M., Trzcinski, T., Strecha, C., Fua, P.: Computing a Local Binary Descriptor Very Fast. IEEE Transactions on Pattern Analysis and Machine Intelligence (2012)
21. Spampinato, G., Bruna, A.: A method and device for stabilizing video sequences, related video capture apparatus and computer program product. Patent US20140204227 (2014)

Adaptive Scale Selection for Multiscale Image Denoising

Federico Angelini[3], Vittoria Bruni[1,3]([✉]), Ivan Selesnick[2],
and Domenico Vitulano[3]

[1] Department of SBAI, University of Rome La Sapienza, Rome, Italy
vittoria.bruni@sbai.uniroma1.it
[2] Electrical and Computer Engineering, Polytechnic Institute of New York
University, New York City, USA
selesi@poly.edu
[3] Istituto per le Applicazioni del Calcolo "M. Picone" — C.N.R., Roma, Italy
d.vitulano@iac.cnr.it

Abstract. Adaptive transforms are required for better signal analysis
and processing. Key issue in finding the optimal expansion basis for a
given signal is the representation of signal information with very few
elements of the basis. In this context a key role is played by the multi-
scale transforms that allow signal representation at different resolutions.
This paper presents a method for building a multiscale transform with
adaptive scale dilation factors. The aim is to promote sparsity and adap-
tiveness both in time and scale. To this aim interscale relationships of
wavelet coefficients are used for the selection of those scales that measure
significant changes in signal information. Then, a wavelet transform with
variable dilation factor is defined accounting for the selected scales and
the properties of coprime numbers. Preliminary experimental results in
image denoising by Wiener filtering show that the adaptive multiscale
transform is able to provide better reconstruction quality with a minimum number of scales and comparable computational effort with the
classical dyadic transform.

1 Introduction

In the last years there has been a huge research work concerning time-frequency
transforms, since many problems of signal and image processing can be successfully solved by expanding the signal in a proper basis where signal features
are emphasized. In general, this property is indicated with the term *sparsity*,
or *sparse representation*, i.e., the signal is represented as a series expansion in
a proper basis where only few coefficients are non zero [1]. A compact representation of the signal is in fact important for compression, denoising, feature
extraction, source separation and more recently, with the advent of compressive
sensing, also for acquisition [6]. However, there is not a unique optimal basis for
each kind of signal or for each kind of problem. That is why the family of bases is
wide; let us think about the family of *...lets*: wavelets, bandelets, brushlets, con-
tourlets, chirplets, curvelets, shearlets, wedgelets and so on [4,5]. These bases are

© Springer International Publishing Switzerland 2015
S. Battiato et al. (Eds.): ACIVS 2015, LNCS 9386, pp. 81–92, 2015.
DOI: 10.1007/978-3-319-25903-1_8

characterized by the class of functions they are able to compactly represent, the existence of a computable inverse transform, a fast algorithm for their discrete implementation. Optimization methods with sparsity constraints like FISTA [7], SALSA[8], MCA [9] etc. can increase the sparsity features of a given basis also allowing the separation of different sources in the signal. Unfortunately, their separation/sparsity properties are strictly dependent on a good selection of the expansion bases and incoherence properties between them. Despite the rich literature on this topic, in general the concept of sparsity is only related to the time axis. Mutiresolution analysis splits signal information into frequency bands whose width increases as the resolution increases with a constant dilation factor. The classical dilation factor is two, giving rise to the dyadic decomposition; on the other hand, there has been a huge work for defining multiresolution with constant dilation factor different from two [2]. Unfortunately, even in this case the partition of the frequency domain is fixed once the number of levels of the transform has been selected, still providing a rigid structure in the scale line. Even though it is possible to select those bands that give a considerable contribution to the signal while discarding the others, these adaptive techniques are dependent on the transform and often are computationally demanding.

The idea of this work is to optimize the choice of the scales of a multiscale transform of a signal that is sparse in time in order to still have a multiresolution decomposition with perfect reconstruction properties and that can be easily implemented through subband coding schemes. The goal is to provide a procedure for the selection of the least number of scales able to represent significant changes in the signal without redundancy. To this aim, the interscale relationship between wavelet coefficients modelled in [15], and the Rational Dilation Wavelet Transform (RDWT) proposed in [2], with variable dilation factor have been employed. In fact, the atomic representation of the wavelet transform presented in [14,15] gives some constraints on the dilation parameters p and q to adopt at each level of the RDWT. More precisely, each signal singularity is modelled as an atom that dilates in the time scale plane and interacts with the atoms of neighbouring singularities. Atoms interference represents the distinct states of the multiscale representation of the signal and the scales at which it occurs are then non redundant. Hence, we are interested in finding those significant scales and to define an invertible multiscale decomposition of the signal that contains only these scales. Since these latter cannot obey to rigid power law, the RDWT with a dilation parameter that changes at each level of the transform can be used. The dilation parameters are selected in order to reproduce the sequence of significant scales. Some preliminary experimental results on image denoising show that the expansion of a signal in the adaptive rational dilation wavelet transform allows us to reach better denoising results than those provided by the dyadic scheme, using a smaller number of scales.

The outline of the paper is the following. Next section gives the motivation of the work through simple examples; it also briefly describes the existing tools that have been employed in the model: the time scale evolution of the wavelet transform [15] and the rational dilation wavelet transform [2]. Section 3 presents the adaptive scale selection procedure and the construction of the dilation parameters to adopt in the rational dilation wavelet transform. Section 4 shows some preliminary experimental results while the last Section draws the conclusions.

2   Motivation of the Work

This section gives the motivations of the work through the three simple examples shown in Fig. 1. The latter shows the wavelet transform at different scales of three piecewise linear signals having respectively two, three and four singularity points. It is evident that for these signals some scales are more important (less redundant) than others; in addition, these significant scales are not the same for the three signals: for the first signal (Fig. 1a) the first 8 scales do not register significant changes in the multiscale profile of the signal; on the contrary, for the second signal (Fig. 1b), scales greater than 8 do not give important additional information; finally, for the third signal (Fig. 1c) the dyadic scales are not the significant ones since they include more than one significant change of the system. It is then evident that the adaptive selection of scales would provide a more proper representation of the multiscale behaviour of the analysed signals.

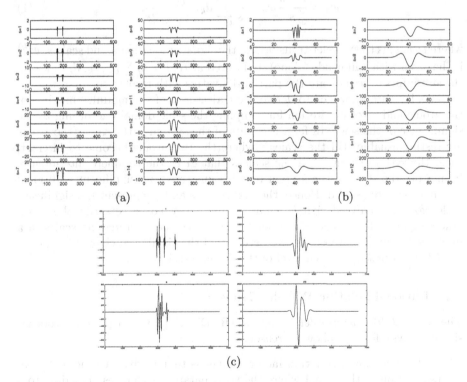

(a)   (b)

(c)

Fig. 1. Wavelet transform at different scales of three piecewise linear signals having respectively two (a), three (b) and four (c) singularity points.

However, this selection would be really useful if it is possible to define an invertible and easy implementable transform providing only those scales. These two goals can be reached using a formal description of the time-scale evolution of the wavelet transform that has been presented in [15] and the Rational dilation wavelet transform as presented in [2].

2.1   Atomic Representation and Time-Scale Evolution

The atomic approximation introduced in [15] allows us to describe the evolution of the wavelet transform of a signal at subsequent scales. Specifically, this evolution is represented as the interference of basic atoms in the scale domain. Each atom corresponds to a singularity in the time domain [14]. If these singularities are far in the time domain, then their corresponding atoms in the wavelet transform dilate as the scale increases and do not influence each other till a given fixed scale where they become to interact. The degree of interaction increases with the scale till the two atoms completely interfere; from this point on it behaves as if they were just one atom (see Fig. 1b). This evolution is properly described by a partial differential equation with diffusive, sourcing and transport terms:

$$w_s = \frac{\bar{t} - u}{s} w_u + \frac{1}{s} \sum_{k=1}^{N} d_k w_u^{(k)} + \frac{w}{2s}, \tag{1}$$

where $w(u, s)$ is the wavelet transform of the signal at location u and scale s, $w^{(k)}$ is the atom with amplitude (slope) α_k located at t_k, $\bar{t} = \frac{1}{N} \sum_{k=1}^{N} t_k$, $d_k = \bar{t} - t_k$, the subscripts of w indicate the partial derivative with respect to s and u.

   This law also allows us to derive the trajectories of the modulus maxima of the atoms and gives a criterion for sampling the scale domain according to the significance of the scale. In fact, the state of the system is the same (the atoms are distinguishable) till the scale $\tilde{s}$, where the two atoms become to interact; then, the system changes till the scale $\bar{s}$ that gives the complete interference; from $\bar{s}$ on, the state of the system remains unaltered: no significant additional information is registered. Hence, the first scale, $\tilde{s}$ and $\bar{s}$ represent the significant scales for the analysed signal. Unfortunately, they not necessarily obey to a power (dyadic) law. Hence, in order to reproduce these interesting scales in a multiresolution decomposition, we need a tool that is able to change the power law (dilation factor) at each level of the decomposition.

2.2   Rational Dilation Wavelet Transform

The *rational-dilation wavelet transform* (RADWT) [2,3] is a powerful tool for signal analysis for the following reasons:

- it allows a tunable dilation factor. It means that it gives a time-scale representation of the signal where the scale parameter changes according to a factor that is smaller than two. Hence, the high frequencies of the signal are analysed with a finer resolution than in the dyadic case;

- it is implemented through a filter bank, as the classical discrete wavelet transform, by using just a couple of filters, respectively low-pass and high pass, that satisfy the perfect reconstruction condition. The same filters are used in both analysis and synthesis steps;
- it involves downsampling (by the parameter p) and upsampling (by the parameter q) operations, even though it has some redundancy with respect to the dyadic case. The redundancy depends on the scale factor (the ratio $\frac{q}{p}$) i.e., the frequency resolution chosen for the analysis;
- it allows a high flexibility in the construction of the involved filters since it is possible to select not only the dilation factor and/or the redundancy, but also the filter decay in the transition band;
- it has a straightforward extension to 2D.

3   Scale Selection

The goal of this Section is to define an adaptive sampling of the scales that better represent the significant interference points given by the evolution law in (1). As mentioned above, atoms interference represents the different states of the system. We are interested in finding those scales where the system changes its state. More formally, let us consider the evolution law for N atoms located at t_k with slopes α_k, then

Theorem 1. *The minimum scale $\bar{s}$ at which N atoms can be represented as one isolated atom (complete interference) is such that*

$$u_k(s) = \bar{t}, \quad \forall\, s > \bar{s}, \quad \forall\, k = 1, \dots, N, \tag{2}$$

where t_k, $\forall\, k = 1, \dots, N$ are atoms locations, $\bar{t} = \frac{1}{N}\sum_{k=1}^{N} t_k$ and $u_k(s)$ is the trajectory of the atom located at t_k and it is the solution of the following problem

$$\begin{cases} \dot{u}_k = -\dfrac{\bar{t}-u_k}{s} - \dfrac{1}{s}\dfrac{\sum_{k=1}^{N} \alpha_k d_k \psi\left(\frac{t_k-u_k}{s}\right)}{\sum_{k=1}^{N} \alpha_k \psi\left(\frac{t_k-u_k}{s}\right)} \\ u_k(1) = t_k \qquad\qquad\qquad\qquad\quad \forall\, k = 1, 2, \dots, N \end{cases} \tag{3}$$

where $d_k = \bar{t} - t_k$ and $\{\alpha_k\}_{1 \le k \le N}$ are the atoms slopes.

This is a straightforward result of the atomic approximation theory in [15] but it would involve expensive numerical schemes for its solution. Since we are interested in finding a fast algorithm for the selection of interesting scales, in the following we will adopt a faster and direct way for the estimation of those scales. In a more simplified setting, we can consider the N interfering and equally spaced (i.e., $t_k - t_{k-1} = d$, $\forall\, k$) atoms having the same slopes, i.e. $\alpha_k = \alpha$ $\forall\, k$. In this case the solution of (3) can be found with a more stable algorithm that looks at the value of the transform rather than at atoms trajectories, i.e. $\bar{s}$ is the minimum scale such that

$$\left\| \sum_{k=1}^{N} w^{(k)}(t_k, u, s) - w_{single}(\bar{t}, u, s) \right\| \le \varepsilon, \tag{4}$$

where $w^{(k)}$ is $k - th$ atom in the packet with slope $\bar{\alpha}$ and w_{single} is the wavelet transform of a signal with one singularity located at $\bar{t}$ and slope $\bar{\alpha}$, and ε is a predefined tolerance. Table 1 provides the values of $\bar{s}$ for a variable number of atoms that have been obtained using (4).

Table 1. Maximum scale of interaction of different number of atoms.

N_i	2	3	4	5	6	7	8	9
$\bar{s}_i$	4.25	7.83	10.81	13.8	18.5	21.24	25.6	30.87

However, in a real signal, the wavelet transform is better represented by groups of interacting atoms and their interaction cannot be neglected, as explained in the next section.

3.1   Packets of Atoms

A packet of atoms is a set of N subsequent adjacent atoms located at $\{t_k\}_{k=1,2,...,N}$ such that

$$|t_{k+1} - t_k| \leq T_2 \quad \forall\, k = 1, 2, \ldots, N - 1$$

where T_2 is the minimum distance between two interfering atoms, i.e. T_2 is the support of the adopted wavelet at the analysed scale.

In other words a packet of atoms is a set of atoms that are adjacent and so close to be in interference. Hence, more in general, each signal can be partitioned into P packets with size $L_1, L_2, ..., L_P$ separated by $P-1$ intervals of size $\overline{L}_1, \overline{L}_2, ..., \overline{L}_{P-1}$, and the following configurations are admissible:

- f has only isolated singularities;
- f contributes in the time-scale domain with just one packet of correlated information;
- f contributes in the time-scale domain with:
  - disjoint packets;
  - joint packets.

For each configuration, we are interested in finding those scales that better represent packets interaction.

Isolated Singularities. Let $\overline{L}_1, \overline{L}_2, .., \overline{L}_{N-1}$ the intervals that separate the N atoms. From the atomic theory they will interfere at $N - 1$ scale levels $s_1, s_2, ..,$ s_{N-1}, not necessarily distinct, that represent the significant scales.

Single Packet. We assume that each packet of size L_i is composed of N_i atoms such that $N_i = L_i/l(s)$, where $l(s)$ is the support of the adopted wavelet at scale s^1. The atoms in the packet will interfere for increasing scales. If we have K available scale levels (budget), they have to be placed in an optimal (in some sense) way in the range of scales $[1, \overline{s}_i]$, where $\overline{s}_i$ is the scale level where all atoms of the packet completely interfere, following the criterion used for isolated singularities.

Disjoint Packets. Disjoint packets are a collection of P packets with sizes $L_1, L_2, .., L_P$ and distances $\overline{L}_1, \overline{L}_2, .., \overline{L}_{P-1}$ such that if $L = max\{L_1, L_2, .., L_P\}$, $\overline{L} = min\{\overline{L}_1, \overline{L}_2, .., \overline{L}_{P-1}\}$, $\overline{s}_L$ the scale where the packet of size L becomes one atom and $\overline{s}_{\overline{L}}$ the scale where the packets at distance $\overline{L}$ begin to interfere, then

$$\overline{s}_L < \overline{s}_{\overline{L}}. \tag{5}$$

This hypothesis assures that all atoms of each packet will go in complete interference before packets will begin to interfere. From that point on, we fall in the case of finding the best allocation of scales with a signal with isolated singularities. More precisely, in case of disjoint packets and for a fixed scale budget K:

- compute the scale $\overline{s}_L$ (corresponding to the largest packet)
- compute the scale $\overline{s}_l$ (corresponding to the smallest packet)
- define the interval of scales as follows $[s_{min}, s_{max}] = [\overline{s}_l, \overline{s}_L]$

This interval contains the significant signal information.

Joint Packets. For joint packets, the condition in eq. (5) does not hold. $L_1, L_2, .., L_P$ are also involved since the lengths $\overline{L}_i$ change as the scale increases, i.e. $\overline{L}_i = \overline{L}_i(s) \quad \forall i$. In particular, they become smaller and smaller for increasing scales and the P scales such that $\overline{L}_i = 0$ become important since they indicate a change in the structure of the signal: two distinct packets become a single one.

3.2   Scale Selection Algorithm

By collecting results and observations of the previous section, we can define the following scale selection algorithm. For a given signal f:

- Compute the continuous wavelet transform of f at scale $s = 1$ using a fixed wavelet;
- Select those coefficients whose modulus overexceeds the threshold value T_1 and determine the *packets decomposition* of the signal as groups of adjacent coefficients in the thresholded vector: P packets of *length* L_i, $i = 1, \ldots, P$;
- For each packet, compute the number of equally spaced atoms in it, i.e. $N_i = L_i/l(i)$. Select the related interesting scales in Table 1 and store them in the vector S_i;

---

[1] This is just a likely and fast approximation of the content of the packet.

- For each couple of subsequent packets, estimate the scale at which the two packets start to interfere ($Sbar_i$ with $i = 1, \ldots, P-1$): assuming the samples between the two packets as a complementary packet.
- For two subsequent packets P_i and P_{i+1}:
  - **if** $Sbar_i > max(max(S_i), max(S_{i+1}))$ [disjoint packets], **then** add S_i and S_{i+1} to the vector of selected scales S
  - **else if** $Sbar_i < min(max(S_i), max(S_{i+1}))$ [joint packets], **then** add S_i^C, the scale of the complementary packet, to the vector of selected scales S
  - **else if** $Sbar_i > min(max(S_i), max(S_{i+1}))$
  AND $Sbar_i < max(max(S_i), max(S_{i+1}))$ [partially joint packets], remove the values greater than $Sbar_i$ from S_i and S_{i+1} and add S_i and S_{i+1} to the vector of selected scales S.

4   Adaptive RDWT

The scale selection algorithm provides a set of significant scales $S = [s_1, s_2, \ldots, s_K]$. It is then necessary to define a transform with K scale levels where the $j-th$ level represents s_j. More precisely, we want to find out the scaling coprime parameters q_j, p_j of a RDWT such that

$$1 \leq p_j < q_j \leq p_{max} \quad \forall j = 1, \ldots, K : \quad \begin{cases} \frac{q_1}{p_1} = s_1 \\ \frac{q_1}{p_1}\frac{q_2}{p_2} = s_2 \\ \ldots \\ \prod_{j=1}^{K} \frac{q_j}{p_j} = s_K \end{cases} \tag{6}$$

where p_{max} is the maximum allowed value for p. By substituting the first equation into the second one, the second equation into the third one and so on, we obtain

$$\begin{cases} \frac{q_1}{p_1} = s_1 \equiv r_1 \\ \frac{q_2}{p_2} = \frac{s_2}{s_1} \equiv r_2 \\ \ldots \\ \frac{q_K}{p_K} = \frac{s_K}{s_{K-1}} \equiv r_K \end{cases} \tag{7}$$

that is a system of K equations with $2K$ variables, where $r_1, r_2, \ldots, r_K$ are rational numbers. Eq. (7) can be easily solved using a binary search in the Stern-Brocot Tree [11] if it is relaxed as follows:

$$1 \leq p_j \leq q_j \leq p_{max} \quad \text{such that}$$

$$\left| r_j - \frac{q_j}{p_j} \right| = \min_{a,b \in \mathbb{N} \cap [1,\ldots,p_{max}]} \left| r_j - \frac{a}{b} \right| \tag{8}$$

In the Stern-Brocot tree each rational number occurs only once and each fraction is *irreducible* [10,12,13] (which means that q and p are coprime). The root of the tree is $\frac{1}{1}$. For each node, the right child is the *mediant*[2] of itself and its

---

[2] The mediant of two fractions $\frac{a}{b}$ and $\frac{c}{d}$ is $\frac{a+c}{b+d}$.

largest and closest ancestor. Hence, the right child is bigger than the father but smaller than the largest and closest father's ancestor. The left child of a node is obtained as the *mediant* of itself and its lowest and closest ancestor. Hence, the left child is lower than the father but greater than the lowest and closest father's ancestor. The Stern-Brocot Tree is then a binary search tree and the search of a specific key requires a logarithmic time. Moreover, since rational numbers with the same integer part are grouped into a specific subtree, it is not necessary to build the entire tree. Hence, by setting $dist_n = a_n - r_j$, $a_0 = \frac{\lceil r_j \rceil}{1}$, $a_1 = \frac{2\lceil r_j \rceil - 1}{2}$, the search path $\{a_n\}_n$ in the Stern-Brocot Tree is:

$$a_{n+1} = \begin{cases} \text{Left child of } a_n & \text{if } dist_n > 0 \\ \text{Right child of } a_n & \text{if } dist_n < 0 \\ \text{stop} & \text{if } dist_n = 0. \end{cases}$$

It is worth observing that the numerator and denominator of a_n are always greater than those of a_{n-1}; so, the lists $\{q_n\}_n$ and $\{p_n\}_n$ are increasing and the elements of the path are gradually closer to r_j. Even in this case, the search can be stopped by introducing a prefixed tolerance on the precision required to the approximation of r_j.

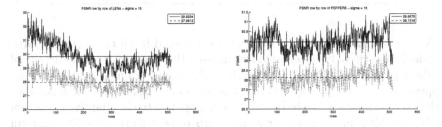

Fig. 2. PSNR results row by row for $512 \times 512 \times 8$ bits Lena (*left*) and Peppers (*right*) images achieved using dyadic (*dashed line*) and adaptive scales (*solid line*).

5   Preliminary Experimental Results

The proposed adaptive RDWT transform has been used for image denoising. To this aim, the empirical Wiener filtering applied to each level of the transform has been selected. The results have been compared with those achieved using the classical dyadic transform with 5 scale levels. In the scale selection algorithm, the threshold T_1 has been fixed equal to the 10% of the energy of the wavelet transform at scale $s = 1$. A 9 taps biorthogonal wavelet has been used since it is the default choice in [15]; the maximum allowed value for the parameters of the RDWT is 64, according to the length of the analysed signals. Due to the 1d nature of atoms' evolution law, the images have been treated as independent 1d signals. We have tested the method by processing the images row by row or

Table 2. PSNR denoising results for the Wiener filter applied to the dyadic and to the adaptive multiscale transform (no. is the average numeber of adopted scales). 1D is referred to the row by row processing; 2D is referred to the block by block processing; the suffix Th means that a constraint on the distance between successive scales has been introduced.

σ	10			15		
Method/scale	Adapt	Dyad	no. of scales	Adapt	Dyad	no. of scales
1D	32.44	30.63	4.05	29.80	27.96	4.24
1D Th=.5	32.20	30.63	3.17	29.48	27.96	3.46
1D Th=1	32.05	30.63	2.17	29.32	27.96	2.33
2D	32.82	30.88	3.92	30.37	28.26	4.20
2D Th=.5	32.38	30.88	3.02	29.81	28.26	3.40
2D Th=1	32.11	30.88	2.05	29.53	28.26	2.27

σ	20			25			30		
Method/scale	Adapt	Dyad	no.	Adapt	Dyad	no.	Adapt	Dyad	no.
1D	28.05	26.28	4.61	26.72	25.07	4.99	25.64	24.11	5.32
1D Th=.5	27.74	26.28	4.01	26.40	25.07	4.51	25.30	24.11	4.91
1D Th=1	27.51	26.28	2.57	26.18	25.07	2.99	25.14	24.11	3.45
2D	28.62	26.60	4.66	27.30	25.40	5.05	26.18	24.46	5.28
2D Th=.5	28.03	26.60	3.97	26.63	25.40	4.38	25.28	24.46	4.53
2D Th=1	27.78	26.60	2.59	26.50	25.40	2.97	25.47	24.46	3.37

block by block (16×16 blocks have been considered in all tests). In the latter case the Peano curve has been used for catching the 2d correlation in a 1d signal.

Fig. 2 provides the PSNR results achieved row by row on 512×512 Lena and Peppers images corrupted by additive independent gaussian noise with standard deviation $\sigma = 15$. As it can be observed, when applied to the adaptive transform, the Wiener filter provides better results with respect to the dyadic transform. The increment of the PSNR value is on average 1.84 db for Lena and 1.81 db for Peppers; the average number of adopted scales respectively is 4.23 and 4.26. Table 2 shows the PSNR results and the average number of scales used for denoising Lena image corrupted by gaussian noise with different standard deviations. As it can be observed, the higher the number of adaptive scales, the higher the PSNR values; however, the increment of PSNR not only depends on the number of adopted scales, but it especially depends on which scales have been selected. It is also worth observing that the use of the Peano Curve (2D) provides better results than the row by row processing (1D).

In order to test the robustness of the proposed method to a smaller number of scales, a further constraint in the distance between successive scales has been introduced. This variant has been indicated with the suffix Th in Table 2. As it can be observed, if the number of adaptive scales decreases, the PSNR decreases too but it is still larger than the one achieved with the dyadic scheme.

The computational cost required by the proposed adaptive transform is moderate. The adaptive RDWT transform has a fast implementation since it involves simple convolutions, upsampling and downsampling operations. In addition,

Fig. 3. $512 \times 512 \times 8$ bits Lena image. *From left to right top to bottom:* original; noisy ($\sigma = 15$); denoised using dyadic scales; denoised using adaptive scales.

these filters have a closed form in the frequency domain, so that their construction does not require additional computational cost. The additional cost of the transform is the one required by the adaptive scale selection algorithm and the binary search in the Stern Brocot tree of the dilation parameters $\frac{q_j}{p_j}$. The binary search requires a logarithmic cost ($O(log_2(p_{max}))$), the scale selection algorithm involves: *i)* a convolution for the computation of the continuous wavelet transform at scale $s = 1$, i.e. $O(N_L)$, where N_L is the length of the analysed signal; *ii)* a thresholding operation for getting the packet decomposition ($O(N_L)$). The determination of the set of scales is a simple search in a look up table that can be precomputed using the iterative algorithm in (4). In a non optimed Matlab code that runs on a processor Intel Core i5-460M,4Gb RAM, the 1D version of the denoising algorithm takes 13 secs while the 2D version requires 22 secs.

6   Conclusions

In this paper an adaptive rational dilation wavelet transform has been presented. It exploits the time-scale relationships of wavelet coefficients for selecting those scales that better represent signal information; then, the dilation parameters that are necessary for defining a multiscale transform having only those scales are estimated and used as dilation factors in the Rational Dilation Wavelet Transform. The latter is invertible and has the nice properties of being implemented through a subband coding scheme. Preliminary experimental results on denoising have shown that the adaptive transform can provide better reconstruction properties than the classical dyadic (or more in general constant dilation factor) transform with a reduced budget of scales and with a negligible additional computational effort. Future research will be oriented to further improve and refine the scale selection algorithm and to test the proposed transform in other applications, like image compression. However, the most interesting development might be the extension of the method to the 2D case. Since the 2D RDWT already exists, it would require the non trivial extension of the evolution law to higher dimensions.

References

1. Mallat, S.: A wavelet tour of signal processing. Academic Press (1998)
2. Bayram, I., Selesnick, I.W.: Overcomplete Discrete Wavelet Transforms with Rational Dilation Factors. IEEE Trans. on Signal Proc. **57**(1), 131–145 (2009)
3. Bayram, I., Selesnick, I.W.: Frequency-Domain Design of Overcomplete Rational-Dilation Wavelet Transforms. IEEE Trans. on Signal Proc. **57**(8), 2957–2972 (2009)
4. Starck, J.L., Candes, E.J., Donoho, D.L.: The Curvelet Transform for Image Denoising. IEEE Trans. on Image Proc. **11**(6) (2002)
5. Do, M.N., Vetterli, M.: The contourlet transform: an efficient directional multiresolution image representation. IEEE Trans. on Image Proc. **14**(12), 2091–2106 (2005)
6. Donoho, D.L.: Compressed sensing. IEEE Trans. on Inf. Theory **52**, 1259–1306 (2006)
7. Beck, A., Teboulle, M.: A Fast Iterative Shrinkage-Thresholding Algorithm for Linear Inverse Problems. SIAM J. Imaging Sciences **2**(1), 183–202 (2009)
8. Afonso, M.V., Bioucas-Dias, J.M., Figueiredo, M.A.T.: Fast image recovery using variable splitting and constrained optimization. IEEE Trans. Image Proc. **19**(9), 2345–2356 (2010)
9. Starck, J.L., Elad, M., Donoho, D.L.: Redundant Multiscale Transforms and their Application for Morphological Component Analysis. Adv. in Imaging and Elect. Phys. **132** (2004)
10. Calkin, N., Wilf, H.S.: Recounting the rationals. The American Mathematical Monthly **107**(4), 360–363 (2000)
11. Brocot, A.: Calcul des rouages par approximation, nouvelle methode. Revue Chronometrique **3**, 186–194 (1861)
12. Northshield, S.: Stern's Diatomic Sequence 0, 1, 1, 2, 1, 3, 2, 3, 1, 4, …. The American Mathematical Monthly **117**(7), 581–598 (2010)
13. Bates, B., Bunder, M., Tognetti, K.: Locating terms in the Stern-Brocot tree. European Journal of Combinatorics **31**(3), 1030–1033 (2010)
14. Bruni, V., Vitulano, D.: Wavelet-based signal de-noising via simple singularities approximation. Signal Processing **86**(4), 859–876 (2006)
15. Bruni, V., Piccoli, B., Vitulano, D.: A fast computation method for time scale signal denoising. Signal, Image and Video Processing **3**(1), 63–83 (2009)

Secure Signal Processing Using Fully Homomorphic Encryption

Thomas Shortell$^{(\boxtimes)}$ and Ali Shokoufandeh

Drexel University, 3141 Chestnut St., Philadelphia, PA 19104, USA
`tms38@drexel.edu, ashokouf@cs.drexel.edu`

Abstract. This paper investigates the problem of performing signal processing via remote execution methods while maintaining the privacy of the data. Primary focus on this problem is a situation where there are two parties; a client with data or a signal that needs to be processed and a server with computational resources. Revealing the signal unencrypted causes a violation of privacy for the client. One solution to this problem is to process the data or signal while encrypted. Problems of this type have been attracting attention recently; particularly with the growing capabilities of cloud computing. We contribute to solving this type of problem by processing the signals in an encrypted form, using fully homomorphic encryption (FHE). Three additional contributions of this manuscript includes (1) extending FHE to real numbers, (2) bounding the error related to the FHE process against the unencrypted variation of the process, and (3) increasing the practicality of FHE as a tool by using graphical processing units (GPU). We demonstrate our contributions by applying these ideas to two classical problems: natural logarithm calculation and signal pr(brightness/contrast filter).

1 Introduction

Privacy is an important part of today's world. Cloud computing is becoming a norm in today's society as a modus operandi of computation ecosystem. Data stored "in the cloud" may not be encrypted and the cloud computer would be able to read this data. If the data contains personal information, then there may be significant privacy concerns associated the environment. However, even if you can assume the server is trust worthy, there is the potential of a security breach to the cloud computer, which would expose data to the attacker.

We focus on a simpler problem in this space: secure signal processing. Signals can be any function of time or space (sounds waves, images, etc.). Signal processing algorithms can be computationally intensive and offloading the computations to a computationally powerful server may be essential. But performing these processes will become a privacy issue if the signal can not be shared with the server. Thus, the problem is of performing computations of a signal processing algorithm in the secure space so that the server does not know what the data is and if possible the server does not know what the algorithm being run is.

© Springer International Publishing Switzerland 2015
S. Battiato et al. (Eds.): ACIVS 2015, LNCS 9386, pp. 93–104, 2015.
DOI: 10.1007/978-3-319-25903-1_9

In 2009, the first fully homomorphic encryption (FHE) scheme was developed [2]. This breakthrough provides a method to encrypt data and then process the data in the encrypted form. The scheme provides capabilities for addition and multiplication, which is very useful for signal processing as two simple building blocks. The contribution of this paper is using FHE as a framework to perform secure signal processing in generic fashions on potentially hostile servers. There are three specific contributions that will make tackling this problem possible. First, as the FHE scheme is integer-only based, a method to perform real number processing is developed. Second, there are numerical errors that can be introduced in the FHE process, and a framework to bound this error is also introduced. Bounding the error will be essential as it requires a trade off between accuracy, performance, and security. Third and finally, focus on making FHE a practical tool was partially tackled by determining the costly processing of FHE was a matrix-matrix multiplication and using the power of a GPU to improve the performance towards a more practical scheme. These contributions are realized by application in two classical problems in function evaluation (natural logarithm) and signal processing (brightness/contrast filter on an image).

2   Related Work

There has been much related work in terms of secure signal processing. Troncoso-Pastoriza and F. Perez-Gonzalez [11] were among the the first to propose the secure signal processing problem and considered its possible solution for a cloud computing model. Important results in this article focus on privacy issues in the cloud that will be important in the years to come particularly related to biometrics and health care information. Signal processing is needed particularly in the biometrics field. Wang et. al. [12] is an example of protecting biometric information that is used as an access control. The authors additionally focus on privacy concerns related to the signal data (biometrics). Others have realized the importance of secure signal processing for images and videos [8].

Knežević et. al. [5] also considered a generalized model on using digital signal processors to perform cryptography. This includes performing encryption and decryption processes on signal processors to speed up the respective processes. This relates to our contribution in that processing is offloaded to an GPU for performing improvements. In contrast, this paper focuses on performing a signal processing algorithm in an encrypted form vice just using the signal processor as a performance improvement.

There is a plethora of secure signal processing applications however, none of them use fully homomorphic encryption as the underlying method. Shashanka and Smaragdis [10] developed a method to classify audio signals via secure multi-party communications by hiding the real signal from the server and the classification parameters from the client. This is different from this work as it assumes there are two parties working together to solve the problem but our situation is the use of the server as a resource vice and interaction. Hsu, Lu, and Pei [4] developed a secure signal processing algorithm using the Paillier encryption

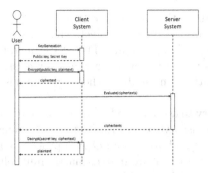

Fig. 1. FHE Scheme Structure and Flow

scheme to extract features from an image using SIFT (Scale Invariant Feature Transform). Paillier encryption scheme is an additive-only homomorphic encryption scheme, meaning that addition is performed on encrypted ciphertexts but multiplication cannot be. Paillier does support constant multiplication as well. The FHE scheme in this paper is a fully homomorphic encryption scheme which provides encrypted multiplication. Others have also worked with the Paillier encryption scheme [6] [7] [1]. Bai et al [1] were able to use Paillier's scheme to implemented an encrypted SURF. While this is closer to the research in this paper, the Paillier scheme only provides homomorphic addition, thus limiting the ability to perform some signal processing algorithms.

3   Fully Homomorphic Encryption

First we wish to go over the basics of fully homomorphic encryption scheme so the capabilities for secure signal processing are available. The scheme we use is a later scheme developed in 2013 by Gentry, Sahai, and Waters [3]. This scheme improved many of the original scheme issues in terms of being a legitimate tool for applications and computationally efficiency. Figure 1 shows how the scheme flows in sequence. As the figure shows, there are four main functions that are used by the user. They are KEYGENERATION, ENCRYPT, DECRYPT, and EVALUATE. KEYGENERATION is the first function and generates the public and secret keys that are used in encrypt and decrypt respectively. At this point, a user can encrypt any number of plaintexts (including a full signal) by using ENCRYPT. The resulting ciphertexts can then be sent to a server that can run the EVALUATE function. While this EVALUATE function is running on the server, it is developed by the user. After EVALUATE finishes, the ciphertexts can be retrieved (or returned to the user). Finally, DECRYPT returns the ciphertexts to their original form.

The public and secret key are generated by the use of a few parameters from the user in KEYGENERATION. The underlying security hardness problem is based on the Learning With Errors (LWE) problem. For brevity, the detailed derivations have been kept out of this paper and refer the reader to the original papers [3] [9]. LWE causes the public key to be a matrix and the secret key to be a vector. This is important as it effects the sizes of ciphertexts and the operations for evaluating. ENCRYPT and DECRYPT operate on integers in the ring $\mathbb{Z}_q$ [3]. We discuss in the following sections our approach to work around this limitation. An additional note about these processes is that ciphertexts are square matrices.

Finally, it is necessary to discuss the EVALUATE capabilities. There were three functions for the user to use (ADD, MULT, MULTCONST). Since ADD is addition of two ciphertexts (matrices), addition is an $O(N^2)$ process of adding the matrices. However, MULT and MULTCONST are matrix matrix multiplication (MULTCONST is a simple value multiplied by the identity matrix and then by the ciphertext matrix). These are obviously $O(N^3)$ processes and a cause of concern since this will require significant computations. This is the primary focus on using a GPU to solve this problem.

4   Encrypted Natural Logarithm

Section 3 provides a scheme that can support addition and multiplication, so now we can consider performing an encrypted natural logarithm. Taylor expansions provide a way to calculate a function around a set point in terms of addition and multiplication (two functions available to us). But this is not the only capability needed to make this work. Natural logarithms are performed over real numbers while the FHE scheme supports integers in a ring. A simple solution would be to just round the integers but this would be inaccurate thus ineffective. Another (but not optimal) solution to this problem is to multiply the fraction part of the real number so it is in the integer space. This solves the problem, but it introduces complexity in the form of unnecessary scaling of the ciphertexts when they are multiplied.

The Taylor expansion of a natural logarithm provides an equation form that the FHE scheme can evaluate. Taylor expansions work around a value $(a \geq 1)$. The following is the Taylor expansion of the natural logarithm of five terms:

$$\ln(x) \approx \ln(a) + \frac{1}{a}(x-a) - \frac{1}{2a^2}(x-a)^2 + \frac{1}{3a^3}(x-a)^3$$
$$- \frac{1}{4a^4}(x-a)^4 + \frac{1}{5a^5}(x-a)^5 \quad (1)$$

This equation is our means to estimate a natural logarithm in a way that can be performed by the FHE scheme. We also need to discuss security and privacy of this construction. It is important to disguise the operation being performed to maintain additional privacy about the data. It is easy to see how the corresponding Taylor expansion is for the natural logarithm. Consider a transform for $\ln(a) \rightarrow in_1$, $x \rightarrow in_2$, and $-a \rightarrow in_3$. Remember these inputs are encrypted. So the processing equation is $out = in_1 + \sum_{i=1}^{5} c_i \cdot (in_2 + in_3)^i$ with c_x for each of the constants of the expansion. Looking at these equations, it may not be immediately obvious that this is a natural logarithm calculation. It may also be hard to distinguish that this is a Taylor expansion. This is partially possible because inputs 2 and 3 are not directly exposed (input 3 is a negative number, which is information not available at the onset to an attacker). The attacker could also be limited by not using constants and actually encrypting the values.

Next, we would like to focus on the issue of quantization that is due to the limitation of FHE in handling real values. By multiplying by a constant factor, a fractional part of a number can be moved into the integer space; similar to a fixed point representation. The difference from an actual fixed point representation is that in fixed point, the fractional part can be contained by performing a division by the constant as part of a multiplication. This is not possible with the FHE scheme - no division capability. Increasing the modulus of the ring will provide additional space to represent the fractional portion of a real number. Consider L multiplication levels and the return factor number is now x^L, with x being the initial factor. This has direct effect on the modulus ($x^L < q$ must be true) and then affects the key and ciphertext sizes as a result. Lastly, we wish to discuss bounding the numerical error that will occur so we can identify a practical, usable scaling factor. We will also bound a to be an integer, since it simplifies the equation and the implementation.

Theorem 1. *Given a natural logarithm Taylor expansion FHE implementation, a value L that is the maximum allowed error, Taylor expansion parameter $a \geq 1$ and $a \in \mathbb{Z}$, then the scaling factor $(\in \mathbb{Z})$ must obey the following equation:*

$$scale \geq \frac{1}{L}\left(1 + \frac{1}{a} + (x-a) - \frac{1}{a^2}(x-a)^2 + (x-a)^2 + \frac{1}{a^3}(x-a)^2 + (x-a)^3 \right.$$
$$\left. -\frac{1}{a^4}(x-a)^3 + (x-a)^4 + \frac{1}{a^5}(x-a)^4 + (x-a)^5\right) \quad (2)$$

Proof. We start by amplifying the Taylor expansion with an additive error value, $\Delta e = \frac{1}{scale}$, to all fractional values $\ln(a) + \Delta e + \left(\frac{1}{a} + \Delta e\right)(x + \Delta e - a) + \cdots$. Next, we will separate the error terms from the main Taylor terms to bound the error. This is a straightforward, but tedious process that is not shown here for brevity. We will also only want to keep first order error terms since higher order terms will be comes negligible quicker than the first order terms. Our next equation shows this remaining first order error.

$$L \geq \Delta e \left(1 + \frac{1}{a} + (x-a) - \frac{1}{a^2}(x-a)^2 + (x-a)^2 + \frac{1}{a^3}(x-a)^2 + (x-a)^3\right.$$
$$\left. -\frac{1}{a^4}(x-a)^3 + (x-a)^4 + \frac{1}{a^5}(x-a)^4 + (x-a)^5\right) \quad (3)$$

If we switch $\Delta e = \frac{1}{scale}$ and rotate terms:

$$scale \geq \frac{1}{L}\left(1 + \frac{1}{a} + (x-a) - \frac{1}{a^2}(x-a)^2 + (x-a)^2 + \frac{1}{a^3}(x-a)^2\right.$$
$$\left. +(x-a)^3 - \frac{1}{a^4}(x-a)^3 + (x-a)^4 + \frac{1}{a^5}(x-a)^4 + (x-a)^5\right) \quad (4)$$

completing the proof.

The usefulness of Theorem 1 should be immediate. If the user knows the desired error bound, then the scaling factor can be selected to meet their needs. The restrictions on the selection is minimizing the difference between x and a. Following the way that Taylor expansions generally work, this should not be an issue.

5   Brightness/Contrast Filter Theory

To realize the idea of a framework for secure signal processing with FHE, a brightness/contrast filter was implemented. By performing this filter via FHE, this validates the framework for secure signal processing. This is a simple example since the brightness/contrast filter operates on individual pixels one by one; with no interaction between the pixels. But the process can handle the entire image.

As part of creating an encrypted brightness/contrast filter, it is necessary to start with the unencrypted version. The basic equation is very simple:

$$g(x) = \alpha f(x) + \beta \qquad (5)$$

where $g(x)$ is the output image and $f(x)$ is the input image. Remember that this filter operates pixel by pixel so two pixels do not directly interact. The only interaction is with the two other parameters in the equation: α and β. α may be known as the gain and β may be know as the bias. It needs to be noted here that α is necessarily a fractional value. This means that to use this equation with an FHE scheme will require us to handle real numbers in some fashion.

The encrypted version of the filter needs to work in the environment of the FHE scheme. The equation itself requires a single multiplication followed by an addition (easily fits in the FHE implementation). Next, the format of the image must be considered because it affects how the α and β parameters are used. Images can be represented in many different formats. One particular format for color images that is used in this paper is representation of pixels as red/green/blue values. Individual colors can take on a variety of formats from a floating point value between 0 and 1 to a discrete value between 0 and 256. This framework was designed to process both potential representations. As a reminder, α and β are not integers and need to be represented as integers using the format discussed in the previous section.

Security aspects of this system need to be considered. First (and always), the FHE parameters need to be set to ensure security. The next item to be considered is whether any information is being given away by the filter itself. From an external perspective the equation looks like this:

$$y_i = c_{(-1)}x_i + c_{(-2)} \qquad (6)$$

where $c_{(-1)}$ and $c_{(-2)}$ are the ciphertext equivalents for α and β. Even though the signal is an image, the evaluator can treat the image as a one dimensional array vice a two dimensional array. This will also limit an attackers ability to get any metadata-like information about the signal from the evaluate processing itself.

From an attackers point of view, this is a simple one-dimensional multiplication by a constant with the addition of another constant.

Finally, the bound of the numerical error that is introduced by the scaling is important to the framework. First, the bound allows a user to identify a scaling factor that can either limit the error in a controllable way or remove it entirely. Second, the bound provides a method to check performance of the implementation.

Theorem 2. *Given a brightness/contrast filter FHE implementation and L, the maximum allowed error, then the scaling factor must obey the following equation:*

$$scale \geq \frac{a+c+1}{L} \qquad (7)$$

where a and c are bounds on the input values α and $f(x)$.

Proof. In the unencrypted world, the basic equation is

$$g(x) = \alpha f(x) + \beta \qquad (8)$$

Moving this equation into the encrypted world, the values α, $f(x)$, and β will have some fractional error as a result of the scaling (Δe). The equation becomes:

$$g(x) = (\alpha + \Delta e) \cdot (f(x) + \Delta e) + (\beta + \Delta e) \qquad (9)$$

then sorting terms:

$$g(x) = (\alpha \cdot f(x) + \beta) + (\alpha + f(x) + 1) \cdot \Delta e + (\Delta e)^2 \qquad (10)$$

where the first grouping is the original calculation, the middle term is the first order error, and the last term is the second order error. Since $(\Delta e)^2$ is less than Δe, this term will be negligible in comparison to the middle term. Additionally, at this point bounds on each of the terms is necessary (looking for maximum amount of error). The Δe term is at most $1/scale$. α and $f(x)$ will be bounded by the actual problem setup that is used for the filter; substituting $a = \alpha$ and $c = f(x)$ for the maximum values. With the value L as the maximum bound for the error, the following must hold:

$$\Delta e \cdot (a + c + 1) \leq L \qquad (11)$$

and since $\Delta e = \frac{1}{scale}$, the terms can be rearranged:

$$scale \geq \frac{a+c+1}{L} \qquad (12)$$

The importance of Theorem 2 is that a user of the framework can use the scaling factor to bound the error. However, there are additional items that can be considered here as well. If the value for any of the parameters is an integer, then there is no error term for that value in the formula. This enables improvements as the scaling factor can be lowered.

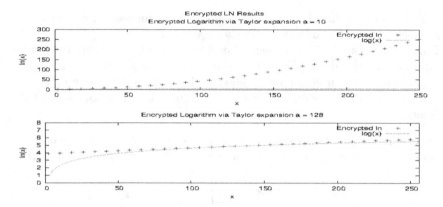

Fig. 2. Encrypted Natural Logarithm via Taylor Expansion Results

6   Experimental Results

In this section, we will evaluate the accuracy of the proposed methods through a set of experimental evaluations. For testing, we worked with input numbers in the ring $\mathbb{Z}_{256}$, a scaling factor of 256 (estimated accuracy of 0.004), and matrices in the size of 390×390. The code was then tested for values of a equal to 10 and 128. Figure 2 shows the results of the testing for values of x at intervals of 8 compared to the actual value. The line represents that actual natural logarithm and the points are the output values of the encrypted natural logarithm. As can be seen in the top diagram, the logarithm value diverges. But comparing the results to actual Taylor expansion of a natural logarithm, the values are actually very close. We show this plot because it is important to remember that there will be trade offs by selecting the value of a in a Taylor expansion. Considering the bottom figure with $a = 128$, it can be seen the accuracy is much better in terms of the value of the natural logarithm. As with the top figure, the results are very closely align to what a five term Taylor expansion would provide (values not shown on the plot). This does remind us that the accuracy will have three parts: a, the number of terms, and any numerical error caused by the scaling factor.

Next, we will present an overview of our implementation for BC filters and evaluate its performance. In our evaluations, we will consider three scenarios. First, comparing the results of running the filter in both domains (encrypted and unencrypted) against a specific image set to determine the total amount of error. Second, comparing the error in the images as a function of their sizes. Third, comparing the affects of different values for α and β.

Starting with the first test, Table 1 shows five images that were processed in both filters (unencrypted and encrypted) with the resulting error. α and β where set to constant values for this test (1.1 and 0.2 respectively). The images themselves were retrieved from the internet from known images used for signal processing. Focusing on the table, the first column is the original image

Table 1. Images Tested Under $\alpha = 1.1$ and $\beta = 0.2$

The first column is the scaled original image. The second column shows the image after being BC filtered in an unencrypted form. The third column shows the image after being BC filtered through the encrypted framework. Images are scaled to sizes on the order of $[100, 200] \times [100, 200]$ pixels.

scaled down to limit the required memory size. The second column is the image run through the unencrypted brightness/contrast filter. The third column is the image run through the FHE scheme's brightness/contrast filter. A naked eye may not easily be able to see the difference between these two columns, but there is some error introduced by the framework. The next paragraph discusses these errors in the second test.

Error introduced into the image by the scheme is an important aspect of whether this framework is a viable approach. Figure 3 shows two perspectives based on total errors that were tallied during testing. Figure 3a shows total error in an image against different sizes of images. Total error obvious increases with image size, which would be expected as there are more and more pixels. Figure 3b focuses the same error data into a per pixel (per color) basis. First, the errors per pixel show that the framework keeps the error below the expected threshold that was specified in Section 5. But there is more to this plot: implicitly, there is a relationship between the error and the type of image. Since the image size was increased from known images, the corresponding points in the x-axis are from equivalent images. This provides an experimental indication that the images' pixels original accuracy will drive how much error is introduced by the scheme. This is aligned with discussion from Section 5.

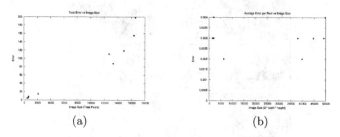

(a)   (b)

Fig. 3. Error Analysis of different sizes. (a) Total error introduced by the encrypted framework for different image sizes. Error increases as the the image size increase. (b) Average per color pixel that was introduced by the encrypted framework for differing image sizes. Errors per color pixel are within the thresholds and that the individual errors do not grow as the size increases.

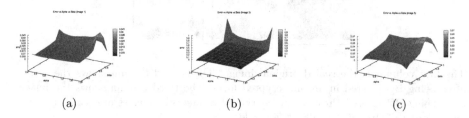

(a)   (b)   (c)

Fig. 4. 3D Plot of Average Errors with Varying α and β. α varied from $[0.5, 1.5]$ in increments of 0.1 and β varied from $[0.0, 1.0]$ in increments of 0.1. Each 3D plot is the averaged individual pixel error per image. The images are scaled down to a smaller range $[20, 30] \times [20, 30]$ from Table 1 sizes. Each plot shows that errors are effected by *alpha* and β and boundary issues begin to occur as β rises closer to one. (a) First image of Table 1. (b) Second image of Table 1. (c) Fifth image of Table 1.

The final test of the framework is varying the values of α and β. Varying these values provides additional insight into the error that can be caused by these two parameters. For the test, $\alpha = [0.5, 1.1]$ and $\beta = [0.0, 1.0]$ at increments of 0.1, respectively. Figure 4 shows the three dimensional plot of these tests. Of particular note immediately is that the values of β at 0.8 and 0.9 are significantly higher than the others and 1.0 is very close $< 10^{-5}$ to zero. This is less of an issue of the scheme itself than of properly handling the boundary conditions: at values of 0.8 and higher for β, this effectively makes the image equal to 1.0 for all pixels. With modular arithmetic, going over 1.0 in the fractional value results in pixels being skewed. In some cases, this was detected and fixed by the framework but it definitely reminds the user that different values of α and β can have unintended affects on the image.

Looking at the individual figures, the obvious artifact is the increase in error as α and β increase. This is a result of the issues discussed in the previous paragraph. Even with the variable caused by going over the limit, much of the error is contained below the error threshold previously setup. In all three tests, if the issues caused at $\beta = 1.0$ are ignored, which is not hard to assume as this is not exactly a useful use of the filter, then the error does hold below the expected threshold. This provides additional experimental evidence for verifying the theoretical work of Section 5. Looking back at these figures, there is evidence that α and β can and do affect the error levels of the results. Previous tests showed that individual images will have different errors and with this latest result, it can be seen that the analytical theory corresponds to the experimental results.

We finish this section by discussing time and space complexity of the schemes. Ciphertexts are matrices so they contribute $N \times N$ space complexity, which expands based on the number of ciphertexts needed (for n: nNN space complexity). For the natural logarithm, our implementation was a constant number of ciphertexts. But the BC filter is effectively an image of $x \times y$ pixels, which translates into $3xy$ ciphertexts for red/green/blue format; a total space complexity of $3xyN^2$. The matrix size is driven by the security parameters of the scheme, so a design decision trade off is needs to be made in all cases between security and complexity. Time complexity is generally going to be driven by the FHE multiplications in an implementation. FHE multiplications are $O(N^3)$ process because matrix-matrix multiplication is the real process inside the scheme. If parallel techniques are not used, this becomes very inefficient compared to an unencrypted version. Because matrix-matrix multiplication is a well known target for parallel computations and in our case with FHE, we were able to use both *openmp* and GPUs to support our needs. Redirecting the *gemm* function of the BLAS allows for significant speed up[1]. For the scaled down image, the processing time drops to less than 15 minutes from an original time of three hours.

7 Conclusion

In this paper, we presented a realization of a FHE protocol for a secure signal processing application. This was achieved by extending FHE to the domain of real numbers by a multiplicative factor, introducing an framework for containing errors introduced for the user to make trade off decisions, and using GPU capabilities to improve the schemes running times. We used two experimental setups to verify the error introduced by the framework. For the future, it will be very important to improve the quality of processing real numbers and continuing to improve the running times of the scheme.

---

[1] We used CUBLAS https://developer.nvidia.com/cublas

References

1. Bai, Y., Zho, L., Cheng, B., Peng, Y.F.: Surf feature extraction in encrypted domain. In: 2014 IEEE International Conference on Multimedia and Expo (ICME), pp. 1–6. IEEE (2014)
2. Gentry, C.: Computing arbitrary functions of encrypted data. Communications of the ACM **53**(3), 97–105 (2010)
3. Gentry, C., Sahai, A., Waters, B.: Homomorphic encryption from learning with errors: conceptually-simpler, asymptotically-faster, attribute-based. In: Canetti, R., Garay, J.A. (eds.) CRYPTO 2013, Part I. LNCS, vol. 8042, pp. 75–92. Springer, Heidelberg (2013)
4. Hsu, C.-Y., Lu, C.-S., Pei, S.-C.: Homomorphic encryption-based secure sift for privacy-preserving feature extraction. In: IS&T/SPIE Electronic Imaging, pp. 788005–788005. International Society for Optics and Photonics (2011)
5. Knežević, M., Batina, L., De Mulder, E., Fan, J., Gierlichs, B., Lee, Y.K., Maes, R., Verbauwhede, I.: Signal processing for cryptograhy and security applications. In: Handbook of Signal Processing Systems, pp. 223–241. Springer (2013)
6. Lathey, A., Atrey, P.K., Joshi, N.: Homomorphic low pass filtering on encrypted multimedia over cloud. newblock. In: 2013 IEEE Seventh International Conference on Semantic Computing (ICSC), pp. 310–313. IEEE (2013)
7. Mohanty, M., Ooi, W.T., Atrey, P.K.: Scale me, crop me, knowme not: Supporting scaling and cropping in secret image sharing. In: 2013 IEEE International Conference on Multimedia and Expo (ICME), pp. 1–6. IEEE (2013)
8. Puech, W., Erkin, Z., Barni, M., Rane, S., Lagendijk, R.L.: Emerging cryptographic challenges in image and video processing. In: 2012 19th IEEE International Conference on Image Processing (ICIP), pp. 2629–2632. IEEE (2012)
9. Regev, O.: On lattices, learning with errors, random linear codes, and cryptography. Journal of the ACM (JACM) **56**(6), 34 (2009)
10. Shashanka, M.V., Smaragdis, P.: Secure sound classification: Gaussian mixture models. In: Proceedings of the 2006 IEEE International Conference on Acoustics, Speech and Signal Processing, ICASSP 2006, vol. 3, pp. III–III. IEEE (2006)
11. Troncoso-Pastoriza, J.R., Perez-Gonzalez, F.: Secure signal processing in the cloud: Enabling technologies for privacy-preserving multimedia cloud processing. IEEE Signal Processing Magazine **30**(2), 29–41 (2013)
12. Wang, Y., Rane, S., Draper, S.C., Ishwar, P.: A theoretical analysis of authentication, privacy, and reusability across secure biometric systems. IEEE Transactions on Information Forensics and Security **7**(6), 1825–1840 (2012)

Video Processing and Camera Networks

Towards a Bayesian Video Denoising Method

Pablo Arias$^{(\boxtimes)}$ and Jean-Michel Morel

CMLA, ENS Cachan, Cachan, France
pariasm@gmail.com, jean-michel.morel@ens-cachan.fr

Abstract. The quality provided by image and video sensors increases steadily, and for a fixed spatial resolution the sensor noise has been gradually reduced over the years. However, modern sensors are also capable of acquiring at higher spatial resolutions which are still affected by noise, specially under low lighting conditions. The situation is even worse in video cameras, where the capture time is bounded by the frame rate. The noise in the video degrades its visual quality and hinders its analysis. In this paper we present a new video denoising method extending the non-local Bayes image denoising algorithm. The method does not require motion estimation, and yet preliminary results show that it compares favourably with the state-of-the-art methods in terms of PSNR.

Keywords: Video denoising · Bayesian methods · Patch-based methods

1 Introduction

Advances in video sensor hardware have steadily improved the acquisition quality. However, due to the reduction in the price of video cameras and data storage, video cameras are being used more each time, and in less favorable situations, such as low lighting conditions. This results in high levels of noise, which negatively affects the visual quality of the video and hinders its use for any application.

In principle, video denoising should be easier than image denoising, due to strong temporal redundancy along motion trajectories. However, there are several challenges: the first one is how to obtain a reliable motion estimate. Motion estimation is a paramount problem in noiseless sequences, and noise makes it much harder. This is why there has always been interest in video denoising methods which do not require motion estimation.

Early works proposed temporal or spatio-temporal filters which either compensate for motion on estimated motion trajectories or used some kind of mechanism to adapt to the changes in the video signal at a fixed location due to the motion. We refer the reader to [2] and references therein for more details. Other video denoising works apply temporal filtering to the wavelet coefficients of the frames [7,23].

Some methods do not distinguish between the temporal and spatial dimensions, and treat the video as a volume, which is denoised in a transformed domain [18–20].

© Springer International Publishing Switzerland 2015
S. Battiato et al. (Eds.): ACIVS 2015, LNCS 9386, pp. 107–117, 2015.
DOI: 10.1007/978-3-319-25903-1_10

Until the advent of patch-based approaches, methods that do not compensate motion failed for sequences with moderate motion, and their main interest resided in their simplicity and low computational cost. First state-of-the-art results obtained without motion estimation were reported in [3], with the non-local means algorithm. The authors argued that for their method, based on averaging similar patches, motion estimation was not only unnecessary but counterproductive: while regions with no texture are problematic for motion estimation, they are a source of a large number of similar patches across different frames. Even if the motion trajectory could be reliably estimated, it makes more sense to use all similar patches, rather than using only the ones on the trajectory. A similar approach was followed by the authors of V-BM3D [4], which extends the BM3D image denoising algorithm [5] to video. This method is based on collaborative filtering of similar patches. The extension to video consists of searching the similar patches in a spatio-temporal neighborhood.

While these methods exploit spatio-temporal redundancy, they do not impose coherence of the trajectories, resulting in flickering artifacts which become noticeable for high levels of noise. This issue was addressed in [16,17] where the authors extend the K-SVD [6] image denoising method to video by learning a dictionary of spatio-temporal 3D patches.

It has been shown by [11] and [13,14] that motion estimation can still be beneficial for patch-based methods. In [11] the authors proposed a method based on non-local means, in which the set of similar patches averaged to denoise each pixel varies smoothly along motion trajectories. This yields results with higher temporal consistency, and permits to handle better structured noise.

In [13,14], the authors introduced a different extension of BM3D to video by collaborative filtering of similar patch trajectories (motion compensated 3D patches). The method was called V-BM4D. Trajectories are computed with a block matching strategy based on the sum of squared differences (SSD) and a temporal regularization term, which favours trajectories with small velocity and low acceleration. The results of this algorithm show higher PSNR and temporal consistency, resulting in a higher overall quality. The authors in [10] propose a framework for video processing by building on top of BM3D. In the case of denoising, their method is similar to V-BM4D with rectangular 3D patches (*i.e.* without motion compensation). Maggioni et al. in [12] use non-motion compensated 3D patches for volumetric images and video.

In this work we present an extension to video of the non-local Bayes image denoising method [8,9], which does not compensate for motion. We show that this algorithm is a valid option for moderate values of noise, due to it simplicity and to the fact that it provides state-of-the-art results in terms of PSNR.

The rest of the paper is structured as follows: in §2 we review the Bayesian patch denoising principle and describe our extension to video. Some results are shown in §3. Concluding remarks are given in §4.

2   Bayesian Video Denoising

Following [8], we adopt a Bayesian model which assumes that the patches similar to a given patch follow a Gaussian distribution. The problem of denoising can then be formulated as a problem of optimal Bayesian inference, where the parameters of the prior are learnt from the noisy data.

2.1   A Nonlocal Bayesian Principle

In the present section we review the formulation of [8], in the context of video. Consider a grayscale video $u : \Omega \times \{1, \cdots, T\} \rightarrow \mathbb{R}$, where Ω is the spatial domain (a rectangular discrete grid). We assume that v is a noisy version of u, contaminated with additive, Gaussian, white noise n of known variance σ^2,

$$v = u + n.$$

Given a square patch $\boldsymbol{q}$ of side s of the noisy video v, and the corresponding patch $\boldsymbol{p}$ of the clean video u, We assume the following Gaussian linear model for $\boldsymbol{p}$ and $\boldsymbol{q}$:

$$\mathbb{P}(\boldsymbol{p}) = \mathcal{N}(\overline{\boldsymbol{p}}, C) \propto \exp\left(-\frac{1}{2}\langle \boldsymbol{p} - \overline{\boldsymbol{p}}, C^{-1}(\boldsymbol{p} - \overline{\boldsymbol{p}})\rangle\right) \tag{1}$$

$$\mathbb{P}(\boldsymbol{q}|\boldsymbol{p}) = \mathcal{N}(\boldsymbol{p}, \sigma I) \propto \exp\left(-\frac{1}{2\sigma^2}\|\boldsymbol{q} - \boldsymbol{p}\|^2\right). \tag{2}$$

Once the mean patch $\overline{\boldsymbol{p}}$ and the covariance matrix C have been estimated from the video itself, the MAP estimate $\widetilde{\boldsymbol{p}}$ given a noisy patch $\boldsymbol{q}$ is obtained as:

$$\widetilde{\boldsymbol{p}} = \arg\max_{\boldsymbol{p}} \mathbb{P}(\boldsymbol{p}|\boldsymbol{q}) = \arg\min_{\boldsymbol{p}} -\log \mathbb{P}(\boldsymbol{p}|\boldsymbol{q}).$$

Since we are working with Gaussian distributions, the log-posterior is a quadratic (positive definite) function and the MAP can be computed explicitly as (see [8])

$$\widetilde{\boldsymbol{p}} = \overline{\boldsymbol{p}} + C(C + \sigma^2 I)^{-1}(\boldsymbol{q} - \overline{\boldsymbol{p}}). \tag{3}$$

This equation is equivalent to a Wiener filter on the projections of the patch over the eigenvectors of C, the principal directions of the Gaussian.

2.2   Learning the *a Priori* Model

The parameters of the *a priori* model, are learnt from the noisy video as follows. For each noisy patch $\boldsymbol{q}$, we select the N_{sim} more similar patches found in a search region centered at $\boldsymbol{q}$. The search region is a spatio-temporal rectangle of size $n_x \times n_x \times n_t$ (n_x, n_t are odd numbers).

Let us note by $\boldsymbol{q}_i$, $i = 1, \ldots, N_{\text{sim}}$ the set of patches similar to $\boldsymbol{q}$ (with $\boldsymbol{q}_1 = \boldsymbol{q}$). We assume that these patches correspond to different noisy observations of the Gaussian linear model (1) and (2). The corresponding marginal distribution is

---

Algorithm 1 Video NL-Bayes

Require: Noisy video v, noise standard deviation σ
Ensure: Estimate of noiseless video $\widetilde{u}$
  for all patches q in v **do**
    Find the N_{sim} most similar patches to q in a search volume centered at q
    Compute $\widehat{\overline{p}}^{(1)}$ and $\widehat{C}^{(1)}$ according to (4)
    Obtain the first stage estimate $\widetilde{p}^{(1)}$ by (3)
  end for
  for all pixel (x,t) in $\Omega \times 1, \ldots, T$ **do**
    Obtain the basic estimate $\widetilde{u}^{(1)}(x,t)$ by averaging the values of all patches
    $\widetilde{p}^{(1)}$ containing (x,t).
  end for
  for all patches q in v **do**
    Find the N_{sim} most similar patches to q in a search volume centered at q
    by comparing the estimates $\widetilde{p}^{(1)}$. We denote them, and their corresponding
    basic estimates as q_i and $\widetilde{p}_i^{(1)}$ respectively.
    Compute $\widehat{\overline{p}}^{(2)}$ and $\widehat{C}^{(2)}$ by applying (4) on the basic estimates $\widetilde{p}_i^{(1)}$ and
    setting $\sigma = 0$.
    Obtain the second stage estimate $\widetilde{p}^{(2)}$ as in (3)
  end for
  for all pixel (x,t) in $\Omega \times 1, \ldots, T$ **do**
    Obtain the final estimate $\widetilde{u}(x,t)$ by averaging the values of all patches $\widetilde{p}^{(2)}$
    containing (x,t).
  end for

---

given by $\mathbb{P}(q) = \mathcal{N}(\overline{p}, C + \sigma^2 I)$. Therefore, the maximum likelihood estimates for $\overline{p}$ and C are given by

$$\widehat{\overline{p}} = \frac{1}{N_{\text{sim}}} \sum_{i=1}^{N_{\text{sim}}} q_i \quad \text{and} \quad \widehat{C} = \frac{1}{N_{\text{sim}}} \sum_{i=1}^{N_{\text{sim}}} q_i^T q_i - \sigma^2 I. \tag{4}$$

Other methods for image denoising have been proposed in the literature based on Gaussian models for the patch density. In [21], the authors introduce a framework for solving inverse problems, based on the assumption that the patches of an image are distributed according to a Gaussian Mixture Model (GMM). A method is proposed to learn the parameters of the model from the image. A GMM is also used in [24], but it is tranined from a database of $2 \cdot 10^6$ patches randomly sampled from the Berkeley database.

In [22] a PCA-based algorithm is introduced which is equivalent to the nonlocal Bayes method. In fact, nonlocal Bayes can be regarded as a Bayesian interpretation of [22].

The BLS-GSM method [15] (Bayes least square estimate of Gaussian scale mixture) models noiseless "wavelet coefficient neighborhoods" with a Gaussian scale mixture defined as a random scaling of a zero-mean Gaussian density.

The wavelet coefficient neighborhood turns out to be a patch of an oriented channel of the image at a given scale.

2.3 Description of the Algorithm

Let us now describe the video denoising algorithm, which follows [8]. As in [4,5,8,14] we perform two stages. In the first stage we compute a *basic* estimate, which we denote $u^{(1)}$.

In the second stage, the basic estimate is used as an oracle. The computation of the patch distances is performed using the patches of the basic estimate instead of the noisy ones. In addition, we assume that the patches of the basic estimate are drawn from the *a priori* Gaussian model and use them to learn the mean and covariance matrix as explained in the Algorithm 1. Note that when computing the covariance matrix in the second stage, we set $\sigma = 0$ since we use the basic estimate as an oracle.

We now discuss some important implementation details.

Handling of Color. In the first stage, we express the video in a luminance-chrominance colorspace, specifically we apply the opponent color transform (see [5,8]). Patch distances are computed using the luminance only. Using the N_{sim} most similar patches, a group is built for each channel. These groups are filtered independently (a Gaussian model is learnt for each of them). In the second stage, the patch distance is computed using the RGB patches, and a single *a priori* Gaussian model is built for the each set of similar RGB patches.

Variance Correction Factor. In practice, when computing the MAP estimate by eq. (3), we introduce a parameter β (with $\beta \approx 1$) multiplying $\sigma^2 I$ to be able to control the amount of filtering.

Patch Distance Threshold. When building the group of similar patches during the second stage, more than N_{sim} patches are allowed if their distances with respect to the reference patch are smaller than a threshold τ. As in [9], we set $\tau = 4$ (the distance between patches is normalized by the number of elements in the patch and the number of channels).

Speed-Ups. To accelerate the computation we apply two tricks considered in [9]. The first one visits a patch each N_{step} patches (similar to [5]). The second trick consists on the following. After filtering the patches in a group, these patches are not considered again as reference patches for a group. In practice we have observe that with these speed-ups the number of groups of patches processed is between a 1% and 2% of the total number of patches, with little reduction in denoising performance.

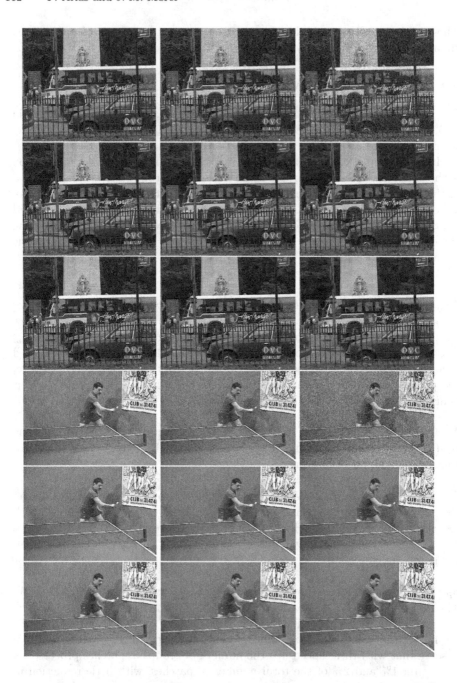

Fig. 1. Some denoising results. The first three rows, correspond to a frame of the bus sequence. From top to bottom: noisy input, VNLB ($n_t = 5$) and V-BM4D-np. The last three rows correspond to the tennis sequence. Each column shows results obtained for $\sigma = 10$, 20 and 40.

2.4 Computational Complexity

Let us consider the complexity associated to the building and filtering of a group of N_{sim} similar patches. Due to the speed-ups described in the previous section, the actual number of groups of similar patches processed might vary, but it is typically a fraction of the number of pixels in the video.

Processing each group of similar patches is of asymptotic order $\mathcal{O}(n_x^2 n_t s^2 + s^6 + N_{\text{sim}} s_x^4)$. The first term comes from the exhaustive search of the N_{sim} most similar patches in the search window. The second term comes from the inversion of the covariance matrix, and the last term contemplates computing the covariance matrix as well as the MAP estimate for each patch in the group (N_{sim} matrix-vector products with a $s^2 \times s^2$ matrix, one for each noisy patch q_i in the group).

3 Results

In this section we present preliminary results obtained with the proposed method. For all experiments shown we used the following parameters.

Patch Size: In both stages, we fixed the patch size at $s = 5$. Better results can be obtained with higher patch sizes, but the computational cost scales considerably (e.g. the inversion of the covariance matrix is of $O(s^6)$).

Number of Similar Patches: For the first stage, we set $N_{\text{sim}}^{(1)} = 3s^2 n_t$ (recall that n_t is the temporal extend of the search region). For the second step we found better results using fewer patches, thus we set $N_{\text{sim}}^{(2)} = 3/4 s^2 n_t$.

Search Region: In both stages, we used $n_x = s^2/2$. For the temporal search region, we found a good trade-off between computational time and quality of the results for $n_t = 5$.

Patch Distance Threshold: When building the group of similar patches in the second stage, more than N_{sim} patches are allowed if their distances with respect to the reference patch are smaller than a threshold τ. As in [9], we set $\tau = 4$ (the distance between patches is normalized by the number of elements in the patch and the number of channels).

We provide results on the classic color test sequences *tennis, coastguard, foreman, bus*. In order to measure the effect of the additional temporal dimension, we tested our method considering temporal search ranges of $1, 3$ and 5 frames. The results are shown in Table 1. The proposed method is labeled VNLB. For these sequences, the best results were obtained with $n_t = 5$ (two frames before and after the frame of the current patch). Larger values of n_t do not necessarily lead to better results. One possible reason for this is that our search does not take motion into account. As a consequence, in the presence of motion, similar patches might exit the search range after a certain number of frames.

For comparison, we also show the result of V-BM3D and three versions of V-BM4D. The method labeled V-BM4D-[14] corresponds to the results reported in [14]. The results labeled V-BM4D-np and V-BM4D-mp were obtained using the

Table 1. PSNRs obtained for the four classic color test sequences used in [14]. See text for details.

σ	Method	Tennis	Coastguard	Foreman	Bus
	V-BM4D [14]	**36.42**	**37.27**	37.92	36.23
	V-BM4D-mp	35.90	36.30	37.21	35.38
10	V-BM4D-np	35.56	36.20	36.90	35.09
	V-BM3D	36.04	36.82	37.52	34.96
	VNLB $n_t = 1$	34.43	36.70	37.21	35.58
	VNLB $n_t = 3$	35.04	37.19	37.88	36.19
	VNLB $n_t = 5$	35.28	**37.30**	**38.11**	**36.37**
	V-BM4D [14]	**32.88**	**33.61**	**34.62**	**32.27**
	V-BM4D-mp	31.98	32.44	33.70	31.34
20	V-BM4D-np	31.67	32.24	33.34	30.95
	V-BM3D	32.54	33.39	34.49	31.03
	VNLB $n_t = 1$	30.65	32.70	33.64	31.39
	VNLB $n_t = 3$	31.26	33.35	34.25	32.11
	VNLB $n_t = 5$	31.49	**33.55**	34.45	**32.35**
	V-BM4D [14]	**29.52**	**30.00**	**31.30**	28.32
	V-BM4D-mp	28.14	28.73	30.09	27.44
40	V-BM4D-np	27.97	28.43	29.69	27.02
	V-BM3D	29.20	**29.99**	31.17	27.34
	VNLB $n_t = 1$	27.43	28.88	30.15	27.60
	VNLB $n_t = 3$	27.97	29.60	30.72	28.23
	VNLB $n_t = 5$	28.11	29.78	30.82	**28.40**

Table 2. PSNRs obtained for the five color sequences from the Middlebury dataset [1]. See text for details.

σ	Method	Army	DogDance	Evergreen	Mequon	Walking
	V-BM4D-np	37.77	35.70	35.40	38.09	38.85
	VNLB $n_t = 1$	36.90	35.42	34.84	38.43	38.86
10	VNLB $n_t = 3$	37.65	35.87	35.38	39.09	39.69
	VNLB $n_t = 5$	**37.88**	**36.01**	**35.53**	**39.20**	**39.74**
	V-BM4D-np	32.91	31.50	30.94	33.60	34.27
	VNLB $n_t = 1$	33.77	32.44	31.68	35.61	35.60
20	VNLB $n_t = 3$	34.45	32.90	32.15	35.89	36.12
	VNLB $n_t = 5$	**34.59**	**33.02**	**32.27**	**35.90**	**36.12**
	V-BM4D-np	30.42	29.29	28.65	31.02	31.64
	VNLB $n_t = 1$	30.55	29.41	28.66	31.78	31.86
40	VNLB $n_t = 3$	**31.02**	29.73	**29.03**	**31.88**	**31.92**
	VNLB $n_t = 5$	**31.06**	**29.74**	**29.08**	31.70	31.74

implementation available online[1]. This implementation provides three parameter profiles of increasing quality and complexity: "low complexity profile", "normal profile" and "modified profile". We show the results obtained with the normal (V-BM4D-np) and modified (V-BM4D-mp) profiles. Let us note that the normal profile has a computation time comparable to our method. Running with a single core in a Intel Xeon X7560 (2.27GHz) CPU, our current implementation takes on average $10s$ per frame for a video of CIF resolution (352×288). V-BM4D takes $13s$ per frame with the normal profile and $44s$ with the modified profile.

In terms of PSNR, the best results for these sequences is obtained by V-BM4D-[14]. Our method seems to do better for $\sigma = 10$, and for the bus sequence, and has problems with the tennis sequence. For $\sigma = 20$ and 40 our method performs similar to V-BM3D (except for the tennis sequence).

We also show quantitative results obtained in for some sequences from the optical flow Middlebury dataset (the sequences have 8 frames each), and compare agaist V-BM4D-np (see table 2). For these sequences, the proposed method outpeforms V-BM4D-np.

For a qualitative analysis we show in Figure 1 results obtained with nonlocal Bayes (setting $n_t = 5$) and V-BM4D-np.[2] Interestingly, for $\sigma = 20$ and 40, V-BM4D-np is able to better recover the wallpaper texture in tennis, but does worse than VNLB for the foliage texture of the trees in bus. For high levels of noise, the wallpaper texture is masked by the noise. It is possible that when comparing 2D patches the noise dominates in the comparison. Using spatio-temporal volumes reduces the distance noise, allowing to find similar patches with the same regular texture pattern.

For $\sigma = 40$ the VNLB method exhibits some noise in flat or over-smoothed regions (e.g. wallpaper in tennis sequence). It seems that the Wiener filter of eq. (3) is not aggressive enough for this noise level.

4   Conclusions

We presented a Bayesian video denoising algorithm assuming a Gaussian model for similar patches. We show preliminary results and compare it with two methods from the state-of-the-art, V-BM3D and V-BM4D. The resulting method does not require motion estimation.In terms of PSNR the results obtained show state-of-the-art performance for low levels of noise. For higher levels of noise the performance is comparable to V-BM3D and improves over the default version of V-BM4D. Current research focuses on extending the method to using spatio-temporal patches and on lowering the computational complexity in the MAP estimation step.

References

1. Baker, S., Scharstein, D., Lewis, J., Roth, S., Black, M., Szeliski, R.: A database and evaluation methodology for optical flow. IJCV **92**(1), 1–31 (2011)

---

[1] http://www.cs.tut.fi/~foi/GCF-BM3D/
[2] The full videos are available at http://dev.ipol.im/~pariasm/video_nlbayes/

2. Brailean, J.C., Kleihorst, R.P., Efstratiadis, S., Katsaggelos, A.K., Lagendijk, R.: Noise Reduction Filters for Dynamic Image Sequences: A Review. Proceedings of the IEEE **83**(9), 1272–1292 (1995)
3. Buades, A., Coll, B., Morel, J.M.: Denoising image sequences does not require motion estimation. In: Proceedings of the IEEE Conference on Advanced Video and Signal Based Surveillance, pp. 70–74 (2005)
4. Dabov, K., Foi, A., Egiazarian, K.: Video denoising by sparse 3D transform-domain collaborative filtering. In: EUSIPCO, pp. 145–149 (2007)
5. Dabov, K., Foi, A., Katkovnik, V., Egiazarian, K.: Image denoising by sparse 3D transform-domain collaborative filtering. IEEE Trans. on IP **16**(8), 2080–2095 (2007)
6. Elad, M., Aharon, M.: Image denoising via sparse and redundant representations over learned dictionaries. IEEE Trans. on IP **15**(12), 3736–3745 (2006)
7. Jin, F., Fieguth, P., Winger, L.: Wavelet video denoising with regularized multiresolution motion estimation. Eurasip Journal on App. Sig. Proc. **2006**, 1–11 (2006)
8. Lebrun, M., Buades, A., Morel, J.M.: A Nonlocal Bayesian Image Denoising Algorithm. SIAM Journal on Imaging Sciences **6**(3), 1665–1688 (2013)
9. Lebrun, M., Buades, A., Morel, J.M.: Implementation of the "Non-Local Bayes" (NL-Bayes) Image Denoising Algorithm. Image Processing on Line **3**, 1–42 (2013)
10. Li, X., Zheng, Y.: Patch-based video processing: A variational Bayesian approach. IEEE Trans. on Circuits and Systems for Video Technology **19**(1), 27–40 (2009)
11. Liu, C., Freeman, W.T.: A high-quality video denoising algorithm based on reliable motion estimation. In: Daniilidis, K., Maragos, P., Paragios, N. (eds.) ECCV 2010, Part III. LNCS, vol. 6313, pp. 706–719. Springer, Heidelberg (2010)
12. Maggioni, M., Katkovnik, V., Egiazarian, K., Foi, A.: Nonlocal transform-domain filter for volumetric data denoising and reconstruction. IEEE Trans. on IP **22**(1), 119–133 (2013)
13. Maggioni, M., Boracchi, G., Foi, A., Egiazarian, K.: Video denoising using separable 4D nonlocal spatiotemporal transforms. In: Proc. of SPIE (2011)
14. Maggioni, M., Boracchi, G., Foi, A., Egiazarian, K.: Video denoising, deblocking, and enhancement through separable 4-D nonlocal spatiotemporal transforms. IEEE Trans. on IP **21**(9), 3952–3966 (2012)
15. Portilla, J., Strela, V., Wainwright, M., Simoncelli, E.: Image denoising using scale mixtures of gaussians in the wavelet domain. IEEE Trans. on IP **12**(11), 1338–1351 (2003)
16. Protter, M., Elad, M.: Sparse and redundant representations and motion-estimation-free algorithm for video denoising. In: Proc. SPIE, pp. 67011D–67011D-12 (2007)
17. Protter, M., Elad, M.: Image sequence denoising via sparse and redundant representations. IEEE Transactions on Image Processing **18**(1), 27–35 (2009)
18. Rajpoot, N.M., Yao, Z., Wilson, R.G.: Adaptive wavelet restoration of noisy video sequences. In: 6th Workshop of Signal Processing in Communications (2003)
19. Selesnick, I.W., Li, K.Y.: Video denoising using 2D and 3D dual-tree complex wavelet transforms. Proceedings of SPIE - The International Society for Optical Engineering **5207**(2), 607–618 (2003)
20. Wilson, R.G., Rajpoot, N.M.: Image volume denoising using a fourier-wavelet basis. In: Proceedings of IEEE International Conference on Image Processing (2004)
21. Yu, G., Sapiro, G., Mallat, S.: Solving inverse problems with piecewise linear estimators: From gaussian mixture models to structured sparsity. IEEE Trans. IP **21**(5), 2481–2499 (2012)

22. Zhang, L., Dong, W., Zhang, D., Shi, G.: Two-stage image denoising by principal component analysis with local pixel grouping. Pattern Recognition **43**(4), 1531–1549 (2010)
23. Zlokolica, V., Pižurica, A., Philips, W.: Wavelet-domain video denoising based on reliability measures. IEEE Transactions on Circuits and Systems for Video Technology **16**(8), 993–1007 (2006)
24. Zoran, D., Weiss, Y.: From learning models of natural image patches to whole image restoration. In: IEEE ICCV, pp. 479–486, November 2011

Collaborative, Context Based Activity Control Method for Camera Networks

Marek Kraft[(✉)], Michał Fularz, and Adam Schmidt

Institute of Control and Information Engineering, Poznan University of Technology,
Piotrowo 3A, 60-965 Poznań, Poland
marek.kraft@put.poznan.pl

Abstract. In this paper, a collaborative method for activity control of
a network of cameras is presented. The method adjusts the activation
level of all nodes in the network according to the observed scene activity,
so that no vital information is missed, and the rate of communication
and power consumption can be reduced. The proposed method is very
flexible as an arbitrary number of activity levels can be defined, and it
is easily adapted to the performed task. The method can be used either
as a standalone solution, or integrated with other algorithms, due to its
relatively low computational cost. The results of preliminary small scale
test confirm its correct operation.

Keywords: Smart camera · Autonomous surveillance · Camera network

1 Introduction

As the costs of cameras and computational platforms decreases and the demand
for large scale surveillance and inspection systems grows, applications of multi-
camera systems are becoming more and more common. Visual data is rich in
information, which on one hand makes it a source of useful, diverse data, but
on the other hand the abundance of data might be overwhelming. In large-
scale systems with tens or hundreds of cameras, analysis of the incoming data
is far beyond the capabilities of a human operator. Moreover, human operators
are susceptible to tiredness and loss of vigilance, as maintaining focus is hard
or even impossible with such a monotonous task [10][11]. These shortcomings
of human-operated large scale systems draw increased attention to automated
surveillance.

Extraction of useful data from raw image streams is considered a computationally intensive task. This is even more true for large-scale systems. The most
common approach for automated processing of images coming from a multi-
camera system is the use of a central server. Such an approach is not without its
limitations. First, the transfer of image data from numerous cameras to the
central processing node needs proper communication infrastructure, whose
deployment might be cumbersome and costly. As the number of cameras
and their resolution in typical applications continuously grows, the bandwidth

S. Battiato et al. (Eds.): ACIVS 2015, LNCS 9386, pp. 118–129, 2015.
DOI: 10.1007/978-3-319-25903-1_11

requirements may become difficult to satisfy. To remedy this problem, increasingly sophisticated video compression algorithms are introduced. On the other hand however, more complex coding requires more computational power both on the transmitter and receiver end and result in an increase in power consumption [15][18]. Moreover, lossy compression may degrade the performance of image processing using decoded images as source data [9][17].

Transition from centralized to distributed processing is regarded as a natural way to overcome the aforementioned limitations. The distributed processing concept is implemented as cloud-based solutions [23] or smart camera networks, in which a significant portion of the processing is delegated to the nodes of the network [21][1][4]. The nodes are to some extent autonomous and capable of communication, which corresponds to the idea of the Internet of Things [3]. The in-place processing ensures, that only the data that is useful from the point of view of the application is transmitted to the central server or other cameras in the network. The load on communication infrastructure is significantly reduced. Furthermore, the ability to perform in-place processing enables adaptation of the nodes to current operating conditions and collaborative, network-wide execution of designated tasks. However, distributed processing is not without its own challenges. Network-wide collaboration, synchronization, task designation and sharing of resource-constrained computational platforms is a complex issue and an area of extensive research.

This paper presents a collaborative method for activity control of a network of cameras. The method is conceptually simple, but effective in constraining the rate of communication and power consumption across the whole sensor network. The activation levels of sensors depend on the activity on the observed scene and the activity of other sensor nodes, linked by spatial or conceptual relations with configurable parameters. This assures, that the attention of the network as a whole is focused only on potentially relevant regions of interest. The method can be used as a standalone solution, but can also be easily integrated with other algorithms performing more complex tasks, such as tracking or recognition, as its computational cost is relatively low.

2 Related Work

Most of the previous work on power management in visual sensor networks is focused on hardware design of individual network nodes, such as very low power, semi-disposable, low cost cameras based on microcontrollers and using low power, low bandwidth protocols for wireless communication [14][20]. The power consumption of such hardware platforms is indeed low, yet on the other hand the interfaces are too slow for the transmission of images at a high framerate, and the performance of computational platforms cannot support sophisticated processing or compression. The data transmitted in such sensor networks is usually constrained to the basic observed scene metadata [22]. Focus on low power is also characteristic to higher performance designs based on application processors or DSPs and is achieved through careful component selection and extensive use of low power sleep modes [7], [16].

As the smart camera networks comprise of multiple nodes, individual cameras will observe different levels of scene activity. Moreover, activity levels change over time, as the content of the observed scene evolves. Adjusting the activity rate of individual sensors as well as the complete sensor network to go hand in hand with the activity on the observed scene opens the way to significant energy savings and enables reduction of the rate of communication. However, this may not come at the cost of the reduction of the quality of results related to the system's primary function. In order to enable such adaptive behavior, dedicated management algorithms must be employed. In [6] an algorithm for adaptive control of the activity of an embedded camera described in [7] is proposed. The active/idle ratio is adjusted based on the presence of the tracked objects in the scene and the speed of their movement. The algorithm is however dedicated to single sensor control only. Network-wide management strategies dedicated to connected smart cameras are relatively uncommon. The management mechanism presented in [24] relies on programmable timeouts, whose length for a given node is dependent on scene activity observed in this node and its direct neighbors. In [8] a distributed camera network management method was proposed, but it is used mainly to control the activity levels of sensors to direct the attention of the network so that no important events on the monitored perimeter are missed or misclassified.

3   The Implemented Algorithm

The activation level of each individual sensor is computed based on the scene motion level by performing background subtraction. The implemented algorithm is derived from the median algorithms, requiring the storing of N image frames preceding the currently processed frame. In such algorithms, the background model is the median value from all the previously stored frames, i.e. the intensity of each pixel in the background model is the median of N intensity values of the corresponding pixels from the stored frames. Although conceptually simple, such methods must accumulate many images to build up history for background estimation. To ease the high memory requirements, the approximate median algorithm was proposed in [19]. The algorithm was implemented in each network node of the presented system. The algorithm for background model update works in the following way:

- if the intensity value $I_{x,y}$ of currently investigated pixel of the current frame I is greater than the value of the corresponding background model pixel $B_{x,y}$, the value of $B_{x,y}$ is incremented by one,
- if the intensity value $I_{x,y}$ of currently investigated pixel of the current frame I is smaller than the value of the corresponding background model pixel $B_{x,y}$, the value of $B_{x,y}$ is decremented by one,
- if the intensity value $I_{x,y}$ of currently investigated pixel of the current frame I has the same value as the corresponding background model pixel $B_{x,y}$, the value of $B_{x,y}$ remains unchanged.

Doing so, the background model converges to an estimate for which the half of the input image pixels is brighter than the corresponding background image pixel, and the other half is darker than the corresponding background image pixel, which corresponds roughly to the median value. The foreground is determined by computing the difference image D as an absolute value of the difference between the current frame I and the background model B. The difference image is filtered with a 3×3 Gaussian, thresholded, and subjected to binary morphological filtering using the closing operation. The algorithm was selected for its speed and simplicity rather than accuracy, but as shown in [2] and [5], the least accurate background subtraction methods are the ones that benefit the most from post-processing, as the additional filtering is efficient at rejecting small spurious responses and making the detected objects more coherent.

The percentage of foreground pixels in the local sensor node and its defined network neighbors are the inputs to the module computing the value of the activation function.

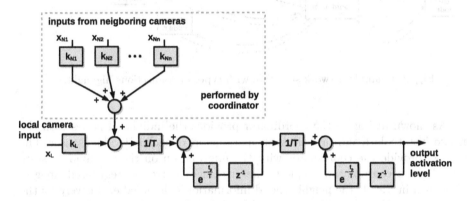

Fig. 1. General internal block diagram of the internal node activation function generator.

As shown in Fig. 1, the weights represented by the local gain k_L and the neighbor gains $k_{N1}, k_{N2}, \cdot, k_{Nn}$ for each input can be adjusted if necessary. The weighted input values are then passed to a block performing discrete low-pass filtering, with the time constant T as another parameter, governing the decay of the activation function's value. The discrete transfer function of a single node in the network is then given by Eq. 1.

$$H(z) = \left(\frac{\frac{1}{T}}{1 - z^{-1}e^{-\frac{T_s}{T}}} \right)^2 [k_L \quad k_{N1} \quad k_{N2} \quad \ldots \quad k_{Nn}] \tag{1}$$

The T_s is the sampling time of the single node. The variable governs the frequency at which the frames constituting the input data for the background subtraction algorithm are acquired and processed. Adjusting the sampling frequency enables adjustment of node activity. In general, the higher the sampling frequency, the more time is spent on processing and more data is transmitted, which also contributes to an increase in power consumption. Lower sampling frequency decreases the power consumption and the amount of transmitted data.

The implemented algorithm assumes, that although the network nodes are capable of autonomous operation, a central coordinator is responsible for the task of network-wide activity coordination based on individual sensor states. However, the amount of processing involved when performing this task does not constitute a significant computational load.

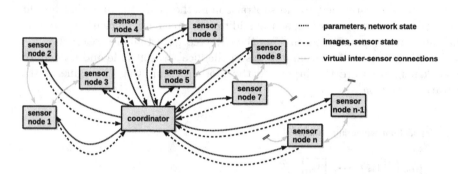

Fig. 2. Example network structure with types of connections highlighted.

As shown in Fig. 2, the coordinator provides the individual nodes with the network state data and can adjust the parameters of each individual sensor. The sensors provide the coordinator with the information on their individual state and, by the coordinators request, the stream of currently registered images. As shown in Fig. 1, the neighborhood information is handled exclusively by the coordinator. The coordinator stores the information on the mutual relations of network nodes (in the form of gain values), forming virtual inter-sensor connections. Based on the received sensor states (the percentage of foreground pixels), the coordinator computes the additional portion of the input value for each node. This information then supplements the locally calculated input coming directly from the node camera observations. Doing so, the coordinator informs all the nodes of the network state and enables the use of network-wide information for collaborative node activity control. Please note, that although the processing scheme is centralized, it operates on a sparse set of sensor data. Moreover, full images are sent only when requested, and all image processing is performed in the network nodes, so the computational load and the amount of data sent is relatively low.

4   The Test Setup

The prototype node solution for performing initial tests of the camera network management algorithm was the PiCam platform. The platform is based on a standard, first generation Raspberry Pi model B single board computer (SBC) running the Arch Linux operating system. The heart of the SBC is a BCM2835 Broadcom System-on-Chip (SoC) with a ARM1176JZF-S CPU. The SoC is equipped with a dedicated MIPI CSI-2 camera serial interface, allowing direct camera module connection. A total of 512MB of RAM is mounted on the SBC. The SBC and the camera module are enclosed in a dedicated housing as shown in Fig. 3 and supplemented with a fisheye lens for a broader field of view. Each node is also equipped with a USB WiFi module for wireless communication and a SD-card for booting the OS. The power source is supplied through a micro-USB connector, enabling the use of a powerbank and making the prototype node portable.

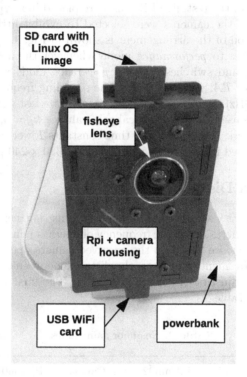

Fig. 3. The PiCam test platform.

The choice of the test platform was dictated mainly by its popularity and availability, good documentation, relatively low price and strong community support, giving access to a wide range of software libraries. The test software was written in Python for easy prototyping, with extensive use of OpenCV library functions. The SBC power governor was configured as shown in Table 1. High computational load switches the CPU and peripherals into *performance* mode. As the SoC does not make any sleep modes available, the *powersave* mode is simply turning the clock frequencies of the CPU and peripherals down to decrease power consumption. Please note, that the camera module itself consumes 0.25 [A].

Table 1. Basic parameters of the two PiCam operating modes.

parameter	*performance* mode	*powersave* mode
CPU clock [MHz]	1,000	300
RAM clock [MHz]	500	150
GPU clock [MHz]	500	150
Current draw [A]	0.5	0.4

For the purpose of the test, five PiCams were placed in a typical office space. The fields of view of the cameras were selected to exhibit little or no overlap. A schematic depiction of the arrangement is shown in Fig. 4.

The node switches to *performance* mode whenever the activation function value is above TA, and switches back to *powersave* mode when the value is equal or drops below TA, with $TA = 15$. The sampling frequency is 10 [Hz] in *performance* and 1 [Hz] in *powersave* mode. To facilitate fast wake-up on activity detection, the nodes use two different local gain values – $k_L = 0.1$ in *performance* mode and $k_L = 2$ *powersave* mode. The time constants T were set to 0.7 [s]. The acquired and processed images have a resolution of 320×240 pixels.

5   Results and Discussion

The actual experiment was preceded by few test runs that helped to adjust the parameters of the cameras. Both the frequency of operation in each mode and the gain were carefully chosen based on the observed camera operation. In addition to the registered movement of objects, the distance between cameras was taken into account while adjusting the neighbors' gains. The final values of neighbor gains are shown in Table 2.

Table 2. Neighbor gain values.

camera	PiCam01	PiCam02	PiCam03	PiCam04	PiCam05
PiCam01	0.0	0.5	0.2	0.0	0.0
PiCam02	0.5	0.0	0.5	0.1	0.0
PiCam03	0.1	0.5	0.0	0.5	0.2
PiCam04	0.0	0.1	0.5	0.0	0.5
PiCam05	0.0	0.0	0.2	0.5	0.0

Each camera affects its direct neighbors with 50% and the more distant cameras with either 20% or 10% of the detected active pixels. It should be

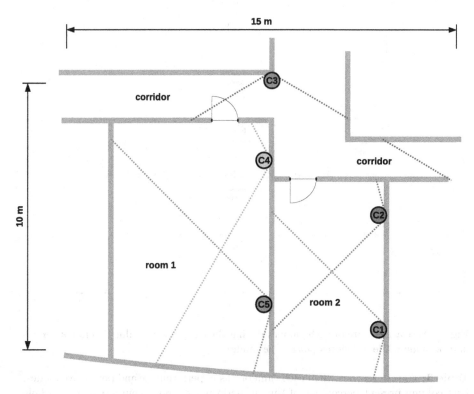

Fig. 4. Schematic depiction of the sensor arrangements in the test setup.

noted that the size of moving objects on the scene has big impact on the camera operation and should always be taken into consideration when tuning the system parameters.

The conducted experiment lasted for six minutes and the results - the activation mode of each camera are shown in Figure 5. At the beginning no movement was observed in the system. After approx. 40 seconds a person moved from the field of view of the camera 1 (room 2) to the corridor and then, at approx. 90 seconds, to the room 1. The person continued to move around the room 2 and traveled back to the starting position in room 2. After a brief period with no movement, a similar trajectory was traveled again.

Both of the described sets of actions are clearly visible in Figure 5 as the cameras turn into the *performance* mode whenever their neighboring cameras detect movement. Such propagation of the cameras activation facilitates observations of fast objects, as it prevents misses due to camera being in the *powersave* mode. In case of the conducted experiment the movement is detected by PiCam01 at the beginning and activates neighboring PiCam02. As object moves the next PiCams are switched into *performance* mode, while previous ones are switched back into *powersave* mode. As both of the sets of actions were almost the same

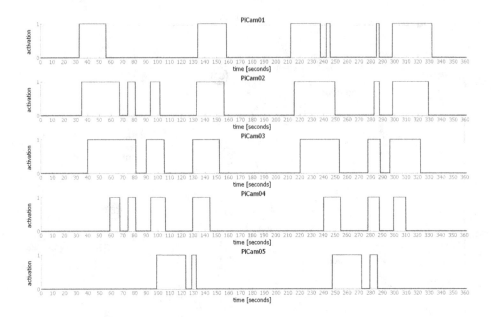

Fig. 5. Activation state of each camera during the experiment (value 1 denotes *performance* mode while 0 denotes *powersave* mode).

Table 3. Time in seconds when each camera was in performance and powersave modes. Last column present percentage of time in performance mode compared to the whole experiment.

camera	*performance* mode	*powersave* mode	% of *perf.* mode
PiCam01	112	249	31.02
PiCam02	140	221	38.78
PiCam03	149	212	41.27
PiCam04	77	284	21.33
PiCam05	59	302	16.34

with only minor differences in duration, the observed activation patterns are similar.

The time spent in each of the modes is shown in Table 3. Additionally, the ratio of time in which the cameras were in the *powersave* mode is presented to highlight the advantages of proposed solution. Thanks to the proposed solution the central PiCam03 camera remained in the low power state for 59% of time while the peripheral PiCam05 camera was in the power saving mode for 84% of time. This reduces the power consumption w.r.t. the full activity mode by 12% and 17%, respectively. Please note, however, that the Raspberri Pi platform is used for prototyping is not designed to enable advanced power management.

6   Conclusions

This paper presents a system for collaborative management of the camera-nodes activity levels aimed at reducing the power consumption of a large-scale, multi-camera surveillance systems. The operation of the system was assessed in an experiment using a camera network consisting of five cameras.

The presented preliminary tests showed, that a multi-camera system using the proposed method was able to successfully keep track of the movement of a person moving across an environment surveyed by a multi-camera movement detection system. The system was able to manage the nodes in order to maintain high activity level in the nodes overlooking busy areas while keeping the other nodes in power-saving mode. The collaborative method presented in the paper clearly has the potential to significantly reduce the power consumption of large-scale, automatic surveillance system without compromising the movement detection efficiency. Moreover, the amount of data transmitted within a network employing the presented solution is also significantly reduced.

In the next stage, the system will be tested in a larger scale experiments. Both using the simulated multi-camera environment proposed by Esterle[12] and in a network of real cameras spread over a large environment. In order to facilitate the second scenario, the proposed method will be integrated with the smart-camera architecture proposed by Fularz et al. in [13]. Moreover, this solution is based on dedicated hardware, so the migration will clearly result in more power reduction, as the differences in power consumption between operating modes will be greater.

The second part of the research will start once the potential for lowering the power consumption of the network and ability to propagate the attention over large networks are confirmed. The work will focus on increasing the autonomy of the system by developing methods for semi-automatic selection of the systems' parameters (the gains and time constants of the state update processes) and the discovery of the networks topology (the gains of the inter-cameras connections).

Acknowledgment. This research was financed by the Polish National Science Centre grant funded according to the decision DEC-2011/03/N/ST6/03022, which is gratefully acknowledged.

References

1. Aghajan, H., Cavallaro, A.: Multi-camera networks: principles and applications. Academic Press (2009)
2. Amer, A.: Memory-based spatio-temporal real-time object segmentation for video surveillance. In: Proceedings of SPIE-IS&T Electronic Imaging Conference on Real-Time Imaging, pp. 10–21 (2003)
3. Atzori, L., Iera, A., Morabito, G.: The Internet of things: A survey. Computer Networks 54(15), 2787–2805 (2010)
4. Bhanu, B., Ravishankar, C., Roy-Chowdhury, A., Aghajan, H., Terzopoulos, D.: Distributed Video Sensor Networks. Springer (2011)

5. Brutzer, S., Hoferlin, B., Heidemann, G.: Evaluation of background subtraction techniques for video surveillance. In: 2011 IEEE Conference on Computer Vision and Pattern Recognition (CVPR), pp. 1937–1944 (2011)
6. Casares, M., Velipasalar, S.: Adaptive methodologies for energy-efficient object detection and tracking with battery-powered embedded smart cameras. IEEE Transactions on Circuits and Systems for Video Technology **21**(10), 1438–1452 (2011)
7. Chen, P., Hong, K., Naikal, N., Sastry, S.S., Tygar, D., Yan, P., Yang, A.Y., Chang, L.C., Lin, L., Wang, S., Lobatón, E., Oh, S., Ahammad, P.: A low-bandwidth camera sensor platform with applications in smart camera networks. ACM Transactions on Sensor Networks **9**(2), 21:1–21:23 (2013)
8. Costa, D.G., Guedes, L.A., Vasques, F., Portugal, P.: Adaptive monitoring relevance in camera networks for critical surveillance applications. International Journal of Distributed Sensor Networks (2013)
9. Cozzolino, A., Flammini, F., Galli, V., Lamberti, M., Poggi, G., Pragliola, C.: Evaluating the effects of MJPEG compression on motion tracking in metro railway surveillance. In: Blanc-Talon, J., Philips, W., Popescu, D., Scheunders, P., Zemčík, P. (eds.) ACIVS 2012. LNCS, vol. 7517, pp. 142–154. Springer, Heidelberg (2012)
10. Dadashi, N., Stedmon, A., Pridmore, T.: Semi-automated CCTV surveillance: The effects of system confidence, system accuracy and task complexity on operator vigilance, reliance and workload. Applied Ergonomics **44**(5), 730–738 (2013)
11. Donald, F.M., Donald, C.H.: Task disengagement and implications for vigilance performance in cctv surveillance. Cognition, Technology & Work **17**(1), 121–130 (2015). http://dx.doi.org/10.1007/s10111-014-0309-8
12. Esterle, L., Lewis, P., Caine, H., Yao, X., Rinner, B.: Camsim: A distributed smart camera network simulator. In: 2013 IEEE 7th International Conference on Self-Adaptation and Self-Organizing Systems Workshops (SASOW), pp. 19–20, September 2013
13. Fularz, M., Kraft, M., Schmidt, A., Kasiński, A.: The architecture of an embedded smart camera for intelligent inspection and surveillance. In: Szewczyk, R., Zieliński, C., Kaliczyńska, M. (eds.) Progress in Automation, Robotics and Measuring Techniques. AISC, vol. 350, pp. 43–52. Springer, Heidelberg (2015)
14. Hengstler, S., Prashanth, D., Fong, S., Aghajan, H.: Mesheye: A hybrid-resolution smart camera mote for applications in distributed intelligent surveillance. In: 6th International Symposium on Information Processing in Sensor Networks, IPSN 2007, pp. 360–369, April 2007
15. Jin, X., Goto, S.: Encoder adaptable difference detection for low power video compression in surveillance system. Signal Processing: Image Communication **26**(3), 130–142 (2011)
16. Kandhalu, A., Rowe, A., Rajkumar, R.: Dspcam: A camera sensor system for surveillance networks. In: Third ACM/IEEE International Conference on Distributed Smart Cameras, ICDSC 2009, pp. 1–7, August 2009
17. Kovesi, P.: Video surveillance: Legally blind? In: Digital Image Computing: Techniques and Applications, DICTA 2009, pp. 204–211, December 2009
18. Ma, T., Hempel, M., Peng, D., Sharif, H.: A survey of energy-efficient compression and communication techniques for multimedia in resource constrained systems. IEEE Communications Surveys Tutorials **15**(3), 963–972 (2013)
19. McFarlane, N., Schofield, C.: Segmentation and tracking of piglets in images. Machine Vision and Applications **8**, 187–193 (1995)

20. Rahimi, M., Baer, R., Iroezi, O.I., Garcia, J.C., Warrior, J., Estrin, D., Srivastava, M.: Cyclops: In situ image sensing and interpretation in wireless sensor networks. In: Proceedings of the 3rd International Conference on Embedded Networked Sensor Systems, SenSys 2005, pp. 192–204. ACM, New York (2005). http://doi.acm.org/10.1145/1098918.1098939
21. Rinner, B., Wolf, W.: An introduction to distributed smart cameras. Proceedings of the IEEE **96**(10), 1565–1575 (2008)
22. Seema, A., Reisslein, M.: Towards efficient wireless video sensor networks: A survey of existing node architectures and proposal for a Flexi-WVSNP design. IEEE Communications Surveys Tutorials **13**(3), 462–486 (2011)
23. Xiong, Y., Wan, S.Y., He, Y., Su, D.: Design and implementation of a prototype cloud video surveillance system. Journal of Advanced Computational Intelligence and Intelligent Informatics **18**(1), 40–47 (2014)
24. Zamora, N., Marculescu, R.: Coordinated distributed power management with video sensor networks: Analysis, simulation, and prototyping. In: First ACM/IEEE International Conference on Distributed Smart Cameras, ICDSC 2007, pp. 4–11, September 2007

EFIC: Edge Based Foreground Background Segmentation and Interior Classification for Dynamic Camera Viewpoints

Gianni Allebosch[✉], Francis Deboeverie, Peter Veelaert, and Wilfried Philips

Department of Telecommunications and Information Processing,
Image Processing and Interpretation, Ghent University - iMinds, Ghent, Belgium
gianni.allebosch@telin.ugent.be

Abstract. Foreground background segmentation algorithms attempt to separate interesting or changing regions from the background in video sequences. Foreground detection is obviously more difficult when the camera viewpoint changes dynamically, such as when the camera undergoes a panning or tilting motion. In this paper, we propose an edge based foreground background estimation method, which can automatically detect and compensate for camera viewpoint changes. We will show that this method significantly outperforms state-of-the-art algorithms for the panning sequences in the ChangeDetection.NET 2014 dataset, while still performing well in the other categories.

Keywords: Foreground background segmentation · Moving edges · Camera motion · Optical flow

1 Introduction

Foreground background segmentation is frequently used as a first step in many computer vision algorithms [3] [4]. Usually, foreground objects coincide with "moving" pixels, so the terms foreground background segmentation and motion detection are often used interchangeably. However, for some applications, static objects could also be of interest, for example if an object is added to the environment (e.g. a backpack left at a crowded station could contain explosives). On the other hand, the motion of some particular objects, such as waving trees, should often not be analyzed in further steps.

State-of-the-art foreground background segmentation methods consider these remarks, such that they can be employed in a wide variety of situations. The method described in [17] e.g. explicitly models both the foreground and background seperately, while the authors of [14] suggest an automatic and dynamic local parameter tuning mechanism. However, one issue which has not received proper attention in foreground background segmentation literature, is that of camera viewpoint changes. Most algorithms assume a fixed camera position. One algorithm that does not make this assumption, by allowing multiple pixelwise background models, shows to outperform other methods when the camera does move with respect to the static scene [13].

© Springer International Publishing Switzerland 2015
S. Battiato et al. (Eds.): ACIVS 2015, LNCS 9386, pp. 130–141, 2015.
DOI: 10.1007/978-3-319-25903-1_12

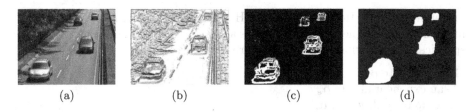

| (a) | (b) | (c) | (d) |

Fig. 1. Overview of the algorithm in static camera environments. (a) Input image, (b) LTP based edge descriptors, (c) foreground edges (d) filled foreground image.

In this paper, we present a novel mechanism to overcome issues caused by camera viewpoint changes, for example panning, tilting or jitter. When compared to our previous work [1], the main contribution is the detection of camera viewpoint changes and the selection of appropriate image transformations. In the following section, a brief overview of the original method and some extensions in the detection step are treated. In Sec. 3 and 4 the main novelties, i.e. camera viewpoint change detection and compensation mechanisms, are explained in depth. Finally, the complete algorithm is tested on the comprehensive ChangeDetection.NET 2014 dataset [18]. We will show that our method EFIC (Edge based Foreground background segmentation with Interior Classification) achieves the best F-measure on 4 out of the 11 video categories, with an especially notable improvement on the Pan-Tilt-Zoom sequences.

2   Edge Based Foreground Background Segmentation

The proposed algorithm is an extension of previous work on foreground background segmentation [1]. This method was shown to be very stable in difficult illumination conditions. In this section, the basic methodology to arrive at a foreground image is explained. This section also covers two small extensions on the original method, while the major contributions are covered in Sec. 3 and 4.

2.1   Previous Work

The original algorithm consists of 3 major steps. First, a stable edge descriptor is calculated, using 8-bit Local Ternary Patters (LTPs) [16]. It was shown in [1] that this descriptor can also be regarded as a two dimensional vector, of which the direction represents the edge orientation. The vector length can be regarded as a confidence measure of the angle. Both inter- and intra-pattern information sources are combined to further increase the robustness of the descriptor.

Secondly, the edge descriptor vectors are compared with a multimodal temporal model. Input vectors which significantly differ from the appropriate background vectors are classified as foreground. Since the LTP-features represent image edges, the determined foreground in this step consists of foreground edges. The temporal model is similar to both a Gaussian Mixture Model [15] and the model proposed by Heikkila et al. [11]. However, the learning rate, which determines how quickly the temporal model is adapted, is adjusted dynamically. More specifically, the learning rate α is comprised of three parts:

1. a base rate α_b
2. an exponential rate α_e
3. an unreliability rate α_u

The base rate, which remains fixed, is typically low, and makes sure that the model is constantly updated slightly in background locations, in order to adapt to slow changes. The exponential rate ensures that the temporal model is updated faster at the beginning of a sequence, as the model generally becomes more reliable over time. If the model does become globally or locally unreliable (e.g. due to a sudden large change in the background or lasting dynamic background), the unreliability rate makes sure that the model is still updated accordingly.

Finally, the algorithm provides a robust contour filling mechanism, which is able to deal with gaps in the object contours. This mechanism treats the foreground edge image as a 4-connected graph, where the edge pixels represent disconnected nodes. The classification of a pixel $\mathbf{p}$ as interior (foreground) or exterior (background) is made with regards to the total "excessive" distance $d_{E,tot}[\mathbf{p}]$ of the shortest paths from the image corners. The distance $d_{E,tot}$ represents the deviation of the shortest paths in the graph, compared to the Manhattan distance d_M between the pixel and the image corners. Formally, given a constant threshold T_E, the edge based foreground image F is defined as follows:

$$F[\mathbf{p}] = \begin{cases} 1 & \text{if } d_{E,tot}[\mathbf{p}] > T_E \ , \\ 0 & \text{otherwise} \ . \end{cases} \tag{1}$$

One can show that the resulting foreground shapes are never larger than the orthogonal hull of the objects, and never smaller than a silhouette obtained by filling only the closed contours. One shortcoming of the previous method is that the proposed filling mechanism is sometimes too strong, in particular when objects contain concavities. Therefore, a novel shape correction method is described below.

2.2   Foreground Shape Correction

In our new method we combine pure edge based features with grayscale information. Besides the LTPs, also the grayscale value is fed into a similar multimodal temporal model as described in the previous section. The grayscale based foreground mask is denoted F_G. The eventual foreground mask F' is now determined through a combination of $d_{E,tot}$ (see Sec. 2.1) and F_G as follows:

$$F'[\mathbf{p}] = \begin{cases} 1 & \text{if } d_{E,tot}[\mathbf{p}] > T_{E,h} \text{ or } (d_{E,tot}[\mathbf{p}] > T_{E,l} \text{ and } F_G[\mathbf{p}] > 0) \\ 0 & \text{otherwise} \ , \end{cases} \tag{2}$$

where $T_{E,h}$ and $T_{E,l}$ are high and low thresholds respectively. The proposed mechanism still ensures the same minimal and maximal size of the silhouettes,

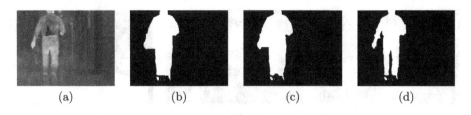

Fig. 2. Example of successive foreground shape correction steps. (a) Input image, (b) Foreground mask using single filling threshold, (c) Foreground mask using double threshold and intensity mask (d) Foreground mask after segmentation refinement of (c).

and now uses F_G as a tiebreaker in ambiguous situations. This partially avoids the unwanted filling of concavities in the silhouette (e.g. between arms or legs).

The shapes of the foreground objects are polished further using a variant of the watershed algorithm, described in [12]. The resulting segments are each investigated individually. If, for a certain segment S, at least half of its corresponding pixels in F' represent foreground, then the entire segment S is considered to be a foreground segment. Conversely, if less than half of the corresponding pixels in F' are foreground pixels, S is regarded as a background segment. An example of the shape correction method is shown in Fig. 2.

2.3 Ghost Removal

An object which is static when the temporal model is being built, but later moves to another location, can leave behind a foreground blob in the foreground image, since, at its original location, the image now appears different from the modelled background. This remaining blob is often called a "ghost". In the proposed algorithm, an adaptation of the ghost removal methodology described in [5] is added.

The ghost removal algorithm is executed only in static regions, i.e., regions where the optical flow vectors are small (explained in detail in Sec. 3.1). First, an edge image is constructed from the LTP features described in 2.1. For every static foreground object, the Chamfer distance between the contour of the foreground object and the edge image is calculated and normalized with respect to the contour length. If the Chamfer distance exceeds a threshold T_C, the contour of the foreground object likely does not coincide with a real object in the image. Such objects are removed from the foreground image. After ghost identification, the temporal model has to be updated locally, which is done by setting a high learning rate for all removed pixels. An example of the ghost removal mechanism is shown in Fig. 3.

Fig. 3. Example of ghost removal. (a) First image in the sequence, (b) input image from further in the sequence, (c) foreground image, where the removed ghost is denoted in red.

3 Camera Motion Detection

If the camera viewpoint is static, reasoning about foreground estimation is generally straightforward. However, as soon as the camera viewpoint changes, the appearance of all pixels might change, even though the background itself does not. In this section we describe how camera motion can be detected. We propose a camera motion detection framework based on optical flow.

3.1 Optical Flow

Optical flow estimation is a widely studied problem in computer vision [10]. It is an image feature which essentially represents the motion of individual pixels between subsequent frames. By assuming a constant brightness, optical flow calculation boils down to the estimation of the displacement $(\Delta x, \Delta y)$ of a pixel at $\mathbf{p} = (x, y)$ [8]. This vector can only be obtained by introducing additional constraints, which is where optical flow methods described in literature differ from one another. These methods can be divided into two main groups: sparse and dense optical flow. Sparse optical flow methods first detect interesting points in the image, and estimate only their motion between successive frames. Dense optical flow methods estimate the motion vectors for all image points.

3.2 Flow Based Camera Motion Detection

If the camera viewpoint is static, it can be expected that the only pixels that appear to move between successive frames come from either foreground objects, or dynamic background otherwise. In most video sequences, the amount of dynamically moving pixels is relatively small compared to the static ones. However, if the camera viewpoint does change, most pixels in the image will also. So, camera motion can be detected by the occurrence of significant optical flow vectors in a large part of the image. In the detection step, dense optical flow is preferred. In sequences with generally smooth backgrounds, not many feature points will be found by sparse flow methods, except on the foreground objects themselves, which could lead to many false positive camera motion detections.

In the proposed method, the dense optical flow vectors are calculated by using the efficient algorithm described in [6]. Let $\mathbf{V}[\mathbf{p}]$ be the flow vector image at pixel $\mathbf{p}$. Now, we define the optical flow mask F_f as follows:

$$F_f[\mathbf{p}] = \begin{cases} 1 & \text{if } ||\mathbf{V}[\mathbf{p}]|| > T_f \\ 0 & \text{otherwise} , \end{cases} \qquad (3)$$

where T_f is a typically low threshold (e.g. 1 pixel). So, F_f represents a significance classification of all flow vectors. If the ratio of significant flow vectors is larger than a second threshold T_n, camera motion is detected.

4   Camera Motion Compensation

In order to compensate for the camera motion, the effect of this motion should be mitigated at every pixel location, while moving foreground objects should still be detected. The next section will explain how the necessary image transformations are executed. Afterwards, we will distinguish two scenarios: one where the camera is undergoing a fairly constant motion away from the original position (e.g pan-tilt-zoom) and one where the camera keeps moving around the same position (jitter).

4.1   Affine Image Transformation

In order to compare a new image with a background model, the image should first be transformed such that coinciding pixels also represent the same objects in the model. However, since the distances to the objects in the scene are not known a priori in most applications, the effects of potential perspective changes on the image formation are difficult to model. Luckily, when a scene's relief is small, relative to the average distance from the objects to the camera, the weak-perspective image formation model can be used to describe the image formation [9]. This model assumes that all objects are at a similar distance from the camera. It is proven in [7] that, assuming a weak-perspective model, all arbitrary projection transformation matrices can be written in the form of an affine matrix.

In this work, the affine transformation between two images is estimated by making use of the Pyramidal implementation of the Lucas Kanade Feature Tracker [2]. The algorithm first detects interest points and then calculates sparse optical flow vectors to detect their individual motion. In the second phase of the algorithm, the robust affine transformation matrix M_{tf} is selected through a RANSAC framework. From this matrix, the expected flow $\mathbf{V_e}$ can now be directly determined. For a certain pixel $\mathbf{p} = (x, y, 1)^T$ in homogeneous coordinates:

$$\mathbf{V_e}[\mathbf{p}] = M_{tf}\mathbf{p} , \qquad (4)$$

4.2   Distinction Between Panning/Tilting and Jitter

If the center pixel is also the origin of the camera's coordinate system, the expected flow at the center pixel $\mathbf{V_e}[\mathbf{0}]$ can be represented by the third column of M_{tf}, also known as a translation vector $\mathbf{t_r} = (t_{r,x}, t_{r,y})$. If the camera viewpoint changes between successive frames, $\mathbf{t_r}$ will be a nonzero vector whose orientation ($\arctan \frac{t_{r,y}}{t_{r,x}}$) represents the direction of the camera shift. If this direction is more or less constant for a longer period, the camera viewpoint obviously moves away from its original position, and a panning (or tilting) camera motion can be detected. Conversely, if the direction of $\mathbf{t_r}$ changes a lot, it is more likely that the camera is jittery, but not necessarily moving away from the original position.

In the proposed method, the distinction between panning and jittery camera's is derived from the reasoning above. Let us define two accumulators: acc_p for panning and acc_j for jitter, both initialized to 0 in the beginning of the sequence. Every time a camera viewpoint change is detected, the current direction of $\mathbf{t_r}$ is compared to the previous one. If the angles differ by more than 90, acc_j is incremented. Otherwise, acc_p is incremented. The camera motion compensation is then executed with regard to the highest corresponding accumulator value.

4.3   Jitter Compensation

If the camera is moving around the same position, the original background model can still be used. By transforming the current image with regard to the most likely background image as described in Sec. 4.1, a pixelwise evaluation of the difference between the current image and background model is feasible, as in the standard case when no camera motion is detected.

There are however some subtle considerations which should be taken into account. Note that the affine transformation estimation can be erroneous, for example due to comparison with interest points coinciding with foreground objects. Furthermore, depending on the camera settings, a moving camera viewpoint might introduce motion blur, which distorts some image structures, especially around edges. In the proposed algorithm, the constant learning rate α_c is therefore raised when jitter is detected, and applied to the entire image, instead of to the background regions.

4.4   Panning/Tilting Compensation

If a panning or tilting camera change is detected, the original background image is no longer usable if the new camera viewpoint has deviated too far from the original one, since pixel-wise comparisons to the original model have become impossible.

However, if the camera motion is relatively slow, such that the spatial relation between successive frames can be established, it becomes possible to build a short-term edge background model $\mathbf{B_s}$. A new frame is compared to this model after using the affine transformation as discussed in the previous sections. Here, $\mathbf{B_s}$ is also transformed after every frame as long as the panning motion continues.

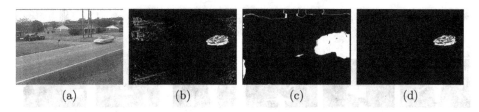

(a)   (b)   (c)   (d)

Fig. 4. Creation of the foreground edges in a sequence with panning camera. (a) Input image, (b) Short-term foreground mask, (c) compensated flow mask, (d) logical AND of short-term foreground mask and compensated flow mask.

Note however, that $\mathbf{B_s}$ in the proposed algorithm is unimodal. Experiments show that using a more complex multimodal background model, as described in Sec. 2.1, does not improve the algorithms performance, likely due to the fact that it is difficult to build a complex model quickly enough. Comparing the LTP feature image $\mathbf{I_{LTP}}$ determined from the input with $\mathbf{B_s}$ results in the short-term foreground mask F_s:

$$F_s[\mathbf{p}] = \begin{cases} 1 & \text{if } ||\mathbf{I_{LTP}}[\mathbf{p}] - \mathbf{B_s}[\mathbf{p}]|| > T_s \\ 0 & \text{otherwise} . \end{cases} \tag{5}$$

Still, the requirement of rapid model construction makes it more likely that parts of the model are unreliable. To overcome the potential decrease in accuracy, the flow vector image $\mathbf{V}$ is used as a secondary decision mechanism. The compensated flow image $\mathbf{V_c}$ is now defined as follows:

$$\mathbf{V_c}[\mathbf{p}] = \mathbf{V}[\mathbf{p}] - \mathbf{V_e}[\mathbf{p}] . \tag{6}$$

Thus, the original flow vectors are compensated with regard to the expected affine image transformation, resulting from the camera viewpoint change. It is expected that for static objects, the corresponding compensated flow vectors should be close to $\mathbf{0}$. However, if an object is moving in the scene, the optical flow vectors will differ from the globally calculated transformation and will locally coincide with nonzero compensated flow vectors. Thus, utilizing a final flow compensation threshold $T_{f,c}$, the compensated foreground flow mask $F_{f,c}$ is now defined as

$$F_{f,c}[\mathbf{p}] = \begin{cases} 1 & \text{if } ||\mathbf{V_c}[\mathbf{p}]|| > T_{f,c} \\ 0 & \text{otherwise} . \end{cases} \tag{7}$$

The resulting foreground (edges) mask now consists of the pixelwise logical AND operation between $F_{f,c}$ and F_s. Fig. 4 shows a visual example of foreground detection in a sequence with a panning camera. Note that the contour filling, shape correction and ghost removal steps described in Sec. 2 are still executed after the foreground edge detection step. Finally, once the panning motion has stopped, the exponential learning rate (Sec. 2.1) is reset, such that the temporal model is quickly rebuilt at the new position.

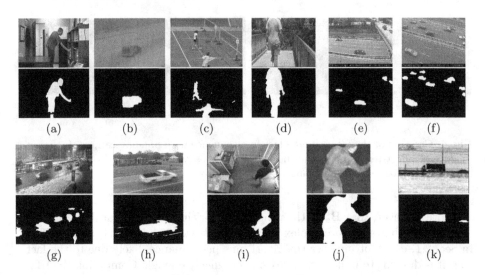

Fig. 5. Performance of our proposed method on a few hand picked frames from the ChangeDetection.NET 2014 dataset [18]. (a) Baseline, (b) Bad Weather, (c) Camera Jitter, (d) Dynamic background, (e) Intermittent Object Motion, (f) Low Framerate, (g) Night Videos, (h) Pan-Tilt-Zoom, (i) Shadows, (j) Thermal, (k) Turbulence.

5 Experiments

The proposed method was tested on the rigorous ChangeDetection.NET 2014 dataset [18]. This dataset comprises of 11 categories of 4 to 6 videos each. The categories are Bad Weather (BW), Low Framerate (LF), Night Videos (NV), Pan-Tilt-Zoom (PTZ), Turbulence (TB), Baseline (BL), Camera Jitter (CJ), Intermittent Object Motion (IOM), Shadows (SH) and Thermal (TH).

The creators of the website also provide ground truth for the majority of the frames, such that 7 performance measures in total can be calculated: Recall, specificity, false positive rate, false negative rate, precision, percentage of wrong classifications and F-Measure. However, as explained in [14] and [13], the F-measure is the most unbiased representation of the performance of a foreground background segmentation algorithm. So, we will focus on this performance measure to compare our proposed method to the state of the art (see Table 1). Note that it is required to use the same parameters and thresholds for all videos, such that optimizing for a particular video or category is discouraged, and only truly versatile methods achieve high scores on this dataset. The values of the thresholds discussed in this paper are given in Table 2.

Smoothing by a 3 by 3 Gaussian kernel was added as a preprocessing step, while the foreground mask were postprocessed by a 5 by 5 median filter. The algorithm runs at about 16 frames per second on a desktop pc with an Intel® Xeon® E5 Quad Core processor for 320 by 240 pixel videos. The proposed method currently achieves the highest F-measure in 4 of the 11 categories.

Table 1. Comparison of the F-Scores of all methods applied to the ChangeDetection.NET 2014 database per category and overall. The highest score is denoted in bold faced numbers. In the categories where the proposed method achieves the highest score, the second highest score is denoted in blue. References to the other methods can be found on the ChangeDetection.NET website [18].

Method	BW	LF	NV	PTZ	TB	BL	DB	CJ	IOM	SH	TH	Over.
EFIC (Proposed)	77.86	**66.32**	**65.48**	**58.42**	67.13	91.72	57.79	71.25	57.83	82.02	**83.88**	70.88
SuBSENSE	86.19	64.45	55.99	34.76	**77.92**	**95.03**	81.77	81.52	65.69	89.86	81.71	**74.08**
FTSG	82.28	62.59	51.30	32.41	71.27	93.30	**87.92**	75.13	**78.91**	88.32	77.68	72.83
SaliencySubsense	85.93	65.15	53.48	33.99	75.12	94.83	81.57	80.71	60.12	**89.94**	68.57	71.76
MBS V0	77.30	62.79	51.58	51.18	56.98	92.87	79.04	**83.67**	70.92	77.84	81.15	71.39
CwisarDH	68.37	64.06	37.35	32.18	72.27	91.45	82.74	78.86	57.53	85.81	78.66	68.12
Spectral-360	75.69	64.37	48.32	36.53	54.29	93.30	77.66	71.42	56.09	85.19	77.64	67.32
Bin Wang Apr 2014	76.73	46.89	38.02	13.48	75.45	88.13	84.36	71.07	72.11	81.28	75.97	65.77
AAPSA	77.42	49.42	41.61	33.02	46.43	91.83	67.06	72.07	50.98	79.53	70.30	61.79
SC_ SOBS	66.20	54.63	45.03	4.09	48.80	93.33	66.86	70.51	59.18	77.86	69.23	59.61
KNN	75.87	54.91	42.00	21.26	51.98	84.11	68.65	68.94	50.26	74.68	60.46	59.37
SOBS_ CF	63.70	51.48	44.82	21.26	47.02	92.99	65.19	71.50	58.10	77.21	71.40	58.83
CP3-online	74.85	47.42	39.19	26.60	37.43	88.56	61.11	52.07	61.77	70.37	79.17	58.05
RMoG	68.26	53.12	42.65	24.70	45.78	78.48	73.52	70.10	54.31	72.12	47.88	57.35
GMM - Stauffer and Grimson	73.80	53.73	40.97	15.22	46.63	82.45	63.30	59.69	52.07	73.70	66.21	57.07
KDE - ElGammal	75.71	54.78	43.65	3.65	44.78	90.92	59.61	57.20	40.88	76.60	74.23	56.88
GraphCutDiff	**87.87**	51.27	46.88	37.23	51.43	71.47	53.91	54.89	40.19	72.28	57.86	56.84
GMM - Zivkovic	74.06	50.65	39.60	10.46	41.69	83.82	63.28	56.70	53.25	73.22	65.48	55.66
Euclidean dist.	67.01	50.15	38.59	3.95	41.35	87.20	50.81	48.74	48.92	67.86	63.13	51.61
Multiscale Spatio-Temporal BG	63.71	33.65	41.64	3.64	52.91	84.50	59.53	50.73	44.97	79.18	51.03	51.41
Mahalanobis dist.	22.12	7.97	13.74	3.74	33.59	46.42	17.98	33.58	22.90	33.53	13.83	22.67

For Night Videos and Pan-Tilt-Zoom, the gaps with the second best scoring methods are especially significant. This can be attributed to the fact that the method is based on the illumination-invariant features described in [1] and that the proposed method is able to cope with slow camera viewpoint changes. However, note that in our experiments the performance on 1 video with a zooming camera was unacceptable. Here, the proposed algorithm failed to detect the changing camera parameters and thus did not compensate for this. A refined zoom detection mechanism could even further improve the performance in this category.

EFIC is also able to provide top performance in the Low Framerate and Thermal videos. For Low Framerate the updating mechanism can quickly learn the correct background, and is not disturbed by rapidly changing foreground objects. Since the Thermal images all consist of single color channel frames and the proposed method does not rely on on chromacity information, the good performance in this category can also be explained.

In the Dynamic Background and Intermittent Object Motion sequences, the proposed method is not yet able to achieve the desired performance. In the other categories, the performance is closer to the state-of-the-art, but not at the very top. As opposed to the Thermal videos, the lack of chromacity information is a limiting factor in videos where the intensity of the foreground objects is similar

Table 2. Threshold values discussed in this paper. Unless stated otherwise, all values are expressed in pixel widths

Threshold	Value
T_E: Single excessive distance	3
$T_{E,l}$: Low excessive distance	1
$T_{E,h}$: High excessive distance	13
T_f: Significant flow	1
T_n: Significant flow ratio	70 (% of total number of pixels)
$T_{f,c}$: Compensated flow	2
T_s: Short-term background model	40 (% of max. LTP vector length)

to that of the background. This effect is especially noticeable in the Dynamic Background videos, where the intensities of the boats are similar to the water intensity, even though the chromacity differs significantly. Utilizing chromacity only when useful through a decision tree approach, could improve the overall results while not harming the performance in categories where EFIC scores best.

It can also be noted that some of these categories present multiple kinds of difficulties. E.g., Bad Weather videos incorporate both difficult illumination conditions, but also dynamic background and thus address both the strengths and weaknesses of the proposed method. We also note that the described ghost removal method did improve the overall results, but still failed in certain sequences with textured background. Improvements could arise from the extension of this method, e.g. through utilization of gradient directional information.

6   Conclusions

In this paper, we propose an edge based foreground background segmentation algorithm, which is able to handle non-static camera viewpoints, using a combination of optical flow and affine image transformations. It was shown that the method achieves good overall performance on the ChangeDetection.NET 2014, while even reaching the best F-measure in 4 out of 11 categories in total. Notably, the addition of color information as an extra feature should help in improving the performance of this method even further.

Acknowledgment. We would like to thank the creators of ChangeDetection.NET, for providing a comprehensive evaluation dataset and all necessary tools to analyze and validate the algorithm's performance.

References

1. Allebosch, G., Van Hamme, D., Deboeverie, F., Veelaert, P., Philips, W.: Edge based foreground background estimation with interior/exterior classification. In: Proceedings of the 10th International Conference on Computer Vision Theory and Applications, vol. 3, pp. 369–375. SCITEPRESS (2015)

2. Bouguet, J.Y.: Pyramidal implementation of the lucas kanade feature tracker description of the algorithm. Intel Corporation Microprocessor Research Labs, Tech. rep. (2000)

3. Bouwmans, T., Baf, F.E., Vachon, B.: Background modeling using mixture of gaussians for foreground detection a survey. Recent Patents on Computer Science, 219–237 (2008)

4. Cristani, M., Farenzena, M., Bloisi, D., Murino, V.: Background subtraction for automated multisensor surveillance: A comprehensive review. EURASIP J. Adv. Sig. Proc. (2010)

5. Evangelio, R., Sikora, T.: Complementary background models for the detection of static and moving objects in crowded environments. In: 2011 8th IEEE International Conference on Advanced Video and Signal-Based Surveillance (AVSS), pp. 71–76, August 2011

6. Farnebäck, G.: Two-frame motion estimation based on polynomial expansion. In: Bigun, J., Gustavsson, T. (eds.) SCIA 2003. LNCS, vol. 2749, pp. 363–370. Springer, Heidelberg (2003)

7. Faugeras, O.D., Luong, Q.T., Papadopoulo, T.: The geometry of multiple images - the laws that govern the formation of multiple images of a scene and some of their applications. MIT Press (2001)

8. Fleet, D.J., Weiss, Y.: Optical flow estimation. In: Handbook of Mathematical Models in Computer Vision, pp. 237–257. Springer US (2006)

9. Forsyth, D.A., Ponce, J.: Geometric camera models. In: Computer Vision: A Modern Approach, 2nd edn., pp. 33–61. Pearson, international edn. (2012)

10. Fortun, D., Bouthemy, P., Kervrann, C.: Optical flow modeling and computation: A survey. Computer Vision and Image Understanding 134(0), 1–21 (2015). image Understanding for Real-world Distributed Video Networks

11. Heikkila, M., Pietikainen, M.: A texture-based method for modeling the background and detecting moving objects. IEEE Transactions on Pattern Analysis and Machine Intelligence 28(4), 657–662 (2006)

12. Meyer, F.: Color image segmentation. In: International Conference on Image Processing and its Applications, pp. 303–306 (1992)

13. Sajid, H., Cheung, S.C.S.: Background subtraction for static and moving camera. In: IEEE International Conference on Image Processing (2015)

14. St-Charles, P.L., Bilodeau, G.A., Bergevin, R.: Subsense: A universal change detection method with local adaptive sensitivity. IEEE Transactions on Image Processing 24(1), 359–373 (2015)

15. Stauffer, C., Grimson, W.E.L.: Adaptive background mixture models for real-time tracking. In: CVPR, pp. 2246–2252 (1999)

16. Tan, X., Triggs, B.: Enhanced local texture feature sets for face recognition under difficult lighting conditions. IEEE Transactions on Image Processing 19(6), 1635–1650 (2010)

17. Wang, R., Bunyak, F., Seetharaman, G., Palaniappan, K.: Static and moving object detection using flux tensor with split gaussian models. In: The IEEE Conference on Computer Vision and Pattern Recognition (CVPR) Workshops, June 2014

18. Wang, Y., Jodoin, P.M., Porikli, F., Konrad, J., Benezeth, Y., Ishwar, P.: Cdnet 2014: An expanded change detection benchmark dataset. In: The IEEE Conference on Computer Vision and Pattern Recognition (CVPR) Workshops, June 2014

A Unified Camera Calibration from Arbitrary Parallelograms and Parallepipeds

Jae-Hean Kim$^{(\boxtimes)}$ and Jin Sung Choi

Content Research Division, Electronics and Telecommunication Research Institute,
218, Gajeong-Ro, Yuseong-Gu, Daejeon 305-700, Republic of Korea
gokjh@etri.re.kr

Abstract. This paper presents a novel approach to calibrate cameras that can use geometric information of parallelograms and parallepipeds simultaneously. The proposed method is a factorization based approach solving the problem linearly by decomposing a measurement matrix into parameters of cameras, parallelograms and parallepipeds. Since the two kinds of geometric constraints can complement each other in general man-made environment, the proposed method can obtain more stable estimation results than the previous approaches that can use geometric constraints only either of parallelograms or of parallelepipeds. The results of the experiments with real images are presented to demonstrate the feasibility of the proposed method.

1 Introduction

This paper concerns the solution to the problem of recovering camera parameters from uncalibrated camera images linearly using scene geometry. This process is known as camera self-calibration. A Euclidean reconstruction from the self-calibration is not possible without any prior information on cameras or on the scene to be recovered. According to the information assumed to be given a priori, there have been many approaches concerning the self-calibration algorithm.

Self-calibration approaches using only the constraints on camera internal parameters are known as auto-calibration and have been widely investigated. These approaches provide great flexibility because they can be applied to views of a generic scene [2,8]. However, to acquire stable estimation results, a large number of images is usually necessary.

There have been many methods to use the constraints from scene geometry: planes [6,9,10], cuboids [1], symmetric polyhedra [4], parallelepipeds [13], parallelograms [5,14]. Due to the geometric information from the scene, these approaches can give more stable estimation results without lengthy image sequences.

In the images captured in man-made environments, there are many primitives giving the geometric information. Among primitives, parallelograms and parallepipeds are frequently present in the scene, such as the architecture.

Wilczkowiak *et al.* suggested an elegant formalism using parallelepipeds of which at least the six vertices are visible in views [13]. This method is a

© Springer International Publishing Switzerland 2015
S. Battiato et al. (Eds.): ACIVS 2015, LNCS 9386, pp. 142–153, 2015.
DOI: 10.1007/978-3-319-25903-1_13

factorization based approach that computes the camera parameters and scene structure parameters linearly and simultaneously in one step. Due to the multiview constraints imposed on a factorization approach, it is possible to obtain the consistency of rigid transformations among cameras. It has been known that the measurements from all images should be used simultaneously to obtain optimal estimates as in the factorization approach [3, 7, 11].

The primitive that can give full affine information is not only a parallelepiped. parallelograms are more basic elements and frequently found than parallelepipeds in man-made environments. Since parallelograms do not always form faces of a parallelepiped, the methods being able to use parallelograms are more useful than the method using only parallelepipeds [5, 14]. However, since the geometric constraint of each parallelogram is 2-dimensional, it is weaker than that of parallelepiped, which is 3-dimensional. The methods being able to use only parallelograms consider a parallelepiped as a set of separate parallelograms. Consequently, when both of two primitives exist in a scene, a novel approach is required being able to use geometric information of parallelograms and parallepipeds simultaneously.

In this paper, we suggest a factorization based framework that can utilize parallelograms and parallelepipeds simultaneously. Since the two kinds of geometric constraints can complement each other, the proposed method can obtain more stable estimation results in practical situations than the previous methods that can use geometric constraints only either of parallelograms or of parallelepipeds.

2   Preliminaries

2.1   Parallelogram Parameterization

A parallelogram is defined by 9 parameters: six extrinsic parameters describing its orientation and position and three intrinsic parameters describing its Euclidean shape: two dimension parameters (edge lengths l_1 and l_2) and one angle between edges (θ). These intrinsic parameters are illustrated in Fig. 1. The parallelogram may be represented by a 2×2 matrix $\bar{\mathbf{L}}$:

$$\bar{\mathbf{L}} = \begin{bmatrix} l_1 & l_2 \cos\theta \\ 0 & l_2 \sin\theta \end{bmatrix}. \tag{1}$$

The matrix $\bar{\mathbf{L}}$ represents the parallelogram's shape (intrinsic parameter). A vertex $\tilde{\mathbf{x}}_\mathbf{s} \equiv (\pm 1, \pm 1)^T$ of the canonic square is mapped, by $\bar{\mathbf{L}}$, to a vertex of parallelogram on its supporting plane.

Let $\mathbf{x}_\mathbf{s}$ be homogeneous coordinates of vertex of the canonic square. Using this representation, the vertex of parallelogram on the world coordinate system is represented as follows:

$$\mathbf{X} \cong \begin{bmatrix} \bar{\mathbf{S}} & \mathbf{v} \\ \mathbf{0}^T & 1 \end{bmatrix} \begin{bmatrix} \bar{\mathbf{L}} & \mathbf{0} \\ \mathbf{0}^T & 1 \end{bmatrix} \begin{bmatrix} \tilde{\mathbf{x}}_\mathbf{s} \\ 1 \end{bmatrix}$$

$$\cong \mathbf{N}\mathbf{x}_\mathbf{s}, \tag{2}$$

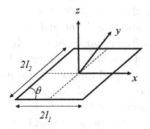

Fig. 1. Parameterization of a parallelogram.

where $\bar{\mathbf{S}}$ is the 3×2 submatrix consisting of the first two columns of the rotation matrix $\mathbf{S}$ representing the parallelogram's orientation and the vector $\mathbf{v}$ its position.

3   Projections of Parallelograms

3.1   Canonic Homography

Consider the projection of a parallelogram's vertices into a camera image plane. Using the results from Section 2, the projection of the corresponding vertex in the image is:

$$\mathbf{x} \cong \mathbf{K} \begin{bmatrix} \mathbf{R}\ \mathbf{t} \end{bmatrix} \begin{bmatrix} \bar{\mathbf{S}}\bar{\mathbf{L}}\ \mathbf{v} \\ \mathbf{0}^T\ 1 \end{bmatrix} \mathbf{x_s}$$
$$= \mathbf{MN}\mathbf{x_s} = \mathbf{H}\mathbf{x_s}, \tag{3}$$

where rotation matrix $\mathbf{R}$ and the vector $\mathbf{t}$ represent the camera's orientation and position, respectively. The 3×3 matrix $\mathbf{K}$ is the camera calibration matrix [2].

The matrix $\mathbf{H}(= \mathbf{MN})$ will be called the *canonic homography*. It represents a perspective projection that maps the vertices of the canonic square onto the vertices of the imaged parallelograms. This is illustrated in Fig 2. Given image points for four vertices, the canonic homography can be computed up to scale, even though we do not know prior knowledge on intrinisic or extrinisic parameters. Our calibration algorithms are based on the link between the canonic homography and the camera's and parallelogram's intrinsic and extrinsic parameters.

3.2   Measurement Matrix of Homographies

Let us now consider the case in which n parallelograms are seen by m cameras. Let $\tilde{\mathbf{H}}_i^j$ be the estimation result of the canonic homography associated with

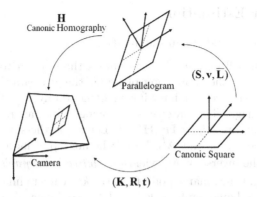

Fig. 2. The projection of the canonic square onto the vertices of the imaged parallelograms.

the projection of the jth parallelogram in the ith camera and λ_i^j a scale factor such that the following equality can be written:

$$
\lambda_i^j \tilde{\mathbf{H}}_i^j = \mathbf{K}_i \begin{bmatrix} \mathbf{R}_i & \mathbf{t}_i \end{bmatrix} \begin{bmatrix} \bar{\mathbf{S}}^j \bar{\mathbf{L}}^j & \mathbf{v}^j \\ \mathbf{0}^T & 1 \end{bmatrix}
$$
$$
= \mathbf{M}_i \mathbf{N}^j = \mathbf{H}_i^j \tag{4}
$$

We may gather the estimated canonic homography for all m cameras and n parallelograms into the following single matrix:

$$
\tilde{\mathbf{W}} = \begin{bmatrix} \tilde{\mathbf{H}}_1^1 & \cdots & \tilde{\mathbf{H}}_1^n \\ \vdots & \ddots & \vdots \\ \tilde{\mathbf{H}}_m^1 & \cdots & \tilde{\mathbf{H}}_m^n \end{bmatrix} \tag{5}
$$

The matrix $\tilde{\mathbf{W}}$ will be called the *measurement matrix*. When the scale factors are recovered, the measurement matrix can be factorized as follows:

$$
\begin{bmatrix} \lambda_1^1 \tilde{\mathbf{H}}_1^1 & \cdots & \lambda_1^n \tilde{\mathbf{H}}_1^n \\ \vdots & \ddots & \vdots \\ \lambda_m^1 \tilde{\mathbf{H}}_m^1 & \cdots & \lambda_m^n \tilde{\mathbf{H}}_m^n \end{bmatrix} = \begin{bmatrix} \mathbf{H}_1^1 & \cdots & \mathbf{H}_1^n \\ \vdots & \ddots & \vdots \\ \mathbf{H}_m^1 & \cdots & \mathbf{H}_m^n \end{bmatrix}
$$
$$
= \begin{bmatrix} \mathbf{M}_1 \\ \vdots \\ \mathbf{M}_m \end{bmatrix} \begin{bmatrix} \mathbf{N}^1 & \cdots & \mathbf{N}^n \end{bmatrix} \tag{6}
$$

However, since the canonic homographies are obtained up to scale, the measurement matrix cannot be factorized as its current form.

4 Parameter Estimation

4.1 Rescaling the Measurement Matrix

In this section, we will describe how to obtain the scale factors mentioned in Section 3.2. Let π^j be the supporting plane for the jth parallelogram. Assume that the plane π^j induces an inter-image homography $\mathbf{A}_{ik}^j$ from the kth to the ith camera image. This inter-image homography can be represented by canonic homograpies as $\mathbf{A}_{ik}^j = \mathbf{H}_i^j(\mathbf{H}_k^j)^{-1}$. Let π^l be the supporting plane for another lth parallelogram and $\mathbf{A}_{ik}^l$ be the homography induced by π^l. Composing $\mathbf{A}_{ik}^l$ with the inverse of $\mathbf{A}_{ik}^j$ yields a *relative homography* represented by $\mathbf{B}_{ik}^{jl} = (\mathbf{A}_{ik}^j)^{-1}\mathbf{A}_{ik}^l$, which map a point from the kth camera image onto the same image. This relative homography is known to be a planar homology having the form $\mathbf{B}_{ik}^{jl} = \mathbf{I} + \mathbf{a}\mathbf{b}^T$, where $\mathbf{a}$ and $\mathbf{b}$ are arbitrary 3-vectors [15]. This means that $\mathbf{B}_{ik}^{jl}$ has an eigenvalue 1 and the multiplicity of that eigenvalue is two.

The relative homography can be computed up to scale from the canonic homographies, which are also up to scale, as follows:

$$\tilde{\mathbf{B}}_{ik}^{jl} = \tilde{\mathbf{H}}_k^j(\tilde{\mathbf{H}}_i^j)^{-1}\tilde{\mathbf{H}}_i^l(\tilde{\mathbf{H}}_k^l)^{-1}$$
$$= (\lambda_i^j\lambda_k^l)/(\lambda_k^j\lambda_i^l)\mathbf{B}_{ik}^{jl}. \tag{7}$$

From Eq. (7) and above property of the relative homography, we can see that the matrix $\tilde{\mathbf{B}}_{ik}^{jl}$ has an eigen value $\rho_{ik}^{jl} = (\lambda_i^j\lambda_k^l)/(\lambda_k^j\lambda_i^l)$ of multiplicity two, which can be extracted from $\tilde{\mathbf{B}}_{ik}^{jl}$.

Now, we can consider $\{\rho_{ik}^{jl}\}$ as alternative scale factors such that the factorization is accomplished. Assume that every canonic homographies in the measurement matrix are rescaled as $\rho_{ik}^{jl}\tilde{\mathbf{H}}_i^j = \lambda_k^l/(\lambda_k^j\lambda_i^l)\mathbf{H}_i^j$. Then, the rescaled measurement matrix can be factorized as follows:

$$\begin{bmatrix} \rho_{1k}^{1l}\tilde{\mathbf{H}}_1^1 & \cdots & \rho_{1k}^{nl}\tilde{\mathbf{H}}_1^n \\ \vdots & \ddots & \vdots \\ \rho_{mk}^{1l}\tilde{\mathbf{H}}_m^1 & \cdots & \rho_{mk}^{nl}\tilde{\mathbf{H}}_m^n \end{bmatrix}$$
$$\cong \begin{bmatrix} \mathbf{M}_1/\lambda_1^l \\ \vdots \\ \mathbf{M}_m/\lambda_m^l \end{bmatrix} \begin{bmatrix} \mathbf{N}^1/\lambda_k^1 \cdots \mathbf{N}^n/\lambda_k^n \end{bmatrix}. \tag{8}$$

However, since the image measurements are always affected by noise, relative homography obtained above cannot has an eigen value of multiplicity two exactly. To obtain an optimal eigen value, we used the method suggested in [12], in which a scalar variable ρ approximating the matrix $\tilde{\mathbf{B}}_{ik}^{jl} - \rho\mathbf{I}$ to rank 1 is selected as the eigen value.

4.2 Factorization

From now on, it is assumed that the measurement matrix is rescaled as above. Let $\bar{\mathbf{H}}$ be the leading 3×2 submatrix of the canonic homography, which can be written as $\bar{\mathbf{H}} = \mathbf{K}\mathbf{R}\bar{\mathbf{S}}\bar{\mathbf{L}}$. Then, the following *reduced measurement matrix* $\bar{\mathbf{W}}$ containing all $\lambda_k^l/(\lambda_k^j\lambda_i^l)\bar{\mathbf{H}}_i^j$ can be factorized as follows:

$$\bar{\mathbf{W}} \cong \begin{bmatrix} \bar{\mathbf{M}}_1/\lambda_1^l \\ \vdots \\ \bar{\mathbf{M}}_m/\lambda_m^l \end{bmatrix} \begin{bmatrix} \bar{\mathbf{N}}^1/\lambda_k^1 \cdots \bar{\mathbf{N}}^n/\lambda_k^n \end{bmatrix}, \tag{9}$$

where $\bar{\mathbf{M}}_i = \mathbf{K}_i\mathbf{R}_i$ and $\bar{\mathbf{N}}^j = \bar{\mathbf{S}}^j\bar{\mathbf{L}}^j$.

As usual in the previous factorization approaches [11,13], the SVD (Singular Value Decomposition) is used to obtain the low-rank factorization of $\bar{\mathbf{W}}$. Let the SVD of $\bar{\mathbf{W}}$ be given as:

$$\bar{\mathbf{W}} = \mathbf{U}_{3m\times3n}\mathbf{D}_{3n\times3n}\mathbf{V}_{2n\times3n}^T. \tag{10}$$

Assume that the diagonal matrix $\mathbf{D}$ contains the singular values of $\bar{\mathbf{W}}$: $\sigma_1 \geq \sigma_2 \geq \ldots \geq \sigma_{3n}$. In the absence of noise, $\bar{\mathbf{W}}$ satisfying Eq. (9) has rank 3 and consequently $\sigma_4 = \sigma_5 = \ldots = \sigma_{3n} = 0$. If noise were present, this would not be the case. If we want to find the rank 3 matrix which is closest to $\bar{\mathbf{W}}$ in the Frobenius norm, such a matrix can be obtained by setting all the singular values, besides the three largest ones, to zero. Then, the rank-3 factorization result can be given as:

$$\begin{aligned} \bar{\mathbf{W}} &= \bar{\mathbf{U}}_{3m\times3}\text{diag}(\sqrt{\sigma_1}, \sqrt{\sigma_2}, \sqrt{\sigma_3}) \cdot \\ &\quad \{\bar{\mathbf{V}}_{2n\times3}\text{diag}(\sqrt{\sigma_1}, \sqrt{\sigma_2}, \sqrt{\sigma_3})\}^T \\ &= \hat{\mathbf{U}}_{3m\times3}\hat{\mathbf{V}}_{2n\times3}^T. \end{aligned} \tag{11}$$

However, the factorization result is not unique because the following is also a valid factorization:

$$\bar{\mathbf{W}} = \left(\hat{\mathbf{U}}_{3m\times3}\mathbf{T}\right)\left(\mathbf{T}^{-1}\hat{\mathbf{V}}_{2n\times3}^T\right), \tag{12}$$

where $\mathbf{T}$ is an arbitrary non-singular 3×3 matrix. The existence of the matrix $\mathbf{T}$ represents the non-translational part of a 3D affine ambiguity. The results obtained up to now are equivalent to 3D reconstruction up to affine transformation. To resolve this affine ambiguity and upgrade the results to the metric ones, we have to impose usual self-calibration constraints and/or geometric constraints on affine reconstruction results. This issue is considered in section 4.3.

4.3 Resolving Affine Ambiguity

To resolve the affine ambiguity, we should find constraints on $\mathbf{T}$. This is equivalent to obtain constraints on the absolute conic Ω_∞^A in affine space. $\mathbf{T}$ can be obtained from $\Omega_\infty^A(=\mathbf{T}^{-T}\mathbf{T}^{-1})$ by Cholesky factorization.

Let the matrices $\hat{\mathbf{U}}_{3m\times3}$ and $\hat{\mathbf{V}}_{2n\times3}$ in Eq. (12) be decomposed in 3×3 and 2×3 submatrices, respectively: $\hat{\mathbf{U}}_{3m\times3}^T = \begin{bmatrix} \mathbf{U}_1^T \cdots \mathbf{U}_m^T \end{bmatrix}$ and $\hat{\mathbf{V}}_{2n\times3}^T = \begin{bmatrix} \mathbf{V}_1^T \cdots \mathbf{V}_n^T \end{bmatrix}$.

Incorporating Self-calibration Constraints. From Eq. (9) and (12), we have $\mathbf{K}_i \mathbf{R}_i \cong \mathbf{U}_i \mathbf{T}$. Using the definition of Ω_∞^A, this can be written as:

$$\omega_i \cong \mathbf{U}_i^{-T} \Omega_\infty^A \mathbf{U}_i^{-1}, \tag{13}$$

where $\omega_i = \mathbf{K}_i^{-T} \mathbf{K}_i^T$ and represents the image of absolute conic (IAC) in ith view.

If the camera's intrinsics do not vary, we can set all $\{\omega_i\}$ to be ω in Eq. (13) and, then, ω can be eliminated using the equations from any pair of views and the constraints on Ω_∞^A can be obtained.

If we know that pixel is square, or principal point is at origin, or aspect ratio is known as r, the constraints on Ω_∞^A can be obtained from Eq. (13).

Using Constraints from Scene Geometry. From Eq. (9) and (12), we have $\mathbf{T}^{-1} \mathbf{V}_j^T \cong \bar{\mathbf{S}}^j \bar{\mathbf{L}}^j$. This can be written as:

$$\mu^j \cong \mathbf{V}_j \Omega_\infty^A \mathbf{V}_j^T, \tag{14}$$

where $\mu^j = \bar{\mathbf{L}}^{jT} \bar{\mathbf{L}}^j$.

If we know θ^j is a right angle, or the ratio of l_1^j to l_2^j is r^j, this information can be used to obtain the constraints on Ω_∞^A from Eq. (14) and (1).

4.4   Computing Camera Parameters

After obtaining $\mathbf{T}$, we can acquire $\mathbf{K}_i$, $\mathbf{R}_i$, and λ_i^l from $\mathbf{U}_i \mathbf{T} (= \bar{\mathbf{M}}_i / \lambda_i^l)$ by QR-decomposition because $(\mathbf{K}_i)_{33} = 1$ and $\det(\mathbf{R}_i) = 1$. Let $\bar{\mathbf{h}}_i^j$ be the third column of the canonic homography $\bar{\mathbf{H}}_i^j$, which can be written as:

$$\bar{\mathbf{h}}_i^j = \frac{1}{\lambda_i^l \lambda_k^j} \left(\mathbf{K}_i \mathbf{R}_i \mathbf{v}^j + \mathbf{K}_i \mathbf{t}_i \right). \tag{15}$$

From Eq. (15), three independent homogeneous equations

$$\left[\mathbf{K}_i \ \mathbf{K}_i \mathbf{R}_i \ -\lambda_i^l \bar{\mathbf{h}}_i^j \right] \begin{bmatrix} \mathbf{t}_i \\ \mathbf{v}^j \\ \lambda_k^j \end{bmatrix} = \mathbf{0} \tag{16}$$

are obtained and these equations for all pairs of camera and parallelogram can be solved linearly to obtain $\mathbf{t}_i$, $\mathbf{v}^j$, and λ_k^j.

5   Merging Information from Parallelepipeds

When there are parallelepipeds in a scene as well as parallelograms, the scene constraints from parallelepipeds can be merged. The *canonic projection matrix* proposed in [13] can be inserted in the measurement matrix $\widetilde{\mathbf{W}}$ of Eq. (5). In this case, it is important to determine the scale factors making the factorization of the new measurement matrix possible because the matrix is obtained also up to scale. In fact, this can be obtaind by using the results of section 4.1.

Let $\mathbf{P}$ be the canonic projection matrix. The canonic projection matrix in [13] is represented as follows:

$$\mathbf{P} = \mathbf{K} \begin{bmatrix} \mathbf{R} \, \mathbf{t} \end{bmatrix} \begin{bmatrix} \mathbf{SL} & \mathbf{v} \\ \mathbf{0}^T & 1 \end{bmatrix}, \tag{17}$$

where $\mathbf{S}$ is a rotation matrix representing a parallelepiped's orientation and the 3×3 matrix $\mathbf{L}$ defined in [13] represents a parallelepiped's shape. We can observe that the upper left 2×2 submatrix of $\mathbf{L}$ is $\bar{\mathbf{L}}$ of Eq. (1) corresponding to the bottom parallelogram of the parallelepiped. Due to this observation, the canonic projection matrix can also be represented as follows:

$$\mathbf{P} = \begin{bmatrix} \mathbf{KRSL} & \mathbf{KRv} + \mathbf{Kt} \end{bmatrix}$$
$$= \begin{bmatrix} \mathbf{KR\bar{S}\bar{L}} & \mathbf{KRSl}_3 & \mathbf{KRv} + \mathbf{Kt} \end{bmatrix}, \tag{18}$$

where l_3 is the third column of $\mathbf{L}$. We can see from Eq. (18) and (3) that if we omit the third column of $\mathbf{P}$, the canonic projection matrix becomes the canonic homography $\mathbf{H}$ corresponding to the bottom parallelogram mentioned above. Since we can obtain the canonic projection matrix from image points of at least any six vertices of a parallelepiped, this canonic homography can be acquired even if that parallelogram cannot be viewed. If an estimated canonic projection matrix is $\tilde{\mathbf{P}}$ and $\mathbf{P}$ can be written as $\lambda \tilde{\mathbf{P}}$, we can also observe that the scale factor of that canonic homography obtained from $\tilde{\mathbf{P}}$ is λ.

Assume that qth parallelepiped is viewed in ith and kth cameras and the estimated canonic projection matrices are $\tilde{\mathbf{P}}_i^q$ and $\tilde{\mathbf{P}}_k^q$, respectively. By using the method in section 4.1, we can obtain the alternative scale factor $\rho_{ik}^{ql} = (\lambda_i^q \lambda_k^l)/(\lambda_k^q \lambda_i^l)$ with the canonic homogrphies $\tilde{\mathbf{H}}_i^q$ and $\tilde{\mathbf{H}}_k^q$, which can be acquired from $\tilde{\mathbf{P}}_i^q$ and $\tilde{\mathbf{P}}_k^q$. Assume that $\tilde{\mathbf{P}}_i^q$, for $i = 1, \cdots, m$, are rescaled with the scale factors ρ_{ik}^{ql}, for $i = 1, \cdots, m$. If we insert the leading 3×3 submatrices of these rescaled matrices into the reduced measurement matrix $\bar{\mathbf{W}}$ defined in section 4.2, it can be factorized as follows:

$$\bar{\mathbf{W}} = \begin{bmatrix} & \vdots & & \vdots & \\ \cdots & \frac{\lambda_k^l}{(\lambda_k^q \lambda_i^l)} \bar{\mathbf{H}}_i^j & \cdots & \frac{\lambda_k^l}{(\lambda_k^q \lambda_i^l)} \bar{\mathbf{P}}_i^q & \cdots \\ & \vdots & & \vdots & \end{bmatrix} \tag{19}$$

$$\cong \begin{bmatrix} \vdots \\ \bar{\mathbf{M}}_i/\lambda_i^l \\ \vdots \end{bmatrix} \begin{bmatrix} \cdots \bar{\mathbf{N}}^j/\lambda_k^j & \cdots \bar{\mathbf{Q}}^q/\lambda_k^q & \cdots \end{bmatrix},$$

where $\bar{\mathbf{P}}_i^q (= \bar{\mathbf{M}}_i \bar{\mathbf{Q}}^q)$ is the leading 3×3 submatirx of $\mathbf{P}_i^q$ and $\bar{\mathbf{Q}}^q = \mathbf{S}^q \mathbf{L}^q$.

The factorization process using SVD is the same as described in section 4.2. However, it is worthwhile noting that if the number of parallelepipeds are p, Eq. (12) is written as:

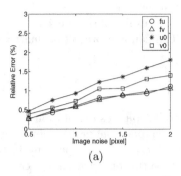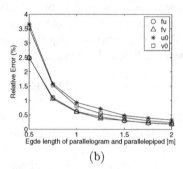

(a)   (b)

Fig. 3. The results from the simulated experiments for analyzing the relation between performance and (a) noise magnitude and (b) parallelogram size.

$$\bar{\mathbf{W}} = \left(\hat{\mathbf{U}}_{3m \times 3}\mathbf{T}\right)\left(\mathbf{T}^{-1}\hat{\mathbf{V}}^T_{(2n+3p) \times 3}\right). \tag{20}$$

$\bar{\mathbf{Q}}^q$ corresponds to the 3×3 submatirx of $\mathbf{T}^{-1}\hat{\mathbf{V}}^T_{(2n+3p) \times 3}$ while $\bar{\mathbf{N}}^j$ corresponds to the 3×2 submatirx. To resolve the affine ambiguity, we can also use the constraint equations from the shape of parallelepipeds, which were proposed in section 4.4.2 of [13], together with the constraint equations described in section 4.3. All the equations are formulated to obtain the same matrix $\mathbf{T}$.

The equations in section 6 of [13] also can be used together with Eq. (16) to acquire the position of cameras and the position and size of parallelograms and parallelepipeds. These equations contain common variables, $\{\mathbf{t}_i, \mathbf{v}^j, \lambda^j_k\}$.

6   Experimental Results

6.1   Simulated Experiment

Before the experiment with real images, simulated experiments were performed in order to make careful analysis of the performance of the algorithm in various size of parallelogram and parallelepiped and noise magnitude. Simulations are performed with synthetic 1600×1200 images, taken by three cameras with the following intrinsic parameters: $(f_u, f_v, s, u_0, v_0,) = (1600, 1600, 0, 800, 600)$. two parallelograms and one parallelepiped were placed in front of the these cameras. The cameras were placed side by side and the distance between the objects and the cameras were about 4m. Zero-mean uniformly-distributed noise over the interval $[-n$ pixel, n pixel$]$, $n = 0.5 \ldots 2.0$, was added to the projections. The constraints used in this experiment were: orthogonality between the edges of the parallelograms and parallelepipeds and zero skew of the cameras. The results are averaged after 1000 runs with each parameters.

First, we tested the calibration performance while varying the noise level from 0.5 to 2.0 pixel. In this experiments, the edge length of the objects was

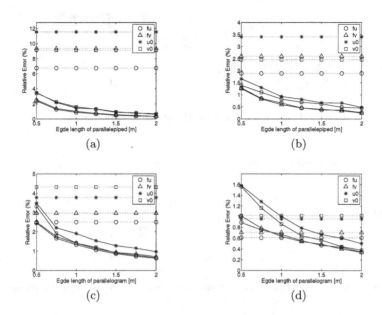

Fig. 4. The results from the simulated experiments for analyzing the complementation effect when using both parallelograms and parallelepipeds. The edge length of parallelograms is set to be (a) 0.5m and (b) 1.0m. The edge length of parallelepipeds is set to be (c) 0.5m and (d) 1.0m. The dotted lines represent the results when using only parallelograms ((a) and (b)) and only parallelepiped ((c) and (d))

set to 1.5m. Fig. 3(a) shows the results. It can be seen from the results that the errors of all calibrated parameters are generally proportional to the input image noise level. When the input noise level increases from 0.5 to 2.0 pixel, the relative error of focal length increases from 0.3 to about 1.0%, and the relative error of principal point increases from 0.5 to about 2.0%.

Second, we tested the calibration performance while varying the edge length of the objects from 0.5m to 2.0m. In this experiments, the noise level was set to 0.5 pixel. Fig. 3(b) shows the results. When the edge length of the objects reaches 0.75m, the relative error of focal length drops to about 1%, and the relative error of principal point drops to about 1.5%

Next, we analyzed the complementation effect when using both parallelograms and parallelepipeds. Fig. 4 shows the results. Fig. 4(a) and 4(a) show that when parallelepipeds are used together, the results become always better regardless of the size than those from using only parallelograms. However, when parallelograms are used together with parallelepipeds, it is not always the case. Fig. 4(c) and 4(d) show that that relatively small parallelograms compared to parallelepipeds give negative effect. The reason is that the geometric constraint of each parallelogram is 2-dimensional and weaker than those of parallelepiped.

(a)   (b)

Fig. 5. Captured images for the two real experiments.

(a)   (b)

Fig. 6. Reconstructed model and camera poses for the two real experiments.

From these results, we can conclude that when both primitives exist in a scene, only the parallelograms larger than parallelepipeds should be used.

6.2   Real Image Experiment

Captured images are shown in Fig. 5. The resolutions of the images were 1024 × 768 (Fig. 5(a)) and 3264 × 2448 (Fig. 5(b)) The cameras were not static. The two parallelograms and one parallelepiped denoted in each Fig. 5(a) and 5(b) with the white dotted lines were used as the input for the algorithms. Metric constraints used in these experiments were: orthogonality of the edge of the objects, zero skew of cameras. Fig. 6 shows the reconstructed model and the camera poses in new view positions.

7   Conclusion

In this paper, a unified calibration method was introduced to use the constraints from both parallelograms and parallelepipeds. Since the two kinds of geometric constraints can complement each other, the proposed method obtained more stable estimation results than the previous approaches that can use geometric constraints only either of parallelograms or of parallelepipeds. It was also shown from the synthetic experiment that when both primitives exist in a scene, only the parallelograms larger than parallelepipeds should be used. The experimental results with real images were also presented to demonstrate the feasibility of the method.

Acknowledgments. This work was supported by ICT R&D program of MSIP/IITP. [R0126-15-1025, Development of 3D printing content creation/authoring/printing technology and its applications in the mobile environment].

References

1. de la Fraga, L.G., Schutze, O.: Direct calibration by fitting of cuboids to a single image using differential evolution. Int. J. Comput. Vision **80**(2), 119–127 (2009)
2. Hartley, R., Zisserman, A.: Multiple View Geometry in Computer Vision, 2nd edn. Cambridge University Press, Cambridge (2003)
3. Jacobs, D.: Linear fitting with missing data: Applications to structure from motion and to characterizing intensity images. In: Proc. IEEE International Conference on Computer Vision and Pattern Recognition, pp. 206–212, San Juan, Puerto Rico, June 1997
4. Jiang, N., Tan, P., Cheong, L.F.: Symmetric architecture modeling with a single image. ACM T. Graphic. (Proc. SIGGRAPH Asia) **28**(5), December 2009
5. Kim, J.H., Koo, B.K.: Linear stratified approach using full geometric constraints for 3D scene reconstruction and camera calibration. Opt. Express **21**(4), 4456–4474 (2013)
6. Malis, E., Cipolla, R.: Camera self-calibration from unknown planar structures enforcing the multiview constraints between collineations. IEEE Trans. Pattern Anal. Mach. Intell. **24**(9), 1268–1272 (2002)
7. Martinec, D., Pajdla, T.: Structure from many perspective images with occlusions. In: Proc. European Conference on Computer Vision, pp. 355–369, Copenhagen, Denmark, May 2002
8. Pollefeys, M., Gool, L.V., Vergauwen, M., Verbiest, F., Cornelis, K., Tops, J., Koch, R.: Visual modeling with a hand-held camera. Int. J. Comput. Vision **59**(3), 207–232 (2004)
9. Rother, C., Carlsson, S.: Linear multi view reconstruction and camera recovery using a reference plane. Int. J. Comput. Vision **49**(2–3), 117–141 (2002)
10. Rother, C., Carlsson, S., Tell, D.: Projective factorization of planes and cameras in multiple views. In: Proc. International Conference on Pattern Recognition, pp. 737–740, Quebec, Canada, August 2002
11. Tomasi, C., Kanade, T.: Shape and motion from image streams under orthography: a factorization method. Int. J. Comput. Vision **9**(2), 137–154 (1992)
12. Ueshiba, T., Tomita, F.: Plane-based calibration algorithm for multi-camera systems via factorization of homography matrices. In: Proc. IEEE International Conference on Computer Vision, pp. 966–973, Nice, France, October 2003
13. Wilczkowiak, M., Sturm, P., Boyer, E.: Using geometric constraints through parallelepipeds for calibration and 3D modelling. IEEE Trans. Pattern Anal. Mach. Intell. **27**(2), 194–207 (2005)
14. Wu, F.C., Duan, F.Q., Hu, Z.Y.: An affine invariant of parallelograms and its application to camera calibration and 3D reconstruction. In: Proc. European Conference on Computer Vision, pp. 191–204, May 2006
15. Zelnik-Manor, L., Irani, M.: Multiview constraints on homographies. IEEE Trans. Pattern Anal. Mach. Intell. **24**(2), 214–223 (2002)

Motion Compensation Based on Robust Global Motion Estimation: Experiments and Applications

Mathieu Pouzet[1,2]([⊠]), Patrick Bonnin[1,2], Jean Laneurit[1], and Cédric Tessier[1]

[1] Effidence, Versailles, France
mathieu.pouzet@effidence.com
http://www.effidence.com
[2] Université de Versailles Saint Quentin, Versailles, France

Abstract. A robust and general method for image alignment is proposed in this paper. The industrial constraints are the possible large and irregular camera motion, some possible occlusions or moving objects in the images and some blur or motion blur. Images are taken from an Unmanned Aerial Vehicle or a long-range camera. Given this context, a similarity transformation is estimated. An hybrid algorithm is proposed, implemented in a pyramidal way, and combining direct and feature-based approaches. Some detailed experiments in this paper show the robustness and efficiency of the proposed algorithm. Results of some applications of this method are given, like image stabilisation, image mosaicing and road surveillance.

Keywords: Motion compensation · Image stabilization · Moving target detection

1 Introduction

This paper focus on the problem of global motion estimation in a sequence of images. The objective is to compensate the motion of a moving camera and then be able to understand the scene more easily. The specification was defined in particular for the image stabilisation, image mosaicing and moving target tracking from a moving camera. As the proposed algorithm is integrated in a product, it must be robust enough to industrial constraints. That is the reason why we propose an experimental framework of evaluation and tests. In a first part, a state of the art about global motion compensation is established (see Sec. 2). Then, we will outline the proposed method (see Sec. 3.1) and give some details about the algorithm (see Sec. 3.2). The experimental framework, the criteria and the obtained results will be given in Section 4. Finally, we will discuss about the tested applications (see Sec. 5) before the conclusion (see Sec. 6).

© Springer International Publishing Switzerland 2015
S. Battiato et al. (Eds.): ACIVS 2015, LNCS 9386, pp. 154–166, 2015.
DOI: 10.1007/978-3-319-25903-1_14

2   Related Work

2.1   Problem Statement

Given two images A and B, the objective is estimate $\mathscr{T}(\Theta)$, the transformation that allows to register A in the frame coordinate of B (the reference image). The camera being mounted on a UAV (Unmanned Aerial Vehicle) or a helicopter ... we can consider a planarity hypothesis in the images. We suppose therefore that the transformation between two images is a similarity [15] :

$$[u, v, 1]_A^T = \mathscr{T}(\Theta) [u, v, 1]_B^T \tag{1}$$

with

$$\mathscr{T}(\Theta) = \begin{bmatrix} s \cos\theta & -s \sin\theta & t_u \\ s \sin\theta & s \cos\theta & t_v \\ 0 & 0 & 1 \end{bmatrix}$$

and with parameters vector $\Theta = [s, \theta, t_u, t_v]^T$ (t_u and t_v are translations along u and v image axes (respectively), θ is the rotation angle around the image origin and s is the zoom parameter).

In order to map pixels X from A to B, a warping function W is used :

$$\mathscr{W}(\Theta, X) = I(\mathscr{T}(\Theta), X)$$

with I the bilinear interpolation function.

Existing approaches about the estimation of $\mathscr{T}(\Theta)$ in order to align two images can be classified in two types : geometric approaches using features matching (most of time points of interest) and direct approaches dealing with the minimisation or maximisation of a similarity criteria between two images. We describe here below the related work of these two approaches.

2.2   Geometric Feature-Based Methods

Main objective of these methods is to match some features : corners [14][24][21], regions [19], edges [8] ... The corner feature is by far the most used, generally associated to a RANSAC [12] algorithm, allowing the rejection of "outliers" i.e. bad matchings.

Negative side of this method is the fact that it needs the extraction of enough corners to work (with a good distribution in the image). As only a small part of the image information is used, the estimation accuracy is most of time not as good as the one from a direct method. But the advantages are the ability to estimate large camera motion and a low time computation.

2.3   Direct Methods

These methods aim at obtaining (in an iterative manner) the transformation between A and B images in such a way that the warped version of A matches with B. Their goal is to find the transformation that will minimize a criteria, in a local (block matching for example) [6][5] or global [23] [4] way.

By initializing the estimated transformation $\mathscr{T}(\hat{\Theta}) = Id$, the minimization methods iteratively estimates $\mathscr{T}(\Theta)$. If we note Δ_Θ the variation of the parameters (must be calculated at each loop) for each iteration, we have :
$\mathscr{T}(\hat{\Theta}) = \mathscr{T}(\hat{\Theta})\mathscr{T}(\Delta_\Theta)$

Generally, a Sum-Squared Difference (SSD) is used as the criteria to minimize, giving the next cost function :

$$f(\Delta_\Theta) = \frac{1}{2} \|\epsilon(\Delta_\Theta))\|^2$$

with $\mathbf{a}$ and $\mathbf{b}$ the vectors gathering the pixel intensities (in gray level images) of A and B , and $\epsilon(\Delta_\Theta) = \mathbf{b} - \mathbf{a}(\mathscr{W}(\hat{\Theta}, \mathscr{W}(\Delta_\Theta, X))))$.

The Gauss-Newton minimization is the most used in the state of the art (Lucas-Kanade [3], [6]). However, in order to get time computation optimization, we will use the ESM method (Efficient Second order Minimization) , proposed by [4].

At each iteration, we get :
$\Delta_\Theta = -(J_{esm}^T J_{esm})^{-1} J_{esm}^T \epsilon(0)$ (see Details in [4]).

Main drawback of this technique is the fact to work around a given point (this is a local technique), that makes impossible to correctly estimate large motion. However, contrarily to geometric methods, direct methods do not depend on the quality of the feature detection.

By observing pros and cons of each approach, we can notice that they are complementary. This leads us to propose the hybrid method detailed in Sec. 3.2.

3   Proposed Method

3.1   Outlines of the Method

We propose a hybrid system, coupling the direct method and the feature based one (see Fig.1). The whole algorithm is implemented in a pyramidal way [6][10]. For a VGA image, a 4 levels pyramid is created, using a Gaussian filter of window 5×5: level L_3: 80×60, L_2: 160×120, L_1: 320×240 and L_0: 640×480.

Inputs of the system are A and B images (A_{L_0} and B_{L_0}). Outputs are the estimated transformation between the two images ($\mathscr{T} = T_{L_0}$) a coefficient of confidence, and the weights W_{L_N} of the M-Estimator (see Sec. 3.4).

Each pyramid level gives the estimated transformation to a lower level (by using a scaling block).

3.2   Detailed Method

We here detail the method for a level L_N of the pyramid ($N \in [0, 3]$).

First, the direct method (ESM M-Estimator) (see Sec. 3.4) iteratively estimates the transformation T_{ESM} for this level. When convergence of the minimization is obtained, the ESM stops and $Conf_{ESM}$ (a confidence coefficient) is calculated using a WZNCC[1] (ZNCC [2] weighted by the M-Estimator weights W_{ESM}).

If the confidence is not good enough ($Conf_{ESM} \leq \tau$), then the feature based method (Harris and RANSAC) is applied and T_{ESM} is rejected. The new confidence coefficient $Conf_{RANSAC}$ is obtained (calculated by using the matching quality and the number of RANSAC inliers, namely the points that respect the model given in Eq. 1) .

If neither the direct method nor the feature-based method work, then output of this level L_N is : $T_{L_N} = \hat{T}_{L_N}$, i.e. the first estimated transformation at the input of the level N.

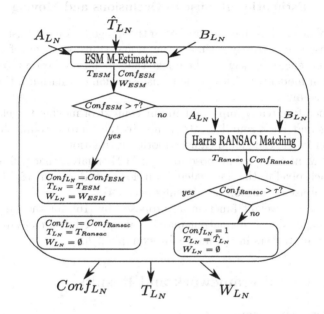

Fig. 1. Image registration algorithm for a level L_N of the pyramid

Contrarily to our system that combines both approaches in a same process, the hybrid method proposed in [20] separately uses each method in a state of their Finite State Machine. Moreover, the confidence system used is based on a ZNCC measure, whereas we propose to use a WZNCC to be robust to moving objects and occlusions.

3.3 A Hybrid Pyramidal Method Robust to Large Motion

As for every direct method using a minimization, the definition domain of ESM is around a given point. It is therefore complex to get good results for large motion of the camera, so a image pyramid is used.

---

[1] WZNCC : Weighted ZNCC
[2] ZNCC : Zero-Mean Normalized Cross-Correlation

Indeed, the transformations for low resolution images of the pyramid will be estimated, in major cases, in the domain definition of the ESM.

However, this is not enough for all cases (see Results Sec. 4.4). That is the reason why we must pair the direct method (ESM) with a geometric feature-based method (Harris corners [14] matched with RANSAC [12]). This allows for estimation of larger camera motion without penalising the computation time. The geometric feature based method is not precise enough, and does not work well in presence of blur (see Results Sec. 4.4). The use of an hybrid algorithm is then justified.

3.4   Motion Estimation Robust to Occlusions and Moving Objects

In presence of occlusions, moving targets in the image ... some robust estimators have to be used to correctly estimate the global transformation of the image. Indeed, the presence of objects in the image that do not correspond to the global camera motion model will disturb the transformation estimation if they are not taken into account.

This is therefore really important in our context of moving target detection and tracking and background creation, not to take into account the residual target motion in the the global camera motion estimation.

About ESM method, we propose to use a M-Estimator, that will modify the weights of each pixel in the final calculation, for each iteration [18]. This allows to obtain a robust estimation (see Results Sec. 4.4).

We will use the weight function w, proposed by [16], for the calculation of the weight image W_{L_N} : this output matrix can be used as a measure to detect potential moving targets in the image for example [22].

4   Experimental Framework and Results

4.1   Problem Statement

The goal is to **qualify** (using a visual expertise) and to **quantify** (mathematically) the obtained results of Sec. 4.4. The major problem is to get the ground truth of the transformations : we have therefore created a simulator allowing to generate image sequences for which the transformation between two successive images is known.

Images of the sequence are obtained from a satellite image (Google Earth), and using known transformation parameters.

The different experiments will allow us to quantify : Accuracy and limits of the compensation, in relation to the different parameters (**Exp1**), robustness to disturbations : in relation to moving targets or occlusions (**Exp2**), and in relation to focus blur and motion blur (**Exp3**)

4.2   Experiments

We propose the three following experiments using VGA images :

Exp1: estimation of t_u, t_v, θ and s, without blur, without moving objects but with **increasing amplitude of the motion**. Between time $t = 0$ and $t = 20$: only translations t_u and t_v are growing from 0 to 180 pixels, between $t = 20$ and $t = 40$: only rotation is growing between 0 and 45 degrees, and between $t = 40$ and $t = 80$, the scale factor is changing ($\pm 40\%$). Finally, from $t = 80$ till the end, a combination of the 4 parameters is randomly used for the transformation.

This experiment allows to compare the features : Harris and SIFT, the estimation : Least Squares and RANSAC of the geometric feature based method, the direct method (ESM) and our proposed hybrid algorithm.

| (a) | (b) | (c) | (d) | (e) |

Fig. 2. Extracts of images for Exp1: (a)Reference image $t = t_1$, (b) with translations: $t = t_{18}$, (c) with rotation: $t = t_{35}$, (d) with zoom: $t = t_{48}$ and (e) with mixed parameters: $t = t_{99}$

Exp2: estimation of $t_v = 5$ pixels , without blur, but with an **increasing number of moving objects**. Moving targets are simulated using moving squares of random color and motion (see Fig. 3).

| (a) | (b) | (c) | (d) |

Fig. 3. Extracts of images for Exp2 : (a) Reference image with 0% of moving objects, (b) Translated image with 0% of moving objects, (c) Reference image with 57% of moving objects, (d) Translated image with 57% of moving objects,

Exp3: estimation of $t_v = 5$ pixels, without moving objects, but with an **increasing focus blur** (on the 50 first images), and with an **increasing motion blur** (on the 50 last images) .

For the focus blur, the image is convolved using a Gaussian filter with an increasing standard deviation sigma. For the motion blur, a vertical camera motion M is simulated with the following kernel of the filter :

$$K = \frac{1}{M} \underbrace{\left[\tfrac{1}{2} \; 1 \cdots 1 \cdots 1 \; \tfrac{1}{2}\right]^T}_{\text{size} : M}$$

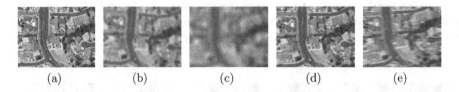

(a)   (b)   (c)   (d)   (e)

Fig. 4. Extracts of images for Exp3 : (a) Reference image at $t = t_1$, (b) using a low focus blur at $t = t_{18}$, (c) using a high focus blur at: $t = t_{35}$, (d) using a low motion blur at : $t = t_{68}$ and (e) using a high motion blur at $t = t_{94}$

4.3   Criteria

In the bibliography, several criteria exist to measure the quality of the transformation estimation :

- the ZNCC score between the two registered images (on the common area)[9]. This criterion gives some good results but can not be used in case of occlusions or in presence of moving targets.
- The comparison between estimated and simulated parameters [2][1]. The parameters t_u, t_v, θ and s have some domains and amplitudes totally different : comparing the global transformation using them is not easy.

Therefore, we prefer to use the following method. Consider two images A and B and T the transformation between them. A grid p of n points is created on image A and transformed by T to know the position of its n points in B image. After transformation, the grid is named p_T. The objective is to compare T and $\hat{T}$: the estimated transformation. So we create as well a grid named $p_{\hat{T}}$. Given $p(1, i)$ and $p(2, i)$ respectively the positions in (u, v) for a point i in a grid p. Our chosen criterion to compare T and $\hat{T}$ is D : the distance norm between p_T and $p_{\hat{T}}$ grids. Lower is this norm of error, better is the transformation estimation :

$$D = \frac{1}{n} \sum_{i=1}^{n} \sqrt{(p_T(1, i) - p_{\hat{T}}(1, i))^2 + (p_T(2, i) - p_{\hat{T}}(2, i))^2}$$

4.4   Results

Exp1 (see Fig. 5) We first notice that for every tested methods (except the SIFT method which intrinsically uses a pyramid for corner detection), the norm of error is lower with an image pyramid (red curves) than without (blue curves). This is really blatant with the ESM and hybrid methods (yellow circles).

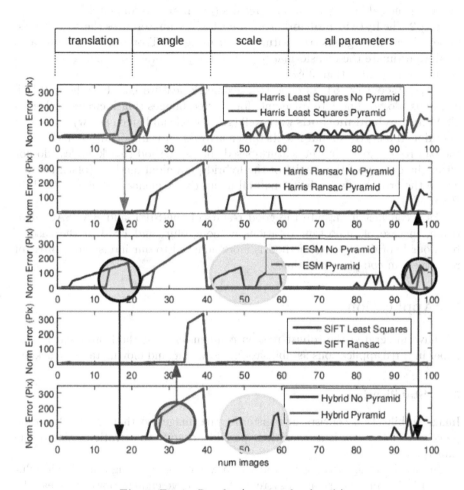

Fig. 5. Exp1 : Results (see text for details)

We observe the importance to use a RANSAC algorithm for Harris corners matching rather than Least Squares. Indeed, even if the images are not noisy and there are no moving objects in the **Exp1** images, when translations are large, a classic Least Squares is not able to correctly estimate the transformation, contrarily to the RANSAC (orange circle).

Black circles show us the images where ESM only is not able to correctly estimate the transformation : the norm of error is very high.

The method using interest corners with RANSAC is adapted to these cases. The hybrid proposed method is then able to give a correct and accurate estimation (black arrows and circles).

At last, we observe that feature-based method using **SIFT** corners matching gives the best results for this experience. Indeed, it allows for the estimation even when the rotation is high (greater than 45 degrees). The hybrid proposed method is not able to get the same results (green arrows and circle).

Exp2 The **hybrid method** using robust M-Estimator gives the best results. Other algorithms (geometric feature-based using SIFT or Harris) are not able at all to estimate the transformation, when the percentage of moving objects in the image is greater than 30%.

Exp3 (see Fig. 6) As expected, geometric feature based methods (SIFT or Harris) do not find interest points for blurred images (black circles), whereas **ESM and hybrid methods** work well (green circle and green arrow). ESM and hybrid methods give similar results (green arrows) : it is important to notice that the bad results given by the feature-based Harris method (black circles) do not affect the quality of the results of the hybrid pyramidal method (black arrow), whose the error norm is almost null all along the sequence (red curve "Hybrid Pyramid").

As a conclusion, despite the good results of the SIFT and RANSAC algorithm, in case of important rotations without blur, and ESM in the case of blur, our hybrid proposed method is more adapted to our industrial context of robustness in complex conditions.

5   Applications

We have integrated the robust motion compensation method proposed in this paper in three applications : stabilisation, mozaicing and moving target tracking.

5.1   Stabilisation

Image stabilisation consists in registering the images so that the final motion perceived by the user is as smooth as possible, despite the erratic motion of the camera..

In last decades, the image stabilisation was designed using a mechanic solution [13], because information systems did not have enough power to treat the problem in an algorithmic way.

Today, state of the art shows that digital stabilisation is possible [11]. We chose to filter high frequencies by a Kalman filter [17], while at the same time keeping a global smooth camera motion.

Some video sequences, results of our work, are available at the following URL: https://www.youtube.com/watch?v=Y9pWEbz0HSc

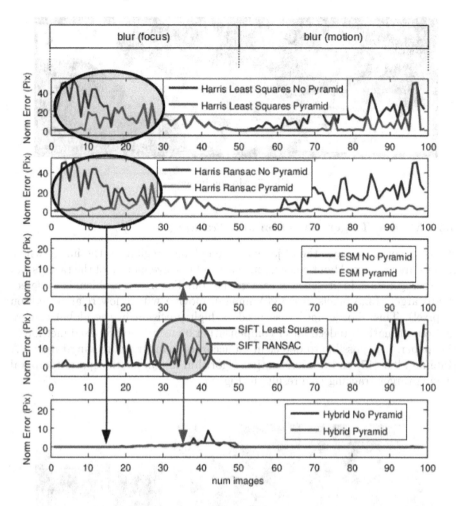

Fig. 6. Exp3 : Results(see text for details)

5.2   Panorama Creation

Panorama creation aims at stitching several images in a unique image (a mozaic image) in order to get an overview of the 2D scene [25][7].

In order to correctly stitch the images in a same frame coordinate, a robust and accurate motion estimation between two successive images is necessary. Because of the noise in the measures, a drift appears inevitably. Therefore, we chose to apply our robust motion estimation hybrid method directly between the current image and the estimated part of the mozaic image where the current image should be stitched : the estimated initial transformation is the multiplication of the successive estimated transformations.

A result is presented in Fig. 7.

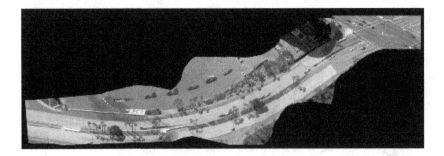

Fig. 7. Mozaic image

5.3 Moving Target Detection and Tracking

By using some overlays, the objective is to enhance regions of the image where targets are moving. About constraints, size and relative motion of the targets can be heterogeneous, in presence of camera motion. The major problem is to detect small targets (3x3 pixels in a VGA image), moving with a low relative motion (1 pixel). This "borderline" case needs a high precision in the global camera motion estimation. Indeed, after compensation by using the proposed method in this paper, it is possible to detect in an accurate manner the moving targets. A Kalman filter [17] and a minimisation algorithm allows for the spatio-temporal moving target tracking (see results in Fig. 8).

| (a) | (b) | (c) |

Fig. 8. Moving target detection, segmentation and tracking

6   Conclusion and Future Work

We propose an image registration method from a moving camera.

It consists in the coupling of an ESM M-Estimator (allowing to get an accurate transformation estimation even in presence of moving targets or with blurred images), and of a feature based method using Harris corners and RANSAC matching (allowing to perform well in case of large camera motion). The whole algorithm is implemented in a pyramidal way.

Getting both advantages of direct and feature-based approaches, the hybrid method proposed is robust and accurate, as shown in some experiments in this paper.

Three applications of this method are proposed in this article : stabilisation, mozaicing and moving target tracking.

We are working now on a GPU implementation of this algorithm, allowing a faster image registration.

References

1. Al Nachar, R., Inaty, E., Bonnin, P.J., Alayli, Y.: A robust edge-based corner detector (EBCD). International Journal of Image and Graphics **14**(04) (2014)
2. Almehio, Y., Bouchafa, S.: Matching images using invariant level-line primitives under projective transformation. In: Proceedings of the 2010 Canadian Conference on CRV, pp. 130–135. IEEE Computer Society (2010)
3. Baker, S., Matthews, I.: Lucas-kanade 20 years on: A unifying framework: Part 1. Tech. Rep. CMU-RI-TR-02-16, Robotics Institute, Pittsburgh, PA, July 2002
4. Benhimane, S., Malis, E.: Real-time image-based tracking of planes using efficient second-order minimization. In: Proceedings of the International Conference on Intelligent Robots and Systems, pp. 943–948 (2004)
5. Boltz, S., Wolsztynski, E., Debreuve, E., Thierry, E., Barlaud, M., Pronzato, L.: A minimum-entropy procedure for robust motion estimation. In: 2006 IEEE International Conference on Image Processing, pp. 1249–1252. IEEE (2006)
6. Bouguet, J.Y.: Pyramidal implementation of the Lucas kanade feature tracker. Intel Corporation, Microprocessor Research Labs (2000)
7. Brown, M., Lowe, D.G.: Automatic panoramic image stitching using invariant features. International Journal of Computer Vision **74**(1), 59–73 (2007)
8. de Cabrol, A., Bonnin, P.J., Hugel, V., Bouchefra, K., Blazevic, P.: Temporally optimized edge segmentation for mobile robotics applications. In: Applications of Digital Image Processing XXVIII. SPIE, vol. 5909, pp. 448–459 (2005)
9. Di Stefano, L., Mattoccia, S., Tombari, F.: ZNCC-based template matching using bounded partial correlation. Pattern Recognition Letters **26**(14), 2129–2134 (2005)
10. Dufaux, F., Konrad, J.: Efficient, robust, and fast global motion estimation for video coding. IEEE Transactions on Image Processing **9**(3), 497–501 (2000)
11. Ertürk, S.: Real-time digital image stabilization using Kalman filters 1 (2002)
12. Fischler, M.A., Bolles, R.C.: Random sample consensus: a paradigm for model fitting with applications to image analysis and automated cartography. Commun. ACM **24**(6), 381–395 (1981). http://doi.acm.org/10.1145/358669.358692
13. Furukawa, H., et al.: Image stabilizing optical system having a variable prism. Tech. rep., U.S. Canon Patent (1976)
14. Harris, C., Stephens, M.: A combined corner and edge detector. In: Proc. of Fourth Alvey Vision Conference, pp. 147–151 (1988)
15. Hartley, R.I., Zisserman, A.: Multiple View Geometry in Computer Vision, 2nd edn. Cambridge University Press (2004). ISBN: 0521540518
16. Huber, P., Wiley, J., InterScience, W.: Robust statistics. Wiley, New York (1981)
17. Kalman, R.E.: A new approach to linear filtering and prediction problems. Transactions of the ASME-Journal of Basic Engineering **82**(Series D), 35–45 (1960)
18. Klose, S., Heise, P., Knoll, A.: Efficient compositional approaches for real-time robust direct visual odometry from RGB-D data. In: IROS. IEEE (2013)

19. Poornima, R.K.: A method to align images using image segmentation. IJCSE **2** (2012)
20. Ladikos, A., Benhimane, S., Navab, N.: A realtime tracking system combining template-based and feature-based approaches. In: VISAPP (2007)
21. Lowe, D.G.: Distinctive image features from scale-invariant keypoints. Int. J. Comput. Vision **60**(2), 91–110 (2004)
22. Pouzet, M., Bonnin, J.L.P., Tessier, C.: Moving target detection from uav based on a robust real-time image registration algorithm. In: ICIP (2014)
23. Odobez, J., Bouthemy, P.: Separation of moving regions from background in an image sequence acquired with a mobile camera. In: Li, H., Sun, S., Derin, H. (eds.) Video Data Compression for Multimedia Computing, chap. 8, pp. 283–311. Kluwer Academic Publisher (1997)
24. Smith, S.M., Brady, J.M.: Susan - a new approach to low level image processing. International Journal of Computer Vision **23**, 45–78 (1995)
25. Szeliski, R.: Image alignment and stitching: A tutorial. Foundations and Trends in Computer Graphics and Vision **2**(1), 1–104 (2006)

Bayesian Fusion of Back Projected Probabilities (BFBP): Co-occurrence Descriptors for Tracking in Complex Environments

Mark Moyou[1]([⊠]), Koffi Eddy Ihou[1], Rana Haber[1], Anthony Smith[1],
Adrian M. Peter[1], Kevin Fox[2], and Ronda Henning[2]

[1] Florida Institute of Technology, Melbourne, FL 32901, USA
{mmoyou,ihouk2002,rhaber2012}@my.fit.edu, {asmith,apeter}@fit.edu
[2] Harris Corporation, Melbourne, FL 32901, USA
{Kevin.Fox,Ronda.Henning}@harris.com

Abstract. Among the multitude of probabilistic tracking techniques, the Continuously Adaptive Mean Shift (CAMSHIFT) algorithm has been one of the most popular. Though several modifications have been proposed to the original formulation of CAMSHIFT, limitations still exist. In particular the algorithm underperforms when tracking textured and patterned objects. In this paper we generalize CAMSHIFT for the purposes of tracking such objects in non-stationary backgrounds. Our extension introduces a novel object modeling technique, while retaining a probabilistic back projection stage similar to the original CAMSHIFT algorithm, but with considerably more discriminative power. The object modeling now evolves beyond a single probability distribution to a more generalized joint density function on localized color patterns. In our framework, multiple co-occurrence density functions are estimated using information from several color channel combinations and these distributions are combined using an intuitive Bayesian approach. We validate our approach on several aerial tracking scenarios and demonstrate its improved performance over the original CAMSHIFT algorithm and one of its most successful variants.

1 Introduction

In our digital media rich environments, many industries are turning to the use of video for a variety of applications, such as enhanced aerial mapping, medical diagnosis, manufacturing quality analysis, and defense targeting. A linchpin of numerous video analytics methodologies is the underlying tracking algorithm. The ideal algorithm must be both computationally scalable and possess the discriminative power needed to localize and tail an object, or region of interest through multiple frames. The key enablers of desirable tracking systems are object modeling, detection, and track association. In this paper, we propose a novel object modeling approach for the popular Continuously Adaptive Mean Shift (CAMSHIFT) algorithm. Our approach utilizes color co-occurrence

© Springer International Publishing Switzerland 2015
S. Battiato et al. (Eds.): ACIVS 2015, LNCS 9386, pp. 167–180, 2015.
DOI: 10.1007/978-3-319-25903-1_15

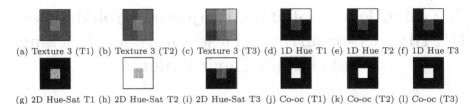

(a) Texture 3 (T1) (b) Texture 3 (T2) (c) Texture 3 (T3) (d) 1D Hue T1 (e) 1D Hue T2 (f) 1D Hue T3

(g) 2D Hue-Sat T1 (h) 2D Hue-Sat T2 (i) 2D Hue-Sat T3 (j) Co-oc (T1) (k) Co-oc (T2) (l) Co-oc (T3)

Fig. 1. (a)-(c) Synthetic textured images with OOI in the center. (d)-(f) Back projected probabilities using 1D hue histograms. (g)-(i) Back projections using 2D hue-saturation histograms. (j)-(l) Back projections using present co-occurrence method. Co-occurrence approach localizes the OOI, other methods fail (see text for details).

probabilistic models to robustly identify textured objects in complex scenes and seamlessly integrates into the overarching CAMSHIFT framework.

The CAMSHIFT algorithm [2] was adapted from the Mean Shift algorithm [3] [7] and is well known for its simplicity and real-time performance as a color-based tracking technique. Its use was primarily geared towards head and face tracking from a stationary camera in a perceptual user interface and has since been altered to track in a variety of scenarios. Even though CAMSHIFT is popular, it has several limitations. First, the algorithm struggles to track when the object color is similar to background colors. This causes false probability peaks in other scene regions besides the object of interest (OOI) and consequently hinders the peak finding mean shift phase of the algorithm. Second the tracking is disturbed when the object is fully or partially occluded by other similar colored foreground objects. This occurs because of the existence of false high probability regions generated by the back projection of the OOI density model. Hence, the defining factor in CAMSHIFT's robustness lies in the object density modeling approach and its ability to discriminate the desired object from the background and other nearby objects. The present effort is motivated by this need for a more flexible and powerful probabilistic modeling approach for the CAMSHIFT algorithm.

To date, there are several other modifications [8] [15] [18] that have also tried to address this issue through the use multi-dimensional histograms. However, the majority still rely on one or more 1D histograms and perhaps linear combinations [9] of them as a density model of the OOI. Given that estimating multi-dimensional histograms increases the computational load, and the limited modeling capabilities of 1D histograms, our framework utilizes the rich descriptive power of pixel co-occurrence modeling to generate 2D joint density functions. This density function encodes the co-occurrence of feature patterns in the OOI, providing the added advantage of encapsulating both color and texture information simultaneously. Essentially, a co-occurrence matrix is a two dimensional histogram, that contains the frequency of pairs of intensity values occurring in a given spatial relationship. (Note: The normalized co-occurrence matrix is our 2D density model, but we will often informally just refer to it as a co-occurrence matrix.)

We parallel the technique of creating co-occurrence matrices initially introduced by [12] and then modified by [1], who proposed a multispectral technique considering correlations between the color bands. We adopt an 8-nearest neighbor scheme on varying combinations of Red-Green-Blue (RGB) and grayscale color bands (alternative color spaces, like HSV, are also possible). Each co-occurrence matrix derived from a color band combination can be used to produce a back projected probability image, just like the original CAMSHIFT. Each of these probability images provides texture and color evidence for the OOI. We then derive a simple, yet powerful, Bayesian combination rule to aggregate these various evidence images into a single probability image. This can then be supplied to the final mean shift phase of CAMSHIFT for localizing and determining the orientation of the OOI. The benefits associated with our approach include:

– The use of co-occurrence modeling on RGB (or any general color-space model) and grayscale intensities allow for complex color and texture information to be encoded in the same probabilistic model.
– Our joint distribution of local patterns is rotation invariant.
– A simple and intuitive Bayesian combination rule that allows us to rigorously fuse probabilistic evidence from multiple co-occurrence images.

Our technique overcomes longstanding deficiencies in the object modeling phase of CAMSHIFT, which is the most critical part that impacts its performance. In Fig. 1 (a)-(c) we have generated synthetic images whose center regions are formed by repeating a 3×3 textured pattern that is made with nine unique colors. The background colors in Fig. 1 (a)-(c) are the colors contained in the textured pattern. We demonstrate three different cases, Fig. 1(a) shows a single color as the background, (b) shows two colors as the background and (c) shows eight colors as the background. The textured center region is selected as the OOI and then used to build the object probability model using: (1) hue values (as in the original 1D CAMSHIFT approach [2]), (2) the current state-of-the-art which builds a 2D histogram on both hue and saturation values [6], and (3) our 2D co-occurrence approach. The 1D hue [(d)-(f)] and 2D hue-saturation histograms [(g)-(i)] are not able to capture the full texture pattern in the center of the image and also contain false back-projections on images with backgrounds that contain more than one of the colors present in the texture pattern. Images (j)-(l) demonstrate the superiority of our approach in isolating textured OOIs.

2   Related Work

The pioneering authors [2] developed CAMSHIFT motivated by the need to have a robust probabilistic tracking method. Robust statistics allowed for rejection of outliers which meant compensation for noise and distractors in visual data. Initially designed as a component of a perceptual user interface, the CAMSHIFT algorithm had to be able to track faces effectively, so a color space that uniquely captured the color of human flesh was desired. The Hue Saturation Value (HSV) color space segments the hue (color) from the saturation (concentration of the color) and the brightness in a colored image. For the creation of an object model, a 1-D histogram of the hue values contained within the target object search region were generated. This normalized histogram was used as a look-up table

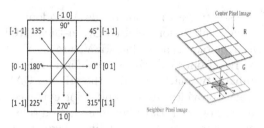

(a) Eight Neighbor Scheme   (b) Two Color Band Image

Fig. 2. (a) Spatial coordinates and angles of neighbor pixels with respect to the center pixel coordinate. (b) An example of a two band color image (Red- Green) construction highlighting the method used to access the neighbor pixels from a center pixel value.

that associated each pixel intensity in the incoming image with a corresponding probability of it being a flesh colored value.

After the inception of CAMSHIFT, a slew of modifications emerged [19] [20] [17] [14], each of which altered some component of the algorithm and provided better tracking results than the original version. In [6], the authors presented a fast and robust improvement to CAMSHIFT which they implemented on the GPU. The approach required multiple views of the object (needed to build the several multi-dimensional histograms) prior to tracking, which is a requirement that often cannot be satisfied, especially in geospatial target tracking applications such as ours. In addition, the use of multiple histograms will still fail to encode any local textural patterns. A stark limitation overcome by our approach.

The approach most closely related to ours was proposed in [15],where the novel tracking algorithm used a joint color-texture histogram as an object model in the mean shift algorithm. Texture features of the object are extracted using the Local Binary Pattern (LBP) technique. The major uniform patterns obtained from the LBP technique are used as a mask for joint color-texture feature selection. Their algorithm essentially extracts the edge and corner features in the target region which lead to better object characterization and representation. However, the reduction of local texture to binary pattern disregards valuable descriptive information offered by using the raw color values to construct the appearance model which we utilize in our approach. By ignoring the minor LBP patterns, the object model loses some of its descriptive capabilities whereas our method utilizes the information contained in full eight neighbor patterns extracted from the grayscale and RGB color band combinations. In [18], the authors propose a modification called the Adaptive Background CAMSHIFT (ABCshift) tracker. The robustness of this approach is achieved through continuous background model learning at each frame based on Bayes' law. However, in this approach both, the foreground and background learning are dependent on color space histograms, which are limited in their discriminating ability; we offset this dependence by encoding the local color texture information.

Finally, [8] used 3D HSV histograms that were weighted based on a convex monotonically decreasing kernel profile [5] that assigns a higher weight to the pixels closer to the center of the search window. Even though the weighted histograms can suppress background pixels which essentially localizes the object, the case may occur where the 3D-histogram of the HSV color space alone does not provide any useful information about the object. Another limitation may arise when tracking multiple objects, the background suppression scheme would need to be altered significantly to have well defined objects, whereas having color-texture models for multiple objects allows each object to be uniquely defined in the probability image.

The rest of this paper is organized as follows. We begin with a discussion on co-occurrence matrices, specifically focusing on their applicability in enhancing the OOI probabilistic modeling for the CAMSHIFT algorithm see §3. After which, §4 details the fusion approach for the back projections generated from multiple co-occurrence matrices. In the experimental evaluations, §5, we compare our method with the original CAMSHIFT algorithm and the current state-of-the art modification in [6]. Finally, §6 conclude with a brief discussion and summary of our efforts.

3   Probabilstic Color Co-occurrence Modeling

Color and texture information play a prominent role in defining the appearance model for both man-made and naturally occurring objects. An ideal mechanism for capturing texture-based image content is a co-occurrence matrix and the associated features one can derive from it. In the canonical work, [12] introduced the use of co-occurrence matrices for classifying terrain features in remote sensing imagery. Essentially, co-occurrence matrices encode the frequency counts of all the pairs of pixel intensities, the most traditional of which is the Gray Level Co-occurrence matrix (GLCM). When applied to color images, which are comprised of individual red, green, and blue bands (or alternative color-space models like HSV), co-occurrence matrices can be designed to utilize the information from the multiple color bands [1], [11]—deftly encoding color and texture in one distribution. To obtain the frequencies of pairs of pixel intensities, a reference and neighbor scheme is used. In our approach we use the standard eight-nearest-neighbor pattern to extract local texture. Given an image I of size $n \times n$, the co-occurrence matrix A can be defined as [12]:

$$A(i,j) = \sum_{y,x=1}^{n} \begin{cases} 1 & \text{if } I(x,y) = i \text{ \& } I(\alpha,\beta) = j \\ 0 & \text{otherwise} \end{cases} \qquad (1)$$

where $(\alpha, \beta) = (x + \bar{x}, y + \bar{y})$ and $(\bar{x}, \bar{y})$ is the offset specifying the distance between each pixel and its nearest neighbor of interest. To construct the eight nearest neighbor scheme, $(\bar{x}, \bar{y})$ are set to unit distances in all directions of a reference pixel (x, y), i.e. $(\bar{x}, \bar{y}) = \{(0, 1), (1, 0), (1, -1), (-1, 1), (0, -1), (-1, 0), (1, 1), (-1, -1)\}$, see Fig. 2. Notice that one can simply obtain a joint distribution function of the intensity co-occurrences by normalizing eq. (1).

By applying this eight neighbor scheme, we produce rotation invariant feature distributions. To simultaneously encode the color and texture information,

[1] modified the standard grayscale co-occurrence matrix. The authors computed six different co-occurrence matrices from the RGB color bands by taking pairwise combinations of the color channels. This yielded the following co-occurrence matrices: the same band co-occurrence matrices (R,R), (G,G), (B,B) and the correlation between the bands (R,B), (R,G), and (G,B). In our approach, in addition to the above co-occurrence matrices we also include the standard grayscale co-occurrence matrix. Once an OOI is selected for tracking, we choose any desired color space model (typically RGB) for the object and then proceed to calculate the seven normalized 2D joint co-occurrence histograms. These seven feature distributions for OOI encode rich discriminative information that surpasses all previous CAMSHIFT modifications. In implementation, a two band image is used for computing the frequency of the pairwise pixel intensities see Fig. 2(b). The image now becomes, a $n \times n \times 2$ matrix, where the first $n \times n$ band (top band) is referred to as the center pixel image and the second $n \times n$ band (bottom band) is referred to as the the neighbor pixel image. For example, in the case of the same color band combination (R,R), the red band would be repeated as both the center pixel and the neighbor pixel image. For the case of different color band combinations, consider the pair (R,G), here the red band is the center pixel image and the green band is the neighbor pixel image. The other combinations are paired similarly.

In order to compute the actual co-occurrence matrix, a pixel is taken from the top band (center pixel image) and the intensity value is recorded, its corresponding position in the bottom band (neighbor pixel image) is located. The intensity values of the eight nearest neighbors of the corresponding center pixel in the bottom band now become the second values in the tuples $(C_p, N_{p,k})$, where $k = 1, .., 8$ and $p = 1, ..n$, where n is the total number of pixels in the image. For each center pixel in the top image we now have eight tuples $(C_p, N_{p,1}), ..., (C_p, N_{p,8})$. The number of reoccurring pairwise intensities is recorded in the co-occurrence matrix. The range of integer intensities $[0, 255]$ for an individual color channel (assuming 8-bit quantization) can be scaled to the desired m number of bins for the co-occurrence histogram. Binning the pixel intensities has a minimal effect on capturing pairwise pixel patterns associated with OOI, as the pattern of these discretized values will also tend to be unique to the appearance of an object. By design, the co-occurrence matrices are square with size equal to $m \times m$. When the same color bands e.g. (R,R) or (G,G) are used to construct the co-occurrence matrix, the resulting matrix is symmetric.

The same is not true for co-occurrence matrices formed from different color band combinations. These different band co-occurrence matrices are equal to the transpose of their opposite combination. For example, the co-occurrence matrix formed from the (R,G) color bands is equal to the transpose of the co-occurrence matrix formed from the (G,R) color bands, i.e. $A_{(R,G)} = A_{(G,R)}^T$. During implementation we only used one of these combinations in the object model. In the literature, co-occurrence matrices are typically cited for the Haralick features[12] that can be generated from the matrix itself. For the purpose of our approach we only focus on the normalized co-occurrence matrices which give us the necessary joint probability densities used for the back projection phase of CAMSHIFT. In implementation the OOI is cropped out and a further interactive polygon selection is used to precisely capture the object pixels, this way background pixels are eliminated as much as possible. A mask is obtained from the polygon selection; the "AND" operation is then applied to the mask and the original search box. This results in an image with only the object pixels which is then used to calculate the co-occurrence histograms. Hence, our model contains very little influence from background pixels.

4   Bayesian Fusion of Multiple Co-occurrence Back Projections

Now, with an understanding of the CAMSHIFT algorithm and our object modeling approach, we explain how to generate a single probability image to be used for tracking. From the co-occurrence scheme previously outlined, we end up with seven joint density functions after co-occurrence matrix normalization. Recall, in standard CAMSHIFT one typically uses a single normalized 1D histogram on the hue channel to model the OOI, and then for each given intensity value in the image, the corresponding probability value from the normalized histogram is back projected to obtain the probability image. In essence, we have assigned each image pixel location (x, y) a probability as to how likely that intensity value $I(x, y)$ is from the OOI, i.e. $P((x, y)|I(x, y)) = P(I(x, y))$. Almost all modifications to CAMSHIFT also adopt this rudimentary intensity to probability mapping, but all these methods neglect the discriminative power that comes from the *local spatial organization* of the intensity values versus just the intensity values themselves. The use of these local co-occurrence patterns is a key discriminator of our methodology. In tracking, for each sequential frame, a probability image is generated based on an initial OOI histogram model, which is then used in the CAMSHIFT framework [2] to localize the OOI within the frame. As previously described in §3, our method encodes the eight neighbor textural and color information contained within the OOI using seven 2D co-occurrence histograms. The end objective is to still a generate a single probability image; to achieve this, we simply have to come up with an efficient way to assign a probability to the image pixel location (x, y), but now under the consideration that there are spatially encoded co-occurrence histograms that capture the distribution of pairwise color patterns around that pixel.

There are two levels to the formulation, first we leverage the power of Bayes' law to fuse the eight pairs of intensity values that correspond to each pixel in the center pixel image, within each color band tuple (e.g. (R, G)). Next, we further extend the scheme across each of the seven color band tuples. Statistical independence is assumed among each of the eight pairs of intensity values and across the seven different color band combinations. Let the set of color band tuples constructed from the Gray, Red, Green and Blue bands be denoted by the set $GrayRGB = \{(Gray, Gray), (R, R), (G, G), (B, B), (R, G), (R, B), (G, B)\}$, the elements of which we also index as $j = \{1, 2, \dots, 7\}$. Recall that for each

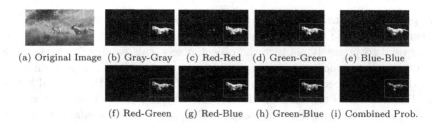

(a) Original Image (b) Gray-Gray   (c) Red-Red   (d) Green-Green   (e) Blue-Blue

(f) Red-Green   (g) Red-Blue   (h) Green-Blue (i) Combined Prob.

Fig. 3. (a) Original image used for back projection. (b)-(h) Co-occurrence probability images derived from the various two color band images. (h) Final combined probability image based off the seven preceding probability images.

color band tuple there is an associated normalized co-occurrence matrix. Therefore the index j is also an index for the co-occurrence matrices corresponding to the elements of $GrayRGB$. For notation purposes, we define the color band tuple as (C, N) where $(C, N) \in GrayRGB$. The C refers to the center pixel color band and the N refers the neighbor pixel color band. At any given position (x, y) in a probability image, the intensities corresponding to the center pixel band are denoted by, $I^C(x, y)$, and its eight directional neighbors by $I^N_{1:8}(x, y)$. For the remainder of this section we refer to $I^C(x, y)$ and $I^N_{1:8}(x, y)$ as I^C and $I^N_{1:8}$ respectively.

We define the posterior probability at any pixel location (x, y) (associated with the jth color band tuple) as $P_j\left((x, y) | I^C, I^N_{1:8}\right)$. This is the probability image that results from the jth co-occurrence histogram corresponding to the jth color band combination. The statistical independence assumption previously stated allows us to compute the probability of a pixel at (x, y) in the final combined probability image as the product of the individual posterior probabilities derived from each color band tuple:

$$P(x, y) = \prod_{j=1}^{7} P_j\left((x, y) | I^C, I^N_{1:8}\right). \tag{2}$$

Now, for any of the jth color band posteriors, we apply Bayes' theorem and simply compute the probability image using the local joint probabilities of the eight intensity value pairs at every pixel location, which we will show can be obtained from the jth co-occurrence histogram. Formally, jth posterior probability (image) is computed as

$$P_j\left((x, y) | I^C, I^N_{1:8}\right) = \frac{P_j\left((x, y)\right) P_j\left(I^C, I^N_{1:8} | (x, y)\right)}{P_j\left(I^C, I^N_{1:8}\right)} \tag{3}$$

where $P_j\left((x, y)\right) = P_j\left(I^C(x, y)\right)$ is the prior probability,
$P_j\left(I^C, I^N_{1:8} | (x, y)\right)$ is the joint neighborhood probability, and $P_j\left(I^C, I^N_{1:8}\right)$ is the total neighborhood probability of the (C, N) color band combination given by:

$$P_j\left(I^C, I^N_{1:8}\right) = \sum_{m=1}^{M} P_j\left((x, y)\right)_m P_j\left(I^C_m, I^N_{1:8} | (x, y)\right) \tag{4}$$

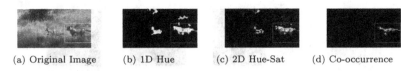

| (a) Original Image | (b) 1D Hue | (c) 2D Hue-Sat | (d) Co-occurrence |

Fig. 4. (a) Original image used for object modeling and back projection. Back projected probability image obtained from: (b) 1D hue histogram (Original CAMSHIFT, [2]), (c) 2D hue-saturation histogram (method from [6]), and (d) Proposed co-occurrence method.

where M is the number of bins in the co-occurrence matrix. We assume the intensity pairs (I^C, I_i^N) in the eight neighbor directions are independent of each other; hence, the full eight neighborhood joint density $P_j\left(I^C, I_{1:8}^N | (x,y)\right)$ can be rewritten as a product of the pairwise probabilities from the co-occurrence histograms:

$$P_j\left(I^C, I_{1:8}^N|\,(x,y)\right) = P_j\left(I^C, I_1^N|(x,y)\right) \times \cdots \times P_j\left(I^C, I_8^N|(x,y)\right) =$$
$$\prod_{i=1}^8 P_j\left(I^C, I_i^N|(x,y)\right) \qquad (5)$$

In summary, the probability image corresponding to the jth co-occurrence density can then be written as

$$P_j\left((x,y)|I^C, I_{1:8}^N\right) = \frac{P_j\left((x,y)\right)\prod_{i=1}^8 P_j\left(I^C, I_i^N|(x,y)\right)}{\sum_{m=1}^M P_j\left((x,y)\right)_m \prod_{i=1}^8 P_j\left(I_m^C, I_i^N|(x,y)\right)} \qquad (6)$$

and the unified single probability image is obtained as a straightforward element-wise product of these seven probability images, i.e.

$$P\left((x,y)\,|I^C, I_{1:8}^N\right) = \prod_{j=1}^7 P_j\left((x,y)|I^C, I_{1:8}^N\right) \qquad (7)$$

It is worth noting that one could adopt a Markov model framework to capture the joint neighborhood clique probabilities. However, the distributions become increasingly more difficult to estimate and the desirable fast performance would also be hindered. As it will be demonstrated in experimental evaluations, see §5, our simplifying pairwise independence still provides rich discriminative power, while retaining computational efficiency.

5   Experimental Evaluations

Practical implementation of the above discussion proceeds as follows: In an initial video frame with the OOI, we select it and estimate the model (2D co-occurrence densities) at a desired intensity discretization specified by the number of bins for the histograms (§3). After the object modeling, for any new incoming RGB frame, we construct seven different two-band images which correspond to the elements of *GrayRGB*. The constructed two-band image (a jth element of

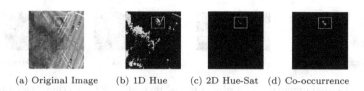

(a) Original Image   (b) 1D Hue   (c) 2D Hue-Sat   (d) Co-occurrence

Fig. 5. (a) Original image used for object modeling and back projection. The red polygon highlights the OOI pixels used to build the model. Back projected probability images obtained from different number of bins of the co-occurrence matrix: (b) 8 bins, (c) 64 bins, and (d) 128 bins.

GrayRGB) is back projected using its corresponding normalized co-occurrence histogram. For example, the (R, R) color band combination is back projected using the co-occurrence histogram constructed from the (R, R) image. When creating the two banded images we pad the bottom band (neighbor pixel band) with an intensity of 256 (does not exist in RGB range), that is one pixel wide on all sides. This ensures that the borders pixels of the top band (center pixel band) will contain a neighbor pixel in the bottom band. The intensity value of 256 ensures that the padded border pixels are not included in the model. For back projection, a mapping from pairs of intensities to indices of the co-occurrence matrix is needed. The intensities obtained from the top band (center pixel) are used as the row indices into the co-occurrence histogram and the intensity from the bottom band (neighbor pixel) are used as the column indices.

By extracting the eight neighbor intensity pairs from each of the two color band images, the corresponding probabilities can be accessed and used to form the final probability image. Since all the two banded image combinations and pairwise probability recalls are independent of each other, our framework is easily parallelizable, making it ideally suited for modern GPU architectures. This maintains the real-time aspect of the original CAMSHIFT algorithm, but now equipped with a more robust probabilistic object model, capable of discriminating low-resolution targets and tracking in complex non-stationary environments (both camera and background may be in motion). Figure 3 illustrates the back projection results for the pairwise color bands and the final probability image, which results from the product of these seven.

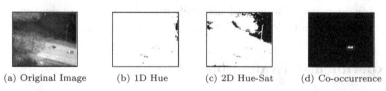

(a) Original Image   (b) 1D Hue   (c) 2D Hue-Sat   (d) Co-occurrence

Fig. 6. (a) Original image used for object modeling and back projection. Back projected probability image obtained from: (b) 1D hue histogram (Original CAMSHIFT, [2]), (c) 2D hue-saturation histogram (method from [6]), and (d) Proposed co-occurrence method.

We validate the proposed approach on several aerial tracking scenarios. This is one of the more challenging tracking environments as the target of interest is moving, the background may be non-stationary, and the camera sensor is also in motion. Keep in mind that the scope of this paper is limited to the object modeling stage and its resulting probability image. As such, the experimental results only focus on the probability images and not the tracking output from the CAMSHIFT algorithm. The modification of the object modeling and/or back projection stages while maintaining the mode seeking component of the CAMSHIFT algorithm is a standard approach taken by many others [9] [13] [8] [16] [10]. It is well known that once a probability image has a sufficient collection of high probability values (object) localized in an area, the CAMSHIFT algorithm would successfully track object.

With this in mind the yellow bounding boxes are displayed to help the reader to identify the object being modeled and is not a result of the mode seeking (Tracking) component of the CAMSHIFT algorithm. For the comparative analysis, we demonstrate our performance against the back-projected probability image generated from the original CAMSHIFT algorithm [2] and one of the most successful variants [6]. For [2], we converted the RGB image into the HSV color space and computed 1D normalized histograms on the hue channel. Since we only focus on probability images, only the object modeling approach was implemented from [6]. The object detection component of their algorithm was not used. Their object modeling approach uses multiple 2D normalized histograms of the hue and saturation bands. In our experiments, we used 40 bins for the 1D hue histograms and 32×6 bins for the 2D hue-saturation histograms. The majority of the aerial tracking video scenes are from the DARPA VIVID data set [4].

(a) Original Image   (b) 1D Hue   (c) 2D Hue-Sat   (d) Co-occurrence

Fig. 7. (a) Original image used for object modeling and back projection. Back projected probability image obtained from: (b) 1D hue histogram (Original CAMSHIFT, [2]), (c) 2D hue-saturation histogram (method from [6]), and (d) Proposed co-occurrence method.

Figure 4(a) shows a cheetah chasing a baby gazelle. The OOI is the cheetah and to generate the object model only the pixels within the red contour were selected. (Note: The bigger yellow bounding box is strictly a visual aid to better identify the entire OOI.) The back projections from the competing methods [2], Fig. 4(b), and the [6], Fig. 4(c) are able to identify the cheetah. However, with both of these methods the gazelle is also assigned approximately the same probabilities as the cheetah, failing to localize just the OOI. This is highly undesirable during tracking as the track may jump on to the other object as they come closer together. Our co-occurrence method is able to uniquely identify the cheetah from the gazelle while suppressing all other background information

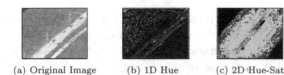

(a) Original Image   (b) 1D Hue   (c) 2D Hue-Sat   (d) Co-occurrence

Fig. 8. (a) Original image used for object modeling and back projection. Back projected probability image obtained from: (b) 1D hue histogram (Original CAMSHIFT, [2]), (c) 2D hue-saturation histogram (method from [6]), and (d) Proposed co-occurrence method.

as well; thus eliminating the possibility of track jumps. The encoding of the differing texture patterns of the cheetah versus the gazelle provides a superior discriminative advantage enabled by the co-occurrence modeling. Even though the all the pixels on the cheetah are not captured in (d), the amount is sufficient enough for the CAMSHIFT algorithm to track the object. Next, Fig. 6(a) shows an Infra-Red (IR) camera image where the color of the vehicles are identical to the color of the background. To compound this, the resolution is low which leads to less rigid pixel patterns within the image. The results show that under these conditions the competing methods in (b) and (c) are not ideally suited for creating discriminative probability images. Once again our method is able to not only identify the object, but also reject all non-object pixels.

Figure 7(a) is another example of tracking using an IR sensor. Once again the resolution is low and the color of the OOI is very similar to the background. Both competing approaches in (b) and (c) yield poor results. We are once again are able to discriminate the OOI from the background effectively with only a small amount of noise. The noise present in the image is not sufficient to warrant track jumps so our method is still superior. The image in Fig. 8(a) shows several cars driving on a desert road. The resolution is of a moderate quality but the amount of pixels available on the object is small. This would typically lead to less descriptive object models. The results in (b) are able to identify the vehicles, but does a poor job at completely discriminating the objects from the background because some background pixels have been assigned high probabilities. This will definitely lead to track jumps and increase the tracking error. Our approach (d) demonstrates its ability as an effective discriminator of non-object pixels.

6 Conclusion

The need for efficient and high-performing tracking remains paramount among video analysis techniques. The CAMSHIFT algorithm is one of the most widely used tracking methodologies due to its simplicity, real-time implementation, and generally good performance on a variety of application domains. The work presented here is a novel contribution to the large number of CAMSHIFT variants that currently exist in the literature. The method extracts and probabilistically encodes texture and color information from the image using color co-occurrence densities. We capture color co-occurrences in pairwise band combinations to obtain a highly discriminative object model. We then propose an efficient combination rule to fuse these multiple co-occurrence densities. Our Bayesian Fusion of Back Projected Probabilities (BFBP) approach combines the probabilities extracted in local eight-neighbor spatial patterns and has the additional benefit of being rotationally invariant. We have demonstrated several experimental scenarios where our method outperforms the current state of the art, on synthetic, natural, and aerial images. The method demonstrated its effectiveness as a general-purpose object modeling approach that can be used to leverage the dynamic mode seeking capabilities of the CAMSHIFT algorithm. Since most of the computations are independent of each other, we plan to develop a GPU parallelized implementation for real-time aerial tracking.

References

1. Arvis, V., et al.: Generalization of the cooccurrence matrix for colour images: application to colour texture classification. Image Analysis & Stereology **23**, 63–72 (2004)
2. Bradski, G.R.: Computer vision face tracking for use in a perceptual user interface. Intel Technology Journal (1998)
3. Cheng, Y.: Mean shift, mode seeking, and clustering. PAMI **17**, 790–799 (1995)
4. Collins, R., Zhou, X., Teh, S.K.: An open source tracking testbed and evaluation web site. In: IEEE Intl. Workshop on Performance Evaluation of Tracking and Surveillance (2005)
5. Comaniciu, D., Meer, P.: Robust analysis of feature spaces: color image segmentation. In: CVPR, pp. 750–755 (1997)
6. Exner, D., Bruns, E., Kurz, D., Grundhofer, A., Bimber, O.: Fast and robust CAMShift tracking. In: CVPR Workshop, pp. 9–16 (2010)
7. Fukunaga, K.: Introduction to Statistical Pattern Recognition. Academic Press, Boston (1990)
8. Allen, J.G., et. al.: Object tracking using CAMSHIFT algorithm and multiple quantized feature spaces. In: Proc. of the Pan-Sydney Area Wkshp on Visual Information Proc., pp. 3–7 (2004)
9. Tian, G., Hu, R., Wang, Z., Fu, Y.: Improved object tracking algorithm based on new HSV color probability model. In: Yu, W., He, H., Zhang, N. (eds.) ISNN 2009, Part II. LNCS, vol. 5552, pp. 1145–1151. Springer, Heidelberg (2009)
10. Ghazali, K., Ma, J., Xiao, R.: Driver's face tracking based on improved CAMSHIFT. Intl. J. of Image Graphics and Signals Processing **5**, 1–7 (2013)
11. Haber, R., Peter, A., et al. C.E.O.: A support vector machine for terrain classification in on-demand deployments of wireless sensor networks. In: IEEE Systems Conference (2013)
12. Haralick, R., Shanmugam, K., Dinstein, I.: Textural features for image classification. IEEE Transactions on Systems Man and Cybernetics **3**, 610–621 (1973)
13. Hidayatullah, P., Konik, H.: CAMSHIFT improvement on multi-hue object and multi-object tracking. In: 3rd European Workshop on Visual Information Processing, pp. 143–148 (2011)
14. Liu, X., Chu, H., Li, P.: Research of the improved CAMSHIFT tracking algorithm. In: Intl. Conf. on Mechanical and Automation Engineering, pp. 968–972 (2007)
15. Ning, J., Zhang, L., Zhang, D., Wu, C.: Robust object tracking using joint color-texture histogram. Intl. J. of PRIA **23**, 1245–1263 (2009)

16. Nouar, O., Ali, G., Raphael, C.: Improved object tracking with CAMSHIFT algorithm. In: IEEE Intl. Conf. on Acoustics Speech and Signal Processing, pp. 11–14 (2006)
17. See, A., Bin, K., Kang, L.Y.: Face detection and tracking utilizing enhanced CAMSHIFT model. Intl. J. of Innovative Computing Innovation and Control **3**, 597–608 (2007)
18. Stolkin, R., et. al.: Efficient visual servoing with the ABCshift tracking algorithm. In: IEEE Intl. Conf. on Robotics and Automation, pp. 3219–3224 (2008)
19. Xia, J., Wu, J., Zhai, H., Cuitis, Z.: Moving vehicle tracking based on double difference and CAMSHIFT. In: Proc. of the Intl. Symposium on Information Processing (2009)
20. Yue, Y., Gao, Y., Zhang, X.: An improved CAMSHIFT based on dynamic background. In: 1st Intl. Conf. on Information Science and Engineering, pp. 1141–1144 (2009)

Embedded System Implementation for Vehicle Around View Monitoring

Wan-Jhen Lo and Daw-Tung Lin$^{(\boxtimes)}$

Department of Computer Science and Information Engineering,
National Taipei University, New Taipei City, Taiwan
dalton@mail.ntpu.edu.tw

Abstract. Traffic safety has become a priority in recent years, and therefore, the field of intelligent transportation surveillance systems has become a major field of research. Among vehicle surveillance systems, the 360° around view monitor (AVM) system is regarded as the development direction recently. In this paper, an approach to constructing a 360° bird's-eye-view around view monitor system is proposed; the approach involves rectifying four fisheye cameras and stitching together the four calibrated images obtained from the cameras into one surrounding view image on a low-cost and high portability Android embedded system. To improve the computation performance, the aforementioned procedures are combined into a single step construction mapping using table lookup mechanism and multithreading technique. Through hardware implementation and experiments evaluation, the proposed AVM system performs satisfactorily with surrounding view video output frame rate 12 fps and the average matching error is as low as 2.89 pixel.

Keywords: AVM · Embedded system · Bird's-eye view

1 Introduction

Today, there is increasing focus on the development of video security surveillance systems such as home and traffic surveillance systems. As surveillance technologies mature, the volume of research on vehicle security surveillance systems is increasing. To reduce drivers' blind spots, Wang proposed a bird's-eye-view vision system [1] in which a polynomial fisheye distortion model [2] is used to calibrate all fisheye cameras. Zhu et al. [3] projected lines of a fisheye image in 3D space onto an image plane to determine the distortion parameters. Devernay and Faugeras [4] proposed a method for obtaining distortion calibration parameters that could minimize the curved extent of mapping from 3D space to an image plane. Tseng et al. [5] calibrated input images by using an FOV model [4] and transformed the images into top-view images by using a homography matrix.

D.-T. Lin—This work is partially supported by a grant (MOST 103-2221-E-305-008-MY2) from the Ministry of Science and Technology, Taiwan.

© Springer International Publishing Switzerland 2015
S. Battiato et al. (Eds.): ACIVS 2015, LNCS 9386, pp. 181–192, 2015.
DOI: 10.1007/978-3-319-25903-1_16

In this experiment, an RF model [6] was used to define the mapping of 3D coordinates of the fisheye camera to 2D image coordinates as a linear combination. The image photomontage method for combining several successive images, proposed by Agarwala, involves using gradient-domain fusion [7][8] to eliminate uneven overlaps between neighboring images and smooth the composited image. Yebes [9] projected the image of each fisheye camera onto a cylinder and then used the feathering technique [10] to construct the surrounding view. However, this method can cause blurring and ghosting in the resulting image. Chen et al. [11] implemented a vehicle surrounding monitor on the dual-core embedded system, in which a technique similar to the pipeline mechanism. Sato [12] obtained a synthesized top-view image through spherical mapping, perspective transformation, and image composition. However, the results showed the presence of seams between images. Another image mosaic method for constructing a panoramic image by using a rotational mosaic representation was proposed by Shum and Szeliski. [13].

To enhance the convenience and safety of drivers while driving and parking, several automobile companies are devoting efforts to developing around view monitor system (AVMS) [14] technologies. To achieve this goal, some companies mount four cameras, one on each side of a car (front, rear, right, and left sides), and combine the images from these cameras to construct a surrounding view image. However, the angle of general cameras is not sufficiently wide, and therefore, some AVMSs have a crevice appearing at the junction of two neighboring camera images (Fig. 1). To solve this problem, in the current study, fisheye cameras were used instead of traditional cameras for achieving a wide angle. However, although the fisheye camera has a wider field of view (FOV), it has serious image distortion. To solve this problem, an image calibration algorithm is first used to adjust the image distortion in the fisheye cameras on each side, and subsequently, bird's-eye-view images are obtained through top-view transformation. Once four top-view images are received, they are stitched together to construct a 360° around view image.

If this technology cannot be implemented in a car, then it has less value. To implement this technology, the proposed algorithm is implemented on an Android embedded system because the Android embedded system has many advantages, such as a low cost [16] , small volume, light weight, high portability, and low power consumption. However, the embedded system's performance is relatively lower than that of a personal computer. This can pose problems in executing a complicated algorithm and displaying the output video in

Fig. 1. Example of a commercial around view monitoring system. [15]

real time. Hence, to reduce calculations, three image-processing steps: distortion rectification, top-view transformation, and image stitching were combined into single step by constructing a coordinate lookup table in the initial state. Each coordinate in the original frames was then mapped to the corresponding coordinate by using the lookup table. In addition, to improve the performance, multithreading [17] was used to optimize the algorithm: the entire algorithm was divided into multiple sections and each thread executed one section synchronously. Since the calculation time was reduced, the device could provide a fluent vehicle surveillance video. In recent years, intelligent transportation systems (ITSs) have been increasingly researched. This method can help drivers see the environment around the vehicle much more clearly. Some car collision accidents are caused by blind spots, for example, a driver opening his or her car door without noticing an approaching motorcycle. The proposed system can be installed on cars to avoid collision accidents. Moreover, this system can be used in parking and backing systems. Thus, the car accident rate can be reduced and vehicle security can be improved.

2   Surrounding Image Construction

This study proposes a thorough and efficient surrounding view construction algorithm. The construction of a surrounding image consists of three parts: fisheye distortion rectification, bird's-eye-view transformation, and image stitching. A system flow diagram is shown in Fig. 2.

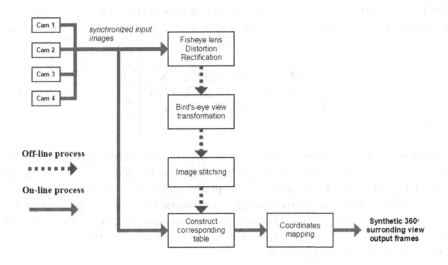

Fig. 2. System flow diagram.

2.1   Rectification

A spherical lens was used for the fisheye camera for achieving a FOV wider than that of a general camera. To solve the distortion problem caused by the wider FOV, a rectification method was used to transform the fisheye input image into an upright and unswerving image. The rectification method involved extracting nine points from the original distorted image (Fig. 3 (a)) and then adjusting the coordinates of these points to their correct values (Fig. 3 (b)).

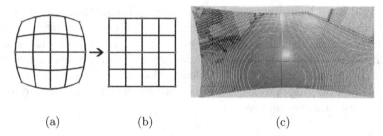

(a)   (b)   (c)

Fig. 3. (a) Original image. (b) After distortion rectification. (c) Holes appeared in the image after calibration.

First, the following formula was used to calculate the calibration parameter C, such that $(x', y') = CF(x, y)$, where (x, y) represents the coordinates of the original image and (x', y') represents the coordinates of the calibrated image. The term $F(x, y)$ can also be expressed in the form $F(x, y) = [x^2, xy, y^2, x, y, 1]^T$. To obtain the matrix C, the positions of the nine points in the calibrated image were conjectured, and their coordinates were substituted into the following equation:

$$\begin{bmatrix} x' \\ y' \\ 1 \end{bmatrix} = \begin{bmatrix} C_{11} & C_{12} & C_{13} & C_{14} & C_{15} & C_{16} \\ C_{21} & C_{22} & C_{23} & C_{24} & C_{25} & C_{26} \\ C_{31} & C_{32} & C_{33} & C_{34} & C_{35} & 1 \end{bmatrix} \begin{bmatrix} x^2 \\ xy \\ y^2 \\ x \\ y \\ 1 \end{bmatrix}. \tag{1}$$

Holes appeared in the resulting image after distortion rectification (Fig. 3 (c)). To fill these holes, the corresponding positions of these holes in the original image should be determined by solving the equation. However, because the matrix C is noninvertible, the corresponding coordinates (x, y) of (x', y') cannot be calculated from the equation. Therefore, the least squares method was adopted for identifying the nearest position of each pixel in the holes; the nearest pixels were then copied to fill the holes.

2.2   Bird's-Eye-View Transformation

This section describes the conversion of the oblique angle of each fisheye camera into a vertical angle (Fig. 4 (a)).

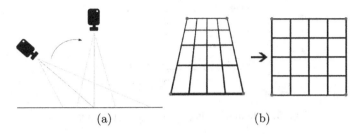

(a)   (b)

Fig. 4. Top-view transformation.

After this transformation, the skew lattice grids can be transformed into squares of the same size (Fig. 4 (b)).

Four points (indicated by red dots in Fig. 4 (b)) were designated on the calibrated image by using a concept similar to that of distortion calibration. These points formed a trapezoid-like pattern that was transformed into a square (Fig. 4 (b)) by using the formula:

$$\begin{bmatrix} x' \\ y' \\ 1 \end{bmatrix} = \begin{bmatrix} t_{11} & t_{12} & t_{13} \\ t_{21} & t_{22} & t_{23} \\ t_{31} & t_{32} & 1 \end{bmatrix} \begin{bmatrix} x \\ y \\ 1 \end{bmatrix} = T \begin{bmatrix} x \\ y \\ 1 \end{bmatrix}. \tag{2}$$

where (x, y) represents the coordinates in the image before the bird's-eye-view transformation, and (x', y') denotes the coordinates after the transformation. The equation can be expanded as follows:

$$x' = \frac{xt_{11} + yt_{12} + t_{13}}{xt_{31} + yt_{32} + 1}, \quad y' = \frac{xt_{21} + yt_{22} + t_{23}}{xt_{31} + yt_{32} + 1}. \tag{3}$$

The coordinates of the four points were then substituted into the polynomials and the matrix T was obtained. Because T is an invertible matrix, Formula (2) can be expressed as $T^{(-1)}X' = X$, which solves the problem of filling the holes.

2.3   Image Stitching

After all camera images were calibrated and transformed into bird's-eye-view images, they were merged together. However, some suture lines appeared in the composite image of images from two cameras. Therefore, the overlap region of two adjacent camera images was used to minimize the occurrence of suture lines.

In Fig. 5, the color of pixel i in the overlap (grey) region was interpolated from images p and q, and therefore, the weight of the color feature of the pixel was defined in terms of its distance from the borders of adjacent images.

Formula (4) was used to calculate the color of pixel i, where h_p and h_q stands for the original R, G, or B color of the pixel in images p and q, respectively, d_p and d_q represents the distance of pixel i from the border of images p and q, respectively.

$$h_i = \frac{d_p}{d_p + d_q} h_p + \frac{d_q}{d_p + d_q} h_q. \tag{4}$$

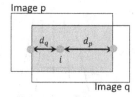

Fig. 5. Schematic diagram of image merging.

3   Embedded System Implementation

This work implemented the aforementioned surrounding view construction procedure (Section 2) on an Android embedded system. This system enables the development of products for the automotive industry. This section introduces the architecture of the Android embedded system and describes the optimization of the system performance.

3.1   Hardware System Architecture

DMA-EIS-620 (Fig. 6 (a)) was used as the embedded platform, and it featured the ARM Cortex-A9 processor. This processor is widely used, and it is a common choice for low-cost, low-power-consumption, or thermally constrained devices. Moreover, it is a multicore processor that can employ up to four cache-coherent cores, and its clock rate is 1.2 GHz. A multicore processor is a single computing component with two or more independent cores coexisting on the same chip. A core is a microprocessor that is used to execute an algorithm. An outline of the entire embedded system hardware architecture is shown in Fig. 6 (b). First four fisheye camera video streams are input, and then the digital videos are decompressed into the H.264 video format by video decoders. Next, the AVMS algorithm introduced in Section 2 is executed on the ARM core. Finally, the resulting video is output to the monitor display.

In the experiment, a model car was constructed to simulate the circumstances of a real car. Four fisheye cameras were mounted on the front, rear, right, and left sides of the model car (Fig. 7 (a)), and each fisheye camera was a 1/4-in CMOS camera. (Fig. 7 (b))

3.2   Performance Optimization

To reduce the calculation time of matrix multiplication, the distortion rectification and bird's-eye-view transformation procedures were combined. Consequently, both the calculation time and the number of hole-filling operations were reduced. The lower the number of hole-filling operations is, the sharper the resulting image. The original calculation formula is $(x', y') = TDCF(x, y)$, where the matrix D is a displacement matrix used to solve the problem of negative coordinates after calibration. The image after calibration can be shifted to the correct

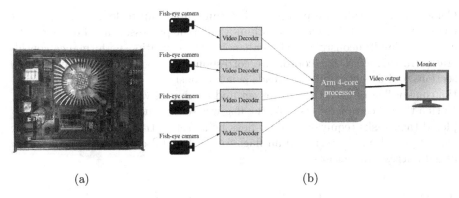

(a)   (b)

Fig. 6. (a) DMA-EIS-620 embedded hardware architecture. (b) The proposed AVM embedded system architecture.

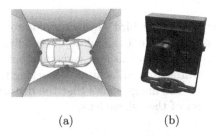

(a)   (b)

Fig. 7. (a) Four fisheye cameras mounting position. (b) Fisheye camera.

position when the coordinates of all points are positive. The preceding formula can also be expressed as follows:

$$
\begin{bmatrix} x' \\ y' \\ 1 \end{bmatrix} = \begin{bmatrix} t_{11} & t_{12} & t_{13} \\ t_{21} & t_{22} & t_{23} \\ t_{31} & t_{32} & 1 \end{bmatrix} \begin{bmatrix} 1 & 0 & d_x \\ 0 & 1 & d_y \\ 0 & 0 & 1 \end{bmatrix} C \begin{bmatrix} x^2 \\ xy \\ y^2 \\ x \\ y \\ 1 \end{bmatrix}. \tag{5}
$$

The joint matrix J of the three matrices T, D, and C is obtained using the following formula: $(x', y') = JF(x, y)$.

Furthermore, in the initialization period, after the completion of image calibration, bird's-eye view transformation, and image stitching, a coordinate corresponding table was constructed. Thereafter, the position of each pixel of camera input images was corrected by referring to the table. Once the coordinate corresponding table is constructed, the aforementioned complex image processing for each input image is not required. This saves computing time and facilitates achieving real-time performance.

To enhance the use of the multiprocessor architecture and performance, the multithreaded process was adopted in the proposed system. Because ARM

Cortex-A9 is a multicore processor that can employ up to four cache-coherent cores, and by executing each thread on a different processor, all threads can be executed simultaneously, thereby enhancing the execution performance considerably. In this work, the coordinate corresponding process was divided into 10 sections and executed by 10 threads synchronously. To avoid data incoherence, the control flag of each thread was set and the initial value was set to be false. Until a thread completed its task, the flag was set to true. Once all threads completed their tasks (equivalent to all flags being set to true), the resultant image was displayed on a screen and all flags were set to false. Thus, the consistency of data access was ensured.

4   Experimental Results

4.1   Calibration Result

The simulated model car with a 360° bird's-eye-view monitor system was steered using a remote controller in a hallway to simulate the conditions of a real vehicle being driven on a road. The original fisheye camera input image is shown in Fig. 8 (a). The grid lines on the ground facilitate observing the fisheye camera's distortion condition clearly. The image shows that the distortion increases with the distance from the center of the fisheye lens.

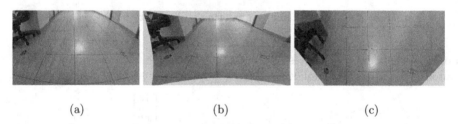

(a)   (b)   (c)

Fig. 8. (a) Original fisheye camera input image. (b) Calibration result. (c) Bird's-eye view result.

In this step, the calibration parameters of each fisheye camera were calculated to transform the curved lines into straight lines. The calibration result is shown in Fig. 8 (b).

4.2   Result of Bird's-Eye-View Transformation

In this step, the curved lines in the calibrated image were transformed into perpendicular lines. In the bird's-eye-view image, pairs of lines are perpendicular to one another. (Fig. 8 (c)).

4.3   Obtaining 360° Surrounding View Image

After the transformation of the visual angle, the four image results were stitched to construct a 360° surrounding view image. The three image-processing steps were combined and a coordinate table was constructed to reduce the algorithm complexity. The entire system was implemented on an Android embedded system and installed on a model car (Fig. 9 (a)).

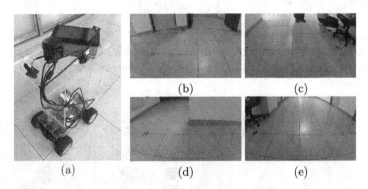

(b)   (c)

(a)   (d)   (e)

Fig. 9. (a) The simulated car with four fisheye cameras. (b) The original input image of the front fisheye camera. (c) The original input image of the rear fisheye camera. (d) The original input image of the right fisheye camera. (e) The original input image of the left fisheye camera.

The original input images (Fig. 9 (b)-(e)) were captured by four fisheye cameras mounted on each side of the model car. After image rectification, bird's-eye-view transformation, and image stitching were completed, the resulting image was output on a monitor. Because the operating matrices were combined, the time required for filling holes was shortened and the resulting image showed reduced blurring (Fig. 10 (a)). Furthermore, in the resulting image, the seams between images from different cameras are smooth. To evaluate the distortion effect of 3D object while projecting the images onto the surrounding view floor plane, we place near the simulated car a teapot and a 31.5 cm×22 cm×22 cm box with a letter R and a chessboard pattern printed on the top side and front side, respectively. As can be observed from Fig. 10(b), the result of the proposed birds-eye-view transformation algorithm shows the 3D objects are elongated a bit, however we can still clearly recognize the objects and patterns. Then we move the 3D objects 15cm far away from the camera (Fig. 10(c)), it can be observed that the farther the object is away from the camera, the longer it will be elongated. Nevertheless, the deformation is still within the acceptable range.

4.4   Real-Time Stitching Performance and Precision

In this implementation, the recording rate of the four fish-eye-cameras was 15 frames per second. After the algorithm execution, the frame rate of the resultant

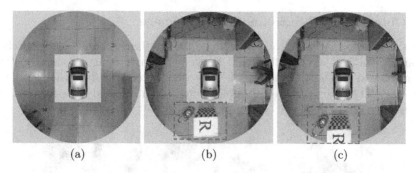

Fig. 10. (a) The 360° surrounding view result. (b) Surrounding view result with 3D objects placed in a nearer position. (c) Surrounding view result with 3D objects placed in a farer position.

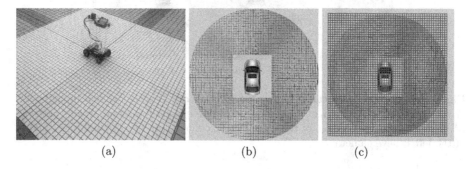

Fig. 11. (a) Measurement environment setting. (b) The resultant surrounding view. (c) Precision measurement of the surrounding view result.

Table 1. Stitching precision of each surrounding ring.

Ring	2nd	4th	6th	8th	10th	12th	14th	16th	18th
# of matching points	127	288	476	665	845	1075	1327	1476	1563
# of total points	133	305	509	745	1013	1304	1569	1779	1919
Correct matching (%)	95.48	94.42	93.51	89.26	83.41	82.43	84.57	82.96	81.44
Average error (pixel)	2.00	2.35	2.55	2.73	2.98	3.25	3.30	3.33	3.51

AVM output was 12 frames per second. A method was developed to measure the precision of the proposed AVMS. A grid poster board was placed on the ground (Fig. 11 (a)) for real environment measure. Each line on the grid poster board was 0.5 cm and each lattice was a 5 cm×5 cm square. The surrounding view embedded system was positioned at the middle of the board (Fig. 11 (a)). The output result is shown in Fig. 11 (b). A 480 pixel×480 pixel blue grid was then placed on the resulting image; each line in the blue grid was 2 pixels (Fig. 11 (c)). Next, the number of points in the resulting image that matched the blue grid was determined for computing the precision. The tolerance of point matching is ± 2 pixels. As shown in Table 1, the number of matching points from the center of the resulting image to the borderline was justified. The correct matching percentage was the number of matching points divided by the number of total points, and it was rounded to the second decimal place. We can observe from Table 1 that the lowest average matching error of the innerest ring of the surrounding view is 2.00 pixel, the highest average error is 3.51 pixel appeared in the outerest ring, and the average of overall error matching is 2.89 pixel, the highest correct matching performance is 95.48 %, the lowest correct matching is 81.44 % and the average correct matching is 87.50 %. The proposed calibration and stitching system performed satisfactorily. It can be concluded that the closer points to the center, the higher matching correct and lower average error it obtained, on the other hand, the farer points from the center, the lower correct matching and higher average error it produced.

5   Conclusion

Traffic security has become an indispensable concern in the car industry. Considerations of cost and space are crucial. This study involved developing a practical, low-cost, low-power-consumption 360° surrounding bird's-eye-view surveillance system for a car; the surveillance system consisted of four fisheye cameras and was simulated on an Android embedded system. The proposed system can provide drivers with an omnidirectional view of the environment around the vehicle and considerably reduces drivers' blind spots.

Currently, there are more and more automotive industries dedicated to develop extended vehicle safety system, but their own developed systems cannot communicate with others. As the result, Android platform is attracting considerable attention in the market for commercial electronic products because of its cross-platform development capabilities. The experimental result shows that the 360° surrounding system can be implemented on an Android embedded system in real time and with high accuracy.

In the future, this system can be combined with monitoring systems in the market and further developed to realize more complete and multifunctional vehicle surveillance systems for additional uses, such as parking path planning [18] and guiding and front collision warning.

References

1. Wang, C., Zhang, H., Yang, M., Wang, X., Ye, L., Guo, C.: Automatic parking based on a bird's eye view vision system. Advances in Mechanical Engineering (1955)
2. Ricolfe-Viala, C., Sanchez-Salmeron, A.J.: Lens distortion models evaluation. Applied Optics 49(30), 5914–5928 (2010)
3. Zhu, H., Wang, X., Yi, C.: An elliptical function model for fisheye camera correction. In: 2011 9th World Congress on Intelligent Control and Automation (WCICA), pp. 248–253, June 2011

4. Devernay, F., Faugeras, O.: Straight lines have to be straight. Machine Vision and Applications **13**(1), 14–24 (2001)
5. Tseng, D.C., Huang, C.C., Chao, T.W.: Vision-based Parking Guidance with Adaptive Isometric Transformation (2013)
6. Claus, D., Fitzgibbon, A.W.: A rational function lens distortion model for general cameras. In: IEEE Computer Society Conference on Computer Vision and Pattern Recognition (CVPR 2005), vol. 1, pp. 213–219, June 2005
7. Agarwala, A., Dontcheva, M., Agrawala, M., Drucker, S., Colburn, A., Curless, B., Salesin, D., Cohen, M.: Interactive digital photomontage. ACM Transactions on Graphics (TOG) **23**(3), 294–302 (2004)
8. Goldman, D.B., Chen, J.H.: Vignette and exposure calibration and compensation. In: Tenth IEEE International Conference on Computer Vision (ICCV 2005), vol. 1, pp. 899–906, October 2005
9. Yebes, J.J., Alcantarilla, P.F., Bergasa, L.M., Gonzalez, A., Almazan, J.: Surrounding view for enhancing safety on vehicles. In: Proceedings of Workshop Perception in Robotics, as part of the IEEE Intelligent Vehicles Symposium (2012)
10. Szeliski, R.: Computer Vision: Algorithms and Applications (2010)
11. Chen, Y.Y., Tu, Y.Y., Chiu, C.H.: An embedded system for vehicle surrounding monitoring. In: 2009 2nd International Conference on Power Electronics and Intelligent Transportation System (PEITS), vol. 2, pp. 92–95, December 2009
12. Sato, T., Moro, A., Sugahara, A., Tasaki, T., Yamashita, A., Asama, H.: Spatio-temporal bird's-eye view images using multiple fish-eye cameras. In: 2013 IEEE/SICE International Symposium on System Integration (SII), pp. 753–758, December 2013
13. Shum, H.Y., Szeliski, R.: Panoramic image mosaics. Technical Report MSR-TR-97-23, Microsoft Research (1997)
14. Ueminami, K., Hayase, K., Sato, E.: Multi-around monitor system. Mitsubishi Motors Technical Review **19**, 55–58 (2007)
15. https://www.youtube.com/watch?v=DyzHAqicA4g
16. Koopman, P.: Embedded system security. Computer **37**(7), 95–97 (2004)
17. Tullsen, D.M., Eggers, S.J., Levy, H.M.: Simultaneous multithreading: Maximizing on-chip parallelism. ACM SIGARCH Computer Architecture News **23**(2), 392–403 (1995)
18. Jung, H.G., Kim, D.S., Yoon, P.J., Kim, J.: Parking slot markings recognition for automatic parking assist system. In: 2006 IEEE on Intelligent Vehicles Symposium, pp. 106–113 (2006)

Motion and Tracking

Cosine-Sine Modulated Filter Banks
for Motion Estimation and Correction

Marco Maass$^{(\boxtimes)}$, Huy Phan, Anita Möller, and Alfred Mertins

Institute for Signal Processing, University of Lübeck, 23562 Lübeck, Germany
{maass,phan,moeller,mertins}@isip.uni-luebeck.de

Abstract. We present a new motion estimation algorithm that uses cosine-sine modulated filter banks to form complex modulated filter banks. The motion estimation is based on phase differences between a template and the reference image. By using a non-downsampled version of the cosine-sine modulated filter bank, our algorithm is able to shift the template image over the reference image in the transform domain by only changing the phases of the template image based on a given motion field. We also show that we can correct small non-rigid motions by directly using the phase difference between the reference and the template images in the transform domain. We also include a first application in magnetic resonance imaging, where the Fourier space is corrupted by motion and we use the phase difference method to correct small motion. This indicates the magnitude invariance for small motions.

Keywords: Motion estimation · Motion correction · Motion invariance · Cosine-sine modulated filter banks · Motion mri

1 Introduction

In the literature, different methods have been proposed for motion field estimation. They can be grouped into direct and indirect methods. For direct methods, block-matching algorithms [9] are most intuitive and traditional. In these algorithms, the template image is splitted into blocks each of which is then used to search the best matching block in the reference image to measure the shift of that block. Methods for capturing the real motion more efficiently are based on optical flow models [6]. With the assumption that the brightness of an image $I(x, y, t)$ at (x, y) is changed only due to the temporal motion, the motion field can be estimated under the assumption of a constant overall brightness [6], in which the total time derivative is constrained to be zero. Indirect methods, on the other hand, utilize different kinds of features and edge detection techniques to estimate the motion field [15]. An overview of different techniques can be found in [13].

Motion estimation can be done in the subband domain of filter banks based on special filter design techniques [4,11]. These methods rely on the principle that a shift in the spatial domain only causes a phase change in the subband

© Springer International Publishing Switzerland 2015
S. Battiato et al. (Eds.): ACIVS 2015, LNCS 9386, pp. 195–204, 2015.
DOI: 10.1007/978-3-319-25903-1_17

domain, and the magnitude is not influenced. In [4], the motion estimation was performed using the complex bandpass Gabor filters which are optimally located in spatial and frequency space. This was then extended in [11] to develop a hierarchical estimation algorithm by using dyadic complex discrete wavelets transform (ℂ-DWT).

It has been shown that a so-called dual-tree complex wavelet transform (DT-ℂ-DWT) can be used as ℂ-DWT [14]. The idea behind the DT-ℂ-DWT is that instead of directly using a ℂ-DWT, we can perform two real-valued normal discrete wavelet transforms (DWT). This is possible if two real-valued filter pairs $\{h_0(n), h_1(n)\}$ and $\{\tilde{h}_0(n), \tilde{h}_1(n)\}$ from the first and second DWT respectively are designed as Hilbert-transform pairs. Then, the complex summation of the first and second filter bank results in a ℂ-DWT [14]. The DT-ℂ-DWT theory was further extended to uniform M-band filter banks [3] and different design methods have been proposed based on this extension [3,2,8].

Our proposed method in this work relies on filter design techniques for cosine-sine modulated filter banks. We employ the M-band DT-ℂ-DWT without DC-leakage proposed in our previous work [10]. The DC-leakage-free property of filter banks is important in image processing to avoid corrupting the higher-order bandpass filtered images by their DC components. The M-band DT-ℂ-DWT was first proposed in [16] in form of a cosine-sine modulated filter bank (CSMFB). The idea behind modulated filter banks is to derive all subband filters from a single real-valued prototype. It was shown that the CSMFB can be interpreted as an M-band DT-ℂ-DWT [8], where the cosine and sine modulated filter banks, respectively, correspond to the real and the imaginary part of the ℂ-DWT. This is illustrated in Fig. 1. In [10], we improved CSMFB to obtain DC-leakage-free property by introducing a lifting factorization to design prototype filters. We will show that, by using the M-band DT-ℂ-DWT without DC-leakage, the coefficient magnitudes are invariant to small motion, and most information about the motion between neighboring frames is contained in the phase differences only. Furthermore, it can be also used for motion estimation and correction with applications in video processing and magnetic resonance imaging.

2   Cosine-Sine Modulated Filter Bank

The one-dimensional CSMFB, illustrated in Fig. 1, has two M-band filter banks, each of which is decimated by N. The system functions $H_k(z)$, $\tilde{H}_k(z)$, $F_k(z)$ and $\tilde{F}_k(z)$ are expressed as cosine- and sine-modulated version of the real-valued prototype $P(z)$ [17]. As proved in [8], the filter bank can also be seen as an M-band DT-ℂ-DWT. The one-dimensional complex analysis filters are obtained by

$$G_k(z) = H_k(z) + j\tilde{H}_k(z)$$
$$G_k^*(z) = H_k(z) - j\tilde{H}_k(z)$$

$$(1)$$

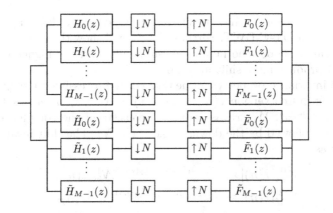

Fig. 1. M-band dual-tree wavelet transform and cosine-sine modulated filter bank.

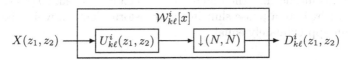

Fig. 2. Processing the image $x(n, m)$ with the transform $\mathcal{W}^i_{k\ell}[x]$ which consists of the complex bandpass filter $u^i_{k\ell}(n, m)$ followed by the downsampler $\downarrow(N, N)$.

with $H_k(z)$ and $\tilde{H}_k(z)$ defined in [10]. For motion estimation, we need the central frequencies of $G_k(e^{j\omega})$ and $G_k^*(e^{j\omega})$. Under the assumption

$$\left(\operatorname*{argmax}_{\omega} \left|P(e^{j\omega})\right|\right) = 0, \tag{2}$$

it can be easily verified that the central frequency for $G_k(e^{j\omega})$ is

$$\omega_k = \operatorname*{argmax}_{\omega} \left|G_k(e^{j\omega})\right| = \left(k + \frac{1}{2}\right)\frac{\pi}{M}. \tag{3}$$

The central frequency ω_k^* for $G_k^*(e^{j\omega})$ can equivalently be calculated.

Following the standard approach [14] for DT-$\mathbb{C}$-DWT, extensions to a two-dimensional M-band DT-$\mathbb{C}$-DWT can be found in the literature [3,7]. For image filtering, the two-dimensional complex bandpass filter will compose two separable bandpass filters, one filter on the columns and the other on the rows. They are defined as

$$U^1_{k\ell}(z_1, z_2) = \left(U^4_{k\ell}(z_1, z_2)\right)^* = G_k(z_1)G_\ell(z_2)$$
$$U^2_{k\ell}(z_1, z_2) = \left(U^3_{k\ell}(z_1, z_2)\right)^* = G_k(z_1)G_\ell^*(z_2). \tag{4}$$

As a consequence, $2M$ filters in one dimension result in $4 \cdot (M \times M)$ two-dimensional bandpass filters. The filtering process on an image $x(n, m)$ with a complex filter $u^i_{k\ell}(n, m)$ is illustrated in Fig. 2.

Complex filters can be completely shift invariant if they have a compact support on one half of the frequency space. However, this can only be achieved with

IIR filters [14]. Therefore, we have to accept that we can only obtain approximate shift invariance for DT-ℂ-DWT. Fortunately, we will show that, for the CSMFB we can arbitrarily choose the number of subbands, and the higher number of bands should produce more shift invariance.

The shift invariance property can be defined by processing an image $x(n) = x(n, m)$ and its shifted version $\hat{x}(n) = x(n + s) = x(n + s_1(n), m + s_2(n))$ with the transform $\mathcal{W}^i_{k\ell}[x]$. $\mathcal{W}^i_{k\ell}[x]$, as in Fig. 2, consists of the complex bandpass filter $u^i_{k\ell}(n, m)$ followed by the downsampler $\downarrow (N, N)$. The shift invariance can be described as

$$\mathcal{W}^1_{k\ell}[\hat{x}(n)] \approx e^{j(\omega_k \tilde{s}_1(m) + \omega_\ell \tilde{s}_2(m))} \mathcal{W}^1_{k\ell}[x(n)],$$
$$\mathcal{W}^2_{k\ell}[\hat{x}(n)] \approx e^{j(\omega_k \tilde{s}_1(m) + \omega_\ell^* \tilde{s}_2(m))} \mathcal{W}^2_{k\ell}[x(n)],$$
(5)

where ω_k, ω_ℓ and ω_ℓ^* are defined by (3) and $\tilde{s}_i(m) = s_i(Nm)$ is the downsampled shift. This means that the difference between $x(n, m)$ and $\hat{x}(n, m)$ can be approximated by only a phase shift in the transform domain, while the magnitudes remain approximately equal.

3   Motion Estimation

3.1   The Error Function

Based on the work in [11], we develop a motion estimation algorithm using the CSMFB. The idea of this algorithm is to obtain the approximate shift invariance on the subband images, as in (5). Let $x(n)$ denote the reference image and $\hat{x}(n) \approx x(n + s)$ denote the current image, respectively. The subband error can be defined as

$$\mathcal{E}^i_{k\ell}(n, s) \approx \left(|\mathcal{W}^i_{k\ell}[x(n)]| - |\mathcal{W}^i_{k\ell}[\hat{x}(n)]| \right)^2$$
$$+ |\mathcal{W}^i_{k\ell}[x(n)]\mathcal{W}^i_{k\ell}[\hat{x}(n)]| \cdot \left\{ \left[\Omega^i_{k\ell} \right]^T \tilde{s}(m) - \theta^i_{k\ell}(m) \right\},$$
(6)

where $\mathcal{W}^i_{k\ell}[x]$ represents the subfilter bank as in Fig. 2 and

$$\theta^i_{kl}(m) = \angle \left[\frac{\mathcal{W}^i_{k\ell}[\hat{x}(n)]}{\mathcal{W}^i_{k\ell}[x(n)]} \right], \quad \tilde{s}(m) = [\tilde{s}_1(m), \tilde{s}_2(m)]^T,$$
$$\Omega^1_{k\ell} = [\omega_k, \omega_\ell]^T, \quad \text{and} \quad \Omega^2_{kl} = [\omega_k, \omega_\ell^*]^T.$$
(7)

Note that in our case the scale of the last quadratic term in (6) is different from that in [11] since on each level M of the motion estimation the transform produces subbands in the complete frequency space. Normally, the images are real-valued, therefore the motion estimation will only be performed on $i = 1, 2$ as formulated in (7). The complete error function for the level M is then determined by

$$\mathcal{E}(n, s) = \sum_i \sum_{k,\ell=1}^{M-2} \mathcal{E}^i_{k\ell}(n, s).$$
(8)

Here, we do not include the suberrors with $k, \ell \in \{0, M-1\}$, because these bands lap into the other frequency quadrants and the shift invariance is not valid anymore.

The combined error is a quadratic function and can be written as

$$\mathcal{E}(\boldsymbol{n}, \boldsymbol{s}) = A\tilde{s}_1^2 + B\tilde{s}_2^2 + C\tilde{s}_1\tilde{s}_2 + D\tilde{s}_1 + E\tilde{s}_2 + G. \tag{9}$$

3.2 Hierarchical Motion Estimation with CSMFB

Our hierarchical motion estimation approach starts with the level $M_{\max} = 2^{J_{\max}}$ and ends with the level $M_{\min} = 2^{J_{\min}}$. Here, M in $\mathcal{W}_{k\ell}^{(i,M)}[x]$ represents both the number of bands and the downsampler in the CSMFB. The algorithm can also include prior knowledge about the motion field $\boldsymbol{s}_0(\boldsymbol{n})$ and has the following steps:

1. Perform the transformation $\mathcal{W}_{k\ell}^{(i,M)}[x]$ for the reference frame $x(\boldsymbol{n})$ and the current frame $\hat{x}(\boldsymbol{n})$ for each level $M = 2^J$ with $J = J_{\min}, \ldots, J_{\max}$ and each subband i, k and ℓ. If the image is real-valued, it is sufficient to perform the transformation only for $i = 1, 2$.
2. For each level M from $M_{\max}$ to $M_{\min}$
   - If there is prior knowledge about the motion included, correct motion on the downsampled grid $\tilde{\boldsymbol{s}}_0(\boldsymbol{m})$ for all subbands $\mathcal{W}_{k\ell}^{(i,M)}[x(\boldsymbol{n})]$ with (5).
   - Calculate $\Delta\tilde{\boldsymbol{s}}_0(\boldsymbol{m}) = \mathrm{argmin}_{\boldsymbol{s}} \, \mathcal{E}(\boldsymbol{n}, \boldsymbol{s})$ by (9).
   - Interpolate $\tilde{\boldsymbol{s}}_0(\boldsymbol{m}) + \Delta\tilde{\boldsymbol{s}}_0(\boldsymbol{m})$ to the next higher level.
   - If there exists prior knowledge about the motion on the higher level, use the mean of the prior motion and the interpolated motion as new prior motion $\tilde{\boldsymbol{s}}_0(\boldsymbol{m})$.
3. Interpolate $\tilde{\boldsymbol{s}}_0(\boldsymbol{m})$ from the last level to $\boldsymbol{s}_0(\boldsymbol{n})$ with the size of $x(\boldsymbol{n})$.
4. Repeat the algorithm with prior motion knowledge $\boldsymbol{s}_0(\boldsymbol{n})$ if necessary.

4   Results

4.1   Motion Estimation

To demonstrate the motion estimation properties of our algorithm under noisy conditions, we consider the Yosemite sequence without clouds, for which the ground truth motion is known[1]. The angular error measure is calculated as in [4]:

$$\psi_e = \arccos\left(\frac{\boldsymbol{v}^T \boldsymbol{v}^{coor}}{\|\boldsymbol{v}\| \cdot \|\boldsymbol{v}^{coor}\|}\right) \tag{10}$$

with $\boldsymbol{v} = [\boldsymbol{s}, 1]^T$ and $\boldsymbol{v}^{coor} = [\boldsymbol{s}^{coor}, 1]^T$. Here, $\boldsymbol{s}$ is the estimated motion vector and $\boldsymbol{s}^{coor}$ is the ground truth motion vector for one spatial position in the image. We calculated the mean $\overline{\psi}_e$ and the standard deviation σ_{ψ_e} of the angular error measures over the whole sequence.

In the estimation algorithm, we set the maximum level to $J_{\max} = 8$ and the minimum level to $J_{\min} = 4$. The frames were extended by zeros at the borders during the downsampling process. When calculating the mean and standard deviation, we took into account only pixel elements that are not in the cloud area of the image. We considered white Gaussian noise with zero mean and different standard deviations σ_g before processing the frames to check the robustness of our algorithm.

The experimental results on the angular error measure are shown in Table 1. As expected, the motion estimation for the noise-free case is relatively good, but it gets worse in noisy conditions. Although the performance of our system in terms of angular error measure is marginally lower than for the best algorithms in [1], it has some significant advantages with regard to motion correction. Our transform has similar properties as the Fourier transform in the sense of shift invariance of the magnitude. With the information being coded in the phase, we can directly calculate the motion field. In contrast to the Fourier transform, our method is able to cope with non-rigid motion and its associated noise.

Table 1. Mean and standard deviation for different noise level of the motion estimation

σ_g	0	10	20	30	40
ψ_e	4.256°	11.642°	17.912°	24.463°	30.216°
σ_{ψ_e}	5.096°	10.596°	13.654°	18.074°	21.532°

4.2   Motion Correction

In this experiment, we perform motion correction between two frames by using the ground truth motion field of the Yosemite sequence without clouds and the filter bank without downsampling step. The downsampling step is not performed because the ground truth motion field can be directly applied by (5) to correct the bandpass filtered images. We used all subbands of the image excluding $\mathcal{W}^1_{0,0}[x]$ and $\mathcal{W}^2_{0,0}[x]$, because they include the DC-component of the image, and correcting the phase here can result in changing the image DC. The other bands do not include DC, because we used filters without DC-leakage [10].

After the correction, we transform the images back into the spatial domain. We measure the error of the correction as $\mathrm{E} = \|X_1 - X_2^{\mathrm{coor}}\|_{\mathrm{F}}$, where X_1 denotes the reference frame and X_2^{coor} denotes the corrected frame. By using the Frobenius norm $\|\cdot\|_{\mathrm{F}}$, we measure the distance between two images. As baseline we also include the error $\|X_1 - X_2\|_{\mathrm{F}}$, where X_2 is the next frame without motion correction. For this experiment, we normalized the pixel values to be in the interval $[0, 1]$. In Fig. 3, we show the error measures between neighboring frames. It can clearly be seen that it is possible to correct motion with a two-dimensional CSMFB for the given motion fields.

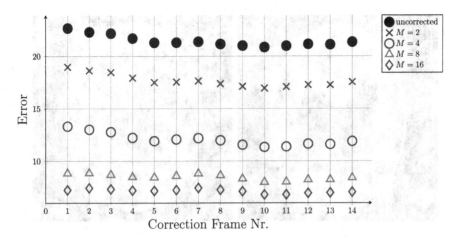

Fig. 3. Error of the motion correction using motion field correction with different number of bands $4M^2$ on the Yosemite sequence.

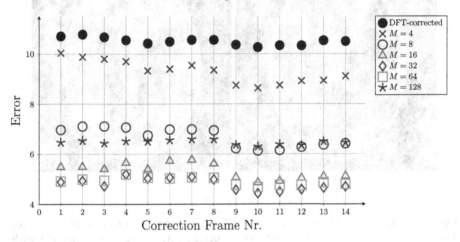

Fig. 4. Error of the motion correction using phase difference correction with different number of bands $4M^2$ on the Yosemite sequence.

4.3 Phase Shift Correction

In this experiment, we want to show that for a two-dimensional CSMFB with downsampling, the difference between the reference and the template frame is only in the phase differences of the subband images $\mathcal{W}_{k\ell}^i[\boldsymbol{x}]$. By correcting the phase differences, we are able to correct the non-rigid motion. As baseline, we used the Fourier transform which is optimal for correcting horizontal and vertical image shifts. In Fig. 4, we show the difference error between neighboring frames. Here, we used the Yosemite sequence with clouds, therefore we are not interested in the ground truth motion. As can be seen in Fig. 4, with increasing number of

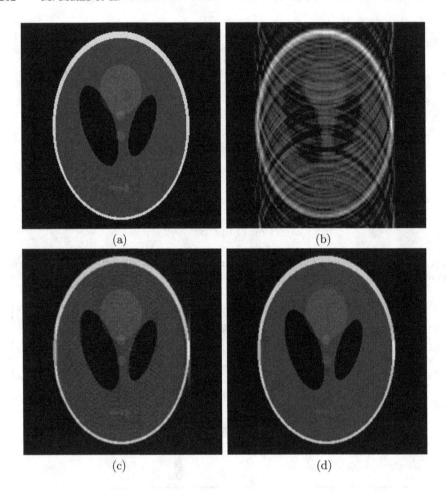

Fig. 5. Example of MR imaging. (a) Original. (b) The motion corrupted phantom. (c) The reconstruction by [12]. (d) The reconstruction with phase shift correction with $M = 16$.

bands, the motion correction becomes better until $M = 32$, which corresponds to $4 \cdot 32^2$ bandpass filtered images. With a reasonable number of bands, the motion information is coded only in the phase, and the motion can be easily corrected by the phase differences. For $M = 64$ and above, the motion correction becomes worse again. The reason is that a too large number of bands causes the two-dimensional CSMFB to become equivalent to the baseline Fourier transform.

4.4   Motion Correction in Magnetic Resonance Imaging

In magnetic resonance imaging the Fourier-space, called k-space, will be sampled directly. If the patient moves during the data acquisition, the movement will result in motion artifacts after the reconstruction. Without any additional phase correction, the sampled medical images could be strongly corrupted by these motion artifacts, and diagnostics are not possible anymore. We extended the blind motion estimation in [18,12] for subpixel motion by a phase-correction step. We simulated the subpixel motion by linear interpolation on the Shepp-Logan phantom (256×256 pixels) by randomly chosen ± 5 pixel translational motion for each k-space line. The motion-corrupted image is denoted by $\boldsymbol{x}_m$. Then, we perform a first motion correction as in [12] to obtain the image $\boldsymbol{x}_s$. After that, we perform a total-variation denoising step with the algorithm in [5] and get the denoised image $\boldsymbol{x}_d$. Between all subbands $\mathcal{W}^i_{k\ell}[\boldsymbol{x}_d]$ and $\mathcal{W}^i_{k\ell}[\boldsymbol{x}_s]$, we calculate the phase differences in the transform-domain $\mathcal{W}$ by (5) and perform the correction for $\mathcal{W}^i_{k\ell}[\boldsymbol{x}_s]$. After the following inverse transform, we obtain the image $\tilde{\boldsymbol{x}}_s$. Finally, we used the Fourier-transform $\mathcal{F}[\hat{\boldsymbol{x}}_s] = |\mathcal{F}[\boldsymbol{x}_m]| \cdot \exp\left(j \cdot \angle(\mathcal{F}[\tilde{\boldsymbol{x}}_s])\right)$ as the new starting point for the iteration. This is repeated until the phase difference between $\mathcal{W}^i_{k\ell}[\tilde{\boldsymbol{x}}_s]$ and $\mathcal{W}^i_{k\ell}[\boldsymbol{x}_s]$ becomes small. We show the results in Fig. 5. An improvement can be clearly seen between the reconstructed image resulted by [12] (Fig. 5 c) and the one obtained by our proposed algorithm (Fig. 5 d).

5 Conclusions

We investigated two-dimensional CSMFBs for motion-field estimation and motion correction. We showed that the motion information is only coded by the phase information of the two-dimensional CSMFB, which significantly facilitates the motion estimation and correction. Furthermore, given a motion field, the motion can be corrected without the need for an external interpolation function. Because of this, we do not need to perform a regridding from images.

Our experimental results on the Yosemite sequence are promising, and further optimization may improve the performance on motion estimation. The main application area of the transform is seen as a building block within image reconstruction methods for capturing image sequences with non-rigid motion, such as in magnetic resonance imaging, where a k-space is corrupted.

References

1. Austvoll, I.: A study of the yosemite sequence used as a test sequence for estimation of optical flow. In: Kalviainen, H., Parkkinen, J., Kaarna, A. (eds.) SCIA 2005. LNCS, vol. 3540, pp. 659–668. Springer, Heidelberg (2005)
2. Bayram, I., Selesnick, I.W.: On the dual-tree complex wavelet packet and m -band transforms. IEEE Transactions on Signal Processing 56(6), 2298–2310 (2008)
3. Chaux, C., Duval, L., Pesquet, J.C.: Image analysis using a dual-tree m-band wavelet transform. IEEE Transactions on Image Processing 15(8), 2397–2412 (2006)
4. Fleet, D.J., Jepson, A.D.: Computation of component image velocity from local phase information. International Journal of Computer Vision 5(1), 77–104 (1990)
5. Goldstein, T., Osher, S.: The split bregman method for L1-regularized problems. SIAM Journal on Imaging Sciences 2(2), 323–343 (2009)

6. Horn, B.K.P., Schunck, B.G.: Determining optical flow. Artificial Intelligence **17**(1–3), 185–203 (1981)
7. Kyochi, S., Suzuki, T., Tanaka, Y.: A directional and shift-invariant transform based on m-channel rational-valued cosine-sine modulated filter banks. In: Proc. Asia-Pacific Signal Information Processing Association Annual Summit and Conference, Hollywood, California, pp. 1–4, December 2012
8. Kyochi, S., Uto, T., Ikehara, M.: Dual-tree complex wavelet transform arising from cosine-sine modulated filter banks. In: Proc. IEEE International Symposium on Circuits and Systems, Taipei, Taiwan, pp. 2189–2192, May 2009
9. Lu, J., Liou, M.L.: A simple and efficient search algorithm for block-matching motion estimation. IEEE Transactions on Circuits and Systems for Video Technology **7**(2), 429–433 (1997)
10. Maaß, M., Phan, H., Mertins, A.: Design of cosine-sine modulated filter banks without dc leakage. In: Proc. International Conference on Digital Signal Processing, Hong Kong, China, pp. 486–491, August 2014
11. Magarey, J., Kingsbury, N.G.: Motion estimation using a complex-valued wavelet transform. IEEE Transactions on Signal Processing **46**(4), 1069–1084 (1998)
12. Möller, A., Maaß, M., Mertins, A.: Blind sparse motion MRI with linear subpixel interpolation. In: Handels, H., Deserno, T.M., Meinzer, H.P., Tolxdorff, T. (eds.) Bildverarbeitung für die Medizin 2015. Informatik aktuell, pp. 510–515. Springer, Heidelberg (2015)
13. Mota, C., Stuke, I., Aach, T., Barth, E.: Divide-and-conquer strategies for estimating multiple transparent motions. In: Jähne, B., Mester, R., Barth, E., Scharr, H. (eds.) IWCM 2004. LNCS, vol. 3417, pp. 66–77. Springer, Heidelberg (2007)
14. Selesnick, I.W., Baraniuk, R.G., Kingsbury, N.G.: The dual-tree complex wavelet transform. IEEE Signal Processing Magazine **22**(6), 123–151 (2005)
15. Torr, P.H.S., Zisserman, A.: Feature based methods for structure and motion estimation. In: Triggs, B., Zisserman, A., Szeliski, R. (eds.) ICCV-WS 1999. LNCS, vol. 1883, pp. 278–294. Springer, Heidelberg (2000)
16. Viholainen, A., Alhava, J., Renfors, M.: Implementation of parallel cosine and sine modulated filter banks for equalized transmultiplexer systems. In: Proc. IEEE International Conference on Acoustics, Speech, and Signal Processing, vol. 6, Salt Lake City, Utah, pp. 3625–3628, May 2001
17. Viholainen, A., Stitz, T.H., Alhava, J., Ihalainen, T., Renfors, M.: Complex modulated critically sampled filter banks based on cosine and sine modulation. In: Proc. IEEE International Symposium on Circuits and Systems, vol. 1, Scottsdale, Arizona, pp. I-833–I-836, May 2002
18. Yang, Z., Zhang, C., Xie, L.: Sparse MRI for motion correction. In: Proc. IEEE International Symposium on Biomedical Imaging, San Francisco, California, pp. 962–965, April 2013

Fast and Robust Variational Optical Flow for High-Resolution Images Using SLIC Superpixels

Simon Donné[✉], Jan Aelterman, Bart Goossens, and Wilfried Philips

iMinds-IPI-UGent, Ghent, Belgium
{Simon.Donne,Jan.Aelterman,Bart.Goossens,philips}@telin.ugent.be

Abstract. We show how pixel-based methods can be applied to a sparse image representation resulting from a superpixel segmentation. On this sparse image representation we only estimate a single motion vector per superpixel, without working on the full-resolution image. This allows the accelerated processing of high-resolution content with existing methods. The use of superpixels in optical flow estimation was studied before, but existing methods typically estimate a dense optical flow field – one motion vector per pixel – using the full-resolution input, which can be slow. Our novel approach offers important speed-ups compared to dense pixel-based methods, without significant loss of accuracy.

Keywords: SLIC superpixels · Segmentation · Optical flow

1 Introduction

The input of high-resolution content to optical flow estimation algorithms is both a curse and a blessing. On the one hand, such images are able to capture details of the scene and its textures – invisible in lower resolutions – which may offer valuable cues for the optical flow estimation. On the flip side, higher resolution content means longer processing times and – specifically for optical flow estimation – a possible aggravation of the aperture problem. The aperture problem states that movement can only be tracked well near gradients, and then only in the direction of the gradient. As a result, large homogeneous regions typically pose problems for optical flow estimation. In high-resolution content, the size of homogeneous areas increases in terms of absolute pixel count: this requires for example an increase in search window or regularisation window size, further increasing processing times.

A typical solution to this problem is to work in a hierarchical way: first estimate the results on a lower-resolution version of the image, and then gradually refine the estimate on higher resolution versions up to the original input resolution.

Part of the research leading to this work was performed within the iMinds HiViz project. Simon Donné is funded by BOF grant 01D21213, and Bart Goossens is a postdoctoral research fellow for FWO.

© Springer International Publishing Switzerland 2015
S. Battiato et al. (Eds.): ACIVS 2015, LNCS 9386, pp. 205–216, 2015.
DOI: 10.1007/978-3-319-25903-1_18

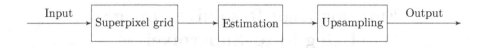

Fig. 1. Overview of the proposed approach: using SLIC, we arrive at a sparse representation of the input image. This sparse representation is processed using a pixel-based methods, and this result is upsampled and scaled to arrive at the final estimate.

We propose a novel framework for optical flow estimation, which allows the exploitation of high-resolution information in the lower resolutions. Contrary to the existing methods, which do content-independent downsampling of the input image, we use SLIC superpixels [1] to arrive at a sparse image representation.

This sparse representation is used as an input to existing dense pixel-based methods. An additional benefit of this novel approach is that superpixels are, to some extent, noise-robust. The output optical flow estimate of those existing methods is then be upsampled using the superpixel information, resulting in the output estimate. Our newly proposed method is shown schematically in Figure 1. As the major interest lies in the speed-up of the dense pixel-based methods, we also implement each of the steps on the GPU, resulting in significant speed-ups.

After a more detailed overview of existing techniques that use (over)segmented images in Section 2, we discuss several superpixel segmentation methods in Section 3, amongst others both the original SLIC algorithm and its adaptation for parallel processing, gSLIC. Our proposed superpixel-based approach is explained in detail in Section 4. To conclude this text we give experimental results, draw our conclusion and outline future work in respectively Section 5 to 7.

2   Existing Work Using (Over)Segmentation

The idea of content-adaptive downscaling from [10], can also be attained through supervoxels, e.g. in MRI [9]. We will use this idea – superpixels as a sparse image representation – and apply it as an initial step before pixel-based methods are applied.

The use of superpixels as a pre-processing step is familiar in object segmentation and recognition, where it is often an initial step [2,12,13]. Optical flow estimation methods that estimate a single motion vector per segment generally segment the scene into objects. This requires specially adapted methods which can work on segmented images instead of pixels [3,14]. Novel to our approach is that we will estimate a single motion vector per superpixel without requiring such segment-based logic.

The alternative use of superpixels in optical flow estimation is the estimation of one motion vector per pixel, a dense pixel-based field, while using a superpixel segmentation to guide this estimation [4,7], for example by performing error

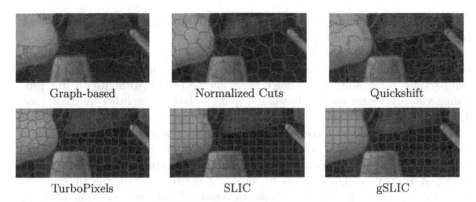

| | Graph-based | | Normalized Cuts | | Quickshift |
| | TurboPixels | | SLIC | | gSLIC |

Fig. 2. Results of various superpixel segmentation methods. The input image was a detail of the Art image from [17].

Table 1. Execution times for the various methods on an image of 1390 × 1110 (Normalized Cuts was run on the half-resolution input). The used implementations were publically available (C++ or MATLAB). gSLIC was implemented using Quasar [8].

Graph Based	Normalized Cuts	Quickshift	TurboPixels	SLIC	gSLIC
1.428 s	7.45 min	15.18 s	71.7 s	0.503 s	45 ms

aggregation over superpixels or by regularising pixels within the same superpixel. These methods still work on the full-resolution input image. In contrast, our new approach applies a pixel-based technique to the superpixel grid, drastically lowering the resolution that is being processed.

3   Existing Superpixel Methods

We take a *superpixel* to be a cluster of pixels that results from oversegmenting an image: groups of pixels that are similar in size (surface area) but not containing major edges. The term *oversegmentation* is used to indicate that they do not correspond with physical objects on a one-to-one basis: the image of a physical object is usually still divided into multiple superpixels. We discuss several algorithms for estimating superpixels, which are illustrated in Figure 2.

Felzenszwalb's graph-based segmentation [6] is an efficient and popular segmentation algorithm. It uses a single scale parameter to influence the segment size. However, the actual size and number of segments varies greatly depending on the local content as seen in Figure 2.

The normalized cuts-approach from [16] is very slow to execute (Table 1). It was unable to process the full-resolution 1390 × 1110 image in an acceptable time, hence results were generated on the half-resolution input.

Quickshift [18] is based on an approximation to kernel-based mean-shift. By processing pixels as points in a five-dimensional space (three colour channels and two location coordinates), mean-shift in this five-dimensional space results in a segmentation of the original image as in Figure 2.

Turbopixels [11] are based on geometric flows, providing boundary-conforming superpixels while keeping under-segmentation in check through a compactness constraint. It is a much faster method than Normalized Cuts, providing visually better results, but is not quite as fast as the other methods (see Table 1).

SLIC (Simple Linear Iterative Clustering [2]) performs k-means clustering in the same five-dimensional color-location space as QuickShift, performing correspondence searches only locally. By controlling the seeds for the k-means clustering, it is very straightforward to impose a desired size on the superpixels, while a compactness parameter handles the trade-off between color and location, as in QuickShift. While the k-means clustering results in superpixels which are connected in the five-dimensional colour-spatial space, superpixels are assumed to be spatially connected. A post-processing step enforces spatial connectivity.

SLIC superpixel estimation is very amenable to parallelisation: an adaptation called gSLIC allows the clustering to be done efficiently on a GPU [15]. The authors of [15] mention a speed up of 10x to 20x, which our findings corroborate. Its results are shown in Figure 2, and visually they appear very similar to the results from the original SLIC (not quite identical because of slight changes for better parallelisation).

We will use the gSLIC estimation of superpixels in our proposed workflow: this is a novel interpretation of the oversegmentation results as a dimensionality reduction resulting in a near-regular grid. gSLIC is an extremely fast segmentation that is of low implementational complexity, and its nature makes it easy to arrive at a superpixel grid of user-specified dimensions (by spawning the k-means seeds along the required grid).

3.1   gSLIC Superpixels

We outline gSLIC's workings and the interpretation of the resulting superpixel grid as a sparse image representation in this section. The image is first divided into a regular grid of the desired size (as in Figure 3 and 4[1]). The position of a superpixel on this grid is used as its label and denoted by (x_s, y_s).

When estimating superpixels using gSLIC, each pixel contains a label indicating which superpixel it belongs to; superpixels are described with a colour and a location, defined as the respective averages all pixels that belong to it.

After the initialisation, k-means clustering is performed: in each iteration, each pixel selects the most fitting label (i.e. the closest cluster center in the 5-dimensional space of colour and location) after which the cluster centers are updated with the new description based on the new labels. A compactness value weights the color distance between a pixel and a prospective cluster against their Euclidean distance in the image plane - because Euclidean distances are used, colours are represented in the CIELAB colour space.

---

[1] Copyright Blender Foundation (www.sintel.org).

Fig. 3. Initialisation for gSLIC.   **Fig. 4.** Detail of the initialisation.

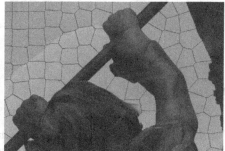

Fig. 5. Final clustering by gSLIC.   **Fig. 6.** Detail of the final clustering.

3.2   (g)SLIC in Our Proposed Workflow

We intend to use SLIC superpixels for dimensionality reduction of the input image. We assume that the superpixels are very small in comparison to the content: this implies that the superpixels will be largely rectangular and uniform as the content is locally uniform/homogeneous. As the resulting segmentations for SLIC and gSLIC are extremely similar, we prefer gSLIC for its faster execution.

We do not enforce label connectivity nor do we fuse small clusters because our superpixels are, by and large, uniform. An example superpixel clustering as we propose to use for the input image is shown in Figure 7. Note that the superpixels form a largely regular grid, except near the content edges, which they adhere to nicely.

4   Variational Optical Flow on the Superpixel Grid

We now outline, in detail, our novel workflow for optical flow estimation on high-resolution images: the superpixel clustering followed by dense pixel-based processing of the superpixel grid, and finally the upsampling using the superpixel labeling information.

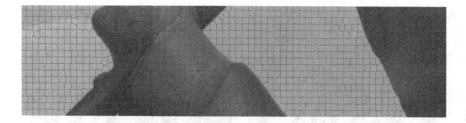

Fig. 7. Example of a superpixel grid such as we propose to use.

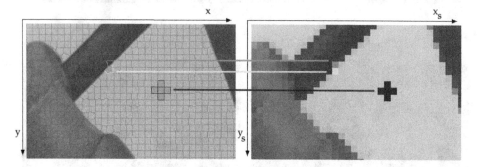

Fig. 8. The full-resolution input image on the left is subdivided into superpixels (red). Each of these superpixels corresponds to a location on the superpixel grid (as indicated by the coloured connections). The superpixel grid is visualized as an image by assigning the colour description of a superpixel to its location in the superpixel grid, resulting in the superpixel grid image shown on the right.

(gSLIC) Superpixel Clustering and Creation of the Superpixel Grid

Each of the superpixels has a two-dimensional coordinate corresponding to its location on the superpixel grid, as well as a colour. After superpixel estimation, each pixel p on the sampling grid of the original input images I_k has a label $(x_{k,s}(p), y_{k,s}(p))$ corresponding to the superpixel it belongs to. This is illustrated in Figure 8: the input image on the left is shown with its estimated superpixels.

The labels of the superpixels (i.e. their initial locations) can be used to create an image of the superpixel grid as in Figure 8: each location in the superpixel grid image has the colour from the description of the corresponding superpixel. The superpixel grid is only a fraction of the size of the original image: if we impose the superpixels to be roughly squares with an area of 2^2, it only has half the width and half the height.

Processing the Superpixel Grid with the Pixel-Based Method

In the case of optical flow estimation, we create a superpixel grid for both input images. We process these two superpixel grids with an existing, pixel-based

| The superpixel grid. | The superpixel grid optical flow estimate. |

| Detail of the original input image. | The upsampled optical flow estimate. |

Fig. 9. Illustration of the proposed method: the superpixel grids (top left) for both input images are processed by a dense pixel-based method, resulting in an optical flow estimate for the superpixel grids (top right). After upsampling (bottom right), we arrive at an optical flow estimate for the original input image (bottom left).

method. For the purpose of this paper, we have chosen a total-variation based optical flow estimation [5]. The output is an estimate of the optical flow between both superpixel grids, as shown in the top right of Figure 9.

Upsampling the Flow Estimate Using the Superpixel Labelling

Finally, the flow estimate on the superpixel grid is upsampled: each pixel in the high-resolution input image has a label which can be used to look up the estimated flow for the superpixel grid. In the case of, e.g., optical flow, the estimate also needs to be scaled (horizontal offsets must be multiplied by the average width of all superpixels, and ditto for vertical offsets).

Note that the sampling grid underlying the superpixel grid is only nearly regular, while the existing pixel-based methods assume a completely regular grid. Because the superpixel grid is very close to regular, and because this irregularity evens out over relatively small neighbourhoods, we expect this to have only a minor influence. Indeed, as the results in Section 5 indicate, the loss of accuracy is small. Furthermore, as we have noted earlier, the superpixels are to some extent noise-robust, and this results in a net gain of accuracy for even small amounts of noise.

Figure 9 shows an example result of the upsampling: the top left shows the superpixel grid, in the top right the superpixel grid flow estimate is shown and in the bottom the original input resolution and the resulting flow estimate are

Fig. 10. Test images for evaluating the proposed method.

shown. We see that the resulting high-resolution output follows the image content well: a more quantitative comparison will be done in the next section.

5   Experiments and Results

We perform both the full-resolution pixel-based approach (i.e. the existing approach on the full-resolution input image) and the superpixel-grid approach on the test images from Figure 10 in full 4K-resolution. The images are perturbed by various levels of noise as shown in Figure 11. The noise is AWGN with a standard deviation of 0.0 to 0.1 when expressing pixel values in the range $[0, 1]$ (with saturation on the boundaries).

We find that SLIC superpixels (and superpixels in general) are noise-robust: Figure 11 shows how the clustering of the input image with an increasing amount of noise changes only slightly - even up to a high noise level (while we have not found it necessary, adjusting the compactness of the superpixels can help as well).

Speed of the Proposed Method

Using segments on a near-regular grid as a sparse image representation, as we propose in this work, has the distinct advantages of reducing the resolution of the input to the pixel-based method and hence its execution time. Figure 12 displays the total execution time of both the existing dense pixel-based method on the original input image, as well as our proposed approach for various superpixel sizes. The total execution times are divided into the three steps of the approach: the superpixel clustering, processing the superpixel grids with the pixel-based methods and finally the upsampling to the original input resolution. We see that the time spent clustering is small, and the time required for upsampling

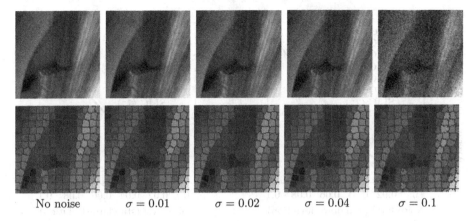

No noise $\sigma = 0.01$ $\sigma = 0.02$ $\sigma = 0.04$ $\sigma = 0.1$

Fig. 11. Illustration of the noise levels and their impact on the estimated superpixels.

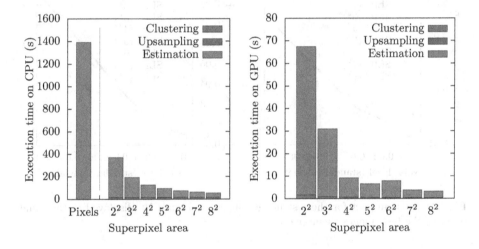

Fig. 12. Timing data for the proposed method in function of superpixel size. The used CPU was an Intel Core i7-980X and the GPU was an nVidia GeForce GTX 770.

is so small as to be invisible on the graph: its impact on the processing time is negligible. As the superpixel size increases, the processing time lowers: as the superpixels grow larger, the dimensions of the superpixel grid image lower – the dense pixel-based optical flow estimation still constitutes the largest part of the processing time.

Thanks to the Quasar platform [8] we have both a CPU and GPU implementation of the approach. Using superpixels about 3 by 3 pixels, we achieve a speed-up factor of more than 40 compared to the existing pixel-based method on the CPU (it was not able to be run on the GPU because of memory restrictions on the used model of GPU).

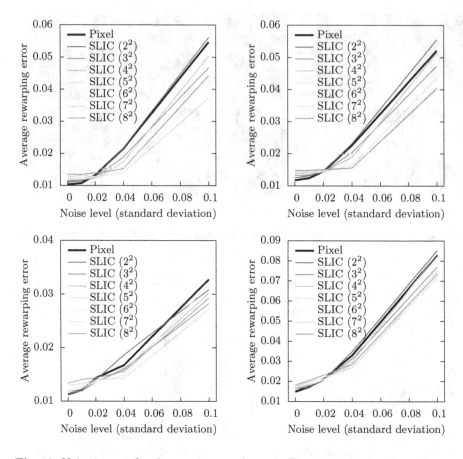

Fig. 13. Noise impact for the test images shown in Figure 10, displayed in the same order as the test images themselves.

Accuracy of the Proposed Method

In order to quantify the accuracy of the proposed methods, the (possibly noisy) inputs are used to estimate an optical flow field between the two views. This optical flow estimate is then used to warp the original (*noise-free*) input images onto each other: the resulting average error is used to evaluate the quality of the estimate. In this way, the actual noise on the input images does not affect the error directly (only through its impact on the optical flow estimate).

The results are shown in Figure 13. We see that the dense pixel-based method has a slight quality advantage over the proposed method based on superpixels, but only in the absence of noise. However, as soon as the input images are perturbed by a small amount of noise, our proposed approach benefits from the robustness of the superpixels, outperforming the pixel-based method. As the superpixel size increases, so does the initial loss of accuracy; this is offset by the increased noise robustness: the error increases less as the noise level is raised.

6   Conclusion

In this paper, we have demonstrated the use of superpixels as a way of reducing the resolution of the input and upsampling the output of an algorithm. We thus showed that the dense pixel-based method can be easily and successfully applied to a superpixel grid, and need not be troubled by the fact that it is now working on a superpixel grid. In this way, we bridge a gap between high-resolution content and (possibly slow or computationally expensive) state of the art techniques.

By limiting ourselves to superpixel grid application of an existing pixelgrid technique, we forfeit the full potential of superpixel-based methods. On the other hand, this approach opens up the full range of existing pixel-based methods. When using superpixels in order to reduce the resolution of the input, the underlying grid is not entirely uniform. However, we illustrate that – given that the superpixels are sufficiently small so that the grid is *close* to regular – this has limited impact on the resulting estimate.

On a final note, this way of processing high-resolution data can be easily expanded to higher-dimensional data. Specifically, high-resolution video data can be processed in the same way. In that case we can either subsample along the temporal dimension or not, depending on the temporal resolution and the temporal content of the input.

7   Future Work

While the proposed workflow allows the continued use of existing methods on high-dimensional data using an abstraction layer which hands the algorithms lower-resolution data, the step will eventually have to be made towards superpixel-based approaches: methods which explicitly take the non-regular grid into account. This will allow those algorithms to process increasingly higher-dimensional data without any additional effort aside from pre-processing by a superpixel method while keeping a theoretically optimal framework and still limiting the amount of data handed to the pixel-based method.

References

1. Achanta, R., Shaji, A., Smith, K., Lucchi, A., Fua, P., Süsstrunk, S.: SLIC Superpixels. Tech. rep, EPFL, EPFL (2010)
2. Achanta, R., Shaji, A., Smith, K., Lucchi, A., Fua, P., Süsstrunk, S.: SLIC Superpixels Compared to State-of-the-art Superpixel Methods. IEEE Transactions on Pattern Analysis and Machine Intelligence (2012)
3. Van den Bergh, M., Van Gool, L.: Real-time stereo and flow-based video segmentation with superpixels. In: 2012 IEEE Workshop on Applications of Computer Vision (WACV), pp. 89–96, January 2012
4. Chang, H.S., Wang, Y.C.: Superpixel-based large displacement optical flow. In: 2013 20th IEEE International Conference on Image Processing (ICIP), September 2013

5. Drulea, M., Nedevschi, S.: Motion estimation using the correlation transform. IEEE Transactions on Image Processing **22**(8), 3260–3270 (2013)
6. Felzenszwalb, P., Huttenlocher, D.: Efficient graph-based image segmentation. International Journal of Computer Vision **59**(2) (2004)
7. Gkamas, T., Nikou, C.: Guiding optical flow estimation using superpixels. In: 2011 17th International Conference on Digital Signal Processing (DSP), pp. 1–6, July 2011
8. Goossens, B., De Vylder, J., Philips, W.: Quasar - A new heterogeneous programming framework for image and video processing algorithms on CPU and GPU. In: 2014 IEEE International Conference on Image Processing, ICIP 2014, Paris, France, October 27 30, 2014, pp. 2183–2185. IEEE (2014). http://quasar.ugent.be
9. Heinrich, M.P., Jenkinson, M., Papież, B.W., Glesson, F.V., Brady, S.M., Schnabel, J.A.: Edge- and detail-preserving sparse image representations for deformable registration of chest MRI and CT Volumes. In: Gee, J.C., Joshi, S., Pohl, K.M., Wells, W.M., Zöllei, L. (eds.) IPMI 2013. LNCS, vol. 7917, pp. 463–474. Springer, Heidelberg (2013)
10. Kopf, J., Shamir, A., Peers, P.: Content-adaptive image downscaling. ACM Trans. Graph. **32**(6) (2013)
11. Levinshtein, A., Stere, A., Kutulakos, K.N., Fleet, D.J., Dickinson, S.J., Siddiqi, K.: Turbopixels: Fast superpixels using geometric flows. IEEE Trans. Pattern Anal. Mach. Intell. **31**(12) (2009)
12. Mori, G.: Guiding model search using segmentation. In: Tenth IEEE International Conference on Computer Vision, ICCV 2005, vol. 2, October 2005
13. Mori, G., Ren, X., Efros, A., Malik, J.: Recovering human body configurations: combining segmentation and recognition. In: Proceedings of the 2004 IEEE Computer Society Conference on Computer Vision and Pattern Recognition, CVPR 2004, vol. 2, June 2004
14. Nishigaki, M.: Color segmentation-based optical flow computation and motion segmentation (2008)
15. Ren, C.Y., Reid, I.: gslic: a real-time implementation of slic superpixe segmentation. University of Oxford, Department of Engineering Science, Tech. rep. (2011)
16. Ren, X., Malik, J.: Learning a classification model for segmentation. In: Proceedings. Ninth IEEE International Conference on Computer Vision, October 2003
17. Scharstein, D., Pal, C.: Learning conditional random fields for stereo. IEEE Conference on Computer Vision and Pattern Recognition, CVPR 2007, pp. 1–8, June 2007
18. Vedaldi, A., Soatto, S.: Quick shift and kernel methods for mode seeking. In: Forsyth, D., Torr, P., Zisserman, A. (eds.) ECCV 2008, Part IV. LNCS, vol. 5305, pp. 705–718. Springer, Heidelberg (2008)

Depth-Based Filtration for Tracking Boost

David Chrapek$^{(\boxtimes)}$, Vitezslav Beran, and Pavel Zemcik

Department of Computer Graphics and Multimedia,
Faculty of Information Technology, Brno University of Technology,
Bozetechova 2, 612 66 Brno, Czech Republic
{ichrapek,beranv,zemcik}@fit.vutbr.cz

Abstract. This paper presents a novel depth information utilization method for performance boosting of tracking in traditional RGB trackers for arbitrary objects (objects not known in advance) by object segmentation/separation supported by depth information. The main focus is on real-time applications, such as robotics or surveillance, where exploitation of depth sensors, that are nowadays affordable, is not only possible but also feasible. The aim is to show that the depth information used for target segmentation significantly helps reducing incorrect model updates caused by occlusion or drifts and improves success rate and precision of traditional RGB tracker while keeping comparably efficient and thus possibly real-time. The paper also presents and discusses the achieved performance results.

Keywords: Real-time · Rgbd · Segmentation · Tracking

1 Introduction

Applications of object tracking, such as surveillance or robotic perception, drive the efforts to make trackers more reliable, robust, and precise; however, tracking still remains a challenging task mainly due to potential occlusions, drifts, or changes in appearance of the target.

Many different approaches have emerged over the years varying especially in object models and their updating schemes. For example the KLT tracker [26] computes transformation of feature points via optical flow [16], whereas NCC tracker [5] matches intensity patches with cross correlation. As occlusions are frequent, the Robust Fragments-based tracker [1] treats the object as a collection of independently tracked patches and Kalman Appearance tracker [20] predicts and matches the intensities for a individual pixels.

Trackers based on gradual updates seem more promising as they account for target changes over time. One way is simply to store multiple instances of the target as in [18,23] where [18] use intensity-based templates to represent the model and L1-optimization to find their linear combination, whereas in [23] multiple instances are kept in leaking memory.

Recently, trackers began utilizing object detectors for tracking. They usually use statistical models which are either generative like WSL [12], Gaussian [17],

© Springer International Publishing Switzerland 2015
S. Battiato et al. (Eds.): ACIVS 2015, LNCS 9386, pp. 217–228, 2015.
DOI: 10.1007/978-3-319-25903-1_19

discriminative, such as SVM [6] and its variations, boosting [10] and its variants, random forests [4] or ferns [21]. MIL [2] is one of the methods, which uses multiple instances as its model. Tracking-Learning-Detection's (TLD) [13] main idea is the independence of the tracker and detector which corrects each other and Context tracker [8] based on TLD distinguish between similar targets by following them and their neighborhood. Partial occlusion is a concern in OSL [15] which uses block matching among its own and difference among neighboring blocks while Struck [11] learns offsets from neighboring patches to avoid labeling of learning data.

Depth data have been used for various tasks [25,14,19,3,22] with convincing results. However, none of them focused on tracking arbitrary objects with no apriori knowledge about the object in video sequences until [24], where depth data are used mainly for occlusion detection and along with RGB data for feature descriptors. In [24] the authors compared their method to state-of-the-art visual-based trackers convincingly beating them in terms of success rate but with massively increased computational time (two magnitudes slower).

The aim of this paper is however use the added depth information for segmentation of the tracked object to prevent incorrect model updates caused by occlusion or drifts, not considering enhancement in depth feature space. By detecting the occluder the tracker is less likely to drift to it and by recentering and resizing the tracked target region to close fit after every frame it prevents the tracker from gradual drifts to background or inclusion of portion of occluder into its model.

The paper is composed as follows: Section 2 describes the proposed solution, Sect. 3 presents the results and conclusion is in Sect. 4.

2   Proposed Approach

We based our solution on TLD [13] for its easily adaptable structure, computational efficiency, and achieved results. First we present the overall schema and the object model and then we describe individual parts.

The system uses combination of Tracking and Detection results and Learns from them as in TLD. The main difference from TLD lies in addition of Pixel filtration, Occlusion handling, and Recenter & Resize (R&R) stages that utilize the depth information. The overall scheme can be seen in Fig. 2. The Pixel filtration stage filters out the pixels that do not belong to the target based on the depth, whereas Occlusion handling determines the target's and occluder's distance from the consecutive frames. The filtered image produced by Pixel filtration stage is used in Tracking and Recenter & Resize stage which, based on depth histograms, relocates the guessed target's position.

We define the status of the tracked object S_t in time t as:

$$S_t = (w_t, h_t, px_t, py_t, d_t, M_t) \ . \tag{1}$$

where w_t and h_t are the object's width and height respectively, px_t and py_t are the object's x and y coordinate, d_t is the distance of the object from the camera,

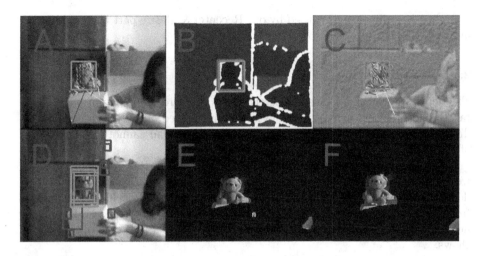

Fig. 1. Visualized system output example: An RGB (A) and normal-based (C) median flow trackers with forward (Green: better, Red: worse) and backward (yellow) checking; (B) depicts the Recenter & Resize strategy (Before: magenta, After: green); (D): cascade detector's output candidates where red resp. green are outputs of early resp. later stages; previous (E) and current (F) filtrated frame used for tracking and Recenter & Resize stages.

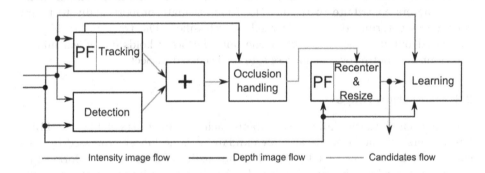

Fig. 2. System schema: Information flow (colored, where candidate means proposed bounding box) used in processing of individual frames (PF: Pixel Filtration stage).

and M_t is the object model defined as in TLD and it consists of patch variance, fern classifier, and collection of positive and negative samples for Nearest Neighbour (NN) classifier (see [13] for details), with our addition of the initial size of the tracked object in meters, estimated from initial bounding box size, and distance of the bounding box from camera. Apart from that, we have opted for Histogram of Oriented Gradients (HOG) features [7] instead of normalized intensity patch for NN classifier (see [13]) because it can deal with changing bounding box dimensions caused by our Recenter & Resize part better than the intensity patches (see Sect. 3).

2.1   Pixel Filtration

The depth information is used to detect pixels that are probably not part of the target and to filter them out. If the pixels are filtered out, they can no longer distract the tracker which reduces the tracking error and cannot affect creation of the depth histograms in Recenter & Resize stage.

In order to filter out the improper pixels in either RGB or depth image, we imply size restrictions in form of maximum depth derivative c_d, which is dependent on the target size, and utilizes the target's and occluder's distances from the camera (see Sect. 2.4); if occluder is in vicinity of the target, the pixels nearer than midpoint between target and occluder are also filtered out as Fig. 3 shows.

2.2   Tracking Stage

Lukas-Kanade optical flow [26] is used as a base tracker in almost the same way as in TLD (see [13] for details); however, the input image is filtered as mentioned in Sect. 2.1, to reduce miss-tracking of points. Another modification is the usage of the same tracker but on the image composed from normal map components. Both trackers contribute to the new location estimate proportionally to their confidences determined by the learned NN classifier. The trackers are highly correlated but in some cases, when one fails the other holds on, which infact contributes to better overall success rate as discussed in Sect. 3.

2.3   Detection Stage

This stage employs the sliding window approach and it consists of 4 layers (TLD has 3 layers); if one layer discards a candidate, it is no longer processed by the consequent layers. The first layer is the same as in TLD and it is in form of a variance filter, where the candidate window is rejected if it is not variable enough in the intensity domain comparing to the object model. The second layer is new and it imposes the restriction on the size of the bounding box depending on the distance of particular patch taken from the depth map based on the assumption that the tracked object size remains constant. The distance of every patch is determined by first significant peak in its depth histogram, similarly to the one in Sect. 2.4. The third layer, represented by fern classifier composed of several ferns, is same as in TLD, where each fern consist of statistics (target/non-target hits) for each binary code composed from several pixel comparison tests. The mean from all ferns is used to determine rejection. If the candidate passes through the earlier layers, it is subject to final NN classifier (see [13] for details) which is in essence collection of positive and negative samples collected so far. The NN

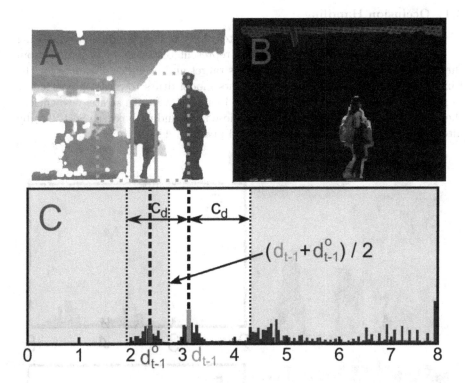

Fig. 3. Pixel filtration: (A) shows depth image with target (green) and the area in which the system searches for occluders (cyan). (B) shows the filtered image, where pixels filtered out are from the red zones of the histogram showed in (C), which depicts depth pixel distribution within the cyan rectangle (Green: target depth, Red: occluder depth, c_d: maximal depth derivative).

classifier is same as in TLD, but since we use different descriptors from TLD the final confidence of this candidate is determined as:

$$\frac{\min\limits_{i=1..m}\left(s_i^- \otimes s^c\right)}{\min\limits_{i=1..m}\left(s_i^- \otimes s^c\right) + \min\limits_{i=1..n}\left(s_i^+ \otimes s^c\right)} = conf^{\mathrm{NN}}(s^c) \ . \tag{2}$$

where n and m are numbers of positive respective negative samples and s_i^+ and s_i^- are i-th positive respective negative samples stored in learned model. s^c is the sample patch being processed and $\otimes$ is error matching operator defined as:

$$(x_1, x_2, ..., x_r) \bigotimes (y_1, y_2, ..., y_r) = \sum_{i=1}^{r}\left(x_i - y_i\right)^2 \ . \tag{3}$$

where $(x_1, x_2, ..., x_r)$ and $(y_1, y_2, ..., y_r)$ are feature vectors of dimension r, in our case the HOGs.

2.4 Occlusion Handling

We devised an Occlusion Handling strategy, inspired by finding newly rising peaks in the depth histogram [24] that represent distances of occluders from the camera. The new strategy determines target and occluder distances for the Pixel Filtration stage, which then prevents model drifts towards the occluders as shown in Fig. 4 and also facilitate the Recenter & Resize strategy to enclose the remaining parts of the target into a close fit bounding box (see Sect. 2.5) by filtering out the occluder and background pixels.

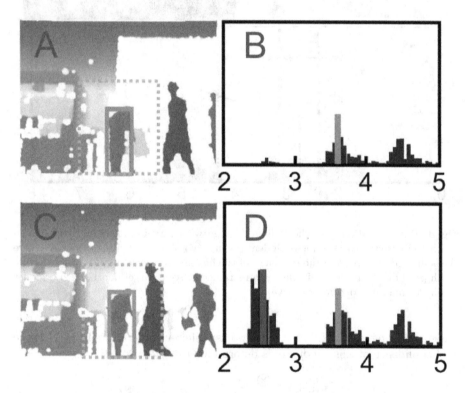

Fig. 4. Occlusion detection: (A) and (C) show frames in time with object's (green) and histogram search area (cyan). (B) and (D) are corresponding depth histograms. In (D), there is new peak (red) in the histogram, which is the occluder.

The goal is to get the target and occluder distance from the camera by finding significant peaks in depth histograms from the area around the target. The target distance from the previous frame is matched with the depth peaks found inside the current bounding box, whereas the occluder distance is matched within extended bounding box to comprise the area around the object. The new target and occluder distances are determined as the closest ones from previous locations, or, if these distances are the same, as the alternative target and occluder depths that minimize the combined distances from previous positions. In the end, the occluder depth is shifted at the closest peak from target's depth, which is closer to camera, to comprise the closest source of occlusion.

2.5 Recenter and Resize

By recentering and resizing the bounding box according to the depth map, as shown in Fig. 5, before learning stage, we ensure that the model is trained in a unified manner, e.g. on close fit bounding boxes, which helps to prevent gradual drifts or inclusion of occluders.

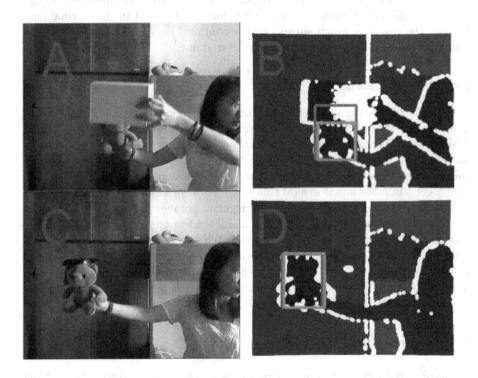

Fig. 5. Recenter & Resize: (B) prevents inclusion of occluder; (D) eliminates gradual drifts (Before: magenta; After: green).

The proposed bounding box is recentered according to depth histogram from current frame containing only object pixels. The filtered depth pixels values are shifted by subtracting the target's distance to disregard the target distance. Normalized depth histograms are then constructed from the proposed patch and shifted patches around it. The best match is then selected as the new position:

$$(x_t^r, y_t^r) = \operatorname*{argmax}_{x \in x_t^P \pm \sigma; y \in y_t^P \pm \sigma} \left(H_t^P \times H(x, y) \right) . \tag{4}$$

where x_t^r and y_t^r are coordinates of the recentered position, x_t^p and y_t^p is position before the recenter, $H(x, y)$ is the depth histogram of the shifted object patch to coordinates x, y and operator $\times$ is defined as:

$$H_1 \times H_2 = \sum_{i=1}^{nbins} cnt_i^{H_1} * cnt_i^{H_2} . \tag{5}$$

where cnt_i^H is the value of $i - th$ bin of the histogram H and $nbins$ is the number of bins of these histograms. The histogram matching is in a form of multiplication because it is computed from and for incomplete/filtered images with the aim of reposition the patch to comprise as much object pixels as possible with the emphasis on those whose depth values are frequent in the original one. Finally, the resulting patch shrinks to not contain blank rows or columns from the borderlines, if they were completely filtered out.

2.6   Learning Stage

It is vital to learn the model often enough to include all possible model states but not if the output is incorrect to prevent drift. We adopted the approach from TLD and the learning takes place when the found target patch is variant enough and confident enough as judged by the NN classifier. It updates both the fern and the NN classifiers with the positive and negative samples. To update the fern, the target patch is warped several times and all of the resulting patches are used to update the ferns statistics. Also the negative patches are randomly gathered from around the target and used to update all the ferns as target misses. The NN classifier is updated with only the target patch as positive example, if it is not too similar to any positive example already stored in the model, to regulate the model size. Randomly sampled negative patches are, on the other hand, stored to negative bag only if they resemble some of the target positive examples at least to a small extent (see [13]), to store only those, that can confuse the detector.

3   Experimental Results

We have tested our solution for success rate, precision, and computational time on the RGBD dataset [24] of 95 indoor scenes. The average success rates across all categories and precision of different variants of our solution are plot to show the advancement of our enhancements. In this section, we first discuss the matter of Success Rate in Sect. 3.1 followed by discussion about Precision in Sect. 3.2 and at the end we comment on the Efficiency of our approach in Sect. 3.3.

3.1   Success Rate

The success rates (results in Table 1) of our approach and the compared approaches were determined by the online evaluation tool of [24] and so it was the fraction of frames, in which the output of the tracker corresponds to the ground truth. It is determined by overlap r, which would have to be at or above (widely accepted) threshold of 0.5. The overlap is determined as:

$$r = \begin{cases} \dfrac{area(BB_\mathrm{T} \cap BB_\mathrm{G})}{area(BB_\mathrm{T} \cup BB_\mathrm{G})}, & \text{if } \exists BB_\mathrm{T} \wedge \exists BB_\mathrm{G} \\ 1, & \text{if } \nexists BB_\mathrm{T} \wedge \nexists BB_\mathrm{G} \\ -1, & \text{otherwise} \end{cases} \tag{6}$$

where BB_T respectively BB_G is the bounding box given by the tracker respectively ground truth bounding box.

Comparing to the best, possibly real-time, RGB solution of Struck [11], our system performs better by 16 % and by whole 24,5 % better than TLD [13], the state-of-the-art RGB tracker our solution is based on as it can bee seen in Table 1. The comparison between our solution and the RGB trackers could seem unfair because the improvements are to be expected based on more informational input data, but we wanted to show that by adding these straightforward depth enhancements we could achieve much more robust tracking in applications where depth data is available and with only modest impact on performance. When comparing our solution to the successful RGBD tracker in [24], ours is approximately 11,5 % less successful; however, [24] uses additional depth features directly in the model and it is nowhere close to real-time (achieves only 0.03 FPS) because of its complex part-based model and learning scheme.

Table 1 also shows that by ommiting the Recenter & Resize, which mainly helps in reducing gradual drifts, the overall success rate drops by 14 %.

Occlusion Detection is, similarly to Recenter & Resize, very important, too. If it is turned off, the performance for sequences where occlusion occurs decreases by 16 %. Interestingly, the success rate also decreases by 5 % when no occlusion occurs in the video because the Occlusion Detection also helps when other objects are in vicinity of the target as it helps filtering them out in Pixel filtration stage (and then they cannot confuse the tracker). Less important is the use of the second normal-based point tracker which boosts the final success rate by 5 % by supplementing the visual-based tracker when it fails.

The TLD from our HOG altered model does not differ much (0.38 vs 0.39) when no depth enhancements are in place but with TLD models not that suitable for resizing, the enhancements boost the original TLD model by 10% only.

3.2   Precision

We tested the precision by the average overlap over matched frames:

$$R_\mathrm{prec} = \frac{1}{\|M_\mathrm{match}\|} \sum_{t \in M_\mathrm{match}} \frac{area(BB_\mathrm{T} \cap BB_\mathrm{G})}{area(BB_\mathrm{T} \cup BB_\mathrm{G})} \tag{7}$$

where M_match is time instances in which the target is positive and matched.

The assumption that Recenter & Resize will improve precision of tracking has been proven by tests. In Table 1, the highest score of around 81 - 83 % for

Table 1. Success rate and precision results (OM = our HOG model, Nt = Tracker based on normals, Pf = Pixel filtration, Oh = Occlusion handling, RR = Recenter & Resize).

Algorithm	AVG. success rate	Precision
RGBDOcc+OF [24]	0.74	-
Struck [11]	0.46	-
TLD [13]	0.38	-
OM+Nt+Pf+Oh+RR	0.62	0.831
OM+Nt+Pf+Oh	0.48	0.738
OM+Nt+Pf+RR	0.51	0.830
OM+Pf+Oh+RR	0.57	0.834
OM	0.39	0.751
TLD+Nt+Pf+Oh+RR	0.48	0.834

precision are indeed in those cases where Recenter & Resize strategy is applied. When Recenter & Resize is turned off, the precision drops about 10 % which clearly shows that the strategy helps significantly both in success rate and precision. While similar drop in success rate can be seen when omitting the Recenter & Resize strategy or Occlusion handling, the same drop in precision caused by switching off the Occlusion handling does not occur. This further supports the claim the Recenter & Resize strategy is the feature that notably enhances the precision of the system.

3.3 Efficiency

With Matlab code, we achieved nearly 5 FPS which is comparable to TLD or Struck ($\approx$ 8 - 12 FPS), while it is whole two orders of magnitude faster than RGBD tracker of [24] ($\approx$ 0,03 FPS), which has quite complex part-based model [9] and so the retraining takes most of the time (opposed to just adding a new template as in our approach) and so the applicability in real-time application is not possible. We believe, by just optimizing the code and paralellizing the whole solution, where tracking and detection parts takes most of the time and are independent of one another and HOG and depth histograms computation is paralellizable, we could get FPS near real-time (>15 FPS) values and so our solution could be used in on-line applications like robotic perception or surveillance, where the sensors are common or possible.

4 Conclusion

In this paper, we have shown that by utilization of depth information for reasoning about possible occlusion and precise position, we outperform current state-of-the-art RGB tracking methods in both success rate and precision with only modest impact on efficiency, while performing only slightly behind the successful RGBD tracker [24] which is two orders of magnitude slower than our approach and thus not applicable for on-line applications. We have proven that each of the proposed depth based enhancements has significant impact on success rate while Recenter & Resize strategy also boosted the precision.

Future work includes efficiency improvement in form of optimization and eventually parallelization to achieve truly real-time performance. We would also like to show that it is useful for robotic perception task such as following objects or collecting samples of unknown objects for offline learning. More suitable object model with depth-based features would also be the focus of our future work as would be movement predictions in 3d space.

Acknowledgement. This work has been funded by IT4Innovations Center of Excellence (Czech Republic MSMT - CZ.1.05/1.1.00/02.0070) and CRAFTERS project (ARTEMIS JU - 295371).

References

1. Adam, A., Rivlin, E., Shimshoni, I.: Robust fragments-based tracking using the integral histogram. In: CVPR, pp. 798–805. IEEE Computer Society (2006)
2. Babenko, B., Yang, M.H., Belongie, S.: Visual tracking with online multiple instance learning. In: Computer Vision and Pattern Recognition (CVPR), pp. 983–990 (2009)
3. Benenson, R., Mathias, M., Timofte, R., Gool, L.V.: Pedestrian detection at 100 frames per second. In: Computer Vision and Pattern Recognition (CVPR), pp. 2903–2910, June 2012
4. Breiman, L.: Random forests. Machine Learning **45**(1), 5–32 (2001)
5. Briechle, K., Hanebeck, U.D.: Template matching using fast normalized cross correlation. Proceedings of SPIE: Optical Pattern Recognition XII **4387**, 95–102 (2001)
6. Cortes, C., Vapnik, V.: Support-vector networks. Machine Learning **20**(3), 273–297 (1995)
7. Dalal, N., Triggs, B.: Histograms of oriented gradients for human detection. Computer Vision and Pattern Recognition (CVPR) **1**, 886–893 (2005)
8. Dinh, T.B., Vo, N., Medioni, G.: Context tracker: exploring supporters and distracters in unconstrained environments. In: CVPR. IEEE (2011)
9. Felzenszwalb, P.F., Girshick, R.B., McAllester, D., Ramanan, D.: Object detection with discriminatively trained part-based models. Pattern Analysis and Machine Intelligence **32**(9), 1627–1645 (2010)
10. Freund, Y., Schapire, R.E.: A decision-theoretic generalization of on-line learning and an application to boosting. Journal of Computer and System Sciences **55**(1), 119–139 (1997)
11. Hare, S., Saffari, A., Torr, P.H.S.: Struck: structured output tracking with kernels. In: Computer Vision (ICCV), pp. 263–270 (2011)
12. Jepson, A.D., Fleet, D.J., El-Maraghi, T.F.: Robust online appearance models for visual tracking. Pattern Analysis and Machine Intelligence **25**(10), 1296–1311 (2003)
13. Kalal, Z., Mikolajczyk, K., Matas, J.: Tracking-learning-detection. In: Pattern Analysis and Machine Intelligence, vol. 34, pp. 1409–1422. IEEE (2012)

14. Keskin, C., Kirac, F., Kara, Y.E., Akarun, L.: Randomized decision forests for static and dynamic hand shape classification. In: Computer Vision and Pattern Recognition Workshops (CVPRW), pp. 31–36, June 2012
15. Liu, L., Xing, J., Ai, H.: Online structure learning for robust object tracking. In: ICIP (2013)
16. Lucas, B.D., Kanade, T.: An iterative image registration technique with an application to stereo vision. In: Hayes, P.J. (ed.) IJCAI, pp. 674–679. William Kaufmann (1981)
17. McKenna, S.J., Raja, Y., Gong, S.: Tracking colour objects using adaptive mixture models. Image and Vision Computing 17(34), 225–231 (1999)
18. Mei, X., Ling, H., Wu, Y., Blasch, E., Bai, L.: Minimum error bounded efficient l1 tracker with occlusion detection. In: Computer Vision and Pattern Recognition (CVPR), pp. 1257–1264 (2011)
19. Mora, K.A.F., Odobez, J.M.: Gaze estimation from multimodal kinect data. In: Computer Vision and Pattern Recognition Workshops (CVPRW), pp. 25–30, June 2012
20. Nguyen, H.T., Smeulders, A.W.M.: Fast occluded object tracking by a robust appearance filter. Pattern Analysis and Machine Intelligence 26(8), 1099–1104 (2004)
21. Ozuysal, M., Calonder, M., Lepetit, V., Fua, P.: Fast keypoint recognition using random ferns. Pattern Analysis and Machine Intelligence 32(3), 448–461 (2010)
22. Ren, C.Y., Prisacariu, V., Murray, D., Reid, I.: Star3d: Simultaneous tracking and reconstruction of 3d objects using rgb-d data. In: 2013 IEEE International Conference on Computer Vision (ICCV), pp. 1561–1568, December 2013
23. Ross, D.A., Lim, J., Lin, R.S., Yang, M.H.: Incremental learning for robust visual tracking. International Journal of Computer Vision 77(1–3), 125–141 (2008)
24. Song, S., Xiao, J.: Tracking revisited using rgbd camera: unified benchmark and baselines. In: ICCV (2013)
25. Sun, M., Kohli, P., Shotton, J.: Conditional regression forests for human pose estimation. In: CVPR. IEEE (2012)
26. Tomasi, C., Kanade, T.: Detection and tracking of point features. Technical Report CMU-CS-91-132, Carnegie Mellon University, April 1991

Robust Fusion of Trackers Using Online Drift Prediction

Isabelle Leang[1]([✉]), Stéphane Herbin[1], Benoît Girard[2,3], and Jacques Droulez[2,3]

[1] ONERA - The French Aerospace Lab, 91761 Palaiseau, France
{isabelle.leang,stephane.herbin}@onera.fr
[2] Sorbonne Universités, UPMC Univ Paris 06, UMR 7222, ISIR, 75005 Paris, France
{girard,droulez}@isir.upmc.fr
[3] CNRS, UMR 7222, ISIR, 75005 Paris, France

Abstract. Visual object tracking is a standard function of computer vision that has been the source of numerous propositions. This diversity of approaches leads to the idea of trying to fuse them and take advantage of the strengths of each of them while controlling the noise they may introduce in some circumstances. The work presented here describes a generic framework for the combination of trackers, where fusion may occur at different levels of the processing chain. The fusion process is governed by the online detection of abnormal behavior either from specific features provided by each tracker, or from out of consensus detection.

The fusion of three trackers exploiting complementary designs and features is evaluated on 72 fusion schemes. Thorough experiments on 12 standard video sequences and on a new set of 13 videos addressing typical difficulties faced by vision systems used in the demanding context of driving assistance, show that using fusion improves greatly the performance of each individual tracker, and reduces by a factor two the probability of drifting.

Keywords: Visual object tracking · Fusion · Algorithm behavior analysis

1 Introduction

Single-object tracking is an elementary computer vision function with a long research history. Indeed, mastering the capacity of pursuing reliably and efficiently a given target, and being robust to various nuisance phenomena, is the key to many offline or online applications exploiting video data.

This research topic produces a huge amount of studies each year, sometimes accompanied by new evaluation benchmarks and metrics. One of the recent outstanding benchmark actions have been the two VOT Challenges in 2013 and 2014[1] that have emphasized the evaluation of single-object short term tracking through two criteria: robustness to drift and localization accuracy. The main

---

[1] http://www.votchallenge.net/

© Springer International Publishing Switzerland 2015
S. Battiato et al. (Eds.): ACIVS 2015, LNCS 9386, pp. 229–240, 2015.
DOI: 10.1007/978-3-319-25903-1_20

conclusions were that "None of the trackers consistently outperformed the others by all measures at all sequence attributes" and that "trackers tend to specialize either for robustness or accuracy" [13]. This means that a generic, robust and reliable solution still seems to be lacking, but also that each tracker has its own domain of expertise. However, a clear causal understanding of tracker behavior when faced with different types of nuisance (illumination change, camera or object motion, object size, aspect and appearance change, occlusion), although globally evaluated in the challenges, is also lacking.

What is proposed in this article is not the description of a new tracking approach relying on new feature extractors, object or background model and online learning, which constitute the core of modern approaches, but to study how an existing repertoire of available trackers can be generically combined in an efficient way.

Tracker combination will be based on the traditional fusion concepts of redundancy — tracker outputs are combined — and complementarity — the repertoire of trackers samples different features and functional structures. Another useful fusion issue is the design of a component able to produce online behavior analysis. Its role is to prevent the propagation of errors during fusion, detect and discard trackers with noisy behaviors, and eventually correct them. It will be shown that possessing such a capacity greatly improves the fusion performances.

The emphasis of the work will be put on drift control. From an operating point of view, losing the tracked target is certainly the most impacting type of error, since it implies also loss of its awareness. Target re-acquisition is possible but is generally less reliable and more costly. The VOT challenge has been one of the first benchmarks to address specifically this question, and our evaluation will follow their methodology.

With this objective, the goal of the behavior analysis will be to predict the occurrence of drift. The idea is to calculate for each tracker, specific clues revealing the uncertainty level they have to deal with, typically object and background likelihoods and features characterizing their geometric distribution. Drift prediction can be used to reinitialize the badly behaving trackers using the output of the others. In this article:

- we propose a generic method of online self-assessment of the trackers based on the score map behavior. This method aims at building a "Drift Predictor" (DP) capable of detecting when a tracker fails.
- we integrate these Drift Predictors in a fusion chain of multiple trackers and test 72 strategies of fusion involving tracker selection and their reinitialization or update, and compare the results to one of the best state of the art trackers, the KCF Tracker (Kernelized Correlation Filters)[9].
- we introduce new video sequences taken in urban context and sampling new types of difficulties in the evaluation.

The paper is organized the following way: Section 2 describes the related work. Section 3 describes in details our approach. The evaluation methodology and results are described in Section 4.

2   Related Work

The online combination and selection of multiple hypotheses and models to control the various sources of perturbations that can affect tracking has been proposed in several studies with various targeted degrees of generality. Fusion of trackers has been addressed at several levels:

Fusion of Models. Tracking algorithms combines basically two types of models: motion models, and observation models.

Historically, the first type of fusion of models studied involved motion models for point tracking, and have given rise to techniques such as Independent Motion Model (IMM) or Multiple Hypothesis Tracking (MHT) typically applied to maneuvering targets, and have been extended to MCMC-like (Markov Chain Monte Carlo) formalism such as particle filtering [2].

In computer vision, tracked objects are extended, usually span regions from tens to hundreds of pixels and require therefore the management of bigger state spaces. One possibility is to add a variable scale or region in the motion model, as it is proposed by Khan et al. [12] where multiple motion models are expected to cover all the possible trajectories of the target.

However, most of the efforts have been made to master the observation model and extract the useful information at the right time. Zhang et al. [21] use object models (SVM classifiers) taken at different instants of the video and select the one that best fits the data. This averts the object model itself to drift (updated by bad training examples) by keeping concurrent and empirically justified object models.

Others use a prior repertoire of image features to describe the appearance of the target. Yoon et al. [20] propose a Bayesian framework using multiple particle filters sampling various image features (HOG, Haar features, intensity). Brasnett et al. [3] improve tracking using particle filters by the fusion of multiple heterogeneous characteristics (colours, textures, contours).

A complete solution is to use all the possible combinations of tracker components (object models, motion models, image features). It is the case of the VTS (Tracking by Sampling Trackers) from Kwon et al. [15].

All those fusion schemes select the current model by maximizing or randomly sampling a score interpreted as a likelihood. However, in all those approaches, the quality of the observation model is not checked online, making the performance depend on the reliability of the likelihoods.

Fusion of Tracker Outputs. One of the simplest way to fuse multiple trackers is to combine directly their outputs, i.e. their pose estimates, without knowledge of their origin. Trackers do not interact with each other. The recent work of Bailer et al. [1] uses strategies of online and offline fusion of bounding boxes produced by the 29 online tracking algorithms presented in [19], and showed clear improvements when using fusion.

Fusion of Functions. Computer vision literature offers many types of processing modules that can be combined in a specific way to build a complex tracker, typically by the association of generic and online learned detectors, and low dimensional state trackers.

Santner et al. [16] combine in a cascade three trackers based on different designs: template correlation, online random forest detectors and optical flow, each tracker correcting the previous one.

Siebel et al. [17] combine modules of detection (movement detector, face detector) and tracking (region-based tracker, shape-based tracker) for people tracking.

Breitenstein et al. [4] propose a tracker-by-detection for multiple people tracking: a generic person detector is used to provide the samples to an online learning specific classifier, which is fed to a particle filter for location prediction.

Kalal et al. [10] describe the cooperation of a flow-based tracker and an online learned detector, which are combined and updated using a low resolution template based detector assessing the quality of each estimate. A very recent version of a similar scheme where the combination law is described as a Hidden Markov Model has been published by Vojir et al. [18].

The fusion approach we propose in this article is closer to the third category than to the first one, which has been abundantly studied in the literature: our goal is to combine a heterogeneous repertoire of trackers, i.e. modules of trackers of variable performances and costs, and allowing a generic level of interaction between them. The combination is controlled through an online assessment of each tracker behavior, which will govern the global dynamics of selection, aggregation and correction (model reinitialization or update) of a pool of trackers. It will also be shown that the simple fusion of tracker outputs have some benefit and can be easily introduced in our framework to discard drifting trackers.

3   Our Approach

Our system is composed of a set of N trackers $T = \{T_1, T_2, ...T_N\}$ running in parallel. At the starting frame, all trackers receive a bounding box B_0 as input, which is the known localization of the target in the first image I_0. For each frame t, each tracker T_i outputs an estimated bounding box $\hat{B}_t^i$, $i \in [1, N]$. A bounding box is defined by its 4 coordinates (x, y, w, h), (x, y) is the coordinate of the top left corner, and (w, h), its width and height. Our approach consists of integrating a dynamic selection of the trackers, as follows (see Fig. 1):

- dynamic selection of the good trackers by detecting drifting trackers, corresponding to steps **1** and **2** in Fig. 1.
- computation of the fusion bounding box, corresponding to step **3** in Fig. 1.
- correction of the good trackers and above all drifting trackers (object model reinitialization or updating), corresponding to step **4** in Fig. 1.

The dynamic selection is performed by a drift indicator as an output of a "Drift Predictor" (DP). A DP is a function of online self-assessment of the correct or poor operation of trackers. At each frame t, for each tracker T_i, $i \in [1, N]$, define the drift indicator D_t^i where $D_t^i = 0$ for a correct operation and 1 when the tracker is drifting. When $D_t^i = 1$, the tracker i is removed from the list of good trackers.

3.1 Drift Predictor

We can differentiate 2 ways of building a DP.

DP from the Individual Behavior of a Tracker: Score Map Analysis. The proposed method builds a DP from score maps (prediction scores) linked to the intrinsic behavior of the tracker.

Score Map. At each frame, a tracker outputs a bounding box corresponding generally to the highest prediction score (correlation, classification, detection) in the search window. This prediction score represents a distance to the object model and is also an indicator of the correct or poor operation of the tracker. Our idea is to exploit the spatial distribution of scores over the image (global) or over a window (local) and not only its maximum value. For example, we can observe if the distribution is rather peaked or flat.

DP from Behavior Features. We assume that the tracker behavior can be characterized by the score map and consider "behavior features" based on the intensity of the response and its spatial distribution. For each frame t, for each tracker T_i, $i \in [1, N]$, we compute a score map and extract behavior features ϕ_t^i from this map (step **1** in Fig. 1). The input of the DP becomes the behavior features ϕ_t^i: $DriftPredictor_i(\phi_t^i) = D_t^i$ (step **2** in Fig. 1).

DP from the Global Behavior of Trackers: Spatial Filtering of the Tracker Outputs. This method builds a DP function from the spatial localization or configuration of the tracker outputs $\hat{\mathbf{B}}_t = (\hat{B}_t^1, \hat{B}_t^2, ...\hat{B}_t^N)$: $DriftPredictor_i(\hat{\mathbf{B}}_t) = D_t^i$ (step **2** in Fig. 1). Vectors are in **bold**. The principle is to remove trackers with an outlier predicted bounding box. For example, a bounding box whose location in the image is incoherent compared with the others, is considered as a drift of the tracker.

We tested 2 spatial filtering methods:

- Distance-based method: removes bounding boxes whose euclidean distance to the previous fusion bounding box is larger than a certain distance threshold.
- Clustering-based method: uses bounding box clustering to filter outlier clusters. Overlapping boxes are placed in the same cluster. If the number of clusters is more than one, then the closest cluster to the previous fusion bounding box is selected whereas the others are removed.

3.2 Computation of the Fusion Bounding Box

The fusion bounding box is computed by merging the outputs of the good trackers (step **3** in Fig. 1): $\hat{B}_t^{fusion} = Fusion(\hat{\mathbf{B}_t}, \mathbf{D_t})$. $\mathbf{D_t} = (D_t^1, D_t^2, ...D_t^N)$.

We tested 2 methods to compute the fusion bounding box:

- Average: the fusion bounding box is the average of the bounding boxes.
- Center of gravity: the fusion bounding box is the combination of M weighted bounding boxes depending on the euclidean distance inter-box d_{ij} with $(i, j) \in [1, M]$ and $j \neq i$. $\hat{B}_t^{fusion} = \sum_{i=1}^{M} w_i * \hat{B}_t^i$ where:

$$w_i = \frac{\frac{1}{\sum_{j \neq i} d_{ij}}}{\sum_{k=1}^{M} \frac{1}{\sum_{j \neq k} d_{kj}}} \tag{1}$$

3.3 Object Model Reinitialization or Update

Reinitialize the object model is necessary when it is noisy, especially when the tracker is drifting to the background, adding noise to the object model. But a reinitialization means starting from scratch, all the past knowledge of the target is erased. A less drastic way is to update the object model by providing the right location to track when the tracker is drifting. But this last solution can be insufficient for large appearance changes. Therefore, we present 2 ways to correct the object model of a tracker (step **4** in Fig. 1):

- Reinitialization: the object model is reinitialized with the fusion bounding box $\hat{B}_t^{fusion}$. This can only be applied to drifting trackers ($D_t^i = 1$).
- Update (no reinitialization): the object model is updated by the right location from $\hat{B}_t^{fusion}$. This can be applied to drifting trackers as well as all the trackers, including good operating trackers.

Define the "corrected bounding boxes" used to reinitialize/update the trackers: $\hat{\mathbf{B}_t^{corrected}} = \left\{ B_t^{i,corrected}, i \in [1, N] \right\}$. $B_t^{i,corrected}$ corresponds to $\hat{B}_t^{fusion}$ (reinitialization or update) or $\hat{B}_t^i$ (no correction).

4 Fusion Experiments and Results

4.1 Video Dataset

To evaluate our trackers, we used videos taken from 3 datasets: 12 videos from the challenge VOT2013 (Visual Object Tracking)[14], 1 video from the challenge KITTI Vision Benchmark Suite[7], and 5 other videos taken from our GoPro Camera; totalling 25 objects to track.

The dataset presents varied objects and scenes in challenging conditions: camera moving, camera zoom, brightness changes, occlusions, deformable objects, fast appearance changes and fast object movements. We produced 5 videos with our onboard GoPro camera (GoPro Hero3+ Black Edition). Videos are taken on the same day: the same camerawork conditions are conserved to enable an homogeneity of the dataset. Situations met are urban traffic scenes such as traffic circle (important appearance changes, object scaling) and crossroads. Most of the targets are cars, bus and motorbikes.

4.2 Evaluation Protocol

Our evaluation protocol is similar to the VOT Challenge Protocol, 2 metrics are used to evaluate our trackers: localization precision and robustness to drift. Precision on a video is measured by the mean overlap between the predicted track (tracker) and the groundtruth track. The overlap between two bounding boxes is defined by their intersection area divided by their union area.

Precision on a dataset is the mean precision on the set of videos of the dataset. Overlap precision is a good measure if the predicted box and the groundtruth box have relatively similar sizes.

Robustness is measured by the total number of drifts in a video. A drift is a total loss of the target: the overlap between the tracker prediction and the groundtruth is null. To count the number of drifts in a video, we reinitialize the tracker 5 frames after each drift, like the VOT challenge protocol.

4.3 Implementation

Our set of trackers is composed of 3 trackers with different levels of complexity and performance (Table 2):

- CT (Compressive Tracking)[22] uses an object model composed of M object-background classifiers, based on Haar-like features. The score map is local (object-size window) with sums of likelihood ratios. The behavior feature used is the proportion of scores higher than a certain threshold.
- STRUCK (Structured Output Tracking with Kernels)[8] is a structured output SVM framework using Haar-like features and gaussian kernels. The score map is local ($radius = 30$) with classification scores in $[-1, 1]$. The behavior features are the variance of the location of the first 10 maxima and the distance between the location of the previous and the current maximum.
- DPM Kalman Tracker (Deformable Part Model)[6] combines an object detector based on trained deformable part models (Dubout and Fleuret's implementation [5]) and a Kalman filter [11]. There is no score map but scores of detections. The behavior features are the difference of scores between the two best detections and an overlap distance between the two best detections. Examples of score map are shown in Fig. 2.

We collected C++ codes of the open source trackers and integrated them into a fusion framework running on an Intel Xeon 4 core 2.80 GHz CPU with 8 GB RAM. To evaluate the performance of the generated drift predictions of a DP, we count a good prediction if the DP predicts a drift 1-15 frames before a true drift of the tracker (use groundtruth), the rest is false alarms. CT performs 44% of good predictions, STRUCK performs 65% and DPM, 84%.

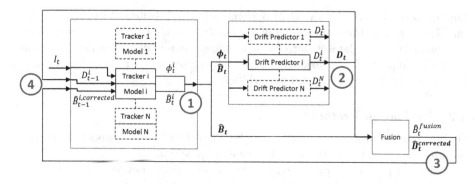

Fig. 1. Our fusion approach. The numbering 1-4 corresponds to different processing steps of fusion detailed in Sect. 3.

Table 1. Results of fusion experiments. See text in Sect. 4 for details.

Exp	Drift Predictor				Fusion		Update Model		Reinit	Performance		
	Map	Ideal	Spatial Filter		Avg	Grav	Drifting	All	Model	Prec	Robust	Speed
			Dist	Clust					Drifting			(fr/s)
1		x			x				x	0.53	2	5.1
2		x		x		x		x		0.48	31	6.2
3						x				0.43	37	5.9
4		x			x				x	0.48	18	5.9
5	x	x			x				x	**0.49**	**18**	**5.9**
6		x				x			x	0.48	25	5.3
7	x		x			x			x	0.47	19	5.4
8	x					x		x		0.51	64	5.8

4.4 Results

The principal experiment results are summarized in Table 1, where only best and worst results are presented. We explored all the possible combinations in fusion according to our approach, totalling 72 experiments:

- DP: Ideal DP (Opt), Score Map Analysis (Map), Spatial Filtering with 2 methods (Distance, Clustering), no DP.
- Fusion (fusion box): Average (Avg) and Center of gravity (Grav) methods.
- Object Model Update: only drifting trackers (Drifting) or all trackers (All).
- Object Model Reinitialization (only drifting trackers).

Simulate an Ideal DP Using Groundtruth. Can we warranty a continuity of the tracks through fusion (no drifts) if we can perfectly predict drift? To answer to the question, we simulate an Ideal DP for each tracker using the groundtruth and see the performance of fusion. The tracker is considered drifting if the overlap between the predicted bounding box and the groundtruth is lower than 0.2.

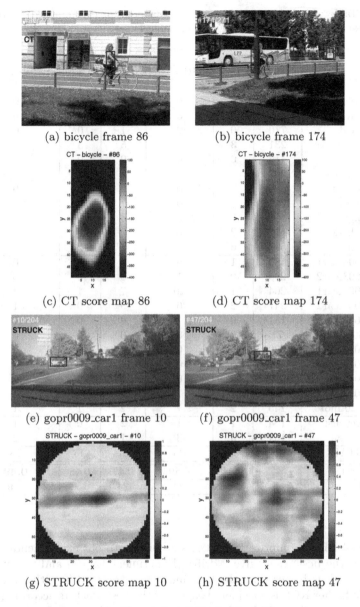

(a) bicycle frame 86

(b) bicycle frame 174

(c) CT score map 86

(d) CT score map 174

(e) gopr0009_car1 frame 10

(f) gopr0009_car1 frame 47

(g) STRUCK score map 10

(h) STRUCK score map 47

Fig. 2. Score maps of CT (c,d) and STRUCK (g,h). (a,b) are two instants of the sequence "bicycle" (VOT2013) tracked by CT. (e,f) are two instants of "gopr0009_car1" (GoPro) tracked by STRUCK. The predicted bounding boxes are the rectangles in blue. The left column (a,e) corresponds to a good behavior of the trackers whereas the right column (b,f) corresponds to a bad one (drifting). The maps (c) and (d) correspond respectively to the image (a) and (b). The maps (g) and (h) correspond respectively to the image (e) and (f). Red corresponds to high scores/responses of the tracker. In (c), the stain with high scores is local and well-centered contrary to (d). (g) shows only one well-centered maximum while (h) presents 4 local maxima.

Table 2. Table of individual performance (robustness, precision, speed) of trackers and the best fusion result in **bold** (Exp 5 in Table 1).

Dataset	#frames	Robustness (#drifts)				
		CT[22]	STRUCK[8]	DPM[6]	KCF[9]	**Fusion (Ours)**
bicycle	271	0	0	0	1	1
bolt	350	9	6	5	0	0
car	374	0	0	1	3	0
david	770	0	2	1	0	0
diving	231	3	1	5	3	2
face	415	0	0	0	0	0
gymnastics	207	3	5	1	2	2
iceskater	500	0	0	2	0	0
jump	228	0	0	7	0	0
singer	351	0	0	3	0	0
sunshade	172	2	0	0	0	0
woman	597	6	0	7	2	1
gopr0008_car1	180	1	0	2	0	0
gopr0008_car2	299	0	1	0	0	0
gopr0009_car1	204	1	10	7	1	4
gopr0009_car2	247	2	6	9	0	1
gopr0009_car3	131	0	1	0	0	1
gopr0011_bus	71	0	0	0	2	0
gopr0013_car1	190	0	0	0	0	0
gopr0013_car2	217	0	0	0	0	0
gopr0013_car3	33	2	0	1	6	1
gopr0013_car4	34	1	1	1	8	1
gopr0020_moto	145	2	1	2	1	1
kitti_cyclist	154	1	1	2	0	1
kitti_van	154	3	3	1	12	2
TOTAL	6525	36	38	57	45	**18**
Precision		0.44	0.49	0.47	0.48	**0.49**
Speed (frames/sec)		28	23	24	150	**5.9**

An Ideal DP can improve robustness according to our experimental results in Table 1, the best result give 2 drifts (Experiment Exp 1) and the worst 31 (Exp 2), which is better than the best individual tracker CT with 36 drifts in Table 2. Whether KCF is considered as one of the best trackers according to the VOT Challenge, CT and STRUCK outperforms in robustness in this dataset. Without DP, the best result obtained is 37 drifts (Exp 3).

These results show that designing a good DP associated with a simple fusion strategy produces an almost perfectly robust tracker.

DP from Score Map Analysis and/or from Spatial Filtering. Using a DP from Score Map Analysis (column Map in Table 1), the best results are obtained in experiments 5 and 7 with 18 and 19 drifts respectively, and outperform the individual trackers CT, STRUCK, DPM and KCF in robustness but not in speed. The worst result is in experiment 8 with 64 drifts. Using only Spatial Filtering (without Score Map Analysis), the best result obtained of 18 drifts is the same as adding a Drift Predictor (Exp 4,5). Drift Prediction from Score Map Analysis works better when combined with a Spatial Filtering (Exp 5,7). Spatial Filtering helps eliminate false alarms generated by Score Map Analysis. But in other cases, Score Map Analysis combined to Spatial Filtering gives better results than using Spatial Filtering only (Exp 6,7): 19 against 25 drifts. Best fusion results are obtained with an Object Model Reinitialization on drifting trackers (Exp 1,4,5,7).

These results show that exploiting multiple levels of fusion have a clear positive impact on performances.

5   Conclusion

Visual object tracking remains a major field of investigation of computer vision. A large number of algorithms are published each year, with increasing average performance when evaluated on standard benchmarks, but also with rather large variations in the way they deal with various types of perturbations. This complementarity is the typical feature allowing fusion techniques to be efficient. The main result of this study is to have assessed the fact through careful experiments that:

- fusing multiple trackers is a profitable trend of investigation for robust single-object tracking;
- fusion can operate at various levels, all levels contributing harmoniously to the global performance;
- the design of a good online tracker behavior analyzer is crucial, but requires careful setting.

References

1. Bailer, C., Pagani, A., Stricker, D.: A superior tracking approach: building a strong tracker through fusion. In: Fleet, D., Pajdla, T., Schiele, B., Tuytelaars, T. (eds.) ECCV 2014, Part VII. LNCS, vol. 8695, pp. 170–185. Springer, Heidelberg (2014)
2. Bar-Shalom, Y., Willett, P.K., Tian, X.: Tracking and data fusion: A Handbook of Algorithms. Yaakov Bar-Shalom (2011)
3. Brasnett, P., Mihaylova, L., Bull, D., Canagarajah, N.: Sequential monte carlo tracking by fusing multiple cues in video sequences. Image and Vision Computing **25**(8), 1217–1227 (2007)
4. Breitenstein, M.D., Reichlin, F., Leibe, B., Koller-Meier, E., Van Gool, L.: Online multiperson tracking-by-detection from a single, uncalibrated camera. IEEE Transactions on Pattern Analysis and Machine Intelligence **33**(9), 1820–1833 (2011)
5. Dubout, C., Fleuret, F.: Exact acceleration of linear object detectors. In: Fitzgibbon, A., Lazebnik, S., Perona, P., Sato, Y., Schmid, C. (eds.) ECCV 2012, Part III. LNCS, vol. 7574, pp. 301–311. Springer, Heidelberg (2012)

6. Felzenszwalb, P.F., Girshick, R.B., McAllester, D., Ramanan, D.: Object detection with discriminatively trained part-based models. IEEE Transactions on Pattern Analysis and Machine Intelligence **32**(9), 1627–1645 (2010)
7. Geiger, A., Lenz, P., Urtasun, R.: Are we ready for autonomous driving? the kitti vision benchmark suite. In: 2012 IEEE Conference on Computer Vision and Pattern Recognition (CVPR), pp. 3354–3361. IEEE (2012)
8. Hare, S., Saffari, A., Torr, P.H.: Struck: structured output tracking with kernels. In: 2011 IEEE International Conference on Computer Vision (ICCV), pp. 263–270. IEEE (2011)
9. Henriques, J.F., Caseiro, R., Martins, P., Batista, J.: High-speed tracking with kernelized correlation filters. IEEE Transactions on Pattern Analysis and Machine Intelligence **37**(3), 583–596 (2015)
10. Kalal, Z., Mikolajczyk, K., Matas, J.: Tracking-learning-detection. IEEE Transactions on Pattern Analysis and Machine Intelligence **34**(7), 1409–1422 (2012)
11. Kalman, R.E.: A new approach to linear filtering and prediction problems. Journal of Fluids Engineering **82**(1), 35–45 (1960)
12. Khan, M.H., Valstar, M.F., Pridmore, T.P.: A generalized search method for multiple competing hypotheses in visual tracking. In: 2014 22nd International Conference on Pattern Recognition (ICPR), pp. 2245–2250. IEEE (2014)
13. Kristan, M., Matas, J., Leonardis, A., Vojir, T., Pflugfelder, R., Fernandez, G., Nebehay, G., Porikli, F., Cehovin, L.: A Novel Performance Evaluation Methodology for Single-Target Trackers, March 2015. ArXiv e-prints
14. Kristan, M., Pflugfelder, R., Leonardis, A., Matas, J., Porikli, F., Cehovin, L., Nebehay, G., Fernandez, G., Vojir, T., Gatt, A., et al.: The visual object tracking vot2013 challenge results. In: 2013 IEEE International Conference on Computer Vision Workshops (ICCVW), pp. 98–111. IEEE (2013)
15. Kwon, J., Lee, K.M.: Tracking by sampling trackers. In: 2011 IEEE International Conference on Computer Vision (ICCV), pp. 1195–1202. IEEE (2011)
16. Santner, J., Leistner, C., Saffari, A., Pock, T., Bischof, H.: Prost: parallel robust online simple tracking. In: 2010 IEEE Conference on Computer Vision and Pattern Recognition (CVPR), pp. 723–730. IEEE (2010)
17. Siebel, N.T., Maybank, S.J.: Fusion of multiple tracking algorithms for robust people tracking. In: Heyden, A., Sparr, G., Nielsen, M., Johansen, P. (eds.) ECCV 2002, Part IV. LNCS, vol. 2353, pp. 373–387. Springer, Heidelberg (2002)
18. Vojir, T., Matas, J., Noskova, J.: Online adaptive hidden markov model for multi-tracker fusion (2015). arXiv preprint arXiv:1504.06103
19. Wu, Y., Lim, J., Yang, M.H.: Online object tracking: a benchmark. In: 2013 IEEE Conference on Computer Vision and Pattern Recognition (CVPR), pp. 2411–2418. IEEE (2013)
20. Yoon, J.H., Kim, D.Y., Yoon, K.-J.: Visual tracking via adaptive tracker selection with multiple features. In: Fitzgibbon, A., Lazebnik, S., Perona, P., Sato, Y., Schmid, C. (eds.) ECCV 2012, Part IV. LNCS, vol. 7575, pp. 28–41. Springer, Heidelberg (2012)
21. Zhang, J., Ma, S., Sclaroff, S.: MEEM: robust tracking via multiple experts using entropy minimization. In: Fleet, D., Pajdla, T., Schiele, B., Tuytelaars, T. (eds.) ECCV 2014, Part VI. LNCS, vol. 8694, pp. 188–203. Springer, Heidelberg (2014)
22. Zhang, K., Zhang, L., Yang, M.-H.: Real-time compressive tracking. In: Fitzgibbon, A., Lazebnik, S., Perona, P., Sato, Y., Schmid, C. (eds.) ECCV 2012, Part III. LNCS, vol. 7574, pp. 864–877. Springer, Heidelberg (2012)

Bootstrapping Computer Vision and Sensor Fusion for Absolute and Relative Vehicle Positioning

Karel Janssen, Erwin Rademakers, Boulaid Boulkroune, Norddin El Ghouti, and Richard Kleihorst[✉]

FlandersMake, Lommel, Belgium
richard.kleihorst@flandersdrive.be

Abstract. With the migration into automated driving for various classes of vehicles, affordable self-positioning upto at least cm accuracy is a goal to be achieved. Commonly used techniques such as GPS are either not accurate enough in their basic variant or accurate but too expensive. In addition, sufficient GPS coverage is in several cases not guaranteed. In this paper we propose positioning of a vehicle based on fusion of several sensor inputs. We consider inputs from improved GPS (with internet based corrections), inertia sensors and vehicle sensors fused with computer vision based positioning. For vision-based positioning, cameras are used for feature-based visual odometry to do relative positioning and beacon-based for absolute positioning. Visual features are brought into a dynamic map which allows sharing information among vehicles and allows us to deal with less robust feautures. This paper does not present final results, yet it is intended to share ideas that are currently being investigated and implemented.

1 Introduction

Autonomy for vehicles allows a positive change for general traffic and construction and agricultural vehicles, in the future it intends to provide mobility for the entire population, avoid accidents and allow round-the-clock working. Self-positioning is crucial for vehicle autonomy and as a general rule decimeter accuracy is aimed at. This allows vehicles to navigate accurately on public roads and agricultural terrains [1–3]. The most commonly known positioning technology is based on Global Navigation Satellite Systems (GNSS) such as GPS. These systems are the perfect example where accuracy and cost are tightly coupled (GPS modules with Real Time Kinematic (RTK) enhancements versus GPS modules as used in smartphones). Unfortunately GPS based absolute positioning is not reliable under all conditions. Also, for affordable systems, the accuracy of a standard system is limited to meters [4]. A common improvement, especially used in agriculture and construction work is to use RTK-GPS which according to its specifications provides the required accuracy. For many opportunistic applications RTK-GPS is either too expensive to incorporate or the GPS reception malfunctions because of urban canyons and foliage. Several approaches exist based

© Springer International Publishing Switzerland 2015
S. Battiato et al. (Eds.): ACIVS 2015, LNCS 9386, pp. 241–248, 2015.
DOI: 10.1007/978-3-319-25903-1_21

on combined GPS and map-matching, often lidar based and made popular by
the DARPA ralley and Google [1]. Lidar being a rotational construction, with
several laser lines, increases the cost more than the price of a regular vehicle.
There are several projects that investigate the use of camera-based navigation for
vehicle positioning on public roads such as Geiger and Van Hamme [5,6]. They
provide an accurate relative positioning strategy using visual odometry where
the ego-motion (relative displacement) of the vehicle is estimated by following
features in space and or on the road surface.

Positioning methods have two flavours: *absolute*, which gives a position with
respect to a map and *relative*, which gives position with respect to a previous
position [7,8]. An overview is given in Figure 1 (already related to our concept)
where along a vehicle track the GPS provides on a regular basis absolute position. A second method to obtain absolute position data is through detection of
(visual) beacons which allow accurate absolute positioning when they are visible.
In between these absolute fixes, relative positioning technology using e.g. inertial
measurement systems, or the previously mentioned visual odometry computer
vision techniques keep track. Besides, vehicle models of different levels of complexity can be used/fused with the mentioned methods to further enhance the
positioning accuracy, reliability and robustness. Despite many reported attempts
to providing low cost and high performing solutions and products, the current
SoA and state of practice suggests that there is ample room for further research
and development to make full use of the potential of what is currently possible
The goals of our approach are to provide accurate vehicle position, parameters

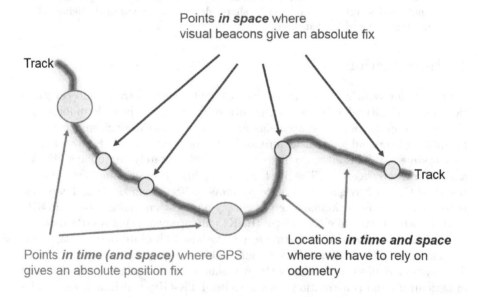

Fig. 1. An overview of our relative and absolute positioning

and state estimates while meeting the robustness and reliability requirements of most applications, at a significantly lower cost of ownership compared to existing state-of-the-art (SoA) solutions, for both on-road and off-road. The challenges we face are the fusion of sensor information with different update rates and varying quality and delays. Overall, accurate estimation of vehicle motion is notoriously difficult due to high noise levels and cross-talk between sensors. In the following we show how the fusion approach is being implemented using a dynamic map as a robust fusion method, and how the various sensing options work. We introduce a bootstrapping approach, our visual beacons and our improved GPS and visual odometry and discuss how all is gathered using a dynamic map. This paper describes the overall concept of our project and highlights certain parts. In Section 2 we discuss the fusion and bootstrapping approach, in Section 3 the visual features we use. Section 4 discusses the improved GPS and Section 5 shows the dynamic map principle.

2   Fusion Approach

All sensor inputs are fused in a bootstrapped system where the intercepting of features and their location goes through a map. Our approach will incorporate several visual features with different properties: Visual beacons that can be positively controlled and have a known position in space and visual features that are detected as salient features of which detection on re-visits cannot be guaranteed. The latter one will group features that can be used for relative positioning. Visual features that are re-visit-able in the sense that they will be recognised based on a signature in subsequent visits. Our input sensor captures several "features" from the environment that can be locked into or used for positioning. Among those features are traffic signs, man-made visual beacons, and the various salient feature points that slamming algorithms [5,6,9,10] choose. As these re-visitable features indeed have the potential of being used for absolute positioning, but as they are anonymous, they are initially not absolutely positioned.

Apart from the man-made visual beacons, the position of the features (viewing angles) are estimated using the current location estimate that the vehicle uses, starting with our GPS and IMU [11]. From a few subsequent estimates while moving, estimates of the x,y,z positions in space of these features are derived. They are stored in a dynamic map together with a signature of the feature. Assuming zero mean noise, with follow-up visits, the estimated location of the features will become more and more accurate. Subsequent visits to the same position with the same viewing position and direction cause re-recognition of certain features. If so, their position in the dynamic map will be refined by robust filtering and the indicator for reliability will be increased. High reliability features will be used for absolute positioning (see later Figure 5). At the top of the reliability index are the visual beacons, followed by the traffic signs and the natural landmarks that the SLAM tool finds. The coordinates used in the dynamic map can be geographical (lat/lon/alt) or cartesian (x/y/z) depending on the application. E.g. for public road applications the former will be more appropriate yet for construction activities and agriculture the latter. The dynamic

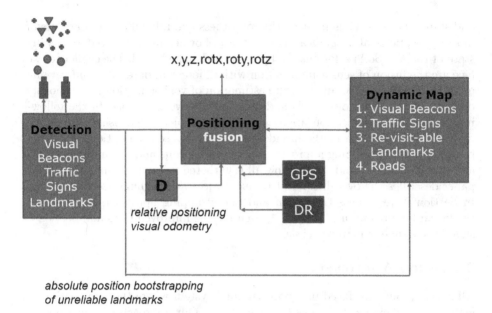

Fig. 2. Overview of the bootstrapping approach

map can be shared among vehicles to arrive to a higher update rate on reliable features.

3 Visual Features

Several visual features are found and tracked with a single distributed vision system. First, the features as found by Libviso2 [5,9,10] with a compound signature for re-recognition. Then, traffic speed signs which are found along the road and last but not least, the omnidirectional visual beacons. Being man-made and man-placed, the location of the visual beacons is known exactly and these are used to give an absolute lock of the position of the vehicle. The concept is similar to the use of light-towers for nautical navigation. The vehicle uniquely identifies the visual beacons in its environment and performs triangulation, either on several beacons visible in the same scene or on a single beacon which is viewed on subsequent locations with dead-reckoning establishing the movement between those locations [12,13]. The visual beacons are positively identified by control from the vehicle. Using an ISM radio link, the vehicle can activate and adjust the frequency of a specific beacon and perform frame differencing for identification. A diagram of the beacon architecture is shown in Figure 3.

The beacons use a ring of white LEDs that illuminate a sphere uniformly, the projection of a sphere on an image plane is always in the shape of an ellipse and can be detected from the frame differenced images by a Hough transform. The center of the detected image region corresponds to the center of the beacon,

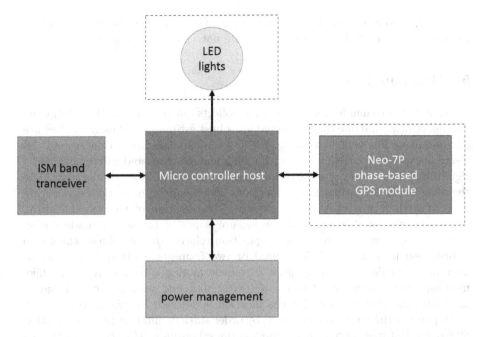

Fig. 3. Architecture plot of the visual beacons

whose location is exactly known. The viewing angles of multiple beacons or of a specific beacon visible from several locations of the vehicle is used for positioning. Visual beacons are very appropriate for off-road applications and applications within a confined region.

4   Improved GPS Method

The vehicle has a GPS module for rough absolute positioning in order to facilitate bootstrapping. With GPS solutions price determines accuracy. A low-cost GPS solution will have an accuracy of 10-15meter, while a high cost RTK solution reaches cm accuracy. In our vehicle we use a Precise Point Positioning (PPP) variant of GPS which uses an off-the-shelve low cost GPS receiver for raw measurements and a 4G cloud connection [4,14,15]. The raw measurements are then corrected for all possible errors caused by ionosphere, troposphere, and errors in clock and satellite orbits. The data for these corrections is retrieved over the internet from a network service. Based on a recursive least square solution an improved position is computed. The PPP algorithm proves more accurate than the SBAS system as the SBAS system only corrects for a few error sources. Note that the network service enabling this PPP is still under development and part of a large scale research project, so it is not yet a stable service. Currently it is free of charge. Our improvement on GPS allows us to achieve an absolute position fix below 1m accuracy in open regions and below 3m accuracy in urban and foliage-covered environments. In this way, GPS will give the absolute fix for the vehicle when reliable visual beacons are not visible (see Figure 1).

5   Dynamic Map

There are two dynamic maps: one that collects (noisy) observations from the various vehicles and one that is filtered for robust estimates and used for absolute position fixes. The vehicle writes to the first map and reads from the second. All visual features that are detected with a high enough threshold will be awarded a signature which allows re-recognition during next visits. Note that, at any time the vehicle has an estimation of location, which can be more or less accurate [16]. At each return visit with a positive identification of the visual feature, the newly estimated location of the feature is added to the list made during previous visits, in order to get a 3D position relative to the vehicle, the stereo information from Libviso2 [5] is used or two frames are taken from different positions with dead-reckoning used as vehicle motion estimate. After a while, multiple feature locations become a scatter plot and with a robust k-means algorithm the best estimate for the location is derived. In this process (which takes place in three dimensions) first, by order statistic filtering in each direction 80% of the features are retained, removing (most) outliers. After this a traditional k-means method is used to establish the 3D coordinates of the center of the remaining group. Basically an alpha-trimmed mean or weighed median filter is used on each coordinate axis, see Figure 4. This coordinate is placed in the

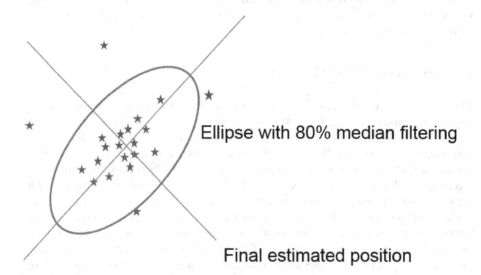

Ellipse with 80% median filtering

Final estimated position

Fig. 4. Robust k-means method to derive the estimate of the (3D) position of a visual feature.

dynamic map which is used for positioning. It is updated whenever a threshold of new revisits has been passed. Also a quality of the feature is added and the final location estimate of the vehicle will be a robust, adaptively weighted mix of all positional information available. In the resulting dynamic map, which is regularly updated by a server based on the information of several vehicles, one can distinguish between the very reliable visual beacons, the relatively reliable traffic signs and the moderately reliable visual landmarks as seen by Libviso2, the map is stored in xml format with different layers, an example of the information on the map is shown in Figure 5.

	reliability	identifier	signature	location
	1.00	1	beacon01	23,34,78
Dependable	1.00	2	beacon02	56,45,91
	1.00	3	beacon03	98,40,23
	...	...	...	...
	0.99	13	EA1678DE	89,67,45
Reliable	0.89	14	DE78A802	12,45,91
	0.87	15	78FA3097	45,93,70
	...	...	...	...
	0.34	890	EE546512	12,98,03
Questionable	0.31	891	0180CBE8	67,89,10
	0.29	892	09EFB405	49,88,73
	...	...	...	...
	0.04	7609	0049EF8B	87,40,49
Noise	0.04	7610	98DD7603	45,28,73
	0.03	7611	89FBA345	98,64,90

Fig. 5. Example of contents of the dynamic map

Acknowledgement. This project is funded by IWT and Flanders'Drive Belgium and is performed in cooperation with Octinion, Dana-Spicer, Tenneco, TomTom and Siemens.

References

1. Stavens, D.M.: Learning to drive: Perception for autonomous cars, tech. rep., Stanford University, Palo Alto, USA, May 2011
2. Scaramuzza, D., Fraundorfer, F.: Visual odometry, part 1: The first 30 years and fundamentals. IEEE Robotics & Automation Magazine, December 2011
3. Fraundorfer, F., Scaramuzza, D.: Visual odometry, part 2: Matching, robustness, optimization, and applications. IEEE Robotics & Automation Magazine, June 2012
4. Tiberius, C., van Bree, R., Buist, P.: Mapping motorway lanes and real-time lane identification with single-frequency precise point positioning. In: InsideGNSS, November/December 2011

5. Geiger, A., Ziegler, J., Stiller, C.: Stereoscan: Dense 3d reconstruction in real-time. In: Intelligent Vehicles Symposium 2011, Baden Baden, Germany, June 2011
6. Van Hamme, D., Veelaert, P., Philips, W.: Robust visual odometry using uncertainty models. In: Blanc-Talon, J., Kleihorst, R., Philips, W., Popescu, D., Scheunders, P. (eds.) ACIVS 2011. LNCS, vol. 6915, pp. 1–12. Springer, Heidelberg (2011)
7. Steinhoff, U., Omerčević, D., Perko, R., Schiele, B., Leonardis, A.: How computer vision can help in outdoor positioning. In: Schiele, B., et al. (eds.) AMI 2007. LNCS, vol. 4794, pp. 124–141. Springer, Heidelberg (2007)
8. Badino, H., Huber, D., Kanade, T.: Visual topometric localization. In: Intelligent Vehicles Symposium 2011, Baden Baden, Germany, June 2011
9. Lategahn, H., Geiger, A., Kitt, B., Stiller, C.: Motion-without-structure: real-time multipose optimization for accurate visual odometry. In: Intelligent Vehicles Symposium 2012, Alcala de Henares, Spain, June 2012
10. Lategahn, H., Beck, J., Kitt, B., Stiller, C.: How to learn an illumination robust image feature for place recognition. In: IEEE Intelligent Vehicles Symposium 2013, Gold Coast, Australia, June 2013
11. S. Micro-Electronics: Inemo inertial module: 3d accelerometer, 3d gyroscope, 3d magnetometer. Datasheet (2013)
12. Yamamoto, Y., Pirjanian, P., Munich, M., DiBernardo, E., Goncalves, E., Ostrowsku, J., Karlsson, N.: Optical sensing for robot perception and localization. In: Proceedings of IEEE Workshop on Advanced Robotics and its Social Impacts, June 2005
13. Olson, E.: Apriltag: a robust and flexible visual fiducial system. In: Proceedings of the IEEE International Conference on Robotics and Automation, Shanghai, China, May 2011
14. uBlox: Neo-7p u-blox 7 precise point positioning gnss module. Datasheet (2014)
15. de Bakker, P., Knoop, V., Tiberius, C., van Arem, B.: Mapping motorway lanes and real-time lane identification with single-frequency precise point positioning. In: Proceedings of the Euroean Navigation Conference (ENC)-GNSS 2014, Rotterdam, The Netherlands, April 2014
16. Brubaker, M.A., Geiger, A., Urtasun, R.: Lost! leveraging the crowd for probabilistic visual self-localization. In: Conference on Computer Vision and Pattern Recognition (CVPR) (2013)

Detection of Social Groups in Pedestrian Crowds Using Computer Vision

Sultan Daud Khan[1]([✉]), Giuseppe Vizzari[1], Stefania Bandini[1], and Saleh Basalamah[2]

[1] Complex Systems and Artificial Intelligence Research Centre, Università degli Studi di Milano–Bicocca, Milano, Italy
sultan.khan@disco.unimib.it
[2] Department of Computer Engineering, Umm Al Qura University, Makkah, Saudi Arabia

Abstract. We present a novel approach for automatic detection of social groups of pedestrians in crowds. Instead of computing pairwise similarity between pedestrian trajectories, followed by clustering of similar pedestrian trajectories into groups, we cluster pedestrians into a groups by considering only start (source) and stop (sink) locations of their trajectories. The paper presents the proposed approach and its evaluation using different datasets: experimental results demonstrate its effectiveness achieving significant accuracy both under dichotomous and trichotomous coding schemes. Experimental results also show that our approach is less computationally expensive than the current state-of-the-art methods.

Keywords: Group detection · Hierarchical clustering · Crowds analysis

1 Introduction

Crowded scenes are composed of large number of people exhibiting different behaviors in a constrained environment. The analysis of the behavior of pedestrians and crowds in video surveillance systems is a topic of growing interest supporting an improved understanding of human behavior and decision making activities through several functions like activity recognition [7], automated analysis of the flow of large crowds, for example through crowd flow segmentation and crowd counting [10], the discovery of frequent pathways [11], the identification of crowd behaviors [21] and abnormal event detection [13,15]. All these studies either focus on individuals or on the overall crowd, considered as large set of pedestrians, not considering the importance of some social interaction among pedestrians: most pedestrians do not really walk alone [16], and researchers observed in most situations pedestrians actually walk in groups. Some interesting forms of social interaction and adaptive behaviors can be observed at the group level and they are growingly investigated in the area of pedestrian and crowd modeling and simulation [16,22]. On the other hand, detecting and analyzing social groups of people is still a less studied topic.

© Springer International Publishing Switzerland 2015
S. Battiato et al. (Eds.): ACIVS 2015, LNCS 9386, pp. 249–260, 2015.
DOI: 10.1007/978-3-319-25903-1_22

A few recent works [2, 26] are aimed at the detection of groups without using future information about the dynamics of the scene. [2] employed Decentralized Particle Filtering (DPF) for group detection while [26] employed unsupervised group detection method based on Dirichlet Process Mixture Model (DPMM) which exploits proxemics to determine group formation. Other approaches like [12, 14, 19] use social forces to analyze motion patterns and recognize groups. These social forces based methods are based on pairwise similarity between trajectories of pedestrians followed by a clustering phase. An approach described in [5] extracts trajectory information from the whole video, then trajectories are temporally analyzed in order to determine the affiliation of each pedestrian to a particular group. Pedestrians are grouped in a bottom-up fashion by employing hierarchical clustering using pairwise proximity and velocity. In [24], both spatial locations and velocities are used within a modified Hausdorff distance to compute trajectory similarities. In [4], Euclidean distance metric is used to cluster vehicle trajectories. [11] measures trajectory similarities using Longest Common Sub-Sequence. [8, 9] use Hausdroff and Dynamic Time Warping metric to measure trajectory similarities. The problems with employing all above pairwise similarity measures are that they are computational expensive and lack probabilistic explanation. On the other hand, instead, recent works are focusing on modeling the distribution of trajectories locations and velocity observations [6, 23].

The approach presented in this paper starts by extracting trajectory information from the whole video and building an *Association Matrix* that captures the joint probability distribution of start and stop locations of all pedestrians to all other pedestrians in the scene and it adopts a bottom-up hierarchical clustering approach similar to the one adopted in [5] to discover social groups. The main contributions of the work are: (i) instead of considering whole trajectories, we consider only two points (start and stop) making the overall group detection process computationally less expensive and more suitable for real-time operation; (ii) our approach does not require training; (iii) the usage of *Association Matrix* for discovering couples and *Adjacency Matrix* for discovering groups; (iv) Our approach requires only one parameter setting.

The paper is organized as follows: in the following we present the overall proposed approach, while Sect. 3 describes the clustering algorithm. Section 4 describes the achieved experimental results, also by comparing the proposed approach with the most relevant existing alternatives. Conclusions and future developments end the paper.

2   Proposed Methodology

The overall framework for automatic detection of pedestrian social groups in crowds is described in Fig. 1; the input is a video sequence in which individual pedestrians are detected: we adopted a semi-automated approach for detecting pedestrians, however, any detector could be used. The second phase is associated to the tracking of the detected pedestrians: once again, we adopted a specific approach, but in principle any tracker could be used. Pedestrians detected in

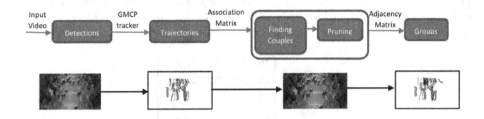

Fig. 1. Proposed Methodology for Group Detection.

first frame are tracked through multiple frames using the Generalized Minimum Clique Graphs (GMCP) [25] method, which is aimed to solve the data association problem by exploiting both motion and appearance in a global manner. The input to GMCP is a graph, in which all the detections in each frame are connected to all other detections in all other frames. The output is the set of several subgraphs, in which the detections belonging to common entities are connected. The trajectory of pedestrian in the scene is a set of tuples (x, y, t), where x and y are the horizontal and vertical coordinates of the location at time t. Therefore, the trajectory of pedestrian is represented by $\{(x_1, y_1, t_1), \ldots (x_n, y_n, t_n)\}$, where n is total length of the trajectory of a pedestrian over a time window T. Once the trajectories are extracted, the next step is to construct an *Association Matrix*, that captures the joint distribution of source and sink locations of all pedestrians to all other pedestrians in the scene.

The first intuition behind this approach is that pedestrians appear and disappear at relatively precise and recurring locations, such as doors, gateways or particular portions of the edges of the scene in videos taken from the fixed camera. We refer to locations where pedestrian appear as *sources* (potential origin of a trajectory) and locations where they disappear as *sinks* (potential destinations of a trajectory). The second consideration is that pedestrian crowd motion is driven by adaptive processes based on local interactions among pedestrians; the latter are more stable and stronger when they move in a group, such as friends or family members, since these individuals exhibit more coherent movements. There are two key characteristics of the members of group: (i) the spatio-temporal relationships of members of group tend to remain stable over time, with members preserving a small distance from one another and avoiding separation unless an obstacle comes in a way; (ii) the velocities of group members are also correlated. We capture the above two characteristics by building an *Association Matrix*. The key notion of our approach is to cluster pedestrians having similar distributions across the source and sink locations.

In order to build an *Association Matrix*, we assume two discrete jointly distributed random variables $\mathbf{X}$, representing "source" locations of the trajectories and $\mathbf{Y}$ representing "sink" locations, where $\mathbf{X} \in \Omega$ and $\mathbf{Y} \in \Omega$ and set Ω represents all the possible scene locations. Let $\mathbf{X}$ and $\mathbf{Y}$ take values in the sets

$\{x_1, x_2, \ldots, x_n\}$ and $\{y_1, y_2, \ldots, y_n\}$ respectively, where x_k and y_k are the start and stop locations of pedestrian's trajectory k. An *Association Matrix* for n trajectories is shown below.

$$P(X,Y) = \left\{ \begin{matrix} p_{11} & p_{12} & p_{13} & \cdots & p_{1n} \\ p_{21} & p_{22} & p_{23} & \cdots & p_{2n} \\ \vdots & \vdots & \vdots & \ddots & \vdots \\ p_{n1} & p_{n2} & p_{n3} & \cdots & p_{nn} \end{matrix} \right\}$$

Each row/column of an *Association Matrix* shows the probability distribution of the source and sink points of single pedestrian P_k over all other n pedestrians in the scene. Let P_k is the distribution of sources and sinks of pedestrian trajectory k with all other n pedestrian trajectories and represented as $\{p_{k1}, p_{k2}, p_{k3}, \ldots, p_{kn}\}$, where $p(k, j)$, is the joint probability of start and stop locations for pedestrian trajectories k and any pedestrian trajectory j. For pedestrian trajectory k, we use a Gaussian likelihood model [18] to compute its probability of its starting from start location of other trajectory j in the scene as equation 1

$$p_x(k, j) = e^{-\| \frac{x_k - x_j}{\sigma} \|} \tag{1}$$

Where x_k is the source location of trajectory k and x_j is the source location of trajectory j. Similarly, probability of stopping for trajectory k from stop location of trajectory j in the scene as equation 2

$$p_y(k, j) = e^{-\| \frac{y_k - y_j}{\sigma} \|} \tag{2}$$

Where y_k is the sink location of trajectory k and y_j is the sink location of trajectory j. Assuming independence among the trajectories, we multiply $p_x(k, j)$ and $p_x(k, j)$ to calculate joint probability $p(k, j)$ for pedestrian trajectories k and j. In the same way, we compute joint probabilities of all other trajectories and after normalization, we obtain an *Association Matrix*. With the detection of new pedestrians, new trajectories are extracted and matrix is updated in the same way.

Association matrix help us in capturing the walking behavior of pedestrians. A single pedestrian (not member of a group) tends to move or stop freely in the environment, changing his/her speed and keep a distance from other pedestrians or obstacles, pursuing is/her own goals. This behavior uniquely identifies his/her source and sink locations. Member of a group generally move and stop together following the notion of group *entitativity* [3], which defines Gestalt psychology of common fate, similarity in appearance and behavior, proximity, and pregnance (patterning). In other words, to a certain extent, a group can be considered as a single entity, as a whole in the environment like, other single pedestrians. Therefore, members of group produce similar distributions and this could be easily detected by looking at the above defined *Association Matrix*. In the next step, we illustrate clustering algorithm that take *Association Matrix* as input.

3   Bottom up Hierarchical Clustering

We adopt a bottom-up hierarchical clustering approach which is a three step process. In the first step, we assign distinct cluster identifiers by treating each pedestrian as a separate cluster. In the second step, our clustering algorithm discovers couples by measuring the difference between distribution of each pedestrian with the distribution of all other pedestrians in the scene by using *Kullback-Leibler (KL) divergence*, also known as relative entropy, denoted by $D_{KL}(P_r||P_k)$, computed by using equation 4 and selects the one that minimizes equation 3. For example, to find a group partner for a pedestrian with distribution P_r, we select a pedestrian with distribution P_k that minimizes the equation 3.

$$\underset{k=1}{\overset{n}{\operatorname{argmin}}}(D_{KL}(P_r||P_k)) \tag{3}$$

$$D_{KL}(P_r||P_k) = \sum_i P_r(i) \ln \frac{P_r(i)}{P_k(i)} \tag{4}$$

This process always proposes for each pedestrian the best possible partner to form a couple, although this candidate partner might even be a bad partner, since the pedestrians do actually not follow similar paths in terms of source and sink in their trajectories. The next step is thus to prune these bad couples. Couples are labeled as bad if the joint probability $p(r, k)$ (computed in section 2), is greater than a specified threshold τ_s.

After pruning, an adjacency matrix is generated which captures the connectivity information among all pedestrians. In order to illustrate the situation with an example, consider the 6 x 6 matrix below that captures the connectivity information among six pedestrians. In matrix A '1' represents an edge between two pedestrians while '0' shows that there is no edge exits between them. As shown in matrix, pedestrian p_1 is adjacent to p_2, p_2 is adjacent to p_4 and p_1, p_3 to p_5, p_4 to p_2 while p_6 is not connected with any other pedestrian.

$$A = \begin{array}{c} \\ p_1 \\ p_2 \\ p_3 \\ p_4 \\ p_5 \\ p_6 \end{array} \overset{\begin{array}{cccccc} p_1 & p_2 & p_3 & p_4 & p_5 & p_6 \end{array}}{\begin{pmatrix} 0 & 1 & 0 & 0 & 0 & 0 \\ 1 & 0 & 0 & 1 & 0 & 0 \\ 0 & 0 & 0 & 0 & 1 & 0 \\ 0 & 1 & 0 & 0 & 0 & 0 \\ 0 & 0 & 1 & 0 & 0 & 0 \\ 0 & 0 & 0 & 0 & 0 & 0 \end{pmatrix}}$$

In the third step of the algorithm, group of couples, those having strong intergroup closeness are merged into a larger group e.g, $G(p_1, p_2)$ have a strong intergroup closeness with $G(p_2, p_4)$ because these two group of couples have one member in common i.e, p_2. Pseudocode of the third step (algorithm 1) automatically discovers groups of pedestrian by taking adjacency matrix as input.

One could take a top-down approach by considering the entire crowd as one group and iteratively splitting into subgroups. We choose the bottom-up approach because it is more efficient in the situations where the crowd is composed

Algorithm 1.. Discovering intergroup closeness and agglomerating couples from adjacency matrix

Input: Adjacency Matrix A

Output: Groups G

```
 1: initialize discovery vector D equal to number of pedestrian to zeros
 2: initialize group G cluster.
 3: idx = 1                                          ▷ ID of the group(cluster)
 4: for all pedestrians n do
 5:     if  n is not discovered then
 6:         D(n) = 1
 7:         insert n in G[idx]
 8:         ptr = 1
 9:         while ptr ≤ length(G[idx]) do
10:             find neighbor n̂ of n in A
11:             if D(n̂)= 0  then
12:                 D(n̂)= 1
13:                 insert n̂ in G[idx]               ▷ insert n̂ in group(cluster)ID idx
14:                 n = n̂                            ▷ update n
15:             end if
16:             increment ptr by 1
17:         end while
18:     end if
19:     increment idx by 1
20: end for
```

of small groups (and this represents the most frequent situation, according to empirical observations [16]). Our clustering algorithm does not require a predefined number of clusters as compared to other traditional clustering algorithms e.g, K-means or spectral clustering. Our algorithm automatically discovers the number of groups by constructing a connectivity graph among pedestrians having similar distributions.

4   Experimental Results

This section presents both quantitative and qualitative analyses of the results obtained from experiments. We carried out our experiments on a PC of 2.6 GHz (Core i5) with 4.0 GB memory, running a Mathlab implementation of the presented algorithm. We validate our proposed group detection approach on video sequences made available from other research groups and acquired through field observations. The overall set of video includes situations including both the so called structured and unstructured crowds with different density conditions. The videos named as *eth* and *hotel* from [17] are recorded in low density situations, *su2* from [5] consists of two 15 minutes sequences, *su2l* and *su2h*. The first sequence, *su2l* has 10-20 pedestrians per frame and covers low density situations, while the second sequence, *su2h*, has more than 50 pedestrians per frame and covers high density situations. The dataset, *gallery* from [1] is

Table 1. Details of datasets: Key-ppf: people per frame

	ETH	HOTEL	GALLERY	SU2-L	SU2-H
Total number of people	360	390	685	639	2678
Number of groups	74	59	85	127	410
Average number of ppf	6	8	12	17	50
Number of Frames	1448	1168	1002	600	600

recorded in a relatively high density situations. Table 1 shows the summary of each analyzed video.

In order to evaluate our proposed approach, we obtain ground truth of all video sequences: a human observer watched a version of video with IDs overlaid on individuals in the scene. For quantitative evaluation of our proposed grouping method, we first compare ground truth and auto-estimated group size for each pedestrian.

Some considerations must be done about the application of the presented group detection approach before discussing results. The overall workflow described in Fig. 1 intrinsically implies a *time window* in which the pedestrians are identified and tracked, in which their sources and sinks are identified and in which all the group detection mechanisms are applied. Therefore, the presented approach produces results that are to be considered valid *within* a time window. The length of the time window, with respect to both general pedestrian dynamics and the overall travel time within a given scene, significantly influences the performance of the group detection: in particular, too short time windows make it difficult to actually perceive differences between genuine groups and simple pedestrians that, for a short time, move in a very similar way, that would represent false positives. A larger time window, close to the length of the average travel time of pedestrians in the scene, would intuitively improve group detection, but it would also reduce the *frequency* of the detection of groups in the scene. While facing this problem is object of current and future works, we will discuss the effect of the choice of a time window size on the precision of group detection.

As previously mentioned, the trajectories were extracted by means of a semi automatic pedestrian detection mechanism; this fact should not hinder or favor the proposed approach compared to existing ones, but this is subject to further analyses. To better discuss the accuracy of the group detection we categorize a member of a group under two coding schemes: *Dichotomous* coding scheme and *Trichotomous* coding scheme. In the former, we checked whether a pedestrian is alone or in group while in the trichotomous coding scheme we determine the size of the group. We compare these coding schemes with the ground truth and from the experiments, we observe that our proposed grouping algorithm achieves 93.6% accuracy in dichotomous while 88.2% accuracy in trichotomous coding scheme on average for all the analyzed videos. As shown in Table 2, the performance of our proposed approach for the first two videos, i.e, *eth* and *hotel*, under dichotomous and trichotomous coding scheme is very high, since these

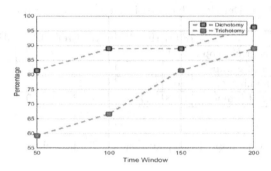

Fig. 2. Effect of Time window on accuracy

videos covers low density situations, where pedestrians are relatively distant one from another, while in the other videos, where the density is relatively high and pedestrians are moving at a short distance, the performance of our algorithm decreases. Further investigations on video sequences reveals that the performance of our proposed approach gradually decreases with the increase in crowd density in general, irrespectively of the adopted video: in high density situations, the available space around the group is reduced and this forces the configuration of the group to change to adapt to the contextual situation, voiding the assumptions behind our approach[1].

From the experiments, we also analyzed how the accuracy of the proposed approach is influenced by the size of the time window. If the time window is shorter than maximum travel time of pedestrian in the scene, this implies that pedestrian trajectories are analyzed for a short duration and the algorithm may lead to false positives. In such situations, two pedestrians walking close to each other for a short period will be detected as couple, although they cease to move together if analyzed for a longer duration. Figure 2, shows the accuracy of dichotomous and trichotomous coding scheme with varying time window for the *gallery* video sequence. In this video sequence, maximum travel time of pedestrian is 200 frames. As it is obvious from Figure that accuracy of our grouping algorithm increases with the increase in duration of time window. Since in general this value is unknown, we can consider a reasonable initialization value to be set according to known data such as the average pedestrian walking speed and the dimension of the observed area

Comparison with State-of-the-Art. We compare our proposed grouping algorithm with the ones that are closest to the present approach, respectively described in [5] and [20]. In [5], the researchers identify small group of pedestrians by combining spatial proximity and velocity cues into a pairwise distance

---

[1] It must be noted that, however, empirical data about the proxemic behavior of groups in relatively high density situation is still lacking, therefore we do not have clear idea of how groups behave in this kind of situation.

Table 2. Dichotomy and Trichotomy on different video sequences

Videos	τ_s	Dichotomoy	Trichotomy
ETH	10^{-10}	100.0%	95.0%
HOTEL	10^{-15}	100.0%	92.0%
GALLERY	10^{-19}	96.3%	89.9%
SU2-L	10^{-12}	90.70%	86.70%
SU2-H	10^{-12}	81.06%	77.24%

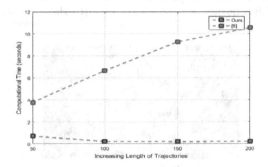

Fig. 3. Time Complexity

computed for the whole trajectory. Intergroup closeness between two groups of pedestrian is measured by symmetric Hausdorff distance. They construct a connectivity graph and adopted bottom-up hierarchical clustering approach that start by treating each individual as separate cluster and gradually discovers large groups by merging two clusters that satisfy intergroup closeness. In contrast, our proposed algorithm does not compute pairwise distance measure for the whole trajectory, instead, we consider only the source (start point of trajectory) and sinks (stop point of trajectory) points of any two trajectories. In order to show the effectiveness of our proposed approach under dichotomous and trichotomous, we compare our approach with [5] using *su2* video sequence as shown in Table 3.

In order to further discuss the quality of the achieved results, we quantitatively compare our approach with [5] in terms of time complexity and shown in Figure 3. The horizontal axis of the Figure shows the increasing mean length of two trajectories belonging to pedestrian couples. Pedestrian couple with mean length of 200 have longer trajectories than pedestrian couple with mean length of 50. The vertical axis of the Figure shows total computational time.

Table 3. Comparison with state-of-the-art method

Data set	Proposed		[5]	
	Dichotomy	Trichotomy	Dichotomy	Trichotomy
SU2-L	**90.70%**	**86.70%**	84.00%	75.00%
SU2-H	**81.06%**	**77.24%**	75.00%	72.00%

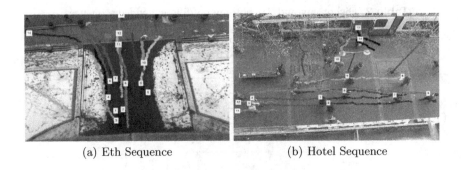

(a) Eth Sequence   (b) Hotel Sequence

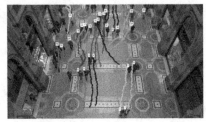

(c) Gallery Sequence

Fig. 4. Qualitative results of different video sequences

The overall computational time is significantly less than [5], for which the cost increases linearly with the increase in length of trajectories, since method [5] computes pairwise distance between all points of the trajectories while in our case the computational time is constant, since we consider only the source and sink point of the trajectories. Our approach is also based on bottom-up hierarchical clustering that also starts by treating each pedestrian as a separate cluster. In the second step, our algorithm tries to find couples and construct a connectivity graph. In the third step, instead of measuring symmetric Hausdorff distance as in [5] (which is widely used for shape matching and trajectory analysis) for merging two groups, we merged two groups of couples into larger group by adopting Algorithm 1.

In [20], instead, the authors proposed a structural SVM-based learning framework that extract Hall's proxemics and Granger's causality as main features from trajectories of pedestrians, then a supervised bottom-up hierarchical clustering approach to discover groups of pedestrians was adopted. This method is very effective and it implied the adoption of an original machine learning method characterized by a plausible model of pedestrian behavior, but it is also computationally expensive, requiring off-line data for learning and training. In contrast, our approach is a relatively simple three step process, it does not require off-line training and learning which makes it suitable for real-time applications, granted that proper pedestrian detection and tracking algorithms are adopted. Figure 4 reports visual examples of our proposed algorithm.

5   Conclusions

We propose a novel approach for automatic detection of social groups of pedestrians in crowds by considering only start (source) and stop (sink) locations of pedestrian trajectories. We build an *Association Matrix* that captures the joint probability distribution of starts and stops locations of all pedestrian trajectories to all other pedestrian trajectories in the scene. Pedestrians exhibiting similar distribution are combine in a group, where as similarity among the distributions is measuread by *Kullback – Leibler(KL)divergence*. We adopt bottom-up hierarchical clustering approach, which is three step process. In first step, we treat all the individuals as independent clusters, In the second step, couples are detected and after pruning of bad couples, *AdjacencyMatrix* is generated. Later on, in step three, using the *AdjacencyMatrix*, groups of couples, those have strong intergroup closeness (similarity) are merged into a larger group. Results of the approach are interesting and promising, future works are aimed, on one hand, at further improving the accuracy of the group detection and, on the other, at clarifying the overall possibility to apply this method (i) respecting real-time constrains or simply (ii) for providing significant data supporting pedestrian modeling and simulation within an integrated approach.

References

1. Bandini, S., Gorrini, A., Vizzari, G.: Towards an integrated approach to crowd analysis and crowd synthesis: A case study and first results. Pattern Recognition Letters **44**, 16–29 (2014)
2. Bazzani, L., Cristani, M., Murino, V.: Decentralized particle filter for joint individual-group tracking. In: 2012 IEEE Conference on Computer Vision and Pattern Recognition (CVPR), pp. 1886–1893. IEEE (2012)
3. Campbell, D.T.: Common fate, similarity, and other indices of the status of aggregates of persons as social entities. Behavioral Science **3**(1), 14–25 (1958)
4. Fu, Z., Hu, W., Tan, T.: Similarity based vehicle trajectory clustering and anomaly detection. In: IEEE International Conference on Image Processing, ICIP 2005, vol. 2, pp. II–602. IEEE (2005)
5. Ge, W., Collins, R.T., Ruback, R.B.: Vision-based analysis of small groups in pedestrian crowds. IEEE Transactions on Pattern Analysis and Machine Intelligence **34**(5), 1003–1016 (2012)
6. Grimson, E., Wang, X., Ng, G.W., Ma, K.T.: Trajectory analysis and semantic region modeling using a nonparametric bayesian model (2008)
7. Hoogs, A., Perera, A.A.: Video activity recognition in the real world. In: AAAI, pp. 1551–1554 (2008)
8. Junejo, I.N., Javed, O., Shah, M.: Multi feature path modeling for video surveillance. In: Proceedings of the 17th International Conference on Pattern Recognition, ICPR 2004, vol. 2, pp. 716–719. IEEE (2004)
9. Keogh, E.J., Pazzani, M.J.: Scaling up dynamic time warping for datamining applications. In: Proceedings of the Sixth ACM SIGKDD International Conference on Knowledge Discovery and Data Mining, pp. 285–289. ACM (2000)
10. Khan, S., Vizzari, G., Bandini, S., Basalamah, S.: Detecting dominant motion flows and people counting in high density crowds. Journal of WSCG **22**(1), 21–30 (2014)

11. Khan, S.D., Vizzari, G., Bandini, S.: Identifying sources and sinks and detecting dominant motion patterns in crowds. Transportation Research Procedia **2**, 195–200 (2014)
12. Leal-Taixé, L., Pons-Moll, G., Rosenhahn, B.: Everybody needs somebody: modeling social and grouping behavior on a linear programming multiple people tracker. In: 2011 IEEE International Conference on Computer Vision Workshops (ICCV Workshops), pp. 120–127. IEEE (2011)
13. Mahadevan, V., Li, W., Bhalodia, V., Vasconcelos, N.: Anomaly detection in crowded scenes. In: 2010 IEEE Conference on Computer Vision and Pattern Recognition (CVPR), pp. 1975–1981. IEEE (2010)
14. Mazzon, R., Poiesi, F., Cavallaro, A.: Detection and tracking of groups in crowd. In: 2013 10th IEEE International Conference on Advanced Video and Signal Based Surveillance (AVSS), pp. 202–207. IEEE (2013)
15. Mehran, R., Oyama, A., Shah, M.: Abnormal crowd behavior detection using social force model. In: IEEE Conference on Computer Vision and Pattern Recognition, CVPR 2009, pp. 935–942. IEEE (2009)
16. Moussaïd, M., Perozo, N., Garnier, S., Helbing, D., Theraulaz, G.: The walking behaviour of pedestrian social groups and its impact on crowd dynamics. PloS One **5**(4), e10047 (2010)
17. Pellegrini, S., Ess, A., Van Gool, L.: Improving data association by joint modeling of pedestrian trajectories and groupings. In: Daniilidis, K., Maragos, P., Paragios, N. (eds.) ECCV 2010, Part I. LNCS, vol. 6311, pp. 452–465. Springer, Heidelberg (2010)
18. Sankaranarayanan, K., Davis, J.W.: Learning directed intention-driven activities using co-clustering. In: AVSS, pp. 400–407 (2010)
19. Sochman, J., Hogg, D.C.: Who knows who-inverting the social force model for finding groups. In: 2011 IEEE International Conference on Computer Vision Workshops (ICCV Workshops), pp. 830–837. IEEE (2011)
20. Solera, F., Calderara, S., Cucchiara, R.: Structured learning for detection of social groups in crowd. In: 2013 10th IEEE International Conference on Advanced Video and Signal Based Surveillance (AVSS), pp. 7–12. IEEE (2013)
21. Solmaz, B., Moore, B.E., Shah, M.: Identifying behaviors in crowd scenes using stability analysis for dynamical systems. IEEE Transactions on Pattern Analysis and Machine Intelligence **34**(10), 2064–2070 (2012)
22. Vizzari, G., Manenti, L., Crociani, L.: Adaptive pedestrian behaviour for the preservation of group cohesion. Complex Adaptive Systems Modeling **1**(1), 1–29 (2013)
23. Wang, X., Ma, K.T., Ng, G.W., Grimson, W.E.L.: Trajectory analysis and semantic region modeling using nonparametric hierarchical bayesian models. International Journal of Computer Vision **95**(3), 287–312 (2011)
24. Wang, X., Tieu, K., Grimson, E.: Learning semantic scene models by trajectory analysis. In: Leonardis, A., Bischof, H., Pinz, A. (eds.) ECCV 2006. LNCS, vol. 3953, pp. 110–123. Springer, Heidelberg (2006)
25. Zamir, A.R., Dehghan, A., Shah, M.: GMCP-tracker: global multi-object tracking using generalized minimum clique graphs. In: Fitzgibbon, A., Lazebnik, S., Perona, P., Sato, Y., Schmid, C. (eds.) ECCV 2012, Part II. LNCS, vol. 7573, pp. 343–356. Springer, Heidelberg (2012)
26. Zanotto, M., Bazzani, L., Cristani, M., Murino, V.: Online bayesian nonparametrics for group detection. In: Proceedings of British Machine Vision Conference, Surrey, p. 111–1 (2012)

Single Image Visual Obstacle Avoidance for Low Power Mobile Sensing

Levente Kovács[✉]

Distributed Events Analysis Research Laboratory,
MTA SZTAKI - Institute for Computer Science and Control,
Hungarian Academy of Sciences, Kende u. 13-17, Budapest 1111, Hungary
levente.kovacs@sztaki.mta.hu
http://web.eee.sztaki.hu

Abstract. In this paper we present a method for low computational complexity single image based obstacle detection and avoidance, with applicability on low power devices and sensors. The method is built on a novel application of single image relative focus map estimation, using localized blind deconvolution, for classifying image regions. For evaluation we use the MSRA datasets and show the method's practical usability by implementation on smartphones.

Keywords: Obstacle avoidance · Mobile sensing · Relative focus maps · Robot navigation

1 Introduction

This paper presents a method for automatic obstacle avoidance, using a single high resolution camera sensor, without the need for additional sensor data ,e.g. range). While classically navigation and obstacle detection and avoidance relies on either stereo camera setups or incorporated range information (sonar, LIDAR, etc.), such an approach has the benefit of simple, more lightweight constructions, lower power and weight requirements, easier setup and lower cost. Research regarding navigation and obstacle avoidance for ground and aerial mobile robots has been producing impressive - in number and in quality - results over the years. Here, we concentrate on obstacle avoidance methods using a single camera sensor, thus we look over some related works in this field.

For outdoor environments, in [1] a single camera based obstacle avoidance was introduced for unmanned ground vehicles using supervised learning to learn depth cues, dividing the images in stripes labeled according to their relative distance and using texture information, followed later by [2], where single image based obstacle avoidance was presented for UAVs, using Markov Random Field classification modeling the obstacles using low level features (color, texture), training the model for obstacle classes with labeled images. In [3] a visual navigation solution was described, following a path of images acquired in a training phase, avoiding new obstacles using the camera (path) and a range scanner

© Springer International Publishing Switzerland 2015
S. Battiato et al. (Eds.): ACIVS 2015, LNCS 9386, pp. 261–272, 2015.
DOI: 10.1007/978-3-319-25903-1_23

(obstacles). For water-based vehicles, in [4] an autonomous watercraft obstacle avoidance approach was presented using a single camera, extracting optical flow to detect and track potential obstacles, based on an occupancy grid approach (using GPS and inertial sensors).

Regarding indoor applications, in [5] an indoor navigation system was presented using a single image for detecting stationary objects and ultrasonic sensing to detect moving objects, using the difference between the current and expected image for detecting stationary obstacles. [6] used low resolution color segmentation and object detection (trained for 8 object classes) for single camera based indoor obstacle avoidance. In [7] obstacle avoidance was created using low resolution images (for color segmentation) to find ground objects and a sonar sensor for extracting depth information, while in [8] indoor obstacle avoidance was produced using optical flow extracted from image series (looking to balance left-right flow quantity) for finding objects and estimating depth.

In some form or another, most single camera obstacle avoidance methods try to extract some sort of saliency information from the images, trying to separate regions that might represent regions to be avoided (obstacles) and regions that contain candidate navigation directions - either not containing obstacles, or containing obstacles which are further away than other obstacles. From this point of view we regard saliency detection approaches as a related field, possibly aiding the obstacle detection/segmentation process. There are several saliency region and object detection approaches, based on segmentation, combining multiple features i.e., contrast, histogram and color distribution [9]; extracting boundaries from natural images using local brightness, color and texture features, using a classifier trained with hand-annotated images [10]; extracting salient regions extracting salient objects including background context that belongs to the images, using features like color, contrast, suppressing frequently occurring features and including some high level information e.g. detected faces [11]; salient region extraction based on multiscale image features (including contrast, color and Gabor filterign) fed into a neural network based region ranking [12]; salient object detection incorporating high level saliency priors with low level (color, edges, superpixel distributions) appearance models using a Markov Random Field construct [13].

The present paper presents a method that does not require a priori scene information or any kind of training, and can work without the use of additional (i.e., range or stereo) sensors. The method builds on our previous work [14], where a method related both to saliency extraction (regarding segmentation, and region of interest selection) and to obstacle avoidance (regarding the detection of near and far objects and regions) was presented. Benefits of the approach include that it produces a so called relative focus map, which is a grayscale index map showing the relative depth of image regions (relative to each other), independent of several factors: the local or global color, the lighting conditions, or the sensitivity of blob extraction or segmentation approaches. It stands close to texture and contrast based approaches in that it incorporates such information, but it is more general, providing more information than traditional saliency estimation techniques, focusing on separating regions based on their conceived relative depth, which is a benefit when we intend to apply it for automatic obstacle avoidance.

The contributions of the paper are the application of the above relative focus map extraction method for automatic obstacle detection using a single camera, the provision of a simple algorithm for detecting candidate navigation directions (in the direction of 'empty' spaces or towards obstacles which are at a further distance than others in the field of view), the evaluation of the proposed approach from a saliency point of view (on the Microsoft Research MSRA Salient Object Database) and from a practical usability point of view (with an implementation on Android smartphones). The presented proof-of-concept method can be incorporated into realtime single camera based navigation systems for mobile robots (a navigation module is not incorporated in the present work).

2   Navigating Around Obstacles

In this section we describe the proposed method for avoiding obstacles using a single image. First, we extract a feature map of the image in Sec. 2.1, which will be used indicate movement directions in Sec. 2.2. The goal is to detect areas on the extracted maps that do not contain immediate obstacles - which means either empty spaces, or obstacles that are further away than others. The result will be that using the proposed method we can roam in spaces without hitting obstacles.

2.1   Relative Focus Maps

For the region detection step we use the relative focus map extraction method presented in [14], which uses a localized, contrast-weighted iterative blind deconvolution procedure to automatically extract regions of interest. In our case, such an approach can be beneficial for its robustness against color and lighting variations and full automatism. Later, we will use the approach in an inverted sense, i.e., we are interested in areas where either there is no obstacle, or in areas which contain obstacles which are further away than others, thus signaling a potential navigation direction. In the following, we will present - very shortly - the main idea behind the relative focus map extraction.

Let g be the observed image, which we consider a convolution $f * h$ of an unknown original image f with an unknown point spread (distortion) function h. In an iterative blind deconvolution process, we think of each image region as a block to be reconstructed, and we are calculating estimates of f and h in each iteration, continuously calculating reconstruction errors vs. the observed image, using the differences between local errors to classify image regions (Fig. 1). Here, calculations are performed in overlapping image blocks, and region classification is performed linearly based on the local reconstruction errors.

For calculating the local reconstruction errors, let $g_k = f_k * h_k$ be an estimation of the observed image produced by the estimated f and h after k deconvolution iteration steps. For local contrast measurement we use the conventional

Fig. 1. Examples for focus extraction on images with various content (top row: input, bottom row: respective focus maps).

contrast definition having the form:

$$C_r(g_r) = (g_{max\{x \in T_r\}} - g_{min\{x \in T_r\}})/(g_{max\{x \in T_r\}} + g_{min\{x \in T_r\}}), \qquad (1)$$

$g_{max\{x \in T_r\}}$ and $g_{min\{x \in T_r\}}$ being the maximum and minimum local image intensities in region T_r at location r. Thus the local error used in the classification has the form [14]:

$$E_r(g, g_k) = |arc\ sin\frac{<g - g_k, g>}{|g - g_k| \cdot |g|}| \cdot \frac{C_r(g_r)}{max_r\{C_r(g_r)\}}. \qquad (2)$$

Fig. 2 shows some examples for images from the MSRA dataset (see Sec. 3) with regions of interest extracted based on this approach, and the generated region boundary rectangles that will be used later in the paper to evaluate the method from a generic saliency detection perspective.

(a)   (b)   (c)   (d)

Fig. 2. Examples for input images from the MSRA dataset (a,c), the extracted maps (b,d), with the selected areas shown with rectangles.

2.2   Obstacle Avoidance

For avoiding obstacles in the field of view of the camera, we first extract the relative focus maps as described in Sec. 2.1. Taking the extracted region image, we divide it into 3×3 regions R_u ($u = 1..9$), and in each region we check the extent of low value classes (dark regions in the extracted maps, e.g., shown in Fig.1 and 2). Since closer regions are represented by higher intensities in the extracted maps, we will assume that the way to go around obstacles is to choose a direction represented by lower intensity regions.

Let w, h be the width and height of the regions, and ϵ be a class threshold (typically 20%). Then.

$$S_u = \sum_{i,j=0}^{i<w,j<h} \begin{cases} 1 & \text{if } R_u(i,j) < \epsilon, \\ 0 & \text{otherwise.} \end{cases} \tag{3}$$

The picked direction to follow will be $D = \underset{u}{\operatorname{argmax}} S_u$, resulting in 10 possible directions: up, right, down, left, 45°, 135°, 225°, 315°, forward (center), and - if undecided - stop (when no direction can be suggested). Since the extracted maps contain relative depth information, situations can occur when we can find the sub-region with the most low-class blocks, but the size of that region is too small to be able to reliably suggest a movement direction. Thus we also have a lower threshold for the amount of low-class blocks in an image region, and a region D will be accepted as a direction candidate only if $D/(N \times M) > 0.05$, where N, M are the input frame dimensions (i.e., the size of the the direction region D is at least 5% of the whole frame), otherwise stopping will be signaled.

Fig. 3. Samples of frames and their extracted maps, white rectangles showing the regions which will be the suggested directions (left, ahead, ahead and right, respectively).eps

We would like to note here, that since the described method is single frame based, it does not matter whether the obstacles are stationary or moving, since the extraction of the feature map is extracted continuously for every frame.

The diagram of the steps of the method is shown in Fig. 4.

2.3 Implementation

For evaluating practical usability, the presented method has been implemented for Android smartphones, with a simple user interface and all algorithmic code written in C++ with OpenMP and compiled into native code (NDK r10). The phones on which the application was tested were: HTC One X (2012, ARM Cortex-A9@1.5GHz), and Moto G (2013, ARM Cortex-A7@1.2GHz). For processing on the mobile devices, the captured images were resized to 320 pixels

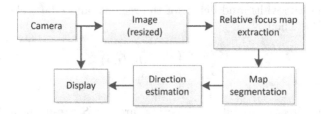

Fig. 4. Overview of the processing steps

width. For all tests, the used block size was fixed to 32×32 pixels with a 16 pixel overlap.

Once the app is started, it continuously processes the camera frames, displays the resulting map in the lower right, and the suggested movement direction in the middle of the view (a green dot for forward motion, a red dot for stopping, and green lines starting from the center for different directions, see Fig. 5 for a few example screenshots).

For testing the method from a saliency point of view (see next section), we created a desktop-PC based version as well, that we can test on a desktop machine over the used saliency dataset.

Fig. 5. Sample app screens showing frame, map, and movement suggestions (ahead, left, right, stop).

3   Evaluation

We show the usability and applicability of the proposed approach in two steps. First, we evaluate the region extraction step from a saliency point of view, using it for region of interest extraction. For this purpose, we use the Microsoft Research MSRA Salient Object Database[1], consisting of Image set A (20840 images labeled by three users) and Image set B (5000 images labeled by nine users) [9]. Secondly, we present results of the smartphone implementation of the obstacle avoidance application of the method.

During the evaluation of the region extractor from the saliency point of view, we first extract the region boundaries with the above described method (Sec. 2.1)

---

[1] http://research.microsoft.com/en-us/um/people/jiansun/salientobject/
salient_object.htm

for each dataset image (which will be referred to as $B2$ below). Then, for each image, we take all the regions created by users (3 and 9 respectively), and we create an average rectangular region for each image (called $B1$), which will be average rectangle of all the user-provided rectangular regions. Then, we will use the similarity between $B1$ and $B2$ to compare the manual and the generated regions, using the two metrics described in the following.

Ley I be an $M \times N$ input image. Let $B1, B2$ be the $N \times M$ manual and automatic boundary images of I, and $n \in \{1, 2\}$ so that:

$$Bn(i,j) = \begin{cases} 1 & \text{if } (i,j) \text{ is a boundary point,} \\ 0 & \text{otherwise.} \end{cases} \tag{4}$$

Let $A()$ denote the area of a region. The Jaccard-index [15] based bounding region similarity will be:

$$J(B1, B2) = \frac{A(B1 \cap B2)}{A(B1 \cup B2)} \in [0; 1], \tag{5}$$

where $A(B1 \cap B2)$ is the area of the intersection of the two boundaries (if any), and $A(B1 \cup B2)$ is the area of the union of the two boundary regions.

If $C1, C2$ denote the centers of mass of regions $B1, B2$, then the condition for accepting an extracted region boundary as a good approximation of the real region of interest (according to the manual user annotations) will be:

$$\begin{cases} J(B1, B2) > 0.25 & \text{and} \\ C2 \in B1, \end{cases} \tag{6}$$

i.e., the common area of $B1, B2$ is at least 25% of the merged area, and $C2$ is inside region $B1$. Fig. 6 shows example images with accepted regions. Please note, that for our purposes (avoiding obstacles, providing a candidate 'way out') we do not need exact region boundaries, only an approximately good direction estimate, thus our premise is a bit different from classical saliency algorithms.

(a) J: 0.92 BDE: 4.3 (b) J: 0.67 BDE: 22.1 (c) J: 0.54 BDE: 37.7 (d) J: 0.29 BDE: 48.2

Fig. 6. MSRA dataset images with accepted regions (black: manual selection; white: automatic selection).

In order to provide a metric in a more general sense about the saliency-related behavior of the relative map extraction, we also provide the Boundary

Displacement Error [16] (BDE) over both datasets. Let $P(Bn)$ ($n \in \{1,2\}$) denote the perimeter of boundary in Bn, $DT(Bn)$ denote the the $N \times M$ distance transform of Bn and '$\circ$' denote the Hadamard matrix product. The Boundary Displacement Error is then calculated as:

$$BDE(B1, B2) = \frac{1}{2} \left(\frac{\sum_{i,j=0}^{i<N,j<M}(B1 \circ DT(B2))_{i,j}}{P(B1)} + \frac{\sum_{i,j=0}^{i<N,j<M}(B2 \circ DT(B1))_{i,j}}{P(B2)} \right). \tag{7}$$

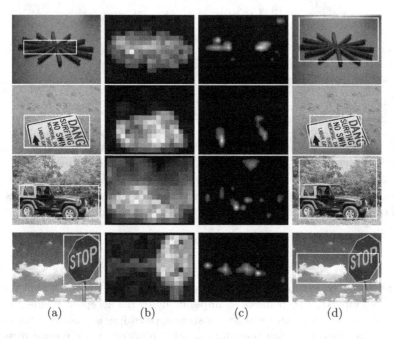

(a)   (b)   (c)   (d)

Fig. 7. Example images with obtained regions based on the extracted maps with the proposed method (a,b) and [12] (c,d).

In Table 1 we include the overall statistics regarding the MSRA datasets, including the number of images and the number of associated manual annotations, the precision over the datasets using the above described approach. Precision in this case is the acceptance percentage of the regions, i.e., the ratio of the accepted generated rectangles (by the above acceptance condition) vs. the total number of images. The table also shows the associated mean BDE and Jaccard-similarity values (with their standard deviations) associated to the produced precision. The table also contains the same results obtained by using the saliency toolbox[2] of [12] to extract the saliency maps, then - similarly to [9] - taking its 'Winner Take All' outputs, keeping the top 90% of the generated map and fitting a rectangle over the obtained map.

---

[2] http://saliencytoolbox.net

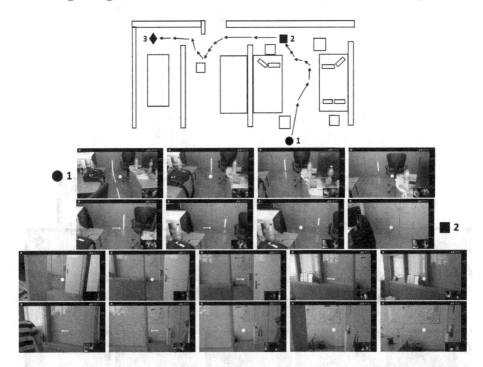

Fig. 8. Example screens and directions during movement with the smartphone app in the office space with its draft plan shown in the top image, from point 1 (start) to point 3 (finish). The order of images follows the sequence of movements.

What this table shows is that the proposed method, when used for generic salient region estimation, can perform fairly well. However, when we take into consideration that for our primary purpose - finding candidate directions for navigation - for which we need well-structured region maps that can be analyzed for obstacles, the proposed method is clearly much more well-suited, providing

Table 1. Precision, mean (μ) and deviance (σ) values of BDE and the Jaccard similarities for MSRA set A and set B using the proposed method (prop.) and [12].

	MSRA set B		MSRA set A	
	prop.	[12]	prop.	[12]
total nr. images	5000		20840	
user labels/image	9		3	
accepted % (precision)	83.3	83.4	84	88.4
μ BDE	45.7	41.3	45	40.2
σ BDE	25.4	19.2	23.5	19.2
μ J	0.45	0.5	0.46	0.51
σ J	0.19	0.16	0.18	0.16

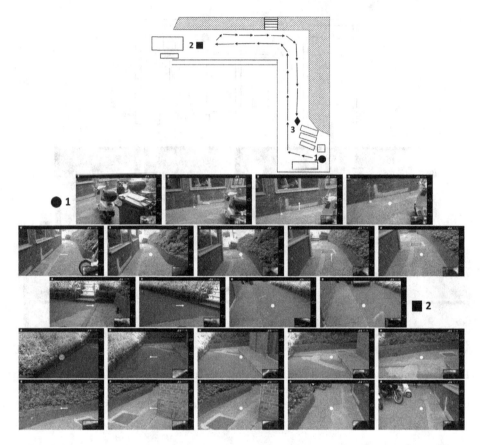

Fig. 9. Example screens and directions during movement with the smartphone app in an outdoor setting with its draft plan shown in the top image, from point 1 (start) to point 2 and 3 (finish). The order of images follows the sequence of movements.

connected regions with estimated relative depth differences, as Fig. 7 also shows for a few examples.

As a second step, we tested the smartphone app in which we implemented the method described above. Since we did not yet implement the method on a mobile robot, the human holding the smartphone emulates the actual navigation, by performing the actual movement in the direction that the app indicates, based on the processing of the captured images. When the app shows a movement direction, the human takes a step in the indicated direction, then waits for the next indication and repeats the process. The directions are shown in the middle of the app screen as a green line going from the center of the image towards an indicated angle, or a large green dot if the indicated directions is straight ahead, or a large red dot, if the method cannot suggest any direction. In such a case the human operator needs to turn slowly around until a direction is indicated again.

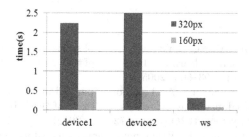

Fig. 10. Average processing times for two internal resolutions for the two used mobile devices (1 and 2) and a desktop workstation (ws).

Fig. 8 shows an example where we used the app to roam around in an office space (whose draft internal plan is shown in the figure). Black rectangles show different obstacles (tables, walls, chairs, computer screens and one human), and the small arrows show the approximate path that the human operator took moving in the directions indicated by the application. Fig. 9 shows another example in an outdoor scenario (with obstacles like walls, bikes, car, vegetation - shown by the hashed areas).

Regarding processing time, Fig. 10 shows processing times on the two above mentioned smartphones (denoted by device1 and device2) and on a Core i7-930@2.8GHz (2010) workstation (denoted by ws), for internal processing in two resolutions (long side being 160 or 320 pixels), in all cases averaged over 50 frames. For practical purposes for a generic device the lowest possible resolution should be selected (based on empirical trials for the specific device) which can provide usable outputs.

You can see examples in color and with more detail at http://web.eee.sztaki.hu/~kla/deb/.

4 Conclusions and Future Work

We presented a single image based obstacle avoidance approach based on the processing of so called relative focus maps, for lightweight moving sensing platforms. The benefits of the approach are that it does not require training, can work indoors and outdoors as well, it is easy to implement and port to different platforms. We showed that the map extraction method performs also fairly well in a pure saliency detection setting, and we have shown implementation results in case of Android smartphones. As next steps, we intend to work on incorporating the method in a complex localization and navigation framework and also on speeding it up with GPGPU/OpenCL implementation for mobile GPUs.

Acknowledgments. This work has been supported by Hungarian Scientific Research Fund (OTKA) grant nr. 106374.

References

1. Michels, J., Saxena, A., Ng, A.Y.: High speed obstacle avoidance using monocular vision and reinforcement learning. In: Proc. of the 21st Intl. Conf. on Machine Learning (ICML), pp. 593–600 (2005)
2. Lenz, I., Gemici, M., Saxena, A.: Low-power parallel algorithms for single image based obstacle avoidance in aerial robots. In: Proc. of IEEE Intl. Conf. on Intelligent Robots and Systems (IROS), pp. 772–779 (2012)
3. Cherubini, A., Chaumette, F.: Visual navigation with obstacle avoidance. In: Proc. of IEEE/RSJ Intl. Conf. on Intelligent Robots and Systems (IROS), pp. 1503–1598 (2011)
4. El-Gaaly, T., Tomaszewski, C., Valada, A., Velagapudi, P., Kannan, B., Scerri, P.: Visual obstacle avoidance for autonomous watercraft using smartphones. In: Proc. of Autonomous Robots and Multirobot Systems workshop (ARMS) (2013)
5. Oh, A., Kosaka, A., Kak, A.: Vision-based navigation of mobile robot with obstacle avoidance by single camera vision and ultrasonic sensing. In: Proc. of IEEE Intl. Conf. on Intelligent Robots and Systems (IROS), pp. 704–711 (1997)
6. Lenser, S., Veloso, M.: Visual sonar: Fast obstacle avoidance using monocular vision. In: Proc. of IEEE/RSJ Intl. Conf. on Intelligent Robots and Systems (IROS) (2013)
7. Viet, C.N., Marshall, I.: Vision-based obstacle avoidance for a small, low-cost robot. In: Proc. of IEEE Intl. Conf. on Advanced Robotics (ICAR) (2007)
8. Souhila, K., Karim, A.: Optical flow based robot obstacle avoidance. International Journal of Advanced Robotic Systems $4(1)$, 13–16 (2007)
9. Liu, T., Sun, J., Zheng, N.N., Tang, X., Shum, H.Y.: Learning to detect a salient object. In: Proc. of IEEE Conf. on Computer Vision and Pattern Recognition (CVPR), pp. 1–8 (2007)
10. Martin, D.R., Fowlkes, C.C., Malik, J.: Learning to detect natural image boundaries using local brightness, color, and texture cues. IEEE Tr. on Pattern Analysis and Machine Intelligence $26(5)$, 530–549 (2004)
11. Goferman, S., Zelnik-Manor, L., Tal, A.: Context-aware saliency detection. IEEE Tr. on Pattern Analysis and Machine Intelligence $34(10)$, 1915–1926 (2012)
12. Itti, L., Koch, C., Niebur, E.: A model of saliency-based visual attention for rapid scene analysis. IEEE Tr. on Pattern Analysis and Machine Intelligence $20(11)$, 1254–1259 (2002)
13. Jia, Y., Han, M.: Category-independent object-level saliency detection. In: Proc. of IEEE Intl. Conf. on Computer Vision (ICCV), pp. 1761–1768 (2013)
14. Kovács, L., Szirányi, T.: Focus area extraction by blind deconvolution for defining regions of interest. IEEE Tr. on Pattern Analysis and Machine Intelligence $29(6)$, 1080–1085 (2007)
15. Levandowsky, M., Winter, D.: Distance between sets. Nature **234**, 34–35 (1971)
16. Freixenet, J., Muñoz, X., Raba, D., Martí, J., Cufí, X.: Yet another survey on image segmentation: region and boundary information integration. In: Heyden, A., Sparr, G., Nielsen, M., Johansen, P. (eds.) ECCV 2002, Part III. LNCS, vol. 2352, pp. 408–422. Springer, Heidelberg (2002)

ROS-Based SLAM for a Gazebo-Simulated Mobile Robot in Image-Based 3D Model of Indoor Environment

Ilya Afanasyev$^{(\boxtimes)}$, Artur Sagitov, and Evgeni Magid

Intelligent Robotic Systems Laboratory (LIRS), Innopolis University,
Universitetskaya, 1, Innopolis 420500, Russian Federation
{i.afanasyev,a.sagitov,e.magid}@innopolis.ru
http://university.innopolis.ru/en/research/robolab/

Abstract. Nowadays robot simulators have robust physics engines, high-quality graphics, and convenient interfaces, affording researchers to substitute physical systems with their simulation models in order to pre-estimate the performance of theoretical findings before applying them to real robots. This paper describes Gazebo simulation approach to simultaneous localization and mapping (SLAM) based on Robot Operating System (ROS) using PR2 robot. The ROS-based SLAM approach applies Rao-Blackwellized particle filters and laser data to locate the PR2 robot in unknown environment and build a map. The real room 3D model was obtained from camera shots and reconstructed with Autodesk 123D Catch and MeshLab software. The results demonstrate the fidelity of the simulated 3D room to the obtained from the robot laser system ROS-calculated map and the feasibility of ROS-based SLAM with a Gazebo-simulated mobile robot to its usage in camera-based 3D environment. This approach will be further extended to ROS-based robotic simulations in Gazebo with a Russian anthropomorphic robot AR-601M.

Keywords: SLAM · ROS · Gazebo · Navigation · Localization and mapping · Image-based 3D model · Laser rangefinder · Robot simulator

1 Introduction

Robot simulators have been playing an important role in mobile robot research as fast, efficient and cheap tools for exhaustive testing of new concepts, methods, and algorithms in the intermediate research stages in order to pre-estimate their performance before applying to a real robot. The most popular robot simulators are Gazebo[1], Microsoft Robotics Developer Studio (MRDS)[2],

---

[1] Gazebo robot simulator, www.gazebosim.org
[2] Microsoft Robotics Developer Studio is a Windows-based environment for robot control and simulation (no longer supported), microsoft.com/robotics/

© Springer International Publishing Switzerland 2015
S. Battiato et al. (Eds.): ACIVS 2015, LNCS 9386, pp. 273–283, 2015.
DOI: 10.1007/978-3-319-25903-1_24

USARSim[3], V-REP[4] and Webots[5].

The usual basic requirements to robot simulators are an accurate physics simulation (such as object velocity, inertia, friction, position and orientation, etc.), high quality rendering (for shape, dimensions, colors, and texture of objects), integration with ROS framework [6] and multi-platform compatibility. It provides great opportunities for modeling robots and their sensors together with developing robot control algorithms, realizing mobile robot simulation, visualization, locomotion and navigation in realistic 3D environments. The high graphical fidelity in a robot simulation is important because the sensory input to the robot perceptual algorithms comes from virtual sensors, which are also provided by the simulation [1]. For example, virtual cameras use the simulator rendering engine to obtain their images. If images from a simulated camera have poor similarity to real camera images, then it is impossible to use them for object recognition and localization. It is also true for other virtual sensors - rangefinders and depth sensors that can provide difficulties for SLAM implementation. To avoid such difficulties we use a robust and high graphical quality robot simulator - Gazebo, which is a ROS-integrated open source robotic simulation package. Gazebo uses the open source OGRE rendering engine, which produces good graphics fidelity, although it also employs the Open Dynamics Engine (ODE) [7], which is estimated as a sufficiently slow physics engine [1].

Integration with ROS gives an access to a large variety of user contributed algorithms. An overview of ROS has been presented in [2]. While various SLAM techniques have been proposed in the past decades, only a few of them are available as implementations to the ROS-community. In [1] authors proposed a two-stage ROS-based SLAM algorithm application. The first stage is a metric based iterative closest point (MBICP) position tracker, which matches successive laser scans to define the position and orientation during the robot motion. These localization data, known as the robot pose, is passed through ROS, running the second stage - an implementation of the FastSLAM algorithm [3], which generates a map of the environment. In [4] authors suggested a ROS-based SLAM algorithm which applies particle filters for a Pioneer 3-DX robot (with a laser sensor mounted on the robot with 390 mm height above the ground) in both real and self-created environments. To implement grid-based SLAM, they used opensource Rao-Blackwellized particle filters [5]. Once mapping and localization are successfully completed the navigation could be achieved. As an example, ROS-based navigation approach for the Willow Garage Personal Robot PR2 (further referred just as PR2) locomotion without collisions, using two costmaps each for the local and global planner is realized in [6].

---

[3] Unified System for Automation and Robot Simulation, usarsim.sourceforge.net/wiki/

[4] V-REP Virtual Robot Experimental Platform, www.coppeliarobotics.com

[5] Cyberbotics Ltd. Webots robot simulator, www.cyberbotics.com/overview

[6] Willow Garage Robot Operating System (ROS) - Robotics middleware for robot software development, providing operating system-like functionality, ros.org

[7] R. Smith, Open Dynamics Engine (ODE), www.ode.org

We are motivated to apply a realistic environment to robot simulation in Gazebo for testing ROS-based mapping, localization and autonomous navigation algorithms for our bipedal robot AR-601M. This work is based on a robust simulation model of AR-601M for robot locomotion [7], which is currently a work-in-progress.

As a first step toward an anthropomorphic AR-601M robot SLAM analysis we use the existing simulation model of the PR2 robot, which has similar characteristics being a human-like android equipped with laser range finders and stereo cameras. We apply the existing ROS-based SLAM software for PR2 robot, simulating the robot locomotion in Gazebo. The realistic indoor environment is obtained by photographing a room with an ordinary camera (or a conventional smartphone), and then combining the images into a 3D model with following meshing and texturizing by Autodesk 123D Catch software.

We consider ROS-based SLAM simulation using OpenSLAM GMapping algorithm[8] based on the particle filters [5]. Our particle filter-based SLAM uses a laser rangefinder LRF_B which is mounted on the PR2 robot base, whereas another LRF (LRF_T) is located on a tilting platform (robot torso) below the pan-tilt robot head and applied for 3D environment visualization. For SLAM task, the robot interprets data from LRF_B sensor in order to produce a map of an unknown environment and performs simultaneous self-localization within this map. The main goal of our paper is to demonstrate the feasibility of ROS-based SLAM which is realized on the particle filters and LRF measurements for a Gazebo-simulated mobile robot locomotion in 3D model of a realistic indoor environment obtained by camera shots.

The paper is organized as following. Section 2 describes the system setup of PR-2 and AR-601M robots for their simulation in Gazebo. Section 3 considers the image-based 3D modeling of indoor environment. Section 4 presents the SLAM for PR2 mobile robot using ROS and Gazebo in camera-based 3D environment. Finally we conclude and discuss the future steps of our research.

2   System Setup

This chapter describes why the PR-2 robot was chosen for simulation in Gazebo, and emphasizes the main features of PR-2 and AR-601M robots, their similarities and differences.

2.1   Choice of a Robot for Simulation in Gazebo

One of our long-term research goals is an application of SLAM algorithm in the Gazebo robot simulator for simulation model of our bipedal robot AR-601M [7] with algorithm's further implementation on the real robot. Being a work-in-progress, a complicated AR-601M simulator is not yet fully compatible with ROS and therefore we are currently testing our localization, mapping and navigation

---

[8] OpenSLAM GMapping algorithm, www.openslam.org/gmapping.html

algorithms with the PR-2 robot, which has the human-like upper parts (a torso, manipulators, and a head), similar sensor system and open-source ROS-based software.

2.2 PR-2 Robot Description and Simulation

The Willow Garage PR2 robot [9] was presented in 2010 as a personal robot, which is still available on the consumer market. It has 2 manipulators with grippers, a head, a spine and an omni directional base on 4 steered and driven casters, which supports a speed of up to 1 m/s. PR2 robot has in total 20 degrees of freedom (DoF). PR2's variety of sensors includes base and tilting lasers; head cameras: wide color stereo camera, narrow monochrome stereo camera, gigabit camera and textured light projector; global shutter camera in every forearm; gripper sensors, etc. Both base and torso lasers (LRF_B and LRF_T respectively) are Hokuyo Top-URG UTM-30LX rangefinders with 30 m and 270 degrees scanning range. LRF_B is used in ROS-based SLAM method (described in Chapter 4). LRF_T is mounted on a tilting platform located just below the head and can sweep the scanning laser through 135 degrees; it is applied for visualization. The total robot weight is 220 kg, the height is 133-165 cm (depending on the particular extension of a telescoping spine). The software on the PR2 is based on ROS. The PR2 robot and its 3D model in RViz software is shown in Fig. 1, where the simulated model of PR2 robot also has Microsoft Kinect sensor[10] attached to the robot head. This Kinect sensor is used to obtain 3D point cloud of environment during the PR2 robot navigation.

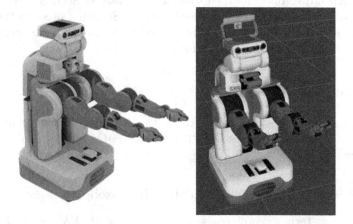

Fig. 1. Willow Garage PR2 robot (left) and its 3D model (right). Courtesy of Willow Garage company.

---

[9] Willow Garage PR2 robot, http://www.willowgarage.com/pages/pr2/overview
[10] Microsoft Kinect, www.microsoft.com/en-us/kinectforwindows/default.aspx

2.3   AR-601M Robot Description and Simulation

The anthropomorphic robot AR-601M (Fig. 2) is being developed by Russian company "Android Technics"[11]. It is a human-like anthropomorphic robot of 144 cm height and 65 kg weight, with 57 DoFs (41 active DoFs). The robot has a torso, a head, two manipulators with gripping fingers and two legs. A built-in multi-sensor system includes a stereo camera, rear-view camera, 2 Hokuyo UTM-30LX sixteen IR sensors located on robot's wrists and feet, feet pressure sensors, and gyroscopes. Detailed specifications of AR-601M robot could be found in [7].

Fig. 2. Android Technics AR-601 robot (left) and its 3D model (right). Courtesy of Android Technics company.

3   Camera-Based 3D Model of Indoor Environment

This chapter presents 3D model building process which was based on camera shooting and multi-image processing technique for indoor environment by Autodesk 123D Catch software.

3.1   Indoor Environment Shooting with Camera

Nowadays, the precise reconstruction of real 3D environment from camera-based dataset using computer vision techniques is widely used in 3D simulators. This image-based 3D modeling technique often applies to low cost or open source software, like Autodesk 123D Catch [12], which is used in our research. This type

---

[11] Androidnaya Tehnika (Android Technics), AR-601M belongs to a AR-600 series of robots, http://en.npo-at.com/products/ar-600
[12] Autodesk 123D Catch software, www.123dapp.com/catch

of web based software (ARC3D, 123D Catch, Hyp3D, my3Dscanner) uses a power of cloud computing to carry out a semi-automatic data processing [8] in the contrast with the elder desktop systems approaches.

It gives the advantage of overcoming the PC slowing-down because of hardware overloading, but as a drawback may be significantly effected by a limited speed of the Internet connection while performing online image processing. Comparison of 3D models from the image-based technique of Autodesk 123D Catch and a terrestrial LIDAR demonstrates encouraging results with the 123D Catch software technology [8]. However, the quality of a 3D model for the camera-based technique strongly depends on image quality (image resolution; brightness homogeneity; constancy of illumination conditions; shadowing; absence of transparent, reflective or glossy objects; presence of multiple color labels, etc.), and photo shooting correctness (photo overlapping; occlusion avoidance; photographing static objects, etc.).

3.2   Image-Based 3D Modeling of Indoor Environment

Depending on results of automatic image processing, the manual correction and 3D model improvements may be required. Such image matching is based on use of image features (e.g., color labels) and usually is time consuming. In the worst case, 3D model may contain significant geometric distortions, which are unacceptable and require to re-shoot the scene completely. Typically, for large and medium scale structures a 3D model after reconstruction has the metric accuracy of 1-2 cm, which depends on mesh quality, resolution of dataset and image quantity [8]. In a room-size environment this accuracy is less than 0.5% which is sufficient for the further use in a 3D robot simulator. Relatively to simple 3D point cloud data the camera-based 3D model reconstruction may contain more information about environment which might be valuable for building 3D semantic maps of indoor household environments for methods of multi-object map creation from sensory data (e.g., [9]).

We are interested in shooting indoor environment and further feeding it into SLAM algorithm implementation. For our research we selected as a trial 3D model the room proposed by Glenn Smooth[13] (from Autodesk 123D image galleries[14]). The room contains of a guitar as an obstacle, which is convenient to use for SLAM purpose. The photo of the room, the 3D view from Autodesk 123D Catch, and 3D view of meshing results in MeshLab[15] are presented in Fig. 3 (from left to right).

---

[13] Glenn Smooth's bass guitar room, www.123dapp.com/obj-Catch/bass-guitar-room/ 1250335

[14] 3D Models gallery from Autodesk 123D Catch, www.123dapp.com/Gallery/catch

[15] MeshLab - an open source 3D mesh processing software, meshlab.sourceforge.net

  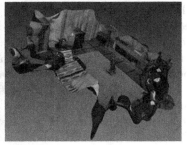

Fig. 3. 3D model of Glenn Smooth's bass guitar room for 3D Gazebo simulation; from left to right: a room photo, 3D view in 123D Catch, and 3D view in MeshLab. Courtesy of Glenn Smooth (www.123dapp.com/obj-Catch/bass-guitar-room/1250335).

4 ROS-Based SLAM Using Gazebo in Image-Based 3D Model of Indoor Environment

This chapter considers the ROS-based SLAM utilizing Rao-Blackwellized particle filter method and laser data to locate the Willow Garage PR2 mobile robot in image-based 3D model of indoor environment and to build a map using Gazebo robot simulator.

4.1 Robot Simulation in Gazebo

Robot simulation is an essential tool of robotics research. A well-designed simulator allows to obtain: 1) the robot and the environment modeling, 2) sensor data and odometry, 3) realistic scenarios of robot locomotion, 4) the implementation of sophisticated algorithms (like SLAM and autonomous navigation), and 5) their fast testing.

Gazebo robot simulator has a number of significant advantages: robust physics engine, high-quality graphics, open-source code, convenient customer and graphical interfaces. It allows to substitute the real robot by its simulation model, providing the calculation of the robot locomotion through odometry and sensor data. Using Gazebo simulator affords to import existing simulated robots and environments, or to create their new 3D model with geometrical primitives.

The simulator's feature is that the environment represents a static model while a robot is a dynamic object. Sensors in Gazebo are the abstract devices with lack of a physical representation, which only give embodiment when they are incorporated into a model. Both passive and active sensors are processed separately from the dynamic simulation in Gazebo – as far as the first only collect data, and the later ones emit and collect data [10]. This feature allows to escape risks of confusion in robot and sensor simulations during robot locomotion. In Gazebo there are three main types of sensor implementation including odometry sensors, ray proximity, and a camera. Odometry is calculated through integration of the traveled distance. The ray proximity sensor returns the contact point of the closest object along the ray's path, that is why it is used to simulate both a scanning laser rangefinder and depth sensor (like Kinect). Finally, the camera renders a scene using OpenGL [10] from the perspective of the model that it is attached to. In SLAM and autonomous navigation we use all three sensor types, performing the sensory data visualization with RViz software[16].

Although it is possible to create a simulated robot model manually with geometric primitives (boxes, spheres, cylinders, planes, etc.), currently a large set of robot models is available in Gazebo, including Willow Garage PR2 robot. The Gazebo-simulated PR2 robot is "equipped" with two Hokuyo laser rangefinders, Kinect sensor, forearm cameras and stereo camera sensors that reasonably replicates a real PR2 robot. The environment modeling could also be created with geometric shapes with appropriate rendering properties such as color, texture, transparency, etc.(e.g., [9]), but we have prepared the real indoor environment based on camera shooting to 3D model for Gazebo simulator.

The results of the Gazebo robot simulation with measurements from a system of two scanning lasers (red lines) and Kinect sensor (a white point cloud) in the room (see Section 3.2) are visualized by RViz and shown in Fig. 4, at the beginning (left) and at the end (right) of SLAM algorithm run.

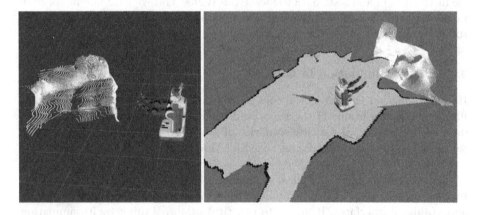

Fig. 4. RViz visualization of Gazebo-simulated PR2 robot locomotion in 3D model of a room at the beginning (left) and at the end (right) of SLAM algorithm run

4.2 ROS-Based SLAM Simulation in Gazebo

The integration of the open-source robot simulator with ROS provides access to a variety of user contributed algorithms. In our study, for SLAM task the PR2 robot must interpret laser data to localize itself and simultaneously produce a map of an unknown environment. The environment to be mapped in this instance is a room with obstacles, shown in Fig. 3.

---

[16] RViz - 3D visualization tool for ROS, wiki.ros.org/rviz

In a cluttered environment, particle filters have been used as an effective solution to the SLAM problem. In this study we implement the OpenSLAM GMapping algorithm based on the Rao-Blackwellized particle filters. The particle filter uses the probabilistic approach with the distribution represented by a set of random particles with associated weights, where each particle has an own weight assigned to represent the probability of that particle being sampled from the probability density function [11]. According to the approach in [5], each particle in the filter carries an individual map of the environment. Therefore the task of particles quantity reduction is really essential. GMapping filter presents adaptive techniques to decrease the number of particles in Rao-Blackwellized particle filter for learning grid maps. It uses an approach to compute an accurate proposal distribution taking into an account not only the robot locomotion but also the observation history. This way it dramatically decreases the uncertainty of the robot's pose in the filter prediction step [5].

Our implementation of ROS-based SLAM method with Gazebo simulation and RViz visualization has the following steps:

1. ROS starts simulation in Gazebo.
2. Gazebo simulates the robot locomotion and sensor measurements, and exports the simulation results to ROS.
3. ROS calculates the robot localization and mapping (SLAM).
4. RViz imports and visualizes the simulation data from ROS (not only immediate robot localization and mapping, but also real-time sensor data).

The laser data is sent via the ROS node running particle filter in OpenSLAM GMapping, and the system produces the robot trajectory (Fig. 5, the red curve) and a map of the simulated environment, which is visualized in RViz (as a plan view).

Figure 5 demonstrates the operating scenario of SLAM algorithm run-time in the static environment. The robot starts from the bottom left corner of the

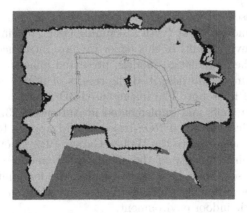

Fig. 5. ROS-based SLAM simulation in Gazebo for the indoor environment 3D model; in the operating scenario the robot has been moving from right to left and back

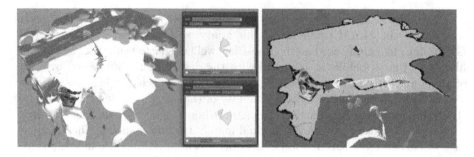

Fig. 6. PR2 robot simulation in Gazebo for 3D model of indoor environment: PR2 loco-motion in the real environment (left), LRF_T scan (top-center), LRF_B scan (bottom-center), RViz visualization (right)

room, bypasses the obstacle (the guitar) in the room center, and targets to reach the bottom right corner. Next, upon the arrival to its destination, the robot navigates itself back to the start (using the obtained at the SLAM stage map) while following the same trajectory within the SLAM-map. Figure 6 (left) represents the Gazebo-simulated PR2 robot locomotion in the real environment together with indications of scanning laser rangefinders (the base laser LRF_B on the top-center and the tilting laser LRF_T at the bottom-center of picture) at the end of the robot path. Figure 6 (right) shows the RViz visualization of the same PR2 robot pose in the simultaneously obtained map of the room environment. Figure 6 qualitatively demonstrates the fidelity of the simulated 3D model of the room with obstacles (at the left) to the sensory map (at the right). That proves the feasibility of ROS-based SLAM of a Gazebo-simulated mobile robot to its usage in camera-based 3D model of a realistic indoor environment.

Conclusions and Future Work

This paper is focused on verifying the feasibility of ROS-based SLAM for a Gazebo-simulated mobile robot (with a scanning laser), moving in 3D model of a realistic indoor environment. In this paper we have introduced AR-601M and PR2 robots with their simulation models, presented image-based 3D model of real indoor environment and described the results of ROS-based SLAM of the Gazebo-simulated PR2 robot. The image-based 3D model of a real room was obtained by camera shots and implemented in Autodesk 123D Catch software with meshing in MeshLab. The ROS-based SLAM applies Rao-Blackwellized particle filters and laser data to the Willow Garage PR2 robot localization and mapping. The obtained fidelity of the simulated 3D model of the room with obstacles to its sensory have demonstrated the feasibility of ROS-based SLAM of the Gazebo-simulated mobile robot to its usage in camera-based 3D model of the realistic indoor environment.

In the next stages of our long term research we will extend the verified ROS-based SLAM approach from Gazebo-simulated PR2 robot model to AR-601M robot model. Also a currently exploited 3D realistic indoor environment will be rebuilt using on-board sensors of AR-601M robot in order to replicate our laboratory environment and investigate sensor data matching of the proposed SLAM approach with new algorithms of autonomous robot navigation.

Acknowledgments. This research has been supported by Russian Ministry of Education and Science as a part of Scientific and Technological Research and Development Program of Russian Federation for 2014-2020 years (agreement 14.609.21.0004, research grant ID RFMEFI60914X0004) and by Android Technics company, the industrial partner of the research.

References

1. Haber, A., McGill, M., Sammut, C.: Jmesim: An open source, multi platform robotics simulator. In: Proc. of Australasian Conference on Robotics and Automation (ACRA), New Zealand, December 3–5, 2012
2. Quigley, M., Conley, K., Gerkey, B.P., Faust, J., Foote, T., Leibs, J., Wheeler, R., Ng, A.Y.: ROS: an open-source robot operating system. In: ICRA Workshop on Open Source Software (2009)
3. Milstein, A., McGill, M., Wiley, T., Salleh, R., Sammut, C.: A method for fast encoder-free mapping in unstructured environments. Journal of Field Robotics **28**, 817–831 (2011)
4. Zaman, S., Slany, W., Steinbauer, G.: ROS-based mapping, localization and autonomous navigation using a Pioneer 3DX robot and their relevant issues. In: Saudi International Electronics, Communications and Photonics Conference (SIECPC), pp. 1–5 (2011)
5. Grisetti, G., Stachniss, C., Burgard, W.: Improved techniques for grid mapping with Rao-Blackwellized particle filters. IEEE Transactions on Robotics **23**, 34–46 (2007)
6. Marder-Eppstein, E., Berger, E., Foote, T., Gerkey, B., Konolige, K.: The office marathon: Robust navigation in an indoor office environment. In: IEEE International Conference on Robotics and Automation (ICRA), pp. 300–307 (2010)
7. Khusainov, R., Shimchik, I., Afanasyev, I., Magid, E.: Toward a human-like locomotion: Modelling dynamically stablel ocomotion of an anthropomorphic robot in Simulink environment. In: Proc. of Int. Conference on Informatics in Control, Automation and Robotics (ICINCO), Alsace, France, July 21–23, vol. 2, pp. 141–148 (2015)
8. Santagati, C., Inzerillo, L., Di Paola, F.: Image-based modeling techniques for architectural heritage 3D digitalization: Limits and potentialities. Int. Archives of the Photogrammetry, Remote Sensing and Spatial. Information Sciences **5**, 555–560 (2013)
9. Marton, Z.C., Blodow, N., Dolha, M., Tenorth, M., Rusu, R.B., Beetz, M.: Autonomous mapping of kitchen environments and applications. In: Proc. of the 1st Int. Workshop on Cognition for Technical Systems, Munich, Germany, October 6–8, 2008
10. Koenig, N., Howard, A.: Design and use paradigms for Gazebo, an open-source multi-robot simulator. In: Proc. of 2004 IEEE/RSJ Int. Conference on Intelligent Robots and Systems (IROS), vol. 3, pp. 2149–2154 (2004)
11. Choset, H.: Principles of robot motion, Theory, Algorithms and Implementations. MIT Press (2006)

Security, Forensics and Biometrics

Full-Body Human Pose Estimation
by Combining Geodesic Distances and 3D-Point
Cloud Registration

Sebastian Handrich[(✉)] and Ayoub Al-Hamadi

Institute of Information Technology and Communications,
Otto-von-Guericke-University Magdeburg, Magdeburg, Germany
{sebastian.handrich,ayoub.al-hamadi}@ovgu.de

Abstract. In this work, we address the problem of recovering the 3D
full-body human pose from depth images. A graph-based representation
of the 3D point cloud data is determined which allows for the measurement of pose-independent geodesic distances on the surface of the human
body. We extend previous approaches based on geodesic distances by
extracting geodesic paths to multiple surface points which are obtained
by adapting a 3D torso model to the point cloud data. This enables us
to distinguish between the different body parts - without having to make
prior assumptions about their locations. Subsequently, a kinematic skeleton model is adapted. Our method does not need any pre-trained pose
classifiers and can therefore estimate arbitrary poses.

1 Introduction

The robust estimation of human poses has a wide range of applications like
human-computer interaction, gaming, and action recognition, but is still a challenging task, since the human body is capable of an enormous range of poses.
Existing techniques can be classified into several categories. Learning based
approaches [1], [2], [3] and [4] are often restricted to previously trained poses
and require a large set of training data. The authors of [3], for example, have
used almost one million training images. Further, the localization of the various body parts is often not very accurate. In contrast, methods without any
prior knowledge [5] can estimate arbitrary human poses but rely on an exact
feature point extraction. Image based methods use feature like silhouettes [6],
skin color [7] or contours [8], but often lack the ability to resolve ambiguities,
e.g. self-occlusion. The recent development of 3d-sensors like Kinect offered the
opportunity to overcome the limits of the image-based approaches. In this work,
we propose an approach that estimates the full-body human pose from depth
images based on geodesic distances. Geodesic distances are independent of the
human pose and therefore suitable for a robust body part segmentation. Geodesic
distances for pose estimation were used before [9]. In this work, we extent prior
works by extracting geodesic paths to multiple surface points which are obtained
by registering a rigid torso model to the depth data. This allows for a labeling
of geodesic paths and is used to robustly segment the body parts.

© Springer International Publishing Switzerland 2015
S. Battiato et al. (Eds.): ACIVS 2015, LNCS 9386, pp. 287–298, 2015.
DOI: 10.1007/978-3-319-25903-1_25

2   Pose Recognition Method

An overview of the suggested method is provided in Fig. 1. At each time stamp t we are given a depth image D_t that contains the depth data of a user in an articulated pose. Depending on the experimental setup, D_t is either captured by a Kinect or contains simulated data which is generated by rendering an animated 3D-character. It is assumed that the user is within the foreground region. User segmentation is therefore limited to applying a depth threshold to D_t. Using a pinhole camera model, we also compute in each frame the corresponding 3D point cloud W_t. Our goal is to estimate the full-body pose $q_t \in \mathbb{H}^K$, with $q_t =$

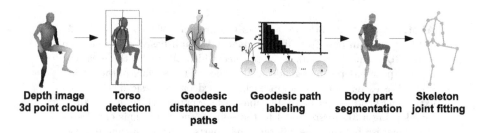

| Depth image
3d point cloud | Torso
detection | Geodesic
distances and
paths | Geodesic path
labeling | Body part
segmentation | Skeleton
joint fitting |

Fig. 1. Suggested method for full-body pose estimation.

$\{q^{to}, q^{ne}, \dots\}$ representing the joint rotations of a hierarchical skeleton model. In each frame, the following steps are performed: a) Fit a 3D-torso model to the torso region (Section 2.1); b) Compute for each 3D-point its geodesic distance to the torso center and extract geodesic paths with maximum length. Determine for each path which limb it represents using a Hidden-Markov-Model (HMM) based approach (2.2); c) Segment individual body parts and fit a kinematic skeleton (2.3).

2.1   3D Torso Model Fitting

In order to determine the position of the limb start point (shoulders, hips, neck), a rigid 3D-torso model is translated and rotated to match with the corresponding points of the point cloud W_t. We detect corresponding points by determining for each model point the closest point in W_t and vice versa. This requires an appropriate initialization of the torso model position and orientation. The torso center is detected based on a distance transformation (Fig. 2a). A point is labeled as being located within the torso region $\mathcal{T}$, if its distance is below the half of the maximum distance: $\mathcal{T} = \{[x, y]^T | I_{DT}(x, y) < 0.5 \max(I_{DT})\}$. The initial position is set to $\bar{\mathcal{T}}$ and the orientation is given by the largest eigenvector U_0 of the covariance matrix of $\mathcal{T}$ (Fig. 2b). Subsequently, the corresponding 3D-point sets X, Y between the model and W_t are determined. The model is then translated by $\Delta p_{to} = \bar{X} - \bar{Y}$. For the rotation, the matrix

$$N = \begin{bmatrix} S_{xx} + S_{yy} + S_{zz} & S_{yz} - S_{zy} & S_{zx} - S_{xz} \\ S_{yz} - S_{zy} & S_{xx} - S_{yy} - S_{zz} & S_{xy} + S_{yx} \\ S_{zx} - S_{xz} & S_{xy} + S_{yx} & S_{yy} - S_{xx} - S_{zz} \\ S_{xy} - S_{yx} & S_{zx} + S_{xz} & S_{yz} + S_{zy} \end{bmatrix}$$

is created with $S = Cov(\boldsymbol{X}, \boldsymbol{Y})$ the covariance matrix. The rotation $\dot{q}$ is given by the largest eigenvector of $\boldsymbol{N}$ and the torso is rotated by $q^{to} = \dot{q} \cdot q^{to}$. The fitting is repeated until the residual error $r = \sum_i ||\boldsymbol{X}(i) - \boldsymbol{Y}(i)||_2$ converges. In each frame the transformation of the previous frame is used. If r is too large, the torso fitting is re-initialized using the aforementioned distance transform based method. For a more detailed description of this approach, see [10].

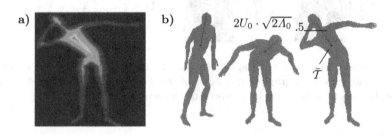

Fig. 2. Torso detection: a) Distance transformation I_{DT}. b) Torso center $\bar{T}$ and initial orientation (red lines).

2.2 Extraction and Labeling of Geodesic Pathes

We proceed by computing the geodesic distances between all 3D-points $\boldsymbol{W_t}$ and the torso center. For this, a graph $\mathcal{G} = (\mathcal{N}, \mathcal{E})$ is constructed. The nodes of the graph are the points of the point cloud $\mathcal{N} = \boldsymbol{W_t}$ and are connected by an edge $\mathcal{E}_{i,j}$, if either an edge criterion $\mathcal{C}_1$ or $\mathcal{C}_2$ is fulfilled. The former connects two nodes if their euclidean distance is below a threshold ϵ_{c1} and if they correspond to adjacent depth pixels (Eq. 1). The second one (Eq. 2) connects two nodes, if all depth image pixels between them have a lower depth value, i.e. are closer to the camera (Fig. 3b).

$$\mathcal{C}_1(i,j) = ||\boldsymbol{w_i} - \boldsymbol{w_j}||_2 \leq \epsilon_{c1} \wedge d(\dot{\boldsymbol{w}}_i, \dot{\boldsymbol{w}}_j) \leq 1, \tag{1}$$

$$\mathcal{C}_2(i,j) = D_t(\dot{\boldsymbol{w}}_k) < \min(D_t(\dot{\boldsymbol{w}}_i), D_t(\dot{\boldsymbol{w}}_j)) \tag{2}$$
$$\forall \dot{\boldsymbol{w}}_k \in \overline{\dot{\boldsymbol{w}}_i \dot{\boldsymbol{w}}_j} \wedge d(\dot{\boldsymbol{w}}_i, \dot{\boldsymbol{w}}_j) > 1,$$

where $d(\cdot)$ is the spatial 2D distance. Each edge has a weight $w(\mathcal{E}_{i,j})$ which is the Euclidean distance between the connected nodes. The shortest connection (path) between two arbitrary graph nodes $\mathbf{a}, \mathbf{b} \in \mathcal{N}$ is determined using the Dijkstra's algorithm [11]. The cumulative weight of all edges that form a geodesic path is denoted as the geodesic distance $g(\mathbf{a}, \mathbf{b}) = \sum_{\mathcal{E} \in \mathcal{P}(\mathbf{a}, \mathbf{b})} w(\mathcal{E})$.

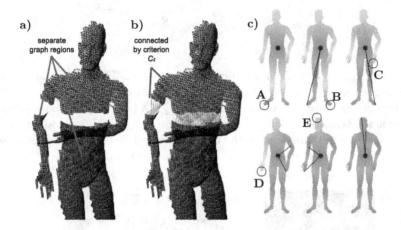

Fig. 3. Geodesic distances: a) Graph with only $\mathcal{C}_1$ applied. b) Graph, if also $\mathcal{C}_2$ is applied, former separated graph region are connected (red lines). c) Detected geodesic maxima, labeled as *A-E*. Black lines represent the zero-weight edges.

Limb end points have high geodesic distances from the torso center (red and orange regions in Fig. 3c) and are extracted as follows: In each pass, the node with the highest distance is detected. In order to prevent a re-detection, we connect the node and the node with half the geodesic distance to the torso center with a zero weight edge $w(\mathcal{E}) = 0$ and re-compute the geodesic distances. This is repeated until all maxima are detected (Fig. 3c).

Once the geodesic maxima $\mathbf{M} = \{m_i\}$ and their paths to the torso center $\mathcal{P}(m_i, \mathbf{p_t})$ are detected, we need to label them as the respective limbs $\{\mathcal{L}_j\}_5$: the left and right arm, the head, and both legs; with their start points $\{\ell_j\}_5 = \{\mathbf{p}_{ls}, \mathbf{p}_{rs}, \mathbf{p}_{lh}, \mathbf{p}_{rh}, \mathbf{p}_{ne}\}$, the positions of the shoulders, hips, and the neck, which are obtained from the torso fitting. Labeling is based on the fact that the paths from the torso center to the ends of the limbs pass the limb start points. For example, the path to the left hand passes the left shoulder.

One could assume that is sufficient for a path labeling to determine for each geodesic path the closest limb start point. This, however, does not work for two reasons. Firstly, there are poses in which the path of a limb is very close or even occludes the start point of another limb. For example, when the right arm occludes the left shoulder. In this case, an incorrect closest limb start point would be detected and the path labeling would fail. Another reason is that, when only single points are used for the path labeling, there is no possibility to reject incorrect geodesic paths.

We therefore propose another approach which is based on the comparisons of complete paths. For each geodesic maximum, five hypotheses are generated (Fig. 4) that it represents limb $\mathcal{L}_j$ (Eq. 3)

$$H_{i,j}: \ \mathcal{P}(\mathbf{p_t}, m_i) \,\hat{=}\, \mathcal{P}(\mathbf{p_t}, \ell_j, m_i), \tag{3}$$

where $\mathcal{P}(\mathbf{p}_t, \ell_j, m_i)$ is the concatenation of two paths starting at the torso center $\mathbf{p}_t$ to the geodesic maximum position m_i via the limb start point ℓ_j.

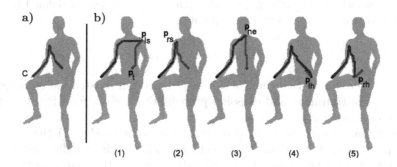

Fig. 4. Detected geodesic path (a) and the hypotheses paths (b).

In order to evaluate the hypotheses, a distance measure is introduced measuring the similarity between two geodesic paths $\mathcal{P}_a$ and $\mathcal{P}_b$. Let $\mathbf{A} = \{a_i\}_N$ and $\mathbf{B} = \{b_k\}_K$ denote the 2D-positions of the elements of $\mathcal{P}_a$ and $\mathcal{P}_b$, respectively. The distance measure is given by Eq. 4.

$$d(\mathcal{P}_a, \mathcal{P}_b) = \frac{1}{N} \sum_{i=0}^{N} e^{-\frac{1}{\sigma}|a_i - b_j|^2}, \; j = h(\mathbf{A}, \mathbf{B}, i). \tag{4}$$

The function $h()$ determines for each element $\mathbf{a}_i$ the index of the corresponding path element in $\mathcal{P}_b$. In a first approach, a nearest-neighbor search was used, but this neglects the sequential order of the path points (Fig. 6a, left). In a second approach (Fig. 6a, right) the sequence of corresponding points is determined using the viterbi algorithm [12]. We define a HMM $\lambda_b = (\phi, \theta, \eta, \pi)$, with $\phi = \{\phi_k\}$ the states, $\theta = \{\theta_{ki}\}$ the transition probability matrix, π the initial state probability matrix and $\eta = \{\eta_k\}$, a set of emission probability functions. The HMM represents path $\mathcal{P}_b$, so there is one state for each path element $\mathbf{B}$. The elements in $\mathbf{A}$ are considered as an observation sequence. The indices of corresponding path points are then given by the most likely sequence of hidden states $\mathbf{q}_\phi$ (viterbi), so that

$$h(\mathbf{A}, \mathbf{B}, i) = \mathbf{q}_\phi(i), \text{ with } \mathbf{q}_\phi \doteq \text{viterbi}(\lambda_b, \mathbf{A}) \tag{5}$$

The HMM is in a left-right form, where each state of λ_b is connected to itself and to the next N_λ states. The transition probability (Eq. 6) decreases for more distant states. This topology considers the sequential order of the path points:

$$\theta_{ki} = \begin{cases} \frac{\exp(-(k-i)^2/N_\lambda)}{\sigma_k}, & i \geq k \wedge i < k + N_\lambda \\ 0, & \text{otherwise} \end{cases}, \tag{6}$$

where σ_k is a normalization term that ensures that the outgoing transition probabilities add up to one.

The emission probability function η determines the probability to observe the path element a_i in state ϕ_k, i.e. at path element b_k and is defined by the Euclidian distance between two path points:

$$\eta_k(a_i) = \exp(-\frac{1}{\sigma}|a_i - b_k|^2). \tag{7}$$

We want to emphasize that the HMM is not trained but constructed out of path $\mathcal{P}_h$, where the transition and emission probabilities are set according to Eq. 6 and Eq. 7, respectively.

Using the distance function (Eq. 4), the hypotheses (Eq. 3) that a path $\mathcal{P}(m_i, p_t)$ represents the limb $\mathcal{L}_j$ are evaluated. This results in a distance matrix Ω^* (Eq. 8). We further assume that limb paths only slightly change between two consecutive frames and compute the path distances w_{ij}^{-1} to previously assigned limb paths $\mathcal{P}_{\mathcal{L}_j}^{t-1}$ (Eq. 9).

$$\Omega^*(i, j) = w_{ij}^* = d(\mathcal{P}(p_t, m_i), \mathcal{P}(p_t, \ell_j, m_i)) \tag{8}$$
$$\Omega^{-1}(i, j) = w_{ij}^{-1} = d(\mathcal{P}(\ell_j, m_i), \mathcal{P}_{\mathcal{L}_j}^{t-1}) \tag{9}$$

Both distances are combined (Eq. 10) as follows: If w_{ij}^{-1} is above a gating threshold $w_G = 1.0$, the path $\mathcal{P}(\ell_j, m_i)$ is too far away from a previously assigned limb path and w_{ij} is set to $w_{max} = 2.0$, which prevents in a subsequent step the path from being labeled as limb $\mathcal{L}_j$. If w_{ij}^{-1} is below the gating threshold, w_{ij}^* is weighted with w_{ij}^{-1}. This ensures that if multiple paths are within the gate interval of the previous assigned limb path $\mathcal{P}_{\mathcal{L}_j}^{t-1}$, it becomes more likely for a path that is closer to the previous one to be labeled as $\mathcal{L}_j$.

$$\Omega(i, j) = w_{ij} = \begin{cases} w_{ij}^*, & \mathcal{P}_{\mathcal{L}_j}^{t-1} \ not \ seen \\ w_{ij}^* w_{ij}^{-1}/w_G, & w_{ij}^{-1} < w_G \\ w_{max}, & w_{ij}^{-1} \geq w_G \end{cases} \tag{10}$$

From all possible assignments α_k between the detected geodesic paths and the limbs $\mathcal{L}_j$, the one $\hat{\alpha}$ that minimizes the total assignment distance is selected (Eq. 11). In Fig. 5, the path distances and assignments for a given set of geodesic paths and their hypotheses are shown.

$$\hat{\alpha} = \underset{\alpha_k \in \{\alpha_0 ... \alpha_K\}}{\operatorname{argmin}} \sum_{j=0}^{4} \Omega(\alpha_k(j), j) \tag{11}$$

2.3 Body Part Segmentation and Skeleton Fitting

The subsequent steps are behind the scope of this work but briefly mentioned. Having labeled the geodesic paths, it would we possible to adapt the bones of

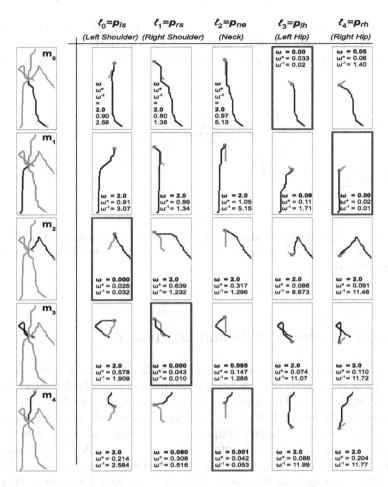

Fig. 5. Detected paths (very left column) towards geodesic maximum positions m_i (red circles) are compared (ω^*) to hypotheses-paths (right columns) defined by the torso center, the geodesic maximum and the limb start point ℓ_j (blue dots). They are also compared (ω^{-1}) to previously labeled limb-paths (not shown). Both distances are combined (ω) and the paths are assigned to the limbs so that the cumulative distance is a minimum (red boxes).

a hierarchical skeleton model to the 3D-points that are located along the paths. This is, however, for two reasons inaccurate. The first reason is that paths only reflect the surface of the human body, whereas the bones should be located inside. The second reason is that the paths describe the shortest connection between the points of the body surface. When a limb is bent, the path thus does not run through the center but close to the border of the limb. This can be seen in Fig. 8. So, instead of fitting a skeleton model to the paths, we utilize them to initialize a watershed based body part segmentation (Fig. 6b). Within each body part, the 3D points are shifted inwards the body using the surface normal, which is obtained from the graph (Fig. 6c). Using the Cyclic coordinate descent method [13], a hierarchical skeleton model is adapted to the shifted points (Fig. 6c) by minimizing the point-to-line distances between the bones and the shifted points.

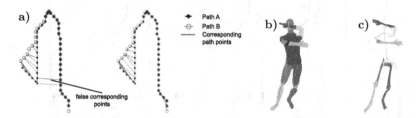

Fig. 6. a) Corresponding path points using nearest neighbor search (left) and viterbi (right) b) Limb paths (white lines) and segmented body parts. c) 3D-points shifted inwards the body.

3   Experimental Results and Discussion

In order to evaluate our pose estimation approach, sequences of synthetic depth images have been generated by rendering an animated 3D-character into an OpenGL depth buffer. The approach has the advantage that the exact ground truth joint positions are known and can therefore be compared to the determined ones. In total, 16 different sequences containing various poses have been created which corresponds to a total number of approx. N=25000 frames. In each sequence, the character is the only rendered object and not more than 45 degrees turned away from the camera. Our skeleton model consists of 16 joints (three for each arm and leg, two for the torso, the neck and the head). Let $z_i(t)$ denote the absolute positions of each joint at frame t. Given the ground truth joint positions $y_i(t)$, we compute in each frame the mean Euclidean distance error (Eq. 12) and the maximum error (Eq. 13).

$$e_m(t) = \frac{1}{16} \sum_{i=1}^{16} |z_i(t) - y_i(t)|_2 \tag{12}$$

$$e_h(t) = \max|z_i(t) - y_i(t)|_2 \, \forall i = 1 \dots 16 \tag{13}$$

$$e_z(i) = \frac{1}{N} \sum_{t=1}^{N} |z_i(t) - y_i(t)|, \forall t = 1 \dots N \tag{14}$$

In Fig. 7, the courses of both errors are shown for a single sequence. It can be seen that the mean distance is about 2cm . The maximum error rises up to 10cm. For other sequences the maximum error raised up to 28cm, which is mainly due to an inaccurate fitted elbow joint position or occurs, when the user's arm points directly to the camera. In this case, there are too few target points for the skeleton fitting and the kinematic chain remains unchanged. For some selected time stamps in 7 the animated 3D-characters are also shown. One can see that the estimated pose (depicted by the blue skeleton) matches the ground truth pose (black skeleton) even in cases of self occlusion.

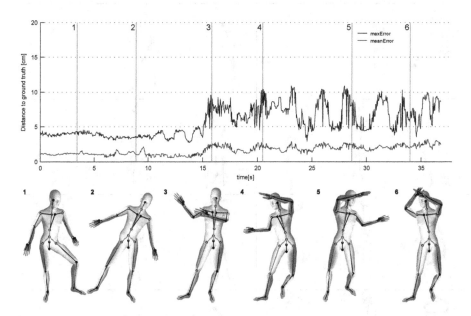

Fig. 7. Top: Mean (blue graph) and maximum (black) joint error for a single sequence. Bottom: Selected poses with ground truth skeleton (black) and the estimated one (blue).

In Fig. 8 more qualitative results of our approach are shown. For several poses, the rendered 3D character together with the estimated and ground truth pose, the geodesic distances and the 3D points of the segmented body parts to which the skeleton is fitted are shown. There are, however, some poses that cannot estimated by our approach. When the user is rotated too far away from the camera, the torso model registration fails. Another case occurs, when the limbs are too close to the torso. In this case, the geodesic paths are not detected. A possible solution would be to perform a local model based search in order to update the skeleton model.

In Fig. 9, we have further computed the per-joint errors (Eq. 14) averaged over all frames. It is between 0.6cm for the head and 3.8cm for the feet and elbows. For comparison, the authors of [9], who have also used geodesic distances, reported averaged per-joint errors between 7cm (shoulders) and 20cm (feets) and an averaged joint distance of $\bar{e}_{Kin} = 10.84$cm. However, these errors are for real depth data. Another graph-based approach was provided by the authors of [14] with reported per-joint distances between 3cm (neck) and 6.8cm (elbow).

Fig. 8. Qualitative results of the pose estimation. The first column for each pose depicts the 3D-character, the ground truth (black) and the estimated pose (blue skeleton). The extracted geodesic paths and distances are shown in the second column. The results of the body part segmentation are shown in the third column.

Our method is suitable for an online processing (20fps). The HMM based path labeling is by far the most computationally expensive step, but can be parallelized for each detected path. Since our approach is a generative approach

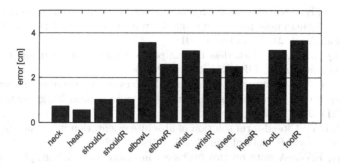

Fig. 9. Per-joint errors averaged over all frames.

that does not need any pre-trained classifiers, the pose estimation is not limited to previously trained poses. A major benefit is that it does not rely on temporal data and as a result cannot get stucked in local minima. Our approach extends prior pose estimation methods based on geodesic distances by extracting the geodesic paths not only to a single but multiple points which are obtained by a torso model registration. As a result, we do not need a specific pose (often T-pose) in which the initial positions of the limbs are determined. Currently, we have extended our method for generating synthetic depth data in order to further examine the influences of parameters like camera position, noise or different character meshes. In a future work, the geodesic distances computed to multiple points will directly be used to segment the individual body parts.

Acknowledgments. This work was supported by Transregional Collaborative Research Centre SFB/TRR 62 (Companion-Technology for Cognitive Technical Systems) funded by the German Research Foundation (DFG).

References

1. Le Ly, D., Saxena, A., Lipson, H.: Pose estimation from a single depth image for arbitrary kinematic skeletons. CoRR (2011)
2. Jaeggli, T., Koller-Meier, E., Gool, L.: Learning generative models for multi-activity body pose estimation. Int. J. Comput. Vision **2**, 121–134 (2009)
3. Shotton, J., Girshick, R., Fitzgibbon, A., Sharp, T., Cook, M., Finocchio, M., Moore, R., Kohli, P., Criminisi, A., Kipman, A., Blake, A.: Efficient human pose estimation from single depth images. IEEE Transactions on Pattern Analysis and Machine Intelligence **35**(12), 2821–2840 (2013)
4. Chang, J.Y., Nam, S.W.: Fast Random-Forest-Based Human Pose Estimation Using a Multi-scale and Cascade Approach **35**(6) (2013)
5. Pons-Moll, G., Baak, A., Helten, T., Muller, M., Seidel, H.-P., Rosenhahn, B.: Multisensor-fusion for 3d full-body human motion capture. In: CVPR, pp. 663–670 (2010)
6. Chen, D.C.Y., Fookes, C.B.: Labelled silhouettes for human pose estimation. In: Int. C. on Inform. Science, Signal Proc. a their App. (2010)

7. Srinivasan, K., Porkumaran, K., Sainarayanan, G.: Skin colour segmentation based 2d and 3d human pose modelling using discrete wavelet transform. Pattern Recognit. Image Anal. **21**(4), 740–753 (2011)
8. Liang, Q., Miao, Z.: Markerless human pose estimation using image features and extremal contour. In: ISPACS, pp. 1–4 (2010)
9. Schwarz, L.A., Mkhitaryan, A., Mateus, D., Navab, N.: Human skeleton tracking from depth data using geodesic distances and optical flow. Image Vision Comput. **30**(3), 217–226 (2012)
10. Horn, B.K.P.: Closed-form solution of absolute orientation using unit quaternions. J. of the Optical Society of America **4**, 629–642 (1987)
11. Dijkstra, E.W.: A note on two problems in connexion with graphs. Numerische Mathematik **1**(1), 269–271 (1959)
12. Viterbi, A.J.: Error bounds for convolutional codes and an asymptotically optimum decoding algorithm. IEEE Transactions on Information Theory **13**(2), 260–269 (1967)
13. Wang, L.-C.T., Chen, C.C.: A combined optimization method for solving the inverse kinematics problems of mechanical manipulators. IEEE Transactions on Robotics and Automation **7**(4), 489–499 (1991)
14. Rther, M., Straka, M., Hauswiesner, S., Bischof, H.: Skeletal graph based human pose estimation in real-time, pp. 69.1–69.12 (2011). doi:10.5244/C.25.69

A Graph Based People Silhouette Segmentation Using Combined Probabilities Extracted from Appearance, Shape Template Prior, and Color Distributions

Christophe Coniglio[1,2]([⊠]), Cyril Meurie[1,2], Olivier Lézoray[3],
and Marion Berbineau[1,2]

[1] Univ Lille Nord de France, 59000 Lille, France
coniglio.christophe@ifsttar.fr
[2] IFSTTAR, COSYS, LEOST, 59650 Villeneuve d'Ascq, France
[3] Normandie Univ., UNICAEN, ENSICAEN, GREYC UMR CNRS 6072,
Caen, France

Abstract. In this paper, we present an approach for the segmentation of people silhouettes in images. Since in real-world images estimating pixel probabilities to belong to people or background is difficult, we propose to optimally combine several ones. A local window classifier based on SVMs with Histograms of Oriented Gradients features estimates probabilities from pixels' appearance. A shape template prior is also computed over a set of training images. From these two probability maps, color distributions relying on color histograms and Gaussian Mixture Models are estimated and the associated probability maps are derived. All these probability maps are optimally combined into a single one with weighting coefficients determined by a genetic algorithm. This final probability map is used within a graph-cut to extract accurately the silhouette. Experimental results are provided on both the INRIA Static Person Dataset and BOSS European project and show the benefit of the approach.

1 Introduction

In video surveillance applications, the extraction of people silhouette is a well-known bottleneck to efficiently perform tasks such as people recognition [1,2]. If such applications have been very popular in the computer vision community, nowadays other application fields also need such a people silhouette segmentation. A recent example comes with clothes segmentation [3,4] that has received much interest from the fashion industry. Indeed, commercially, it can be used in online cloth retail portals where people can search various clothes from image examples. In a more general way, since people silhouettes describe human appearance, it is an important step towards understanding the human-based content in images. Anyway, to well operate, all these applications need precise people silhouette extraction. Indeed, any object not belonging to people but incorporated in the extracted silhouette can strongly degrade the performance of the intended applications.

© Springer International Publishing Switzerland 2015
S. Battiato et al. (Eds.): ACIVS 2015, LNCS 9386, pp. 299–310, 2015.
DOI: 10.1007/978-3-319-25903-1_26

Traditionally, people silhouette segmentation is performed in videos with standard motion-based background subtraction strategies [5]. With static images, detection-oriented methods have emerged and make extensive use of machine learning together with efficient appearance representations (such as Histograms of Oriented Gradients -HOG) [6,7]. The result of such a detection is a bounding-box (BB) with the detected people inside. However, this does not directly provide the silhouette segmentation that has to be further estimated inside the obtained bounding box. Such an extraction of people silhouette is therefore less easy than with videos [8]. In [9] the authors propose a global approach that consists in analyzing links between structural elements in images formed by regions of pixels. A process based on color and texture features allowing to link these structural elements is also proposed. In [10,11] the authors propose to use several characteristics of bounding boxes (such as the fact that people are centered in BB images). Thus, it is easier to define a template driven to delimit the position of people. In [11] the authors propose to extend the previous method with part-based templates and extract the person silhouette with combined graph-cuts. In [10], a local window SVM classifier from HOG features is combined with edge detection to enhance an iterative graph-cut segmentation. To conclude, in the context of video-surveillance, one can notice that very few studies deal with people silhouette segmentation but solely focus on the re-identification step. This is probably explained by the fact that realizing a ground truth silhouette segmentation dataset is tedious and costly in time. Thus, few ground truths are available in the literature, that is why, it seems important to point out that we have achieved a consequent ground truth of people silhouettes for the BOSS database [12]. In this paper, we propose an approach towards the automatic extraction of people silhouette from bounding box images with a graph based segmentation using combined probabilities extracted from appearance, shape template prior, and color distributions all optimized with a genetic algorithm (GA).

2   Proposed Method

Our method is designed to extract precisely people silhouettes in images in the form of a bounding box and obtained using basic techniques of person detection (such as Histograms of Oriented Gradients -HOG) [6]. To perform the segmentation, we need to estimate a probability map that provides the class memberships of each pixel for the two classes people/background to discriminate. This probability map is used to initialize the capacities in a graph-cut segmentation. As we already mentioned it, estimating an accurate probability map is difficult. Therefore, on the one hand, our contribution consists in developing a new method to estimate probability maps based on local small windows probability appearance (as illustrated in Figure 2). Each local small window is described by its own learned classification characterized by optimized HOG features. On the other hand, we propose to combine our probability maps with those obtained by the following standard techniques: template shape prior probabilities that are estimated from a learning database in the form of a mean shape and two color distribution probabilities obtained by color histograms and Gaussian Mixture Models (initialized by our probability map and the probability obtained by the template shape prior). The resulting six probability maps are combined altogether with weighting factors optimally determined with a genetic algorithm (GA). Figure 1 sums up the whole approach. Contrary to the works presented in [11], our method does not only use one information (part based templates) but the previous six cues to initialize the graph cut segmentation. In opposition to [10], we prefer to detect a probability to belong to people or background, instead of detecting possible edges of people in local small windows.

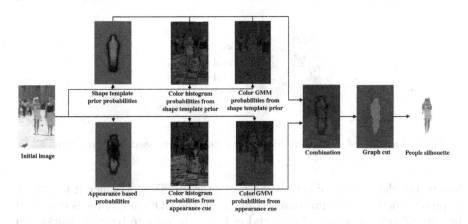

Fig. 1. Synopsis of the proposed approach.

2.1 Appearance Based Probabilities

In [6], the authors have proposed to classify local windows inside a bounding-box into two classes (people or not people) using HOG descriptor combined with a single SVM classifier. We will use a similar but different method and we will classify local windows inside the bounding-box using several SVM classifiers (one per considered local window). With such an approach, the classification process is not anymore performed globally but at the local window level in order to classify any piece of people as being or not a piece of the persons silhouette (see Figure 3). Given the estimations from the local windows' classifications, we can obtain an appearance based probability map by averaging the predictions of overlapping local windows for each image pixel. In order to have the finest probability results per pixel, we consider all the possible local windows with an offset of one pixel. To build the HOG descriptor, each local window is divided into blocks and each block is divided into cells (see Figure 2). HOG features are extracted from cells and a HOG descriptor is the vector of the cells' HOGs features. To obtain better HOG descriptors, we consider an overlapping between cells, so that each cell contributes to several blocks' descriptors. A SVM classifier classifies each HOG descriptor extracted from local windows, therefore it is necessary to have an individual training for each local window. During these training steps, a particular attention is necessary for the background label. Indeed in the case where the person to extract is surrounded by other people (for example in a crowed environment), it is preferable to ignore this example during the training since this can lower the generalization capabilities of the SVM classifier. Given all the obtained classifications from the overlapping local windows, an average of all pixel class memberships is performed to determine the final labeling. In this paper we will show such results with colors ranging from blue (background class) to red (people class). In order to reduce the changes of HOG descriptors due to brightness changes between images, a pre-processing step normalizes the HOG descriptor per block. Finally, since we do not have any preconceived

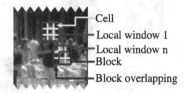

Fig. 2. Example of cut into local windows, cells, blocks, and block overlapping.

idea on the ideal setting of both HOG descriptor and SVM classifier, it is difficult to predict the best configuration setting. First, the HOG descriptor is described by sizes of local windows, blocks, and cells, by the overlap between blocks and by the number of bins of the HOG feature and the type of normalization (L_1 or L_2 Norms). Second, a SVM classifier can use different kernels (linear, polynomial, Gaussian) that have several parameters. We could arbitrarily fix all these parameters but this does not ensure that we will have the best possible configuration. In addition, if we use large HOG descriptors this amounts to use larger local windows and because of the final averaging, the classification is much less efficient on edges. A compromise has to be found. To optimally determine the latter, we have determined the best parameters by the use of a genetic algorithm. For the SVM, each training is performed with cross-validation and grid-search to determine the best parameters. To compare the different possible configurations of the HOG descriptor, we perform a segmentation with graph cuts (see section 2.5 for details) from the estimated probability map to obtain a final segmentation in two classes (people or background). Figure 3 shows the approach. The obtained segmentations are compared with the $F_{measure}$ score and are shown in Table 1. Table 1 resumes the five best settings for the local windows HOG based classifier. The best size of cell turns to be of 5 pixels with 9-bins histograms. Block overlapping is not of interest and mid-size local windows and blocks are sufficient. This is in concordance with the remark we made before on the blurring effect obtained with too large HOG descriptors that are averaged. We have retained finally the best parameter configuration shown in Table 1. An example of result is shown in Figure 4.

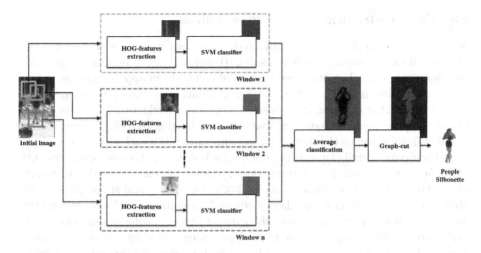

Fig. 3. Synopsis of the strategy employed to evaluate the best parameter settings of local windows HOG based classifier.

Table 1. The five best parameter settings for the estimation of appearance based probabilities with local windows classifier. Training realized on training set and scores obtained on the test set of the *INRIA Static Person Dataset*.

SVM kernel	local-window size	block size	block overlap size	Cell size	HOG #Bins	Type of Normalization	Recall	Precision	$F_{measure}$
RBF	8	8	∅	4	9	∅	0.765	0.865	0.806
RBF	10	10	∅	5	9	L_2 Norm	0.76	0.865	0.804
RBF	5	∅	∅	5	9	L_2 Norm	0.757	0.862	0.802
RBF	15	10	5	5	9	L_2 Norm	0.792	0.823	0.799
RBF	12	12	∅	6	9	L_2 Norm	0.756	0.858	0.798

2.2 Shape Template Prior Based Probabilities

The use of shape template priors is common in literature [13,14]. Indeed, we can notice that images of people, in the form of bounding-boxes, are generally centered on the person. This comes from the fact that bounding-boxes are mostly results of a people detection process based on machine learning trained with positives images for people in the center of the image. We propose to use a shape template prior based probability template in contrast to a binary shape template. In the case of binary shape template, one applies directly the template on the image as a mask. The use of a probability shape template is more appropriate for our choice of segmentation method using graph cuts that needs such a membership information. Our shape template prior based probabilities is obtained from an averaging of all the ground-truth shapes in the training set of the *INRIA Static Person Dataset*, see Figure 4. This prior is therefore computed only once.

2.3 Color Distributions Based Probabilities

As it can be seen in Figure 4, the obtained appearance and shape prior probability maps do not provide very fine results. To enhance these results, we propose to rely on color distributions given the initial results from appearance and shape prior probability maps.These two latter probability maps are used to make two lists of pixels that describe two classes (people and background). To be added to a list, a pixel needs to have a probability of belonging to a class upper than a thresholding defined by the final genetic optimization. For each given list, we estimate their color distributions using both color histograms (one per color channel with 256 bins) or Gaussian Mixture Models (using 5 Gaussians to describe each class). Given these two distributions for both appearance and shape prior probability maps, we estimate the class memberships using the color distributions. This provides four additional probability maps: two with color distributions estimated from color histograms for both appearance and shape prior probability maps and two with GMMs estimated for both appearance and shape prior probability maps. Figure 4 shows an example of the obtained color distributions based probabilities. One can see that the obtained results are much more fine than with the appearance and shape prior probability maps. However since only color is used, the colors that describe a person can also be found in the background and identified as people. This shows that not a single probability map is sufficient and we have to make the most of all of them.

Fig. 4. Example of probability map estimation. From left to right: initial image, appearance based probabilities, color histogram based probabilities from appearance based probabilities, Color GMM based probabilities from appearance based probabilities, shape template prior based probabilities, color histogram based probabilities from shape template prior based probabilities and GMM based probabilities from shape template prior based probabilities.

2.4 Combination of the Probability Maps

Thanks to previous steps, we have six probability maps about the position of people (appearance and shape prior probability maps and four derived color distributions based probabilities). In this step, we propose to combine these six informations into a single one. We affect a coefficient $C(k)$ for each probability map and we calculate the final pixels probabilities of the two classes (people and background) by:

$$P^{class}(p_i) = \sum_{k=1}^{6} C(k) \cdot P_k^{class}(p_i) \text{ with } \sum_{k=1}^{6} C(k) = 1 \tag{1}$$

where $P_k^{class}(p_i)$ denotes the conditional estimated probability from the k-th map for a given *class* among background and people. As our method needs a training step to define the shape template and train all the SVM classifiers with local windows, we also use this training step to set the weighting coefficients on the same training set. To ensure that the coefficients we obtain are optimally chosen, we use a genetic algorithm. With such an algorithm, we represent the coefficient setting problem as an optimization problem. The genetic algorithm is based on three steps (crossover, mutation and selection) that execute in loops with random initialization for the start. These steps are performed on a population of chromosomes. A chromosome correspond to the coding of the six coefficients $C(k)$ of our proposed method. We have used the $F_{measure}$ score as a fitness measure to evaluate each chromosome in the selection step. Our method is fast, the chromosome being relatively small, and the optimization loop quickly converges with a population of almost 100 chromosomes. Results of best selected chromosomes will be presented in Section 3.

2.5   Graph Cut Segmentation

The final step consists to classify into two classes (people and background) the image given the estimation of probabilities obtained from the combination of probability maps. To do so, we use graph cuts [15]. Graph-cut techniques are among the most powerful methods that extract foreground from background. Graph-cuts enable object segmentation with the optimization of a discrete energy function defined on a binary label set $L = \{0, 1\}$ by computing a minimum cut on the graph associated to the image. The key task is the proper definition of this energy in order to capture the properties of object regions and those of boundaries between them. We consider a graph $G = (V, E)$ witch is composed of $|V|$ nodes (the pixels of the image), where each node p_i is assigned a label $l_i \in L$ and $|E|$ edges (inferred from 8-connectivity between pixels). To classify each node of the graph into two classes, we consider the following energy:

$$\hat{i} = \underset{l \in F}{\arg\min} \left(\sum_{p_i \in V} W^{l_i}(p_i) + t \sum_{p_i \in V} \sum_{p_j \in N_{p_i}} S(p_i, p_j) \cdot \delta_{l_i \neq l_j} \right) \tag{2}$$

The best segmentation (clustering into the two classes people and background) corresponds to the minimum of the energy $\hat{i}$, in the set F of all possible labeling solutions. The first term of the energy is defined as $W^{l_i}(p_i) = -\log(P^{l_i}(p_i))$. It uses the probabilities of each pixel to belong to the l_i class (people or background), and is obtained from the weighted combination of six different probability maps. The second term is obtained from the product of two terms.

The term $\delta_{l_i \neq l_j}$ is the Potts prior that encourages piecewise-constant labeling, and N_{p_i} is the set of 8-connected neighbors of p_i in the grid graph associated to the image. The term $S(p_i, p_j)$ expresses a similarity measure between both pixels p_i and p_j and is given by:

$$S(p_i, p_j) = exp\left(-\frac{d(p_i, p_j)}{2\theta^2}\right) \cdot \frac{1}{dist(p_i, p_j)} \text{ and } d(p_i, p_j) = \sqrt{\sum_{c=1}^{3}(p_i^c - p_j^c)^2} \quad (3)$$

where the $dist(pi, pj)$ is the Euclidean distance between the pixels p_i and p_j. The coefficient θ is a parameter genetically optimized to adjusting the sensitivity to intensity difference between neighboring pixels and $d(p_i, p_j)$ denotes the sum of distance between the color channels p_i^c and p_j^c associated to pixels p_i and p_j. The optimization is done with the min-cut/max-flow implementation of [16]. The result of graph cut labeling is a binary image where each pixel has been assigned to one class among background and people. Therefore, we obtain the final people silhouette.

3   Experimental Results

Our method has been evaluated on two databases. Each database was separated into two sets of images with 2/3 of positive image for the training set and 1/3 positive image for the test set. The first database is composed of 390 positive images (bounding-boxes of 96×160 pixels with a people in the center with a wide range of different background such as crowded environments) and 150 negative images (bounding-boxes of 96×160 pixels without people inside) from the INRIA Static Person Dataset [17] (this database contains only static images). We have used the people ground-truth segmentation provided by [13] to define the reference people segmentations. The second database is from the BOSS European project database [12] and contains video sequences. We have selected a video sequence that contains several difficulties due to real-world transportation systems such as strong brightness changes or many shadows. On the chosen sequence, there are twelve persons that move in front of the camera inside a train. We have used the Dalal's algorithm [6] (with parameters tuned by a genetic algorithm) to extract people bounding-boxes from the video sequence. Our database contain 453 positive images (bounding-boxes of 96×160 pixels) and 200 negative images (bounding-boxes of 96×160 pixels without people, taken in the same video sequence).

The proposed method contains three separate training (shape template prior, local windows classifier and genetic algorithm for probabilities combination). We begin by training separately on the training set, the shape template and the local windows classifier. For the local windows classifier, we have already defined the best parameters settings for the HOG descriptor, and the training step consists only to train each SVM classifier on local windows. Then we use the genetic algorithm on the obtained (and derived from color distributions) probability maps with the training set.

Table 2 shows parameters and weighting coefficients defined by the genetic algorithm. We can see several differences on the results between the two databases (INRIA and BOSS). In case of INRIA database, probability maps are close altogether. Concerning the BOSS database, the most important probability maps are those obtained from HOG local windows and the two GMM. Then the derived color histogram probabilities are not as much essential. These differences are certainly due to the facility to detect the background in the BOSS database.

Table 2. Parameters and weighting coefficients given by genetic algorithm for combination step

	Database	
	INRIA	BOSS
Appearance based probabilities	17.6%	27.5%
Color histograms probabilities from Appearance based probabilities	10.5%	2.3%
GMM probabilities from Appearance based probabilities	20.7%	24.8%
Shape template prior Probability	24.7%	14.3%
Color histograms probabilities from Shape template prior Probability	15.3%	3.5 %
Color GMM probabilities from Shape template prior Probability	11.2%	27.5%
Thresholding for color distribution (% of belonging probabilities)	18%	25%
Coefficient θ in graph-cut segmentation	56.6	22.6

The processing time obtained with a non-optimized C++ program is a full process of 180ms by image on a 1.8 GHz Intel Core i5. Table 3 shows the $F_{measure}$ results with our method compared to recent literature [10, 11, 18]. The fitness measure used to perform the genetic optimization is the $F_{measure}$ score:

$$F_{measure} = 2 \cdot \frac{\text{precision} \cdot \text{recall}}{\text{precision} + \text{recall}} \tag{4}$$

$$\text{recall} = \frac{TP}{TP + FN} \text{ and precision} = \frac{TP}{TP + FP} \tag{5}$$

Where TP is true positive pixels, FN is false negative pixels and FP is false positive pixels of the initial image.

First of all, on INRIA database, our method obtains a good score ($F_{measure}$ of 0.860) upper than [10] ($F_{measure}$ of 0.841) which uses only one appearance based feature. This confirms our interest to combine different cues to estimate the position of people and initialize the graph-cut. The method proposed in [11] uses a part-based template combined with a graph cut results for each part. This method allows to increase the precision of the people template. Even if our proposed method obtains a close score ($F_{measure}$ of 0.860) compared to [11] ($F_{measure}$ of 0.885), our future works will consist to use a similar technique to improve our template-driven method and further increase our results. We also think it is important to mention that there is hardly very few works on segmentation of people silhouette with quantitative results on static images. In [19], we

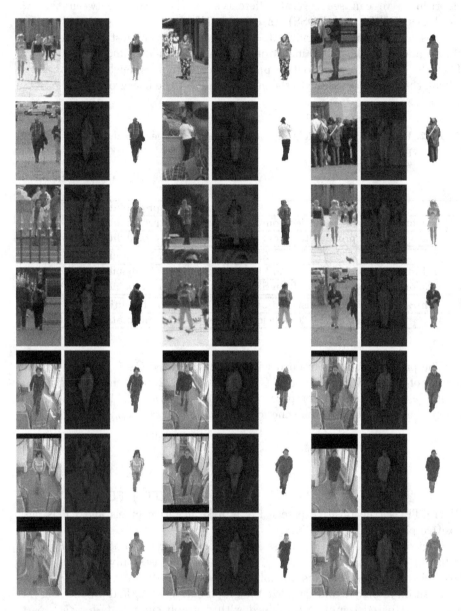

Fig. 5. Four first rows present results on INRIA Static Dataset and last rows on BOSS Dataset. Each row presents three silhouette extraction results. Each result shows the initial image (left), the combined probability map (people in red and background in blue) in the middle and the segmentation obtained with the proposed method (right).

have proposed another approach exploiting the video information, for which the $F_{measure}$ was 0.89. Our proposed approach performs better without any temporal information use. The gap between the $F_{measure}$ score on the INRIA and the BOSS databases can be explained by the uniformity and the complexity of the background. Figure 5 shows segmentation results on the two databases. We see that people silhouettes are well segmented even in crowded environments. Nevertheless, the border delineation between people and background is not always perfect and there is still some room for improvement.

Table 3. Segmentation results ($F_{measure}$) on INRIA and BOSS databases

	Database	
	INRIA	BOSS
MIGNIOT 2011[11]	0.885	-
MIGNIOT 2013[10]	0.841	-
SHARMA 2007[18]	0.820	-
Proposed method	**0.860**	**0.911**

4   Conclusion

In this paper, we have proposed to use a graph based segmentation to extract the silhouette of people from bounding boxes. To do so we have proposed to combine several probability maps estimated from cues relying on appearance (with HOG descriptors extracted on local windows classified by different SVM classifiers), on a shape template prior and on derived probabilities from color distribution (color histograms or GMMs). The weighting coefficients as well as the parameters of the appearance local window classifiers have been optimally determined with a genetic algorithm. Experimental results have shown good results comparable to the actual state-of-the-art on the standard INRIA Static person dataset, and very good results on the real-world BOSS dataset. Future works will aim at enhancing the people silhouette border delineation by improving our template-driven method and integrating a superpixel segmentation into the graph-cut clustering.

References

1. Mori, G., Ren, X., Efros, A.A., Malik, J.: Recovering human body configurations: combining segmentation and recognition. In: Computer Society Conference on Computer Vision and Pattern Recognition, ser. CVPR 2004, pp. 326–333 (2004)
2. Farenzena, M., Bazzani, L., Perina, A., Murino, V., Cristani, M.: Person re-identification by symmetry-driven accumulation of local features. In: IEEE Conference on Computer Vision and Pattern Recognition (CVPR), June 2010
3. Yang, M., Yu, K.: Real-time clothing recognition in surveillance videos. In: ICIP, pp. 2937–2940. IEEE (2011)

4. Gallagher, A., Chen, T.: Clothing cosegmentation for recognizing people. In: IEEE Conference on Computer Vision and Pattern Recognition, pp. 1–8, June 2008
5. Stauffer, C., Grimson, W.E.L.: Adaptive background mixture models forreal-time tracking. In: Computer Vision and Pattern Recognition, vol. 2, pp. 2246–2252 (1999)
6. Dalal, N., Triggs, B.: Histograms of oriented gradients for human detection. In: International Conference on Computer Vision & Pattern Recognition, vol. 2, pp. 886–893 (2005)
7. Zhu, Q., Avidan, S., Yeh, M.-C., Cheng, K.-T.: Fast human detection using a cascade of histograms of oriented gradients. In: CVPR 2006, pp. 1491–1498 (2006)
8. Gong, S., Cristanio, M., Yan, S., Loy, C.: Person re-identification. Springer (2014)
9. Jojic, N., Perina, A., Cristani, M., Murino, V., Frey, B.: Stel component analysis: modeling spatial correlations in image class structure. In: IEEE Conference on Computer Vision and Pattern Recognition, CVPR 2009, pp. 2044–2051 (2009)
10. Migniot, C., Bertolino, P., Chassery, J.-M.: Iterative human segmentation from detection windows using contour segment analysis. In: VISAPP 2013 - Proceedings of the International Conference on Computer Vision Theory and Applications, pp. 405–412 (2013)
11. Migniot, C., Bertolino, P., Chassery, J.-M.: Automatic people segmentation with a template-driven graph cut. In: International Conference on Image Processing (2011)
12. Boss europeen project (on bord wireless secured video surveillance). http://www.multitel.be/image/research-development/research-projects/boss.php
13. Migniot, C., Bertolino, P., Chassery, J.-M.: Contour segment analysis for human silhouette pre-segmentation. In: 5th International Conference on Computer Vision Theory and Applications (VISAPP 2010), Angers, France, May 2010
14. Lin, Z., Davis, L.S.: Shape-based human detection and segmentation via hierarchical part-template matching. IEEE Trans. Pattern Anal. Mach. Intell., pp. 604–618 (2010)
15. Boykov, Y., Jolly, M.: Interactive graph cuts for optimal boundary region segmentation of objects in n-d images. In: IEEE International Conference on Computer Vision, vol. 1, pp. 105–112 (2001)
16. Boykov, Y., Kolmogorov, V.: An experimental comparison of min-cut/max-flow algorithms for energy minimization in vision. IEEE Transactions on Pattern Analysis and Machine Intelligence **26**(9), 1124–1137 (2004)
17. Inria person dataset. http://pascal.inrialpes.fr/data/human/
18. Sharma, V., Davis, J.: Integrating appearance and motion cues for simultaneous detection and segmentation of pedestrians. In: Computer Vision ICCV IEEE, pp. 1–8. IEEE (2007)
19. Coniglio, C., Meurie, C., Lzoray, O., Berbineau, M.: A genetically optimized graph-based people extraction method for embedded transportation systems real conditions. In: 17th International Conference on Intelligent Transportation Systems, pp. 1589–1595 (2014)

Improved Region-Based Kalman Filter for Tracking Body Joints and Evaluating Gait in Surveillance Videos

Binu M. Nair[(✉)] and Kimberly D. Kendricks

College of Sciences, University of Nevada-Las Vegas, Las Vegas, NV, USA
{binu.nair,kimberly.kendricks}@unlv.edu

Abstract. We propose an Improved Region-based Kalman filter to estimate fine precise body joint trajectories to facilitate gait analysis from
low resolution surveillance cameras. This is important because existing
pose estimation and tracking techniques obtain noisy and discrete trajectories which are insufficient for gait analysis. Our objective is to obtain
a close approximation to the true sinusoidal/non-linear transition of the
body joint locations between consecutive time instants. The proposed
filter models the non-linear transitions along the sinusoidal trajectory,
and incorporates a refining technique to determine the fine precision
estimates of the body joint location using prior information from the
individual's rough pose. The proposed technique is evaluated on an outdoor low-resolution gait dataset categorized by individuals wearing a
weighted vest (simulating a threat) or no weighted vest. Experimental
results and comparisons with similar representative methods prove the
accuracy and precision of the proposed filter for fine-precision body joint
tracking. With respect to analyzing gait for threat identification, the proposed scheme exhibits better accuracy than state of the art pose discrete
estimates.

Keywords: Fine precision tracking · Gait analysis · Surveillance ·
Kalman filter

1 Introduction

Research in gait analysis from video sequences in recent years have primarily
been focused on computing efficient gait signatures for person identification.
These signatures are often computed from silhouettes or binary masks obtained
from segmentation of video sequences having stationary background [9]. But, in
real world scenarios, the extraction of silhouettes require complex foreground segmentation and may contain noise which affects gait features. In contrast, another
approach considers the human pose at every frame and estimates continuous
joint trajectories, from which gait features can be extracted. This is possible
with marker-less motion capture systems or VICON capture data where pose
estimates are accurate and joint trajectories are smooth enough for potential

© Springer International Publishing Switzerland 2015
S. Battiato et al. (Eds.): ACIVS 2015, LNCS 9386, pp. 311–322, 2015.
DOI: 10.1007/978-3-319-25903-1_27

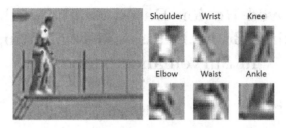

Fig. 1. Illustration of specific joints on the human body to be tracked [11].

analysis of an individual's gait cycle for person identification or clinical studies. However, when low resolution surveillance footage is considered, the pose estimates obtained, tend to be very noisy and highly discretized, due to view-point variation, camera motion, blurred pixel regions and scale of person, thereby making them insufficient for further gait analysis [11].

In this manuscript, we propose a fine-tuning and tracking mechanism by which continuous body joint trajectories can be estimated from low resolution imagery with prior information of a rough estimate of the individual's pose at each frame. The end result will lead to joint trajectories which are analogous to those obtained using marker-less motion capture data. This would facilitate the extraction of gait features and its analysis for different applications. The application presented here, is that of classifying threats (simulated by a person wearing a hidden weighted vest) and non-threats by analyzing gait features extracted from these trajectories. Our contribution is as follows:

- Development of the prediction phase of the Improved Region-based Kalman filter (IRKF) to predict the transitions of a body joint by updating the state of the filter using non-linear region matching criteria.
- Development of the correction phase of the Improved Region-based Kalman filter to characterize the non-linear transitions of a body joint between consecutive frames using a Gaussian distribution model.
- Development of a novel framework using the Improved Region-based Kalman filter to estimate the spatial image coordinates of the body joint using the discrete pose estimates as prior information.

To illustrate the tracking mechanism, we track six relevant body joints such as the shoulder, elbow,wrist, hip, knee and ankle across the low-resolution scene as shown in Figure 1.

2   Related Work

Similar work in the area of pose tracking has been researched and implemented in markerless motion capture systems, most of them are restricted to indoor scenarios which use either 3D sensors such as the Kinect [14] or a multi-camera environment where 3D joint locations can be estimated accurately [7].

These primarily have been restricted to usage in clinical studies and other indoor gait analysis applications. However, since these techniques require high resolution imagery or depth information associated with each pixel, their use in outdoor scenarios has been limited. So, a pose estimation algorithm based purely on image and video sequences is required.

In image-based pose estimation techniques, one of most popular and state of art method is the Flexible mixture of parts model, proposed by Yang and Ramanan [16] where a variety of oriented body parts are modeled by a family of affine-warped templates with each template consisting of non-oriented pictorial structures. When the parts model is applied on very low resolution body image using pre-trained models, the body region needs to be scaled at least two to three times more in order to get a acceptable pose estimate. Often, these pose estimates are very discrete in nature and noisy, and provide only a rough indicator where the body joints are located [11]. Pose estimation in video sequences have also been considered in Ramakrishna et al. [12] where an occlusion aware algorithm tracked human body pose by considering symmetrical pairs to account for occlusion. Although these state of the art techniques show an increased accuracy on datasets such as the Buffy Dataset [5] and the Image Parse dataset [13], the performance on very low-resolution imagery is not yet evaluated and their use is limited to high resolution imagery. Xavier et al. [3] proposed a pose-Kmeans algorithm by which multiple pose estimates taken over time are merged to obtain accurate pose estimates at each frame of the sequence. This post-processing technique is not suitable for surveillance which requires computation online and in a streaming fashion.

Recent analysis on the tracking of body joints in low resolution was done [10,11] where multiple variations of the Kalman filter were used to refine the discrete pose estimates in real time. However, the algorithm approximated the transition between body joints in successive frames as a linear function and updated measurements based on the optical flow or a region-based matching scheme. In this work, we propose an improved version of the region-based Kalman filter which models the transition as a gaussian distribution.

3   Improved Region-Based Kalman Filter (IRKF)

The Improved Region-based Kalman filter, like the Region based Kalman filter [11], has a prediction phase and a correction phase. For modeling the transition of a particular body joint, the state of the filter should be updated in a non-linear fashion and this corresponds to finding the appropriate state transition and measurement matrix. This non-linear prediction operation can be approximated by a linear search area followed by non-linear region matching scheme. The correction of the filter is similar to standard techniques, except here, we use a Gaussian weight function to find the appropriate measurement. This Gaussian weight function is computed by using both the non-linear region matching estimate and the discrete joint location estimate (from a pose detector). The non-linearity required in the correction phase is approximated by computing

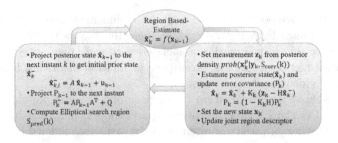

Fig. 2. Joint tracking algorithm using Improved Region-based Kalman Filter.

the Maximum Likelihood Estimate (MLE) within the Gaussian weight function and using a linear measurement function for state and covariance matrix update. Unlike other versions of the kalman filter such as Extended Kalman Filter (EKF), Unscented Kalman filter or the Invariant Extended Kalman filter which either requires prior information of the non-linear motion model or the underlying distribution model before tracking, the IRFK determines the non-linear state transition and measurement functions at run time based on the image region matching and estimation operations.

3.1 Prediction Phase of Improved Region-Based Kalman Filter

The state $\mathbf{x}_k \in \mathbb{R}^4$ of the non-linear process of the body joint region at instant k is taken as its centroid given by (x, y) along with its velocity (v_x, v_y). By approximating the motion of a joint in a small time interval by a linear function, we can design the transition matrix A so that the next state is a linear function of the previous states. As done by Kohler [8], to account for non-constant velocity often associated with accelerating image structures, we use the process noise co-variance matrix Q defined as

$$Q = \frac{a_i^2 \triangle t}{6} \begin{bmatrix} 2(\triangle t)^2 & 0 & 3\triangle t & 0 \\ 0 & 2(\triangle t)^2 & 0 & 3\triangle t \\ 3\triangle t & 0 & 6 & 0 \\ 0 & 3\triangle t & 0 & 6 \end{bmatrix} \tag{1}$$

where a is the acceleration and $\triangle t$ is the time step determined by the frame rate of the camera. However, the linear approximation of the state vector does not provide us a good predicted estimate. Therefore, to account for the non-linear state changes, we first predict a search region where the body joint location can be found. This is done by assuming a linear state change and computing the elliptical region $S_{pred}(k)$ by considering $\hat{\mathbf{x}}_{k-1}$ and $\hat{\mathbf{x}}_{k,i}^-$ as two foci of an ellipse with the standard deviations provided by the pre-error covariance matrix P_k^-. Then, we obtain a region-based match $f(\hat{\mathbf{x}}_{k-1})$ by comparing the corresponding descriptors at each point of the search region $\mathbf{f}_j$ to the one computed at the detected location $\mathbf{f}_p$ at instant $k - 1$. The state prediction phase is shown in Equation 3.

$$\hat{\mathbf{x}}_{k,i}^- = A\hat{\mathbf{x}}_{k-1} + \mathbf{u}_{k-1} + f(\hat{\mathbf{x}}_{k-1})$$

$$P_k^- = AP_{k-1}A^T + Q \tag{2}$$

$$\hat{\mathbf{x}}_k^- = f(\hat{\mathbf{x}}_{k-1}) \approx argmin_{p \in S_{pred}(t)} \chi^2(\mathbf{f}_j, \mathbf{f}_p) \tag{3}$$

3.2   Correction Phase of the Improved Region-Based Kalman Filter

The correction phase of the RKF includes the use of the discrete pose estimates as the measurement vector. But, unlike the traditional linear Kalman filter with Kalman gain K_k and measurement matrix H, a non-linear observation model is used. Similar to the computation of search region $S_{pred}(k)$, a second search region $S_{corr}(k)$ is computed using the detected pose estimate $\hat{\mathbf{y}}_k$ and the predicted state $\hat{\mathbf{x}}_k^-$ as two foci of the ellipse. The correction phase is given by Equation 4 where the measurement vector $\hat{\mathbf{z}}_k$ is estimated by maximizing the posterior distribution of the discrete pose estimate $\hat{\mathbf{y}}_k$ and the possible state at locations $\hat{\mathbf{x}}_k^p$.

$$\hat{\mathbf{x}}_k = \hat{\mathbf{x}}_k^- + K_k(\hat{\mathbf{z}}_k - H\hat{\mathbf{x}}_k^-)$$

$$\hat{\mathbf{z}}_k = g(\hat{\mathbf{x}}_k^-, \hat{\mathbf{y}}_k) \approx argmax_{p \in S_{corr}(k)} prob(\hat{\mathbf{y}}_k | \hat{\mathbf{x}}_k^p) \tag{4}$$

Let the discrete pose estimate and the possible location estimate be represented as $\hat{\mathbf{y}}_k \approx \mathbf{y} = [y_1, y_2, y_3]$ and $\hat{\mathbf{x}}_k^p \approx \mathbf{x} = [x_1^p, x_2^p, x_3^p]$ for ease of illustration where (y_1^p, y_2^p) and (x_1^p, x_2^p) are the corresponding locations in image space and $\{x_3^p, y_3^p\}$ are the corresponding distance between the region descriptors computed at those locations. Then, the effective measurement vector to correct the Kalman filter is given in Equation 5.

$$(\hat{y}_1, \hat{y}_2) = argmax_{p \in S_{corr}(k)} prob(\mathbf{x}_k^p | \mathbf{y}_k, S_{corr}(k))$$

$$prob(\mathbf{x}_k^p | \mathbf{y}_k) \sim \exp(\frac{(x_1^p - y_1)}{\delta_1^2} + \frac{(x_2^p - y_2)}{\delta_2^2} + \frac{(x_3^p - y_3)}{\delta_3^2}) \tag{5}$$

By maximizing this posterior density, we aim to find the best measurement estimate which is not only close to the discrete pose estimate in terms of image coordinates but also in the region descriptor space. The modification of the Kalman Filter recursive algorithm used for the joint tracking is shown in Figure 2 where the measurement is obtained from the region based estimate computed within the elliptical search region.

3.3   Tracking Algorithm

A block schematic of the tracking scheme is shown in Figure 3. As we traverse across each time step, each joint region will be described by a region descriptor. In this manuscript, we evaluate different types of descriptors such as HOG, SIFT, SURF, LBP, BRIEF, BRISK and ORB. The tracking algorithm is given below:

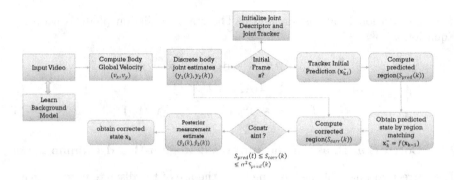

Fig. 3. Block schematic of the tracking scheme for a specific body joint.

1: Compute the median global velocity of body through optical flow.
2: Compute discrete pose estimates $(y_1(k), y_2(k))$ of individual using state of the art techniques at instant k.
3: If $k < T$ where $1 \leq k \leq T$ is the first set of frames, then initialize Kalman filter and body joint descriptor.
4: If $k \geq T$, then make an initial linear prediction $\hat{\mathbf{x}}_{k,i}^-$ and compute the search region $S_{pred}(k)$.
5: Compute the non-linear prediction $\hat{\mathbf{x}}_k^- = f(\hat{\mathbf{x}}_{k-1})$
6: Compute the search region $S_{corr}(k)$
7: Check for constraint on search region sizes $S_{pred}(k) \leq S_{corr}(k) \leq \alpha^2 S_{pred}(k)$ and if true, use Equation 4 to obtain the measurement.
8: If above condition is false, check the condition $S_{pred}(k) \geq S_{corr}(k)$ and if true, use region-based matching scheme in $S_{corr}(k)$ to obtain measurement.
9: If above condition is false, check the condition $\alpha^2 * S_{pred}(k) \leq S_{corr}(k)$, use the discrete pose estimates as measurement.
10: Obtain corrected state $\hat{\mathbf{x}}_k$ and update $k \to k + 1$

The constraint, parameterized by α, is used to restrict the size of the search regions in both prediction and corrected phase, where the two extremes $(S_{pred}(k) \geq S_{corr}(k)$ and $\alpha^2 * S_{pred}(k) \leq S_{corr}(k))$ are countered by using the appropriate measurement. The running time of the tracking algorithm excluding the optical flow computation and discrete pose estimation depends on the joint region (size $M \times M$), the computation of the descriptor $\mathbf{f}$, the computation of the search regions, the matching mechanism (Equation 3 and 4), and maximization of the posterior density (Equation 5). If we consider the running time of descriptor computation on a image of size $N \times N$ to be $f(N)$, then the overall running time of the tracking algorithm for a single joint is $\mathcal{O}(M^2 \cdot f(M))$.

4   Results and Experiments

The tracking scheme was tested on a private dataset by the Air Force Institute of Technology (AFIT) at Wright Patterson Air Force Base, OH. It consisted of the

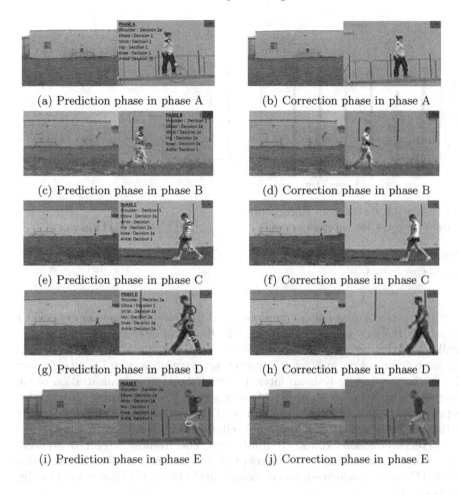

(a) Prediction phase in phase A   (b) Correction phase in phase A

(c) Prediction phase in phase B   (d) Correction phase in phase B

(e) Prediction phase in phase C   (f) Correction phase in phase C

(g) Prediction phase in phase D   (h) Correction phase in phase D

(i) Prediction phase in phase E   (j) Correction phase in phase E

Fig. 4. Illustration of elliptical search regions before tracking and joint location estimates after tracking.

walking activity of 12 individuals on an outdoor circular track that included flat grass, a staircase attached to a raised platform, and a down ramp. The subjects walked clockwise and counterclockwise around the track to collect a total of 100 video sequences in each direction. Subjects wore civilian clothes and shoes during the experiment. The video sequences were captured using two Canon GL cameras that faced the track at a distance of 50 ft. Each sequence was divided into 5 phases A, B, C, D, and E, a sequence of each phase was selected from either the left camera or right camera depending on what part of the track the walking activity was taking place. For the purposes of our analysis, we don't consider which camera the sequence was shot from. There are two variations of the sequences; one which contains an individual wearing a weighted vest of around 3-5 Kg and the other the same individual not wearing this heavy weighted

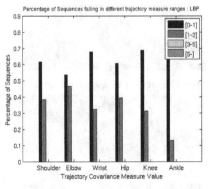

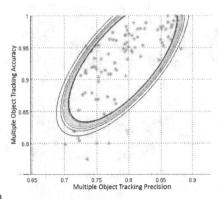

(a) Histogram of sequences falling within certain ranges of the closeness measure.

(b) MOTA/MOTP scores

Fig. 5. Experimental results obtained with the Improved Region-based Kalman tracking scheme using LBP.

vest. We perform our analysis on phases A,B,C,D, and E of the sequence which simulates different walking conditions. The frames of interest are of the subject walking on the cross over platform. We set equal neighborhood sizes of 17×17 for each joint region and set a constant acceleration $a = 0.1 \, pixels/frame^2$ for the corresponding Kalman filter. Figure 4 shows sample illustration of the proposed scheme in certain frames of the sequence. The coarse pose estimates are represented by purple color in each frame. The search regions and the finer joint estimates are given as shoulder(blue), elbow(green), wrist (red), waist(cyan), knee (yellow) and ankle(pink). To illustrate its effectiveness in terms of accuracy and precision, we provide two different types of measures as done in our earlier work [11], one a covariance-based measure and the other, multiple object tracking accuracy/precision.

4.1   Co-variance-Based Trajectory Measure

It is a statistical measure [6] which provides the closeness of the tracked joint locations to the coarse estimates for each sequence of an individual. This is given by Equation 6 where $K \in \mathbb{R}^{3 \times 3}$ is the co-variance of the tracked points, $K_m \in \mathbb{R}^{3 \times 3}$ is the co-variance matrix of the coarse joint locations, λ_i is the ith Eigen value associated with $|\lambda K - K_m| = 0$ and n being the number of eigenvalues.

$$d(K, K_m) = \sqrt{\sum_{i=1}^{n} (\log(\lambda_i(K, K_m)))^2} \tag{6}$$

The lower the value, the closer are the tracked points to the coarse joint locations. This measure although does not provide us with the precision of the tracking scheme, it gives an indication whether the tracked joint trajectory was located

Table 1. Median score of the covariance based measures (Overall).

Tracking Method	Descriptors	Shoulder	Elbow	Wrist	Hip	Knee	Ankle
Image-based	KLT	1.9771	2.1303	3.2899	2.9514	3.9265	2.7857
	HOG	3.9456	3.1325	2.8431	3.5799	2.3995	2.0461
	LBP	4.3486	3.3483	3.1029	3.8681	2.5546	1.9740
	SIFT	3.0621	3.2595	3.7534	3.3791	3.5910	2.9401
Local region-based	SURF	1.9769	2.4254	3.0824	2.3119	2.7704	2.0538
	BRIEF	2.5592	2.7796	3.4463	2.4422	3.1828	2.7194
	BRISK	2.6526	3.0258	3.3661	2.7184	2.9127	3.7850
	ORB	3.1826	2.9223	3.2247	2.4770	2.9240	3.1314
	HOG	1.4602	1.0966	1.0464	1.2853	0.9732	0.8363
	LBP	0.9152	0.9435	0.7766	0.9289	0.7695	0.5643
	SIFT	0.9941	1.3501	0.7199	1.1046	0.7360	0.4749
Proposed	SURF	0.8891	1.0024	0.7354	1.0362	0.6612	0.4401
	BRIEF	0.8696	1.4314	0.6906	0.9889	0.7426	0.4727
	BRISK	0.9181	1.2683	0.7302	1.0519	0.7270	0.4843
	ORB	0.9040	1.2766	0.7846	1.0018	0.7370	0.4727

within the spatial-temporal neighborhood of the coarse joint trajectory. Table 1 provides the covariance matrix scores obtained using different combinations of various region descriptors and the tracking scheme. We see that the proposed tracking scheme (with different types of decriptors) obtains much lower values than the local region-based matching with similar region descriptors. We can empirically determine different ranges of the trajectory discrepancy measures over which we can evaluate the finer estimates obtained by the tracking scheme through verification by visual inspection. Using these pre-defined ranges, we compute the percentage of sequences whose trajectory discrepancy measure falls within the specified ranges. Figure 5a illustrates the histogram of sequences falling within specified regions of the trajectory discrepancy. Under the proposed scheme, we see a large percentage of sequences of around $50 - 60\%$ falling within the first measure range $d \in [0, 1]$ and around $40 - 50\%$ falling within the region $d \in [1, 3)$ for the shoulder and elbow joint. For all the other joints, around 90% of the sequences fall within the region $d \in [0, 1]$. This shows that the estimates provided by the non-linear region tracking scheme are consistent with the coarse joint location estimates and the trajectories do not move away from their true path.

4.2   Multiple Object Tracking Precision/Accuracy (MOTP/MOTA)

As done in our previous work [11], the MOTP/MOTA [1, 2] metric has been used to compute the precision and accuracy of the tracked points. Multiple object tracking precision (MOTP) refers to the closeness of a tracked point location to its true location (given as ground truth). We measure the closeness by computing the overlap between the neighborhood region occupied by the tracked joint location and the discrete body joint location. The higher the value of this

Table 2. Multiple object tracking precision (MOTP), accuracy (MOTA) scores.

		HOG	*LBP*	*SIFT*	*SURF*	*BRIEF*	*BRISK*	*ORB*
Region-based	*MOTP*	0.6585	0.6561	0.6938	0.6907	0.6762	0.7068	0.7001
	MOTA	0.2698	0.2500	0.5237	0.5173	0.5781	0.6074	0.5724
Kalman Filter	*MOTP*	0.6850	0.6528	0.7172	0.7195	0.7141	0.7259	0.7160
	MOTA	0.1823	0.2013	0.3981	0.4192	0.4495	0.4531	0.4017
RKF (Proposed)	*MOTP*	0.7015	0.7925	0.7936	0.7892	0.7907	0.7902	0.7865
	MOTA	0.7027	0.9554	0.9559	0.9537	0.9524	0.9537	0.9524

overlap, the more precise is the estimated location of the point. Multiple object tracking accuracy (MOTA) gives the accumulated accuracy in terms of the fraction of the tracked joints matched correctly without any misses or mismatches. We computed the MOTP,MOTA, false positive rate and false negative rate for each sequence by setting the threshold $T = 0.5$ with same acceleration parameter $a = 0.1$ and a neighborhood size of 17×17 for each body joint. We also used the coarse joint location estimates as the reference joint locations since no appropriate ground truth about the true continuous joint locations corresponding to the sinusoidal trajectory was provided with this dataset. In Figure 5b, we see that all of the sequences have moderately high precision of around 75% and a high accuracy of around 90%. Table 2 provides the MOTP and MOTA scores for the proposed tracking schemes and other methods using different types of region descriptors. We see that the proposed tracking schemes outperforms the other methods in terms of precision and accuracy. Moreover, the LBP region descriptor shows high values of precision and accuracy when compared to the other region descriptors using the proposed tracking scheme. This shows that the proposed tracking scheme is less noisy and the reduction in precision is due to the slight variation of the estimated joint locations with respect to the coarse joint location estimates.

4.3 Threat Detection Using Trajectories Obtained by Proposed Tracker

The computed joint trajectories from the tracking scheme and other methods can further be evaluated as a gait signature, and in this manuscript, we use these trajectories to distinguish individuals wearing a weighted vest and those not wearing a weighted vest. The above mentioned AFIT dataset contains sequences of individuals wearing a weighted test that simulates the threat of an improvised explosive device. The aim is to associate a set of joint trajectories of an individual into a threat or non-threat (weighted vest or no weighted vest). We ran two experiments of the proposed algorithm on the dataset, one which uses the manual annotation joint locations obtained from the proprietary Point light software and the other which uses the human pose estimation algorithm computed at every frame of the sequence [16]. The feature descriptor used to represent the joint trajectories is the "shape trajectory" descriptor defined in [15] and use the Kernel

SVM with a Chi-Squared kernel as the classifer [4]. We set the maximum length of sub-trajectory at 25 frames to compute this shape descriptor. Thus, for a single video sequence containing on an average of 5 secs, we computed shape trajectory descriptors for every 15 frames with a stride of one frame. The dataset will then contain around 3000 descriptors for evaluation. We employ a randomized train-

Table 3. Comparison of threat classification with other tracking mechanism.

Tracking Mechanism	Region Description	Percent Accuracy
Discrete Pose Estimates		51.3725
Kalman Filter on Discrete Pose Estimates		50.9728
Kanade Lucas Tracker	Optical Flow	51.5686
SIFT tracker	SIFT descriptor	52.1984
Optical flow + Kalman filter [10]	HOG+LBP	51.463
Non-Linear Region based Kalman Filter	LBP	58.0517

test split which uses $(2/3)^{rd}$ of the data for training and $(1/3)^{rd}$ for testing and run monte-carlo simulations of around 1000 iterations. The results are then averaged across the iterations. Table 3 shows the comparison of the classification accuracies obtained with the proposed and other tracking schemes. The accuracy obtained by just using the human pose estimates without any tracking scheme is only $50 - 52\%$. Those obtained from trajectories computed with other tracking schemes obtained an average accuracy of 54%. The proposed tracking scheme, however obtained an accuracy of around 58%. The SVM classifier trained with trajectories obtained from the proposed scheme was able to distinguish between individuals wearing a vest and no vest more accurately than the one trained with only the pose estimates. This validates our proposed tracking scheme in the context for analyzing gait patterns from body joint trajectories for threat identification.

5   Conclusion

We have seen that the Improved Region-based Kalman filter plays a crucial role in obtaining finer body joint location estimates from the discrete pose on low resolution imagery. This non-linear refining technique computes continuous body joint trajectories which can be used for analyzing the gait patterns for threat identification. The trajectories obtained by the proposed scheme using the LBP descriptor provided more information about the gait than other similar representative techniques, and is more accurate in analyzing the trajectories for gait-based threat identification.

Acknowledgments. This work was done in collaboration with University of Nevada, Las Vegas and is supported by the National Science Foundation grant No: 1240734. We would like to thank the National Signature Program and the Air Force Institute of Technology for the dataset used in this research.

References

1. Bagdanov, A., Del Bimbo, A., Dini, F., Lisanti, G., Masi, I.: Posterity logging of face imagery for video surveillance. IEEE MultiMedia **19**(4), 48–59 (2012)
2. Bernardin, K., Stiefelhagen, R.: Evaluating multiple object tracking performance: The clear mot metrics. J. Image Video Process. **2008**, 1:1–1:10 (2008)
3. Burgos-Artizzu, X., Hall, D., Perona, P., Dollar, P.: Merging pose estimates across space and time. In: Proceedings of the British Machine Vision Conference. BMVA Press (2013)
4. Chang, C.C., Lin, C.J.: LIBSVM: A library for support vector machines. ACM Transactions on Intelligent Systems and Technology **2**, 27:1–27:27 (2011)
5. Ferrari, V., Marin-Jimenez, M., Zisserman, A.: Progressive search space reduction for human pose estimation. In: IEEE Conference on Computer Vision and Pattern Recognition, CVPR 2008, pp. 1–8, June 2008
6. Forstner, W., Moonen, B.: A metric for covariance matrices (1999)
7. Huang, C.H., Boyer, E., Ilic, S.: Robust human body shape and pose tracking. In: 2013 International Conference on 3DV-Conference, pp. 287–294 (2013)
8. Kohler, M.: Using the Kalman Filter to Track Human Interactive Motion: Modelling and Initialization of the Kalman Filter for Translational Motion. Forschungsberichte des Fachbereichs Informatik der Universität Dortmund, Dekanat Informatik, Univ. (1997)
9. Mansur, A., Makihara, Y., Aqmar, R., Yagi, Y.: Gait recognition under speed transition. In: 2014 IEEE Conference on Computer Vision and Pattern Recognition (CVPR), pp. 2521–2528, June 2014
10. Nair, B.M., Kendricks, K.D., Asari, V.K., Tuttle, R.F.: Optical flow based kalman filter for body joint prediction and tracking using hog-lbp matching. In: Proceedings of SPIE, Video Surveillance and Transportation Imaging Applications, vol. 9026, pp. 90260H–90260H-14 (2014)
11. Nair, B.M., Kendricks, K.D., Asari, V.K., Tuttle, R.F.: Body Joint tracking in low resolution video using region-based filtering. In: Bebis, G., et al. (eds.) ISVC 2014, Part I. LNCS, vol. 8887, pp. 619–628. Springer, Heidelberg (2014)
12. Ramakrishna, V., Kanade, T., Sheikh, Y.: Tracking human pose by tracking symmetric parts. In: 2013 IEEE Conference on Computer Vision and Pattern Recognition (CVPR), pp. 3728–3735 (2013)
13. Ramanan, D.: Learning to parse images of articulated bodies. In: Schölkopf, B., Platt, J., Hoffman, T. (eds.) Advances in Neural Information Processing Systems, vol. 19, pp. 1129–1136. MIT Press (2007)
14. Shotton, J., Fitzgibbon, A., Cook, M., Sharp, T., Finocchio, M., Moore, R., Kipman, A., Blake, A.: Real-time human pose recognition in parts from single depth images. In: 2011 IEEE Conference on Computer Vision and Pattern Recognition (CVPR), pp. 1297–1304 (2011)
15. Wang, H., Klser, A., Schmid, C., Liu, C.L.: Dense trajectories and motion boundary descriptors for action recognition. International Journal of Computer Vision **103**(1), 60–79 (2013)
16. Yang, Y., Ramanan, D.: Articulated pose estimation with flexible mixtures-of-parts. In: 2011 IEEE Conference on Computer Vision and Pattern Recognition (CVPR), pp. 1385–1392, June 2011

A Predictive Model for Human Activity Recognition by Observing Actions and Context

Dennis G. Romero[1]($\boxtimes$), Anselmo Frizera[2], Angel D. Sappa[1,3],
Boris X. Vintimilla[1], and Teodiano F. Bastos[2]

[1] Facultad de Ingeniería en Electricidad y Computación, Escuela Superior Politécnica del Litoral, ESPOL, Campus Gustavo Galindo Km 30.5 Vía Perimetral, P.O. Box 09-01-5863, Guayaquil, Ecuador
{dgromero,boris.vintimilla}@espol.edu.ec

[2] Universidade Federal do Espírito Santo, Av. Fernando Ferrari 514, Campus Goiabeiras, Vitória, ES, Brazil
{anselmo,tfbastos}@ele.ufes.br

[3] Computer Vision Center, Edifici O, Campus UAB, 08193 Bellaterra, Barcelona, Spain
asappa@cvc.uab.es

Abstract. This paper presents a novel model to estimate human activities — *a human activity is defined by a set of human actions*. The proposed approach is based on the usage of Recurrent Neural Networks (RNN) and Bayesian inference through the continuous monitoring of human actions and its surrounding environment. In the current work human activities are inferred considering not only visual analysis but also additional resources; external sources of information, such as context information, are incorporated to contribute to the activity estimation. The novelty of the proposed approach lies in the way the information is encoded, so that it can be later associated according to a predefined semantic structure. Hence, a pattern representing a given activity can be defined by a set of actions, plus contextual information or other kind of information that could be relevant to describe the activity. Experimental results with real data are provided showing the validity of the proposed approach.

1 Introduction

Human-Machine interaction is an attractive research field in the human assistance domain. One of the main goals is to develop methods for automatic human activities recognition in order to guarantee an easy communication. Actually, the automatic human activity recognition is not just needed for human-machine interaction, but also for tasks related to human behavior understanding in the health context; suspicious behavior detection in the context of video surveillance; or activity registration in the context of pattern recognition can be benefited from it. This ever growing research field finds also applications in the assistance to elderly persons, where a continuous activity recognition is needed to help elder people in their everyday life [1].

© Springer International Publishing Switzerland 2015
S. Battiato et al. (Eds.): ACIVS 2015, LNCS 9386, pp. 323–333, 2015.
DOI: 10.1007/978-3-319-25903-1_28

The automatic recognition of human activities, expressions and intentions are multimodal problems; hence, the recognition process may use different sources of information to improve their results. Examples of such multimodal sources of information are facial or bodily expressions, voice or audio-visual signals, among other. Different studies have been published exploiting such a multimodality nature; for instance [2] introduces a learning framework to identify emotions from speech using a discriminant function based on Gaussian mixture models. The authors in [3] propose a multimodal approach for recognizing emotions from an ensemble of features. It involves face detection, followed by key-point identification and feature generation, which are finally used by the emotion recognition. Finally, in [4] the cross-modality information is explored in an audiovisual emotion recognition system. The authors study the relationship between acoustic features of the speaker and facial expressions of the interlocutor during dyadic interactions.

Due to the problem complexity, different taxonomies have been proposed in the literature related with motion recognition. One of the most widely accepted has been presented in [5]; it is also considered in the current work and consists of the following categories: *primitive action*, *action* and *activity*. A primitive action is an atomic movement that can be described at the level of the human body parts. An action consists of a set of primitive actions and describes a complex movement or full corporal expression. Finally, an activity consists of a set of consecutive actions performed by the person. Examples of the previous definitions are as follow: *i*) "putting the right arm in fron" is a primitive action; *ii*) "moving an object" is an action; *iii*) "playing chess" is an activity that involves primitive action, movement of objects and other actions related to the rules of the game.

During the last five decades different studies have been carried out to tackle problems related with the human activities inference. The main goal and motivation of current research in this field is to reach a human-machine interaction similar to human-human interaction. An interesting review can be found in [6]. Several approaches have been proposed to solve problems related with the activity understanding of human everyday life. For instance, in the pedestrian detection domain it is possible to empirically identify safe/unsafe activities of a person crossing a street. In this case, an automatic system can predict risky situations due to the recklessness of a pedestrian. In order to develop applications like the previous one, or some other that involves understanding of human actions, it is necessary to develop models. These models should cover the full description of these actions, considering the different variables that affect them (object, culture, environment, among other) together with their temporal and non-temporal surrounding framework. The current paper proposes a novel model to recognize human activities. It is based on RNN and Bayesian inference considering human movements together with contextual information. The manuscript is organized as follow: The proposed model is presented in Section 2. Experimental results and comparisons are provided in Section 3. Finally, conclusions are given in Section 4.

2   Proposed Approach

In the proposed approach the actions or human bodily expressions are considered as input data. They are obtained using a computer vision system like the one presented in [7]. Therefore, each identified action or human bodily expression are sent to the inference engine; this inference engine is responsible for encoding, tracking and activity estimation according to an *actions-context-activity* association previously defined. The idea behind the proposed approach lies on the observation of human movements, which were already identified, together with the context information in order to predict possible interactions of the subject. In a general way, the proposed inference model can be represented as shown in Fig. 1.

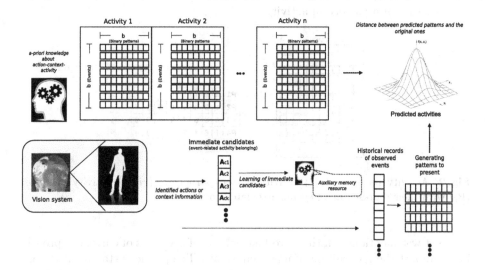

Fig. 1. General illustration of the proposed approach.

Human bodily expressions are important elements in the observation of human behavior. These expressions correspond to both movements of the body limbs (global level analysis) and facial expressions (detailed analysis). In order to reach the final goal, the information is encoded in such a way that it can be associated, later on, according to a predefined semantic structure. Hence, an encoded pattern representing an activity can be defined by a set of actions, contextual information or other kind of information that could be relevant to describe the given activity. Next, the three main elements of the proposed approach are described. First, the methodology to generate patterns that encode the information is introduced in Section 2.1. Then, the inference engine based on recurrent neural network is presented in Section 2.2. Finally, the architecture used for tracking identified events is summarized in Section 2.3.

2.1 *Actions-Activity-Context* Patterns

One of the first problems to solve after recognizing actions and context is to abstract their representation. In the current work it is proposed a model that uses RNN as resources of *Associative Memory*, considering binary patterns and two *Hopfield* Neural Networks [8] [9] in a long and short term approach.

In this sense, let $Ac = \{ac_1^{(b)}, \ldots, ac_k^{(b)}\}$ be a set of actions, where k is the number of actions or context information that can be identified by the recognition system, and b is the set of bits, representing an associated event. Assuming a *Hopfield* recurrent neural network is used, then, the total number of neurons in the network will be $I = b^2$. In other words, an activity can be represented by a matrix $x_n^{(b \times b)}$, where $x_n \subset Ac$ and $n = \{1, 2, \ldots \lfloor 0.138I \rfloor\}$ (0.138 represents the theoretical storage capacity as will be defined in eq (3)). Figure 2(*left*) illustrates the structure of a pattern of activity.

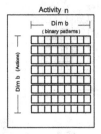

P1	e	e	f	9	c	f	9	f
P2	f	9	c	e	9	8	9	7
P3	6	c	6	f	9	e	9	9
P4	f	6	f	9	8	7	9	e
P5	e	9	f	f	f	5	9	9

Fig. 2. Activity pattern: (*left*) activity pattern structure; (*right*) activity patterns (P$_i$) with their representative events associated to them.

As it was mentioned in the introduction, one of the goals of current approach is to support the recognition of unsorted events. The previous statement means that it could exist a semantic similarity between a set of events, which have been observed in a different order. Additionally, this provides to the system the capability to estimate an activity even in those cases where the observed events are related with some other activity already known.

In this context, the neural network takes into account representative observations within a given activity, and then the probability of the candidate activities could change as soon as a new event occurs. In the "retrieval" phase an observation will induce to a known state, converging in each new observation to some trained pattern. The resulting patterns could have variations that can be measured using the *Hamming distance* [10] at each new observation presented to the network.

In the current work, the inputs and outputs of the neural network correspond to binary patterns $(x_n^{(I)})$, which represent a combination of observable events (each event is encoded using 8 bits). Initially, these combinations are randomly defined using *Linux Pseudo-Random Number Generator* (LRNG) [11] [12]. The initial combinations, randomly generated, are used to define a set of observable events k, without semantic relationships between them. Hence, in order to have a balance between the resulting patterns (*unbias*), they are discriminated so that $P(x_i(j) = 1) = P(x_i(j) = -1) = 1/2$, where $j = \{1, 2, \ldots, I\}$.

Unfortunately, the process presented above for the random generation of patterns and posterior discrimination, do not provide enough information regarding the correlation between them. For this reason, each activity (semantic relationship between events) will be assigned to the less correlated patterns, which are selected by means of a *cross-correlation* criterion based on the *Pearson's* correlation (PPMCC or PCC) [13,14]. The *Pearson's* correlation coefficient (r_{xy}) is defined as the covariance of two variables divided by the product of their standard deviations; it is expressed as:

$$r_{xy} = \frac{n \sum x_i y_i - \sum x_i y_i}{\sqrt{n \sum x_i^2 - (\sum x_i)^2} \sqrt{n \sum y_i^2 - (\sum y_i)^2}}. \tag{1}$$

The correlation coefficient spans $[-1, 1]$, where 1 means that the linear equation perfectly describes the relation between X and Y, with all the data lying on a straight line where X and Y increase. On the contrary, -1 means that all the data lie on the straight line where X and Y decrease. Hence, the 0 value represents the lack of linear correlation between the variables. Figure 2(*right*) shows five activity patterns with their corresponding associated events (i.e., actions or context), where each alphanumeric character represents a binary code according with the 8-bits ASCII table.

Once all the patterns have been defined, a semantic annotation is given to them according to a specific application (e.g., events representing actions or context information and patterns representing activities). Table 1 shows the results of the selection process based on the *Pearson's* correlation.

Table 1. Cross-correlation using the Pearson's correlation.

	P1	P2	P3	P4	P5	P6	P7	P8	P9	P10
P1	1	0.25	0.188	0.5	0.312	0.5	0.375	0.562	0.312	0.438
P2	0.25	1	0.375	0.438	0.438	0.125	0.562	0.312	0.25	0.5
P3	0.188	0.375	1	0.312	0.438	0.438	0.438	0.25	0.562	0.125
P4	0.5	0.438	0.312	1	0.312	0.438	0.375	0.5	0.562	0.438
P5	0.312	0.438	0.438	0.312	1	0.375	0.625	0.188	0.188	0.562
P6	0.5	0.125	0.438	0.438	0.375	1	0.312	0.312	0.688	0.188
P7	0.375	0.562	0.438	0.375	0.625	0.312	1	0.062	0.25	0.5
P8	0.562	0.312	0.25	0.5	0.188	0.312	0.062	1	0.5	0.375
P9	0.312	0.25	0.562	0.562	0.188	0.688	0.25	0.5	1	0.062
P10	0.438	0.5	0.125	0.438	0.562	0.188	0.5	0.375	0.062	1

2.2 Recurrent Neural Network Based Approach

The *Hopfield* neural network has two main applications. In the first one they are used as *associative memories*, while in the second one they are used to solve *optimization problems*. On the other hand, the inference process in the context of recurrent neural networks could be faced in two ways: the first one is by considering the internal probabilistic constitution of the neural network, while the second one, is focused on the probabilistic meaning of the results, being the latter one the approach considered in the current work.

According to [15], there is a difference between the theoretical storage capacity and the experimental one, both using the Hebbian learning rule as well as the pseudo-inverse rule (also referred to as projection learning rule) [16]; the main reasons for these differences [9] are:

- The high correlation between training patterns; the correlation between patterns reduces the performance of the network.
- The storage capacity of Hopfield networks is related to the sparsity of training patterns.
- The *global inibition* is another factor that can affect the storage capacity.

The number of patterns to be stored can be increased if a small error is accepted. In the current work a storage of $N = 8$ patterns, of $I = 64$ bits, is considered. Hence, the theoretical error due to bit swapping in the first iteration is about 0.2%; this error will be larger if next iterations are considered.

Regarding the rate between the number of stored patterns and the number of neurons N/I, [17] states that the maximum number of patters to be stored, with an acceptable maximum error value, is defined by the following expression (this statement is shared by [18]):

$$N_{max} \simeq \frac{I}{4lnI + 2ln(1/\epsilon)},\qquad(2)$$

actually, in [18] a critical limit is presented, which considers the abrupt drop in the performance of the network with the increase of the ratio N/I; this critical limit is defined as:

$$N_{crit} = 0.138I.\qquad(3)$$

As presented above, the balanced combination of each pattern and the selection of those with the lowest correlation are intended to reach a fair initial distribution of the probabilities of each state. Later on, during the training of the network, these probabilities are biased toward the most active state. In other words, if in the activity "$activ_1$" the event "a_1" is performed more than one time, this event will have a higher weight in the given activity, which will be reflected in the neural network. In the same way, activities that have been trained using the proposed model, will be tolerant to the presence of events that may belong to other activities, or events identified by the system (computer vision or other systems).

2.3   Tracking of Identified Events

Initially, all the set of actions-activity-context patterns (x_n) are stored in the main associative memory block (long-term), considering the limit of n defined in the previous section (see Fig. 1). Then, as soon as a new event is identified, the second block of memory (shot-term) stores all the patterns x_n that contain a new action, these selected patterns are referred to as immediate candidates:

$$X_{sel} = \{\forall x_n \in X | ac_k \in x_n, n = \{1, 2, \ldots, \lfloor 0.138I \rfloor\}\}. \tag{4}$$

The new set of patterns X_{sel} ($X_{sel} \subset X$) is temporally stored, so that the recurrent network responsible of storing these patterns will behave like a short-term memory. In this way, the patterns in time $t - 1$ could be "forgotten" when a new event appears (Fig. 3).

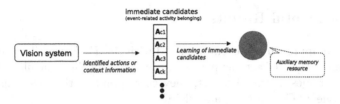

Fig. 3. Temporal storing of immediate candidates.

Considering the constraints in the storage capacity of activity patterns, the probability of a candidate activity being one of the learned activities, given the appearance of a new action, can be determined using the Bayes theorem (assuming that $ac_k \in X$):

$$P(x_n | ac_k) = \frac{P(x_n) P(ac_k | x_n)}{P(ac_k)}. \tag{5}$$

The aim of the short-term resource is to provide the system with a knowledge base to be used during the appearance of the first actions.

After storing (memorizing) the immediate candidates, the observed event is kept in a historical register $hist(ac_j)$; for each new observed event, a new set of patterns H to be presented to the network is created from $hist$, fulfilling $x_n(i) = H(ac_j)$, for $\forall i \in \Re| \leq b$ and $\forall j \in \Re| j \leq k$.

In this way, at least one of the patterns from H will be an *incomplete* and/or partially wrong version of x_n. Hence, for every new observation, considering a 64-bits activity pattern (8 observable events of 8 bits), it will exist a pattern to be presented to the network with an overlap of at least $1/8$ with some of the patterns initially learned. Once the neural network returns the estimated activity (with an acceptance rate based on the mean and variance of Hamming distance values between the stored patterns in long-term memory x_n and those retrieved from it x_{des}), the total content in the historical register $hist$ is deleted; starting again with a new and continuous loop of analysis. In a particular situation, if the information presented to the long-term memory is not enough, the patterns in H will be presented to the short-term memory, the probability of retrieving a correct patterns could be obtained from the equation (5) when $ac_k \in X$. Although the short term memory tends to give a strong conclusion (due to the reduced number of stored patterns), it is not reliable. For instance, it could give an answer even in the case when an observed event does not belong to some learned patterns, in this particular case, the obtained conclusion would be wrong (false positive).

The proposed model allows the estimation of an activity from $1/b$ of the actions that define it, considering the theoretical limit of storage capacity of Hopfield neural networks (assuming a correlation between patterns ($r_{x,y} \rightarrow 0$)), fixed as $N_{max} = \lfloor 0.138I \rfloor$.

3   Experimental Results

The proposed approach has been evaluated with the *Hollywood* data set [19]. It contains annotations of actions performed in scenes of different films. Figure 4 shows some frames of this data set; they correspond to the following actions: "AnswerPhone"; "GetOutCar" and "Kiss".

Fig. 4. Frames from the Hollywood data set, corresponding to the following actions: (*left*) AnswerPhone; (*middle*) GetOutCar; (*right*) Kiss.

Table 2 shows the annotations of identified actions in different time intervals for different films (they are provided by [19] and are used as ground truth). In the current work these annotations have been used to estimate the titles of the video sequences during the actions observation.

Table 2. Annotated actions, provided by [19], of different films.

Video Sequence	Time	Annotation	Video Sequence	Time	Annotation
"As Good As It Gets – 00259.avi"?	(10-125)	$< SitDown >$	"LOR-FellowshipOfTheRing – 01181.avi"?	(10-96)	$< StandUp >$
"As Good As It Gets – 01311.avi"?	(1-180)	$< StandUp >$	"LOR-FellowshipOfTheRing – 01181.avi"?	(1796-1875)	$< SitUp >$
"As Good As It Gets – 01400.avi"?	(620-730)	$< Kiss >$	"LOR-FellowshipOfTheRing – 01286.avi"?	(1-80)	$< SitUp >$
"As Good As It Gets – 01619.avi"?	(1-50)	$< Kiss >$	"LOR-FellowshipOfTheRing – 01494.avi"?	(25-232)	$< SitUp >$
"As Good As It Gets – 01834.avi"?	(150-450)	$< SitDown >$	"LOR-FellowshipOfTheRing – 01712.avi"?	(246-372)	$< Kiss >$
"As Good As It Gets – 01935.avi"?	(1-209)	$< StandUp >$	"LOR-FellowshipOfTheRing – 02501.avi"?	(65-93)	$< SitUp >$
"As Good As It Gets – 02002.avi"?	(1-664)	$< Kiss >$	"LOR-FellowshipOfTheRing – 02707.avi"?	(1-410)	$< HugPerson >$
"Erin Brockovich – 00816.avi"?	(1-50)	$< StandUp >$	"Dead Poets Society – 00068.avi"?	(18-55)	$< SitDown >$
"Erin Brockovich – 01233.avi"?	(450-530)	$< StandUp >$	"Dead Poets Society – 00148.avi"?	(163-233)	$< HandShake >$
"Erin Brockovich – 01768.avi"?	(43-141)	$< AnswerPhone >$	"Dead Poets Society – 00205.avi"?	(1-89)	$< HandShake >$
"Erin Brockovich – 01916.avi"?	(1-91)	$< StandUp >$	"Dead Poets Society – 01587.avi"?	(1-377)	$< SitDown >$
"Erin Brockovich – 02110.avi"?	(1-180)	$< SitDown >$	"Dead Poets Society – 01587.avi"?	(1-377)	$< Kiss >$
"Erin Brockovich – 02137.avi"?	(1-180)	$< StandUp >$	"Dead Poets Society – 01741.avi"?	(144-195)	$< AnswerPhone >$
"Erin Brockovich – 02262.avi"?	(130-241)	$< SitDown >$	"Dead Poets Society – 02590.avi"?	(148-230)	$< SitUp >$
"Pianist, The – 01525.avi"?	(1-141)	$< HandShake >$			
"Pianist, The – 01285.avi"?	(1-150)	$< StandUp >$	"Pianist, The – 01285.avi"?	(360-445)	$< GetOutCar >$
"Pianist, The – 00926.avi"?	(100-367)	$< HugPerson >$	"Pianist, The – 01255.avi"?	(450-716)	$< HugPerson >$
"Pianist, The – 01334.avi"?	(350-530)	$< SitDown >$	"Pianist, The – 01285.avi"?	(925-995)	$< HandShake >$

Each action has been encoded and selected according to the lowest *Pearson's* correlation. Table 3 shows patterns (in ASCII format) corresponding to the annotated actions according to the video sequences presented in Table 2. Each set of patterns defines an activity representing the title of the film. The annotated actions corresponds to: $f=< SitDown >$; $Y=< StandUP >$; $R=< Kiss >$; $K=< AnswerPhone >$; $q=< HandShake >$; $|=< SitUP >$ and $g=< HugPerson >$. The Figure 5 depicts the codified patterns corresponding to the defined activities in Table 3.

Table 3. Titles (*activities*) in *Hollywood* data set [19] with their corresponding codified annotations (*actions*).

Title	Codified Annotations
As Good As It Gets	$fYRRfYR$
Pianist, The	$ggYXqfq$
Dead Poets Society	$fqqYRK|$
Erin Brockovich	$YYKYfYf$
LOR-FellowshipOfTheRing	$Y|||R|g$

Fig. 5. Activities defined in Table 3 (left to right corresponds to films from top to bottom).

As soon as a new action is observed, the different stages of the proposed model are performed: selection of possible activities, generation of candidate patterns, presentation of candidates to the network; and finally, selection of the highest probability answer. Table 4 presents the results estimated by the model, using the annotations of the film "As Good As It Gets". Each row in the "Obs. Actions" column corresponds to the set of actions that have been identified in different pieces of the film. The inference process is shown to the extent that actions are observed. It can be appreciated that in the second observation the obtained conclusion corresponds with the activity that has the most representative action (see the activities defined in Table 3), considering all the previous actions associated to the activities. In this example, the correct result can be obtained just when a new action is observed. This fact is also appreciated in Table 5, where an action that do not belong to the activity of interest (AOI) is observed; a similar trend is observed, but in this case due to the previous wrong information, showing the influence of the learning process (associative reinforcement between events and activities) in the results given by the model.

Table 4. Inference of films' titles according to observed actions.

Obs.	Obs. Actions	Films titles			
		Good... (AOI)	Pianist...	Poets...	Erin...
1	f	**35.29%**	–	17.65%	17.65%
2	fY	70.59%	17.65%	17.65%	**82.35%**
3	fYR	**100%**	17.65%	29.41%	82.35%
4	fYRR	**100%**	17.65%	29.41%	82.35%

Table 5. Inference of films' titles according to observed actions and by inserting a wrong observation (q).

Obs.	Obs. Actions	Films titles			
		Good... (AOI)	Pianist...	Poets...	Erin...
1	f	**40.0%**	–	30%	30%
2	fq	14.29%	7.14%	**21.43%**	–
3	fqY	**72.22%**	27.78%	44.44%	22.22%
4	fqYR	**100%**	82.35%	58.82%	82.35%

4   Conclusions

The current work presents an approach for events tracking captured by a vision system and other sensors that can provide contextual information towards the automatic inference of human activities. The usage of states in a recurrent neural network for representing human actions and context information has been formulated. Additionally, it proposes a cyclic model for tracking actions and inferring activities, which consider predominant actions that influence it. In this way, it was possible to incorporate two common properties present in everyday life: first, the fact that different persons can do different set of actions during the performance of a given activity; second, the inclusion of contextual information, which affect the decision criteria during the automatic inference of activities as an association of movements or corporal expressions. The model proposed for the activity inference has been described supporting the selected options.

The results obtained with the *Hopfield* network opens the possibility to incorporate other recurrent neural networks working as associative memory within the proposed cyclic model. Finally, the state of the art on recurrent neural networks, shows the potential of these techniques for applications related with associative memory. The current computational capability represents an appealing factor for implementing techniques as the ones proposed in the current work.

Acknowledgments. This work has been partially supported by the Escuela Superior Politécnica del Litoral, ESPOL. The work of A. Sappa has been partially supported by the Spanish Government under Project TIN2014-56919-C3-2-R and PROMETEO Project of the "Secretaría Nacional de Educación Superior, Ciencia, Tecnología e Innovación de la República del Ecuador".

References

1. Zhang, M., Sawchuk, A.A.: Manifold learning and recognition of human activity using body-area sensors. In: International Conference on Machine Learning and Applications (ICMLA), vol. 2, pp. 7–13 (2011)
2. Yun, S., Yoo, C.: Loss-scaled large-margin gaussian mixture models for speech emotion classification. IEEE Transactions on Audio, Speech, and Language Processing **20**, 585–598 (2012)
3. Tariq, U., Lin, K.H., Li, Z., Zhou, X., Wang, Z., Le, V., Huang, T., Lv, X., Han, T.: Recognizing emotions from an ensemble of features. IEEE Transactions on Systems, Man, and Cybernetics, Part B: Cybernetics **42**, 1017–1026 (2012)
4. Mariooryad, S., Busso, C.: Exploring cross-modality affective reactions for audio-visual emotion recognition. IEEE Transactions on Affective Computing **4**, 183–196 (2013)
5. Moeslund, T.B., Hilton, A., Kruger, V.: A survey of advances in vision-based human motion capture and analysis. Computer Vision and Image Understanding **104**, 90–126 (2006)
6. Saygin, A.P., Cicekli, I., Akman, V.: Turing test: 50 years later. Minds and Machines **10**, 12–20 (2000)
7. López, D.R., Neto, A.F., Bastos, T.F.: Reconocimiento en-línea de acciones humanas basado en patrones de rwe aplicado en ventanas dinámicas de momentos invariantes. Revista Iberoamericana de Automática e Informática Industrial RIAI **11**, 202–211 (2014)
8. Hopfield, J.J.: Neural networks and physical systems with emergent collective computational abilities. Proceedings of the National Academy of Sciences **79**, 2554–2558 (1982)
9. Trappenberg, T.: Fundamentals of computational neuroscience. Oxford University Press (2010)
10. Mandic, D.P., Chambers, J.: Recurrent neural networks for prediction: Learning algorithms, architectures and stability. John Wiley & Sons, Inc. (2001)
11. Gutterman, Z., Pinkas, B., Reinman, T.: Analysis of the linux random number generator. In: Symposium on Security and Privacy, pp. 371–385. IEEE (2006)
12. Vadhan, S.P.: Pseudorandomness, vol. 7 (2012)
13. Goh, K.I., Cusick, M.E., Valle, D., Childs, B., Vidal, M., Barabasi, A.L.: The human disease network. Proceedings of the National Academy of Sciences **104**, 8685–8690 (2007)
14. Nikolić, D., Mureşan, R.C., Feng, W., Singer, W.: Scaled correlation analysis: a better way to compute a cross-correlogram. European Journal of Neuroscience **35**, 742–762 (2012)
15. Wu, Y., Hu, J., Wu, W., Zhou, Y., Du, K.L.: Storage capacity of the Hopfield network associative memory. In: International Conference on Intelligent Computation Technology and Automation (ICICTA), pp. 330–336 (2012)
16. Valiant, L.G.: Projection learning. Machine Learning **37**, 115–130 (1999)
17. MacKay, D.J.: Information theory, inference and learning algorithms. Cambridge University Press (2003)
18. McEliece, R., Posner, E.C., Rodemich, E.R., Venkatesh, S.: The capacity of the Hopfield associative memory. IEEE Transactions on Information Theory **33**, 461–482 (1987)
19. Marszalek, M., Laptev, I., Schmid, C.: Actions in context. In: IEEE Conference on Computer Vision and Pattern Recognition (CVPR), pp. 2929–2936. IEEE (2009)

Direct Image Alignment for Active Near Infrared Image Differencing

Jinwoo Kang[1(✉)], David V. Anderson[1], and Monson H. Hayes[2]

[1] Georgia Institute of Technology, Atlanta, GA 30332, USA
jinwoo@gatech.edu
[2] George Mason University, Fairfax, VA 22030, USA

Abstract. One of the difficult challenges in face recognition is dealing with the illumination variations that occur in varying environments. A practical and efficient way to address harsh illumination variations is to use active image differencing in near-infrared frequency range. In this method, two types of image frames are taken: an illuminated frame is taken with near infrared illumination, and an ambient frame is taken without the illumination. The difference between face regions of these frames reveals the face image illuminated only by the illumination. Therefore the image is not affected by the ambient illumination and illumination robust face recognition can be achieved. But the method assumes that there is no motion between two frames. Faces in different locations on the two frames introduces a motion artifact. To compensate for motion between two frames, a motion interpolation method has been proposed; but it has limitations, including an assumption that the face motion is linear. In this paper, we propose a new image alignment method that directly aligns the actively illuminated and ambient frames. The method is based on Lucas-Kanade parametric image alignment method and involves a new definition of errors based on the properties of the two types of frames. Experimental results show that the direct method outperforms the motion interpolation method in terms of face recognition rates.

1 Introduction

Image differencing with active near infrared (NIR) illumination shows promise to remove ambient illuminations effectively from face images and increase the robustness of subsequent face recognition algorithms in the presence of ambient illumination changes [8,9,20,23]. In the image differencing method, two image frames are taken within a short time interval: an *illuminated* frame (called "I-frame") is taken with active NIR illumination, and an *ambient* frame (called "A-frame") is taken without active NIR illumination. Then the *difference* between the I-frame and the A-frame (called "D-frame") would ideally correspond to a face image illuminated only by the active NIR illumination. In order for this to be approximately true, it is necessary that the image preprocessing of the camera is linear in pixel intensities and there is no motion between two images. Example

© Springer International Publishing Switzerland 2015
S. Battiato et al. (Eds.): ACIVS 2015, LNCS 9386, pp. 334–344, 2015.
DOI: 10.1007/978-3-319-25903-1_29

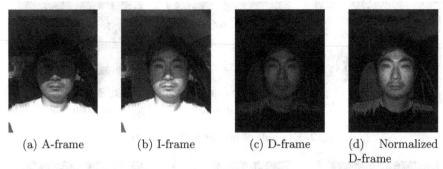

(a) A-frame   (b) I-frame   (c) D-frame   (d)   Normalized
                                                                       D-frame

Fig. 1. Example ambient, illuminated and difference frames are shown. Only the image in (d) was normalized to be visualized in proper contrast.

images are shown in Fig. 1. Figure 1(a) shows an A-frame with strong shadow. The contrast between shadowed region and unshadowed region is reduced by the active NIR illumination in the I-frame of Fig. 1(b). The D-frame is shown in Fig. 1(c) and the same image is shown in Fig. 1(d) with intensity normalization for the visual purpose. The D-frame shows the image illuminated only by the active NIR illumination as expected.

For the visible band, there have been many computer vision and computational photography applications developed using flash and non-flash images. Dicarlo, *et al.*, introduced an active imaging method to measure ambient illumination using flash and non-flash image pairs [5]. Petschnigg, *et al.*, proposed the joint bilateral filter combining flash and non-flash images to achieve better exposure and color balance and to reduce noise [15]. In [7], Eisemann and Durand presented an alternative algorithm that shares some of the same basic concepts of [15]. Agrawal, *et al.*, presented a gradient projection and flash-exposure sampling scheme to remove photography artifacts [1]. In [6], shadows from color images were removed using flash/no-flash image edges. Sun, *et al.*, proposed an approach for foreground layer extraction using flash/no-flash image pairs[17]. Zhuo, *et al.*, developed an image deblurring approach to remove camera motion blur using a pair of blurred and flash images [22]. In [16], an iterative improvement of the guided image filter for flash/no-flash photography was presented. Li, *et al.*, introduced a hand-held multispectral camera to capture a pair of blurred image and NIR flash image simultaneously and analyze the correlation between the pair of images for blind motion deblurring [11]. Mikami, *et al.*, captured color and near-infrared images with different exposure times for image enhancement under extremely low-light scene [14]. Yoon, *et al.*, presented an image enhancement method with flash and no-flash pairs based on adaptive total variation minimization [21].

One assumption shared with the works mentioned above is that there is no motion between two images. Since the methods are based on the pixel-to-pixel correspondence, misalignment between images can cause artifacts and decrease performance. When the algorithm involves the difference between two pixels, even a very small misalignment can lead to significant artifacts on the result.

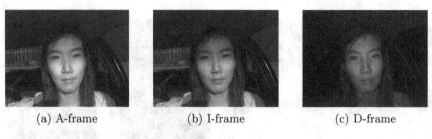

(a) A-frame   (b) I-frame   (c) D-frame

Fig. 2. Example of images without motion.

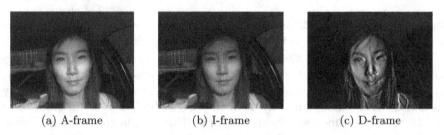

(a) A-frame   (b) I-frame   (c) D-frame

Fig. 3. Example of images with motion.

Figure 2 shows an example of an A-frame, an I-frame and a D-frame where there is no motion between the A-frame and the I-frame, and Fig. 3 shows an example an A-frame, an I-frame and a D-frame where there is motion between the A-frame and the I-frame. The D-frame in Fig. 3(c) shows artifacts introduced by the motion between the A-frame and the I-frame.

Therefore, very accurate image registration or motion compensation is necessary. To compensate such motion, Zou, Kittler and Messer [24] applied the optical flow estimation method by Black and Anandan [4] to consecutive I-frames in video where active NIR illumination is turned on and off alternately. Then image differencing is applied to the interpolated image and the A-frame that is in the middle of the I-frames. But the interpolation method has some problems. Since the motion between an I-frame and an A-frame is estimated from the motion between two I-frames, there is a possibility of errors when the face is not moving at the same speed in the same direction. And since the information that we are interested in is in the I-frames, interpolation on I-frames will smooth out the details in I-frame and also resulting D-frame. In addition, the optical flow method by Black and Anandan is slow and not viable in real-time applications.

In this work, we present novel parametric image registration methods to directly compensate motions between an I-frame and an A-frame. From the method, more accurate image registration is achieved. In addition, the warping and interpolation can be applied to A-frames to avoid smoothing on I-frames. The algorithms are based on the parametric image alignment method proposed by Lucas and Kanade [2,13]. To make the algorithm work on the I-frame and A-frame pairs under different illumination conditions, we define a new energy minimization criterion and derive a new formula.

The rest of the paper is organized as follows: the original Lucas-Kanade image registration algorithm is summarized in Section 2. Section 3 describes the proposed image registration algorithm with a new energy minimization criterion for active image differencing. The details and results of the experiments carried out are presented in Section 4. Conclusions are presented in Section 5.

2   Lucas-Kanade Algorithm

The original Lucas-Kanade algorithm is a parametric and iterative image alignment method based on gradient descent. It finds an image region in an input image $I(\mathbf{x})$ that best matches a template image $T(\mathbf{x})$, where $\mathbf{x} = (x, y)^{\mathrm{T}}$ is the pixel coordinates.

For active illumination applications, we have two images to align: an I-frame that is taken with the active illumination and an A-frame that is taken without the active illumination. Because detection and tracking algorithms are known to work better under regularized illumination condition, the template $T(\mathbf{x})$ is a detected face region in the I-frame, and the input image $I(\mathbf{x})$ is set to be the A-frame. In this section, the notations and derivations of equations are based on [2].

The vector $\mathbf{p} = (p_1, ..., p_n)^{\mathrm{T}}$ is the parameter vector and $\mathbf{W}(\mathbf{x}; \mathbf{p})$ is the warping function that maps pixels in the template T to the locations in the image I. The choice of the warp can be arbitrary including a translation, scaling, affine, piecewise affine or homography. Then the difference image D is the difference between two images, the template T and the warped image $I(\mathbf{W}(\mathbf{x}; \mathbf{p}))$:

$$D(\mathbf{x}; \mathbf{p}) = T(\mathbf{x}) - I(\mathbf{W}(\mathbf{x}; \mathbf{p})). \tag{1}$$

The difference image is the error that should be minimized in general applications. The Lucas-Kanade algorithm finds the parameters that minimize the energy $E(\mathbf{p})$:

$$\operatorname*{argmin}_{\mathbf{p}} E(\mathbf{p}) \tag{2}$$

where the energy $E(\mathbf{p})$ is defined by the sum of squared error of pixel intensities in the difference image:

$$E(\mathbf{p}) = \sum_{\mathbf{x}} [D(\mathbf{x}; \mathbf{p})]^2. \tag{3}$$

Minimizing the energy $E(\mathbf{p})$ is a non-linear optimization problem. In the Lucas-Kanade algorithm, the non-linear optimization is iteratively calculated using the Gauss-Newton gradient descent method. Starting with an initial guess of $\mathbf{p}$, the method proceeds by the iterations

$$\mathbf{p} \leftarrow \mathbf{p} + \Delta\mathbf{p}, \tag{4}$$

where the increment $\Delta\mathbf{p}$ is the solution to minimize the approximated energy $\hat{E}(\mathbf{p} + \Delta\mathbf{p})$:

$$\operatorname*{argmin}_{\Delta\mathbf{p}} \hat{E}(\mathbf{p} + \Delta\mathbf{p}) \tag{5}$$

where the approximated energy $\hat{E}(p + \Delta p)$ is defined by the first order Taylor expansion of $I(\mathbf{W}(\mathbf{x}; p+\Delta p))$:

$$\hat{E}(p + \Delta p) = \sum_{\mathbf{x}} \left[T(\mathbf{x}) - I(\mathbf{W}(\mathbf{x}; p)) - \left(\nabla I \frac{\partial \mathbf{W}}{\partial p} \right) \Delta p \right]^2. \tag{6}$$

In this equation, the term $\nabla I = \left(\frac{\partial I}{\partial x}, \frac{\partial I}{\partial y} \right)$ is the gradient of the image I and $\frac{\partial \mathbf{W}}{\partial p}$ is the Jacobian of the warp. The gradient ∇I is evaluated at $\mathbf{W}(\mathbf{x}; p)$ and the Jacobian $\frac{\partial \mathbf{W}}{\partial p}$ is evaluated at the particular values of $\mathbf{x}$ and p. The problem of finding the increment Δp that minimizes Eq.(6) is a least squares problem and it can be solved by setting $\frac{\partial \hat{E}(p+\Delta p)}{\partial \Delta p} = 0$:

$$\Delta p = H^{-1} \sum_{\mathbf{x}} \left[\nabla I \frac{\partial \mathbf{W}}{\partial p} \right]^{\mathrm{T}} [T(\mathbf{x}) - I(\mathbf{W}(\mathbf{x}; p))] \tag{7}$$

where H is the *Hessian* matrix:

$$H = \sum_{\mathbf{x}} \left[\nabla I \frac{\partial \mathbf{W}}{\partial p} \right]^{\mathrm{T}} \left[\nabla I \frac{\partial \mathbf{W}}{\partial p} \right]. \tag{8}$$

3   Proposed Image Alignment Method for Active Image Differencing

In this section, we introduce a new parametric image registration method for active image differencing based on the Lucas-Kanade alignment method. In most image alignment applications, the difference image D is the error that should be minimized. But in the active image differencing method, the difference image D is the desired output image. Since the I-frame is taken with additional illumination, the pixel intensities in the I-frame should be greater than or equal to the corresponding pixel intensities in the A-frame assuming that pixel intensities corresponding to the ambient illumination do not change between the two images. Therefore positive pixel values are considered as the desired output, and negative pixel values are considered as error or noise. Consequently we modified the total cost function so that only negative intensities are considered as errors.

First, we generalize the energy term in Eq.(2) by introducing an error function $\rho(x){:}\mathbb{R} \to \mathbb{R}$ instead of the Euclidean L2 norm. The goal is then to minimize this energy:

$$E(p) = \sum_{\mathbf{x}} \rho(D(\mathbf{x}; p)) \tag{9}$$

To penalize negative values in the difference image, we choose the error function as

$$\rho(x) = \begin{cases} \frac{1}{2}x^2 & ; \quad x < 0 \\ 0 & ; \quad x \geq 0. \end{cases} \tag{10}$$

L2 norm error function is chosen for negative values as in the original Lucas Kanade method. For positive values, it is set to be zero since the positive values are not errors. And the $\frac{1}{2}$ factor is used to simplify the following equations. The first and second derivatives of the error function $\rho(x)$ are as follows:

$$\rho'(x) = \begin{cases} x & ; \quad x < 0 \\ 0 & ; \quad x \geq 0, \end{cases} \tag{11}$$

$$\rho''(x) = \begin{cases} 1 & ; \quad x < 0 \\ 0 & ; \quad x \geq 0. \end{cases} \tag{12}$$

Then, the approximated energy $\hat{\mathrm{E}}(\mathbf{p} + \Delta\mathbf{p})$ is defined by the first order Taylor expansion of $I(\mathbf{W}(\mathbf{x}; \mathbf{p}+\Delta\mathbf{p}))$ as in Eq.(6):

$$\hat{\mathrm{E}}(\mathbf{p} + \Delta\mathbf{p}) = \sum_{\mathbf{x}} \rho\left(T(\mathbf{x}) - I(\mathbf{W}(\mathbf{x}; \mathbf{p})) - \left(\nabla I \frac{\partial \mathbf{W}}{\partial \mathbf{p}}\right) \Delta\mathbf{p} \right) \tag{13}$$

$$= \sum_{\mathbf{x}} \rho\left(\hat{D}(\mathbf{x}; \mathbf{p} + \Delta\mathbf{p}) \right),$$

where $\hat{D}(\mathbf{x}; \mathbf{p} + \Delta\mathbf{p})$ is the difference that is linearly approximated by the first order Taylor expansion:

$$\hat{D}(\mathbf{x}; \mathbf{p} + \Delta\mathbf{p}) = T(\mathbf{x}) - I(\mathbf{W}(\mathbf{x}; \mathbf{p})) - \left(\nabla I \frac{\partial \mathbf{W}}{\partial \mathbf{p}}\right) \Delta\mathbf{p}. \tag{14}$$

To solve the minimization problem in Eq.(5), we calculate the partial derivative of the approximated energy on $\Delta\mathbf{p}$ and find the solution to make the equation to be equal to zero:

$$\frac{\partial \hat{\mathrm{E}}(\mathbf{p} + \Delta\mathbf{p})}{\partial \Delta\mathbf{p}} = -\sum_{\mathbf{x}} \left[\nabla I \frac{\partial \mathbf{W}}{\partial \mathbf{p}}\right]^{\mathrm{T}} \rho'\left(\hat{D}(\mathbf{x}; \mathbf{p} + \Delta\mathbf{p})\right) \tag{15}$$

$$= -\sum_{\{\mathbf{x}:\hat{D}(\mathbf{x};\mathbf{p}+\Delta\mathbf{p})<0\}} \left[\nabla I \frac{\partial \mathbf{W}}{\partial \mathbf{p}}\right]^{\mathrm{T}} \hat{D}(\mathbf{x}; \mathbf{p} + \Delta\mathbf{p})$$

$$= -\sum_{\mathbf{x}} \rho''(\hat{D}(\mathbf{x}; \mathbf{p} + \Delta\mathbf{p})) \left[\nabla I \frac{\partial \mathbf{W}}{\partial \mathbf{p}}\right]^{\mathrm{T}} \hat{D}(\mathbf{x}; \mathbf{p} + \Delta\mathbf{p}) = 0.$$

The problem is that this equation cannot be solved analytically because of the nonlinear function $\rho''(D(\mathbf{x}; \mathbf{p}+\Delta\mathbf{p}))$ that depends on $\Delta\mathbf{p}$. To solve the equation, we assume that

$$\rho''(\hat{D}(\mathbf{x}; \mathbf{p} + \Delta\mathbf{p})) \approx \rho''(D(\mathbf{x}; \mathbf{p})) \tag{16}$$

for small $\Delta\mathbf{p}$. Then Eq.(15) can be solved by replacing $\hat{D}(\mathbf{x}; \mathbf{p}+\Delta\mathbf{p})$ with Eq.(14):

$$\Delta \mathbf{p} = H^{-1} \sum_{\{\mathbf{x}:D(\mathbf{x};\mathbf{p})<0\}} \left[\nabla I \frac{\partial \mathbf{W}}{\partial \mathbf{p}} \right]^{\mathrm{T}} D(\mathbf{W}(\mathbf{x};\mathbf{p})) \tag{17}$$

$$= H^{-1} \sum_{\mathbf{x}} \rho''(D(\mathbf{x};\mathbf{p})) \left[\nabla I \frac{\partial \mathbf{W}}{\partial \mathbf{p}} \right]^{\mathrm{T}} D(\mathbf{W}(\mathbf{x};\mathbf{p})),$$

where

$$H = \sum_{\{\mathbf{x}:D(\mathbf{x};\mathbf{p})<0\}} \left[\nabla I \frac{\partial \mathbf{W}}{\partial \mathbf{p}} \right]^{\mathrm{T}} \left[\nabla I \frac{\partial \mathbf{W}}{\partial \mathbf{p}} \right] \tag{18}$$

$$= \sum_{\mathbf{x}} \rho''(D(\mathbf{x};\mathbf{p})) \left[\nabla I \frac{\partial \mathbf{W}}{\partial \mathbf{p}} \right]^{\mathrm{T}} \left[\nabla I \frac{\partial \mathbf{W}}{\partial \mathbf{p}} \right].$$

Note that the terms in Eqs.(17) and (18) are included in the summations only if the difference $D(\mathbf{x};\mathbf{p})$ is negative. That means the updates are driven by the negative values which are the artifacts of the misalignments. Therefore this algorithm works directly to remove the misalignment artifacts on every iteration.

Figure 4 shows an example of the results with no motion compensation, motion interpolation method by [24], and our direct alignment method. As seen in the figure, the positive difference image with no motion compensation shows severe motion artifacts especially around edges and facial features. The negative difference image with no motion compensation has significant pixel intensities around edges and facial features. The motion interpolation method reduces the motion artifacts on the positive difference image and the pixel intensities on the negative difference image. Our proposed method further reduces those noises in both positive and negative difference images.

4   Experiments

We used the GT NIR database [9] to test our proposed image alignment method. The database consists of videos of drivers in vehicles taken with active NIR image differencing. Figure 5 shows the camera and illuminator hardware setup installed in a vehicle. The camera is Point Grey Research Flea2 IEEE1394a with Sony ICX424AL monochrome CCD. The image size is 640 by 480 pixels. The camera is equipped with an 880 nm optical band pass filter in front of the lens to take only near-IR frequency. The illuminator has 42 Fairchild Semiconductor QED223 NIR LEDs around the camera. The illuminator is controlled by a probe signal from the camera so that it is alternately turned on and off in even and odd frames respectively. The database contains 194 videos of 40 drivers. Videos were taken with various number of LEDs turned on (6, 12, 18, 24 LEDs) in diverse outdoor illumination conditions including windows open, windows closed, direct sunlight, cast shadows, daytime and nighttime.

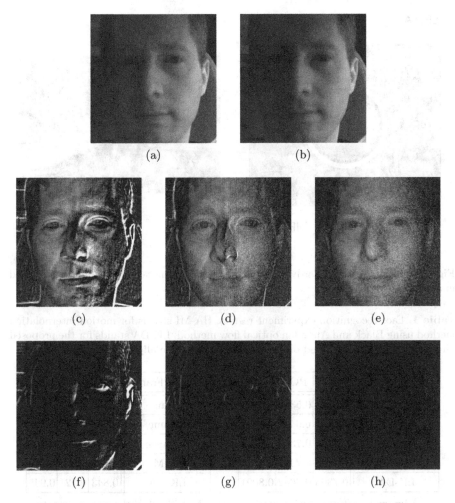

Fig. 4. Experimental comparison of image alignment methods: (a) detected face region in the I-frame (b) corresponding face region in the A-frame (c) positive difference image without alignment (d) positive difference image with motion interpolation (e) positive difference image with proposed alignment method (f) negative difference image without alignment (g) negative difference image with motion interpolation (h) negative difference image with proposed alignment method.

Face regions in I-frames of the videos are detected by the modified version of the boosted classifier proposed by Viola Jones [12,19]. Corresponding face regions in A-frames are found and aligned by our proposed method and the difference face images are calculated. And also the motion interpolation method is applied to consecutive I-frames to compare the face recognition results to ours. Then the difference face images go through a preprocessing stage including masking and pixel value normalization. Masking is used to consider only the

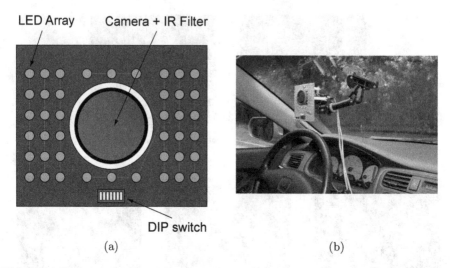

(a)   (b)

Fig. 5. (a) Illustration of hardware components (b) Camera and illuminator installed in a vehicle

Table 1. Face recognition experiment results. BA-MI stands for motion interpolation method using Black and Anandan optical flow method. LK-DA stands for the proposed direct image alignment based on the Lucas Kande image alignment mehtod.

Type of Frames	RAW	PCA	LDA
A-frame	0.5173	0.5352	0.5791
I-frame	0.6131	0.6412	0.6647
D-image	0.7109	0.7327	0.7390
BA-MI	0.7149	0.7416	0.7651
LK-DA	0.7366	0.7682	0.8091

(a) Image-based recognition rate.

Type of Frames	RAW	PCA	LDA
A-frame	0.531	0.551	0.612
I-frame	0.632	0.664	0.745
D-image	0.767	0.788	0.796
BA-MI	0.812	0.901	0.912
LK-DA	0.843	0.921	0.945

(b) Video-based recognition rate.

pixels inside the face boundary. The pixel values are then normalized to have zero mean and a unit standard deviation. Then two popular dimension reduction methods are applied: Principal Component Analysis (PCA) [18] and Linear Discriminant Analysis (LDA) [3]. PCA and LDA subspaces are trained by CBSR NIR database [10] which has 3,940 NIR face images of 197 subjects.

To test the effectiveness of the proposed direct image alignment method on face recognition, image and video-based face identification experiments were performed. Fist, 10 subjects are randomly selected from the GT NIR database. And a gallery video and a probe video are randomly selected for each subject. Then each found face image in each probe video are compared with all the found face images in the 10 gallery videos, and the face identity is determined by the minimum distance between two images in three subspace domains: raw, PCA and LDA. Then the same experiment is repeated 100 times with other randomly selected probe and gallery video of other randomly selected 10 subjects. The results in Table 1 (a) show that active NIR image differencing improves face recognition performance, and motion interpolation method using Black and Anandan optical flow method further improves the result. Furthermore, our proposed direct image alignment method based on Lucas-Kanade outperforms the both in raw, PCA and LDA domain. For video-based face identification experiment, the image-based result for a probe video are summed up by majority voting. Table 1 (b) shows the results and it also shows that our method outperformed the previous methods in raw, PCA and LDA domain.

5 Conclusion

Active NIR image diffenencing improves robustness of face recognition by generating images only lit by active NIR illumination. But the motion between frames introduces motion artifacts and reduces face recognition performance. A motion interpolation method was proposed to deal with the problem, but the method is not successful when the motion is not linear between frames. In this paper, we proposed an approach that can align the face image in I-frame and the face image in A-frame directly. The experimental result shows that the method outperforms the motion interpolation method. Since both NIR and visible lights are reflected on the surface and share the same physical properties, the proposed direct image alignment method can also be applied to flash and no-flash image pair applications where the motion is not linear.

References

1. Agrawal, A., Raskar, R., Nayar, S.K., Li, Y.: Removing photography artifacts using gradient projection and flash-exposure sampling. ACM Transactions on Graphics **24**(3), 828–835 (2005)
2. Baker, S., Matthews, I.: Lucas-Kanade 20 years on: A unifying framework. International Journal of Computer Vision **56**(3), 221–255 (2004)
3. Belhumeur, P., Hespanha, J., Kriegman, D., et al.: Eigenfaces vs. Fisherfaces: recognition using class specific linear projection. IEEE Transactions on Pattern Analysis and Machine Intelligence **19**(7), 711–720 (1997)
4. Black, M.J., Anandan, P.: The robust estimation of multiple motions: Parametric and piecewise-smooth flow fields. Computer Vision and Image Understanding **63**(1), 75–104 (1996)
5. DiCarlo, J.M., Xiao, F., Wandell, B.A.: Illuminating illumination. In: Color and Imaging Conference, vol. 2001, pp. 27–34. Society for Imaging Science and Technology (2001)
6. Drew, M.S., Lu, C., Finlayson, G.D.: Removing shadows using flash/noflash image edges. In: IEEE International Conference on Multimedia and Expo, pp. 257–260. IEEE (2006)
7. Eisemann, E., Durand, F.: Flash photography enhancement via intrinsic relighting. ACM Transactions on Graphics **23**(3), 673–678 (2004)
8. Hizem, W., Krichen, E., Ni, Y., Dorizzi, B., Garcia-Salicetti, S.: Specific sensors for face recognition. In: Zhang, D., Jain, A.K. (eds.) ICB 2005. LNCS, vol. 3832, pp. 47–54. Springer, Heidelberg (2005)

9. Kang, J., Hayes III, M.H.: Face recognition for vehicle personalization with near-IR frame differencing and pose clustering. In: IEEE International Conference on Consumer Electronics, pp. 455–456. IEEE (2015)

10. Li, S., Chu, R., Liao, S., Zhang, L.: Illumination Invariant Face Recognition Using Near-Infrared Images. IEEE Transactions on Pattern Analysis and Machine Intelligence **29**(4), 627–639 (2007)

11. Li, W., Zhang, J., Dai, Q.: Robust blind motion deblurring using near-infrared flash image. Journal of Visual Communication and Image Representation **24**(8), 1394–1413 (2013)

12. Lienhart, R., Maydt, J.: An extended set of haar-like features for rapid object detection. In: Proceedings of International Conference on Image Processing, vol. 1, p. I-900. IEEE (2002)

13. Lucas, B.D., Kanade, T.: An iterative image registration technique with an application to stereo vision. International Joint Conference on Artificial Intelligence **81**, 674–679 (1981)

14. Mikami, T., Sugimura, D., Hamamoto, T.: Capturing color and near-infrared images with different exposure times for image enhancement under extremely low-light scene. In: IEEE International Conference on Image Processing, pp. 669–673. IEEE (2014)

15. Petschnigg, G., Szeliski, R., Agrawala, M., Cohen, M., Hoppe, H., Toyama, K.: Digital photography with flash and no-flash image pairs. ACM Transactions on Graphics **23**(3), 664–672 (2004)

16. Seo, H.J., Milanfar, P.: Iteratively merging information from a pair of flash/no-flash images using nonlinear diffusion. In: IEEE International Conference on Computer Vision Workshops, pp. 1324–1331. IEEE (2011)

17. Sun, J., Sun, J., Kang, S.B., Xu, Z.B., Tang, X., Shum, H.Y.: Flash cut: foreground extraction with flash and no-flash image pairs. In: IEEE Conference on Computer Vision and Pattern Recognition, pp. 1–8. IEEE (2007)

18. Turk, M., Pentland, A.: Eigenfaces for recognition. Journal of Cognitive Neuroscience **3**(1), 71–86 (1991)

19. Viola, P., Jones, M.: Rapid object detection using a boosted cascade of simple features. In: Proceedings of Computer Vision and Pattern Recognition, vol. 1, p. I-511. IEEE (2001)

20. Yi, D., Liu, R., Chu, R.F., Wang, R., Liu, D., Li, S.Z.: Outdoor face recognition using enhanced near infrared imaging. In: Lee, S.-W., Li, S.Z. (eds.) ICB 2007. LNCS, vol. 4642, pp. 415–423. Springer, Heidelberg (2007)

21. Yoon, S.M., Lee, Y.J., Yoon, G.J., Yoon, J.: Adaptive total variation minimization-based image enhancement from flash and no-flash pairs. The Scientific World Journal 2014 (2014)

22. Zhuo, S., Guo, D., Sim, T.: Robust flash deblurring. In: IEEE Conference on Computer Vision and Pattern Recognition, pp. 2440–2447. IEEE (2010)

23. Zou, X., Kittler, J., Messer, K.: Ambient illumination variation removal by active near-IR imaging. In: Zhang, D., Jain, A.K. (eds.) ICB 2005. LNCS, vol. 3832, pp. 19–25. Springer, Heidelberg (2005)

24. Zou, X., Kittler, J., Messer, K.: Motion compensation for face recognition based on active differential imaging. In: Lee, S.-W., Li, S.Z. (eds.) ICB 2007. LNCS, vol. 4642, pp. 39–48. Springer, Heidelberg (2007)

Two-Stage Filtering Scheme for Sparse Representation Based Interest Point Matching for Person Re-identification

Mohamed Ibn Khedher[✉] and Mounim A. El Yacoubi

Institut Mines-Telecom, Telecom SudParis: CEA Saclay Nano-Innov,
91191 Gif sur Yvette Cedex, France
{mohamed.ibn_khedher,mounim.el_yacoubi}@telecom-sudparis.eu

Abstract. The objective of this paper is to study Interest Points (IP) filtering in video-based human re-identification tasks. The problem is that having a large number of IPs to describe person, Re-identification grows into a much time consuming task and IPs become redundant. In this context, we propose a Two-Stage filtering step. The first stage reduces the number of IP to be matched and the second ignores weak matched IPs participating in the re-identification decision. The proposed approach is based on the supervision of SVM, learned on training dataset. Our approach is evaluated on the dataset PRID-2011 and results show that it is fast and compare favorably with the state of the art.

Keywords: Person re-identification · Sparse representation · Filtering · SVM · Interest point

1 Introduction

Person re-identification is an important video surveillance task for tracking people over multiple cameras. It consists of finding people that leaves the view field of camera A and reappears in the view field of camera B. It is typical for video surveillance in shopping centers or hospitals where tracking a person for access control or following some incident could be cast into a re-identification problem.

Although the first re-identification systems were launched about one decade ago, the re-identification task is still a challenge due to some variability factors. The latter are mainly related to uncontrolled acquisition conditions and to the amount of data available on each camera. Indeed, on one hand, only one image or one video sequence is available for each person and each camera. On the other hand, the same person may have very different appearances under uncontrolled acquisition conditions, owing to lighting conditions, change of view angle and partial or total occlusions (Fig.1). These factors explain the relatively low performance of existing re-identification systems compared to standard biometric systems that identify people from their faces, iris, gaits, etc. Figure 1 gives some examples of the challenges raised by the re-identification task.

© Springer International Publishing Switzerland 2015
S. Battiato et al. (Eds.): ACIVS 2015, LNCS 9386, pp. 345–356, 2015.
DOI: 10.1007/978-3-319-25903-1_30

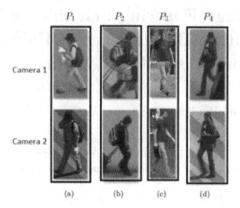

Fig. 1. Examples of re-identification challenges showing changes across two cameras in (a) lighting conditions, (c) view angles and (b,d) presence of other people or objects.

Re-identification methods are based either on single image (single-shot scheme) [8] or on a set of images (multi-shot scheme) [7,9]. The latter may consist of the whole video sequence or of few frames that are usually not ordered. For both schemes, performance improvement would be relevant if it is associated with increasing the re-identification rate or reducing the re-identification running time. This paper aims at reducing the running time of a multi-shot re-identification approach based on local features matching.

A re-identification system consists usually of two stages: features extraction and matching. In this work, Interest Points (IPs) are used as local descriptors. These features are able to make a tradeoff between extracting only salient feature points and keeping sufficient information to describe a person. The use of IPs is also motivated by their robustness to change of acquisition conditions. The IPs matching proposed in this paper is performed via Sparse Representation (SR), rather than classical similarity techniques used in the state of the art as the former is better at tackling IP variability across two different camera settings. The idea behind SR in the IP matching context is to express each query IP as a linear combination vector of reference IPs. This representation corresponds to a sparse vector whose nonzero entries correspond to the weights of reference IPs. The SR is used to determine the identity of the query IP. In fact, a reconstruction error is calculated for each reference identity using only the coefficients corresponding to this identity. The query IP is identified as the reference identity minimizing the reconstruction error of the sparse representation. Finally, the reference person obtaining the majority of votes is claimed as the re-identified person.

In spite of the superiority of the SR matching over similarity-based matching, the former suffers from computing speed issues as building a SR for each query IP over closest subset of the IP reference set turns out to be a costly operation. To alleviates such a burden, we propose to add a filtering step that aims at rejecting matched IPs pairs that are probably less reliable. Such matched pairs may result, for instance, from: 1) matching of a background's IP to a foreground's IP (silhouette), 2) matching of IPs associated with different parts of the silhouette and 3) matching of IPs associated with different people. The proposed method is based on two filtering stages for each test video sequence after IPs extraction: the first, named pre-SR filter, is carried out prior to performing SR-based matching while the second, named post-SR filter, is performed after the SR-based matching is over. The pre-SR filter consists of filtering IPs that are relatively dissimilar to their closest reference IPs. Our motivation is the following: if a query IP is significantly dissimilar to its closest reference IP, its set of k-closest reference IPs are even much more dissimilar. Since this set represents the input to SR-based matching, it is reasonable to discard the query IP before SR matching takes place as the latter is likely to be unreliable. The post-SR filtering consists of filtering query IPs whose SR-based matching turns out to be ambiguous. Such an ambiguity can be inferred by analyzing whether non-null SR coefficients are are associated with several persons in the reference dataset. For both filtering stages, the filtering mechanism is learned through a binary SVM (Support Vector Machine) learned on the target training dataset. The first SVM takes as input pairs of IPs (query IP, closest reference IP), while the second SVM takes as input the sparse representation output vector the components of which correspond to the reconstruction errors associated with non-null coefficients.

The rest of the paper is organized as follows. In section 2, a state of the art is presented. The principle of our approach is presented in section 3. Sections 4, 5 and 6 present respectively the major steps of the re-identification system: feature extraction, filtering and matching. The section 8 includes the experimental part and finally a conclusion and perspectives are presented.

2   State of the Art

Several taxonomies of recent re-identification approaches are presented in [1,3]. Re-identification approaches can be classified as unsupervised or supervised depending on whether a learning phase is called for or not: .

Unsupervised Approaches: This category mainly focuses on feature design. Usually, an image is represented by a set of IPs or is divided into a set of strips or regions (usually corresponding to body parts). Regarding approaches based on IP features, the authors in [9] describe the person by a set of IPs, namely SURF, extracted from a short video sequence. In [11], a SIFT descriptor is combined with a geometric description related to the IP position. IPs are matched locally via 1-NN (1-Nearest Neighbor) using the Euclidean distance in [9] and globally via a Bag of Features (BoF) representation in [11]. Among region based approaches, Farenzena et al. [5] propose the Symmetry-Driven Accumulation of Local Features (SDALF) by exploiting the symmetry property of the human body. The latter is decomposed, via two horizontals axes into three parts. Each part is represented by a combination of three features related to color and texture.

Supervised Methods: The learning phase allows learning parameters to optimize the re-identification accuracy. This learning phase can be related to parameters of the metric used to compare images, or to the discriminant descriptors selected among the extracted features. Regarding learning metrics, the authors of [8] combine a weighted "Ensemble of Localized Features" (ELF) to represent a person. The weights are learned using the Adaboost algorithm. In [4], authors learn the parameters of the Mahalanobis distance; the matching step is performed via the kNN algorithm. In [19], the re-identification task is considered as a problem of "Probabilistic Relative Distance Comparison" (PRDC); the distance probabilities are learned on a training dataset. Prosser et al. [14] formulated the person re-identification task as a ranking problem. The authors used different ranking algorithms such as RankBoost or RankSVM to learn pairwise similarities. As far as discriminative methods are concerned, most of the works found in the literature are based on dimensionality reduction. The authors in [15,16] introduce a graph-based approach for a non-linear dimensionality reduction.

Regarding IPs filtering methods, only few are proposed in the state of the art. In [9] an empirically preset number of the best matched IPs is chosen. In [13], two interest points p_0 and p_1 ($p_0 \in$ Reference and $p_1 \in$ Query) are matched if $d(p_1,p_0) < c.d(p_1,p_i) \ \forall \ p_i \in$ Reference, where c is a preset coefficient ($c < 1$ and $d(.,.)$ is the Euclidean distance). In [12], a method of acceptance and rejection of SURF correspondence is proposed; it is based on the likelihood ratio of two GMMs learned on the reference set. The filtering methods proposed in [9,13] are based on empirical setting, while in [12] the GMM-based filtering lacks modeling power since it learns only the uni-variate distance between matched IP pairs.

Our approach lies in the supervised category as it harnesses a training dataset to learn the post-SR filtering SVM model. Our two-stage filtering method is automatic and does not depend on empirically parameters. Moreover, contrary to the filtering methods above, it has stronger modeling power since it learns relatively high dimensional vectors as detailed in next sections.

3   Proposed Approach

Our approach consists basically of four stages: 1) Feature extraction, 2) Two stage IP Filtering: a) pre sparse representation (pre-SR filtering) and b) post sparse representation (post-SR filtering); 3) IPs Matching via sparse representation and 4) Person re-identification based on majority vote rule. Figure 2 shows the flowchart of our approach.

First, for each input test video, IP features, namely SURF, are extracted to provide the person's signature. Then the first filtering is applied. After matching each test SURF to the closest reference one, we generate a difference vector, obtained by component-wise difference of the matched IP pair descriptors. The pre-SR SVM, pre-learned on a training dataset, accepts the test SURF IP for subsequent SR matching or rejects it depending on the winning SVM class. Next, for each retained SURF, a SR is calculated. The SR coefficients are used as input of the post-SR pre-learned SVM to accept or reject the test SURF. Finally, for each retained SURF and using its SR coefficients, a vote is added to the reference identity minimizing its reconstruction. In this way, a vote vector of dimension

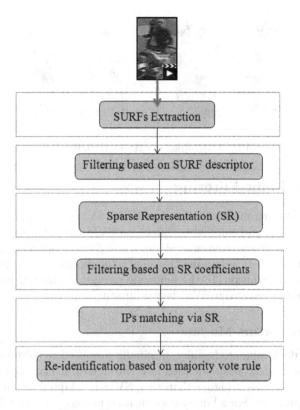

Fig. 2. Flowchart of our approach.

equal to the number of reference identities is generated. The reference person obtaining the majority of votes is claimed as the re-identified person.

4   Features Extraction

SURF is a popular IP descriptor proposed by [2], and used for several tasks including person re-identification. SURF is robust to geometric transformations (view angle and scale) and lighting variations. It presents a good compromise between the robustness to geometric transformations and the computation time.

The computation of SURF descriptor for an image involves two major steps: interest points detection and descriptor extraction. The detection step is based on the approximation of the determinant of the Hessian matrix by using a convolution of the image with a set of box filters; while the descriptor is based on the Haar wavelet. The SURF descriptor considers a square region around the IP, oriented according to a predefined orientation. This region is divided into 4x4 grids to form 16 sub-regions. Within each sub-region, four components related to Haar-wavelet x-responses and y-responses are calculated. To ensure illumination invariance, the descriptor is normalized to unit length. Figure 3 shows the detected SURF points within a samples from image silhouettes.

Fig. 3. Samples of extracted SURFs.

5 Interest Point Filtering

The proposed filtering method is based on SVM. SVM is used to classify IPs into two classes: reliable and unreliable. Based on SVM output, the filtering model discards unreliable IPs and retains reliable ones. SVM is often used in computer vision applications such as handwritten character recognition, pedestrian detection and action recognition. In the following paragraph, we introduce the SVM principle an then present our SVM-based filtering approach.

5.1 Support Vectors Machine

SVM [17] is a discriminant classifier, originally proposed to solve binary classification problems .i.e. data classification into two classes. In classification problems with a number of classes higher than two, SVM is adapted to solve the multi-class decision problem. For a binary classification problem, assume that we have a series of input d-dimension vectors x_i with corresponding labels $y_i \in \{-1, +1\}$, where $+1$ and -1 indicate the two classes. The goal of SVM is to divide the training data $(x_1, y_1), (x_2, y_2), ...(x_N, y_N)$ into two classes. The idea is to estimate an objective function $f : x_i \longmapsto y_i$ able to assign each vector x_i to one of the two classes. Usually, samples from different classes cannot be linearly separated by a hyperplane. To tackle this problem, SVM projects the input vectors, $\{x_i, 1 \leq i \leq N\}$, into a high dimensional feature space $\phi(x_i) \in H$ where data become linearly separately by a hyperplane: $w \cdot \phi(x) + b = 0$. The mapped function ϕ is implicitly defined by a Kernel function $K(x_i, x_j)$ which defines an inner product between x_i and x_j in the space H. The objective function that defines the SVM model is defined as following (Eq.1):

$$g(x) = \text{sign}\left(\sum_i y_i \alpha_i K(x_i, x) + b \right) \tag{1}$$

where α_i and b are found by using the SVC learning algorithm [17] and K is the RBF Kernel $(K(x_i, x_j) = \exp(-\gamma \|x_i - x_j\|^2)$, γ being a kernel parameter).

5.2 Filtering Method

To use SVM, two steps are needed: 1) Model Estimation and 2) Class prediction. First, a model is constructed from a training dataset consisting of people filmed

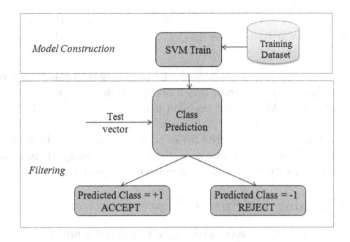

Fig. 4. Filtering flowchart using SVM

by two cameras A and B. Then for each query vector, SVM assign it to one from the two classes. Figure 4 shows the principle of filtering using SVM.

Model Estimation. To train the pre-SR and post-SR filtering models, SVM takes as input two vector sets: S_{Same} (positive vectors associated with class $+1$) and S_{Diff} (negative vectors associated with class -1). S_{Same} and S_{Diff} model respectively reliable and unreliable IPs. We explain below the construction of S_{Diff} and S_{Same} in both filtering. For the first filtering, we consider all training IPs. Then, IPs corresponding to camera A are matched to those corresponding to camera B to form IP pairs. Two cases are possible:

1. If the matched pair is associated with the same person, the difference vector between the pair descriptors is added to S_{Same}.
2. If the matched pair is associated with two different persons, the difference vector between the pair descriptors is added to S_{Diff}.

For the second filter, only IPs retained from the first filtering are used. To form S_{Same} and S_{Diff}, we consider the SRs of retained IPs. Two cases are possible :

1. If the query IP and the reference identity minimizing its reconstruction are associated with the same person, then the SR vector is added to S_{Same}.
2. If the query IP and the reference identity minimizing its reconstruction are associated with two different persons, then the SR vector is added to S_{Diff}.

After sets S_{Same} and S_{Diff} are generated in this way for either filter, the associated SVM model is estimated by computing the hyperplane separating S_{Same} and S_{Diff} in the non-linear space defined by the RBF kernel . The parameter γ of the latter is automatically optimized using a cross-validation method.

Class Prediction. This step consists of assigning a query IP to one of the two classes using the SVM-based filter model. The Acceptation/Rejection decision is performed as following:

- In the first filtering stage, each query IP is matched to the closest reference IP. Then, the matched IP pair difference descriptor is input into the pre-SR SVM model. If SVM's output decision is class +1, the query IP is retained, otherwise it is rejected.
- In the second filtering stage, the SR of each IP is input to the post-SR SVM model. If SVM's output decision is class +1, the query IP is retained for subsequent majority votes rule, otherwise it is rejected.

6   IPs Matching via Sparse Representation

Sparse representation has been studied since two decades but it became popular in vision only recently after its successful application in face recognition [18]. The main idea of sparse representation is to find a representation of a signal (a query IP, y, in our case) involving the smallest number of elements of a preselected dictionary A (in our case, A is a subset of reference IPs) by solving the Eq. 2:

$$y = A\alpha \tag{2}$$

To match one query IP q via SR, three steps are applied: 1) Dictionary construction, 2) Sparse representation and 3) Identity assignment.

- **Dictionary construction:** to reduce the running time of SR, the dictionary A is composed of the N closest IPs from the reference dataset. The dimension of A is (DxN) where each column represents an IP's descriptor ($D = 64$, dimension of SURF descriptor) and N is empirically set to 200.
- **Sparse Representation:** the goal of SR consists of finding the sparsest representation α_s of Eq.2. In this work, we use the Coordinate Descent Algorithm [6] to solve Eq.2 as following :

$$\alpha_s = \min_{\alpha}(\|\Phi\alpha - y\|_2^2 + \lambda\|\alpha\|_1) \tag{3}$$

The advantage of this solution is the use of a tuning parameter λ, to adjust the tradeoff between sparsity term $\|\alpha\|_1$ and error reconstruction term $\|\Phi\alpha - y\|_2^2$.
- **Identity Assignment:** the non-zero coefficients of α_s are used to identify the query IP. In fact, a residual r_i is calculated for each reference identity i having at least one non-zero coefficient:

$$r_i = \|Ax_i - q\|_2^2 \tag{4}$$

where x_i is a coefficient vector obtained from α_s with all zero elements except those associated with the identity i. The query IP is identified as person j minimizing r_i ($1 \leq i \leq M$, where M is the number of reference identities) and a vote equal to 1 is added to the identity j. Finally, the query person is claimed as the person has the majority of votes.

7   Experimental Results

We evaluated our approach on the public dataset PRID-2011. PRID-2011 was obtained from two cameras (A and B) located on street. 385 people were filmed by camera-A and 749 people were filmed by Camera-B, 200 being common to the two cameras. A is used for query and B as reference. All images were normalized to 64x128 pixels. On average, 80 images are available per person. PRID-2011 is evaluated with two protocols: supervised protocol to evaluate directly our approach and unsupervised protocol to compare with the state of the art.

- Supervised Protocol: the dataset is divided into two parts: training and test. The training set contains video sequences of the first 100 people that appear both in Cameras A and B. Each person has one sequence per camera. The test set contains the remaining 649 people from Camera-B as reference and the remaining 100 common people in Camera-A for query.
- Unsupervised Protocol: the evaluation consists of searching the common 200 people filmed by Camera-A in the gallery set (Camera-B) of 749 people.

In the rest of this paper, the standard approach means non filtering is applied.

7.1   Supervised Protocol

We evaluated our approach on the PRID-2011 dataset using the supervised protocol. Table 1 compares our approach with the standard one according to two performance indicators: re-identification rate and running time per image.

Table 1. Results of our approach on PRID-2011 (Supervised Protocol)

Filtering Rate	Re-identification Rate	Running Time / Image
80.55%	37%	0.94(s)
No Filtering	36%	1.86(s)

This shows that our filtering scheme is able to maintain accuracy (even slightly outperforming the one obtained by the standard one) while significantly increasing speed since it basically halves the processing time. As SVM actually computes a score for each class and assigns the query IP to the class with the maximum score, we can investigate more deeply the tradeoff between filtering and re-identification rate. This is carried out by varying the ratio of the two classes scores under which to filter or accept an IP i.e. accepting an IP if score(+1) $>$ c.score(-1), where c is a preset coefficient and score(.) is a function returning the score of input class. The results shown in Tab.1 correspond to $c = 1$. Taking the first filtering (pre-SR) stage as an example, Fig.5 shows the evolution of re-identification and filtering rates according to coefficient c.

Figure 5 shows that the default value of parameter $c = 1$ used by SVM is optimal and gives a good tradeoff between maintaining accuracy and increasing

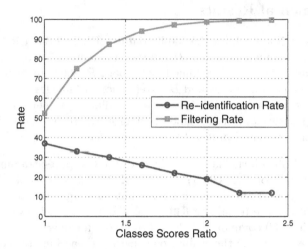

Fig. 5. Performances on PRID-2011 according to classes scores ratio

speed. For $c = 1$, 80.55% of IPs are automatically filtered. However, when we increase the filtering rate, the re-identification rate decreases. Hence, our filtering scheme does not need any empirical threshold as it relies on selecting directly the winning class, $+1$ or -1.

7.2 Unsupervised Protocol

PRID-2011 is evaluated in the state of the art only using the unsupervised protocol where all the dataset is used in test. Our standard approach, where no filtering is applied, achieves an improvement of 5% compared to [12] and an improvement of 9.82% compared to [10]. This improvement is significant given the large size of the dataset and proves that the sparse representation can provide richer information compared to other interest point matching like [12]. To overcome the issue of missing training data for filtering in this protocol, we use two external datasets as training datasets: CAVIAR4REID and WARD. Figure 6 shows samples of the two datasets.

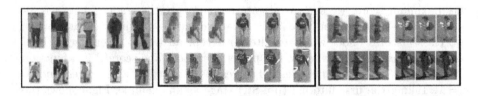

Fig. 6. Samples from datasets: CAVIAR4REID (Left); WARD (Middle); PRID-2011 (Right)

Table 2 shows the obtained results using CAVIAR4REID and WARD compared to the standard approach (first row of Tab.2).

Table 2. Results of our approach on PRID-2011

Training dataset	Filtering Rate	Re-identification Rate	Running Time
—	No Filtering	27%	1.86(s)
CAVIAR4REID	73.11%	27.5%	1.28(s)
WARD	77.97%	26.5%	0.92(s)

Table 2 shows that despite the use of other training datasets, we can correctly estimate the SVM-based filtering models. This may be explained by the fact that CAVIAR4REID and WARD have the same characteristics and variability between the two cameras as in PRID-2011 (lighting variation, view angle change, etc) (See Fig.6). On the other hand, the results confirm the benefits of filtering. Indeed, by filtering 73.11% using CAVIAR4REID or 77.97% using WARD, our approach achieves an improvement in running time of about 51% while maintaining the re-identification rate obtained with the standard approach.

8 Conclusion

This paper has studied the importance of Interest Point filtering in re-identification tasks. It proposed a two filtering stage scheme based on SVM for estimating the reliability of IPs and discarding them accordingly. The first stage consisted of filtering IPs that are significantly dissimilar from their closest reference IPs. The second stage consisted of filtering IPs that have a noisy sparse representation. The experiment results on the large dataset PRID-2011 show that our approach leads to significant reduction in re-identification processing time and outperforms the state of the art. In the future, we will focus on other filtering scheme that better harnesses the rich information stemming from sparse representation. One direction in this respect is to analyze the set of person identities retrieved from SR and filter an IP depending on whether such an SR is generated mainly by one reference person (retain the IP) or rather by many (filter the IP).

References

1. Bak, S., Corvee, E., Bremond, F., Thonnat, M.: Boosted human re-identification using Riemannian manifolds. Image and Vision Computing **30**, 443–452 (2011)
2. Bay, H., Tuytelaars, T., Gool, L.V.: Surf: Speeded up robust features. In: European Conference on Computer Vision, pp. 404–417 (2006)
3. Bazzani, L., Cristani, M., Murino, V.: Symmetry-driven accumulation of local features for human characterization and re-identification. Computer Vision and Image Understanding **117**, 130–144 (2013)

4. Dikmen, M., Akbas, E., Huang, T., Ahuja, N.: Pedestrian recognition with a learned metric. In: Asian Conference on Computer Vision (2010)
5. Farenzena, M., Bazzani, L., Perina, A., Murino, V., Cristani, M.: Person re-identification by symmetry-driven accumulation of local features. In: Conference on Computer Vision and Pattern Recognition, pp. 2360–2367 (2010)
6. Friedman, J.H., Hastie, T., Tibshirani, R.: Regularization paths for generalized linear models via coordinate descent. Journal of Statistical Software **33**, 1–22 (2010)
7. Gheissari, N., Sebastian, T.B., Hartley, R.: Person reidentification using spatiotemporal appearance. In: Computer Society Conference on Computer Vision and Pattern Recognition, pp. 1528–1535 (2006)
8. Gray, D., Tao, H.: Viewpoint invariant pedestrian recognition with an ensemble of localized features. In: Proceedings of the 10th European Conference on Computer Vision, vol. Part I, pp. 262–275 (2008)
9. Hamdoun, O., Moutarde, F., Stanciulescu, B., Steux, B.: Person re-identification in multi-camera system by signature based on interest point descriptors collected on short video sequences. In: International Conference on Distributed Smart Cameras, pp. 1–6 (2008)
10. Hirzer, M., Beleznai, C., Roth, P.M., Bischof, H.: Person re-identification by descriptive and discriminative classification. In: Scandinavian conference on Image analysis, pp. 91–102 (2011)
11. Jungling, K., Arens, M.: View-invariant person re-identification with an implicit shape model. In: International Conference on Advanced Video and Signal-Based Surveillance, pp. 197–202 (2011)
12. Khedher, M.I., El-Yacoubi, M.A., Dorizzi, B.: Probabilistic matching pair selection for surf-based person re-identification. In: International Conference of Biometrics Special Interest Group, pp. 1–6 (2012)
13. de Oliveira, I.O., de Souza Pio, J.L.: People reidentification in a camera network. In: International Conference on Dependable, Autonomic and Secure Computing, pp. 461–466 (2009)
14. Prosser, B., Zheng, W.S., Gong, S., Xiang, T.: Person re-identification by support vector ranking. In: British Machine Vision Conference, pp. 21.1–21.11 (2010)
15. Truong Cong, D.N., Khoudour, L., Achard, C., Meurie, C., Lezoray, O.: People re-identification by spectral classification of silhouettes. Signal Processing **90**, 2362–2374 (2010)
16. Truong Cong, D.N., Achard, C., Khoudour, L., Douadi, L.: Video sequences association for people re-identification across multiple non-overlapping cameras. In: International Conference on Image Analysis and Processing, pp. 179–189 (2009)
17. Vapnik, V.N.: Statistical Learning Theory. Wiley-Interscience (1998)
18. Wright, J., Yang, A.Y., Ganesh, A., Sastry, S.S., Ma, Y.: Robust face recognition via sparse representation. IEEE Transactions on Pattern Analysis and Machine Intelligence **31**, 210–227 (2009)
19. Zheng, W.S., Gong, S., Xiang, T.: Person re-identification by probabilistic relative distance comparison. In: Conference on Computer Vision and Pattern Recognition, pp. 649–656 (2011)

Distance-Based Descriptors
for Pedestrian Detection

Radovan Fusek$^{(\boxtimes)}$ and Eduard Sojka

Department of Computer Science, Technical University of Ostrava,
FEECS, 17. listopadu 15, 708 33 Ostrava-Poruba, Czech Republic
{radovan.fusek,eduard.sojka}@vsb.cz

Abstract. In this paper, we propose an improvement of the detection approach that is based on the distance function. In the method, the distance values are computed inside the image to describe the properties of objects. The appropriately chosen distance values are used in the feature vector that is utilized as an input for the SVM classifier. The key challenge is to find the right way in which the distance values should be used to describe the appearance of objects effectively. The basic version of this method was proposed to solve the face detection problem. As we observed from the experiments, the method in the basic form is not suitable for pedestrian detection. Therefore, the goal of this paper is to improve this method, and create the pedestrian detector that outperforms the state-of-the-art detectors. The experiments show that the proposed improvement overcomes the accuracy of the basic version by approximately 10%.

Keywords: Object detection · Sliding window · Distance function · SVM

1 Introduction

In the process of detection, we use the sliding window technique that represents the popular and successful approach for object detection. The main idea of this approach is that the input image is scanned by a rectangular window at multiple scales. Many windows represent the result of the scanning process. A vector of features is obtained for each window. The vector is then used as an input for the classifier (in our case, the SVM classifier). During the classification process, some windows are marked as containing the object. Using the sliding window approach, multiple positive detections may appear, especially around the objects. The detections are merged into the final bounding box that represents the resulting detection. The classifier that determines whether or not the window contains the object is trained over the training set that consists of positive and negative images. The key point is to find which quantities should be used to effectively encode the image inside the sliding window.

In the method we propose, the geodesic distances are computed inside the sliding window to describe the objects. The preliminary version of this approach

© Springer International Publishing Switzerland 2015
S. Battiato et al. (Eds.): ACIVS 2015, LNCS 9386, pp. 357–368, 2015.
DOI: 10.1007/978-3-319-25903-1_31

was presented in [9], where the properties of the method were shown in the area of face detection. The image inside the sliding window is divided into the cells in which the distances are computed. The distance values are used to create the feature vector. This vector is then used as an input for the SVM classifier. Unfortunately, only one way of how to encode the distance values inside the image is shown in [9]. We experimented with this detector, and we observed that the method (in the version from [9]) is not suitable for describing the pedestrians. Therefore, we propose an extension of the method, thanks to which the method can be effectively used in the area of pedestrian detection. The improvement is based on extending the way of how the distance values are encoded. Using this improvement, we are able to outperform the basic version of the distance detector as well as the state-of-the-art detectors in the area.

The rest of this paper is organized as follows. In the next section, we provide the overview of the features that can be extracted from images. We focus on the methods that use the sliding window technique. Thereafter, we describe the main idea of the proposed improvement. Finally, we show the experiment results. The last section is a conclusion.

2 Related Work

The Haar-like features represent a popular and famous approach that is very often used for object description. The main idea behind the Haar-like features is that the features can encode the differences of mean intensities between the rectangular areas. For instance, in the problem of face detection, the regions around the eyes are brighter than the areas of the eyes; the regions bellow or on top of the eyes have different intensities that the eyes itself. These specific characteristics can be encoded by one two-rectangular feature, and the value of this feature can be calculated as the difference between the sum of the pixel values inside the rectangles. The Haar-like features were proposed by Papageorgiou and Poggio [16]. In their paper, the Haar-like features are combined with the SVM classifier to create the face, car, and pedestrian detectors. Viola and Jones [20] proposed the very efficient way of how these features can be used in the combination of the integral image and AdaBoost algorithm. An extension of the Haar feature set was presented by Lienhart et al.[14]. The authors proposed the 45 ° rotated features. The rotated features are able to reduce false detections and achieve more accurate results. A comparison of face and facial feature detectors based on the Viola-Jones general object detection framework was presented in [2]. Recently, the improvement of Haar-like features for efficient object detection under a wide range of illumination conditions was proposed in [18].

The local binary patterns (LBP) represent an another way of how to encode the shape of objects. The LBP operator was proposed by Ojala et al.[15] for texture analysis. Since then, due to their positive properties (e.g. invariance to lighting changes), LBP were used in many detection tasks, especially for facial analysis. For example, LBP were used to create the face detector in low-resolution images in [10]. In [22], multi-block local binary patterns (MB-LBP) for face detection were proposed. In this method, the authors encode the rectangular regions by the local binary pattern operator and the gentle AdaBoost is used for feature selection. The authors showed that MB-LBP are more distinctive than the Haar-like features and the original LBP features. The comprehensive study of facial expression recognition methods using LBP was proposed in [19]. The survey of facial analysis methods using LBP was presented in [11].

The histograms of oriented gradients (HOG) proposed in [5] are considered as the state-of-the-art method in the area of pedestrian detection. In HOG, the gradient magnitudes and orientations are computed and composed into the feature vector that is used as an input for the SVM classifier. Many methods and applications based on HOG were presented in recent years. The method that combines principal component analysis (PCA) with the HOG features was proposed in [12]. Co-occurrence histograms of oriented gradients (CoHOG) that encode the spatial relationship between the pairs of pixels were proposed in [21]. The face recognition method using the HOG features was proposed in [6].

Due to the fact that the geodesic distance is used in the paper, we mention the works in which this distance was used in the area of image processing. Image segmentation and object detection methods based on the geodesic distance were presented in [1,4,7,17].

3 Proposed Method

The main idea of the presented detector is based on the fact that the shape (appearance) of objects can be described using the distance values. If we speak about the distance values in this paper, we have in mind the geodesic distance. However, any appropriate distance function can be used (e.g. resistance distance, diffusion distance).

Consider the image that consists of one object of constant brightness. Suppose the point located in the mentioned object. From this point, the distances are computed inside the whole image. After that, the distance values can be investigated. Since the object has constant brightness, the distances inside the object are shorter than the distances investigated outside the object, which is the fact that the edges of the object create the barrier, and this barrier is reflected in the distance values. Therefore, we can conclude that the values of distances are different inside and outside of object and this assumption can be used to encode the properties of objects.

In the real images (e.g pedestrian images), the situation is more complicated. One point placed inside the objects will not probably be enough to cover all areas and important places of objects. Therefore, the image inside the sliding window is divided into the small cells. Inside each cell, the center point of the cell is determined. From this point, the distances are calculated to all remaining points within the cell. In [9], the authors proposed only one pattern how to encode the distance values. This pattern is shown in Fig. 1. The red point represents the center point of cell. The green points represent the places around the center point that are taken into account; i.e. the distances from the center point to

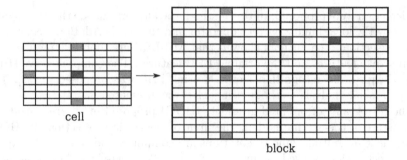

Fig. 1. An example of 9 × 9 cells that are grouped into one block. In this particular case, four values are used in the feature vector (depicted by green color) from each cell. The centers of cells are represented by red color. From the centers, the distances are computed.

these places are than used in the feature vector. To achieve better resistance to illumination changes, the cells are grouped into the larger blocks (similarly to HOG) and the distance values are normalized within the blocks.

We experimented with this pattern and we observed (as can be seen in Section 4) that this pattern is not suitable for pedestrian detection. The four values that are used in each cell are not enough to describe the shape of pedestrians. Therefore, we propose the extended versions of this pattern. The proposed patterns can be seen in Fig. 2.

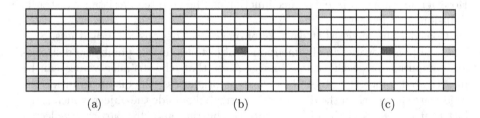

(a)   (b)   (c)

Fig. 2. An example of three 11 × 11 cell patterns that are used inside the blocks. In this particular case, eight values (areas) are used in the feature vector (depicted by green color). The centers of cells are represented by red color. From the centers, the distances are computed.

All proposed patterns use eight values from each cell in the feature vector. In the patterns (a) and (b), the averages of distance values are calculated inside the green areas. In the pattern (c), one value from each green point is used. In the next section, we propose the pedestrian detectors based on the original pattern and the new patterns to compare these detectors with the state-of-the-art approaches.

4   Pedestrian Detection

For the training phase, we collected 2500 positive images and 10000 negative images. We combined the pedestrian images from the CBCL Pedestrian Database [3] with the images from the Daimler benchmark [8] for the positive set. For the negative set, the images were randomly sampled from the INRIA Person Dataset [5].

Fig. 3. The visualization of the distance function values inside each cell of the $Dist_2$ configuration. The values of distance function are depicted by the level of brightness.

To find the optimal sizes of sliding windows, cells, and blocks, we experimented with the following three configurations: $Dist_1$, $Dist_2$, $Dist_3$. The configurations use the original pattern from Fig. 1. Some examples of the values of distance function are shown in Fig. 3.

The parameters of the $Dist_1$ configuration are as follows. The size of sliding window is 70 × 140, the size of blocks is 14 × 14, the size of cells is 7 × 7, the horizontal block step size is 7. The detector using this configuration has 2736 descriptors for one position of sliding window; each window consists of 171 overlapping blocks and each block consists of 4 cells, i.e. 684 cells are defined in each window. Finally, each cell is described using 4 distance values, i.e. 2736 descriptors are used (684×4).

The parameters of the $Dist_2$ configuration are as follows. The size of sliding window is 72 × 144, the size of blocks is 18 × 18, the size of cells is 9 × 9, the horizontal block step size is 9. The detector using this configuration has 1680 descriptors for one position of sliding window; each window consists of 105 overlapping blocks and each block consists of 4 cells, i.e. 196 cells are defined in each window. Finally, each cell is described using 4 distance values, i.e. 1680 descriptors are used (420×4).

The parameters of the $Dist_3$ configuration are as follows. The size of sliding window is 88 × 176, the size of blocks is 22 × 22, the size of cells is 11 × 11, the horizontal block step size is 11. The detector using this configuration has 1680 descriptors for one position of sliding window; each window consists of 105 overlapping blocks and each block consists of 4 cells, i.e. 420 cells are defined in each window. Finally, each cell is described using 4 distance values, i.e. 1680 descriptors are used (420×4).

Let us compare these configurations. For the test, we collected 85 images from [5]. In the detection stage, the sliding window scanned 10 different resolutions of input image. Before the process of performance calculation, the positive detections were merged to one if at least 3 positive detections hit approximately one place in image. In Table 1, the detection performances are shown. For evaluation, we use the following quantities; Precision = TP/(TP+FP), Sensitivity = TP/(TP+FN), F1 score (harmonic mean of precision and sensitivity) = 2 × Precision × Sensitivity/(Precision + Sensitivity); TP = number of true positives, FP = number of false positives, FN = number of false negatives.

Table 1. The pedestrian detection results of the $Dist_1$, $Dist_2$, and $Dist_3$ configurations.

	Precision	Sensitivity	F1 score
$Dist_1$	81.21%	77.91%	79.53%
$Dist_2$	88.98%	68.48%	77.40%
$Dist_3$	79.89%	84.24%	82.01%

From Table 1, it can be seen that the detection results are not convincing. As we mentioned in the previous section, this experiment shows that if only the four values from each cell are included into the feature vector, it is non sufficient to describe the shape of pedestrian properly. However, due to the fact that the best detection results achieved the detector that used the $Dist_3$ configuration (F1 82.01%), the further experiments were based on this detector, because we wanted to verify whether this detector could be improved using the proposed extended patterns.

Let us consider the detector $Dist_{3(a)}$ with the same settings like in $Dist_3$, however with the change that the pattern is from Fig. 2(a). Similarly, the pattern from Fig. 2(b) is used in $Dist_{3(b)}$, and the pattern from Fig. 2(c) is used in $Dist_{3(c)}$. The new detectors have 3360 descriptors for one position of sliding window; each window consists of 105 overlapping blocks and each block consists of 4 cells, i.e. 420 cells are defined in each window. Finally, each cell is described using 8 distance values, i.e. 3360 descriptors are used (420×8). The detection results of these detectors are shown in Table 2.

From this table, it can be seen that with the use of the proposed patterns, the detectors are more efficient (by approximately 10%) than the original proposed

Table 2. The pedestrian detection results of the $Dist_{3(a)}$, $Dist_{3(b)}$, and $Dist_{3(c)}$ configurations.

	Precision	Sensitivity	F1 score
$Dist_{3(a)}$	87.95%	88.48%	88.22%
$Dist_{3(b)}$	90.12%	88.48%	89.30%
$Dist_{3(c)}$	94.27%	89.70%	**91.93%**

pattern. The best detection results were achieved by the detector that used the $Dist_{3(c)}$ configuration with the pattern from Fig. 2(c). On the basis of the results, we can conclude that (in this particular application) using a simple distance value of each green area (in Fig. 2(c)) seems to be a more efficient approach than using the mean of the distance values.

Table 3. The summary of pedestrian detection results.

	Precision	Sensitivity	F1 score
$Dist_{3(c)}$	94.27%	89.70%	**91.93%**
HOG	82.82%	81.82%	82.32%
$Haar$	88.55%	89.09%	88.82%
LBP	86.93%	80.61%	83.65%

To compare the proposed $Dist_{3(c)}$ detector that achieved the best detection results with the state-of-the-art methods in the area of sliding window detectors, we used the detectors that are based on the HOG features, LBP (Local Binary Patterns) features [13] and Haar features (Viola-Jones detection framework). For HOG, we created the detector with the classical settings of HOG. The detector is denoted as HOG. The parameters of HOG are as follows. The size of block is 16×16, the size of cell is 8×8, the horizontal step size is 8, the number of bins is 8. The detector based on these parameters gives 3360 descriptors for one position of sliding window. The training images (for the HOG detector) were resized to 64×128 pixels (the size of sliding window was also set to this size).

For the detectors based on the Viola-Jones detection framework with the Haar features and with the features that are based on LBP, we created the cascade classifiers. For these classifiers, we resized the training images to 24×48 pixels. The cascade classifier of LBP features had 21 stages; the cascade classifier of Haar features had 24 stages. The detectors are denoted as LBP and $Haar$. We used the same training and testing images for all methods. In Table 3, the detection performances are shown.

Similarly as in the previous tests, the detector based on the geodesic distance achieved the best detection result in the test (F1 91.93%). This detector even overcame all tested detectors that use HOG, Haar, and LBP features. From these non-proposed detectors, the Haar-based detector achieved the best detection result (F1 88.82%), despite the fact that this detector is usually used in the

$Haar$ $Dist_{3(c)}$

Fig. 4. The differences between the detection results of *Haar* detector and the proposed detector that uses the $Dist_{3(c)}$ configuration. The results are without the postprocessing (the detection results are not merged).

Fig. 5. The pedestrian detection results of the $Dist_{3(c)}$ configuration. The results are with the postprocessing (the detection results are merged).

Fig. 6. The pedestrian detection results of the $Dist_{3(c)}$ configuration in that the method fails. The results are with the postprocessing (the detection results are merged).

face detection area. Nevertheless, it is important to note that the Haar-based detector with the AdaBoost classifier was trained for 45 hours on the 16-core CPU (2× Intel Xeon CPU E5-2640 v2); all cores were used. HOG and the proposed method (SVM classifiers with RBF kernels) were trained for approximately 5-10 minutes (depending on the dimensionality of the feature vectors). In the proposed method, the calculation of geodesic distance and composing the feature vector took approximately 0.5 milliseconds for one position of sliding window on the 16-core CPU (2× Intel Xeon CPU E5-2640 v2); all cores were used. The recognition time depends on the chosen classifier.

The differences between the detection results of the Haar-based detector and the proposed distance-based detector can be seen in Fig. 4. The examples of pedestrian detection results of the proposed distance-based method are shown in Fig. 5. The examples in which this method failed are shown in Fig. 6.

5 Conclusion

In this paper, we presented an improvement of the distance-based object detector in which the distance values are used in the feature vector that is used as an input for the SVM classifier. The improvement is based on the extension of the basic pattern that was proposed in the first version of this detector. The newly proposed patterns outperformed the basic pattern by approximately 10%. The new version of detector also outperformed the state-of-the-art detectors in the area of pedestrian detection. In the current version of the presented approach, the geodetic distance is used. We leave the experiments with another distances for future work.

Acknowledgments. This work was supported by SGS in VSB - Technical University of Ostrava, Czech Republic, under the grant No. SP2015/141.

References

1. Bai, X., Sapiro, G.: A geodesic framework for fast interactive image and video segmentation and matting. In: IEEE 11th International Conference on Computer Vision. ICCV 2007, pp. 1–8, October 2007
2. Castrilln, M., Dniz, O., Hernndez, D., Lorenzo, J.: A comparison of face and facial feature detectors based on the viola-jones general object detection framework. Machine Vision and Applications **22**(3), 481–494 (2011)
3. Center for Biological and Computational Learning: MIT CBCL Pedestrian Database #1 (2013). http://cbcl.mit.edu/software-datasets/PedestrianData.html
4. Criminisi, A., Sharp, T., Blake, A.: GeoS: geodesic image segmentation. In: Forsyth, D., Torr, P., Zisserman, A. (eds.) ECCV 2008, Part I. LNCS, vol. 5302, pp. 99–112. Springer, Heidelberg (2008)
5. Dalal, N., Triggs, B.: Histograms of oriented gradients for human detection. In: IEEE Computer Society Conference on Computer Vision and Pattern Recognition. CVPR 2005, vol. 1, pp. 886–893, June 2005
6. Dniz, O., Bueno, G., Salido, J., la Torre, F.D.: Face recognition using histograms of oriented gradients. Pattern Recognition Letters **32**(12), 1598–1603 (2011)
7. Economou, G., Pothos, V., Ifantis, A.: Geodesic distance and MST based image segmentation. In: European Signal Processing Conf., pp. 941–944 (2004)
8. Enzweiler, M., Gavrila, D.: Monocular pedestrian detection: Survey and experiments. IEEE Trans. on Patt. Anal. and Mach. Intell. **31**(12), 2179–2195 (2009)
9. Fusek, R., Sojka, E.: Distance-based descriptors and their application in the task of object detection. In: Jiang, X., Hornegger, J., Koch, R. (eds.) GCPR 2014. LNCS, vol. 8753, pp. 488–498. Springer, Heidelberg (2014)
10. Hadid, A., Pietikainen, M., Ahonen, T.: A discriminative feature space for detecting and recognizing faces. In: Proceedings of the 2004 IEEE Computer Society Conference on Computer Vision and Pattern Recognition. CVPR 2004, vol. 2, pp. II-797–II-804 (2004)

11. Huang, D., Shan, C., Ardabilian, M., Wang, Y., Chen, L.: Local binary patterns and its application to facial image analysis: A survey. IEEE Trans. on Systems, Man, and Cybernetics, Part C: Applications and Reviews **41**(6), 765–781 (2011)
12. Kobayashi, T., Hidaka, A., Kurita, T.: Selection of histograms of oriented gradients features for pedestrian detection. In: Ishikawa, M., Doya, K., Miyamoto, H., Yamakawa, T. (eds.) ICONIP 2007, Part II. LNCS, vol. 4985, pp. 598–607. Springer, Heidelberg (2008)
13. Liao, S.C., Zhu, X.X., Lei, Z., Zhang, L., Li, S.Z.: Learning multi-scale block local binary patterns for face recognition. In: Lee, S.-W., Li, S.Z. (eds.) ICB 2007. LNCS, vol. 4642, pp. 828–837. Springer, Heidelberg (2007)
14. Lienhart, R., Maydt, J.: An extended set of haar-like features for rapid object detection. In: Proceedings of the 2002 International Conference on Image Processing, vol. 1, pp. I-900–I-903 (2002)
15. Ojala, T., Pietikäinen, M., Harwood, D.: A comparative study of texture measures with classification based on featured distributions. Pattern Recognition **29**(1), 51–59 (1996)
16. Papageorgiou, C., Poggio, T.: A trainable system for object detection. Int. J. Comput. Vision **38**(1), 15–33 (2000)
17. Paragios, N., Deriche, R.: Geodesic active contours and level sets for the detection and tracking of moving objects. IEEE Transactions on Pattern Analysis and Machine Intelligence **22**(3), 266–280 (2000)
18. Park, K.Y., Hwang, S.Y.: An improved haar-like feature for efficient object detection. Pattern Recognition Letters **42**, 148–153 (2014)
19. Shan, C., Gong, S., McOwan, P.W.: Facial expression recognition based on local binary patterns: A comprehensive study. Image Vision Comput. **27**(6), 803–816 (2009)
20. Viola, P., Jones, M.: Rapid object detection using a boosted cascade of simple features. In: Proceedings of the 2001 IEEE Computer Society Conference on Computer Vision and Pattern Recognition. CVPR 2001, vol. 1, pp. I-511–I-518 (2001)
21. Watanabe, T., Ito, S., Yokoi, K.: Co-occurrence histograms of oriented gradients for pedestrian detection. In: Wada, T., Huang, F., Lin, S. (eds.) Advances in Image and Video Technology. Lecture Notes in Computer Science, vol. 5414, pp. 37–47. Springer, Berlin Heidelberg (2009)
22. Zhang, L., Chu, R.F., Xiang, S., Liao, S.C., Li, S.Z.: Face detection based on multi-block LBP representation. In: Lee, S.-W., Li, S.Z. (eds.) ICB 2007. LNCS, vol. 4642, pp. 11–18. Springer, Heidelberg (2007)

Spatiotemporal Integration of Optical Flow Vectors for Micro-expression Detection

Devangini Patel$^{(\boxtimes)}$, Guoying Zhao, and Matti Pietikäinen

Center for Machine Vision Research,
Department of Computer Science and Engineering, University of Oulu, Oulu, Finland
{dpatel,gyzhao,mkp}@ee.oulu.fi

Abstract. Micro-expressions are brief involuntary facial expressions. Detecting micro-expressions consists of finding the occurrence of micro-expressions in video sequences by locating the onset, peak and offset frames. This paper proposes an algorithm to detect micro-expressions by utilizing the motion features to capture direction continuity. It computes the optical flow vector for small local spatial regions and integrates them in local spatiotemporal regions. It uses heuristics to filter non-micro expressions and find the appropriate onset and offset times. Promising results are obtained on a challenging spontaneous micro-expression database. The main contribution of this paper is to find not only the peak but also the onset and offset frames for spotted micro-expressions which has not been explored before.

Keywords: Affective computing · Facial expression recognition · Micro-expression detection · Optical flow

1 Introduction

Micro-expressions are brief involuntary facial expressions created when a person is trying to suppress true feelings or repress the inside emotion. In 1970, Ekman reported finding micro-expressions when he was trying to find possible signals of lying in a recorded film of a patient, who was planning to commit suicide [3]. Since then micro-expressions have attracted lots of interest in psychological studies. There are many potential applications for detecting and recognizing micro-expressions, e.g., doctors can understand the situation of patients indirectly, police can detect potential crimes by analyzing the behaviour of people and business negotiators can find if deal is good [2]. In real life situations, people might not be able to detect micro-expressions because of the short duration and subtle movement. Due to inaccuracy and time consumed in human evaluation, a computer program for micro-expression detection would be more favored. Such a real-time software could be used in surveillance, Human Computer Interaction (HCI) and Human Robot Interaction (HRI) systems.

Micro-expressions can be used for affect analysis as these portray the person's real emotions. But unlike facial expressions, they are brief, subtle, unsymmetrical and appear in a few face regions. Thus, micro-expression analysis is

© Springer International Publishing Switzerland 2015
S. Battiato et al. (Eds.): ACIVS 2015, LNCS 9386, pp. 369–380, 2015.
DOI: 10.1007/978-3-319-25903-1_32

much more challenging than facial expression analysis. In the field of Computer vision, micro-expression research has started recently. Most of the work has mainly focused on micro-expression recognition [9] [15] [12] [11] i.e. recognizing the emotional label of well-segmented video containing micro-expression from onset to offset. Onset is the frame when the micro-expression first appears, peak is the frame when it reaches maximum muscular contraction and offset is the frame when it disappears [5]. For micro-expressions to be recognized in real world applications, they must be detected i.e. micro-expression is segmented in the video from onset frame to offset frame.

Some of the research work on micro-expression detection has been conducted on posed micro-expressions. Wu et al. [15] extracted Gabor features and used GentleSVM to spot posed micro-expressions. Polikovsky et al. [12] developed a 3D gradient descriptor and used k-means algorithm to classify the onset, apex and offset frames of posed micro-expressions. But there are considerable differences between posed and spontaneous micro-expressions in terms of motion intensity, muscle activations and duration. Moilanen et al. [10] spotted spontaneous micro-expressions by thresholding Chi-Squared distance of Local Binary Pattern (LBP) of center frame and average of first and last frames of a fixed sized sliding window. Yan et al. [17] quantified spontaneous micro-expressions using Constrained Local Model (CLM) and LBP on manually decided facial regions to spot the peak frames. Little work has been done on spontaneous micro-expression detection and only peaks are detected. No previous work has been done on spotting the onset and offset and this work is the first exploration.

This paper introduces a method that uses motion features and direction continuity to detect spontaneous micro-expressions while giving less attention to pre-processing. Optical flow vectors are computed in small region of interest (ROI) around facial landmarks. These motion features are spatiotemporally integrated across variable sized sliding windows. The peak, group, onset and offset are detected by using a simple search algorithm in the average magnitude of resultant optical flow versus frame graph. Finally, the false detections are removed by thresholding, removing head movements, eye blinks and eye gaze changes.

The structure of this paper is as follows: Section 2 discusses the database used, Section 3 explains the detection algorithm in detail, Section 4 presents the results for micro-expression detection and Section 5 concludes the paper.

2   Background

The publicly available spontaneous micro-expression databases for the task of detection are: SMIC-VIS-E extracted from SMIC-VIS [9], CASME [19] and CASME II [16]. In this paper, the experiments are carried out using SMIC-VIS-E database because the participants are of different ethnicity. This database consists 71 positive, negative and surprise micro-expressions videos with image size 640x480px recorded at 25fps. It contains a total of 76 micro-expressions. The participants were shown emotional clips and were instructed to suppress their feelings and not to move their heads during the experiment. These videos are annotated with onset and offset frames. The maximum duration of a micro-expression is 13 frames which is consistent with the research conducted by [18].

3 Detection Algorithm

Optical flow is an indicator of the motion occurring between the frames. It can capture the movements of the face and their direction at every frame instance. Due to the controlled set-up of the SMIC database collection procedure, there is slight head movement during micro-expressions. So, it is possible to learn about trajectory change of points at the FACS Action Units (AU) [4] i.e. the motion vectors from onset to peak follows a smooth trajectory and traverses this trajectory in opposite direction from peak to offset. [14] propose Greedy-Exchange algorithm to track points of non-rigid objects using direction continuity and velocity continuity. Direction continuity is the normalized dot product of motion vectors of two successive frames i.e. $(V_{i,t-1} \cdot V_{i,t})/(|V_{i,t-1}||V_{i,t}|) = \cos\theta$ where θ is the angle between the vectors. $0 < \cos\theta \le 1$ for $0° \le \theta < 90°$, $-1 \le \cos\theta \le 0$ for $90° \le \theta \le 180°$ and so it can represent the direction changes during micro-expressions. The drawback of this term is that it is converted to a scalar value for two consecutive frames therefore can not work for detecting direction changes which take place in non-adjacent frames. So, this concept has to be extended to a vector stores the current motion vector history.

The proposed flow of detection algorithm, as shown in Fig. 1, consists of three main stages: (1) Feature Extraction, (2) Spatiotemporal integration and detection, (3) Micro-expression filtering.

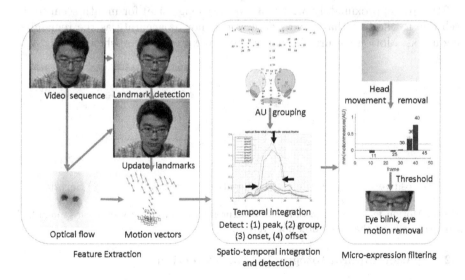

Fig. 1. Algorithm for detecting micro-expressions

3.1 Feature Extraction

Facial Landmark Detection and Tracking. Discriminative Response Map Fitting (DRMF) [1] method detects facial landmarks in the first image of the sequence. Figure 3 shows the 49 landmarks detected by DMRF. Detecting facial landmarks across multiple frames does not guarantee correspondence. So, tracking facial points is achieved by updating the facial landmarks using optical flow i.e. the x and y co-ordinates of the landmarks are incremented by the optical flow vector's horizontal and vertical components respectively.

Optical Flow. Generally, micro-expression and facial expression analysis methods don not consider the raw images for optical flow computation. Usually, face regions are cropped, registered with a face model then optical flow is computed for these processed images. These pre-processing steps are carried out to address the pose and face variations but they can alter the trajectory of the landmarks. So, in our method, optical flow is computed from raw images using TV-L1 optical flow estimation [13] method and head motion is removed as post-processing.

Motion Features. Small regions of interest are created around the facial landmarks and the mean optical flow in these regions is the motion feature of the frame. The ROIs are created to balance the inaccuracy of the landmark detection algorithm. If they are too small then the window might not cover the exact location of the point. If they are too big then they might contain a lot of noise and be smoothed out. By exhaustive testing, window size of 11x11px (approximately 1.7%x2.3% of the image size) for the eyebrows, eyes and nose and window size of 21x21px (approximately 3.2%x4.3% of the image size) for mouth seem to do well due to the fact that mouth detection is not as accurate as the remaining landmarks. Motion features for various micro-expressions are shown in Fig. 2.

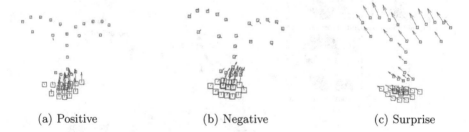

(a) Positive   (b) Negative   (c) Surprise

Fig. 2. Motion features for various micro-expressions (The flow vectors are magnified proportionally so that they don not overlap)

3.2 Spatiotemporal Integration and Detection

Spatial Integration. The optical flow vectors of each landmark can be grouped using FACS system [4] to detect the activated micro-expression AU which corresponds to the maximum motion and then detect the onset, peak and offset from the pattern of the activated AU group. Fig. 3 shows Venn diagram illustrating the grouping of landmarks for the detection of various AUs. Some AUs have been split into left and right groups because micro-expressions could be asymmetrical. These left and right groups are called similar groups i.e. $1 \approx 2, 3 \approx 4, 7 \approx 8$.

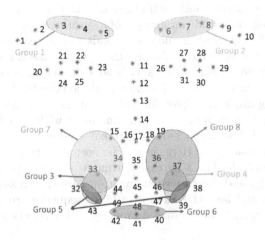

Fig. 3. Venn diagram of landmark groups for detecting AU activation

Temporal Integration. Vector addition of two vectors $A = \{a_1, ..., a_n\}$ and $B = \{b_1, ..., b_n\}$ produces a vector $C(= A + B)$ by adding the respective components i.e. $C = \{c_1, ..., c_n\} = \{a_1 + b_1, ..., a_n + b_n\}$. Parallelogram law states that if vectors A and B represent the two sides of a parallelogram then the diagonal represents the vector sum C. For landmark i, let A be the motion vector at time t, B be the motion vector at time $t+1$ then C represents the cumulative motion from time t to $t+2$. In theory, if A and B have similar trajectory, then $|C| > |A|$ as shown in Fig. 4a and if A and B have opposite trajectory at peak frame, then $|C| < |A|$ (provided that B_1 is small) as shown in Fig. 4b.

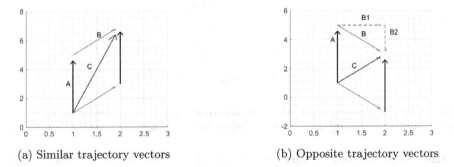

(a) Similar trajectory vectors   (b) Opposite trajectory vectors

Fig. 4. Law of parallelogram for 2D vector addition in different cases

Peak and Group Detection. This concept of vector addition is extended to spot the peak frame in a video sequence as follows: (1) Initialize the resultant motion vector as the motion vector of the first frame, (2) find magnitude for each landmark, (3) find the average magnitude for each AU group, (3) update the resultant motion vector for each landmark by adding the next frame's motion vector, (4) go to step 2 and continue till the end. The images, motion vectors and their corresponding magnitude for group 2 of a surprise micro-expression sample is shown in Fig. 5. The peak frame corresponds to the peak in the magnitude plot. (Note: if peak is detected at frame i then peak frame is $i+1$)

This approach accumulates previous head motions, micro-expressions and facial expressions which might lead to false peak detections. To circumvent this problem, the magnitude-time plot for video sequence is constructed for variable window sizes from minimum 3 to maximum 11 with step 1. Fig. 6a shows an example optical flow graph plot of different landmarks for surprise micro-expression for $window = 8$. Here, it can be seen clearly that the AU group 2 has higher magnitude. For a particular window size, the peaks in the maximum of magnitudes and the corresponding group are chosen as detections. The peaks in the first and last 11 frames of a video sequence are ignored because their magnitudes can not be compared properly and it rejects incomplete facial expressions.

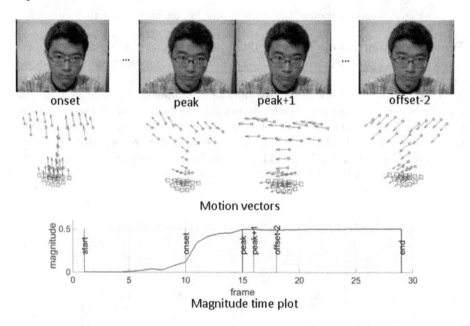

Fig. 5. Image, motion vector and magnitude for group 2 in a surprise micro-expression video sequence (Scaling of the motion vectors for each frame are done independently.)

Onset Calculation. Computing the onset given the detected peak is an optimization problem. Suppose frame k is the peak for some activated AU, $k - n + 1$

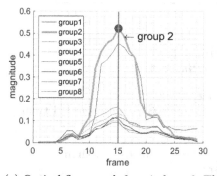 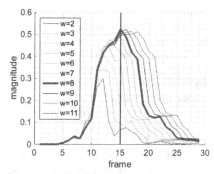

(a) Optical flow graph for window=8. The detection is marked with a colored circle. The detected peak at frame 15 corresponds to group 2.

(b) Comparison of optical flow graphs for different window sizes of group 2 and the optimal onset time corresponds to the window with maximum magnitude at the peak

Fig. 6. Detection of peaks, group and onset

is the ground truth onset frame and the average magnitude of resultant motion vectors from frame i to frame k is $magnitude_k(i)(i \le k)$. Suppose, $window = 2$, then $magnitude_k(k-1) \ge magnitude_k(k)$ because motion vectors at frames k and $k+1$, follow the same trajectory. Similarly, the magnitude will increase till $i = n$ after which it should decrease. Fig. 6b illustrates how the magnitude differs with window size and the maximum magnitude corresponds to $window = 8$ which also occurs at peak frame. Pseudo-code 1 computes a list of (peaks, onset) given list of (potential peaks, window sizes, AU group). It is possible that the micro-expression has less duration and there is some head motion before the onset and after the offset due to which the peaks corresponding to bigger window sizes have more magnitude in comparison to the micro-expression peak. This case is indirectly handled by the change of group condition.

Offset Calculation. The motion vectors from the peak to offset frames have less motion and inconsistent trajectory, so both vector sum and dot product operations are used to approximate the offset. The starting offset frame is defined as the first frame after peak which has negative normalized dot product with the first onset frame. The potential offset should lie between starting offset to peak+windowsize-1 and it is incremented till: (1) magnitude of resultant vector from starting offset to potential offset increases and (2) normalized dot product of the onset vector and potential offset is less than or equal to $cos(70°)$. $70°$ is enough to show opposite direction motion while allowing some amount of noise.

3.3   Filtering Micro-Expressions

Head Movement Removal. Many detections which do not correspond to ground truth onset, offset are caused by head motion and illumination changes.

Algorithm 1. Onset Calculation

1: **Inputs:**
     $peaks, windows, groups$
2: **Initialize:**
     $peaklist \leftarrow peaks[windows = 2], rejectlist \leftarrow [],$
     $timelist \leftarrow windows[windows = 2], rejecttime \leftarrow []$
3: **for** $windowsize = 3$ to 11 **do**
4:    **for** $peak_i \in peaks[windows = windowsize]$ **do**
5:       **if** $peak_i \in rejectlist - rejecttime + 1 : rejectlist + rejecttime - 1$ **then**
6:          continue
7:       **end if**
8:       **if** $peak_i \in peaklist - timelist + 1 : peaklist + timelist - 1$ **then**
9:          $oldpeak \leftarrow$ matched peaklist entry
10:         **if** $group[peak_i] \approx group[oldpeak]$ and magnitude increases **then**
11:           $timelist[oldpeak] + +;$
12:         **else**
13:           $rejectlist.append(peak_i), rejecttime.append(windowsize);$
14:         **end if**
15:       **else**
16:         $peaklist.append(peak_i), timelist.append(windowsize);$
17:       **end if**
18:    **end for**
19: **end for**

This step is used to remove such false detections and remove the head movement during the micro-expression. Optical flow between the onset and peak frames can be used to confirm motion at the AU landmarks. Consider the face plane as the bounding box containing all the AU landmarks. Head movement can be considered as the dominant motion in the face plane and micro-expression can be considered as the independent motion. Inspired from [8], the dominant motion of the head is removed by performing hierarchical dense affine registration of the face plane of the peak frame with respect to onset frame then motion measure is computed between them at each landmark as the average magnitude of optical flow in 11x11px window. The median motion measure of the video sample is subtracted from the motion measure to remove the effects of the face variations.

Threshold. Motion measure should be high for activated AU and low for the remaining points. A peak frame is considered as true detection if all the points of the AU group (or similar) have motion measure greater than a particular threshold. Fig. 7 shows detections for a positive micro-expression sample.

Eye Blink and Eye Glance Removal. Many eye blinks and gaze changes are detected even after thresholding. Emotions change the eye blink frequency [6] and the viewing of gaze [7]. It is observed that many facial movements occur in the eyebrow and mouth areas when these events occur. If the detections fall

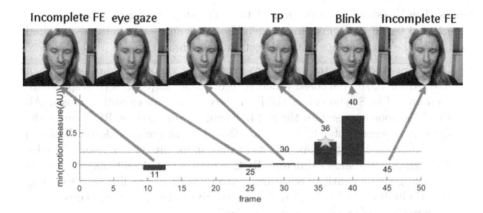

Fig. 7. Micro-expression detection of positive sample for threshold=0.2, TP marked by yellow star. Peaks 11 (incomplete facial expression), 40 and 45 are ignored since they occur at first/end 11 frames.

within eye blinks and eye gaze changes onset and offset annotation extended by 2 frames, then they are removed from false positives.

4   Results

4.1   Execution Time

Since spotting micro-expressions needs to be performed in real time, the computational time is an important aspect of this method. The code has been implemented in Matlab and executed on a Intel Core i5-3750 CPU running at 3.4GHz, using 64-bit Windows OS and 8GB RAM. The most time consuming parts are: (1) landmark detection ($\sim 3.5s$), (2) optical flow ($\sim 10s$). Since they take a lot of time, they are used when required i.e. landmarks are detected only in first frame of the video but optical flow is an essential part and can not be compromised. An average video sample is of 151 frames ($\sim 6s$) in the SMIC-VIS-E database. It takes (1) $\sim 1600s$ to detect landmarks, calculate optical flow and track landmarks, (2) $\sim 20s$ to compute motion features, construct optical flow graph and find potential peaks with their onset, offset, (3) $\sim 1.5s$ to find the motion measure for every potential peak. There is a trade-off between accuracy and computational time. The code has not been optimized but it can be expected to be real time if implemented in C++ and executed on GPU.

4.2   Experimental Analysis

A peak is said to be correctly detected if it is within [-2,+2] range of the ground truth onset and offset. This follows the standard set by [10], assuming N is the average micro-expression length(10). Sample counts are used for the TP and FP values. The threshold is varied from -1 to 5. The step size for threshold is 0.005 in [0,1] and 0.1 in the remaining range. The following parameters are explored for tuning the performance of the detection algorithm:

- Duration: According to [18], micro-expressions should not be longer than 0.5s, so for SMIC database which is recorded at 25fps, 0.5s corresponds to 13 frames. Fig. 8a shows how the FP reduces when this condition is used. All the detections are used for the red ROC curve. For the blue ROC curve, the detections whose total time (onset-offset+1)≤ 13 are considered. It shows the importance of onset and offset calculation for proper detection of peaks. This graph also shows different ROC curves when detections are filtered according to their ratio of onset frames to total time. The line corresponding to ratio limit of 0.6 has similar ROC curve to total time curve, so onset time is more than offset time for most of the TP.
- Same versus similar groups: Fig. 8b shows how the performance slightly improves when similar group is used instead of same group. The concept of similar group is used in various steps to establish the almost symmetrical motion during micro-expression: (1) in onset detection, similarity of groups is checked while incrementing the onset time, (2) motion measures of similar groups can be used while thresholding. Here, the similarity of groups is explored in the thresholding step.

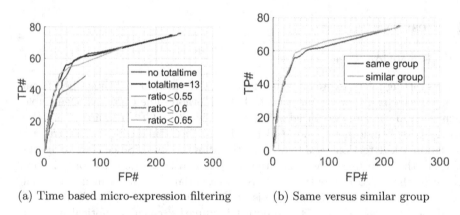

(a) Time based micro-expression filtering   (b) Same versus similar group

Fig. 8. Experimental analysis

4.3   Detection Results

Micro-expression detection consists of: (1) peak detection, (2) onset detection, (3) offset detection. These component detections are explored separately:

- Peak Detection: Fig. 9a shows how this method compares to the baseline method for SMIC database in terms of samples [10]. This method has a higher elbow point (41, 59) than the baseline method's elbow point (23, 53) at the cost of higher amounts of FP. It has a higher area under the curve (AUC) of 95% in comparison to the baseline method's AUC of 90% because it reaches maximum TP for less FP.

– Onset and offset detection: Fig. 9b shows histogram of errors for both onset and offset of the TP of elbow point. The mean onset error is 1.14 and standard deviation is 3.68. The mean offset error is -0.55 and standard deviation is 3.52. Thus, for most detections, the onset is detected later than the ground truth onset and the offset is detected earlier than the ground truth offset.

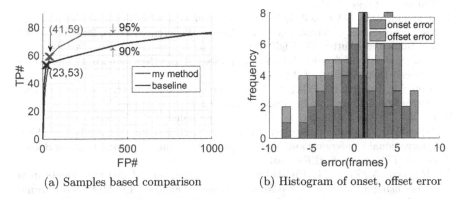

(a) Samples based comparison   (b) Histogram of onset, offset error

Fig. 9. Detection results

5 Conclusion

This paper presented an algorithm to (1) detect micro-expressions from onset to offset (2) using motion features which have not been explored for spontaneous micro-expressions. This method uses landmark detection and optical flow to compute optical flow vectors in certain spatial locations and uses motion continuity to locate peak, onset and offset. Finally, it thresholds the effective displacement i.e. motion measure to detect the real detections. However it does not remove all non-emotional eye blinks and eye gaze changes. The use of landmarks and AU groups suggests that emotion recognition might play an important role for better detection. In the future, an approach combining recognition and detection would be developed to find AU as well as reduce false positive rate and test it on AU annotated databases. In addition, this approach should work for less constrained micro-expression videos and execute in real time.

Acknowledgments. This work was sponsored by the Academy of Finland, Infotech Oulu and Tekes Fidipro program.

References

1. Asthana, A., Zafeiriou, S., Cheng, S., Pantic, M.: Incremental face alignment in the wild. In: 2014 IEEE Conference on Computer Vision and Pattern Recognition (CVPR), pp. 1859–1866. IEEE (2014)
2. Ekman, P.: Telling Lies: Clues to Deceit in the Marketplace, Politics, and Marriage (Revised Edition). WW Norton & Company (2009)

3. Ekman, P., Friesen, W.V.: Nonverbal leakage and clues to deception. Tech. rep, DTIC Document (1969)
4. Ekman, P., Friesen, W.V.: Facial Action Coding System: A Technique for the Measurement of Facial Movement. Consulting Psychologists Press, Stanford University, Palo Alto (1978)
5. Ekman, P., Rosenberg, E.L.: What the face reveals: Basic and applied studies of spontaneous expression using the Facial Action Coding System (FACS). Oxford University Press (1997)
6. Harrigan, J.A., O'Connell, D.M.: How do you look when feeling anxious? facial displays of anxiety. Personality and Individual Differences **21**(2), 205–212 (1996)
7. van Honk, J., Schutter, D.: Vigilant and avoidant responses to angry facial expressions. Social Neuroscience: Integrating Biological and Psychological Explanations of Social Behavior, 197–223 (2007)
8. Irani, M., Rousso, B., Peleg, S.: Computing occluding and transparent motions. International Journal of Computer Vision **12**(1), 5–16 (1994)
9. Li, X., Pfister, T., Huang, X., Zhao, G., Pietikäinen, M.: A spontaneous micro-expression database: inducement, collection and baseline. In: 2013 10th IEEE International Conference and Workshops on Automatic Face and Gesture Recognition (FG), pp. 1–6. IEEE (2013)
10. Moilanen, A., Zhao, G., Pietikäinen, M.: Spotting rapid facial movements from videos using appearance-based feature difference analysis. In: 2014 22nd International Conference on Pattern Recognition (ICPR), pp. 1722–1727. IEEE (2014)
11. Pfister, T., Li, X., Zhao, G., Pietikäinen, M.: Recognising spontaneous facial micro-expressions. In: 2011 IEEE International Conference on Computer Vision (ICCV), pp. 1449–1456. IEEE (2011)
12. Polikovsky, S., Kameda, Y., Ohta, Y.: Facial micro-expressions recognition using high speed camera and 3d-gradient descriptor. In: 3rd International Conference on Crime Detection and Prevention (ICDP 2009), pp. 1–6. IET (2009)
13. Sánchez, J., Meinhardt-Llopis, E., Facciolo, G.: Tv-l1 optical flow estimation. Image Processing On Line **3**, 137–150 (2013)
14. Sethi, I.K., Jain, R.: Finding trajectories of feature points in a monocular image sequence. IEEE Transactions on Pattern Analysis and Machine Intelligence **1**(1), 56–73 (1987)
15. Wu, Q., Shen, X., Fu, X.: The machine knows what you are hiding: an automatic micro-expression recognition system. In: D'Mello, S., Graesser, A., Schuller, B., Martin, J.-C. (eds.) ACII 2011, Part II. LNCS, vol. 6975, pp. 152–162. Springer, Heidelberg (2011)
16. Yan, W.J., Li, X., Wang, S.J., Zhao, G., Liu, Y.J., Chen, Y.H., Fu, X.: Casme ii: An improved spontaneous micro-expression database and the baseline evaluation. PloS One **9**(1), e86041 (2014)
17. Yan, W.-J., Wang, S.-J., Chen, Y.-H., Zhao, G., Fu, X.: 3D hand pose detection in egocentric RGB-D images. In: Agapito, L., Bronstein, M.M., Rother, C. (eds.) ECCV 2014 Workshops. LNCS, vol. 8925, pp. 356–371. Springer, Heidelberg (2015)
18. Yan, W.J., Wu, Q., Liang, J., Chen, Y.H., Fu, X.: How fast are the leaked facial expressions: The duration of micro-expressions. Journal of Nonverbal Behavior **37**(4), 217–230 (2013)
19. Yan, W.J., Wu, Q., Liu, Y.J., Wang, S.J., Fu, X.: Casme database: a dataset of spontaneous micro-expressions collected from neutralized faces. In: 2013 10th IEEE International Conference and Workshops on Automatic Face and Gesture Recognition (FG), pp. 1–7. IEEE (2013)

Unified System for Visual Speech Recognition and Speaker Identification

Ahmed Rekik[1]([✉]), Achraf Ben-Hamadou[2], and Walid Mahdi[1,3]

[1] Multimedia InfoRmation Systems and Advanced Computing Laboratory
(MIRACL), Sfax University Pôle technologique de Sfax,
BP 242, route de Tunis Km 10, 3021 Sfax, Tunisia
rekikamed@gmail.com, w.mahdi@tu.edu.sa

[2] Driving Assistance Research Center, Valeo 34 rue St-André Z.I. des Vignes,
93012 Bobigny, France
achraf.ben-hamadou@valeo.com

[3] Department of Computer Science, College of Computers and Information
Technology, Taif University, P.O.Box 888, Hawiyah Taif 21974,
Kingdom of Saudi Arabia

Abstract. This paper proposes a unified system for both visual speech
recognition and speaker identification. The proposed system can handle
image and depth data if they are available. The proposed system consists
of four consecutive steps, namely, 3D face pose tracking, mouth region
extraction, features computing, and classification using the Support Vector Machine method. The system is experimentally evaluated on three
public datasets, namely, MIRACL-VC1, OuluVS, and CUAVE. In one
hand, the visual speech recognition module achieves up to 96 % and
79.2 % for speaker dependent and speaker independent settings, respectively. On the other hand, speaker identification performs up to 98.9 %
of recognition rate. Additionally, the obtained results demonstrate the
importance of the depth data to resolve the subject dependency issue.

Keywords: Mouth feature extraction · Biometry · Lip-reading ·
Speaker identification · Visual speech recognition

1 Introduction

Mouth features extraction is a process used traditionally for speech recognition (*i.e.,* called also lip-reading) [15,16] and recently for speaker identification
[7,17,22]. Two main issues have been recently tackled regarding lips' feature
extraction[22]. First, there could be various head poses in the captured visual
data. Since the appearance of a talking mouth could vary significantly in images
due to the view change, pose variation presents a challenge to speech recognition and speaker identification systems. Second, only the spatial analysis of the
provided visual data is not sufficient for a robust lip-reading [20,23] and speaker
identification [6,18]. Temporal information has been proven to be useful for discriminating visual speech and identities and hybrid system combining static and

© Springer International Publishing Switzerland 2015
S. Battiato et al. (Eds.): ACIVS 2015, LNCS 9386, pp. 381–390, 2015.
DOI: 10.1007/978-3-319-25903-1_33

temporal features not only improve recognition results but also offer robustness to variation, such as caused by illumination [2].

The main difference between visual speech recognition and speaker identification is handling of the speaker dependency issue. Indeed, speech recognition techniques attempt to represent only speech information and suppress the speaker-dependent information in visual feature. Conversely, speaker identification techniques attempt to represent only speaker-dependent information in visual features and suppress other sources of variation.

In this paper, we propose a unified system for both lip-reading and speaker identification. The proposed system uses a 3D face pose tracking to extract a normalized mouth region. For each frame of the input video sequence, the speaker's face pose is estimated using a 3D face model including a rectangular mouth patch. This mouth patch is projected on the video data to extract the normalized mouth regions. Moreover, we compute both of appearance and temporal features on the extracted regions for visual feature extraction. The appearance features are used to model the mouth shape at each single frame data, and the temporal features are used to capture mouth deformations. Additionally, the importance of all involved visual features is studied for a better understanding of the contribution of each one for each module (i.e., visual speech recognition and speaker identification).

The remaining of this paper is organized as follows. First, we present an overview of the proposed system. Then, the different steps of the mouth region extraction process are described. In section 4, we present different features used to encode the lips' deformation. Finally, experimental results are provided to evaluate of the proposed system for both configurations, lip-reading and speaker identification.

2   Problem Definition and Framework Overview

The proposed system is inspired from the mouth feature extraction approach proposed by Rekik et al. in [14]. As illustrated in Figure 1, the proposed system takes as input an RGB-D video sequence covering the uttered speech where the speaker's face is supposed to be in the frustum of the camera. Then, we perform sequentially four main steps as follows. In the first step, the speaker's face is detected and its 3D pose is tracked over the input video sequence. Second, we extract the mouth region using a rectangular 3D mouth patch automatically positioned in front of the mouth. For each frame, the mouth patch is then projected into the RGB-D data to extract 2D and depth normalized mouth regions. In the third step, appearance and temporal features are computed on the extracted regions, separately, for each frame. Then, these features are combined and normalized to obtain a final feature vector describing the uttered speech and the speaker identity. In the final step, the obtained feature vector is used to recognize the uttered speech or the speaker identity using a Support Vector Machine (SVM) trained off-line on a training samples.

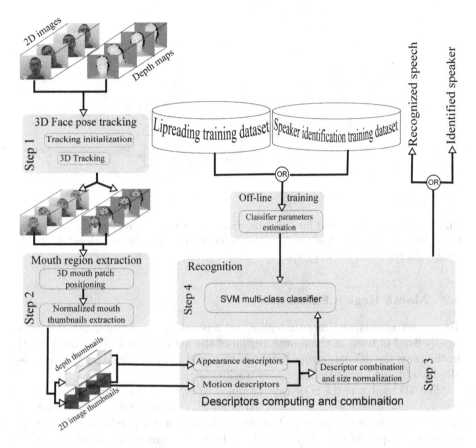

Fig. 1. General overview of our lip-reading and speaker identification systems.

3 Mouth Region Extraction

In this section, we describe the mouth region extraction process. The challenge is to make this extraction invariant to the orientation and the motion of the speaker's head. The mouth region extraction process is performed following steps 1 and 2 of the illustration in figure 1.

3.1 Face Pose Tracking

To extract the mouth region, the existing methods that use 2D/3D information perform a deformable mouth tracking or detect lip landmarks points using only the 2D images. These techniques are very complicated, sensitive to illumination changes and above all need a good resolution of the mouth region. To this end, we proposed to use a rigid face pose tracking method proposed in [13]. This method is based on a modified version of the Candide model [1] where only rigid parts of the face are considered (see figure 2(a)).

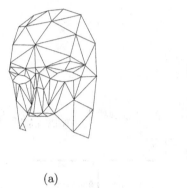

(a)   (b)

Fig. 2. 3D face model used for face pose tracking and mouth region extraction. 2(a) Rigid 3D face model used in the face pose tracking step. 2(b) 3D mouth patch used in the mouth region extraction step.

3.2   Mouth Region Extraction

To extract normalized mouth region, we have define a rectangular 3D patch rigidly fixed in front of the mouth region of the 3D face model (see figure 2(b)). In this way, the 3D patch rigidly follows the head motion using the 3D face pose already obtained from the face pose tracking step.

The 3D mouth patch is densely sampled to $n_h \times n_w$ 3D points $\{P_{u,v}\}$ where $u = 1, \ldots, n_h$ and $v = 1, \ldots, n_w$. A 3D point $P_{u,v}$ corresponds to one thumbnail pixel of coordinate u, v as well. The size of the 3D mouth patch is automatically scaled to adapt the size of the speaker's face. The size of the speaker's face is obtained in the initialisation step of the face tracking (see [14] and [13] for more details).

The definition of a 3D mouth patch simplifies the mouth region extraction and normalization in terms of position, orientation, and size. Indeed, for a given face pose, each patch point $P_{u,v}$ is projected into the 2D image and the depth map yielding two normalized thumbnails (see figure 3). To make the depth thumbnail extraction process less sensitive to the speaker-camera distance, we normalize the depth thumbnail values relative to the nose tip of the speaker.

4   Mouth Feature Extraction and Classification

Like [14], we have encoded the visual speech segment using appearance and temporal features computed on the extracted mouth thumbnails. Since the appearance feature describes the mouth shape in each frame, the temporal feature computes the mouth deformation over the uttered speech. To encode the mouth shape, we computed the Histogram of Oriented Gradient (HOG) descriptor [4] on the 2D and the depth thumbnails of each frame. We denoted by HOG_{2D} and HOG_{depth} the HOG descriptor computed on the 2D and the depth thumbnail,

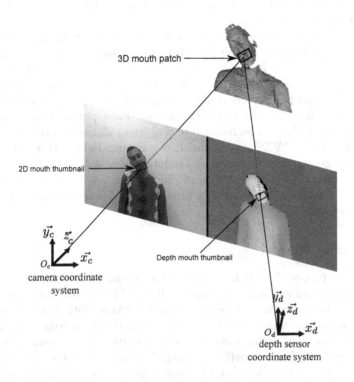

Fig. 3. 3D mouth patch projection. The 3D mouth patch is projected on the 2D image and the depth map to extract a normalized mouth thumbnail.

respectively. Moreover, used the Motion Boundary Histograms (MBH) [5] to encode the temporal lips' deformation. Since appearance and temporal descriptors are computed for each frame, all the computed feature vectors are concatenated on a final single vector encoding the uttered speech. To recognize the speech or the speaker identity, we have trained two multi-class SVMs. Each class of the speech recognition SVM refers to an utterance, therefore, is trained using a set of speech instances of the same utterance pronounced by different speakers. Inversely, each class of the speaker identification SVM refers to a speaker, and trained using a speech instances set of different utterances pronounced by a single speaker.

5 Experiments and Results

In this section, we evaluate the proposed system for lip-reading and speaker identification. To show the importance of 2D images and depth, we have used different type of input data (*i.e.,* RGB-D data, 2D data). To evaluate our system on RGB-D data, we have used the public dataset MIRACL-VC1 originally presented in [14]. Additionally, we have used the OuluVS [20] and CUAVE [11] datasets containing only 2D data.

The MIRACL-VC1 [1] dataset consists of a new speech recognition dataset containing 1500 words (15 persons×10 words×10 instances) and 1500 phrases (15 persons×10 phrases×10 instances). All speech sequences are acquired using a Kinect sensor with a resolution of 640×480 pixels and at an acquisition rate of 15 fps. The calibration parameters could be provided using [3,19] The OuluVS dataset consists of ten different everyday phrases. Each phrase is uttered by 20 subjects up to five times. The frame rate was set to 25 fps at a resolution of 720×576 pixels. The CUAVE dataset consists of a speaker-independent corpus of over 7000 utterances of both connected and isolated digits spoken by 37 subjects. The dataset was recorded at a resolution of 720×480 with a frame rate of 29.97 fps. The OuluVS and CUAVE datasets provide only 2D images are for each visual speech sequence.

5.1   Lip-Reading Results

We evaluate the proposed system on lip-reading under two settings, namely, speaker dependent and speaker independent. In the Speaker Independent (SI) setting, leave-one-speaker-out strategy is utilized where data from a single speaker are used as the validation data, and the remaining speakers are used as the training data. The same procedure was repeated for all speakers in the dataset. In the Speaker Dependent(SD) setting, the training and the testing data are from the same speaker. For each of speakers in the dataset, the leave-one-video-out cross validation was carried out, that is, two videos are used for testing and the rest for training.

The proposed system is evaluated using RGB-D data from MIRACL-VC1 dataset with different descriptor combinations. In these experiments, MIRACL-VC1 dataset is split into two sub-datasets where the first contain phrases, and the second contains words. Table 1 shows the obtained recognition rates for different descriptors (rows) for phrases and words with **SD** and **SI** settings(columns).

For **SD** setting, results show that the best performance is obtained for the combination $HOG_{2D} + HOG_{depth}$ (96.0% for phrases and 95.4% for words). That is, when we added MBH (*i.e.*, $HOG_{2D}+HOG_{depth}+MBH$) in row 6), we improve the **SI** setting results (*i.e.*, gain of 12.5% and 3.3% of recognition rate) while keeping the same recognition rates for **SD** setting. By comparing results in rows 5 and 6, we can see that the use of depth data improves slightly the **SD** performances (gain of 3.1% for phrases and 3.9% for words) and significantly the **SI** performances (gain of 17.4% for phrases and 6.9% for words). Consequently, we can conclude that the use of depth data can reduce the problem of speaker-dependency in a lip-reading system.

The proposed system is also evaluated on two 2D datasets and compered with the recent lip-reading works [2,20,21,23,24]. Table 2 shows the obtained

---

[1] MIRACL-VC1 is accessible following :
   https://sites.google.com/site/achrafbenhamadou/-datasets/miracl-vc1

Table 1. Lip-reading performances of speaker dependent (**SD**) and speaker independent (**SI**) experiments on MIRACL-VC1 dataset

Descriptors	Phrases		Words	
	SD	**SI**	**SD**	**SI**
HOG_{2D}	95.4%	54.4%	92.8%	48.1%
HOG_{depth}	94.2%	64.7%	94.2%	54.5%
$HOG_{2D}+HOG_{depth}$	96.0%	66.7%	95.4%	59.8%
MBH	87.4%	49.4%	86.2%	45.1%
$HOG_{2D} + MBH$	92.9%	61.8%	91.4%	56.2%
$HOG_{2D}+HOG_{depth}+MBH$	96.0%	79.2%	95.3%	63.1%

recognition rates (row 1) and other works on the OuluVS dataset. Our system outperforms all the other works for **SD** configuration with 93.2% against 64.2%, 73.5%, 85.1%, and 90.6% for [20], [2],[23], and [24] respectively. For **SI** setting, our system is better than [20] and [2], while [23] and [21] outperform our system by 2.3% and 8.3% respectively.

Table 2. Lip-reading performances of speaker dependent (**SD**) and speaker independent (**SI**) experiments on OuluVS dataset and comparison with other recent works

	SD	SI
Our system	93.2%	68.3%
[20]	64.2%	58.6%
[2]	73.5%	62.3%
[23]	85.1%	70.6%
[21]	N/A	76.6%
[24]	90.6%	N/A

Our system is evaluated on the CUAVE dataset and compared with other works [8–10,12] that used the same dataset (see Table 3). Authors of [8–10] have not presented the results for **SD** setting since they presented in their works a solution for the speaker dependency problem. In [12], only two samples on CUAVE where used for evaluation. They obtained 100% of recognition rate for the **SD** setting. For the same two samples and the same setting, we obtained 97.0%. For **SI** setting, our system outperform works in [8] and [9] by 3.9% and 8.9% respectively. [10] presents better results with 74% against 70.1% for **SI** in our work.

5.2   Speaker Identification Results

Our system is evaluated on speaker identification using the three public datasets MIRACL-VC1, OuluVS and CUAVE. This evaluation is performed using a speech independent setting where the data from a single speech are used as

Table 3. Lip-reading performances of speaker dependent (**SD**) and speaker independent (**SI**) experiments on CUAVE dataset and comparison with other works

	SD	SI
Our system	90.0%	70.1%
[8]	N/A	66.2%
[9]	N/A	61.2%
[10]	N/A	74%
[12]	100%	N/A

the validation data, and the remaining speech segments are used as the training data. This procedure is repeated for all speech segments in the dataset. We tested the same mouth combinations of features witch used in the lip-reading evaluation. The obtained results on RGB-D data from the MIRACL-VC1 dataset (see table 4) show that the best speaker identification performances are obtained with the appearance feature HOG_{2D}. The best combination of features for lip-reading (Table 1 row 6) gives, also, good results for speaker identification (Table 4 row 6). Consequently, the combination of features $HOG_{2D} + HOG_{depth} + MBH$ can be used simultaneously for lip-reading and speaker identification. By comparing the results in row 3 of table 1 and 4, we can see that the features computed on depth data improves lip-reading performance with **SI** setting and decrease the performance of speaker identification. This difference is explained by the certain independence of depth data to the speaker identity mainly because depth data does not include skin color and texture.

Table 4. Speaker identification performances with different features combination on MIRACL-VC1 dataset

	Phrases	Words
HOG_{2D}	98.9%	98.4%
HOG_{depth}	85.32%	85.2%
$HOG_{2D}+HOG_{depth}$	98.4%	98.7%
MBH	61.0%	49.0%
$HOG_{2D} + MBH$	96.7%	94.4%
$HOG_{2D}+HOG_{depth}+MBH$	97.6%	97.3%

Moreover, our system is evaluated on the two 2D datasets OuluVS and CUAVE. Since depth data are not provided, we have computed only HOG_{2D} and MBH descriptors. Table 5 shows the speakers identification rates on the OuluVS and the CUAVE datasets. The HOG descriptor is more discriminant on the speaker identity than MBH. The combination of this two descriptors (see row 3 of table 3) does not improve the recognition rates.

Table 5. Speaker identification performances with different features combination on OuluVS dataset

Descriptors	OuluVS	CUAVE
HOG_{2D}	98.6%	98.5 %
MBH	63.9%	58.4 %
$HOG_{2D} + MBH$	97.7%	97.4 %

6 Conclusion and Perspectives

This paper proposes a new system for both lip-reading and speaker identification. The feature extraction process of the proposed system is based on three main steps. First, 3D face pose tracking is performed on the input video to robustly extract the mouth region. The 3D poses are then used in the second step to position a 3D rectangular path on the mouth region to extract normalized mouth thumbnails. Next step, appearance and temporal features are computed on the extracted thumbnails to generate a set of visual feature vectors. The proposed system is evaluated on lip-reading and speaker identification using three public datasets (*i.e.*, MIRACL-VC1, OuluVS and CUAVE). The obtained results show the importance of the depth data for lip-reading and that a same combination of mouth features can be used for lip-reading and speaker identification. The proposed system can be used for a biometric system to both identify the speaker and interact with a machine in a spontaneous way. In feature work, we will focus on spotting speech portions in continuous video flow for a human-machine interaction application.

References

1. Ahlberg, J.: Candide-3 - an updated parameterised face. Technical report, Department of Electrical Engineering, Linköping University, Sweden (2001)
2. Bakry, A., Elgammal, A.: Mkpls: manifold kernel partial least squares for lipreading and speaker identification. In: International Conference on Computer Vision and Pattern Recognition, pp. 684–691 (2013)
3. Ben-Hamadou, A., Soussen, C., Daul, C., Blondel, W., Wolf, D.: Flexible calibration of structured-light systems projecting point patterns. Computer Vision and Image Understanding **117**(10), 1468–1481 (2013)
4. Dalal, N., Triggs, B.: Histograms of oriented gradients for human detection. International Conference on Computer Vision and Pattern Recognition **1**, 886–893 (2005)
5. Dalal, N., Triggs, B., Schmid, C.: Human detection using oriented histograms of flow and appearance. In: Leonardis, A., Bischof, H., Pinz, A. (eds.) ECCV 2006. LNCS, vol. 3952, pp. 428–441. Springer, Heidelberg (2006)
6. de la Cuesta, A.G., Zhang, J., Miller, P.: Biometric identification using motion history images of a speaker's lip movements. In: International Machine Vision and Image Processing Conference, IMVIP 2008, pp. 83–88. IEEE (2008)

7. Liu, Y.-F., Lin, C.-Y., Guo, J.-M.: Impact of the lips for biometrics. IEEE Transactions on Image Processing **21**(6), 3092–3101 (2012)
8. Lucey, P., Sridharan, S.: Patch-based representation of visual speech. In: Proceedings of the HCSNet Workshop on Use of Vision in Human-Computer Interaction, pp. 79–85 (2006)
9. Lucey, P., Sridharan, S., Dean, D.: Continuous pose-invariant lipreading. In: INTERSPEECH 2008, 9th Annual Conference of the International Speech Communication Association, Brisbane, Australia, pp. 2679–2682, September 22–26, 2008
10. Papandreou, G., Katsamanis, A., Pitsikalis, V., Maragos, P.: Adaptive multimodal fusion by uncertainty compensation with application to audiovisual speech recognition. Audio, Speech, and Language Processing **17**(3), 423–435 (2009)
11. Patterson, E.K., Gurbuz, S., Tufekci, Z., Gowdy, J.: Cuave: a new audio-visual database for multimodal human-computer interface research. In: Acoustics, Speech, and Signal Processing, vol. 2, pp. 2017–2020 (2002)
12. Pei, Y., Kim, T.-k., Zha, H.: Unsupervised random forest manifold alignment for lipreading. In: International Conference on Computer Vision, pp. 129–136 (2013)
13. Rekik, A., Ben-Hamadou, A., Mahdi, W.: Face pose tracking under arbitrary illumination changes. In: International Conference on Computer Vision, Imaging and Computer Graphics Theory and Applications (2014)
14. Rekik, A., Ben-Hamadou, A., Mahdi, W.: A new visual speech recognition approach for RGB-D cameras. In: Campilho, A., Kamel, M. (eds.) ICIAR 2014, Part II. LNCS, vol. 8815, pp. 21–28. Springer, Heidelberg (2014)
15. Rekik, A., Ben-Hamadou, A., Mahdi, W.: An adaptive approach for lip-reading using image and depth data. Multimedia Tools and Applications, 1–28 (2015)
16. Rekik, A., Ben-Hamadou, A., Mahdi, W.: Human machine interaction via visual speech spotting. In: Proc. of Advanced Concepts for Intelligent Vision Systems (ACIVS) (2015)
17. Saeed, U.: Comparative analysis of lip features for person identification. In: Proceedings of the 8th International Conference on Frontiers of Information Technology, pp. 20. ACM (2010)
18. Saeed, U.: Person identification using behavioral features from lip motion. In: 2011 IEEE International Conference on Automatic Face & Gesture Recognition and Workshops (FG 2011), pp. 131–136. IEEE (2011)
19. Zhang, Z.: A flexible new technique for camera calibration. Pattern Analysis and Machine Intelligence **22**(11), 1330–1334 (2000)
20. Zhao, G., Barnard, M., Pietikainen, M.: Lipreading with local spatiotemporal descriptors. Multimedia, IEEE Transactions **11**(7), 1254–1265 (2009)
21. Zhou, Z., Hong, X., Zhao, G., Pietikainen, M.: A compact representation of visual speech data using latent variables. IEEE Transactions on Pattern Analysis and Machine Intelligence **36**(1), 181–187 (2014)
22. Zhou, Z., Zhao, G., Hong, X., Pietikäinen, M.: A review of recent advances in visual speech decoding. Image and Vision Computing (2014)
23. Zhou, Z., Zhao, G. and Pietikainen, M.: Towards a practical lipreading system. In: International Conference on Computer Vision and Pattern Recognition, pp. 137–144 (2011)
24. Zhou, Z., Zhao, G., Pietikainen, M.: Lipreading: a graph embedding approach. In: International Conference on Pattern Recognition, pp. 523–526 (2010)

Soft Biometrics by Modeling Temporal Series of Gaze Cues Extracted in the Wild

Dario Cazzato[2]([⊠]), Marco Leo[1], Andrea Evangelista[2], and Cosimo Distante[1]

[1] National Research Council of Italy - Institute of Optics, Arnesano, LE, Italy
[2] Faculty of Engineering, University of Salento, Lecce, Italy
dario.cazzato@ino.it

Abstract. Soft biometric systems have spread among recent years, both for powering classical biometrics, as well as stand alone solutions with several application scopes ranging from digital signage to human-robot interaction. Among all, in the recent years emerged the possibility to consider as a soft biometrics also the temporal evolution of the human gaze and some recent works in the literature explored this exciting research line by using expensive and (perhaps) unsafe devices which, moreover, require user cooperation to be calibrated. By our knowledge the use of a low-cost, non-invasive, safe and calibration-free gaze estimator to get soft-biometrics data has not been investigated yet. This paper fills this gap by analyzing the soft-biometrics performances obtained by modeling the series of gaze estimated by exploiting the combination of head poses and eyes' pupil locations on data acquired by an off-the-shelf RGB-D device.

1 Introduction

Biometrics is the science of establishing the identity of an individual basing on physical, chemical or behavioral attributes of the person. In the literature, several features have been employed in order to achieve the recognition task, like palmprint [14], iris [22] or fingerprint [24], as well as DNA, face, retina and so on. The diffusion of large-scale biometric systems in both commercial and government applications have increased the researcher's awareness of this technology. As a consequence of this rapid growth, also the challenges associated with designing and deploying biometric systems have been highlighted. Hard biometric systems raise many security and privacy issues, since they are based on personal, physiological and behavioral data that could be stolen and misused [3]. Moreover, they need to process information that could not be always accessible, or available only by means of intrusive devices in order to obtain the required reliability and precision for the particular application context. In large-scale identification applications, due to the larger number of comparisons to be performed, these systems may not yet be extremely accurate [11], as well as due to noise in the data, intra-class variation and non-universality of the biometrics. To improve reliability, different biometrics can be merged in the same solution: at this aim, the work of [9] formulates the problem of multiple biometrics,

© Springer International Publishing Switzerland 2015
S. Battiato et al. (Eds.): ACIVS 2015, LNCS 9386, pp. 391–402, 2015.
DOI: 10.1007/978-3-319-25903-1_34

showing the potential improvement of multibiometrics. However, requirements of such solution increase in terms of computational needs, as well as the overall intrusiveness. At this purpose, the concept of soft biometrics has spread in the literature. In [10] soft biometrics are defined as characteristics that provide some information about the individual, but such that they lack of the distinctiveness and permanence to sufficiently differentiate any two individuals. Example of soft biometric estimations by computer vision algorithms are age estimation [7] or gender recognition [1], but also the race, the height, the color of the hair or the shape of the face are classified as soft biometrics. These features can be merged in an easier way to provide multiple label classification [8], or in such a way that a set of biometrics can enhance another estimation problem, like in [21].

Among well consolidated soft biometrics, the idea of gaze analysis as a personal distinctive feature has been also taken into account. The milestone of this research area is a series of works which make use of an head mounted eye tracker, based on the detection of infrared light reflection, to temporally analyze the eye movements during predefined stimuli. The final aims of the data analysis range from the evaluation of student behavioral skills [2] to the identification of users among a set of predefined ones ([13], [6]). Instead of analyzing eye movement, more recently, the work in [4] proposes to consider the temporal evolution of the gaze direction as a soft-biometrics. The study was based on data acquired by a Tobii 1750[1] remote eye tracker that is expensive, it requires the user cooperation to achieve an initial calibration and it employs infrared light concentrated on the eye pupils whose safety is still under discussion (as demonstrate the recent updates of required standards for commercial devices[2]). The work demonstrated that the gaze direction is able to distinguish among users but its real applicability is limited by its operating modes and hardware requirements.

By our knowledge the use of a low-cost, non-invasive, safe and calibration-free gaze estimator to get soft-biometrics data has not been investigated yet.

This paper fills this gap by analyzing the soft-biometrics performances obtained by modeling the series of gaze estimated by an innovative framework exploiting the combination of head poses and eyes' pupil locations on data acquired by an off-the-shelf RGB-D device. The gaze estimation approach does not require any initial person dependent calibration, it allows the user to freely rotate the head in the field of view of the sensor and it is insensitive to the presence of eyeglasses, beard or hairstyle. Gaze estimation series are probabilistically modelled by using Hidden Markov Models [17] and their suitability for biometrics purposes has been demonstrated by acquiring in the wild different persons watching a benchmark video. The use of HMM for the classification of gaze cues is another important contribution of the paper. Although HMMs have been largely exploited for the classification of biometrics traits ([18], [16]), there is only one work that uses HMM to build a personalized gaze profile from data acquired by a commercial eye-tracker [25].

---

[1] http://www.tobii.com/

[2] http://www.tobii.com/en/eye-tracking-research/global/support-and-downloads/faqs/501a0000000zX3c/

The rest of the paper is organized as follows: Section 2 introduces the proposed gaze estimation framework, while Section 3 deals with the problem of human gaze as a possible soft biometric. Experimental setup and results are presented in Section 4. Section 5 concludes the paper.

2   Gaze Estimation in the Wild

Fig. 1 gives an overall view of the proposed solution. The proposed gaze estimation method works on depth and RGB images extracted from commercial depth sensors e.g., Microsoft Kinect[3] and ASUS Xtion Pro Live[4]. The acquired data are processed by a multistep approach performing, at first, head pose estimation using both depth and RGB streams. The head pose estimation algorithm computes the exact position of the head with regards to the sensor, in terms of yaw, pitch and roll angles. Head pose information, integrated with the 3D positions of the user, can supply a rough estimation of the human gaze: this can be carried out by computing the intersection between the sensor plane and a straight line whose direction in the 3D space is defined by head pose angles [5] but, unfortunately, any gaze estimation that does not take into account the localization of the eye centers is highly inaccurate [19], especially for some kinds of application. For this reason the proposed approach, as a second step, computes pupils localization over the RGB data, using differential geometry and local self-similarity matching that assures a suitable accuracy in detection even under critical acquisition conditions [15]. The information about pupils is then used to refine the initial gaze estimation and this is done by computing a correction factor for the angles of the 3D model.

For the estimation of the rough gaze only the 3D position of the eye center[5] and the head pose information angles are used . The gaze track is computed as the straight line passing through the eye center with direction defined by the available head pose angles and finally the rough point of regard (POR) is estimated as the intersection of the line with a a vertical plane with regard to the ground and passing from the center of the sensor.

Fig. 2 schematizes this procedural step and it helps to understand the underlying equations which are stated basing on a right-handed coordinate system (with the origin at the sensor, z axis pointed towards the user and y axis pointed up). The depth sensor directly gives the length of the segment $\overline{AC}$, i.e. the distance between the eye of the observer and the considered target plane. The right-angled triangle $\widehat{ABC}$ can be then completely solved as: $\overline{AB} = \frac{\overline{AC}}{\cos \omega_y}$ and

$\overline{BC} = \sqrt{\overline{AB}^2 - \overline{AC}^2}$. and using the same coordinate system, it is possible to

---

[3] www.microsoft.com/en-us/kinectforwindows/

[4] www.asus.com/Multimedia/

[5] Only the gaze track passing though one eye is considered since taking into account both eyes would require additional knowledge about how, for each specific person, the eye are aligned and moreover a mutual error compensation scheme should be introduced.

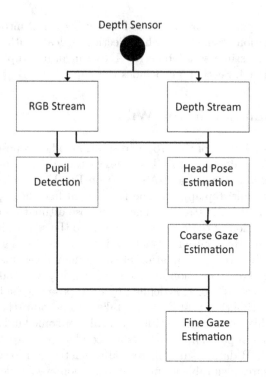

Fig. 1. A block diagram of the proposed solution.

compute also the cartesian equation of the gaze ray as the straight line passing for points $A = (x_A, y_A, z_A)$ and $B = (x_B, y_B, z_B)$ expressed as:

$$r : \begin{cases} \frac{x - x_A}{x_B - x_A} = \frac{y - y_A}{y_B - y_A} \\ \frac{y - y_A}{y_B - y_A} = \frac{z - z_A}{z_B - z_A} \end{cases} \tag{1}$$

with $z_A = 0$ since the sensor lies on the target plane.

The translations of the observer, on the x and y axes, with regard to the sensor, are easily handled by a posteriori algebraical sums.

At this point the rough gaze estimation, i.e. the gaze based only on head pose information, is available and it has to be refined by integrating the information extracted by the pupil locator. To do that a 3D geometric model of the eye has to be introduced [20] and, in particular, the used model is defined by the following three parameters:

- Eye Center, derived from the 3D overlapped mask (denoted by $EyeCenter = (x_{EyeCenter}, y_{EyeCenter}, z_{EyeCenter})$);
- Pupil Center, derived from the pupil detection module (denoted by $EyePupilCenter = (x_{EyePupilCenter}, y_{EyePupilCenter}, z_{EyePupilCenter})$);

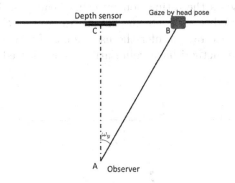

Fig. 2. Gaze estimation by head pose.

– Eyeball Center, a variable that is not visible by the system, and whose position can only be estimated
$(EyeballCenter = (x_{EyeballCenter}, y_{EyeballCenter}, z_{EyeballCenter}))$;

The Eyeball Center parameter ($EyeballCenter$) is firstly computed: the eye is modeled as a perfect sphere, with an estimated radius of 12 mm [23] since the low camera resolution does not allow to consider more accurate models. The parameter $EyeballCenter$ is then estimated as the point that lies 12 mm behind the eye center, in the direction (meant as the straight line) previously computed. Indicating with $Radius_{EB}$ this value, it follows that:

$$EyeballCenter = \begin{cases} x = x_{EyeCenter} \pm |Radius_{EB} \cos \omega_x \sin \omega_y| \\ y = y_{EyeCenter} \pm |Radius_{EB} \cos \omega_y \sin \omega_x| \\ z = Radius_{EB} \cos \omega_x \cos \omega_y + z_{EyeCenter} \end{cases} \quad (2)$$

where the sign $\pm$ depends on a, respectively, negative or positive pitch (yaw) angle of the specified coordinate system.

This 3D point represents the center of the sphere of the considered eye. From this point, it is possible to compute the straight line that passes through $EyePupilCenter$ and $EyeballCenter$ with Equation 1. Thus, the x_{tp} and y_{tp} coordinates on the target plan tp (with $z = 0$) are:

$$\begin{cases} x_{tp} = \frac{z_{EyeballCenter}}{z_{EyeballCenter} - z_{EyePupilCenter}} (x_{EyePupilCenter} - x_{EyeballCenter}) + \\ + x_{EyeballCenter} \\ y_{tp} = \frac{z_{EyeballCenter}}{z_{EyeballCenter} - z_{EyePupilCenter}} (y_{EyePupilCenter} - y_{EyeballCenter}) + \\ + y_{EyeballCenter} \end{cases} \quad (3)$$

and this is the finer gaze estimation that is the outcome of this procedural step.

Fig. 3 gives an overall view of the proposed method: the straight line r (replicated with the parallel straight line r' passing for the nose, for clarity to the reader) represents the estimation by using head pose information only. This information is used to estimate the 3D coordinates of *EyeballCenter*, and thus to use the new gaze ray to infer the user point of view. Note that all the key parameters of the method have voluntarily been enlarged in the figure, for the sake of clarity.

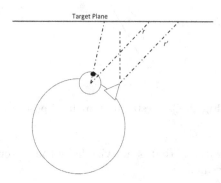

Fig. 3. Overall view of the gaze estimation model.

3   Gaze as Soft-Biometrics

This section describes how the gaze outcomes have been used as soft-biometrics, i.e. to build a temporal pattern that can be exploited to recognize a target person. In order to represent the real intersection point with the environment and to realize experimental tests, coordinates are normalized to image plane coordinates with the generic formula, valid for both coordinates x and y of the image plane:

$$c_{norm} = c - \frac{bound_{low}}{bound_{upp} - bound_{low}} \cdot size(I) \tag{4}$$

where $bound_{upp}$ and $bound_{low}$ are the two bounds, in meters, of the space, and $size(I)$ is the width (or height, depending on the coordinate under consideration), expressed in pixels. After that, a mapping from continuous to discrete outcomes is performed: this helps addressing distortions in the gaze estimation process. The aforementioned mapping is achieved in practice by partitioning the target scene (i.e. a screen) in a suitable number of regions labeled with predefined symbols (e.g., numbers or letters). This way, every time a subject is observed, a series of symbols is associated to his gaze behavior and it represents the pattern to be modeled for biometric scopes. To this end, a HMM is associated to each involved subject obtaining this way a HMM bank. Each HMM is then trained using one or more series associated to the subject. After training, learned HMMs are used to get the likelihoods that, given an unknown series in input, it belongs to each of the subjects in the training group. The maximum likelihood score is then considered and the label corresponding to the subject associated to the winning HMM is finally attached to the unknown series under investigation. The above mentioned procedural steps are resumed in Fig. 4.

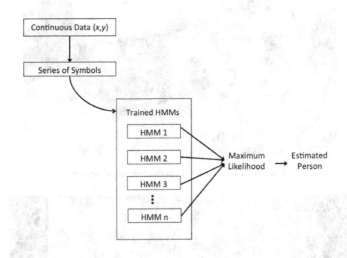

Fig. 4. The performed Soft-Biometrics authentication by HMM.

4   Experimental Results

In order to evaluate the proposed framework, the experimental environment in Fig. 5 has been setup. In particular, a screen of dimensions 70×22.5 cm was used.

Each user was asked to sit down on a chair at a distance of 60 cm from the screen and the depth sensor was placed on top of the screen, pointing at the user. A Microsoft Kinect sensor has been employed in order to acquire input data.

The screen has been split into 15 equal rectangles of size of 512×360 pixels each one, labeled from 1 to 15, as shown in Fig. 6. For each gaze point, the rectangle to which it belongs is stored and then a series of symbols is collected for each test session. All the hits lying out of the screen were automatically replaced with the coordinates of the closest pixel on the screen, and thus associated to the respective rectangle.

To map world coordinates into screen coordinates, the Equation 4 (that refers to the center of a generic rectangular target) was slightly modified by considering a translation parameter among the y axis equal to the distance between the actual sensor position and the center of the screen. Experiments were carried out on 7 participants that were asked to look at the same video while the system

Fig. 5. The realized environmental setup.

Fig. 6. The used subdivision of the watching area in an example frame of the benchmark video.

recorded and stored their gaze tracks. For each person, 5 different acquisition sessions were performed. Each session was carried out in different days (spread in 15 days) experiencing different lightning conditions and without imposing any constraint to the users in terms of head rotations, beards and eyeglasses.

During each session the same benchmark video run on the screen: the video shows a session of F1 cars test and presents a large variability of the position of relevant objects (the cars) on the screen due also to a frequent change of camera views. The video is coupled with the audio of the engines and this is an external feature that somehow could influence the users' behavior. The video is available on [26]. Fig. 7 shows three frames of the selected video. The video lasts 199 seconds but only the first 170 seconds has been considered. The video has a resolution of 1280 × 720 pixels, a frame rate of 25fps and it was shown at a

Fig. 7. Three frames of the benchmark video.

fullscreen resolution on a screen of 2560×1080 pixels[6]. This causes a black border of $7.7cm$ on both left and right side of the screen that was anyway recorded.

The synchronization between the gaze estimator and the actual frame shown on the screen was made by means of the timing functions of the operative system[7]. For each gaze estimation the x and y coordinates, computed as described in Equations 3 and 4, were stored.

As expected the gaze was not estimated in each frame of the video due to computational delay and missed detections of the face/pupil. Missing data were then filled by Kalman Filter predictions [12]. Anyway, on average, an actual estimate was available every 2.89 frames.

This way, a vector of size 1×4252 components have been created for each session of each participant. In order to evaluate recognition accuracy, to each participant a label has been manually associated, from 1 to 7.

The gaze estimation system has been implemented using Microsoft Visual C++ developing environment, with RGB and depth images taken at a resolution of 640×480, 30 fps.

In order to accomplish the aim of discovering if the used framework is suitable for biometrics purposes, the analysis of acquired data was performed as follows. First of all, in order to evaluate the optimal number of hidden states for HMMs, different configurations (from 2 to 24 states) were considered and trained using the first series of observations for each involved subject. Then the output likelihoods (when the same series is given as input) were added together and the configuration reporting the maximization of the achieved score was retained for the subsequent experiments. Fig. 8 shows the Log-likelihood values while varying HMM's configuration. As can be observed, the best value was obtained when a configuration with 16 hidden states was used. In the second experimental phase the bank of 7 HMMs with 16 hidden states was exploited for soft-biometrics issues. In order to evaluate how accurate the predictive model will performs in practice, the experiment was done on the available data performing N-times $(N = 10)$ a k-fold $(k = 5)$ cross-validation. This way each example was classified 10-times by using 10 different training sets built at each iteration on the 30 examples which did not belong to the same fold of the test examples. The relative confusion matrix is reported in Table 1 from where the following parameters of performances can be extracted:

---

[6] Philips 298P4

[7] Microsoft Windows 8.1

$$precision_M^{k-fold} = 0.739;$$

$$recall_M^{k-fold} = 0.737.$$

These data are very encouraging and they demonstrate that it is possible to find a strong relationship between the identity of a person and its gaze behavior during the projection of a specified video on a screen in front at it. This study demonstrated that this is true even if the gaze behavior is recorded by using not-invasive, calibration free and low-cost system as the proposed one.

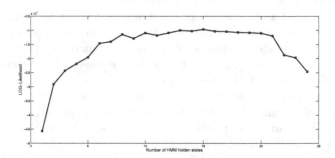

Fig. 8. Log-likelihood values for different HMM lengths.

Table 1. Confusion matrix using the proposed framework and k-fold cross-validation.

	Estimated labels						
	p#1	p#2	p#3	p#4	p#5	p#6	p#7
p#1	**37**	2	5	2	1	3	
p#2		**41**	1	1	4		3
p#3	4	1	**40**		4	1	
p#4		3		**35**	6		6
p#5	3	1		8	**34**		4
p#6	5		5			**40**	
p#7				6	7	6	**31**

5   Conclusions

This work introduced a preliminary study to evaluate biometric identification of individuals on the basis of data acquired by a low-cost, non-invasive, safe and calibration-free gaze estimation framework consisting of two main components conveniently combined and performing user's head pose estimation and eyes' pupil localization on data acquired by a RGB-D device. The experimental evidence of the feasibility of using the proposed framework as soft-biometrics has been given on a set of users watching a benchmark video in an unconstrained environment. Future works will validate the system by comparisons with a commercial eye tracker, in order to provide quantitative measurements of the system reliability. Moreover, an evaluation of the possibility to combine both eye information in order to enhance the system will be performed.

References

1. Bekios-Calfa, J., Buenaposada, J.M., Baumela, L.: Robust gender recognition by exploiting facial attributes dependencies. Pattern Recognition Letters **36**, 228–234 (2014)
2. Busjahn, T., Schulte, C., Sharif, B., Begel, A., Hansen, M., Bednarik, R., Orlov, P., Ihantola, P., Shchekotova, G., Antropova, M., et al.: Eye tracking in computing education. In: Proceedings of the Tenth Annual Conference on International Computing Education Research, pp. 3–10. ACM (2014)
3. Campisi, P.: Security and Privacy in Biometrics. Springer (2013)
4. Cantoni, V., Galdi, C., Nappi, M., Porta, M., Riccio, D.: Gant: Gaze analysis technique for human identification. Pattern Recognition **48**(4), 1027–1038 (2015)
5. Cazzato, D., Leo, M., Distante, C.: An investigation on the feasibility of uncalibrated and unconstrained gaze tracking for human assistive applications by using head pose estimation. Sensors **14**(5), 8363–8379 (2014)
6. Deravi, F., Guness, S.P.: Gaze trajectory as a biometric modality. In: BIOSIGNALS, pp. 335–341 (2011)
7. Fernández, C., Huerta, I., Prati, A.: A comparative evaluation of regression learning algorithms for facial age estimation. In: Ji, Q., B. Moeslund, T., Hua, G., Nasrollahi, K. (eds.) FFER 2014. LNCS, vol. 8912, pp. 133–144. Springer, Heidelberg (2015)
8. Guo, G., Mu, G.: Joint estimation of age, gender and ethnicity: CCA vs. PLS. In: 2013 10th IEEE International Conference and Workshops on Automatic Face and Gesture Recognition (FG), pp. 1–6. IEEE (2013)
9. Hong, L., Jain, A.K., Pankanti, S.: Can multibiometrics improve performance? In: Proceedings AutoID, vol. 99, pp. 59–64. Citeseer (1999)
10. Jain, A.K., Dass, S.C., Nandakumar, K.: Soft biometric traits for personal recognition systems. In: Zhang, D., Jain, A.K. (eds.) ICBA 2004. LNCS, vol. 3072, pp. 731–738. Springer, Heidelberg (2004)
11. Jain, A.K., Ross, A., Prabhakar, S.: An introduction to biometric recognition. IEEE Transactions on Circuits and Systems for Video Technology **14**(1), 4–20 (2004)
12. Kalman, R.E.: A new approach to linear filtering and prediction problems. Journal of Fluids Engineering **82**(1), 35–45 (1960)
13. Kasprowski, P., Komogortsev, O.V., Karpov, A.: First eye movement verification and identification competition at BTAS 2012. In: 2012 IEEE Fifth International Conference on Biometrics: Theory, Applications and Systems (BTAS), pp. 195–202. IEEE (2012)
14. Kumar, A., Wong, D.C., Shen, H.C., Jain, A.K.: Personal verification using palmprint and hand geometry biometric. In: Kittler, J., Nixon, M.S. (eds.) AVBPA 2003. LNCS, vol. 2688, pp. 668–678. Springer, Heidelberg (2003)
15. Leo, M., Cazzato, D., De Marco, T., Distante, C.: Unsupervised eye pupil localization through differential geometry and local self-similarity matching. PloS one **9**(8), e102829 (2014)
16. Parris, E.S., Carey, M.J.: Language independent gender identification. In: Proceedings of the 1996 IEEE International Conference on Acoustics, Speech, and Signal Processing. ICASSP 1996, vol. 2, pp. 685–688. IEEE (1996)
17. Rabiner, L.: A tutorial on hidden Markov models and selected applications in speech recognition. Proceedings of the IEEE **77**(2), 257–286 (1989)

18. Roy, A., Halevi, T., Memon, N.: An HMM-based behavior modeling approach for continuous mobile authentication. In: 2014 IEEE International Conference on Acoustics, Speech and Signal Processing (ICASSP), pp. 3789–3793. IEEE (2014)
19. Stiefelhagen, R., Zhu, J.: Head orientation and gaze direction in meetings. In: CHI 2002 Extended Abstracts on Human Factors in Computing Systems, pp. 858–859. ACM (2002)
20. Sun, L., Liu, Z., Sun, M.T.: Real time gaze estimation with a consumer depth camera. Information Sciences (2015)
21. Wang, X., Ly, V., Lu, G., Kambhamettu, C.: Can we minimize the influence due to gender and race in age estimation? In: 2013 12th International Conference on Machine Learning and Applications (ICMLA), vol. 2, pp. 309–314. IEEE (2013)
22. Wildes, R.P.: Iris recognition: an emerging biometric technology. Proceedings of the IEEE **85**(9), 1348–1363 (1997)
23. Xiong, X., Cai, Q., Liu, Z., Zhang, Z.: Eye gaze tracking using an RGBD camera: a comparison with a RGB solution. In: Proceedings of the 2014 ACM International Joint Conference on Pervasive and Ubiquitous Computing: Adjunct Publication, pp. 1113–1121. ACM (2014)
24. Ye, Z., Mohamadian, H., Ye, Y.: Information measures for biometric identification via 2d discrete wavelet transform. In: IEEE International Conference on Automation Science and Engineering. CASE 2007, pp. 835–840. IEEE (2007)
25. Yoon, H.J., Carmichael, T.R., Tourassi, G.: Gaze as a biometric. In: SPIE Medical Imaging, pp. 903707–903707. International Society for Optics and Photonics (2014)
26. YouTube: Video (2015). https://www.youtube.com/watch?v=KnJtsZzMJ8Y

Online Face Recognition System Based on Local Binary Patterns and Facial Landmark Tracking

Marko Linna[✉], Juho Kannala, and Esa Rahtu

Department of Computer Science and Engineering, University of Oulu, P.O. Box
4500, 90014 Oulu, Finland
marko.linna@student.oulu.fi

Abstract. This paper presents a system for real-time face recognition.
The system learns and recognizes faces from a video on the fly and it
doesn't need already trained database. The system consists of the following sub-methods: face detection and tracking, face alignment, key frame
selection, face description and face matching. The system detects face
tracks from a video, which are used in learning and recognition. Facial
landmark tracking is utilized to detect changes in facial pose and expression in order to select key frames from a face track. Faces in key frames
are represented using local binary patterns (LBP) histograms. These histograms are stored into the database. Nearest neighbor classifier is used
in face matching. The system achieved recognition rate of 98.6% in offline
test and 95.9% in online test.

1 Introduction

Majority of the state-of-the-art face recognition methods focus on a specific
sub-problem and are usually computationally intensive [5–8]. Therefore it is not
straightforward to use them in online face recognition systems, where learning
and recognition must happen in real-time while processing a video. They may
not be suitable for applications, which require short response times (e.g. human-
robot interaction).

In this paper, we present real-time face recognition system for practical application. We don't focus on a specific sub-problem, but consider the whole system.
Our method is a complete package including learning, recognition and database
update. The method operates in real-time while processing a video. Already
trained database is not mandatory, because the method learns on the fly. Possible cases for our method are human-robot interaction, door camera, greeter,
home security and home entertainment systems (e.g. integrated on a TV). The
software implementation of our method is publicly available.

For real-time video based face recognition the computational lightness, as
well as accuracy, is very important. To cope with this, we selected LBP for face
descriptor [3] and fast facial landmark tracker [13] for tracking detected faces,
omitting the need of computationally heavy face detection for every frame.

Our method detects face tracks from a video. Face tracks are used in recognition and learning. In the recognition, face representations of n frames from the

© Springer International Publishing Switzerland 2015
S. Battiato et al. (Eds.): ACIVS 2015, LNCS 9386, pp. 403–414, 2015.
DOI: 10.1007/978-3-319-25903-1_35

beginning of the face track are used to find out nearest match from the database. Nearest neighbor classifier is used in matching. Distances between face representations are measured using weighted Chi-square. In the learning, key frames are selected from the face track so that they represent the face in different poses and expressions. Then face representations are extracted from the key frames and stored into the database.

2   Related Work

Face recognition may typically consist of sub-problems like face detection, face alignment, facial landmark tracking, face description and face matching. Most common face detection methods use Haar-like features and AdaBoost [17]. Some face recognition methods focus on alignment [9], [5]. Several methods are introduced for facial landmark tracking [11], [13], [15]. Common methods used in face description are principal component analysis (PCA) [1], linear discriminant analysis (LDA) [2] and local binary patterns (LBP) [3]. Lately deep learning has been studied a lot and methods based on it seem to give most promising results [5–7].

The face recognition studies usually focus on a specific sub-problem and don't consider the face recognition at a system level. Few works focus on purely real-time or online face recognition systems. Most related to our work is [4], which provides real-time face recognition and online learning. The method increases the separability of the classes by maximizing the inter-class and minimizing the intra-class variations. Only the most representative samples are selected in order to gain robustness against illumination and pose changes. Additionally, to allow for classification of unknown faces, the method finds the relation between the distance of classification and the certainty of that classification. To further improve recognition performance multiple frames are used in classification. The method uses class-weighted average PCA (CAPCA) for face description, while our method uses LBP. The CAPCA uses feature size of 4096, while our LBP descriptor size is 2301. Our descriptor size is roughly half of the CAPCA size, which means that our method is potentially faster in face matching and requires a smaller database. In addition, LBP is known to be more robust against illumination and pose changes than holistic approaches like PCA [3] based methods, so our method is likely to perform better in challenging environments.

It is not trivial to compare our method against state-of-the-art methods, because their software may not be available or it might be very difficult to implement them to work in real-time. Therefore, we don't compare our method to other methods.

3   Method

The usage the method is best understood with a practical example, which follows. The method is running in a greeter robot. The robot is "just born" and doesn't know anybody. Then, a boy comes to say hello to the robot. Robot detects the face of the boy, then it asks name and the boy answers. The robot starts to memorize the face until the boy leaves. Time passes and several other persons visit the robot. Next day, the same boy comes to greet the robot. Now the robot remembers the face of the boy and says hello with the name of the boy.

Our method consists of *recognition* and *learning*, which both needs face tracks. These face tracks are detected from a video by our method. In the recognition, the beginning of the detected face track is used to find nearest match, meaning that n frames from the beginning of the face track are used in database search. The n is determined by the search time and the video frame rate. If the total frame count in the face track is smaller than the search time multiplied with the video frame rate, the n is the total frame count. Further, the n decreases while the database gets larger, because it takes more time to find nearest match for a single frame. The search and matching is explained in more detail in Section 3.5. Face representation is extracted from each frame used in the search. This representation is in form of LBP histogram and is explained in more detail in Section 3.4. The database search is started immediately when a new face track is detected and it happens in real-time while tracking a face. It lasts for a specified time, after which the person identity is either known or not known (see Fig. 1).

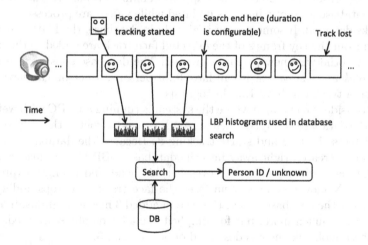

Fig. 1. Recognition: n subsequent frames from the beginning of a track are used in classification. If multiple classes returned, the one with shortest distance is taken.

In the learning, the key frames are selected from the detected face track so that they represent the face in different pose and expression (e.g. person is talking or turning head). The selection of key frames is explained in more detail in Section 3.3. Face representations are extracted from the key frames and stored into the database as LBP histograms. Learning happens in real-time while tracking a face (see Fig. 2).

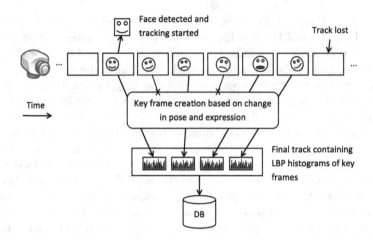

Fig. 2. Learning: face representations of the selected key frames of a track are stored into the database. Selection happens if there is large enough change in pose and expression compared to the last key frame.

The recognition and the learning happens in online fashion. At the beginning the face database is empty, but gets updated while videos are processed and new face tracks detected. If some person is already in database, the LBP histograms extracted from the key frames of the detected face track are added to the person in question, otherwise new person is created. The database consists of entities: *person*, *track* and *histogram*. It can have 0...n persons, a person can have 1...m tracks and a track can have 1...k histograms.

Let's consider an example where the system is running on a PC with webcam. Initially the database is empty. Then person X comes to front of the webcam. The system detects the face and starts tracking it. Because the database is empty, new person is created right away into the database. LBP histograms are added to the database while person X moves her/his head and changes expression. Now person X moves away, system loses the face track and stops adding new histograms to the database. So far the system added 3 new histograms. In reality there would be much more, but for simplicity smaller numbers are used. What the database looks like now is described on left in Fig. 3.

Now person Y comes to front of the webcam. The face is detected and database search initialized. The search uses all the available frames (not only key frames) from the beginning of the face track to find close enough match. The search continues for a specific time (or until whole database is gone through), then the classification is done. The *unknown* class is returned and new person is added into the database along with the histograms of the key frames of the detected face track so far. Histograms are added until suddenly person Y changes head pose so that the system loses track of the face. Then she/he watches again directly to webcam and a new track is initialized for the same person. The search is started and now it finds the *person id* of the person Y. New track is added for

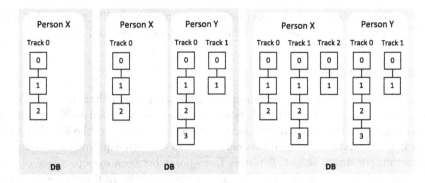

Fig. 3. Database state where squares are LBP histograms of key frames. Left: after adding person X. Center: after adding person Y. Right: after updating person X.

person Y and following histograms are added to it. After person Y moves away, the database looks like what is described in center in Fig. 3.

For next, person X comes again in front of the camera. The search finds *person id* of the person X correctly and the following histograms are added for it. Then the person X looks away for a while and then back to camera, so that the track is lost and new one started. Also this time search found correct *person id* and just adds next histograms to it. After the person X moves away, she/he has 3 tracks in the database. What the database looks at the end, is described on right in Fig. 3.

Our method consists of the following key components: *face detection and tracking, face alignment, key frame selection, face description* and *face descriptor matching*. These all are explained in their own sub-sections below.

3.1   Face Detection and Tracking

We considered two facial feature detection methods for locating and tracking facial landmarks. The first one was using conditional regression forest [11] and the second one was based on updating a discriminative facial deformable model [13]. The software, [12] and [14] respectively, was available for both methods. According to our experiments, the second method turned out to be faster and more robust with big head rotations so it was selected for the final experiments reported in section 4. The software of the selected method is called Chehra. Chehra provides 49 facial landmark points and 3D head-pose estimation when a face is detected. After initial detection, Chehra starts tracking already found landmarks, until they are lost. After losing landmarks, Chehra starts detecting faces again. This detection phase turned out to be computationally very slow compared to the tracking phase. Internally Chehra uses OpenCV's Viola-Jones face detection algorithm [17].

In addition, a third method, using an ensemble of regression trees to estimate face's landmark positions [15] has been recently published. This method is reported to achieve real-time performance with high quality predictions and could be used in our system, but we have not yet experimented with it.

3.2 Face Alignment

Alignment of the face image and landmarks are used for geometric normalization of the input image. The landmark points of the eyes are used to determine a region of interest (ROI) around the face. For every facial frame, the ROI is found out by first calculating distance between eyes and then multiplying that distance with certain constants to get distances from point between eyes to edges of the ROI, thus giving 4 corner points. The corner points of the ROI are then rotated according to the head-pose (see Fig. 4). The aim is to size ROI to get minimum amount of background pixels, and exclude hair. This way of getting ROI, from eye points only, works well if there are no very big out-of-plane head rotations. From the face ROI, the transformation matrix T is calculated. Then it is used to do perspective transformation for the landmark points and the face image in order to get rid of rotation, scaling and translation.

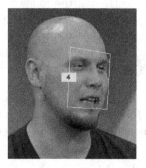

Fig. 4. A frame with facial landmarks and face ROI.

There are three factors in 3D head-pose: *yaw, pitch* and *roll*. The roll is in-plane rotation and is easily compensated. The yaw and pitch are out-of-plane and more problematic because the face will be partially occluded when the rotation angle is high. So aligning using only perspective transformation doesn't give good results with highly out-of-plane rotated faces. However, a small rotation is not a problem. Alternative, more complicated, alignment method was presented by Taigman et al. in their paper [5]. They use 3D model of a face for alignment.

Because LBP is not very robust to noise [10], aligned face image is smoothed with median filter using kernel size 3. This blurs the image only a little and gives better results than without smoothing, especially with noisy source images. After smoothing, the face image is converted into grayscale, thus giving the final normalized face image. See Fig. 5 for illustration of the alignment and normalization.

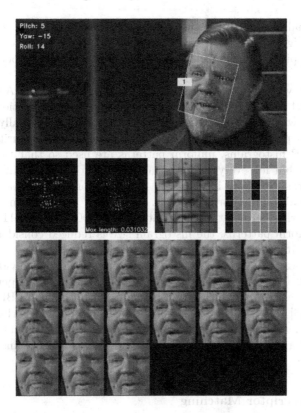

Fig. 5. Normalization and key frame creation. Top: a frame with facial landmarks and face ROI. Center: normalized landmarks, delta vectors of landmarks, normalized face image on 7x7 grid and weight map where black square has weight 0, dark gray 1, light gray 2 and white 4. bottom: Subsequent key frames of a track while expression and pose are changing.

3.3 Key Frame Selection

Our method uses facial landmark tracking to detect changes in facial pose and expression. This is important when selecting the key frames from a face track. The key frames should represent the face in different pose and expression, which can lead to better performance. For each facial frame, a delta vector is calculated for every landmark. The delta vectors show landmark movement between current frame and the last key frame. If at least one delta vector length exceeds a certain limit, a new key frame is selected. See Fig. 5 for illustration of the key frame selection.

3.4 Face Description

We selected LBP for face description, because it has proven to work both fast and accurate in face recognition tasks. The LBP image and histogram is created from the normalized face image using so called *extended LBP operator* [3]. It defines local neighborhood as a set of sampling points evenly spaced on a circle centered at the pixel to be labeled, allowing any radius R and number of sampling points P.

In addition, we selected another extension, *uniform patterns*. A local binary pattern is called uniform if it contains at most two bitwise transitions from 0 to 1 or vice versa when the bit pattern is considered circular. Basically this means that a uniform pattern has no transitions or precisely two transitions. When computing LBP histograms, uniform patterns are used so that the histogram has a separate bin for every uniform pattern, and one extra bin for all non-uniform patterns. So there is $P(P-1)+2$ bins for uniform patterns and 1 shared bin for all non-uniform patterns. The added two uniform pattern bins are cases when there are no transitions at all. E.g. 00000000 and 11111111, if P is 8. With uniform patterns, the histogram size is reduced considerably and it can still detect important features.

The face image, from which the LBP histogram is created, is divided into 7×7 regions (see Fig. 5) using region size 18×21 in pixels. The $\text{LBP}_{8,2}^{u2}$ operator is used separately to each region, which are combined to form the final LBP histogram. According to [3] this is a good trade-off between recognition performance and feature vector length. The $\text{LBP}_{8,2}^{u2}$ operator has 8 sampling points, radius of 2 and it use uniform patterns. Thus there are $8(8-1)+3=59$ bins for a single region.

3.5   Face Descriptor Matching

Our method uses nearest neighbor classifier in LBP histogram matching. To measure distances between LBP histograms, weighted Chi-square (χ^2) is used. It is defined as

$$\chi_w^2(S, M) = \sum_{i,j} w_j \frac{(S_{i,j} - M_{i,j})^2}{S_{i,j} + M_{i,j}} \tag{1}$$

where S and M are histograms to be compared, indices i and j refer to ith bin in histogram corresponding to the jth region and w_j is the weight for region j. We selected weights based on the experiments made by Ahonen et al. [3]. Their method emphasize eye, eyebrow, mouth and temple regions and ignore parts of cheeks and bridge of the nose.

Classification is done for n frames in a detected face track. For each frame, the method starts to calculated distances between the LBP histogram in the frame and histograms in the database, consecutively. The order is such that subsequent histograms are from different person. Distances are calculated until under some histogram the distance is below the *distance threshold* or all histograms are gone through and all distances are above the threshold. In the first case, classification to the person owning the histogram in question happens. Otherwise classification to unknown class happens. If different frames results in different classes, the one with the shortest distance is selected.

4   Experiments

4.1   Dataset

We tested the method on the videos of the Honda/UCSD video database [16]. The dataset contains 20 persons and each person (except one) has at least two videos. Videos are recorded indoor at 15 frames per second. All the videos contain significant in-plane and out-of-plane head rotations. In addition, some videos contain changes in expression and partial occlusions. Videos are separated into training and testing videos.

4.2   Offline test

In the offline test, we used training videos of the dataset to create training database. The training database contains 20 persons, 96 tracks and 2888 histograms (about 144 histograms/person). For testing we used testing videos of the dataset. During testing the database was not updated so every face track was tested against the same database. All frames from a face track were used in testing. In testing videos, there were 278 detected face tracks. The average frame count of the detected face tracks were 47.

The results with three different distance thresholds 0.57, 0.27 and 0.42 are presented in Fig. 6 and Fig. 7 as confusion matrices. Recognition rates with different thresholds were 62.2%, 64.0% and 98.6% respectively. Recognition rate was calculated by dividing all the correct classifications (values in diagonal of a confusion matrix) with the total number of the tested tracks, which is 278 in this case.

4.3   Online test

In the online test, the database was initially empty and was updated every time when new face track were tested. Every later track was tested against a bigger database. Both training and testing videos of the dataset were used in testing. In videos, there were 389 detected face tracks. The average number of frames used in database search were 17 for every detected face track. The search time was 1.5 seconds and distance threshold 0.37 was used. A little stricter threshold 0.37 was selected (0.42 in offline test), because it performed better in online test. Two things were tested. First, what is systems ability to detect new persons. Second, does the system recognize already trained persons.

The new person detection rate was 100%. It was calculated by considering only the first tracks from the persons, which were not already trained. There were 21 of these tracks (note there were extra unknown person in testing videos in the background resulting a face track creation). Then it was find out how many of these track resulted in unknown class. That value was divided with 21, giving the new person detection rate. The recognition rate was 95.9%. It was calculated by considering all the face tracks excluding the first track from each person. The number of these tracks were $389 - 21 = 368$. By dividing the

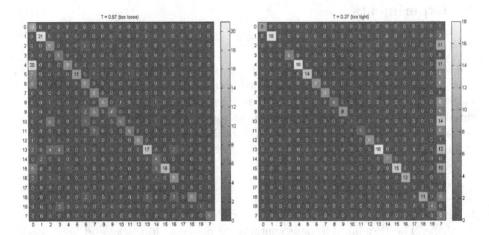

Fig. 6. Confusion matrices showing offline test results. In y-axis are actual persons and in x-axis recognized persons. Left: threshold 0.57 (too loose). The first trained person is emphasized because it is searched first and the search stops when the distance is below the threshold. Right: threshold 0.27 (too tight). The unknown class is emphasized, because there are less histograms whose distance is below the threshold.

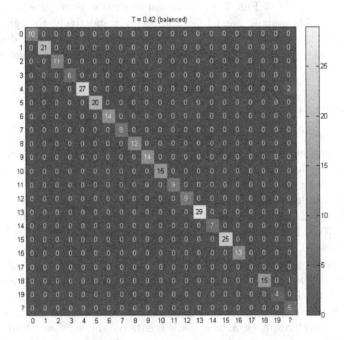

Fig. 7. Confusion matrix showing offline results. In y-axis are actual persons and in x-axis recognized persons. Threshold 0.42. Based on recognition rate, this was the best choice.

number of correct recognitions with this track count, the recognition rate was calculated. The number of false recognitions (classification to wrong/unknown class) in the tracks were 15. The number of the correct recognitions were then $368 - 15 = 353$. It can be seen that the recognition rate 95.9% is a bit worse compared to 98.6% in offline test. This is due to fact that the accuracy is better the more frames from the detected face track were used in the search. In online test this was 17 and in offline test 47. It can be figured out that longer search time results in better recognition rate.

The size of the database was 8623 histograms (about 80 megabytes) at the end of the test. The database can grow even bigger and the method would still perform well, but the search strategy have to be improved for very large databases or search will get inefficient. Tests were ran on 6 years old PC with Intel Core i7 920 2.66 GHz processor and 6 gigabytes memory. Results from the both tests are summarized in the Table 1.

Table 1. Test results

Test name	Database updated	Tracks tested	Average frame count	Recognition rate	New person detection rate
Offline test	No	278	47	98.6%	-
Online test	Yes	389	17	95.9%	100%

5   Conclusion

We introduced online face recognition method based on LBP and facial landmark tracking. The method is a system including real-time face recognition and learning. The method detects face tracks from a video. In learning, key frames are selected from a face track by using facial landmark tracking so that they represent the face in different pose and expression. Faces in key frames are represented by using LBP histograms. The database is updated with LBP histograms on the fly while processing videos. Already trained database is not required. The method uses nearest neighbor classifier in LBP histogram matching.

Our method is computationally efficient and achieved good results. These originate from the use of LBP and fast facial landmark tracking, which omits the need to detect faces from every frame. We carried out two tests on the Honda/UCSD video database: *offline test* and *online test*. They resulted in recognition rates of 98.6% and 95.9% respectively. In addition, the software implementation of our method is publicly available.

References

1. Turk, M., Pentland, A.: Eigenfaces for Recognition. Journal of Cognitive Neuroscience **3**(1), 71–86 (2006)

2. Belhumeur, P.N., Hespanha, J.P., Kriegman, D.: Eigenfaces vs. Fisherfaces: recognition using class specific linear projection. IEEE Transactions on Pattern Analysis and Machine Intelligence **19**(7), 711–720 (1997)

3. Ahonen, T., Hadid, A., Pietikäinen, M.: Face Description with Local Binary Patterns: Application to Face Recognition. IEEE Transactions on Pattern Analysis and Machine Intelligence **28**(12), 2037–2041 (2006)

4. Gaisser, F., Rudinac, M., Jonker, P.P., Tax, D.: Online face recognition and learning for cognitive robots. In: 2013 16th International Conference on Advanced Robotics (ICAR), pp. 1–9 (2013)

5. Taigman, Y., Yang, M., Ranzato, M.A., Wolf, L.: DeepFace: closing the gap to human-level performance in face verification. In: 2014 IEEE Conference on Computer Vision and Pattern Recognition (CVPR), pp. 1701–1708 (2014)

6. Sun, Y., Wang, X., Tang, X.: Deeply learned face representations are sparse, selective, and robust. In: 2015 IEEE Conference on Computer Vision and Pattern Recognition (CVPR), pp. 2892–2900 (2015)

7. Schroff, F., Kalenichenko, D., Philbin, J.: FaceNet: a Unied embedding for face recognition and clustering. In: 2015 IEEE Conference on Computer Vision and Pattern Recognition (CVPR), pp. 815–823 (2015)

8. Lu, C., Tang, X.: Surpassing human-level face verification performance on LFW with GaussianFace. In: Proc. 29th AAAI Conference on Artificial Intelligence (AAAI), pp. 3811–3819 (2015)

9. Wagner, A., Wright, J., Ganesh, A., Zhou, Z., Mobahi, H., Ma, Y.: Toward a Practical Face Recognition System: Robust Alignment and Illumination by Sparse Representation. IEEE Transactions on Pattern Analysis and Machine Intelligence **34**(2), 372–386 (2012)

10. Chen, J., Kellokumpu, V., Zhao, G., Pietikäinen, M.: RLBP: Robust Local Binary Pattern. In: Proc. British Machine Vision Conference (BMVC), pp. 1–10 (2013)

11. Dantone, M., Gall, J., Fanelli, G., Van Gool, L.: Real-time facial feature detection using conditional regression forests. In: 2012 IEEE Conference on Computer Vision and Pattern Recognition (CVPR), pp. 2578–2585 (2012)

12. Dantone, M., Gall, J., Fanelli, G., van Gool, L.: Facial Feature Detection. http://www.dantone.me/projects-2/facial-feature-detection/

13. Asthana, A., Zafeiriou, S., Cheng, S., Pantic, M.: Incremental face alignment in the wild. In: 2014 IEEE Conference on Computer Vision and Pattern Recognition (CVPR), pp. 1859–1866 (2014)

14. Asthana, A., Zafeiriou, S.: Chehra. https://sites.google.com/site/chehrahome/home/

15. Kazemi, V., Sullivan, J.: One millisecond face alignment with an ensemble of regression trees. In: 2014 IEEE Conference on Computer Vision and Pattern Recognition (CVPR), pp. 1867–1874 (2014)

16. Lee, K.C., Ho, J., Yang, M.H., Kriegman, D.: Visual Tracking and Recognition Using Probabilistic Appearance Manifolds. Computer Vision and Image Understanding **99**(3), 303–331 (2005)

17. Viola, P., Jones, M.: Rapid object detection using a boosted cascade of simple features. In: Proc. 2001 IEEE Computer Society Conference on Computer Vision and Pattern Recognition (CVPR), vol. 1, pp. 511–518 (2001)

A Minimax Framework for Gender Classification Based on Small-Sized Datasets

Marco Del Coco$^{(\boxtimes)}$, Pierluigi Carcagnì, Marco Leo, and Cosimo Distante

National Research Council of Italy, Institute of Applied Sciences and Intelligent
Systems - UOS Lecce, Lecce, Italy
marco.delcoco84@gmail.com

Abstract. Gender recognition is a topic of high interest especially in
the growing field of audience measurement techniques for digital signage applications. Usually, supervised approaches are employed and they
require a preliminary training phase performed on large datasets of annotated facial images that are expensive (e.g. MORPH) and, anyhow, they
cannot be updated to keep track of the continuous mutation of persons' appearance due to changes of fashions and styles (e.g. hairstyles or
makeup). The use of small-sized (and then updatable in a easier way)
datasets is thus high desirable but, unfortunately, when few examples
are used for training, the gender recognition performances dramatically
decrease since the state-of-art classifiers are unable to handle, in a reliable
way, the inherent data uncertainty by explicitly modeling encountered
distortions. To face this drawback, in this work an innovative classification scheme for gender recognition has been introduced: its core is the
Minimax approach, i.e. a smart classification framework that, including
a number of existing regularized regression models, allows a robust classification even when few examples are used for training. This has been
experimentally proved by comparing the proposed classification scheme
with state of the art classifiers (SVM, kNN and Random Forests) under
various pre-processing methods.

Keywords: Gender classification · Minimax · Soft biometrics

1 Introduction

Biometrics have attracted a lot of attention over the past decade, considering
the numerous applications they can lead in both industry and academia [11].
Soft biometrics can be defined as characteristics that provide information about
the individual, but such that they lack of the distinctiveness and permanence to
sufficiently differentiate any two individuals [9] (i.e. they are useful in order to
recognize a face [11] and to extract generic appearance information but not to
recognize a specific subject). The soft biometric traits can either be continuous
(e.g., height and weight) or discrete (e.g., gender, eye color, ethnicity, etc.).

Soft biometrics applications lead into the fields of security, digital signage,
domotics, home rehabilitation, artificial intelligence and so on. Even socially

© Springer International Publishing Switzerland 2015
S. Battiato et al. (Eds.): ACIVS 2015, LNCS 9386, pp. 415–427, 2015.
DOI: 10.1007/978-3-319-25903-1_36

assistive technologies are a new and emerging field where these solutions could considerably improve the overall human-machine interaction level for example with autistic individuals [4], as well as with people with dementia [20] and, generally, for elderly care [2].

Gender is the most debated issue in literature and two exhaustive surveys can be found in [12] and [14]. A first study in this research field was done by Brunelli and Poggio [3] who investigated the use of geometrical features to train two competing HyperBF networks to classify according to gender. An alternative approach was proposed in [1] where the ability of a statistical/neural network to classify faces by sex by means of a pixel-based representation was investigated. More recently Seetci at al. [13] used features extracted by a trained AAM to construct support vector machine (SVM) classifiers arranged into a cascade structure in order to optimise overall recognition performance. The use of Weber's Local Descriptor (WLD) for gender recognition was investigated in [21] whereas in [15] a procedure to learn discriminative LBP-Histogram (LBPH) bins, as compact facial representation for gender classification, was presented. In [19] the use of feature selection based on mutual information and feature fusion to improve gender classification of face images was addressed.

Preliminary studies about the performance of different classifiers and features were proposed in [18] and [17]: four different classifiers (Bayes, Neural Network, Support Vector Machine and LDA) were compared using LBP or genetic feature subset selection.

Datasets, usually used to train classifiers, cover a central point. To obtain good results, usually large datasets are necessary even with commonly used classifiers (e.g. SVM, Random Forest, K-nearest neighbors). Anyway, the use of large datasets makes difficult to keep track of the continuous mutation of persons' appearance due to changes of fashions and styles (e.g. hairstyles or makeup). The use of small-sized datasets would make the update process more feasible but, unfortunately, when few examples are used for training, the gender recognition performance dramatically decrease since the state-of-art classifiers are unable to handle in a reliable way the inherent data uncertainty by explicitly modeling encountered distortions.

In order to overcome these limitations, in this work an innovative classification scheme, exploiting for the first time the Minimax framework proposed in [6], has been introduced to achieve automatic gender recognition. An exhaustive experimental session has proven the superiority of the proposed methodology, with respect to convectional classification approaches, when small-sized training datasets are employed. The rest of the paper is organized as in the following: in section 2 the proposed methodology is detailed; in section 3 the experimental setup and results are discussed. Conclusions are summarized in section 4.

2   Gender Prediction Pipeline

Gender recognition from generic images requires an algorithmic pipeline that involves different operative blocks. In this work three main steps have been

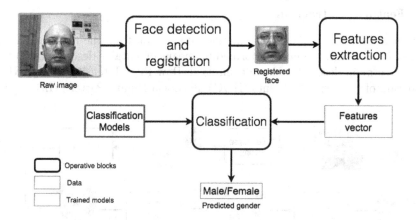

Fig. 1. Used gender prediction pipeline: faces are registered and then feature extraction is performed in order to build a data vector that is finally provided as input to a classification block.

considered. The *face detection and registration* is the first step that detects the human faces in the image under investigation and then it registers the face to a standard shape/size [5]. These preliminary operations allow to get the quite similar position for eyes and this way the subsequent features descriptor may be applied using a coherent spatial reference. Successively, a *features extraction* step is performed in order to obtain a features vector useful to describe the main facial characteristics. As a last step, the gender decision is made by means of a trained *classification* algorithm. A schematic representation of the used gender prediction pipeline is represented in Fig. 1 whereas each aforementioned operating step is detailed in the following.

2.1 Face Detection and Registration

In this step, human faces are detected in the input images and then a registration operation, inspired to the work of [5], is performed. The registration is a fundamental preprocessing step since the subsequent algorithms improve their accuracy if they evaluate input faces with predefined size and pose.

Firstly, face detection is performed by means of the general frontal face detector proposed by [23] which combines increasingly more complex classifiers in a cascade. Whenever a face is detected, the face registration is performed by the following operations: as a first step, the system heuristically fits an ellipse to the face blob (exploiting facial features color models) in order to rotate it to a vertical position. Hence, a Viola-Jones based eye detector searches the eyes and, finally, eye positions, if detected, provide a measure to crop and scale the frontal face candidate to a standard size of 65×59 pixels as illustrated in Fig. 2. Finally, the registered face is given as input to the subsequent *features extraction* step.

2.2 Features Extraction

In order to highlight the most distinctive information from the registered facial images, *features extraction* is performed by means of suitable descriptors. In this work three main descriptors have been used: Raw Pixel Intensity values (RPI); Histogram of Oriented Gradients (HOG) [8]; Local Binary Pattern (LBP) [7].

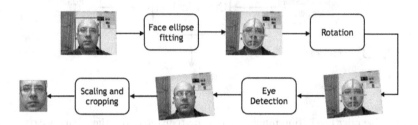

Fig. 2. Face registration: the detected face is fitted in an ellipse used to rotate the face in a perfectly vertical position; successively eyes are detected and used to scale the image and crop the zone of interest.

RPI is the simplest descriptor for an image: it works by concatenating the gray scale intensity values of the image pixels into a single vector. However, although this approach is computationally inexpensive, the resulting vector brings along a huge amount of useless information that could affect the subsequent classification step. In the specific case of the registered facial patches the corresponding vector counts 3835 elements.

HOG technique exploits local object appearance and shape by analysing the distribution of local intensity gradients or edge directions. This technique has been used in its mature form in Scale Invariant Features Transformation [10] and it has been widely exploited in human detection [8]. HOG descriptor is based on the accumulation of gradient directions over the pixels of a small spatial region referred as "cell" and in the subsequent construction of a series of 1D histograms which are finally concatenated to achieve the features vector. Let L be the image to be analysed. The image is divided into cells of size $N \times N$ pixels (as in Fig. 3 (a)) and the orientation $\theta_{x,y}$ of the gradient in each pixel is computed (Fig. 3 (b-c)) by means of the following rule:

$$\theta_{x,y} = \tan^{-1} \frac{L(x, y+1) - L(x, y-1)}{L(x+1, y) - L(x-1, y)} \tag{1}$$

Successively, the orientations θ_i^j $i = 1...N^2$, i.e. belonging to the same cell j are quantized and accumulated in a M-bins histogram (Fig. 3 (d-e)). Finally, all the achieved histograms are ordered and concatenated in a unique HOG histogram (Fig. 3 (f)) that is the final outcome of this algorithmic step, i.e. the features vector to be considered for the subsequent processing. HOG has been employed on registered facial images with a cell size of 4×4 pixels and 9 orientation

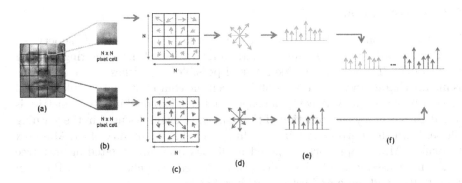

Fig. 3. HOG extraction features process: image is divided into cells of size $N \times N$ pixels. The orientation of all pixels is accumulated in an M-bins histogram of orientations. Finally, all cell histograms are concatenated in order to construct the final features vector. The example reports a cell size of 4 pixels and 9 orientation bins for the cell histograms.

bins and, under these choices, the corresponding features vector consists of 2016 elements. The *VLFeat library* has been used for HOG operator[1].

LBP is a local features descriptor widely used for texture description in pattern recognition. The original LBP assigns a label to each pixel. Each pixel is used as a threshold and compared with its neighbor. If the neighbor is higher it takes value 1 otherwise it takes value 0. Finally, the thresholded neighbor pixel values are concatenated and considered as a binary number that becomes the label for the central pixel. A graphical representation is showed in Fig. 4 (a) and defined as follows

$$LBP_{P,R}(x_c) = \sum_{p=0}^{P-1} u(x_p - x_c)2^p \tag{2}$$

where $u(y)$ is the step function, x_p the neighbor pixels, x_c the central pixel, P the number of neighbors and R the radius. To account for the spatial information, the image is then divided in sub-regions. LBP is applied to each sub-region and an histogram of L bins is generated from the pixel labels. Then the histograms of different regions are concatenated in a single higher dimensional histogram as represented in Fig. 4. LBP has been spatially processed over a 5×5 grid of the image with 8 neighbors and 1 pixel radius (256 bins). The online implementation of LBP[2] has been employed in the experimental session. These implementation strategies, when LBP is applied on the registered facial images, lead to a LBP features vector of 6400 elements.

---

[1] www.vlfeat.org

[2] www.bytefish.de

2.3   Classification

The classification step is the last and key step of the whole pipeline. In supervised learning, in order to classify unseen data, a model is built by exploiting training labeled data. There exists a wide range of possible approaches whose difference is mainly characterised by a trade off between the computational complexity and the reachable accuracy. Anyway, an aspect not well explored in soft biometrics is about the accuracy as a function of the number of examples used in the learning phase. With this purpose in mind, in this paper the potentiality of the Minimax Classifier (MMC) approach proposed in [6] has been investigated against tree of the most used classification methods: K-Nearest Neighbor (K-NN), Random Forest (RF) and Support Vector Machines (SVM).

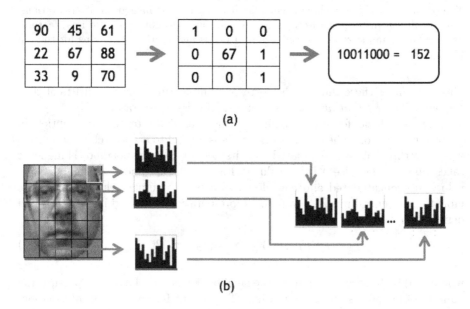

(a)

(b)

Fig. 4. LBP labeling procedure (a) and spatial LBP histogram concatenation (b).

K-NN is probably the simplest discriminative classifier. Training data are stored with respective labels to build up the model. Then, the classification on a new data point is done according to the majority vote of its K nearest other data points (in a Euclidean sense of nearness). It is often effective but its computational complexity and amount of needed memory is proportional to the amount of training data. The Matlab (2014a) implementation of K-NN has been used in the experimental session with default parameters.

RF is based on a discriminative forest of many decision trees, where each tree is built down to a large or maximal splitting depth. In the learning procedure, each node of each tree is allowed to choose splitting variables only from a random subset of the data features. This helps to ensure that each tree becomes a statistically independent decision maker. In run mode, each tree gets an unweighted vote. In the experimental session, the RF implemented in Matlab (2014a) with a forest depth of 50 has been employed.

SVM is a discriminative classifier defined by a separating hyperplane. Given a set of labelled training data (supervised learning), the algorithm computes an optimal hyperplane (the trained model) which categorizes new examples in the right class. The main advantage of SVM with respect to previously mentioned algorithms is given by the use of a kernel function that projects data in an higher-dimensional space. This step allows to find the optimal linear separator between classes. In the experimental session, the Matlab (2014a) implementation of SVM with Radial Basis Function kernel and default parameters have been used.

MMC proposed in [6] estimates a representation model that minimizes the fitting errors under a class of distortions of interest to an application, and deriving subsequent categorical information based on the estimated model.

The most significant advantage of the MMC approach is the ability to compute a reliable classification model by means of a small number of training examples by accounting for a generic class of distortions.

Traditional cases involve large-sample datasets where the number of samples n is much greater then the vector size p $(n \gg p)$, whereas a limited number of examples could lead to the opposite situation $n \ll p$. MMC imposes no restriction on n or p and consequently is applicable to general data including large-sample and high-dimensional data. MMC approach demonstrates comparable accuracy to the SVM when working with large datasets whereas, when the vector size increases and the number of training examples is limited, MMC guarantees the best performance.

More specifically, Generalized Multiplicative Distortion MMC (GMD-MMC) has been used in order to manage the multiplicative type of distortions. As an instance, the image brightness may be described using multiplicative models of illumination if referred to a camera device acquisition. Moreover, gamma correction is applied in order to enhance image quality correction (based on the relationship between the sensation of color and spectral power at different wavelengths) and is observed to follow multiplicative power laws as suggested also by the Stevens power law[16]. Similar considerations are still true for other distortion components in the image processing field. In order to model these behaviors, the above mentioned generalized-multiplicative-distortion (GMD) model is introduced.

GMD model assumes that each observation may incur a distortion proportional to q degrees of the energy of the signal, with the scaling factor uniformly upper bounded by λ. Moreover, it includes plain multiplicative scaling which is often used in signal processing.

In detail, the algorithm works in the following manner. Let $A = [x_1, \cdots, x_n] \in R^{p \times n}$ the matrix of training examples, $y = [y_1, \cdots y_n]$ (where $y_k \in 1, \cdots, M$) the labels vector for training examples and $x \in R^p$ the test example. The first step is to solve the minimization problem:

$$\min_{\omega \in R^n} \{\omega^T K \omega - 2\omega^T K_x + \lambda \sum_{i=1}^{n} |\omega_i| k^{q/2}(x_i, x_i)\} \tag{3}$$

where $k(\cdot, \cdot)$ is the kernel function, $K_x = [k(x, x_1), \cdot, k(x, x_n)]^T$, $K = (k(x_i, x_j))_{i,j=1}^n$.

Once ω^* is found, the final statistic is computed:

$$\rho_i^\phi = \omega^*|_{C_i}^T K \omega^*|_{C_i} + \omega^*|_{\overline{C}_i}^T K \omega^*|_{\overline{C}_i} - 2\omega^*|_{C_i}^T K_x \tag{4}$$

where $\omega^*|_{C_i}$ represent restricting ω^* onto the sub-space of the ith class C_i and $\overline{C}_i = \cup_{k=1, k \neq i}^M C_k$.

Finally the predicted class is obtained as:

$$\hat{i} = \operatorname*{argmax}_{i \in \{1, \cdots, M\}} \{\rho_i\} \tag{5}$$

More specifically, in the experimental session a RBF kernel with a $\sigma = 31$ has been used.

3   Experimental Results

In this section, the experimental setup is introduced and, successively, the obtained results are discussed.

The key point of this work is the performance in gender classification by adopting few training examples of facial images. In this context, the testing methodology, as well as the construction of the dataset, is very important.

All the tests have been performed on a dataset of 17000 images built as a subset of the well-known Morph database [22], a collection of facial images largely used for benchmark purpose in gender, age or race recognition problems. Unfortunately the Morph dataset suffers of an unpleasant and non-neglectable unbalancing among male and female subjects and, this drawback, prevents the researchers using it as a whole. When dealing with issues related to gender classification it is therefore better to consider a subset of the images in the Morph dataset and, in general, this subset is constructed taking under consideration the balancing of the cardinality among genders. Following this common practice, a subset of the Morph images was selected and used in the following experimental sessions: in particular the subset contained 8500 male entries and 8500 female entries. Notice that 8500 is the maximum number of available subjects for the smaller class (female) in the Morph dataset: this means that all the female subjects were retained.

Classification strategies, based on supervised learning solutions, are usually tested by means of a k-fold approach, a testing procedure that splits the available dataset into k folds (preferably keeping the balancing among classes in each fold) and iteratively uses k-1 folds for training purpose and the remaining fold for the test phase. This kind of procedure does not fit the goal of this work because would lead to too much large training sets. To accomplish the goal an alternative solution was then implemented: k-1 folds were used for testing and just the remaining fold for training. Anyway, the selection of a small sized fold would imply the increase of the number of iterations. For instance, in order to obtain a fold of 50 entries, the dataset should be splitted into 340 folds and, consequentially 340 training and testing iterations would be needed for each experiment. Unfortunately, due to the novelty of the adopted classifier (not yet optimized), this approach has proved to be unfeasible in terms of computational cost. In order to overcome these drawbacks while working in the fairest way, the following ad-hoc cross validation procedure has been introduced: N subjects (N/2 males and N/2 females) were randomly selected from the built dataset in order to obtain the training set needed to build-up the *classification model*, whereas the remaining elements were exploited as testing samples.

The procedure described in Fig. 5 was then applied at each iteration: training set images were processed by the descriptor and the obtained training vectors (with the associate class labels) were employed for the construction of the classification model. Testing set images were, in the same way, processed by the descriptor and the carried out feature vectors were classified with the previously computed *classification model*. Finally the gender recognition accuracy was computed by comparing estimated and ground-truth labels. The procedure was repeated 10 times (with the constrain of not selecting, as the training set, entries already selected for testing in the previous iterations) and the average accuracy was finally accounted.

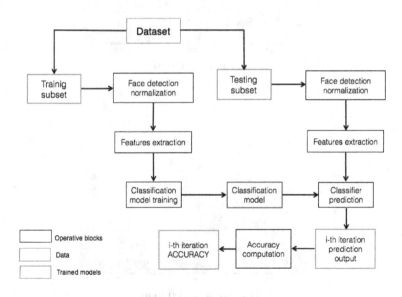

Fig. 5. Testing procedure: a cross validation procedure was used for accuracy evaluation; the model was trained using a N randomly selected subjects and successively tested on the remaining entries.

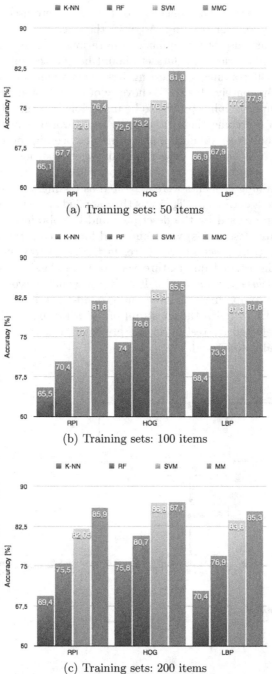

(a) Training sets: 50 items

(b) Training sets: 100 items

(c) Training sets: 200 items

Fig. 6. Bar diagrams of accuracy for different sizes of the training sets: 50 training samples for diagram (a), 100 training samples for diagram (b) and 200 training samples for diagram (c). It is evident that as training size increased the advantage of using the Minimax became less remarkable.

The tests were performed for each possible combination of descriptor/classification approaches and using three different values of the training set size N, i.e. 50, 100 and 200 elements.

Results are reported in Fig. 6 where the bar diagrams of the experienced average accuracies are shown. Already at first glance the superiority of MMC classifier against all the competitors is evident: more specifically when few training examples were used, the MMC was able to better generalize knowledge from data than K-NN, RF and SVM. MMC was also able to discard useless information from large features vector as demonstrated by the much higher MMC classification performances when using RPI features. It is worth noting that the gap between the MMC and the SVM classification accuracy rapidly decreased as the number of training elements increased. This was even more evident when HOG features were supplied as input and this was due, on the one side, to the smaller vector length (i.e. 2016 elements) to be handled and, on the other side, to the ability of HOG features to very-well represent the data distribution. On the contrary, the gap does not significantly change when LBP (6400 elements) and RPI (3830 elements) descriptors were used and this was probably due to the larger vector size that continues to exploits the MMC advantages also when the training set increases. This behaviour is quite reasonable given that the employed MMC is particularly suitable when the cardinality of each example is particularly high. The worst results were carried out by the use of th KNN classifier. Indeed, as previously discussed, it works by a voting system based on the Euclidean distance between the test sample and its neighbors; when the number of possible neighbors is pretty poor, the number of misclassifications dramatically increases. The presented results confirm that MMC is a suitable solution for gender classification in that kind of situations where the subject appearance, or image quality, is highly variable and new training sessions are frequently necessary.

4   Conclusions

In this work the use of a classification algorithm has been introduced for gender recognition. In particular its ability to get satisfying accuracy expecially with small-sized datasets has been demonstrated. Experimental sessions have been performed by means of a pipeline involving a face detector, a features extraction strategy and, as a final step, the classification block. The classification performances of the Minimax have been compared with those obtained with tree commonly used classifiers (K-NN, RF and SVM) and, in addition, three different preprocessing methodologies have been used in order to better investigate the capability to handle different data lengths and with different approaches to encode data distributions. Experiments show the superiority of the MMC approach, in terms of recognition accuracy, in contexts characterized by small sized datasets. These promising results open new prospectives towards the possibility to work with updated appearance information that is a demanding requirement in video analytics for audience measurement. Future works will be addressed to an accurate investigation of the asymptotic (respect to dataset sizes) behavior of the MMC algorithm in gender as well as in other prediction problems.

References

1. Abdi, H., Valentin, D., Edelman, B., O'Toole, A.: More about the difference between men and women: evidence from linear neural networks and the principal-component approach. Neural Comput. **7**(6), 1160–1164 (1995)
2. Bemelmans, R., Gelderblom, G.J., Jonker, P., De Witte, L.: Socially assistive robots in elderly care: a systematic review into effects and effectiveness. Journal of the American Medical Directors Association **13**(2), 114–120 (2012)
3. Brunelli, R., Poggio, T.: Hyberbf networks for gender classification. In: Proc. DARPA Image Understanding Workshop, pp. 311–314 (1995)
4. Carcagnì, P., Cazzato, D., Del Coco, M., Leo, M.: Visual interaction including biometrics information for a socially assistive robotics platform. In: Second Workshop on Assistive Computer Vision and Robotics (ACVR) in conjunction with European Conference on Computer Vision (ECCV), September 2014
5. Castrillón, M., Déniz, O., Guerra, C., Hernández, M.: Encara2: Real-time detection of multiple faces at different resolutions in video streams. Journal of Visual Communication and Image Representation **18**(2), 130–140 (2007)
6. Cheng, Q., Zhou, H., Cheng, J., Li, H.: A minimax framework for classification with applications to images and high dimensional data. IEEE Transactions on Pattern Analysis and Machine Intelligence **36**(11), 2117–2130 (2014)
7. Da, B., Sang, N.: Local binary pattern based face recognition by estimation of facial distinctive information distribution. Optical Engineering **48**(11), 117203-1-117203-7 (2009)
8. Dalal, N., Triggs, B.: Histograms of oriented gradients for human detection. In: IEEE Computer Society Conference on Computer Vision and Pattern Recognition (CVPR), vol. 1, pp. 886–893, June 2005
9. Jain, A.K., Dass, S.C., Nandakumar, K.: Soft biometric traits for personal recognition systems. In: Zhang, D., Jain, A.K. (eds.) ICBA 2004. LNCS, vol. 3072, pp. 731–738. Springer, Heidelberg (2004)
10. Lowe, D.G.: Distinctive image features from scale-invariant keypoints. Int. J. Comput. Vision **60**(2), 91–110 (2004)
11. Martiriggiano, T., Leo, M., D'Orazio, T., Distante, A.: Face Recognition by Kernel Independent Component Analysis. In: Ali, M., Esposito, F. (eds.) IEA/AIE 2005. LNCS (LNAI), vol. 3533, pp. 55–58. Springer, Heidelberg (2005)
12. Mkinen, E., Raisamo, R.: An experimental comparison of gender classification methods. Pattern Recognition Letters **29**(10), 1544–1556 (2008)
13. Saatci, Y., Town, C.: Cascaded classification of gender and facial expression using active appearance models. In: 7th International Conference on Automatic Face and Gesture Recognition (FGR), pp. 393–398, April 2006
14. Sakarkaya, M., Yanbol, F., Kurt, Z.: Comparison of several classification algorithms for gender recognition from face images. In: IEEE 16th International Conference on Intelligent Engineering Systems (INES), pp. 97–101, June 2012
15. Shan, C.: Learning local binary patterns for gender classification on real-world face images. Pattern Recognition Letters **33**(4), 431–437 (2012). Intelligent Multimedia Interactivity
16. Stevens, S.S.: On the psychophysical law. Psychological Review **64**, 153–181 (1957)

17. Sun, N., Zheng, W., Sun, C., Zou, C., Zhao, L.: Gender Classification Based on Boosting Local Binary Pattern. In: Wang, J., Yi, Z., Żurada, J.M., Lu, B.-L., Yin, H. (eds.) ISNN 2006. LNCS, vol. 3972, pp. 194–201. Springer, Heidelberg (2006)
18. Sun, Z., Bebis, G., Yuan, X., Louis, S.J.: Genetic feature subset selection for gender classification: a comparison study. In: IEEE Workshop on Applications of Computer Vision, pp. 165–170 (2002)
19. Tapia, J., Perez, C.: Gender classification based on fusion of different spatial scale features selected by mutual information from histogram of lbp, intensity, and shape. IEEE Transactions on Information Forensics and Security 8(3), 488–499 (2013)
20. Tapus, A., Tapus, C., Mataric, M.J.: The use of socially assistive robots in the design of intelligent cognitive therapies for people with dementia. In: IEEE International Conference on Rehabilitation Robotics (ICORR), pp. 924–929. IEEE (2009)
21. Ullah, I., Hussain, M., Muhammad, G., Aboalsamh, H., Bebis, G., Mirza, A.: Gender recognition from face images with local wld descriptor. In: 19th International Conference on Systems, Signals and Image Processing (IWSSIP), pp. 417–420, April 2012
22. University of North Carolina Wilmington: Morph noncommercial face dataset (2015). www.faceaginggroup.com/morph/
23. Viola, P., Jones, M.: Robust real-time face detection. International Journal of omputer Vision 57(2), 137–154 (2004)

Age and Gender Characterization Through a Two Layer Clustering of Online Handwriting

Gabriel Marzinotto, José C. Rosales,
Mounim A. El-Yacoubi[⊠], and Sonia Garcia-Salicetti

Institut Mines-Telecom Télécom SudParis, CNRS UMR 5157 SAMOVAR,
CEA Saclay Nano-Innov, PC176 Bât. 861, 91191 Gif Sur Yvette Cedex, France
{gabriel.marzinotto_cos,jose.rosales_nunez,mounim.el_yacoubi,
sonia.garcia}@telecom-sudparis.eu

Abstract. Age characterization through handwriting is an important research field with several potential applications. It can, for instance, characterize normal aging process on one hand and detect significant handwriting degradation possibly related to early pathological states. In this work, we propose a novel approach to characterize age and gender from online handwriting styles. Contrary to previous works on handwriting style characterization, our contribution consists of a two-layer clustering scheme. At the first layer, we perform a writer-independent clustering on handwritten words, described by global features. At the second layer, we perform a clustering that considers style variation at the previous level for each writer, to provide a measure of his/her handwriting stability across words. We investigated different clustering algorithms and their effectiveness for each layer. The handwriting style patterns inferred by our novel technique show interesting correlations between handwriting, age and gender.

Keywords: Handwriting styles · Two layer clustering · Age · Gender

1 Introduction

Handwriting style classification is a research field that has been extensively investigated for both online [1] and offline [2] handwriting recognition and writer authentication tasks. In this context, it is used as a first processing layer to split these complex tasks into simpler ones by considering specific style-based models that grant higher performance. Handwriting analysis can also be used for health applications, including pathology detection [3], age and gender characterization [12].

Automatic inference of handwriting styles is a difficult task as there are no *a priori* rules to define or label a handwriting style. For this reason, a clustering algorithm is usually required. Indeed, works on this topic commonly use Gaussian Mixture Models (GMMs) [2], *K*-means algorithm [5], Self-Organizing Maps [1] and Agglomerative Hierarchical Clustering [4]. Previous works for clustering handwriting styles, either on offline or online input, have tackled the problem at the stroke level [4], the character level [5], or the word level [6]. The first level consists of clustering strokes and

© Springer International Publishing Switzerland 2015
S. Battiato et al. (Eds.): ACIVS 2015, LNCS 9386, pp. 428–439, 2015.
DOI: 10.1007/978-3-319-25903-1_37

defining handwriting styles according to the empirical distribution of stroke clusters. The second performs a series of clustering over isolated character representations and considers a handwriting style as a combination of isolated character styles. The third extracts word global spatial parameters and cluster similar words to define styles.

In this paper, we address the problem of age and gender characterization through online handwriting style analysis. The objective is to automatically detect handwriting styles using an unsupervised criterion and study their correlation with age and gender, based on the analysis of dynamic and spatial handwriting parameters. This study could lead to an age and gender recognition system from online handwritten samples or to handwriting degradation analysis for early pathology detection.

Handwriting style is usually characterized based on word appearance (inclination, curvature, *etc.*) and on the writing process dynamics (speed, acceleration, jerk). We believe, however, that style characterization should not rely only on this raw signal information but should take into account high-level information associated with the variability observed across the writer words. We propose, in this work, an original approach for handwriting style characterization based on a *two-level* clustering scheme. The first level allows generating writer-independent word clusters according to raw signal information. At the second level, the handwritten words produced by a person are converted into a Bag of Prototype Words (*BPW*) [14] by assigning each word to its closest cluster and subsequently generating the person's cluster frequency histogram. The set of *BPWs* is then input to the second clustering to generate handwriting styles based on two kinds of information, raw spatiotemporal word similarities, and handwriting variability similarities between different writers.

Such a two-level clustering scheme might be more effective for characterizing handwriting styles and especially for analyzing their correlation with age and gender. Indeed, the variability observed when producing different words is highly informative of meaningful writer categories. Our experiments on a large database of online handwriting words, the IRONOFF database [7], asserts this assumption and show that our two level clustering approach is able to find interesting correlations between age and handwriting style on one side and sex and handwriting style on the other.

Our paper is organized as follows. Section 2 presents the proposed approach including extraction of spatiotemporal features, feature-based word visualization and the two-level clustering scheme. Section 3 describes the experiments and gives an analysis of the detected writer categories and their correlation with age and gender. Section 4 concludes the paper and envisages future directions of this work.

2   Proposed Approach

The online handwritten words are each described as a sequence of three temporal functions $(x(t), y(t), p(t))$ representing the coordinates of the pen trajectory and pen pressure when writing on a digitizer. Our aim is to characterize styles based not only on the word visual aspect, but also on the writing process dynamics. This is especially important when we address age and gender characterization, as important correlation between age and handwriting dynamics is a well-established fact [12]. The section below describes the word feature extraction phase, the output of which is a global spatiotemporal feature vector that is input to the two-layer clustering scheme.

2.1   Feature Extraction

For each handwritten word, we extract two feature types: dynamic and spatial. The first gathers local dynamic information, such as speed, acceleration and jerk [4], while the second describes the static shape of local pen trajectories by measures such as local stroke angles and curvatures [8], or inter-character spaces [6]. As dynamic parameters, we consider horizontal and vertical speed computed locally at point n as $V_x=|\Delta x/\Delta t|$ and $V_y=|\Delta y/\Delta t|$ where $\Delta x(n)=x(n+1)-x(n-1)$, $\Delta y(n)=y(n+1)-y(n-1)$ and $\Delta t(n)=t(n+1)-t(n-1)$. These values are computed along the word and used to build a histogram of 4 bins, the binning being automatically derived through quantification. A similar process is used to extract local acceleration and jerk values, associated respectively with horizontal and vertical derivatives of speed and acceleration. In addition, pen pressure, its derivative, and the pen-up duration ratio, computed as $PR=(Pen\text{-}up\ Duration)/(Total\ Duration)$ [12], are considered, thus obtaining 33 global dynamic features. For spatial parameters, a resampling process is first performed to ensure that consecutive word points are equidistant, so as the parameter values at each point become equally representative, regardless of speed. After resampling, local direction and curvature angles are extracted as in [8] and used to build a histogram of 8 quantified bins. We also consider the number of pen-ups, the horizontal in-air distance, the number of strokes and their average lengths, a stroke being defined as a writing movement between two local minima of speed. We obtain, in this way, 22 spatial features. The list of all features, dynamic and spatial, is given in Table 1.

Table 1. Word description by the 55 global spatial and dynamic features

Dynamic Parameters	Spatial Parameters
(F1-F4) Histogram of Speed on X axis	(F34-F41) Histogram of Direction [0° to 180°]
(F5-F8) Histogram of Speed on Y axis	(F42-F49) Histogram of Curvature [0° to 180°]
(F9-F12) Histogram of Accel. on X axis	(F50) Number of Pen ups
(F13-F16) Histogram of Accel. on Y axis	(F51) Number of Strokes
(F17-F20) Histogram of Jerk on X axis	(F52) Average Stroke length on X
(F21-F24) Histogram of Jerk on Y axis	(F53) Average Stroke length on Y
(F25-F28) Histogram of Pressure	(F54) Average Stroke length
(F29-F32) Histogram of Pressure var.	(F55) In air distance along the X axis
(F33) Pen up time ratio	

2.2   Visualization of Dynamic and Spatial Local Features

While it is quite straightforward to visualize handwritten words from the appearance (spatial) viewpoint, it is no longer the case for dynamic information. For this reason, we propose a color-based visualization technique to highlight local writing dynamics. To visualize parameters such as speed, acceleration, jerk, pressure and pressure variation, we use a color scale that reflects the parameter value along the word. This scale goes from blue (small parameter values) to red (large parameter values). Figure 1 displays speed information of a word written quickly and slowly respectively.

Fig. 1. Visualization of Speed parameter evolution (a) The word "rugby" written quickly; (b) The same word "rugby" written slowly

This visualization scheme is also exploited for spatial parameters, as it better highlights local stroke direction and curvature information. Figure 2 displays the curvature information on two words written with high and low curvatures.

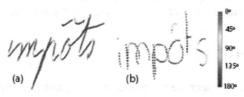

Fig. 2. Color visualization of the curvature at each resampled point (a) Word with large curvature (b) Word with small curvature

2.3   Clustering

As stated in Section 1, handwriting style detection is a complex problem with no *a priori* knowledge on the styles to be found. This explains why style classification is usually performed in an unsupervised way through a clustering technique. The styles detected by any clustering algorithm will obviously depend on the static and dynamic features extracted from words. However, when a person writes, there is no reason why the above features will not fluctuate across words. These fluctuations may actually be relevant information for characterizing handwriting styles, particularly in terms of age [12]. For this reason, we propose a novel two-level approach for clustering words. The first one, denoted as "first layer", is related to raw signal information (spatial and dynamic parameters), while the second, or "second layer", is related to high-level information associated with fluctuations observed across words.

In the first layer, we propose to cluster all words of all persons, each word being described by a global feature vector composed of the 55 parameters listed in Table 1. The aim here is to generate word clusters regardless of person identity. Each cluster will group words of similar global descriptors. This first layer clustering is carried out with the K-means algorithm. In the second layer, the clustering is performed at the writer level. The set of handwritten words of a given writer is converted into a Bag of Prototype Words (*BPW*) [14] by assigning each word to its closest (1st layer) cluster and subsequently generating the person's cluster frequency histogram. The set of *BPWs* is then given as input to the (2nd layer) clustering stage to generate handwriting styles that take into account two kinds of information: spatiotemporal word similarities and handwriting variability similarities between different writers. This second layer of clustering is based on Agglomerative Hierarchical Clustering [13]. The latter is considered as it does not assume spherical clusters, unlike *K*-means algorithm. Since there is no fixed number of handwriting styles, the number of clusters in each layer is estimated using two criteria: the Silhouette criterion proposed by Rosseeuw [10] and the Calinski-Harabasz [11] criterion.

Clustering Visualization
To visualize clustering results, two dimensionality reduction techniques, Principal Component Analysis (*PCA*) and Stochastic Neighbor Embedding (*SNE*), are used. *PCA also* allows computing the correlations between features and their relevance for style characterization. *SNE*, proposed by *Hinton et al.* [9], is a non-linear method that projects the points from a high dimensional space onto a two-dimensional space while preserving distance relations between points as much as possible.

3   Experiments

In this section, we first present the experimental setup, and then the results of the two-layer clustering approach. We pay special attention to writer-independent styles retrieved at the first layer and to the demographic data distribution of the population in the second layer, by analyzing its relation to the clusters obtained in the first layer.

3.1   Database

The database used consists of the 794 writers from the IRONOFF database[1] [7], and contains online samples of words in both English and French. The words were extracted using a pressure sensitive Wacom tablet, by a sampling of *x*, *y* positions and pen pressure at 100Hz. The IRONOFF database contains, for each word, writer's age and sex information. We extracted from each person 20 to 50 words, chosen long enough to characterize handwriting styles. This led to a total of 23.826 words, which is large enough to statistically validate our approach.

3.2   Protocol

First we apply Calinski-Harabasz [11] and Silhouette criteria [10] to determine the optimal number of clusters for the first layer clustering algorithm. Then, we cluster all

---

[1] Actually, IRONOFF consists of 700 writers but the word samples of 94 writers are given two different identifiers. These writers are thus duplicated without affecting the study.

words of all persons using the *K*-means algorithm. *PCA* is used to visualize the distribution of clusters and for highlighting the main differences between them. Indeed, analyzing the correlation circle allows retrieving which parameters are significant to characterize the handwriting styles associated with different clusters, and also to study correlations between parameters. Finally, in order to understand the meaning of the clusters found, we visualize, in each cluster, the closest words to its center.

For the second layer clustering, we compute the percentage of each writer's words on each cluster. In this way, handwritten word samples of each writer are converted into a Bag of Prototype Words (*BPW*) [14]. The 2nd layer clustering algorithm takes as input *BPWs* of writers and groups them into clusters each consisting of similar writer patterns of variation across the "primary" (1st layer) handwriting styles. Clusters are found through Agglomerative Hierarchical Clustering [13], in order to take into account the non-spherical nature of clusters that emerge in this layer. In this context, the optimal number of clusters is estimated through dendrogram analysis.

3.3   Demographic Data Visualization.

To analyze and represent demographic data (age and gender) of the population inside each cluster, several techniques were implemented. In order to interpret clustering results in terms of age, the population is divided into 6 groups, according to previous works on the field [12]:

- Children: 7 -13 years old (A1)
- Teenagers: 14-19 years old (A2)
- Young Adults: 20-30 years old (A3)
- Adults: 31-45 years old (A4)
- Old Adults: 46-59 years old (A5)
- Elders: 60 -77 years old (A6)

The age distribution of the whole database is shown in Figure 3.a. To represent the age distribution in each cluster, we compute a series of histograms (one per cluster) that display, the relative frequency of each age group with respect to the whole database. This is achieved through a double normalization: we first compute the histogram of age distribution inside a cluster and we normalize it with respect to the size of the cluster, dividing it by the number of persons inside the cluster. Then a second normalization is applied to compensate for the non-uniform age distribution in the database: this time we divide, inside a cluster, each age group by its appearance frequency on the whole database; equation (2) summarizes the normalization process:

$$NormHist_{A_i-C_j} = \frac{Hist_{A_i-C_j}}{Size(C_j) \cdot Size(A_i)} \times N \qquad (2)$$

where C_j stands for the *j*-th cluster, A_i for the *i*-th age group, and N is the number of persons in the database. When a histogram bar is above 1, the cluster contains a higher percentage of persons in that age group than the percentage they represent in the whole database. On the other hand, values below 1 represent the opposite. An example of a normalized age distribution within a cluster is shown in Figure 3.b.

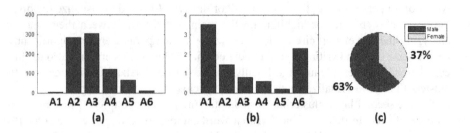

Fig. 3. (a) Histogram of age distributions on the database (b) Normalized histogram of age distribution within a cluster (c) Pie chart displaying the gender distribution on the database

To interpret the clustering results in terms of sex distribution, a series of pie charts are used, displaying the percentage of male and female writers, in blue and red respectively. Figure 3.c. displays the percentage of men and women in the whole database: men represent 63% of writers while women represent 37%.

3.4   First Layer Clustering Results

The optimal number of clusters found through both Silhouette and Calinski-Harabasz methods was 6. All 23.826 words of 794 persons were clustered into 6 groups through the K-means algorithm. The obtained clusters are visualized in Figure 4.

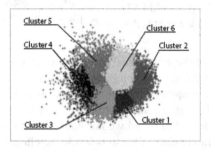

Fig. 4. PCA on the two first axes for the First Layer Clustering

Figure 5 displays several words near the centers of some of the clusters found. Using this in conjunction with information retrieved through PCA (as explained in Section 2.3), we can observe main handwriting styles clustered among all words. The color scale introduced in Section 2.2 shows, for instance, a clear difference between the two clusters in Figure 5. We observe that writer-independent clusters are characterized by three main criteria. The first one is dynamic information; words are separated based on speed, acceleration and jerk (highly correlated parameters). The second criterion is word slant; words are clustered according to whether they are inclined to the left, to the right, or are straight. The third criterion separates words rather written in a script style from those rather written in a cursive style. Combinations of these factors characterize the six clusters, as described in Table 2, each with its corresponding color.

Fig. 5. Speed intensity values in words near clusters' centers in the first layer

Table 1. Analysis of the first layer clustering results

	Associated Dynamics	**Inclination**	**Script-Cursive**
Cluster 1	Med. Velocity/Accel/Jerk	Straight Writing	Mixed Writing
Cluster 2	Slow Velocity/Accel/Jerk	Straight Writing	Script Writing
Cluster 3	Fast Velocity/Accel/Jerk	Straight Writing	Mixed Writing
Cluster 4	Fast Velocity/Accel/Jerk	Inclined to Right	Cursive Writing
Cluster 5	Med. Velocity/Accel/Jerk	Inclined to Right	Mixed Writing
Cluster 6	Slow Velocity/Accel/Jerk	Inclined to Left	Script Writing

3.5   Results of Second Layer Clustering

In the second layer, Agglomerative Hierarchical Clustering was performed using average linkage criteria. The number of clusters was derived by the analysis of the dendrogram. Several cluster sizes were tested and the best results in terms of style correlation with age/sex were obtained using 12 clusters. As the parameters are highly uncorrelated and *PCA* was not effective in reducing data dimensionality, keeping only 43% of the variance on the first two axes, we use the *SNE* technique to visualize the clusters as shown in Figure 6. In Figure 9, we display the distribution of each of the 12 second layer clusters w.r.t the 6 first layer clusters, to better interpret the results.

To study the effects of age on handwriting, we analyze the clusters gathering a particular age group; such information appears in Figure 10 through intra-cluster age histograms. The first and twelfth clusters have the largest concentration of children (from 7 to 13 years old). The first cluster is the most evenly distributed in terms of the 6 handwritten word styles clusters that emerged from the first clustering. This may be explained by the fact that children do not have a mature and well-defined handwriting style, thus tending to mix different well-defined types of handwriting across the population. At the opposite, cluster 12, that shows the largest concentration of children and a high proportion of aged people (from 60 to 80 years old), is a

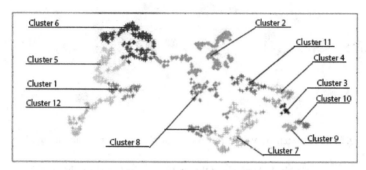

Fig. 6. The 12 clusters of the second layer visualized using *SNE*

highly stable cluster in terms of dynamic parameters: Figure 7 displays some words representative of persons in this cluster, that write with slow velocity (see color scale). Moreover, this cluster contains few average-aged adults; this could indicate the existence of a slow and script-style writing pattern due to initial steps in children's handwriting, or a possible loss of capabilities for elders. Also, the type of handwriting in such clusters are mostly "script" (clusters 1, 2 and 6 of the first clustering layer, see Table 2), possibly due to a lack of higher handwriting capabilities involved in cursive-style handwriting.

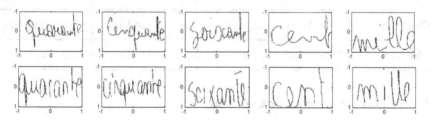

Fig. 7. Representative handwriting styles for infants with color scale for jerk intensity

Clusters 3 and 10 present the largest concentration of aged people: The latter are respectively 6 and 15 times overrepresented w.r.t the proportion of aged people within the whole population. The third and tenth clusters are composed of medium and high velocities, inclined to right and mostly cursive handwriting styles. Both clusters present high values and a more variable behavior of the jerk parameter; Figure 8 displays jerk intensity on 5 words in each of the 2 clusters of elders. This result is in perfect accordance with previous works, since jerk is widely known as a health-discriminative feature, high jerk values reflecting some loss of handwriting capabilities. On the other hand, the two layer clustering scheme reveals that handwriting stability is higher within the aged population, as some aged persons probably need to write more carefully to compensate for loss of coordination skills.

Also, Figure 11 illustrates the evolution of jerk through ages: for cluster 2 that is composed of average young people (from 20 to 40 years old), we find smaller values of jerk than in clusters 4, 7 and 9, composed of average old population (from 45 to 60 years old), as shown in Figure 11. This reflects a progressive change in the dynamics of handwriting through age, possibly related to some loss of psycho-motor capabilities that is normal in the aging process.

Fig. 8. Jerk intensity (color scale) in handwriting styles of aged persons

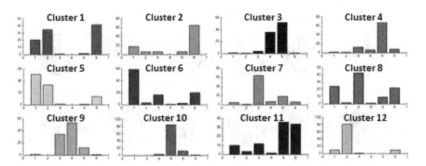

Fig. 9. The distribution of 12 second layer clusters in terms of the 6 primary first layer styles

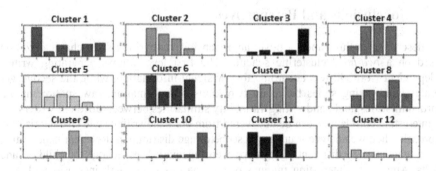

Fig. 10. Age histogram in each of the 12 clusters (2nd layer)

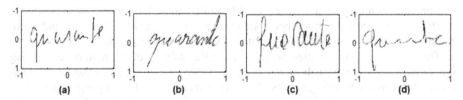

Fig. 11. The evolution of jerk (color scale) through ages: (a) Cluster 2 (young adults)   (b) Cluster 4 (mostly 45-60) (c) Cluster 7 (mostly 45-60)   (d) Cluster 9 (mostly 45-60)

Considering gender (Figure 12), the gender distribution inside most clusters does not vary much from the initial distribution of 63% of men and 37% of women. Yet, Clusters 1, 4, 6, 8 and 11 partially gather men while Clusters 2, 9, 10 and 12 partially gather women. Among the clusters dominated by a gender, there are actually several variations. Therefore, it is impossible to attribute a handwriting style to a single gender, or to separate men from women according to the styles that appeared at the first layer. Some interesting tendencies, nonetheless, can be retrieved from such clusters: men tend to have a medium speed writing style, and tend to write by mixing "cursive" and "script" styles. On the other hand, women write either very fast or very slow, and do not tend to mix "cursive" and "script" styles.

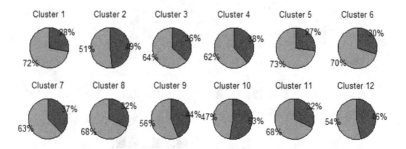

Fig. 12. Gender distribution on each cluster (Men: blue, Women: red)

4   Conclusions and Perspectives

We described, in this paper, a novel approach for handwriting style characterization based on a *two-level* clustering scheme. The first level allows generating writer-independent word clusters according to raw signal information, while the second generates handwriting styles based on two kinds of information, raw spatiotemporal word similarities, and handwriting variability similarities between different writers.

Interesting correlations can be uncovered from our handwriting style characterization approach when we analyze it under the scope of age distribution. Relevant handwriting styles associated to different age groups were uncovered, especially for children and adults. Among the interesting findings of our analysis is that jerk increases with age. Also, we were able to extract handwriting prototypes that represent the population of children and elder persons. When it comes to gender characterization, results are not as encouraging as for age, but we are still able to find some tendencies that characterize gender. For instance, our study reveals that men tend to use mixed cursive and script handwriting, while women tend to use either script or cursive writing.

The proposed approach attempts to measure the stability of the writers considering the variations they present between clusters at the first layer. Even though this approach has given interesting results, there are situations in which a person may show inter-word stability while having his words classified into different clusters. This is the reason why new stability measures should be added in order to improve results.

To confirm our results, we intend to run experiments on a database with a homogeneous age distribution that ensures a higher children and elder population coverage than IRONOFF. Finally, gender and age characterization could be approached using supervised learning techniques for classifying age groups and gender based on handwriting or even for inferring the writer age from his/her handwriting style.

Acknowledgments. This work was partially funded by Fondation MAIF through project "Biométrie et santé sur tablette". For more information, please refer to:http://www.fondation-maif.fr/notre-action.php?rub=1&sous_rub=3&id=269.

References

1. Vuori, V.: Clustering writing styles with a self-organizing map. IWFHR (2002)
2. Sarkar, P., Nagy, G.: Style Consistent Classification of Isogenous Patterns. IEEE PAMI, **27**(1) (2005)
3. Teulings, H.-L., Contreras-Vidal, J.L., Stelmach, G.E., Adler, C.H.: Adaptation of handwriting size under distorted visual feedback in patients with Parkinson's disease and elderly and young controls. J. Neurol. Neurosurg. Psychiatry **72**, 315–324 (2002)
4. Bharath, A., Deepu, V., Madhvanath, S.: An approach to identify unique styles in online handwriting recognition. ICDAR (2005)
5. Chan, S.-K., Tay, Y.-H., Viard-Gaudin, C.: Online Text Independent Writer Identification Using Character Prototypes Distribution. SPIE Electronic Imaging (2007)
6. Crettez, J.-P.: A set of handwriting families: style recognition. ICDAR (1995)
7. Viard-Gaudin, C., Lallican, P.M., Knerr, S., Binter, P.: The IRESTE on/off (IRONOFF) dual handwriting database. ICDAR (1999)
8. Guyon, I., Albrecht, P., Le Cun, Y., Denker, J., Hubbard, W.: Design of a neural network character recognizer for a touch terminal. Pattern Recognition **24** (1991)
9. Hinton, G., Roweis, S.: Stochastic Neighbor Embedding. NIPS **15**, 833–840 (2002)
10. Rousseeuw, P.: Silhouettes: a graphical aid to the interpretation and validation of cluster analysis. J. of Computational and Applied Mathematics (1987)
11. Calinski, R.B., Harabasz, J.: A dendrite method for cluster analysis. Communications in Statistics - Theory and Methods **41**, 2279–2280 (2012)
12. Rosenblum, S., Engel-Yeger, B., Fogel, Y.: Age-related changes in executive control and their relationships with activity performance in handwriting. Human Movement Science **32**, 1056–1069 (2013)
13. Jain, A.K., Murty, M.N., Flynn, P.J.: Data Clustering: a review. ACM Computing Surveys **31**, 264–323 (1999)
14. Sivic, J.: Efficient visual search of videos cast as text retrieval. IEEE Trans. on PAMI **31**(4), 591–605 (2009)

Head Roll Estimation Using Horizontal Energy Maximization

Nam-Jun Pyun[1,2]([⊠]) and Nicole Vincent[1]

[1] Université de Paris Descartes, LIPADE, 45 rue des Saints-Pères,
75006 Paris, France
[2] Konbini, 20 Rue du Faubourg du Temple, 75011 Paris, France
namjun_fr@hotmail.com

Abstract. Head Pose estimation is often a necessary step for many applications using human face, for example in human-computer interaction systems, in face recognition or in face tracking. Here we present a new method to estimate face roll by maximizing a horizontal global energy. The main idea is face salient elements such as nose basis, eyes and mouth have an approximate horizontal direction. According to roll orientation, several local maximums are extracted. A further step of validation using a score computed on relative positions, sizes, and patterns of eyes, nose and mouth allow choosing one of the local maximums. This method is evaluated on BioID and Color Feret databases and achieves roll estimation with a mean absolute error of approximately 4 deg.

Keywords: Head pose estimation · Roll · Horizontal energy · Haar · Maximization · Eyes nose mouth extraction

1 Introduction

Many methods and applications relative to human face analysis, such as face recognition, tracking or human-computer interactions are not rotation invariant. These methods need to estimate the head pose in order to get a frontal face before applying algorithms on it. Even most of the yaw estimation methods need to have a roll close to zero. Therefore, roll estimation should be the first task of many applications which involve faces.

Template Based Methods. A test face image is compared to each image of a sample database. Each sample image is labeled with a discrete pose. These methods try to find the most similar image such as in [1] or in [2]. These methods strongly depend on the quality of the samples.

Geometric Methods. They use some spatial properties of faces to estimate the pose. For example, in [3], vanishing points are used whereas in [4], projective geometry is used. These methods are very fast, but are very sensitive to occlusion and noise and, generally, estimate the pose as an quite interval and not an accurate value.

Methods Based on Classification. A descriptor characterizes the face appearance. Machine learning techniques link the descriptor to the space of

© Springer International Publishing Switzerland 2015
S. Battiato et al. (Eds.): ACIVS 2015, LNCS 9386, pp. 440–451, 2015.
DOI: 10.1007/978-3-319-25903-1_38

poses [5]. In [6], Haar-like features and AdaBoost are used to learn the face pose. Other machine techniques can be used such as SVM in [7] or multiclass Linear Discriminant Analysis in [8] or neural networks in [9]. These methods are efficient. Not only they learn what a face according to the pose variation is, but they also learn to ignore other illumination or occlusion variations. However, these methods have a significant drawback; they need a huge database of face samples where all poses are labeled.

Flexible Model Methods. Classification methods try to map a rectangular area with a pose, flexible models still use machine learning, but try to learn the face deformation according to the pose. Active Appearance Models (AAM) [10] try to learn the deformation of the visage from a set of control points. PCA is applied on positions and texture information of these control points. AAM are used for pose estimation in [11] and in [12]. These methods are robust to partial occlusion and give impressive visual results. However, they need to acquire a database of faces where all control points are positioned.

Methods Based on Linear or Nonlinear Regression. The pose is estimated by learning a function between face images and discrete poses. Support Vector Regressors (SVRs) are widely used, such as in [13], [14] and [15] as well as many other functions such as in [16]. These methods require a well distributed training data with lot of images and are not robust to noise.

Manifold Embedding Methods. They assume pose variation can be represented in a low-dimensional space. The challenge here is to create a model of the manifold as well as an embedding technique which recover head pose and ignore other variations, such as in [17] and in [18]. However, in reality, training data is heterogeneous, variations in face images are not only due to pose. Therefore, finding a low dimensional space correlated with pose variation is difficult.

Our method will evaluate the face roll. We assume face has been extracted in a face window of size L. This is essentially a geometrical method, inspired by some basic knowledge of the face. To solve the problem, we will rely on the previous study presented in [19] where salient face elements are extracted in their bounding boxes. In this previous work, the main assumption is that the roll had almost a null value. Here, the idea is that when roll estimation is not correct, the face elements extraction should not reliable. Therefore, if we extract face elements for each of the roll discrete values, the most reliable extraction will give the roll of the face. However, in order to obtain an accurate roll value, the computation time would be too long. Thus, we introduce a first step which will select only a few possible roll values. This selection is based on the detection of horizontal regions of the face, since all face salient elements, such as eyes, nose and mouth have an approximate horizontal direction.

Figure 1 shows an overview of the proposed method. So, first, we will present a measure of face local and global horizontal energies enabling to extract some candidate roll values of the test face image. Then, using a credibility score among the selected candidate roll values, the final roll value can be estimated. Finally, our method will be evaluated in BioID and Color Feret databases.

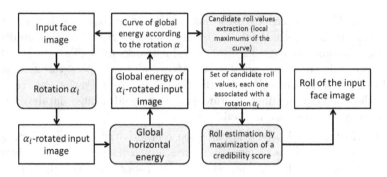

Fig. 1. Global scheme of the proposed method.

2 Horizontal Energy of a Face

In this section, we will present how we compute a measure of local and global horizontal energy. Here, we choose to use the horizontal mirror pattern of Haar-like features $H(w, h) = W \cup B$. There are two main benefits in choosing Haar features. First, if we know the scale of the face image, in other words, if we know the size of the face window, we will be able to choose a suitable width and height for the Haar pattern. Second, Haar-like features are extremely fast to compute. Integral image, defined by Viola and Jones [20], allows the computation of a Haar value in constant time, whatever the size of Haar pattern is.

2.1 Fixing the Size of the Pattern

In order to compute the local energy map, we must choose a suitable width and height for the horizontal Haar pattern. We assume that face is correctly found in a square window of size L. Since all faces are detected in this square window, L gives the order of magnitude of the face. Hence, the width w and height h of Haar pattern will be expressed as a percentage of L. When Haar filter size is small, the energy map is still sensitive to vertical directions. On the other hand, when the filter size is too large, the filter is not enough local compare to the face window. A good compromise is when w and h are almost the size of an eye. With this size, the filter is local enough and is less sensitive to vertical direction lines. Moreover, the other face salient parts, such as nose basis or mouth have a size of the same order of magnitude. Therefore a suitable size for the Haar filter should be $w = 15\%$ and $h = 5\%$. Figure 2 shows our local horizontal energy maps according to Haar pattern width w and height h as well as the binarisation of these maps. As we expected, the local horizontal energy map using a Haar filter with the mentioned size is still local and is less sensitive to noise.

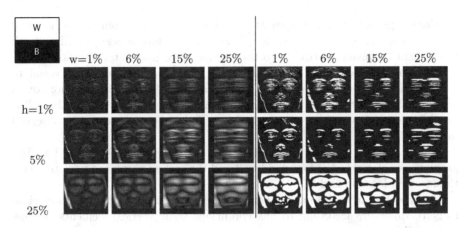

Fig. 2. Left: Local horizontal energy according to the filter width w and height h as a percentage of face window length L. Right: Binarization of the left part images.

2.2 Expression of the Local Energy

Given a Haar filter $H(w, h)$ of width w and height h and $i(x, y)$ the intensity at position (x, y), we define the value of this Haar feature at the central pixel of position (X, Y) by the equation 1.

$$f_{H(w,h)}(X, Y) = \sum_{(x,y) \in W} i(x, y) - \sum_{(x,y) \in B} i(x, y) \tag{1}$$

The local horizontal energy $E_{H(w,h)}$ is then the absolute value of $f_{H(w,h)}$ as shown in equation 2.

$$E_{H(w,h)}(X, Y) = \left| f_{H(w,h)}(X, Y) \right| \tag{2}$$

In this generated horizontal energy map, the higher a value is, the more confident in the presence of an approximate horizontal line in the neighborhood of this pixel we are.

2.3 Face Global Horizontal Energy

Here, we propose to express face global horizontal energy. Although this energy should be computed on all pixels of the face, segmenting the face is not an easy task. We propose a simple circle of which the center is also the center of the square face window (Figure 3). This mask will include most of the face elements.

Given E_H the local horizontal energy, given Ω the mask and $Ro(\alpha, \Omega, I)$ the roll rotation operator of α using the mask Ω applied on the face window I, we define the global horizontal energy $E_G(\alpha)$ by the equation 3.

$$E_G(\alpha) = \iint\limits_{Ro(\alpha,\Omega,I)} E_H(x, y) \, dx \, dy \tag{3}$$

Here, a positive roll corresponds to a clockwise rotation whereas a negative one is a counter clockwise rotation. When a face has almost a null roll, all face salient elements contribute to the formation of horizontal lines and hence generate a maximum in E_G. On the other hand, when face roll is equal to ± 90 deg, nose borders, face contours will be highlighted and will form horizontal lines too. Hence, we expect to see a local maximums in a face where the roll is around 0 deg and eventually around ± 90 deg. These phenomenon can be observed in Figure 3.

Figure 4 shows E_G according to the roll α of images of Figure 3. The first graph is associated to the face window 3 and the second graph is associated with the face windows 3b and 3c.

As expected, in both images, there is a local maximum with a roll value close to zero. However, according to line conditions some vertical elements become more visible and produce also a local maximum.

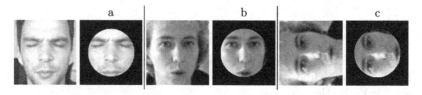

Fig. 3. Original face window and application of the circular mask on the face window.

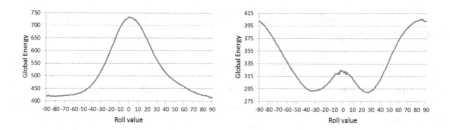

Fig. 4. Examples of the global horizontal energy E_G according to the roll α: left graph is extracted from the Figure 3a whereas the right graph is computed from the Figure 3b and 3c.

3   Face Role Estimation

From a face window of which the roll is unknown, we will, first compute the global energy of this face window. Then, we apply a rotation on the face window image of ± 1 deg of which the center is the face window center. Thus, we simulate a roll rotation. After each rotation, the couple composed by the value of the global energy E_G and the roll value α are saved. Hence, the global energy graph according to the roll α is generated. From this energy measures, local maximums are extracted. Since each local maximum is associated to a roll value α, finally, we get a set $\Theta =$ of n possible rolls $\Theta = \{\alpha_1, \alpha_2, \cdots, \alpha_n\}$ for this test face window. One of these angles should be the roll estimation.

3.1   Face Salient Element Extraction

In [19], we introduce a method which extracts face salient elements. Actually, we assumed that with a non-negligible roll, the face elements extraction will fail.

Brief Description of the Method. In the previous method, the local energy map gives the measure of confidence in the presence of horizontal lines in every pixel neighborhood. However, illumination conditions can vary a lot within the same face window; a global threshold will not be efficient. Therefore, we choose to use 18 different thresholds on the horizontal energy map to get binarized images. This method extracts bounding boxes of each eye, nose basis and mouth using each threshold. As expected, since 18 thresholds are used, each of them generating at most 4 bounding boxes, we have at most 72 candidate regions generated.

A final multi-threshold analysis select a threshold per salient region, The final results is the association of all the bounding boxes corresponding to the selected threshold and region (Figure 5). Here, to estimate the face roll, this step of multi-threshold analysis will not be used.

$$t^*_{LE} = 0.88 \quad t^*_{RE} = 0.80 \quad t^*_N = 0.80 \quad t^*_M = 0.76 \qquad \text{multi}$$

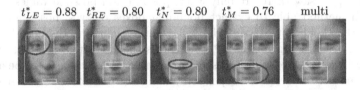

Fig. 5. Selected thresholds respectively for left eye, right eye, nose, and mouth as well as their associated candidate regions. The image "multi" on the right is the final result; it is a association of all selected candidate regions.

Reliability of the Face Element Extraction Method. Our method of salient face element is quite different from the others. Although it is not the main issue of this paper, the roll detection depends on this method of face salient elements extraction. Therefore, we will present here only some main results to prove the reliability of the method.

In order to evaluate the extraction, Jesorsky measure [21] is used. it relies on d_r the distance between the estimated and real right iris, on d_l the distance between the estimated and real left iris and on d_{rl}, the distance between the real right and left iris, Jesorsky measure quantifies the error err of both eyes position by the equation 4.

$$err = \frac{max(d_r, d_l)}{d_{rl}} \tag{4}$$

A couple of eyes are considered as correctly detected if $err < 0.25$. Here, the iris are simply estimated as the center of eye bounding box. Table 1 compares our method to Li et al [22] and to Asteriadis et al.[23].

Table 1. Comparison of Li et al. and Asteriadis et al. methods to ours in BioID database.

Method	Correctness(%)	Relative mean-error
Li et al.	96	0.1004
Asteriadis et al.	96	Not given
Our method	97.23	0.1130

Our method has a better correctness that the others, but a worse mean error. As a reminder, we do not really estimate the position of the center of the iris, contrary to Li et al..

3.2   Choosing the Roll Value among Candidates

In section 2, we saw there are only a few possible roll possible values. We also describe a method able to extract bounding boxes of eyes, nose and mouth. For each threshold t, it extracts the left eye, the right eye, the nose basis and the mouth in bounding boxes. Figure 6 shows the extracted candidate regions according to some thresholds and some rolls value. What appears to be a drawback is used here to select a proper roll among the candidate set Θ. A scoring system able to select the roll is built on this assumption. An extracted face region of each threshold which satisfies some criteria will add a point to the score $SC(\alpha)$. Therefore, the searched roll α^* will be the roll which maximizes the score as shown in equation 5.

$$- \alpha^* \in \Theta / SC(\alpha^*) = \max_{\alpha_i \in \Theta} SC(\alpha_i) \tag{5}$$

These criteria may vary from a face element to another. Other criteria concern relative position of two regions when they exist.

1. A region must be significant: the bounding box area should be greater than 1% of the face window area.
2. A region bounding box should have a greater width than the height, since it should be an horizontal object when the roll is null.
3. An eye width should be smaller than half of the face window width.
4. Mouth and nose tip should be smaller than 60% of the face window width.

5. In a null roll face, both eyes must be almost at the same ordinate. In other words, both eye bounding box projections on y-axis must have a common part.
6. Mouth and nose basis must be in the face symmetry axis. The intersection of their projections on x-axis should not be empty.

A score is computed only on the face windows according the roll corresponding to a local maximum of E_G. The upper limit of the score is 72. Each time, an eye candidate region verifies all criteria 1, 2 and 3, a point is added to the score SC. Each time, a nose or mouth candidate region verifies all criteria 1, 2 and 4, a point is also added to the score SC. However, when criteria 5 is not satisfied, it means, that one the eyes regions is wrong. Similarly, when criterion 6 is not satisfied, it means that the mouth or nose region is wrong. Therefore, whenever conditions 5 or 6 is not satisfied, a point is subtracted on the score SC.

Each candidate roll belonging to the set Θ are now associated with a score. As shown in equation 5, the roll with the highest score will give the final and selected roll of the face window.

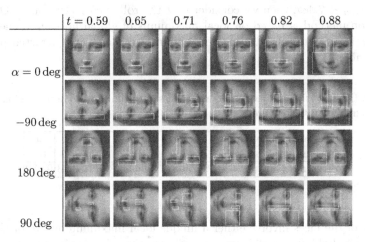

Fig. 6. Candidate anatomic regions according to the threshold applied on local horizontal energy map.

4 Evaluation

BioID does not annotate the roll whereas Color Feret does. Both databases contain faces with glasses or a beard or a mustache in various illumination conditions.

α_R denotes the real roll, and α_E represents the estimated roll. Figure 7 shows the percentages of correct yaw estimation using the method described in [19]. As we can expect, this yaw estimation method is sensitive to face roll and have a best estimation rate for a null roll.

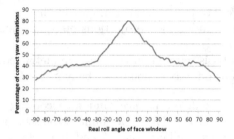

Fig. 7. Percentage of correct yaw estimation using the method described in [19] according to the real roll of faces images in Color Feret database.

In order to give a more accurate evaluation of the roll estimation method, we also define the error measure err_{roll} by equation 6.

$$err_{roll} = |\alpha_R - \alpha_E| \tag{6}$$

If $err_{roll} < 7$ deg, then we consider that the roll is correctly found. Our role estimation method is based on local maximums of global horizontal energy. In all Color Feret database, five local maximums, at most, are extracted per face image (table 2).

Table 2. Disctribution of faces and correctness according to the number of extracted local maximums in Color Feret.

Local maximums number	1	2	3	4	5	all
Distribution of faces(%)	76.12	9.16	10.42	1.97	0.33	100
Correctness(%)	99.59	87.72	96.05	86.11	83.33	97.80

Most of the faces involve either a unique local maximum or two or three. It shows the global horizontal energy according to the roll α is piecewise monotone.

Our method is also based on a scoring system at local maximums of the global horizontal energy. It means that each local maximum is associated, obviously with a roll α, but also with the score $SC(\alpha)$. Given $SC(\alpha_{M1})$ the highest score and $SC(\alpha_{M2})$ the second highest score, we define the difference operator Δ by the equation 7. We assume that when only one maximum is detected, $SC(\alpha_{M2}) = 0$

$$\Delta = |SC(\alpha_{M1}) - SC(\alpha_{M2})| \tag{7}$$

Figure 8a shows the distribution according to the difference operator Δ and Figure 8b shows the correctness in percentage according to the difference operator Δ. There are two parts in this distribution and correctness according to Δ. First, almost all the faces (generating at least, two local maximums) are located at the left part of the curve. Face images with a single maximum are mainly in the right part of the curves. Generally, we can see in the correctness curve that the higher Δ is, the better is the correctness. In the first part of the curve, almost all correctness are greater than 80.0%.

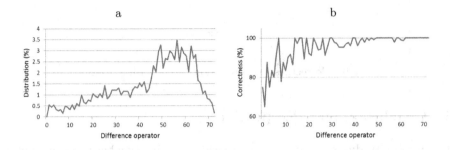

Fig. 8. a) Distribution of face images (%) according to the difference operator Δ. b) Correctness (%) according to Δ.

To improve the correctness, we propose to introduce a rejection rule. As the results are better when Δ is higher, we propose to use Δ as a rejection threshold. We define correctness with rejection $C_R(T)$ by the equation 8.

$$C_R(T) = \frac{\text{number of face windows with } \Delta > T \text{ and } err_{roll} < 7\deg}{\text{number of face windows with } \Delta > T} \quad (8)$$

Figure 9 shows the correctness with rejection. When all image are taken into account, the correctness is equal to 97, 80%.

Similar tests were done in BioID database and gives similar results. Table 3 gives the correctness (%), the mean absolute error and standard deviation of the roll estimation in Color Feret and BioID databases. All images, even those where Δ is low ($T = 0$), are taken into account.

Table 3. Correctness(%), mean absolute error and standard deviation of the roll estimation in Color Feret and BioID. All face images are taken into account.

Database	Correctness (%)	Mean absolute error (deg)	Standard deviation (deg)
Color Feret	97.80	4.07	8.54
BioID	98.23	4.00	8.35

The mean absolute error is quite good, but the standard deviation is quite high. In our method, when estimation fails, it is often about 90 deg error. However, it also means that when the roll is correctly estimated, the error is less than 4 deg.

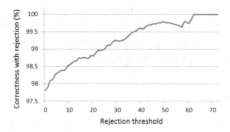

Fig. 9. Correctness with rejection (%) according to Δ.

5   Conclusion and Perspective

This paper introduces a new method for head roll estimation based on horizontal global energy maximization. It uses a method which is able to extract bounding boxes of eyes, nose and mouth. We introduce a simple scoring system based on relative positions and sizes of these face elements. In order to evaluate, we also add a correctness roll measure based on the absolute error. Our roll estimation method presents good results in terms of mean absolute error or correctness.

The standard deviation has a non-negligible value compared to the mean. This method can be used in the context of head pose estimation in video analysis where the range of possible roll values is small. Indeed, the difference of roll of the same face between two consecutive frames will be considerably less than 90 deg.

Besides, this method can be added to other methods dealing with faces in computer vision. For example, this method can be introduced in Viola and Jones face detector to make it invariant to roll variation.

References

1. Sherrah, J., Gong, S., Ong, E.J.: Face distributions in similarity space under varying head pose. Image and Vision Computing **19**, 807–819 (2001)
2. Niyogi, S., Freeman, W.: Example-based head tracking. In: Intern. Conf. on Autom. Face and Gesture Recog., pp. 374–378 (1996)
3. Wang, J.-G., Sung, E.: EM enhancement of 3D head pose estimated by point at infinity. Image and Vision Computing **25**, 1864–1874 (2007)
4. Horprasert, T., Yacoob, Y., Davis, L.: Computing 3-d head orientation from a monocular image sequence. In: Conf. on Autom. Face and Gesture Recog., pp. 242–247 (1996)
5. Wu, J., Trivedi, M.: A two-stage head pose estimation framework and evaluation. Pattern Recognition **41**, 1138–1158 (2008)
6. Jones, M., Viola., P.: Fast multi-view face detection. Mitsubishi Electric Research Laboratories, Tech. Rep. 096 (2003)
7. Li, S., Fu, Q., Gu, L., Scholkopf, B., Zhang, J.: Kernel machine based learning for multi-view face detection and pose estimation. In: ICCV, pp. 674–679 (2001)

8. Hoffken, M., Wang, T., Wiest, J., Kressel, U., Dietmayer, K.: Synchronized sub-manifold embedding for robust and real-time capable head pose detection based on range images. In: Intern. Conf. on 3D Vision, pp. 167–174 (2013)
9. Balasubramanian, V.N., Ye, J., Panchanathan, S.: Biased manifold embedding: a framework for person-independent head pose estimation. In: CVPR, pp. 1–7 (2007)
10. Cootes, T.F., Edwards, G.J., Taylor, C.J.: Active appearance models. Trans. on Pattern Anal. and Mach. Intel. **23**, 681–685 (2001)
11. Martins, P., Batista, J.: Single view head pose estimation. In: ICIP, pp. 1652–1655 (2008)
12. Xiao, J., Baker, S., Matthews, I., Kanade, T.: Real-time combined 2D+3D active appearance models. In: CVPR, vol. 2, pp. 525–542 (2004)
13. Murphy-Chutorian, E., Trivedi, M.M.: Head Pose Estimation and Augmented Reality Tracking: An Integrated System and Evaluation for Monitoring Driver Awareness. Trans. on Intel. Transportation Systems **11**, 300–311 (2010)
14. Moon, H., Miller, M.: Estimating facial pose from a sparse representation. In: Intern. Conf. Image Processing, pp. 75–78 (2004)
15. Ma, Y., Konishi, Y., Lao, S., Kawade, M.: Sparse Bayesian regression for head pose estimation. In: ICPR, pp. 507–510 (2006)
16. Ji, H., Liu, R., Su, F., Su, Z., Tian, Y.: Robust head pose estimation via convex regularized sparse regression. In: ICIP, pp. 3617–3620 (2011)
17. Raytchev, B., Yoda, I., Sakaue, K.: Head pose estimation by nonlinear manifold learning. In: ICPR, vol. 4, pp. 462–466 (2004)
18. Hoffken, M., Wang, T., Wiest, J., Kressel, U., Dietmayer, K.: Synchronized sub-manifold embedding for robust and real-time capable head pose detection based on range images. In: Intern. Conf. on 3D Vision, pp. 167–174 (2013)
19. Pyun, N.-J., Sayah, H., Vincent, N.: Adaptive haar-like features for head pose estimation. In: Campilho, A., Kamel, M. (eds.) ICIAR 2014, Part II. LNCS, vol. 8815, pp. 94–101. Springer, Heidelberg (2014)
20. Viola, P., Jones, M.: Rapid object detection using a boosted cascade of simple features. In: CVPR, vol. 1, pp. 511–418 (2001)
21. Jesorsky, O., Kirchberg, K.J., Frischholz, R.W.: Robust face detection using the Hausdorff distance. In: Bigun, J., Smeraldi, F. (eds.) AVBPA 2001. LNCS, vol. 2091, p. 90. Springer, Heidelberg (2001)
22. Li, Y., Zhao, P., Wan, B., Ming, D.: An improved hybrid projection function for eye precision location. In: Gao, X., Müller, H., Loomes, M.J., Comley, R., Luo, S. (eds.) MIMI 2007. LNCS, vol. 4987, pp. 312–321. Springer, Heidelberg (2008)
23. Asteriadis, S., Nikolaidis, N., Pitas, I.: Facial feature detection using distance vector fields. Pattern Recognition **42**, 1388–1398 (2009)

Tooth Segmentation Algorithm
for Age Estimation

Mauro Bacaloni[1]($\boxtimes$), Pierluigi Maponi[1], and Roberto Cameriere[2]

[1] Division of Mathematics, University of Camerino, 62032 Camerino, Mc, Italy
{mauro.bacaloni,pierluigi.maponi}@unicam.it
[2] AgEstimation Project, University of Macerata, 62100 Macerata, Mc, Italy
r.cameriere@unimc.it

Abstract. The estimation of age of adult subjects usually is based on age-related changes in skeleton. An interesting non invasive method, recently developed, involves teeth parameters achievable from peri-apical X-ray. Specifically, this procedure estimates age of adults through the changes of the tooth due to the apposition of secondary dentine, using pulp and tooth area as fundamental parameters. Aim of this study is to define an algorithm able to detect the boundary of the interested tooth in order to apply an automatic procedure for age estimation. The algorithm is based on classical segmentation methods as thresholding and shape analysis. Furthermore, our early results obtained on a small sample, are encouraging to proceed on this path.

Keywords: Forensic science · Age estimation · Pulp/tooth ratio · Canine · Segmentation

1 Introduction

Age estimation is a strongly interesting field of research for both archaeology and forensic studies, despite the different aims of the two studies. Age estimation is fundamental in archaeology and in physical anthropology studies for the determination of demographic parameters as growth rates, life expectancies and establishment of mortality patterns [13]. In the forensic context, this parameter is useful for the identification of victims and living subjects for investigating crimes, mass disaster or war crimes [21, 26]. Although age estimation is a widely studied problem for subjects under the legal age, it means still an hard task for adults living. A particular growing problem regards the case of subjects, often immigrants, who can not say with exactness their date of birth and therefore their chronological age. In order to maintain their employment or to ask for retirement, age estimation is required.

Classical methods for estimate age of subjects are based on the observation of the bones: in particular, development stage of bones is analyzed in case of minor subjects, while for adults the stage of degeneration process is the key to identify age. Details of skeleton most analyzed are the degenerative changes in

© Springer International Publishing Switzerland 2015
S. Battiato et al. (Eds.): ACIVS 2015, LNCS 9386, pp. 452–463, 2015.
DOI: 10.1007/978-3-319-25903-1_39

the pubic symphysis [28], sternal rib ends [12], auricular surface of the ilium [18], endo- and ecto- cranial sutures [7] and the clavicle [30]. However, two kind of problems are encountered in the study of the bones for age estimation. The first one is represented by the taphonomic processes that too often damage the skeletons hopelessly. Secondly, degenerative changes in bones structure strongly depends on the lifestyle of the subjects: therefore bones study for age estimation requires the knowledge of the subject's habits.

Alternatively, development of teeth is practically independent from habits and their degeneration do not depend from habits and lifestyle as much as other tissues [15,19]. More important, taphonomic processes have no big impact on them and,for last but not least, they are often the only body part available for archaeologic study [19]. Most of the proposed methods for teeth are based on macroscopic, microscopic and biochemical analysis of teeth themselves. These methods apply to various forms of tooth modification as wear [2], root dentine transparency [17], tooth cementum annulation [31], racemization of aspartic acid [20]. Most of those methods are invasive and can not be applied to living subjects. Different case regards methods based on the apposition of secondary dentine.

Dental pulp is a mesenchymal tissue surrounded by a pulp canal. Outside the pulp are some odontoblast lines, which release dentine during the subject's life and reduce the size of the pulp canal. Changes in its size caused by the apposition of secondary dentine are the best morphometric parameters for estimating age by X-rays. This process is a continuous and regular one, modified only by caries or particular abrasions. In [1] the correlation between the apposition of secondary dentine and chronological age has firstly been observed, while the pattern and rate of apposition of secondary dentine have been deeply studied in [24,25].

Secondary dentine can be studied by several methods, both sectioning and X-rays. A successful tool for age estimation in adults based on the relationship between age and pulp size on peri-apical X-rays[16,22]. Such method has strongly been improved in later years, obtaining a quite accurate formula for estimate age through analysis of biometrical data from peri-apical X-ray of the maxillary canine [4].

The privileged teeth for this method are the canines for many reasons: usually they are the oldest teeth (i.e. they are more commonly found on skeletons from excavating), they less undergo into the effect of diet with respect to posterior teeth, their wear is less damaged then the anterior teeth and, especially, they are the one-single root teeth with the largest pulp area, making them easier to analyze.

Other different information could be obtain, mainly using the computerized tomography (CT) [32], improving the method, but they usually can not be applied since they require the extraction of the tooth.

Aim of this study is to define an algorithm that automatically compute the canine parameters necessary for age estimation. In particular, two parameters are needed: the area of tooth region, and area of pulp region. Two scenario are possible: the case of an already extracted tooth and the case of not-extracted one. We already analyzed the case of extracted tooth in [5]. The present work is focused on the algorithm for not-extracted teeth.

The main advantage of a singular method for both living and deceased subjects as the one applied in this work is its completeness. As a matter of fact, solution to age estimation problem based on this method can be implemented on a unique tool usable on several fields of research.

While in [5] we analyzed both edge detection and pulp boundary detection algorithms, for not extracted teeth only tooth edge detection represent a challenge, in fact, once such goal is achieved, the pulp area is easily found in the same way as in the case of extracted tooth.

2 Materials

Panoramic dental X-rays have been taken from Spanish white Caucasian patients. Subjects have been chosen from collection stored at the private radiology department in Bilbao (Spain) and the Faculty of Odontology of the University of Granada (Spain). Protocols to collect orthopantomograms for human subjects were approved by the Ethics Committee for Research Involving Human Subjects of the University of Granada (Spain), and the study was conducted in accordance with the ethical standards of the Declaration of Helsinki. Patient's medical history was not taken into account when selecting the X-rays. The World Medical Association (WMA) has developed the Declaration of Helsinki as a statement of ethical principles for medical research involving human subjects, including research on identifiable human material and data.

This paper presents the preliminary results of an automatic method for age estimation, so only patients without root fillings, crown restorations or any abnormal dental anatomy have been selected.

3 Methodology

Starting from work [16], several statistical methods have been studied for age determination of adults. In general, such methods establish a relationship between the individual age (the dependent variable) and some meaningful tooth parameters obtained by analyzing the digitalized X-ray. Although several regression methods have been proposed to define such a relation, Cameriere [3] established a successful formula through a linear regression statistical process. In particular, from the ratio RA between the area of the pulp and area of same tooth (canine), age is determined through formulas

$$Age_u = 101.3 - 556.68RA_u, \tag{1}$$

$$Age_l = 93.27 - 492.05RA_l, \tag{2}$$

where formula (1) refers to upper canines, while formula (2) refers to lower canines.

Accuracy of formulas (1) and (2) is deeply investigated in [3, 8, 29].

3.1   The Extracted Tooth Case

In order to build an algorithm able to automatically detect the tooth and the pulp edges from an extracted canine's X-ray standard techniques of image analysis have been used.

Hence we need to solve two segmentation problems: the detection of the tooth pixels, and the detection of the pulp pixels. Moreover, the second problem must be solved after the first one; in fact pulp pixels must be retrieved from the tooth pixels. These two segmentation problems are very different, so appropriate methods must be used to solve each one of them efficiently. In particular, the main difference is that the intensity of the pixels is much greater in the tooth than in the background, and so we can solve the first problem through usual thresholding techniques [9,27]. However, these techniques are usually inadequate for the second problem [9], the detection of the pulp pixels, because the grey levels of the pulp pixels are not very different from those of the tooth pixels. In [5], we proposed a shape analysis algorithm [33] for the solution of the pulp segmentation problem. In the following, both those segmentation methods are briefly described for the convenience of the readers.

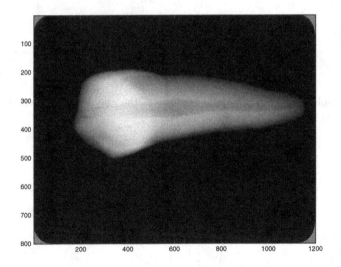

Fig. 1. Peri-apical X-ray of an extracted canine tooth.

The Segmentation of the Tooth. The intensity of the pixels is greater in the tooth than in the background, so we call T the tooth area and τ_T a suitable threshold. Therefore the pixels $(i, j) \in T$ could be detected by the test $I(i, j) > \tau_T$, where I is the matrix corresponding to the digital X-ray image of the extracted canine. Figure 1 shows an example of the image handled by the algorithm.

Actually, the previous test could select also spare pixels due to image noise. Hence, T is computed as the maximal connected component [14] of the set described by the previous test.

The edge of the tooth is computed by a linear approximation of the boundary of T.

The Segmentation of the Pulp. Shape analysis constitutes the basics for the pulp segmentation algorithm. More precisely, shape analysis is applied to all transversal sections of the tooth.

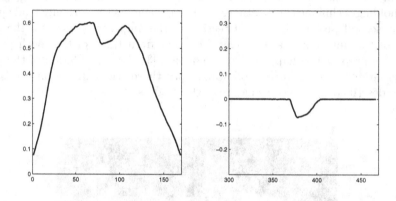

Fig. 2. Example of the characteristic M-shape of the gray level function (left) and its filtered version (right).

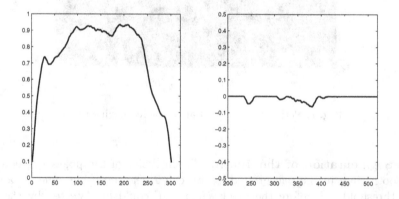

Fig. 3. Example of degenerative profile (left) and its filtered version (right).

As it is shown in the left-hand side of Fig. 2, grey level profiles of the transversal sections are characterized by an M-shape function. Roughly speaking, section of the pulp area is bounded by the two local maxima in this grey level function. Therefore simple techniques of signal analysis seem to be effective to solve the problem. Actually, image noises and presence of eventual degenerate cases, as in left-hand side of Fig. 3, increase the difficulty of such issue.

In order to overcome to previous complications, grey level profile are refined by a suitable spatial filter, resembling the filter of minimum, see [5] for details. In Figs 2 and 3, on the right-hand side, filtered version of profiles in Figs 2 and 3, left-hand side, are displayed. This filtering operation simplifies the grey level function; in fact the filtered section is represented by a flat background perturbed by a parabolic pattern. All perturbations of the filtered section can be used to describe pulp area. For degenerate cases, where multiple parabolic perturbations appear as in Figs 3, the largest perturbation usually corresponds to pulp area.

Such estimation of pulp boundary usually is larger then the real edges; therefore a proper reduction sub-algorithm is used to reduce the resulting interval in each section.

The implementation of the segmentation procedure is realized starting from the transverse section of the middle of the tooth, where usually the pulp area is better defined. Tooth sections are processed until five consecutive sections provide similar interval for pulp area. A mean interval is then obtained by taking the mean of the upper and lower bounds of these five intervals. This procedure starts from the middle of the tooth to the end of the root, analyzing each transverse section as explained above. Whenever a section produces a valid interval for the pulp area, such boundary values are stored and the mean interval is updated. Note that the interval computed from a generic section is valid when it is near to the mean interval.

Finally, the procedure starts again from the middle of the tooth to the end of the crown in an analogous way.

In this last phase, the detection of the pulp end is based on a simple observation: the intensity of the pixels is greater in the boundary of the pulp than in the middle of it. Therefore, for all transverse sections, the arithmetic mean of the grey levels of pixels around the middle of the pulp area are compared to the one of pixels around the boundary of the pulp area. When their difference is lower then a given threshold, the pulp ending is fixed and this concludes the analysis of transverse sections.

A piecewise linear approximation of the points of the pulp boundary is obtained by a least square polyline of points stored during the analysis of the vertical sections. From the knowledge of the boundary, area of tooth and area of pulp are computed as the number of pixel inside the corresponding region, age is estimated by formula (1) or (2) according to the canine tooth taken into account.

3.2   The Not-Extracted Tooth Case

The segmentation of a not-extracted canine in an X-ray image has another challenging step, that is the segmentation of tooth in images arising from orthopanto-
mographes. Note that, when this problem is solved, the procedure for extracted
teeth, described in section 1, can be used for age estimation.

For sake of simplicity, without any loss of generality, we consider images with
teeth horizontally aligned, with the crown on the left-hand side of the image and
the root on the right-hand side, see Fig. 4 for an example.

Images of non-extracted teeth usually show two or three teeth, as in Fig. 4.
Our algorithm requires a-priori information about which tooth is the canine, so,
from a practical point of view, the operator has to click on the canine crown to
start the segmentation procedure.

In order to reduce the domain of the image where the canine is contained,
we define a parametric model as follows:

$$
\begin{cases}
x(t) = p \sin^4 \left(\dfrac{t}{2} \right) + \tau_x, & t \in [-\pi, \pi), \\
y(t) = q \sin(t) + \tau_y, & t \in [-\pi, \pi),
\end{cases}
\tag{3}
$$

where p, q are real positive numbers representing the dimension of the canine on
the digitalized image, and τ_x, τ_y are integers representing a translation in the
image space. Parameters of model (3) can be determined by the model fitting to
pixels in the tooth. The above model is not accurate for a precise tooth boundary
description. Its scope is only to reduce the image space of investigation for the
searched edge. So, a preliminary step, needs for the detection of some pixels in
the tooth.

Two different kinds of tooth pixels are considered in this parameter identification problem: boundary pixels and inner pixels.

The Detection of Boundary Pixels. A set of boundary pixels that can be
quite easily recognized are given by the ones on the boundary of the crown,
where the pixels on the background have very different gray level value. As a
matter of fact, such points are detected through thresholding techniques, where
the threshold value ν is computed through an analysis of the grey level histogram
function of the image. The detection procedure starts from the point clicked by
the operator moving to left direction; then it starts again from the apex of the
crown to right direction until a column with no values less then ν is found. For
every column of the image, the thresholding provides all the possible intervals
for the crown area, but only the nearest one to previous selected intervals is
registered.

This algorithm may produce wrong results for image regions corresponding
to the teeth intersection and eventual shattered jaw. So, in order to avoid such
mistake, we applied a check filter similar to one used in the pulp segmentation.
More precisely, for each image column, the interval for the crown area is accepted
only if it is near to the areas obtained for the neighbor columns.

The Detection of Inner Pixels. The pixels in the canine region are characterized by grey levels more uniform then the ones of background pixels.So a minimum filter is used to enhance the tooth region. More precisely, the filtered image I' is computed starting from image I through a simple procedure: pixel $(r, c) \in I'$ is the minimum value of the sub-matrix $[r - \delta, r + \delta] \times [c - \delta, c + \delta] \in I$, where $\delta > 0$ is the half-width of the filter. The filtered image is shown in Fig. 5.

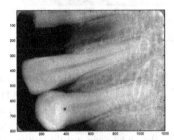

Fig. 4. Example of a peri-apical X-ray of not extracted canine.

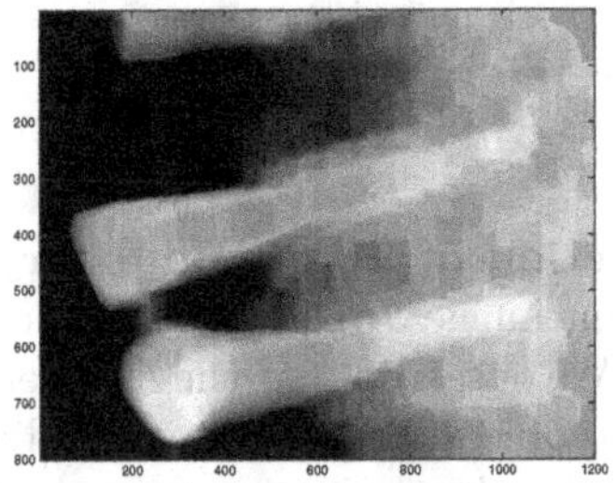

Fig. 5. Representation of the output of the minimum filter.

A new suitable thresholding value is automatically found from an analysis of grey level histogram function. All selected pixels belonging to the selected regions are marked as inner points.

At this stage, the proper longitudinal axe can be easily detected through a linear regression of all boundary and inner pixels detected previously described. Values τ_x and τ_y of model (3) are estimated through observation on crown boundary pixels. An initial value for parameter p is guessed as the maximal distance among all the selected pixels.

Let $\{(V_{1,j}, V_{2,j}), j = 1, 2, \ldots, n\}$ be selected pixels (either boundary pixels or inner pixels). From the parametric model (3) we define the corresponding implicit form $\tilde{F}(x, y, p, q, \theta) = 0$, where

$$\tilde{F}(x, y, p, q, \theta) = y'^2 - \left(q \sin \left(2 \operatorname{asin} \sqrt[4]{\frac{x'}{p}} \right) \right)^2,$$

and (x', y') is obtained by (x, y) through a translation by vector $(-\tau_x, -\tau_y)$ and a rotation of an angle θ.

Finally the minimizer of the problem

$$\min_{p,q,\theta} \sum_{j=1}^{n} \tilde{F}(V_{1,j}, V_{2,j}, p, q, \theta) \tag{4}$$

defines the region J containing the interested tooth, see Fig. 6.

We abuse the notation J also to denote the image of all zero grey level with exception of the pixels arising from problem (4). Image J is shown in Fig. 7

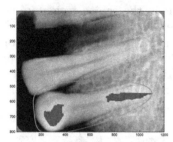

Fig. 6. Plot of minimum $\tilde{F}$.   **Fig. 7.** Output of the minimization.

Detection of Tooth Boundary. The final step of the algorithm takes into account image J. Detection of the tooth boundary is based on a simple observation. We observed that the first derivative and second order derivative of the grey level profile along the transversal sections have common features. In particular, the first order derivative around an edge point is closer to zero, while the second order derivative considered in absolute value has a local minimum around that point.

Such considerations have been implied in the algorithm that start from the apex of the crown and proceed to right-hand side until the width of the edge detected is smaller then a given values, determining the end of the root. Figure 8 shows the result of this procedure.

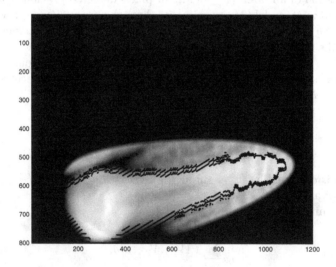

Fig. 8. Final step of the boundary detection.

4 Discussion

Age estimation in adults is a strongly significant problem in forensic and archaeological science. Although several macroscopic techniques have been developed, analysis of the apposition of the secondary dentine is one of the most reliable principle.

This work intends to propose image analysis methods to provide a semi-automatic procedure for age estimation. Advantages of a semi-automatic procedure are various: among all of them, the consistency of the results repeating the age estimation at different time and by different operators.

This paper is a continuation of [5], where the algorithm for extracted were proposed. In the present paper, the problem for not-extracted teeth is considered. The proposed algorithm still requires some adjustment, and a wider sample of X-rays is required to test our procedure on a large scale. However, the proposed algorithm seems to be quite robust and able to deal with general cases. In fact, its implementation in a Matlab code usually provides satisfactory results.

Accordingly to our analysis and our early results, our approach, applied to the analyzed kind of images, gave better results then ones obtained by other classic methods as region growing [9,11,23], Markov random field models [23] or deformable models [6,23]. We do not expect that our procedure is the final solution to age estimation problem by peri-apical X-rays of canine teeth, but this procedure can be provided as a good initial guess for a find refinement by using the above cited methods.

A point we will focus on immediately future work is the image noise. Particularly, image noise arising from the bones has a big impact on tooth boundary detection. This problem has been avoided by the shape analysis of gray-scale vertical profiles of the image as follow. However, use of classical and original models for noise in medical images, as [9,10], are under study.

Since the described method regarding the not-extracted case is a new one, a statistical analysis on the results from its implementation has not been realized yet. This work claims only on a early presentation of the method. Improvements of its steps, pre-processing statistical noise analysis and reduction and a strong statistical analysis on its results will be the cornerstone of our future works.

Several other improvements are already under study. Among them, a linear regression of the estimated age error to chronological age, and different trials to enhancement the software robustness.

References

1. Bodecker, C.F.: A consideration of some of the changes in the teeth from young to old age. Dent Cosm **67**, 543–549 (1925)
2. Brothwell, D.: The relationship of tooth wear to aging. In: Iscan, M.Y. (ed.) Age Markers in Human Skeletons, pp. 303–316. Charles C. Thomas Ltd., Springfield (1989)
3. Cameriere, R., Cunha, E., Sassaroli, E., Nuzzolese, E., Ferrante, L.: Age estimation by pulp/tooth area ratio in canines: study of a portuguese sample to test cameriere's method. Forensic Sci. Int. **193**(1–3), 128e1–128e6 (2009)

4. Cameriere, R., Ferrante, L., Belcastro, M.G., Bonfiglioli, B., Rastelli, E., Cingolani, M.: Age estimation by pulp/tooth ratio in canines by peri-apical x-rays. J. Forensic Sci. **52**(1), 166–170 (2007)
5. Cameriere, R., Luca, S.D., Egidi, N., Bacaloni, M., Maponi, P., Ferrante, L., Cingolani, M.: Automatic age estimation in adults by analysis of canine pulp/tooth ratio: preliminary results. J. Forensic Radiology and Imaging (2014)
6. Cootes, T.F., Taylor, C.J.: Statistical models of appearance for computer vision, May 2004
7. Galera, V., Ubelaker, D.H., Hayek, C.: Comparison of macroscopic cranial methods of age estimation applied to skeletons from the terry collection. J. Forensic Sci. **43**, 933–939 (1998)
8. Galić, I., Vodanović, M., Cameriere, R., Nakaš, E., Galić, E., Selimović, E., Brkić, H.: Accuracy of cameriere, haavikko, and willems radiographic methods on age estimation on bosnian-herzegovian children age groups 6–13. Int. J. Legal Med. **125**, 315–321 (2011)
9. Gonzales, R.C., Woods, R.E.: Digital image processing, 2nd edn. Prentice Hall, Upper Saddle River (2002)
10. Gravel, P., Beaudoin, G., Guise, J.A.D.: A method for modeling nooise in medical images. IEEE Trans. Med. Imaging **23**(10), 1221–1232 (2004)
11. Hojjatoleslami, S.A., Kittler, J.: Region growing: a new approach. IEEE Trans. Image Processing **7**(7), 1079–1084 (1998)
12. Iscan, M.Y., Loth, S.: Osteological manifestation of age in the adult. In: Kennedy, K.A.R. (ed.) Reconstruction of Life from the Skeleton, pp. 23–40. Wiley-Liss, New York (1989)
13. Jackes, M.: Building the bases for paleodemographic analysis: adult age determination, New York, NY (2000)
14. Kong, T.Y., Rosenfeld, A.: Digital topology: Introduction and survey. Computer Vision, Graphics and Image Processing **48**, 357–393 (1989)
15. Kullman, L.: Acuracy of two dental and one skeletal age estimation methods in swedish adolescents. Forensic Sci. Int. **75**, 225–236 (1995)
16. Kvaal, S.I., Kolltveit, K.M., Thomsen, O., Solheim, T.: Age estimation of adults from dental radiographs. Forensic Sci. Int. **74**, 175–185 (1995)
17. Lamendin, H., Baccino, E., Humpert, J.F., Tavernier, J.C., Nossintchouk, R.M., Zerilli, A.: A simple technique for age estimation in adult corpses: the two criteria dental method. J. Forensic Sci. **37**(5), 1373–1379 (1993)
18. Lovejoy, C.O., Meindul, R.S., Pryzback, T.R., Mensforth, P.: Chronological metamorphosis of the auricular surgace of the ilium: A new method for the determination of adult skeletal age at death. Am. J. Phys. Antrhropol. **68**, 15–28 (1985)
19. Lucy, D., Pollard, A.M., Roberts, C.A.: A comparison of three dental techniques for estimating age at death in humans. J. Archaeol. Sci. **22**, 417–428 (1995)
20. Ohtani, S.: Studies on age estimation using racemization of aspartic acid in cementum. J. Forensic. Sci. **40**, 805–807 (1995)
21. Ousley, S.: Should we estimate biological or forensic stature? J. Forensic Sci. **40**(5), 768–773 (1995)
22. Paewinsky, E., Pfeiffer, H., Brinkmann, B.: Quantification of secondary dentine formation from orthopantomograms: A contribution to forensic age estimation methods in adults. Int. J. Legal. Med. **119**, 27–30 (2005)
23. Pham, D.L., Xu, C., Prince, J.L.: Current methods in medical image segmentation. Annu. Rev. Biomed. Eng. **02**, 315–337 (2000)
24. Philippas, G.G., Applebaum, E.: Age changes in the permanent upper lateral incisor. J. Dent. Res. **46**, 1002–1009 (1967)

25. Philippas, G.G., Applebaum, E.: Age changes in the permanent upper canine teeth. J. Dent. Res. **47**, 411–417 (1968)
26. Ritz-Timme, R., Cattaneo, C., Collins, M.J., Waite, E.R., Shultz, H.W., Kaatsch, H.J.: Age estimation: the state of the art in relation to the specific demands of forensic practice. Int. J. Legal. Med. **113**, 129–136 (2000)
27. Sahoo, P.K., Soltani, S., Wong, A.K.C.: A survey of thresholding techniques. Computer Vision, Graphics and Image Processing **41**, 233–260 (1988)
28. Suchey, J.M., Katz, D.: Application of pubic age determination in a forensic setting. In: Reichs, K.J. (ed.) Forensic Osteology. Advances in Identification of Human Remains, pp. 204–236. Thomas Publisher, Springfield (1998)
29. Vodanović, M., Dumančić, J., Galić, I., Pavičin, I.S., Petrovečki, M., Cameriere, R., Brkić, H.: Age estimation in archaelogical skeletal remains: evaluation of four non-destructive age calculation methods. J. Forensic Odontostomatol **29**(2), 14–21 (2011)
30. Walker, R.A., Lovejoy, C.O.: Radiographic changes in the clavicle and proximal femur and their use in the determination of skeletal age at death. Am. J. Phys. Antrhropol. **68**, 67–78 (1985)
31. Wittwer-Backofen, U., Gampe, J., Vaupel, J.W.: Tooth cementum annulation for age estimation: results form a large known-age validation study. Am. J. Phys. Antrhropol. **123**, 119–129 (2004)
32. Yang, F., Jacobs, R., Willems, G.: Dental age estimation through volume matching of teeth imaged by cone-beam ct. Forensic Sci. Int. **159**(suppl. 1), S78–S83 (2006)
33. Zhang, D., Lu, G.: Review of shape representation and description techniques. Pattern Recognition **37**, 1–19 (2004)

On Blind Source Camera Identification

G.M. Farinella, M.V. Giuffrida$^{(\boxtimes)}$, V. Digiacomo, and S. Battiato

Image Processing Laboratory, Dipartimento di Matematica e Informatica, University
of Catania, Catania, Italy
{gfarinella,battiato}@dmi.unict.it,
{valerio.giuffrida88,vinc.digiacomo}@gmail.com

Abstract. An interesting and challenging problem in digital image
forensics is the identification of the device used to acquire an image.
Although the source imaging device can be retrieved exploiting the file's
header (e.g., EXIF), this information can be easily tampered. This lead
to the necessity of blind techniques to infer the acquisition device, by
processing the content of a given image. Recent studies are concentrated
on exploiting sensor pattern noise, or extracting a signature from the
set of pictures. In this paper we compare two popular algorithms for
the blind camera identification. The first approach extracts a fingerprint
from a training set of images, by exploiting the camera sensor's defects.
The second one is based on image features extraction and it assumes that
images can be affected by color processing and transformations operated
by the camera prior to the storage. For the comparison we used two
representative dataset of images acquired, using consumer and mobile
cameras respectively. Considering both type of cameras this study is
useful to understand whether the theories designed for classic consumer
cameras maintain their performances on mobile domain.

Keyword: Blind source camera identification

1 Introduction

Since the increasing use of low cost imaging devices embedded in different consumer products (e.g., digital cameras, smartphones, tablet, etc.), thousands of
pictures are shot everyday and most of them are posted on the Internet through
social networks. Among the questions, Image Forensics aim to answer the following one during investigation: is the image under consideration generated by
the device being claimed to be acquired with? In examining the history of a picture, the identification of the device used for its acquisition is a key ingredient.
Indeed, in a court of law, the origin of a particular image may represent a crucial
evidence; the validity of this evidence might be compromised by the (reasonable) doubt that the image has not been captured from the claimed device [1].
Figuring out what devices was used to take a particular picture could be so
important to overturn the court's decision on a trial. Sometimes, one can be
lucky to find EXIF metadata inside an image file and can trivially detect the

© Springer International Publishing Switzerland 2015
S. Battiato et al. (Eds.): ACIVS 2015, LNCS 9386, pp. 464–473, 2015.
DOI: 10.1007/978-3-319-25903-1_40

model of camera used to take a picture [2]. However, EXIFs cannot be used during a trial, because can be easily manipulated. Therefore, particular attention was made by the research community to design algorithms able to infer the camera device using the only available visual information: the input image itself.

Blind source camera identification methods attempt to infer the device using the information extracted from the images. In literature, different solutions were proposed for this purpose. The methods can be grouped in two main categories: sensor's defects based and pipeline based. In building the fingerprint, the first kind of algorithms usually exploits the noise generated by camera sensor, whereas the latter one is based on features extracted from the image. For a survey of the different techniques the reader can refer [1,3].

We tested two popular source camera identification algorithms, belonging to the aforementioned categories. Specifically, we have considered the camera identification through the sensor noise [4] and the feature based method [5,6]. The contribution of this study is to test those approaches on images acquired by mobile phone devices. This allows to understand the performances of the involved methods (which were designed for images acquired with consumer digital cameras), perform well in the mobile domain. We aim to prove how those methods are able to solve two source camera identification's scenarios. The former one detects which camera device shot a particular picture, whereas the latter one discriminates among different camera models.

The remainder of this paper is organized as follows: Section 2 discusses the camera identification based on sensor noise, whereas Section 3 introduces the approach based on feature extraction. Section 4 reports experimental settings and the results. Finally, Section 5 concludes the paper.

2   Camera Identification Based on Sensor Noise

Any image can contain different kinds of noise, which can be classified how they are generated from. The *shot noise* is a random electronic signal perturbation produced by the integrated circuits. Another noise source are due to faulty pixels (dead or saturated), which alter significantly the RGB value of a cell in the camera sensor. The remaining part of the noise is almost a regular signal and it is imprinted at each camera shot, called *pattern noise* [7,8]. And in fact, it is the *pattern noise* the signal we look for to generate the camera fingerprint. Figure 1 shows the two components included in the *patter noise*: *Fixed Pattern Noise* (FPN), and *Photo Response Non-Uniformity* (PRNU). A small amount of the pattern noise is given by the FPN and it is caused by dark currents in the circuit and also depends on exposure and temperature. Most of the pattern noise is due to the *Photo Response Non-Uniformity*, which is given in part by the *Pixel Non-Uniformity* (PNU) noise, and in part by *Low Frequency Defects* (LFD).

To extract the PNU signature component of a specific camera, N pictures have to be considered [4,9–11]. The residual noise of each image is obtained by the following relation:

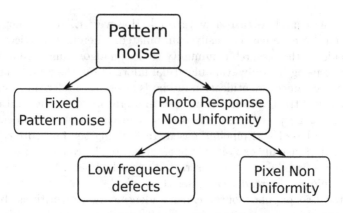

Fig. 1. Pattern noise hierarchy.

Table 1. List of features used in [12].

Color Features	IQM features
Pixel intensity mean value	Minkowsky measures
R-G, R-B, G-B channel correlation	Correlation measures
Pixel neighbor center of mass	Spectral distances
Frequency-domain statistics	

$$n_c^{(k)} = p_c^{(k)} - F(p_c^{(k)}) \qquad (1)$$

where $p_c^{(k)}$ denotes the kth image acquired with a camera c and $F(\cdot)$ is a denoising filter. Given a camera c, the PNU fingerprint P_c is obtained by averaging all the $n_c^{(k)}$'s. When the fingerprints for each camera P_c, $c = 1\ldots,C$ are extracted, the identification of an image is done correlating the pattern noise, extracted from the query image, and all of the fingerprints. The correlation is computed as follows:

$$\rho_c(p) = \frac{(n - \overline{n})(P_c - \overline{P_c})}{\|n - \overline{n}\|\|P_c - \overline{P_c}\|} \qquad (2)$$

where the $\overline{n}$ and $\overline{P_c}$ denotes mean values respectively of the picture residual noise and fingerprint of the camera c. Refinements of this method employ the *Maximum-Likelihood* approach to estimate the fingerprint [9], or specifically designed correlation method [10] to improve the classification performances.

3 Camera Identification Based on Features

Another family of source camera identification methods is based on the extraction of a set of features to build up a descriptor for the specific camera. The

Table 2. Selected camera model from the *Dresden database*.

Model	Symb.	# Devices	# Pictures
Canon Ixus 70	I70	3	567
Casio EX-Z150	EX	3	555
Kodak M1063	M	3	603
Nikon Coolpix S710	S710	3	566
Olympus μ1050SW	μ	3	631
Pratika DCZ 5.9	DCZ	3	614
Rollei RCP-7325XS	RCP	3	589
Samsung NV15	NV	3	645
TOTAL		**24**	**4770**

discrimination is performed by analyzing differences on model-dependent characteristics. The basic idea resides in looking at differences in the *Image Generation Pipeline* (IGP), where the image is processes by different algorithms (e.g., demosaicing, white balancing, color correction, etc.) [13]. Since many types of camera use different algorithms/parameters in the IGP, features on the image can be properly extracted to set up a descriptor for the camera model.

The employed method considers a set of features [5,6,12,14,15], which can be grouped into two families, as it is shown in Table 1: *features based on color* and

Table 3. List of mobile phones in [16] dataset.

Model	Symb.	# Pictures
LG 5600	L	200
Motorola V3	V3	200
Motorola V500	V5	231
Nokia 5140i	N5	200
Nokia 6230i	N62	216
Nokia 6600 (1)	A66	235
Nokia 6600 (2)	B66	200
Nokia 7270	N7	219
Samsung D500	S5	200
Samsung D600	S6	200
Samsung E720	S7	200
Sony K700i (1)	AK7	275
Sony K700i (2)	BK7	200
Sony K750	K75	204
Sony P800	P8	209
Sony P910	P9	200
PalmOne Treo	PO	200
TOTAL		**3589**

Table 4. Confusion matrix from the first test on Dresden database (cf. Section 4.1), for the algorithm based on sensor noise.

				Inferred as				
	I70	EX	M	S710	μ	DCZ	RCP	NV
I70	14.65	10.21	9.89	**20.16**	11.07	7.58	12.51	13.92
EX	1.08	**86.88**	1.79	2.52	2.70	1.43	1.81	1.79
M	8.45	8.79	**28.18**	9.44	11.77	10.82	10.80	11.76
S710	3.37	2.32	2.69	**79.69**	2.47	4.63	2.147	2.69
μ	6.70	9.10	9.76	10.84	**40.22**	8.13	7.60	7.67
DCZ	7.48	9.16	12.72	17.27	11.06	**22.78**	10.10	9.43
RCP	2.72	3.56	3.05	5.61	5.27	1.70	**73.67**	4.41
NV	9.90	9.79	13.00	**18.30**	10.40	9.31	12.39	16.91

Table 5. Confusion matrix from the first test on Dresden database (cf. Section 4.1), for the algorithm based on features extraction.

				Inferred as				
	I70	EX	M	S710	μ	DCZ	RCP	NV
I70	**82.25**	7.15	0.18	0	1.24	2.13	0	7.06
EX	14.62	**80.93**	0	0.53	2.14	0.18	0.36	1.25
M	0	0	**99.83**	0	0.17	0	0	0
S710	0.34	0.53	0	**94.20**	4.08	0	0	0.85
μ	0.96	1.80	1.28	1.46	**66.28**	0	3.11	25.12
DCZ	2.93	0.64	0	0	0	**78.71**	17.06	0.65
RCP	0	1.68	0	0	10.27	19.70	**67.34**	1.01
NV	4.63	1.69	0	1.85	17.29	0.61	9.97	**63.96**

image quality metrics (IQM) features. The set of features can be improved by adding new measurement for similarity between two images [16]. Other features include the dependencies between the average values of the colour channels [16]; additional features characterising white point correction have been also included considering twelve new features belonging to two groups [5,6]: *white balancing* and *wavelets measurement.* Classification is performed by training a *Support Vector Machine* [17], using the radial basis kernel function.

4   Experimental Setup and Results

The methods discussed in Section 2 and Section 3 have been considered and tested on two different datasets: the well-known *Dresden database* [18] and a cellular mobile phone dataset [16]. The *Dresden database* collects more than 14,000 pictures of 47 different scenes, using 73 consumer camera devices of 25 different models. The second dataset [16] collects more than 3,000 pictures, using 17 mobile phones of 15 different models. Table 2 and Table 3 show in detail the two datasets respectively.

Table 6. Results for the second test, using sensor noise based algorithm.

	I70	EX	M	S710	μ	DCZ	RCP	NV
			Inferred as					
I70	**100**	0	0	0	0	0	0	0
EX	0	**99.86**	0	0	0.14	0	0	0
M	0.28	0	**99.17**	0.28	0	0	0	0.28
S710	0	0	0	**100**	0	0	0	0
μ	1.03	1.16	0.90	1.55	**90.48**	1.67	1.54	1.67
DCZ	0	0	0	0.13	0	**99.73**	0	0.13
RCP	0	0	0	0	0	0	**100**	0
NV	0	0.26	0	0.26	0	0	0	**99.48**

Table 7. Results for the second test, using features extraction algorithm.

	I70	EX	M	S710	μ	DCZ	RCP	NV
			Inferred as					
I70	**54.90**	0.96	0	0	0.55	14.80	2.73	21.55	4.51
EX	13.34	**51.31**	0	0.84	7.78	4.33	21.97	0.42
M	1.11	7.21	**90.57**	0.28	0.69	0	0.14	0
S710	0	2.66	0	**81.32**	3.11	0	12.16	0.75
μ	0.39	0	1.81	4.65	**58.25**	0.51	31.31	3.08
DCZ	17.57	4.78	0	0	9.07	**47.02**	11.48	10.08
RCP	0.40	0.71	0	0	**54.16**	0.42	34.12	10.18
NV	2.42	0.26	0	2.77	**35.07**	0.65	29.31	29.52

4.1 First Test on Dresden Database

For this test we considered the problem of recognizing the camera model. Hence, we are not interested to detect the exactly device, but its model. We selected a subset of the *Dresden dataset* such that the same scene was taken from all the devices. With this setup, testing dataset contains 4,470 images coming from 24 camera devices of 8 different models (see Table 2). We performed the test, using picture from 2 devices as training set and the last one as validation set. Final results are obtained by averaging the outcomes of each test. In Table 4 we report the results using the sensor noise method, whereas in Table 5 we report the results for the feature based method.

Results show that the algorithm based on sensor noise do not perform well in this case. This is due to the fact that fingerprints cannot be generalized for different devices, even if they belong to the same model. Specifically, an average accuracy of 45.37% (Table 4) was obtained for the method based on sensor noise, whereas the feature based method obtained an average accuracy of 79.19% (Table 5).

Table 8. Results for the second test for the algorithm based on features extraction (Section 3) by using leave-one-out cross-validation.

| | \multicolumn{8}{c}{**Inferred as**} | | | | | | | |
	I70	EX	M	S710	μ	DCZ	RCP	NV
I70	**78.99**	1.91	0	0	0.70	16.68	0.77	0.95
EX	6.28	**81.79**	0.11	3.14	0.45	5.84	1.90	0.47
M	0	0.99	**99.01**	0	0	0	0	0
S710	0	1.07	0	**96.92**	0.47	0	0.47	1.06
μ	7.06	0.71	2.01	0	**40.94**	0	10.57	38.70
DCZ	0.57	0.11	0	0	0.51	**91.69**	6.21	0.91
RCP	0	0	0	0	0.83	0.35	**98.82**	0
NV	5.58	0.83	0	0.19	18.13	1.55	6.11	**67.62**

4.2 Second Test on Dresden Database

As a follow-up of the previous test, we selected randomly 2/3 of the pictures for each of camera data models, independently from the acquisition device. With this setup, we obtained an average accuracy of 98.59% (Table 6) for the method based on sensor noise. Instead, feature based method we obtained an average accuracy of 55.87%. Considering sensor noise from many pictures, selected randomly from three different devices of the same model, makes the resulting fingerprint more sensitive for the blind camera identification. Nevertheless, the drop in accuracy for features based methods is due to cameras parameters variability. Even if we tested among the same camera model, each device had different photometric setting (focus, white balancing, and so forth), which makes the classification task harder. To confirm our theory, we performed another test with feature based algorithm, using leave-one-out cross validation [19]. In this case, accuracy of the feature based method was 81.97%, as it is shown in Table 8.

4.3 Third Test on Dresden Database

The third test is devoted to assess the performances of the identification of a specific camera device. Differently than before, we tested how those algorithms perform in identifying the device that took a specific picture. In this case, the *Dresden dataset* was randomly sampled, in such a way 29 scenes were used as training set and the remaining 18 as validation set. This experiment was repeated three times as before, and we reported the average performances. In Table 9 we shows that sensor based method outperforms the feature one, with an overall accuracy of about 99%.

4.4 Test on Mobile Phones Database

The tests presented so far have been performed considering a dataset composed by images acquired with consumer digital camera. However, nowadays most of the images are acquired with mobile phones and are becoming more and more

Table 9. Third test results.

	Device 0		Device 1		Device 2	
Models	*Sensor Noise*	*Features*	*Sensor Noise*	*Features*	*Sensor Noise*	*Features*
I70	**100%**	60.73%	**100%**	41.45%	**100%**	16.86%
EX	**99.12%**	30.51%	**99.58%**	33.10%	**99.18%**	45.57%
M	**99.16%**	30.91%	**98.27%**	59.18%	**99.60%**	28.69%
S710	**100%**	27.08%	**100%**	61.30%	**100%**	24.11%
μ	**93.03%**	9.98%	**95.34%**	54.04%	**93.43 %**	41.29%
DCZ	**100%**	52.27%	**100%**	37.25%	**100%**	23.30%
RCP	**100%**	51.86%	**100%**	20.35%	**100%**	36.22%
NV	**100%**	33.41%	**100%**	35.99%	**100%**	33.72%

Table 10. Confusion matrix for the algorithm based on sensor noise, tested with the mobile phone dataset [16].

							Inferred as									
	L	V3	V5	N5	N62	A66	B66	N7	S5	S6	S7	AK7	BK7	K75	P8	P9	PO
L	**100**	0	0	0	0	0	0	0	0	0	0	0	0	0	0	0	0
V3	0	**99.67**	0	0	0	0	0	0	0	0	0.33	0	0	0	0	0	0
V5	0.87	2.33	**84.30**	0.58	0.58	1.17	1.45	0.29	0.29	0.87	2.33	0	1.17	0	0.58	0.58	2.61
N5	0	0	0	**100**	0	0	0	0	0	0	0	0	0	0	0	0	0
N62	0	0	0	0	**100**	0	0	0	0	0	0	0	0	0	0	0	0
A66	0	0.28	0.57	0.28	0	**98.01**	0	0	0	0	0.29	0	0.57	0	0	0	0
B66	0	0	0	0	0	0	**99.67**	0	0	0	0	0	0	0	0	0.33	0
N7	0	0	0	0	0	0.31	0.31	**99.38**	0	0	0	0	0	0	0	0	0
S5	0	0	0	0	0	0	0	0	**100**	0	0	0	0	0	0	0	0
S6	0	0	0	0	0	0	0	0	0	**99.33**	0	0.66	0	0	0	0	0
S7	0	0	0	0	0	0	0	0	0	0	**100**	0	0	0	0	0	0
AK7	0	0	0	0	0	0	0	0	0	0	0	**100**	0	0	0	0	0
BK7	0	0	0	0	0	0	0	0	0	0	0	0	**100**	0	0	0	0
K75	1.96	0	0.33	0.65	0	0.33	0.33	1.30	0.33	0.65	0.98	0	0	**91.19**	0.65	0.65	0.65
P8	0	0	0	0	0	0	0	0	0	0	0	0	0	0	**100**	0	0
P9	0	0	0	0	0	0	0	0	0	0	0	0	0	0	0	**100**	0
PO	0	0	0	0	0	0	0	0	0	0.33	0	0	0	0	0	0	**99.67**

recurring in digital investigation. We used the dataset in [16], that is listed in Table 3. Because of the data we have, we considered the device detection task, as it was done in Section 4.3 for the *Dresden dataset*. Devices belonging to the same model (e.g., Nokia 6600) are treated as different cameras.

We perfomed three experiments, splitting each time the dataset in three groups. Table 10 shows the results obtained from the sensor noise based method, whereas Table 11 we report the results obtained from feature based approach. Experimental results show that sensor noise method outperforms the feature based on. Cameras found in a mobile phone has a worse optic than the cameras used in the *Dresden database*. This means that the amount of noise released by the devices in the pictures is higher, resulting in a stronger fingerprint able to discriminate better among different devices.

Table 11. Confusion matrix for the algorithm based on features, tested with the mobile phone dataset [16].

	L	V3	V5	N5	N62	A66	B66	N7	S5	S6	S7	AK7	BK7	K75	P8	P9	PO
								Inferred as									
L	**72.34**	0	0.33	0	0	0	27.33	0	0	0	0	0	0	0	0	0	0
V3	0	**66.67**	31.33	0	0	1	1	0	0	0	0	0	0	0	0	0	0
V5	0	18.02	**80.82**	0	0	1.16	0	0	0	0	0	0	0	0	0	0	0
N5	21.67	1	0.33	**22.67**	21	9.67	18	1	0.33	0.33	2	0	0	2	0	0	0
N62	0.93	9.24	5.87	0	**73.78**	2.16	7.71	0	0.31	0	0	0	0	0	0	0	0
A66	0	15.10	7.98	0	0	**72.08**	4.84	0	0	0	0	0	0	0	0	0	0
B66	0	4.33	0.67	0	0	11.67	**83.33**	0	0	0	0	0	0	0	0	0	0
N7	1.26	6.92	2.83	3.77	11.95	4.09	0	**65.10**	0.63	0	0.31	0	0	0.31	1.57	0.63	0.63
S5	0.67	19.67	0.67	0.33	20.67	0.33	0.33	3.67	**49.66**	0	2.33	0	0	0.33	0.67	0	0.67
S6	0	0	0	0	0.34	0	0.67	0	0	**99**	0	0	0	0	0	0	0
S7	3.33	4.67	1.33	0.33	42.67	0.33	2	0	5	0	**40.33**	0	0	0	0	0	0
AK7	0	0	0	0	0	0.49	0	0	0	0	0.49	**97.81**	1.21	0	0	0	0
BK7	1	0.67	0	1	0	2	0	0	0	0	0	**80**	15.33	0	0	0	0
K75	1.31	3.92	0	7.52	7.19	4.25	3.92	2.29	0.98	0.98	0.98	0	0	**66.33**	0	0.33	0
P8	0	27.24	8.01	0	0.32	16.67	7.05	0	0	0	0.64	0	0	0	**30.45**	4.49	5.13
P9	0	4.67	1.67	0	0.33	10	2	0	0	0	0.33	0	0	0	20.67	**51**	9.33
PO	0	**43**	9	0	0	16.34	1	0	0	0	0	0	0	0	0	0.33	30.33

5 Conclusions

In this paper we have presented a comparative study of two popular methods for source camera identification: sensor noise extraction method [4] and features extraction method [6,18]. We tested the performances of those two approaches with two dataset: the *Dresden dataset* [20] and the mobile phone dataset proposed by [16]. Our tests show the sensor noise approach outperforms the feature one. The reason in that the pattern noise imprinted on the pictures is more discriminative than the extracted features. Our finding are more evident in the mobile phones dataset. Optic in these devices are worse than the devices used to make the *Dresden Dataset*, resulting in a more evident and sensible fingerprint for the classification task. The only case the features based method outperformed the sensor noise one is discussed in Section 4.1, where the camera model has to be recognized. In the performed experiments, feature based methods are not able to classify the devices correctly, when the images taken for the same camera devices are grouped altogether. Morever, for the device identification problem, the feature methods was not able to provide a reliable response. Future works could focus on combining the methods to improve the results, as well as in extending these methods in order to perform blind source camera identification in video domain.

Acknowledgments. We would like to thank the authors of [12] for providing us their original implementation for feature extraction, as well as the authors of [16] who allowed us to use their database to perform the experimental comparison on mobile images.

References

1. Redi, J.A., Taktak, W., Dugelay, J.-L.: Digital image forensics: a booklet for beginners. Multimedia Tools and Applications **51**(1), 133–162 (2010)
2. Kee, E., Johnson, M.K., Farid, H.: Digital image authentication from JPEG headers. IEEE Transactions on Information Forensics and Security **6**(3), 1066–1075 (2011)
3. Piva, A.: An overview on image forensics. ISRN Signal Processing, Article ID 496701, 22 (2013)
4. Lukáš, J., Fridrich, J., Goljan, M.: Digital camera identification from sensor pattern noise. IEEE Transactions on Information Forensics and Security **1**(2), 205–214 (2006)
5. Gloe, T., Borowka, K., Winkler, A.: Feature-based camera model identification works in practice. In: Katzenbeisser, S., Sadeghi, A.-R. (eds.) IH 2009. LNCS, vol. 5806, pp. 262–276. Springer, Heidelberg (2009)
6. Gloe, T.: Feature-based forensic camera model identification. Transactions on Data Hiding and Multimedia Security **8**, 42–62 (2012)
7. Holst, G.C.: CCD arrays, cameras, and displays, 2nd edn. JCD Publishing & SPIE Press, USA (1998)
8. Janesick, J.R.: Scientic Charge-Coupled Devices. SPIE Press, USA (2001)
9. Chen, M., Fridrich, J., Goljan, M.: Digital imaging sensor identification (further study). In: Delp III, E.J., Wong, P.W. (ed.) Security, Steganography, and Watermarking of Multimedia Contents IX. Proceedings of the SPIE, vol. 6505 (2007)
10. Goljan, M., Fridrich, J., Filler, T.: Large scale test of sensor fingerprint camera identification. In: Proc. SPIE, Electronic Imaging, Security and Forensics of Multimedia Contents XI, pp. 18–22
11. Cooper, A.J.: Improved photo response non-uniformity (PRNU) based source camera identification. Forensic Science International **226**(1–3), 132–141 (2013)
12. Kharrazi, M., Sencar, H.T., Memon, N.: Blind source camera identification. In: 2004 International Conference on Image Processing, ICIP 2004, vol. 1, pp. 709–712 (2004)
13. Battiato, S., Bruna, A.R., Messina, G., Puglisi, G.: Image Processing for Embedded Devices. Bentham Science Publisher (2010)
14. Avcibas, I., Memon, N., Sankur, B.: Steganalysis using image quality metrics. Transaction on Image Processing **12**(2), 221–229 (2003)
15. Ismail, A., Bülent, S., Khalid, S.: Statistical evaluation of image quality measures. Journal of Electronic Imaging **12**(2), 221–229 (2003)
16. Celiktutan, O., Sankur, B., Avcibas, I.: Blind identification of source cell-phone model. IEEE Transactions on Information Forensics and Security **3**(3), 553–566 (2008)
17. Cristianini, N., Shawe-Taylor, J.: An introduction to support Vector Machines: and other kernel-based learning methods. Cambridge University Press, New York (2000)
18. Gloe, T., Böhme, R.: The dresden image database for benchmarking digital image forensics. In: Proceedings of the 25th Symposium on Applied Computing (ACM SAC 2010), vol. 2, pp. 1585–1591 (2010)
19. Webb, A.R.: Statistical Pattern Recognition, 2nd edn. John Wiley & Sons Ltd., November 2002
20. Gloe, T., Böhme, R.: The dresden image database for benchmarking digital image forensics. In: Proceedings of the 2010 ACM Symposium on Applied Computing, pp. 1584–1590 (2010)

Content-Fragile Commutative Watermarking-Encryption Based on Pixel Entropy

Roland Schmitz[1][✉], Shujun Li[2], Christos Grecos[3], and Xinpeng Zhang[4]

[1] Stuttgart Media University, Stuttgart, Germany
schmitz@hdm-stuttgart.de
[2] University of Surrey, Guildford, UK
[3] Sohar University, Sohar, Oman
[4] Shanghai University, Shanghai, China

Abstract. Content-fragile commutative watermarking-encryption requires that both the content-fragile image signature and the watermarking process are invariant under encryption. The pixel entropy, being dependent on first-order image statistics only, is invariant under permutations. In the present paper we embed semi-fragile signatures based on pixel entropy by using a histogram-based watermarking algorithm, which is also invariant to permutations. We also show how the problem of collisions, i.e. different images having the same signature, can be overcome in this approach, if embedder and encryptor share a common secret.

Keywords: Commutative watermarking-encryption · Content-fragile watermarking · Pixel entropy

1 Introduction

Encryption and watermarking are important techniques for the protection of digital media. While encryption serves to provide confidentiality, watermarks can be used to provide various security services ranging from integrity protection to source authentication and copyright protection. Content-fragile (or semi-fragile) watermarks try to strike the middle ground between exact authentication as provided by cryptographic hash functions or digital signatures, and robust watermarks that are hard to destroy by any image modification. They are supposed to survive benign operations like compression, but should be destroyed by modifications of the image content. In the most common way of content-fragile watermarking, the first step is to compute a content-fragile signature value, which is to represent the semantics of the image. The content-fragile signature is then embedded by some robust watermarking scheme. In the verification process, the watermark is extracted from the marked image and compared to the signature value computed from the marked image. Therefore, care must be taken that the watermarking proces does not influence the signature value. Very often, these watermarks are applied separately to small image parts, so that content modifications can be localized.

S. Battiato et al. (Eds.): ACIVS 2015, LNCS 9386, pp. 474–485, 2015.
DOI: 10.1007/978-3-319-25903-1_41

While there has beem some work in recent years on the problem of combining watermarking and encryption (CWE, see for example [1], [2], [4], [5],[6], and [8]), to the best of our knowledge no content-related watermarks commutative with encryption have been proposed so far. At first glance, however, it seems to be paradoxical to search for a content-fragile watermark that is commutative with encryption. After all, the encryption process is supposed to destroy the visual information from an image, so how can a content-related watermark survive this operation? However, in the past, there have been attempts to define content-fragile signatures which only involve first-order statistics of the image, but no localization information, like the mean histogram value [9] and the pixel entropy [11]. Obviously, this kind of signatures will be invariant under permutation ciphers. The same is true for watermarking strategies that are purely histogram based. In order to be able to combine these two approaches, the watermarking process must not change the histogram in such a way that the content-fragile signature is affected. This paper presents a feasible way to combine a special kind of content-related signature and a watermarking algorithm commutative with permutation ciphers, where the signature is based on the pixel entropy. A common problem with content-related signatures are collisions, i.e., different images having the same content-related signature. Particularly if the signature is based on the histogram alone, collisions are quite easy to find. We show how this problem can be avoided by involving secret information into the signature computation.

The rest of the paper is organized as follows: In Section 2 we discuss some basic properties of the pixel entropy we use in our CWE scheme. Section 3 describes the watermarking process with its three variants: The *localized version* is able to detect and localize content-related changes, the *collision-resistant version* trades localization for collision-resistance, and the *combined version* combines the features of the former two versions. In Section 4 we discuss commutativity of the three versions with encryption, and Section 5 gives some experimental results. Section 6 concludes the paper and gives directions for future research.

2   Properties of Pixel Entropy

In [11], the classical Shannon entropy of an information source [10] is re-defined as pixel entropy of the color channel c of an input image I:

$$PE(I,c) = \sum_{k=0}^{L} p_k \cdot \log_2(p_k),$$ (1)

where p_k ia the probability of the grey level k within the color channel c and L is the maximum pixel value. The pixel entropy has three interesting properties which make it useful for content-related commutative watermarking-encryption. Obviously, it is invariant under pixel permutations, meaning it does not change if the image undergoes a permutation-based cipher (**Property 1**). It is also invariant under permutations of the histogram bins of a colour channel (**Property 2**), because permuting the hi)stogram bins will permute the order of summation in (1), but will not change the pixel entropy. This implies that that the pixel entropy is invariant under the watermarking process described in Section 3.

Finally, the sensitivity of the pixel entropy with respect to changes in the grey values of single pixels is governed by the total number N of pixels in the image I (**Property 3**). In order to verify this, we assume that a single pixel has changed its grey value from j to i. Then the new probabilities are $\tilde{p}_i = \frac{n_i+1}{N}$ and $\tilde{p}_j = \frac{n_j-1}{N}$. A direct computation shows that the corresponding change in the pixel entropy is given by

$$\Delta PE = \frac{1}{N}\left(\log\left(\frac{n_i}{n_j}\right) + (n_i+1)\log\left(1+\frac{1}{n_i}\right) + (n_j-1)\log\left(1-\frac{1}{n_j}\right)\right)$$
$$\approx \frac{1}{N}\left(\log\left(\frac{n_i}{n_j}\right) + \frac{1}{n_i} + \frac{1}{n_j}\right), \tag{2}$$

as $\log(1+x) \approx x$ for small x.

As mentioned above, content-related signatures can be applied to small subimages to localize content modifications. If the pixel entropy is used for this purpose, the size of the subimages should be minimized for maximum sensitivity, because we have no control over n_i or n_j.

Note that invariance under permutation ciphers does not hold for the second order pixel entropy,

$$PE^2(I,c) = \sum_{i=0}^{L}\sum_{j=0}^{L} p_{ij} \cdot \log_2(p_{ij}), \tag{3}$$

where p_{ij} is the probability of ocurrence of the pair (i,j) of grey values within the colour channel c, because PE^2 is also a function of the pixel's scanning order.

3   Watermarking Process

The basic watermarking process closely follows the approach taken in [8] and [7] and is based on the idea of swapping histogram bins according to a secret watermarking key W_K [3]: For each watermark bit $w_i \in \{-1,1\}$, the algorithm randomly selects a certain histogram bin a_i and another bin b_i within a d-neighbourhood of a_i, taking W_K as initial seed. Here, d is a fixed parameter governing the tradeoff between robustness and transparency of the watermark. Histogram bins of equal height are not selected. Now, if $w_i = 1$, $hist(a_i) > hist(b_i)$ should hold, and if $w_i = -1$, $hist(a_i) < hist(b_i)$ should hold. If this is not the case, the two bins are swapped. For watermark extraction, the bins at the positions specified by W_K are compared. If a reference watermark is known before extraction, the authenticity of the image can be verified by computing the linear correlation of the reference mark and the extracted mark.

Here, a reference mark m is provided by the pixel entropies of the color channels. For embedding purposes, each pixel entropy is turned into an integer by first multiplying it by 10^4 and then quantizing it with a quantization factor q. More specifically, for a given input image I and colour channel c, the signature is calculated as follows:

$$m(I,c) = \left\lceil \frac{10^4 \times PE(I,c)}{q} \right\rceil \times q \qquad (4)$$

In the following embedding examples q has been set to 2. The 16 most significant bits of $m(I,c)$ are converted into a 16-bit bipolar bitstring $w(I,c)$ and embedded into the corresponding colour channel c by the procedure described above. It is important to note that this procedure does not affect the pixel entropy according to Property 2 given in Section 2. After detection, the three extracted 16-bit integers are concatenated and compared to the concatenated pixel entropies found in the color channels of the marked image by computing the linear correlation. An image is deemed unauthentic, if the linear correlation is below a certain threshold T. Assuming a balanced distribution of the bipolar bits in $w(I,c)$, the corresponding False Positive probability is [7]:

$$p(\text{False Positive}) = \left(\frac{1}{2}\right)^N \cdot \sum_{k=\lceil \frac{N}{2}(T+1)\rceil}^{N} \binom{N}{k}, \qquad (5)$$

where N is the length of the embedded mark. In what follows, we have set $T = 0.8$, while $N = 3 \times 16 = 48$ as discussed above. This gives a false positive probability of 7.57×10^{-10}. For a grey-scale image, we have $N = 16$ and a false positive probability of 2.59×10^{-4}. False negative probabilities, on the other hand, are notoriously difficult to estimate as it is not clear which attacks are performed on a marked image.

In what follows, we describe three variants of the general watermarking scheme described above. While in all variants certain subimages are marked, the variants differ in the way the subimages are formed.

3.1   Localized Version

The aim of the localized version is to identify subimages where image modifications have taken place. To this end, square subimages with a side length s are formed in a regular, non-overlapping fashion, then marked with their respective pixel entropies. Experience has shown that the minimum subimage size that can provide meaningful histograms and a sufficient embedding capacity is $s = 32$. This size therefore offers the most fine-grained localization of changes and the highest sensitivity to changes. As an example, the upper row of Figure 1 shows a plaintext image and the corresponding marked image in the localized version with a subimage size $s = 32$. The visual quality of the marked image is assessed by computing the Peak Signal to Noise Ratio (PSNR) and the Structural Similarity Index (SSIM, [12]). Next, the marked Lenna image was modified setting the grey values of 20 random pixels in the area between upper lip and nose to 0. Figure 1 (c) and (d) show the modified image and verified image, indicating the two subimages where the modifications have taken place. Specifically, in Figure 1(d), a regular subimage is rendered white if one of the random sub-subimages yields a correlation value $T < 0.8$.

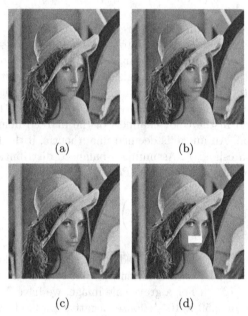

(a)   (b)

(c)   (d)

Fig. 1. (a) Original image; (b) Marked image (PSNR 43.82 db, SSIM 0.98); (c) Modified marked Lenna image; (d) Verified Lenna image.

3.2   Collision-Resistant Version

It is relatively easy to generate collisions, i.e. to generate different images that have the same pixel entropy. In principle, any permutation of the histogram bins will produce an image version with the same pixel entropy as the original image. While most of these permutations will destroy the watermark because embedder and detector are de-synchronized, the watermarking process can be made robust against cyclic shifts by a suitable calibration of the embedding and detection process [7]. In a cyclic shift of the histogram, the grey values of the pixels in the three colour channels undergo the following transformation:

$$P_{\text{attacked}}(i,j) = (P(i,j) + x) \mod 256, \tag{6}$$

where x is a positive or negative integer. Due to the wrap-up at the end of the histogram, cyclic histogram shifting may lead to visible changes of the image content, as Figure 2 shows, where two subimages of the Lenna image have been cyclically shifted by an amount of $x = 20$. The localized version introduced in the last subsection is unable to detect the different image contents, because of the

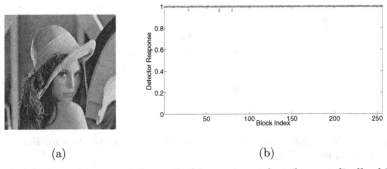

(a)   (b)

Fig. 2. (a) Two subimages of the marked Lenna image have been cyclically shifted; (b) Cyclic shifting goes unnoticed by the detector in the localized version.

unchanged pixel entropy of the subblocks and the robustness of the underlying watermarking process.

In order to cope with the collision problem, some secret information needs to be introduced into the pixel entropy computation. More specifically, let I be an original image of size $H \times W$. We generate an $m \times n$ array of subimages of size s, where $m = H/s$, $n = W/s$, by pseudo-randomly choosing pixels from the original image and assigning them to the subimages in turn, under control of a secret SplitKey. The resulting subimages are marked separately with their pixel entropy. After marking, the subimages are merged back to form the watermarked image. The complete Split-and-Merge process is described in Section 4 in greater detail, where we investigate its interplay with encryption.

Through the Split process, any local change in the watermarked image will be randomly distributed over the subimages and lead to corresponding changes of the pixel entropy, which cannot be foreseen by an attacker, unless she knows SplitKey. This fact is illustrated in Figure 3, where we compare the correlation values of the subimages of Figures 1(c) and 2(a) for the localized version and the collision-resistant version. Because of the distribution over subimages, however, localization information of changes is lost in this approach. Here, we have used $m = n = 2$, but different values for m and n are possible as well, especially if the original image is not square. In any case, s must be common divisor of H and W (see Section 5).

3.3   Combined Version

It is possible to combine the virtues of the localized and the collision-resistant version by splitting the image in a regular fashion first and applying the collision-resistant approach to the resulting subimages. This means that the subimages are split again randomly into a 2×2 array of sub-subimages. If we maintain the minimum size of $s = 32$ for the irregular sub-subimages, the regular subimages have a minimum size of $s_{reg} = 64$ in the combined version. The modified Lenna

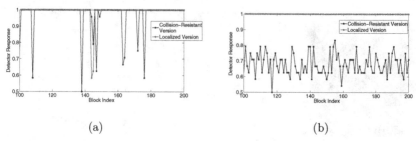

(a)   (b)

Fig. 3. (a) Detector Responses for modified Lenna image 1(c); (b) Detector Responses for modified Lenna image 2(a).

image shown in Figure 4(a), for example, has been split into an 8×8 array of regular subimages of size $s_{reg} = 64$ each. The subimages were further split into an 2×2 array of randomly formed sub-subimages which were watermarked afterwards. Both entropy-preserving and non-entropy preserving image modifications can be localized on subimage level (see Figure 4).

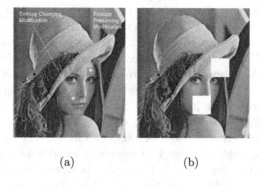

(a)   (b)

Fig. 4. (a) Modified marked Lenna image; (b) Verified Lenna image (Combined Version).

4   Commutativity with Encryption

Commutativity of the marking process with encryption means that

$$\mathcal{M}(\mathcal{E}_K(I), m) = \mathcal{E}_K(\mathcal{M}(I, m)) \tag{7}$$

holds, where $\mathcal{E}$ is the encryption function, K is the encryption key, I is the plaintext media data, $\mathcal{M}$ is the marking function and m is the mark to be embedded. In the next subsections, we discuss the issue of commutativity with encryption for the three watermarking variants introduced in Section 3.

4.1   Localized Version

The localized version is commutative to encryption, if the encryption function $\mathcal{E}$ is permutation based and is confined to the same regular subimages of size s as the watermarking process (see Fig. 5 (a)). In this case, encryption and watermarking commute at subimage level, because the watermarking process is purely histogram-based and does not include any components which are changeable by applying a permutation.

4.2   Collision-Resistant and Combined Version

The collision-resistant version splits the whole image randomly into subimages, while in the combined version first regular subimages are formed, which are split randomly afterwards. As both methods differ only in the size of subimages they are applied to (actually, the collision-resistant version can be seen as an instance of the combined method using a single large subimage), we can restrict our discussion to the collision-resistant method.

As in the localized version, one has to make sure, that the watermarking and encryption processes act on the same subimages. To this end, both marking function $\mathcal{M}$ and encryption function $\mathcal{E}$ have to use a common secret SplitKey which governs the random split process. More specifically, the encryption process has to include the same Split-and-Merge cycle as the marking process. As embedding and watermarking are not completely independent of each other anymore in this case, they may be called *quasi-commutative* instead.

To check whether encryption and watermarking actually commute if they share SplitKey, let us go through the encryption and marking processes for an original image I in detail:

- **Encrypt-then-Mark**
  A pixel P at position (r_I, c_I) within I with a pixel value g is selected by the random number generator and assigned to row r_A, column c_A in subimage A. Permuting subimage A sends the pixel to a different position (r_e, c_e) within A. The merging process will asssign this pixel to some position (i, j) within I, thus $\mathcal{E}(I)(i, j) = g$. When marking $\mathcal{E}(I)$, the split process will first assign position (i, j) to position (r_e, c_e) within subimage A. Marking A may change the pixel value to g_M, and merging back yields $\mathcal{M}(\mathcal{E}(I))(i, j) = g_M$.
- **Mark-then-Encrypt**
  The Split process assigns P to position (r_A, c_A) within subimage A. Marking changes P'spixel value to g_M. Merging back into I gives $\mathcal{M}(I)(r_I, c_I) = g_M$. Encryption assigns this pixel first to (r_A, c_A) within A by the Split process and then to (r_e, c_e) by permuting A. Merging back into I yields $\mathcal{E}(\mathcal{M}(I))(i, j) = g_M$.

Figure 5 shows the results of appliying a permutation cipher to the marked subimages for the three described versions of the marking process, i.e. the right-hand side of Eq. 7. The mark can be extracted from the encrypted image in the

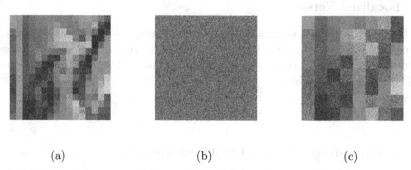

       (a)   (b)   (c)

Fig. 5. Marked, then encrypted Lenna image: (a) Localized version; (b) Collision resistant version; (c) Combined version.

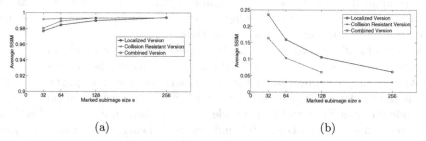

                (a)   (b)

Fig. 6. Average SSIM values for (a) watermarked images and (b) watermarked encrypted images with different subimage sizes

same way as from the plaintext image. In the collision-resistant and combined versions, however, `SplitKey` has to be known to the detector as well.

Note that although only the marked subimages are permuted, the random process used for splitting into subimages in Figures 5 (b) and (c) distributes the permutation further into the image. It is clearly visible that there is a tradeoff between cipher security on one hand (both in terms of key space and opacity of image features) and sensitivity and the ability to localize image changes on the other.

5   Experimental Results

In this section we report the results of applying the three versions of the watermarking process to a set of 25 test images with three different formats, namely $512 \times 768, 768 \times 512$ and 512×512. One of the test images is the Lenna image, the other 24 come from the Kodak true-color image database. As the subimage size must be a common divisor of height and width of the images, we investigated the influence of the possible subimages sizes $s \in \{32, 64, 128, 256\}$ on transparency of the watermark, opacity of the marked, encrypted images and on sensitivity of the mark with respect to pixel value changes within marked images.

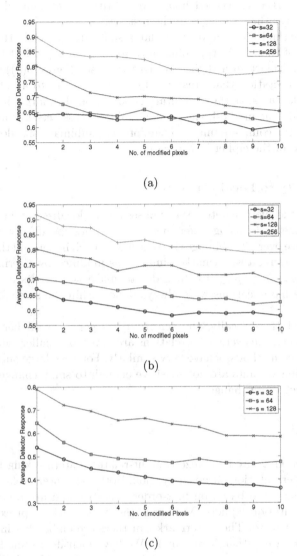

(a)

(b)

(c)

Fig. 7. Average detector responses for watermarked and modified images: (a) Localized Method; (b) Collision Resistant Method; (c) Combined Method

5.1 Visual Quality of Watermarked Images and Effectivity of Encryption

For Fig. 6, the 25 images of the test set were watermarked by the three variants, using different values for the subimage size s. The plot shows the resulting SSIM values, computed by comparing the original image to the watermarked image and the watermarked encrypted image, respectively. The plotted values have been averaged over the 25 images in the test set.

All three methods have a very similar visual quality, while the additional randomization of changes in the collision resistant seems to affect the perceptibility of the watermark in a slighty positive way (see Figure 6(a)). Figure 6(b) confirms the expectation that greater subimage sizes lead to a better concealment of visual features, as the permutations are applied to larger subimages. In the collision resistant method, the random split process acts like an additional permutation of the complete image. Therefore, the subimage size does not affect the effectiveness of the cipher in this case.

5.2 Sensitivity to Local Changes

Figure 7 shows the average detector responses for the localized and the combined watermarking methods, using different s-values. More specifically, the minimal detector response over all subimages is recorded for each image and then averaged over all images. Here, a watermarked image was modified by altering a number of pixels p, where $1 \leq p \leq 10$. In order to make the results as comparable as possible, the modifications were always done within the same 32×32 pixel subimage.

As predicted theoretically, the sensitivity is generally higher for smaller subimage sizes, i.e., the average correlations are lower for smaller subimage sizes. Overall, the three methods behave very similarly. For very large subimage sizes, the watermarking variants are not sensitive enough to small changes to be able to reliably detect those changes.

6 Conclusion

We have presented a way to realize content-related watermarking that is commutative with permutation based encryption. Both the content-related signature and the watermark are based on first-order statistics and are therefore invariant under permutation ciphers. Moreover, the watermarking process does not influence the signature. The watermark can therefore embedded into the same subimages which are authenticated by it. We have identified some fundamental tradeoffs between collision resistance and cipher security hand and the ability to locate content changes within the image. Our further research will focus on the question of robustness of the presented scheme against benign, content-preserving operations in the plaintext domain.

References

1. Battisti, F., Cancellaro, M., Boato, G., Carli, M., Neri, A.: Joint watermarking and encryption of color images in the Fibonacci-Haar domain. EURASIP J. Advances in Signal Processing, Article ID 938515 (2009)
2. Boato, G., Conotter, V., De Natale, F.G.B., Fontanari, C.: A joint asymmetric watermarking and image encryption scheme. In: Security, Forensics, Steganography, and Watermarking of Multimedia Contents X. Proc. SPIE, vol. 6819, p. 68191A (2008)
3. Chrysochos, E., Fotopoulos, V., Skodras, A.N., Xenos, M.: Reversible image watermarking based on histogram modification. In: Proc. 11th Panhellenic Conf. Informatics (PCI 2007), pp. 93–104 (2007)
4. Guo, J., Zheng, P., Huang, J.: Secure watermarking scheme against watermark attacks in the encrypted domain. Journal of Visual Communication and Image Representation 30, 125–135 (2015)
5. Lemma, A., Katzenbeisser, S., Celik, M.U., van der Veen, M.: Secure watermark embedding through partial encryption. In: Shi, Y.Q., Jeon, B. (eds.) IWDW 2006. LNCS, vol. 4283, pp. 433–445. Springer, Heidelberg (2006)
6. Lian, S.: Quasi-commutative watermarking and encryption for secure media content distribution. Multimedia Tools and Applications 43(1), 91–107 (2009)
7. Schmitz, R., Li, S., Grecos, C., Zhang, X.: Towards more robust commutative watermarking-encryption of images. In: 2013 IEEE International Symposium on Multimedia (ISM), pp. 283–286, December 2013
8. Schmitz, R., Li, S., Grecos, C., Zhang, X.: A new approach to commutative watermarking-encryption. In: De Decker, B., Chadwick, D.W. (eds.) CMS 2012. LNCS, vol. 7394, pp. 117–130. Springer, Heidelberg (2012)
9. Schneider, M., Chang, S.F.: A robust content based digital signature for image authentication. In: Proceedings of the International Conference on Image Processing, vol. 3, pp. 227–230, September 1996
10. Shannon, C.E.: A mathematical theory of communication. Bell System Technical Journal 27, 379–423 (1948)
11. Thiemert, S., Sahbi, H., Steinebach, M.: Using entropy for image and video authentication watermarks. In: Proc. SPIE, vol. 6072, pp. 607218-1–607218-10 (2006)
12. Wang, Z., Bovik, A.C., Sheikh, H.R., Simoncelli, E.P.: Image quality assessment: from error visibility to structural similarity. IEEE Transactions on Image Processing 13(4), 600–612 (2004)

A PNU-Based Technique to Detect Forged Regions in Digital Images

Giuseppe Cattaneo[1], Umberto Ferraro Petrillo[2],
Gianluca Roscigno[1(✉)], and Carmine De Fusco[1]

[1] Dipartimento di Informatica,
Università degli Studi di Salerno, 84084 Fisciano, SA, Italy
{cattaneo,giroscigno}@unisa.it, c.defusco1@studenti.unisa.it
[2] Dipartimento di Scienze Statistiche,
Università di Roma "La Sapienza", 00185 Roma, Italy
umberto.ferraro@uniroma1.it

Abstract. In this paper we propose a non-blind passive technique for image forgery detection. Our technique is a variant of a method presented in [8] and it is based on the analysis of the *Sensor Pattern Noise* (SPN). Its main features are the ability to detect small forged regions and to run in an automatic way. Our technique works by extracting the SPN from the image under scrutiny and, then, by correlating it with the reference SPN of a target camera. The two noises are partitioned into non-overlapping blocks before evaluating their correlation. Then, a set of operators is applied on the resulting *Correlations Map* to highlight forged regions and remove noise spikes. The result is processed using a multi-level segmentation algorithm to determine which blocks should be considered forged. We analyzed the performance of our technique by using a dataset of 4,000 images.

Keywords: Digital image forensics · Image integrity · Image forgery detection · Forgery localization · Pixel non-uniformity noise

1 Introduction

Nowadays, there are plenty of tools that allows even an inexperienced user to modify the content of a digital image without leaving a visible trace of alternation (i.e., *digital image forgery*). This practice may be harmful if used, e.g., to alter the digital evidences in a criminal trial or to support the spread of false news for political propaganda.

Several techniques have been proposed in the past years for detecting forged images. These typically work by searching for tracks released during the forgery process. Most of these techniques can determine if an image has been forged or not, but are not able to identify which parts of an image have been forged or require some sort of human intervention for this purpose (e.g. select a possibly forged area or its shape in advance).

S. Battiato et al. (Eds.): ACIVS 2015, LNCS 9386, pp. 486–498, 2015.
DOI: 10.1007/978-3-319-25903-1_42

In this paper we present a technique that is able to determine whether an image has been forged or not and, in case of forgery, it is able to automatically locate areas of the image that are likely to have been forged, provided that the camera originally used to take the image is available. It is a variant of the technique originally presented by Fridrich *et al.* in [8] and it is based on the analysis of the *Pixel Non-Uniformity* (PNU) noise, i.e., a characteristic noise of every camera. The ability of our technique for operating in an automatic and adaptive way has been obtained through a clever use of the multi-level segmentation process proposed by Otsu [12] and exploiting an accurate experimental calibration phase. Our technique supports the identification of *splicing*, *copy-move* and *inpainting* forgery operations.

Organization of the Paper. The rest of the paper is organized as follows. In Section 2 we briefly review the state of the art in the field of image forgery detection. In Section 3 we present and detail our technique. The assignment of several parameters for our technique has been done with an experimental calibration phase discussed in Section 4. In Section 5 we present the results of an experimental analysis involving our technique. Finally, in Section 6 we give some concluding remarks for our work.

2   State of the Art

The digital image forgery detection research field is concerned with the development of automatic or semi-automatic techniques able to determine any forgery of an image. These techniques can be *active* or *passive*. In the case of active techniques, a watermark placed initially in the image is useful to determine the authenticity of an image. Passive techniques cannot rely on the existence of any explicit signature on the image under scrutiny and, for this reason, they are often called *blind* techniques. In this paper we focus our attention on passive techniques.

Following the description presented in [13], we distinguish three general types of digital artifacts that can be used to detect the forgery of a digital image, regardless from the type of alteration: compression artifacts, alterations in the camera *Sensor Pattern Noise* (SPN) and re-sampling traces. Compression artifacts are caused by the encoding of a digital image through a *lossy* compression format, like the JPEG format. In this last case, we can detect forgeries by checking for the existence of the *Double Quantization* (DQ) effect in the histograms of the *Discrete Cosine Transform* (DCT) coefficients. Many of the algorithms using the DQ effect rely on the fact that the presence of this effect is caused by the initial compression that an image has undergone when saved for the first time, and by the second compression, performed when saving again the image after having forged it. One popular algorithm based on this approach is the one presented by Lin *et al.* in [11] and further discussed in [2,3]. This algorithm determines the authenticity of an image and it locates any forged region through a *probability map*; this is used to mark each 8×8 block of a target image with a probability of being forged. The algorithm then extracts from this map some features needed to train a dichotomous *Support Vector Machine* (SVM) classifier used to determine if the overall image is likely forged or not.

The sensor pattern noise (SPN) is the noise left by digital sensors on the images they capture. This noise is mainly due to some imperfections derived from the manufacturing process of the sensor and, thus, can be used to recognize the images that have been captured using a particular digital camera. The analysis of this noise has been extensively used for solving problems related to identification of the digital camera used to take a picture (see, e.g., [1,4,9]). However, there are also several forgery detection approaches based on the analysis of this noise. These typically work by calculating the statistical correlation between the SPN extracted from the image under scrutiny and the *reference sensor pattern noise*, which is a sort of fingerprint of a digital camera. Forged areas can be localized as those lacking the corresponding SPN. The most relevant contribution is the one presented by Fridrich *et al.* in [8]. This method assumes that either the camera that took the image is available to the analyst or at least some other non-forged images taken by the camera are available. The method comes in two variants. The first variant requires the investigator to manually select in advance the region of the image that is suspected of having being forged, then it is calculated the statistical evidence that the region was tampered. The second variant attempts to automatically determine the forged region without assuming any a priori knowledge about its location, shape, or size. This region is determined as the area with the lowest pattern noise presence in the image. This is achieved by sliding over the image a set of basic shapes with different orientations and size, and accumulating the lowest correlation values. Once the region is localized, it is inspected using the original algorithm. The computational cost of this variant is proportional to the number of shapes and sizes used for locating the tampered region. An improvement of this method has been presented by Fridrich *et al.* in [5]. Here the authors introduced a correlation predictor working on small blocks and trained by taking into account the intensity of the images taken with a given camera, the textures existing in the images being analyzed and the flattened areas existing in these images due to image processing operations. The predictor is obtained from blocks coming from a few non-forged images from the same camera. The same authors in [6] have presented another improved version of the previous method, while Chierchia *et al.* in [7] have recently proposed a strategy to improve the resolution of SPN-based forgery detection techniques. Namely, they used a spatially adaptive filtering technique with weights computed over a suitable pilot image to improve the resolution of the technique when evaluating the correlation between the SPN of an input image with the reference SPN. In particular, a guided filtering approach is adopted, obtaining performance much superior to the reference technique when small forgery areas are involved.

3   Our Technique

Our technique is inspired from the method presented by Fridrich *et al.* in [8] and it is based on the analysis of a particular type of *Sensor Pattern Noise*, the *Pixel*

Non-Uniformity (PNU) noise. Let I be an image under investigation and C the camera that has been used to take it, our technique works by first extracting the PNU noise from I and by correlating it with an estimation of the reference sensor pattern noise (*Reference Pattern, RP*) of C. The correlation is evaluated by first partitioning the two noise images into non-overlapping blocks. Then, a *Correlations Map* is built by correlating the corresponding pair of blocks of the two images. The out coming map may be very noisy and may incorrectly consider as forged small boundary regions. To overcome these problems we first apply a smoothing filter to remove *noise spikes* (i.e., isolated pixels with exceptionally high or low intensity). Then, we use an *opening operator* to further highlight large regions having homogeneous correlation values while leaving out smaller boundary regions. Once the Correlations Map has been post-processed, we use a multi-level segmentation algorithm to adaptively compute a set of thresholds that will be used, in turns, to determine which blocks should be considered forged. More details about this technique are provided in the rest of this section, while a set of pictures showing the different steps of our technique on three sample images is available in Figure 1.

Camera Sensor Pattern Noise Extraction (Setup). In this initial step we calculate the reference pattern of the camera C using the technique presented in [9]. Let $\mathcal{D}_C$ be a set of authentic images taken with C, called enrollment set. We extract the PNU noise estimation RN_e existing in each image $e \in \mathcal{D}_C$ and, then, we apply a pixel-by-pixel average operation on these noises to obtain an approximation of the reference pattern RP_C. The PNU noise is extracted from an image by first denoising it and, then, by subtracting from the input image the denoised one.

In the rest of the paper, unless stated otherwise, we assume that all the considered images have the same resolution. In addition, we only work on the green channel of the RGB color space.

Correlations Map Extraction (Step 1). In this step we first partition RN_I (i.e. the PNU noise estimation of the image I under scrutiny) and RP_C in blocks of size $s \times s$ pixels. Thus, if the two images have initially size $M \times N$, the partitioning will return two matrices RN'_I and RP'_C, composed of $M/s \times N/s$ blocks each. Then, we calculate the Bravais-Pearson Correlations Map between RN'_I and RP'_C using the approach defined in [9]:

$$corr(RN'_I(i,j), RP'_C(i,j)) = \frac{(RN'_I(i,j) - \overline{RN'_I(i,j)})(RP'_C(i,j) - \overline{RP'_C(i,j)})}{\|RN'_I(i,j) - \overline{RN'_I(i,j)}\| \, \|RP'_C(i,j) - \overline{RP'_C(i,j)}\|} \quad (1)$$

In Equation 1, the numerator is the covariance of $RN'_I(i,j)$ and $RP'_C(i,j)$, while the denominator is the product of their two standard deviations. The resulting index is in the range $[-1; +1]$, where values tending to $+1$ indicate that the block at index (i, j) has been taken by using C, while values tending to -1 indicate that it is not from C. This correlation is evaluated for each pair of blocks $b(i,j)$ of RN'_I and RP'_C, where $i \in \{1, ..., M/s\}$ and $j \in \{1, ..., N/s\}$. The resulting values will be used to fill a Correlations Map matrix (CM).

Smoothing (Step 2). Since the Correlations Map is noisy, in this step, we apply a mean filter to reduce the noise in CM. This filter replaces each pixel value in an image with the average value of its neighbors, including itself (for details, see [15]). We call CM_{filt} the resulting Correlations Map.

Homogeneous Regions Highlighting (Step 3) In this step, we apply an *opening operation* [10] to remove some of the foreground (bright) pixels from the edges of regions of foreground pixels existing in CM_{filt}. This operation preserves foreground regions that have a shape that is similar to the chosen structuring element, or that can completely contain the structuring element, while eliminating all other regions of foreground pixels. In our case, the opening operation uses a *disk structuring element.* We define CM_{open} the Correlations Map resulting from the application of the opening operation to CM_{filt}.

Multi-level Segmentation (Step 4). In this step, we mark the regions of I that are considered to be forged by analyzing the content of CM_{open}. For this purpose, we first determine the correlation threshold below which blocks have to be considered forged, using the multi-level segmentation process proposed by Otsu [12]. Let l the number of distinct levels, the multi-level segmentation returns a vector T, sorted in ascending order, containing l different thresholds. We select among these thresholds the smallest, $l_{min} = min(T)$. Then, for each block $b(i,j)$, we mark it as 0 (i.e., forged), if $CM_{open}(i,j) \le l_{min}$, and 1 (i.e., authentic), otherwise. The binary map obtained in this way is called $BinaryImage$. The benefit of using the multi-level segmentation algorithm is that a single fixed global threshold classifying the whole image in a binary way, could label as forged even blocks that are authentic, only because adjacent to forged blocks.

4   Experimental Calibration

The general technique presented in Section 3 required the calibration of several parameters. In our case, the assignment for these parameters was estimated through an empirical assessment conducted on a set of reference images.

4.1   Spatial Filter

The Correlations Map obtained during Step 1 may be very noisy. This may either be due to random noise or to other factors such as an oversaturated image or the presence of a strong texture in the portrayed scene. To overcome this problem we tried different smoothing filters and kernels. In the first case, we evaluated three different smoothing filters: gaussian filter (Figure 2b), median filter (Figure 2c) and mean filter (Figure 2d). The gaussian filter modifies the input signal by convolution with a gaussian function. The mean filter replaces

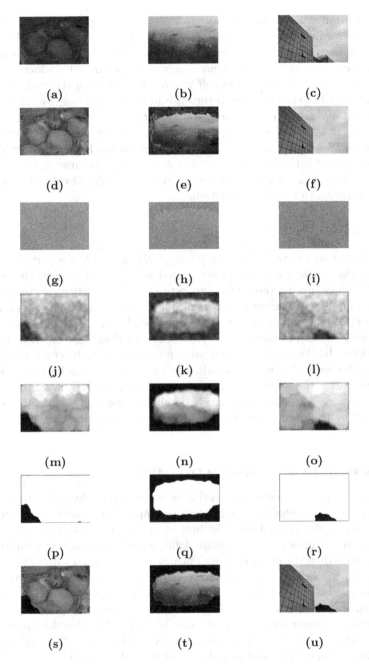

Fig. 1. (a, b, c) Authentic images. (d, e, f) Forged images with copy-move, splicing and inpainting respectively. (g, h, i) Correlations Maps (CMs). (j, k, l) Filtered Correlations Maps with mean filter (CMs_{filt}). (m, n, o) Filtered Correlations Maps after opening (CMs_{open}). (p, q, r) Binary Maps ($BinaryImages$). (s, t, u) Marked forged images ($MarkedImages$).

each pixel in an image with the average value of its neighbors, including itself. Finally, the median filter does the same, but by using the median value of the neighboring pixels. A qualitative analysis revealed that the median filter was the most effective in denoising the input image, but introduced artifacts near the edges of the image. The best trade-off was reached by using the mean filter.

Concerning the choice of the kernel size in the mean filter, we tried several different squared sizes for this parameter (i.e., 8×8, 16×16, 32×32 and 64×64). The results, presented in Figures 2e, 2f, 2g and 2h, show that when using values up to 16×16, the resulting map is still too noisy. If we use, instead, high values like 64×64, the resulting map is too smoothed because of the excessive approximation of the edges of the forged areas. Therefore we fixed 32×32 as the size of kernel to use in mean filtering.

4.2   Block Size

We recall that in our technique the pixels of RP and RN are partitioned into square blocks of size $s \times s$, before being analyzed. This introduces the problem about the block size to choose for this purpose. We investigated this problem through a qualitative analysis. We tried different assignments for s as reported in Figures 2i, 2j, 2k and 2l. Here we show the Correlations Maps obtained in Step 2 using various sizes of blocks ($s = 4, 8, 16, 32$). In these figures, each resulting Correlations Map has been denoised using a mean filter with kernel size 32×32. As it can be seen, if s is very small, the resulting Correlations Map is very noisy, even after the application of the mean filter. Instead, if s is very large, the Correlations Map loses too much detail because of the smoothing effect introduced by the mean filter. We found that the size giving the best results is $s = 8$.

4.3   Mathematical Morphology Operation

We decided to use the opening operation in our technique for separating objects that are poorly connected in the Correlations Maps while removing small regions. In our case, we determined that the best morphology operator to use is a disk kernel because it allows a more precise definition of the boundaries and of large forged regions than the other kernels. Then, we experimented with different sizes for this kernel, roughly equivalent to the radius of the disk kernel. According to our experimental results, shown in Figures 3a, 3b, 3c, 3d, 3e and 3f, the best performance are achieved when using a disk with radius 32. Using larger values would let the structuring element consider as part of the forged even adjoining regions that are not. Conversely, using values smaller than 32 would raise the probability of excluding some forged regions from the detection.

4.4   Segmentation Process

The multi-level segmentation algorithm used by our technique requires the indication of the number of levels to be used for partitioning the CM_{open}. We found

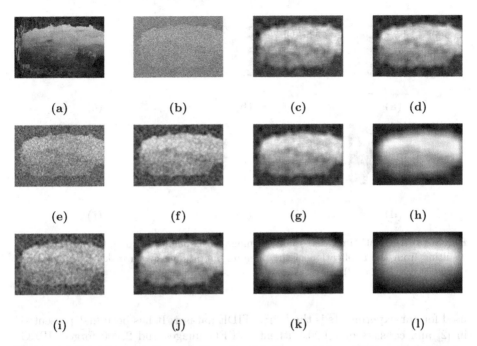

Fig. 2. (a) Forged image. (b, c, d) Gaussian, Median and Mean filter on Correlations Map. (e, f, g, h) Mean filters with kernel size $k \times k$, $k = 8, 16, 32, 64$. (i, j, k, l) Block size $s \times s$ of mean filtered Correlations Map with $s = 4, 8, 16, 32$.

in our experiments that a small number of levels (e.g., $l = 3$) is enough to obtain better performance that when using a single global threshold, but tends to give rise to false positives. We then tried using an increasing number of levels and found that, in our tests, the good partitioning is obtained with $l = 10$. Figure 4a shows an authentic image, while its forged counterpart is presented in 4b. Figures 4c, 4d, 4e and 4f show how the output, i.e. *BinaryImage*, changes according to the number of levels used to partition the input image.

5   Experimental Study

In this section we present the results of an experimental study we conducted to evaluate the effectiveness of our technique[1]. The study has been organized in two stages. In the first stage, we analyzed the localization performance of the technique by *per se*. In the second stage, we compared the performance of our technique to detect authentic and forged images with the one of the Lin *et al.* algorithm [11], a popular method used to detect the image forgery exploiting DQ effect.

The PNU filter used during the experiments is based on the one presented in [9] and it uses the Daubechies wavelet 16 with 8 vanishing moments. The dataset

---

[1] A reference implementation of our technique is available upon request.

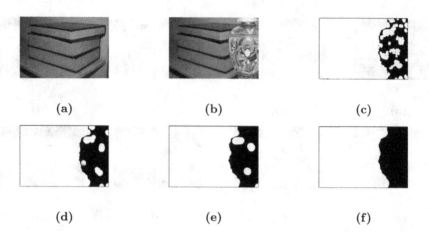

Fig. 3. (a) Authentic image. (b) Forged image with splicing. (c, d, e, f) Binary images resulting from the application of the opening operation using a disk with increasing radius ($r = 8, 16, 24, 32$).

used for our experiments is the UniSa TIDE dataset. It has been first presented in [2] and consists of 2,000 authentic JPEG images and 2,000 forged JPEG images. It was assembled from a set of 200 authentic raw images taken by using two digital cameras, Nikon D5100 and Nikon D600, and compressed in JPEG employing the following quality factors: $QF = \{100, 98, 95, 90, 85, 80, 75, 70, 65, 60\}$ (obtaining 2,000 authentic JPEG images). At this point, 200 of these images were chosen uniformly at random and were forged using splicing operations. The objects were pasted either from the same picture, from another image from the same digital camera, or from an image from a completely different camera. The resulting images were compressed again in JPEG employing the previous quality factors, obtaining 2,000 forged JPEG images. In our tests, for each of the two considered digital cameras, we used a first batch of 50 authentic images with low compression rate to calculate the reference pattern. We then used a second batch of 1,000 authentic images and 1,000 forged images for evaluating our technique in the experiments presented in this section.

5.1 Test 1: Forged Blocks Detection

In this test we investigate the ability of the proposed technique to correctly detect the forged blocks belonging to a set of reference images coming from the UniSa TIDE dataset. We report in Table 1 the outcome of the test. The overall performance of the technique seems to be very good as over the 74% of total forged blocks (True Positive Rate, TPR) and over the 87% of the total authentic blocks (True Negative Rate, TNR) were correctly classified. Conversely, the amount of authentic blocks erroneously classified as forged (False Positive Rate, FPR) and the amount of forged blocks erroneously classified as authentic (False Negative Rate, FNR) is relatively small. In sums, the *accuracy* (ACC) of the technique,

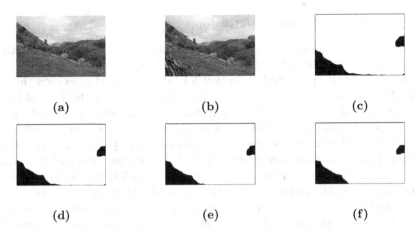

(a)   (b)   (c)

(d)   (e)   (f)

Fig. 4. (a) Authentic image. (b) Forged image using splicing. (c, d, e, f) *BinaryImages* resulting from partitioning using an increasing number of levels ($l = 5, 10, 15, 20$).

Table 1. Performance evaluation of our technique on a dataset made of $1,000$ authentic images and $1,000$ forged images. Performance is measured by considering the rate of blocks successfully classified as forged or not, grouped according to their quality factors. Concerning forged images, the quality factor (QF) indication refers to the one used to recompress them after the digital forgery.

Test	ACC	BAC	TPR	FPR	TNR	FNR
Images $_{QF \leq 75}$	0.79	0.76	0.72	0.20	0.80	0.28
Images $_{75 < QF \leq 90}$	0.89	0.82	0.72	0.08	0.92	0.28
Images $_{90 < QF \leq 100}$	0.90	0.85	0.79	0.08	0.92	0.21
Images $_{All}$	0.85	0.80	0.74	0.13	0.87	0.26

measured as the ratio between the number of correctly classified blocks and the total number of blocks, is good as it reaches the 85%. Since the number of authentic blocks in our dataset is, in the average, larger than the number of forged blocks, we also estimated the *balanced accuracy* (BAC) of our technique, as defined in [14]. Even in this case, the performance is good, as the balanced accuracy is approximately the 80%.

We further investigated the performance of our technique by examining how it changed according to the quality factors of the images being analyzed. The results, reported in the same table, suggest a strong correlation between the quality of the images and the ability to correctly classify authentic and forged blocks. Conversely, we analyzed the blocks that were not correctly recognized and found that some errors were due to oversaturated images or to pictures portraying outdoor environments with very complex subjects, like the foliage of trees. Many of these errors were due to blocks covering boundary regions between forged areas and authentic areas.

5.2   Test 2: Forged Images Detection

In this second test, we faced the more general problem of determining whether an input image is authentic or not. Since our technique operates at block-level and given the results presented in Section 5.1, we introduced a decision threshold so that we consider an image to be forged if more than the 10% of them blocks are classified as forged by our technique. The outcoming results have been compared with those of the Lin *et al.* algorithm [11], a popular technique for determining if an image is forged by exploiting the DQ effect (see Section 2). The two approaches have been evaluated on 2,000 testing images of the UniSa TIDE dataset (1,000 authentic and 1,000 forged) plus 2,000 other images used for training the SVM classifier used by the Lin *et al.* algorithm. The results show that our technique is able to correctly classify the 74% of the considered images, against the 55% achieved by the Lin *et al.* algorithm. If we leave out from the dataset all the images with a $QF \leq 75$, the recognition rate of our technique reaches the 83% of the images against the 59% of the Lin *et al.* algorithm.

6   Conclusion and Future Work

In this paper we proposed a non-blind passive image forgery detection technique based on the analysis of the Pixel Non-Uniformity noise, under the assumption that the camera used to take the image under investigation is available. Our proposal is based on the technique first proposed by Fridrich *et al.* in [8]. Differently other methods, such as [5,6], our technique does not require a preliminary training phase. In addition, our technique is able to operate on forged areas that are smaller than the ones used by other methods like [5–8].

We conducted a thorough experimental analysis of our technique using a reference dataset of 4,000 forged and authentic JPEG images. In the general case, our technique exhibits a very high accuracy, and easily outperforms the popular detection algorithm by Lin *et al.*. However, its performance deteriorates when working with images that are oversaturated, that have been saved using a low quality factor or that portray outdoor environments with very complex subjects. In fact, the SPN is absent in completely saturated regions and largely suppressed in dark areas. In addition, the denoising filter is less effective in removing the SPN in highly textured areas with many fine edges. Therefore, in these areas, the correlation will be naturally lower and care must be taken not to misinterpret such regions as forged. Moreover, our technique is only able to identify *splicing*, *copy-move* and *inpainting* forgery operations, while it does not support alterations of digital images like compensations (e.g., changing the color of an image), affine transforms (e.g., rotating and translating an image) and recompressions.

There are several directions worth to be investigated from here on. It could be explored the possibility to further improve the performance of our technique when locating the forged regions of an image by adopting graph-cut methods in order to better detect the boundaries of the forged regions. Similarly, it should be investigated the possibility to evaluate the results at a single-pixel level rather than at block-level. Moreover, it would be interesting to consider in our experimentation other approaches based on SPN, and to develop a very large scale data set of images featuring forgeries of different shapes and sizes.

References

1. Cattaneo, G., Faruolo, P., Ferraro Petrillo, U.: Experiments on improving sensor pattern noise extraction for source camera identification. In: Sixth International Conference on Innovative Mobile and Internet Services in Ubiquitous Computing (IMIS), pp. 609–616. IEEE (2012)
2. Cattaneo, G., Roscigno, G.: A possible pitfall in the experimental analysis of tampering detection algorithms. In: 17th International Conference on Network-Based Information Systems (NBiS), pp. 279–286 (2014)
3. Cattaneo, G., Roscigno, G., Ferraro Petrillo, U.: Experimental evaluation of an algorithm for the detection of tampered JPEG images. In: Linawati, Mahendra, M.S., Neuhold, E.J., Tjoa, A.M., You, I. (eds.) ICT-EurAsia 2014. LNCS, vol. 8407, pp. 643–652. Springer, Heidelberg (2014)
4. Cattaneo, G., Roscigno, G., Ferraro Petrillo, U.: A scalable approach to source camera identification over Hadoop. In: IEEE 28th International Conference on Advanced Information Networking and Applications (AINA), pp. 366–373. IEEE (2014)
5. Chen, M., Fridrich, J., Lukáš, J., Goljan, M.: Imaging sensor noise as digital X-ray for revealing forgeries. In: Furon, T., Cayre, F., Doërr, G., Bas, P. (eds.) IH 2007. LNCS, vol. 4567, pp. 342–358. Springer, Heidelberg (2008)
6. Chen, M., Fridrich, J., Goljan, M., Lukáš, J.: Determining image origin and integrity using sensor noise. IEEE Transactions on Information Forensics and Security 3(1), 74–90 (2008)
7. Chierchia, G., Cozzolino, D., Poggi, G., Sansone, C., Verdoliva, L.: Guided filtering for PRNU-based localization of small-size image forgeries. In: International Conference on Acoustics, Speech and Signal Processing (ICASSP) 2014, pp. 6231–6235. IEEE (2014)
8. Fridrich, J., Goljan, M., Lukáš, J.: Detecting digital image forgeries using sensor pattern noise. SPIE, Electronic Imaging, Security, Steganography, and Watermarking of Multimedia Contents VIII. 6072, 1–11 (2006)
9. Fridrich, J., Goljan, M., Lukáš, J.: Digital camera identification from sensor pattern noise. IEEE Transactions on Information Forensics and Security 1(2), 205–214 (2006)
10. Haralick, R.M., Sternberg, S.R., Zhuang, X.: Image analysis using mathematical morphology. IEEE Transactions on Pattern Analysis and Machine Intelligence 9(4), 532–550 (1987)
11. Lin, Z., He, J., Tang, X., Tang, C.K.: Fast, automatic and fine-grained tampered JPEG image detection via DCT coefficient analysis. Pattern Recognition 42(11), 2492–2501 (2009)
12. Otsu, N.: A threshold selection method from gray-level histograms. Automatica 11(285–296), 23–27 (1975)

13. Redi, J.A., Taktak, W., Dugelay, J.L.: Digital image forensics: a booklet for beginners. Multimedia Tools and Applications **51**(1), 133–162 (2011)
14. Sokolova, M.V., Japkowicz, N., Szpakowicz, S.: Beyond accuracy, F-Score and ROC: A family of discriminant measures for performance evaluation. In: Sattar, A., Kang, B.-H. (eds.) AI 2006. LNCS (LNAI), vol. 4304, pp. 1015–1021. Springer, Heidelberg (2006)
15. Yadav, P., Yadav, A.: Digital Image Processing. University Science Press, New Delhi (2010)

Depth and 3D

What Does One Image of One Ball Tell Us About the Focal Length?

Rudi Penne[1,2]($\boxtimes$), Bart Ribbens[1], Luc Mertens[1], and Paul Levrie[1]

[1] Faculty of Applied Engineering, University of Antwerp,
Salesianenlaan 90, 2660 Antwerp, Belgium
rudi.penne@uantwerpen.be
[2] Department of Mathematics, University of Antwerp, Antwerp, Belgium

Abstract. We reanimate the (sometimes forgotten) Belgian Theorems, and show how the *balls of Dandelin* can give us elegant proofs for geometric properties of perspective ball projections. As a consequence, we derive a new formula for computing the focal length by means of 1 image of 1 ball. By means of simulations we show the sensitivity of our formula in function of the ratio of the major axis to the minor axis of the elliptic ball image. This provides a measure of reliability and enables us to select the most appropriate ball image.

1 Introduction

It has been observed by other authors that images of balls (spheres) can be used for an intrinsic calibration of the used camera, as an alternative to the popular methods with planar grid patterns relying on [12] (Zhang's method). Mostly, knowledge about the size of the imaged balls is not needed, nor the spatial position of these balls, making these ball calibration methods rather user friendly. However, the user could be bothered by disturbing elements in the image (ball shadow, supporting table, suspending cable, etc...) that cause obstacles in the extraction of the elliptic edge of the ball image. However, nowadays there are good ellipse fitting algorithms on the market. We use [5] in our experiments, but we also want to mention [1,6,9,10].

Once the elliptic borders of one or more ball images are available, some or all camera intrinsics may be deduced from geometric properties of perspective ball projections. One of the first ball image calibrations can be found in [3], where the authors used the property that the line though the major axis of an elliptic ball image always contains the principal point. No proof for this property was provided in [3], but we will show that it is an immediate consequence of a classical theorem (Proposition 3). In [7] it is shown how to deduce the aspect ratio from ball images, and in [4] sphere images are used to calibrate a catadioptric camera.

The most complete ball image procedures for calibration that we met are [11], using 3 balls, and [8], using only one ball. Both articles rely on the determination of the image of the absolute conic (IAC).

The first objective of this paper is to make publicity for the Belgian Theorem (*balls of Dandelin*) (Theorem 1) by showing that this theorem enables us to

© Springer International Publishing Switzerland 2015
S. Battiato et al. (Eds.): ACIVS 2015, LNCS 9386, pp. 501–509, 2015.
DOI: 10.1007/978-3-319-25903-1_43

understand and prove the several geometric properties of ball projections that are used in several calibration publications in a uniform way. But our main contribution is to present a new formula to compute the focal length by means of one image of one ball (Proposition 5 in Section 3).

We evaluated this formula in Section 4 by means of simulations. We confirmed the following observation made by other authors [3,8,11]:
The sensitivity of the computation of the focal length strongly depends on the position of the ball image(s).
More precisely, we discovered that the quality measure for our formula is given by the ratio a/b of the main axes of the elliptic ball images. As a matter of fact $a/b = 1.03$ seems to be an experimentally based threshold, below which results become unreliable.

Camera lenses with a large field of view are able to capture ball images with a large a/b ratio, implying that they might be suitable for our focal length formula. This has been confirmed by real experiments.

2   Fundamental Facts of Elliptic Cone Sections

Let $\mathcal{B}$ be a ball centered at P with radius R. A pinhole camera captures that ball by a perspective projection of this ball from the camera centre O upon the sensor plane γ. This perspective image $\mathcal{E}$ is obtained by intersecting this plane γ with the cone $\mathcal{K}$ with top O, cone axis OP, and tangent to the ball. Notice that we may reduce $\mathcal{K}$ to the half cone that emanates from the camera centre O, directed toward the scene (ball). We also assume that we have a complete image of the ball, and hence that the sensor plane γ separates the camera O from the viewed ball. It was already observed by Apollonius in his *Konika* (225 A.D) that the conic section obtained in this way is an ellipse.

The reader should realize that this claim is not evident if one defines an ellipse (like Apollonius did) by means of two foci, or by means of one focus and a *directrix* (Figure 1). In Konika also other positions of the intersecting plane are considered, yielding hyperbolic and parabolic sections, but these are not relevant in this article.

By symmetry it is easily seen that the points of tangency where the tangents from O meet the ball $\mathcal{B}$ form a circle on this ball in a plane perpendicular to the cone axis OP. This implies that $\mathcal{K}$ effectively is a **circular** cone (the type considered by Apollonius). Furthermore, the *Theorem of Dandelin-Quételet* applies. This theorem, sometimes called the "Theorem of the Belgians", is probably the most elegant tool to prove the conic section result of Apollonius ([2]).

Theorem 1. *Let γ be a plane that intersects a circular cone $\mathcal{K}$ in a closed curve $\mathcal{E}$, and $\mathcal{B}_1$ and $\mathcal{B}_2$ be the two spheres (Dandelin balls) that are simultaneously tangent to the cone $\mathcal{K}$ and the plane γ (see Figure 2). Then $\mathcal{E}$ is an ellipse and the Dandelin balls touch the plane γ in the two foci of $\mathcal{E}$. Furthermore, the plane β_i that contains the circle $\mathcal{C}_i = \mathcal{K} \cap \mathcal{B}_i$, intersects the plane γ in a directrix of $\mathcal{E}$.*

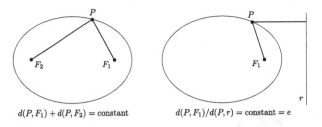

$$d(P, F_1) + d(P, F_2) = \text{constant} \qquad\qquad d(P, F_1)/d(P, r) = \text{constant} = e$$

Fig. 1. In the left diagram, an ellipse is defined as the locus of points having a constant sum of distances to two fixed foci. In the right diagram, we define an ellipse as the set of points such that the ratio of the distance to a fixed focus relative to the distance to a fixed directrix is a constant number (called the *excentricity e*, with $e < 1$ for ellipses).

Proof. Figure 2 should suffice.

This Belgian theorem has similar formulations concerning hyperbolic and parabolic sections, but we only need this version. As a start, it provides a simple proof for a fundamental but important property of ball images.

Proposition 2. *Let γ be a plane that intersects the circular cone $\mathcal{K}$ in an elliptic section $\mathcal{E}$. If α is the plane through s, being the cone axis of $\mathcal{K}$, and perpendicular to γ, then α contains the major axis of the ellipse $\mathcal{E}$.*

Proof. Let $\mathcal{B}_1$ be one of both Dandelin balls associated with the cone $\mathcal{K}$ and the elliptic section $\mathcal{E}$ (right diagram of Figure 2). Further, let β_1 denote the plane through $\mathcal{C}_1$, the circle of tangency where $\mathcal{K}$ touches $\mathcal{B}_1$. So, β_1 meets the intersecting plane γ in the directrix r of the ellipse $\mathcal{E}$. Since α contains the cone axis s, that is perpendicular to the plane β_1, we know that $\alpha \perp \beta_1$. Furthermore, $\alpha \perp \gamma$, implying that α is perpendicular to the directrix $r = \beta_1 \cap \gamma$.

On the other hand, α contains the centre M_1 of the ball $\mathcal{B}_1$, because this centre belongs to the cone axis s. Consequently, α contains the line l through M_1 perpendicular to the plane γ, which is tangent to the ball $\mathcal{B}_1$. So, l meets γ in the point of tangency, being F_1, whence α contains F_1 as well.

Finally, because we deduced that α contains a focus of $\mathcal{E}$ and is perpendicular to a directrix of $\mathcal{E}$, the plane α intersects γ in a line that carries the major axis of $\mathcal{E}$.

An important consequence for computer vision can easily be deduced now. This result already appeared in [3], but without a proof (and nowhere else, to our best knowledge):

Proposition 3. *Let $\mathcal{E}$ be the image of a ball with centre P by a pinhole camera with centre O. Further, let C denote the principal point in the sensor plane γ, and let Q denotes the intersection of the line OP with γ. Then the line w carrying the major axis of $\mathcal{E}$ contains both Q and C.*

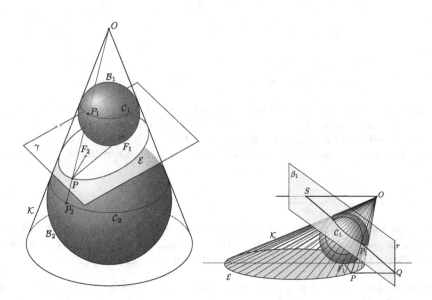

Fig. 2. The proof of Theorem 1. In the left diagram one can see that $d(P,F_1) = d(P,P_1)$ and $d(P,F_2) = d(P,P_2)$, whence $d(P,F_1) + d(P,F_2) = d(P_1,P_2) = $ constant. The right diagram shows that $d(P,F_1)/d(P,r) = d(P,P_1)/d(P,Q)$, and from triangle similarity we observe that $d(P,P_1)/d(P,Q) = D(O,P_1)/D(O,S) = $ constant.

Proof. Consider the plane α of Proposition 2. So, the line of intersection w of α with the sensor plane γ contains the major axis of $\mathcal{E}$. Clearly, w also contains $Q = OP \cap \gamma$ because OP is exactly the axis of the cone $\mathcal{K}$, belonging to α. Futhermore, by construction $\alpha \perp \gamma$, so α contains the focal axis Z (as it is perpendicular to γ), and therefore $C = Z \cap \gamma \in \alpha \cap \gamma = w$.

3   A Closed form Formula for the Focal Length from One Image of One Ball

Another curious consequence of Theorem 1 and Proposition 2 restricts the camera position O for a given ball image $\mathcal{E}$ to the "reciprocal hyperbola" of $\mathcal{E}$ (Figure 3).

Proposition 4. *Let $\mathcal{E}$ be the image of a ball, captured in the sensor plane γ by a pinhole camera with centre O. Then O belongs to the reciprocal hyperbola $\mathcal{H}$ of $\mathcal{E}$. More precisely, if α is the plane through the major axis of $\mathcal{E}$ and perpendicular to γ, then $\mathcal{H}$ lies in α, with foci equal to the major tops of $\mathcal{E}$, and with tops equal to the foci of $\mathcal{E}$.*

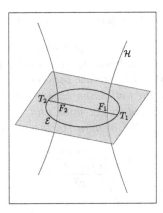

Fig. 3. An ellipse and the associated reciprocal hyperbola.

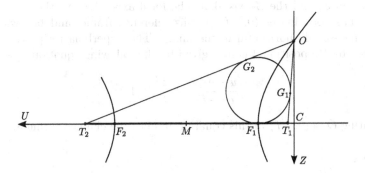

Fig. 4. The camera centre O is constrained to lie on a hyperbola with foci equal to the ellipse tops T_1 and T_2. Indeed, the difference $d = |OT_2| - |OT_1|$ is a constant determined by the ellipse.

Proof. The argument is in fact completely covered by Figure 4, that represents the plane α that meets the sensor plane γ perpendicularly in the major axis (with tops T_1 and T_2) of $\mathcal{E}$. From Proposition 2 we know that α contains the axis s of the cone with top the camera centre O that is tangent to the viewed ball. The part of this cone above the sensor plane intersects the plane α in the triangle OT_1T_2. Furthermore, the intersection of α with the upper Dandelin ball gives the inner tangent circle for this triangle (*incircle*), touching the major axis $[T_1, T_2]$ in focus F_1 (Theorem 1). The other points of tangency of this incircle are called G_1 (on $[O, T_1]$) and G_2 (on $[O, T_2]$). From an elementary circle property we see that

$$|OG_1| = |OG_2|, \ |T_1F_1| = |T_1G_1|, \ |T_2G_2| = |T_2F_2|$$

implying that $|OT_2| - |OT_1| = d$ where $d = |T_2F_1| - |F_1T_1|$ is a constant determined by the elliptic image $\mathcal{E}$. By definition, O lies on the hyperbola with foci T_1 and T_2, more precisely on the component with top F_1.

As a consequence, we can now prove the main result of this paper.

Proposition 5. *Assume an elliptic image $\mathcal{E}$ of a ball by a perfect pinhole camera with square pixels (removed non-linear lense distortions, corrected aspect ratio, no skewness). Let δ_M denotes the distance between the principal point C and the centre M of $\mathcal{E}$, let a denote the half major axis and b denote the half minor axis of $\mathcal{E}$ (all three of them measured in the same unit, e.g. in pixels). Then we can compute the focal length f of the camera (in the chosen unit) by means of the following formula:*

$$f = b\sqrt{\frac{\delta_M^2 - a^2 + b^2}{a^2 - b^2}}$$

Proof. In the plane α represented by Figure 4 we can choose a reference frame (U, Z) with the origin in the principal point C, the positive U-axis containing the major axis of $\mathcal{E}$, and the Z-axis along the focal axis. Observe that the camera centre O has coordinates $(0, -f)$ in this reference frame, and be aware that U is not necessarily horizontal in the image. The hyperbola reciprocal to $\mathcal{E}$ as introduced by Proposition 4 is now given by the following equation:

$$\frac{(u - \delta_M)^2}{a^2 - b^2} - \frac{z^2}{b^2} = 1$$

Substituting $O = (0, -f)$ in this equation implies the claimed formula.

Remarks

- Of course, one focal length formula does not provide a complete calibration procedure. However, it might be useful in applications with varying focal length but more or less fixed aspect ratio and principal point. This requires the presence of "reliable balls" in the image. In Section 4 we will evaluate our formula and circumscribe the conditions imposed on the ball image for obtaining accurate and precise results for the focal length f.
- We suggest to use our focal length formula as a module in a more complete calibration procedure based on the image of one or more balls, in the same spirit as [3,8,11]. As a matter of fact, our formula is suitable to be plugged in the procedure of [3]:
  1. If we have at least three (preferably non-overlapping) balls in the given image, then the aspect ratio can be recovered as the vertical dilatation factor that guarantees that the carriers of the major ellipse axes are concurrent (which should, according to Proposition 3).
  2. Once again due to Proposition 3, the principal point is computed as the common point of intersection of the major axes of the available ball images.
  3. Finally, the focal length is computed by the formula of Proposition 5.

4   Evaluation of the Focal Length Formula

We simulated a 2000×2000 camera with $f = 2000$ (in pixel units say). The elliptic images are obtained by means of the perspective projection of a given ball on the sensor plane. Without loss of generality we can restrict to ball images with centres in the first quadrant of the image. Edge uncertainties and quantization pixel errors are modelled by isotropic Gaussian noise.

A first observation is that the quality of the recovered (accuracy and stability) strongly depends on the position of the projected ball in the image. Figure 5 illustrates that the spread and the mean value of repeated computations of the focal value both become cumbersome in case the image of the ball lies close to the principal point. For each position and noise level, the mean value and the standard deviation of the computed f has been considered for a run of 100 trials. The principal point was assumed to be known. The ellipse fitting through the noisy ball image was carried out by the algorithm of [5].

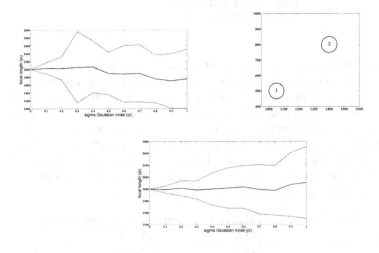

Fig. 5. These two graphs plot the recovered $f = 2000$ for both ball images separately as function of increasing noise level: the mean value plus and minus 1 standard deviation. The computation of f by means of the ball closest to the principal point (left graph) appears to be unreliable.

The reason for the significant difference in performance is the fact that the formula of Proposition 5 is sensitive for small ratios a/b (ratio of major axis to minor axis of the elliptic image). For ball 1 in Figure 5 we have $a/b = 1.0016$, for ball 2 we have $a/b = 1.0393$. Table 1 shows the increasing quality of the recovered focal length for increasing ratio a/b. This table has been composed by experiment with the described simulated camera. Observe that a ratio a/b close to 1 corresponds to a ball image that tends to be a circle, which takes place when the focal axis is directed toward the centre of the viewed ball.

Table 1. Accuracy and precision of the recovered focal length for increasing a/b ratio.

a/b	σ	mean(f)	std(f)
1.0003	0.5	992.3	280.2
1.0003	1.0	681.6	288.8
1.0016	0.5	1979.1	490.3
1.0016	1.0	1589.1	516.7
1.0050	0.5	1994.7	297.4
1.0050	1.0	1996.2	376.0
1.0062	0.5	1973.4	182.7
1.0062	1.0	2017.5	415.5
1.0124	0.5	2014.1	99.1
1.0124	1.0	1999.4	155.7
1.0210	0.5	2006.4	47.7
1.0210	1.0	2015.4	135.5
1.0308	0.5	1999.7	38.8
1.0308	1.0	2017.1	83.5
1.0393	0.5	2000.3	34.1
1.0393	1.0	2019.8	67.7

Testing our formula in a real experiment is more difficult, because then the focal length computation interferes with other procedures (principal point detection, aspect ratio correction, radial distortion removal). Simulations show that our formule is sensitive in misplacements of the principal point, more precisely, the error in f seems to be proportional to the error on the principal point relative to the distance δ_M, as suggested by the formula (Proposition 5). Not surprisingly, the best results have been obtained by a camera lens with a broad field of view (uEye UI-2230RE-M-GL, 1024 × 768, with a 3.5mm lens). We give the results for four ball images that realize the ratio $a/b \approx 1.06$:

	manufacturer (mm)	Zhang calib (mm)	our formula (mm)
Ball 1	3.5	3.65	3.6117
Ball 2	3.5	3.65	3.6044
Ball 3	3.5	3.65	3.6035
Ball 4	3.5	3.65	3.6157

5   Conclusions and Future Work

We blew the dust away from the old theorem of the Belgians, and showed the use of the balls of Dandelin in understanding the geometry of ball projections. As a consequence we gave a new elegant proof for the fact that the line through the major axis of the elliptic image of a given ball always contains the principal point.

Furthermore, we deduced an easy formula for computing the focal length from this elliptic image. In order to apply this theoretical result in practice, it should be incorporated in a global procedure, because we need a priori knowledge of the aspect ratio and the principal point. As future research we plan to design such a complete procedure, using one or more balls in one image. At the moment it is clear that the performance of our formula improves if the distance of the ball image to the principal point increases. Decentered positions minimize the effect of errors on the principal point as well as the effect of noise on the edge pixels. This second observation is explained by the larger a/b ratio realized by balls that are viewed away from the image centre. We suggest to select ball images with a a/b ratio of at least 1.03. As a consequence, our formula is best suitable for lenses with a large field of view. The impact of non-linear lens distortions will also be investigated in the future.

Another trajectory for further research is to investigate how we can avoid to compute the fitting ellipse, and how certain stable characteristics of the ball image (such as the ellipse centre) can be directly derived to serve in reconstruction and calibration applications.

References

1. Ballard, D.H.: Generalizing the hough transform to detect arbitrary shapes. Pattern Recognition **13**(2), 111–122 (1981)
2. Dandelin, G.P.: Mémoire sur quelques propriétés remarquables de la focale parabolique. Nouveaux mémoires de l'Académie Royale des Sciences et Belles-Lettres de Bruxelles, T. **II**, 171–202 (1822)
3. Daucher, D., Dhome, M., Lapreste, J.: Camera calibration from spheres images. In: Eklundh, J.-O. (ed.) ECCV 1994. LNCS, vol. 800, pp. 449–454. Springer, Heidelberg (1994)
4. Duan, H., Yihong, W.: A calibration method for paracatadioptric camera from sphere images. Pattern Recogn. Lett. **33**(6), 677–684 (2012)
5. Fitzgibbon, A., Pilu, M., Fisher, R.: Direct least-square fitting of ellipses. In: Proceedings International Conference on Pattern Recognition, pp. 253–257 (1996)
6. Ho, C.T., Chen, L.H.: A fast ellipse/circle detector using geometric symmetry. Pattern Recognition **28**(1), 117–124 (1995)
7. Penna, M.A.: Camera calibration: A quick and easy way to determine the scale factor. IEEE Trans. Pattern Analysis and Machine Intelligence **13**(12), 1240–1245 (1991)
8. Teramoto, H., Xu, G.: Camera calibration by a single image of balls: From conics to the absolute conic. In: Asian Conference on Computer Vision, pp. 499–506 (2002)
9. Xie, Y., Ji, Q.: A new efficient ellipse detection method. In: Int. Conf. on Pattern Recognition, pp. 957–960 (2002)
10. Yin, P.Y., Chen, L.H.: A new method for ellipse detection using symmetry. J. Electronic Imaging **3**, 20–29 (1994)
11. Zhang, H., Wong, K.K., Zhang, G.: Camera calibration from images of spheres. IEEE Trans. on Pattern Analysis and Machine Intelligence **29**(3), 499–503 (2007)
12. Zhang, Z.: Flexible camera calibration by viewing a plane from unknown orientations. In: Proceedings of the Fifth International Conference on Computer Vision, pp. 666–673 (1999)

Visual Localisation
from Structureless Rigid Models

Guido Manfredi[1,2]([⊠]), Michel Devy[1,2], and Daniel Sidobre[1,2]

[1] CNRS, LAAS, 7 Avenue du Colonel Roche, 31400 Toulouse, France
gmanfred@laas.fr
[2] University de Toulouse, UPS, LAAS, 31400 Toulouse, France

Abstract. Visual rigid localisation algorithms can be described by their model/sensor input couple, where model and input can either be 2-D or 3-D sets of points. While Perspective-N-Point (PnP) solvers directly solve the 3-D/2-D case, to the best of our knowledge there is no localisation method to directly solve the 2-D/3-D case. This work proposes to handle the 2-D/3-D case by expressing it as two successive PnP problems which can be dealt with using classical solvers. Results suggest the overall method has comparable or better precision and robustness than state of the art PnP solvers. The approach is demonstrated on an object localisation application.

Keywords: Modelling · Localisation · Motion · Structure · PnP · RGB-D

1 Introduction

Visual rigid localisation methods, hereafter shortened to localisation methods, compare a scene's known model to a sensor input and compute the motion between the scene frame and the sensor frame. The model and input are made of 2-D or 3-D points.

Depending on the type of points, 2-D or 3-D, used as model/input, localisation methods can be arranged in four families. In the following, the four families are presented and illustrated through representative works. Table 1 sums up the families and associated works.

In the 2-D/2-D case, the model and input points are 2-D projections of unknown 3-D reference points. The classical approaches are based on finding the fundamental matrix [7], in the uncalibrated case, or the essential matrix [10], in the calibrated case. However, these methods lack precision and they may have mathematical flaws which introduce degenerate cases [1].

The 3-D/3-D methods use two different sets of 3-D points, with different frames, as model and input. Such localisation problem can be solved, for example, with the Iterative Closest Point (ICP) approach [9]. In the ICP method, the pose of a set of 3-D points to another is determined iteratively by matching closest

© Springer International Publishing Switzerland 2015
S. Battiato et al. (Eds.): ACIVS 2015, LNCS 9386, pp. 510–520, 2015.
DOI: 10.1007/978-3-319-25903-1_44

points. These approaches are computationally intensive and building a model with 3-D points can prove challenging, even with 3-D sensors.

According to [11], combining 3-D and 2-D data yields greater robustness and precision than those of the two previous families, so the rest of this work focuses on mixed families.

In the 3-D/2-D case, the model is composed of 3-D reference points and the 2-D input points are projections of the reference points on a camera image plane. This localisation family requires solving the Perspective-N-Point (PnP) problem. Various solutions to this problem will be presented in the next section.

The 2-D/3-D case has gained importance with the advent of cheap RGB-D cameras providing 3-D input. In this case, the model is made of 2-D projections of unknown 3-D reference points, and the input is a set of 3-D points in the camera frame. The principal benefit of such approach is that a single image is sufficient to build the model. The main obstacle stems from the fact that no 3-D frame is initially associated to the scene, thus it is not possible to find a motion between the scene frame and camera frame. To the best of our knowledge, there is no localisation algorithm available to directly solve this case.

This paper proposes a localisation algorithm for the 2-D/3-D case, with a calibrated or uncalibrated sensor. The problem is expressed as two successive PnP problems and solved with classical PnP solvers. The proposed solution robustness and precision are compared with 3-D/2-D localisation methods based on state of the art PnP solvers.

Next section presents the state of the art in PnP solvers. Section 3 introduces the proposed localisation method. An experimental setup is described in Section 4 to compare our approach with classical methods based on PnP solvers. Section 5 presents and discusses the results. Finally, Section 6 concludes this article and opens on future work.

Table 1. Works illustrating the use of the four families of localisation techniques and their hypothesis.

Work	Model	Input	Calibrated
[7]	2-D	2-D	Yes
[10]	2-D	2-D	No
[9]	3-D	3-D	No
[8]	3-D	2-D	Yes/No
Our	**2-D**	**3-D**	**Yes**

2 Related Work

When a set of 3-D reference points, expressed in a reference frame, and their 2-D projections on a camera image plane are available, with known calibration, a PnP solver allows retrieving the motion between the reference frame and the camera frames. Solvers can be separated into iterative and non-iterative methods.

This work focuses on non-iterative methods as they are faster and thus more appropriate for real-time applications [8].

Nevertheless, this comparison considers one popular iterative method developed by Lu et al. [6] which computes iteratively the rotation and translation using SVD.

In their work [4], Li et al. introduce the RPnP solver. They propose to divide the 3-D reference points into 3-points subsets, express the problem for each subset as a polynomial and then create a cost function from the sum of squares of these polynomials. The solution correspond to the optimum of this cost function.

Zheng et al. suggest a more precise method dubbed OPnP [14]. In this method, the rotation is expressed as a non-unit quaternion, thus relaxing the optimization problem constraints. The whole problem can then be solved with a Grobner basis solver. The main benefit is that it is a global optimization which can handle any singular case and will find all possible solutions. The main drawback being that when various solutions are available, it is not possible to tell which is the correct one. It is interesting to note that in their results, when various solutions are available, the authors select the solution closest to the ground truth in a L2 norm sense. This is not possible for an actual problem.

Finally, the authors of [3] show that a Direct Least Square (DLS) approach can be applied. They propose to use a Cayley-Gibbs-Rodriguez parametrization for the rotation. Relaxing scale constraints, it is possible to express the scale and translation as a function of the rotation. It is then possible to find the rotation with a least square approach and, from it, compute the translation and scale.

The aforementioned methods work well in the 3-D/2-D case. However, they are not applicable directly in the 2-D/3-D case. The next section shows how a 2-D/3-D problem can be formulated as two successive PnP problems and solved with any of the previous solvers.

3   Localisation with a Structureless Model

In the 2-D/3-D case, no scene frame, nor 3-D points, are initially available in the model, hence the term structureless model. The first step is to create a scene frame S, once and for all, with a first 3-D input. Then, localisation is possible for subsequent inputs.

Consider a set of 2-D points in the image plane of a perspective camera C_1. Then, a depth camera C_2 provides a set of corresponding 3-D points, for example by matching natural features from C_1 and C_2, with coordinates expressed in C_2. The goal here is to find the SC_2 motion. However, as explained earlier, there is no frame S associated to the scene, so localisation is not possible.

In order to make localisation possible, the 3-D points from C_2 are used to arbitrarily define S. By construction, the SC_2 motion is known. Then, the 3-D points from C_2 are expressed in frame S. Thereupon, the scene has an associated frame and 3-D points expressed in it. With corresponding 2-D points from C_1, it is now possible to use a PnP solver to determine the SC_1 motion once and for all.

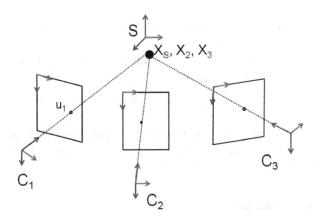

Fig. 1. Illustration of the proposed localisation method. Though various points are necessary for motion computation, for clarity a single 3-D point X_S and its projection u_1 are considered. The point u_1, on C_1's image plane, form the model. The input is made of X_2, the point X_S expressed in C_2, and X_3, the point X_S expressed in C_3. First, a frame S is created from X_2. Then, the motion SC_1 is estimated using u_1 and X_2. Finally, the motion C_3C_1 is computed using u_1 and X_3. With SC_1 and C_3C_1, one can retrieve the desired motion SC_3

When a new set of 3-D points is available from a new depth camera C_3, one finds the corresponding 2-D points in C_1's image plane. These 3-D/2-D correspondences allow solving a PnP problem to obtain the C_3C_1 motion. Since the SC_1 motion is known, computing the SC_3 motion is straightforward. The whole process is illustrated in Figure 1.

From a computational point of view, the process can be split in three steps. First, offline modelling, where 2-D points from the first image plane are computed and added to the model. As only 2-D data is required to build the model, it can be built from any camera or from the Internet, provided calibration data is available. Second, online modelling, where a camera input allows defining a scene frame and computing the SC_1 motion. Third, online localisation, where a new camera input allows computing the motion between the scene and this new camera. In the following, each step is described in more detail.

3.1   Offline Modeling

The starting data is a set u_1 of 2-D points. In the pinhole camera model, u_1 verifies the projective relationship,

$$u_1 = KP_1X_S, \tag{1}$$

where K is C_1's intrinsic parameters matrix, P_1 is the SC_1 motion and X_S is the set of 3-D points corresponding to u_1, expressed in the S frame. In this equation, K is known but P_1 and X_S are unknown, they will be determined in the next step.

3.2   Online Modeling

A new depth camera C_2 provides a set X_2 of 3-D points expressed in C_2, associated to 2-D points u_1 learned in the previous step. A scene frame is arbitrarily defined at the barycentre of X_2 and for simplicity the SC_2 rotation is set to identity. With P_2 being the SC_2 motion,

$$X_S = (P_2)^{-1}X_2, \tag{2}$$

This equation allows computing X_S, the 3-D points in the scene frame, from X_2. Then any PnP method allows solving Equation 1 to get P_1. The matrix P_1 is saved in the model and represents the SC_1 motion.

3.3   Online Localisation

Now that P_1 is known, it is possible to localise a new depth camera C_3, from which a set of points X_3 is acquired. Let's suppose the correspondences between u_1 and X_3 are known, then adapting Equation 2 to this new camera and combining it with Equation 1 gives the localisation formula,

$$u_1 = KP_1(P_3)^{-1}X_3, \tag{3}$$

where P_3 is the SC_3 motion, the u_1 are known from the offline model, K is known a priori, P_1 is known from the online modelling step and the X_3 are a set of input points expressed in C_3 frame. Again, any PnP method allows computing $P_1(P_3)^{-1}$. Then, P_3 can be directly obtained.

Note that only K, the intrinsic parameters of C_1, are needed. Calibration data from cameras C_2 and C_3 are not necessary.

3.4   Uncalibrated Case

When K is not available, for example when the image is taken from the internet with no EXIF data available, the intrinsic parameters must be determined on the fly. This is done at the online modelling step. Instead of using a PnP solver to recover P_1, an auto-calibration method is used to compute $T_1 = KP_1$. Then, T is decomposed into K and P_1 and the online localisation step can be done normally. In order to compute T_1, the most general approach is the Direct Linear Transform (DLT) [2] which uses a least-square approach to approximate the coefficients of T_1. However, under some hypothesis other methods can be used. For example, if the optical center position can be approximated from the images dimensions in pixels, then Tsai's method provides an efficient solver. Finally, there is a direct relationship which allows recovering exactly K and P_1 from T_1 The precision loss due to the approximation of T_1 is evaluated below.

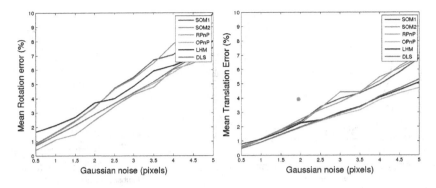

Fig. 2. Mean rotation and translation errors for six points and a noise with standard deviation varying between 0.5 and 5 pixels.

This approach allows using as model a simple image, calibrated or uncalibrated. It enables to use the billions of images available online to build a partial or full model of almost any textured object.

4   Experimental Setup

To assess the robustness and precision of the proposed localisation method, four simulation experiments are set-up. Two of them estimate the robustness against noise and the precision when the number of corresponding points (u_1,X_2) and (u_1,X_3) vary. The third experiment compares the precision of the uncalibrated solution with the precision of the calibrated one.

In order to simulate data as close as possible to real ones, the 3-D reference points should be realistically projected on camera's image planes. To ensure this, the general idea is to define a cuboid in space from which the 3-D points will be picked. Then, cameras are created at random poses such that they see the whole cuboid. Finally, points are randomly picked in the cuboid and projected with noise onto the camera image planes.

The first step is the computation of the minimum distance z, between the camera and the cuboid's center so that the cuboid is engulfed in the camera's field of view. A maximum distance Z, is chosen arbitrarily while keeping it low enough to avoid the planar case due to distance. To ensure random pose, while keeping the camera oriented to the cuboid, a random point A is picked inside the cuboid and a random point B between the spheres of diameter z and Z centred on the cuboid center. To obtain the camera frame, an orthonormal basis is created from $\mathbf{BA}$. This process is done for each required camera, three in this case. Finally, n points are randomly created inside the cuboid and projected on each camera plane with a certain amount of zero-mean Gaussian noise. The points and their projections constitute the simulation data.

In these experiments, the cuboid is a cube of side 2 and $Z = 10$. To be consistent with previous work's experiments [14], in the first experiment n is set

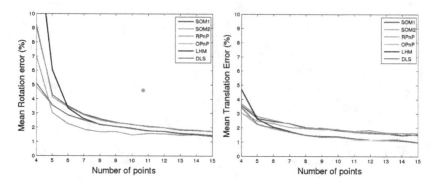

Fig. 3. Mean rotation and translation errors for a noise with standard deviation of two pixels and a number of points going from 4 to 15.

to 6 while the noise standard deviation σ varies between 0.5 and 5. In the second experiment, $\sigma = 2$ and n varies between 4 and 15. Each experiment is run 1000 times and the results show the mean error over all runs.

In the real world case, the test object is chosen with an arbitrary shape. The object is modelled from a single image taken with a calibrated RGB camera. This image is described with sift features [5]. The SiftGPU library [13] is used in order to speed up the computation. The matching is done by brute force on gpu and only mutual matches are considered. A Xtion Pro live sensor is used to acquire RGB-D images of the object under different points of view. No calibration data are needed for this sensor. Again, sift features are extracted from the images. All points having a NaN depth are filtered out and the remaining ones are matched against the object's model. The first RGB-D view is used for the online modelling step, this step needs to be done only once. All subsequent views can be used for online localisation, they allow computing the object-camera pose. For online modelling and online localisation, transforms are computed using the EPnP algorithm [8], as it is readily available in OpenCV, and refining the result with an iterative Levenberg-Marquardt. Processing one frame on a consumer grade laptop takes a mean time of 200ms.

For all the experiments, the precision of the proposed methods are compared with the state of the art PnP solvers : RPnP, OPnP, DLS and LHM. For the two calibrated experiments, our approach is based on solving two PnP problems, both are solved using the RPnP solver, as it is the only non-iterative method providing a single solution. Indeed, OPnP and DLS can provide various solutions with no way to discriminate the correct one. For more insight into the working of our method two results are provided: the online modelling error SOM1 and the online localisation error SOM2. For the two uncalibrated experiments, our approach is based on solving an uncalibrated problem, with Tsai's autocalibration method [12] method and a PnP problem using the RPnP solver, as for the calibrated case.

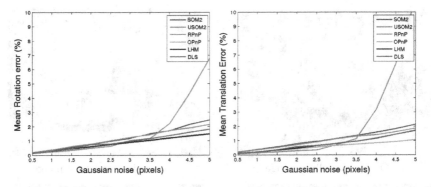

Fig. 4. Mean rotation and translation errors for fifty points and a noise with standard deviation varying between 0.5 and 5 pixels.

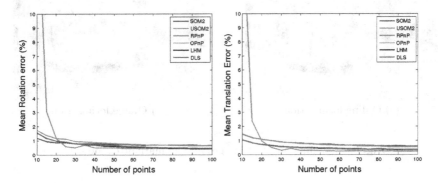

Fig. 5. Mean rotation and translation errors for a noise with standard deviation of two pixels and a number of points going from 10 to 100.

5   Results and Discussion

5.1   Calibrated Case

The results in Figure 3 and 2 show that SOM1, the modelling error, follows the behaviour of RPnP, the underlying PnP solver. Globally, the error decreases with the number of points available and increases with the noise. Regarding SOM2, the online localisation error, its translation error closely follows RPnP performances. However, when increasing the number of points or the noise, the rotation error is lower than the ones of the other solvers.

One could expect our method to perform at best as well as the underlying PnP solver, which is the case for the translation error. However, the rotation error is significantly lower than the one of the underlying PnP method and lower than the ones of state of the art solvers. This could be explained empirically by the fact that our method uses more data than a single PnP solver: a scene-camera transform, a set of 3-D points and a set of 2-D points, are required for the calculus. Moreover, it seems reasonable to think that when a PnP solver is

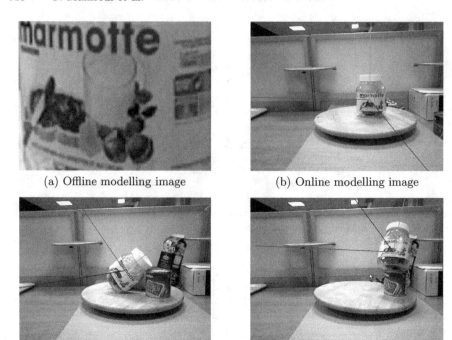

(a) Offline modelling image   (b) Online modelling image

(c) Online localisation   (d) Online localisation

Fig. 6. Modelling and test images for the marmottela object.

applied to the result of a previous PnP solver, the result is further refined. Finally, the fact that the frame associated to the scene is the 3-D points barycentre may provide some normalisation to the points coordinates, thus reducing numerical approximations.

5.2   Uncalibrated Case

In the first uncalibrated experiment (Figure 4), the rotation and translation errors remain low, lower than the PnP solver's for $\sigma < 3.5$. Then, for $\sigma > 3.5$, it quickly grows and at $\sigma = 3.75$ it is higher than the error of any other method. It keeps raising as noise increases. In the second uncalibrated experiment (Figure 5), the errors are high with less than twenty points. With twenty points and more, the error quickly diminish to an error lower to the state of the art PnP solver's.

Note that none of these methods use a noise reduction approach, like RANSAC for example. However, the autocalibration method computes a new camera intrinsic parameter from noisy points, i.e. which takes into account the noise. The autocalibration process can be understood as finding the image-to-camera pose that minimize reprojection error. So the resulting camera suffers from less noise. This can explain why USOM2 has lower error than the other methods. And this points to the fact that autocalibration can be used to diminish noise influence. However, these results also put forward the limits of such methods. Indeed, when there are not enough points ($n < 20$) or too much noise ($\sigma > 3.5$), the autocalibration approach can't find a noise reducing solution.

5.3   Modelling with a Calibrated Camera

To illustrate the proposed method in a concrete object localisation case, we proceed to an experiment on regular objects with a calibrated camera. Figure 6 (a) (b) are the two images needed to build and complete the model. Figure 6 (c) (d) show localisation examples. Note in Figure 6 (b) that the object frame which is set up at this online modelling stage is not necessarily aligned with the object shape. Nevertheless, it allows estimating the object motion as long as the current image matches the offline modelling image.

6   Conclusion

This paper tackles the localisation problem when the model is made of 2-D points and the input of 3-D points. Though finding a direct solution seems hard, this work shows that it is possible to express the problem as two PnP problems which can be solved with classical PnP solvers. The benefits of this approach are twofold, the model can be built from calibrated still images only and the overall precision is comparable or better than state of the art PnP solvers. Future work includes bridging the gap between image categorisation and object localisation. Image categorisation learning is done on images, if the same images allow localisation, then it is possible to use advanced categorisation algorithm to recognise objects and then localise them with the presented method.

References

1. Basta, T., Rudas, I., Mastorakis, N.: Mathematical flaws in the essential matrix theory. In: Proceedings of the WSEAS International Conference on Recent Advances in Computer Engineering, WSEAS (2009)
2. Faugeras, O.D., Luong, Q.T., Maybank, S.J.: Camera self-calibration: theory and experiments. In: Sandini, G. (ed.) ECCV 1992. LNCS, vol. 588, pp. 321–334. Springer, Heidelberg (1992)
3. Hesch, J.A., Roumeliotis, S.I.: A direct least-squares (DLS) method for PnP. In: 2011 IEEE International Conference on Computer Vision (ICCV), pp. 383–390. IEEE (2011)
4. Li, S., Xu, C., Xie, M.: A robust O(n) solution to the perspective-n-point problem. IEEE Trans. Pattern Anal. Mach. Intell. **34**(7), 1444–1450 (2012)
5. Lowe, D.G.: Object recognition from local scale-invariant features. In: The Proceedings of the Seventh IEEE International Conference on Computer Vision, vol. 2, pp. 1150–1157. IEEE (1999)
6. Lu, C.P., Hager, G.D., Mjolsness, E.: Fast and globally convergent pose estimation from video images. IEEE Trans. Pattern Anal. Mach. Intell. **22**(6), 610–622 (2000)

7. Luong, Q.T., Faugeras, O.D.: The fundamental matrix: theory, algorithms, and stability analysis. Int. J. Comput. Vis. **17**(1), 43–75 (1996)
8. Moreno-Noguer, F., Lepetit, V., Fua, P.: Accurate non-iterative O(n) solution to the PnP problem. In: IEEE 11th International Conference on Computer Vision, ICCV 2007, pp. 1–8, October 2007
9. Newcombe, R.A., Davison, A.J., Izadi, S., Kohli, P., Hilliges, O., Shotton, J., Molyneaux, D., Hodges, S., Kim, D., Fitzgibbon, A.: Kinectfusion: real-time dense surface mapping and tracking. In: 2011 10th IEEE International Symposium on Mixed and Augmented Reality (ISMAR), pp. 127–136. IEEE (2011)
10. Nistér, D.: An efficient solution to the five-point relative pose problem. IEEE Trans. Pattern Anal. Mach. Intell. **26**(6), 756–770 (2004)
11. Scaramuzza, D., Fraundorfer, F.: Visual odometry [tutorial]. IEEE Robot. Autom. Mag. **18**(4), 80–92 (2011)
12. Tsai, R.Y.: A versatile camera calibration technique for high-accuracy 3d machine vision metrology using off-the-shelf tv cameras and lenses. IEEE J. Robot. Autom. **3**(4), 323–344 (1987)
13. Wu, C.: SiftGPU: a GPU implementation of scale invariant feature transform (SIFT) (2007). http://cs.unc.edu/~ccwu/siftgpu
14. Zheng, Y., Kuang, Y., Sugimoto, S., Astrom, K., Okutomi, M.: Revisiting the PnP problem: a fast, general and optimal solution. In: 2013 IEEE International Conference on Computer Vision (ICCV), pp. 2344–2351. IEEE (2013)

Optical Sensor Tracking and 3D-Reconstruction of Hydrogen-Induced Cracking

Christian Freye, Christian Bendicks,
Erik Lilienblum, and Ayoub Al-Hamadi[⊠]

Institute for Information Technology and Communications,
Otto von Guericke University, 39106 Magdeburg, Germany
ayoub.al-hamadi@ovgu.de

Abstract. This paper presents an approach, which combines a stereo-camera unit and ultrasonic sensors to reconstruct hydrogen-induced crack (HIC) three-dimensional locations. The sensor probes are tracked in the images and their 3D position is triangulated. The combination with the ultrasonic measurement leads to a determination of the crack position in the material. To detect varying crack characteristics, different probes have to be used. Their measurements are combined in a common coordinate system. To evaluate the method, a milled reference block was examined and the results are compared to the ground-truth of the block model.

Keywords: Sensor-tracking · 3D-Reconstruction · Material inspection

1 Introduction

Since many years ultrasonic testing is an important utility to detect flaws in different sound-conducting materials. It is a non-destructive testing technique, which is based on the propagation of ultrasonic waves in the object. The main advantages are high accuracy, absence of hazardous radiation, flexibility of the measurement devices and the inspection of integrated components. In particular, the examination of components is important, in which the opposite side is not accessible (e.g. corrosion detection in pipes).

Ultrasonic testing has been extensively studied in recent years, which results in a great number of ISO/CEN standards for a wide field of application. Beside the two "classical" methods, which are pulse-echo and through-transmission, there are about 50 special testing methods. Especially, in the field of automated measuring of great areas (e.g. in automobile or aviation industry) large technological progress was made. In [1] an algorithm for automated defect classification was presented. The author(s) used pulse-echo ultrasonic testing and a Bayes classifier to detect defects in adhesively bonded joints. An automated approach for phased array ultrasonic testing (PAUT) of nozzle welds was presented in [2]. A comparison of PAUT and single beam measurements in an automated system

© Springer International Publishing Switzerland 2015
S. Battiato et al. (Eds.): ACIVS 2015, LNCS 9386, pp. 521–529, 2015.
DOI: 10.1007/978-3-319-25903-1_45

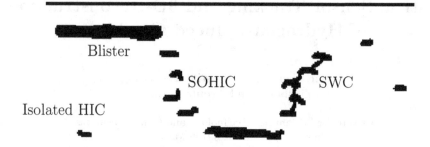

Fig. 1. Schematic representation of Hydrogen Induced Cracking (HIC), Stress Oriented HIC (SOHIC) and Stepwise Cracking (SWC) and Blisters.

for testing bars can be found in [3]. An automated air-coupled robot ultrasonic imaging system is introduced in [4], which works without water coupling.

For the detection of Hydrogen-Induced Cracking (HIC) their different characteristics have to be known. Fig. 1 gives an schematic overview of possible cracks. Blisters are a planar cavity formed as the result of hydrogen charging. Stress Oriented HIC is made up of a series of HIC cracks that are stacked perpendicularly in the direction of through wall cracks. They can easily lead to failure if the individual cracks get connected. The result will be a step-wise cracking (SWC), which can affect the stability of the material. To detect these cracks, the pulse echo method can be used. Horizontal cracks are detected by vertical probes and SWC/SOHIC cracks can be detected by 45° shear wave probes. The analysis of A-scans gives an overview for the appearance of hydrogen-induced cracks.

A method for tracking a hand-held sensor in combination with pulse-echo measurements of the wall-thickness of pipes was presented in [5]. An other approach is the use of PAUT probes [6]. There are different measuring systems available on the market from brands like Olympus, GE or United NDT. A PAUT probe consists of many ultrasonic transducer. Each of them can be pulsed independently, which allows the testing with varying beam angles. The advantage of this technique is, that many beams are reflected from potential cracks back to the transducer. This leads to a good detection rate of HIC at manual inspection. But on the other side, the signal processing is very complex and the evaluation requires high experienced technicians. The obtained results of PAUT consist mostly of S-scan or sectorial scan images. These images represent a two-dimensional cross-sectional view from a series of A-scans with respect to time delay and refracted angle. The vertical axis represents the depth and the horizontal axis the width of the test object. The evaluation of the measurement results in different two-dimensional views, which were created by the examiner. Both, TOFD and PAUT systems lead to a vague statement about the exact positioning of cracks in the material, because the sensor position is not located precisely. Furthermore, the examination of crack growth over a long time is difficult to manage. Because of lacking accurate position data of cracks, it is hard to make conclusions about the crack growth.

The main purpose of the present paper is to show the feasibility of crack detection with multiple single beam ultrasonic probes and store their position in a defined 3D coordinate system. Therefore, we extend the classical ultrasonic examination with a stereo camera system as mentioned in [5]. This is used for optical tracking of ultrasonic probes and triangulation of their position in the world frame. The position of the probes and their ultrasonic measurements are combined in a local coordinate system of the test object and lead to a novel three-dimensional view of defects in the material. Furthermore, the use of a fixed local coordinate system facilitates the comparison of different measurements, which allows the analysis of crack growth in time.

2   Experimental Procedure

The following section describes the consecutive steps for HIC reconstruction. The used camera model is introduced and the triangulation of 3D points is explained. Then, the local coordinate system is defined and the calculation of crack locations is illustrated.

2.1   Calibration and World Coordinate System

A pinhole camera model was used for this approach. To determine the relationship between 3D world coordinates and their projection on the image plane, the internal and external camera parameters have to be estimated. Therefore, the two cameras were calibrated separately with a test field and Tsai's method for the bundle block adjustment [7]. The result was a 3×3 calibration matrix K, which encapsulates the intrinsic camera parameters. The relationship between the homogeneous images coordinates $\tilde{x}$ and the camera coordinates $\boldsymbol{X_C} = (X_C, Y_C, Z_C)^T$ can be described as follows [8]:

$$\tilde{x} = (u, v, w)^T = K \cdot \boldsymbol{X_C} \tag{1}$$

The extrinsic camera parameters correspond to a rotation matrix R and a translation vector t, because in general the world coordinate frame and the camera coordinate frame are not aligned. Let $\boldsymbol{X_W} = (X_W, Y_W, Z_W)^T$ be a three-dimensional point in the world reference frame, then the corresponding point X_C in the camera coordinate frame is calculated with:

$$X_C = R \cdot X_W + t \tag{2}$$

Now, the mapping of a 3D object point on the image plane can be described by the combination of Eqs. 1 and 2 as:

$$\tilde{x} = P \cdot \widetilde{X_W} \tag{3}$$

with $P = K \cdot [R|t]$ as the 3×4 projection matrix [8]. In order to compute three-dimensional object points from image coordinates, an ambiguity along the Z-axis of the camera coordinate system exists. To solve this problem, corresponding points in the images of two cameras are needed.

2.2 Feature Detection and Tracking

Feature detection is used to find corresponding points p and p' in two images. In this approach circular markers were applied but also other features, which can be detected robustly, could be appropriate. To find circular markers on the image plane, the Förstner operator [9] was used. The algorithm extracts circular points from gray value images with sub-pixel accuracy. This is important for the later reconstruction of 3D coordinates. Correspondences between two camera images $\mathcal{I}$ and $\mathcal{I}'$ are found with the help of epipolar geometry. The ray from the projection center O through p is re-projected on $\mathcal{I}'$, known as epipolar line. The corresponding point p' lies on that line, which reduces the search space ideally to one dimension. The found correspondences p and p' are utilized to triangulate 3D points in the world frame. The two rays back-projected from image points p and p' lie in a common epipolar plane, which is passing through the two projection centers. Thus, the two rays will intersect in a point X_W, which correlate to the feature points in the world frame. The resulting 3D points are used for further calculation.

In the next step, the transformation $T_{LW} = \{q_{LW}, t_{LW}\}$ between the local object frame and the world frame is determined. T_{LW} consists of the rotation quaternion $q_{LW} = a + bi + cj + dk$ and the translation vector t_{LW}. As seen in Fig. 2 the test object is a block with attached markers on the top. Their positions x_i in a defined local object frame are well known. With the found marker in the images, the corresponding 3D coordinates X_i in the world frame are triangulated. The mapping between x_i and X_i can be described as follows:

$$\begin{aligned}
X_i &= (b^2 + a^2 - c^2 + d^2)x_i + 2(bc - ad)y_i + 2(bd + ac)z_i + t_x \\
Y_i &= 2(ad + bc)x_i + (a^2 - b^2 + c^2 - d^2)y_i + 2(cd - ab)z_i + t_y \\
Z_i &= 2(bd - ac)x_i + 2(ab - cd)y_i + (a^2 - b^2 - c^2 + d^2)z_i + t_z \\
1 &= a^2 + b^2 + c^2 + d^2
\end{aligned} \tag{4}$$

The unknown transformation parameters can be estimated by least square minimization (Gauss-Markov theorem). The resulting transformation T_{LW} is used to map the calculated sensor positions in a common coordinate system, which is bonded to the test object.

In this approach, circular markers were also attached on the top of the ultrasonic sensors to facilitate accurate tracking of the probes. The vertical probe had one marker to determine its support point s. The shear wave probe had three markers attached to compute an additional direction vector v. They are detected with the same method mentioned above and their positions in the local object

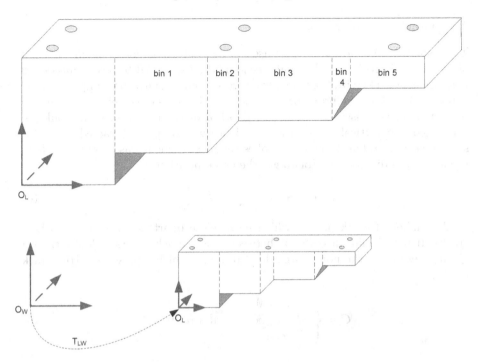

Fig. 2. Top: Local object frame with well known marker coordinates. Bottom: Marker coordinates in world frame and transformation of object frame.

frame are calculated. There is an initialization phase and a tracking phase. The first phase contains the following steps:

1. marker detection in the images,
2. assign IDs to markers,
3. correspondence analysis,
4. triangulation of 3D coordinates in the world frame,
5. transform coordinates to local object frame,
6. compute support point of the probe.

After the initialization the algorithm goes into the tracking mode. In the following images, small regions of interest around the latest marker coordinates were inspected. The tracking of the markers was realized with the Lucas-Kanade method [10] for optical flow estimation. The results were pixel-based coordinates of the actual marker position in the images. In an optimization step, ellipses were fitted again to achieve sub-pixel accurate coordinates. The IDs of the marker were used to determine the corresponding points in the two images. The remaining steps were identical to the initialization phase. This leads to a robust method for tracking the ultrasonic probes.

2.3   Crack Reconstruction

The achieved 3D coordinates were used to compute crack locations in the local object frame in real time. The pulse echo method was used to record ultrasonic measurements. Thereby, the transceiver probe sends an ultrasonic impulse which is reflected back to the probe or gets lost. On the basis of the elapsed time, the projected surface distance $\bar{r}$ and flaw depth $\bar{d}$ of the reflection point could be calculated. On vertical probes the flaw depth was simply subtracted along the surface normal n. On shear wave probes the measurement was subtracted along the computed direction vector to get the crack position c:

$$c = s + \bar{r} \cdot \frac{v}{\|v\|} - \bar{d} \cdot \frac{n}{\|n\|} \tag{5}$$

A number of crack points, which lie at close quarters are merged to HIC cracks. If the Euclidean distance between single crack points is lower than a given threshold d, the points are added to a set, which represents a HIC crack C:

$$C = \begin{cases} c \mid C = \emptyset \\ C \cup c \mid \exists \hat{c} \in C : dist(\hat{c}, c) < d \\ C \mid else \end{cases} \tag{6}$$

3   Experiments

In the following section the proposed method is validated with experiments. We used a milled reference block with well known structure (see Fig. 3). The model of the block serves as ground-truth data for the coordinates of the ultrasonic measurements. On top of the block, circular markers are attached, which define the described local object frame. As seen in Fig. 2 the point of origin is defined at the lower right corner of the block. To investigate the accuracy of the 3D point reconstruction, the probes are guided consecutively over the reference block. The computed 3D coordinates of the "cracks" in the local object frame are then compared to the ground-truth data and the deviations are analyzed as quality criterion.

For the experiment two monochrome cameras with 10 mm lenses are combined to a stereo camera system. It is placed 150 cm above the reference block with a base width of 50 cm. In a prior step, the system was calibrated to determine its intrinsic and extrinsic parameter. The image acquisition is controlled by a hardware trigger. It has an integrated clock generator, which creates the trigger signals for both cameras. The recorded images are transferred to the computer via Fast-Ethernet. The ultrasonic device is also connected to the computer and measurements are recorded simultaneously with the images. If the amplitude of the ultrasonic measurement is below 60% of the maximum intensity of the reflected signal, the measurement is discarded. That helps to reduce the presence of noise, especially while using the shear beam probe.

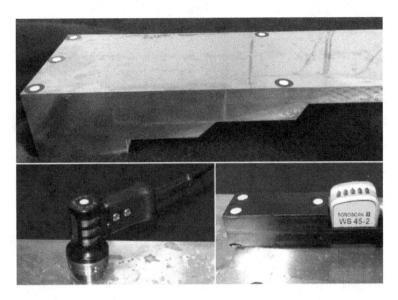

Fig. 3. Top: Section of the prepared reference block with well defined back plane structure in different depths and varied angles. Lower left: Vertical probe with marker on top. Lower right: 45° shear wave probe with adapter and three markers.

The results are binned and compared to different layers of the reference block. Their extent is given in x-direction according to the local object frame and the depth relates to the surface of the reference block. In table 1 the results and an overview of the bins are presented. The mean absolute error refers to the difference in depth of the reconstructed "cracks" and the ground-truth of the model. The results show, that the reconstruction of horizontal segments is more accurate than sloped layers. One reason is, that at the borders of Bin2 and Bin4 also measurements are included, that arise from the vertical probe. These measurements are inaccurate, because the ultrasonic beam is only reflected partially.

Table 1. Overview of the different layers in the reference block and the mean error of the reconstructed "cracks" according to the ground-truth of the model.

	bin 1	bin 2 (45°)	bin 3	bin 4 (60°)	bin 5
Extent (mm)	50-90	90-100	100-145	145-150	150-200
Depth (mm)	30	20-30	20	10-20	10
# of samples	367	55	543	31	238
Abs. mean error (mm)	0.17	1.12	0.17	1.8	0.34
Std. dev. (mm)	0.14	1.23	0.19	2.16	0.31

The results in Fig. 4 show the feasibility of the approach to reconstruct certain cracks in 3D. The vertical layers and the 45° layer were identified correct and

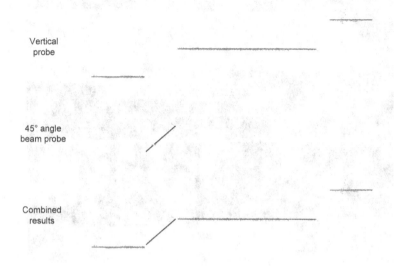

Vertical
probe

45° angle
beam probe

Combined
results

Fig. 4. Resulting crack positions and reconstructed HICs, achieved by the different sensor probes. At the bottom the combined results are visualized.

with adequate accuracy. The layer with the 60° slope was not recognized correct, because the ultrasonic signal was not reflected back to the angle beam probe. However, the three-dimensional localization of cracks could offer a benefit for material inspection. Because up to now the results of an examination is a coarse 2D overview of the surface area, which shows assumed defects. It is possible that our results might facilitate a more objective analysis of HIC occurrence or crack growth.

4   Conclusion

In this paper, we presented an approach for the reconstruction of hydrogen-induced cracking. Therefore, the classical pulse-echo ultrasonic testing method was extended with an optical sensor tracking. We used a stereo camera system, to determine three-dimensional sensor positions. The examined area was prepared with circular markers, to define a local object coordinate system, which was used to merge multiple measurements with different ultrasonic probes.

The examination of crack borders yielded measurements, which were difficult to interpret. This arose from the cone-shaped sound propagation, which could be problematic at small lateral cracks. Furthermore, the recognition is limited to the used angle beam probes. The detection of real hydrogen-induced cracks is the next step to evaluate the proposed method. Another idea could be the application of PAUT probes to cover a wider range of crack orientations.

Acknowledgement. This work was funded by the German Federation of Industrial Research Associations (KF3300801EB4).

References

1. Hajian, M.: Defect Classification of Adhesively Bonded Joints Using Pulse-Echo Ultrasonic Testing in Automotive Industries. SAE International, SAE Technical Paper 2015–01-0592 (2015)
2. Liaptsis, D., Yan, D., Cooper, I.: Development of an automated scanner and phased array ultrasonic testing technique for the inspection of nozzle welds in the nuclear industry. In: 51st Annual Conference of the British Institute for Non-destructive Testing (2012)
3. Deutsch, W. A., Joswig, M., Kattwinkel, R., Roye, W., Maxam, K., Razeng, M.: Automated ultrasonic testing systems for bars and tubes, examples with mono-element and phased array probes. In: 11th European Conference on Non-destructive Testing (2014)
4. Hillger, W., Bhling, L., Ilse, D.: Air-coupled ultrasonic testing-method, system and practical applications. In: 11th European Conference on Non-destructive Testing (2014)
5. Bendicks, C., Lilienblum, E., Freye, C., Al-Hamadi, A.: Tracking of a handheld ultrasonic sensor for corrosion control on pipe segment surfaces. In: Blanc-Talon, J., Kasinski, A., Philips, W., Popescu, D., Scheunders, P. (eds.) ACIVS 2013. LNCS, vol. 8192, pp. 342–353. Springer, Heidelberg (2013)
6. Farzam, M., Malekinejad, P., Khorashadizadeh, M.: Hydrogen induced cracking analysis of a pressure vessel made of SA 516 grade 70 steel by the use of phased array technology. In: 12th International Conference on Fracture, pp. 3500–3509 (2009)
7. Tsai, R.Y.: A Versatile Camera Calibration Technique for High-accuracy 3D Machine Vision Metrology Using Off-the-shelf TV Cameras and Lenses. IEEE Journal of Robotics and Automation **34**, 133–148 (1987)
8. Hartley, R., Zisserman, A.: Multiple View Geometry in computer vision, 2nd edn. Cambridge University Press (2008)
9. Förstner, M.A., Gülch, E.: A fast operator for detection and precise location of distinct points, corners and centers of circular features. In: Proceedings of the ISPRS Intercommission Workshop on Fast Processing of Photogrammetric Data, pp. 281–305 (1987)
10. Bouguet, J.: Pyramidal Implementation of the Lucas Kanade Feature Tracker Description of the algorithm. Intel Corporation Microprocessor Research Labs (2000)

Plane Extraction for Indoor Place Recognition

Ciro Potena[(✉)], Alberto Pretto, Domenico D. Bloisi, and Daniele Nardi

Department of Computer, Control and Management Engineering, Sapienza University of Rome, via Ariosto 25, 00185 Rome, Italy
cirpote@gmail.com

Abstract. In this paper, we present an image based plane extraction method well suited for real-time operations. Our approach exploits the assumption that the surrounding scene is mainly composed by planes disposed in known directions. Planes are detected from a single image exploiting a voting scheme that takes into account the vanishing lines. Then, candidate planes are validated and merged using a region growing based approach to detect in real-time planes inside an unknown indoor environment. Using the related plane homographies is possible to remove the perspective distortion, enabling standard place recognition algorithms to work in an invariant point of view setup. Quantitative Experiments performed with real world images show the effectiveness of our approach compared with a very popular method.

1 Introduction

Place recognition is the problem of identifying from images a place already seen before, or a place represented by a set of images included in a given database. The place recognition problem is often referred to as the "loop closure detection" problem, and it has been addressed in a number of works (e.g., [4,9,12]).

However, most of these methods assume that same places are seen at multiple times with approximately the same position and orientation. This means that, if the same place is seen more times from different points of view, using a perspective camera no loops closure are usually detected. This is due to the perspective distortion of the camera that, for different points of view, projects the same scene in different ways.

A possible solution is to employ an omni-directional camera, which provides a rotational invariant snapshot of the surrounding scene in a single frame. If an omni-directional camera is not available, a solution is to remove the perspective distortion from the images, at least where the three dimensional (3D) structure of the scene allows this process. An example is shown in Fig. 1, where two images of the same room are captured from opposite points of view (the black bounding boxes represent the same plane into the two views). Even if the two images represent the same place, they cannot be used directly as input for common place recognition techniques, since they are captured with very different view angles.

Fig. 1c and Fig. 1d show the two planes highlighted in the input images after removing the perspective distortion: they can be used for robust place

© Springer International Publishing Switzerland 2015
S. Battiato et al. (Eds.): ACIVS 2015, LNCS 9386, pp. 530–540, 2015.
DOI: 10.1007/978-3-319-25903-1_46

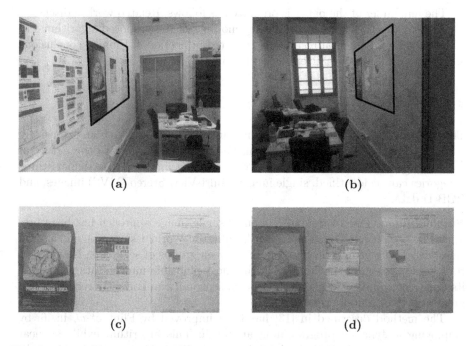

Fig. 1. a) and b) two images of a room captured from opposite points of view. The black boxes highlight a plane seen from both views. c) and d) the two planes highlighted in black after removing the perspective distortion.

recognition purposes. The capability to recognize planar surfaces in the environment enables to obtain a canonical, point of view invariant, visual representation of the places of interest.

In this work, we present a robust and fast plane recognition method that works with single images. We exploit the Manhattan World assumption [3], considering three mutually orthogonal directions as possible orientations. This hypothesis is well justified by the fact that most indoor environments meet this assumption. In order to extract the planes, the vanishing points are calculated from the line segments detected in the images. This represents a starting point for successive information extraction about the 3D structure of the scene. The image is then segmented to obtain three regions, representing mutually orthogonal directions. Finally, contextual information and a region growing technique are used to refine the result. From the extracted planes, it is possible to recover the related homographies that enable to re-project the plane in a canonical way (i.e., to remove the perspective distortion), independently from the initial point of view (see Fig. 1). These planes can be used to solve the place recognition problem by using conventional methods. Quantitative experiments show that our method outperforms the line-sweep approach presented by Lee *et al.* in [13].

The remainder of the paper is organized as follows. Related work is discussed in Section 2. Section 3 describes the key modules of the proposed algorithm and quantitative experimental results are reported in Section 4. Finally, conclusions and future directions are given in Section 5.

2   Related Work

The problem of recovering a model for indoor scenes from images is an extensively studied problem. Existing methods can be grouped according to the nature of the input data that are processed to compute the model. In particular, three categories can be identified: single image, Multi-View Stereo (MVS) images, and RGB-D data.

Single Image. One of the most popular single image approach has been presented by Lee *et al.* in [13]. The Indoor Manhattan World assumption and a set of rules, describing geometric constraints between groups of segments, is exploited to generate a scene hypothesis with the most plausible interpretation. Despite its apparent simplicity, this method is efficient and can correctly reconstruct a great variety of indoor scenes.

The method described in [13] has been improved by Flint *et al.* in [6] by employing a dynamic programming approach: This algorithm exhibits linear computational complexity in both model complexity and image size, and it works also with partially occluded scenes.

Saxena *et al.* in [16] propose to segment the image into small homogeneous regions (i.e., superpixels). Their orientations and 3D positions are then inferred inside a Markov Random Field framework.

Hoiem *et al.* in [11] use learning appearance-based models of geometric classes to estimate planes in the scene structure, providing also a confidence value for each inferred geometric label.

Multi-view Stereo. Baker *et al.* in [1] propose a MVS approach that starts from a photo consistency estimate and then refines it by using a re-synthesis algorithm, which takes into account both occlusions and mixed pixels. The output represents the scene as a collection of approximately planar layers.

Fukurawa *et al.* in [8] use stereo pairs to reconstruct textured regions. Dominant plane directions are extracted, generating a set of plane hypotheses. Per-view depth maps are finally recovered by using Markov Random Fields.

All the above-listed MVS algorithms often require textured regions in order to give accurate results. Therefore, they can work poorly for many architectural scenes (e.g., for building interiors with textureless regions, painted walls). Actually, they give no relevant improvements with respect to a monocular set up.

RGB-D Data. Silberman *et al.* [17] propose to use a Conditional Random Field (CRF) based model to evaluate a range of different representations for depth information and a novel prior on 3D location. In Guan *et al.* [10], the image is segmented in an initial number of planes, followed by a pixel-to-plane assignment. Plane equations are iteratively refined.

A common limitation of the depth based algorithms is that they suffer in presence of crowded places. In addition, depth sensors (e.g., Kinect) can have a limited field of view.

Our aim is to extract planes in a robust way, avoiding corruptions provided by obstacles near walls or people in common environment, and in real-time. Given the limitations of MVS and RGB-D algorithms, we have decided to follow a single camera approach.

3   Indoor Manhattan World Plane Extraction

Given a single image of a scene, our goal is to calculate the orientation of each pixel. A perfectly uncluttered indoor environment can be represented exactly by an indoor Manhattan model, though, in general, we expect to encounter clutter and, in such cases we aim to recovering the orientation of the environment in spite of this distraction. We aim to ignore completely all the objects within the environment and to reconstruct only the main structure of the scene, in contrast to most previous approaches that aim to reconstruct the entire scene. This choice is due to our intention of using the models as input for successive higher-level reasoning steps.

The Manhattan World assumption, as described in [3], states that world surfaces are oriented in one of three mutually orthogonal directions. In case of indoor scenes, it also states that the environment consists of a floor plane, a ceiling plane, and a set of walls extending vertically between them. In addition, indoor environments usually have a single floor plane and a single ceiling plane with constant ceiling height.

With these simplifying hypothesis an indoor scene can often be fully represented by corners, thus geometric constraints on corners will guarantee the entire structure to be valid.

Indoor Manhattan models are very interesting because they can represent many indoor and outdoor environments, with an adequate level of precision. Indeed, with this kind of geometric model, it is possible to reconstruct the indoor world, as done in [13], or make a decomposition of the scene, as described in [6,7].

The two above cited approaches require an initial orientation hypothesis, on which the method proposed in this paper rests. The entire pipeline of our approach to reconstruct indoor Manhattan environment is shown in Fig. 2. The computer steps are given in Algorithm 1.

3.1   Vanishing Point Extraction

We extract the three vanishing points from the detected lines. This extraction process is highly influenced by the illumination of the environment. In order to reduce this effect, i.e., for recovering edge and contours in the part of the image where there are variations in the illumination conditions, we carry out an image

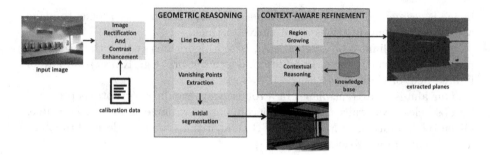

Fig. 2. Overall functional architecture of the proposed algorithm for plane extraction from single images.

Algorithm 1: Plane extraction from single image.

---

input : $m \times n$ RGB image I
data : $m \times n$ RGB images R, E, and T; vector of lines D; vectors of
points $CurrModel$ and $BestModel$; scalar $Score$
output: $m \times n$ RGB image S

$R \leftarrow \texttt{ImageRectification}(I)$
$E \leftarrow \texttt{Enhancing}(R)$
$D \leftarrow \texttt{LineExtraction}(E)$
initialize $BestScore$
for $i = 1$ **to** max_iter **do**
    D←$\texttt{LineSampling}(D)$
    $Score \leftarrow \texttt{ScoringFunction}(CurrModel)$
    if $Score \geq BestScore$ **then**
        $BestModel = CurrModel$
        $BestScore = Score$

$T \leftarrow \texttt{SweepRegion}(BestModel)$
$S \leftarrow \texttt{OrientationRefinment}(T)$

---

contrast enhancement based on two main steps: First, by using a histogram equalization and then, by increasing the contrast of the image. In particular, the contrast is increased by mapping the values of the input intensity image to new values such that, by default, 1% of the data are saturated at low and high intensities of the input data. The lines are then extracted by using a standard Canny edge detector [2] with a probabilistic Hough lines extractor [14]. The line segments that belong to the same lines are linked together, while short lines are filtered out, since they often corrupt the plane estimation process.

We adopt the method proposed by Rother [15] to find three orthogonal vanishing points. Two pairs of lines are randomly sampled in a RANSAC fashion and the intersection of each pair of lines generates a candidate vanishing point. A voting scheme, with a cost function that takes into account the number of classified lines, is used for choosing the best model. The third vanishing point

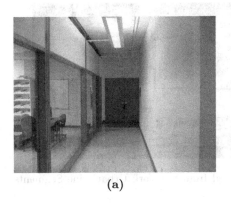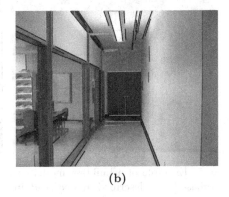

(a)   (b)

Fig. 3. An example of vanishing line extraction. a) Input image. b) Detected, mutually orthogonal, vanishing lines.

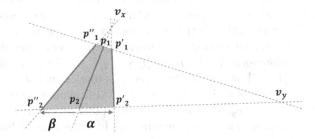

Fig. 4. The shaded area denotes the sweep $S(l_{x,i}, v_y, \alpha)$ of a line l towards and backwards vanishing point v_y by amount α and β. It potentially supports the region to be orthogonal to v_x and v_y.

is computed to be orthogonal to the two previous calculated vanishing points. From the three vanishing points, we can recover the orientation of the three principal axis of the 3D structure. All the extracted planes will have one of these three orientation.

Is important to note that the proposed technique can fail in some particular cases, e.g., when there are no lines in one of the three direction, or when many lines don't belong to the principal directions. To avoid these problems, we simply discard the estimated model if the error is greater than a fixed threshold. An example of the final line labelling is shown in Fig. 3.

3.2 Initial Building Orientation

Once the vanishing points have been estimated, we generate an initial segmentation, also denoted as the building hypothesis, which represents an initial estimate of the indoor structure. For this initial estimation, we use the approach described in [13], called geometric reasoning, due to its robustness and efficiency. The geometric reasoning approach , in fact, uses only the detected lines because they

Fig. 5. Example of a building model extracted from the York Urban Line Segments Database [5] as described by Lee *et al.* in [13].

give a strong indication about local orientation in the image. In other words, if a pixel is supported by two line segments with different orientation, there is a strong probability that it has a perpendicular orientation with respect to two line segments. This assumption is true in a world with all mutually orthogonal lines too, usually producing accurate orientation map, except around occluding objects or people. More formally, let $L_x = \{l_{x,1}, l_{x,2}, ..., l_{x,n}\}$ the set of extracted lines, where $x \in \{1, 2, 3\}$ is one of the three possible orientations among the calculated vanishing points and n represents the total number of the extracted lines. The "sweep" $S(l_{x,i}, v_y, \alpha)$ of a line $l_{x,i}$ is a pixel region with the normal along the third vanishing point z and extends up to a the nearest line with the same orientation, going toward the vanishing point v_y. α is the the width of this region, called "amount". For the same line $l_{x,i}$ is computed another "sweep" away from the vanishing point v_y, in this case with amount β. An example is shown in Fig. 4. The total set of pixels supported by L_x swept towards v_y is:

$$\bigcup_{l_{x,i} \in L_x} S(l_{x,i}, v_y, \hat{\alpha}_{x,i}) \cup S(l_{x,i}, v_y, \hat{\beta}_{x,i}).$$

A pixel is labeled with orientation z when two lines of different orientation x and y exclusively support it, i.e., the pixel can have a possible orientation only. The complete initial building model is:

$$R_z = P_{x,y,z} \cap P_{y,x,z}$$
$$O_z = R_z \cap R_x \cap R_y.$$

An example of building model generation is shown in Fig. 5.

3.3 3D Structure Hypothesis Refinement

The initial structure model can result inaccurate when too few lines can be extracted or if the scene contains many occluding objects. This negatively affects directly also higher-level processes, like navigation, scene recognition or 3D

| Image index | Input image | Ground truth | Lee et al. algorithm | Our approach |

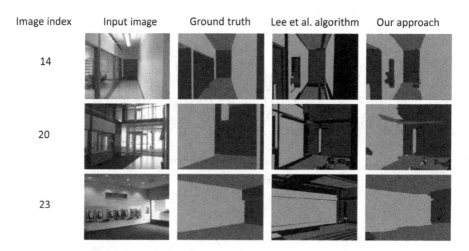

Fig. 6. Some sample images with the pixels orientation estimated by our method. Each row contains four images: the input image, the ground truth image, the initial orientation estimate by lee et al. [13], and the final output generated by our method.

indoor scene reconstruction. Actually, the line extraction process highly depends on the lighting conditions and the resolution of the camera.

As a consequence, in many cases of indoor scenes the lines on the floor and on the ceiling are badly extracted. Thus, the sweep regions $S(l_{x,i}, v_y, \alpha)$, where x is the orientation of the floor or ceiling lines and v_y is the direction of the vanishing point orthogonal to v_x and to the vertical orientation, support only few pixels and the amount of pixel with orientation R_z will be very small.

We propose a solution for this problem, that uses contextual information. In particular the indoor Manhattan scene has exactly one floor and one ceiling plane, both with orientation z. First, we find the unlabeled region of the initial segmentation that can probably belong to the floor or ceiling regions. For this purpose, a floor or a ceiling always has as boundary at least two vertical walls. If these regions are supported by one of the two sweeps of R_z, we classify them as a floor or a ceiling. The second step we propose is a region growing algorithm. The aim is to classify the pixels that are not yet labeled with an orientation, e.g. to occluding objects. Formally, for every unlabeled pixel in the image with position (u, v) we define the sum of its neighborhood as:

$$\beta_{u,v,i} = f(u \pm 1, v \pm 1)$$

where f is a linear filter and the index $i = \{x, y, z\}$ is the orientation along the three vanishing points in which the sum is computed. Repeating the above operation for the three orientation images R_x, R_y, R_z , we are able to classify the unlabeled pixels with the following rule:

$$d(u, v) = \arg \max_{u,v}\{\beta_{u,v,x}, \beta_{u,v,y}, \beta_{u,v,z}\}$$

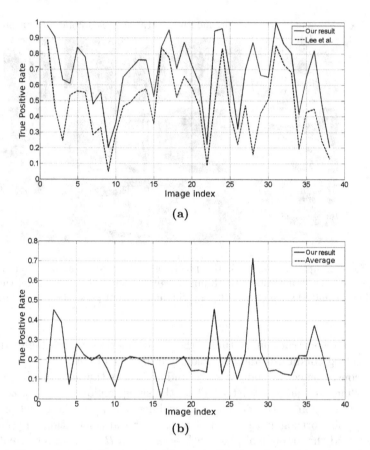

Fig. 7. a) Comparison of the true positive rate for the pixel with orientation z. b) Difference of the true positive rate between the two approaches.

$$l_{u,v} = \begin{cases} x \ \ if \ \ d(u,v) > 3 \ \ \wedge \ \ d(u,v) = \beta_{u,v,x} \\ y \ \ if \ \ d(u,v) > 3 \ \ \wedge \ \ d(u,v) = \beta_{u,v,y} \\ z \ \ if \ \ d(u,v) > 3 \ \ \wedge \ \ d(u,v) = \beta_{u,v,z} \end{cases}$$

where $l_{u,v}$ is the orientation assigned to the unlabeled pixel at hand in position (u,v).

4   Experimental Results

For evaluating our method we used the publicly available York Urban Line Segment Database [5]. It is a compilation of 102 images (45 indoor, 57 outdoor) of urban environments. Most of them consist of scenes from the campus of York University and downtown Toronto, Canada. The images are 640 x 480 in size and have been taken with a calibrated Panasonic Lumix DMC-LC80 digital camera.

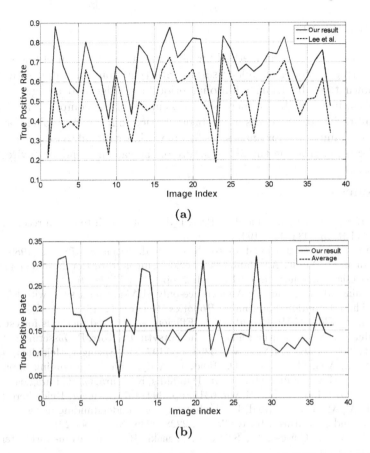

Fig. 8. a) True positive rate for all the three orientations. b) Difference of the true positive rate between the two approaches.

We have manually labeled every pixel with three orientation values in all the indoor scenes, ignoring the occluding object, in order to create the ground truth images. Qualitative results on three sample frames from the York Urban data set are shown in Fig. 6. The results of our method are compared with the output generated by the algorithm of Lee et al. [13] with respect to corresponding ground truth images. As quality metric, we have used the True Positive Rate between the labeled pixel with respect to the ground truth. Fig. 7 shows the high percentage of correctly labeled pixel with orientation z of our approach, due to the indoor assumptions. The average percentage of improvement is around 20% and, in a few cases, it is higher than the 50%.

Fig. 8 shows the True Positive rate among all labeled pixel of the input images. Also in this case, the percentage of correctly labeled pixel is increased significantly with an average of 16% by our method.

5   Conclusions

We have proposed a novel method for interpreting a collection of line segments for recovering a model of indoor scenes. Starting from an initial estimate we have shown that, by using additional prior knowledge and a region growing mechanism, it is possible to increase the accuracy of the computed model.

Quantitative experiments have been carried out on a publicly available dataset, containing indoor images. As future work, we intend to use the computed model for reconstructing the 3D structure of the captured indoor environment.

References

1. Baker, S., Szeliski, R., Anandan, P.: A layered approach to stereo reconstruction. In: CVPR, pp. 434–441 (1998)
2. Canny, J.: A computational approach to edge detection **8**, 679–697 (1986)
3. Coughlan, J., Yuille, A.: Manhattan world: compass direction from a single image by bayesian inference. In: CVPR, vol. 2, pp. 941–947 (1999)
4. Cummins, M., Newman, P.: Appearance-only SLAM at large scale with FAB-MAP 2.0. The International Journal of Robotics Research (2010)
5. Denis, P., Elder, J.H., Estrada, F.J.: Efficient edge-based methods for estimating manhattan frames in urban imagery. In: Forsyth, D., Torr, P., Zisserman, A. (eds.) ECCV 2008, Part II. LNCS, vol. 5303, pp. 197–210. Springer, Heidelberg (2008)
6. Flint, A., Mei, C., Murray, D., Reid, I.: A dynamic programming approach to reconstructing building interiors. In: Daniilidis, K., Maragos, P., Paragios, N. (eds.) ECCV 2010, Part V. LNCS, vol. 6315, pp. 394–407. Springer, Heidelberg (2010)
7. Flint, A., Murray, D., Reid, I.: Manhattan scene understanding using monocular, stereo, and 3d features. In: ICCV, pp. 2228–2235, November 2011
8. Furukawa, Y., Curless, B., Seitz, S., Szeliski, R.: Manhattan-world stereo. In: CVPR (2009)
9. Galvez-Lopez, D., Tardos, J.: Real-time loop detection with bags of binary words. In: IROS, pp. 51–58, September 2011
10. Guan, L., Yu, T., Tu, P., Lim, S.N.: Simultaneous image segmentation and 3d plane fitting for rgb-d sensors — an iterative framework. In: CVPR Workshops, pp. 49–56 (2012)
11. Hoiem, D., Efros, A., Hebert, M.: Geometric context from a single image. In: ICCV, vol. 1, pp. 654–661 (2005)
12. Labbe, M., Michaud, F.: Appearance-based loop closure detection for online large-scale and long-term operation. IEEE Transactions on Robotics **29**(3), 734–745 (2013)
13. Lee, D., Hebert, M., Kanade, T.: Geometric reasoning for single image structure recovery. In: CVPR, pp. 2136–2143 (2009)
14. Matas, J., Galambos, C., Kittler, J.: Robust detection of lines using the progressive probabilistic hough transform. In: CVIU, April 2000
15. Rother, C.: A new approach for vanishing point detection in architectural environments. In: BMVC, pp. 382–391 (2000)
16. Saxena, A., Sun, M., Ng, A.: Make3d: learning 3d scene structure from a single still image. In: PAMI, pp. 824–840 (2009)
17. Silberman, N., Fergus, R.: Indoor scene segmentation using a structured light sensor. In: ICCV Workshops, pp. 601–608 (2011)

A Trust Region Optimization Method for Fast 3D Spherical Configuration in Morphing Processes

Naziha Dhibi[(✉)], Akram Elkefi, Wajdi Bellil, and Chokri Ben Amar

REGIM Laboratory, ENIS, University of Sfax, Sfax, Tunisia
{dhibi.naziha,elkefi}@gmail.com,
{wajdi.bellil,chokri.benamar}@ieee.org

Abstract. This paper addressed the problem of Spherical Mesh parameterization. The main contribution of this work was to propose an effective optimization scheme to compute such parameterization, and to have an algorithm exposing a property of global convergence This is the case of trust region spherical parameterization (TRSP) to minimizing the ratio of inverted triangle, have an efficient spherical parameterization, and to generate bijective and lowly distorted mapping results so the faces have the correct orientation, thus creating a 3d spherical geometry object. Simulation results show that it is possible to achieve a considerable correspondence between the angle and area perspective distortion.

Keywords: Spherical parameterization · Mesh processing · Inverted triangle · 3D mesh morphing

1 Introduction

3D mesh parameterization is a powerful method assisting geometric modeling and geometry processing in many applications of computer graphics. The objective of mesh parameterization is to create a map between the source mesh and a triangultion of the domain. An important goal of parameterization is to develop a bijective map, where for each vertex in the source mesh there is only one correspondent vertex in the target parameterization domain, Other fields that benefit from parameterization include detail mapping, detail synthesis, detail transfer, mesh fixing, mesh editing, object database creation, mesh compression, surface fitting, modeling from material sheets, medical visualization, filtering, texture mapping, remeshing, and morphing.

Planar parameterization for high genus meshes usually introduce mesh segmentation or seam cutting, and mapping these piecewise onto a planar domain [1], [2], [3] . The disadvantage of this technique is the existence of visible seams on the surface. For such objects which can generate discontinuities and distortions. For the simplicial complex domain, it is difficult to optimize the parameterization globally in most cases. Topologically, closed manifold, genus-zero meshes, are correspondent to a sphere, the sphere is the most natural parameterization, genus-zero surfaces, i.e. deformed spheres. Spherical mapping is a key permitting technology in modeling and

© Springer International Publishing Switzerland 2015
S. Battiato et al. (Eds.): ACIVS 2015, LNCS 9386, pp. 541–552, 2015.
DOI: 10.1007/978-3-319-25903-1_47

processing genus-0 close surfaces. So a spherical base surface is the natural parameterization domain for these meshes. Compared to the planar and simplicial domains, the advantage of spherical parameterization is that it allows smooth, seamless and continuous parameterization of genus zero models. Thus, much research attention has been devoted to the spherical domain in the past few years. Parameterizing a 3D triangle mesh onto the 3D sphere means assigning a 3D position on the unit sphere to each of the mesh vertices, such that the spherical triangles induced by the mesh connectivity do not overlap. This is called a spherical triangulation. Aside from the topological similarity, there is typically quite a large geometric difference between the source mesh and the parameterization domain, which almost always introduces distortions existing in either angles or areas. The goal of a good parameterization algorithm is to minimize these distortions for the entire mesh. In morphing processes a spherical   parameterization represents a mandatory and important and they condition the overall quality of the metamorphosis for this we introduce a robust technique for directly parameterizing a genus-zero surfaces onto a spherical domain. The objective is to present an effective flowing computation using a spherical parameterization with bounded distortion and localized boundary constraints and an effective optimization scheme to compute such a parameterizations, minimizing a ratio of inverted triangle then a balancing angle and area distortions and we used this parameterization in morphing processes. Then we formulate and solve an optimization procedure to produce spherical triangulations which reproduce the geometric properties of a given 3D mesh in various ways.

2   Basic Concepts

Geometric objects are frequently described by closed, genus-zero surfaces, i.e. deformed spheres. For such models, the sphere is the most natural parameterizations domain, and then it does not need cutting the surface into disk(s).

Though we may later resample the surface signal onto a piecewise continuous do main, these domain boundaries can be resolute more conveniently and a posteriorion the sphere. Three-dimensional modeling requires a step of parameterization of the sphere while preserving the topology of the mesh (neighborhood, edges, and faces).

Spherical parameterizations search for a bijective map $f: M \rightarrow S$ between a closed genus-0 surface M and a unit spherical domain S. The angle distortion per triangle can be measured [4] on the map of each triangle $fT \rightarrow t$: by

$$D(T) = \cot \alpha \, |a|^2 + \cot \beta |b|^2 + \cot \gamma |c|^2 \qquad (1)$$

Where T and t are the triangle of mesh M and its image on the parametric sphere S respectively; α, β, γ are the angles in T and a, b, c are the corresponding opposite edge-lengths in t. The area distorsion can be measured by

$$EA(T) = \frac{Area(t)}{Area(T)} \qquad (2)$$

For low distortion the superlative parameterization is isometric, i.e. it completely preserves areas and angles. Then this is not possible in the general case, low-distortion parameterization are necessary. Parameterizations giving low distortions are obviously more practical. Then a spherical parameterization proves to be challenging in practice, for two reasons. First, for the algorithm to be robust it must prevent parametric "foldovers" and thus guarantee a 1-to-1 spherical map. Second, though all genus-zero surfaces are in essence sphere-shaped, several can be highly deformed, and generating a parameterization that adequately samples all surface regions is difficult: figure(1).

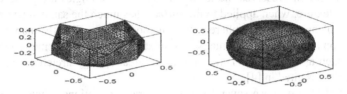

Fig. 1. Sample spherical parameterization [29]

3   Problem of Spherical Parameterization

The parameterization of a genus-zero mesh over some standard domain is needed. usually the triangles in given meshes are with good shape, i.e., that the three edges of the triangle do not change dramatically in their lengths. In order to obtain good fitting results, we need the triangles in the parameterization domain to be with good shapes as well. Hence, we should propose a mapping from the given mesh to a unit sphere preserving the shapes of the triangles.

Spherical parameterization causes distortion. Distortion can be measured in many ways, including how well angles or areas are preserved, or how much parametric distances are stretched. Very few cases admit isometric parameterization (zero distortion). Based on the type of distortion minimization methodology, most parameterizations can be classified as two groups of mappings. Maps that attempt to minimize the angle distortions are named 'conformal' and maps that minimize the area distortion are referred as 'authalic'. High dimensional parameterization domains are actively being researched and many different algorithms and methodologies have been developed. Based on the type of mapping domain causes distortion. The distortion energy introduced in the mapping of each triangle is nonlinear and nonconvex. Usually, directly optimizing the energy will get trapped in local minima inevitably. There are numerous optimization methods for vertex repositioning. Most of them are based on the idea of local optimization and need an improvement of such mesh quality parameters as aspect ratio, area, etc. Our method generates a bijective and lowly-distorted mapping, and converges efficiently. Therefore, our algorithm can be applied on large geometric models with complex geometry robustly.

4   Related Work

Some previous works on mesh parameterization exist, it is a major challenge to produce that which best fits the geometry of the 3D mesh, minimizing some measure of distortion. Most of the recent works on the subject of parameterization ([5], [6], [24]) have focused on defining the distortion, and viewing how to minimize it. In this section, we have described a general method for mapping certain surfaces to the sphere in a manner which preserves the local geometry. Since angles are preserved by this mapping, a texture, when applied to the surface, has much the same appearance that is has in the plane or on the sphere. Most methods are to directly map the mesh to spherical domain, which is habitually, formulated as a spherical energy minimization problem, such as conformal, Tutte, Dirichlet, area, spring, stretch energies, or their combinations, as cited in [4].

Kent et al [10] propose several spherical parameterizations schemes. For general shapes, they simulate a balloon inflation process, but are not able to guarantee a 1-to-1 map. Alexa [11] uses a spring-like relaxation process. The relaxation solutions may collapse to a point, or experience foldovers, de-pending on the starting state. He demonstrates several heuristics that help the solution converge to valid maps. Grimm [12] partitions the surface into 6 charts, and maps these to faces of a cube, and from there to a sphere. Schemes based on a priori chart partitions constrain the spherical parameterization. Haker et al [13] find conformal approximations of meshes over the sphere. Conceptually, they remove a single point from the surface, harmonically map the remaining surface onto an infinite plane, and finally map that infinite plane onto the sphere using stereographic projection.

Sheffer et al [14] find the angles of a spherical embedding as a constrained nonlinear system, and show results for simple meshes. Gotsman et al [15] show a nice relationship between spectral graph theory and spherical parameterization, and embed simple meshes on the sphere by solving a quadratic system. Quicken et al [16] parameterize the surface of a voxel volume onto a sphere. Their nonlinear objective functional exploits the uniform quadrilateral structure of the voxel surface; it seeks to equalize areas and preserve right-angles of surface elements. Their scheme is not applicable to general triangle meshes. Rhaleb and Christian [17] present a novel approach to spherical parameterization, where computation time is dominated by solving only linear systems. Their method relies on setting the problem in a curvilinear coordinates system, hence reducing it to a two dimensional problem.

Zayer et al [18] proposed a Curvilinear Spherical Parameterization which better reduces area distortion efficiently. Praun and Hoppe [9] they used the progressive mesh to iteratively optimize the L^2 stretching energy [19] defined piecewise on the mesh of M. Such a coarse-to-fine solving scheme can effectively overcome the local minima issue existing in most spherical mapping formulations that aim to minimize angle and area distortion together.[20, 21] propose a conformal harmonic spherical map. The resultant mapping is angle-preserving. However, its area distortion could be very large, especially in the long and thin protrusion regions. The optimization process is to relax the initial map to reach no-foldovers under specified distortion metric. In this case, since many parameterizations exist, it is a major challenge to produce that which best fits the geometry of the 3D mesh, minimizing some measure of distortion Kent et al[22] develop an effective progressive optimization scheme to compute such a parameterization, minimizing a nonlinear energy balancing angle and area distortions. These previous schemes cannot parameterize a complex mesh robustly and with the low scale-distortion necessary for good 3D modeling remeshing, morphing, smoothing.

5   Spherical Parameterization for 3D Morphing Processes

Morphing is a creating a morph between two models becomes easier once their spherical settings are achieved (figure 2).The word morphing is derived from the word "metamorphosis". All quaternion specifies a rigid alignment of the two do mains of the sphere. Then, both can be crossed to form spherical triangultions mutual paving can interpolate models [26].Morphing methods are today extensively used in computer graphics to simulate the transformation between two completely different objects or to create new shapes by a combination of other existing shapes; it has a variety of applications ranging from special effects in film industry and other visual arts to medical imaging and scientific purposes. The objective of a morphing method is to compute a transformation ensuring a visually pleasant transiton between the two, source and target shapes.

Fig. 2. Morphing with alignment but no feature point matching: fish (4994 faces) to duck (1926 faces) [23].

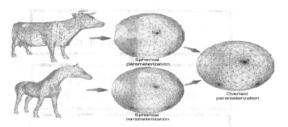

Fig. 3. Overlaid parameterization of two spherical mappings [27]

The parameterization represents a mandatory and important step in the morphing process and they condition the overall quality of the metamorphosis.

Feature alignment process is necessary in order to guarantee a successful morphing process. This comes to define a set of features of interest on both source and target models and apply a warping/deformation of the parametric domain in order to guarantee that the parametric position of the corresponding features are as closed as possible for both models. We speak in this case of overlaid parameterztions (figure 3).

6   Our Proposed Trust Region Spherical Parametrization Algorithm (TRSP)

We develop an effective optimization scheme to compute such parameterization, based on energy minimization. Reduce an optimization problem, it be interesting to have an algorithm exposing a property of global convergence. This is the case of trust region method that we have implemented in our approach to minimizing the ratio of inverted triangle and an efficient spherical parameterization to have a good spherical geometry object. Our method uses a number of optimization methods combined with an algebraic multigrid technique. With these, we are able to spherically parameterize meshes containing up to a hundred thousand vertices in a matter of minutes, our idea is to use the trust region method for nonlinear minimization ratio of inverted triangles when mapping each triangle of surface during parameterization of the object on the sphere to have a good system by minimizing angle area distortion. The main idea of our trust region method is to transform the original optimization problem by a series of sub-optimization problems, easier to solve. In each sub-problem, the objective function is transformed by a model function, to a current iterate. A trust region is inspired as the region within which trust is given to the model function about its quality to give a good approximation (low distortion) of the objective function and consequently the rate of inverted triangle is reduced. Our approach exposed ensures effective and bijective parameterization.

We start by creating a smoothing operator:

1.   First load and display the mesh.
2.   Compute the weights, the weights should be positive for the method to work.
3.   Compute the normalized weight matrix such that its rows sums to 1.

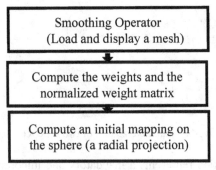

Fig. 4. Smoothing operator

4.   Spherical Relaxation is obtained by:

Smoothing the positions of the mesh on the sphere and projecting back on the sphere and check which faces have the correct orientation, for this we used an effective optimization scheme to compute such parameterization.

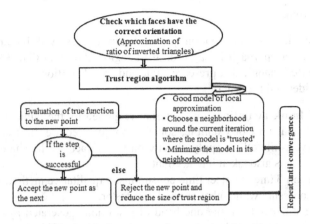

Fig. 5. Spherical Relaxation used trust region algorithm

The goal of this approach is used to:

- Presents an easy to implement feature-compatible method for mapping 3D objects on the sphere using an optimization technique that achieves a mapping geometrically similar to the original object while preserving connectivity and topology
- An efficient computation using a spherical parameterization with bounded distortion and localized boundary constraints.
- Minimize the rate of inverted triangle: for a bijective parameterization, it should not be any inverted triangles.
- Creating a good spherical geometry image.

7   Implementation and Results

For our part, we used the spherical parameterization in 3D mesh morphing; significantly reduce the computation distortion required for the procedure on the parameterization of the mesh in a sphere, since all calculations are performed in the space of the sphere to reduce the distortion angle and region: ratio of inverted triangle (IT) at mapping each of the triangles. The following figure shows the original objects that we used:

Horse.off   *bunny.off*   *Elephant.off*

Fig. 6. Original Objects

7.1 Approach

Spherical energy minimization problem can be resolved by an algorithm of optimization our approach is based on trust region algorithm (TRSP) to minimize a ratio of inverted triangle that preserve angle and area distortion.

We considered three criteria:

- **Ease of Implementation:** this criterion is guided by the number and number of method to put up (for example, some techniques require the establishment of a progressive while others apply directly on the surface mesh).The difficulty of implementation is also taken into account
- **Calculation Time:** to meet time constraints, a qualitative method relied represent a slow processing while other methods are faster.
- **Quality:** it depends on the one hand of distortions generated by the method and other a visual quality to have a good spherical geometry Object.

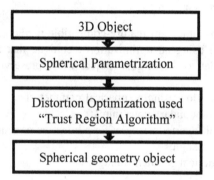

Fig. 7. The main steps of our approach

7.2 Simulation Result

The following equation shows the ratio of inverted triangle for each vertex:

$$IT = \sum_{f=1}^{n} \frac{C * normal\ f}{m} \tag{3}$$

When C is the center of the faces, $normal\ f$ is the normal to the faces and m is the size of the faces, n is the number of faces.

Table1 presents a comparative study that describes the ratio of the inverted triangle using a simple spherical parameterization (SP) and the proposed approach (TRSP).

Table 1. Comparative study based on Ratio of inverted triangle

| | | | SP | TRSP |
Model	Faces	Vertex	Ratio of IT	Ratio of IT
Bunny	69473	34835	0.0979%	0%
Elephant	49918	24955	0.225%	0%
Horse	1420	712	0.224%	0%

- It was found that the ratio of inverted triangle in our approach converges to zero, there should not be any inverted triangle therefore the angle distortion is very low so we have a bijective parameterization.

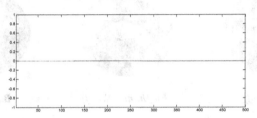

Fig. 8. The evolution of the Ratio of inverted triangle

- Pinkall and Polthier [25] wrote the Dirichlet energy(DE) for discrete conformal mappings between triangles as a function of Dirichlet energy that preserves the angles for each triangle:

$$E_{dirichlet} = d_{min}^{-2} \cdot (cot\alpha \cdot (B - C)^2 + cot\beta \cdot (A - C)^2 + cot\gamma \cdot (A - B)^2 \quad (4)$$

- The following table shows a comparison of different results depending the Dirichlet energy (DE) using by simple spherical parameterization (SP) and that our approach TRSP.

Table 2. Comparative study based on Dirichlet Energy

| | SP | | TRSP | |
Model	D E	Time(s)	DE	Time(s)
Bunny	32.04	143	2.77.e+05	168
Elephant	33.67	82.83	1.99e+05	113
Horse	30.24	3.32	5.64e+03	12.75

Numerically, the spherical mapping results of Bunny, Elephant and Horse, computed by [26], are compared with our approach in Table.2 our method generates a bijective and lowly-distorted mapping, and converges efficiently. We see that the energy is increased from 32.04 to 2.77e+05. In other hand we see that the execution time is increased in our approach, because the search space is increased with the appearance of the optimization algorithm: "trust region" which an algorithm exposing a property of global convergence. In this figure we observe for 500 iterations the energy drops severely in the beginning and the slope of the graph asymptotically goes towards zero with increasing number of iterations. This indicates our approach finally converges.

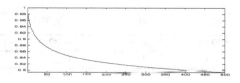

Fig. 9. The decay of the evolution of the Dirichlet energy

Horse.off   *Elephant-50kv.off*   *Bunny.off*

Fig. 10. Parameterized objects on the sphere

This is an example of 3D objects parameterization of the sphere using our approach.

In Figure 11 (b) using our approach we can see that the faces have the correct orientation in comparison with the object in Figure 11 (a) [26].

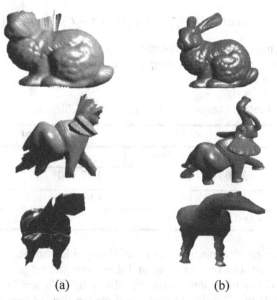

(a)   (b)

Fig. 11. Comparative study of Spherical geometry image

- To have the correspondence between the angle and area perspective distortion we present a framework for fast spherical configuration using an optimization algorithm to generate bijective and lowly distorted mapping results so the faces have the correct orientation, thus creating a good spherical geometry image.

8   Conclusion and Perspectives

In this paper, we present an effective spherical mapping algorithm using trust re gion optimization scheme minimizing angle and area distortions which guarantee a bijective spherical parameterization 3d mesh thus creating a good spherical geometry image. Compared with other state-of-the-art spherical mapping algorithms, our me thod generates a bijective and lowly-distorted mapping, and converges efficiently. The parameterization represents a mandatory and important step in the morphing process also a feature alignment process is necessary in order to guarantee a success-ful morphing process.As future work we propose to use Spherical Parameterization (TRSP) to feature-based 3D Morphing and we build a new direct manipulation tech-nique for free form deformations, based on Wavelet network approximation to:

- Features Alignment
- Corresponding features
- Optimize to align feature and minimize distorsion with fixed features

References

1. Maillot, J., Yahia, H., Verroust, A.: ACM SIGGRAPH (1993)
2. Cignoni, P., Montani, C., Rocchni, C., Scopigno, R.: A general method for recovering attributes values on simplified meshes. In: IEEE Visualisation (1998)
3. Sander, P., Snyder, J., Gortler, S., Hoppe, H.: Texture mapping progressive meshes. In: ACM SIGGRAPH (2001)
4. Floater, M.S, Hormann, K.: Surface parameterization: a tutorial and survey (2005)
5. Floater, M.S.: Parameterization and smooth approximation of surface triangulation. Computer Aided Geometric Design 14 (1997)
6. Levy, B., Petitjean, S.: Least squares conformal maps for automatic texture atlas genera-tion. In: Proceedings of ACM SIGGRAPH (2002)
7. Isenburg, M., Gumhold, S., Gotsman, C.: Connectivity Shapes. In: Proceedings of IEEE Visualization (2001)
8. Gu, X., Gortler, S., Hoppe, H.: Geometry images. In: ACM SIGGRAPH (2002)
9. Praun, Hoppe, H.: Spherical parametrization and remeshing. In: SIGGRAPH 2003 (2003)
10. Kent, J., Carlson, W., Parent, R.: Shape transformation for polyhedral objects. In: ACM SIGGRAPH 92 (1992)
11. Alexa, M.: Recent advances in mesh morphing. Computer Graphics Forum (2002)
12. Grimm, C.: Simple manifolds for surface modeling and parametrization. Shape Modeling International (2002)
13. Haker, S., Angenent, S., Tannenbaum, S., Kikinis, R., Sapiro, G., Halle, M.: Conformal surface parametrization for texture mapping. In: IEEE TVCG (2000)

14. Sheffer, A., Gotsman, C., Dyn, N.: Robust spherical parameterization of triangular meshes. In: 4th Israel-Korea Bi-National Conf. on Geometric Modeling and Computer Graphics (2003)
15. Gotsman, C., Gu, X., Sheffer, A.: Fundamentals of spherical parameterization for 3D meshes. In: ACM SIGGRAPH (2003)
16. Quicken, M., Brechbuhler, C., Hug, J., Blattmann, H., Székely, G.: Parametrization of closed surfaces for parametric surface description. In: CVPR (2000)
17. Zayer, R., Rossl, C., Seidel, H.P.: Curvilinear spherical parameterization. In: Proc. IEEE International Conf. on Shape Modeling and Applications (2006)
18. Sander, P., Snyder, J., Gortler, S., Hoppe: Texture mapping progressive meshes. In: Proceedings of SIGGRAPH (2001)
19. Gu, X., Yau, S.T.: Global conformal surface parameterization. In: Proc. Symp. of Geometry Processing (2003)
20. Li, X., He, Y., Gu, X., Qin, H.: Curves-on-surface: a general shape comparison framework. In: Proc. IEEE International Conf. on Shape Modeling and Applications (2006)
21. Wa, S., Ye, T., Li, M., Zh, H., Li, X., Hu, S.-M., Martin, R.R.: CVM. LNCS. Springer-Verlag, Heidelberg (2012)
22. Theodoris, A., Ioannis, F., Christophoros, N.: Feature-based 3D Morphing based on Geometrically Constrained Sphere Mapping Optimization (2010)
23. Sheffer, A., de Sturler, E.: Parameterization of faceted surfaces for meshing using angle based flattening. Engineering with Computers (2001)
24. Pinkall, U., Polthier, K.: Computing Discrete Minimal Surfaces and Their Conjugates
25. https://www.ceremade.dauphine.fr/~peyre/numericaltour/tours/meshdeform_2_parameterization_sphere/
26. Bogdan, CM., Titus, Z.: IA3D Mesh Morphing
27. Li, S., Moo, C.: Large-Scale Modeling of Parametric Surfaces using Spherical Harmonics

On Optimal Illumination for DOVID Description Using Photometric Stereo

Daniel Soukup$^{(\boxtimes)}$, Svorad Štolc, and Reinhold Huber-Mörk

Digital Safety & Security Department, AIT Austrian Institute of Technology GmbH,
Donau-City-Straße 1, 1220 Vienna, Austria
`daniel.soukup@ait.ac.at`

Abstract. Diffractive optically variable image devices (DOVIDs) are popular security features used to protect security documents such as banknotes, ID cards, passports, etc. Nevertheless, checking authenticity of these security features on both user as well as forensic level still remains a challenging task, requiring sophisticated hardware tools and expert knowledge. Based on a photometric acquisition setup comprised of 32 illumination sources from different directions and a recently proposed descriptor capturing the illumination dependent behavior, we investigate the information content, illumination pattern shape and clustering properties of the descriptor. We studied shape and discriminative power of reduced illumination configurations for the task of discrimination applied to DOVIDs using a sample of Euro banknotes.

Keywords: Optimal illumination directions · Photometric stereo · Diffractive optically variable image devices (DOVID) industrial inspection

1 Introduction

DOVID security features are state-of-the-art means for protecting security documents (e.g., banknotes, ID cards, passports, etc.) as well as for brand protection [5]. In most of these use cases, the possibility of automating the inspection/verification process is crucial and highly appreciated. Nevertheless, in practice, checking authenticity of DOVIDs remains a challenging task, that still requires sophisticated hardware tools based either on microscopic analysis of the DOVID's grating structure or sparse point-wise projection and recording of the diffraction patterns [5]. Currently, the state-of-the-art tool for hologram verification used in forensic investigations is the *Universal Hologram Scanner* (UHS) [4]. The UHS records diffraction patterns at discrete steps over the hologram area and performs an orientation vs. frequency analysis on the recorded data [6]. Methods for non-forensic analysis using mobile devices were suggested recently,

We Would Like to Thank the National Bank of Austria (OeNB), Test Center, Vienna for Providing Us with Samples and Expertise in the Field of Banknote Authentication.

© Springer International Publishing Switzerland 2015
S. Battiato et al. (Eds.): ACIVS 2015, LNCS 9386, pp. 553–565, 2015.
DOI: 10.1007/978-3-319-25903-1_48

where user performance evaluation w.r.t. guided navigation to image capture positions [2] as well as hologram detection and tracking [1] was presented.

The use of different viewpoints and/or different illumination directions provides an insight into the material properties by estimation of the *bidirectional reflectance distribution function* (BRDF). The optimal configuration of light patterns was investigated for the task of material classification, where machine learning was used to determine optimal illumination patters [3]. Material classification from 2-D BRDF slices using different combinations of illuminations was also discussed in [11]. Up to our knowledge, there exists no work on studying illumination pattern shapes for DOVID analysis from 2-D BRDF slices.

In previous work, a descriptor for DOVID characterization based on photometric acquisitions of DOVIDs on genuine and counterfeited Euro banknotes was developed [9]. Those photometric acquisitions comprised 32 color images for every DOVID, each corresponding with a different illumination direction. The resulting DOVID descriptor is a highly compressed vector representation of DOVID areas, which showed impressive performance in classification of DOVIDs of various Euro denominations and counterfeit detection [10]. Moreover, invariance properties of this descriptor w.r.t. perturbations such as shift and tilt of the DOVID within the analysis device, wear&tear, or crease testified in favor of the descriptor's robustness.

In this study, we analyze possibilities of reducing the number of illumination directions while still retaining the discriminating power of the derived DOVID descriptor. In Section 2, we present the acquisition setup and explain the DOVID descriptor and the sample data set is described in Section 3. Section 4 gives an overview over alternative illumination patterns. The actual analysis comprises three different aspects. In the first part (Section 5), we approach the problem from an information theoretic point of view. In the second and third part (Sections 6 and 7), actual classification performance and discriminative power of the DOVID descriptors are investigated for the different illumination patterns. Finally, we summarize and conclude on the results in Section 8.

2   Photometric DOVID Descriptor

For DOVID acquisitions, we employed a photometric acquisition rig composed of an area-scan color camera and a photometric light dome – *NUSTEP Light-Dome32D* (see Fig. 1). The NUSTEP LightDome32D consists of 32 individually operated high-power LEDs (each approx. 10 W, 1000 lm). The LEDs are distributed uniformly over three height levels (by 8, 12, and 12 LEDs placed respectively at approx. 25°, 43°, and 61° circles from the dome's central axis). Moreover, the dome is equipped with an internal diffuser in order to provide uniform illumination for a larger field of view. The inner diameter of the dome is approx. 30 cm facilitating a minimum working distance of about 5 cm (depending on the lens size). The employed color camera provided a spatial resolution of 63 μm/px at the working distance of approx. 6 cm.

In the acquisition procedure, an object area comprising DOVID is acquired 32 times, one image for each illumination direction. Those 32 acquisitions of the

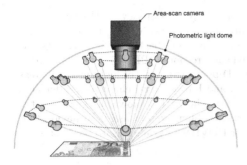

Fig. 1. Schematic drawing of the photometric setup used in this study for acquiring DOVIDs. The employed photometric light dome comprised of 32 high-power LEDs depicted as yellow bulbs at three levels.

DOVID capture a 2-D slice of the BRDF, which will be hereinafter referred to as the BRDF. Due to specific reflection properties of diffraction gratings such as those used in DOVIDs, it is possible to associate between the BRDF and the diffraction pattern itself [9].

From the aforementioned 32 images, one can derive a strongly compressed vector descriptor characterizing the entire DOVID area [10]. This descriptor proved to be a suitable DOVID representation in tasks such as characterizing banknote denominations, detecting counterfeits, etc. It was shown, that the DOVID descriptor is vastly robust to rotation, shift, tilt, and even crease of the banknotes.

Although DOVID points may exhibit very complex diffraction behaviors, they can be quite efficiently characterized by means of the eccentricity and orientation of the spatial response pattern. This phenomenon is especially pronounced in Euro banknotes. Considering a single DOVID point (i.e., a specific pixel position in the 32 DOVID images), there are 32 color samples available for that point, each corresponding with a different illumination direction. By associating each color sample with the corresponding illumination direction and interpolating directions in between, we get to an estimate of a densely sampled BRDF in that particular DOVID point. Fig. 2 depicts such a BRDF estimate for one DOVID point on a genuine EUR20 banknote. Note, that in this case, color responses are strong mostly along vertical direction, which results in a high eccentricity of the color response and a characteristic orientation. Due to the highly structured nature of diffraction gratings used in DOVIDs, it can be assumed that, in general, BRDFs of DOVID points exhibit either a specific orientation or additionally also a high eccentricity (such as in Euro banknotes). On the other hand, BRDFs of non-DOVID points lack both a characteristic orientation as well as a high eccentricity of the color responses.

In order to capture these BRDF characteristics, in each DOVID point, we represent the general shape of the associated BRDF by means of its alignment angle $\alpha \in [-\frac{pi}{2}, \frac{pi}{2}]$ and the eccentricity value $e \in [0, 1]$ (i.e., oblongness of the distribution of bright color responses).

For describing the entire DOVID area, a histogram h_e of eccentricities over all DOVID points as well as a corresponding histogram h_α of alignment angles

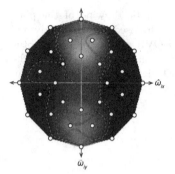

Fig. 2. Schematic top down view of the light dome, where white points indicate the respective light positions and the color background represents the interpolated color response (BRDF) associated with a single DOVID point. Contours of high-intensity areas in red, green and blue spectral channels are depicted as dashed lines. The BRDF shown here exhibits the unique (vertical) oblong color changing behavior, that is typical for DOVIDs of genuine Euro banknotes.

are generated. Since the eccentricity value is implicitly rotational, shift, and tilt invariant w.r.t. banknote pose during acquisition, so is the associated histogram h_e. Unfortunately, this is not the case for the alignment angle as well as its histogram, especially regarding the rotational invariance. Nevertheless, as h_α is periodic w.r.t. the alignment angle, we apply Fourier transform to it to obtain $\hat{h}_\alpha$. The transformed $\hat{h}_\alpha$ represents the alignment angle distribution as amplitudes in the frequency domain that is rotationally invariant after all. We define the concatenated descriptor by:

$$H := [h_e, \hat{h}_\alpha]. \tag{1}$$

3   Data Set

The data set used in this paper consisted of a representative set of 30 Euro banknotes (2002 design) of various denominations. All banknotes were acquired using our photometric acquisition rig, described in Section 2. In the case of EUR5 banknotes, we had access to a set of 16 banknotes comprising several defined levels of crease. All EUR5 banknotes were acquired under standard conditions, i.e. not rotated, shifted or tilted. The data set of EUR10 banknotes consisted of a single EUR10 banknote acquired under different standard and non-standard conditions. Besides one standard acquisition, we considered 7 additional non-standard conditions:

1. DOVID rotated by 20° to the left,
2. DOVID rotated by 40° to the left,
3. DOVID rotated by 20° to the right,
4. DOVID rotated by 40° to the right,
5. DOVID shifted downwards by 1 cm (viewing angle changed by approx. 10°),
6. DOVID tilted to the left by 5°,
7. DOVID tilted to the right by 5°.

Additionally, we considered also three samples of EUR20 and another three of EUR50 banknotes, all acquired under standard conditions.

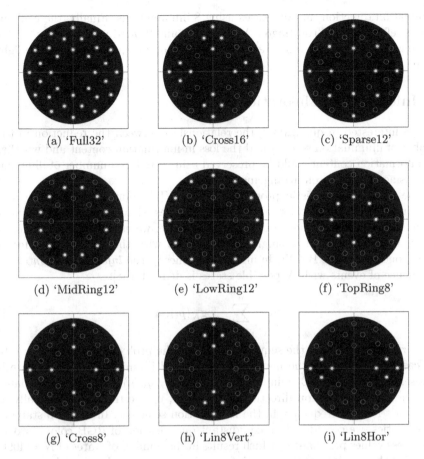

Fig. 3. Schematic top down views of the light dome, depicting 9 illumination patterns we analyzed w.r.t. their suitability for a robust DOVID description. The 32 circles mark illumination positions available in the light dome, while full circles indicate the actual illumination pattern used in each tested configuration.eps

4   Alternative Illumination Configurations

We will study several sparse illumination patterns (i.e., subsets of 32 illuminations available in the light dome) of different shape in detail.

Fig. 3 shows schematic top down views of the light dome, depicting 9 illumination patterns considered in this study. The configuration abbreviated as 'Full32' is the original setup comprising all 32 illuminations. The configuration denoted as 'Sparse12' contains a sparse but still quite homogeneous pattern with only 12 illuminations. In the 'Cross16' and 'Cross8' configurations, only two main illumination directions (i.e., horizontal and vertical) are covered with 16 and 8 illuminations, respectively. In the 'Lin8Hor' and 'Lin8Vert' configurations, the sparsification goes further to considering only horizontal or vertical illumination direction, in both cases using 8 illuminations. Finally, the configurations referred to as 'TopRing8', 'MidRing12', and 'LowRing12' represent three full ring patterns, that associate with the three illumination levels of the light dome.

5   Information Theoretic Analysis

We are interested in quantifying the relationship between the reduction in the number of illumination sources and the loss in information content and whether the information content could be preserved using a reduced number of illuminations using a well-chosen arrangement pattern.

The most characteristic property of a DOVID point in contrast to normal print is that its color appearance changes significantly when illuminated/observed from various directions. Therefore, we associate the amount of information contained in a single DOVID point with the amount of different colors contained in its BRDF. In information theory, the *information content* of a sequence of events with N possible states is defined as[8]:

$$I = \sum_{i=1}^{n} -\log_N(p_i), \tag{2}$$

where n is the length of the sequence and p_i is the probability for the state. In our case, n is given by the number of considered illuminations and a state is represented by a DOVID point's color sample $(r_i, g_i, b_i) \in [0, 255]^3$ associated with the i-th illumination direction. In practice, p_i is estimated empirically as the color's relative frequency in the illumination sequence. In order to stabilize the statistics, we considered an equidistant quantization of RGB colors into 16 brightness values per channel, which results in the number of states of $N = 4096$.

Fig. 4 shows an example of the information content analysis conducted on a genuine EUR20 DOVID for three illumination patterns 'Full32', 'Sparse12', and 'Cross16'. One can see that, in the case of 'Full32', DOVID points throughout the entire DOVID area contain a lot of information. Although the general tendency remains the same in both remaining cases, the absolute amount of information is significantly lower in these cases. Interestingly, the illumination pattern 'Cross16' seems to contain more information than 'Sparse12' despite the lack of diagonal illumination directions. On the other hand, the obvious result of the missing diagonal illuminations is that DOVID points exhibiting high information content tend to group predominantly in the center around number '20' and fade out towards margins.

In order to get the information content for the entire DOVID area, we introduce the histogram h_I of pixel-wise information contents collected over all DOVID points (see Fig. 4, d-f). Furthermore, we express the *global information content* comprised in the DOVID by means of the median value $\tilde{h}_I$ of the information content histogram.

The theoretical maximum information content that can be encoded in a sequence of n events is achieved when the sequence is comprised of exactly n

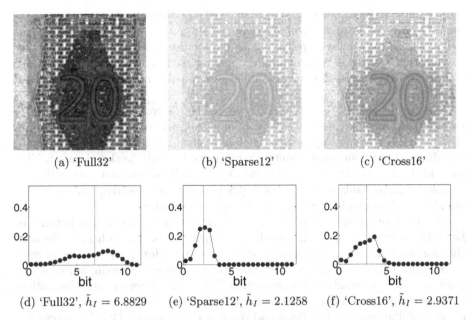

(a) 'Full32'   (b) 'Sparse12'   (c) 'Cross16'

(d) 'Full32', $\tilde{h}_I = 6.8829$ (e) 'Sparse12', $\tilde{h}_I = 2.1258$ (f) 'Cross16', $\tilde{h}_I = 2.9371$

Fig. 4. (a-c) Images of pixel-wise information content obtained for a genuine EUR20 DOVID using three different illumination patterns (darker means higher information content). (d-f) Corresponding information content histograms h_I over all DOVID points in (a-c), respectively. The vertical lines mark the global information content represented by the median value $\tilde{h}_I$ of h_I.

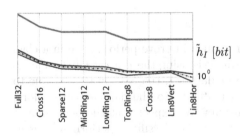

Fig. 5. Global information content $\tilde{h}_I$ for different illumination patterns analyzing DOVIDs of all 30 banknotes. The bold solid line marks the theoretical maximum information content for each individual illumination pattern. The dotted line indicates the average information content over all analyzed banknotes, the solid lines mark minimum and maximum values.

different states. In Fig. 5, the theoretical maximum information content of each considered illumination pattern is compared with the actual values obtained for a sample of 30 DOVIDs on banknotes. Rather small difference between minimum and maximum values observed in the database confirms that the average global information content can be taken as a representative for the entire database.

The fact, that the actual global information content obtained in all configurations (even 'Full32') is lower than the theoretical maximum, gives an indication of a certain redundancy in the underlying data, which also suggests that the illumination configurations could be optimized. On the other hand, the proportional drop of the obtained information content with the theoretical maximum shows that the proportion of the contained information w.r.t. the theoretical maximum remains constant, regardless of the illumination configuration. This would suggest that, whatever illumination configuration is considered, the amount of preserved information is mostly influenced by the number of illumination directions.

One exceptional case is 'Lin8Hor', where the information content drops to almost 0, which indicates especially poor performance of this configuration. Given the fact there is no principle difference between 'Lin8Hor' and 'Lin8Vert', the observed behavior must admittedly originate from the testing data set. The most likely reason why 'Lin8Hor' performed so badly on our data set is that it consists of Euro banknotes only, DOVIDs of which are sensitive mostly to the illumination/observation changes in the vertical direction.

From the obtained results it is not yet clear which illumination pattern is favorable over the others. The conclusion which can be drawn here is the fact that for most illumination patterns (except for 'Lin8Hor'), the amount of preserved information remains proportional to the theoretical maximum, which is given just by the number of illumination directions. However, an information theoretic investigation does not consider the dependencies between states in the domain of illumination directions and the fact that the used DOVID descriptor uses eccentricity and orientation derived from of the entire BRDF (instead as spatially uncorrelated color samples). Therefore, we conducted further investigations, described respectively in Sections 6 and 7, where discriminant and cluster analysis approaches are pursued, making direct use of the DOVID descriptor.

6   Discriminant Analysis

In order to identify illumination patterns which improve performance in a classification task, we applied discriminant analysis using the *nearest-neighbor classifier* (NNC). Given the limitations of our data set, the NNC was used due to its favorable asymptotic properties, strict affinity to the data and, therefore, straightforward interpretability of the results. We expect that the performance of the illumination pattern will be reflected in the classifier's performance, generating different numbers of incorrect predictions.

As for the NNC dissimilarity measure, we employed the *cosine dissimilarity* defined as follows, were H_i are descriptors as defined in Eq. 1:

$$D_{\cos}(H_1, H_2) = 1 - \frac{\langle H_1, H_2 \rangle}{||H_1|| \, ||H_2||} \in [0, 1]. \qquad (3)$$

$D_{\cos}(H_1, H_2) = 1$ if H_1 and H_2 are orthogonal, i.e. maximally dissimilar, and $D_{\cos}(H_1, H_2) = 0$ if H_1 and H_2 are parallel, i.e., maximally similar.

For each illumination pattern, we performed the NNC on the respective 30 DOVID descriptors using the *leave-one-out cross-validation* scheme (i.e., the training set comprises all available data except for the one classified sample).

Table 1. Confusion matrices associated with different illumination patterns obtained by the nearest-neighbor classification of DOVID descriptors. Correct predictions are marked in gray color, while black color stands for errors.

Class \Pred.	(a) 'Full32' 'Cross16' 'Sparse12' 'MidRing12' 'LowRing12'				(b) 'TopRing8'				(c) 'Cross8'				(d) 'Lin8Vert'				(e) 'Lin8Hor'			
	EUR5	EUR10	EUR20	EUR50	EUR5	EUR10	EUR20	EUR50	EUR5	EUR10	EUR20	EUR50	EUR5	EUR10	EUR20	EUR50	EUR5	EUR10	EUR20	EUR50
EUR5	16	0	0	0	16	0	0	0	16	0	0	0	14	0	2	0	16	0	0	0
EUR10	0	8	0	0	0	8	0	0	0	8	0	0	0	8	0	0	0	8	0	0
EUR20	0	0	3	0	0	1	2	0	1	0	2	0	3	0	0	0	2	1	0	0
EUR50	0	0	0	3	0	0	0	3	0	0	0	3	0	0	0	3	2	0	0	1

The obtained results were summarized in a form of *confusion matrices*, where all correct and incorrect predictions are clearly visible (see Table 1).

As can be seen in Table 1 (a), for five illumination patterns (i.e., 'Full32', 'Cross16', 'Sparse12', 'MidRing12', 'LowRing12'), the NNC generate no error suggesting that there is enough information preserved with all illumination patterns to perform perfect classification of our tiny data set. In accordance with conclusions of the information theoretic analysis from Section 5, only one mistake was made in both cases of 'TopRing8' and 'Cross8' (see Table 1, b-c), regardless of the fact that 'TopRing8' considers 8 azimuths on one height level, while 'Cross8' considers only 4 azimuths on two height levels. On the other hand, contrary to the information theoretic analysis, the discriminant analysis gives a clear evidence that different illumination patterns with the same number of illumination directions may after all perform differently, despite an equal amount of preserved information content. This fact is well demonstrated with the 'TopRing8', 'Cross8', 'Lin8Vert' and 'Lin8Hor' configurations (see Table 1, b-e), which all use eight illuminations, however former two perform much better than latter two (i.e., one vs. five errors per 30 classified DOVIDs).

It is perceivable that illumination patterns covering densely various azimuths, but not necessarily height levels, (i.e., patterns with ≥ 12 illuminations) perform better in the DOVID classification task than the others. Using these illumination patterns, all DOVIDs in our limited data set were classified perfectly, regardless from the number of illuminations in each pattern. This observation strongly suggests that some reduction of illumination directions is reasonable, but it is still unclear if a simple ring illumination would suffice or if a more complicated illumination pattern (e.g., 'Sparse12') would be a better choice.

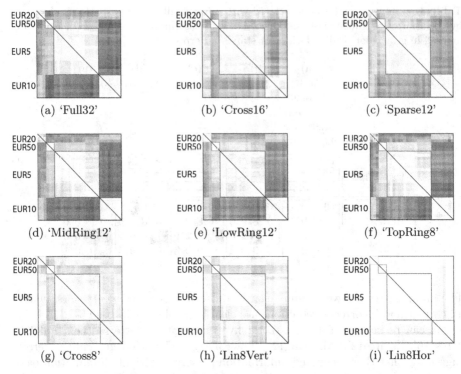

Fig. 6. Cosine dissimilarity matrices associated with different illumination patterns obtained for DOVIDs of 30 sample banknotes. The matrices depict mutual cosine distances between individual DOVID samples (darker means more distance), where each row and column refer to one particular sample. The lines and columns are sorted equally denomination-wise, so that squares marked along the diagonal correspond with DOVIDs of the same denomination and enclose within-cluster dissimilarities. All values found outside of these squares represent between-cluster dissimilarities.

7   Cluster Analysis

In some sense, the analysis conducted in this section is similar to the discriminant analysis from Section 6, as also here we make use of the cosine dissimilarity measure. In contrast to the NNC approach taken there, here we investigate the actual topology of the banknote denomination clusters in the DOVID descriptor spaces obtained for different illumination patterns instead of looking just into the numbers of errors. We determine how compact are the data clusters and how well they separate from each other. This approach should enable to see much gentler differences between analyzed illumination patterns than what was possible with the discriminant analysis.

In Fig. 6, *dissimilarity matrices* obtained for the different illumination patterns are shown. The matrices depict mutual cosine dissimilarities between individual DOVID samples comprised in our data set (where dark cells correspond

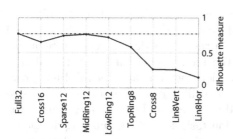

Fig. 7. Averaged cluster silhouette coefficients over all sample banknotes for the different illumination patterns.

to high dissimilarity, and vice versa). In order for the DOVID descriptors to accurately discriminate between denomination clusters, we expect that within-cluster dissimilarities should be smaller than those between members of different clusters. Visually one can already see that this criterion is quite well reflected in the cases of 'Full32', 'Sparse12', 'MidRing12', 'LowRing12', as well as 'TopRing8' (see Fig. 6, a and d-f). On the other hand, illumination patterns with a sparser coverage of azimuths (i.e. 'Cross16', 'Cross8', 'Lin8Vert', and 'Lin8Hor') seem to provide worse separation of clusters w.r.t. the within-cluster dissimilarities.

Quantitatively, such an evaluation can be implemented by means of any technique for validating the quality of cluster analysis results. In our case, we employed the *silhouette coefficient* [7] which puts in contrast average distances to elements of the same cluster and average distances to elements of the next nearest cluster. Fig. 7 shows a plot of the silhouette coefficients we obtained for each illumination pattern, where the silhouette values of the individual banknotes were averaged. The result confirms the impression formulated beforehand, that illumination patterns with a dense coverage of the azimuth angles perform better. Only 'TopRing8' performs distinctly worse among those ring illuminations, probably due to its inappropriate height level. Nevertheless, generally, it can be concluded that ring illumination setups comprise more distinctly separated denomination clusters.

Based on these observations, we conclude that covering many different azimuths is more important than considering multiple height levels. Moreover, the ring illumination pattern at the appropriate height level is equally good as the configuration comprising all LEDs in a sense of better discriminability of denomination clusters in the DOVID descriptor space.

8   Conclusions

We have analyzed different illumination patterns of a photometric illumination setup w.r.t. their suitability for characterizing DOVIDs. The analysis captured three different aspects: (i) an analysis of the information theoretic viewpoint, (ii) a discriminant analysis, and finally (iii) a detailed cluster analysis for better understanding the discriminant power of the DOVID descriptor. Although the presented experiments have been based just on a sample of 30 DOVIDs on genuine Euro banknotes of various denominations, we believe that the obtained results and conclusions have more general validity and extend to different DOVID types too. By means of the information theoretic approach, we could only show that the information content in the acquisitions is reduced by a certain amount mostly corresponding to the reduction of the number of illumination directions. Therefore, the information theoretic approach did not prove to be a suitable tool for identifying optimal illumination patterns. In the discriminant analysis, we attempted to address this problem by formulating the selection criteria through the classification task using NNC, making direct use of the DOVID descriptor. From this analysis we could see that illumination patterns with a dense coverage of illumination angles perform equally well as dense patterns with more height levels. On the other hand, patterns with poor coverage of illumination azimuths failed in the classification task. Only finally, the detailed investigation of banknote denomination clusters confirmed that the dense ring illumination at the appropriate height level may provide equal performance than configurations with more height levels. Regarding the future work, we will address a more elaborate statistical analysis of the classification performance using the DOVID descriptor on the basis of larger data sets, as well as investigate capabilities of counterfeit detection in more detail.

References

1. Hartl, A., Arth, C., Schmalstieg, D.: AR-based hologram detection on security documents using a mobile phone. In: Bebis, G., Boyle, R., Parvin, B., Koracin, D., McMahan, R., Jerald, J., Zhang, H., Drucker, S.M., Kambhamettu, C., El Choubassi, M., Deng, Z., Carlson, M. (eds.) ISVC 2014, Part II. LNCS, vol. 8888, pp. 335–346. Springer, Heidelberg (2014)
2. Hartl, A., Grubert, J., Schmalstieg, D., Reitmayr, G.: Mobile interactive hologram verification. In: Proc. of International Symposium on Mixed and Augmented Reality (ISMAR), pp. 75–82. Adelaide, AU, October 2013
3. Jehle, M., Jähne, B.: Optimal lighting for defect detection: illumination systems, machine learning, and practical verification. In: Forum Bildverarbeitung, pp. 241–252. KIT Scientific Publishing (2010)
4. McGrew, S.P.: Method and apparatus for reading and verifying holograms. U.S. Patent No. 6,263,104, July 2001
5. van Renesse, R.L.: Optical document security, 3rd edn. Artech House, Boston (2005)
6. van Renesse, R.L.: Testing the universal hologram scanner: a picture can speak a thousand words. Keesing Journal of Documents & Identity 12, 7–10 (2005)
7. Rousseeuw, P.J.: Silhouettes: a graphical aid to the interpretation and validation of cluster analysis. Journal of Computational and Applied Mathematics 20, 53–65 (1987)
8. Shannon, C.E.: A mathematical theory of communication. Bell System Technical Journal 27, 379–423 (1948)
9. Soukup, D., Štolc, S., Huber-Mörk, R.: Analysis of optically variable devices using a photometric light-field approach. In: Proc. of SPIE-IS&T Electronic Imaging - Media Watermarking, Security, and Forensics (to appear). San Francisco, CA, USA, February 2015

10. Štolc, S., Soukup, D., Huber-Mörk, R.: Invariant characterization of dovid security features using a photometric descriptor. In: Proc. of ICIP 2015 IEEE International Conference on Image Processing (SUBMITTED). Quebec City, Canada (2015)
11. Wang, O., Gunawardane, P., Scher, S., Davis, J.: Material classification using brdf slices, pp. 2805–2811, June 2009

Human Machine Interaction via Visual Speech Spotting

Ahmed Rekik[1](✉), Achraf Ben-Hamadou[2], and Walid Mahdi[1,3]

[1] Multimedia InfoRmation Systems and Advanced Computing Laboratory
(MIRACL), Sfax University Pôle technologique de Sfax,
BP 242, Route de Tunis Km 10, 3021 Sfax, Tunisia
rekikamed@gmail.com

[2] Driving Assistance Research Center, Valeo, 34 Rue St-André Z.I. des Vignes,
93012 Bobigny, Bobigny, France
achraf.ben-hamadou@valeo.com

[3] Department of Computer Science, College of Computers and Information
Technology, Taif University, 888, Hawiyah Taif 21974, Kingdom of Saudi Arabia
w.mahdi@tu.edu.sa

Abstract. In this paper, we propose an automatic visual speech spotting system adapted for RGB-D cameras and based on Hidden Markov Models (HMMs). Our system is based on two main processing blocks, namely, visual feature extraction and speech spotting and recognition. In feature extraction step, the speaker's face pose is estimated using a 3D face model including a rectangular 3D mouth patch used to precisely extract the mouth region. Then, spatio-temporal features are computed on the extracted mouth region. In the second step, the speech video is segmented by finding the starting and the ending points of meaningful utterances and recognized using Viterbi algorithm. The proposed system is mainly evaluated on an extended version of the MIRACL-VC1 dataset. Experimental results demonstrate that the proposed system can segment and recognize key utterances with a recognition rates of 83 % and a reliability of 81.4 %.

Keywords: Human machine interaction · Visual speech spotting · Visual speech features · RGB-camera · Kinect

1 Introduction

Visual speech recognition (VSR) is an active research area in the computer vision computing that can assist several applications like Human-Machine-Interaction (HMI) and biometrics [11,12,16]. Visual speech recognition system could provide an intuitive basis for Human-Machine-Interaction especially in a noisy environment (*e.g.,* noisy factory, car cockpit, *etc.*). Nevertheless, visual speech recognition is a challenging problem since the extracted visual features should be sufficiently informative regarding the uttered speech and must show a certain

© Springer International Publishing Switzerland 2015
S. Battiato et al. (Eds.): ACIVS 2015, LNCS 9386, pp. 566–574, 2015.
DOI: 10.1007/978-3-319-25903-1_49

level of invariance against the pose variation of the speaker's head [10]. In addition to the mouth shape, the visual features must encode the temporal deformation of a speaking mouth.

Several works in VSR are proposed these last years, especially with the arrival of RGB-D cameras which boosted the Human-Face-Analysis research field in general [1,5,13]. In contrast to gesture spotting [4,6,14], the visual speech spotting in a continuous stream has largely been ignored by researchers [16].

An important step in a Visual Speech Spotting (VSS) system consists of the segmentation of some meaningful speech segments from a continuous speech stream, which is highly difficult for three major reasons. First, it is difficult to determine when a speech segment (word, digit, *etc.*) starts and when it ends. Second, the duration of a speech segment can vary, even uttered by a same person. Lastly, unlike a VSR system working on isolated data, a VSS system should handle in addition non-meaningful utterances (*i.e.,* negative samples).

Since [5,9] present systems for isolated speech recognition, the main contribution of this paper is to introduce a visual speech spotting system that performs continuous speech segmentation and recognition simultaneously. Similarly to [5,9,10], we used RGB-D cameras for data acquisition and to cope with the latest advances in the field.

The proposed method uses a spotting network based on HMMs where we considered the Left-Right-Banded LRB topology to model each meaningful utterance and an ergodic topology model to model non-meaningful utterances. In addition, our method is based on [10] to extract mouth region and compute visual speech features with handling speakers' face pose variation.

The remaining of this paper is organized as follows. First, we present an overview of the proposed method. The different steps of the mouth region extraction and feature computing process are described in section 3. Finally, experimental results are provided to evaluate the performances of the proposed approach in case of continuous speech stream and also isolated speech.

2   General Framework

We propose a visual speech recognition and spotting system that detects and recognizes meaningful utterances in an RGB-D video sequence using Hidden Markov Models (HMMs) [7].

As illustrated in figure 1, the proposed system consists of two main steps. First, the input video sequence is preprocessed to extract visual speech features. In this step, we estimate, for each frame, the 3D face pose of the speaker using a 3D face model including a rectangular 3D mouth patch (see figure 2(a)). This mouth patch is projected to the frame data (2D image and depth map) to extract the mouth region. Then, mouth features are computed on the extracted mouth region. In the second step, the meaningful utterance are detected in the input video and recognized using the Viterbi algorithm [7].

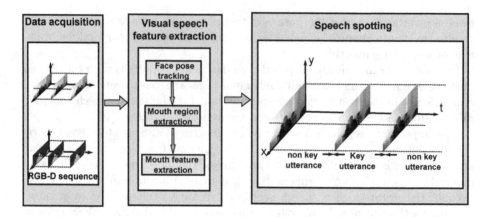

Fig. 1. General overview of our speech recognition and spotting system.

3   Visual Speech Feature Extraction

In the feature extraction process, it is unreasonable to assume that users face is fixed in front of the camera all the time during speaking. Therefore, there could be various head poses in the captured data. Since the visual appearance of a talking mouth could vary significantly in images due to the view change, pose variation poses a serious challenge to the features extraction step.

To reduce the effect of speakers face pose variation, we have used a feature extraction method proposed in [9]. This method is based on a 3D face pose tracking method [8] that can robustly estimate the speakers face pose with handling illumination condition changes. For each frame, the face pose tracking process estimates the optimal face pose involving the six degrees of freedom (*i.e.*, three translations and three rotation angles). As shown in figure 2(a), the mouth region is presented by a 3D rectangular patch. This patch rigidly follows the face motion by means of the estimated face poses. The size of the mouth patch is automatically scaled to adapt the speaker's face size [1]. The patch is densely sampled to $n_h \times n_w$ 3D points $\{P_{i,j}|i = 1, \ldots, n_h, j = 1, \ldots, n_w\}$. These points $P_{i,j}$ are then projected into the 2D image and the depth map yielding two rectified thumbnails (see figures 2(b) and 2(c)).

To describe the mouth shape and deformation during a visual speech sequence, we have computed appearance and motion descriptors on the extracted mouth regions. To model the mouth appearance, we have computed the Histogram of Oriented Gradient (HOG) descriptor [3] on extracted depth and the color mouth regions. We denote by HOG_c and HOG_d the HOG descriptor computed on the color and depth mouth region respectively. To model the temporal

---

[1] We note that the mouth patch size is fixed experimentally to $n_h = \frac{d_e}{7}, n_w = d_e$, where d_e represents the distance between speaker eyes center in the Candide face model (see [8] for more details).

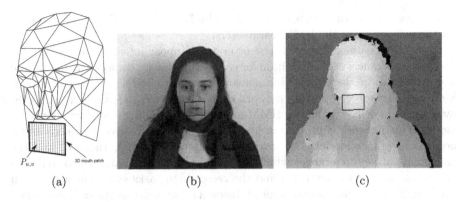

(a)   (b)   (c)

Fig. 2. Mouth region extraction. 2(a): 3D model used for 3D face tracking. The rectangular mesh corresponds to the mouth patch rigidly fixed to the face model. 2(b) and 2(c): Projection of the 3D mouth patch in the 2D image and the depth map, respectively.

mouth deformation we have used the Motion Boundary Histograms (MBH). For more details about mouth region extraction and feature computing see [9].

4 Visual Speech Recognition and Spotting

The task of spotting key utterances from a stream of input sequence is to find the start and end points of a meaningful utterance while ignoring the rest. Here, we discuss how to model key utterance patterns discriminately and how to model non-command patterns effectively. Each reference pattern for a key utterance is modelled by a HMM and all other patterns are modelled by a single HMM called a non key utterance model (garbage model), however, it is not easy to obtain the set of non key utterance patterns because there are infinite varieties of meaningless utterance.

For each key utterance model, each HMM state represents the local visual speech part, while the states transition represent the sequential order structure of an utterance. The number of HMM states is an important parameter because the excessive number of states can generate the over-fitting problem if the number of training samples is insufficient compared to the model parameters.

The number of states in our visual speech spotting system is based on the complexity of each key utterance. We considered the Left-Right Banded topology (LRB) for the following reasons. Since each state in Ergodic topology has many transitions than LeftRight (LR) and LRB topologies, the structure data can be lost easily. On the other hand, LRB topology has no backward transition where the state index either increases or stays the same as time increases. In addition, LRB topology is more restricted rather than LR topology and simple for training data that will be able to match the data to the model. To model the non key utterance pattern, we considered an ergodic topology trained on a set of non-key utterances. The feature vectors are trained by Baum-Welch (BW) algorithm [7] for the estimation of the HMM parameters.

In continuous visual speech, key utterances appear intermittently with pre- and post-utterances (*i.e.,* transition for connecting key utterances). To spot these key utterances, a speech spotting network is constructed as shown in figure 3. Moreover, the speech spotting network can be easily expanded the vocabularies by adding a new key utterance HMM model and rebuilding a non key utterance model. This network contains ten gesture models for ten key utterances and a non key utterance model. The speech spotting network finds the start and the end points of key utterances which are embedded in the input video sequence and performs the segmentation and the recognition tasks simultaneously. Each HMM in figure 3 contains two kinds of states: a set of emitting states (solid circle) and a non-emitting states (dashed circle). The emitting states are associated with observations, while the non-emitting states are not associated with any observation. The transitions from an non-emitting state to the an emitting state is denoted by dashed lines and the rest of transitions are denoted by solid lines.

5   Experiments and Results

The proposed system is mainly evaluated using RGB-D sequences of speakers from the MIRACL-VC1 dataset [2].

The MIRACL-VC1 dataset consists of 1500 word data(15 persons×10 words×10 times/word) and 1500 phrases (15 persons×10 phrases×10 times/phrase). The dataset covers words like *navigation, connection, etc.* and phrases like *Nice to meet you, I love this game, etc.*. The Kinect sensor is used to acquire 2D images and depth maps with a resolution of 640 × 480 and at an acquisition rate of 15 fps. The distance between the speaker and the Kinect is about 1 *m*. The calibration parameters of the Kinect camera can be obtained using [2,15].

In this section, we start by evaluating the performances of our system to recognize isolated visual speech segments. Then, we present the robustness of our system to detect key utterances in a continuous speech sequence.

5.1   Results of Isolated Visual Speech Recognition

In this experiment, we adopt two configurations for visual speech recognition: speaker independent and speaker dependent.

 - In the speaker independent (SI) experiment, the training and the query data are from different speakers. We employ the leave-one-out strategy where data from a single speaker are used as the validation data, and the remaining speakers are used as the training data. This is repeated for each speaker in the dataset.

---

[2] MIRACL-VC1 is accessible following
https://sites.google.com/site/achrafbenhamadou/-datasets/miracl-vc1

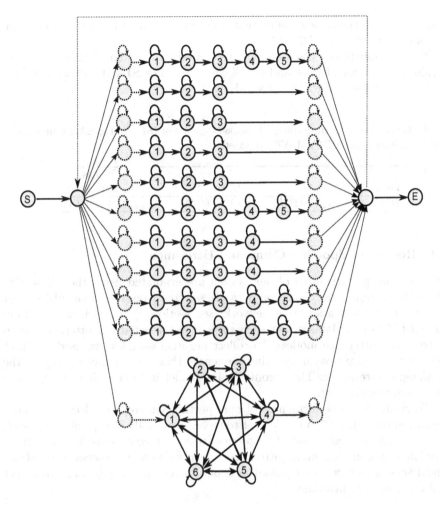

Fig. 3. The visual speech spotting network which contains ten key utterance models and the non meaningful utterance model. The key utterances are modeled by an LRB topology (ten first models) and the non key utterances are modeled using an ergodic topology.

- In the speaker dependent(SD) experiment, the training and the testing data are from the same speaker.

To evaluate the recognition of isolated speech segments on the MIRACL-VC1 dataset, we have considered all words and phrases of the dataset as isolated utterance, then, we have applied our method to compute different descriptors on the extracted mouth regions. In [9], a lip reading system is evaluated with different combination of appearance and motion descriptors using a support vector machine (SVM) classifier and the presented results show that the best performance is obtained for the combination HOG_c+HOG_d+MBH. Based on these results, we used the same combination of descriptors to evaluate the recognition of isolated speech using HMMs.

Table 1 illustrates the obtained recognition rates. For **SD** settings, we obtained 95.1% for phrases and 93.4% for words. For **SI** settings, we obtained 69.7% for phrases and 62.1% for words.

Table 1. Lipreading performances of speaker dependent (SD) and speaker independent (SI) experiments on MIRACL-VC1 dataset.

	Phrases		Words	
Descriptors	**SD**	**SI**	**SD**	**SI**
$HOG_c + HOG_d + MBH$	95.1%	69.7%	93.4%	62.1%

5.2   Results of Spotting Command Utterance

The spotting performances of our system are evaluated using the SD setting where the training and validation data are selected from the same subject. For this, we have built a spotting network (see section 4) for each subject from the MIRACL-VC1 dataset. For each subject, we selected ten utterances from to train key utterance models. To collect negative samples, we used a Kinect camera to acquire several speaking sequences that do not include any of the meaningful utterances. The ergodic HMM model is then trained using these additional negative data.

To evaluate the performances of our spotting system, we selected five subjects from the MIRACL-VC1 dataset to record new RGB-D sequences. For each sequence, the subject is asked to pronounce a text containing key utterances separated by non meaningful utterances. Each video is preprocessed to extract visual speech features, and passed as input to the spotting network to detect and recognize key utterances.

Table 2. visual speech spotting performances.

Test	True	Deletion	Substitution	Insertion	recognition	reliability
40	34	1	5	0	85 %	85 %
40	31	1	8	1	77.5%	75.6%
40	32	1	7	2	80 %	76.1%
40	34	2	4	0	85 %	85%
40	35	2	3	1	87.5 %	85.3%

In table 2, we present the obtained performances of spotting where three types of errors are considered (insertion, substitution and deletion). The insertion error is occurred when the spotter detects a non existent utterance. A substitution error occurs when the key utterance is classified falsely (*i.e.,* classifies the utterance as another utterance). This error is usually happened when the extracted features are falsely quantized to other speech. The deletion error happens when the spotter fails to detect a key utterance. In order to calculate the recognition ratio (see equation 1), insertion errors are totally not considered.

$$recognition = \frac{recognized\ utterances}{test\ utterances} \times 100 \tag{1}$$

Deletion errors directly affect the recognition ratio whereas insertion errors do not. However, the insertion errors affect the speech spotting ratio directly. To take into consideration the effect of insertion errors, another performance measure called reliability (Rel) is proposed by the following equation:

$$Reliability = \frac{correctly\ recognized\ utterances}{test\ utterances\ +\ Insertion\ error} \times 100 \tag{2}$$

6 Conclusion and Perspectives

In this paper, we have proposed a visual speech spotting and recognition system in continuous RGB-D video sequences.

The proposed system is performed within two main steps. First, mouth feature extraction is performed based on a 3D face pose tracking on the input video to robustly extract the mouth region. The 3D poses are then used to position a 3D rectangular patch to extract the normalized mouth region. Then, motion and appearance descriptors are computed on the extracted mouth regions and combined to generate a set of visual feature vectors. In the second step, we performed a key utterance spotting and recognition based on HMMs. To this end, we have proposed a spotting network containing ten key utterance models and a single non key utterance model.

We have evaluated our system on the MIRACL-VC1 dataset. The obtained results show that our system can recognize isolated phrases with 95.1 % of recognition rate using SD configuration. The results of spotting key utterances show that our system can detect and recognize key utterances in continuous video flow with a mean of 83 % of recognition rate and 81.4 % of reliability.

The proposed system can be adapted to Human-Machine-Interaction applications were a set of key utterances can be set to activate a set of corresponding commands such as for devices in car-cockpit or a machine in a noisy factory.

References

1. Bakry, A., Elgammal, A.: Mkpls: manifold kernel partial least squares for lipreading and speaker identification. In: International Conference on Computer Vision and Pattern Recognition, pp. 684–691 (2013)
2. Ben-Hamadou, A., Soussen, C., Daul, C., Blondel, W., Wolf, D.: Flexible calibration of structured-light systems projecting point patterns. Computer Vision and Image Understanding 117(10), 1468–1481 (2013)

3. Dalal, N., Triggs, B.: Histograms of oriented gradients for human detection. International Conference on Computer Vision and Pattern Recognition **1**, 886–893 (2005)
4. Hoste, L., De Rooms, B., Signer, B.: Declarative gesture spotting using inferred and refined control points. In: ICPRAM, pp. 144–150 (2013)
5. Pei, Y., Kim, T.-K., Zha, H.: Unsupervised random forest manifold alignment for lipreading. In: International Conference on Computer Vision, pp. 129–136 (2013)
6. Peng, B., Qian, G.: Online gesture spotting from visual hull data. Pattern Analysis and Machine Intelligence, IEEE Transactions on **33**(6), 1175–1188 (2011)
7. Rabiner, L.: A tutorial on hidden markov models and selected applications in speech recognition. Proceedings of the IEEE **77**(2), 257–286 (1989)
8. Rekik, A., Ben-Hamadou, A., Mahdi, W.: Face pose tracking under arbitrary illumination changes. In: International Conference on Computer Vision, Imaging and Computer Graphics Theory and Applications (2014)
9. Rekik, A., Ben-Hamadou, A., Mahdi, W.: A new visual speech recognition approach for RGB-D cameras. In: Campilho, A., Kamel, M. (eds.) ICIAR 2014, Part II. LNCS, vol. 8815, pp. 21–28. Springer, Heidelberg (2014)
10. Rekik, A., Ben-Hamadou, A., Mahdi, W.: An adaptive approach for lip-reading using image and depth data. Multimedia Tools and Applications, pp. 1–28 (2015)
11. Rekik, A., Ben-Hamadou, A., Mahdi, W.: Unified system for visual speech recognition and speaker identification. In: Proc. of Advanced Concepts for Intelligent Vision Systems (ACIVS) (2015)
12. Shiell, D.J., Terry, L.H., Aleksic, P.S., Katsaggelos, A.K.: Audio-visual and visual-only speech and speaker recognition: Issues about theory, system design. Visual speech recognition: lip segmentation and mapping 1–38 (2009)
13. Shin, J., Lee, J., Kim, D.: Real-time lip reading system for isolated korean word recognition. Pattern Recognition **44**(3), 559–571 (2011)
14. Yang, S.-E., Park, K.-H., Bien, Z.: Gesture spotting using fuzzy garbage model and user adaptation. Contemporary Theory and Pragmatic Approaches in Fuzzy Computing Utilization 120 (2012)
15. Zhang, Z.: A flexible new technique for camera calibration. Pattern Analysis and Machine Intelligence **22**(11), 1330–1334 (2000)
16. Zhou, Z., Zhao, G., Hong, X., Pietikäinen, M.: A review of recent advances in visual speech decoding. Image and Vision Computing (2014)

Improving Kinect-Skeleton Estimation

Jakub Valcik$^{(\boxtimes)}$, Jan Sedmidubsky, and Pavel Zezula

Masaryk University, Botanicka 68a, 60200 Brno, Czech Republic
xvalcik@fi.muni.cz

Abstract. Capturing human movement activities through various sensor technologies is becoming more and more important in entertainment, film industry, military, healthcare or sports. The Microsoft Kinect is an example of low-cost capturing technology that enables to digitize human movement into a 3D motion representation. However, the accuracy of this representation is often underestimated which results in decreasing effectiveness of Kinect applications. In this paper, we propose advanced post-processing methods to improve the accuracy of the Kinect skeleton estimation. By evaluating these methods on real-life data we decrease the error in accuracy of measured lengths of bones more than two times.

1 Introduction

The Microsoft Kinect is probably the most popular low-cost motion capturing device with more than 24 million units sold as of February 2013. A new version of this device, called the Microsoft Kinect v2 (see Figure 1), was introduced in 2014. Both the versions provide users with a Software Development Kit (SDK) which enables to transform input camera streams into 3D motion data in real-time. Real-time tracking has brought a lot of sophisticated human-computer interaction ideas to be employed in various application fields. For example, the Kinect has been examined in healthcare to monitor and improve the process of physical therapy and rehabilitation [4,20], at smarthomes and public places to detect falls of elderly people [3,12], in computer games to enhance the user-computer interaction [6,16], in security to identify special-interest persons [11, 15], or in robotics to navigate a robot using hand gestures [19].

Disregarding the specific application domain, motion data captured by the Kinect are usually preprocessed by extracting high-dimensional features which are then compared by distance-based functions [17] or machine-learning methods [2,9]. Although a lot of endeavor is devoted to design the most suitable features and comparison methods, effectiveness of the application is highly influenced by the *accuracy* of input motion data. For example, to be able to differentiate subjects based on their lengths of bones only, the 3D positions of skeleton joints have to be captured with the accuracy on the level of millimeters. Unfortunately, the accuracy of the Kinect joint estimation is about 10 cm [13]. Such a high inaccuracy can be only used to assess general trends in the movement, but for quantitative estimation an improved skeletonization is needed.

P. Zezula—Supported by the Czech Science Foundation project No. P103/12/G084.

S. Battiato et al. (Eds.): ACIVS 2015, LNCS 9386, pp. 575–587, 2015.
DOI: 10.1007/978-3-319-25903-1_50

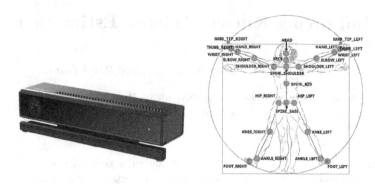

Fig. 1. Kinect v2 device (left) and Kinect v2 human-body model (right).

The inaccuracy of the Kinect skeleton estimation motivates us to propose advanced post-processing methods that highly improve the estimation of skeleton proportions from captured motion data. In particular, we propose and compare a number of methods to estimate skeleton proportions more accurately in real-life scenarios, e.g., from ordinary walking during a medical examination. We hope that the proposed methods can improve a wide range of Kinect applications relaying on the accuracy of skeleton proportions. In summary, the main contributions of this paper are:

- definition of aspects that highly influence the accuracy of skeletonization;
- proposal of 8 variants of advanced methods to estimate skeleton proportions;
- experimental comparison of the proposed methods against 25 variants of simple approaches on real-life Kinect data.

2   Related Work

The principles of motion data acquisition and a basic comparison of both Kinect v1 and v2 properties is given in an extensive survey [10]. The low-level accuracy of Kinect v1 depth data is analyzed in [8] to show the need of a proper camera calibration in order to achieve the accuracy of depth reconstruction of approximately 4 cm at a distance of 5 m. The rotational accuracy of both Kinect versions is evaluated and compared with provided manufacturer specifications in [1]. This evaluation shows an improvement in the rotational accuracy of the Kinect v2, however, the average rotational accuracy error still ranges from 1 to 3.2 . These findings support the need of a more accurate skeleton estimation.

The accuracy of the Kinect v1 skeleton estimation is evaluated in several studies. Obdržálek et al. [13] compare joint estimation of the Kinect v1 and more precise marker-based optical device Impulse[1] in the context of coaching of elderly population. Fernández-Baena et al. [7] develop an application for guided rehabilitation treatments and evaluate the Kinect v1 usability against another professional marker-based optical device Vicon MX[2]. A similar analysis is con-

---

[1] PhaseSpace, http://www.phasespace.com [accessed 30/04/2015].

[2] Vicon, http://www.vicon.com [accessed 30/04/2015].

ducted in [5] where the accuracy and robustnes of Microsoft Kinect SDK and opensource OpenNI NITE[3] is compared to the precise Vicon device. All the presented approaches provide information about the estimated accuracy in comparison with more precise devices. However, analyses are conducted only on the Kinect v1 and no techniques for the skeletonization improvements are proposed.

3 Skeleton Tracking by Kinect v2

The Kinect v2 enables to digitize movement of up to 6 human subjects in the view range of 0.5–4.5 m from the camera source. The movement is digitized with frequency of 30 frames per second in the following four steps [10]: (1) retrieving the stream of depth frames containing one or more human subjects, (2) performing background subtraction from depth frames, (3) matching the extracted subject against an extensive trained model to estimate the current skeleton configuration, and (4) inferring the joint positions once the current skeleton configuration is estimated.

The digitized movement is then represented by a stream of skeleton configurations, called *poses*. Each pose describes the positions of 25 human-body *joints* which are visualized in Figure 1. Formally, motion m is defined as a sequence $(p_1, \ldots, p_n)$ of poses p_i $(i \in [1, n])$ where n equals to the motion length (i.e., the number of captured frames). Each pose p_i is a 25-dimensional vector $(j_1, \ldots, j_{25})$ of 3-dimensional real-world coordinates $j_i \in \mathbb{R}^3$ $(i \in [1, 25])$ that correspond to the specific body joints.

Based on the joint positions, we can measure lengths of individual *bones* in each pose – simply by calculating the Euclidean distance between the positions of the given pair of joints. In an ideal case, the length of the given bone should not vary over time. However, Figure 2 depicts how the length of left-tibia bone varies over 90 consecutive poses in standing and walking scenarios. Both the scenarios are repeated three times where individual repetitions are visualized by red, blue and violet color. Even if the bone length varies up to 2 cm during stationary standing, the error during walking is more than 10 cm, which is also confirmed by results in [13]. Such a high inaccuracy is primarily caused by fitting an unsuitable trained body model and imprecise estimation of joint coordinates. This situation motivates us to propose statistical methods to estimate lengths of bones much more accurately.

4 Improving Skeleton Proportions Estimation

Skeleton proportions vary over time because of an inaccurate estimation of joint coordinates, as is demonstrated in the previous section on a floating length of the left-tibia bone. In addition, the variability increases when a subject is moving (e.g., during walking) in contrast to a stationary stance. This is the reason why it is highly risky to determine lengths of bones of the given subject just by taking

---

[3] OpenNI, http://structure.io/openni [accessed 30/04/2015].

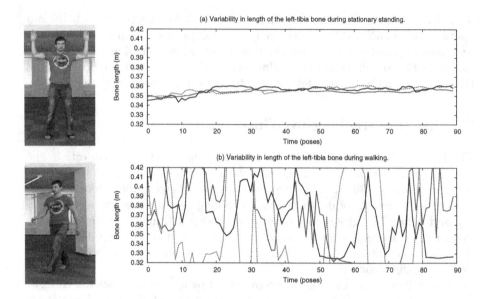

Fig. 2. Variability in length of the left-tibia bone measured over 90 poses. The bone length is measured three times independently – visualized by red, blue and violet color – for both (a) standing and (b) walking scenarios.

skeleton configurations from the first (or randomly chosen) motion pose. To get closer to the "real ground-truth" of the subject, we propose to consider the four following aspects which can highly improve the accuracy of skeletonization.

1. **Measures** – application of statistical measures, such as average, median or standard deviation, to estimate lengths of bones in a sufficiently representative set of poses rather than considering a single randomly chosen pose.
2. **Motion Scope** – detection of semantically interesting movement segments, such as left/right footsteps or walk cycles, which can carry more accurate information about skeleton proportions than randomly chosen poses.
3. **Movement Repetitions** – aggregation of multiple segments of the same type within a single motion. Multiple movement instances can carry more accurate information than only a single movement.
4. **Movement Direction** – determination of movement direction with respect to the Kinect location. The lengths of the specific bones vary much more in one direction than in the others, with respect to the camera source.

By considering these aspects, we propose simple and advanced ways of skeleton estimation, with a special focus on a walking scenario. Before introducing individual methods, we describe the above mentioned aspects in more detail.

4.1 Aspects of Improved Skeletonization

This subsection introduces supporting techniques within the specific aspects to be utilized by the proposed simple as well as advanced skeletonization methods.

Measures. To simply estimate skeleton proportions of the given subject, (1) the *first* or (2) a *random* motion pose is chosen from which lengths of bones are calculated. As the first or random pose can contain misleading information about skeleton proportions, we propose to calculate lengths of bones in each pose and apply common statistical measures, such as (3) *average*, (4) *median* and (5) *mode*, on the computed distances. Although these measures are easy to implement and do not require any special preprocessing, they themselves cannot profit from the knowledge of a performed movement type nor its repetitions.

Motion Scope. We propose to analyze an input motion to identify its semantically interesting movement segments, such as footsteps and walk cycles, and use them in a favor of a more accurate skeleton estimation. We use the term "motion scope" to denote the level of motion which is used for estimating proportions. In particular, we estimate proportions on the level of (1) the whole *motion*, (2) left or right *footsteps* and (3) the whole *walk cycle*, i.e., the left and successive right footstep, extracted from the walking motion. To automatically extract footsteps/walk cycles, we apply an enhanced version of the walk cycle detection algorithm [18]. By applying this algorithm to the whole motion, we obtain a number of movement segments with the following advantages:

- detected segments do not already consist of marginal or deformed poses where body-model fitting and joint coordinates estimation is very poor, due to body-part occlusions and bad light conditions;
- advanced skeletonization methods can benefit from the knowledge of the specific segment type and its multiple occurrences within a single motion.

Movement Repetitions. Multiple occurrences of movements of the same type enable to determine "average" and "outlying" motion segments. By filtering out the outliers, advanced methods are believed to estimate lengths of bones from more similar segments more accurately. To analyze segments of walk cycles more deeply, we further normalize each walk cycle to a fixed length of $\bar{n}$ poses, where $\bar{n} = 32$ corresponds to the average walk-cycle length. This is implemented by shortening or prolonging each walk cycle of length n in a way that its i-th pose corresponds to the $\lfloor i \cdot \frac{\bar{n}}{n} \rfloor$-th pose of the normalized segment, similarly as in [14].

Movement Direction. By studying characteristics of many walk cycles we find out that the direction in which a subject walks relatively to the Kinect highly influences the accuracy of skeletonization. In addition, the length of some bones floats much more in one direction in contrast to other bones, and vice versa in the opposite direction. Based on these findings we define the walk cycle direction as a vector between skeleton coordinates of the root joint in the first pose and in the last pose. This simplification is based on the assumption that the subject walks more or less straight and if there is a significant turn during walking, then such walk cycle is not probably identified. The resulting vector is finally quantized into four directions (north, east, south, and west), where the Kinect is heading to the north. By analyzing experimental data, we recommend to measure the 9 skeleton proportions with respect to the directions presented in Figure 4.

4.2   Advanced Skeletonization Methods

We use the term "simple methods" to denote skeletonization approaches that apply the specific measure to the motion of the given scope, without considering movement repetitions nor its direction. The set of 25 variants of simple methods is introduced and evaluated against 8 variants of advanced methods.

The advanced methods primarily estimate skeleton proportions based on analyzing normalized walk-cycle segments detected within walking motions. Due to the same length of each normalized walk cycle, lengths of the given bone in the same movement phase can be compared across multiple walk cycles, instead of analyzing the bone within each walk cycle independently. Formally, we denote $m = (p_1, \ldots, p_{\bar{n}})$ as a walk cycle consisting of exactly $\bar{n}$ poses. Having the given bone specified by a pair of joint indexes j_1 and j_2, we compute its length in the f-th pose by the following function:

$$pose\_bone\_length^{j_1, j_2}(p_f) = ||c_{j_1}, c_{j_2}||,$$

where $j_1, j_2 \in [1, 25], f \in [1, \bar{n}]$ and c_{j_1}, c_{j_2} are 3D joint coordinates of pose $p_f = (c_1, \ldots, c_{25})$ between which the bone length is computed on the basis of the Euclidean distance. In this way, we can compute the bone length for each walk cycle in the same movement phase. By computing the bone length across the set $M = \{m_1, \ldots, m_l\}$ of l normalized walk cycles, we obtain the set $B^{j_1, j_2}(f, M)$ of bone lengths in the f-th pose as:

$$B^{j_1, j_2}(f, M) = \{pose\_bone\_length^{j_1, j_2}(p_f) \,|\, \forall m \in M : p_f \in m\}.$$

The lengths of the specific bone in each B set should be ideally equal since they are calculated in the same movement phase across several instances of walk cycles. However, this is faraway from true – Figure 3 illustrates the variability in length of the left-tibia bone measured on 8 instances of walk cycles which are normalized to $\bar{n} = 32$ poses. To determine the bone length as much accurately as possible, we consider the set F of only k *important* movement phases $F = \{f_1, \ldots, f_k\}$ $(k \in [1, \bar{n}])$ where the variability should be small. The resulting bone length is finally calculated by averaging bone lengths in all important movement phases as:

$$bone\_length^{j_1, j_2}(F, M) = \frac{\sum_{f \in F} \sum_{b \in B^{j_1, j_2}(f, M)} b}{|F| \cdot |M|}.$$

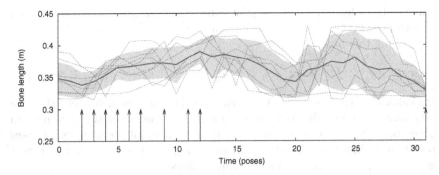

Fig. 3. Variability in length of the left-tibia bone measured in 8 instances of walk cycles which are normalized to 32 poses. The variability of each walk cycle is visualized by the gray dashed line, wheras the red line denotes the average value with corresponding standard deviations in form of pink bars. Blue arrows denote the ten ($k = 10$) detected important movement phases where standard deviation is the smallest.

To determine k important movement phases, we introduce the following two approaches based on minimization of standard deviation of bone lengths and minimization of joint velocities.

Minimization of Standard Deviation in Multiple Walk Cycles

This approach selects the desired k poses based on calculating standard deviation on bone lengths for each of $\bar{n}$ bone sets B. The objective is to consider only such bone sets where the standard deviation is minimal. The smaller the standard deviation is, the higher probability of the correctly determined bone length is. Standard deviation of the bone between joints j_1 and j_2 in the f-th pose is computed as:

$$bone\_std\_dev^{j_1,j_2}(f, M) = \sqrt{\frac{\sum_{b \in B^{j_1,j_2}(f,M)} (b - b_{avg})^2}{|M|}},$$

where b_{avg} is the average bone length within the input bone set $B^{j_1,j_2}(f, M)$. As standard deviation is computed for each bone set, these sets are sorted according to their standard deviation in ascending order. Then the first k sets corresponding to the specific poses are considered as the important movement phases. In Figure 3, $k = 10$ important phases are identified from 8 walk-cycle instances.

Minimization of Joint Velocities in Multiple Walk Cycles

Another approach to select the k important movement phases is based on measuring joint velocities. The motivation is to determine the moments where the measured bone moves the most slowly. The slower the bone is moving, the more accurate Kinect joint estimation is considered. To calculate the *joint velocity*, we measure the Euclidean distance the joint travels over one pose. The *bone velocity* in the f-th pose is then defined as a maximum of velocities of both joints j_1 and j_2 determining this bone:

$$bone\_velocity^{j_1,j_2}(f) = \max\{||c_{j_1} \in p_f, c_{j_1} \in p_{f+1}||, ||c_{j_2} \in p_f, c_{j_2} \in p_{f+1}||\}.$$

Having calculated the bone velocity for each motion pose, we determine the *pose velocity* over multiple walk cycles as the median of bone velocities measured in the given pose. Similarly as in the previous approach, all the walk-cycle poses are sorted according to their velocity in ascending order and the first k slowest poses are chosen as the important movement phases.

5   Experimental Evaluation

We evaluate a number of variants of the proposed simple and advanced methods that estimate skeleton proportions from walking motions. These methods combine different aspects of measures, motion scopes, movement repetitions and directions. The evaluation is based on comparing the results of individual methods against the skeleton ground-truth, which is measured for each subject.

5.1   Dataset

All the experiments are evaluated on our own dataset captured by the Microsoft Kinect v2 device. The dataset consists of 270 motion sequences performed by 10 subjects (9 males and 1 female of age 25–67 and height of 164–188 cm). Each subject is recorded in 7 different movement scenarios which focus on measuring proportions during standing and walking in different distances and directions from the Kinect. All the scenarios are presented in Table 1, where direction values are abbreviations for north (N), east (E), south (S) and west (W). Individual scenarios constitute three different motion types: (1) *T-pose* is the standing subject with legs slightly apart and outstretched hands bent in elbows so the fingers point up, (2) *U-turn* represents walking directly towards the device and approximately 0.5 m in front of it U-turn (right or left) is performed and walking continues in the opposite direction, and (3) *diagonal walking* is performed by walking from one of distant corners of the Kinect field-view to the opposite corner nearer to the device, i.e., from the NE corner to the SW corner and from the NW corner to the SE corner.

5.2   Ground Truth

The ground truth we create consists of skeleton proportions – lengths of bones – for each subject. In particular, we focus only on the 9 main bones: L/R tibia, L/R femur, L/R humerus, L/R radius, and hip width. Measuring lengths of bones exactly is a non-trivial task since the centers of most joints are inside the body. It is the reason we construct the ground truth directly from data acquired by

Table 1. Movement scenarios performed by each of 10 recorded subjects.

Motion Type	Direction	Distance	# of Repetitions
T-pose	S	1.5 m	3
T-pose	S	2 m	3
T-pose	S	2.5 m	3
U-turn right	S, N	0.5–4.5 m	3
U-turn left	S, N	0.5–4.5 m	3
Diagonal walking	SE	0.5–4.5 m	6
Diagonal walking	SW	0.5–4.5 m	6

the Kinect. To achieve low variance of bone lengths over time, the ground truth is calculated only from T-poses (see Table 1). The average standard deviation of the left-tibia length in the T-poses is 0.022 m, in contrast to U-turn and diagonal walking where average standard deviation is 0.064 m and 0.084 m, respectively.

However, standard deviation of 2.2 cm in T-poses is still not satisfactory. This error is mainly caused by an inaccurate skeleton fitting in the beginning of capturing. To further improve measured lengths of bones, we propose to go through an approximately 10-seconds T-pose scenario and locate its 3-seconds part where the specific bone length changes much less. The choice of such suitable part is implemented by a 3-seconds long sliding window that searches for the movement part with the smallest standard deviation. After locating these parts for individual bones, the specific bone length is calculated as the median value within its corresponding localized window. Having T-pose standing scenarios recorded nine times (three repetitions for three different distances from the Kinect), the ground-truth bone length is determined as the median value over these 9 measurements. In this way, the ground-truth skeleton proportions

5.3 Evaluation of Simple and Advanced Skeletonization Methods

The proposed variants of simple and advanced methods are evaluated by measuring mean absolute error (MAE) and mean relative error (MRE) between estimated and ground-truth skeleton proportions. The results are presented in Table 2 which combines different variants of measures, motion scopes, movement repetitions and directions, and also a *tracking status*. Since the Kinect provides us with the information whether a given joint is properly tracked, or not, we extend the proposed methods to omit poses where joints are not properly tracked, with respect to the specific bone estimation. This behavior corresponds to the flag "Tracked=yes" in Table 2. The results show a high error of simple methods, e.g., estimating skeleton proportions in the first and random motion pose achieves MAE of 0.041 m and 0.038 m, respectively. Moreover, the absolute error of simple methods varies quite a lot with the average MAE higher than 0.030m. The best simple method which averages lengths of bones over all motion poses, reaches MAE of 0.021 m with relative error of 8.5 %. On the other hand, MAE of advanced methods (detecting $k = 10$ and $k = 16$ important phases for

Table 2. Mean absolute (MAE) and relative (MRE) errors of skeleton proportions estimated by 33 variants of simple and advanced methods, with respect to the ground-truth skeleton proportions of each subject.

Measure	Scope	Tracked	Repetitions	Direction	MAE (m)	MRE (%)
First	Motion	Yes	Single	No	0.041	14.4%
First	Motion	No	Single	No	0.041	14.5%
First	NWC	No	Single	No	0.032	11.8%
First	LF	No	Single	No	0.033	12.2%
First	RF	No	Single	No	0.033	12.5%
Random	Motion	Yes	Single	No	0.034	12.7%
Random	Motion	No	Single	No	0.038	14.4%
Random	NWC	No	Single	No	0.034	12.8%
Random	LF	No	Single	No	0.035	12.8%
Random	RF	No	Single	No	0.036	13.3%
Mode	Motion	Yes	Single	No	0.034	12.5%
Mode	Motion	No	Single	No	0.037	13.7%
Mode	NWC	No	Single	No	0.034	12.8%
Mode	LF	No	Single	No	0.035	13.0%
Mode	RF	No	Single	No	0.037	13.6%
Median	Motion	Yes	Single	No	0.023	9.3%
Median	Motion	No	Single	No	0.025	9.9%
Median	NWC	No	Single	No	0.028	11.0%
Median	LF	No	Single	No	0.030	11.6%
Median	RF	No	Single	No	0.032	12.0%
Average	Motion	Yes	Single	No	0.021	8.5%
Average	Motion	No	Single	No	0.022	8.9%
Average	NWC	No	Single	No	0.025	10.0%
Average	LF	No	Single	No	0.028	10.7%
Average	RF	No	Single	No	0.028	11.1%
Stddev minimization	NWC	Yes	Multiple	No	0.021	8.6%
Stddev minimization	NWC	No	Multiple	No	0.022	9.0%
Stddev minimization	NWC	Yes	Multiple	Yes	0.018	6.7%
Stddev minimization	NWC	No	Multiple	Yes	0.018	6.8%
Velocity minimization	NWC	Yes	Multiple	No	0.022	8.7%
Velocity minimization	NWC	No	Multiple	No	0.021	8.5%
Velocity minimization	NWC	Yes	Multiple	Yes	0.017	6.5%
Velocity minimization	NWC	No	Multiple	Yes	0.017	6.6%

methods of standard deviation minimization and velocity minimization, respectively) varies much less with the average MAE around 0.020 m. The best results are achieved by considering the walking direction, tracked poses, and multiple instances of walk cycles – both standard deviation minimization and velocity minimization methods reach similar MAE of 0.017 m and MRE below 7%.

We further analyze advanced methods to determine walk cycle phases which are the most suitable for skeleton estimation, with respect to individual bones. By analyzing the velocity minimization method (with setting "Direction=Yes" and "Tracked=Yes"), we visualize the positions of important movement phases detected within the normalized walk cycle in Figure 4. This figure visualizes the 10 most important movement phases (i.e., $|F| = k = 10$) detected independently for each subject with respect to individual bones. We can observe that important phases are generally concentrated in three parts of the walk cycle where

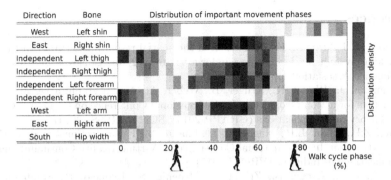

Fig. 4. Distribution of important movement phases within the normalized walk cycle for individual bones. Each bone is also associated with the walking direction in which the error in measurement is the lowest.

feet meet and pass by, i.e., they do not occur within double-support poses and their close surroundings. We can also see that left and right bone pairs usually form complement-like distribution, e.g., important phases of right forearm are localized at the beginning and ending part of the walk cycle while important phases of left forearm are concentrated in the middle. In summary, this figure illustrates the direction and walk-cycle phase in which the specific bone should be measured so that the measurement is accurate as much as possible.

6   Conclusions

We concentrate on the accuracy of skeleton proportions estimated by the Microsoft Kinect v2 device. By analyzing data in standing and walking scenarios, we define the four aspects that highly influence effectiveness of skeletonization. The defined aspects allow us to propose several variants of advanced skeletonization methods. These methods are experimentally compared against simple ones and show more than two times better effectiveness – by taking simply the first or random pose, the absolute bone-length error is about 4 cm, whereas advanced methods achieve the error of only 1.7 cm. In addition, we analyze the properties of advanced methods and visualize the important walk-cycle phases in which the specific bone should be measured. As a result, we highly recommend to consider the movement direction, left and right bone pairs, and walk-cycle phases where feet meet in order to estimate lengths of bones much more accurately. In the future, we plan to statistically model bone-length error distributions to enhance skeleton estimation and analyze robustness of the proposed methods in different movement scenarios, e.g., by changing walking speeds.

References

1. Amon, C., Fuhrmann, F.: Evaluation of the spatial resolution accuracy of the face tracking system for kinect for windows v1 and v2. In: Congress of Alps-Adria Acoustics Assosiation, pp. 9–12 (2014)
2. Baumann, J., Wessel, R., Krüger, B., Weber, A.: Action graph: a versatile data structure for action recognition. In: International Conference on Computer Graphics Theory and Applications (GRAPP 2014). SCITEPRESS (2014)
3. Bian, Z.P., Chau, L.P., Magnenat-Thalmann, N.: Fall detection based on skeleton extraction. In: International Conference on Virtual-Reality Continuum and its Applications in Industry (VRCAI 2012), pp. 91–94. ACM, USA (2012)
4. Chang, C.Y., Lange, B., Zhang, M., Koenig, S., Requejo, P., Somboon, N., Sawchuk, A., Rizzo, A.: Towards pervasive physical rehabilitation using microsoft kinect. In: 6th International Conference on Pervasive Computing Technologies for Healthcare (PervasiveHealth 2012), pp. 159–162 (2012)
5. Cosgun, A., Bünger, M., Christensen, H.I.: Accuracy Analysis of Skeleton Trackers for Safety in HRI. Tech. rep, Georgia Tech, Atlanta, GA, USA (2013)
6. Farhadi-Niaki, F., GhasemAghaei, R., Arya, A.: Empirical study of a vision-based depth-sensitive human-computer interaction system. In: 10th Asia Pacific Conference on Computer Human Interaction (APCHI 2012), pp. 101–108. ACM (2012)
7. Fernandez-Baena, A., Susin, A., Lligadas, X.: Biomechanical validation of upperbody and lower-body joint movements of kinect motion capture data for rehabilitation treatments. In: 4th Int. Conf. on Intelligent Networking and Collaborative Systems (INCoS 2012), pp. 656–661. IEEE Comp. Soc. (2012)
8. Khoshelham, K., Elberink, S.O.: Accuracy and Resolution of Kinect Depth Data for Indoor Mapping Applications. Sensors 12(2), 1437–1454 (2012)
9. Liang, Y., Lu, W., Liang, W., Wang, Y.: Action recognition using local joints structure and histograms of 3D joints. In: Computational Intelligence and Security (CIS), pp. 185–188 (2014)
10. Lun, R., Zhao, W.: A Survey of Applications and Human Motion Recognition with Microsoft Kinect. Int. Journal of Pattern Rec. and Artificial Intelligence (2015)
11. Milovanovic, M., Minovic, M., Starcevic, D.: Walking in colors: human gait recognition using kinect and CBIR. IEEE MultiMedia 20(4), 28–36 (2013)
12. Ni, B., Dat, N.C., Moulin, P.: RGBD-camera based get-up event detection for hospital fall prevention. In: International Conference on Acoustics, Speech and Signal Processing (ICASSP 2012), pp. 1405–1408 (2012)
13. Obdržálek, S., Kurillo, G., Ofli, F., Bajcsy, R., Seto, E., Jimison, H., Pavel, M.: Accuracy and robustness of kinect pose estimation in the context of coaching of elderly population. In: Engineering in Medicine and Biology Society (EMBC 2012), pp. 1188–1193. IEEE Computer Society (2012)
14. Park, J.P., Lee, K.H., Lee, J.: Finding Syntactic Structures from Human Motion Data. Computer Graphics Forum 30(8), 2183–2193 (2011)
15. Preis, J., Kessel, M., Werner, M., Linnhoff-Popien, C.: Gait recognition with kinect. In: 1st International Workshop on Kinect in Pervasive Computing (2012)
16. Raj, M., Creem-Regehr, S.H., Rand, K.M., Stefanucci, J.K., Thompson, W.B.: Kinect based 3d object manipulation on a desktop display. In: ACM Symposium on Applied Perception (SAP 2012), pp. 99–102. ACM, New York (2012)
17. Sedmidubsky, J., Valcik, J., Balazia, M., Zezula, P.: Gait recognition based on normalized walk cycles. In: Bebis, G., Boyle, R., Parvin, B., Koracin, D., Fowlkes, C., Wang, S., Choi, M.-H., Mantler, S., et al. (eds.) ISVC 2012, Part II. LNCS, vol. 7432, pp. 11–20. Springer, Heidelberg (2012)

18. Valcik, J., Sedmidubsky, J., Balazia, M., Zezula, P.: Identifying walk cycles for human recognition. In: Chau, M., Wang, G.A., Yue, W.T., Chen, H. (eds.) PAISI 2012. LNCS, vol. 7299, pp. 127–135. Springer, Heidelberg (2012)
19. Xu, D., Chen, Y.L., Lin, C., Kong, X., Wu, X.: Real-time dynamic gesture recognition system based on depth perception for robot navigation. In: International Conference on Robotics and Biomimetics (ROBIO 2012), pp. 689–694 (2012)
20. Zhao, W., Lun, R., Espy, D., Reinthal, M.: Rule based realtime motion assessment for rehabilitation exercises. In: IEEE Symposium on Computational Intelligence in Healthcare and e-health (CICARE 2014), pp. 133–140 (2014)

Image Quality Improvement
and Assessment

Color Image Quality Assessment Based on Gradient Similarity and Distance Transform

Zianou Ahmed Seghir[1]($\boxtimes$) and Fella Hachouf[2]

[1] Faculty ST, ICOSI Lab., Khenchela University,
BP 1252 El Houria, 40004 Khenchela, Algeria
zianou_ahmed_seghir@yahoo.fr
[2] Laboratoire dAutomatique et de Robotique,
Université des fréres Mentouri Constantine, Constantine, Algeria

Abstract. In this paper, a new full-reference image quality assessment (IQA) metric is proposed. It is based on a Distance transform (DT) and a gradient similarity. The gradient images are sensitive to image distortions. Consequently, investigations have been carried out using the global variation of the gradient and the image skeleton for computing an overall image quality prediction. First, color image is transformed to YIQ space. Secondly, the gradient images and DT are identified from Y component. Thirdly, color distortion is computed from I and Q components. Then, the maximum DT similarity of the reference and test images is defined. Finally, combining the previous metrics the difference between test and references images is derived. The obtained results have shown the efficiency of the suggested measure.

Keywords: DT · Gradient similarity · IQA · Color space

1 Introduction

Image quality assessment (IQA) [15] plays a main function in appraising and enhancing the effectiveness of image processing systems. They are proposed for human consumers, so the evaluation of image quality must be consistent with perceived quality of digital images and video. Several measures have been designed. And it is essential to estimate the performance of these methods in a comparative manner and to study the power and failings of these metrics. IQA can be divided into subjective and objective methods. A subjective evaluation method is the most consistent judgment of the image quality assessment. It is carried out by the human observers. Objective image quality algorithms evaluate the difference between the reference and test images. Most methods that have been proposed for image quality assessment in an objective manner can be categorized into three groups; full-reference measures (FR), no-reference measures (NR) and reduced-reference measures (RR). In this paper, the discussion is confined in FR metrics where the reference images are available. The most popular method for full reference image quality assessment is the Structural Similarity Index [1] ($SSIM$). It contains three parts: Luminance, Contrast and

© Springer International Publishing Switzerland 2015
S. Battiato et al. (Eds.): ACIVS 2015, LNCS 9386, pp. 591–603, 2015.
DOI: 10.1007/978-3-319-25903-1_51

Structure Comparison. However, it fails in measuring the badly blurred images [2]. In [3], an approach based on edge-region information, distorted and displaced pixels (*ERDDM*) has been developed. Initially, the test and reference images are divided into blocks of 11×11 pixels, then distorted and displacement pixels are calculated to produce the global error. In [4], *DTex* metric is proposed with consideration of the texture masking effect and contrast sensitivity function. In [5], it has been shown that the masking effect and the visibility threshold can be combined with structure, luminance and contrast comparison to create the image quality measure (gradient similarity measure (*GSM*)). Most Apparent Distortion (*MAD*) designed in [6,7] yields two quality scores, i.e., visibility-weighted error and the differences in log-Gabor subbands statistics. In [16] the authors proposed a quality measure using a phase congruency [17]. However, this measure correlates well with the subjective quality. And it is very time consuming method. In [28], Zianou et al. proposed a gradient similarity based Color distortion measure (*GSCDM*) which was an extension of Gradient magnitude similarity deviation (*GMSD*) [29] to take color distortion in consideration.

In this work, it is assumed that the important information of images is mainly represented by the edge [30]-[32]. So, the gradient and *DT* transform are analyzed. Also, color distortions are used. The proposed measure combines these structural and color information. Its goal is to give scores values which are closer to a human judgment. This image quality measure can eliminate the expensive study of the subjective assessment.

The rest of the paper is organized as follows. In Section 2, the proposed image quality measure is presented. In section 3, this method is compared with well established methods in the literature using different types of distortion. Finally, some conclusions are given in section 4.

2   Proposed Method

The principal function of the human eye is to take out the structure information from the vision field. Hence, the human vision system (HVS) is completely adapted to scene recognition. The main idea of the proposed method is to determine the contribution of the image structural information in the quality assessment. So, a new image quality assessment metric based the gradient similarity and the distance transform is developed. Reference and test images are represented by *Ref* and *Dis* respectively. In addition, all variables used in the proposed method are defined next:

Ref: reference image.
Dis: test image.
$M \times N$: the image size.
G_1: gradient image of *Ref*.
G_2 : gradient image of *Dis*.
Gradient_map: the gradient similarity map of G_1 and G_2.
DT_1: Distance transform of *Ref*.
DT_2 : Distance transform of *Dis*.

DT_max: the maximum of DT_1 and DT_2.

DT_map: Distance transform map.

CFI_map and CFQ_map : chromatic features.

C_1, C_2, C_3, α, β: positive constants.

$GSDTM$: Gradient similarity and Distance transform measure.

2.1 Color Space Transformation

In this step, color image coded in RGB color space is transformed to YIQ color space. As a result, this formula approximate the conversion between the RGB color space and YIQ [10]

$$\begin{bmatrix} Y \\ I \\ Q \end{bmatrix} = \begin{bmatrix} 0.299 & 0.587 & 0.144 \\ 0.596 & -0.275 & -0.321 \\ 0.212 & -0.528 & 0.311 \end{bmatrix} \begin{bmatrix} R \\ G \\ B \end{bmatrix} \tag{1}$$

The YIQ is intended to take advantage of human color-response characteristics. The eye is more sensitive to changes in the orange-blue (I) range than in the purple-green range (Q). Therefore less bandwidth is required for Q than for I. The choice of the color space will be discussed in next section.

2.2 Distance Transforms (DT)

Distance transforms (DT) plays a central role in images comparison, particularly for images resulting from local feature detection techniques such as edges or corner detection. In the proposed method, DT is used as a feature when computing the quality map of the test image. Then, it is utilized as a weighting function to reflect the significance of a local area in the pooling function. Furthermore, DT map contains the most information.

We have used the developed algorithm in [25, 26] to compute the DT image. This latter is calculated using the gray component Y of YIQ space. The function $DT()$ gives the distance transform of an image by calling $DTA()$. The definition of the two-dimensional DT for an input image Y and output image D is

```
Algorithm DT(Y)
for i = 1to M
   D(i ,1.. N) = DTA(Y(i , 1.. N))
end
for j =1 to N
   D(1.. M, j) = DTA(D(1.. M, j))
end
```

Where:

Y(i , 1.. N) and D(i ,1.. N) are the row vectors of Y and D.

Y(1.. M, j) and D(1.. M, j) are the column vectors of Y and D.

M and N are the row and column size of Y, respectively.

Algorithm $DTA(f)$

1. $k \leftarrow 0$ (*Index of rightmost parabola in lower envelope *)
2. $v[0] \leftarrow 0$ (*Locations of parabolas in lower envelope *)
3. $z[0] \leftarrow -\infty$ (*Locations of boundaries between parabolas *)
4. $z[1] \leftarrow +\infty$
5. for $q = 1$ to n - 1 (*Compute lower envelope *)
6. $s \leftarrow ((f(q) + q^2) - (f(v[k]) + v[k]^2))/(2q - 2v[k])$
7. if $s \leq z[k]$
8. then $k \leftarrow k$ - 1
9. goto 6
10. else $k \leftarrow k + 1$
11. $v[k] \leftarrow q$
12. $z[k] \leftarrow s$
13. $z[k + 1] \leftarrow +\infty$
14. $k \leftarrow 0$
15. for $q = 0$ to n - 1 (* Fill in values of distance transform *)
16. while $z[k + 1] < q$
17. $k \leftarrow k + 1$
18. $D_f(q) \leftarrow (q - v[k])^2 + f(v[k])$

DT_1 and DT_2 of the reference and test images are produced, respectively. In order to compute the DT map (DT_map), the following formula is used:

$$DT\_map(I, J) = \frac{2|DT_1|.|DT_2| + C_2}{DT_1{}^2 + DT_2{}^2 + C_2} \qquad (2)$$

Where $| . |$ is absolute function. C_2 is a positive constant to increase the stability of DT_map. The same concept was also employed in $SSIM$ [1]. Equations (2), (5), (6) and (7) are used to describe the similarity of two positive numbers [1] and its result ranges within $[0, 1]$.

Then, the maximum of the distance transform (DT_Max) is computed

$$DT\_Max = \max(DT_1, DT_2) \qquad (3)$$

Dissimilarities between two images are already quantified in the distance transform map. Given a reference image and a deformed image, then the sum of the coefficients in the distance transform map can represent the transformation evaluation between the compared images.

2.3 Gradient Similarity

Gradient can be employed to take out information from images. Prewitt mask is introduced to generate gradient images. This later consists of a pair of 3×3 convolution kernels and it is used for detecting vertical and horizontal edges in image. The gradient magnitude is given by:

$$G = \sqrt{Gradientx_1{}^2 + Gradienty_2{}^2} \qquad (4)$$

The gradient operators (G) of the reference and test images are computed. As a result, the G_1 and G_2 of the test and reference images are produced, respectively. The gradient similarity is computed in the proposed method. Hence the Gradient map $(Gradient\_map)$ is formed as:

$$Gradient\_map = \frac{2G_1.G_2 + C_1}{G_1{}^2 + G_2{}^2 + C_1} \tag{5}$$

The G_2 and G_1 of the test and reference images are computed from Y_1 and Y_2 of YIQ color space respectively.

2.4   Color Space Transformation

The color distortion cannot be differentiated by gradient. Hence, to make the image quality assessment measures possess the ability to deal with color distortions, special considerations are given to chrominance information. Let I_1 (I_2) and Q_1 (Q_2) be the I and Q chromatic channels of the image Ref (Dis), respectively. Similar to the definitions of CFI_map and CFQ_map, the similarity between chromatic features is defined as follows:

$$CFI\_map = \frac{2I_1.I_2 + C_3}{I_1{}^2 + I_2{}^2 + C_3} \tag{6}$$

$$CFQ\_map = \frac{2Q_1.Q_2 + C_3}{Q_1{}^2 + Q_2{}^2 + C_3} \tag{7}$$

2.5   Structural Pooling

In this step, the map is merged into a single quality value using a spatial pooling approach [11]. In the proposed method, a structural pooling measure is introduced given by:

$$F = \frac{\sum_u v_u f_u}{\sum_u v_u} \tag{8}$$

where u is an index, f_u is the quality measure, and v_u is a structural weight with large value indicating substantial structural information. The pooling approach of the proposed method is given in (9) where the quality value is computed as actually the average of $GSDT\_map$ (gradient similarity, color distortion and Distance transform map) with DT_Max as weight. The total gradient similarity distance transform measure $(GSDTM)$ is defined as:

$$GSDTM = \frac{\sum_{i=1}^{M} \sum_{j=1}^{N} DT\_Max\,(i,j)\,.GSDT\_map\,(i,j)}{\sum_{i=1}^{M} \sum_{j=1}^{N} DT\_Max\,(i,j)} \tag{9}$$

Where

$$GSDT\_map = DT\_map.(Gradient\_map)^\alpha.(CFI\_map.CFQ\_map)^\beta \tag{10}$$

i and j index the pixels and $M \times N$ denote the total number of pixels. $GSDT\_map$ is a multiplicative model. The proposed measure is closer to one when the test image has the best quality and closer to zero in the other case. Fig. 1 is Flowchart depicting computation of the proposed measure.

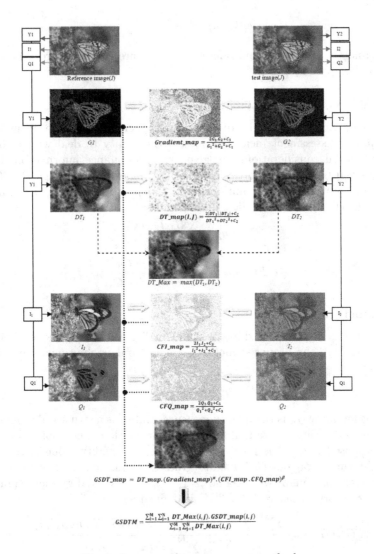

Fig. 1. Image quality assessment method

3   Results

To test the proposed method efficiency, experiments have been carried on images set. The standard performance assessment procedures utilized in the video quality experts group (VQEG) [18] have been followed. Objective scores are fitted to the subjective using logistic function [18]. This function is based on five parameters (θ_1, θ_2, θ_3, θ_4 and θ_5) to set the objective quality measures to a set of the predicted Difference Mean Opinion Score ($DMOS/MOS$) values ($DMOS_P/MOS_P$). In equation (11), the logistic regression function which is employed for the nonlinear regression is introduced.

$$DMOS_p = \theta_1 \left(\frac{1}{2} - \frac{1}{\exp\left(\theta_2 \left(VQR - \theta_3\right)\right)} \right) + \theta_4 VQR + \theta_5 \qquad (11)$$

Where VQR is the value of the objective method and θ_1, θ_2, θ_3, θ_4, θ_5 are selected for the most excellent fit. In this test, four metrics are used: the Root mean square prediction error ($RMSE$), the Spearman rank-order correlations coefficient ($ROCC$), Kendall rank-order correla-tion coefficient ($KROCC$) and Pearson linear correlation coefficient (CC). $ROCC$ and $KROCC$ evaluate the prediction monotonicity. CC and $RMSE$ assess the prediction accuracy. $ROCC$, $KROCC$ and CC are better with values closer to 1 or -1. $RMSE$ is better when its values are small. To judge the performance of the proposed approach, four kinds of databases are used: TID2008 database [12], CSIQ database [13], LIVE database [14] and TID2013 database [27]. The performance of $GSDTM$ metric is compared with $PSNR$, $SSIM$ [1,24], Multiscale-SSIM (MS-$SSIM$) [19,24], Visual Singal-to-Noise Ratio ($VSNR$) [20,24], Visual Information Fidelity (VIF) [21,24], Information Fidelity Criterion (IFC) [22,24], Noise Quality Measure (NQM) [23, 24], $DTex$ [4], GSM [5], MAD [6,7], $ERDDM$ [3] and $Fsim$ [16].

A comparative study using Sobel [8], Prewitt[8] and Scharr [9] edge detections is presented in Table 1 (TID2008 database is used in this experience), noticed that Prewitt operator performs better performance than the others. Furthermore, the choice of YIQ color space needs to be proved. To this goal, we run the proposed method with different four color spaces. The results are summarized in table 2.

Table 1. $ROCC$ and $KROCC$ values using three gradient operators

Gradient operator	Sobel	Prewitt	Scharr
$ROCC$	0.8923	**0.8931**	0.8908
$KROCC$	0.7071	**0.7093**	0.7039

Table 2. $ROCC$ and $KROCC$ values using four color spaces

Color space	Lab	ycbcr	HSV	YIQ
$ROCC$	0.8225	0.8898	0.793	**0.8931**
$KROCC$	0.6331	0.7056	0.6084	**0.7093**

Table 7 summaries the performance classification of the used methods according to their *ROCC* values. Tables 3, 4, 5 and 6 show the obtained results. The top three measures for each assessment measure are highlighted in bold. It is observed that the top methods are mostly *GSDTM*, *FSIM* and *MAD*. And the *GSDTM* correlates much better with the subjective results (i.e. *DMOS/MOS* is generated by averaging the human subjects results of a set of subjective test and act as an indicator for the perceived image quality) than the other measures. From Table 7, it can be seen that *GSDTM* performs well on almost databases. Specially, it performs better than the others measures on the three databases, CSIQ, TID2008 and TID2013. On LIVE database, even it is not the best, *GSDTM* ranks in the five place compared to the best results. In the other hand, for the other methods, they can work well on some database but fail on other databases. From Table 7, although *MAD* and *VIF* give the best results on LIVE, they fail to give the best scores on TID2008 and TID2013.

Curves of Fig. 2 indicate that *GSDTM* values are very close to *DMOS* and *MOS*, assessing the efficiency of this measure. Moreover, an interesting result is obtained from the comparison of the *GSDTM* with *GSM*, *DTex* and *MAD* in Table 4. The values of *ROOC* are close to 1; this means that *GSDTM* has a similar performance as the existing methods. These results clearly indicate that the proposed measure performs quite well. And it is competitive with other *IQA* measures.

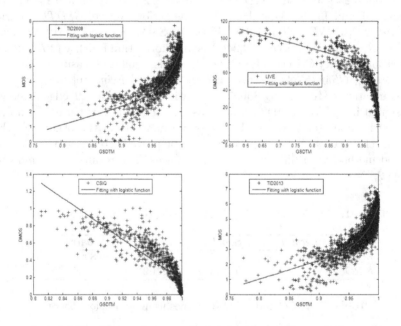

Fig. 2. Scatter plots of subjective scores versus scores from the proposed scheme on IQA databases

In addition, to compare the efficiency of different models, the average execution time required an image of size 512×384 is calculated. All metrics were run on a TOSHIBA Satetillete T130-11U notebook with Intel Core U4100 CPU@1.30 GHz and 3G RAM. The software platform used to run all metrics was MAT-LAB R2007a (7.4.0). Table 8 shows the required time in seconds per image. It is shown in Table 8 that the proposed measure is faster than *Fsim. VIF, VSNR, IFC, GSM, MAD, NQM* and *ERDDM*. And it takes more time than the *PSNR*, the *SSIM*, the *DCTex*, and *MS-SSIM*.

Table 3. Performance comparison for IQA measures on live database

Method	ROCC	KROCC	CC	RMSE
PSNR	0.8756	0.6865	0.8723	13.3597
SSIM	0.9479	0.7963	0.9449	8.9454
MS-SSIM	0.9513	0.8044	0.9409	9.2593
VSNR	0.9280	0.7625	0.9237	0.4694
VIF	**0.9632**	**0.8270**	**0.9598**	**7.6670**
IFC	0.9259	0.7579	0.9268	10.2643
NQM	0.9086	0.7413	0.9122	11.1926
ERDDM	0.9496	0.8128	0.9619	6.3204
DCTex	0.9483	0.8066	0.9443	8.9897
GSM	0.9554	0.8131	0.9437	9.0376
MAD	**0.9669**	**0.8421**	**0.9674**	**6.9235**
Fsim	**0.9645**	**0.8363**	**0.9613**	**7.5296**
GSDTM	0.9548	0.8129	0.9495	8.5751

Table 4. Performance comparison for IQA measures on TID2008 database

Method	ROCC	KROCC	CC	RMSE
PSNR	0.5794	0.4210	0.5726	1.1003
SSIM	0.7749	0.5768	0.7710	0.8546
MS-SSIM	0.8542	0.6568	0.8451	0.7173
VSNR	0.7049	0.5345	0.6823	0.9810
VIF	0.7496	0.5868	0.8090	0.7888
IFC	0.5675	0.4236	0.7340	0.9113
NQM	0.6243	0.4608	0.6142	1.0590
ERDDM	0.5961	0.4411	0.6685	0.998
DCTex	0.4973	0.4095	0.5605	1.1113
GSM	**0.8554**	**0.6651**	**0.8462**	**0.7151**
MAD	0.8340	0.6445	0.8306	0.7474
Fsim	**0.8840**	**0.6991**	**0.8762**	**0.6468**
GSDTM	**0.8931**	**0.7093**	**0.8769**	**0.6449**

Moreover, the parameters have been adjusted based on TID2008 and TID2013 databases. For each *GSDTM* evaluated, the related parameters were tuned experimentally. The parameters values that give the higher *ROCC* values have been chosen. The parameters required in the proposed method have been set to: $C_1 = 180$, $C_2 = 2.4$, $C_3 = 290$, $\alpha = 0.30$, $\beta = 0.03$.

Table 5. Performance comparison for IQA measures on TID2013 database

Method	ROCC	KROCC	CC	RMSE
PSNR	0.6396	0.4698	0.669	0.9214
SSIM	0.7417	0.5588	0.7895	0.7608
MS-SSIM	0.7859	0.6047	0.8329	0.6861
VSNR	0.6812	0.5084	0.7402	0.8392
VIF	0.6769	0.5147	0.7720	0.7880
IFC	0.5389	0.3939	0.5538	1.0322
NQM	0.6432	0.474	0.6858	0.9023
ERDDM	0.5623	0.4124	0.6352	1.230
DCTex	0.5863	0.4573	0.6495	0.9425
GSM	**0.7946**	**0.6255**	**0.8464**	**0.6603**
MAD	0.7807	0.6035	0.8267	0.6975
Fsim	**0.8510**	**0.6665**	**0.8769**	**0.5959**
GSDTM	**0.8720**	**0.6893**	**0.8858**	**0.5752**

Table 6. Performance comparison for IQA measures on CSIQ database

Method	ROCC	KROCC	CC	RMSE
PSNR	0.8005	0.5984	0.7998	0.1576
SSIM	0.8756	0.6907	0.8612	0.1334
MS-SSIM	0.9133	0.7393	0.8990	0.1150
VSNR	0.8104	0.6237	0.7993	0.1578
VIF	0.9195	0.7537	0.9277	0.0980
IFC	0.7671	0.5897	0.8384	0.1431
NQM	0.7402	0.5638	0.7433	0.1756
ERDDM	0.8626	0.6781	0.8295	0.1466
DCTex	0.8042	0.6420	0.7915	0.1605
GSM	0.9126	0.7403	0.8979	0.1156
MAD	**0.9467**	**0.7970**	**0.9502**	**0.0818**
Fsim	**0.9310**	**0.7690**	**0.9192**	**0.1034**
GSDTM	**0.9531**	**0.8086**	**0.9431**	**0.0873**

Table 7. Ranking of IQA metrics performance on four databases

Method	Live	TID2008	TID2013	CSIQ
PSNR	13	11	11	11
SSIM	9	6	6	7
MS-SSIM	6	4	4	5
VSNR	10	8	7	9
VIF	2	7	8	4
IFC	11	12	9	12
NQM	12	9	10	13
ERDDM	7	10	13	8
DCTex	8	13	12	10
GSM	4	3	3	6
MAD	1	5	5	2
Fsim	3	2	2	3
GSDTM	5	1	1	1

Table 8. Running time of the competing IQA models

Method	Time (second)	Method	Time (second)
PSNR	0.0493	ERDDM	9.6089
SSIM	0.1917	DCTex	0.5327
MS-SSIM	1.1304	GSM	1.4003
VSNR	1.5018	MAD	15.6235
VIF	5.1429	Fsim	2.4990
IFC	4.6738		
NQM	1.8846	GSDTM	1.3584

4 Conclusion

In this paper, a new measure for assessing a color image quality has been presented. In addition to color distortions parameters, the proposed method uses two structural information, namely the images edges and the image transform distance. Compared with existing methods, the proposed measure yields competitive results. Future works will include more studies on color components distortions.

References

1. Wang, Z., Bovik, A.C., Sheikh, H.R., Simocelli, E.P.: Image quality assessment: From error measurement to structural similarity. IEEE Trans. Image Processing **13**(4), 600–612 (2004)
2. Guan-Hao, C., Chun-Ling, Y., Sheng-Li, X.: Gradient-based structural similarity for image quality assessment. In: Proc. ICIP 2006, pp. 2929–2932 (2006)

3. Seghir, Z.A., Hachouf, F.: Edge-region information measure based on deformed and displaced pixel for Image quality assessment. Signal Processing: Image Communication **26**(8–9), 534–549 (2011)

4. Zhang, F., Ma, L., Li, S.: Practical image quality metric applied to image coding. IEEE Trans. Multimedia **13**, 615–624 (2011)

5. Liu, A., Lin, W., Narwaria, M.: Image quality assessment based on gradient similarity. IEEE Transactions on Image Processing **21**(4), 1500–1512 (2012)

6. Larson, E.C., Chandler, D.M.: Most apparent distortion: Full-reference image quality assessment and the role of strategy. J. Electron. Imaging **19**(1), 011006:1–011006:21 (2010)

7. Larson, E., Chandler, D.: Full-Reference Image Quality Assessment and the Role of Strategy: The Most Apparent Distortion. http://vision.okstate.edu/mad/

8. Jain, R., Kasturi, R., Schunck, B.G.: Machine Vision. McGraw-Hill, NewYork (1995)

9. Jhne, B., Haubecker, H., Geibler, P.: Handbook of Computer Vision and Applications. Academic, New York (1999)

10. Yang, C., Kwok, S.H.: Efficient gamut clipping for color image processing using LHS and YIQ. Opt. Eng. **42**(3), 701–711 (2003)

11. Wang, Z., Shang, X.: Spatial pooling strategies for perceptual image quality assessment. In: Proc. ICIP 2006, pp. 2945–2948 (2006)

12. Ponomarenko, N., Lukin, V., Zelensky, A., Egiazarian, K., Carli, M., Battisti, F.: TID2008A database for evaluation of full-reference visual quality assessment metrics. Adv. Modern Radioelectron **10**, 30–45 (2009)

13. Larson, C., Chandler, D.M.: Categorical Image Quality (CSIQ) Database (2009). http://vision.okstate.edu/csiq

14. Sheikh, H.R., Seshadrinathan, K., Moorthy, A.K., Wang, Z., Bovik, A.C., Cormack, L.K.: Image and Video Quality Assessment Research at LIVE 2004 (2004). http://live.ece.utexas.edu/research/quality

15. Zhang, X., Feng, X., Wang, W., Xue, W.: Edge Strength Similarity for Image Quality As-sessment. IEEE Signal Processing Letters **20**(4), 319–322 (2013)

16. Zhang, L., Zhang, L., Mou, X., Zhang, D.: FSIM: a feature similarity index for image quality assessment. IEEE Transactions on Image Processing **20**(8), 1–26 (2011)

17. Kovesi, P.: Image features from phase congruency. Videre: Journal of Computer Vision Research **1**(3), 1–26 (1999)

18. VQEG report. http://www.its.bldrdoc.gov/vqeg/about-vqeg.aspx

19. Wang, Z., Simoncelli, E.P., Bovik, A.C.: Multi-scale structural similarity for image qualityassessment. In: Proc. IEEE Asilomar Conf. Signals, Syst., Comput., Pacific Grove, CA, pp. 1398–1402, November 2003

20. Chandler, D.M., Hemami, S.S.: VSNR: a wavelet-based visual signal-to-noise-ratio for natural images. IEEE Trans. Image Process. **16**(9), 2284–2298 (2007)

21. Sheikh, H.R., Bovik, A.C.: Image information and visual quality. IEEE Trans. Image Process. **15**(2), 430–444 (2006)

22. Sheikh, H.R., Bovik, A.C., de Veciana, G.: An information fidelity criterion for image quality assessment using natural scene statistics. IEEE Trans. on Image Processing **14**(12), 2117–2128 (2005)

23. Damera-Venkata, N., Kite, T.D., Geisler, W.S., Evans, B.L., Bovik, A.C.: Image quality assessment based on degradation model. IEEE Trans. on Image Processing **9**(4), 636–650 (2000)

24. Gaubatz, M.: Metrix MUX Visual Quality Assessment Package: MSE, PSNR, SSIM, MSSIM, VSNR, VIF, VIFP, UQI, IFC, NQM, WSNR, SNR. http://foulard.ece.cornell.edu/gaubatz/metrix_mux/
25. Felzenszwalb, P.F., Huttenlocher, D.P.: Distance Transforms of Sampled Functions. Theory of Computing **8**, 415–428 (2012)
26. Felzenszwalb, P.F., Huttenlocher, D.P. : Distance Transforms of Sampled Functions. Cornell Computing and Information Science Technical Report TR2004-1963, September 2004
27. Ponomarenko, N., et al.: Color image database TID2013: peculiarities and preliminary results. In: Proc. 4th Eur. Workshop Vis. Inf. Process., pp. 106–111, June 2013
28. Seghir, Z.A., Hachouf, F.: Full-reference image quality assessment measure based on color distortion. In: Amine, A., Bellatreche, L., Elberrichi, Z., Neuhold, E.J., Wrembel, R. (eds.) CIIA 2015, vol. 456, pp. 66–77. Springer, Heidelberg (2015)
29. Xue, W., Zhang, L., Mou, X., Bovik, A.C. : Gradient Magnitude Similarity Deviation: A Highly Efficient Perceptual Image Quality Index. IEEE Trans. on Image Processing, 684–695 (2014)
30. Marr, D.: Vision. Freeman, New York (1980)
31. Marr, D., Hildreth, E.: Theory of edge detection. Proc. R. Soc. Lond. B **207**(1167), 187–217 (1980)
32. Morrone, M.C., Burr, D.C.: Feature detection in human vision: A phase-dependent energy model. Proc. R. Soc. Lond. B **235**(1280), 221–245 (1988)

Toward a Universal Stereoscopic Image Quality Metric Without Reference

Aladine Chetouani[✉]

Polytech'Orléans, Université d'Orléans, 12 rue de Blois, 45067 Orléans, France
aladine.chetouani@univ-orleans.fr

Abstract. Stereoscopic Image becomes an attractive tool in image processing area. However, such as in 2D, this kind of images can be also affected by some types of degradations. In this paper, we are interesting by the impact of some of these degradation types on the perceived quality and we propose a new framework for Stereoscopic Image Quality Metric without reference (SNR-IQM) based on a degradation identification and features fusion steps. Support Vector Machine (SVM) models have been here used. The aptitude of our method to predict the subjective judgments has been evaluated using the 3D LIVE Image Quality Dataset and compared with some recent methods considered as the state-of-the-art. The obtained experimental results show the relevance of our work.

Keywords: Stereoscopic Image Quality · Degradation identification · Subjective judgments · Fusion

1 Introduction

Due to the emergence of the 3D displays, more and more researchers in image quality domain focus their works on the development of quality measures that are adapted to this kind of images [1]. As for 2D images, stereoscopic images can be also affected by some common types of degradations (blocking and ringing effects, noise, blur and so on). Indeed, the transmission process remains relatively the same (coding, compression, transmission and so on). Three main approaches exist: Full-Reference (FR) [2] where the original and the degraded images are used, Reduced-Reference (RR) [3] where only some features of the original image are exploited and No-Reference (NR) [4] where just the degraded image is utilized. Note that only few metrics without reference are actually proposed in the literature.

As mentioned in [5], we distinguish currently two main strategies to estimate the quality of stereoscopic images. The first one consists to exploit and to combine some selected 2D IQMs without adding any other information [6]. The second one is to consider the disparity information in the quality estimation process. It should be noted that even in this case, 2D IQMs are generally often used [7].

In this study, we focus our attention on Stereoscopic Image Quality Metric without reference by developing a new framework. We propose to derive from some selected

S. Battiato et al. (Eds.): ACIVS 2015, LNCS 9386, pp. 604–612, 2015.
DOI: 10.1007/978-3-319-25903-1_52

metrics, a quality measure per degradation type. Each of these metrics is here obtained by a combining step. In order to select automatically one of these metrics according to the degradation contained in a given stereoscopic image, a degradation identification step has been firstly applied. The performance of our method has been compared to some recent methods in terms of correlation with subjective judgments.

This paper is organized as follows: Section 2 describes the used 3D dataset. Our method is presented in Section 3. Experimental results are then exposed and discussed in section 4, followed by some conclusions and remarks in section 5.

2   Used 3D Image Database

Our method has been tested and evaluated using the 3D LIVE Image Quality Database [8]. Note that some other databases are also available [9]. Our choice was essentially motivated by the number of degradation types. This database is composed of 20 pairs of reference images, from which 365 pairs of degraded images have been obtained. Five different degradation types are proposed: JPEG2000 compressed stereo images (80 pairs of images, Kakadu encoder), JPEG compressed stereo images (80 pairs of images, MATLAB's JPEG compression tool: imwrite), white noise (80 pairs of images, MATLAB function: imnoise), blur (45 pairs of images, MATLAB function: imfilter) and fast fading (80 pairs of images, JPEG2000 compressed image transmitted by a Rayleigh fading channel).

Left image   Right image

Superposed image

Fig. 1. Sample of stereoscopic reference images.

Subjective scores (DMOS), which are considered as the ground truth measures and used to evaluate the efficiency of the developed metrics, are also provided. A sample of images is shown in Fig. 1.

3　Proposed Method

As mentioned above, the goal of this study is to develop a blind metric that is able to predict the quality of a given pairs of images. Here, only the more encountered degradation types are considered. This method is based on two main steps (see Fig. 2).

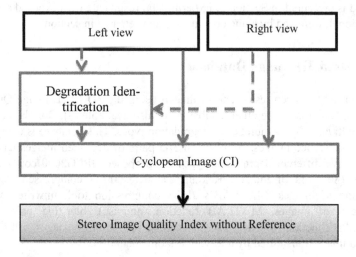

Fig. 2. Flowchart of the proposed framework.

1. **Degradation Type Detection:** during this step, some features are first extracted from the left and the right images. These features are then used as input to a Support Vector Machine (SVM) model.
2. **Stereoscopic Image Quality Metric Per Degradation Type:** For each considered degradation type, some adapted features are selected and are extracted from the Cyclopean Image computed from both left and right images. One stereo image quality metrics without reference per degradation type is then derived from a combination step.

3.1　Degradation Identification

The goal of this step is to identify the degradation type contained in a given degraded stereoscopic image. For that, some features are first extracted and are then used as input to a classifier. A lot of features are available in the literature. These features must be able to well characterize each type of degradation. Here, we propose to use several common 2D metrics that are initially developed to predict the perceived quality for a given degradation. Some of them are frequency-based, while some others are computed in the spatial domain (see Table 1).

Table 1. Used features during the identification step.

Degradation type	Number of features	Based on
Noise	3	Spatial [10]
		DCT [11]
		Spatial [12]
Blur	1	Spatial [13]
Blocking	1	FFT [14]
Ringing	1	Wavelet [15]

In order to identify and to select the more adapted metric, a multiclass (one against all) SVM classifier with a Gaussian function as kernel has been used and can be accessed in [16]. The 5-fold cross validation method has been applied. The number of inputs is thus equal to 6. The obtained results are presented and discussed in section 4.

3.2   Stereoscopic Image Quality Metric Per Degradation Type

Once the type of degradation is identified, the quality of each stereoscopic image is estimated using the appropriate metric. Further, in order to increase their performances, several selected metrics have been combined. A metric per degradation type, which is more adapted and more efficient than the others, is thus obtained. Note that the index values are here computed from the cyclopean image. Cyclopean image computation process and the selected metrics for all considered degradation types are presented in this section.

3.2.1   Cyclopean Image (CI)

Binocular rivalry is a well-known visual perception phenomenon that appears when two sufficiently different images are presented to the left and the right eyes simultaneously. Only one image is visualized at a time (one is dominant and the other is suppressed). Several CI models have been proposed in the literature. In this paper, the one proposed in [5] has been used. The authors propose an improved version of the Levelt's model [17] that takes into account the local weighting and the strength of the two views. This image is computed as follows:

$$CI(x,y) = W_L(x,y) . I_L(x,y) + W_R(x+d,y) . I_R(x+d,y) \quad (1)$$

where CI denotes the Cyclopean Image, I_L and I_R are respectively the left and right views. W_L and W_R are the weighting coefficients computed from the normalized Gabor filter magnitude responses and d represents the disparity index.

3.2.2   Combination Step

Table 2 shows the selected features for each considered degradation type. One SVM model has been used for each degradation type to combine these selected features. As the identification step, a 5-fold cross validation method has been also applied with the same type of kernel function.

Finally, the global architecture of our method is composed of 5 SVM models (1 for classification and 4 for the combination). Each of them has different number of inputs.

Table 2. Used 2D No-Reference image quality metrics

Degradation type	Number of features per degradation type	Based on
Noise	4	Spatial [10]
		DCT [11]
		Spatial [12]
		Spatial [18]
Blur	1	Spatial [19]
Blocking	2	FFT [20]
		FFT [14]
Ringing	3	Wavelet [15]
		FFT [21]
		Spatial [13]

4   Experimental Results

Our method is compared to some common stereoscopic measures. Each of them is briefly described below:

- **Akhter et al [2]:** A no reference image quality assessment for JPEG coded stereoscopic images has been proposed. This measure is based on local information extraction of artifacts and disparity (edge, blockiness, blur and so on).
- **Benoit et al. [22]:** this method is based on the combination of 2D quality metrics (the difference between original and degraded images) and the depth information (the difference between its corresponding disparity maps). The SSIM [23] and C4 [24] metrics have been selected as 2D IQMs.
- **Hewage et al. [4]:** A reduced reference image quality metric based on PSNR has been proposed. The disparity information was here also exploited. Edges are first extracted from the reference depth map and its distorted version. The obtained binary edge maps are then compared and used to achieve a quality index.
- **You et al. [25]:** The authors propose to study the capacities of 2D IQMs to estimate the quality of stereo images by integrating the disparity information. Eleven 2D IQMs have been used.

- **Hachicha et al. [26]:** The authors propose a Stereoscopic Image Quality Assessment measure based on some Human Visual System (HVS) characteristics. Perceptual versions of the reference and distorted images are first computed using some common HVS models (Contrast Sensitivity Function, cortex transform and masking model as enounced in [27]). A Binocular Just Noticeable Difference (BJND) models are then calculated and used to derive a quality index

In this section, we first show in this section the classification rate, and then the obtained correlations with subjective judgments are shown.

4.1 Classification Rate

Table 3 shows the obtained confusion matrix. The obtained classification values are high for all the degradation types and are superior to 80%. However, some confusions can be observed for ringing, fast fading and blur distortion types. These confusions are essentially due to the similarity of these degradations. Indeed, Ringing effect can be defined as oscillations around high contrast regions. However, depending on the bite rate blur can appear, which justify the high confusion between the ringing and the blur than the ringing and the fast fading. The same observations can be done for the fast fading distortion. Note that the fast fading degradation type has been also considered because it is composed by blur and ringing effect. Thus, we could characterize it using the selected features.

Table 3. Confusion Matrix

	Class	Noise	Blocking	Ringing	Fast Fading	Blur
				Estimated classes (%)		
True	Noise	100	0	0	0	0
	Blocking	0	100	0	0	0
Classes	Ringing	0	0	92,5	2,5	5
(%)	Fast Fading	0	0	6,25	85	8,75
	Blur	4,44	0	8,88	4,44	82,22

We can also see that the blur is confused with different classes (Noise, Ringing, Fast Fading). For noise, this is maybe due to the selected features that not permit to separate completely the classes. The overall classification rate is equal to 92.88%, which is higher and is efficient.

4.2 Correlation Results

To evaluate our method in terms of correlation with subjective scores, the 5-fold cross validation principle has been used (80% during the training and 20% during the test).

As evaluation criteria, the Pearson Linear Correlation Coefficient (PCC) is used and is computed as follows:

$$CORR_i = \frac{\sum_{k=1}^{K} (SFRIQM(k)_i - \overline{SFRIQM_i}).(DMOS(k)_i - \overline{DMOS_i})}{\sqrt{\sum_{k=1}^{K} (SFRIQM(k)_i - \overline{SFRIQM_i})^2} . \sqrt{\sum_{k=1}^{K} (DMOS(k)_i - \overline{DMOS_i})^2}} \tag{2}$$

where i stands for the ith degradation. The index k stands for the kth image, and K is the total number of pairs of images considered in the experiment. SFRIQM corresponds to the objective score, while DMOS is the subjective score.

Table 4 shows the obtained PCCs for each considered type of degradation. For the NR and the FR approaches, the best PCC is shown in red and blue colors respectively, while the best method whatever the approach is represented by a black background. The obtained values are high, except for blocking effect where the correlation is low. For the fast fading, the obtained result is closed to the best metric (Hachicha's method).

Table 4. Obtained Pearson Correlation Coefficients (PCC) for each considered degradation type.

		Degradation type				
	Method	Noise	Blur	Blocking	Ring-ing	Fast Fading
NR	*Our method*	0.9612	0.9718	0.6657	0.9563	0.8345
	Akther	0.9047	0.6177	0.7294	0.9059	0.6603
FR	Hewage	0.9253	0.9488	0.6405	0.9398	0.7472
	You	0.8955	0.7984	0.5305	0.9043	0.6698
	Benoit	0.9412	0.9198	0.4874	0.8778	0.7300
	Hachicha	**0.9502**	**0.9624**	**0.6565**	**0.9402**	

Compared to the NR metric (Akhter's method), our method provides better results, except for the blocking effect (0.7294), where the PCC value is lower (0.6657). Note that this metric (Akhter's method) has been developed for this specific degradation type (blocking effect). Moreover, for all compared metrics (NR & FR approaches) poor PCC values are also obtained. For the other degradation types, high correlations are obtained.

Compared to the FR metrics, better results are obtained for noise, blur, blocking and ringing degradations. For the fast fading, our method is better than all the compared method except for Hachicha's method. The obtained PCC value is slightly lower than Hachicha's method. It 's important to remember that this kind of metrics (FR) predicts the quality using the original image, while the NR metrics (our approach) use only the degraded image.

5   Conclusion and Perspectives

In this paper, a new Stereoscopic Image Quality metric without reference based on a classification and fusion steps is proposed. Our method was evaluated in terms of classification and correlations with the subjective scores. The obtained correlations show the relevance of the proposed framework and are better than the majority of the compared measures.

As perspective, we will consider other types of degradations and try to use a feature selection method in order to improve the performance.

References

1. http://www.its.bldrdoc.gov/vqeg/projects/3dtv/3dtv.aspx
2. Ryu, S., Kim, D.H., Sohn, K.: Stereoscopic image quality metric based on binocular perception model. In: IEEE International Conference on Image Processing, pp. 609–612 (2012)
3. Hewage, C.T.E.R., Martini, M.G.: Reduced-reference quality metric for 3d depth map transmission. In: 3DTV-CON, pp. 1–4 (2010)
4. Akhter, R., Sazzad, Z.M.P., Horita, Y., Baltes, J.: No reference stereoscopic image quality assessment. In: IS&T/SPIE Electronic Imaging, vol. 7524 (2010)
5. Chen, M.J., Su, C.C., Kwon, D.K., Cormack, L.K., Bovik, A.C.: Full-reference quality assessment of stereopairs accounting for rivalry. Signal Processing: Image Communication **28**, 1143–1155 (2013)
6. Gorley, P., Holliman, N.: Stereoscopic image quality metrics and compression. In: SPIE 6803, Stereoscopic Displays and Applications XIX (2008)
7. You, J., Xing, L., Perkis, A., Wang, X.: Perceptual quality assessment for stereoscopic images based on 2d image quality metrics and disparity analysis. In: International Workshop on Video Processing and Quality Metrics (2010)
8. Moorthy, A.K., Su, C.-C., Mittal, A., Bovik, A.C.: Subjective evaluation of stereoscopic image quality. Signal Processing: Image Communication **28**, 870–883 (2012)
9. http://stefan.winkler.net/resources.html#3D
10. Van de Ville, D., Kocher, M.: SURE-Based Non-Local Means. IEEE Signal Processing Letters **16**, 973–976 (2009)
11. Buclkey, M.J.: Fast computation of a discretized thin-plate smoothing spline for image data. Biometrika **81**, 247–258 (1994)
12. D'Errico, J.: http://www.mathworks.com/matlabcentral/fileexchange/16683-estimatenoise
13. Ferzli, R., Karam, J.L.: A No-Reference Objective Image Sharpness Metric Based on the Notion of Just Noticeable Blur. IEEE Transactions on Image Processing **18**(4), 717–728 (2009)
14. Wang, Z., Sheikh, H.R., Bovik, A.C.: 'No-Reference Perceptual Quality Assessment of JPEG Compressed Images. In: IEEE International Conference on Image Processing, vol. 1, pp. 477–480 (2002)
15. Sheikh, H.R., Bovik, A.C., Cormack, L.K.: No-Reference Quality Assessment Using Natural Scene Statistics: JPEG2000. IEEE Transactions on Image Processing **14**(12) (2005)
16. http://asi.insa-rouen.fr/enseignants/~arakoto/toolbox/
17. Levelt, W.J.M.: On Binocular Rivalry. Mouton, The Hague, Paris (1968)

18. Farias, M.: No-reference and reduced reference video quality metrics: new contributions. Thesis report
19. Narvekar, N.D., Karam, L.J.: A no-reference perceptual image sharpness metric based on a cumulative probability of blur detection. In: IEEE International Workshop on Quality of Multimedia Experience, pp. 87–91 (2009)
20. Wang, Z., Bovik, A.C., Evans, B.L.: Blind measurement of blocking artifacts in images. IEEE International Conferecne on Image Processing **3**, 981–984 (2000)
21. Chetouani, A., Beghdadi, A., Deriche, M.: A new free reference image quality index for blur estimation in the frequency domain. IEEE ISSPIT (2009)
22. Benoit, A., Le Callet, P., Campisi, P.: Quality assessment of stereoscopic images. EURASIP Journal on Image and Video Processing **2008** (2009)
23. Wang, Z., Bovik, A.C., Sheikh, H.R., Simoncelli, E.P.: Image Quality Assessment: From Error Visibility to Structural Similarity. IEEE Transactions on Image Processing **13**, 600–612 (2004)
24. Carnec, M., Le Callet, P., Barba, D.: An image quality assessment method based on perception of structural information. IEEE International Conference on Image Processing **2**, 185–188 (2003)
25. You, J., Xing, L., Perkis, A., Wang, X.: Perceptual quality assessment for stereoscopic images based on 2d image quality metrics and disparity analysis. In: International Workshop on Video Processing and Quality Metrics (2010)
26. Hachicha, W., Beghdadi, A., Alaya, F.C.: Stereo image quality assessment using a binocular just noticeable difference model. In: IEEE International Conference on Image Processing (2013)
27. Daly, S.: The visible differences predictor: an algorithm for the assessment of image fidelity. Digital Images and Human Vision **4**, 124–125 (1993)

Analysis of HVS-Metrics' Properties Using Color Image Database TID2013

Nikolay Ponomarenko[1], Vladimir Lukin[1(✉)], Jaakko Astola[2], and Karen Egiazarian[2]

[1] Department of Transmitters, Receivers and Signal Processing, National Aerospace University,
17 Chkalova St, Kharkiv 61070, Ukraine
nikolay@ponomarenko.info, lukin@ai.kharkov.com
[2] Institute of Signal Processing, Tampere University of Technology,
P.O. Box-553, 33101 Tampere, Finland
{jaakko.astola,karen.egiazarian}@tut.fi

Abstract. Various full-reference (FR) image quality metrics (indices) that take into account peculiarities of human vision system (HVS) have been proposed during last decade. Most of them have been already tested on several image databases including TID2013, a recently proposed database of distorted color images. Metrics performance is usually characterized by the rank order correlation coefficients of the considered metric and a mean opinion score (MOS). In this paper, we characterize HVS-metrics from another practically important viewpoint. We determine and analyze image statistics such as mean and standard deviation for several state of the art quality metrics on classes of images with multiple or particular types of distortions. This allows setting threshold value(s) for a given metric and application.

Keywords: Full reference metrics · Visual quality · Color image database · Mean opinion score · Threshold values

1 Introduction

Full-reference metrics have been widely used for assessing image quality in several applications of digital image processing [1-4]. In particular, among typical applications there are watermarking [5], lossy compression of still images and video [3,6], image denoising [7], multimedia [2,4], etc. Standard metrics such as mean square error, signal-to-noise ratio, etc. have been criticized for being not adequate enough to human perception. Due to this, many efforts were spent on designing so-called HVS-metrics [1,4,7,8] which are able to take into account peculiarities of human vision system.

Many full-reference metrics (i.e., the metrics calculated for a distorted image and a sample one, often called also as etalon, undistorted, or reference image) have been designed and intensively tested [1,8-12]. For testing purposes, several image databases have been developed and exploited [11,13-15]. These databases have served several purposes including the following: checking metric adequacy for all types of distortions present in a database or for a particular group of distortions; comparison of metrics' performance for

© Springer International Publishing Switzerland 2015
S. Battiato et al. (Eds.): ACIVS 2015, LNCS 9386, pp. 613–624, 2015.
DOI: 10.1007/978-3-319-25903-1_53

all types of distortions or groups; determination of drawbacks of a given metric, i.e. the types of distortions for which this metric does not perform well enough. As a result, it has been established that currently there is no universal metric that is able to correspond to human perception perfectly [1,15,16]. Meanwhile, usually there exist a few quite good full-reference metrics for each group of distortion types. In particular, this takes place for such types of distortions as noise, distortions due to lossy compression, blur and image filtering [15,16]. These groups of distortions were collected into the subset 'Actual' specially analyzed in [15]. There are several HVS-metrics for which Spearman rank order correlation coefficient [17] between these metrics and mean opinion score exceeds 0.9 (which can be considered high enough). Among these metrics, there are the following: color version of the metric FSIM (further denoted as FSIMc) [18] and the component-wise version of this metric (denoted as FSIM) [18], the component-wise metrics PSNR-HVS [19] and PSNR-HVS-M [20], the combined metric BMMF [21], the metrics PSNR-HMA and PSNR-HA [22], the metric SR SIM [23] and few others (see Table 4 in [15]). The metric MSSIM [24] produces good results as well for this subset.

However, there is one more problem in exploiting the aforementioned and other HVS-metrics. On one hand, it is usually known what are the limits of their variation (e.g., from 0 to 1 for the metrics FSIM and MSSIM) or that larger values of a given metric relate, in general, to a better visual quality (this happens for the most of metrics). On the other hand, it is often unknown what value of a considered metric corresponds to a desired visual quality. A research on this is, to the best of our knowledge, very limited. In particular, it has been stated in [25, 26] that the values of PSNR-HVS-M about 40 dB or MSSIM about 0.99 correspond to almost invisible distortions (if these distortions are more or less uniformly spread over the entire image). In other words, it is difficult for an inexperienced user to imagine how good is an image visual quality if, e.g., PSNR-HVS-M for it is about 30 dB or MSSIM is about 0.90. Thus, a certain correspondence between the metric values (or thresholds) and image visual quality perceived by humans and described by a certain scale is required.

The goal of this paper is to establish such a correspondence. To reach this goal, we have considered MOS values for 3000 distorted color images in the database TID2013 [15, 16] as well as additional information from experiment participants such as detection of images with practically invisible distortions, verbal characterization of visual quality for the analyzed images, etc.

2   Brief Description of TID2013

The database TID2013 (Tampere image database, available at http://ponomarenko. info/tid2013.htm) was designed two years ago as a modification of the earlier database TID2008. TID2013 includes the same 25 reference color images as its predecessor TID2008. 24 distortion-free images were obtained from the Kodak database http://r0k.us/graphics/kodak/ by cropping them, the last reference image was artificially created. All the images used in both databases (both reference and distorted) have the same size of 512x384 pixels. Totally, the database TID2013 contains 3000 distorted images. For each reference image, there are 120 distorted images. More in detail, there are five levels of distortions that approximately correspond to peak signal-to-noise ratio (PSNR) equal to 33, 30, 27, 24, and 21 dB. There are also twenty four types of distortions where seventeen of them were in TID2008 and seven new types are added in TID2013. The types of distortions are the following: additive white Gaussian noise (#1), additive white Gaussian noise which is more intensive in color components than in the luminance component (#2), additive Gaussian spatially correlated noise (#3), masked noise (#4), high frequency noise (#5), impulse noise (#6), quantization noise (#7), Gaussian blur (#8), image denoising (residual noise, #9), JPEG lossy compression (#10), JPEG2000 lossy compression (#11), JPEG transmission errors (#12), JPEG2000 transmission errors (#13), non-eccentricity pattern noise (#14), local block-wise distortions of different intensity (#15), mean shift (#16), contrast change (#17), change of color saturation (#18), multiplicative Gaussian noise (#19), comfort noise (#20), lossy compression of noisy images (#21), image color quantization with dither (#22), chromatic aberrations (#23), sparse sampling and reconstruction (#24).

Recall now how experiments were carried out. Three images were displayed simultaneously where a reference image was placed below and two distorted ones obtained on basis of the given reference were put together in the upper part of the monitor screen. Pair-wise comparisons were performed where each distorted image participated in nine comparisons and a winner was getting one point. Thus, each distorted image was able to get the maximal sum of 9 points in one experiment. Results of experiments carried out by observers were processed with removing abnormal results and averaging the remaining ones. Therefore, the maximal MOS could be equal to 9. However, this did not happen for any distorted image. The distribution of the obtained MOS values is presented in Fig. 1 and it is seen that the largest MOS only slightly exceeds 7. There are the following reasons for this. First, there were, at least, several images among 120 distorted ones that had approximately the same and high visual quality (distortions for them were hardly noticeable or practically invisible). Second, in each situation (pair-wise comparison) an observer had to undertake a decision and these decisions were subjective.

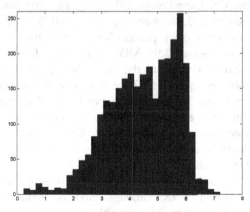

Fig. 1. Histogram of MOS values for TID2013

For TID2013, people from five countries (Ukraine, Finland, Italy, France, USA) participated in experiments and good agreement was observed for results coming from different countries. Totally, almost one thousand experiments were performed in laboratory conditions under tutor's control and distantly via Internet. For each reference image, practically equal number of experiments was performed. This provided the variance of MOS estimates for the distorted images about 0.69. Other data on experiments and their results can be found in [15, 16].

3   Gradations of Image Visual Quality

Analysis of image visual quality was often done using a certain number of gradations. For example, the designers of the database LIVE have used five gradations in their experiments, namely, "Bad", "Poor", "Fair", "Good", and "Excellent" (or, equivalently, with a score from 1 to 5). It is possible to use other number of gradations (categories) and names for them as, e.g., "Excellent", "Good", "Middle", and "Bad" visual quality. A special case useful for practice can be also a category "Images with invisible distortions".

For the database TID2013, we have MOS values and additional information from observers (participants of experiments) such as: a set of images for which distortions are considered invisible (213 images), verbally expressed opinions (gradations) concerning visual quality of analyzed images. Then, we can rely on MOS values in determining the groups in images in them. The following four groups have been formed:

- images of excellent quality for which either the distortions are invisible or their visual quality is perceived as very high; this group includes images with 200 top rank values of MOS;
- images of good quality for which MOS have the ranks from 201 to 1000;
- images of middle (fair) quality for which MOS have ranks from 1001 to 2000;
- images of bad quality which have the lowest 1000 ranks (from 2001 to 3000, ranking is done in the order of descending MOS).

It is possible to describe these groups differently. The first group contains the images with MOS exceeding 6.05, the second group has MOS in the limits from 5.25 to 6.05, the images of the third group possess MOS values from 3.94 to 5.25 and the fourth group have MOS less than 3.94. MOS mean values for these groups are equal to 6.28, 5.66, 4.60, and 3.04, respectively. Interestingly, the MOS mean for images with invisible distortions is equal to 5.87, i.e. it is smaller than for the images of the first group. This is not very surprising since visibility of distortions depend upon many factors including image structure complexity. For textural images, there are more chances that distortions are invisible. Due to this, we had more distorted images with invisible distortions for such reference images as #13 or #5 and less for reference images with simpler structures as, e.g., #3.

People of image processing community usually have some experience of dealing with images having different PSNR. Although PSNR is, obviously, not adequate metric to describe well visual quality, its mean values can provide some imagination on the quality of images in the aforementioned groups. The mean values of PSNR for groups are equal to 30.9, 30.5, 26.8, and 23.2 dB, respectively. Mean MOS for images with invisible distortions is equal to 32.0. Images of excellent quality and with invisible distortions mainly relate to the upper level (about 33 dB, see the scatter-plot in Fig. 2, points that correspond to images with invisible distortions are shown by blue circles). In turn, images of Bad quality mainly relate to the two lower levels of PSNR (21 and 24 dB). These results are also in a good agreement with the results in [25]. For example, distortions are often not seen in lossy compressed images if PSNR for them is about 31...33 dB. Lossy compressed images that are characterized by PSNR about 21...24 dB really have obvious distortions.

To get more imagination what is appearance of distorted images referred to different groups, Fig. 3 presents four distorted images (for the same reference image #1) that have MOS approximately equal to mean MOS for the aforementioned groups. As it is seen, the image in Fig. 3,a has a perfect quality whilst the quality of the image in Fig. 3,d is obviously bad.

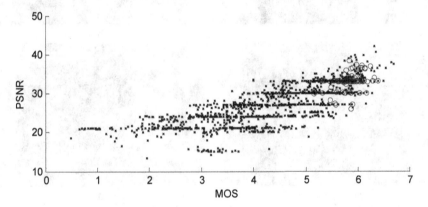

Fig. 2. Scatter-plot of PSNR vs MOS, blue circles relate to images with invisible distortions

4   Performance Analysis for Different HVS-Metrics

Before starting to analyse the obtained results, let us explain what are the requirements to a good HVS-metric. Conventional requirements [1, 15] are adequateness to MOS (which is characterized and controlled by Spearman or Kendal rank order correlation coefficients), universality (applicability to different types of distortions) and high computational efficiency (simplicity of metric's calculation).

The latter two requirements are not obligatory in some applications but desirable. For a given application, a universality of a metric can be neglected. It should be enough if a metric has an appropriate adequateness for this particular type or several close types of distortions. Keeping this in mind, we have decided to analyze statistics of the considered metrics for all types of distortions (denoted as 'Full') to characterize a metric's universality and for two particular subsets of distortions. The first subset has been earlier mentioned. The subset called 'Actual' includes images with the following types of distortions: additive white Gaussian noise (#1), additive Gaussian spatially correlated noise (#3), masked noise (#4), high frequency noise (#5), impulse noise (#6), Gaussian blur (#8), image denoising (residual noise, #9), JPEG lossy compression (#10), JPEG2000 lossy compression (#11), multiplicative Gaussian noise (#19), lossy compression of noisy images (#21). The second subset (denoted as 'Compr') includes only images with distortions due to JPEG lossy compression (#10) and JPEG2000 lossy compression (#11), i.e. relates to a particular application.

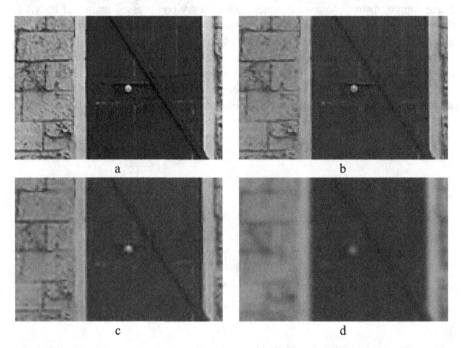

Fig. 3. Examples of fragments of distorted images with different MOS (a – i01_17_4, MOS=6.24, b – i01_11_2, MOS=5.68, c – i01_11_3, MOS=4.69, d – i01_08_4, MOS=3.00)

Additional requirement to HVS-metrics can be the following: to have some fixed (recommended threshold) values that allows distinguishing (dividing) images of different visual quality to the aforementioned or other groups. A theory of solving such tasks (e.g., detection theory) states that misclassification errors can be minimized if class centers are separated well (have rather large distance D) and inner-class standard deviations (STD_1 and STD_2) are small enough [27]. Then, a separability of classes (image groups in our case) can be roughly characterized by $S = D / \sqrt{STD_1 \times STD_2}$.

Statistics (mean MOS, mean values for three subsets and five groups) for the conventional metric PSNR is presented in Table 1. Here and below we present data for additional group of images called 'Invisible'. Note that the subsets 'Actual' and 'Compr' for each group include those distorted images that have MOS in the limits given above.

The first interesting observation is that mean PSNR for the set 'Full' (that includes all distorted images) and the subsets 'Actual' and 'Compr' are quite close for each group. Meanwhile, standard deviations for the set 'Full' are considerably larger than STDs for the subsets 'Actual' and 'Compr'. We attribute this to a variability of distortions for the set 'Full' and problems of designing universal quality metrics.

As a case study, consider separability of the groups Excellent and Good Quality for the subset 'Actual' - $S = 2.6 / \sqrt{2.71 \times 2.87} \approx 0.94$. Separability for other neighbour groups (e.g., Middle and Bad quality) is better (S is larger).

Table 1. Statistics of PSNR for the considered classes

Images quality	mean MOS	Mean metric value			STD of metric values		
		Full	Actual	Compr	Full	Actual	Compr
Invisible	5.87	32.0	32.9	33.5	2.78	2.23	2.39
Excellent	6.28	30.9	34.4	35.3	4.17	2.71	1.60
Good	5.66	30.5	31.8	32.4	3.69	2.87	2.32
Middle	4.60	26.8	27.6	28.4	4.05	3.73	2.42
Bad	3.04	23.2	22.8	23.5	2.87	3.07	2.35

Consider now the results for the metric PSNR-HVS-M (this metric is expressed in dB) given in Table 2. Mean values for the considered sets are all larger than the corresponding PSNR values. Moreover, they differ more than for PSNR. For example, whilst mean PSNR for the subset Actual vary from 22.8 to 34.4 dB, PSNR-HVS-M vary from 25.4 to 45.5 dB. Meanwhile, separability of the classes Excellent and Good for the metric PSNR-HVS is characterized by $S = 2.0 / \sqrt{5.21 \times 5.77} \approx 0.37$, i.e. it is worse that for the metric PSNR.

Table 2. Statistics of PSNR-HVS-M for the considered classes

Images quality	Mean MOS	Mean metric value			STD of metric values		
		Full	Actual	Compr	Full	Actual	Compr
Invisible	5.87	46.7	49.2	48.7	6.55	4.86	3.65
Excellent	6.28	36.7	45.5	49.7	10.4	5.21	2.38
Good	5.66	39.7	43.5	44.5	8.63	5.77	5.29
Middle	4.60	32.6	35.1	35.0	6.88	4.15	3.80
Bad	3.04	24.7	25.4	23.7	6.40	4.11	3.34

The scatter-plot of PSNR-HVS-M vs MOS is presented in Fig. 4. Images with invisible distortions concentrate around MOS≈6 and have PSNR-HVS-M from about 35 dB to almost 60 dB. It is possible to set the threshold T≈42 dB for detecting images with invisible distortions, but, as it is seen, there can be many false detections in this case.

An interesting outlier has happened for the set 'Full' for the classes Excellent and Good. Mean PSNR-HVS-M for the latter class is higher than for the class Excellent. This is because quite many images with the distortion type #17 (Contrast change) that have enhanced contrast have got high MOS and were addressed to the class Excellent. Meanwhile, PSNR-HVS-M for them is not high and this fact has shifted mean PSNR-

HVS-M to smaller values. Note that a similar effect is observed for the metric PSNR (see data in Table 1, the set 'Full') where mean PSNR are practically equal for the classes Excellent and Good.

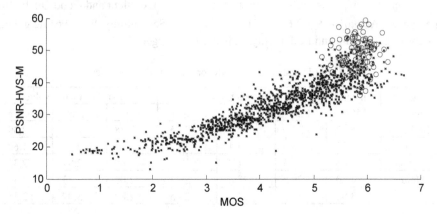

Fig. 4. Scatter-plot of PSNR-HVS-M vs MOS, blue circles relate to images with invisible distortions

The results for the metric PSNR-HMA are given in Table 3. This metric is also expressed in dB and the range of its variation is also wider than for PSNR. One good point for this metric is that the mean values for a given class are close to each other for the set 'Full' and the subsets 'Actual' and 'Compr'. This evidences in favor of higher universality of this metric compared to the metric PSNR-HVS-M. As for the previously analyzed metrics, STD values for the subset 'Compr' are the smallest whilst they are the largest for the set 'Full'. Concerning separability of classes, let us again determine the parameter S for the classes Excellent and Good of the subset Actual: $S = 2.1/\sqrt{3.62 \times 3.97} \approx 0.56$ This means that the classes can be separated better than using the metric PSNR-HVS-M. The results presented as a scatter-plot in Fig. 5 show that the threshold of distortions invisibility can be set as T≈40 dB.

The results for the metrics PSNR-HVS and PSNR-HA are very similar to those for the metric PSNR-HMA. The recommendation on setting the "invisibility threshold" is the same.

Table 3. Statistics of PSNR-HMA for the considered classes

Images quality	Mean MOS	Mean metric value			STD of metric values		
		Full	Actual	Compr	Full	Actual	Compr
Invisible	5.87	41.9	44.6	42.0	5.34	3.96	2.14
Excellent	6.28	41.3	44.1	43.0	5.57	3.62	1.18
Good	5.66	39.9	42.0	40.5	5.04	3.97	2.48
Middle	4.60	34.2	35.3	34.8	4.42	3.33	2.24
Bad	3.04	26.9	27.2	25.7	4.03	3.20	2.90

Consider now another group of metrics that includes MSSIM, FSIM, and FSIMc. Their common peculiarity is that these metrics vary from zero to unity where the latter value corresponds to a perfect quality. The data obtained for the metric MSSIM are presented in Table 4. The data for the metrics FSIM and FSIMc are represented in Tables 5 and 6, respectively. The mean values of all three metrics that correspond to each other in these Tables are quite close. Starting from values for the classes Invisible and Excellent that are very close to unity (of the order 0.996), they gradually reduce and reach 0.83...0.88 for the class Bad. This means that the range of possible variation of these metrics is not exploited fully. Mostly their values concentrate between 0.9 and 1.0. This is a drawback of these metrics.

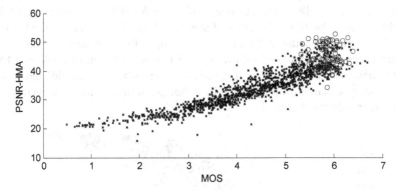

Fig. 5. Scatter-plot of PSNR-HMA vs MOS, blue circles relate to images with invisible distortions

Table 4. Statistics of the metric MSSIM for the considered classes

Images quality	Mean MOS	Mean metric value			STD of metric values		
		Full	Actual	Compr	Full	Actual	Compr
Invisible	5.87	0.996	0.996	0.995	0.00362	0.00330	0.0023
Excellent	6.28	0.991	0.994	0.996	0.0119	0.00389	0.0014
Good	5.66	0.990	0.990	0.992	0.0100	0.00799	0.0061
Middle	4.60	0.969	0.969	0.978	0.0264	0.0241	0.0117
Bad	3.04	0.881	0.878	0.854	0.0843	0.0718	0.0879

Table 5. Statistics of the metric FSIM for the considered classes

Images quality	Mean MOS	Mean metric value			STD of metric values		
		Full	Actual	Compr	Full	Actual	Compr
Invisible	5.87	0.996	0.997	0.997	0.0030	0.00220	0.00133
Excellent	6.28	0.991	0.995	0.998	0.0112	0.00400	0.00072
Good	5.66	0.992	0.992	0.993	0.0081	0.00629	0.00532
Middle	4.60	0.974	0.974	0.976	0.0193	0.0170	0.0126
Bad	3.04	0.891	0.887	0.847	0.0728	0.0657	0.0770

Table 6. Statistics of the metric FSIMc for the considered classes

Images quality	Mean MOS	Mean metric value			STD of metric values		
		Full	Actual	Compr	Full	Actual	Compr
Invisible	5.87	0.995	0.996	0.996	0.0038	0.0026	0.0016
Excellent	6.28	0.990	0.994	0.997	0.0126	0.0048	0.0008
Good	5.66	0.989	0.991	0.992	0.0093	0.0075	0.0062
Middle	4.60	0.968	0.968	0.971	0.0214	0.0201	0.0142
Bad	3.04	0.876	0.871	0.829	0.0763	0.0695	0.0809

Meanwhile, class separability is not bad. The values of S for the subset 'Actual' and the classes Excellent and Good are of the order 0.5...0.73 (the largest is for MSSIM). This is due to small values of standard deviations which are the largest for the set 'Full' and the smallest for the subset 'Compr'. Fig. 6 presents the most important part of the scatter-plot of MSSIM vs MOS (the scatter-plots of FSIM and FSIMc vs MOS have similar properties). It is seen that "Invisibility threshold" has to be set approximately equal to 0.993 (Fig. 6,b) although, similarly to other metrics, fault detections are observed well.

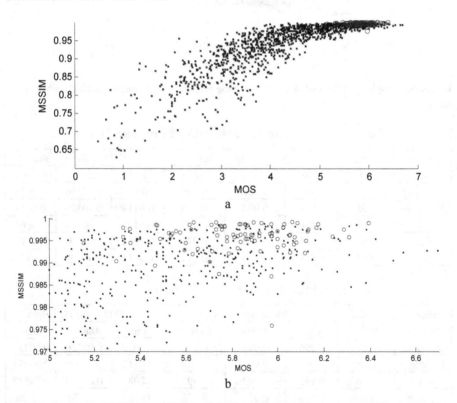

Fig. 6. Scatter-plot of MSSIM vs MOS for full (a) and limited (b) range of MOS variation, blue circles relate to images with invisible distortions

5   Conclusions

We have divided distorted images contained in the database TID2013 into several classes according to their visual quality characterized by MOS. This has allowed determining statistical characteristics for several HVS-metrics that are among the best according to the SROCC values between the quality metrics and MOS. The determined mean values describe quality classes centers and the obtained standard deviations characterize class variability. It is shown that this variability is smaller if only distortions of a limited number of types are considered. This means that universality of HVS-metrics is still not good enough. We have also analyzed separability of classes and have demonstrated that it is a difficult task to separate classes by a simple thresholding of metric values. Better separation is provided by HVS-metrics that take into account color. Approximate values of "distortion invisibility thresholds" are given for the considered metrics based on analysis for a large number of tested color images.

References

1. Chandler, D.M.: Seven Challenges in Image Quality Assessment: Past, Present and Future Research. ISNR Signal Processing **2913**, 1–53 (2013)
2. Wu, H.R., Lin, W., Karam, L.: An overview of perceptual processing for digital pictures. In: Proceedings of International Conference on Multimedia and Expo Workshops, Melbourne, pp. 113–120 (2012)
3. Larson, E.C., Chandler, D.M.: Most apparent distortion: full-reference image quality assessment and the role of strategy. Journal of Electronic Imaging **19**(1), 011006 (2010)
4. Moorthy, A.K., Bovik, A.C.: Visual quality assessment algorithms: what does the future hold? Multimedia Tools and Applications **51**(2), 675–696 (2011). Springer
5. Carli, M.: Perceptual Aspects in Data Hiding. Thesis for the degree of Doctor of Technology, Tampere University of Technology (2008)
6. Ponomarenko, N., Krivenko, S., Lukin, V., Egiazarian, K.: Lossy compression of noisy images based on visual quality: a comprehensive study. EURASIP Journal on Advances in Signal Processingm 13 (2010). doi:10.1155/2010/976436
7. Fevralev, D., Lukin, V., Ponomarenko, N., Abramov, S., Egiazarian, K., Astola, J.: Efficiency analysis of DCT-based filters for color image database. In: Proceedings of SPIE Conference Image Processing: Algorithms and Systems VII, San Francisco, vol. 7870 (2011)
8. Wang, Z., Bovik, A., Sheikh, H., Simoncelli, E.: Image quality assessment: from error visibility to structural similarity. IEEE Transactions on Image Processing **13**(4), 600–612 (2004). New York
9. Keelan, B.W.: Handbook of Image Quality. Marcel Dekker Inc, New York (2002)
10. Jin, L., Egiazarian, K., Jay Kuo, C-C.: Perceptual image quality assessment using Block-Based Milti-Metric Fusion (BMMF). In: Proceedings of ICASSP, Kyoto, Japan, pp. 1145–1148 (2012)
11. Sheikh, H.R., Wang, Z., Cormack, L., Bovik, A.C.: LIVE Image Quality Assessment Database Release 2, http://live.ece.utexas.edu/research/quality/subjective.htm
12. Sheikh, H.R., Sabir, M.F., Bovik, A.C.: A Statistical Evaluation of Recent Full Reference Image Quality Assessment Algorithms. IEEE Transactions on Image Processing **15**(11), 3441–3452 (2006)

13. Horita, Y., Shibata, K., Parvez Saddad, Z.M.: Subjective quality assessment toyama database. http://mict.eng.u-toyama.ac.jp/mict/
14. Ponomarenko, N., Lukin, V., Zelensky, A., Egiazarian, K., Carli, M., Battisti, F.: TID2008 - A Database for Evaluation of Full-Reference Visual Quality Assessment Metrics. Advances of Modern Radioelectronics **10**, 30–45 (2009)
15. Ponomarenko, N., Ieremeiev, O., Lukin, V., Egiazarian, K., Jin, L., Astola, J., Vozel, B., Chehdi, K., Carli, M., Battisti, F., Kuo, C.-C.J.: Image Database TID2013: Peculiarities, Results and Perspectives. Signal Processing: Image Communication **30**(1), 57–77 (2015)
16. Ponomarenko, N., Ieremeiev, O., Lukin, V., Jin, L., Egiazarian, K., Astola, J., Vozel, B., Chehdi, K., Carli, M., Battisti, F., Kuo, C.-C.: A new color image database TID2013: innovations and results. In: Blanc-Talon, J., Kasinski, A., Philips, W., Popescu, D., Scheunders, P. (eds.) ACIVS 2013. LNCS, vol. 8192, pp. 402–413. Springer, Heidelberg (2013)
17. Kendall, M.G.: The advanced theory of statistics, vol. 1. Charles Griffin & Company Limited, London (1945)
18. Zhang, L., Mou, X., Zhang, D.: FSIM: a feature similarity index for image quality assessment. IEEE Transactions on Image Processing **20**(5), 2378–2386 (2011)
19. Egiazarian, K., Astola, J., Ponomarenko, N., Lukin, V., Battisti, F., Carli, M.: New full-reference quality metrics based on HVS. In: Proceedings of the Second International Workshop on Video Processing and Quality Metrics, 4 p., Scottsdale (2006)
20. Ponomarenko, N., Silvestri, F., Egiazarian, K., Carli, M., Astola, J., Lukin, V.: On between-coefficient contrast masking of DCT basis functions. In: Proc. of the Third International Workshop on Video Processing and Quality Metrics, USA, 4 p. (2007)
21. Jin, L. Egiazarian, K., Kuo, C.-C.J.: Performance comparison of decision fusion strategies in BMMF-based image quality assessment. In: Proceedings of APSIPA, Hollywood, pp. 1–4 (2012)
22. Ponomarenko, N., Eremeev, O., Lukin, V., Egiazarian, K., Carli, M.: Modified image visual quality metrics for contrast change and mean shift accounting. In: Proceedings of CADSM, Polyana-Svalyava, pp. 305–311 (2011)
23. Zhang, L., Li, H.: SR-SIM: a fast and high performance IQA index based on spectral residual. In: 19th IEEE International Conference on Image Processing (ICIP), Orlando, USA, pp. 1473–1476 (2012)
24. Wang, Z., Simoncelli, E.P., Bovik, A.C.: Multi-scale structural similarity for image quality assessment. In: IEEE Asilomar Conference on Signals, Systems and Computers, pp. 1398–1402 (2003)
25. Lukin, V., Zriakhov, M., Krivenko, S., Ponomarenko, N., Miao, Z.: Lossy compression of images without visible distortions and its applications. In: Proceedings of ICSP 2010, Beijing, China, pp. 694–697 (2010)
26. Ponomarenko, N., Zemlyachenko, A., Lukin, V., Egiazarian, K., Astola, J.: Performance Analysis of Visually Lossless Image Compression. In: Proceedings of VPQM, Scottsdale, USA, 6 p. (2012)
27. Van Trees, H.L.: Detection, Estimation, and Modulation Theory (Part 1). John Wiley & Sons, New York (2004)

Solidarity Filter for Noise Reduction of 3D Edges in Depth Images

Hani Javan Hemmat$^{(\boxtimes)}$, Egor Bondarev, and Peter H.N. de With

Eindhoven University of Technology, Den Dolech 2, 5612 AZ Eindhoven,
The Netherlands
{h.javan.hemmat,e.bondarev,p.h.n.de.with}@tue.nl
http://vca.ele.tue.nl/

Abstract. 3D applications processing depth images significantly benefit from 3D-edge extraction techniques. Intrinsic sensor noise in depth images is largely inherited to the extracted 3D edges. Conventional denoising algorithms remove some of this noise, but also weaken narrow edges, amplify noisy pixels and introduce false edges. We therefore propose a novel solidarity filter for noise removal in 3D edge images without artefacts such as false edges. The proposed filter is defining neighbouring pixels with similar properties and connecting those into larger segments beyond the size of a conventional filter aperture. The experimental results show that the solidarity filter outperforms the median and morphological close filters with 42 % and 69 % higher PSNR, respectively. In terms of the mean SSIM metric, the solidarity filter provides results that are 11 % and 21 % closer to the ground truth than the corresponding results obtained by the median and close filters, respectively.

Keywords: Solidarity filter · Noise removal · 3D edges · Depth images · Peak Signal-to-Noise Ratio · Structural SIMilarity

1 Introduction

Various types of noise and corresponding denoising and restoration techniques have been widely studied in the literature [1–12]. 3D image processing has obtained a significant benefit from the introduction of low-cost depth sensors (e.g. Kinect and Xtion). Unfortunately, the limited resolution applied in these sensors results in the appearance of significant noise in the resulting depth images. This noise incorporates both blur (especially on edges) and salt-and-pepper noise (mostly on flat surfaces), depending on the shape, material and pose of objects in a scene. Any type of depth data processing will include these types of noise in the finally obtained result. For instance, in our recent work on 3D edge extraction within depth images [15,16], we have observed that such noise types occurred in the extracted 3D edges. In this paper, we propose a novel filter to remove noise on 3D edges extracted from depth images.

To remove the above-mentioned noise types, we have first evaluated several conventional algorithms at both pre- and post-processing stages, applying them

© Springer International Publishing Switzerland 2015
S. Battiato et al. (Eds.): ACIVS 2015, LNCS 9386, pp. 625–636, 2015.
DOI: 10.1007/978-3-319-25903-1_54

to the depth images and to the extracted 3D edge images, respectively. Considering a depth image as a 2D intensity image and applying the conventional denoising algorithms results in a poor performance because of the following reasons. First, in depth images, spatial distribution of range data can be irregular, which requires adaptive processing with respect to the shape and size of the objects in a scene. Second, the traditional algorithms are limited by orientation and scale and, therefore, perform poorly on blurred edges of depth images. In addition to this, there are no broadly accepted algorithms to handle depth images as 3D data (e.g. pointcloud). On the other hand, applying conventional denoising algorithms to the obtained 3D edges at a post-processing stage produces more acceptable results, when compared to the previously mentioned pre-processing approach. Let us have a closer look to the type of algorithm that may be applied to 3D edge images.

It should be noticed that the 3D edge images resulting from depth data are binary images, where each pixel indicates whether the corresponding pixel in the depth image is located on a 3D edge or not. To reduce the noise in such 3D edge images, we have utilized morphological erosion, dilation, opening and closing, as well as median, bilateral, and Gaussian filters [15,16]. Although each individual filter can handle part of the noise, it cannot solve the dominant noise completely, so that the following main challenges still remain. First of all, these methods process 3D edge images as normal images to which a window-based filter is applied, irrespective of the special contents of the window. In other words, the filters process the data within the aperture without looking to the information of neighbouring areas. Accordingly, these methods are window-dependent and their outcome depends on the size and shape of the windows, while 3D edges are connected objects spreading throughout the image. As a consequence, when applying these filters to 3D edge images, the size of the filtering window directly affects the resulting edges. Small-sized windows may boost the noise, while large-sized windows may destroy the 3D edges. Finally, these methods are based on recomputing the image data, which may result in converting an actual edge pixel into a non-edge pixel (missed edges) and vice versa (false edges). Missed and false edges can affect the outcome of the algorithms in a crucial way, which are dependent on 3D edge images such as our planar segmentation algorithm [15,16].

Inspired by the fact that 3D edges are connected pixels spreading all over the image, we have come to a novel concept of a solidarity filter. The solidarity filter attempts to connect all *similar* pixels in an image, in order to form groups of connected pixels. The *similarity* between pixels is determined based on a user-defined metric. For example, in the scope of 3D edges, the *similarity* is defined as follows: two pixels are similar if both are either edge pixels or non-edge pixels. A solidarity value is assigned to each group of pixels based on its population (number of pixels) and the level of similarity (according to the user definition). Inside a group, each pixel has a share in the solidarity value and therefore, has an effect on all other connected pixels, accordingly. The effect of noise in 3D edge images resembles a conversion of an edge-pixel to a non-edge-pixel or vice-versa. Therefore, noisy pixels become *dissimilar* to their neighbours. Due to this dissimilarity, the corresponding solidarity value for noisy pixels is very small, when compared to the connected edge pixels similar to each other. With the solidarity filter, for removing noise from 3D edge images, we sort groups with connected pixels based on the solidarity value and then discard any group with the solidarity value less than a user-defined threshold. According to our experiments, edge pixels are much more robust to noise reduction by a solidarity filter in comparison with outliers. This is due to the similarity between connected pixels inside a group, which increases the solidarity value to reach the user-defined threshold. The solidarity filter features two major benefits: (a) it has a global influence rather than a local influence, and thereby, it is a completely window-independent algorithm, and (b) the data manipulation is minimal, when compared to the conventional algorithms.

This paper is structured as follows. Section 2 describes the proposed algorithm in detail. Experimental results and evaluation are presented and discussed in Section 3. Finally, Section 4 concludes the paper.

2 Solidarity Filter

This section specifies a formal definition of the solidarity filter. Besides this, an algorithmic processing architecture for filtering steps is provided. The solidarity filter is defined as

$$S(P_{ij}) = \begin{cases} P_{ij} & \text{if } Solidarity_{value}(P_{ij}) \geq T_{solidarity}, \\ 0 & \text{otherwise}. \end{cases} \quad (1)$$

Thus the solidarity filter discards pixels with $Solidarity_{value}$ less than a user-defined threshold represented by $T_{solidarity}$ (the granularity level of the filter). Equation (1) has been defined based on the following five definitions. First,

$$P_{ij} = \text{a pixel located on column } i \text{ and row } j \text{ of a given image}, \quad (2)$$

and second, a binary neighbouring indicator specifies neighbouring pixels, giving

$$F_{nb}(P_{ij}, P_{i'j'}) = \begin{cases} 1 & \text{if } |i - i'| \leq T_{dist} \text{ AND } |j - j'| \leq T_{dist}, \\ 0 & \text{otherwise}. \end{cases} \quad (3)$$

The binary indicator is true if a pixel is within a certain distance T_{dist} ($= 1$, by default). Third, a similarity flag is defined based on a user-defined metric as

$$F_{sim}(P_{ij}, P_{i'j'}) = \begin{cases} 1 & \text{if } P_{ij} \text{ is } similar \text{ to } P_{i'j'}, \\ 0 & \text{otherwise}, \end{cases} \quad (4)$$

where the function *similar* is for example, being on an edge or not, as discussed earlier. Fourth, we define pixels to be connected directly (the first term), or indirectly connected (the second term) to a common pixel $P_{i''j''}$ that was already a connected neighbour, hence

$$
\begin{aligned}
F_{conn}(P_{ij}, P_{i'j'}) = \\
(F_{nb}(P_{ij}, P_{i'j'}) = 1 \quad \text{AND} \quad F_{sim}(P_{ij}, P_{i'j'}) = 1) \quad \text{OR} \\
(F_{conn}(P_{ij}, P_{i''j''}) = 1 \quad \text{AND} \quad F_{conn}(P_{i'j'}, P_{i''j''}) = 1).
\end{aligned} \tag{5}
$$

Fifth, the amount of pixels connected in an image is defined by

$$
N_{conn}(P_{ij}) = \sum_{c=1}^{N_{cols}} \sum_{r=1}^{N_{rows}} F_{conn}(P_{ij}, P_{cr}). \tag{6}
$$

The parameter N_{conn} defines the number of pixels connected to a given pixel based on the connectivity flag specified by Equation (5). Finally, we compute

$$
Solidarity_{value}(P_{ij}) = Solidarity_{itself} + \left(N_{conn}(P_{ij}) \times Solidarity_{effect}\right). \tag{7}
$$

In Equation (7), the solidarity value for a pixel is calculated based on the number of similar pixels connected to it. The parameters $Solidarity_{itself}$ and $Solidarity_{effect}$ are user-defined constants (by default, both equal to 1), representing the weights for a pixel itself and its neighbours, respectively.

Focusing specifically on the denoising of 3D edge images, the concept of *similarity* is defined as a binary function with the following definition: two pixels are *similar* if they both are either edge pixels or non-edge pixels. Algorithm 1 illustrates the denoising process via the solidarity filter for a given image containing 3D edges. First, it generates the $\boldsymbol{Solidarity_{value}}$ matrix (bold notation

---

Algorithm 1. applies the solidarity filter to a given image.

1: **function** SOLIDARITYFILTER(I, $Solidarity_{effect}$, $T_{solidarity}$)
Input:
　　– I is a given image to which the solidarity filter is apply,
　　– $Solidarity_{effect}$ is the effect of each pixel to other pixels in I,
　　– $T_{Solidarity}$ is a user-defined threshold.
Output:
　　– $I_{filtered}$ is the corresponding filtered image of I.

2:　　$\boldsymbol{Solidarity_{value}}$ = GENERATESOLIDARIYVALUEMATRIX(I, $Solidarity_{effect}$)
3:　　**for each** pixel P in I **do**
4:　　　　**if** $Solidarity_{value}(P) \geq T_{solidarity}$ **then**
5:　　　　　　$I_{filtered}(P) \leftarrow I(P)$
6:　　　　**else**
7:　　　　　　$I_{filtered}(P) \leftarrow 0$
8:　　　　**end if**
9:　　**end for**
10:　　**return** ($I_{filtered}$)
11: **end function**

Algorithm 2. generates the $Solidarity_{value}$ matrix for a given image.

1: **function** GENERATESOLIDARIYVALUEMATRIX(I, $Solidarity_{effect}$)

Input:

    – I is a given image for generating the $Solidarity_{value}$ matrix,

    – $Solidarity_{effect}$ is the effect of each pixel to other pixels in I.

Output:

    – **$Solidarity_{value}$** is a matrix containing the solidarity values for each pixel of I.

2:      Initialize **$Solidarity_{value}$** by $Solidarity_{itself}$.

3:      **for each** pixel P in I **do**

4:         Initialize all elements of the **flag_matrix** to `False`

5:         SCATTERPIXELEFFECT(P, $Solidarity_{value}$, $Solidarity_{effect}$, flag_matrix)

6:      **end for**

7:      **return** ($Solidarity_{value}$)

8: **end function**

---

is used for matrices) for the input image (Line 2), and then filters the image pixels, accordingly (Lines 3 to 9). As specified by Algorithm 2, in order to generate the $Solidarity_{value}$ matrix for a given image, we scatter the effect of each pixel throughout the whole image. The scattering function is shown by Algorithm 3. Since it is a recursive function, a flag for each pixel (*flag_matrix*) is required to ensure that all other pixels are affected by each individual pixel only once (Lines 2 and 3). Finally, Algorithm 4 defines the similarity function for 3D edge images. The source code of the algorithms is publicly available at http://vca.ele. tue.nl/demos/SolidarityFilter/solidarityfilter.html.

Algorithm 3. scatters the effect of a pixel throughout its containing image.

1: **function** SCATTERPIXELEFFECT(P, **$Solidarity_{value}$**, $Solidarity_{effect}$, **flag_matrix**)

Input:

    – P is the pixel to scatter its effect throughout the image,

    – **$Solidarity_{value}$** is the matrix containing the solidarity value for each pixel,

    – $Solidarity_{effect}$ is the effect of each pixel to the others,

    – **flag_matrix** is a boolean matrix to evaluate if a pixel has already been effected.

2:      **if** ($flag\_matrix(P)$ = `True`) **then**

3:         **return**

4:      **else**

5:         $flag\_matrix(P) \leftarrow$ `True`

6:         **for each** pixel $P_{nb} \in \{neighbours\ of\ P\}$ **do**

7:            **if** SIMILARPIXELS(P,P_{nb}) = `True` **then**

8:               $Solidarity_{value}(P_{nb}) \leftarrow Solidarity_{effect} + Solidarity_{value}(P_{nb})$

9:               SCATTERPIXELEFFECT(P_{nb}, **$Solidarity_{value}$**, $Solidarity_{effect}$, **flag_matrix**)

10:            **end if**

11:         **end for**

12:      **end if**

13: **end function**

Algorithm 4. defines the similarity function for 3D edge images.

1: **function** BINARY3DEDGESIMILARPIXELS(P_i, P_j)
Input: P_i and P_j are any pair of pixels of a given image containing 3D edges.
2:     **if** $P_i = 1$ and $P_j = 1$ **then return** (True)
3:         **else return** (False)
4:     **end if**
5: **end function**

---

3   Results and Discussion

To evaluate the quality of the proposed algorithm for denoising of 3D edge images, we have collected five datasets, each containing 49 images. Besides this, a dataset of 25 ground-truth images has been manually generated (http://vca.ele.tue.nl/demos/SolidarityFilter/solidarityfilter.html). We have applied the proposed solidarity filter to the dataset collection and report the results in this section. All the results have been obtained utilizing a PC with a CPU of Xeon(R) W3550 @3.07GHz (4 cores) and 20 GB of RAM. We have compared the solidarity filter to the *median* and *morphological close* filters. To evaluate the quality, we have computed the Peak Signal-to-Noise Ratio (PSNR) and mean Structural SIMilarity (mSSIM) metrics. The OpenCV library has been used for both the conventional denoising filters and similarity assessment functions.

Figure 1 and Figure 2 show the resulting PSNR and mSSIM metrics for various values of the solidarity threshold, $T_{solidarity}$. Both metrics indicate a consistent pattern, where the maximum similarity between the ground-truth and filtered images occurs for a value of $T_{solidarity} = 50$. By increasing this threshold, the similarity indicator decreases for both PSNR and mSSIM metrics. As shown in Table 1, on the average, the solidarity filter yields a PSNR of 23.5 dB and 97.4% of similarity with the mSSIM metric. The lower the solidarity threshold is, the better it preserves the smaller edge segments.

3.1   Solidarity vs. Median

Although the median filter is widely used as a denoising tool in digital image processing [1], it gives problems when applied to 3D edge images. As depicted in Figures 3c-3e, the median filter output depends on the window size. The smaller the window size, the less successful the median filter handles the noise and the larger amount of noise remains. For instance, a window size of 4×4 pixels

Table 1. Comparing the solidarity filter to the median and morphological close filters. The window size is expressed in pixels.

Similarity metric	Solidarity	Median (window size)			Close (dilation/erosion size)	
		4 × 4	6 × 6	8 × 8	5 × 5/3 × 3	3 × 3/3 × 3
PSNR (dB)	23.5	16.6	13.7	12.9	8.2	13.9
mSSIM (%)	97.4	88.0	81.1	78.3	58.9	80.3

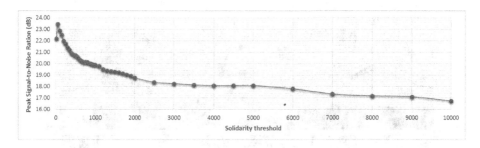

Fig. 1. Average PSNR values with respect to the ground-truth images for various settings of threshold $T_{solidarity}$.

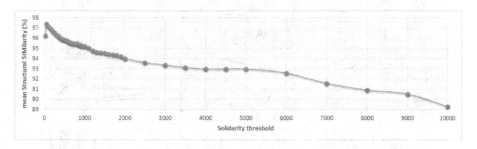

Fig. 2. Average mSSIM values with respect to the ground-truth images for various settings of threshold $T_{solidarity}$.

(Figure 3c) results in more noise, when compared to a window size of 6×6 pixels (Figure 3d). The same observation holds when comparing window sizes of 6×6 and 8×8 pixels (Figure 3d and Figure 3e, respectively). Despite the fact that larger window sizes can remove more noisy pixels, the edge pixels themselves (more specifically pixels on narrow edges) also suffer from larger window sizes. Comparing Figure 3c to Figure 3d and Figure 3e, it is obvious that more edges are disappearing by increasing the window size. On the other hand, the solidarity mask, as shown in Figure 3f, provides satisfactory results in both aspects: first, it removes most of the noise and second, it preserves all the connected edge pixels without any losses and it is independent of edge thickness.

As illustrated by Table 1, the proposed solidarity filter provides better results in terms of both PSNR and mSSIM metrics, when compared to the median filter. The solidarity filter outperforms the median filter with a 42% better PSNR value. In terms of the mSSIM metric, the result of the solidarity filter is 11% closer to the ground truth compared to the result of the median filter.

Figure 4 shows that for both PSNR and mSSIM metrics, the proposed algorithm outperforms the median filter.

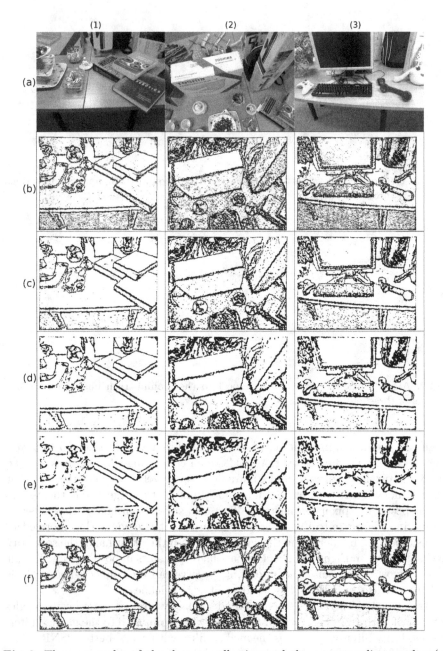

Fig. 3. Three examples of the dataset collection and the corresponding results: (a) RGB images of the scenes; (b) input binary 3D edge images; (c)–(e) denoising results by a median filter for the window sizes of 4×4, 6×6 and 8×8 pixels, respectively; and (f) *Solidarity$_{value}$* for the edge images depicted as intensity images (the darker, the stronger solidarity). Note that the lighter pixels are related to the noisy pixels which have a smaller solidarity value and can be removed by the solidarity filter.

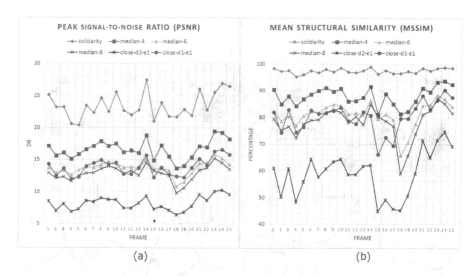

Fig. 4. Comparison of the solidarity filter, median and close filters in terms of (a) PSNR and (b) mSSIM metrics (applying to 25 frames of the dataset vs. groundtruth).

3.2   Solidarity vs. Morphological Close

The *close* and *open* morphological operators are used as powerful filter tools [2] to remove the noise in the 3D edge images. Applying the *morphological open* filter to an image removes small objects, while the *morphological close* filter removes small holes. Being applied to 3D edge images, the open filter removes noisy pixels, while it also destroys narrow edges. On the other hand, the close filter strengthens the narrow edges, while it makes the noisy pixels stronger as well. Since the 3D edges are mostly narrow objects, they are widely affected by the open filter. As a consequence, the open filter converts a continuous 3D edge into a set of smaller discrete edges, which is not acceptable for edge-detection applications [15, 16]. For this reason, we have compared the proposed solidarity filter only to the morphological close filter. As depicted in Figure 5, applying the close filter produces more continuous and thicker edges. The obtained level of thickness is related to the dilation window size: the larger the window, the thicker the edges become. Unfortunately, the close filter strengthens noisy pixels along with the 3D edges, which is far from effective noise removal. The proposed solidarity filter does not manipulate the original data and, therefore, does not strengthen edges nor produce solid edges, but desirably weakens noisy pixels.

As shown in Table 1, the proposed solidarity filter provides better results in terms of both PSNR and mSSIM metrics, when compared to the morphological close filter. The solidarity filter outperforms the close filter with a 69% higher PSNR value. In terms of mSSIM metric, the result of the solidarity filter is 21% closer to the ground truth compared to the result of the close filter.

As depicted in Figure 4, the solidarity filter outperforms the morphological close filter in terms of both PSNR and mSSIM metrics.

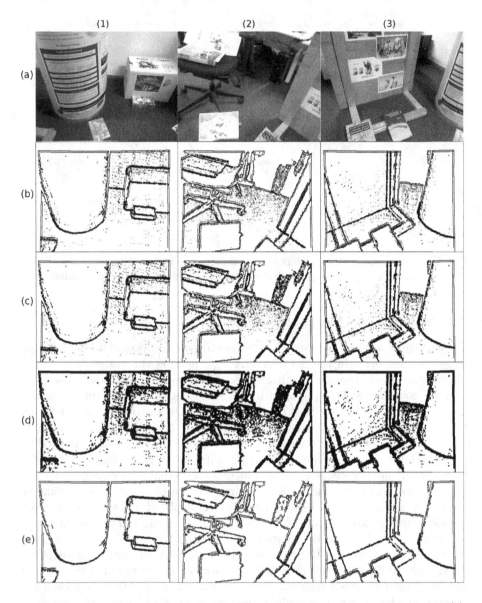

Fig. 5. Three examples of the dataset collection and the corresponding results: (a) RGB images of the scenes; (b) the input binary 3D edge images; (c) denoising results obtained by the morphological closing filter with both erosion and dilation window sizes of 3×3 pixels; (d) denoising results obtained by the morphological closing filter with the erosion and dilation window sizes of 3×3 and 5×5 pixels, respectively; and (e) filtered 3D edge images obtained via the proposed solidarity filter.

Table 2. Detailed execution times of the proposed solidarity filter applied to five datasets. Each dataset contains 49 images with 3D edges (all values in seconds).

dataset	average	median	std. dev.	min	max
1	6.61	5.93	1.85	5.24	13.90
2	5.73	5.65	0.48	5.11	7.16
3	5.21	5.15	0.24	4.95	6.17
4	4.96	4.95	0.05	4.85	5.09
5	18.85	16.03	10.09	7.19	55.30
avg.	**8.27**	**7.54**	**2.54**	**5.47**	**17.52**

3.3   Performance Assessment

The current implementation of the proposed algorithm concentrates only on functionality evaluation and therefore, optimization has not yet been performed. The detailed timing for the single-threaded execution of the solidarity filter applying to VGA-resolution 3D edge images is shown in Table 2. Looking to median execution time, being the most robust for outliers, the solidarity filter, on the average, executes in 7.5 seconds per 3D edge image. Due to the loops, which are performing independently for each pixel provided in Algorithm 1 (Line 3), Algorithm 2 (Line 3) and Algorithm 3 (Line 6), there is a high potential for enhancing the pipelined execution time by utilizing GPU-based implementations.

4   Conclusions

The recently introduced low-cost depth sensors provide depth images for 3D image processing. Due to limited system parameters of the applied sensors, these depth images become noisy which leads to noisy objects such as extracted 3D edges [15,16]. In order to denoise 3D edge images, we have evaluated conventional filters, but each individual filter can only combat a part of the noise while leaving several remaining challenges. These involve: (a) manipulation of source data resulting in false edges, (b) weakening and destroying narrow edges and (c) amplifying noisy pixels. To solve these challenges, we have proposed the solidarity filter for denoising the 3D edge images. The promising results show that the solidarity filter can denoise 3D edge images directly without any data manipulation. The filter is based on ranking principles such as defining neighbouring pixels with similar properties and connecting those into larger segments beyond the size of a conventional filter aperture. With respect to performance, the proposed filter prevents any occurrence of false edges, while it preserves narrow edges and does not amplify noisy pixels. We have also compared the solidarity filter to the median and morphological close filter. The solidarity filter outperforms the median and close filters with 42% and 69% higher PSNR values, respectively. In terms of mSSIM metric, the results of the solidarity filter are 11% and 21% closer to the ground truth compared to the results of median and close filters, respectively. According to the above aspects and performance, we expect satisfactory results when applying the solidarity filter to images containing larger connected objects, such as ultra sound images [13,14].

Acknowledgement. This research has been performed within the PANORAMA project, co-funded by grants from Belgium, Italy, France, the Netherlands, the United Kingdom, and the ENIAC Joint Undertaking.

References

1. Lagendijk, R.L., Biemond, J.: Iterative Identification and Restoration of Images. Kulwer Academic, Boston (1991)
2. Dougherty, E.R.: An introduction to morphological image processing. SPIE Optical Engineering Press (1992)
3. Gautam, A.: Image Denoising Using Switching Adaptive Decision Based Algorithm: Easy Removal of Salt and Pepper Impulsive Noise, ISBN: 9783846528853. Lap Lambert Acadademic Publication, GmbH KG (2012)
4. Peng, H.: Automatic Denoising and Unmixing in Hyperspectral Image Processing, Ph.D. thesis, Rochester Institute of Technology (2014)
5. Khare, A.: Wavelet Transform Based Techniques for Denoising of Medical Images, ISBN: 9783843362603, Lambert Academic Publishing (2010)
6. Uddin, J., Shahjahan, M.: Image Denoising and Qualiy Enhancement of Corrupted Images. Lap Lambert Acad. Pub, GmbH KG (2012)
7. Reddy, G.J., Prasad, T.J., Giriprasad, N.: Enhancement of Image Compression and Denoising by Curvelet Transform, LAP Lambert Acad. Publ. (2011)
8. Saxena, C., Kourav, D.: Noises and Image Denoising Techniques: A Brief Survey. Int. Jour. of Emerging Tech. and Advanced Eng. **4**, 878–885 (2014)
9. Pathak, M., Sinha, G.R.: A Survey of Fuzzy Based Image Denoising Techniques. IOSR Journal of Electronics and Communication Engineering (IOSR-JECE) **9**(4), 27–36 (2014). p-ISSN: 2278–8735, Ver. I, Jul-Aug 2014
10. Gayathri, R.S., Sabeenian, G.R.: A Survey on Image Denoising Algorithms. International Journal of Advanced Research in Electrical, Electronics and Instrumentation Engineering **1**(5), 456–462 (2012)
11. Buades, A., Coll, B., Morel, J.M.: A Review of Image Denoising Algorithms, with a New One. SIAM Journal on Multiscale Modeling and Simulation: A SIAM Interdisciplinary Journal **4**(2), 490–530 (2005)
12. Roy, S., Sinha, N., Sen, A.K.: A New Hybrid Image Denoising Method. Int. Jour. of Info. Tech. and Knowledge Management **2**, 491–497 (2010)
13. Luizou, C.P., Pattichis, C.S., Christodouluo, C.I., Istepanian, R.S.H., Pantziaris, M., Nicolaides, A.: Comparative Evaluation of Despecle Filtering In Ultrasound Imaging of the Carotid Artery. IEEE Transactions on Ultrasonics, Ferroelectrics and Frequency Control **52**(10), 1653–1669 (2005)
14. Finn, S., Glavin, M., Jones, E.: Echocardiographic Speckle Reduction Comparison. IEEE Transactions on Ultrasonics, Ferroelectrics, and Frequency Control **58**(1), 82–101 (2011)
15. Javan Hemmat, H., Pourtaherian, A., Bondarev, E., de With, P.H.N.: Fast planar segmentation of depth images. In: Egiazarian, K.O., Agaian, S.S., Gotchev, A.P. (Eds.) Image Processing: Algorithms and Systems XIII. Proceedings of SPIE Vol. 9399, pp. 93990I. SPIE, Bellingham (2015)
16. Javan Hemmat, H.A., Bondarev, E., de With, P.H.N.: Real-time planar-segmentation of depth images: from 3D-edges to segmented planes. accepted to SPIE Journal of Electronic Imaging (2015)

A Task-Driven Eye Tracking Dataset for Visual Attention Analysis

Yingyue Xu[⊠], Xiaopeng Hong, Qiuhai He, Guoying Zhao,
and Matti Pietikäinen

Department of Computer Science and Engineering, University of Oulu, Oulu, Finland
{yixu,xhong,qhe,gyzhao,mkp}@ee.oulu.fi

Abstract. To facilitate the research in visual attention analysis, we design and establish a new task-driven eye tracking dataset of 47 subjects. Inspired by psychological findings that human visual behavior is tightly dependent on the executed tasks, we carefully design specific tasks in accordance with the contents of 111 images covering various semantic categories, such as text, facial expression, texture, pose, and gaze. It results in a dataset of 111 fixation density maps and over 5,000 scanpaths. Moreover, we provide baseline results of thirteen state-of-the-art saliency models. Furthermore, we hold discussions on important clues on how tasks and image contents influence human visual behavior. This task-driven eye tracking dataset with the fixation density maps and scanpaths will be made publicly available.

Keywords: Eye tracking dataset · Fixation · Scanpath · Saliency · Visual attention

1 Introduction

As a promising technology, visual attention analysis contributes to various computer vision and image processing based applications, such as object detection and image segmentation. Since eye movement reveals the regions of interest (ROI) of the human visual system, it is widely utilized in researches regarding visual attention understanding.

Two modalities of eye movement, namely fixations and saccades [28], are widely analyzed and studied. Fixations indicate the positions where the observer fixates for a long enough duration. It shows how the regions catch the observer's attention on a scene. Saccades are movements between fixations. A sequence of fixations and saccades form a scanpath, which visualizes the sequence of ROIs and thus provides an insight into individual visual behavior.

Data preparation becomes one of the most fundamental problems for most recent computer vision researches as it forms a basis for evaluating the performance of computational models and algorithms. Not surprisingly, eye movement data is essential to the research in visual attention analysis. As a result, several eye tracking datasets, as briefly summarized in Table 1, were established in the

© Springer International Publishing Switzerland 2015
S. Battiato et al. (Eds.): ACIVS 2015, LNCS 9386, pp. 637–648, 2015.
DOI: 10.1007/978-3-319-25903-1_55

Table 1. A brief comparison between our dataset and seven popular eye tracking datasets. All datasets provide fixations obtained by eye tracking devices.

Datasets	#Subject	#Image	Image Size (px)	Tasks	Image Semantics
MIT [19]	15	1003	up to 1024 × 1024	No	Landscape, portrait
Eye Crowd [16]	16	500	1024 × 768	No	Crowd in various de-nsities
KTH [20]	31	99	1024 × 768	No	Symmetrical natural objects, animals, bu-ildings, natural envi-ronment
NUSEF [27]	25	758	1024 × 728	No	Face, portrait, nude, action, affect variant group, etc.
Toronto [5]	20	120	681 × 511	No	Images without cert-ain particular regions of interest.
POET [26]	28	6270	up to 1680 × 1020	Yes	10 classes in 5 pairs: cat/dog, bicycle/motorbike, boat/airplane, horse/cow, sofa/diningtable in Pascal VOC 2012 [11]
Ehinger [9]	14	912	800 × 600	Yes	Urban environment (half with pedestria-ns).
Ours	**47**	111	**1920×1200px**	Yes	Text, facial expressi-on, texture, pose, ga-ze, vehicle, pedestria-n, motion, landscape, etc.

past few years. Some early ones were built using a collection of images without particular semantics [19] [5]. Then, scientists noticed that images with certain semantics assist visual attention analysis in specific fields. Thus, a few semantic-driven datasets were established. For example, the Eye Crowd dataset [16] con-sists of images with crowd in various densities; the NUSEF dataset [27] collects images with faces, portraits, actions, affect variants, etc.

On most of the existing datasets, the participants observed the images in a free viewing manner, without performing any specific task. However, as previous psychological studies suggest, human viewing behavior is tightly dependent on the executed tasks [32]. Thus, researchers began to concern the influence of tasks on visual attention analysis [17][33]. It is also reported that visual searching tasks result in faster fixations and reduce distractions [26] [7]. Therefore a task-driven eye tracking dataset can provide more targeted data for visual attention analysis. To our best knowledge, only few recently published datasets such as

POET dataset [26] and Ehinger dataset [9] are established in this manner. Hence, more task-driven datasets are desired for visual attention analysis.

To further facilitate the research in visual attention, in this paper we design and establish a new task-driven eye tracking dataset. It is different from previous datasets with the following aspects: Firstly, most materials in our dataset are designed with specific tasks, which makes in-depth investigation in the human visual behavior possible. Secondly, the sematic materials cover a few hot computer vision topics, such as text, facial expression, texture, pose, and gaze. Thirdly, it involves more participants (up to 47 subjects) and higher resolution images (WUXGA: 1920 × 1200 px) as watching materials. Moreover, we provide baseline results by evaluating several popular saliency models. Furthermore, we hold discussions about the influence of tasks and image semantics on human visual behavior and provide suggestions for the scanpath estimation research in future.

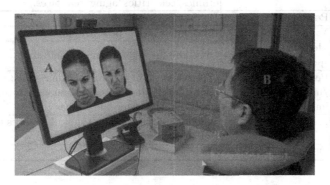

Fig. 1. Illustration of a scene where a participant was fulfilling the task of indicating an angry face on the screen.

2   Eye Tracking Dataset

In this section, we describe the construction and data collecting process of our eye tracking dataset. Firstly, we specify the image contents and the corresponding tasks designed for the observers. Secondly, we depict the data collection environment and the eye tracking experiment in details.

2.1   Image Materials with Specific Tasks

We collected hundreds of raw images from Google and Flickr. They were processed and merged into 111 WUXGA images as watching materials. The watching materials covered various semantic categories, among which 102 images were designed with a specific task based on different semantic implications and 9 were free viewing materials. The tasks, fueled by currently active computer vision problems (e.g., micro/normal facial expression recognition and pedestrian detection), are designed in line with the image semantics. For instance, the image on the computer display in Figure 1 belongs to the normal facial expression category, and the corresponding task is to find out an angry face; the fourth image of the first row in Figure 2 belongs to vehicle/pedestrian category, and the task is to detect pedestrians. Table 2 lists the image categorization and the corresponding tasks.

Table 2. Image contents and corresponding tasks.

Number	Semantics	Tasks
7	Text/map	Read texts; watch maps.
13	Normal/micro expressions	Distinguish facial expressions.
21	Face images	Compare similar faces; distinguish gender/ ethnics/celebrities/aging/real faces.
15	Pose/gaze	Distinguish pose/gaze/directions.
6	Vehicle/pedestrian	Find out vehicles/pedestrians.
15	Motion/blurring/ special lighting	Observe blur/lighting/motion effects.
16	Periodity/symmetry /material/mosaic images	Observe periodity/symmetry/materials; find out main objects and distinguish main categories in small patches in mosaic images.
9	Landscape/scenes	Watch landscape images; spot differences between similar scenes.
9	Others	Free view.

2.2 Data Collection

47 students and staffs in institution were invited regardless of gender, age, and nationality. Conditions like eye colors, glasses, and contact lenses were not restricted. The myGaze eye tracker[1], which was proved to be robust in challenging environment, was utilized to collect the fixation data.

The collection process was divided into two sections. 57 images were displayed in the first section while the rest were shown in the second, with a 15 min. break between them. Figure 1 shows the data collection environment. At the beginning of each section, the eye tracker (Figure 1.C) was calibrated by a five-point algorithm. Before displaying an image, the screen showed the assigned task. Then the image was displayed for a certain duration in line with the complexity of the task. Each participant (Figure 1.B) was asked to sit in front of a 1920×1200 display (Figure 1.A) to watch the provided images and to finish each task only by watching the images, without explicitly indicating the answers. The eye tracker recorded the eye movement data and the Logitech C930 web camera (Figure 1.D) captured the videos of observers' eye movements for future studies.

---

[1] Information about myGaze eye tracker can be found at http://www.mygaze.com.

3   Ground Truth and Dataset Statistics

3.1   Ground Truth

For each image, we aggregated all fixation data collected from the subjects, and used the Gaussian Mixture Model [24] with 10 components to obtain a "ground truth" fixation density map. Only fixation data within an accuracy of 1° visual angle was taken into account. Meanwhile, we provide heatmaps of fixation density maps for visualization. Figure 2 visualizes some examples of the fixation data.

To indicate how the fixation shifts when each subject was watching an image, we generated the corresponding scanpath using fixation data as the "ground truth" scanpath. Figure 3 is a snapshot of the last frame of the scanpath animation when a subject was asked to distinguish the real face from the synthetic one.

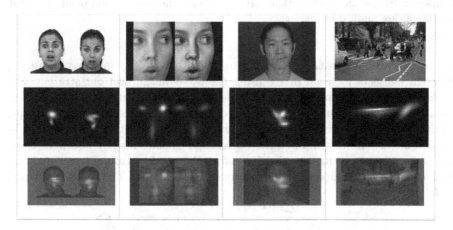

Fig. 2. Visualizations of fixations. The first row shows examples of watching materials; the second row illustrates the created fixation density maps; the third row presents the corresponding heatmaps.

3.2   Fixation Statistics

Compared to previous datasets, our dataset indicates a much weaker center bias thanks to the executed visual tasks. By mapping all the fixations of all the images to one image coordinate, we found that 12% of the fixations are in the top 20% center area, while 60% of the fixations are in the top 50% center area, which are much lower than the statistics given in previous findings [19] [16]. The red curve in Figure 4(a) presents the proportion of fixations in the top center areas. The relatively smooth increase indicates that our dataset is only slightly center biased.

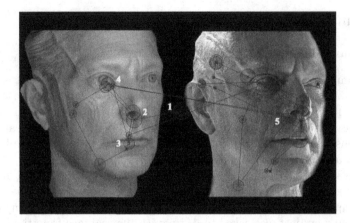

Fig. 3. Example of a scanpath. The circles are fixation positions and the length of radius correlates to the duration between fixations. The line shows the direction of fixation shifts and the circle without cross symbol is the first fixation point. The first 5 fixations are marked in this image.

We carried out correlation analysis to evaluate how the fixations vary among different subjects for each image using the leave-one-subject-out strategy. For each subject, we computed a fixation density map without using the fixation data gathered from that subject (leave-one-subject-out fixation density map), in the same way as we computed the "ground truth" fixation density maps in Section 3.1. Then, we computed the Correlation Coefficients (CC) between these leave-one-subject-out fixation density maps (F) and the "ground truth" fixation density maps (G) computed from fixations of all subjects. The CC is calculated as follows:

$$CC = \frac{\sum_{i,j}(F(i,j) - \bar{F})(G(i,j) - \bar{G})}{\sqrt{\sum_{i,j}(F(i,j) - \bar{F})^2}\sqrt{\sum_{i,j}(G(i,j) - \bar{G})^2}} \tag{1}$$

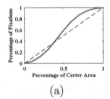 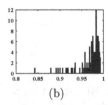 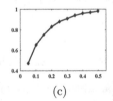

(a)   (b)   (c)

Fig. 4. Illustration of fixation statistics: (a) Proportion of fixations in the center area of the images. (b) Histogram of the distribution of the average CC for each image. (c) The horizon axis indicates the percentage of the most salient regions of the leave-one-subject-out fixation density maps; the vertical axis indicates the proportion of fixations from the left-out subject falling in the salient regions of the leave-one-subject-out fixation density maps.

where $F(i,j)$ and $G(i,j)$ denote the pixels on location (i,j) of F and G respectively, $\bar{F}$ and $\bar{G}$ are mean values of F and G.

Figure 4(b) presents the histogram of the average CC for each image. We observed an average CC for all images of 0.97. It shows that the fixations are highly consistent across subjects. Thus, the obtained fixation density maps well represent the ROI of the majority of the subjects. We also noticed that 3.6% of the CC are within the range of [0.84 0.90] with 0.84 the lowest, which indicates that the individual attention regions slightly vary.

Additionally, we calculated the average proportion of the fixations from the left-out subject falling within the salient regions of the fixation density map from the remaining subjects. As shown in Figure 4(c), 47% of the fixations from the left-out subject were within the top 5% salient regions of the leave-one-subject-out fixation density map and over 90% in the top 30% salient regions.

The above observations indicate that the fixation density maps provided in our dataset are consistent with the visual attentions of the majority of the subjects. These observations also suggest the feasibility to carry out subject-independent saliency detection studies on our dataset.

4   Baseline Results of Saliency Models

Saliency is an important item in visual attention analysis, as it describes how certain pixels or regions stand out from their neighbours in the image. Saliency models are computational models predicting possible salient regions in the image. Currently, there is no clear or restricted definition for saliency modeling. However, all the saliency models result in outputs of saliency maps which present the spatial distribution of the scalar quantity of predicted salient regions on the image. Thus, saliency modeling is believed to reflect ROI in the human visual system.

In general, the existing approaches can be categorized into two types: bottom-up and top-down. Bottom-up models are computed based on low level features of images, such as color, orientation, etc., while top-down saliency models are obtained dependent on prior information, such as semantics and tasks. To provide the baseline results for saliency detection, we evaluated thirteen state-of-the-art saliency models on our dataset, among which three models are constructed with distinct image features, (Itti et al. [15] with color, intensity contrast, and orientation features, Vikram et al. [29] with color feature in CIE color space, SWD [8] with color and luminance features). Six models are based on various image properties: GBVS [13] focuses on graph computations, Murray et al. [25] induct wavelet transformations, Hou & Zhang [14] concentrate on log-spectrum based features, Achanta et al. [1] utilize features in frequency domain, Margolin et al. [23] apply self-defined pixel operations, and SUN [34] explores saliency based on information theory. Moreover, there are three models constructing the saliency map with different operations on feature maps: Cheng et al. [6] propose a region contrast (RC) based method, CovSal [10] uses region covariance matrices of the image features, Walther & Koch [30] utilize a 4-connected neighbourhood

Table 3. Illustration of mean and standard deviations of CC and AUC of thirteen saliency models.

Model	CC		AUC	
	Ours	MIT	Ours	MIT
Hou & Zhang [14]	0.34 ± 0.22	–	0.68 ± 0.11	–
Walther & Koch [30]	0.05 ± 0.15	0.14	0.50 ± 0.04	0.54
GBVS [13]	0.47 ± 0.17	0.48	0.74 ± 0.09	0.80
Itti et al. [15]	0.36 ± 0.21	0.37	0.69 ± 0.10	0.74
Achanta et al. [1]	0.05 ± 0.30	0.04	0.49 ± 0.13	0.52
Judd et al. [19]	0.44 ± 0.16	0.47	0.75 ± 0.08	0.80
CovSal [10]	0.39 ± 0.21	0.45	0.72 ± 0.09	0.67
SWD [8]	0.50 ± 0.19	0.49	0.76 ± 0.09	0.80
Margolin et al. [23]	0.41 ± 0.16	0.43	0.71 ± 0.08	0.76
Vikrama et al. [29]	0.30 ± 0.19	0.38	0.67 ± 0.07	0.74
Murray et al. [25]	0.28 ± 0.19	0.27	0.65 ± 0.09	0.66
SUN, 2008 [34]	0.30 ± 0.17	0.25	0.68 ± 0.09	0.66
Cheng et al., 2011 [6]	0.33 ± 0.16	0.47	0.68 ± 0.09	0.78

approach. Among all the tested saliency models, Judd et al. [19] model inducts top-down image features.

Two evaluation metrics are utilized to measure the performance of saliency models on our dataset: (1) Correlation Coefficient: computing the CC between the "ground truth" fixation density map and the resulted saliency map, (2) Area Under the ROC Curve (AUC) [4]: the resulted saliency map is thresholded as a binary classifier with positive and negative samples. By plotting the true positive rate vs. false positive rate, an ROC curve is obtained and the underneath area is AUC.

Table 3 reports the performance of the tested saliency models on our dataset. To evaluate whether the various image semantics in our dataset increase the difficulty in saliency detection, we also list the corresponding reported records on MIT saliency benchmark [18] as a reference, which is a dataset of natural images. Most methods under consideration work consistently well on both datasets. Thus, we consider our dataset applicable. However, the slightly inferior performance on our dataset also implies that ours is challenging. Novel saliency models are encouraged to be evaluated on our dataset.

As a reference, we also plot the average CC categorized by image semantics in Figure 5, such that the performances of the thirteen saliency models over different image semantic groups can be compared. It can be observed that SWD model outstands other saliency models in most image semantic categories. However, for image categories like expressions, faces, pose and gaze, Judd et al. model results in the best performance.

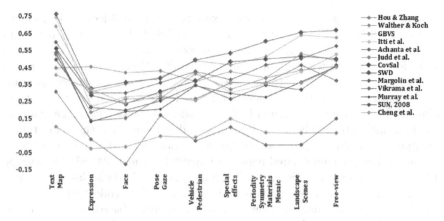

Fig. 5. Average CC categorized by image contents.

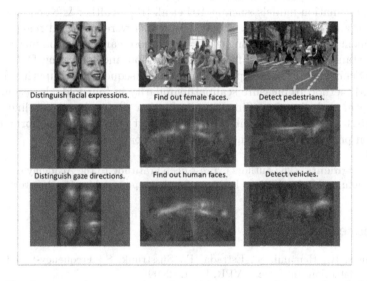

Fig. 6. The first row gives examples of watching images; the second and third rows illustrate the heatmaps computed under different tasks.

5   Discussion and Future Work

In this paper, we established a task-driven eye tracking dataset for visual attention analysis. Besides, we provide baseline results from thirteen widely used saliency modeling methods.

Unlike most existing datasets, which only provide fixation data, our task-driven eye tracking dataset also provides an opportunity of exploring the intrinsic relation between tasks and human visual behavior. According to the obtained fixation density maps and scanpaths, we have some interesting observations. Given the same image as watching material but different tasks, as shown in

Figure 6, although the observers mainly fixate on the same objects (a.k.a. salient objects [2,3,6,22]), their focusing regions are different. For instance, observers tend to focus on whole facial regions when recognizing facial expressions, but mainly focus on eyes when distinguishing gaze directions. We also designed a pair of images captured from the same scene but with different camera focuses. The scanpaths indicate that observers tend to fixate prior on clear objects in an image. The above phenomenon indicate that both tasks and image contents are significant factors influencing human visual behavior. By the same token, we suppose that with appropriate image semantics and tasks, it is possible to guide observers fixate on desired regions to facilitate salient detection in specific fields. Thus, we hope to raise critical thinking about the task design strategy and image contents selection criteria for eye tracking data collection.

Future work may involve visual behavior analysis based on comparison of individual scanpaths, designing evaluation protocol, and providing baseline results for scanpath estimation. We will further test our dataset with existing scanpath estimation models, such as Itti et al. [15], Walther & Koch [30], Wang et al. [31], and Liu et al. [21]. So far, few works were proposed regarding fair measurement of scanpaths. Wang et al. [31] proposed an evaluation method comparing distance of scanpaths, fixation distribution and forgetting factor. Foerster and Schneider [12] developed a functionally sequenced scanpath similarity (FuncSim) method to measure scanpath similarity in four folds: location, duration, length, and direction. Since the evaluation protocol and baseline results for scanpath estimation are still desired, the next step will be the formation of evaluation protocol and baseline results for scanpath estimation.

Acknowledgments. The authors express deep gratitude to the Academy of Finland, Infotech Oulu and Tekes Fidipro Program for their sponsorships for this work.

References

1. Achanta, R., Hemami, S., Estrada, F., Susstrunk, S.: Frequency-tuned salient region detection. In: Proc. CVPR. IEEE (2009)
2. Ardizzone, E., Bruno, A., Mazzola, G.: Visual saliency by keypoints distribution analysis. In: Maino, G., Foresti, G.L. (eds.) ICIAP 2011, Part I. LNCS, vol. 6978, pp. 691–699. Springer, Heidelberg (2011)
3. Borji, A., Sihite, D.N., Itti, L.: Salient object detection: a benchmark. In: Fitzgibbon, A., Lazebnik, S., Perona, P., Sato, Y., Schmid, C. (eds.) ECCV 2012, Part II. LNCS, vol. 7573, pp. 414–429. Springer, Heidelberg (2012)
4. Borji, A., Tavakoli, H., Sihite, D., Itti, L.: Analysis of scores, datasets, and models in visual saliency prediction. In: Proc. ICCV. IEEE (2013)
5. Bruce, N., Tsotsos, J.: Saliency based on information maximization. In: Proc. NIPS (2005)
6. Cheng, M.M., Zhang, G.X., Mitra, N.J., Huang, X., Hu, S.M.: Global contrast based salient region detectionl. In: Proc. CVPR. IEEE (2011)
7. Doshi, A., Trivedi, M.: Head and gaze dynamics in visual attention and context learning. In: Proc. CVPR Joint Workshop for Visual and Contextual Learning and Visual Scene Understanding. IEEE (2009)

8. Duan, L., Wu, C., Miao, J., Qing, L., Fu, Y.: Visual saliency detection by spatially weighted dissimilarity. In: Proc. CVPR. IEEE (2011)
9. Ehinger, K., Hidalgo-Sotelo, B., Torralba, A., Oliva, A.: Modelling search for people in 900 scenes: a combined source model of eye guidance. Visual Cognition **17**, 945–978 (2009)
10. Erdem, E., Erdem, A.: Visual saliency estimation by nonlinearly integrating features using region covariances. Journal of Vision **13**, 11 (2013)
11. Everingham, M., Gool, L., Williams, C., Winn, J., Zisserman, A.: The pascal visual object classes challenge 2012 (voc2012) results (2012). http://pascallin.ecs.soton.ac.uk/challenges/VOC/voc2012/
12. Foerster, R., Schneider, W.: Functionally sequenced scanpath similarity method (funcsim): Comparing and evaluating scanpath similarity based on a task's inherent sequence of functional (action) units. Journal of Eye Movement Research, June 2013
13. Harel, J., Koch, C., Perona, P.: Graph-based visual saliency. In: Proc. NIPS (2006)
14. Hou, X., Zhang, L.: Saliency detection: A spectral residual approach. In: Proc. CVPR. IEEE (2007)
15. Itti, L., Koch, C., Niebur, E.: A model of saliency-based visual attention for rapid scene analysis. IEEE Trans. PAMI **20**, 1254–1259 (1998)
16. Jiang, M., Xu, J., Zhao, Q.: Saliency in crowd. In: Fleet, D., Pajdla, T., Schiele, B., Tuytelaars, T. (eds.) ECCV 2014, Part VII. LNCS, vol. 8695, pp. 17–32. Springer, Heidelberg (2014)
17. Johansson, R., Westling, G., Backstrom, A., Flanagan, J.: Eye-hand coordination in object manipulation. Journal of Neuroscience **21**, 6917–6932 (2001)
18. Judd, T., Durand, F., Torralba, A.: A benchmark of computational models of saliency to predict human fixations. MIT Technical report (2012)
19. Judd, T., Ehinger, K., Durand, F., Torralba, A.: Learning to predict where humans look. In: Proc. ICCV. IEEE (2009)
20. Koostra, G., Boer, B., Schomaker, L.R.B.: Predicting eye fixations on complex visual stimuli using local symmetry. Cognitive Computation III, pp. 223–240, March 2011
21. Liu, H., Xu, D., Huang, Q., Li, W., Xu, M., Lin, S.: Semantically-based human scanpath estimation with hmms. In: Proc. ICCV. IEEE (1998)
22. Liu, T., Yuan, Z., Sun, J., Wang, J., Zheng, N., Tang, X., Shum, H.: Learning to detect a salient object. IEEE Trans. PAMI **33**, 353–367 (2011)
23. Margolin, R., Zelnik-Manor, L., Tal, A.: Saliency for image manipulation. The Visual Computer **29**, 381–392 (2013)
24. McLachlan, G., Peel, D.: Finite mixture models. John Wiley & Sons, Inc., Hoboken (2000)
25. Murray, N., Vanrell, M., Otazu, X., Parraga, C.A.: Saliency estimation using a non-parametric low-level vision model. In: Proc. CVPR. IEEE (2011)
26. Papadopoulos, D.P., Clarke, A.D.F., Keller, F., Ferrari, V.: Training object class detectors from eye tracking data. In: Fleet, D., Pajdla, T., Schiele, B., Tuytelaars, T. (eds.) ECCV 2014, Part V. LNCS, vol. 8693, pp. 361–376. Springer, Heidelberg (2014)
27. Ramanathan, S., Katti, H., Sebe, N., Kankanhalli, M., Chua, T.-S.: An eye fixation database for saliency detection in images. In: Daniilidis, K., Maragos, P., Paragios, N. (eds.) ECCV 2010, Part IV. LNCS, vol. 6314, pp. 30–43. Springer, Heidelberg (2010)
28. Salvucci, D., Goldberg, J.: Identifying fixations and saccades in eye-tracking protocols. In: Proc. Symp. ETRA. ACM (2000)

29. Vikram, T.N., Tscherepanow, M., Wrede, B.: A saliency map based on sampling an image into random rectangular regions of interest. Pattern Recognition **45**, 3114–3124 (2012)
30. Walther, D., Koch, C.: Modeling attention to salient proto-objects. Neural Networks **19**, 1395–1407 (2006)
31. Wang, W., Chen, C., Wang, Y., Jiang, T., Fang, F., Yao, Y.: Simulating human saccadic scanpaths on natural images. In: Proc. CVPR. IEEE (2011)
32. Yarbus, A.: Eye Movements and Vision. Plenum Press, New York (1967)
33. Ye, B., Sugano, Y., Sato, Y.: Influence of stimulus and viewing task types on a learning-based visual saliency model. In: Proc. Symp. ETRA. ACM (2014)
34. Zhang, L., Tong, M.H., Marks, T.K., Shan, H., Cottrell, G.W.: Sun: A bayesian framework for saliency using natural statistics. Journal of Vision **8**, 7 (2008)

Classification and Recognition

Image Analysis and Microscopy in Food Science: Computer Vision and Visual Inspection

Gaetano Impoco[✉]

CoRFiLaC, S.P.25 Ragusa-Mare, 97100 Ragusa, Italy
impoco@corfilac.it

Abstract. Rheological properties of food products are strongly related to their microstructure. Microscopy is thus a preferred tool in food research. In food science, microscopy has long been used for visual inspection. Recently, however, quantitative analysis has become the new trend. In spite of this, only a few experts in computer vision are actively involved into image analysis projects, applied to food microscopy. Microscopists tend to use simple tools, without bothering whether they are appropriate for their application. As a consequence, most published work in food science journals lacks scientific rigour, when it comes to analysing images. On the other hand, image analysis experts tend to undervalue microscopists' needs and opinions, which can be surprisingly different from what most people in the computer vision community might think. Drawing upon our experience, we try to highlight microscopists' perspective on image segmentation and, at the same time, show a few examples of collaborative projects that compute interesting measures for the food science community, that do not rely on segmentation accuracy.

Keywords: Image analysis · Microscopy · Food · Geometry

1 Image Analysis and Food Microscopy

Rheological properties of complex food products, such as taste, consistency, and texture, are closely related to their microstructure. Food research takes advantage from microscopy to study microstructural features in food samples, such as porosity, protein and fat aggregates, and so on. Although microscopy has long been used only for visual inspection by expert users, the potential of quantitative analysis of microscopic features has only recently been recognised by some influential researchers [1], objective quantification and rapid data handling being the most prominent advantages over visual inspection.

Clearly, the accuracy of quantitative measurements computed on food micrographs are deeply influenced by the segmentation accuracy, especially when shape descriptors of features are involved. In the food science community, segmentation is mostly carried out with time-consuming user interaction, by means of techniques as simple as thresholding and basic morphology operators [13–15,17]. Automatic or more advanced techniques are rarely used in the lab practice. This is mainly due to the lack of knowledge of state-of-the-art segmentation techniques, designed by the image processing community.

© Springer International Publishing Switzerland 2015
S. Battiato et al. (Eds.): ACIVS 2015, LNCS 9386, pp. 651–660, 2015.
DOI: 10.1007/978-3-319-25903-1_56

In order to fill this gap, some authors reviewed state-of-the-art techniques applied to digital micrographs [2, 3, 10] and to food quality inspection [4]. However, these papers are targeted to a public of experts in computer vision and offer no practical guidance to microscopists. Only a few of the reviewed techniques are implemented in commercial or free image analysis software tools. When confronted with state-of-the-art methods, microscopists perceive them as slow, tricky and difficult to learn compared, e.g., to straightforward thresholding. Moreover, the quality of results often does not pay for the increased time and difficulty of use.

In this context, only a few experts in computer vision are actively involved into image analysis projects applied to food microscopy. As a consequence, most published work in food science journals lacks scientific rigour, when it comes to analysing images. Results and even experimental methods are often questionable. Ramírez and colleagues [16] point out that most scientific papers do not adequately present the image processing techniques used, as well as the composition and extent of the image set used in experiments. They conclude that "images have become a *sui generis* type of data in scientific research". That is, images do not undergo the same rigorous experimentation standards as other data. This is a strong argument against the relaxed use of image analysis. Even when careful descriptions of experiments are provided, results are often accepted without any validation or critical analysis.

In this paper we address two aspects of the analysis of microscopy imagery, namely the user perspective about segmentation approaches, and the difficulties arising in quantification and measuring. This is not strictly a survey nor a review. Going through our personal experience in this field, our aim is to discuss, in the context of the computer vision community, problems and possible developments of image analysis in food microscopy.

The excerpt "computer vision and visual inspection" from the title of this contribution is meant to highlight the dual role of computer vision as a support to visual inspection, and as a means to go beyond it. Both aspects are discussed, each in one of the following sections.

2   Segmentation

When imaging specialists evaluate segmentation algorithms, they mostly focus on segmentation quality, robustness against noise, speed, applicability on different imagery, and so on [2, 3]. On the other hand, microscopists are more concerned with simplicity and interactivity, that is, user-friendliness. Surprisingly, a few users are demanding about segmentation quality. True enough, this is partly due to the belief that computer output is always right. Being unbiased and deterministic, computers and algorithms are often deemed as infallible or, at the very worst, much better and faster than human operators. As a result of this attitude, segmentation quality is often taken for granted. In fact, most people in food microscopy do not even bother to check whether image statistics are biased by noisy binarisations.

There is another reason, though. In our experience, most microscopists feel uncomfortable with segmentation tools that do not allow some degree of inter-action. During image acquisition, they turn knobs back and forth to adjust lens focus, illumination, beam power, and the like. It is quite natural for them to manipulate simple parameters to adjust segmentation results. For this purpose, however, manipulation must be simple and fast enough to be interactive. This is probably one of the main reasons why thresholding is so popular, the other being its conceptual simplicity.

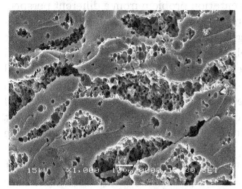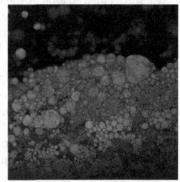

(a) Scanning Electron Microscope (SEM).

(b) Confocal Light Scanning Microscope (CLSM).

Fig. 1. Two cheese samples acquired with different microscopy technologies.

In the last decade, most of our efforts have been devoted to devise effective segmentation approaches, often sacrificing elegance and novelty, for images like those in Figure 1. Here, user needs are simply stated: segment images into a number of meaningful "phases", where the meaning is defined by the specific application at hand.

The first attempt that probably comes to every expert's mind is to suggest a very simple processing chain, involving separation of colour channels, noise reduction, thresholding, and morphological manipulations. Even these simple steps, however, proved to require too much strong image processing skills than most people have or are willing to acquire. That is the main reason why, in 2006, we published one such chain for scanning electron micrographs of cheese samples, such as that in Figure 1(a), with the help of expert microscopists [5]. Being accompanied by a piece of software in the public domain, this paper received what, in our opinion, was an undeserved attention from communities ranging from food to medical sciences, although it had no novelty for an audience of imaging experts.

The unexpected success of this paper convinced us that microscopists have much need of simple and effective segmentation tools for their experiments with images. Giving fair results on a reasonable variety of Scanning Electron Microscope (SEM) images, the simple algorithm described in the paper was a significant improvement on simple thresholding. Later on, much later indeed, we came to think that one of the reasons of the warm acceptance reserved to our paper was the clear and compact presentation of key ideas on quantitative analysis and measurement. That is, microscopists cannot be asked to become proficient image processing professionals, especially about image segmentation. Rather, the computer vision community should provide simple tools and simple guides to deal with the most typical applications. That is what we inadvertently did in our paper, even if we did not realise this until very recently.

Now, armed with our belief that simplicity and ease-of-use were the keys to success, we decided to look at the segmentation problem from a different perspective. Namely, since most microscopists are interested in features such as holes and spherical blobs, in isolation or aggregated, we tried to design a sort of smart selection tool to segment regions by clicking inside each region [7]. It was based on an integer approximation of level sets to make it fast enough to be considered interactive. When we proposed this tool to a few microscopists, they found it too slow and scarcely interactive. Moreover, since each click was considered the seed to start level set evolution, the shape of selected regions could vary with respect to the position of the mouse in the interest region. Needless to say, users where upset by this 'feature' of our software. Finally, and somehow surprisingly, when presented with an image to segment they were somehow confused and did not understand where to start from. Their final question was why they should use such a tricky tool to select features one by one when they could use our previous algorithm to select them all at once. Our objections about segmentation quality did not persuaded them at all. Disarming.

Up to this point, we had learned that most microscopists prefer simple, fast, interactive tools, provided that there is not too much interaction, even if this means to sacrifice segmentation quality. We then went back to non-interactive tools. Who needs interaction if results are acceptable, after all. Due to the difficulty of clearly identifying well-defined sample features, we tried with brute-force supervised statistical classifiers [9]. This was probably our biggest mistake. Microscopists never accepted the workload needed to label training images, although we demonstrated that much better results could be obtained even with straightforward Bayesian learning and trivial filter banks. Worst of all, we were unable to convince them of the usefulness of training. One of their most keen observations was why training could not be hard-coded into the program. They perceived all this training stuff as tricky and unnecessarily complicating a simple thing, such as image segmentation.

The next step was thus to try and simplify training. We moved along a few guidelines:

1. the operator should be aware of the usefulness of training as soon as possible
2. she should be provided a simple method to modify or refine learned data
3. labelling must be as little painful as it can be
4. a fast and self-explanatory bootstrap should be provided (i.e., the operator should not be left "alone" at the beginning)

We came up with a training scheme divided into two distinct phases [8]. At a first bootstrap stage, a weakly-supervised clustering method is used, where cluster centroids are set by the user by clicking into one image of the training set. Each image of the training set is classified using the same centroids. Classified images are used as labellings for further stages, i.e. the classification of each pixel is regarded as if it was a label provided by the operator. These labellings are used to learn density functions for each class and for each filter in the bank. The learned model is then used to segment images in the training set.

The second phase involves iterative re-labelling. The operator is presented all images in the training set, in a sequence, together with tentative segmentations. For each image, she is asked to correct segmentation by selecting image regions and changing their label. When the operator is satisfied with the new segmentation, the new labellings are used to update the model. This model, in turn, is used to compute new labellings. The process can be repeated iteratively until the user is satisfied (i.e., the model explains data sufficiently well).

This scheme satisfies all criteria defined above. The initial bootstrap only requires that one exemplar pixel is selected for each cluster, giving as a result a partially-correct labelling for each training image. Labelling is much simplified since the user can re-label a few regions per iteration, with no need to be precise. The iterative nature of this scheme guarantees that the model can be refined and evolved whenever new images are added to the training set. Finally, it allows the user to evaluate model fitness at each step, giving the operator more awareness of what is being done.

This time we promptly asked a few microscopists to discuss and evaluate our new tool. A brief discussion is reported in the original paper [8]. Here, we summarise our main findings. Our framework shares most of the drawbacks of segmentation systems based on supervised learning: the training phase is perceived as tricky and its usefulness is not fully understood, the learn/classify structure is not intuitive, the training procedure is considered boring and burdensome, the classification phase is slow if it takes more than a few seconds. On the other hand, common segmentation tools are considered simple, intuitive, and fast. In this framework, however, the training phase is faster and can be carried out in shorter steps. This is perceived as a great improvement. The bootstrap phase makes it more user-friendly since it presents roughly-labelled images. The incremental framework is more intuitive and assures a greater control over learning. These features make it easier to accept. This is more true since it drops the requirement that labelling must be precise, thus allowing much less attention to be put on the labelling task.

Despite these improvements, however, the microscopists we worked with are not satisfied, yet. They still prefer to use our first tool or other standard tools available in their processing software. They still think that the improved segmentation quality is not worth the increased time and burden of using such tools. How much user involvement in the segmentation process is acceptable for microscopists remains an open question. The message, here, is that much more experimentation should be carried out to really understand user needs, in the very first phases, when designing new segmentation algorithms.

Obviously several other papers deal with interactive micrograph segmentation. We do not report them here. Let us discuss just one example to show what we believe the problem is with most of them. In [11], a cost function for active contours is learnt from manually annotated examples. Users just provide a few contours bounding interest objects. Then, the parameters of the cost function are set using a probabilistic classifier. It is not clear how many contours must be provided to initialise the functions, and if their number has an impact on segmentation quality or on convergence speed. Also, the authors do not report information about training time, both for annotating images and to learn the cost function, and about execution time. Finally, and most important for our discussion, it is not clear whether their method can be easily accepted by microscopists and is ready to be used in the lab practice.

An attempt to account for user needs during evaluation is made in [12]. The author argues that segmentation error should be rated with respect to how much effort it takes to correct it, by a human operator. It is suggested, for example, that over-segmentation should be preferred to under-segmentation, since manually merging two regions is much faster than breaking a region into parts. It is not clear how segmentation algorithms should be designed to reduce post-processing efforts. Another open question is how should we measure human efforts. As we tried to demonstrate above, this is not an easy issue. Nonetheless, this perspective is probably an interesting one and it is worth further exploration.

3   Quantification and Measurement

The main objective of image analysis in microscopy is measurement. Microscopists are often interested in measuring the shape of features in the imaged sample. In this context, accurate segmentation is of paramount importance.

There are applications, however, where segmentation accuracy has a lower impact on measurement quality. Some applications do not involve direct measurements on image regions, i.e., they do not require those measurements as the final output. In those cases, the user does not expect exact measurements on the shape of features. She might not even know that images are being segmented. On extreme cases, measurements could be taken on the raw input image, not drawing upon segmentation at all. On the other hand, measurement quality is required at a different level, e.g., when evaluating global image characteristics, such as the density of some particles. Here, accurate measurements can be guaranteed, provided that the descriptors used to measure image characteristics are robust against poor segmentations, or are robustly measured on raw images.

One such application is the analysis of suspensions, such as milk. Figure 2 shows micrographs of milk samples during different phases of cheese making, acquired using a Confocal Light Scanning Microscope (CLSM). One of the most important aspects microscopists observe in this sequence is the evolution of the fat phase, i.e. of the globular features (stained in red, in the figure).

(a) Milk fermentation. (b) Begin of curding. (c) End of curding.

Fig. 2. Milk samples in different phases of cheese making, acquired with Confocal Light Scanning Microscope (CLSM). Fat phase (globular structures, stained in red) and compact protein matrix (stained in green) are shown.

Isolating fat in Figure 2 amounts to removing all colour channels, save for the red channel. Then, fat droplets can be easily segmented using simple thresholding algorithms. Finally, watershed allows to separate touching features. Although this standard processing method is simple and effective enough in several cases, it may badly fail in case images are noisy or simply acquired with low magnification (i.e., fat droplets are tiny). If we are to take measurements that are sensitive to droplets' shape, a certain amount of error must be taken into account. On the other hand, global measures are less prone to segmentation errors since they act on a statistical basis. Badly segmented features can be easily treated as outliers.

Microscopists, however, tend not to accept global measures. They have been extensively trained on qualitative visual inspection of micrographs. Image analysis is often simply deemed as a way to automate their activities, mostly selecting (i.e., segmenting) features and measuring their area and perimeter. Conversely, being confronted with measurements that describe the whole image is perceived as a strong viewpoint shift. That is why only a few microscopists are willing to explore new processing and analysis algorithms.

When this happens, however, a serious problem still remains open. Namely, global measures often do not accurately model what microscopists are looking for. This is exactly what happened in [6]. We devised several simple descriptors for modelling spatial patterns generated by fat droplets. Then, we asked a number of experts and laypersons to rate the images in a dataset with respect to some indicators, provided by expert microscopists. We expected to find some descriptors giving the same answers as one or more indicators, on the same images. It was not so. None of our descriptors matched any of the indicators suggested by microscopists. Somehow surprisingly, though, when we compared the feature spaces induced by our descriptors and by microscopists' indicators, two well-distinguished groups appeared, and the very same. Hence, although our descriptors did not mimic human observation, they were able, as a whole, to induce the same groupings as human observers did. Moreover, a simple Bayesian learning approach was able to correctly identify more then 90% of unseen images.

In spite of this success, microscopists have since been uneasy with this method. Some still keep asking why, if our method was successful to give a comprehensive answer, we are unable to mimic simple indicators such as droplet density.

Another fundamental point, here, is the one we started with. Namely, this method is completely forgetful of segmentation quality. Obviously, the ability of our descriptors to give reasonable answers is still dependent on segmentation success. However, this is clearly true at a much lesser degree as opposed to shape descriptors, mainly due to the statistical nature of the measurements. Moreover, the answers users get are of a higher abstraction level compared to simple geometric measurements.

The price microscopists have to pay for this better quality is an effort to shift their point of view with respect to requirements and possibilities offered by image analysis. This is probably a cultural gap that we, as computer vision experts, should work hard to fill.

One of the main points in image analysis is assessing descriptors against user needs. In the method sketched above, we chose to compare experimental results from descriptors and from visual inspection. This method gives strong support to the employment of these descriptors to explain biological phenomena.

In a more recent paper, Silva et al. [18] recognise the importance of collecting more abstract measurements and, at the same time, to assess their results. They use a different method to validate their descriptors, not relying on human observers. Basically, a golden standard is artificially constructed by rendering images that should somehow reproduce the statistical properties and microscopic arrangement of particles, observed in real micrographs. Synthetic volumes representing the arrangements of casein micelles in milk were built. For each volume, a number of slices were cut, with fixed, finite depth. Each slice was flattened (i.e., projected on a planar surface) and rendered as a binary image. The collected images constituted a reference database. Then, descriptors were computed both for synthetic and real micrographs. Since comparisons showed close values and similar trends, the authors are enabled to use their measurements to draw conclusions about their samples.

4   Summing Up

When computer vision experts evaluate algorithms, they often focus on segmentation quality and optimisation of resources. On the other hand, they often neglect simplicity and interactivity. In our experience, these two features are most appreciated by microscopy experts, and there is reason to believe that this applies to most users in different fields. Still, little attention is devoted to systematically analyse user needs and cultural limitations.

This is mostly true for segmentation algorithms. There is a plethora of methods, using the most diverse technologies. Several review papers compare these algorithms using different criteria but, again, with little or no account for the user perspective. In the preceding pages, we showed what a mistake this can be by drawing episodes from our personal scientific experience.

On the other hand, people in food science often overlook the importance of assessing their image analysis methods. There are a few cases, however, where image analysis experts try to overcome this limitation. What the two methods sketched in Section 3 have in common is that they recognise the need for validation and assessment of descriptors. Thorough experiments are run, comparing numerical results on synthetic and real data, or comparing performances of computer vision descriptors against visual observation. Only then, validated measures can be safely used to analyse micrographs and draw conclusions.

This way of constructing image analysis tools and experiments is novel and still far from being commonplace in food science. Nonetheless, in this community there is now a diffused feeling that image analysis deserves more rigorous experimental protocols. It is up to computer vision specialists to help building such protocols, workflows and tools, like it is being done in the medical sciences.

Acknowledgments. I am grateful to Nicoletta Fucà, former CLSM microscopist at CoRFiLaC, and to Catia Pasta for the many stimulating discussions and for carefully revising the manuscript. Financial support was provided by the Assessorato Agricoltura e Foreste della Regione Siciliana, Palermo, Italy.

References

1. Aguilera, J.M., Stanley, D.W.: Microstructural principles of food processing and engineering, 2nd edn. Aspen (1999)
2. Beneš, M., Zitová, B.: Performance evaluation of image segmentation algorithms on microscopic image data. Journal of Microscopy **257**(1), 65–85 (2015)
3. Dima, A.A., Elliott, J.T., Filliben, J.J., Halter, M., Peskin, A., Bernal, J., Kociolek, M., Brady, M.C., Tang, H.C., Plant, A.L.: Comparison of segmentation algorithms for fluorescence microscopy images of cells. Cytometry. Part A: The Journal of the International Society for Analytical Cytology **79**(7), 545–559 (2011)
4. Du, C.J., Sun, D.W.: Learning techniques used in computer vision for food quality evaluation: a review. Journal of Food Engineering **72**(1), 39–55 (2006)
5. Impoco, G., Carrato, S., Caccamo, M., Tuminello, L.: Quantitative analysis of cheese microstructure using SEM imagery. In: SIMAI 2006. Minisymposium: Image Analysis Methods for Industrial Application, May 2006
6. Impoco, G., Fucà, N., Pasta, C., Caccamo, M., Licitra, G.: Quantitative analysis of nanostructures' shape and distribution in micrographs using image analysis. Computers and Electronics in Agriculture **84**, 26–35 (2012)
7. Impoco, G., Licitra, G.: An interactive level set approach to semi-automatic detection of features in food micrographs. In: Jiang, X., Petkov, N. (eds.) CAIP 2009. LNCS, vol. 5702, pp. 914–921. Springer, Heidelberg (2009)
8. Impoco, G., Tuminello, L.: Incremental learning to segment micrographs. Computer Vision and Image Understanding (2015)
9. Impoco, G., Tuminello, L., Fucà, N., Caccamo, M., Licitra, G.: Segmentation of structural features in cheese micrographs using pixel statistics. Computers and Electronics in Agriculture **79**(2), 199–206 (2011)

10. Nattkemper, T.W.: Automatic segmentation of digital micrographs: a survey. Studies in Health Technology and Informatics **107**(2), 847–851 (2004)
11. Nilufar, S., Perkins, T.J.: Learning a cost function for interactive microscope image segmentation. In: AAAI Workshop on Modern Artificial Intelligence for Health Analytics, July, 27th 2014
12. Parag, T.: What properties are desirable from an electron microscopy segmentation algorithm. Computing Research Repository (CoRR) (2015). abs/1503.05430
13. Pastorino, A.J., Hansen, C.L., McMahon, D.J.: Effect of salt on structure function relationships of cheese. Journal of Dairy Science **86**, 60–69 (2003)
14. Pastorino, A.J., Ricks, N.P., Hansen, C.L., McMahon, D.J.: Effect of calcium and water injection on structure function relationships of cheese. Journal of Dairy Science **86**, 105–113 (2003)
15. Rajbhandari, P., Kindstedt, P.S.: Development and application of image analysis to quantify calcium lactate crystals on the surface of smoked cheddar cheese. Journal of Dairy Science **88**, 4157–4164 (2005)
16. Ramírez, C., Germain, J.C., Aguilera, J.M.: Image analysis of representative food structures: application of the bootstrap method. Journal of Food Science **74**(6), R65–R72 (2009)
17. Russ, J.C.: Image Analysis of Food Microstructure. CRC Press, November 15, 2004
18. Silva, J.V.C., Legland, D., Cauty, C., Kolotuev, I., Floury, J.: Characterization of the microstructure of dairy systems using automated image analysis. Food Hydrocolloids **44**, 360–371 (2015)

Semantic Shape Models for Leaf Species Identification

Olfa Mzoughi[1,3]([✉]), Itheri Yahiaoui[2], Nozha Boujemaa[1],
and Ezzeddine Zagrouba[3]

[1] INRIA Saclay, Palaiseau, France
olfa.mzoughi@inria.fr
[2] CReSTIC Université de Reims CReSTIC, Champagne-Ardenne, France
[3] SIIVA/RIADI, Intitut Supérieur d'Informatique,
Université de Tunis El Manar, Tunis, Tunisia

Abstract. We present two complementary botanical-inspired leaf shape representation models for the classification of simple leaf species (leaves with one compact blade). The first representation is based on some linear measurements that characterise variations of the overall shape, while the second consists of semantic part-based segment models. These representations have two main advantages: First, they only require the extraction of two points: the base and apex, which are the key characterisation points of simple leaves. The second advantage is the complementary of the proposed model representations, which provides robustness against large leaf species variations as well as high inter-species and low intra-class similarity that occurs for some species. For the decision procedure, we use a two-stage Bayesian framework: the first concerns each shape model separately and the second is a combination of classification scores (posterior probabilities) obtained from each shape model. Experiments carried out on real world leaf images, the simple leaves of the Pl@ntLeaves scan images (46 species), show an increase in performance compared to previous related work.

Keywords: Leaf contour · Botany · Semantic segment-based representation · Naive Bayesian classifier · Fusion

1 Introduction

Plants are universally recognized as being the central components of the nature's cycle of life, as they maintain the Earth's environmental balance and the ecosystem functionality. Moreover, they represent the main source of many products (such as food, fibre, fuel and medicine), that are essential for human well-being. Nowadays, plants are threatened by over-exploitation, pollution, rapid urban development and global climatic change. The resulting ecological crisis presents one of the greatest challenges faced by the world community. Therefore, there is a crucial need to deepen knowledge about the diversity of the plant community and to aggregate and share it with a large scale of people (scientists, industrials

© Springer International Publishing Switzerland 2015
S. Battiato et al. (Eds.): ACIVS 2015, LNCS 9386, pp. 661–671, 2015.
DOI: 10.1007/978-3-319-25903-1_57

and amateurs). To achieve these goals, a suitable solution is to use computer vision techniques for constructing rapid and reliable plant classification systems. In the last few years, several researches have been conducted in this direction, yielding to successful plant identification systems (for instance, LeafSnap [10] and Pl@ntNet [6]). However, this problem is still challenging mainly if new species are involved or when dealing with the high inter-class and the low intra-class similarity that characterize some species.

Previous plant identification approaches have mainly relied on leaves since they are the most readily apparent organs on many plants [4] (i.e, they are available for much of the year, unlike reproductive organs such as fruits or flowers which are seasonal). Moreover, they provide an important amount of key information characteristic to plant species [8].

Fundamental features, that have been used to represent leaves, are the texture and shape which describe, respectively, variations within the vein pattern and the global and margin shape, the main key indicators of leaf species [8]. In this paper, we focus mainly on the study of the shape and particularly its contour, because of two main reasons: (1) It is easier to extract and analyse, unlike texture, which mostly requires a high image resolution and sophisticated texture analysis techniques [1,4]. (2) A valuable content of foliar characteristics, that were extensively used by botanists, is located on the contour [8].

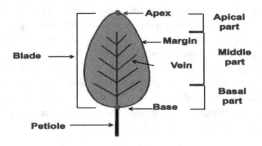

Fig. 1. Simple leaf parts

Most existing leaf-based identification approaches have relied mainly on standard global representation of the contour (for example, histograms [9,20], multi-scale representations [5,11,14], transforms [17], etc). However, such approaches suffer from the lack of expertise knowledge, which make them insufficient to deal with such a complex problem (a large species variability, low intra-species similarity, etc.). As an alternative, we propose, in this paper, two simple and complementary botanical-inspired model representations. The definition of these representations require the extraction of two particular semantic key points: the base and apex. This was performed automatically, using the method [15]. Models are described below:

- The first model focus on the overall shape variations. It is composed from some simple measurements computed using positions of the base and apex.

They are the base and apex angles, the position of the broadest region, the length/width ratio, the asymmetry ratio and the elongation.

– The second model focus on local variations of the shape contour. It consists of segments that correspond to open contours of semantic parts of the leaf. The definition of semantic parts is done with regard to the position of the base and apex. In fact, according to the Manual of Leaf Architecture [8], simple leaves may be partitioned into three semantic regions: the apical, basal and middle parts (see Figure 1, obtained as follows: after aligning the leaf blade according to the line that joins the base and apex, the apical, basal and middle parts are defined as respectively the 25% upper, the 25% lower and the in-between part of the blade (see Figure 1). Segments are defined as the open contours of these regions. Notice that the middle region corresponds to two separate segments (see Figure 4).

This representation was chosen for two main reasons: (1) The first is that it simplifies the shape normalisation and correspondence problem. Each part segment model is represented by its two endpoints and the rest of landmarks as well as the set of similarity transformations, required to construct the part segment model, are defined with regard to these two endpoints.

(2) The second reason is that it enables the identification of query shapes that have partial similarities with a part segment model of a given class but not similar if the model of this class is constructed using the whole closed contour shapes. This makes this representation robust to occlusion or partial damage. Moreover, this semantic part-based representation is particularly efficient mainly in the case of intra-species non-similarity (in terms of certain parts). For instance, leaves of the salix caprea species may hold differences in their margins while they have similar basal parts (see [15] and Figure 2 on the left). Moreover, the Corylus Avellena may hold variable forms of apical parts (see Figure 2 on the right) unlike the others. We consider leaf species as a random

Fig. 2. Intra-variation within leaf parts: from right to left: 4 specimens of the corylus Avellena with variable forms of the apical parts, 2 specimens of the Salix caprea with different margins and similar basal parts [15].

variables on each part manifold and characterize them with normal probability densities. Finally, notice that the part-based segment model is analysed in the Principal Component Space in order to provide an interpretable model of the variation of part segments across all species.

The rest of the paper is organized as follows: An overview of related work is presented in Section 2. The method is described in Section 3. Experimental results and evaluations are presented in Section 4.

2 Related Work

Several standard contour-based shape descriptors have been applied in the context of leaf shape retrieval. Basic descriptors are the Curvature Scale Space, which is a multi-scale representation of the inflection points of the contour (at different smoothing scales) [12,13], the inner shape context, which combines the Inner Distance and the shape context [2], the Contour Centroid descriptor (CCD), which is a set of distances from the centroid to the point of the contour [19]. Such representations express variations in the descriptor space, which may cause a loss or an emphasize of non discriminative information. Thus, using a direct representation within the shape space, by defining a model (prototype), for example, the mean shape, would be more representative, but require domain-specific information about the shape contour. An attempt to realise this goal, is achieved in this paper, in which we propose a semantic model representation of the global and part-based variations of leaves.

3 Proposed Work

3.1 Leaf Shape Representation

We present two complementary shape modelling representations. They are described as follows:

– Overall leaf shape description The first way to represent leaves is to quantify their overall shape variations using the following simple linear measurements (see Figure 3). These measurements are computed after aligning the shape along the line that joins the base and apex.

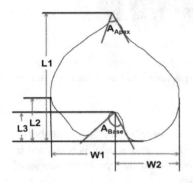

- Apex angle: A_{Apex}
- Base angle: B_{Base}
- Height/width ratio: $\frac{L1-L3}{W1}$
- Elongation: $\frac{L1}{W1}$
- Position of the broadest width of the leaf: $\frac{L2}{L1}$
- Asymmetry ratio: $\frac{W2}{W1-W2}$

Fig. 3. Overall leaf shape representation

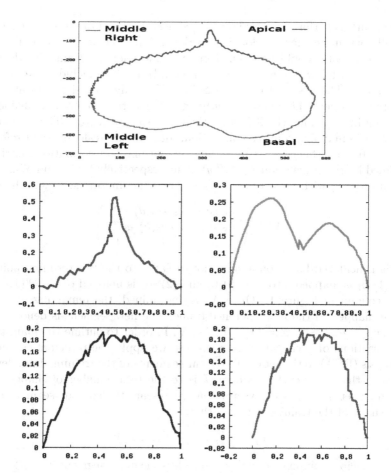

Fig. 4. Semantic segment-based leaf: 1st line: Original image, 2nd and 3rd line: The four normalised segments)

– Semantic segment-based leaf representation We associate to the leaf shape four representations corresponding respectively to the contour segments of the apical, basal, margin right and margin left parts (see respectively, red, green, blue and violet coloured segments in Figure 4). The extraction of these parts from the image requires the localisation of the basic key structures of the leaf, which are the petiole and the base and apex points. We perform this task automatically based on the study of variation of the local translational symmetry of widths, for the petiole extraction and the local symmetry of concavity depths (after petiole removal) for the base and apex localization, as proposed in [15].

Let $\mathcal{S}$, denote a contour segment. $\mathcal{S}$ may correspond to the apical, basal, right margin or left margin parts. The definition of a contour segment model, of a given part, is performed based on analysing statistics of the coordinates points of all contour segments belonging to the training set of that part. For that, these segments should be aligned in the same reference frame. To do so, in practice, we follow the method presented in [18], which includes the following two steps: The first is to sample S into $\mathcal{N}$ evenly spaced points along the contour segment. Let $p_i = (x_i, y_i)|i < \mathcal{N}$, denote a point of S defined by its coordinates along the X,Y axis, then $S = \{p_1, p_2, ..., p_{\mathcal{N}}\}$. The second step consists in mapping S into a translation, rotation and scale invariant reference frame. In fact, this consists in finding the optimal transformation matrix $\mathcal{M}$, defined by the translation $T(T_x, Ty)$ along respectively the X and Y axis, the rotation $R(\theta)$ with regard to the angle θ and the uniform scale s such as:

$$\mathcal{M} = \begin{pmatrix} s\ cos(\theta) & -s\ sin(\theta) & s\ T_x \\ s\ sin(\theta) & s\ cos(\theta) & s\ T_y \\ 0 & 0 & 1 \end{pmatrix}$$

This is achieved based on assumptions related to the two terminal points of S: (1) p_1 is mapped into $p'_1 = (0,0)$ and (2) $p_{\mathcal{N}}$ is mapped to $p'_{\mathcal{N}} = (1,0)$ (see 2nd column in Figure 4). Once $\mathcal{M}$ is determined, the remaining points are then mapped in the new reference frame. The new segment is denoted $S' = \{p'_1, p'_2, ..., p'_{\mathcal{N}}\}$ with $p'_i = (x'_i, y'_i) \mid i < \mathcal{N}$. In order to outline the main trends of variations of each part across species, we apply the principal component analysis (PCA) to the set of all contour segments of the training data, denoted V such that $V = \{v_j\}_{j=1}^{\mathcal{J}}$ where $\mathcal{J}$ is to the total number of shapes of the training set and v_j is the vector that represents the contour segment of the jth shape of the training set such that:

$$v_j = (x'_1, ..., x'_{\mathcal{N}}, y'_1, ..., y'_{\mathcal{N}})^T$$

The principal component analysis considers the mean segment $\bar{v} = \frac{1}{\mathcal{J}} \sum_{j=1}^{\mathcal{J}} v_j$ and the covariance matrix $C = \frac{1}{\mathcal{J}} \sum_{j=1}^{\mathcal{J}} (v_j - \bar{v})(v_j - \bar{v})^T$. It defines the principal axes that define the principal modes of variation of segments as the unit eigenvectors d_k of the covariance matrix C such that: $Sd_k = \lambda_k d_k$, where λ_k is the kth eigenvalue, $\lambda_k \leq \lambda_{k+1}$, $k < 2\mathcal{N}$). Now, we consider $D = [d_1, ..., d_K]$ as the matrix of the K ($K < 2\mathcal{N}$) first eigenvectors. The contour segment representation, denoted vm_j, that corresponds to the projection of v_j into the PCA space is defined as follows:

$$vm_j = (v_j - \bar{v})D^T$$

Notice that this procedure (normalisation into the invariant reference frame and the projection into the eigenspace computed using the training set) is also computed for segments of the test set.

3.2   Shape Classification

Our aim is to associate to each species a prototype and a probability distribution. A given shape will be assigned to the class maximizing the probability.

Furthermore, since we propose different shape models depending on the source of information considered (overall shape or semantic parts), we accordingly define different classifiers followed by an aggregation (or fusion) strategy to determine the species identity.

3.2.1 Naive Bayes Classifier

As a classifier, we use the Naive Bayes Classifier, which is one of the most simple, rapid and efficient classification algorithms. Consider $\mathcal{F} = \{f_l\}_{l=1}^{L}$ the feature vector composed from components of the shape model (either the set of linear measurements or the coordinates of one of the part segment model). The Bayes Classifier employs the Bayes' rule in order to define the posterior probability of each species C:

$$P(C|\mathcal{F}) = \frac{P(C)P(\mathcal{F}|C)}{P(F)}$$

The "naive" assumption implies that the components of the feature vector are statistically independent between each others, which is correct in our context. Hence, the likelihood term of the posterior probability can be obtained by the product of the individual conditional probabilities of each component of the feature vector. Thus, the posterior probability is expressed as follows:

$$P(C|\mathcal{F}) \propto P(C) \prod_{l=1}^{L} P(f_l|C)$$

We assume that the individual conditional probabilities of each component of the feature vector follows a Gaussian distribution. Let μ_c^l and $(\sigma_c^l)^2$ be, respectively, the mean and the variance of the components f_l associated with a class C:

$$P(f_l|C) = \frac{1}{\sigma_c^l\sqrt{2\Pi}} \exp -\frac{(f_l - \mu_c^l)^2}{2(\sigma_c^l)^2}$$

As for the prior probability, it is estimated based on the training set by computing the ratio of the number of sample in a class C with regard to the total number of samples in the training set.

3.2.2 Multiple Classifiers Aggregation

The shape model representations, presented in this paper, are designed in a way they give a complementary information about the shape species, thus, a combination of the corresponding classifiers is expected to be efficient in species identification. Recall that we constructed five classifiers, based, respectively, on the overall shape model, the apical, basal, margin right and margin left segment models. The output from each of these classifiers (denoted m, with $m \leq 5$) is a list of posterior probabilities that quantifies the similarity of an input shape g to a class C. In this paper, we evaluate two fusion strategies, where the outputs are also given in term posterior probability:

– The Bayes Average (BA). It consists in computing an average of the posterior probability taken from all classifiers:

$$P_{fusion}(g \in C|(F_g)) = \frac{1}{5}\sum_{m}^{5} P_m(g \in C|(F_g))$$

– The Weighted Bayes Average (WBA):

$$P_{fusion}(g \in C|(F_g)) = \frac{1}{5}\sum_{m}^{5} w_m \ P_m(g \subset C|(F_g))$$

where $\sum_{k}^{5} w_m = 1$. The principle is to give specific relevance scores per classifier (for example, using the confusion matrix). Here, since the number of classifiers implied is limited (only five), we choose the weights (among a set of possible combinations of predefined values) in a way they correspond to the best combination, using a simple cross-validation process among the training set images. From that, we realize that both left and right margins are the most informative (with the highest weights), but the use of the apical, basal part as well as the morphological ratios-based models allow to enhance identification results.

4   Experimental Results

4.1   The Pl@ntLeaves Dataset

Experiments were carried out on a subset including simple leaves of the Pl@ntLeaves Scan pictures dataset [6]. This subset contains 2438 images belonging to 46 plant species (see some examples in Figure 5). This dataset was chosen because it affords a good representation of the challenging real world leaf images (mainly in terms of the diversity across species and the variability intra-species) [6]. Moreover, it presents a good evaluation base since there are many approaches that were tested on this dataset, in the framework of the ImageCLEF 2011 [7] leaf species identification competition and particularly for simple leaves [16].

Fig. 5. Some simple leaf species of the Pl@ntleaves dataset

4.2   Results and Evaluation

In our experiments, we follow the ImageCLEF 2011 framework for the test and evaluation [7]. In fact, the simple leaves of the Scan Pictures of the pl@ntLeaves dataset are divided into a train and test sets. Moreover, the effectiveness of the approach is measured using the normalized classification score S, an adapted identification score, defined as the Average Classification Score (where the score is 0 if correct and 1 if incorrect), normalized over all test images, all users and all individual plants:

$$S = \frac{1}{N} \sum_{u=1}^{U} \frac{1}{P_u} \sum_{p=1}^{P_u} \frac{1}{N_{u,p}} \sum_{n=1}^{N_{u,p}} s_{u,p,n},$$

where U is the number of users (who have at least one image in the test data), P_u is the number of individual plants observed by the $u - th$ user, $N_{u,p}$ is the number of pictures taken from the $p - th$ plant observed by the $u - th$ user and $s_{u,p,n}$ is the classification score (1 or 0) for the $n - th$ picture taken from the $p - th$ plant observed by the $u - th$ users.

We evaluate the 5 shape model representations, proposed in this paper, using both classifier aggregation strategies: the Bayes Average (BA) and the Weighted Bayes Average (WBA), by comparing their performances, with regard to the top-3 methods that have participated on the ImageCLEF 2011 leaf classification task [7] as well as to a more recent approach [16]. This latter holds the particularity that it also uses the positions of the base of apex to represent leaves, such as what we have done. However, these points are used to define some local (HSV, Hough, EOH and Fourier) histograms computed on a vantage point frame. The computation of the base and apex positions as well as the features are performed, using a coarse-to-fine strategy, based on SVM scores associated with a likelihood framework. Results obtained by different approaches are illustrated in Table 1. We can see that our approach outperforms all previous methods. This proves the representativeness and the effectiveness of such simple overall and segments-based shape models for successful leaf retrieval. Moreover, as expected, the use of different weights per classifier (the Weighted Bayes Average (WBA)) gives better results than the Bayes Average (BA), which treats different classifiers equally.

Table 1. Normalized classification scores of simple leaves of the SCAN pictures of the Pl@ntLeaves dataset, BA (Bayes Average), WBA (Weighted Bayes Average)

Sabanci-run1 [21]	66.52%
LIRIS-run3 [3]	64.48 %
LIRIS-run1 [3]	64.16 %
Vantage Feature Frame [16]	67,00 %
BA (5 models)	**67.83 %**
WBA(5 models)	**68.94 %**

5   Conclusion

We propose two botanical-inspired leaf shape representation models, dedicated to simple leaves. The first representation is based on some geometric measurements that describe the overall shape. The second representation is computed on semantic part segments of leaves. Both representations are directly obtained by only defining the two key characterisation points of simple leaves: the base and apex. The complementary between different models make the proposed approach more robust to the high inter-species and low intra-species similarity (a main problem in the plant identification task). The classification is performed in two stages: In the first stage, we use a Bayesian classification for each model representation. Then, outputs from each classifiers, that are expressed in terms of terms posteriors probabilities are then averaged uniformly or using different weights per classifier, in order to make the final decision a given sample species. Experiments results, obtained on the simple leaves of the P@ntLeaves dataset and using the evaluation framework of the ImageCLEF 2011 classification task, outperforms different entry runs as well as a recent nearby related work (dedicated to simple leaves only). This confirms the efficiency and the robustness of our approach for the classification of simple leaves. The success of this work encourage us to focus on other specific modelling representation, depending for example, on particular leaf categories such as lobed or compound leaves.

References

1. Backes, A.R., Bruno, O.M.: Plant leaf identification using color and multi-scale fractal dimension. Computer Science **6134**, 463–470 (2010)
2. Belhumeur, P.N., Chen, D., Feiner, S.K., Jacobs, D.W., Kress, W.J., Ling, H., Lopez, I., Ramamoorthi, R., Sheorey, S., White, S., Zhang, L.: Searching the world's Herbaria: a system for visual identification of plant species. In: Forsyth, D., Torr, P., Zisserman, A. (eds.) ECCV 2008, Part IV. LNCS, vol. 5305, pp. 116–129. Springer, Heidelberg (2008)
3. Cerutti, G., Tougne, L., Mille, J., Vacavant, A., Coquin, D.: Guiding Active Contours for Tree Leaf Segmentation and Identification (2011)
4. Cope, J.S., Corney, D., Clark, J.Y., Remagnino, P., Wilkin, P.: Review: Plant species identification using digital morphometrics: A review. Expert Syst. Appl., 7562–7573 (2012)
5. Florindo, J.B., Backes, A.R., Bruno, O.M.: Leaves shape classification using curvature and fractal dimension. Computer Science **6134**, 456–462 (2010)
6. Goëau, H., Joly, A., Selmi, S., Bonnet, P., Mouysset, E., Joyeux, L.: Visual-based plant species identification from crowdsourced data. ACM Multimedia (2011)
7. Goëau, H., Bonnet, P., Joly, A., Boujemaa, N., Barthelemy, D., Molino, J.F., Birnbaum, P., Mouysset, E., Picard, M.: The clef 2011 plant images classification task. In: Working Notes of CLEF 2011 Conference (2011)
8. Group. 65p, L.A.W.: Manual of Leaf Architecture. Department of Paleobiology Smithsonian Institution, Cornell University Press (1999–2000)
9. Haibin, G.A., Agarwal, G., Ling, H., Jacobs, D., Shirdhonkar, S., Kress, W.J., Russell, R., Belhumeur, P., Dixit, A., Feiner, S., Mahajan, D., Sunkavalli, K.,

Ramamoorthi, R., White, S.: First steps toward an electronic field guide for plants. Taxon **55**, 597–610 (2006)

10. Kumar, N., Belhumeur, P.N., Biswas, A., Jacobs, D.W., Kress, W.J., Lopez, I.C., Soares, J.V.B.: Leafsnap: a computer vision system for automatic plant species identification. In: Fitzgibbon, A., Lazebnik, S., Perona, P., Sato, Y., Schmid, C. (eds.) ECCV 2012, Part II. LNCS, vol. 7573, pp. 502–516. Springer, Heidelberg (2012)

11. Mokhtarian, F., Abbasi, S.: Matching shapes with self-intersections:application to leaf classification. IEEE Transactions on Image Processing **13**, 653–661 (2004)

12. Mokhtarian, F., Mackworth, A.: Scale-based description and recognition of planar curves and two-dimensional shapes. IEEE Transactions on Pattern Analysis and Machine Intelligence PAMI **8**, 34–43 (1986)

13. Mokhtarian, F., Mackworth, A.K.: A theory of multiscale, curvature-based shape representation for planar curves. IEEE Transactions on Pattern Analysis and Machine Intelligence **14**, 789–805 (1992)

14. Mouine, S., Yahiaoui, I., Verroust-Blondet, A.: A shape-based approach for leaf classification using multiscaletriangular representation. In: ICMR (2013)

15. Mzoughi, O., Yahiaoui, I., Boujemaa, N., Zagrouba, E.: Advanced tree species identification using multiple leaf parts image queries. In: IEEE International Conference on Image Processing (ICIP) (2013)

16. Sfar, A.R., Boujemaa, N., Geman, D.: Vantage feature frames for fine-grained categorization. In: CVPR. IEEE (2013)

17. Suk, T., Flusser, J., Novotný, P.: Comparison of leaf recognition by moments and Fourier descriptors. In: Wilson, R., Hancock, E., Bors, A., Smith, W. (eds.) CAIP 2013, Part I. LNCS, vol. 8047, pp. 221–228. Springer, Heidelberg (2013)

18. Sun, K., Super, B.: Classification of contour shapes using class segment sets. In: 2005 IEEE Computer Society Conference on Computer Vision and Pattern Recognition, CVPR 2005 (2005)

19. Wang, Z., Chi, Z., Feng, D.: Shape based leaf image retrieval. In: VISP, pp. 34–43 (2003)

20. Yahiaoui, I., Mzoughi, O., Boujemaa, N.: Leaf shape descriptor for tree species identification. In: ICME2012 (2012)

21. Yanikoglu, B.A., Aptoula, E., Tirkaz, C.: Sabanci-okan system at imageclef 2011: Plant identification task. In: CLEF (Notebook Papers/Labs/Workshop) (2011)

Multi-distinctive MSER Features and Their Descriptors: A Low-Complexity Tool for Image Matching

Andrzej Śluzek[✉]

Khalifa University, VSAP Center, Abu Dhabi, UAE
andrzej.sluzek@kustar.ac.ae

Abstract. The paper proposes *multi-distinctive MSER features* (*md*-MSER) which are MSER keypoints combined with a number of encompassed keypoints of another type, which should also be affine-invariants (e.g. Harris-Affine keypoints) to maintain the invariance of the proposed method. Such a *bundle of keypoints* is jointly represented by the corresponding number of SIFT-based descriptors which characterize both visual and spatial properties of *md*-MSERs. Therefore, matches between individual *md*-MSER features indicate both visual and configurational similarities so that true feature correspondences can be established (at least in some applications) without the verification of spatial consistencies (i.e. the computational costs of detecting contents visually similar in a wider context are significantly reduced). The paper briefly presents the principles of building and representing *md*-MSER features. Then, performances of *md*-MSER-based algorithms are experimentally evaluated in two benchmark scenarios of image matching and retrieval. In particular, *md*-MSER algorithms are compared to typical alternatives based on other affine-invariant keypoints.

Keywords: MSER · Harris-Affine · SIFT · Keypoint matching · Visual words

1 Introduction and Motivation

1.1 MSER Keypoints

MSER algorithm of keypoint/keyregion detection, proposed by Matas *et al.* in [6] and improved by Nistér and Stewénius in [9], is one of popular tools for image matching/retrieval and for object tracking. MSER's are approximately affine invariant which makes them particularly suitable for the analysis of images of 3D real worlds. Compared to other similar detectors, MSER scheme performs well (the analysis presented in [8]) and has a favorable computational structure allowing hardware implementations, e.g. [4,11].

Additionally, MSERs are generally believed to be less numerous and larger than other affine-invariant keypoints, although our tests only partially support

© Springer International Publishing Switzerland 2015
S. Battiato et al. (Eds.): ACIVS 2015, LNCS 9386, pp. 672–680, 2015.
DOI: 10.1007/978-3-319-25903-1_58

this opinion. We have found (using standard setups of the detectors over many thousands of random images) that, in average, MSER keypoints are 48% less numerous than Harris-Affine (*haraff*) keypoints, and 32% less numerous than Hessian-Affine (*hesaff*) keypoints. Regarding the average size of keypoints, however, the results are inconclusive. Surprisingly, the average area of MSER keypoint ellipses is approx. FOUR times smaller than the average area of *haraff* or *hesaff* ellipses. The paradigm of larger and less numerous MSERs holds only with the additional assumption that too small MSERs (which are particularly numerous in textured parts of images) are discarded. This is often assummed in applications of MSER detectors: (e.g. in [16]). It is also indirectly assumed in this paper (as discussed later).

1.2 Image Matching Using Keypoints

Performances of image matching based on individual keypoint correspondences are generally very poor, especially in larger collections of images. While *recall* of keypoint matching can exceed 50% (see results on the popular dataset[1] in [7,8]) if highly repeatable detectors and reliable descriptors are applied (e.g. MSER keypoints represented by SIFT descriptors, [5]) *precision* depends primarily just on the number of images in the dataset. For example, in the same benchmark set of 48 images, *precision* is approx. 10% (for MSER, *haraff* and *hesaff* keypoints described by SIFT) even if the most reliable *mutual-nearest-neighbor* scheme is used. However, when 100 random images are added to the dataset *precision* falls to 3% , and it further deteriorates to 0.35% with 1,000 images added (see the statistics provided in [12]).

Therefore, the second step of image matching operations, i.e. verification of spatial constraints, is usually required. In the large-scale image retrieval, it becomes the bottleneck so that many attempts have been reported to minimize complexity of spatial verification without compromising excessively the retrieval accuracy (e.g. [2,3,14–16]). Some works go even further and suggest no spatial verification at all (e.g. [12] and partially [15]), e.g. by pre-embedding geometric data needed for such a verification into descriptions of individual keypoints. A similar idea is explored and further developed in this paper.

1.3 Overview of the Proposed Approach

One of the popular ideas to reduce complexity of geometric verification is *feature bundling* (e.g. [10,16,17]. There, keypoints are preliminarily grouped (using various criteria) so that the subsequent spatial verification is performed between such groups of keypoints. In this paper, we actually also create a kind of bundles. Following [16], we create bundles formed by MSER keypoints encompassing at least two keypoints of the other type used (e.g. *haraff*). Then, the whole feature (i.e. the bundle consisting of MSER keypoint and the encompassed *haraff* keypoints) is represented by a number of so-called contextual SIFT (CONSIFT)

---

[1] http://www.robots.ox.ac.uk/~vgg/research/affine/

descriptors (proposed in [12] and [13]). CONSIFTs jointly represent photometry and geometry of the central MSER keypoint and the bundled *haraff* keypoints (more details are provided in Section 2). Eventually, matches between individual features (using CONSIFT descriptors quantized into visual words) indicate not only the overall visual similarity between the MSER keypoints but also consistent spatial distributions on finer details within those keypoints. Since both MSER and *haraff* keypoints are (approximately) affine-invariant, the proposed approach also satisfies the requirements of affine invariance.

We argue that such a representation of image contents offers several advantages. First, visual contents can be matched with high *precision* without any kind of geometric verification, because spatial configurations are (at least partially) pre-embedded into the feature descriptors so that the similarity of descriptors indicates not only similarities between visual contents but also similar distributions of those contents within the images. Secondly, much larger visual vocabularies can be built (details also in Section 2) without compromising *recall*. Finally, the numbers of MSER keypoints which can be bundled in the proposed manner are rather limited so that the retrieval of visual contents, especially at the level of sub-image retrieval, can be performed at much lower computational costs. Nevertheless, because those bundled MSER keypoints are highly informative, performances of the retrieval are generally not compromised.

Several experimental evaluations of the proposed method, including typical examples of visual content matching and image retrieval, are contained in Section 3.

2   Multi-distinctive MSER Features

The proposed idea of building *multi-disctinctive* MSER (*md*-MSER) features is based on the following principles (partially following [16]):

1. Keypoints are extracted by both MSER detector and by another detector. The other detector can be MSER as well, but it is recommended to use detectors extracting keypoints of different characteristics. Following comments from Section 1.1, we use Harris-Affine detector as the other one (Hessian-Affine detector can be used as an almost equivalent alternative).
2. MSER keypoints are considered *multi-distinctive* if their contents are sufficiently complex to ensure visual prominence of not only the keypoint itself but also of its fragments (i.e. there are keypoints of the other type encompassed within the MSER of interest).
3. Thus, a MSER keypoint becomes a *md*-MSER feature if its ellipse encompasses at least 2 keypoints of the other type (i.e. *haraff*). For practical reasons, an encompassed *haraff* keypoint is accepted if it is not too large (e.g. its area is at most 50% of the MSER ellipse) and not too small (e.g. at least 10% of the MSER ellipse). The second condition becomes important if the images of interest are available in diversified scales. When the corresponding MSER is detected in a significantly downscaled image, the encompassed *haraff* may disappear (quantization effects) if originally it is too small.

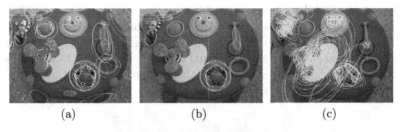

(a)   (b)   (c)

Fig. 1. Exemplary image with all MSERs (a) and only *md*-MSERs (b) shown. The distribution of *haraff* keypoints in the same image is given as a reference in (c).

A comparison between MSER and *md*-MSER features is illustrated in Fig. 1. It shows that the number of *md*-MSERs is significantly smaller than the number of originally detected MSERs (normally only approx.10 − 12% of original MSERs become *md*-MSERs. Nevertheless (as discussed in Section 2.1) the amount of visual data contained in *md*-MSER features is actually even higher than in the original MSERs (because of the *haraff* keypoints encompassed in MSERs) and those data are concentrated in the visually diversified parts of images.

2.1   Description of Multi-distinctive MSERs

Description of *md*-MSERs are built using jointly the MSER keypoint and the encompassed *haraff* keypoints (including spatial characteristics of such a bundle of keypoints). Therefore, matches between two *md*-MSER features indicate much deeper visual similarities than matches between ordinary MSERs.

To build descriptions of *md*-MSER, we propose to use so-called CONSIFT (*contextual* SIFT) descriptors, [13], which can be briefly explained (with some simple modifications proposed for the purpose of the discussed problem) as follows:

Given a MSER keypoint K with E_K ellipse, and a *haraff* keypoint L with E_L ellipse (encompassed within E_K) a $384D$ CONSIFT descriptor of K in the context of L is obtained by concatenating three $128D$ SIFT vectors (actually, we use RootSIFT modification of SIFT because of its superior performances, [1]). The first part (the *absolute* component of CONSIFT) is just an ordinary SIFT computed over E_K ellipse. The second and the third part (the *relative* components of CONSIFT) are SIFT descriptors computed over E_K and over E_L, using $\overline{(K,L)}$ vector and $\overline{(L,K)}$ vector as the respective reference orientation. Thus CONSIFT descriptors contain a mixture of pictorial and geometric characteristics of a larger MSER keypoint and its smaller fragments represented by the encompassed *haraffs*.

Md-MSER features are, therefore, represented by N CONSIFT descriptors, where N corresponds to the number of *haraffs* encompassed within the MSER keypoint. Fig. 2 shows an example of a *md*-MSER feature incorporating two *haraffs*. Most *md*-MSERs, however, have more encompassed *haraffs*, i.e. they are represented by larger numbers of CONSIFT descriptors. Therefore, even though only $10 - 12\%$ of MSERs become md-MSERs, the total numbers of CONSIFT descriptors in the whole images are often larger than the numbers of original MSER keypoints. Thus, the image description becomes richer and concentrated primarily in the areas of the highest visual diversity because CONSIFT descriptors represent only image fragments contained in md-MSER features.

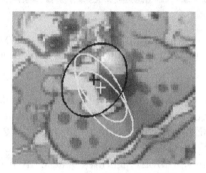

Fig. 2. Exemplary md-MSER keypoint (blue ellipse) with two encompassed *haraffs* (yellow ellipses).

Dimensionality of CONSIFT descriptors is high ($384D$ CONSIFT vectors are concatenations of three $128D$ SIFTs) so that feature matching based directly on CONSIFT vectors is obviously inefficient. Instead, CONSIFTs can be easily quantized into visual words using any vocabulary of SIFT words. The three sections of a CONSIFT vector can be quantized separately using the original SIFT vocabulary, and the results are from a Cartesian product of three SIFT vocabularies (which might be identical). Thus, a SIFT vocabulary of K words generates the corresponding CONSIFT vocabulary of K^3 words. However, each section of CONSIFT vectors can be quantized using a different SIFT vocabulary, which provides even more flexibility in building CONSIFT vocabularies.

3   Experimental Verification

The experiments have been conducted using CONSIFT descriptors quantized into words (from vocabularies built as outlined in Section 1.2). Not only because of the high dimensionality of CONSIFTs, but also because the *mutual-NN* scheme does not work properly in case of matching features represented by a number of descriptors of the same type. Thus, we use a simple formula that two md-MSER features match if they share some identical CONSIFT words. The number NS of shared words is used as an additional parameter defining the *strength-of-match*. We use $NS = 2$, i.e. the minimum number of encompassed *haraffs* required to build a md-MSER feature.

Two schemes of CONSIFT vocabulary building have been eventually adopted. In Scheme A, we use a larger SIFT vocabulary ($64k$ words) to quantize the absolute part of CONSIFT (i.e. the original SIFT of the MSER keypoint) while the relative parts of CONSIFT vectors are quantized using only 128 words (see notes at the end of Section 2.1). In Scheme B, all SIFTs contributing to CONSIFT vectors are quantized using the same vocabulary of 1024 words. Note that both schemes generate the same large number of the CONSIFT words (2^{30}, i.e. over one billion) since $64k \times 128 \times 128 = 1k \times 1k \times 1k$. Vocabularies of such sizes are recommended for CONSIFT descriptors in [13].

In the first experiment, md-MSERs are tested for the standard performance parameters of features matching, i.e. *precision* and *recall*. The popular benchmark dataset mentioned in Section 1.2 is used. However, unlike in most experiments reported for this dataset, we match all pairs of images (most of them obviously irrelevant) so that *precision* values are rather low. Table 1 shows the results compared to popular affine-invariant alternatives (i.e. *haraff*, *hesaff* and MSER detectors, all of them represented by SIFTs quantized into words from two exemplary vocabularies). Superior performances of of md-MSERs features represented by CONSIFTs are clearly seen. *Recall* remains at a similar level, but *precision* is two orders of magnitude higher. Additionally, it can be noticed that the average number of md-MSER features in an individual image is small (compared to the numbers returned by the other tested keypoint detectors) which makes these results particularly encouraging.

Exemplary matches for relevant and irrelevant image pairs are shown in Fig. 3 as an illustration.

Table 1. Feature matching results (using SIFT and CONSIFT visual words).

Features (descriptor)	Average no of features	Vocabulary size	recall	precision
haraff (SIFT)	2110	2^{10}	0.5834	0.0025
		2^{16}	0.2671	0.0040
hesaff (SIFT)	1758	2^{10}	0.6067	0.0016
		2^{16}	0.2813	0.0032
MSER(SIFT)	1099	2^{10}	0.5160	0.0026
		2^{16}	0.212	0.0034
md-MSER(CONSIFT)	119	2^{30} (A)	0.4839	0.2284
		2^{30} (B)	0.4695	0.2452

In the second experiment, the practicality of md-MSERs in image retrieval has been tested. The simplest variant of *bag-of-words* method (i.e. the cardinality of BoWs intersection) has been applied to obtained as unbiased results as possible. As an example, a popular UKB benchmark dataset, [9] has been selected, and performances are compared using a standard *mean average precision* measure (where the results for a 2^{16}-word SIFT vocabulary over *haraff* keypoints are considered the reference). As shown in Table 2, the md-MSER features provide a significant improvement, although not that spectacular as in case of feature matching experiment.

Fig. 3. Feature correspondences found in relevant (a,c) and irrelevant (b,d) image pairs. The top row shows *hesaff* matches (using 2^{16} SIFT words), the bottom row shows *md*-MSER matches (using 2^{30} CONSIFT words).

An example illustrating superior performances of *md*-MSER-based retrieval is shown in Fig. 4.

Table 2. *Mean average precision* (mAP) values for UKB dataset retrieval using a simple BoW scheme (the results for *haraff* keypoints with 2^{16}-word SIFT vocabulary are considered the reference).

Feature (descriptor - vocabulary)	relative *mAP* value
haraff (SIFT - 2^{16} words)	100%
hesaff (SIFT - 2^{16} words)	98%
haraff (SIFT - 2^{20} words)	122%
MSER (SIFT - 2^{20} words)	118%
md-MSER (CONSIFT - 2^{30} words)	171%

In typical works on image retrieval, the results similar to those in Table 2 are considered preliminary (pre-retrieval phase) and they are subsequently refined using more advanced algorithms (e.g. geometric consistency verification). The *md*-MSER results, nevertheless, can be refined (or improved in the pre-retrieval phase) without applying those additional algorithms. Instead, we can just take into account only those feature matches which have a sufficiently high *strength-of-match* (see the first paragraph of this section). For example, if the required *strength-of-match* is increased to $N = 4$ (the default value used in the proposed method is $N = 2$), the relative value of *mAP* measure in Table 2 would be increased to 238%. It should be noted that the computational costs of such modifications are negligible (compared, for example, to high costs of spatial consistency verification).

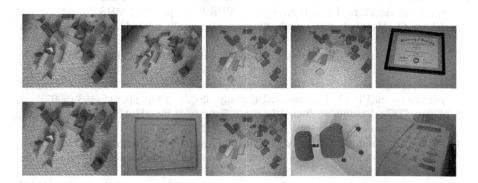

Fig. 4. Exemplary top retrievals with BoW using CONSIFT words built over *md*-MSER features (top row) and using SIFT words built over *haraff* keypoints (bottom). The vocabulary size is, correspondingly, 2^{30} and 2^{20}. Note that in UKB each query has only THREE relevant images.

4   Summary

The paper introduces the concept of multi-distinctive MSER features (*md*-MSER) which are bundles of several *haraff* keypoints encompassed by a single MSER keypoint. Such features can be represented by CONSIFT vectors (concatenation of three SIFT vectors, [12, 13]) jointly describing photometric and geometric properties of the features. CONSIFT vectors can be easily quantized into huge vocabularies (Cartesian products of the original SIFT vocabularies) which, obviously, can provide high *precision* but also, more surprisingly, high *recall*.

The proposed tool seems particularly suitable for a visual retrieval (including retrievals of partially similar images) in system of limited computational power, because it can substitute (to a certain extent) the spatial consistency verification of keypoint configurations (which is computationally complex) by simple matches between *md*-MSER features.

Additionally, *md*-MSER features are much less numerous then the original MSER keypoints (which is another advantage for limited-capabilities systems) but they provide the same (or larger) amount of visual data. Morover, those data are concentrated in the most diversified fragments of images (because this is where *md*-MSERs are formed) so that image matching and retrieval can be focused on the most significant fragments of images without a need to detect such fragments by alternative algorithms (e.g. without a need to analyze *saliency* of images).

More specific applications of of *md*-MSER features are currently under development and will be reported in future papers.

References

1. Arandjelovic, R., Zisserman, A.: Three things everyone should know to improve object retrieval. In: Proc. IEEE Conf. CVPR 2012, pp. 2911–2918 (2012)
2. Chum, O., Matas, J.: Large-scale discovery of spatially related images. IEEE PAMI **32**(2), 371–377 (2010)
3. Chum, O., Perdoch, M., Matas, J.: Geometric min-hashing: finding a (thick) needle in a haystack. In: Proc. IEEE Conf. CVPR 2009, pp. 17–24 (2009)
4. Kristensen, F., MacLean, W.: Real-time extraction of maximally stable extremal regions on an FPGA. In: Proc. IEEE Symp. ISCAS 2007, pp. 165–168 (2007)
5. Lowe, D.G.: Distinctive image features from scale-invariant keypoints. International Journal of Computer Vision **60**(2), 91–110 (2004)
6. Matas, J., Chum, O., Urban, M., Pajdla, T.: Robust wide baseline stereo from maximally stable extremal regions. In: British Machine Vision Conference, pp. 384–393 (2002)
7. Mikolajczyk, K., Schmid, C.: A performance evaluation of local descriptors. IEEE Trans. PAMI **27**, 1615–1630 (2005)
8. Mikolajczyk, K., Tuytelaars, T., Schmid, C., Zisserman, A., Matas, J., Schaffalitzky, F., Kadir, T., Gool, L.V.: A comparison of affine region detectors. International Journal of Computer Vision **65**, 43–72 (2005)
9. Nistér, D., Stewénius, H.: Scalable recognition with a vocabulary tree. In: Proc. IEEE Conf. CVPR 2006, vol. 2, pp. 2161–2168 (2006)
10. Romberg, S., August, M., Ries, C.X., Lienhart, R.: Robust feature bundling. In: Lin, W., Xu, D., Ho, A., Wu, J., He, Y., Cai, J., Kankanhalli, M., Sun, M.-T. (eds.) PCM 2012. LNCS, vol. 7674, pp. 45–56. Springer, Heidelberg (2012)
11. Salahat, E., Saleh, H., Sluzek, A., Al-Qutayri, M., Mohammed, B., Ismail, M.: Architecture and method for real-time parallel detection and extraction of maximally stable extremal regions (MSERS). U.S. Patent Application No. 14/482,629 (2014)
12. Śluzek, A.: Contextual descriptors improving credibility of keypoint matching. In: Proc. 13th Int. Conf. ICARCV 2014, pp. 117–122 (2014)
13. Śluzek, A.: Extended keypoint description and the corresponding improvements in image retrieval. In: Jawahar, C.V., Shan, S. (eds.) ACCV 2014 Workshops. LNCS, vol. 9008, pp. 698–709. Springer, Heidelberg (2015)
14. Stewénius, H., Gunderson, S.H., Pilet, J.: Size matters: exhaustive geometric verification for image retrieval accepted for ECCV 2012. In: Fitzgibbon, A., Lazebnik, S., Perona, P., Sato, Y., Schmid, C. (eds.) ECCV 2012, Part II. LNCS, vol. 7573, pp. 674–687. Springer, Heidelberg (2012)
15. Tolias, M., Jegou, H.: Visual query expansion with or without geometry: refining local descriptors by feature aggregation. Pattern Recognition **47**, 3466–3476 (2014)
16. Wu, Z., Ke, Q., Isard, M., Sun, J.: Bundling features for large scale partial-duplicate web image search. In: Proc. IEEE Conf. CVPR 2009, pp. 25–32. Miami Beach (2009)
17. Zhang, Y., Jia, Z., Chen, T.: Image retrieval with geometry-preserving visual phrases. In: Proc. IEEE Conf. CVPR 2011, pp. 809–816 (2011)

Spatio-Temporal Object Recognition

Roeland De Geest[1,3]($\boxtimes$), Francis Deboeverie[2,3], Wilfried Philips[2,3],
and Tinne Tuytelaars[1,3]

[1] KU Leuven ESAT - PSI, Leuven, Belgium
Roeland.DeGeest@esat.kuleuven.be
[2] UGent TELIN - IPI, Ghent, Belgium
[3] iMinds, Ledeberg, Belgium

Abstract. Object recognition in video is in most cases solved by extracting keyframes from the video and then applying still image recognition methods on these keyframes only. This procedure largely ignores the temporal dimension. Nevertheless, the way an object moves may hold valuable information on its class. Therefore, in this work, we analyze the effectiveness of different motion descriptors, originally developed for action recognition, in the context of action-invariant object recognition. We conclude that a higher classification accuracy can be obtained when motion descriptors (specifically, HOG and MBH around trajectories) are used in combination with standard static descriptors extracted from keyframes. Since currently no suitable dataset for this problem exists, we introduce two new datasets and make them publicly available.

1 Introduction

Object recognition is one of the main topics of interest in computer vision. In still images, it has been extensively covered (e.g., [4,11]) and various competitions such as Pascal VOC [3] and ImageNet [16] have encouraged research and provided datasets for evaluation and comparison of the developed methods. Far fewer object recognition methods have been published for video data, however. In most cases (e.g., [17,18]) keyframes are extracted from the video. These frames are chosen in such a way that they represent the whole video, preserving the information (i.e., the object appearance) in the video as much as possible. Afterwards, standard image object recognition methods are applied on these keyframes only. As a consequence, the video object recognition problem is reduced to static object recognition in the keyframes, and temporal information is left unexploited.

In this work, we investigate whether the motion of dynamic objects (and by extension, animals) can be used to improve their recognition. To this end, we evaluate object recognition methods that build on spatio-temporal

This work was financially supported by the project "Multi-camera human behavior monitoring and unusual event detection" (FWO G.0.398.11.N.10) and the PARIS project (IWT-SBO Nr. 110067).

© Springer International Publishing Switzerland 2015
S. Battiato et al. (Eds.): ACIVS 2015, LNCS 9386, pp. 681–692, 2015.
DOI: 10.1007/978-3-319-25903-1_59

representations, as typically used for action recognition. We start from two observations. First, video is a different domain than still images: Kalogeiton et al. [6] show that an object detector for video is best trained on video data as well. If we train on video anyway, it makes sense to exploit as much motion information as possible. Second, some object classes are dynamic: they change over time due to non-rigid deformations (e.g., a tree in the wind), manipulation (e.g., a driving car) or actions (e.g., a sleeping or walking lion). Because of this extra variability, these kinds of objects are more difficult to recognize. By using spatio-temporal features, we can capture these variations for a better recognition.

One issue that may have hampered the development of spatio-temporal object recognition methods is the lack of good datasets. Therefore, we introduce two new datasets for our experiments.

We start our discussion in the next section with a review of related work. In Section 3, we introduce our new datasets. Section 4 describes our experiments and the results are discussed in Section 5. Section 6 concludes the paper.

2   Related Work

Video Object Recognition. There is only a limited amount of work on learning object detectors directly from video and/or applying them to videos as such (i.e., without falling back to the sampling of keyframes from the video and applying static detectors to these). While at first sight video seems a far richer format than still images, video comes with its own challenges, such as (typically) lower resolutions, interlacing effects, motion blur and compression artifacts. For these reasons, it has been argued that video is actually a different domain than still images [6,15]. Instead of just applying classifiers trained on static images to video data, one should then compensate for the domain shift using domain adaptation methods.

Obviously, directly training models from video data avoids this issue. At the same time, as we argued earlier, this allows to exploit the richer information contained in video, including typical motion patterns and temporal continuity. Collecting ground truth annotations for video data is cumbersome, however, even when using specialized annotation tools such as [23]. Therefore, not many good datasets for learning object classifiers from video are available to date, except for action recognition (where the motion component is judged critical), surveillance (often with a static camera and hence limited background variation) or traffic sequences (mostly with very specific scene constraints that provide strong cues for detection). None of these seem suitable for evaluating object recognition methods exploiting motion cues in an unconstrained setting, as is the goal in this paper.

As one of a few exceptions that do train models directly from video data, we should mention the work of Viola et al. [19], who designed a pedestrian detector that uses both appearance and motion features. They calculate the absolute difference of the intensities of two consecutive frames and use it for their rectangle filters. This work is most closely related to our work. It starts with the same observation that motion is characteristic for the moving actor or object. However, we use information over more frames and different, more modern descriptors. Moreover, we show the validity of this assumption for other, non-human, animals and objects.

Liu et al. [10] developed a method to recognize static, non-moving objects in videos. The representation of an object changes when the camera moves. They map these representations on a manifold and perform manifold-to-manifold matching for recognition. By using a moving camera, they get multiple views from the object and some insight in its depth structure. Their objects are static. We, however, focus on what can be learned from the motion of the object itself. Moreover, they only want to recognize specific objects, not object classes as we do. Finally, they test on videos with a homogenous background. We use realistic user-generated YouTube content.

A related problem is **gait recognition** (see [8] for a survey). In this topic, the aim is to recognize human individuals based on the way they walk. We, on the other hand, focus on category-level recognition.

Several methods have recently been proposed focusing on **video segmentation**, e.g., [1,5]. These methods exploit motion information in video, either in the form of optical flow or through a set of points tracked over a small fragment of the video (trajectories), to discover which pixels belong to the same object. Most recently, Oneata et al. [14] proposed a 'tube' (bounding box of an object over time) detection method starting from a graph of superpixels. However, instead of recognizing particular object categories, these methods at best detect and locate unknown objects (and with low precision).

Prest et al. [15] build on the approach of [1] to find objects in videos and use these as additional data for training an object detector for images. We show results on the dataset they compiled from YouTube videos, but the reader should note its small scale, with only about ten example videos for some of the categories.

Action Recognition. has been intensively studied over the last years, and several powerful motion descriptors have been proposed in this context. In practice, the distinction between recognizing actions and recognizing objects can sometimes be diffuse: a *pedestrian* is often considered a different object category than the more general *person*. Likewise, one could consider *human playing tennis* and *human walking* as two different objects. However, this is a very constrained formulation. Objects and animals not only show variation between instances, but they can also perform multiple actions and therefore have multiple motion patterns. Learning a separate classifier for each object/action combination is not desirable as it further increases the amount of training data needed.

There are two main approaches for feature extraction in videos. In the first, the video is considered as a 3D image, with time as a third dimension, and 2D interest point detectors are extended to 3D (e.g., [2,7,22]). In the second approach, points are tracked over time and the resulting trajectories are used as features (e.g., [12,13,20]). In our experiments, we use the dense trajectories of Wang et al. [20].

3   Savanna Datasets

Since currently no suitable video object recognition dataset is publicly available, we collected our own data and intend to share it with anyone interested. We sampled 86 videos from YouTube with African animals, such as elephants, giraffes and lions. We divided these videos in three-second fragments (75 frames at a frame rate of 25 Hz). We select the fragments where only one species of animal is present (there can be multiple individuals of the same species, however), the animal or a part of it is moving and the camera focal length is not changed drastically (i.e., not heavily zooming in or out) to make tracking of (parts of) the animals easier.

The fragments are labeled according to their species. More videos are available for some animals than for others, but evaluation on a balanced dataset is easier to interpret. Therefore, we create two datasets. The first consists of approximately 100 fragments from each of four animal classes; we call it **Savanna4**. The second, **Savanna7**, has about 60 fragments from seven species. The species, number of videos and number of fragments for both datasets can be found in Table 1. For evaluation, we divide the fragments of a dataset in five groups with a similar number of fragments per class and perform leave-one-group-out cross validation. Fragments from the same YouTube video are kept in the same group to avoid contamination between fragments for training and fragments for testing. The final classification score is obtained by averaging the accuracies of all classes.

Table 1. Classes of the Savanna4 and Savanna7 datasets with their numbers of videos and fragments.

	Savanna4		Savanna7	
	Videos	Fragm.	Videos	Fragm.
Giraffe	21	106	21	60
Lion	12	99	12	60
Rhinoceros	15	90	15	60
Elephant	16	106	14	60
Antelope			14	61
Baboon			13	55
Zebra			9	47
Total	55	401	82	403

Recognition of the species in these datasets is challenging for multiple reasons. First, the animal is not always completely visible due to occlusion or bad image composition; on the other hand, some fragments contain complete herds. Second, the pose and activity of the animal can differ: some animals are standing or walking, others eating or drinking. Third, the appearance of animals varies within the species: a male lion is clearly different from the female or juvenile. Finally, compression artefacts are clearly visible. The image quality is often significantly lower than what one finds in static image datasets. An extra challenge for video-based methods lies in the moving camera: most videos were recorded by amateurs on safari. While we avoid strong zooming effects, the camera may follow the animal, or may be unstable since it is hand held. Figure 1 shows some snapshots of fragments in our datasets.

Fig. 1. Frames from our Savanna datasets. The first four species are in both datasets, the last three only in Savanna7.

4   Experimental Setup

4.1   Datasets

We conduct experiments on four datasets. **Savanna4** and **Savanna7** are already described in Section 3. Our third dataset is based on the **Wild8** dataset from Liu et al. [9]. This dataset consists of 100 videos of African landscape and animals. It was collected for video object segmentation and has eight categories: bird, lion, elephant, sky, tree, grass, sand and water. Each video comprises three seconds at a sample rate of 10 Hz. Only the three animals move sufficiently to be considered for our application. This way, we have 47 videos of birds, 15 videos of lions and 11 videos of elephants. We split them in five groups to be able to evaluate with leave-one-group-out cross validation and still have a decent (albeit small) number of training examples. The final classification score is obtained by averaging the accuracies of all classes. Figure 2 shows some frames of the dataset.

Our fourth dataset is an adaptation of the **Youtube Objects** dataset collected by Prest et al. [15]. This dataset consists of videos (split in shots) of ten object and animal categories (examples in Fig. 3). We only know the object is present somewhere in each video. Therefore, we check for each shot whether the object is visible while no other classes of the dataset are; otherwise, the shot is removed. Next, we split the shots in 30-frame fragments. We divide the fragments in four groups. Fragments coming from the same video are in the same group. Here too, we evaluate with leave-one-group-out cross validation and average accuracy. Table 2 shows the classes with their numbers of videos and fragments. We should emphasize that some videos generate hundreds of fragments, while

Fig. 2. Example frames of the classes in the Wild8 dataset.

others have only one valid fragment. Videos with many fragments have a high influence on the trained model, even though it is plausible that they contain very limited motion and appearance information. In that case, the model does not generalize well and unseen object instances are classified wrongly.

Fig. 3. Example frames of the classes in the YouTube Objects dataset.

Table 2. Classes of the adapted YouTube Objects dataset with their numbers of videos and fragments.

	Videos	Fragments		Videos	Fragments
Airplane	13	1854	Bird	16	784
Boat	17	2114	Cat	21	1303
Car	9	374	Cow	22	1679
Motorbike	14	1081	Dog	36	2696
Train	30	5873	Horse	29	4300

4.2   Features and Classifier

The motion features we use are the HOG, HOF and MBH descriptors around a trajectory as well as the motion of the trajectory itself, as in [20]. We use their setup with one exception: to reduce the calculation time, we set the sampling step size to $W = 10$. Only on the Wild8 dataset, where the amount of data is limited, we take $W = 5$. We also experimented with improved trajectories [21] that try to compensate for the camera motion of the video. Our object recognition results were slightly better, but with a similar improvement (about 2%) in all possible settings. We kept using the basic dense trajectories for the rest of our experiments, because their effect has been more extensively researched in all kinds of video processing applications.

As a baseline, we implement a keyframe-based approach. For this, we calculate dense 128-bin SIFT descriptors [11] with the same spatial density W as the trajectories over the same eight scales. We take a frame every $L = 15$ frames. This way, we ensure that the number of SIFT descriptors is roughly equal to the maximum number of trajectories. In practice, however, on average many more SIFT descriptors than trajectories are extracted, since trajectories are not started in homogeneous regions and can still be discarded after they finish. Note that a SIFT detector instead of dense SIFT would not improve recognition results, since the background of the videos has enough texture to let the detector fire.

Next, we train a codebook for each descriptor type and collect the quantized descriptors in a bag-of-words representation. Finally, we train a multi-channel one-against-all support vector machine with χ^2-kernel as in [20]. The recognized object category is the one with the highest probability. We take the average of the accuracies of all classes as final performance criterion.

This is a very basic setup: higher accuracies can easily be obtained with more sophisticated methods. The advantage of this scheme is that features and descriptors have a high influence on the classification accuracy, therefore making it well-suited to examine the effectiveness of descriptors.

5   Results and Discussion

Table 3 shows the average classification accuracy for all datasets for multiple descriptor combinations. On Savanna4, Savanna7 and Wild8, we conduct the experiments five times and report the average performance and the standard deviation. We experiment only once on YouTube Objects, because calculations on this dataset are more time-consuming.

When we use only one descriptor, SIFT is a good choice. It has top performance on the Savanna4 and Wild8 datasets and decent scores on the others; moreover, it is fast to calculate. Of the motion-containing descriptors, HOG and MBH are the best. These two descriptors preserve some appearance information: HOG directly, MBH by focusing on the boundaries of a moving object. The trajectory descriptor, the uncoded motion of the trajectory, is the least effective descriptor, probably because it is most affected by the camera ego-motion.

The classification accuracy increases with well-chosen descriptor combinations. Recognition with SIFT and either HOG or MBH is already better than SIFT alone. The best results are obtained by combining HOG, MBH and SIFT, with an improvement of 7% over the keyframe approach on the Savanna datasets and 14% on YouTube Objects. Configurations with the pure trajectory

Table 3. Average accuracy on Savanna4, Savanna7, Wild8 and YouTube Objects datasets for different descriptor combinations. 'All trajectory' is short for 'Trajectory+HOG+HOF+MBH'.

	Savanna4	Savanna7	Wild8	YouTube Obj.
SIFT	$61.9\% \pm 0.6\%$	$41.6\% \pm 1.0\%$	**$62.3\% \pm 4.5\%$**	44.3%
Trajectory	$33.1\% \pm 2.0\%$	$16.9\% \pm 1.2\%$	$41.3\% \pm 1.6\%$	23.9%
HOG	$61.9\% \pm 1.3\%$	$48.4\% \pm 1.1\%$	$53.5\% \pm 1.7\%$	36.0%
HOF	$39.6\% \pm 1.3\%$	$19.0\% \pm 0.8\%$	$39.7\% \pm 2.6\%$	27.9%
MBH	$52.2\% \pm 0.8\%$	$36.1\% \pm 0.7\%$	$47.8\% \pm 1.7\%$	45.3%
HOG+MBH	$65.7\% \pm 1.3\%$	$47.2\% \pm 2.7\%$	$49.2\% \pm 4.8\%$	47.7%
All trajectory	$60.1\% \pm 2.3\%$	$40.8\% \pm 1.1\%$	$50.4\% \pm 3.3\%$	51.4%
SIFT+HOG	$65.2\% \pm 0.9\%$	$44.9\% \pm 0.6\%$	$59.0\% \pm 6.7\%$	52.8%
SIFT+MBH	$67.0\% \pm 0.5\%$	$46.0\% \pm 0.7\%$	$54.9\% \pm 4.9\%$	55.9%
SIFT+HOG+MBH	**$68.6\% \pm 0.9\%$**	**$49.6\% \pm 0.4\%$**	$56.7\% \pm 3.4\%$	**58.1%**
SIFT+All trajectory	$66.6\%, \pm 0.7\%$	$43.3\%, \pm 0.9\%$	$49.8\%, \pm 2.0\%$	57.1%

descriptors and HOF, however, yield lower results than the ones without them. On Wild8, the single SIFT descriptor works best. This dataset is too small to draw conclusions: the instability of the results is indicated by the large values of the standard deviation in Table 3.

Some objects are not suited for recognition by motion. Figure 4 shows the confusion matrix of the Savanna7 dataset with only SIFT and only MBH. Zebras are often confused with antelopes with MBH, but not with SIFT: the appearance is very discriminative here. On the other hand, antelopes have a score three times higher with MBH. The dataset includes seven species of antelope, making the appearance more variable, while the motion is still similar. The different types of cats, dogs and birds in YouTube Objects give rise to a similar effect.

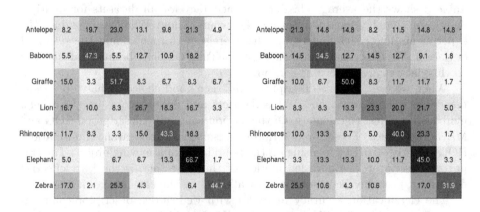

Fig. 4. Confusion matrices for Savanna7 dataset with SIFT (left) and MBH (right) descriptor.

To find out whether appearance or motion is more easily learned, we train models on the Savanna4 dataset with a varying number of training samples. The classification accuracies can be found in Fig. 5. All descriptors start levelling out around the same time, so we conclude there is no significant difference in learning difficulty.

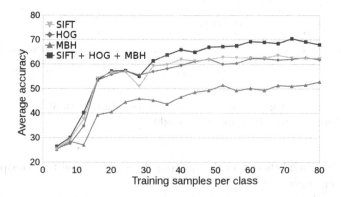

Fig. 5. Average classification accuracy as a function of the number of training samples per class for the Savanna4 dataset.

Another interesting observation is that HOG and SIFT combined are better than either of them separately, though they are both based on appearance. The difference lies in two aspects. First, the HOG descriptor is only centered on the moving points, not on a static background. Second, the descriptor is constructed differently. A HOG descriptor has some time information, not only because it is calculated over the 15 frames of a trajectory, but also because it is subdivided in spatio-temporal cells. These cells manage to preserve more structure in the HOG. The SIFT descriptor, however, has 32 more dimensions, so it can store its information at a finer scale. To investigate the effect of these two differences, we calculate a SIFT descriptor around the middle point of each trajectory and train a model on Savanna4 with these descriptors. The first difference is now neutralized. With this configuration, we obtain a score of 43.0%. This is significantly lower than the 61.9% of HOG and the 61.9% of standard SIFT. We can conclude that the main advantage of HOG is its structure-preserving descriptor, while SIFT makes efficiently use of a larger number of features.

Savanna4, Savanna7 and Wild8 contain only animal classes. YouTube Objects has some objects (means of transportation) as well, and for these too adding motion information benefits the recognition accuracy (as can be seen in the confusion matrices of Fig. 6). With SIFT descriptors, the average accuracy of the objects only is equal to 48.4%. When we add HOG and MBH, it increases to 65.9%. We observe four quadrants in the confusion matrix of the comined HOG, MBH and SIFT descriptors. Animals and means of transportation are less easily

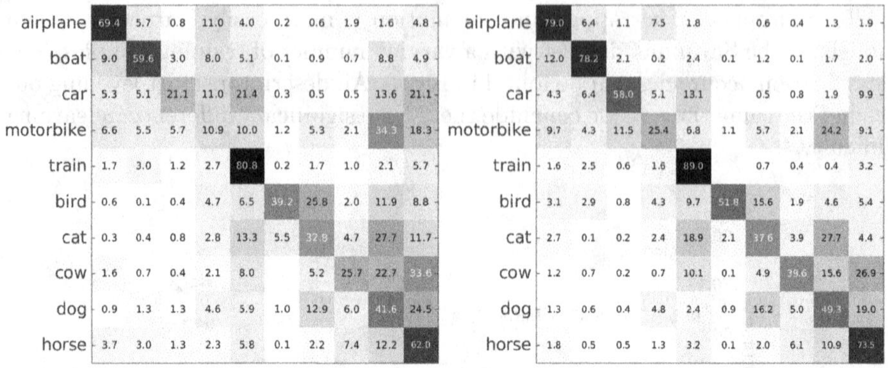

Confusion matrix with SIFT (left):

	airplane	boat	car	motorbike	train	bird	cat	cow	dog	horse
airplane	69.4	5.7	0.8	11.0	4.0	0.2	0.6	1.9	1.6	4.8
boat	9.0	59.6	3.0	8.0	5.1	0.1	0.9	0.7	8.8	4.9
car	5.3	5.1	21.1	11.0	21.4	0.3	0.5	0.5	13.6	21.1
motorbike	6.6	5.5	5.7	10.9	10.0	1.2	5.3	2.1	34.3	18.3
train	1.7	3.0	1.2	2.7	80.8	0.2	1.7	1.0	2.1	5.7
bird	0.6	0.1	0.4	4.7	6.5	39.2	25.8	2.0	11.9	8.8
cat	0.3	0.4	0.8	2.8	13.3	5.5	32.9	4.7	27.7	11.7
cow	1.6	0.7	0.4	2.1	8.0		5.2	25.7	22.7	33.6
dog	0.9	1.3	1.3	4.6	5.9	1.0	12.9	6.0	41.6	24.5
horse	3.7	3.0	1.3	2.3	5.8	0.1	2.2	7.4	12.2	62.0

Confusion matrix with combined descriptors HOG, MBH and SIFT (right):

	airplane	boat	car	motorbike	train	bird	cat	cow	dog	horse
airplane	79.0	6.4	1.1	7.5	1.8		0.6	0.4	1.3	1.9
boat	12.0	78.2	2.1	0.2	2.4	0.1	1.2	0.1	1.7	2.0
car	4.3	6.4	58.0	5.1	13.1		0.5	0.8	1.9	9.9
motorbike	9.7	4.3	11.5	25.4	6.8	1.1	5.7	2.1	24.2	9.1
train	1.6	2.5	0.6	1.8	89.0		0.7	0.4	0.4	3.2
bird	3.1	2.9	0.8	4.3	9.7	51.8	15.6	1.9	4.6	5.4
cat	2.7	0.1	0.2	2.4	18.9	2.1	37.6	3.9	27.7	4.4
cow	1.2	0.7	0.2	0.7	10.1	0.1	4.9	29.6	15.6	26.9
dog	1.3	0.6	0.4	4.8	2.4	0.9	16.2	5.0	49.3	19.0
horse	1.8	0.5	0.5	1.3	3.2	0.1	2.0	6.1	10.9	73.5

Fig. 6. Confusion matrix for the YouTube Objects dataset with SIFT (left) and combined descriptors HOG, MBH and SIFT (right).

confused with each other than the different types of animal (or transportation) are with each other.

As a disadvantage, use of motion descriptors increases calculation time, mainly because the optical flow has to be calculated in order to track points and obtain MBH and HOF.

6   Conclusion

Motion is often discarded in video object recognition. We have shown that a higher accuracy can be obtained when it is taken into account. In particular, combining HOG and MBH descriptors around a trajectory with a standard dense SIFT method results in significantly higher performance than using only SIFT. We have introduced two new datasets and adapted two existing datasets to the problem. These datasets will be made publicly available to stimulate and help further research on this topic.

References

1. Brox, T., Malik, J.: Object segmentation by long term analysis of point trajectories. In: Daniilidis, K., Maragos, P., Paragios, N. (eds.) ECCV 2010, Part V. LNCS, vol. 6315, pp. 282–295. Springer, Heidelberg (2010)
2. Dollár, P., Rabaud, V., Cottrell, G., Belongie, S.: Behavior recognition via sparse spatio-temporal features. In: 2005 2nd Joint IEEE International Workshop on Visual Surveillance and Performance Evaluation of Tracking and Surveillance, pp. 65–72. IEEE (2005)
3. Everingham, M., Van Gool, L., Williams, C.K.I., Winn, J., Zisserman, A.: The Pascal visual object classes (VOC) challenge. International Journal of Computer Vision 88(2), 303–338 (2010)

4. Felzenszwalb, P., McAllester, D., Ramanan, D.: A discriminatively trained, multi-scale, deformable part model. In: 2008 IEEE Conference on Computer Vision and Pattern Recognition, CVPR 2008, pp. 1–8. IEEE (2008)
5. Grundmann, M., Kwatra, V., Han, M., Essa, I.: Efficient hierarchical graph-based video segmentation. In: 2010 IEEE Conference on Computer Vision and Pattern Recognition (CVPR), pp. 2141–2148. IEEE (2010)
6. Kalogeiton, V., Ferrari, V., Schmid, C.: Analysing domain shift factors between videos and images for object detection (2015)
7. Laptev, I., Lindeberg, T.: Space-time interest points. In: 2003 Proceedings of the Ninth IEEE International Conference on Computer Vision, pp. 432–439. IEEE (2003)
8. Liu, L.-F., Jia, W., Zhu, Y.-H.: Survey of gait recognition. In: Huang, D.-S., Jo, K.-H., Lee, H.-H., Kang, H.-J., Bevilacqua, V. (eds.) ICIC 2009. LNCS, vol. 5755, pp. 652–659. Springer, Heidelberg (2009)
9. Liu, X., Tao, D., Song, M., Ruan, Y., Chen, C., Bu, J.: Weakly supervised multiclass video segmentation. In: Proceedings of the IEEE Conference on Computer Vision and Pattern Recognition, pp. 57–64 (2013)
10. Liu, Y., Jang, Y., Woo, W., Kim, T.K.: Video-based object recognition using novel set-of-sets representations. In: 2014 IEEE Conference on Computer Vision and Pattern Recognition Workshops (CVPRW), pp. 533–540 (2014)
11. Lowe, D.G.: Object recognition from local scale-invariant features. In: 1999 Proceedings of the Seventh IEEE International Conference on Computer vision, vol. 2, pp. 1150–1157. IEEE (1999)
12. Matikainen, P., Hebert, M., Sukthankar, R.: Trajectons: Action recognition through the motion analysis of tracked features. In: 2009 IEEE 12th International Conference on Computer Vision Workshops (ICCV Workshops), pp. 514–521. IEEE (2009)
13. Messing, R., Pal, C., Kautz, H.: Activity recognition using the velocity histories of tracked keypoints. In: 2009 IEEE 12th International Conference on Computer Vision, pp. 104–111. IEEE (2009)
14. Oneata, D., Revaud, J., Verbeek, J., Schmid, C.: Spatio-temporal object detection proposals. In: Fleet, D., Pajdla, T., Schiele, B., Tuytelaars, T. (eds.) ECCV 2014, Part III. LNCS, vol. 8691, pp. 737–752. Springer, Heidelberg (2014)
15. Prest, A., Leistner, C., Civera, J., Schmid, C., Ferrari, V.: Learning object class detectors from weakly annotated video. In: IEEE Conference on Computer Vision and Pattern Recognition, pp. 3282–3289, June 2012
16. Russakovsky, O., Deng, J., Su, H., Krause, J., Satheesh, S., Ma, S., Huang, Z., Karpathy, A., Khosla, A., Bernstein, M., Berg, A.C., Fei-Fei, L.: ImageNet large scale visual recognition challenge (2014)
17. Sivic, J., Zisserman, A.: Video Google: a text retrieval approach to object matching in videos. In: 2003 Proceedings of the Ninth IEEE International Conference on Computer Vision, pp. 1470–1477. IEEE (2003)
18. Snoek, C., Sande, K., Rooij, O., Huurnink, B., Uijlings, J., Liempt, M., Bugalhoy, M., Trancosoy, I., Yan, F., Tahir, M., et al.: The MediaMill TRECVID 2009 semantic video search engine. In: TRECVID Workshop (2009)
19. Viola, P., Jones, M.J., Snow, D.: Detecting pedestrians using patterns of motion and appearance. In: 2003 Proceedings of the Ninth IEEE International Conference on Computer Vision, pp. 734–741. IEEE (2003)
20. Wang, H., Klaser, A., Schmid, C., Liu, C.L.: Action recognition by dense trajectories. In: 2011 IEEE Conference on Computer Vision and Pattern Recognition (CVPR), pp. 3169–3176. IEEE (2011)

21. Wang, H., Schmid, C.: Action recognition with improved trajectories. In: 2013 IEEE International Conference on Computer Vision (ICCV), pp. 3551–3558. IEEE (2013)
22. Willems, G., Tuytelaars, T., Van Gool, L.: An efficient dense and scale-invariant spatio-temporal interest point detector. In: Forsyth, D., Torr, P., Zisserman, A. (eds.) ECCV 2008, Part II. LNCS, vol. 5303, pp. 650–663. Springer, Heidelberg (2008)
23. Yuen, J., Russell, B., Liu, C., Torralba, A.: Labelme video: building a video database with human annotations. In: 2009 IEEE 12th International Conference on Computer Vision, pp. 1451–1458. IEEE (2009)

Image Recognition in UAV Application Based on Texture Analysis

Dan Popescu[✉] and Loretta Ichim

Faculty of Automatic Control and Computers, University Politehnica of Bucharest,
Bucharest, Romania
dan.popescu@upb.ro, loretta.ichim@aii.pub.ro

Abstract. In this paper we propose a simple and efficient method of image classification in UAV monitoring application. Taking into consideration the color distribution two types of texture feature are considered: statistical and fractal characteristics. In the learning phase four different and efficient features were selected: energy, correlation, mean intensity and lacunarity on different color channel (R, G and B). Also, four classes of aerial images were considered (forest, buildings, grassland and flooding zone). The method of comparison, based on sub-images, average and the Minkovski distance, improves the performance of the texture-based classification. A set of 100 aerial images from UAV was tested for establishing the rate of correct classification.

Keywords: Aerial images · Image recognition · Lacunarity · Texture features

1 Introduction

A Drone or Unmanned Aerial Vehicle (UAV) is an aircraft without pilot which can be maneuvered automatically. Nowadays, UAV has various applications in civil surveillance [1], military actions [2] etc.

The main advantages of the unmanned aerial vehicles are: the reduced cost of the flights and timers shorter times for mission. The traditional classification of aerial images is expensive for the monitoring of the evolution for specific area regions. In this case, the UAV has many advantages in comparison with classical system [3]: the cost of monitoring the interest zone is reduced, the control of flying is better and the possibility of collecting various parameters due to attached sensors. In transportations systems and mapping applications it is important to identify the regions of interest.

In transportations systems, the UAV role for the roads area identifications [4,5] is important for traffic data collection. The actualization of the satellite images in modern mapping systems is expensive and limited. The UAV permits us to offer more details to user from satellite images due to low cost and high resolutions of the attached camera.

© Springer International Publishing Switzerland 2015
S. Battiato et al. (Eds.): ACIVS 2015, LNCS 9386, pp. 693–704, 2015.
DOI: 10.1007/978-3-319-25903-1_60

In Digital Aerial Imagery (DAI) process [3], the images are acquired from a small video camera attached to the aircraft. One economical alternative to reduce the price of the DAI acquisitions is to use an UAV system. This is an aircraft without pilot which can be automatically maneuvered.

In [6] the authors present a video surveillance method based on the consideration of the flood overflow as a monitoring object. The detection of flooding and waterlogging areas is produced by the processing of the images acquired by a remote cyber surveillance system.

Taken into account the motion detection, in [7] a solution for early flood and fire detection is presented. The method is simple and efficient and is based on real time video processing.

The regions of interest from aerial images can be detected and classified by the aid of the feature extraction and interpretation. At different scales, images can be considered as multi-textured type. Therefore, texture analysis of sub-images can be used to image classification or segmentation. Although direct color texture analysis was reported [8], we considered that color decomposition followed by selection of efficient features on each color channel give best results concerning the processing time and computing complexity.

The paper proposes a methodology for classification of images in order to highlight the flooding zone in different context like urban and non urban areas. The images are acquired from an UAV based system and are considered as static type. The classification process takes into account the average of features of the sub-images and Minkovski distance between the vectors of these features. As a consequence of a selection process in the RGB color space, three types of efficient features are used. Thus, from Gray Level Co-occurrence Matrix we extract statistical features and combine them with first statistic order and fractal features like lacunarity to improve the classification process.

2   Methodology for Image Acquisition

2.1   Characteristics of UAV System

For image acquisition an UAV Hirrus system [9] was used (Fig. 1). It is a hybrid system with a structure based on two main component parts: the fix part (or ground components) and the mobile part (the Unmanned Aerial Vehicle – UAV) – Fig. 2. The ground components are the following: GCS (Ground Control Station – with the task of data and control management), GDT (Ground Data Transmission – which represents the communication node between GCS and UAV) and the Launcher (the launching mechanism for the UAV). The UAV platform contains a retractable payload with camera equipment, stabilized for vibrations. The acquired images are transmitted to GCS via GTD by corresponding blocks (telemetry and video).

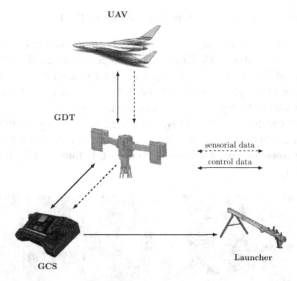

Fig. 1. Hirrus system

The main features and technical specification are presented below.

— High resolution imagery;
— GIS support;
— Automatic navigation;
— Antenna tracking system;
— Retractable gyro-stabilized payload;
— Mission planning software application;
— Application: critical infrastructures, photography, cartography; recognition missions and so on;
— Maximum cruise speed: 130 km/h;
— Maximum camera weight: 0.7 kg;
— Maximum altitude: 3000 m;
— Operating range: 15 km in classical regime; 30 km in autopilot regime.

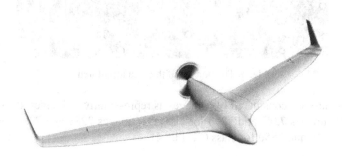

Fig. 2. UAV – aerial platform Hirrus

2.2   Aerial Photo Acquisition and Grouping Method

Images were taken concatenated from a digital orthophotography in a predetermined area created by the aid of UAV Hirrus. Each image has attached an ID.

The analyzed images were taken by a compact system camera. The images were analyzed in the RGB space and HSV in order to select the proper features, color space and color channels which give the best classification accuracy.

In Fig. 3 it can be seen that ID was allocated sequentially in order of lanes, from monitoring area. Four classes of images were considered. The representatives of the classes are shown in Fig. 4 (flooding zones – C1, forest – C2, grassland – C3 and buildings – C4).

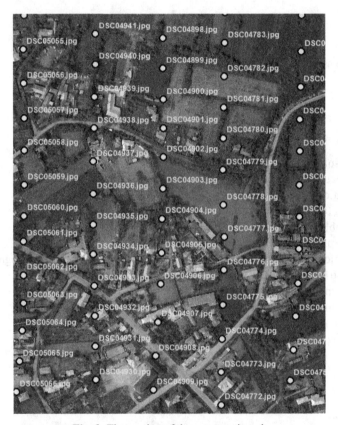

Fig. 3. The portion of the area monitored

For each class we considered two images as representatives: images 4881 and 4904 for class C1; images 7342 and 7290 for class C2; images 7281 and 7386 for class C3 and images 7526 and 7550 for class C4 (Fig. 4).

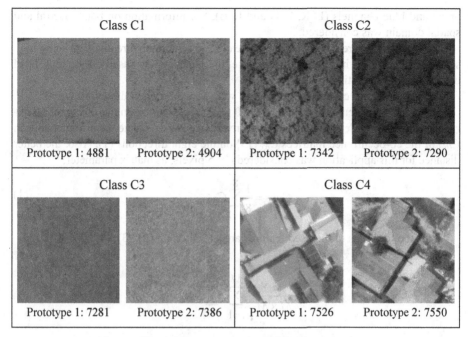

Fig. 4. The representatives of the classes

2.3 Texture Selection for Image Classification

For the classification process, the choice of features aims to select of highly discriminate features. In other words, it was selected the features that are able of discriminating between different classes. For the problem of features selection for classification, a significant number of different features were tested on 100 color images and then each relevant feature was assessed. With the aim of classification, the analyzed images were grouped into four classes (flooding zones, forest, grassland and buildings). The features with extremely high difference values between classes and low difference values inside the classes are considered.

Evaluation of features was made experimentally in RGB and HSV color space. We tested different categories of feature: statistics of order one, statistics of order two, extracted from gray level co-occurrence matrices – GLCM [10], statistics from difference image and fractal type [11,12,13]. The features tested were: mean intensity, standard deviation, entropy, energy, homogeneity, contrast, correlation, variance, mean intensity of image difference, fractal dimension and lacunarity on R, G, B and H component of color spaces. All the formulas for these features are well known and are presented in common literature [10], [13], [14].

With respect to the above considerations we select the basic color channels R, G, B and the following features: mean intensity on red and green channels (Im_R and Im_G) two textural features extracted from GLCM matrix, namely energy on red, green and blue channels (En_R, En_G and En_B) and correlation on red and green channels (Cor_R and Cor_G), and one from fractal category, lacunarity [13], on red, green and blue channels (L_R, L_G and L_B). So, information on both spectral and spatial domain was considered.

The lacunarity were a complementary feature in remote texture analysis being high sensitive to the gaps in images. In our case, the lacunarity is based on the gray level differential box-counting approach.

The features from co-occurrence matrix were tested on eight directions ($i = 0°$, $45°$, ..., $315°$) and on different distances (1 to 10 pixels), depending on the texture characteristics. Finally, in order to obtain rotation invariance, we calculate the arithmetic mean Cm_d of the co-occurrence matrices $C_{d,i}$ [15] on the eight directions (1). Also, the better distance for this application was considered $d = 5$ pixels, as matrix parameter:

$$Cm_5 = \frac{1}{8} \sum_{i=1}^{8} C_{5,i} \tag{1}$$

Thus, the formulas of the used features are as following (2), (3), (4), (5).
Mean intensity:

$$Im = \frac{1}{M \times M} \sum_{i=1}^{M} \sum_{j=1}^{M} I(i,j) \tag{2}$$

Energy:

$$En = \sum_{i=1}^{L} \sum_{j=1}^{L} Cm_5(i,j)^2 \tag{3}$$

Correlation:

$$Cor = \sum_{i=1}^{L} \sum_{j=1}^{L} ij Cm_5(i,j) \tag{4}$$

Lacunarity:

$$L(r) = \frac{\sum_N N^2 \cdot P(N,r)}{[\sum_N N \cdot P(N,r)]^2}, \quad N = \sum_u \sum_v n_r(u,v) \tag{5}$$

In equation (5) the lacunarity $L(r)$ depends from a division factor r. The term $n_r(u,v)$ represents the difference between the maximum value and the minimum value of the intensity on the box in the (u,v) position of the squared grid obtained by division factor r [13].

The lacunarity notations L_R, L_G and L_B represent the averages of $L(r)$ on the channels R, G and B, respectively, for all possible values of r.

In the above formulas, $M{\times}M$ is the image dimension, $I(i,j)$ is the value of the pixel (i,j) on a specific color channel (R, G or B), L represents the number of intensity level on a color channel.

Because there are great differences between the values of the features, in order to correctly evaluate the distance, a normalized process of these features is necessary.

We tested three well known distances between two vectors as: Chebyshev, Euclidian and Minkovski distances [16]. Chebyshev distance gives more errors in the classification process (20 errors from 100 test images) than Euclidian distance or Minkovski distance with $p = 1$ (2 errors from 100 test images). Because Minkovski distance ($p = 1$) needs less computing effort than Euclidian distance we choose Minkovski distance in our application. Thus, the Minkovski distance between two vectors x and y as classification criterion is given by the following formula (6):

$$D_M(x,y) = \left(\sum_{i=1}^{n} |x_i - y_i|^p \right)^{\frac{1}{p}} \tag{6}$$

Let I_1 and I_2 be two images which are characterized by the following features mentioned above. We consider the Minkovski distance D_M of order $p = 1$ between images I_1 and I_2 as distance between the feature vectors (7):

$$\begin{aligned}
D_M(I_1, I_2) = & \left| Im\_R_i - Im\_R_j \right| + \left| Im\_G_i - Im\_G_j \right| + \\
& \left| En\_R_i - En\_R_j \right| + \left| En\_G_i - En\_G_j \right| + \left| En\_B_i - En\_B_j \right| + \\
& \left| Cor\_R_i - Con\_R_j \right| + \left| Cor\_G_i - Con\_G_j \right| + \left| L\_R_i - L\_R_j \right| + \\
& \left| L\_G_i - L\_G_j \right| + \left| L\_B_i - L\_B_j \right|
\end{aligned} \tag{7}$$

The images captured by the UAV are classified according to prototypes of the classes considered. We considered two images as prototypes for each class.

The images to be analyzed are also split into non-overlapping sub-images, which are characterized in the feature space, of size 10. The splitting of the image is necessary for improving the image recognition process in terms of computing time. It allows the parallel computing of the features for each sub-image. Also, the principle of the Minkovski distance method allows the parallel computing of the elements of the distance involved in the classification process. These two elements lower the overall processing time. The image features in equation (7) are considered as average of the same features of sub-images.

In fact, the distances between acquired images and the classes are needed to be evaluated. The features of the classes are considered as the average of the same features of all sub-images of the prototypes.

The method used to compute the lacunarity was implemented using FracLac [17], which is a plug-in of ImageJ, a public domain Java image processing program. Several other MATLAB programs were subsequently used for image processing and for computing the other texture features.

3   Experimental Results

In order to evaluate the efficiency of the method, a number of 100 aerial images were selected to be classified. Both the learning images (prototypes) and test images were taken by a camera Sony Nex7, objective 50 mm, 24.3 megapixels, 10 fps; flight speed of 70 km/h and flight level 300 m. In order to select small representative areas, from the initial images were cropped windows of size 512×512 pixels.

The image prototypes were chosen such as to be representative for one of the four considered classes (Fig. 4). Some of the test images are presented in Fig. 5.

Fig. 5. Images for classification test

The values of the features for the classes and test images are presented in Table 1. These are considered as average on the columns and the results are underlined by gray color.

Table 1. The values of the image features.

Image ID	Sub-image	En_R	En_G	En_B	Im_R	Im_G	Cor_R	Cor_G	L_R	L_G	L_B
Representative of the classes											
4881	1	0.966	0.366	0.960	0.576	0.493	0.838	0.424	0.792	0.776	0.722
	2	0.973	0.952	0.941	0.556	0.482	0.730	0.035	0.798	0.784	0.742
	3	0.926	0.784	0.675	0.581	0.480	0.092	0.185	0.669	0.681	0.663
	4	0.819	0.874	0.483	0.594	0.460	0.082	0.623	0.997	0.953	0.869
4904	1	0.355	0.410	0.891	0.635	0.475	0.383	0.249	0.363	0.426	0.455
	2	0.341	0.443	0.897	0.635	0.472	0.443	0.404	0.356	0.411	0.444
	3	0.393	0.629	0.919	0.634	0.474	0.405	0.158	0.363	0.410	0.424
	4	0.310	0.553	0.859	0.616	0.464	0.444	0.426	0.281	0.285	0.287

Table 1. (*Continued*)

Image ID	Sub-image	En_R	En_G	En_B	Im_R	Im_G	Cor_R	Cor_G	L_R	L_G	L_B
Class C1 – flooding zones	-	0.635	0.626	0.828	0.603	0.474	0.427	0.313	0.580	0.594	0.578
7342	1	0.158	0.116	0.204	0.280	0.366	0.421	0.511	0.186	0.188	0.177
	2	0.175	0.131	0.214	0.266	0.354	0.540	0.619	0.185	0.192	0.182
	3	0.104	0.084	0.185	0.350	0.455	0.497	0.541	0.171	0.170	0.164
	4	0.217	0.162	0.230	0.301	0.395	0.411	0.480	0.186	0.188	0.181
7290	1	0.458	0.343	0.737	0.156	0.220	0.541	0.581	0.208	0.224	0.194
	2	0.490	0.418	0.763	0.151	0.213	0.549	0.609	0.183	0.215	0.176
	3	0.442	0.313	0.722	0.164	0.231	0.649	0.701	0.175	0.186	0.167
	4	0.525	0.480	0.855	0.151	0.215	0.481	0.519	0.156	0.175	0.155
Class C2 – forest	-	0.321	0.255	0.488	0.227	0.306	0.515	0.570	0.181	0.192	0.174
7281	1	0.796	0.581	0.880	0.418	0.470	0.208	0.332	0.214	0.214	0.211
	2	0.580	0.893	0.948	0.399	0.450	0.235	0.142	0.208	0.205	0.203
	3	0.870	0.608	0.899	0.426	0.474	0.274	0.180	0.282	0.267	0.275
	4	0.457	0.903	0.834	0.391	0.446	0.462	0.094	0.217	0.219	0.212
7386	1	0.587	0.332	0.273	0.564	0.608	0.120	0.111	0.200	0.198	0.198
	2	0.678	0.315	0.294	0.575	0.614	0.111	0.119	0.208	0.211	0.207
	3	0.479	0.254	0.356	0.575	0.617	0.139	0.121	0.194	0.194	0.196
	4	0.393	0.248	0.486	0.599	0.631	0.390	0.249	0.185	0.183	0.183
Class C3 – grassland	-	0.605	0.516	0.621	0.493	0.538	0.242	0.168	0.213	0.211	0.210
7526	1	0.559	0.157	0.249	0.906	0.555	0.909	0.913	0.781	0.771	0.757
	2	0.213	0.126	0.108	0.734	0.647	0.870	0.903	0.801	0.971	0.759
	3	0.229	0.195	0.117	0.783	0.640	0.871	0.881	0.589	0.533	0.961
	4	0.129	0.158	0.153	0.678	0.470	0.922	0.815	0.609	0.537	0.515
7550	1	0.102	0.119	0.126	0.666	0.555	0.881	0.801	0.570	0.562	0.537
	2	0.083	0.108	0.124	0.593	0.557	0.879	0.790	0.569	0.584	0.543
	3	0.122	0.157	0.133	0.660	0.568	0.851	0.788	0.721	0.671	0.657
	4	0.101	0.096	0.089	0.661	0.596	0.890	0.861	0.582	0.561	0.537
Class C4 – buildings		0.192	0.139	0.137	0.710	0.573	0.886	0.844	0.653	0.648	0.657
Test images											
4902 (flooding zones)	1	0.464	0.905	0.983	0.513	0.422	0.285	0.092	0.366	0.376	0.365
	2	0.402	0.849	0.982	0.510	0.420	0.415	0.138	0.269	0.273	0.265
	3	0.517	0.632	0.952	0.474	0.399	0.698	0.363	0.413	0.421	0.399
	4	0.312	0.796	0.968	0.491	0.413	0.539	0.328	0.591	0.598	0.591
Image features	-	0.424	0.795	0.971	0.497	0.414	0.484	0.230	0.409	0.417	0.405
7333 (forest)	1	0.409	0.255	0.615	0.154	0.233	0.531	0.581	0.177	0.187	0.174
	2	0.561	0.309	0.804	0.162	0.220	0.419	0.498	0.158	0.164	0.155
	3	0.501	0.274	0.724	0.168	0.236	0.429	0.551	0.151	0.157	0.145
	4	0.525	0.271	0.708	0.174	0.246	0.421	0.560	0.136	0.144	0.135

702   D. Popescu and L. Ichim

Table 1. (*Continued*)

Image features	-	0.498	0.277	0.713	0.165	0.234	0.450	0.550	0.156	0.163	0.152
7354 (grassland)	1	0.493	0.276	0.440	0.578	0.648	0.121	0.181	0.210	0.206	0.219
	2	0.446	0.282	0.463	0.574	0.650	0.201	0.217	0.224	0.219	0.229
	3	0.431	0.298	0.431	0.576	0.652	0.197	0.233	0.213	0.211	0.224
	4	0.464	0.322	0.598	0.559	0.647	0.302	0321	0.215	0.212	0.227
Image features	-	0.458	0.295	0.483	0.572	0.649	0.210	0.240	0.215	0.212	0.225
7537 (buildings)	1	0.159	0.115	0.133	0.766	0.547	0.841	0.881	0.520	0.531	0.505
	2	0.073	0.058	0.062	0.689	0.629	0.822	0.762	0.507	0.476	0.460
	3	0.133	0.167	0.317	0.485	0.627	0.807	0.836	0.611	0.651	0.641
	4	0.231	0.083	0.086	0.805	0.643	0.890	0.841	0.435	0.439	0.402
Image features	-	0.149	0.106	0.149	0.689	0.611	0.840	0.830	0.518	0.524	0.502
4903 (flooding zones)	1	0.707	0.949	0.965	0.965	0.990	0.705	0.271	0.576	0.597	0.456
	2	0.192	0.420	0.513	0.839	0.997	0.781	0.619	0.702	0.703	0.699
	3	0.732	0.985	0.997	0.967	0.910	0.681	0.264	0.436	0.428	0.376
	4	0.656	0.922	0.975	0.921	0.981	0.272	0.062	0.433	0.406	0.398
Image features	-	0.572	0.819	0.862	0.496	0.403	0.609	0.304	0.536	0.533	0.482
7287 (forest)	1	0.376	0.259	0.331	0.195	0.275	0.580	0.661	0.218	0.200	0.213
	2	0.311	0.266	0.311	0.208	0.297	0.611	0.674	0.222	0.230	0.208
	3	0.341	0.251	0.292	0.215	0.302	0.553	0.665	0.235	0.216	0.225
	4	0.306	0.239	0.315	0.200	0.285	0.606	0.690	0.269	0.235	0.267
Image features	-	0.334	0.254	0.312	0.205	0.289	0.590	0.670	0.219	0.220	0.214
7353 (grassland)	1	0.791	0.674	0.801	0.550	0.596	0.441	0.161	0.320	0.303	0.337
	2	0.620	0.454	0.707	0.551	0.599	0.440	0.280	0.319	0.312	0.349
	3	0.518	0.652	0.730	0.537	0.578	0.352	0.319	0.336	0.294	0.325
	4	0.716	0.373	0.681	0.566	0.610	0.481	0.341	0.313	0.306	0.333
Image features	-	0.661	0.538	0.729	0.550	0.595	0.420	0.280	0.322	0.304	0.336
7536 (buildings)	1	0.249	0.177	0.185	0.813	0.547	0.861	0.920	0.971	0.871	0.872
	2	0.221	0.125	0.148	0.814	0.737	0.863	0.871	0.701	0.870	0.678
	3	0.110	0.112	0.138	0.666	0.645	0.835	0.837	0.528	0.435	0.524
	4	0.469	0.145	0.205	0.885	0.536	0.881	0.912	0.957	0.635	0.864
Image features	-	0.282	0.159	0.157	0.775	0.578	0.86	0.880	0.789	0.773	0.734

In Table 2 we present the Minkovski distance between the test images and classes, the class assigned as consequence of process classification and the classification score considered as 1 for correct assign and 0 for incorrect. In this table all tested images are correctly classified. Overall, 98 images from 100 were correctly classified.

The running time for classification of an image was 9.7 s on a computer with processor Intel Pentium Dual CPU E2200, 2.20 GHz, 3 GB of RAM using Matlab R2013a.

Table 2. Distances between test images and classes.

Class / Image	C1	C2	C3	C4	Class assigned	Classification score
4902	**1.35**	2.56	1.84	3.84	C1	1
4903	**0.86**	2.92	2.13	3.39	C1	1
7333	2,82	**0.72**	1.82	4.12	C2	1
7287	3.39	**0.51**	2.25	2.99	C2	1
7354	2.45	1.61	**0.82**	3.57	C3	1
7353	3.23	2.28	**0.92**	3.67	C3	1
7537	3.05	3.01	3.78	**0.62**	C4	1
7536	3.31	3.39	4.46	**0.60**	C4	1

4   Conclusions

In this paper we present a simple and efficient method for aerial image classification based on three types of textural features: statistic order one (mean intensity), statistical order two (extracted from mean co-occurrence matrix) and fractal type (lacunarity). The images are obtained by the over-flight of an UAV and are grouped in four categories. The classification algorithm takes into consideration the partitioning of the images into sub-images and comparing the vectors of the feature average. The method of comparison based on Minkovski distance offers good results in this classification process.

Acknowledgements. The work has been funded by National Research Program STAR, project 71/2013: Multisensory robotic system for aerial monitoring of critical infrastructure systems - MUROS.

References

1. Pahsa, A., Kaya, P., Alat, G., Baykal, B.: Integrating navigation amp; surveillance of unmanned air vehicles into the civilian national airspaces by using ADS-B applications. In: Integrated Communications, Navigation and Surveilance Conference (ICNS 2011), pp. J7–1–J7–7 H (2011)
2. Dufrene Jr., W.R.: Mobile military security with concentration on unmanned aerial vehicles. In: 24th Conference in Digital Avionics Systems (DASC 2005), vol. 2, 8D.3, pp. 1–8 (2005)
3. Ahmad, A., Tahar, K.N., Udin, W.S., Hashim, K.A., Darwin, N., Hafis, M., Room, M., Hamid, N.F.A., Azhar, N.A.M., Azmi, S.M.: Digital aerial imagery of unmanned aerial vehicle for various applications. In: IEEE International Conference on Control System, Computing and Engineering (ICCSCE 2013), pp. 535–540 (2013)
4. He, Y., Wang, H., Zhang, B.: Color-based road detection in urban traffic scenes. IEEE Trans. Intell. Transp. Syst. **5**, 309–318 (2004)

5. Zhou, H., Kong, H., Wei, L., Creighton, D., Nahavandi, S.: Efficient road detection and tracking for Unmanned Aerial Vehicle. IEEE Trans. Intell. Transp. Syst. **16**, 297–309 (2015)
6. Lo, S.-W., Wu, J.-H., Lin, F.-P., Hsu, C.-H.: Cyber surveillance for flood disasters. Sensors **15**, 2369–2387 (2015)
7. Lai, C.L., Yang, J.C., Chen, Y.H.: A real time video processing based surveillance system for early fire and flood detection. In: Instrumentation and Measurement Technology Conference (IMTC 2007), Warsaw, Poland, pp. 1–6 (2007)
8. Losson, O., Porebski, A., Vandenbroucke, N., Macaire, L.: Color texture analysis using CFA chromatic co-occurrence matrices. Computer Vision and Image Understanding **117**, 747–763 (2013)
9. www.aft.ro/bro.pdf
10. Haralick, R., Shanmugam, K., Dinstein, I.: Textural Features for Image Classification. IEEE Transactions on Systems, Man, and Cybernetics **SMC-3**, 610–620 (1973)
11. Sarker, N., Chaudhuri, B.B.: An efficient differential box-counting approach to compute fractal dimension of image. IEEE Transactions on Systems, Man, and Cybernetics **24**, 115–120 (1994)
12. Chaudhuri, B.B., Sarker, N.: Texture segmentation using fractal dimension. IEEE Transactions on Pattern Analysis and Machine Intelligence **17**, 72–77 (1995)
13. Barros Filho, M.N., Sobreira, F.J.A.: Accuracy of lacunarity algorithms in texture classification of high spatial resolution images from urban areas. In: XXI Congress of International Society of Photogrammetry and Remote Sensing (ISPRS 2008), Beijing, China, pp. 417–422 (2008)
14. Pratt, W.: Digital Image Processing: PIKS Inside, 3rd edn. John Wiley & Sons, Inc. (2001)
15. Popescu, D., Dobrescu, R., Angelescu, N.: Statistical texture analysis of road for moving objectives. U.P.B. Sci. Bull. Series C. **70**, 75–84 (2008)
16. Deza, E. Deza M.: Dictionary of Distances. Elsevier (2006)
17. Karperien, A.: FracLac for ImageJ, available on line at: http://rsb.info.nih.gov/ij/plugins/fraclac/FLHelp/Introduction.htm

Cascaded Regressions of Learning Features for Face Alignment

Ngoc-Trung Tran[1,2]([✉]), Fakhreddine Ababsa[2], Sarra Ben Fredj[3],
and Maurice Charbit[1]

[1] LTCI-CNRS, Telecom ParisTECH, 37-39, Rue Dareau, 75014 Paris, France
tntrung@gmail.com
[2] IBISC, University of Evry, 40, Rue du Pelvoux, 91020 Evry, France
[3] UFE, Paris Observatory, 5, Place Jules Janssen, 92195 Meudon, France

Abstract. Face alignment is a fundamental problem in computer vision to localize the landmarks of eyes, nose or mouth in 2D images. In this paper, our method for face alignment integrates three aspects not seen in previous approaches: First, learning local descriptors using Restricted Boltzmann Machine (RBM) to model the local appearance of each facial points independently. Second, proposing the coarse-to-fine regression to localize the landmarks after the estimation of the shape configuration via global regression. Third, and using synthetic data as training data to enable our approach to work better with the profile view, and to forego the need of increasing the number of annotations for training. Our results on challenging datasets compare favorably with state of the art results. The combination with the synthetic data allows our method yielding good results in profile alignment. That highlights the potential of using synthetic data for in-the-wild face alignment.

Keywords: Face alignment · Cascaded regression · Face tracking · Learning feature

1 Introduction

Face alignment is a fundamental problem in computer vision that has received considerable attention. It aims to localize the landmarks of eyes, nose or mouth in 2D images. A lot of studies over the last decade has provided significant progress (Belhumeur et al. [2011]; Cootes et al. [2001]; Cristinacce and Cootes [2006]; Wang et al. [2008]; X. Zhu [2012]), but it still remains as a difficult problem because of many challenging conditions, such as: the pose variation, face expression and illumination conditions. In recent years, cascaded regression has become the leading approach for accurate and robust face alignment, in which most of them has achieved state-of-the-art performance. The basic idea of this approach is to use a sequence of weak regressors, which are learned sequentially. The pioneer works of cascaded regression have been proposed in (Dollar et al. [2010]; M. F. Valstar and Pantic [2010]) for object alignment, then

© Springer International Publishing Switzerland 2015
S. Battiato et al. (Eds.): ACIVS 2015, LNCS 9386, pp. 705–716, 2015.
DOI: 10.1007/978-3-319-25903-1_61

improved in (Cao et al. [2012]) and applied successfully for face alignment. (Burgos-Artizzu et al. [2013]) inherited the framework of (Dollar et al. [2010]) to use the extra information (visible or invisible) of landmarks to work robustly with occlusions. (Xiong and la Torre Frade [2013]) proposed Supervised Descent Method (SDM) explaining naturally and precisely the cascaded manner, which used simple linear regressors to achieve superior performances. (Ren et al. [2014]) sped up SDM using learned local binary features. (Kazemi and Sullivan [2014]) also used a set of regression trees to accelerate the cascaded process. (Sun et al. [2013]; Zhang et al. [2014]; Zhou et al. [2013]) used deep networks to learn features at multi-scale sizes from coarse to fine. (Zhao et al. [2013]) proposed a cascaded pruning method to remove incorrect landmark candidates. (Yan et al. [2013]) improved the sensitive initialization of SDM by learning the combination of multiple hypotheses with ranking.

Through observation and experiment, we find out that cascaded regression has some specific problems. First, the later regressors tend to be over-weaker than early regressors. This problem has been mentioned in (Cao et al. [2012]; Sun et al. [2013]), but none of efficient method has been proposed for this problem. Second, it is sensitive to initialization. (Cao et al. [2012]; Yan et al. [2013]) analyzed deeply this problem and proposed good solutions. Third, the local descriptor is a critical factor needs to be well-designed to obtain a robust alignment, and a large amount of works focused on this problem, (Cao et al. [2012]; Kazemi and Sullivan [2014]; Ren et al. [2014]; Xiong and la Torre Frade [2013]). Fourth, the capability of strong generalization of facial variations and the flexibility with data scale. Unlike discriminative approach, for example, Constrained Local Model (CLM) (Saragih et al. [2011]; Wang et al. [2008]) using linear SVMs (non-linear SVM is too expensive) to train patch models that is difficult to capture well patch variations on large scale data. Otherwise, if having more training data, the cascaded method still models well by simply increasing the number of regressors while the time consuming is not more significantly consumed. However, the campaign of ground-truth is too expensive, particularly for the profile view.

In this study, we focus on the first, third and fourth problems. We first propose the use of learning feature to represent discriminating local region. We then propose a coarse-to-fine regression in order to localize more accurate landmark locations. Finally, we propose the use of synthetic data to verify if it is possible to have good performances while saving time and human resources. The synthetic data is an adequate tool to build a robust profile alignment system. Validated on challenging databases our method, compared to some others from the state-of-the-art, provides significant improvements and more robustness.

The remaining sections are organized as follows: Section 2 presents the method in detail. Empirical experiments are performed and analyzed in Section 3. The conclusion and further works are discussed in Section 4.

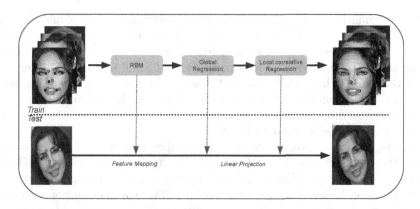

Fig. 1. The overview of our approach. In training, we learn sequentially RBM models, coarse-to-find regression (global and correlative regression).

2   Our Method

2.1   Cascaded Regression

Let the shape $\mathbf{S} \in R^{2p \times 1}$ be the coordinate vector of p facial landmarks. Let $\widehat{\mathbf{S}}$ be true shape. The goal of face alignment is to align the shape $\mathbf{S}$ as closely as the true shape by minimizing $\|\widehat{\mathbf{S}} - \mathbf{S}\|$. To estimate the shape, we use a sequence of T weak regressors $(\mathbf{r}(1), \mathbf{r}(2), ..., \mathbf{r}(T))$, $\mathbf{r}(t) \in R^{2p \times pd}$, pd is the dimension of feature $\Phi \in R^{pd \times 1}$ extracted from the image, d is the feature size of one landmark:

$$\mathbf{S}(t) = \mathbf{S}(t-1) + \mathbf{r}(t)\Phi(I, \mathbf{S}(t-1)), \quad t = 1, ..., T \qquad (1)$$

Given the facial image I and the initial face shape $\mathbf{S}(0)$, one weak regressor $\mathbf{r}(t)$ estimates the new shape $\mathbf{S}(t)$ at time t from image features $\Phi(I, \mathbf{S}(t-1))$ computed using the previous shape $\mathbf{S}(t-1)$ on the image I. The sequential training of the weak regressors $\mathbf{r}(t)$ is based on N examples $\{(I_i, \widehat{\mathbf{S}}_i)\}_{i=1}^{N}$ by minimization as:

$$\arg\min_{\mathbf{r}(t)} \sum_{i=1}^{N} \left\| \widehat{\mathbf{S}}_i - (\mathbf{S}_i(t-1) + \mathbf{r}(t)\Phi(I_i, \mathbf{S}_i(t-1))) \right\|_2^2 \qquad (2)$$

The initial shape $\mathbf{S}(0)$ is simply the mean shape aligned in the area detected by the face detectors. This minimization is a linear regression problem whose solution is in closed-form. We use the same way like (Xiong and la Torre Frade [2013]) to train the sequence of weak regressors and use SIFT as its features.

2.2   Local Learning Feature

In addition to weak regressor learning, the facial representation via $\Phi(I, \mathbf{S}(t-1))$ is important. Largely, Φ is usually a concatenation vector of p landmark descriptors $\Phi = [\phi_1^T ... \phi_p^T]^T$. Hence, the local descriptor $\phi_i \in R^{d \times 1}$

of i-th landmark is critical to have good performances. It could be the designed features (Dalal and Triggs [2005]; Xiong and la Torre Frade [2013]) or the learning features (Cao et al. [2012]; Ren et al. [2014]). For example, (Xiong and la Torre Frade [2013]) learned PCA of SIFT (Lowe [2004]) descriptors of random patches. (Cao et al. [2012]) learned ferns from difference of pixel intensities and (Kazemi and Sullivan [2014]) improved this feature by exponential that regressed by regression trees. (Ren et al. [2014]) proposed local binary features using regression random forest.

In this study, we propose to use an unsupervised method to learn efficiently the representation of local patches. We find out the Restricted Boltzmann Machine (RBM) (Hinton and Salakhutdinov [2006]) is a good approach for our purpose. In addition, we can consider RBM as a dimensional reduction method if we state a number of hidden units smaller than of visible units. To learn the appearance model of l-th landmark using RBM, N_{rand} points are randomly sampled in its local region to localize training patches where then local features are extracted from. The normalized intensity pixels is considered as the feature from patch size $(N_{size} \times N_{size})$. The RBM model is then trained from these random patches. In our method, RBM models are trained independently for landmarks. ϕ now is considered as the output vector of top layer (dimension N_{hidden}) of RBM that used as local features in stages of cascaded regression.

2.3   Coarse-to-Fine Cascaded Regression (CCR)

In cascaded regression, the later regressors tend to be over-weaker than earlier regressors. Through empirical experiments, we found that in the behavior of cascaded regression training, each pair of landmarks has a particular relationship with the constraint of global shape configuration. In this section, we would propose a new way, local coarse-to-fine regression, to avoid partly this problem. The main idea is to use a set of N_c random landmarks to localize one specific landmark with the constraint of shape. In other words, one landmark position can be localized by using its descriptor and descriptors of other landmarks. The value N_c will gradually be reduced in later regression stages. However, the question is which landmarks should be chosen for each subset? {Fig. 5} shows the performance examples of each pair of landmarks using cross-validation reported in Experimental section. It turns out that there is not much difference when detecting one landmark using its self-descriptor or other landmark descriptors in the cascaded regression training behavior. Let others landmark to detect one specific landmark be correlative landmarks. It seems the performance belongs only to landmarks that need to be detected. For example, the performance when detecting 4-th landmark seems better than 18-th landmark even whatever correlative landmark was used. It means they are likely equal to be chosen to detect other facial landmarks. Notice that in Fig. 5 the horizontal axis is the Root Mean Square (RMS) error normalized by eye pupil distance. The vertical axis is the percentage of image numbers has the RMS error lower than each specific thresholds indicated from horizontal axis.

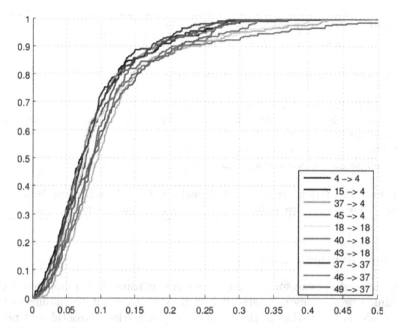

Fig. 2. Sample evaluation of local correlative regression. Example of using i-th to detect jth landmarks, $i \rightarrow j$.

The equality of correlative landmarks as above allows to choose the subset of landmarks by randomly sampling the correlative landmarks for a specific landmark. The l-th landmark has N_c correlative landmarks whose indices are chosen randomly. Notice that correlative landmarks are re-sampled at every stage of regression. These landmarks (including l-th landmark) become a group G_l used to localize the new position of l-th landmarks. The local correlative regression at stage t is a linear regression problem:

$$\arg\min_{r_{G_l}} \sum_{i=1}^{N} \left\| \pi_{G_l} \circ \Delta \widehat{\mathbf{S}}_i(t) - \mathbf{r}_{G_l}(t) \phi\left(I_i, \pi_{G_l} \circ \mathbf{S}_i(t-1)\right) \right\|_2^2 \qquad (3)$$

where i is the index of the training sample, the operator $\pi_{G_l} \circ \Delta \widehat{\mathbf{S}}_i(t)$ extracts the 2D positions of G_l landmarks from ground-truth shape increment $\Delta \widehat{\mathbf{S}}_i(t) = \widehat{\mathbf{S}}_i(t) - \mathbf{S}_i(t-1)$, and $\phi\left(I_i, \pi_{G_l} \circ \mathbf{S}_i(t-1)\right)$ is the local descriptors of G_l landmarks on image I_i. The weak regressor $\mathbf{r}_{G_l}$ learned to localize the incremental of l-th landmark position. However, only the l-th landmark position are updated for the next stage of regression. At the first regression, G_l is the group of all landmarks. Except the first stage, the k-th landmark is computed as average of the same landmark positions estimated from groups because k-th is chosen randomly in other groups. The learning of coarse-to-fine regression is reported in {Algorithm 1}.

Algorithm 1. Learning weak regressors at stage t.

INPUT: The training data $\{I_i, \hat{\mathbf{S}}_i(t-1), \mathbf{S}_i(t-1), \Phi(I_i, \mathbf{S}_i(t-1))\}$. N_c landmarks for one group.
OUTPUT: Local regressors $\mathbf{r}_{G_l}(t)$ and $\{\hat{\mathbf{S}}_i(t)\}$.

1: **for** $l = 1 : p$ (the number of landmarks) **do**
2:    Choose randomly N_c landmark $(l_0, l_1, l_2, \ldots l_{N_m-1})$ for group G_l to learn correlative regression. $l_0 \equiv l$.
3:    Learn the regressor $\mathbf{r}_{G_l}(t)$ using {Eqn. 3}.
4:    Compute the incremental $\pi_{G_l} \circ \Delta\hat{\mathbf{S}}_i(t)$.
5: **end for**
6: Computing $\{\hat{\mathbf{S}}_i(t)\}$ using $\pi_{G_l} \circ \Delta\hat{\mathbf{S}}_i(t)$ and $\{\hat{\mathbf{S}}_i(t-1)\}$. Notice one landmark is computed as the average of its positions chosen randomly in many groups G_l.

2.4   Using Synthetic Data

Building a good dataset for face alignment is expensive. It is more challenging if containing profile views, because it is impossible to annotate landmarks that people could not see. Hence, the number of landmarks of frontal and profile faces are always differently annotated in available datasets (Gross et al. [2010]; Koestinger et al. [2011]). That makes a gap of how to align multi-views using one single model. Indeed, the view-based models are the possible solution for this problem (Cootes et al. [2002]; X. Zhu [2012]); however, it requires the pose detectors to determine which view needs to be used. This is why most of cascaded methods are not good for non-frontal views. In contrast, if using synthetic data, the same number of points at all views enable the alignment performed exactly the same. The use of synthetic data is likely a good approach to work with profiles, so we include the extra mount of synthetic images into the real dataset to train the alignment models.

The 3D Morphable Model (3DMM) (Blanz and Vetter [1999]) is implemented to create the synthetic images. We annotated once 51 inner landmarks (similar to 300-W dataset), Fig. 4. The boundary landmarks are not considered because the their textures are not usually good at 3D face reconstruction. Despite that the 3DMM of our implementation has no facial expression yet, but showing the possibility of using synthetic for face alignment with neutral faces are still valuable.

3   Experimental Results

3.1   Datasets

We work mainly on 300-W dataset (Sagonas et al. [2013]) created from existing datasets, which are re-annotated in the same 68 landmark, including LFPW (Belhumeur et al. [2011]), AFW (X. Zhu [2012]), Helen (Le et al. [2012]), XM2VTS (Messer et al. [1999]) and one new IBUG dataset. Since it is created as a challenge and the official testing set is not publicly available. We follow (Ren et al. [2014]) to split data into three sets: training set, common subset and challenging subset. The training set with 3148 images in total, including AFW, the training sets of LFPW, and the training set of Helen. The common subset with 689 images in total, including the testing set of LFPW and the testing set of Helen. The challenging set is IBUG subset. We use the training set of LFPW (811 images) for cross-validation, where 566 first images for training and the others for cross-validating. The performance is measured by Root Mean Square (RMS) of all landmarks normalized by pupil distance.

3.2 Results

To be fair and comparable with SDM algorithm, we use the same parameters similar to (Xiong and la Torre Frade [2013]), for example, the local patch size $N_{size} = 32 \times 32$, the number of random samples for data argument $N_{rand} = 10$ to train RBM models, the number of regressors $N_{reg} = 5$. We set $N_{hidden} = 128$ of RBM to have the same feature dimension like SIFT used in SDM. To avoid overfitting when using linear regression, the regularization term is considered as the number of training images like (Yan et al. [2013]). Notice that the face region is always normalized to reference size 200×200 before extracting local features.

The first experiment evaluates the performance of SIFT and RBM features using based on (Xiong and la Torre Frade [2013]). The cross-validation shown in Fig. 3. The horizontal axis is the Root Mean Square (RMS) error normalized by eye pupil distance. The vertical axis is the percentage of image numbers has the RMS error lower than each specific threshold from horizontal axis. In this experiment, we also propose to verify the effects of inner and boundary landmarks. In the same figure, the performances of 17 boundary points using both RBM and SIFT are low, in which RBM are worse than SIFT. However, if using only 51 inner points, RBM has a better performance. When using 68 landmarks, the boundary points degrades more performance with RBM than SIFT. It turns out that using RBM is good to learn the inner points but bad for boundary points compared to SIFT.

To compare to state-of-the-art methods, *we propose the use of RBM (for inner points) and SIFT (for boundary points)*. Table. 1 is the results when testing on 68 landmarks compared to state-of-the-art methods on reported datasets. The numbers in the table are the average normalized RMS errors of all test images. We are the best at common set, but worse than LBF (Ren et al. [2014]) at challenging set. The performance of 51 landmarks on the same dataset is also reported Table. 2. Because of no information of state-of-the-art methods for this case, we only compare our method with SDM. It shows our method outperforms SDM.

The second experiment uses RBM features in the first one and coarse-to-fine cascaded regression (CCR), the performance is more improved as Table. 1. In our implementation, the number of correlative landmarks is reduced by two times at each stage. By the combination of RBM (or RBM + SIFT for 68 landmarks) features and correlative regression, we achieve the best result on common subset

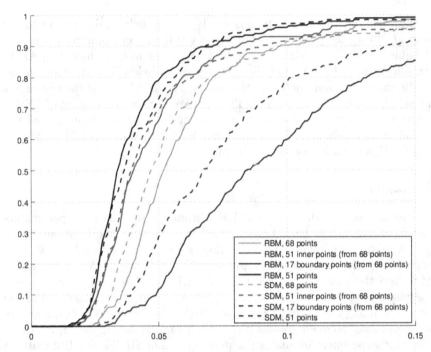

Fig. 3. The cross-validation of inner and boundary points. The horizontal axis is the Root Mean Square (RMS) error normalized by eye pupil distance. The vertical axis is the percentage of image numbers has the RMS error lower than each specific threshold from horizontal axis.

Table 1. Compare to state-of-the-art methods on 300-W dataset using 68 landmarks. SIFT is for 17 boundary points.

300-W (68 landmarks)

Method	Common set	Challenging set
ESR (Cao et al., 2012)	5.28	17.00
SDM (Xiong and la Torre Frade, 2013)	5.60	15.50
LBF (Ren et al., 2014)	4.95	**11.98**
LBF-fast (Ren et al., 2014)	5.38	15.50
Ours (RBM + SIFT)	**4.91**	14.40
Ours (RBM + SIFT + CCR)	**4.85**	12.50

Table 2. Compare to state-of-the-art methods on 300-W dataset using 51 landmarks.

300-W (51 landmarks)

Method	Common set	Challenging set
SDM (Xiong and la Torre Frade, 2013)	4.04	11.20
Ours (RBM)	**3.48**	10.13
Ours (RBM + CCR)	**3.45**	**9.80**

and the comparable result on challenging subset of 300-W dataset compared to the state-of-the-art.

The third experiment investigate the possibility of using synthetic data for large rotations using the method in the second experiment. i) First, we generate about 3000 synthetic data of random poses using 3DMM at both frontal and profile views. We train our method using this dataset and test on synthetic and real samples. Fig. 4 shows some examples using synthetic data. The method can align well the synthetic profile samples, as well as the frontal real images although the synthetic and real textures are quite different. ii) The synthetic set is included into the training part of common set of 300-W (about 2000 frontal images) to train our model, and we develop a tracker to track profile faces based our method used on single frame. See the video demo of our tracking here[1]. The tracker works robustly with the profile thanks to the synthetic profile images. Although the face is sometimes lost when the face turns too fast or moves to the edges of video, or occlusion happening, this result confirms the potential of synthetic data. Based on synthetic data, we simply build a single model to track efficiently face at multi-views.

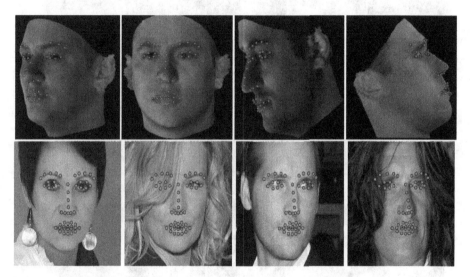

Fig. 4. Landmark detection on synthetic and real images.

It is possible to improve more if we have better synthetic images, for example (Hassner [2013]). One technical problem, our program is not real-time because of Matlab implementation. In addition, a number of correlative regressors needs to be run each time that slows down the speed. The current frame rate of our method is 1 frame (or image)/second.

---

[1] See our demo at: http://youtu.be/46EQReuoXKo.

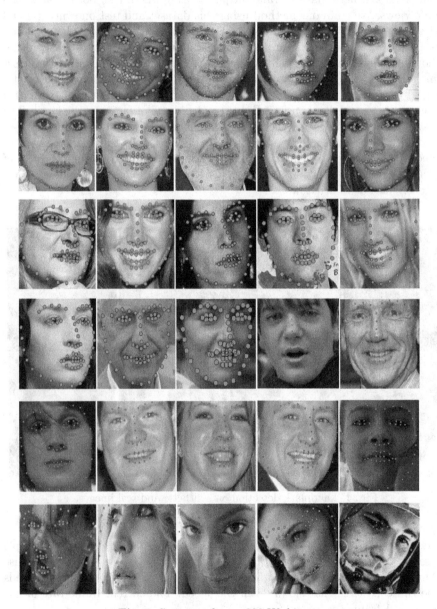

Fig. 5. Some results on 300-W dataset.

4   Conclusion

In this work, we have presented a new method through a combination of local and global regression for face alignment. The locality via correlative regression allows the later regressors stronger and more flexible. The proposition of using RBM also improved a lot the performance. We tested our hypothesis on the synthetic data to obtain the good results in term of developing a face tracking framework for large pose rotation; however, we believe that the result could be much better if we have a better synthetic data (texture, expression,...). That confirms that our method or cascaded regression can work efficiently at profile if enough data are provided. Experimental results demonstrate the advantages of our proposed aspects in building a robust face alignment. Some drawbacks need to be solved in the future and a better 3DMM model perhaps is a possible solution.

References

Belhumeur, P.N., Jacobs, D.W., Kriegman, D.J., Kumar, N.: Localizing parts of faces using a consensus of exemplars. In: CVPR (2011)

Blanz, V., Vetter, T.: A morphable model for the synthesis of 3D faces. In: SIGGRAPH, pp. 187–194, New York (1999)

Burgos-Artizzu, X., Perona, P., Dollár, P.: Robust face landmark estimation under occlusion. In: ICCV (2013)

Cao, X., Wei, Y., Wen, F., Sun, J.: Face alignment by explicit shape regression. In: CVPR (2012)

Cootes, T.F., Edwards, G.J., Taylor, C.J.: Active appearance models. TPAMI **23**(6), 681–685 (2001)

Cootes, T.F., Wheeler, G.V., Walker, K.N., Taylor, C.J.: View-based active appearance models. IVC **20**(9–10), 657–664 (2002)

Cristinacce, D., Cootes, T.F.: Feature detection and tracking with constrained local models. In: BMVC (2006)

Dalal, N., Triggs, B.: Histograms of oriented gradients for human detection. In: CVPR (2005)

Dollar, P., Welinder, P., Perona, P.: Cascaded pose regression. In: CVPR (2010)

Gross, R., Matthews, I., Cohn, J.F., Kanade, T., Baker, S.: Multi-pie. IVC **28**(5), 807–813 (2010)

Hassner, T.: Viewing real-world faces in 3D. In: ICCV (2013)

Hinton, G., Salakhutdinov, R.: Reducing the dimensionality of data with neural networks (2006)

Kazemi, V., Sullivan, J.: One millisecond face alignment with an ensemble of regression trees. In: CVPR (2014)

Koestinger, M., Wohlhart, P., Roth, P. M., Bischof, H.: Annotated facial landmarks in the wild: a large-scale, real-world database for facial landmark localization. In: First IEEE International Workshop on Benchmarking Facial Image Analysis Technologies (2011)

Le, V., Brandt, J., Lin, Z., Bourdev, L., Huang, T.S.: Interactive facial feature localization. In: Fitzgibbon, A., Lazebnik, S., Perona, P., Sato, Y., Schmid, C. (eds.) ECCV 2012, Part III. LNCS, vol. 7574, pp. 679–692. Springer, Heidelberg (2012)

Lowe, D.G.: Distinctive image features from scale-invariant keypoints. IJCV **60**, 91–110 (2004)

Valstar, M.F., Martinez, B., Binefa, X., Pantic, M.: Facial point detection using boosted regression and graph models. In: CVPR, pp. 2729–2736 (2010)

Messer, K., Matas, J., Kittler, J., Luettin, J., Maitre, G.: XM2VTSDB: the extended M2VTS database. In: Second International Conference on Audio and Video-based Biometric Person Authentication (1999)

Ren, S., Cao, X., Wei, Y., Sun, J. : Face alignment at 3000 FPS via regressing local binary features (2014)

Sagonas, C., Tzimiropoulos, G., Zafeiriou, S., Pantic, M.: 300 faces in-the-wild challenge: the first facial landmark localization challenge. In: ICCV Workshops (2013)

Saragih, J.M., Lucey, S., Cohn, J.F.: Deformable model fitting by regularized landmark mean-shift. IJCV **91**, 200–215 (2011)

Sun, Y., Wang, X., Tang, X.: Deep convolutional network cascade for facial point detection. In: CVPR (2013)

Wang, Y., Lucey, S., Cohn, J.: Enforcing convexity for improved alignment with constrained local models. In: CVPR (2008)

Zhu, X., Ramanan, D.: Face detection, pose estimation, and landmark localization in the wild. In: CVPR (2012)

Xiong, X., la Torre Frade, F.D.: Supervised descent method and its applications to face alignment. In: CVPR (2013)

Yan et al., 2013]yan-iccvw-2013 Yan, J., Lei, Z., Yi, D., Li, S.Z.: Learn to combine multiple hypotheses for accurate face alignment. In: ICCV Workshops (2013)

Zhang, J., Shan, S., Kan, M., Chen, X.: Coarse-to-Fine Auto-Encoder Networks (CFAN) for real-time face alignment. In: Fleet, D., Pajdla, T., Schiele, B., Tuytelaars, T. (eds.) ECCV 2014, Part II. LNCS, vol. 8690, pp. 1–16. Springer, Heidelberg (2014)

Zhao, X., Shan, S., Chai, X., Chen, X.: Cascaded shape space pruning for robust facial landmark detection. In: ICCV (2013)

Zhou, E., Fan, H., Cao, Z., Jiang, Y., Yin, Q.: Extensive facial landmark localization with coarse-to-fine convolutional network cascade. In: ICCV Workshops (2013)

A Generic Feature Selection Method for Background Subtraction Using Global Foreground Models

Marc Braham$^{(\boxtimes)}$ and Marc Van Droogenbroeck

INTELSIG Laboratory, Department of Electrical Engineering
and Computer Science, University of Liège, Liège, Belgium
{m.braham,M.VanDroogenbroeck}@ulg.ac.be

Abstract. Over the last few years, a wide variety of background subtraction algorithms have been proposed for the detection of moving
objects in videos acquired with a static camera. While much effort have
been devoted to the development of robust background models, the automatic spatial selection of useful features for representing the background
has been neglected. In this paper, we propose a generic and tractable
feature selection method. Interesting contributions of this work are the
proposal of a selection process coherent with the segmentation process
and the exploitation of global foreground models in the selection strategy. Experiments conducted on the ViBe algorithm show that our feature
selection technique improves the segmentation results.

Keywords: Background subtraction · Feature selection · Foreground
modeling · Change detection · ViBe

1 Introduction

Detecting moving objects in video sequences provides a valuable information for
various applications such as video coding [1], depth extraction from video [2], or
intelligent vision systems [3]. A straightforward approach for motion detection
is background subtraction, typically used in tracking systems, for its ability to
detect moving objects without any assumption about their appearance, size or
orientation [4,5]. The process consists in building a model of the static scene,
which is named *background*, and updating this model over time to account for
luminance and structural changes in the scene. The background model is subtracted from the current frame, and pixels or regions with a noticeable difference
are assumed to belong to moving objects (the *foreground*). A background sub-
tractor is thus a two-class classifier (foreground or background).

While conceptually simple, background subtraction still remains a difficult
task because of the variety of challenging situations that occur in real world
scenes. For instance, pixels may be erroneously classified as foreground in the
presence of camera jitter, dynamic background (such as swaying trees or sea

© Springer International Publishing Switzerland 2015
S. Battiato et al. (Eds.): ACIVS 2015, LNCS 9386, pp. 717–728, 2015.
DOI: 10.1007/978-3-319-25903-1_62

waves) or illumination changes. On the other hand, camouflage (*i.e.* foreground and background sharing similar colors) generate many false negative detections.

To deal with these challenging situations, a plethora of background subtraction techniques have been proposed (see [6] or [7] for a recent and comprehensive classification of these techniques including more than 300 references). They differ, among other things, in the features chosen to build the background model. According to Bouwmans [7], five categories of features are frequently used: color features, edge features, texture features, motion features, and stereo features. Color features refer mainly to the color components of color spaces which can be processed separately or jointly. The RGB domain is the most popular [8,9], but some authors exploit other color spaces such as HSV [10] or YCbCr [11] in order to increase invariance with respect to brightness changes, and thus illumination changes and shadows. Gradient features [12] and texture features such as LBP histogram [13] or its variants [14,15] offer a robust solution to illumination changes but might be unsuitable in image areas with poor texture. Motion features, such as optical flow [16], should be particularly interesting for scenes where the foreground is moving continuously (absence of temporarily stopped objects) and depth features acquired with range cameras such as the Kinect camera [17] are (to some degree) insensitive to lighting conditions but cannot be computed when objects are far from the camera.

In conclusion, there seems to be no agreement on a unique feature performing better than any other feature independently of the background and foreground properties. Surprisingly, this is not considered in practice. Almost all existing background subtraction techniques operate with a uniform feature map in the sense that the features used to model the background and perform the detection are the same for all pixels of the image, thus ignoring the non-uniformity of the spatial distribution of background properties and neglecting the foreground properties. Recently, Bouwmans concluded in a comprehensive survey paper [7] that feature selection in background subtraction is still an open problem and may be one of the main future developments in this field.

In this paper, we propose a generic method for the spatial selection of the most significant features and we assess it for the ViBe technique. The main novelties of our work are: (1) a dedicated feature selection process that is coherent with the background subtraction process, and (2) the use of global foreground models in the selection strategy. The rest of the paper is organized as follows. Section 2 reviews the related work and presents the main limitations of existing selection methods. We provide the details of our method in Section 3. Experiments showing the benefits of our method are described in Section 4. Finally, Section 5 concludes the paper.

2   Related Work

Li *et al.* [18] were among the first to express the need for modeling distinct part of the image with different features. They describe the background image as consisting of two pixel categories, static pixels and dynamic pixels, and incorporate this model in a Bayesian framework. Static pixels belong to stationary objects such as walls or room furniture whereas dynamic pixels refer to non stationary objects such as swaying trees or sea waves. Color and gradient statistics are used to describe static pixels while color co-occurrence statistics describe dynamic pixels. As the correspondence between a pixel category and the features used to describe it is fixed, the selection strategy reduces to an identification process of static and dynamic pixels. A temporal difference between two consecutive video frames is used for this purpose. Unfortunately, this method lacks of generality as the cardinality of the feature set, *i.e.* the number of candidate features or group of features, is limited to two (one group of features for static pixels and one other for dynamic pixels).

Parag *et al.* [19] introduced a more general feature selection framework requiring a set of training images free of foreground objects. The set of training images is divided into two parts. The first one generates a background statistical model for each feature of the feature set. These statistical models are used for the computation of background probability estimates (for each candidate feature) with the Kernel Density Estimation (KDE) [8] on the remaining part of the training set and on synthetic foreground examples. The computed estimates feed the training of a RealBoost classifier [20]. The resulting classifier selects the most useful features for each pixel and assigns a confidence weight to each of them. While this framework can be used with an arbitrary number of candidate features, it has a serious drawback. Indeed, the synthetic foreground examples used for boosting are generated randomly from a uniform distribution. In other words, all candidate features are assumed to be uniformly distributed for foreground objects. This assumption is not valid because of the wide variety of foreground statistical distributions among different features. For instance, gradient has a foreground probability density function (FG-pdf) concentrated around low values while RGB color components have a wider FG-pdf. This may explain why the classification performance of Parag's framework [19] decreases when gradient features are added to the feature set. In our work, we overcome this major limitation by means of global statistical foreground models.

Another boosting-based approach for feature selection was proposed by Grabner *et al.* [21, 22]. The main novelty of their work is the spatio-temporal nature of the selection through on-line boosting. However, since the method is based on self-learning (*i.e.* classifier predictions feed model updates), the background model can end up in catastrophic state, as mentioned in [23]. Once again, unrealistic assumptions about the statistical distributions of foreground features are used (a uniform distribution is assumed for the gray value of foreground objects and serves as a basis for computing other feature distributions).

Recently, Javed *et al.* [24] included a dynamic feature selection strategy for background subtraction in an *Online Robust Principal Component Analysis* (OR-PCA) framework. Feature statistics, in terms of means and variances, are used as a selection criterion. Unlike aforementioned purely spatial or spatio-temporal selection approaches, their method is exclusively temporal-based, which means that all pixels use the same features for the foreground segmentation. The non-uniformity of the spatial distribution of background properties is thus ignored.

3   Proposed Selection Strategy

A schematic view of our feature selection strategy is given in Fig. 1. Like in Parag's work [19], our selection process occurs during a training phase, which allows to avoid extra computations during normal background subtraction operations. This training phase is divided into three parts, represented by boxes [1], [2], and [3] in Fig. 1. The first part consists to accumulate images free of foreground objects, typically a few hundreds at a framerate of 30 frames per second, which are further processed to build local background statistical models. The second training part requires another sequence of images, this time including foreground objects. These images are not saved into memory, but processed by a background subtraction algorithm in order to build a global foreground statistical model for each candidate feature of the feature set. The third part of the training phase selects the best feature/threshold combination; this process is *local*, meaning that it is performed for each pixel individually. The goal of the selection process consists to detect which feature is most appropriate to discriminate between the local background and the foreground at the frame level. To guarantee some consistency with the segmentation process, the selection step is fed by supplementary information relating to the background model of the segmentation algorithm, and to the application performance metric (see box [4] in Fig. 1). All these steps are detailed in the following subsections.

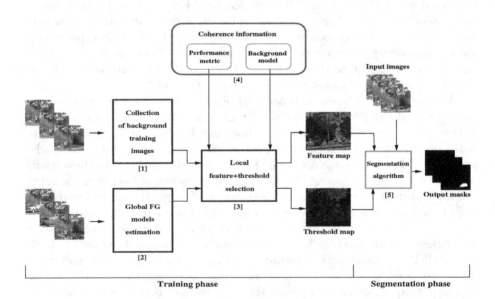

Fig. 1. Schematic representation of the proposed feature selection framework.

3.1 Estimation of the Foreground: Local vs Global Foreground Models

Background subtraction is a classification problem between the background or foreground classes. It is well known that the classification performance of a classifier is dependent on the discriminating power of the used features. Therefore, an optimal classifier should select the best feature locally, that is for each pixel separately, to maximize its capability to distinguish between the local background values and the local foreground values, which indirectly implies that we are able to estimate the corresponding statistical distributions for any feature.

Obtaining reliable local background statistical models is realistic and common. Indeed, local background feature values are relatively stable (or at least predictable). Moreover, the pixel-wise probability to observe a background sample (we name this as the local BG-prior) is much higher than the local FG-prior. Subsequently, it suffices to collect a small set of background training images to estimate the local BG feature distributions. However, estimating local foreground distributions is more complex. The two main difficulties are that (1) most features have a wide FG-pdf, and (2) local FG-priors are often low with respect to BG-priors, which means that foreground might not be encountered locally during the training phase. In fact, estimating the local foreground distributions reliably would require an extremely long observation period, which is clearly intractable. There is thus an imbalance between the estimation of local background or foreground characteristics.

To overcome this estimation problem, we assume that the *local* foreground distribution of a feature can be approximated by its *global* foreground distribution. There is an important advantage to assume this. Indeed, it might be that a moving object is very different from the background for some areas of the image, but close for other areas. A global estimation will help to learn from the foreground values detected in the easiest areas of the scene. Mathematically, assuming that the distributions are represented by histograms of observed values, and denoting by $\mathbf{LH_f}$ the matrix of local histograms for a feature f, the *global* histogram $\mathbf{GH_f}$ of feature f is given by:

$$\mathbf{GH_f}(b) = \sum_{(x,y)} \mathbf{LH_f}(x, y, b) \ , \tag{1}$$

where b is a particular bin and (x, y) refers to the coordinates in the image. For a multi-dimensional feature (for instance the RGB feature which is a tri-dimensional feature, to the contrary of the individual color components: R,G, or B), equation (1) becomes:

$$\mathbf{GH_f}(b_1, b_2, ..., b_D) = \sum_{(x,y)} \mathbf{LH_f}(x, y, b_1, b_2, ..., b_D) \ , \tag{2}$$

where D is the number of dimensions of the feature. Note that our assumption of a uniform spatial distribution of foreground feature values is not perfectly true, especially because of the modification of geometrical and colorimetric properties of foreground objects in the image as they move across the scene. Despite that, we believe that the approach is appropriate. The main benefit results from the considerable reduction of the observation time required for estimating the local foreground distributions. A practical estimation becomes thus feasible.

In summary, the second training stage (named "Global FG models estimation" in Fig. 1) is performed as follows. We feed a background subtraction algorithm (named "estimator" in the remainder of the paper) with a sequence of training images including foreground objects. The choice of the estimator is not critical; state-of-the-art techniques, such as SuBSENSE [25] or PAWCS [26], are good candidates to segment foreground objects. Note that a fast estimator is not necessary because there is no real-time requirement during the training phase. The segmentation masks of the estimator are processed to build the $\#_f$ global foreground models, $\#_f$ denoting the cardinality of the feature set.

3.2   Coherence Between Selection, Segmentation, and Application

While some authors have expressed the need for modeling distinct part of the image with different features for background subtraction [18,19,21], none of them noticed that the best feature map may depend on elements unrelated to background or foreground statistical properties. We innovate in this paper by considering the type of background model used by the segmentation algorithm (see box [5] in Fig. 1). Some features may be adapted to specific background models, while performing badly for others. This statement was confirmed recently by López-Rubio *et al.* [27]. They showed that, while Haar-like features [28] were reported to be adapted to KDE background models in the context of feature combination [29], they have an insufficient discriminating power in a probabilistic mixture-based approach. A generic algorithm should therefore select, locally, the most discriminating feature *for each background model individually*.

Another important element of our framework is the inclusion of coherence with respect to the application. Some applications require to minimize the false alarm rate while maintaining a desired recall, whereas others need to maximize the recall while maintaining a relatively low false alarm rate. As each feature choice tends to favor particular metrics, the performance metric of the application should be considered during the selection process. Therefore, we use the application performance metric to evaluate the capability of a feature to discriminate between local background samples and global foreground samples. Note however that the framework is incompatible with prior-dependent performance metrics, such as the popular F_1 measure. The origin of this limitation is the modification of the local FG-prior due to the construction of the global foreground histograms. Indeed, the number of global foreground samples collected during the second step of the learning phase (see box [2] in Fig. 1) is much higher than the number of local background samples of a pixel (in fact equal to the number of background training images). Therefore, as the selection process introduces a large bias in the estimation of the local FG-prior, it is strongly recommended to use prior-independent metrics, such as the geometrical mean [30] or the Euclidean distance in ROC space introduced in [31].

3.3 Local Feature/Threshold Selection Process

Our generic feature selection method for background subtraction is presented in Algorithm 1. This algorithm is implemented in the [3] box of Fig. 1. Note that the background subtraction step involves the choice of matching thresholds (one threshold per feature) for comparing current input feature values with local background feature values. For instance, in the case of ViBe [9], the radius of the color sphere is the matching threshold used to compare RGB feature values. These thresholds affect the results of the corresponding features. For this reason, we feed the generic selection algorithm with $\#_f$ sets of $\#_t$ candidate thresholds (one set of candidate thresholds per feature), where $\#_t$ denotes the cardinality of the threshold sets (assumed equal for each threshold set, for convenience) and let the algorithm select the best feature/threshold combination, locally.

The selection process consists in a simulation of the target background model for each feature. Firstly, the simulated local feature background models are build. In the case of ViBe's background model [9], this is performed by selecting, randomly and for each feature, 20 values among the K background feature values available at coordinates (x, y), K denoting the number of background training images. Then, each model is assessed for its capability to predict the correct class of input samples, these one being both (1) all local samples of the background training images, and (2) all global samples collected in the corresponding global FG histogram. As the predictions depend on the matching threshold, this capability is assessed for all candidate thresholds of a given feature, and described by a confusion matrix [32]. The performance metric is computed from the confusion matrix and the best feature/threshold combination is selected.

4 Experiments

4.1 Description of the Methodology

We particularized our generic method for the ViBe background subtraction algorithm [9], and evaluated it for the CDnet 2012 dataset [33]. The feature set contains 9 individual color components ($\#_f = 9$), taken from the 3 common color spaces RGB, HSV, and YCbCr:

$$CF = \{R, G, B, H, S, V, Y, Cb, Cr\}, \ \#_f = 9 \ . \tag{3}$$

Each feature is quantized into 256 bins. For this purpose, the saturation S and the value V (resp. the hue H) are rescaled linearly from the range $[0, 1]$ (resp. $[0, 360)$) to the range $[0, 255]$. The pre-defined set of possible thresholds is

$$CT^f = \{2, ..., 10, 12, 14, 16, 18, 20, 25, 30, 35, 40, 45, 50\} \ \forall f, \ \#_t = 20 \ . \tag{4}$$

The Euclidean distance in the ROC space, introduced in [31] and defined as

$$d_{euc} = \sqrt{FNR^2 + FPR^2}, \tag{5}$$

Algorithm 1. Generic algorithm for local feature/threshold selection.

Inputs

(1) A set of $\#_f$ candidate features $CF = \{F_1, F_2, ..., F_{\#_f}\}$

(2) $\#_f$ sets of $\#_t$ candidate thresholds $CT^f = \{T_1^f, T_2^f, ..., T_{\#_t}^f\}$

(3) A performance metric P

(4) A target background model BM

(5) A table of K background training images **BTI** where **BTI**(x,y,k) is the background RGB value at pixel coordinates (x,y) and training image k

(6) A table **FGGH** where **FGGH**(f,b) is the global FG histogram value for bin b of feature F_f (see Section 3.1 for more details)

Outputs

(1) A feature map $\mathbf{F}_{map}$ with $\mathbf{F}_{map}(x, y) \in CF$, $\forall$(x,y)

(2) A threshold map $\mathbf{T}_{map}$ with $\mathbf{T}_{map}(x, y) \in CT^{F_{map}(x,y)}$, $\forall$(x,y)

Internal data

(1) $\#_f$ tables **Class**$_f$ where **Class**$_f$(b) is a class assigned to bin b of feature F_f

(2) A confusion matrix **CM**

(3) A table **PT** where **PT**(f,t) is a performance assigned to the combination F_f / T_t^f

(4) $\#_f$ feature background models FBM_f

Pseudo-code of the selection algorithm

for each (x,y) do
    for each $F_f \in$ CF do
        Build the feature background model FBM_f using BM and **BTI**(x,y,:) ;
        for each $T_t^f \in CT^f$ do
            for each bin b of feature F_f do
                Predict **Class**$_f$(b) given FBM_f and T_t^f ;
            end
            Compute **CM** given **Class**$_f$(:), **BTI**(x,y,:), and **FGGH**(f,:) ;
            Compute **PT**(f,t) given **CM** and P ;
        end
    end
    Find (f*,t*) optimizing **PT**(f,t) ;
    If several f optimize **PT**(f,t), then select f* randomly among the optimum f ;
    If several t optimize **PT**(f*,t), then select t corresponding to the lowest $T_t^{f^*}$ as t* ;
    $\mathbf{F}_{map}$(x,y) $= F_{f^*}$; $\mathbf{T}_{map}$(x,y) $= T_{t^*}^{f^*}$;
end

---

where FNR and FPR denote respectively the false negative rate and the false positive rate, is our prior-independent performance metric. Its behavior is close to that of the geometrical mean of Barandela et al. [30], but it is easier to interpret because it measures the distance between a classifier and the theoretically best classifier, also called *oracle* (top left corner of the ROC space). We want to minimize this distance, because lower distances mean being closer to the oracle.

For the purposes of our analysis, we have selected three categories of videos of CDnet [33]: "*Baseline*", "*Camera jitter*", and "*Dynamic background*". Other categories are less relevant, because either they are inappropriate ("*Thermal*" only contains grayscale images), or because our algorithm is not designed to deal with the particularities of that category ("*Shadow*" for example). In fact, it is designed to be robust against camouflage and against background changes that occur during the first part of the training phase (see box [1] in Fig. 1), such as camera jitter, dynamic backgrounds, or illumination changes. Intermittent object motion and shadows are related to foreground objects, and thus cannot be learned during the background learning step.

CDnet [33] provides videos split for the needs of two phases: (1) an initialization phase (ground-truth images are not provided) and (2) an evaluation phase (ground-truth images are provided). Images of the initialization phase are used to train the background model. For videos containing moving objects during this phase, we have manually selected background images, when it was possible. Otherwise, we have manually defined bounding boxes around moving objects and their shadows, to help discarding these areas for building the background models. The first half of images of the evaluation phase is used to estimate the global foreground models, using PAWCS [26] as an estimator. After this step, we perform the local feature/threshold selection. The computed feature and threshold maps are provided to ViBe (designated by ViBe-FT), which then detects the foreground for the second half of images of the evaluation phase. We evaluate the segmentation masks of ViBe-FT on this second half.

4.2   Results and Discussion

The results of ViBe-FT are compared to those of the original ViBe [9] algorithm when applied on the 9 color components separately, *i.e.* with uniform feature and threshold maps, denoted by {ViBe-R, ViBe-G, ..., ViBe-Cb, ViBe-Cr}. The uniform thresholds have been set to {11,11,11,11,11,11,11,3,3} (these values were found to be well suited to the corresponding features). Moreover, we report the results of ViBe when only the feature selection process of Algorithm 1 is activated (thresholds are fixed to the aforementioned values), designated by ViBe-F.

Results displayed in Fig. 2 show that the proposed local feature selection framework significantly improves the detection results. For each category, our feature and threshold maps reduce the mean Euclidean distance of ViBe. This means that our framework pushes the background subtraction algorithm towards the oracle of the ROC space, and thus improves the detection. The conclusion is similar when the threshold selection mechanism is deactivated (denoted by "ViBe-F" on the graphic), which proves the robustness of the local feature selection process with respect to the threshold values.

Fig. 3 shows several feature maps obtained after the local feature selection process, as well as the resulting improved segmentation masks. Note that these improvements are significant despite that (1) a small set of candidate features was used, and (2) the number of training frames used to estimate the global foreground distributions is relatively small (744 on average), which confirms the importance of a *global* estimation for obtaining reliable foreground distributions. The computational complexity of the selection process is $O(\#_f\#_t)$. Note however that, as this process occurs during an off-line training phase, it does not affect the computational complexity of the detection task.

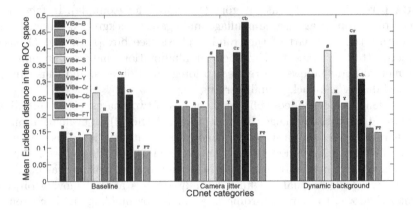

Fig. 2. Mean Euclidean distances in the ROC space for relevant CDnet [33] categories.

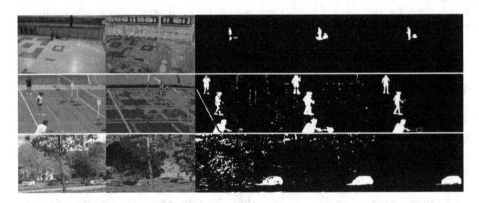

Fig. 3. Improvements obtained with our selection framework for three videos of CDnet [33]. Columns from left to right show: the input images, the computed feature maps (see legend of Fig. 2 for the color-feature matching), the results of ViBe-G (lowest mean d_{euc} among the uniform feature maps), the results of ViBe-FT, and the ground-truths. Note that both ViBe-G and ViBe-FT are post-processed by a 9x9 median filter.

5   Conclusions

In this paper, we present a generic feature selection method for background subtraction. Unlike previous approaches, we estimate the foreground feature statistical distributions *at the frame level*. Features are selected locally depending on their capability to discriminate between *local* background samples and *global* foreground samples *for a specific background model* and *for a chosen performance metric*. Experiments led for the ViBe algorithm show that our method significantly improves the performance in the ROC space.

Acknowledgments. Marc BRAHAM has a grant funded by the FRIA (www.frs-fnrs. be). We are also grateful to Jean-François FOULON for his help.

References

1. Xiao, J., Liao, L., Hu, J., Chen, Y., Hu, R.: Exploiting Global Redundancy in Big Surveillance Video Data for Efficient Coding. Cluster Computing **18**(2), 531–540 (2015)
2. Karsch, K., Liu, C., Kang, S.B.: DepthTransfer: Depth Extraction from Video Using Non-Parametric Sampling. IEEE Trans. Pattern Anal. Mach. Intell. **36**(11), 2144–2158 (2014)
3. Oliver, N.M., Rosario, B., Pentland, A.P.: A Bayesian Computer Vision System for Modeling Human Interactions. IEEE Trans. Pattern Anal. Mach. Intell. **22**(8), 831–843 (2000)
4. Kim, Z.: Real time object tracking based on dynamic feature grouping with background subtraction. In: IEEE Int. Conf. Comput. Vision and Pattern Recognition (CVPR), pp. 1–8 (2008)
5. Jodoin, J.-P., Bilodeau, G.-A., Saunier, N.: Urban tracker: multiple object tracking in urban mixed traffic. In: IEEE Winter Conference on Applications of Computer Vision (WACV), pp. 885–892 (2014)
6. Jodoin, P.-M., Piérard, S., Wang, Y., Van Droogenbroeck, M.: Overview and benchmarking of motion detection methods. In: Bouwmans, T., Porikli, F., Hoferlin, B., Vacavant, A. (eds.) Background Modeling and Foreground Detection for Video Surveillance, chap. 24. Chapman and Hall/CRC (2014)
7. Bouwmans, T.: Traditional and Recent Approaches in Background Modeling for Foreground Detection: An Overview. Computer Science Review **11**, 31–66 (2014)
8. Elgammal, A., Harwood, D., Davis, L.: Non-parametric model for background subtraction. In: Vernon, D. (ed.) ECCV 2000. LNCS, vol. 1843, pp. 751–767. Springer, Heidelberg (2000)
9. Barnich, O., Van Droogenbroeck, M.: ViBe: A Universal Background Subtraction Algorithm for Video Sequences. IEEE Trans. Image Process. **20**(6), 1709–1724 (2011)
10. Cucchiara, R., Grana, C., Piccardi, M., Prati, A.: Detecting Moving Objects, Ghosts, and Shadows in Video Streams. IEEE Trans. Pattern Anal. Mach. Intell. **25**(10), 1337–1342 (2003)
11. Kristensen, F., Nilsson, P., Öwall, V.: Background segmentation beyond RGB. In: Narayanan, P.J., Nayar, S.K., Shum, H.-Y. (eds.) ACCV 2006. LNCS, vol. 3852, pp. 602–612. Springer, Heidelberg (2006)
12. Gruenwedel, S., Van Hese, P., Philips, W.: An edge-based approach for robust foreground detection. In: Blanc-Talon, J., Kleihorst, R., Philips, W., Popescu, D., Scheunders, P. (eds.) ACIVS 2011. LNCS, vol. 6915, pp. 554–565. Springer, Heidelberg (2011)
13. Heikkilä, M., Pietikäinen, M.: A Texture-Based Method for Modeling the Background and Detecting Moving Objects. IEEE Trans. Pattern Anal. Mach. Intell. **28**(4), 657–662 (2006)
14. Bilodeau, G.-A., Jodoin, J.-P., Saunier, N.: Change detection in feature space using local binary similarity patterns. In: International Conference on Computer and Robot Vision (CRV), pp. 106–112 (2013)
15. Silva, C., Bouwmans, T., Frélicot, C.: An extended center-symmetric local binary pattern for background modeling and subtraction in videos. In: Int. Conf. Comput. Vision Theory and Applicat. (VISAPP), pp. 395–402 (2015)

16. Chen, M., Yang, Q., Li, Q., Wang, G., Yang, M.-H.: Spatiotemporal background subtraction using minimum spanning tree and optical flow. In: Fleet, D., Pajdla, T., Schiele, B., Tuytelaars, T. (eds.) ECCV 2014, Part VII. LNCS, vol. 8695, pp. 521–534. Springer, Heidelberg (2014)

17. Freedman, B., Shpunt, A., Machline, M., Arieli, Y.: Depth Mapping Using Projected Patterns, US patent 8150142 (2012)

18. Li, L., Huang, W., Gu, Y.-H., Tian, Q.: Statistical Modeling of Complex Backgrounds for Foreground Object Detection. IEEE Trans. Image Process. **13**(11), 1459–1472 (2004)

19. Parag, T., Elgammal, A., Mittal, A.: A framework for feature selection for background subtraction. In: IEEE Int. Conf. Comput. Vision and Pattern Recognition (CVPR). vol. 2, pp. 1916–1923 (2006)

20. Schapire, R.E., Singer, Y.: Improved Boosting Algorithms Using Confidence-rated Predictions. Machine Learning **37**(3), 297–336 (1999)

21. Grabner, H., Bischof, H.: On-line boosting and vision. In: IEEE Int. Conf. Comput. Vision and Pattern Recognition (CVPR), vol. 1, pp. 260–267 (2006)

22. Grabner, H., Roth, P., Grabner, M., Bischof, H.: Autonomous learning of a robust background model for change detection. In: IEEE Int. Workshop on Performance Evaluation of Tracking and Surveillance (PETS), pp. 39–46 (2006)

23. Grabner, H., Leistner, C., Bischof, H.: Time dependent on-line boosting for robust background modeling. In: Int. Conf. Comput. Vision Theory and Applicat. (VISAPP), pp. 612–618 (2007)

24. Javed, S., Sobral, A., Bouwmans, T., Jung, S.: OR-PCA with dynamic feature selection for robust background subtraction. In: ACM Symposium on Applied Computing, pp. 86–91. ACM, New York (2015)

25. St-Charles, P.-L., Bilodeau, G.-A., Bergevin, R.: SuBSENSE: A Universal Change Detection Method with Local Adaptive Sensitivity. IEEE Trans. Image Process. **24**(1), 359–373 (2015)

26. St-Charles, P.-L., Bilodeau, G.-A., Bergevin, R.: A self-adjusting approach to change detection based on background word consensus. In: IEEE Winter Conference on Applications of Computer Vision (WACV), pp. 990–997 (2015)

27. López-Rubio, F., López-Rubio, E.: Features for Stochastic Approximation Based Foreground Detection. Comp. Vision and Image Understanding **133**, 30–50 (2015)

28. Viola, P., Jones, M.: Rapid object detection using a boosted cascade of simple features. In: IEEE Int. Conf. Comput. Vision and Pattern Recognition (CVPR), vol. 1, pp. 511–518 (2001)

29. Han, B., Davis, L.S.: Density-Based Multifeature Background Subtraction with Support Vector Machine. IEEE Trans. Pattern Anal. Mach. Intell. **34**(5), 1017–1023 (2012)

30. Barandela, R., Sánchez, J., García, V., Rangel, E.: Strategies for Learning in Class Imbalance Problems. Pattern Recognition **36**(3), 849–851 (2003)

31. Braham, M., Lejeune, A., Van Droogenbroeck, M.: A physically motivated pixel-based model for background subtraction in 3D images. In: International Conference on 3D Imaging (IC3D), pp. 1–8 (2014)

32. Fawcett, T.: An Introduction to ROC Analysis. Pattern Recognition Letters **27**(8), 861–874 (2006)

33. Goyette, N., Jodoin, P.-M., Porikli, F., Konrad, J., Ishwar, P.: changedetection.net: a new change detection benchmark dataset. In: IEEE Int. Conf. Comput. Vision and Pattern Recognition Workshop (CVPRW), pp. 1–8 (2012)

Towards More Natural Social Interactions of Visually Impaired Persons

Sergio Carrato, Gianfranco Fenu, Eric Medvet, Enzo Mumolo,
Felice Andrea Pellegrino, and Giovanni Ramponi^(✉)

DIA, University of Trieste, Trieste, Italy
{carrato,fenu,emedvet,mumolo,fapellegrino,ramponi}@units.it

Abstract. We review recent computer vision techniques with reference
to the specific goal of assisting the social interactions of a person affected
by very severe visual impairment or by total blindness. We consider a
scenario in which a sequence of images is acquired and processed by a
wearable device, and we focus on the basic tasks of detecting and recognizing people and their facial expression. We review some methodologies
of Visual Domain Adaptation that could be employed to adapt existing
classification strategies to the specific scenario. We also consider other
sources of information that could be exploited to improve the performance of the system.

1 Introduction

The realization of tools for improving the quality of life of blind people has always
been a very active topic of both academic research and industry development.
Modern ICT technologies have opened new interesting possibilities; for example,
the large available communication bandwidth has made feasible a project such as
BeMyEyes [1], where volunteers, using a live video connection, help blind people
by answering questions they make, e.g., the expiry date printed on some food,
or by giving information about the surroundings, so that they can easily move
around. Many other initiatives exist, such as FaceSpeaker [2], a wearable face
recognition system which can help the social interaction of a blind person by
identifying those who are close to him or her, Horus [3], which relies on video to
audio information conversion, or vEyes [4], a non-profit organization which aims
at boosting the development of simple application-specific tools for the blind.
However, the fact that none of these has received universal acceptance in the
blind people community, as it instead happened to the Braille systems almost
200 years ago, seems to suggest that they have not been able to provide solutions
with a sufficient degree of efficacy, efficiency and ease of use.

In terms of personal interactions, in particular, the everyday life of persons
with a visual impairment brings a number of situations in which "naturalness"
is affected. The person with disability and his/her interlocutor are aware that
many commonly used non-verbal interaction channels are not available; as a
consequence, they are compelled to modify their behaviour to partially compensate for this deficiency. Non-verbal communication includes physical movements

© Springer International Publishing Switzerland 2015
S. Battiato et al. (Eds.): ACIVS 2015, LNCS 9386, pp. 729–740, 2015.
DOI: 10.1007/978-3-319-25903-1_63

(hand and eyes movements, posture, face expressions), the speaker's appearance (clothes, accessories, make-up) and the distance between communicators. Blind people would feel uncomfortable asking other people to report non-verbal information. According to the focus group of the project "Social Interaction Assistant" [5,6] the most important non-verbal cues that visually impaired people may need to access are the number and the identity of present people, where a specific person is directing his/her attention, hand and body motions, if someone is behaving inappropriately, and the appearance of a person and how it has changed since the last encounter.

A research project has recently started, funded by the University of Trieste and a private donation, aiming to devise user-friendly vision-based techniques that assist the social interaction of a person affected by a very severe visual impairment or a total blindness. In this paper, we review some recent computer vision techniques, and revisit them according to the requirements of our goal. The originality of this contribution is related to the specific application we refer to. We consider a scenario in which a sequence of images is acquired by a wearable device and is processed by a smartphone in real-time. The number, the identity and the apparent emotional state of the present people have to be discovered and communicated (for instance verbally) to the visually impaired person. It seems obvious to rely on the face appearance to recognize people and infer their emotional state; as a consequence, face detection is a necessary preliminary step. Given the limited computational power at disposal, it seems reasonable to use the same face detector for both detecting and counting people (of course, a drawback of the mentioned approach is that people whose face is not visible in the acquired image will not be detected and counted.) Thus, the sequence of processing steps will be (i) face detection, (ii) recognition of each detected face, and (iii) facial expression recognition on each detected face; indeed, steps ii and iii could be performed in parallel. We refer the reader to [7] for a discussion of some relevant low-level vision issues specific to the described scenario. Here, we deal with computer vision tools at a higher abstraction level, namely those related to the use of classifiers (notice that all the mentioned processing steps require the use of some sort of classifier.) In particular, Section 2 discusses some methodologies of Visual Domain Adaptation that could be used to adapt existing classification strategies to the specific scenario. It is focused on face detection and recognition, but the same techniques can be applied to face expression recognition problems, treated in Section 3. Section 4 finally considers other sources of information that could be exploited to improve the performance of the overall system.

2   Visual Domain Adaptation

When a classifier is tested against data that possess a distribution different from the training data, a performance degradation usually occurs. For instance, a face detector trained to detect adult faces may fail to detect faces of babies and infants [8]. In pattern recognition, *domain adaptation* refers to a number of techniques aimed at mitigating the performance degradation of a classifier when it is applied to instances belonging to a domain (called *target domain*) different from that employed during the training phase (called *source domain*). A survey of the recent developments of domain adaptation for visual recognition (i.e., *Visual Domain Adaptation, VDA*) is provided in [9]. Basically, VDA methods try to exploit a few (possibly unlabelled) instances $\mathcal{T}$ of the target domain, along with the whole training set $\mathcal{S}$ of the source domain, to train a classifier capable of working in the target domain. A couple of notable exceptions, that do not rely on the knowledge of $\mathcal{S}$, are [8,10] as we will explain later on.

2.1   Feature Augmentation

Feature augmentation is probably the simplest approach to domain adaptation and is based on the seminal work [11]. If N is the number of features of the original domain, a new vector of features of dimension $3N$ is constructed by duplicating the features and stacking up a null vector 0_N of dimension N. More precisely, given $x_i^s \in \mathcal{S}$ and $x_i^t \in \mathcal{T}$, the corresponding augmented feature vectors, that belong to the new training set, will be $[(x_i^s)^T \ (x_i^s)^T \ 0_N^T]^T$ and $[(x_i^t)^T \ 0_N^T \ (x_i^t)^T]^T$. This simple approach, that exploits the commonalities of source and target domains (first block of the augmented feature space) and the specificity of the source (second block) and the target (third block) is shown to be surprisingly effective in [11], where a kernel version is also proposed. To allow the source and target domain to have a different feature dimensionality (respectively N and M), a projection-based approach has been proposed in [12]. Precisely, the extended feature vectors are $[(W_1 x_i^s)^T \ (x_i^s)^T \ 0_M^T]^T$ and $[(W_2 x_i^t)^T \ 0_N^T \ (x_i^t)^T]^T$ where the projection matrices W_1 and W_2 have the same number l of rows, resulting in an augmented feature space of dimension $l+N+M$. The projection matrices are learned during the training of the adapted classifier. Other feature augmentation approaches are [13,14], where a manifold of intermediate domains is employed, instead of a single augmented feature space. The feature augmentation approach amounts to building a new training set. As a consequence, the methods could be applied, in principle, to any kind of classifier (a new classifier is trained in a standard way based on the new training set) and in particular on cascade classifiers. Hence these methods are attractive for the considered scenario. Cascade classifiers, indeed, are known to be fast and reliable in object detection, see for instance [15].

2.2   Feature Transformation

Instead of augmenting the features, other approaches try to learn a suitable transformation from $\mathcal{T}$ to $\mathcal{S}$. In [16], a transformation is sought such that the instances of the target are mapped close to the instances of the same class belonging to the source and far from those of different class. The transformation is found by solving a constrained optimization problem. If $y = W x^t$ is the linearly transformed instance, the inner product $(x^s)^T y = (x^s)^T W x^t$ may be viewed as a similarity measure between x^s and the mapped instance. Based on the known labels of x^s and x^t, a proper constraint is added to the optimization problem to force similarity or dissimilarity. To prevent overfitting, the objective function is a regularizer $r(W)$, precisely $r(W) = \text{trace}(W) - \log \det(W)$. A kernelized version of the approach is provided in [17] to learn nonlinear transformations. Another feature transformation approach is reported in [18], where a transformation from $\mathcal{S}$ to $\mathcal{T}$ is learnt. More precisely, each instance x_i^s belonging to $\mathcal{S}$ undergoes a rigid transformation $W x_i^s - e_i$ where W is an orthonormal matrix and e_i is a translation term. In other words, all the source instances are rotated by the same amount and translated by a possibly different amount. The matrix W is found by solving an optimization problem whose goal is to satisfy the constraints $W x_i^s = [x_1^t \ x_2^t \cdots] Z + e_i$, $\forall i$, by keeping small the rank of Z and the error e_i. The idea is that of expressing the transformed source instances as a combination of few target instances. The transformed source data are then mixed to the target data to train a new classifier. As for feature augmentation approach, the method is not classifier-specific.

2.3   Parameter Adaptation

In the parameter adaptation approach, a new decision function for the target domain is formulated, based on a proper perturbation of the original one: $\text{sgn}(f_{\mathcal{T}}(x)) = \text{sgn}(f_{\mathcal{S}}(x) + \delta f(x))$. This approach has been pursued in the Support Vector Machine (SVM) context in [19] and in [20]. The main idea is that of formulating an optimization problem (whose decision variable, in the primal formulation, is w) similar to the standard SVM problem for the target domain, with an additional term in the objective function. The additional term is $||w - w_{\mathcal{S}}||^2$ meaning that a parameter w *close to the parameter $w_{\mathcal{S}}$ of the source classifier* has to be found. Notice that $\mathcal{S}$ does not need to be known explicitly, being encoded in $w_{\mathcal{S}}$. Despite the simplicity of the approach, the methods are reported to be effective in visual domain adaptation (for instance, in the task of adapting a classifier trained on bicycles to detect motorbikes). The parameter adaptation approach is suitable for those classifiers whose training amounts to finding a proper vector w of parameters, for instance multilayer perceptrons and SVMs. The new classifier is trained in a non-standard way (because of the additional cost $||w - w_{\mathcal{S}}||^2$) hence a specific code for training has to be written (off-the-shelf SVM implementations are not suitable, for instance), this being a possible drawback.

2.4   Cascade-Specific Methods

In [8,10] two VDA approaches are proposed that are particularly relevant for the scenario considered in the present paper. The mentioned approaches are structure-specific, in particular they are suitable for cascade classifiers. Cascade classifiers (see for instance [21]) are composed by a sequence of classifiers that usually have increasing complexity. An instance to be classified may be rejected at any stage of the sequence, being thus classified as negative; it is classified as positive only if it passes through all the stages of the sequence. Perhaps, the most known cascade classifier is the celebrated face detector by Viola and Jones

[22], hence the approaches [8,10] are relevant for the problem at hand. Furthermore, as opposite to the majority of the other domain adaptation methods, they do not require the knowledge of S. In [10], the following idea is pursued: given a binary classifier whose decision function is sgn $(f(x))$, the smaller is the prediction value $|f(x)|$, the more uncertain is the assigned class. For the face detection problem, the pre-trained classifier will confidently accept unoccluded, well-illuminated faces, and reject many non-face regions in a given image. Hence it will generate large prediction values for these easy acceptances and rejections. The difficult-to-detect faces will produce smaller prediction values. In [10] it is proposed to update the prediction values of the instances with low prediction from the pre-trained classifier by enforcing the smoothness of $f(x)$ (similar instances are encouraged to produce similar prediction values). In other words, a new function $f'(x)$ is found by enforcing $f(x)$ to be smooth *in the new domain*. The authors of [10] report good results in online adaptation (the classifier is adapted to each image, considered as a new domain). In a sense, detected faces in the image "attract" the difficult images toward themselves. Of course, an underlying assumption is that more faces of similar appearance (for instance, under the same lighting condition) appear in the image. In [8] the cascade classifier is adapted off-line, based on few positive instances from the target domain. In brief, the first stages of the pre-trained cascade (those responsible for the rejection of easy-to-reject instances) are replaced by some stages trained from scratch, based on the few target samples. The remaining stages are selected in order to remove those stages that are responsible of false negatives on the target domain. In [8] the approach is applied to the task of detection of baby faces. The reported results show that the adapted cascade outperforms both the original cascade (trained on human adults faces) and a new cascade, trained from scratch based on the few instances of the target domain.

3   Facial Expression Recognition

Facial expression recognition is performed by extracting from the face image the features connected to facial expressions and by classifying them. It is a challenging problem because in real environments there are variations in illumination and view angle and because there can be occlusions of the face image, like glasses, or long hair. Moreover, face recognition is generally based on a 2-D face imaging while the face is a 3-D object. However, using 3-D representation of the face images only alleviates the problems.

When benchmarking an algorithm it is recommendable to use a standard testing data set in order to directly compare the results. Therefore, similarly to what has happened for the face detection and recognition problems, many researchers dealing with automatic recognition of facial expressions have developed public datasets. The most popular are the Yale Face Database, which contains 165 grayscale images of 15 individuals with different facial expressions, the Cohn-Kanade Facial Expression Database, which contains 2105 digitized images from male and female subjects, and the Japanese Female Facial Expression (JAFFE) Database, which contains 213 images of 7 facial expressions by 10 Japanese female models.

3.1   Features for Facial Expression Recognition

The features employed for facial expression recognition can be roughly classified in two main categories, namely geometric features and appearance features. Geometric features can be extracted from the shape of the face or from the location of important facial components such as mouth and eyes. Patil et al. [23] suggest the use of active contour model, called snakes, for tracking lips in face images.

Appearance-based methods use some kind of image processing technique on the facial image in order to extract changes in facial appearance. Appearance features include Gabor [24] and Local Binary Pattern (LBP) [25] features. Gabor features are the output of Gabor filters, which are bandpass filters selective for orientation, and LBP features are local image descriptors which label each pixel on the basis of thresholding of its neighborhoods. It turns out that LBP features are able to statistically describe face characteristics. Among Gabor and LBP methods, LBP is the most commonly used technique for facial expression recognition.

3.2   Classifiers for Facial Expression Recognition

SVM are very popular classifiers for facial recognition. For example, Xiaoming and Shiqing in [26] propose a method based on LBP features and SVM. They achieved 78.57% on the JAFFE database. Using Gabor features and pseudo 2D Hidden Markov Model, He et al. [27], obtained a 96% accuracy on the JAFFE database. Piparsaniyan et al. describe in [28] a facial expression recognition system based on Gabor feature and simple Bayesian discriminating classifier based on principal component analysis (PCA). They obtain an accuracy of 96.7% on the JAFFE database.

3.3   Real Time Recognition of Facial Expression

Since in the application described in the present paper facial expression recognition is executed by devices of low computational power, tipically smartphones, the development of algorithms which are accurate but at the same time require low computational power is particular important. The real-time system described in [29] is based on a Haar cascade face detector, high-level facial shape features generated from facial landmarks, and a SVM classifier with linear kernel. Accuracy results on two different smartphones (Nexus 4 and Galaxy S3) is 77.5% on the extended Cohn-Kanade dataset. In [30] a real-time system for human-robot interaction based on Gabor filter with a set of morphological and convolutional filters to reduce the noise and the light dependence, and a Dynamic Bayesian Network classifier is described. The authors achieved average emotion detection accuracy of about 94% on a dataset developed by the authors themselves.

Novel Techniques Based on Deep Learning. The deep neural network (DNN) is an emerging technology that has recently demonstrated dramatic success in many applications. These structures need a particular way beyond back propagation to learn the weights of the connections, called Deep Learning. In [31] a facial emotion recognizer based on a convolutional neural network with 65 000 neurons and 5 hidden layers is described. With the extended Cohn-Kanade dataset the authors obtain an accuracy of 99.2% while with LBP features and SVM classifier on the same dataset they obtain 93%. The problem of this kind of algorithm is that the training phase is very computationally intensive, and this is the reason why they use a CUDA machine for training the network. The usage of the network is instead quite fast. The execution of the algorithm on a currently available smartphone takes less than 100 ms.

A fully connected Convolutional Neural Network or cascades of more Convolutional Neural Networks gives rise to Deep Convolutional Neural Networks. The deep CNN has been shown to achieve a strong success for image recognition [32].

4 Context-Aware Techniques

Social interactions among persons occur, in general, in uncontrolled environments, which may result in low quality information available for the aid machinery, e.g., unoptimal pose, illumination, and so on [7]. On the other hand, other kinds of information could be exploited besides image and video acquired by the device. This supplementary information is often referred to as *context*.

Contextual information may be roughly classified in two categories: (i) low-level data which can be acquired by device sensors other than a camera, and (ii) high-level data which can be acquired by other sources such as Online Social Networks (OSN). Several studies have been carried out which focus on how to better solve specific tasks (mainly face recognition) by using contextual information. Here we review some recent and significant works and highlight how their findings can apply in the scenario considered in this paper.

4.1 Low-Level Contextual Data

The vast majority of today smartphones are equipped with sensors which allow the system to obtain an estimate of its location—i.e., the spatial context: the estimate can be obtained from GPS, or, indirectly, from other sensor readings (opportunistic location). Moreover, all devices are able to determine the current time and hence infer the temporal context. The spatial and temporal contexts have been widely used to improve the accuracy of person identification systems: several noteworthy papers that follow this approach are described below.

The authors of [33] show a method for exploiting spatial and temporal context for improving the accuracy of face recognition applied to images captured by smartphone cameras. They report a remarkable improvement in accuracy (+40%) when using contextual information. Interestingly, this also includes the cell ID—a generally unique number used to identify each Base transceiver station

(BTS), to which the smartphone is connected—which can be used to provide a raw estimate of the location even when the GPS sensor does not operate.

In [34], a similar method is proposed to perform person identification within photo collections. The proposed system gathers three types of contextual information which the authors call temporal proximity, spatial proximity, and co-occurrence. Co-occurrence is the information related to the presence of two or more subjects in the same photo: in the cited work, it is obtained from the Bluetooth signal of nearby devices, when available, with respect to the device which captured the image. The authors conclude that it is possible to improve performance by considering contextual information; besides, they find that temporal proximity is more helpful than spatial proximity and co-occurrence.

A more general framework is proposed in [35], where the availability of location and temporal information is incorporated in a system which is experimentally shown to be effective for person identification in photo collections. The experimental evaluation is carried out using actual GPS readings.

Notwithstanding the cited works seem to suggest that great benefit can be obtained from low-level contextual data (namely, location and temporal information) for real-world person identification, we argue that the actual applicability of this finding to the scenario considered in this paper deserves further investigation. Indeed, the works mentioned above focus on the managing of photo collections, a task that can be performed offline. For instance, consider the case in which a photo P_2 exists in a photo collection in which the persons A and B can be easily identified with a content-only technique, since image conditions are optimal (e.g., pose, illumination); if a photo P_1 exists which has been acquired before P_2 and P_1 and P_2 share the context, then the identification of A and B in P_1 could be aided, even in case of nonoptimal image conditions, by using the context. On the other hand, a system aiming at improving naturalness of social interactions of a visually impaired person should be able to precisely identify persons also when the context (in terms of location and time) is "new", and hence no previous contextual information can be exploited: e.g., the impaired user enters a room where some persons have to be identified.

A radically different kind of low-level data which can be used to perform face recognition is the data coming from 3-D and infrared (IR) sensors. Despite it is known that this data can positively affect face recognition effectiveness, we believe that its impact on the scenario considered in this paper is currently limited, since common devices do not include the related sensors yet. We refer the reader to [36] for a recent survey on techniques which build also on 3-D and IR, also known as multimodal face recognition.

Finally, non visual information can be used also in tasks other than person identification. In [37], a method is presented for real-time, user independent classification of emotions from webcam quality video and audio. The authors shows that the classification accuracy can be improved by considering features derived from audio signal, w.r.t. using only those deriving from video signal. We think that this finding could be of interest also for the scenario considered in this paper, despite the fact that visually impaired persons are likely good in estimating people emotions from audio. In particular, merging information of audio and video could be useful in the learning phase, when the emotion of a "new" subject can be heard by the user who may then make the system associate the subject's current appearance with that emotion.

4.2   High-Level Contextual Data

The ever increasing ubiquitousness of network-enabled devices able to capture images (e.g., smartphones) and the large adoption of OSN web sites as a tool to store and share those images lead to the existence of large-scale knowledge bases about people appearance and social connections. This high-level information made possible, in the recent past, to reach new milestones of effectiveness and/or practicality in the task of person identification from images. The improvements have been obtained mainly in two ways: (i) by exploiting, in the learning phase, the big (possibly labeled) data available in OSN without significant modifications of existing methods, or (ii) by directly leveraging OSN data to refine the outcome of an identification method. It is worth to note, though, that exploiting web-available information for moving the person identification effectiveness beyond the level that a human would achieve autonomously is perceived as controversial and raises privacy issues. For instance, the authors of [38] highlight the implications of the convergence of face recognition technology and increasing online self-disclosure: they perform two experiments to illustrate the ability to identify strangers online (on a dating site where individuals protect their identities by using pseudonyms) and offline (in a public space), based on photos made publicly available on a social network site.

Researchers of Facebook AI Research show in [39] how they obtained a remarkable improvements in face recognition accuracy on unconstrained environments. To this end, the authors revisit the alignment and representation steps of a conventional face recognition pipeline by including a piecewise affine transformation and a deep neural network, which they train on a dataset including four million facial images.

Many approaches have been proposed for exploiting the social context to refine the results of face recognition methods. For instance, in [40], social cues learnt from large collection of annotated photos by means of association rule mining techniques are used to re-rank face recognition output for the input photo, which results in improved face identification performance with marginal computational overhead. The availability in the web of loosely annotated images of persons can be exploited to build unsupervised face recognition systems. Tools with this aim, possibly tailored to specific kinds of images or persons, have been proposed in [41,42].

Finally, a fully automatic end-to-end system for face augmentation on mobile devices is proposed in [43]: a smartphone user can point his/her device to a person and the system identifies the person and overlays, in near real-time, a box with his/her information. The tracking algorithm runs on the mobile client, while the recognition runs on a server: people information is obtained offline from OSNs. The cited paper shows the feasibility of a face recognition system which runs on commodity mobile hardware, a proposal which fits the scenario considered in this paper.

5   Conclusions

We have examined a set of computer vision techniques, revisiting them with the aim of devising the core of a vision-based system able to assist the blind in his/her social interactions. We discussed several visual domain adaptation techniques, which aim at reducing the differences between the training and testing images. Moreover, the emerging deep neural network architectures for image and facial expression recognition have been briefly described. Finally, several approaches for better solving specific tasks using contextual information have been discussed.

Further studies will be devoted to the tools needed to transmit the extracted information to the user. Tactile sensations or sound could be used for this purpose. Moreover, together with the Users' Group of our project, we will realize a set of benchmark sequences to test the various system components. Indeed, even if many datasets exist for the study of face detection and recognition techniques (some have been cited above), none of them is suited to our context and goals.

Acknowledgement. This work has been supported by the University of Trieste - Finanziamento di Ateneo per progetti di ricerca scientifica - FRA 2014, and by a private donation in memory of Angelo Soranzo (1939-2012).

References

1. Be My Eyes: Web site. http://www.bemyeyes.org/ (accessed August 5, 2015)
2. FaceSpeaker: Web site. http://www.facespeaker.org/ (accessed August 5, 2015)
3. Horus Technology: Web site. http://horus.technology/en/ (accessed August 5, 2015)
4. vEyes: Web site. http://www.veyes.it/ (accessed August 5, 2015)
5. Krishna, S., Little, G., Black, J., Panchanathan, S.: A wearable face recognition system for individuals with visual impairments. In: Proceedings of the 7th international ACM SIGACCESS conference on Computers and accessibility, pp. 106–113. ACM (2005)
6. McDaniel, T., Krishna, S., Balasubramanian, V., Colbry, D., Panchanathan, S.: Using a haptic belt to convey non-verbal communication cues during social interactions to individuals who are blind. In: IEEE International Workshop on Haptic Audio visual Environments and Games, HAVE 2008, pp. 13–18. IEEE (2008)
7. Bonetto, M., Carrato, S., Fenu, G., Medvet, E., Mumolo, E., Pellegrino, F.A., Ramponi, G.: Image processing issues in a social assistive system for the blind. In: 9th International Symposium on Image and Signal Processing and Analysis (ISPA), September 2015
8. Jain, V., Farfade, S.S.: Adapting classification cascades to new domains. In: IEEE International Conference on Computer Vision (ICCV), pp. 105–112. IEEE (2013)
9. Patel, V., Gopalan, R., Li, R., Chellappa, R.: Visual domain adaptation: A survey of recent advances. IEEE Signal Processing Magazine **32**(3), 53–69 (2015)

10. Jain, V., Learned-Miller, E.: Online domain adaptation of a pre-trained cascade of classifiers. In: IEEE Conference on Computer Vision and Pattern Recognition (CVPR), pp. 577–584. IEEE (2011)

11. Daumé III, H.: Frustratingly easy domain adaptation. In: Proceedings of the 45th Annual Meeting of the Association of Computational Linguistics, pp. 256–263 (2007)

12. Li, W., Duan, L., Xu, D., Tsang, I.W.: Learning with augmented features for supervised and semi-supervised heterogeneous domain adaptation. IEEE Transactions on Pattern Analysis and Machine Intelligence 36(6), 1134–1148 (2014)

13. Gopalan, R., Li, R., Chellappa, R.: Domain adaptation for object recognition: An unsupervised approach. In: IEEE International Conference on Computer Vision (ICCV), pp. 999–1006. IEEE (2011)

14. Gopalan, R., Li, R., Chellappa, R.: Unsupervised adaptation across domain shifts by generating intermediate data representations. IEEE Transactions on Pattern Analysis and Machine Intelligence 36(11), 2288–2302 (2014)

15. Zhang, C., Zhang, Z.: A survey of recent advances in face detection. Microsoft Research, Technical report MSR-TR-2010-66 (2010)

16. Saenko, K., Kulis, B., Fritz, M., Darrell, T.: Adapting visual category models to new domains. In: Daniilidis, K., Maragos, P., Paragios, N. (eds.) ECCV 2010, Part IV. LNCS, vol. 6314, pp. 213–226. Springer, Heidelberg (2010)

17. Kulis, B., Saenko, K., Darrell, T.: What you saw is not what you get: Domain adaptation using asymmetric kernel transforms. In: IEEE Conference on Computer Vision and Pattern Recognition (CVPR), pp. 1785–1792. IEEE (2011)

18. Jhuo, I.H., Liu, D., Lee, D., Chang, S.F.: Robust visual domain adaptation with low-rank reconstruction. In: IEEE Conference on Computer Vision and Pattern Recognition (CVPR), pp. 2168–2175. IEEE (2012)

19. Yang, J., Yan, R., Hauptmann, A.G.: Cross-domain video concept detection using adaptive SVMs. In: Proceedings of the 15th international conference on Multimedia, pp. 188–197. ACM (2007)

20. Aytar, Y., Zisserman, A.: Tabula rasa: Model transfer for object category detection. In: IEEE International Conference on Computer Vision (ICCV), pp. 2252–2259. IEEE (2011)

21. Dal Col, L., Pellegrino, F.A.: Fast and accurate object detection by means of recursive monomial feature elimination and cascade of SVM. In: Fanti, M., Giua, A. (eds.) Proceedings of the IEEE Conference on Automation Science and Engineering, pp. 304–309, Trieste (2011)

22. Viola, P., Jones, M.J.: Robust real-time face detection. International Journal of Computer Vision 57(2), 137–154 (2004)

23. Patil, R., Vineet, S., Mandal, A.S.: Facial expression recognition in image sequences using active shape model and svm. In: Proceedings of the UKSim 5th European Symposium on Computer Modeling and Simulation, pp. 16–18, December 2011

24. Gu, W., Xiang, C., Venkatesh, Y., Huang, D., Lin, H.: Facial expression recognition using radial encoding of local gabor features and classifier synthesis. Pattern Recognition, pp. 80–91 (2012)

25. Zhang, S., Zhao, X., Lei, B.: Facial expression recognition based on local binary patterns and local fisher discriminant analysis. WSEAS Trans. Signal Process, pp. 21–31 (2012)

26. Xiaoming, Z., Shiqing, Z.: Facial expression recognition based on local binary patterns and least squares support vector machines. Lecture Notes in Electrical Engineering 140, 707–712 (2012)

27. He, L., Wang, X., Yu, C., Wu, K.: Facial expression recognition using embedded hidden markov model. In: IEEE International Conference on Systems, Man and Cybernetics, pp. 1568–1572 (2009)
28. Piparsaniyan, Y., Sharma, V.K., Mahapatr, K.K.: Robust facial expression recognition using Gabor feature and bayesian discriminating classifier. In: Proc. of Int. Conf. on Comm. and Signal Processing, pp. 538–541 (2014)
29. Suk, M., Prabhakaran, B.: Real-time facial expression recognition on smartphones. In: Proc. of IEEE Winter Conference on Applications of Computer Vision, pp. 1054–1059 (2015)
30. Cid, F., Prado, J., Bustos, P., Nunez, P.: A real time and robust facial expression recognition and imitation approach for affective human-robot interaction using Gabor filtering. In: Proc. of IROS, pp. 2188–2193 (2013)
31. Song, I., Kim, H.J., Jeon, P.B.: Deep learning for real-time robust facial expression recognition on a smartphone. In: Proc. of IEEE Int. Conf. on Cons. Electronics (2014)
32. Krizhevsky, A., Sutskever, I., Hinton, G.: Imagenet classification with deep convolutional neural networks. In: Advances in neural information processing systems, pp. 1097–1105 (2012)
33. Davis, M., Smith, M., Canny, J., Good, N., King, S., Janakiraman, R.: Towards context-aware face recognition. In: Proceedings of the 13th annual ACM international conference on Multimedia, pp. 483–486. ACM (2005)
34. O'Hare, N., Smeaton, A.F.: Context-aware person identification in personal photo collections. IEEE Transactions on Multimedia 11(2), 220–228 (2009)
35. Kapoor, A., Lin, D., Baker, S., Hua, G., Akbarzadeh, A.: How to make face recognition work: The power of modeling context. AAAI Work (2012)
36. Zhou, H., Mian, A., Wei, L., Creighton, D., Hossny, M., Nahavandi, S.: Recent advances on singlemodal and multimodal face recognition: A survey. IEEE Transactions on Human-Machine Systems 44(6), 701–716 (2014)
37. Paleari, M., Huet, B., Chellali, R.: Towards multimodal emotion recognition: a new approach. In: Proceedings of the ACM International Conference on Image and Video Retrieval, pp. 174–181. ACM (2010)
38. Acquisti, A., Gross, R., Stutzman, F.: Face recognition and privacy in the age of augmented reality. Journal of Privacy and Confidentiality 6(2), 1 (2014)
39. Taigman, Y., Yang, M., Ranzato, M., Wolf, L.: Deepface: closing the gap to human-level performance in face verification. In: IEEE Conference on Computer Vision and Pattern Recognition (CVPR), pp. 1701–1708. IEEE (2014)
40. Bharadwaj, S., Vatsa, M., Singh, R.: Aiding face recognition with social context association rule based re-ranking. In: IEEE International Joint Conference on Biometrics (IJCB), pp. 1–8. IEEE (2014)
41. Medvet, E., Bartoli, A., Davanzo, G., De Lorenzo, A.: Automatic face annotation in news images by mining the web. In: Proceedings of the 2011 IEEE/WIC/ACM International Conferences on Web Intelligence and Intelligent Agent Technology, vol. 01, pp. 47–54. IEEE Computer Society (2011)
42. Wang, D., Hoi, S.C.H., He, Y.: A unified learning framework for auto face annotation by mining web facial images. In: Proceedings of the 21st ACM international conference on Information and knowledge management, pp. 1392–1401. ACM (2012)
43. Dantone, M., Bossard, L., Quack, T., Van Gool, L.: Augmented faces. In: IEEE International Conference on Computer Vision Workshops (ICCV Workshops), pp. 24–31. IEEE (2011)

A Mobile Application for Braille to Black Conversion

Giovanni Maria Farinella, Paolo Leonardi, and Filippo Stanco[✉]

Dipartimento di Matematica e Informatica, University of Catania, Catania, Italy
{gfarinella,pleonardi,fstanco}@dmi.unict.it
http://iplab.dmi.unict.it

Abstract. This work aims to the production of inclusive technologies to help people affected by diseases. In particular, we present a pipeline to convert Braille documents, acquired with a mobile device, into classic printed text. The mobile application has been thought as support for assistants (e.g., in the education domain) and parents of blind and partially sighted persons (e.g., children and elderly) for the reading of Braille written documents. The software has been developed and tested thanks to the collaboration with experts in the field [2]. Experimental results confirm the effectiveness of the proposed imaging pipeline in terms of conversion accuracy, punctuation, and final page layout.

Keywords: Braille · Optical character recognition · Blind · Visually impaired · Mobile devices · iOS

1 Introduction and Motivation

The creation of new technologies to support people with diseases is one of the most important challenges posed by modern society to the research community. Among the diseases that can affect the humans, the visual impairment is increasing. The World Health Organization (WHO) estimated that there were more than 160 millions visually impaired people in the world in 2002, which means more than 2.5% of the total population. Specifically, the study of WHO reported that there were 124 millions of people with low vision capacity and 37 millions were blind [3].

Today, the society has a high attention for the blind and partially sighted people (e.g., suitable books are available, medications and city maps report information for blind, tactile museums exist, etc.). Industry has produced dedicated hardware (e.g., printers and keyboards) and software (e.g., pdf readers by text to sound transduction, cash machine readers, etc.) for the people with low vision ability. Computer Vision products (e.g., Orcam [1]) are in the market to help blind and partially sighted to read newspapers, recognize objects, localize and recognize faces. Despite these efforts, too few tools have been developed to support assistants and parents of blind and partially sighted people for the reading of documents written for the blind.

© Springer International Publishing Switzerland 2015
S. Battiato et al. (Eds.): ACIVS 2015, LNCS 9386, pp. 741–751, 2015.
DOI: 10.1007/978-3-319-25903-1_64

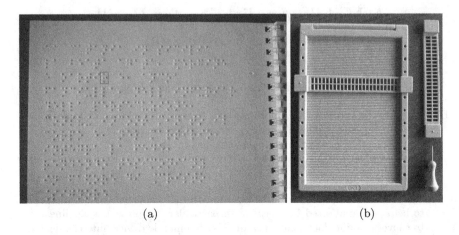

Fig. 1. (a) Example of Braille document. Each character consists of a maximum of six dots arranged in a 3 × 2 grid (as example see the Braille letter "r" in region indicated by the red bounding box). (b) Example of tablet for writing in Braille. On the right the awl used to produce the dots on the paper.

The writing system used by blind and partially sighted people is called "Braille" (Fig. 1(a)). It is a tactile writing system invented by Louis Braille in the middle of 19th century. The Braille characters are small rectangular blocks containing tiny palpable dots. Each character consists of a maximum of six dots arranged in a 3 × 2 grid (Fig. 2).

The number and arrangement of the dots discriminate one character from another (i.e., the different letter of the alphabet and the symbols of punctuation). Some other rules are coded by coupling Braille characters in order to reproduce the classic writing (e.g., an uppercase character is preceded by another Braille symbol with the dots in the first and third row of the first column). Braille-users can write with a portable braille note-taker like the one shown in Fig. 1(b). The Braille characters are produced with an awl which is used to impress the dots composing the letters. Braille characters are written from the right to the left in the rear of the Braille page. The reader scrolls the fingertip on the face of the sheet to perceive the dots in relief. The classic printed letters (i.e., the ones written with classic ink) are referred as "black" letters in the slang of blind people.

The present work has been inspired and supported by the Unione Italiana Ciechi e Ipovedenti (Italian Union of the Blind and Partially Sighted) [2] who expressed the need to have technologies useful for non-impaired people (e.g., assistants and parents of blind people) who wish to help blind and partially sighted in the context of education and more in general in other contexts of the public domain. Specifically, in the education context an automatic Braille to black conversion software is useful to help not-impaired volunteers to interact with visually impaired people (e.g., in particular children and elderly) when a Braille document have to be read. Indeed, to read a document written for the

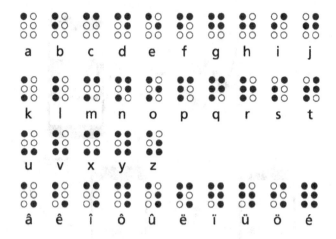

Fig. 2. The Braille alphabet.

blind and visually impaired, the Braille system should be known. Despite experts can easily read a Braille document, this is not the case for most of parents of blind persons. As indicated by experts of [2], a tool for Braille to black conversion is extremely useful to solve, for instance, disputes between teachers and parents of a blind person. Those disputes usually happen in the context of education when the parents of a blind (who usually do not know the Braille system) do not agree with the outcome of the exams of their children. The problems above have motivated the development of the proposed Braille to black conversion software.

Although similar works have been proposed in literature [5–9], most of them have been tested on few Braille documents, and no one seems have been assessed with the support of blind and non blind experts [2] who provided a set of Braille documents considering the different encoding aspects of the Braille writing system. Moreover, the developed software has been properly tested taking into account the different rules encoded in the Braille documents, as well as page layout and punctuation (e.g., the uppercase characters are preceded by a specific Braille code).

The present work is an extension of our previous Braille to black conversion software [13] to the mobile devices domain. The algorithms have been revised and improved to work considering affine transformations of the point of view. The application has been developed for iOS touch devices.

The paper is organized as follows: Section 2 details the proposed Braille to black conversion method, whereas in Section 3 the experimental phase and the obtained results are reported. Finally, conclusions and hints for future works are given in Section 4.

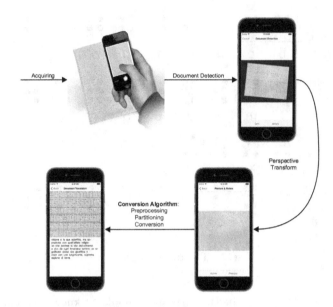

Fig. 3. Pipeline to convert a Braille document into classic printed text.

2   Braille to Black Conversion

The aim of the proposed image processing pipeline is the conversion of a Braille document acquired with a mobile device into text. The overall pipeline is composed by four main steps as shown on Fig. 3.

After the image acquisition, a document detection procedure and a perspective transform are performed to find and extract the portion of the image related to the Braille document. Then, a pre-processing step is applied to remove the noise and to enhance the signal information in correspondence of the Braille characters. At this stage a detection procedure to locate the positions of the dots is employed and the document is partitioned obtaining lines and Braille cells. Finally, starting from the association of the dots to the grid layout and considering the rules of the Braille writing system, the conversion from Braille to black is performed.

The main steps involved in the proposed Braille to black conversion procedure are detailed in the following sub-sections.

2.1   Document Detection and Transform

Once the image is acquired with the mobile device (Fig. 4(a)), the edges related to the document are detected. We start searching for all the edges from the image using the algorithm proposed in [14]. Then the close areas found are sorted by their size. The largest area that contains all the edges is approximated with four points that we assume to be the corners of the document in the image.

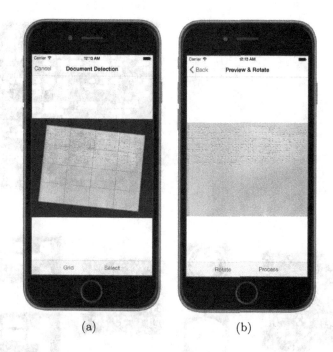

          (a)   (b)

Fig. 4. (a) The acquired document. (b) The document after the affine transforms.

We assume that the document to be acquired with the mobile device is the main focus of the image and the document is rectangular.

The next operation is to take the four points representing the corners of the document to make geometrical trasformations to obtain a top-down image. In particular, a perspective transform [14] is performed to obtain a rectangular area to be used in the next steps (Fig. 4(b)).

2.2 Preprocessing

In the preprocessing step different operations are performed in order to remove the noise and to enhance the information related to the dots.

The image is first binarized using a proper threshold (Fig. 5(b)). A flood fill operation is then executed to fill the holes in the dots and a Gaussian filter is applied to improve the structure of the image (Fig. 5(c)). As last steps are sequentially performed the morphological operations of erosion and dilation [14] (Fig. 5(d)).

2.3 Braille Document Partitioning

This step is devoted to locate the Braille cells. As first part of the step, the lines of the Braille document are detected and then each line is partitioned in cells.

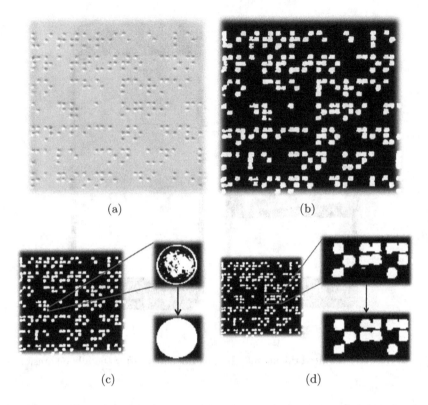

(a)

(b)

(c)

(d)

Fig. 5. (a) Original image. (b) Binary image. (c) Flood fill operation. (d) Erosion and dilation morphological operators.

The values on the previous binarized image are summarized with an histogram along the vertical side to obtain a column vector where each component is equal to the sum of the binary values (Fig. 6(a)). From the column vector are obtained the initial and the end positions of the Braille lines. The values in the vertical histogram is related to the number of dots present in the line (Fig. 7(a)). Since a Braille cell is composed by 3×2 dots, 3 peaks in the histogram correspond to one Braille line. The values on every lines are hence summed along the columns. We obtain a row vector and two peaks of the horizontal histogram correspond to one 3×2 Braille cell (Fig. 7(b)).

2.4   Conversion

The Braille cells obtained in the previous step are divided in 3×2 grid shown in Fig. 6(b). The number of white pixel in each of the six areas of the grid is considered and if this number is below a threshold the value 1 is assigned to the area, otherwise the value 0 is associated to that area. So, for each Braille cell a six-bits code who describes the position of the dots un the cell is obtained

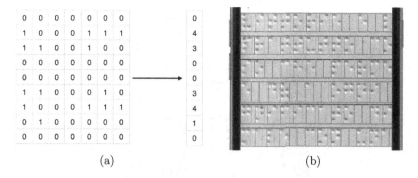

Fig. 6. (a) Conversion of image matrix in column vector. (b) Example of partitioning.

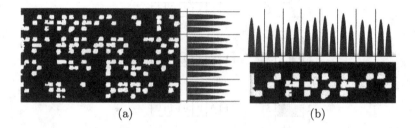

Fig. 7. (a) Partitioning the image in lines. (b) Partitioning the lines in Braille cells.

Fig. 9. The conversion took place finding the text character corresponding to the obtained binary code by exploiting a standard conversion table (Fig. 8).

3   Experimental Results

For testing purpose we have used the dataset previously exploited in [13]. The dataset is composed by 55 Braille documents coming from journals and books. It contains both geometric and photometric variability (i.e., variability in terms of rotation, page dimensions, color of pages, contrast).

The Braille documents have been selected by experts from [2] by considering the different encoding aspects of the Braille writing system to properly test the proposed imaging pipeline with respect to the different rules embedded in the Braille documents (e.g., the number and position of the Braille dots related to the letter "a" and to the number "1" are identical. An extra Braille symbol, with three dots in the first column and just one dot in the lower row of the second column, precedes the one representing a number). Five random documents have been chosen and each dot within those documents has been manually labeled to have a ground truth to set the parameters involved into the Braille to black conversion pipeline. The remaining 50 Braille documents have been used for testing purposes. The average number of Braille characters in the test set is 774

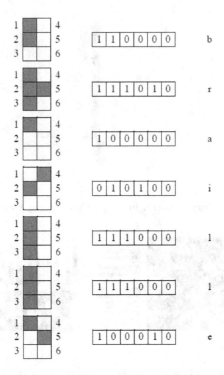

Fig. 8. A part of standard conversion table.

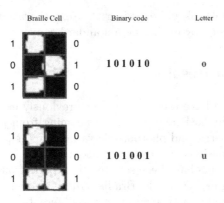

Fig. 9. Examples of conversion.

characters per document. Each document has been acquired with an iPhone 6 with a 1,4 GHz dual core processor, 1GB RAM and 8 megapixel rear camera. The assessment of the conversion has been done with the help of experts (both blind and not blind) of the Unione Italiana Ciechi e Ipovedenti (Italian Union of the Blind and Partially Sighted) [2], who read each Braille document in order

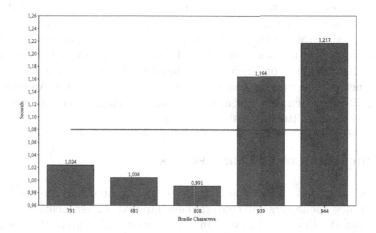

Fig. 10. Average speed of the algorithm with the test configuration.

Fig. 11. A Braille document and the related text obtained with the developed software.

to have a ground truth to be compared with the documents produced by the automatic conversion. The comparison between the document transcription and the text obtained with our software has given an accuracy of 91% in terms of characters recognition. This results is similar to the one we have obtained in our previous work [13] where a scanner was imployed for the acquisition. As in [13] most of the unrecognized characters were found in old and worn Braille documents. No errors in terms of page layout and punctuation (i.e., structure and organization of the text) have been found in the converted documents. In Fig. 10 is reported the conversion time related to the five document used to set the parameters. The average conversion time is about 1 second. An example of a part of Braille document given as input to our application with the related black conversion (in Italian) is shown in Fig. 11.

4   Conclusion and Future Works

This paper describes an imaging pipeline to be exploited in a mobile device to acquire Braille documents and convert them into text. Experiments have demonstrated that the developed algorithm can acquire and convert the documents with good accuracy and in real time. Future works will be devoted to implement a dictionary correction over the converted text to improve the conversion accuracy. We plan to make the application available also for other operating systems (i.e., Android, Windows Phone).

Acknowledgments. The authors would like to thank the Unione Italiana Ciechi e Ipovedenti (Italian Union of the Blind and Partially Sighted) [2] for inspiring, supporting and testing this work.

References

1. www.orcam.com
2. Unione Italiana Ciechi e Ipovedenti (Italian Union of the Blind and Partially Sighted). http://www.uiciechi.it/
3. Kocur, I., Parajasegaram, R., Pokharel, G.: Global Data on Visual Impairment in the Year 2002. Bulletin of the World Health Organization **82** (2004)
4. Mennens, J., Van Tichelen, L., Francois, G., Engelen, J.J.: Optical recognition of Braille writing using standard equipment. IEEE Transactions on Rehabilitation Engineering **2**(4), 207–212 (1994)
5. Ng, C.M., Ng, V., Lau, Y.: Regular feature extraction for recognition of Braille. In: Proceedings of the Third International Conference on Computational Intelligence and Multimedia Applications, pp. 302–306 (1999)
6. Hentzschel, T.W., Blenkhorn, P.: An optical reading system for embossed Braille characters using a twin shadows approach. International Journal of Microcomputer Applications **18**(4), 341–354 (1995)
7. Wong, L., Abdulla, W., Hussmann, S.: A software algorithm prototype for optical recognition of embossed Braille. In: Proceedings of the International Conference on Pattern Recognition, Vol. 2, pp. 586–589 (2004)
8. Tai, Z., Cheng, S., Verma, P., Zhai, Y.: Braille document recognition using Belief Propagation. Journal of Visual Communication and Image Representation **21**(7), 722–730 (2010)

 9. Schmid, C.: Constructing models for content-based image retrieval. In Proceedings of the IEEE Conference on Computer Vision and Pattern Recognition (2001)
10. Sezgin, M., Sankur, B.: Survey over image thresholding techniques and quantitative performance evaluation. Journal of Electronic Imaging **13**(1), 146–168 (2004)
11. Atherton, T.J., Kerbyson, D.J.: Size invariant circle detection. Image and Vision Computing **17**(11) (1999)
12. Suzuki, S., Abe, K.: Topological Structural Analysis of Digitized Binary Images by Border Following. Computer Vision, Graphics, and Image Processing CVGIP **30**(1), 32–46 (1985)
13. Stanco, F., Buffa, M., Farinella, G.M.: Automatic braille to black conversion. In: Baldoni, M., Baroglio, C., Boella, G., Micalizio, R. (eds.) AI*IA 2013. LNCS, vol. 8249, pp. 517–526. Springer, Heidelberg (2013)
14. Gonzalez, R.C., Woods, R.E.: Digital Image Processing, 3rd edn. Prentice-Hall Inc, Upper Saddle River (2006)

Unsupervised Salient Object Matting

Jaehwan Kim[✉] and Jongyoul Park

Electronics and Telecommunications Research Institute, Daejeon, Republic of Korea
{jh.kim,jongyoul}@etri.re.kr

Abstract. In this paper, we present a new, easy-to-generate method that is capable of precisely matting salient objects in a large-scale image set in an unsupervised way. Our method extracts only salient object without any user-specified constraints or a manual-thresholding of the saliency-map, which are essentially required in the image matting or saliency-map based segmentation, respectively. In order to provide a more balanced visual saliency as a response to both local features and global contrast, we propose a new, coupled saliency-map based on a linearly combined conspicuity map. Also, we introduce an adaptive tri-map as a refined segmented image of the coupled saliency-map for a more precise object extraction. The proposed method improves the segmentation performance, compared to image matting based on two existing saliency detection measures. Numerical experiments and visual comparisons with large-scale real image set confirm the useful behavior of the proposed method.

Keywords: Unsupervised matting · Object segmentation · Saliency-map

1 Introduction

Unsupervised matting or object segmentation, the goal of which is to extract interesting foreground components from natural background regions in the absence of any additional information, plays an important role in a variety of areas such as computer vision and graphics. The conventional matting has been widely used in contents production in order to provide an efficient way of dealing with a complicated composition [10,16,19] or an extraction process in application such as an object-oriented reconstruction [8,18]. Especially, performing unsupervised segmentation with any level of significant accuracy can be useful for automatic generation of large-scale annotated training sets with more accuracy, and improving the performance of object recognition or content-based image retrieval. The actual unsupervised matting was introduced by [11] under the name of spectral matting which is an extension of spectral segmentation [21]. The spectral matting is to estimate a complete foreground alpha matte under an assumption that a set of matting components of whole image as well as minimal user intervention is given in advance. Image matting including the unsupervised matting is intrinsically ill-posed so that it is hard to generate a clean segmented object matte from a given image without any prior constraints. This additional constraints are usually fed by means of a tri-map which

© Springer International Publishing Switzerland 2015
S. Battiato et al. (Eds.): ACIVS 2015, LNCS 9386, pp. 752–763, 2015.
DOI: 10.1007/978-3-319-25903-1_65

is a rough pre-segmented image consisting of three subregions of foreground, background and unknown. When such matting process is applied to the object collections in a large-scale image set, the requirement for manually specifying every tri-map for each of independent input images can be a serious drawback definitely. Meanwhile, automatic detection of salient object regions in images has been widely researched in computer vision tasks including image segmentation, object recognition, salient object segmentation and so on [1–7,12,13,15]. Although there are many different types of proposal measures in methodology under the common perceptual assumption of a salient region standing out its surrounding neighbors and capturing the attention of a human observer, most final saliency-maps having lots of noises are not sufficient to take advantage of the consequent computational processes of highly accurate low-level representation of images. Within the framework of human perception system in [9], the saliency-map is also considered as a linearly combined information of a variety of individual conspicuity maps such as orientation of edges, color, disparity, etc.

Motivated by existing works [1,4,5,9,10], in this paper we introduce a novel object extraction method, whereby it is possible to segment more precisely salient objects in a large-scale image set in an unsupervised manner. The method is referred to as 'unsupervised salient object matting', where the procedure is performed by incorporating a saliency estimation into a matting process. We also introduce a new, coupled saliency-map based on fused information from different saliency-maps into one coherent whole, as well as an adaptive tri-map as a refined segmented image of the coupled saliency-map.

This paper is organized as follows: section 2 handles technical details, section 3 validates the proposed method by performing several experiments, and finally we conclude in section 4 with summarizing the main contributions.

2   Unsupervised Salient Object Matting

We begin with revisiting the salient object detection solutions. Then, we illustrate how to construct the coupled saliency-map, how to apply the tri-map adaptation from the obtained saliency-map, and finally, how to simulate our method while comparing with the results obtained from matting solution based on each of two well-known saliency-maps. In Fig. 1, our systematic flow is briefly illustrated.

2.1   Coupled Saliency-Map

We propose a new coupled saliency-map as a linearly combined feature map under the physiological assumption that a topographical saliency-map includes a variety of different features encoding the global conspicuity of objects [9] in order to consider a visual saliency as a balanced response to both local features(e.g., edges, color, and luminance) and global contrast(e.g., regions and shapes). The frequency tuned method proposed by [1] is capable of extracting a uniformly highlighted salient regions with well-defined boundaries by using difference of Gaussian. The frequency tuned method evaluates the saliency based

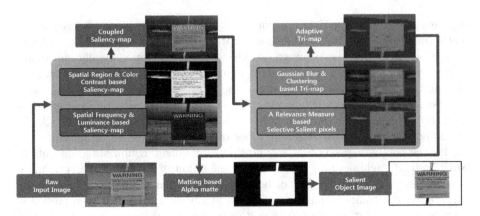

Fig. 1. Overview of our system: data flows for the saliency measure and matting process are denoted by red & blue colored lines, respectively.

on the low-level features of color and luminance. Moreover, the global contrast based approach introduced by [4] estimates the saliency-map measured by image segmentation, region-level contrast, and spatial distances to other regions in the image.

The c channel color original image is denoted as $\mathcal{I}$, and $\mathcal{I}_i$ represents the color vector of the ith pixel. Our coupled saliency-map of involving a spatially weighted region contrast computed in the RGB color space, $\mathcal{S}^g$, and the difference of Gaussian based a salient region evaluated in the CIELab color space, $\mathcal{S}^f$, which can be defined as:

$$
\begin{aligned}
\mathcal{S}^c = \mathcal{S}^f + \mathcal{S}^g &= \sum_{j=1}^{N} \mathcal{S}_j^f + \sum_{p=1}^{K} \mathcal{S}_{c_p}^g \\
&= \sum_{j=1}^{N} \| \mathcal{I}_\mu - (G_\sigma * \mathcal{I}_j) \| + \\
&\quad \sum_{p=1}^{K} \sum_{c_q \neq c_p} exp \left(\frac{D_s(c_q, c_p)}{-\sigma_s^2} \right) \cdot \omega_{c_q} \cdot D_r(c_q, c_p),
\end{aligned}
\tag{1}
$$

where the first term, $\mathcal{S}^g$ is defined as an integration of region-based contrast and spatial relationships after a Gaussian mixture model based representation having K components $\{c_p\}_{p=1}^{K}$. $N = \sum_{p=1}^{K} |c_p|$, $|c_p|$ is the number of pixels of a component region c_p. $D_s(c_q, c_p)$ is a spatial distance between component regions c_q and c_p. The stiffness parameter σ_s controls the strength of spatial distance weighting. ω_{c_q} is defined by the number of pixels in component c_q as a weight value, $D_r(c_q, c_p)$ is a color distance between the two component regions, which is defined as the Euclidean metric. After the spectral-based image clustering [14] in [4], each pixel color $\mathcal{I}_j$ is represented as a weighted combination of several Gaussian components, with its probability of belonging to a component c_p.

They weight the contrast by the spatial distances in the image under an assumption that high contrast to surrounding regions is usually a more remarkable evidence for saliency of a region than high contrast to far-away regions. The second term, S^f is determined as the Euclidean distance between the mean image feature vector $\mathcal{I}_\mu$ and the Gaussian blurred vector of N pixels, $(G_\sigma * \mathcal{I}_j)$. [1] employ the difference of Gaussian filter to retain the desired spatial frequencies from the image, and use a Gaussian kernel to eliminate high frequency artifacts.

For qualitative visual evaluation, we present comparison with our saliency-map, S^c, against the global contrast based saliency-map, S^g, and the frequency tuned saliency-map, S^f, shown in Fig. 2. Results in Fig. 2 show experimental comparison of the saliency-maps for randomly selected data from the publicly available MSRA [1,12]. As shown in Fig. 2, we empirically confirm that both of the measures have a tendency to be complementary to each other in that the frequency tuned method provides better accuracy for the global saliency-map than the color contrast based method in a local luminance change condition, while the global contrast based approach is very sensitive to the pixel-wise luminance differences. Meanwhile, the global contrast based method generates the local salient object detection with better accuracy in dominant color contrast regions. As illustrated in Fig. 1, given a saliency-map for each image, we next compute the adaptive tri-map based matting process in order to obtain a segmented salient object with any level of significant accuracy.

2.2   Adaptive Tri-Map Based Matting

The matting problem is to estimate the opacity, called the alpha matte, under an assumption of a linear combination of the corresponding foreground and background colors, which is typically expressed as the following equation [10,19]:

$$\mathcal{I}_i = \alpha_i \mathcal{F}_i + (1 - \alpha_i)\mathcal{B}_i, \tag{2}$$

where $\alpha_i \in [0,1]$ represents the pixel's foreground opacity. $\mathcal{F}_i$ and $\mathcal{B}_i$ are $c \times 1$ vectors representing foreground and background colors of the ith pixel, respectively.

In our unsupervised salient object matting, we use the closed-form matting solution [10] instead of the GrabCut [17] usually employed in saliency detection based segmentation methods [4,13]. [17] is one of popular algorithms for image segmentation, however, it has difficulty in segmentation of a precise salient object for a complex salient region containing lots of holes and thin components since the method performs border matting by fitting a parametric alpha profile in a narrow strip around the hard boundary. The closed-form formulation using matting Laplacian [10] has been proven to be very effective in a variety of natural images [20]. The closed-form solution leads a well-defined quadratic cost function from a inherently underconstrained matting problem, also yields an accurate soft matte. In [10], two main assumptions on which they rely are that foreground and background color elements are approximately constant over a local window around each pixel, and that each of $\mathcal{F}_i$ and $\mathcal{B}_i$ pixels is a mixture of colors.

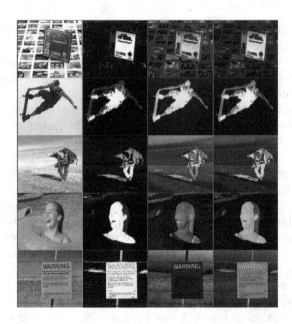

Fig. 2. Some typical results: from left to right, original image, $\mathcal{S}^g$, $\mathcal{S}^f$, and our $\mathcal{S}^c$.

Then, the quadratic cost function of α can be defined by:

$$\mathcal{J}(\boldsymbol{\alpha}) = \boldsymbol{\alpha}^\top \boldsymbol{L} \boldsymbol{\alpha}, \tag{3}$$

where $\boldsymbol{\alpha} = [\alpha_1 \cdots \alpha_N]^\top$ and $\boldsymbol{L} \in \mathbb{R}^{N \times N}$ is a matting Laplacian. This Laplacian can also be written as $\boldsymbol{L} = \boldsymbol{D} - \boldsymbol{A}$, where $\boldsymbol{A}$ is referred to as a matting affinity [10] and $\boldsymbol{D}$ is a diagonal matrix which consists of diagonal elements $\boldsymbol{D}_{ii} = \sum_j \boldsymbol{A}_{ij}$. The affinity's element $\boldsymbol{A}_{ij}$ is

$$\sum_{k|(i,j)\in w_k} \frac{1}{|w_k|} \left\{ 1 + (\mathcal{I}_i - \boldsymbol{\mu}_k)(\boldsymbol{\Sigma}_k + \frac{\epsilon}{|w_k|}\boldsymbol{I}_c)^{-1}(\mathcal{I}_j - \boldsymbol{\mu}_k) \right\},$$

where $\boldsymbol{\mu}_k$ and $\boldsymbol{\Sigma}_k$ denote a $c \times 1$ mean vector and a $c \times c$ covariance matrix of color vectors in the kth local window w_k, respectively. $\boldsymbol{I}_c$ is a $c \times c$ identity matrix, and ϵ represents a regulation parameter. The above objective function is then incorporated with constraints provided by a tri-map which discriminates between foreground and background pixels through definitely assigning an alpha matte to the two different regions. As a result, the constrained quadratic cost function can be expressed as follows:

$$\begin{aligned} \arg\min_{\boldsymbol{\alpha}} \ & \boldsymbol{\alpha}^\top \boldsymbol{L} \boldsymbol{\alpha}, \\ \text{s.t.} \quad & \boldsymbol{W}_v \boldsymbol{\alpha} = \hat{\alpha}_v, \\ & 0 \preceq \boldsymbol{\alpha} \preceq 1, \quad \forall v \in \mathcal{V}, \end{aligned} \tag{4}$$

where $\mathcal{V}$ is the group of constrained pixels, and $\boldsymbol{W}_v$ is a diagonal matrix penalizing α from $\hat{\alpha}_v$ which is a vector with predefined alpha values for all constrained pixels. The predefined alpha values consist of a tri-map, $\mathcal{T}$, as an indicator vector in Eq.(5).

$$\hat{\alpha}_v = \begin{cases} 1, & \text{if } v \in \mathcal{T}^{\mathcal{F}} \\ 0, & \text{if } v \in \mathcal{T}^{\mathcal{B}} \end{cases}, \quad \forall v \in \mathcal{V}, \text{ and } \mathcal{T} = \{\mathcal{T}^{\mathcal{F}}, \mathcal{T}^{\mathcal{B}}, \mathcal{T}^{\mathcal{U}}\}, \tag{5}$$

where $\mathcal{F}$ and $\mathcal{B}$ indicate the set of pixels of the foreground and background images. $\mathcal{T}^{\mathcal{F}}$, $\mathcal{T}^{\mathcal{B}}$, and $\mathcal{T}^{\mathcal{U}}$ are the set of alpha values for the constrained three subregions of foreground, background, and unknown, respectively. As we describe in Fig. 1, the tri-map, $\mathcal{T}$, is generated from the already constructed the coupled saliency-map, $\mathcal{S}^c$, through Gaussian blur and clustering [14] with three groups. We also propose an adaptive tri-map for tackling small and thin subregions in the saliency-map. The quality of alpha matte results depends on the accuracy of the tri-map, in general, the more accuracy the tri-map is, the better matting results are produced.

The adaptive tri-map is generated according to our procedure described in Algorithm 1. The main property of the procedure is that the closer the color of distance between tri-map's foreground and salient subregions in the same unknown, the greater the contribution to the region of the salient object-of-interest. Results in Fig. 3 show experimental comparison of the tri-maps for the data set. Finally, an optimal alpha matte solution, enforcing $\alpha_i = 1$ for $\mathcal{F}_i \in \mathcal{F}$ and $\alpha_i = 0$ for $\mathcal{B}_i \in \mathcal{B}$, can be obtained through propagation the constraints to the entire image by minimizing the Lagrangian of Eg.(4). We denote the extracted alpha matte set for each of the saliency detection based matting methods as $\mathcal{A}^g$ for $\mathcal{S}^g$, $\mathcal{A}^f$ for $\mathcal{S}^f$, and $\mathcal{A}^c$ for $\mathcal{S}^c$, respectively. As shown in Fig. 3, the adaptive tri-map regards salient pixels to surrounding the already computed foreground region, $\mathcal{T}^{\mathcal{F}}$, in the tri-map as more important than the salient pixels far away from the $\mathcal{T}^{\mathcal{F}}$. Moreover, the adaptive tri-map retains salient pixels missing from some thin salient subregions due to the Gaussian blur effect.

Fig. 3. Some typical results: from left to right, tri-map $\mathcal{T}$ set(1-3 columns) and our adaptive tri-map $\mathcal{T}^a$ set(4-6 columns).

Algorithm 1. Procedure for an adaptive tri-map construction

Data: $\mathcal{T} = \{\mathcal{T}^{\mathcal{F}}, \mathcal{T}^{\mathcal{B}}, \mathcal{T}^{\mathcal{U}}\}$ and $\{\mathcal{S}_n^c\}_{n=1}^N \in \mathcal{S}^c$

Result: $\{\mathcal{T}_n^a\}_{n=1}^N \in \mathcal{T}^a$

begin

$\quad$ $\mathcal{T}_\mu^{\mathcal{F}} \longleftarrow \frac{1}{|\mathcal{T}^{\mathcal{F}}|} \sum_i \mathcal{T}_i^{\mathcal{F}}$, $\mathcal{T}_\mu^{\mathcal{B}} \longleftarrow \frac{1}{|\mathcal{T}^{\mathcal{B}}|} \sum_i \mathcal{T}_i^{\mathcal{B}}$, $\mathcal{T}_\mu^{\mathcal{U}} \longleftarrow \frac{1}{|\mathcal{T}^{\mathcal{U}}|} \sum_i \mathcal{T}_i^{\mathcal{U}}$

$\quad$ $\mathcal{T}^a \longleftarrow \mathcal{T}$

$\quad$ **for** $n \leftarrow 1$ **to** N the number of pixels in $\mathcal{T}$ **do**

$\quad\quad$ $D_r^f \longleftarrow \|\mathcal{T}_\mu^{\mathcal{F}} - \mathcal{S}_n^c\|$, $D_r^b \longleftarrow \|\mathcal{T}_\mu^{\mathcal{B}} - \mathcal{S}_n^c\|$, $D_r^u \longleftarrow \|\mathcal{T}_\mu^{\mathcal{U}} - \mathcal{S}_n^c\|$

$\quad\quad$ **if** $\arg\min_{\mathcal{T}_\mu^*} (D_r^f, D_r^b, D_r^u) \equiv \mathcal{T}_\mu^{\mathcal{F}}$ **then**

$\quad\quad\quad$ $Stack.Push(n)$

$\quad\quad\quad$ **while** $Stack \neq \emptyset$ **do**

$\quad\quad\quad\quad$ $i \longleftarrow Stack.Pop$

$\quad\quad\quad\quad$ **if** $\mathcal{T}_i^a \equiv \mathcal{T}_\mu^{\mathcal{F}}$ **then**

$\quad\quad\quad\quad\quad$ $Break$

$\quad\quad\quad\quad$ **if** $\mathcal{T}_i^a \equiv \mathcal{T}_\mu^{\mathcal{U}}$ **then**

$\quad\quad\quad\quad\quad$ $\mathcal{T}_i^a \longleftarrow \mathcal{T}_\mu^{\mathcal{F}}$

$\quad\quad\quad\quad\quad$ $Stack.Push(i + (0,1))$ $\quad$ $Stack.Push(i - (0,1))$

$\quad\quad\quad\quad\quad$ $Stack.Push(i + (1,0))$ $\quad$ $Stack.Push(i - (1,0))$

---

3 Experiments

In this section, we show the usefulness of the proposed method, 'unsupervised salient object matting', through the empirical comparison with segmented set obtained from the closed-form matting solution based on two current saliency measures. We applied our method to some randomly selected data from the publicly available MSRA [1,12] and ECSSD data set [22]. For a more balanced comparisons, we carry out a variety of performance evaluations including the mean absolute error, the average values of precision, recall, F-measure, and accuracy, as well as visual comparison over the ground truth data set [1].

$$MAE = \frac{1}{|\mathcal{I}|} \sum_i |\mathcal{A}_i^* - \mathcal{G}_i| \in [0,1],$$

$$F_\beta = (1 + \beta^2) \cdot \frac{Precision \cdot Recall}{\beta^2 \cdot Precision + Recall} \in [0,1], \tag{6}$$

where $\mathcal{G}_i$ and $\mathcal{A}_i^*$ represent the ground truth data of the ith pixel and the matte data of the ith pixel for each of different types of alpha mattes, respectively. The F-measure is defined as Eq.6 with $\beta^2 = 1$ for the harmonic mean of precision and recall. In Table 1, we present the performance comparisons between ours and two other result set, namely the global-contrast and the frequency-tune based final matting outcomes for the data set used for Fig. 5 and Fig. 7. Each experiment in Table 1 is carried out on both the tri-map, $\mathcal{T}$ and the adaptive tri-map,

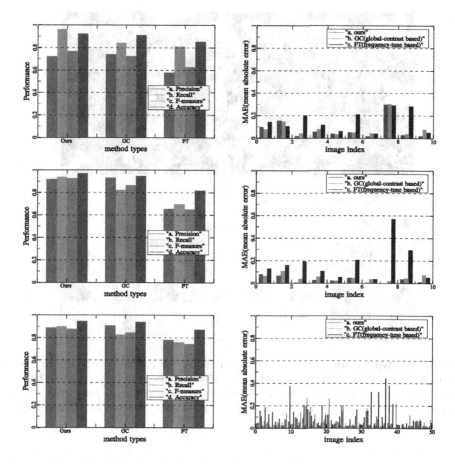

Fig. 4. Performance comparison of the average precision, recall, F-measure, accuracy, and mean absolute error of each method for the data set used in Table 1.(a)-(c): Ours($\mathcal{A}^c$ on $\mathcal{T}^a$), GC(global-contrast)($\mathcal{A}^g$ on $\mathcal{T}$), and FT(frequency-tune)($\mathcal{A}^f$ on $\mathcal{T}$) based matting. Images are indexed in column-major order. Top: Performance against the ground truth[1](see Table 1.(a)). Mid: Performance against the new ground truth samples in Fig. 6 for the same data(see Table 1.(b)). Bottom: Performance against the ground truth[1](see Table 1.(c))

$\mathcal{T}^a$. For each case, we performed 10 independent experiments in terms of the mean absolute error and the F-measure for statistical analysis of the outcomes, moreover, their averaged results are summarized in Table 1. As shown in Table 1, results of our method but the values in Table 1.(a) outperform two other methods under the condition of using of adaptive tri-maps, $\mathcal{T}^a$. Furthermore, the two methods also provide better numerical values when using the adaptive tri-maps (see Table 1.(b)-(c)). However, Both Table 1.(a) and $\mathcal{A}^f$ based on $\mathcal{S}^f$ show better results for the tri-map $\mathcal{T}$ rather than for the adaptive tri-map $\mathcal{T}^a$, which is considered to be caused by the adaptive tri-map's property of retaining salient

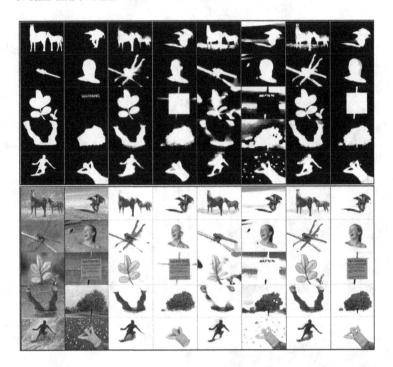

Fig. 5. Some typical results: from the 1st row to the 5th row, ground truth set(gray), set of alpha mattes of the $\mathcal{A}^g$(green) based on $\mathcal{T}$, $\mathcal{A}^f$(blue) based on $\mathcal{T}$, and $\mathcal{A}^c$(red) based on $\mathcal{T}^a$, respectively. From the 6th row to the 10th row, original image set(black), set of salient object segmentation images for $\mathcal{A}^g$(yellow), for $\mathcal{A}^f$(cyan), and for $\mathcal{A}^c$(magenta), respectively.

pixels as many as possible. As illustrated in Fig. 3, the adaptive tri-map is more suitable for segmentation of the salient object having lots of thin components. Moreover, the ground truth set could be biased towards a particular algorithm used to evaluate it or be subjective. For instance, a few ground truth data of the red dragonfly, warning sign, and tree images in Fig. 5(index 2, 8, and 9

Table 1. Performance on segmentation with data images in Fig. 5-7.

		$\mathcal{A}^g$ based on $\mathcal{S}^g$		$\mathcal{A}^f$ based on $\mathcal{S}^f$		our $\mathcal{A}^c$ based on $\mathcal{S}^c$	
		MAE(avg)	F_1(avg)	MAE(avg)	F_1(avg)	MAE(avg)	F_1(avg)
(a) Set	$\mathcal{T}$	0.0906	0.7282	0.1517	0.6299	**0.0762**	**0.7764**
in Fig. 5	$\mathcal{T}^a$	0.0951	0.7279	0.1646	0.6267	0.0792	0.7710
(b) Set in	$\mathcal{T}$	0.0533	0.8673	0.1817	0.6530	0.0405	0.9052
Fig. 5 & Fig. 6	$\mathcal{T}^a$	0.0479	0.8855	0.1924	0.6537	**0.0312**	**0.9264**
(c) Set	$\mathcal{T}$	0.0655	0.8483	0.1307	0.7445	0.0600	0.8688
in Fig. 7	$\mathcal{T}^a$	0.0618	0.8562	0.1308	0.7607	**0.0565**	**0.8772**

Fig. 6. Ground truth set obtained from matting process with tri-maps specified by user-manually for the data in Fig. 5

Fig. 7. Visual comparisons of alpha mattes and salient object segmentation images: from the 1st row to the 10th row, ground truth set(gray), set of alpha mattes of the $\mathcal{A}^g$(green) based on $\mathcal{T}$, $\mathcal{A}^f$(blue) based on $\mathcal{T}$, and $\mathcal{A}^c$(red) based on $\mathcal{T}^a$, respectively. From the 11th row to the 20th row, original image set(black), set of salient object segmentation images for $\mathcal{A}^g$(yellow), for $\mathcal{A}^f$(cyan), and for $\mathcal{A}^c$(magenta), respectively.

in Fig. 4.Top-Mid) do not match with visual evaluations by a human. In order to provide more objective comparison for the data used in Fig. 5, we perform an experiment against the ground truth samples in Fig. 6 generated from matting with manually defined tri-maps (see Table 1.(b) and Fig. 4). Due to the subjective nature of choosing ground truth set and performance measurements, it is difficult to compare the superiority of methods over a ground truth set.

In order to support more reliable qualitative evaluations, we show the results of the extensive visual comparisons in Fig. 5 and Fig. 7. The final extracted images present that our proposed method yields more accurate salient object segmentation results. From several experimental results, we can notice that the performance of our method is more prominent. Such a good result is due to the consideration of our coupled saliency-map, adaptive tri-map, and closed-form matting processes. Our segmentation method is developed in C++ with Qt SDK for providing an effective, integrated process over large-scale image set.

4   Conclusions

We have presented a salient object matting method, where we employ the closed-form matting solution incorporating with our proposed coupled saliency-map and adaptive tri-map. Useful aspects of our proposed method could be summarized as follows: (a) The proposed coupled saliency-map provides complementary information from the linearly combined feature map of the global contrast and the frequency tuned saliency-maps; (b) The proposed adaptive tri-map yields more precise pre-segmentation of a complicated salient object consisting of lots of holes and thin components as a prior knowledge for matting; (c) Our segmentation method is capable of extracting only salient objects in an unsupervised way. The above features can provide an efficient way of collecting the salient object-of-interest images for large-scale image set, automatically. Our proposed method is expected to be very useful for a variety of applications including image classification, content-based image retrieval, etc, as an effective preprocessing system.

Acknowledgments. This work was supported by Institute of Information & communications Technology Promotion(IITP) grant funded by the Korea government(MSIP)[No.B0101-15-0266, Development of High Performance Visual Big-Data Discovery Platform for Large-Scale Realtime Data Analysis]

References

1. Achanta, R., Hemami, S., Estrada, F., Susstrunk, S.: Frequency-tuned salient region detection. In: Proc. Int'l Conf. Computer Vision and Pattern Recognition, pp. 1597–1604 (2009)
2. Ardizzone, E., Bruno, A., Mazzola, G.: Visual saliency by keypoints distribution analsis. In: Proc. Int'l Conf. Image Analysis and Processing, pp. 691–699 (2011)

3. Borji, A., Sihite, D.N., Itti, L.: Salient object detection: a benchmark. In: Fitzgibbon, A., Lazebnik, S., Perona, P., Sato, Y., Schmid, C. (eds.) Computer Vision – ECCV 2012. LNCS, pp. 414–429. Springer, Heidelberg (2012)
4. Cheng, M.M., Mitra, N.J., Huang, X., Torr, P.H.S., Hu, S.M.: Global contrast based salient region detection. IEEE Trans. Pattern Analysis and Machine Intelligence 37(3), 569–582 (2015)
5. Cheng, M.M., Warrell, J., Lin, W.Y., Zheng, S., Vineet, V., Crook, N.: Efficient salient region detection with soft image abstraction. In: Proc. Int'l Conf. Computer Vision, pp. 1529–1536 (2013)
6. Itti, L., Koch, C., Niebur, E.: A model of saliency-based visual attention for rapid scene analysis. IEEE Trans. Pattern Analysis and Machine Intelligence 20(11), 1254–1259 (1998)
7. Judd, T., Ehinger, K., Durand, F., Torralb, A.: Learning to predict where humans look. In: Proc. Int'l Conf. Computer Vision, pp. 2106–2113 (2009)
8. Kim, J., Jeong, I.: Single image based 3d tree and growth models reconstruction. ETRI Journal 36(3), 450–459 (2014)
9. Kock, C., Ullman, S.: Shifts in selective visual attention: Towards the underlying neural circuitry. Human Neurobiology 4, 219–227 (1985)
10. Levin, A., Lischinski, D., Weiss, Y.: A closed form solution to natural image matting. IEEE Trans. Pattern Analysis and Machine Intelligence 30(2), 228–242 (2008)
11. Levin, A., Rav-Acha, A., Lischinski, D.: Spectral matting. IEEE Trans. Pattern Analysis and Machine Intelligence 30(10), 1699–1712 (2008)
12. Liu, T., Yuan, Z., Sun, J., Wang, J., Zheng, N., Tang, X., Shum, H.Y.: Learning to detect a salient object. IEEE Trans. Pattern Analysis and Machine Intelligence 33(2), 353–367 (2011)
13. Mehrani, P., Veksler, O.: Saliency segmentation based on learning and graph cut refinement. In: Proc. of British Mchine Vision Conference, pp. 110.1–110.12 (2011)
14. Orchard, M., Bouman, C.: Color quantization of images. IEEE Trans. Signal Processing 39(12), 2677–2690 (1991)
15. Perazzi, F., Pritch, Y., Hornung, A.: Saliency filters: contrast based filtering for salient region detection. In: Proc. Int'l Conf. Computer Vision and Pattern Recognition, pp. 733–740 (2012)
16. Rhemann, C., Rother, C., Wang, J., Gelautz, M., Kohli, P., Rott, P.: A perceptually motivated online benchmark for image matting. In: Proc. Int'l Conf. Computer Vision and Pattern Recognition, pp. 1826–1833 (2009)
17. Rother, C., Kolmogorov, V., Blake, A.: Grabcut: interactive foreground extraction using iterated graph cuts. ACM Transactions on Graphics 23(3), 309–314 (2004)
18. Tan, P., Zeng, G., Wang, J., Kang, S.B., Quan, L.: Image-based tree modeling. ACM Transactions on Graphics 26(3), 108:1–108:7 (2007)
19. Wang, J., Cohen, M.F.: An iterative optimization approach for unified image segmentation and matting. In: Proc. Int'l Conf. Computer Vision, pp. 936–943 (2005)
20. Wang, J., Cohen, M.F.: Image and video matting: a survey. Foundations and Trends in Computer Graphics and Vision 3(2), 97–175 (2007)
21. Weiss, Y.: Segmentation using eigenvectors: a unifying view. In: Proc. Int'l Conf. Computer Vision, pp. 975–982 (1999)
22. Yan, Q., Xu, L., Shi, J., Jia, J.: Hierarchical saliency detection. In: Proc. Int'l Conf. Computer Vision and Pattern Recognition, pp. 1155–1162 (2013)

A Comparison of Multi-scale Local Binary Pattern Variants for Bark Image Retrieval

Safia Boudra[1(✉)], Itheri Yahiaoui[2], and Ali Behloul[1]

[1] LaSTIC, Université de Batna, Batna, Algérie
{safia.boudra,ali.behloul}@gmail.com
[2] CReSTIC, Université de Reims Champagne-Ardenne, Reims, France
itheri.yahiaoui@univ-reims.fr

Abstract. With the growing interest in identifying plant species and the availability of digital collections, many automated methods based on bark images have been proposed. Bark identification is often formulated as a texture analysis problem. Among numerous approaches, Local Binary Pattern (LBP) based texture description has achieved good performances. Bark structure appearance is subject to resolution variations which can be due to a number of factors (environment, age, acquisition conditions, etc). Thus it remains a very challenging problem. In this paper, we implement and study the efficiency of different multi-scale LBP descriptors: Multi-resolution LBP (MResLBP), Multi-Block LBP (MBLBP), LBP-Filtering (LBPF), Multi-Scale LBP (MSLBP), and Pyramid based LBP (PLBP). These descriptors are compared on two bark datasets: AFF and Trunk12. The descriptors are evaluated under increasing levels of scale space. The performances are assessed using the Mean Average Precision and Recall\Precision curves. The results show that multi-scale LBP descriptors outperform the basic LBP and MResLBP. In our tests, we observe that the best results of LBPF and PLBP are obtained under low scale space levels. We also observe similar results for MSLBP and MBLBP across the six scales considered.

Keywords: Plant identification · Multi-scale LBP · Texture description · Bark species recognition · Image retrieval

1   Introduction

Plants play an essential role in sustaining life on our planet. In addition to providing a natural habitat, they are a constant source of oxygen, food, and medicine. Given the vast diversity and variety of plant species, there is understandably increasing interest in indentifying new and existing species in order to improve agriculture and plant production, while adding to the proof of knowledge available to researchers in the field of botany.

The classical approach to identifying and classifying plant species requires specialist domain knowledge meaning that only a taxonomist or botanist can distinguish between various species.

© Springer International Publishing Switzerland 2015
S. Battiato et al. (Eds.): ACIVS 2015, LNCS 9386, pp. 764–775, 2015.
DOI: 10.1007/978-3-319-25903-1_66

However, ever a domain expert cannot be expected to know of all plant species, and recent years have seen increasing interest in automated plant species identification and classification.

Over the last decade, many automated plant species identification methods based on low-level features extracted from images of organs (leaf, flower, fruit, stem, bark ...) have been proposed; [1,2,3,4,5]. Mobile applications, Leafsnap and Pl@ntNet, have been developed aiming to achieve accurate real time identification. Recently, many studies based on bark (or stem) images have appeared [3, 4] [6,7,8,9,10].

The appearance and morphology of the bark are used by foresters and botanists to distinguish between plant species and to estimate plant age [11]. The Bark has the advantage of being the only part of the tree that is available throughout the year and it is present for almost all plant's lifetime. As bark is a rigid 3D object, its 2D image acquisition is straightforward.

Since bark shows texture properties, its automated identification is formally defined as a texture analysis problem, and researchers aim to develop relative methods to extract highly discriminative features for an accurate identification. Nonetheless, it remains a challenging problem in the image processing and computer vision field.

Bark appearance often depends on environmental conditions, tree age and the effects of plant diseases. Additionally, acquisition conditions like rescaling, uncontrolled illumination changes, branch shadow clutter can alter the image quality and the texture properties. Fig. 1 illustrates some examples.

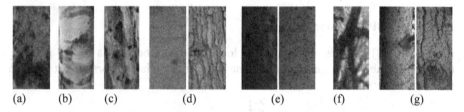

(a)   (b)   (c)   (d)   (e)   (f)   (g)

Fig. 1. Examples of the visual diversity of the surface of bark: (a) lichen, (b) peeled bark, (c) scars, (d) tree age deformation, (e) illumination change, (f) shadow clutters, (g) different texture structures at different scales.

The most significant image transformation problem in bark images is scale changes, due to the fact that image samples are taken at distinct distances from the tree trunk: texture structures taken close to the trunk are of high resolution while those far from the trunk are of low resolution. To handle this disparity, many features need to be extracted to capture texture properties at different scale levels.

Several texture descriptors [12] have been used for bark image classification and identification. Statistical features such as co-occurrence distribution were used by [7]. Huang et al. [8], [13, 14] proposed different approaches, respectively, based on contourlet filter, Gabor filters, and Discrete Wavelet Decomposition (DW). In [4], a bag of words model was constructed with SIFT interest points. Recently, structural features such as LBP variants have been used [9, 10], [15, 16].

Sixta et al. [9], used Multi-Block Local Binary Pattern where mean filter with different sizes is applied to input images. MBLBP was the first multi-scale LBP variant used for bark texture analysis. Sulc et al. [10] proposed a Multi-Scale LBP. Input images are Gaussian Filtered prior to the LBP operator with increasing radii. In both, histograms of all the scales considered are concatenated to form the final texture descriptor.

Motivated by the high performances achieved in the two last studies, we want to focus more closely on multi-scale LBP as efficient texture descriptor for bark texture identification.

Our work aims to quantitatively discuss and compare four different multi scale LBP approaches with filters for bark texture analysis, namely: (1) Multi-Block LBP (MBLBP) [17]with a mean filter, (2) LBP Filtering (LBPF) [18] and (3) Multl-Scale LBP (MSLBP) [10]with a low pass Gaussian filter, and (4) Pyramid-based LBP (PLPB) [19]with a pyramid transform. These methods are implemented and compared to the conventional Multi Resolution LBP (MResLBP) [20] where texture information is simply collected from single pixels at different scales rather than using filter's responses.

The remainder of this paper is structured as follows: the LBP operator and its multi-scale variants are presented in Section 2. In Section 3, a detailed description of bark datasets is given. Our bark image retrieval experiments and results are set out and discussed in Section 4. Finally, the conclusion is given in Section 5.

2   The LBP Operator and Its Multi-scale Variants

2.1   The LBP Operator

Basic LBP [20] encodes the sign of the local difference between a central pixel p_c and its P neighbors p_i, evenly spaced on a circle of radius R. Formally, it is given by:

$$LBP_{P,R} = \sum_{i=0}^{P-1} s(p_i - p_c)2^i \tag{1}$$

Where $s(x)$ is a step function; $s(x) = 1$, if $x >= 0$; 0 otherwise.
Once the LBP codes have been computed, a histogram is built to represent the texture image.

Another extension to the basic LBP operator considers *uniform patterns;* the uniformity measure was first defined by [21] as "the number of bitwise 0/1 and 1/0 changes when the pattern is considered circular". Based on this definition, a local binary pattern is said to be uniform if its uniformity measure takes that form $U \leq 2$.

Using this mapping, denoted by LBPu2, every uniform pattern is assigned to a single bin in the histogram and all non uniform patterns are assigned to a unique bin.
It is formally defined by:

$$LBP_{P,R}^{u2} = \sum_{i=0}^{P-1} s(p_i - p_c), \text{ if } U\left(LBP_{P,R}\right) \leq 2, P+1 \; otherwise \tag{2}$$

The uniform patterns are shown to provide fundamental local texture information properties [20]. Furthermore, it can significantly reduce the histogram length: only 59 bins with 8 samples in the local neighborhood instead of 256.

Multi Resolution LBP (MRes-LBP).

Bark texture images are captured at various scales. Therefore, large-scale structures cannot be defined within the 3×3 space area of the original LBP.

An intuitive and efficient way to capture large-scale structures is to combine different LBP operators with increasing values of (P, R), i.e. (8, 1), (16, 2), (24, 3).

Ojala's [20] multi resolution LBP (MResLBP) is based on the concatenation of three uniform LBP histograms, $LBP_{8,1}^{u2} + LBP_{16,2}^{u2} + LBP_{24,3}^{u2}$. Fig. 2 shows LBP operators with different configurations of (P, R).

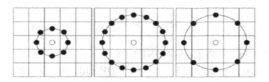

Fig. 2. LBP operator with different values of (P, R): (8, 1), (16, 2) and (8, 2).

Using different LBP operators with increasing radii causes an aliasing effect and leads to noise sensitivity since the texture information is collected from a single pixel at different levels. To overcome this issue, several multi-scale LBP schemes have been proposed [10], [17, 18, 19] mainly based on filter responses to collect texture information from large areas at different scales. Therefore, it captures microstructures as well as macrostructures with reduced noise.

2.2   Multi-scale LBP

Multi-Block Local Binary Pattern (MBLBP).

Liao [17] applied a set of mean filters at different scales to the input image. The simple point to point comparison in basic LBP was extended to a comparison between mean intensity values of square sub-blocks. The size of the filter s×s denotes the scale of the MBLBP operators. Each filter is divided into 9 sub blocks as shown in Fig. 3. Therefore its size must be a multiple of 3.

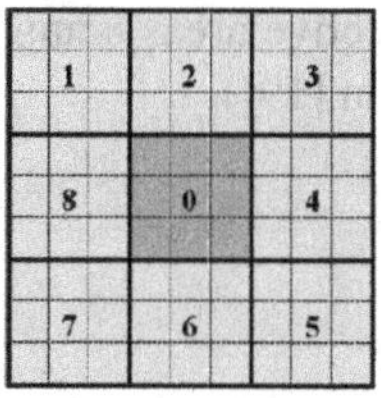

1	2	3
8	0	4
7	6	5

Fig. 3. MBLBP operator of size 9*9 [17]

In their work, [17] stated a new uniformity definition based on percentage distribution. The n patterns (n = 63) with a high percentage distribution are labeled as uniform and the remaining patterns are labeled as non uniform.

Local Binary Pattern Filtering (LBPF).
Following a multi-scale approach, in [18] large-scale texture patterns are detected by combining exponentially growing neighborhood radii with Gaussian low-pass filtering. Gaussian low-pass filtering is used to collect information from an area larger than a single pixel, named the "effective area". Solid circles in Fig. 4 (a) indicate a constant number of effective areas over different scales. The P circles (P=8) are tangent and have the same size.

Exponentially growing radii of the LBP operator, R_s , indicated by dotted circles in Fig. 4 (a) at level s, are given by:

$$R_s = \frac{r_s + r_{s-1}}{2} \tag{3}$$

Multi-scale Local Binary Pattern (MSLBP).
In contrast to the scale space in [18] where LBP radii are designed so that the effective areas at different levels are tangent, in MSLBP [10] a finer scale with a step of $\sqrt{2}$ is used between LBP radii, i.e.

$$R_s = R_{s-1} \sqrt{2} \ and \ R_1 = 1 \tag{4}$$

Pyramid-Based Local Binary Patterns (PLBP).
Qian et al. [19] proposed Pyramid-based LBP. Each image at level s of the pyramid representation is obtained by convolving it with a Gaussian low pass filter, $G(x, y)$, followed by down sampling of the s-1th level image. Formally $f_s (x, y)$ is obtained as follows, where $f_0 (x, y)$ is the original image:

$$f_s(x, y) = G(x, y) * f_{s-1}(R_x x + m, R_y y + n), for \ level \ s > 1 \tag{5}$$

Where R_x, R_y are the down-sampling ratios in x and y directions respectively, and the Gaussian filter, G(x, y), is given by:

$$G(x, y) = \frac{1}{2\pi\sigma^2} \ exp \left(\frac{x^2 + y^2}{2\sigma^2}\right) \tag{6}$$

PLBP can be seen as a general case of LBPF and MSLBP differing in that is sampling or no sampling; that the effective areas being tangent or not; and low pass filter types, (more details can be found in [19]).

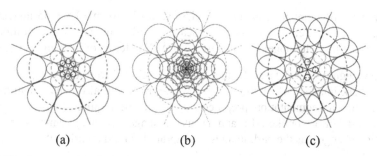

(a)   (b)   (c)

Fig. 4. Effective areas. (a)LBPF, (b)MSLBP Finer scale space, (c) PLBP with different LBP bits at each scale [19], [10].

3   Bark Datasets

Two bark image datasets (AFF[1] [4] and Trunk12[2] [16]) were used to evaluate the multi-scale LBP descriptors. These datasets differ with regard to the number of classes, the number of samples per class, image transformation i.e. scale, pose and illumination changes. Fig. 5 shows samples from each class of the two datasets.

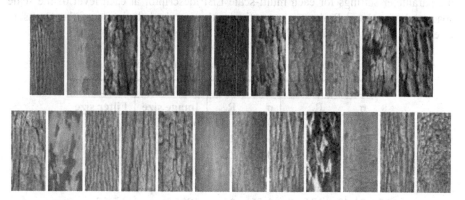

Fig. 5. Bark image samples; Top row, AFF dataset, bottom row, Trunk12 dataset.

- **AFF Dataset:** The AFF bark dataset provided by "Osterreichische Bundesforste", Austrian Federal Forests (AFF) was first used in [4]. It is a collection of the most common Austrian trees and the dataset contains 1182 bark samples belonging to 11 classes, the size of each class varying between 16 and 213 images. AFF samples are captured at different scales, and under different illumination conditions.

- **Trunk12 Dataset:** Trunk12 was the first publicly available bark dataset. It contains 393 images of tree barks belonging to 12 different trees that are found in

---

[1]   We are grateful to the computer vision Lab, TU, Vienna for allowing us access to the AFF dataset for scientific use.

[2]   http://www.vicos.si/Downloads/TRUNK12

Slovenia. The number of images per class varies between 30 and 45 images. Bark images are captured under controlled scale, illumination and pose conditions. The classes are more homogenous than those of AFF in terms of imaging conditions.

A challenging bark dataset, ImageClef, was excluded from this comparison study since its bark images do not show only the tree trunk, but also contain natural background. Thus a segmentation preprocessing would be required to extract the bark regions. In addition, unlike AFF and Trunk12, ImageClef image samples are subject to rotation changes, as the bark images are captured at random orientations.

4   Experimental Results and Evaluation

Bark images in the AFF dataset and the Trunk12 dataset are of high resolution and processing the samples with their original pixel resolution slows down the task. Therefore, all the images are resized to 600×400 px and converted to gray level.

LBP histograms at level s are normalized to unit length, and then concatenated. Thus the final multi-scale histogram length is $2^P \times s$ where P is set to 8 neighbors for all scales and $s \in \{1, ... , S\}$ where $S=6$, is the scale space level. Table 1 summarizes the parameter settings for each multi-scale LBP descriptor at each level of the scale space, where σ, and R_s denote respectively, the standard deviation of the Gaussian filter and the LBP radius at level s (see [10, 18] for details).

Table 1. Multi-scale LBP descriptor parameters over different scales.

	LBPF		MSLBP		PLBP	MBLBP
s	σ	R_s	σ	R_s	Image size	Filter size
1	0.38	2.43	0.28	1.41	600×400	3×3
2	0.85	5.44	0.39	2	300×200	9×9
3	1.91	12.19	0.55	2.83	150×100	15×15
4	4.27	27.3	0.78	4	75×50	21×21
5	9.56	61.16	1.1	5.66	38×25	27×27
6	21.42	136.98	1.56	8	19×13	33×33

To evaluate the descriptors presented above, we use the Mean Average Precision and the Precision\Recall curves. The Precision (Pre) and the Recall (Rec) are given by:

$$Pre = \frac{\#relevant\ images}{\#retrieved\ images} \; ; Rec = \frac{\#retrieved\ relevant\ images}{\#relevant\ images} \qquad (7)$$

The Mean Average Precision (MAP) is the mean of the Average Precision (AP) of a set of queries Q, and is defined by:

$$MAP = \frac{\sum_{q=1}^{Q} AP(q)}{Q} \;, where \quad AP(q) = \frac{\sum_{k=1}^{n} Pre(k) \times f(k)}{\#retrieved\ relevant\ images\ for\ q} \qquad (8)$$

Where *Pre (k)* is the precision at a given cut-off, and *f (k)* is set to 1 if the retrieved image at rank k is relevant; zero otherwise.

In what follows, we highlight the max values of MAP in bold and min values in italics.

Table 2. Mean Average Precision of LBP variants without filtering.

	LBP	LBPu2	MResLBP
AFF	31.46	*31.00*	**32.69**
Trunk12	**31.42**	*29.69*	30.03

Table 2 reports the MAP values of LBP, LBPu2, and MResLBP. We can see that the LBP and LBPu2 results are very close. The MResLBP, which is the concatenation of three uniform LBPs slightly exceeds the uniform LBP performance. One reason for this slight improvement of MResLBP, is the aliasing effect in the second and third scales.

Table 3. Mean Average Precision of multi-scale LBP variants on the AFF dataset.

AFF	MBLBP			LBPF		MSLPB		PLBP	
s	*org*	*u2*	*n*	*org*	*u2*	*org*	*u2*	*org*	*u2*
1	32.12	*30.28*	26.39	34.1	33.95	*32.14*	31.66	34.99	33.69
2	**33.86**	31.75	29.4	35.62	34.96	33.25	33.08	**35.17**	34.18
3	33.40	**31.9**	29.98	**36.6**	**35.39**	34.09	33.74	34.68	**34.78**
4	32.74	31.72	**30.04**	35.5	34.19	34.87	34.53	32.93	32.78
5	32.17	31.65	30	29.75	28.44	35.33	34.71	27.82	27.91
6	*31.67*	31.53	29.93	*18.97*	*19.91*	**35.8**	**34.77**	*22.71*	22.98

Table 4. Mean Average Precision of multi-scale LBP variants on the Trunk12 dataset.

Trunk12	MBLBP			LBPF		MSLPB		PLBP	
s	*org*	*u2*	*n*	*org*	*u2*	*org*	*u2*	*org*	*u2*
1	*32.34*	28.32	*24.76*	32.85	31.11	*31.3*	28.75	36.23	34.74
2	34.43	29.16	28.75	37.44	35.51	31.62	29.43	40.93	39.67
3	35.8	29.84	31.22	42.8	40.14	32.68	30.59	45.05	44.29
4	36.46	30.74	32.58	**47.66**	**44.28**	35.09	33.15	**47.1**	**46.74**
5	**36.66**	31.22	33.32	39.07	36.64	37.38	35.01	37.6	38.27
6	36.57	**31.79**	**33.77**	*17.38*	*18.2*	**39.59**	**36.66**	*23.45*	*24.85*

Table 3 and Table 4 show MAP values for the multi-scale LBP descriptors on the AFF and the Trunk12 datasets respectively with increasing scale space levels. The uniform extension of multi-scale LBP variants, noted *u2,* as well as the original patterns i.e. all possible patterns (256), noted *org*, are also considered. Note that for

772   S. Boudra et al.

MBLBP, the uniformity measure defined in [17] is also tested in this study, noted by MBLBPn. Fig 6 illustrates Recall\Precision curves. The multi-scale LBP descriptors are chosen at their best scale according to the highest MAP value in Table 3 and Table 4 for the AFF and Trunk 12 datasets respectively.

The above results suggest that all multi-scale descriptors at the proper scale outperform MResLBP and basic LBP. That is because in multi-scale LBP descriptors, macro-texture information captured at the high level, contributes to increasing MAP value.

Moreover, the information\is collected from regions (effective areas) and not from single pixels, as is performed in MResLBP. Thus reduces noise sensitivity and increases performances.

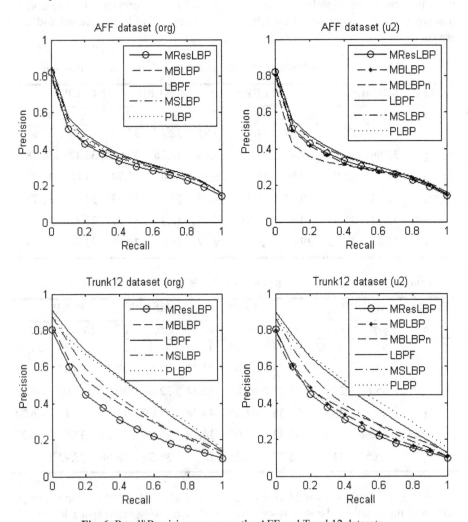

Fig. 6. Recall\Precision curves on the AFF and Trunk12 datasets.

It is clear that more LBP scales lead to increased MAP values on both datasets. However, multi-scale descriptors do not behave in a similar way at different scales. It is worth noting that all the multi-scale LBP descriptors on the Trunk12 dataset behave as well as, or better than they do for the AFF dataset. One reason for this may be that Trunk12 classes are more homogenous than those of AFF regarding both imaging conditions and botanical factors.

One reason why all multi-scale descriptors with only *u2* patterns perform slightly lower than *org* patterns, is the part of information that is roughly described by the last bin of the non-uniform histogram.

MBLBPn has the lowest MAP value and the worst Recall\Precision curve on the AFF dataset, but not on the Trunk12 dataset. Note, however, that MBLBPn is based on a statistical distribution of patterns and not on fundamental local texture properties. Consequently, the comparison of two histograms can match completely different patterns together. This can explain the AFF results. For the Trunk12 dataset, we suppose that the matching between different patterns coincides with space projection.

MBLBP has the lowest performances on the AFF dataset and the Trunk12 dataset. We believe that this came from low pass filtering used, i.e. mean filter in MBLBP.

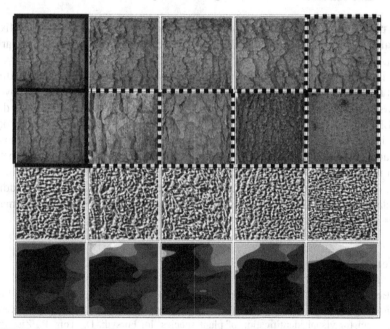

Fig. 7. LBPF descriptor behavior. Request image highlighted in solid square, false positive in dotted square, from top to bottom; first five returned images at level 3, second row, returned images et level 6; third row: LBP images at level 3, with high inter-class variation; bottom row, LBP images at level 6, high inter-class similarity.

For MSLBP, the best MAP values are obtained at scale 6 on both datasets. MSLBP MAP values increase slowly compared to other variants. Indeed, a finer scale with step of $\sqrt{2}$ is used between LBP radii (see Table 1) and Gaussian smoothing is applied firstly at scale 4 (more details in [10]). The best results for LBPF are obtained at scale 3 with LBP radius equal to 12.19, which is higher than the MSLBP radius at scale 6 (R_6 =8). Based on these remarks, we believe that MSLBP reaches its optimal performance at scales higher than 6. However, it results in a longer histogram compared to LBPF.

The sharp drop in MAP values for the LBPF descriptor on both, AFF and Trunk 12 from scales 3 and 4 respectively can be explained as follows: With increasing values of σ over the scales (details in Table 1), images are increasingly smooth, and local texture information is lost and subject to noise sensitivity. Thus the descriptor loses its discriminative power. Fig. 7 shows an example of an image request and the first 5 images returned, the LBPF descriptor, cannot distinguish between different classes at scale level 6.

The deterioration in PLBP performances on the two datasets is due to the fact that images at coarse pyramid levels are of very low resolution, as reported in Table 1, and do not provide enough structure information.

5   Conclusion

This paper reports on the evaluation results of basic LBP, uniform LBP, and five multi-scale LBP descriptors. These descriptors are tested and compared on two bark datasets (AFF and Trunk12).

It is worth noticing that multi-scale LBP provides more discriminative texture features than basic and uniform LBP. Therefore, multi-scale information improves LBP results. LBPF gives the best results over all the descriptors tested on both datasets. MBLBPn produced less satisfying results than we had expected for both datasets. This is due to its uniformity definition. Using a distribution percentage does not take into account the local structure properties, and the uniqueness of the relative patterns.

In this work, we focused on the multi-scale problem. It would be interesting to explore other LBP configurations with different neighborhood topologies in addition to the classic circular one, and to combine other complementary texture information in order to boost performances.

References

1. Belhumeur, P.N., Chen, D., Feiner, S.K., Jacobs, D.W., Kress, W., Ling, H., Lopez, I., Ramamoorthi, R., Sheorey, S., White, S., Zhang, L.: Searching the world's Herbaria: a system for visual identification of plant species. In: Forsyth, D., Torr, P., Zisserman, A. (eds.) ECCV 2008, Part IV. LNCS, vol. 5305, pp. 116–129. Springer, Heidelberg (2008)
2. Nilsback, M.E.: An automatic visual flora: Segmentation and classification of flower images (2009). http://www.robots.ox.ac.uk/~vgg/publications/2009/Nilsback09/
3. Chi, Z., Houqiang, L., Chao, W.: Plant species recognition based on bark patterns using novel Gabor filter banks. In: Proceedings of the 2003 International Conference on Neural Networks and Signal Processing, vol. 2, pp. 1035–1038 (2003)
4. Fiel, S., Sablatnig, R.: Automated identification of tree species from images of the bark, leaves and needles. In: Proceedings of the 16th Computer Vision Winter Workshop, pp. 67–74. Andreas Wendel, Sabine Sternig, Martin Godec, Mitterberg (2011)

5. Goëau, H., Bonnet, P., Barbe, J., Bakic, V., Joly, A., Molino, J.-F., Barthelemy, D., Boujemaa, N.: Multi-organ plant identification. In: Proceedings of the 1st ACM International Workshop on Multimedia Analysis for Ecological Data, pp. 41–44. ACM, New York (2012)

6. Song, J., Chi, Z., Liu, J., Fu, H.: Bark classification by combining grayscale and binary texture features. In: Proceedings of 2004 International Symposium on Intelligent Multimedia, Video and Speech Processing, pp. 450–453 (2004)

7. Wan, Y.-Y., Du, J., Huang, D.-S., Chi, Z., Cheung, Y., Wang, X.-F., Zhang, G.-J.: Bark texture feature extraction based on statistical texture analysis. In: Proceedings of 2004 International Symposium on Intelligent Multimedia, Video and Speech Processing, pp. 482–485 (2004)

8. Huang, Z.-K., Quan, Z.-H., Du, J.-X.: Bark classification based on contourlet filter features using RBPNN. In: Huang, D.-S., Li, K., Irwin, G.W. (eds.) ICIC 2006. LNCS, vol. 4113, pp. 1121–1126. Springer, Heidelberg (2006)

9. Sixta, T.: Image and Video-based Recognition of Natural Objects, Diploma Thesis, Prague: Czech Technical University (2011)

10. Sulc, M., Matas, J.: Kernel-mapped histograms of multi-scale LBPs for tree bark recognition. In: 2013 28th International Conference of Image and Vision Computing New Zealand (IVCNZ), pp. 82–87 (2013)

11. Whitmore, T.C.: Studies in Systematic Bark Morphology. I. Bark Morphology in Dipterocarpaceae. New Phytol. **61**, 191–207 (1962)

12. Mirmehdi, M., Xie, X., Suri, J.: Handbook of Texture Analysis. Imperial College Press, London (2009)

13. Huang, Z.-K., Huang, D.-S., Lyu, M.R., Lok, T.-M.: Classification based on Gabor filter using RBPNN classification. In: 2006 International Conference on Computational Intelligence and Security, pp. 759–762 (2006)

14. Huang, Z.-K.: Bark Classification Using RBPNN Based on Both Color and Texture Feature (2006)

15. Goëau, H., Joly, A., Bonnet, P., Selmi, S., Molino, J.-F., Barthélémy, D., Boujemaa, N.: LifeCLEF plant identification task 2014. In: Cappellato, L., Ferro, N., Halvey, M., and Kraaij, W. (eds.) CLEF2014 Working Notes. Working Notes for CLEF 2014 Conference, Sheffield, UK, September 15–18, pp. 598–615. CEUR-WS (2014)

16. Švab, M.: Computer-vision-based tree trunk recognition , Bsc Thesis, (Mentor: doc. dr. Matej Kristan), Fakulteta za racunalništvo in informatiko, Univerza v Ljubljani (2014)

17. Liao, S., Zhu, X., Lei, Z., Zhang, L., Li, S.Z.: Learning multi-scale block local binary patterns for face recognition. In: Lee, S.-W., Li, S.Z. (eds.) ICB 2007. LNCS, vol. 4642, pp. 828–837. Springer, Heidelberg (2007)

18. Mäenpää, T., Pietikäinen, M.: Multi-scale binary patterns for texture analysis. In: Bigun, J., Gustavsson, T. (eds.) SCIA 2003. LNCS, vol. 2749, pp. 885–892. Springer, Heidelberg (2003)

19. Qian, X., Hua, X.-S., Chen, P., Ke, L.: PLBP: An effective local binary patterns texture descriptor with pyramid representation. Pattern Recognit. **44**, 2502–2515 (2011)

20. Ojala, T., Pietikäinen, M., Mäenpää, T.: Multiresolution Gray-Scale and Rotation Invariant Texture Classification with Local Binary Patterns. IEEE Trans. Pattern Anal. Mach. Intell. **24**, 971–987 (2002)

21. Topi, M., Timo, O., Matti, P., Maricor, S.: Robust texture classification by subsets of local binary patterns. In: Proceedings of the 15th International Conference on Pattern Recognition, vol. 3, pp. 935–938 (2000)

Multidimensional Signal Processing

Improvement of a Wavelet-Tensor Denoising Algorithm by Automatic Rank Estimation

Julien Marot[⊠] and Salah Bourennane

Ecole Centrale Marseille, Institut Fresnel, Aix Marseille University,
D.U. de Saint Jérôme Av. escadrille Normandie-Niemen, 13397 Marseille, France
julien.marot@fresnel.fr

Abstract. This paper focuses on the denoising of multidimensional data by a tensor subspace-based method. In a seminal work, multiway Wiener filtering was developed to minimize the mean square error between an expected signal tensor and the estimated tensor. It was then placed in a wavelet framework. The reliable estimation of the subspace rank for each mode and wavelet decomposition level is still pending. For the first time in this paper, we aim at estimating the subspace ranks for all modes of the tensor data by minimizing a least squares criterion. To solve this problem, we adapt particle swarm optimization. An application involving an RGB image and hyperspectral images exemplifies our method: we compare the results obtained in terms of signal to noise ratio with a slice-by-slice ForWaRD denoising.

Keywords: MWF · Rank · PSO · Wavelets

1 Introduction

Hyperspectral images (HSI) are now currently used in remote sensing applications, for instance for aerial survey [1]. Most of HSIs, acquired by Hyperspectral Digital Imagery Collection Experiment (HYDICE) and Airborne Visible/ Infrared Imaging Spectrometer (AVIRIS) sensors, are impaired by noise from solar radiation, or atmospheric scattering [2]. Hence the interest of denoising HSIs, before applying further processings such as target detection.

Relation with Previous Work in the Field. A seminal work consisted in adapting Wiener filtering in a tensor framework, yielding the Multiway Wiener Filtering (MWF) [3], a subspace-based method requiring the estimation of ranks, usually performed with the statistical Akaike information criterion (AIC) [4], working best with a very high number of signal realizations. Recently, the MWPT-MWF (Multidimensional Wavelet Packet Transform-Multiway Wiener Filtering) method has been proposed [1,5], yielding good results in terms of signal to noise ratio (SNR) and classification accuracy. The drawback of this method is that a large number of subspace rank values must be estimated to ensure accurate denoising results. In [1], a study about the accurate depth of

© Springer International Publishing Switzerland 2015
S. Battiato et al. (Eds.): ACIVS 2015, LNCS 9386, pp. 779–790, 2015.
DOI: 10.1007/978-3-319-25903-1_67

the wavelet decomposition has been performed, but the subspace ranks are still estimated with AIC.

Goal and Contributions. In this paper, we propose a criterion and an optimization strategy based on particle swarm optimization (PSO) [6] to estimate the subspace ranks in MWF. We extend this strategy to the case where MWF is included in a wavelet framework. We infer from the large number of rank values to be thereby estimated that an accurate estimation has even more influence on the denoising quality.

Outline. Section 2 sets the problem of the subspace rank estimation in MWF and propose a criterion to minimize. In Section 3 we adapt PSO to rank estimation. In Section 4, we integrate rank estimation in a wavelet framework. In Section 5, the denoising results obtained with PSO or AIC are compared with truncation of HOSVD, MWF, or ForWaRD method [7].

2   Problem Setting

We consider a noisy multidimensional signal, also called tensor: a signal $\mathcal{X}$ impaired by a multidimensional additive white noise $\mathcal{N}$ [8]. The additive case generally holds for hyperspectral images [4,9]. As concerns the white noise assumption, it is also generally adopted for multidimensional images [8], and permits to focus on the main issue of this paper. In the case where the noise is not white, a prewhitening process could be applied as proposed in [10]. Thus, this tensor can be a model for an HSI, expressed as : $\mathcal{R} = \mathcal{X} + \mathcal{N}$. Tensors $\mathcal{R}$, $\mathcal{X}$, and $\mathcal{N}$ are of size $I_1 \times I_2 \times I_3$. For each spectral band indexed by $i = 1, \ldots, I_3$, the noise $\mathbf{N}(:,:,i)$ is assumed stationary zero-mean. We aim at denoising tensor $\mathcal{R}$ with a subspace-based method. Subspace-based methods have been shown to exhibit good denoising results when applied to data with salient main orientations in the image [11]. They provide an estimated signal tensor which, generally in the literature and in the remainder of this paper, is denoted by $\hat{\mathcal{X}}$. This estimate depends on the so-called 'subspace ranks' $\{K1, K2, K3\}$ which must be estimated. In the literature, the method which is proposed to estimate the subspace ranks is the AIC (Akaike Information Criterion) [8]. AIC estimates correctly the number of sources in an array processing problem. However, a large number of realizations of the same random signal are then available, hence the good behavior of AIC. Usually, in the frame of HSI processing, through a stationarity hypothesis, a covariance matrix is computed from the column vectors of the unfolded matrix obtained from the HSI, which are considered as realizations of the same random signal. AIC is applied to the eigenvalues of the covariance matrix obtained for each mode of the HSI [4]. However, it has been shown empirically that there is no clear domination of a subset of eigenvalues with high magnitude with respect to the others [4]. Hence, evaluating the best subspace ranks based on the eigenvalues only is not reliable. We propose to estimate the rank values through the minimization of a least squares criterion. MWF minimizes the MSE (mean square error) between expected and estimated tensor. So, we propose to minimize an MSE criterion to estimate the subspace ranks. It should increase the SNR values compared to an estimation with AIC. As a scalar criterion to estimate the subspace ranks $K1, K2, K3$, we choose:

$$J(K1, K2, K3) = ||\mathcal{R} - \hat{\mathcal{X}}||^2, \qquad (1)$$

where $||.||$ represents the Frobenius norm. The criterion J is a nonlinear function of the parameters $K1, K2, K3$, hence the need for an adequate optimization method, which must be global.

3   Particle Swarm Optimization for Rank Estimation

Some global optimization methods may be available to minimize the criterion J of Eq. (1), but they exhibit some drawbacks: the DIRECT method [12], for instance, would assume J to be a Lipschitzian function of the ranks, which may not handle. The Nelder-Mead Simplex Method [13] is meant to minimize a scalar-valued nonlinear function of several real variables, without any derivative information. However, as specified in [13], the global convergence of the Nelder-Mead method is ensured only in a one-dimensional problem, and only if some conditions about the parameters involved in the method are respected. On the contrary, particle swarm optimization [6] provides the global minimum of a scalar function of several variables and is gradient-free. The basic PSO algorithm consists, for the current iteration number it, in computing the velocity:

$$\mathbf{v}_q^{K1,K2,K3}(\text{it}+1) = W \ \mathbf{v}_q^{K1,K2,K3}(\text{it})...$$
$$... + \gamma_{1q} \ r1_q(\mathbf{p}_q^{K1,K2,K3} - \mathbf{y}_q^{K1,K2,K3}(\text{it}))$$
$$... + \gamma_{2q} \ r2_q(\mathbf{G}^{K1,K2,K3} - \mathbf{y}_q^{K1,K2,K3}(\text{it})) \qquad (2)$$

and the position:

$$\mathbf{y}_q^{K1,K2,K3}(\text{it}+1) = \mathbf{y}_q^{K1,K2,K3}(\text{it})$$
$$... + \mathbf{v}_q^{K1,K2,K3}(\text{it}+1) \qquad (3)$$

In (2) and (3), $\mathbf{v}_q^{K1,K2,K3}(\text{it})$ is the velocity of particle q at iteration it in a 3-dimensional space because there are 3 unknowns, W is the inertia weight, γ_{1q} and γ_{2q} are the acceleration constants encouraging a local and a global search respectively, $r1_q$ and $r2_q$ are random numbers between 0 and 1, applied to the qth particle, $\mathbf{p}_q^{K1,K2,K3}$ is the best position found for particle q, $\mathbf{G}^{K1,K2,K3}$ is the best position found over the whole group, and $\mathbf{y}_q^{K1,K2,K3}(\text{it})$ is the current position of particle q at iteration it. A large inertia weight (W) facilitates a global search while a small inertia weight facilitates a local search. We look forward to encourage a global search for the first iterations, and a local search for the last iterations. Hence, we fix an initial value W_{Init} and a final value W_{Final} for the weighting coefficient. At the iteration it, the weighting coefficient is computed as: $W = W_{Init} - \frac{(W_{Init} - W_{Final}) * \text{it}}{\text{maxit}}$, where maxit is the final iteration number. When this last iteration number is attained, the position vector $\mathbf{y}^{K1,K2,K3}(\text{maxit})$ contains the final estimated values $\hat{K}1, \hat{K}2, \hat{K}3$, of the signal subspace ranks.

4   Extension to the Wavelet Framework

We wish to adapt rank estimation to the most recent version of MWF, that is, its implementation in a wavelet framework [1]. This makes a reliable rank estimation method even more relevant: one triplet of rank values must be estimated for each wavelet coefficient. Following [1], minimizing the MSE between $\mathcal{X}$ and its estimate $\hat{\mathcal{X}}$ is equivalent to minimizing the MSE between $\mathcal{C}^{\mathcal{X}}_{1,\mathbf{m}}$ and $\hat{\mathcal{C}}^{\mathcal{X}}_{1,\mathbf{m}}$ for each $\mathbf{m}$:

$$\|\mathcal{X} - \hat{\mathcal{X}}\|^2 - \|\mathcal{C}^{\mathcal{X}}_1 - \hat{\mathcal{C}}^{\mathcal{X}}_1\|^2 = \sum_{\mathbf{m}} \|\mathcal{C}^{\mathcal{X}}_{1,\mathbf{m}} - \hat{\mathcal{C}}^{\mathcal{X}}_{1,\mathbf{m}}\|^2 \tag{4}$$

where $\mathcal{C}^{\mathcal{X}}_1$ is the wavelet packet coefficient tensor for levels in $\mathbf{l} = [l_1, l_2, l_3]^T$, $\mathcal{C}^{\mathcal{X}}_{1,\mathbf{m}}$ is the coefficient subtensor of $\mathcal{C}^{\mathcal{X}}_1$ where $\mathbf{m} = [m_1, m_2, m_3]^T$ is the index vector, $1 \le m_k \le 2^{l_k} - 1$, $k = 1, \ldots, 3$.

We wish to minimize all terms of the summation in Eq. (4), knowing that the noise-free tensor $\mathcal{X}$ is not available. For this we propose Algorithm 1, *multidimensional wavelet packet transform and multiway Wiener filtering with rank estimation by particle swarm optimization* (MWPT-MWF-PSO). In Algorithm 1, $\mathbf{H}_{1,\mathbf{m}}, \mathbf{H}_{2,\mathbf{m}}, \mathbf{H}_{3,\mathbf{m}}$ denote the n-mode filters of MWF, which depend on rank values (K1,K2,K3) [1,8]; $\mathcal{C}^{\mathcal{R}}_{1,\mathbf{m}}$ denote the wavelet coefficients of $\mathcal{R}$.

Algorithm 1 MWPT-MWF-PSO

Input: noisy tensor $\mathcal{R}$.
• compute the wavelet decomposition of the noisy tensor $\mathcal{R}$: $\mathcal{C}^{\mathcal{R}}_1 = \mathcal{R} \times_1 \mathbf{W}_1 \times_2 \mathbf{W}_2 \times_3 \mathbf{W}_3$
• extract the wavelet coefficients [1]:
$\mathcal{C}^{\mathcal{R}}_{1,\mathbf{m}} = \mathcal{C}^{\mathcal{R}}_1 \times_1 \mathbf{E}_{m_1} \times_2 \mathbf{E}_{m_2} \times_3 \mathbf{E}_{m_3}$,
• for each wavelet coefficient $\mathcal{C}^{\mathcal{R}}_{1,\mathbf{m}}$:
i) estimate with PSO the optimal rank values $\hat{K}1, \hat{K}2, \hat{K}3$ in terms of the criterion:
$J_{\mathbf{m}}(K1, K2, K3) = \|\mathcal{C}^{\mathcal{R}}_{1,\mathbf{m}} - \hat{\mathcal{C}}^{\mathcal{X}}_{1,\mathbf{m}}\|^2$
where $\hat{\mathcal{C}}^{\mathcal{X}}_{1,\mathbf{m}} = \mathcal{C}^{\mathcal{R}}_{1,\mathbf{m}} \times_1 \mathbf{H}_{1,\mathbf{m}} \times_2 \mathbf{H}_{2,\mathbf{m}} \times_3 \mathbf{H}_{3,\mathbf{m}}$.
As PSO is a global optimization method, algorithm 1 is supposed to converge asymptotically towards the best set of rank values. In practice, the total number of iterations, that is, the parameter maxit is fixed automatically: the algorithm stops when the criterion $J_{\mathbf{m}}(K1, K2, K3)$ does not vary from an iteration to another by a small factor ϵ set by the user.
ii) apply MWF to each coefficient subtensor $\mathcal{C}^{\mathcal{R}}_{1,\mathbf{m}}$, with the optimal rank values.
• obtain $\hat{\mathcal{C}}^{\mathcal{X}}_1$ by concatenating all coefficients $\hat{\mathcal{C}}^{\mathcal{X}}_{1,\mathbf{m}}$.
• reconstruct the final estimated tensor by inverse wavelet transform: $\hat{\mathcal{X}} = \hat{\mathcal{C}}^{\mathcal{X}}_1 \times_1 \mathbf{W}^T_1 \times_2 \mathbf{W}^T_2 \times_3 \mathbf{W}^T_3$
Output: denoised tensor $\hat{\mathcal{X}}$.

---

5   Results

In this section, we apply the proposed method based on multiway Wiener filtering, multidimensional wavelet packet transform and particle swarm optimization, and comparative methods such as ForWaRD [7] on an RGB image and on real-world HSIs acquired by an AVIRIS sensor. ForWaRD is originally a deconvolution and denoising method. It includes first a Fourier Wiener filtering step and secondly a Wavelet filtering step. In the first step, a deconvolution process is proposed in the original paper [7]. In this paper, we avoid deconvolution as it is not required for the processed data, and use ForWaRD strictly as a denoising method. Programmes were written in $Matlab^{®}$ language, and executed on a PC computer running Windows, with a 3GHz double core and 3GB RAM. The images are artificially impaired with white, identically distributed random noise. The denoising performance will be evaluated through SNR and $PSNR$: $SNR = 10 \, log(\frac{||\mathcal{X}||^2}{||\mathcal{X}-\hat{\mathcal{X}}||^2})$ and $PSNR = 10 \, log(\frac{||\max(\mathcal{X})||^2}{||\mathcal{X}-\hat{\mathcal{X}}||^2})$, where max denotes maximum value. The numerical results are computed from images truncated to the size $200 \times 200 \times 64$ to avoid the border issues. In the wavelet decomposition, following the recommendations in [1] we choose Coiflets and Daubechies wavelet functions. To choose adequately the number of decomposition levels for the considered noise level, we tested the two combinations proposed in [1]: either two or three decomposition levels for the space modes and no decomposition in the wavelength mode. Choosing $\mathbf{l} = [2, 2, 0]^T$, the results obtained with PSO are slightly better than with three decomposition levels, and those obtained with AIC hardly change. This yields 16 wavelet coefficients (4 coefficients for each level), which are 3rd-order tensors of size $64 \times 64 \times 64$ for which the rank for each mode must be estimated. We initialize the ranks with a random value between 8 and 64. For this purpose we run the PSO algorithm with a swarm size 25 and a parameter $\epsilon = 10^{-6}$. This generally yields maxit = 150 iterations. The acceleration constants γ_{1i} and γ_{2i} are set to 2 and 3 respectively; the initial and final values of W are set to 0.9 and 0.4. ForWaRD is implemented with Daubechies wavelets, and two decomposition levels [7]. In the following subsections we present the numerical and visual results obtained with either ForWaRD algorithm [7], the truncation of HOSVD [8], or MWF [8] with the rank values which have been empirically found to yield the best results in terms of SNR; and MWF-MWPT in two configurations: the subspace ranks being estimated by AIC, and the subspace ranks being estimated with PSO (the proposed algorithm). As specified throughout the section, the input SNR is set to 10 dB for the first experiments, and then to 5, and 15 dB. For the RGB display of the hypespectral images throughout the section, we select 3 representative bands in the red, green, and blue wavelength domains respectively.

5.1   RGB Image

We apply denoising to the standard three-channel color image 'Lena' truncated to size 256×256. First, Table 1 provides the numerical results obtained when we impair the image in such a way that the input SNR is 10 dB. The original noise-free, noisy, and denoised images are displayed in Fig 1. Table 1 and Fig. 1

Table 1. SNR and PSNR values for the noised image; MWF with ranks fixed to 50, 50, 3; MWF of the multidimensional wavelet packet coefficients with rank estimation by AIC or by PSO (proposed method).

Criterion Method	SNR	PSNR
Noised image	10.00	20.20
MWF	14.17	19.06
MWF-MWPT:		
• AIC	14.85	19.75
• PSO	17.00	21.90

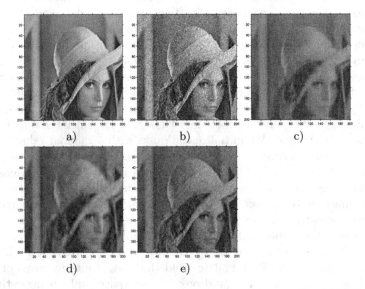

Fig. 1. a) Raw image; b) Noised image (10 dB); Denoising result: c) MWF, d) AIC, e) PSO.

show that the proposed method performs well on a color image, compared to MWF and the case where AIC criterion is used to estimate the ranks in a wavelet framework. Indeed for an input SNR of 10 dB the proposed method provides a denoised image with an output SNR of 17.00 dB, MWF provides 14.17 dB and AIC 14.85 dB. In the next two subsections, hyperspectral images are considered.

5.2   Hyperspectral Image AVIRIS 1

The HSI AVIRIS 1 is of size $256 \times 256 \times 64$, containing 64 wavelength channels. It contains rather straight orientations crossing the image. Hence, we expect that the original MWF, which applies a subspace-based filtering on the whole image, without wavelet decomposition, will provide rather good results. The ranks for the truncation of HOSVD and MWF are fixed to 50,50,20. The numerical results are provided in Table 2.

Table 2. AVIRIS 1: SNR and PSNR values for the noised image; Truncation of the HOSVD; MWF; MWF of the multidimensional wavelet packet coefficients with rank estimation by AIC or by PSO (proposed method).

Method \ Criterion	SNR	PSNR
Noised image	10.00	20.20
Truncation HOSVD	21.20	30.68
MWF	22.72	32.83
MWF-MWPT:		
• AIC	15.96	26.07
• PSO	21.30	31.41

When PSO is used, along the spatial modes, the ranks obtained for the approximation coefficients are between 20 and 64 (the maximum possible value), decreasing to 8 for the detail coefficients; along the wavelength mode, the rank is 8 (the smallest possible value). When AIC is used, along the spatial modes, the rank values vary from 1 to 64 without distinguishing between approximation and detail coefficients; along the wavelength mode, the rank values vary between 47 and 64, therefore much more elevated than in the case where PSO is used. Hence the lower noise magnitude in the case where PSO is used. Table 2 shows that, in the particular case of this image, MWF performs slightly better, in terms of SNR, than the proposed method. We notice however that estimating the rank values with PSO yields a better result than when AIC is used. However, the proposed method based on PSO provides the best visual result, as shown in Fig. 2 which presents the original noise-free (a), the noised (b), and denoised images for the comparative methods from c) to e) and the proposed method (f). Particularly, the contours are better preserved. See for instance the region between rows 120 to 140 and columns 30 to 80. A zoom on these regions is provided in Fig. 3. We infer from Fig. 3 that the proposed method better preserves the grey level values of each band in small regions.

The results obtained on the HSI AVIRIS 1 yields the following overall comments: when horizontal and vertical contours are present, there is no improvement -in terms of SNR- provided by the combination of wavelet decomposition and a subspace-based method such as MWF. However, the visual aspect is improved when the wavelet decomposition is performed. For the HSI AVIRIS

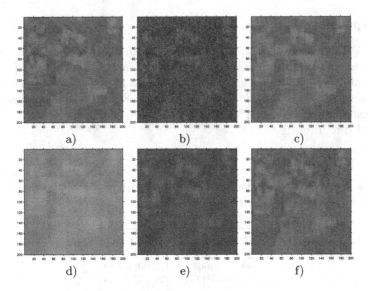

Fig. 2. AVIRIS 1: a) Raw image; b) Noised image (SNR 10 dB); Denoising result: c) Truncation of HOSVD, d) MWF, e) AIC, f) PSO.

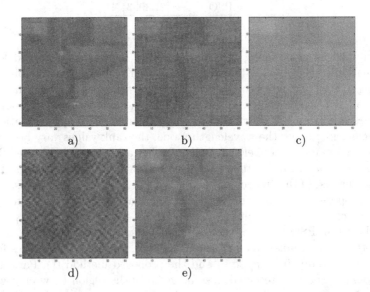

Fig. 3. Zoom on AVIRIS 1: a) Raw image, b) truncation of the HOSVD, c) MWF, d) AIC, e) PSO.

1, MWF takes advantage of the vertical and horizontal features present along the two spatial modes [8]. When small features are present instead, the interest of wavelet decomposition and of a correct subspace rank value in each mode will be emphasized.

5.3   Hyperspectral Image AVIRIS 2

In this subsection, we present results obtained on the HSI AVIRIS 2, of size $256 \times 256 \times 64$, where the relevant features are localized on some regions of the image. From the presence of such small local features we expect methods based on wavelet decomposition to provide better results compared to subspace-based methods, because wavelet decomposition permits to separate the processing of high frequency and low frequency features. We compare the results obtained with the wavelet-based ForWaRD algorithm [7] and MWF with ranks fixed to 50, 50, 20.

Input SNR 10 dB: Numerical and Visual Results. First, we impair the image with an input SNR 10 dB. We obtain the numerical results (SNR and PSNR) presented in Table 3.

Table 3. AVIRIS 2: SNR and PSNR values for the noised image; comparative For-WaRD method; MWF; MWF of the multidimensional wavelet packet coefficients with rank estimation by AIC or by PSO (proposed method).

Method \ Criterion	SNR	PSNR
Noised image	10.00	23.13
ForWaRD	11.58	24.52
MWF	12.21	25.85
MWF-MWPT:		
• AIC	14.61	28.24
• PSO	18.58	32.21

Table 3 shows the superiority of the proposed method combining wavelet decomposition and rank estimation by PSO. The comparison with ForWaRD algorithm, which also works in the wavelet domain, shows that the proposed method is more appropriate to denoise such an HSI. Indeed, each spectral band is processed independently from the others with ForWaRD, whereas the tensor based methods using AIC or PSO take into account the relationships between bands. The original noise-free, noisy, and denoised images are displayed in Fig. 4. They show firstly that the result provided by MWF enhances some of the rows and columns which results in blurring the contours which are neither horizontal nor vertical. Also, they show that the homogeneous regions are better denoised with PSO than with AIC, or ForWaRD. In Fig. 5 we focus on the region containing the building and its frontiers (between rows 50 to 120 and columns 70 to 140 of AVIRIS 2). Comparing the result obtained by MWF and wavelet decomposition with rank estimation by PSO, we notice that the frontiers are much less blurred and that the details are better preserved when wavelet decomposition is used, and that the homogeneous regions are better denoised when PSO is used compared to the case where AIC is used. In this experiment, a close examination of the estimated rank values shows that, for the third mode, AIC tends to overestimate the ranks. We remind that the wavelet packet decomposition is performed with 2 levels on the two space modes, and that no decomposition is performed on the wavelength mode. When PSO is used, along the spatial modes, the rank values obtained are between 59 and 64; along the wavelength mode, the rank is always 8 (the smallest possible value). When AIC is used, along the spatial modes, the rank values vary from 2 to 64 with a much higher variability than in the case where PSO is used; along the wavelength mode, AIC yields elevated rank values between 51 and 64. PSO yields a stronger denoising in the wavelength mode and hence, overall, a better preservation of the spatial details and a higher output SNR.

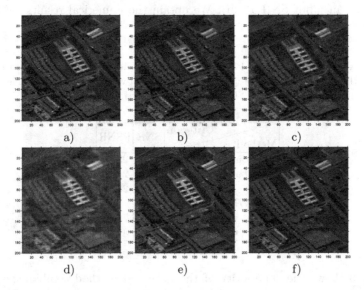

Fig. 4. AVIRIS 2: a) Raw image; b) Noised image (SNR 10 dB); Denoising result: c) ForWaRD, d) MWF, e) AIC, f) PSO.

The results obtained on AVIRIS 2 show the superiority of the proposed method not only in terms of image quality but also in terms of output SNR. To confirm this good behavior, we present, in the following, the results obtained on AVIRIS 2 with two other values of input SNR: 5 and 15 dB.

Input SNR 5 and 15 dB: Numerical Results. Here are some numerical results obtained with the image AVIRIS 2 and SNR=5 dB and SNR=15 dB in Table 4.

As a balance for the numerical results presented in Tables 3 and 4, we can assert that the rank values chosen by PSO yield the best denoising result in terms of SNR and PSNR at least when AVIRIS 2 is considered. We infer from these results that it is important to perform Wiener filtering in the wavelet domain,

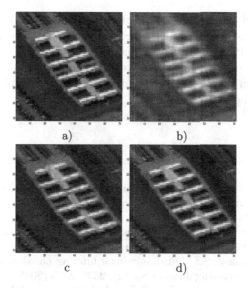

Fig. 5. Zoom on AVIRIS 2: a) Raw image, b) MWF, c) AIC, d) PSO.

Table 4. SNR and PSNR values for the noised image; comparative MWF; MWF-MWPT with rank estimation by AIC or by PSO (proposed method).

Criterion Method	SNR	PSNR	SNR	PSNR
	5.00 dB		15.00 dB	
Noised image	5.00	19.22	15.00	28.73
MWF	10.61	24.23	12.99	26.62
MWF-MWPT:				
• AIC	11.17	24.79	18.98	32.60
• PSO	13.73	27.36	22.56	36.18

but also to use appropriate rank values to reach the best possible result in terms of SNR. This is the case as for AVIRIS 2 when the processed image contains small features such as buildings in aerial images, but also any small objects of interest. This appears very often in the case of other multidimensional images such as medical ones. Other experiments were performed with different images and SNR values. The corresponding numerical and visual results are provided at: www.fresnel.fr/perso/marot/Documents/Resultsacivs.html.

6   Conclusion

Recently, a common framework was proposed for multiway Wiener filtering and multidimensional wavelet decomposition, where a rank parameter must be available for each mode of the processed tensor, that is, 3 for an HSI, and for each decomposition level. This makes an automatic rank estimation method very valuable. AIC overestimates the expected values. We propose a novel approach which consists in minimizing a least squares criterion with particle swarm optimization, for each coefficient of the wavelet decomposition of the noisy tensor. Results obtained on an RGB image and noisy HSIs containing small features and details show the superiority of the proposed approach compared to AIC, FoRwaRD, HOSVD or MWF algorithms.

References

1. Lin, T., Bourennane, S.: Hyperspectral image processing by jointly filtering wavelet component tensor. IEEE Transactions on Geoscience and Remote Sensing **51**(6), 3529–3541 (2013)
2. Kerekes, J.P., Baum, J.E.: Full spectrum spectral imaging system analytical model. IEEE Trans. on Geosc. and Remote Sensing **43**(3), 571–580 (2005)
3. Muti, D., Bourennane, S.: Multidimensional filtering based on a tensor approach. Elsevier Signal Proceesing Journal **85**(12), 2338–2353 (2005)
4. Renard, N., Bourennane, S., Blanc-Talon, J.: Denoising and dimensionality reduction using multilinear tools for hyperspectral images. IEEE Geoscience and Remote Sensing Letters **5**(2), 138–142 (2008)
5. Lin, T., Marot, J., Bourennane, S.: Small target detection improvement in hyperspectral image. In: Blanc-Talon, J., Kasinski, A., Philips, W., Popescu, D., Scheunders, P. (eds.) ACIVS 2013. LNCS, vol. 8192, pp. 460–469. Springer, Heidelberg (2013)
6. Kennedy, J., Eberhart, R.: Particle swarm optimization. In: IEEE International Conference on Neural Networks, Perth, pp. 1942–1948 (1995)
7. Neelamani, R., Choi, H., Baraniuk, R.: Forward: Fourier-wavelet regularized deconvolution for ill-conditioned systems. IEEE Trans. on Signal Processing **52**(2), 418–433 (2004)
8. Muti, D., Bourennane, S., Marot, J.: Lower-rank tensor approximation and multiway filtering. SIAM Journal on Matrix Analysis and Applications **30**(3), 1172–1204 (2008)
9. Parra, L., Spence, C., Sajda, P., Ziehe, A., Müller, K.: Unmixing hyperspectral data. In: Advances in Neural Information Processing Systems, vol. 12, pp. 942–948 (2000)
10. Liu, X., Bourennane, S., Fossati, C.: Nonwhite Noise Reduction in Hyperspectral Images. IEEE Geoscience and Remote Sensing Letters **9**(3), 368–372 (2012)
11. Letexier, D., Bourennane, S., Blanc-Talon, J.: Main flattening directions and quadtree decomposition for multi-way wiener filtering. Signal, Image and Video Processing **1**(3), 253–256 (2007)
12. Jones, D.R., Pertunen, C.D., Stuckman, B.E.: Lipschitzian optimization without the lipschitz constant. Journal of Optimization Theory and Application **79**(1), 157–181 (1993)
13. Lagarias, J.C., Reeds, J.A., Wright, M.H., Wright, P.E.: Convergence properties of the nelder-mead simplex method in low dimensions. SIAM Journal of Optimization **9**(1), 112–147 (1998)

Minimizing the Impact of Signal-Dependent Noise on Hyperspectral Target Detection

Josselin Juan, Salah Bourennane$^{(\boxtimes)}$, and Caroline Fossati

Centrale Marseille, Aix-Marseille Université, CNRS,
Institut Fresnel UMR 7249, 13013 Marseille, France
`salah.bourennane@fresnel.fr`

Abstract. Multilinear algebra based method for noise reduction in hyperspectral images (HSI) is proposed to minimize negative impacts on target detection of signal-dependent noise. A parametric model, suitable for HSIs that the photon noise is dominant compared to the electronic noise contribution, is used to describe the noise. To diminish the data noise from hyperspectral images distorted by both signal-dependent (SD) and signal-independent (SI) noise, a tensorial method, which reduces noise by exploiting the different statistical properties of those two types of noise, is proposed in this paper. This method uses a parallel factor analysis (PARAFAC) decomposition to remove jointly SI and SD noises. The performances of the proposed method are assessed on simulated HSIs. The results on the real-world airborne hyperspectral image HYDICE (Hyperspectral Digital Imagery Collection Experiment) are also presented and analyzed. These experiments have demonstrated the benefits arising from using the pre-whitening procedure in mitigating the impact of the SD in different detection algorithms for hyperspectral images.

1 Introduction

Hyperspectral images consist of a considerably large number of narrow spectral bands which are uniformly distributed over a wide spectral range [1]. The hyperspectral signatures offer the possibility to detect and discriminate ground cover types. Specific processing methods, for instance, spectral signatures unmixing [2], target detection [3] and classification [4] etc., have been developed. Generally, these methods operate well in the presence of a high signal-to-noise ratio (SNR).

The noise in HSIs can be regrouped into two classes: Photon and electronic noises are examples of random noise in HSIs. For new-generation hyperspectral sensors the photon noise, which depends on the spatially varying signal level, is not negligible. The widely accepted SI noise model is white Gaussian one [5–8]. In [9–11], it was shown that the SI noise in some HSIs is colored, *i.e.* spectrally non-white. Therefore, in this paper we use the widely accepted noise model in [5,7,8] including both SD and SI noise. By exploiting the different statistical properties of SI and SD noise, in this paper, we propose a multilinear algebra

© Springer International Publishing Switzerland 2015
S. Battiato et al. (Eds.): ACIVS 2015, LNCS 9386, pp. 791–802, 2015.
DOI: 10.1007/978-3-319-25903-1_68

method to improve the SNR of HSI before detection algorithm execution. We propose to estimate the noise by PARAFAC decomposition method from HSIs distorted by both SD and white or colored SI noise firstly. Then, a non-stationary transform noise pre-whitening aimed at reducing the noise spatial variability is applied.

Our proposed method is applied to the simulated HSIs in order to evaluate its performances in a controlled environment. The results obtained on the real-world HYDICE HSIs are also presented and discussed. To compare the denoising performance to other methods, Multiway Wiener Filtering (MWF) [3], Pre-whitening Multiway Wiener Filtering (PMWF) [11], two well-known 2D denoising methods, minimum noise fraction (MNF) and noise-adjusted principal components analysis (PCA) [10, 12, 13] are used in the simulations. The experimental results show that the proposed method is efficient in the reduction of both SI and SD noise in HSIs.

The remainder of the paper is organized as follows: some multilinear algebra tools are introduced in section 2. Section 3 gives the data model of HSIs distorted by both SD and SI noise. Section 4 overviews PARAFAC decomposition. Section 5 presents the detailed description of our proposed method for the reduction of both SI and SD noise in HSIs; some denoising and comparative results are contained in section 6 and section 7 concludes the paper.

2 Multilinear Algebra Tools

2.1 Overview of Noise Reduction Methods Based on Tensor Models

During the last decade, multilinear algebra based methods are developed to HSI processing, for instance, for denoising applications, where a tensor is defined as a multidimensional array [14] and HSI is modelled as tensor data. Conversely to the conventional methods, they consider the spectral relationships among bands and process tensor data as a whole entity [15, 16]. Two main decomposition models for tensors are: Tucker3 decomposition [17] and CANDECOMP/PARAFAC (Canonical Decomposition / Parallel Factor Analysis) decomposition [18] [19]. Tucker3 decomposition decomposes a tensor into a core tensor multiplied by a matrix along each mode. From signal processing point of view, subspace-based methods project the data on the signal subspace which is spanned by the eigenvectors associated with the largest eigenvalues of the covariance matrix of data. The subspace-based approach can be extended to multidimensional data when noise is independent from the signal tensor [20]. Multidimensional Wiener filtering method (MWF) is an extension of the subspace-based approach to tensorial case based on Tucker3 model decomposition [15, 16]. However, MWF method can only deal with the signal-independent white noise [15]. Since Tucker3 decomposition was used in MWF method and discussed in [15] , we will not discuss Tucker3 decomposition in this paper. PARAFAC decomposition has the distinguishing uniqueness characteristics, i.e. low-rank PARAFAC decomposition can be unique for rank values higher than one. Based on this property, in this paper, PARAFAC decomposition is proposed to denoise HSI and the experimental results showed its promising performance in the reduction both SI white/color noise and SD noise. In the following, some basic multilinear algebra tools used in tensor decompositions are introduced.

2.2 Rank-One Tensor

N-mode tensor $\mathcal{Y} \in \mathbb{R}^{I_1 \times I_2 \times \cdots \times I_N}$ being rank 1 means that it can be written as the outer product of N vectors [14,21], that is

$$\mathcal{Y} = \boldsymbol{a}^{(1)} \circ \boldsymbol{a}^{(2)} \circ \cdots \circ \boldsymbol{a}^{(N)} \tag{1}$$

So, each element of $\mathcal{Y}$ is the product of the corresponding vector elements: $y_{i_1,i_2,\ldots,i_N} = a_{i_1}^{(1)} a_{i_2}^{(2)} \ldots a_{i_N}^{(N)}$ for all $1 \leq i_n \leq I_n$.

2.3 n-Mode Unfolding

To transfer a n-mode tensor $\mathcal{Y} \in \mathbb{R}^{I_1 \times \cdots \times I_N}$ to a matrix, the n-mode fibers must be arranged to be the columns of the resulting matrix [14]. The n-mode unfolding matrix of a tensor $\mathcal{Y}$ is denoted by $\mathbf{Y}_n$ which is a $I_n \times M_n$ matrix with:

$$M_n = I_1 \cdots I_{n-1} I_{n+1} \cdots I_N \tag{2}$$

2.4 n-Mode Product

The n-mode product is defined as the product of a data tensor $\mathcal{Y} \in \mathbb{R}^{I_1 \times \cdots \times I_N}$ and a matrix $\mathbf{B} \in \mathbb{R}^{J \times I_n}$ in mode n and is used to extend matrix SVD (singular value decomposition) [22]. It is of size $I_1 \times \cdots \times I_{n-1} \times J \times I_{n+1} \times \cdots \times I_N$ and denoted by $\mathcal{Y} \times_n \mathbf{B}$. Elementwise, it is

$$(\mathcal{Y} \times_n \mathbf{B})_{i_1 \cdots i_{n-1} j i_{n+1} \cdots i_N} = \sum_{i_n=1}^{I_n} y_{i_1 i_2 \cdots i_N} b_{j i_n} \tag{3}$$

3 Signal Model

A noisy HSI can be represented as a third order tensor $\mathcal{R} \in \mathbb{R}^{I_1 \times I_2 \times I_3}$ composed of a signal tensor $\mathcal{X} \in \mathbb{R}^{I_1 \times I_2 \times I_3}$ impaired by an additive random noise tensor $\mathcal{N}(\mathcal{X}) \in \mathbb{R}^{I_1 \times I_2 \times I_3}$:

$$\mathcal{R} = \mathcal{X} + \mathcal{N}(\mathcal{X}) \tag{4}$$

where $\mathcal{N}(\mathcal{X})$ accounts for both SI and SD noise and its variance depends on the pixel x_{i_1,i_2,i_3} in the useful signal $\mathcal{X}$. Elementwise, the data model is [8]

$$r_{i_1,i_2,i_3} = x_{i_1,i_2,i_3} + \sqrt{x_{i_1,i_2,i_3}} \cdot s_{i_1,i_2,i_3} + w_{i_1,i_2,i_3} \tag{5}$$

where s_{i_1,i_2,i_3} is a stationary, zero-mean uncorrelated random process independent of x_{i_1,i_2,i_3} with variance σ_{s,i_3}^2 and w_{i_1,i_2,i_3} is SI noise which is zero-mean white Gaussian noise in each band with variance σ_{w,i_3}^2. The additive term $\sqrt{x} \cdot s$ is the generalized SD noise and denoted as SD noise, w is the SI noise component and is generally assumed to be Gaussian distribution in each band. Then, we can define $\mathcal{N}(\mathcal{X}) = \mathcal{N}_{SD}(\mathcal{X}) + \mathcal{N}_{SI} = \mathcal{N}_{SD}(\mathcal{X}) + \mathcal{W}$, and (4) can be correspondingly rewritten as

$$\mathcal{R} = \mathcal{X} + \mathcal{N}_{SD}(\mathcal{X}) + \mathcal{W}. \tag{6}$$

With the assumption that x, s and w are independent and both s and w are zero mean and are stationary, the noise variance of each entry $n(\mathcal{X})_{i_1,i_2,i_3} = \sqrt{x_{i_1,i_2,i_3}} \cdot s_{i_1,i_2,i_3} + w_{i_1,i_2,i_3}$ of $\mathcal{N}(\mathcal{X})$ can be written as: [5,7,8,23] :

$$\sigma_{\mathcal{N}(\mathcal{X}),i_1,i_2,i_3}^2 = x_{i_1,i_2,i_3} \cdot \sigma_{u,i_3}^2 + \sigma_{w,i_3}^2 \tag{7}$$

The unfolding matrix $\mathbf{R}_3 \in \mathbb{R}^{I_3 \times M_3}$ of the HSI data tensor $\mathcal{R} \in \mathbb{R}^{I_1 \times I_2 \times I_3}$ (with $M_3 = I_1 I_2$ defined in (2)) can be expressed as :

$$\mathbf{R}_3 = \mathbf{X}_3 + \mathbf{N}(\mathcal{X})_3 \tag{8}$$

where $\mathbf{X}_3$ is the 3-mode unfolding matrix of the multidimensional signal tensor $\mathcal{X}$ and

$$\mathbf{N}(\mathcal{X})_3 = \mathbf{N}_{SD}(\mathcal{X})_3 + \mathbf{W}_3 \tag{9}$$

with $\mathbf{N}_{SD}(\mathcal{X})_3$ and $\mathbf{W}_3$ being the 3-mode unfolding matrices of $\mathcal{N}_{SD}(\mathcal{X})$ and $\mathcal{W}$ respectively.

Using the mean noise variance of the i_3th spectral band defined as $\frac{1}{I_1 I_2} \sum_{i_1=1}^{I_1} \sum_{i_2=1}^{I_2} \sigma_{\mathcal{N}(\mathcal{X}),i_1,i_2,i_3}^2 = \mu_{i_3} \sigma_{s,i_3}^2 + \sigma_{w,i_3}^2$ where $\mu_{i_3} = \frac{1}{I_1 I_2} \sum_{i_1=1}^{I_1} \sum_{i_2=1}^{I_2} x_{i_1,i_2,i_3}$ is the mean of all x_{i_1,i_2,i_3} in the i_3th band of $\mathcal{X}$ with $i_3 = 1, \cdots, I_3$, the covariance matrix of the 3-mode unfolding matrix $\mathbf{W}_3$ of the SI noise tensor $\mathcal{W}$ can be written as a diagonal matrix:

$$\mathbf{C}_{\mathcal{W}}^{(3)} = diag(\sigma_{w,1}^2, \sigma_{w,2}^2, \cdots, \sigma_{w,I_3}^2) \tag{10}$$

Based on the assumption of the independence of x and s, where s is zero-mean and independent between spectral bands, the covariance matrix of the 3-mode unfolding matrix $\mathbf{N}_{SD}(\mathcal{X})_3$ can be expressed as:

$$\mathbf{C}_{\mathcal{N}_{SD}(\mathcal{X})}^{(3)} = diag(\mu_1 \sigma_{s,1}^2, \mu_2 \sigma_{s,2}^2, \cdots, \mu_{I_3} \sigma_{s,I_3}^2) \tag{11}$$

where $\mu_{i_3} \sigma_{s,i_3}^2 = \frac{1}{I_1 I_2} \sum_{i_1=1}^{I_1} \sum_{i_2=1}^{I_2} x_{i_1,i_2,i_3} \sigma_{s,i_3}^2$ with $i_3 = 1, \cdots, I_3$.

4   Noise Estimation Based on PARAFAC Model

The PARAFAC model factorizes a tensor into a sum of rank-1 tensors [14]. For instance, tensor $\mathcal{R} \in \mathbb{R}^{I_1 \times I_2 \times I_3}$ can be expressed as

$$\mathcal{R} \approx \hat{\mathcal{R}} = \sum_{k=1}^{K} \mathcal{R}_k = \sum_{k=1}^{K} \lambda_k a_k^{(1)} \circ a_k^{(2)} \circ a_k^{(3)} \tag{12}$$

where K is the rank, $\hat{\mathcal{R}}$ is the rank-K approximation of $\mathcal{R}$; $\mathcal{R}_k \in \mathbb{R}^{I_1 \times I_2 \times I_3}$ is rank-1 tensor; $\boldsymbol{a}_k^{(1)}, \boldsymbol{a}_k^{(2)}, \boldsymbol{a}_k^{(3)} \in \mathbb{R}^{I_n}$ are normalized vectors of the n-mode space of $\mathcal{R}$ normalized by $\boldsymbol{a}_k^{(n)} = \boldsymbol{a}_k^{(n)} / \|\boldsymbol{a}_k^{(n)}\|$, $n = 1, 2, 3$; and $\lambda_k = \|\boldsymbol{a}_k^{(1)}\| \|\boldsymbol{a}_k^{(2)}\| \|\boldsymbol{a}_k^{(3)}\|$, $k = 1, 2, \cdots, K$. Elementwise, (12) is written as

$$\hat{r}_{i_1, i_2, i_3} = \sum_{k=1}^{K} \lambda_k a_{i_1 k}^{(1)} a_{i_2 k}^{(2)} a_{i_3 k}^{(3)} \tag{13}$$

with $i_1 = 1, \ldots, I_1$, $i_2 = 1, \ldots, I_2$, $i_3 = 1, \ldots, I_3$.

The PARAFAC decomposition is used to compute $\hat{\mathcal{R}}$ with K components that approximate the best value of $\mathcal{R}$ by minimizing the square error $e = \|\mathcal{R} - \hat{\mathcal{R}}\|^2$. Using Khatri-Rao product, the n-mode unfolding matrix [14] of $\mathcal{R}$ is given by:

$$\hat{\mathbf{R}}_1 = \mathbf{A}^{(1)} \boldsymbol{\Lambda} (\mathbf{A}^{(3)} \odot \mathbf{A}^{(2)})^{\mathrm{T}}$$
$$\hat{\mathbf{R}}_2 = \mathbf{A}^{(2)} \boldsymbol{\Lambda} (\mathbf{A}^{(3)} \odot \mathbf{A}^{(1)})^{\mathrm{T}} \tag{14}$$
$$\hat{\mathbf{R}}_3 = \mathbf{A}^{(3)} \boldsymbol{\Lambda} (\mathbf{A}^{(2)} \odot \mathbf{A}^{(1)})^{\mathrm{T}}$$

where $\mathbf{A}^{(n)} = [\boldsymbol{a}_1^{(n)}, \ldots, \boldsymbol{a}_K^{(n)}]$ $(n = 1, 2, 3)$, $\boldsymbol{\Lambda} = \mathrm{diag}(\lambda_1, \cdots, \lambda_K)$. Thus, minimizing $e = \|\mathcal{R} - \hat{\mathcal{R}}\|^2$ is transformed to find $\mathbf{A}^{(n)}$ where:

$$\mathbf{A}^{(n)} = \arg\min |e_t - e_{t+1}| \tag{15}$$

with t means the t-th iteration to estimate $\mathbf{A}^{(n)}$ in the "PARAFAC ALS algorithm" [14]. If HSIs are contaminated by non-white SI noise, the noise $\mathcal{W}$ in (6) will be colored, $i.e.$ the noise variance σ_{w,i_3}^2 is different from band to band. With the assumption that the noisy tensor $\mathcal{R}$ can be exactly expressed by sum of T $(T > K)$ rank-1 tensors, then

$$\mathcal{R} = \sum_{k=1}^{K} \lambda_k \boldsymbol{a}_k^{(1)} \circ \boldsymbol{a}_k^{(2)} \circ \boldsymbol{a}_k^{(3)} + \sum_{k=K+1}^{T} \lambda_k \boldsymbol{a}_k^{(1)} \circ \boldsymbol{a}_k^{(2)} \circ \boldsymbol{a}_k^{(3)} \tag{16}$$

by using $\mathcal{G}_k = \boldsymbol{a}_k^{(1)} \circ \boldsymbol{a}_k^{(2)} \circ \boldsymbol{a}_k^{(3)}$, we can get $\lambda_k = <\mathcal{R}, \mathcal{G}_k>$, then $\mathrm{E}[<\mathcal{R}, \mathcal{G}_k>^2] = \mathrm{E}[\lambda_k^2] = \lambda_k^2$.

With the assumption that x, s and w are independent, and both s and w are zero-mean, therefore

$$\lambda_k^2 = \mathrm{E}[<\mathcal{R}, \mathcal{G}_k>^2] = \mathrm{E}[<\mathcal{X} + \mathcal{N}, \mathcal{G}_k>^2] = \mathrm{E}[(<\mathcal{X}, \mathcal{G}_k> + <\mathcal{N}, \mathcal{G}_k>)^2]$$
$$= \mathrm{E}[<\mathcal{X}, \mathcal{G}_k>^2 + 2 <\mathcal{X}, \mathcal{G}_k><\mathcal{N}, \mathcal{G}_k> + <\mathcal{N}, \mathcal{G}_k>^2]$$
$$= <\mathcal{X}, \mathcal{G}_k>^2 + 2 <\mathcal{X}, \mathcal{G}_k>< \mathrm{E}[\mathcal{N}], \mathcal{G}_k> + \mathrm{E}[<\mathcal{N}, \mathcal{G}_k>^2]. \tag{17}$$

Without loss of generality, the noise $\mathcal{N}$ can be assumed to be zero-mean, $i.e.$ $\mathrm{E}[\mathcal{N}] = 0$, then

$$\lambda_k^2 = <\mathcal{X}, \mathcal{G}_k>^2 + \mathrm{E}[<\mathcal{N}, \mathcal{G}_k>^2]$$
$$= \lambda_{\mathcal{X},k}^2 + \lambda_{\mathcal{N},k}^2.$$

So

$$\min \|\mathcal{R} - \hat{\mathcal{R}}\|^2 \Longleftrightarrow \{\lambda_{\mathcal{X},k}^2 + \lambda_{\mathcal{N},k}^2 \mid k = K+1,\cdots,T\}$$

are $T - K$ smallest terms among

$$\{\lambda_{\mathcal{X},k}^2 + \lambda_{\mathcal{N},k}^2 \mid k = 1,\cdots,T\}.$$

In practice, the observed real-world HSI has SNR$\geq$ 35dB [24–26], the signal $\mathcal{X}$ is the dominant part in the noisy HSI $\mathcal{R}$. Therefore,

$$\min \|\mathcal{R} - \hat{\mathcal{R}}\|^2 \Longrightarrow \{\lambda_{\mathcal{X},k}^2 \mid k = K+1,\cdots,T\}$$

are $T - K$ smallest terms among

$$\{\lambda_{\mathcal{X},k}^2 \mid k = 1,\cdots,T\}.$$

Therefore, the minimum of the square error $\|\mathcal{R} - \hat{\mathcal{R}}\|^2$ corresponds to throw away other smaller terms from $K + 1$ to T of PARAFAC decomposition where both signal and noise components exist. With the assumption that x, s and w are independent and the criterion of minimizing the square error $\|\mathcal{R} - \hat{\mathcal{R}}\|^2$, the signal components in the smallest terms from $K + 1$ to T are the smallest ones among all the signal components from 1 to T of PARAFAC decomposition. Therefore, for fixed K, PARAFAC decomposition can reduce the noise at the cost of lowest loss of signal and be unrelated to the noise character, for instance white or non-white, that is to say that the rank-K PARAFAC approximation of a noisy tensor results in an estimation of the signal. Since the denoising by PARAFAC decomposition is based on skipping smaller terms from $K + 1$ to T where SD noise components exist, so PARAFAC decomposition has the effect of the reduction of SD noise. In this paper, we take the residual parts of PARAFAC decomposition, *i.e.* $\mathcal{R} - \hat{\mathcal{R}}$, as the estimation of the noise.

5   Proposed Algorithm

In practice, the mean value of the expected signal $\mathcal{X}$ is unknown. Based on the assumption of independence of x, s and w and both s and w being zero-mean, from (5) we know that $E[r_{i_1,i_2,i_3}] = E[x_{i_1,i_2,i_3}] + E[\sqrt{x_{i_1,i_2,i_3}} \cdot s_{i_1,i_2,i_3}] + E[w_{i_1,i_2,i_3}] = E[x_{i_1,i_2,i_3}] + E[\sqrt{x_{i_1,i_2,i_3}}] \cdot E[s_{i_1,i_2,i_3}] = E[x_{i_1,i_2,i_3}]$, so the mean value of the noisy data $\mathcal{R}$ can be used instead of the mean value of the expected signal $\mathcal{X}$. As shown in Section 3, the SI noise in (4) and (5) is generally assumed as zero-mean Gaussian noise whose covariance matrix is given in (10), so PARAFAC decomposition can reduce the noise by selecting appropriate rank. Each diagonal entry of the covariance matrix of the SD noise in (11) can be expressed $\sigma_{\mathcal{N}(\mathcal{X}),i_3}^2 \approx \hat{\sigma}_{s,i_3}^2 \cdot \hat{\mu}_{i_3}$.

Therefore, the covariance matrix $\mathbf{C}_{\hat{N}(\mathcal{X})}^{(3)}$ of the 3-mode unfolding matrix of the removed noise $\hat{\mathbf{N}}(\mathcal{X})_{(3)} = \mathbf{R}_{(3)} - \hat{\mathbf{R}}_{(3)}$ should approach a diagonal matrix $diag(\sigma_{w,1}^2 + \hat{\sigma}_{s,1}^2, \sigma_{w,2}^2, \cdots, \sigma_{w,I_3}^2 + \hat{\sigma}_{s,I_3}^2)$, where σ_{w,i_3}^2 being the variance of SI noise in the i_3 band of HSI and $i_3 = 1, \cdots, I_3$. If the squared norm of the covariance $\|\mathbf{C}_{\hat{\mathcal{N}}(\mathcal{X})}^{(3)}\|^2$ is quite close to the sum of the diagonal elements $\sum_{i_3=1}^{I_3} c_{i_3,i_3}^2$, then this $\mathbf{C}_{\hat{\mathcal{N}}(\mathcal{X})}^{(3)}$ can be considered approaching a diagonal matrix. This criterion can be used to estimate the noise. Therefore, the reduction of the noise by PARAFAC decomposition consists of the following steps:

1. unfold the estimated noise tensor to n-mode unfolding matrix with $n = 1, 2, 3$.
2. calculate the covariance matrix of the n-mode unfolding matrix of the estimated noise tensor.
3. use the criterion above to assess the result matrix obtained from step 2) approaching a diagonal matrix.

Then, the rank K of PARAFAC decomposition for the reduction of the noise can be obtained from these three steps.

6 Experiments

One of the most important applications of HSI is target detection. In this paper, we focus on the improvement of target detection using the adaptive coherence/cosine estimator (ACE) [3,27] which is largely applied to HSI data. The results of ACE target detection of both simulated and real data desnoised by the proposed PARAFAC method and other considered methods are shown and discussed in this section.

For the HSI described in (4), the ACE detector can be expressed as:

$$D(\mathbf{r}_m) = \frac{(\mathbf{u}^\mathrm{T} \boldsymbol{\Gamma}^{-1} \mathbf{r}_m)^2}{(\mathbf{u}^\mathrm{T} \boldsymbol{\Gamma}^{-1} \mathbf{u})(\mathbf{r}_m^\mathrm{T} \boldsymbol{\Gamma}^{-1} \mathbf{r}_m)} \tag{18}$$

where $\mathbf{r}_m = [r_{1,m}, r_{2,m}, \cdots, r_{I_3,m}]^\mathrm{T}$ is the vector in the unfolding matrix $\mathbf{R}_3$ of tensor $\mathcal{R}$ with $m = 1, \cdots, M_3$ and $M_3 = I_1 I_2$, $\mathbf{u}$ is the target spectrum template which is assumed a priori known or computed by a supervised method directly on the initial HSI, $\boldsymbol{\Gamma}$ is the covariance matrix calculated by $\boldsymbol{\Gamma} = \frac{1}{M_3} \sum_{m=1}^{M_3} (\mathbf{r}_m - \boldsymbol{\gamma})(\mathbf{r}_m - \boldsymbol{\gamma})^\mathrm{T}$ with $\boldsymbol{\gamma} = \frac{1}{M_3} \sum_{m=1}^{M_3} \mathbf{r}_m$ being the sample mean value vector. Thus, when $D(\mathbf{r}_m) > \eta$ the target is present, otherwise the target is absent, where η is a detection threshold that sets the probability of detection (Pd) and the false alarm rate.

6.1 Results on Simulated Data

According to the data model in (4), synthetic HSI without noise, *i.e.* the signal $\mathcal{X}$, having size $100 \times 100 \times 148$ and holding 6 target types and two different spatial sizes (9×9) and (3×3) are generated. The targets are mixed to the background with respect to the linear mixing model[28,29] when target abundance is 90%. Figure 1 shows the simulated HSI without noise (the signal $\mathcal{X}$) and spectral signatures of targets. The random noise is generated with a variance depending on the value of the useful signal according to (7) and added into the signal $\mathcal{X}$ as (5) to create the simulated HSI data $\mathcal{R}$.

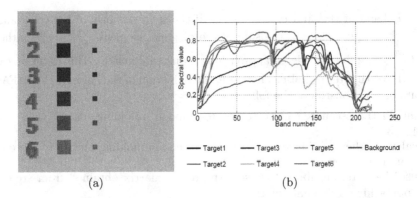

(a)   (b)

Fig. 1. (a) Simulated HSI without noise, from top to bottom the index of targets is 1 to 6 respectively. (b) Spectral signatures of the simulated targets and background.

Probability of Detection: In this experiment, we focus on the detection results obtained from images denoised by the noise reduction methods described above. Figure 2 shows the Pd of ACE target detection for simulated HSI denoised by the considered methods in this paper, and the Pd values are obtained when the probability of false alarm (Pfa) is 10^{-3}.

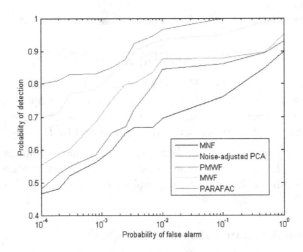

Fig. 2. Probability of detection of simulated HSI denoised by different methods. SNR=30dB.

In Fig. 2, the Pd values of ACE target detection of denoised HSIs by different methods show that the ACE target detection of denoised HSIs by PARAFAC method outperforms other methods. The quality of the denoised HSI is ameliorated so much that the ACE target detection of the denoised HSI is improved greatly. Therefore, PMWF [11], MNF and noise-adjusted PCA [10,13] methods are not suitable for SD noise reduction.

6.2 Results on Real-World Data

The real-world HYDICE HSI, referred to as $HSI0$, with 210 spectral bands is considered in this experiment. Several wavelengths were removed regarding the low signal / high noise bands and water vapor absorption bands. Thus the HYDICE data in Fig. 3(a) have 150 rows and 140 columns and 148 spectral channels out of 210 with 0.75 m spatial and 10 nm spectral resolution. It can be represented as a tensor data, denoted by $\mathcal{R} \in \mathbb{R}^{150 \times 140 \times 148}$. Six targets are added into the $HSI0$ image and each row of targets in Fig. 3(a) has the same target spectral signature (spectral reflectance) illustrated in Fig. 3(b), which is taken from the image itself. The target size is 8×8 pixels along the first column, 5×5 pixels along the second one and 2×2 pixels along the last one.

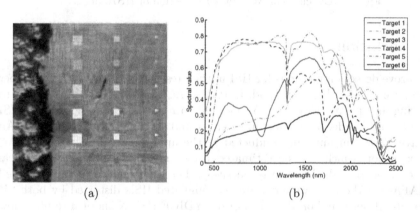

(a) (b)

Fig. 3. (a) $HSI0$ image, from top to bottom the index of targets is $1, 2, \cdots, 6$ respectively. (b) Spectral signatures of the targets.

It is worth noting that, for the real-world HYDICE HSI image, the real values of σ_{s,i_3}^2 and σ_{w,i_3}^2 are not available. To estimate the results obtained by the PARAFAC method, we can only resort to other indirect ways. Therefore, the receiver operating characteristic (ROC) curves of ACE target detection is plotted in Fig. 4.

It is clear in Fig. 4 that the Pd values of ACE target detection of denoised $HSI0$ image by MWF and PARAFAC methods are improved significantly and are superior to the other considered methods in the reduction of both SD and SI noise. The PMWF, noise-adjusted PCA and MNF methods are not designed for SD noise reduction, so their denoising performance are not ideal, which is reflected indirectly by the target detection results in these ROC curves in Fig. 4.

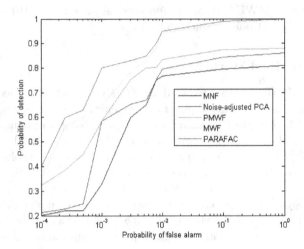

Fig. 4. ROC curve of ACE target detection of $HSI0$ image.

7   Conclusion

To improve detection methods for HSI in the presence of SD noise in this paper we propose a tensor-based method. In PARAFAC model is firstly introduced to denoising and proved to be a good method to reduce additive noise from HSI by exploiting its decomposition uniqueness and its single rank character. An iterative algorithm must be conducted at the appropriate rank of PARAFAC approximation which can be estimated according to the different statistical properties of SI and SD noise respectively. The performance of the proposed PARAFAC method are validated on the simulated HSIs distorted by both SD and white SI noise and on the real-world HYDICE HSI. Numerical results show that PARAFAC model performs much better than other considered methods as a denoising procedure for the detection in HSI. From the analysis and the comparative study against other similar methods in the experiments, it can be concluded that PARAFAC method can effectively reduce both SD and white or colored SI noise from HSI. It is also necessary to take into account the noise signal-dependency hypothesis when dealing with HYDICE data. If HSIs are distorted by both SD and white SI noise, the MWF method is also a considerable choice for the noise reduction. These promising results encourage us to extend our experiments on the HSIs distorted by both SD and spectrally correlated SI noise and on other hyperspectral data, for instance HSIs obtained from new-generation high-resolution hyperspectral sensors.

References

1. Chang, C.-I.: Hyperspectral Imaging : Techniques for spectral detection and classification. Kluwer Academic/Plenum Publishers, New York (2003)
2. Nascimento, J.M.P., Bioucas-Dias, J.M.: Hyperspectral unmixing based on mixtures of dirichlet components. IEEE Trans. on Geosc. and Remote Sensing **50**(3), 863–878 (2012)
3. Renard, N., Bourennane, S.: Improvement of target detection methods by multiway filtering. IEEE Trans. on Geosc. and Remote Sensing **46**(8), 2407–2417 (2008)
4. Archibald, R., Fann, G.: Feature selection and classification of hyperspectral images with support vector machines. IEEE Trans. on Geosc. and Remote Sensing **4**(8), 674–677 (2007)
5. Acito, N., Diani, M., Corsini, G.: Signal-dependent noise modeling and model parameter estimation in hyperspectral images. IEEE Trans. on Geosc. and Remote Sensing **49**(8), 2957–2971 (2011)
6. Joyeux, F., Letexier, D., Bourennane, S., Blanc-Talon, J.: Multidimensional noise removal method based on PARAFAC decomposition. In: Blanc-Talon, J., Bourennane, S., Philips, W., Popescu, D., Scheunders, P. (eds.) ACIVS 2008. LNCS, vol. 5259, pp. 465–473. Springer, Heidelberg (2008)
7. Uss, M., Vozel, B., Lukin, V., Chehdi, K.: Local signal-dependent noise variance estimation from hyperspectral textural images. IEEE Jounal of Selected Topics in Signal Proc. **5**, 469–486 (2011)
8. Alparone, L., Selva, M., Aiazzi, B., Baronti, S., Butera, F., Chiarantini, L.: Signal-dependent noise modelling and estimation of new-generation imaging spectrometers. In: First Workshop on Hyperspectral Image and Signal Proc.: Evolution in Remote Sensing (2009)
9. Roger, R.E.: Principal components transform with simple, automatic noise ajustment. INT. J. Remote Sensing **17**, 2719–2727 (1996)
10. Chang, C.-I., Du, Q.: Interference and noise adjusted principal components analysis. IEEE Transactions on Geoscience and Remote Sensing **37**, 2387–2396 (1999)
11. Liu, X., Bourennane, S., Fossati, C.: Nonwhite noise reduction in hyperspec tral images. IEEE Geosc. and Remote Sensing Letters **9**(3), 368–372 (2012)
12. Bourennane, S., Fossati, C., Cailly, A.: Improvement of target-detection algorithms based on adaptive three-dimensional filtering. IEEE Trans. Geosci. Remote Sens. **49**, 1383–1395 (2011)
13. Lee, J., Woodyatt, A., Berman, M.: Enhancement of high spectral resolution remote-sensing data by a noise-adjusted principal components transform. IEEE Trans. on Geosc. and Remote Sensing **28**(3), 295–304 (1990)
14. Kolda, T.G., Bader, B.W.: Tensor decompositions and applications. SIAM Review **51**(3), 455–500 (2009)
15. Marot, J., Fossati, C., Bourennane, S.: About advances in tensor data denoising methods. EURASIP Journal on Advances in Signal Processing **2008** (2008)
16. Muti, D., Bourennane, S.: Multidimensional filtering based on a tensor approach. Signal Processing **85**, 2338–2353 (2005)
17. Tucker, L.R.: Some mathematical notes on three-mode factor analysis. Psychometrika **31**, 279–311 (1966)
18. Carroll, J.D., Chang, J.J.: Analysis of individual differences in multidimensional scaling via an n-way generalization of 'Eckart-Young' decomposition. Psychometrika **35**, 283–319 (1970)

19. Harshman, R.A.: Foundations of the PARAFAC procedure: Models and conditions for an "explanatory" multi-modal factor analysis. UCLA Working Papers in Phonetics **16**, 1–84 (1970)
20. Bourennane, S., Fossati, C., Cailly, A.: Improvement of classification for hyperspectral images based on tensor modeling. IEEE Geosci. Remote Sens. Lett. **7**, 801–805 (2010)
21. De Silva, V., Lim, L.: Tensor rank and the ill-posedness of the best low-rank approximation problem. SIAM Journal on Matrix Analysis and Applications **30**(3), 1084–1127 (2008)
22. Muti, D., Bourennane, S.: Survey on tensor signal algebraic filtering. Signal Processing **87**, 237–249 (2007)
23. Bourennane, S., Fossati, C.: Dimensionality reduction and colored noise removal from hyperspectral images. Remote Sensing Lett. **6**(10), 765–774 (2015)
24. Letexier, D., Bourennane, S.: Noise removal from hyperspectral images by multidimensional filtering. IEEE Trans. on Geosc. and Remote Sensing **46**(7), 2061–2069 (2008)
25. Othman, H., Qian, S.-E.: Noise reduction of hyperspectral imagery using hybrid spatial-spectral derivative-domain wavelet shrinkage. IEEE Trans. on Geosc. and Remote Sensing **44**(2), 397–408 (2006)
26. Chen, G., Qian, S.-E.: Denoising of hyperspectral imagery using principal component analysis and wavelet shrinkage. IEEE Trans. on Geosc. and Remote Sensing **49**(3), 973–980 (2011)
27. Manolakis, D., Shaw, G.: Detection algorithms for hyperspectral imaging applications. IEEE Signal Processing Magazine **19**(1), 29–43 (2002)
28. Liu, X., Bourennane, S., Fossati, C.: Reduction of signal-dependent noise from hyperspectral images for target detection. IEEE Trans. Geoscience and Remote Sensing **52**(9), 5396–5411 (2014)
29. Haertel, V., Shimabukuro, Y.: Spectral linear mixing model in low spatial resolution image data. IEEE Transactions on Geoscience and Remote Sensing **43**(11), 2555–2562 (2005)

Edge Detection Method Based on Signal Subspace Dimension for Hyperspectral Images

Caroline Fossati[✉], Salah Bourennane, and Alexis Cailly

Centrale Marseille, Aix-Marseille Universite, CNRS,
Institut Fresnel UMR 7249, 13013 Marseille, France
caroline.fossati@fresnel.fr

Abstract. One of the objectives of image processing is to detect the region of interest (ROI) in the given application, and then perform characterization and classification of these regions. In HyperSpectral Images (HSI) the detection of targets in an image is of great interest for several applications. Generally, when ROI containing targets is previously selected, the detection results are better. In this paper we propose to select the ROI with a new edge detection method for large HSI containing objects with large and small sizes, based on tensorial modeling, and an estimation of local rank variations.

1 Introduction

In HSI, edge detection is not considered by the community, which instead focuses on applications related to remote sensing such as target detection, classification or spectral unmixing. Moreover, it is less easy to define what can be a contour in a HSI than in a conventional image where the edges are defined as a rapid change in the intensity of the pixels. In fact, because the spectral data (hyperspectral pixels) consist of several hundreds of values, it becomes more difficult to define the variations between two pixels. One can found in the literature a few edge detection works on multi or hyperspectral images, based on statistical similarity criteria (maximum likelihood, Mahalanobis distance) [1,2], or based on a geometric measurement approach (study of distances or angles between pixel vectors) [3], some works also adapt to multispectral data some classical convolution filters (Sobel gradient, etc.) [4], or mathematical morphology methods [5,6]. But all these methods are more suited to the multi-spectral than the hyperspectral data because they are put in difficulty by the large amount of information known as Hugues phenomenom [7].

In this paper we propose a new multidimensional method, based on tensor modeling of HSI, and using a local approach thanks to subtensors rank estimation to perform edge detection. This could be a good way to predifine regions of interest which are known to be useful when small target detection is needed [8,9].

The remainder of this paper is organized as follows : section 2 introduces the tensorial data model and a way to estimate the tensor or subtensor rank.

© Springer International Publishing Switzerland 2015
S. Battiato et al. (Eds.): ACIVS 2015, LNCS 9386, pp. 803–815, 2015.
DOI: 10.1007/978-3-319-25903-1_69

Section 3 outlines the limitations of classical segmentation methods. Then the proposed method is given in section 4 and section 5 presents experimental results on simulated and real-world data.

2 Tensorial Data Model and Rank Estimation

Usually for HSI, the data are modeled as a tensor $\mathcal{Z}^{I_1 \times I_2 \times I_3}$ which is a three-dimensional array where I_1 and I_2 correspond to the spatial dimensions and I_3 corresponds to the spectral dimension.

2.1 Hyperspectral Data Flattening in the Spectral Mode

The flattening in the spectral mode of the tensor $\mathcal{Z}^{I_1 \times I_2 \times I_3}$ is performed to obtain the data matrix $\mathbf{Z} \in \mathbb{R}^{I_3 \times n}$ with $n = I_1 \times I_2$, (see Fig. 1). The obtained

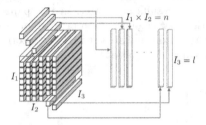

Fig. 1. Tensor flattening in the spectral mode.

matrix $\mathbf{Z}^{I_3 \times n}$ is a column-matrix where each column of the matrix corresponds to a spectral pixel vector $\{\mathbf{z}_i\}_{i=1..n}$.

2.2 Linear Mixture Model

In practice, the observed data vector $\{\mathbf{z}_i\}_{i=1,...,n}$ are assumed to satisfy the following linear model [10–12]:

$$\mathbf{z}_i = \mathbf{x}_i + \mathbf{n}_i \tag{1}$$

where $\mathbf{z}_i \in \mathbb{R}^{I_3}$ is the observed random vector containing the signal vector $\mathbf{x}_i \in \mathbb{R}^{I_3}$ and the additive noise vector $\mathbf{n}_i \in \mathbb{R}^{I_3}$. Usually, the signal vector $\mathbf{x}_i$ is defined as the linear combination between k pure material spectra represented by the endmember matrix $\mathbf{A} \in \mathbb{R}^{I_3 \times k}$ and $\mathbf{s}_i \in \mathbb{R}^k$ their corresponding abundances [13]:

$$\mathbf{z}_i = \mathbf{A}\mathbf{s}_i + \mathbf{n}_i \tag{2}$$

In matrix formulation (2) can be written:

$$\mathbf{Z} = \mathbf{X} + \mathbf{N} = \mathbf{A}\mathbf{S} + \mathbf{N} \tag{3}$$

where $\mathbf{Z} \in \mathbb{R}^{I_3 \times n}$ is a column-matrix of all $\{\mathbf{z}_i\}_{i=1,\ldots,n}$, $\mathbf{X} \in \mathbb{R}^{I_3 \times n}$ is a column-matrix of the signal vectors which can be written as: $\mathbf{X}=\mathbf{AS}$ where $\mathbf{A} \in \mathbb{R}^{I_3 \times k}$ is the mixing matrix containing the signatures of the endmembers present in the covered area, and $\mathbf{S} \in \mathbb{R}^{k \times n}$ is the fractional abundance matrix. $\mathbf{N} \in \mathbb{R}^{I_3 \times n}$ is an additive perturbation (e.g. noise and modeling error) matrix composed of all $\{\mathbf{n}_i\}_{i=1..n}$ vectors.

2.3   Signal Subspace and Rank Estimation

The signal subspace engendered by $\mathbf{X}$ is unknown and is attempted to be estimated from $\mathbf{Z}$.

Classical Approach. According to the classical SVD (singular value decomposition) approach, the signal subspace $\mathcal{E}_k$, rank $\mathcal{E}_k = k$, is estimated by minimizing the l_2 norm of the residuals [14,15]:

$$\hat{\mathcal{E}}_k = \arg\min_{\mathcal{L}} \|\mathbf{Z} - \mathbf{P}_{\mathcal{L}}\mathbf{Z}\|_2^2 = \arg\min_{\mathcal{L}} \left\|\mathbf{P}_{\mathcal{L}}^{\perp}\mathbf{Z}\right\|_2^2 \tag{4}$$

$$\hat{\mathcal{E}}_k = \arg\min_{\mathcal{L}} \|\mathbf{R}\|_2^2 \tag{5}$$

where $\|.\|_2$ denotes the l_2 norm (or Frobenius norm), and $P_{\mathcal{L}}$ denotes an orthogonal projection onto subspace $\mathcal{L}$. The projector $\mathbf{P}_{\mathcal{L}}$ is obtained via SVD of the observation matrix $\mathbf{Z}$ as $\mathbf{Z} = \hat{\mathbf{U}}\hat{\mathbf{\Sigma}}\hat{\mathbf{V}}^*$, where $\hat{\mathbf{U}}$ is a $I_3 \times I_3$ matrix, $\hat{\mathbf{V}}$ is a $n \times I_3$ matrix, and $\hat{\mathbf{\Sigma}}$ is a diagonal matrix containing $\hat{\lambda}_1 \geq \ldots \geq \hat{\lambda}_{I_3}$ the singular values. The projector $\mathbf{P}_{\mathcal{L}}$ is equal to $\hat{\mathbf{U}}_k\hat{\mathbf{U}}_k^*$ where $\hat{\mathbf{U}}_k$ contains the first k columns of $\hat{\mathbf{U}}$. So, $\mathbf{P}_{\mathcal{L}}^{\perp}$ is the projector on the orthogonal subspace of $\mathcal{L}$, and $\mathbf{R}$ is the residual matrix of $\mathbf{Z}$ projected on $\mathcal{L}^{\perp}$ by $\mathbf{P}_{\mathcal{L}}^{\perp}$. For an accurate estimation $\mathcal{L} = \mathcal{E}_k$, the residual matrix $\mathbf{R}$ corresponds to the noise matrix $\mathbf{N}$.

It is interesting to note that usually, this approach applied on large data tends to underestimate the signal subspace in the presence of rare signals by assimilating their rare pixel vectors to the noise, [15,16]. Consequently the signal subspace promotes only the abundant signals.

Local Approach via Local Residuals. In this paper we propose to process with a local approach for noisy signals containing rare pixel vectors, based on the study of local blocks (subtensors). This could help to balance the number of rare vectors and abundant ones for target detection application, and will mainly be usefull for the segmentation method proposed in section 4. Let's divide the observed matrix data $\mathbf{Z}$ into m blocks : $\mathbf{Z} = [\mathbf{Z}_1|\ldots|\mathbf{Z}_i|\ldots|\mathbf{Z}_m]$ where each $\mathbf{Z}_i$ is a $I_3 \times p_i$ matrix. For each $\mathbf{Z}_i$, a local linear model is defined as:

$$\mathbf{Z}_i = \mathbf{X}_i + \mathbf{N}_i \tag{6}$$

where $\mathbf{X}_i$ and $\mathbf{N}_i$ are $I_3 \times p_i$ matrices corresponding to the associated signal block and noise block, respectively. Considering the residual $\mathbf{R}_i$ of (5) applied to a matrix block $\mathbf{Z}_i = \mathbf{X}_i + \mathbf{N}_i$:

$$\mathbf{R}_i = \mathbf{P}_{\mathcal{L}}^{\perp_i}\mathbf{Z}_i \tag{7}$$

If the subspace $\mathcal{L}_i$ underestimates the rare vectors of the accurate signal-subspace $\mathcal{E}_{k_i}^{(i)}$, the residual $\mathbf{R}_i$ contains some rare signal data and noise as:

$$\|\mathbf{R}_i\|_2^2 = \|\mathbf{X}_{r_i} + \mathbf{N}_i\|_2^2 \neq \|\mathbf{N}_i\|_2^2 \tag{8}$$

where $\mathbf{X}_{r_i}$ is the part of signal not estimated with the subspace $\mathcal{L}_i$. The local approach tends to skew the following approximation: $\|\mathbf{R}_i\|_2^2 = \|\mathbf{X}_{r_i} + \mathbf{N}\|_2^2 \approx \|\mathbf{N}_i\|_2^2$.

Determination of the Signal Subspace $\hat{\mathcal{E}}_k$. We propose an iterative method based on successive update of the estimated signal subspace $\hat{\mathcal{E}}_k$ of $\mathbf{Z}$ from the m blocks $\{\mathbf{Z}_i\}_{i=1,\ldots,m}$ while considering a possible redundancy of information between the matrix blocks. Let the matrix of observations be divided into m blocks : $\mathbf{Z} = [\mathbf{Z}_1, \ldots, \mathbf{Z}_i, \ldots, \mathbf{Z}_m]$. The current subspace $\mathcal{L}^{(i)}$ will be updated with the iterations for $i = 1, \ldots, m$. Let consider any iteration i, the current subspace is spanned by an orthonormal basis vectors as $\mathcal{L}^{(i)} = \{\mathbf{u}_1, \ldots, \mathbf{u}_{k_i}\}$ estimated during the first iterations. Redundancy information between the block $\mathbf{Z}_i$ and the first blocks, $\{\mathbf{Z}_1, \ldots, \mathbf{Z}_{i-1}\}$, is removed by the projection of $\mathbf{Z}_i$ on the current subspace $\mathcal{L}^{(i)^\perp}$ such that:

$$\mathbf{Z}_{f_i} = \mathbf{Z}_i - \mathbf{P}_{\mathcal{L}^{(i)}} \mathbf{Z}_i = \mathbf{P}_{\mathcal{L}^{(i)\perp}} \mathbf{Z}_i \tag{9}$$

where $\mathbf{P}_{\mathcal{L}^{(i)}} = [\mathbf{u}_1, \ldots, \mathbf{u}_{k_i}] [\mathbf{u}_1, \ldots, \mathbf{u}_{k_i}]^T$. According to (9), the matrix $\mathbf{Z}_{f_i}$ contains only the new vectors related to $\mathbf{Z}_i$ not contained in the first blocks and not yet estimated in the subspace $\mathcal{L}^{(i)}$ ensuring the removal of the redundancy between the blocks for the large number of same vectors spread throughout $\mathbf{Z}$ (ex : background, road, grass...). According to $\mathbf{Z}_{f_i}$, two cases remain :

1. The matrix block $\mathbf{Z}_i$ contains no additional vectors compared to earlier matrices $\{\mathbf{Z}_1, \ldots, \mathbf{Z}_{i-1}\}$. The current subspace can generate the set of vectors of $\mathbf{X}_i$, according to (9) in this case $\mathbf{Z}_{f_i}$ corresponding to $\mathbf{N}_i$. The subspace is not updated and remains unchanged for the next iteration : $\mathcal{L}^{(i+1)} = \mathcal{L}^{(i)}$.
2. The matrix bloc $\mathbf{Z}_i$ contains additional data from earlier matrices. According to (9), $\mathbf{Z}_{f_i}$ can be expressed as :$\mathbf{Z}_{f_i} = \mathbf{X}_{f_i} + \mathbf{N}_{f_i}$, where $\mathbf{X}_{f_i}$ corresponds to the additional data not yet included in the subspace $\mathcal{L}^{(i)}$. The signal subspace $\mathcal{E}_{k_i}^{(i)}$ associated to $\mathbf{X}_{f_i}$ is estimated from (4) thanks to the SVD of $\mathbf{Z}_{f_i}$:

$$\hat{\mathcal{E}}_{k_i}^{(i)} = \left\{\mathbf{u}_1^{(i)}, \ldots, \mathbf{u}_{k_i}^{(i)}\right\} \tag{10}$$

where $\left\{\mathbf{u}_1^{(i)}, \ldots, \mathbf{u}_{k_i}^{(i)}\right\}$ correspond to the first singular vectors from the matrix $\mathbf{U}_{f_i}$ following the SVD of $\mathbf{Z}_{f_i} = \mathbf{U}_{f_i} \mathbf{\Sigma}_{f_i} \mathbf{V}_{f_i}^T$. For the next iteration, the current subspace $\mathcal{L}^{(i+1)}$ is updated as :

$$\mathcal{L}^{(i+1)} = \mathcal{L}^{(i)} \bigoplus \hat{\mathcal{E}}_{k_i}^{(i)} \tag{11}$$

$$\mathcal{L}^{(i+1)} = \left\{\mathbf{u}_1, \ldots, \mathbf{u}_k, \mathbf{u}_1^{(i)}, \ldots, \mathbf{u}_{k_i}^{(i)}\right\} \tag{12}$$

The algorithm is initialized with $\mathcal{L}^2 = \hat{\mathcal{E}}_{k_1}^{(1)}$ where $\hat{\mathcal{E}}_{k_1}^{(1)}$ is the signal subspace of $\mathbf{Z}_1$. The signal subspace $\hat{\mathcal{E}}_k$ of $\mathbf{Z}$ is obtained when the set of matrix blocks for $i = m : \hat{\mathcal{E}}_k = \mathcal{L}^{(m)}$ are processed. Algorithm 1 summarizes this procedure.

Algorithm 1 $\mathcal{E}_k$ estimation

- **Initialisation :** $\mathbf{Z} = [\mathbf{Z}_1|\ldots|\mathbf{Z}_m]$
  - $\mathbf{U} \leftarrow SVD(\mathbf{Z}_1)$
  - $\mathcal{E}_{k_1}^{(1)} \leftarrow \arg\min_{\mathcal{L}} \left\| \mathbf{Z}_1 - \mathbf{P}_{\mathcal{L}}^{\perp} \mathbf{Z} \right\|_2^2$
  - $\mathcal{E}_{k_1}^{(1)} \leftarrow \left\{ \mathbf{u}_1^{(1)}, \ldots, \mathbf{u}_{k_1}^{(1)} \right\}$
  - $\mathcal{L}^{(1)} \leftarrow \left\{ \mathbf{u}_1^{(1)}, \ldots, \mathbf{u}_{k_1}^{(1)} \right\}$
- **For:** i from 2 to m
  - "filtering" $\mathbf{Z}_{f_i} \leftarrow \mathbf{Z}_i - \mathbf{P}_{\mathcal{L}^{(i)}}^{\perp} \mathbf{Z}_i$
  - **If** $\mathbf{Z}_{f_i} \neq \mathbf{N}_i$ **Then**
    * $\mathbf{U} \leftarrow SVD(\mathbf{Z}_{f_i})$
    * $\mathcal{E}_{k_i}^{(i)} \leftarrow \arg\min_{\mathcal{L}} \left\| \mathbf{Z}_{f_i} - \mathbf{P}_{\mathcal{L}}^{\perp} \mathbf{Z}_{f_i} \right\|_2^2$
    * $\mathcal{E}_{k_i}^{(i)} \leftarrow \left\{ \mathbf{u}_1^{(i)}, \ldots, \mathbf{u}_{k_i}^{(i)} \right\}$
    * $\mathcal{L}^{(i)} \leftarrow \left\{ \{\mathbf{u}_1, \ldots, \mathbf{u}_k\}, \left\{ \mathbf{u}_1^{(i)}, \ldots, \mathbf{u}_{k_i}^{(i)} \right\} \right\}$
  - **End IF**
- **EndFor**
- **Output :** $\mathcal{E}_k \leftarrow \mathcal{L}$

Residual Analysis. In the estimation procedure, the filtered block $\mathbf{Z}_{f_i}$ is analysed in order to determine whether there are new data not yet involved in the current signal subspace. Considering a Gaussian noise, we propose to study the covariance matrix of $\mathbf{Z}_{f_i}$ approaching a diagonal matrix in which $\mathbf{Z}_{f_i}$ corresponding to the noise. For this, we define a normalized diagonal criterion (Dc) of the covariance matrix of $\mathbf{Z}_{f_i}$ as :

$$\mathrm{Dc} = \frac{\left\| \mathbf{\Gamma}_{f_i} - \mathrm{diag}(\mathbf{\Gamma}_{f_i}) \right\|_2^2}{\left\| \mathbf{\Gamma}_{f_i} \right\|_2^2} \tag{13}$$

where $\mathbf{\Gamma}_{f_i}$ is the covariance matrix associated to $\mathbf{Z}_{f_i}$, and diag(.) is an operator for extracting the matrix diagonal. When, $\mathbf{Z}_{f_i}$ contains no new information criterion tends to zero. In practice, the null value is never reached. The criterion Dc being normalized, a threshold has to be set to decide if the matrix contains new relevant information.

3 Classical Segmentation Method Limitations

Conventional methods are based on the study of an intensity variation between pixels. Let consider the example of a low natural variation between pixels of the same object, thus forming no edge. In the case of conventional images, these pixels will be considered without difficulty as similar, and therefore forming any contour. It is more complicated for hyperspectral data where even a little variation will affect a hundred of coordinate values in the pixel vector, greatly reducing the similarity of pixels which can induce false detection of edges. One can see that by considering the case of a criterion based on the evaluation of a distance or angle. Let's consider two neighboring pixel vectors representing the same signal $\mathbf{x}$ corresponding to the same object with only a short variation $\mathbf{n}$ between the two pixels, that is to say : $\mathbf{z}_1 = \mathbf{x} + \mathbf{n}_1 \in \mathbb{R}^{I_3}$ and $\mathbf{z}_2 = \mathbf{x} + \mathbf{n}_2 \in \mathbb{R}^{I_3}$. The Euclidian distance between those two pixels is given by : $\|\mathbf{z}_1 - \mathbf{z}_2\|^2 = \|\mathbf{n}_1 - \mathbf{n}_2\|^2$.

In the conventional case where the variation follows a Gaussian distribution with zero mean, then: $\|\mathbf{z}_1 - \mathbf{z}_2\|^2 \approx I_3 \sigma^2$, where σ^2 is the variance of $\mathbf{n}_1 - \mathbf{n}_2$ The distance between the two pixel vectors tends to enlarge with the spectral dimension I_3, decreasing the similarity of the two pixels representing a same object. This is true regardless of the similarity criterion : statistical or geometric. The difficulty to define the similarity of two objects from a large data set is known as "Hughes Phenomenon" or "Scourge of the large size" this is why one generally process to a band selection before these kinds of treatment.

4   Edge Detection Based on Local Rank Variations Evaluation

We propose in this paper, taking into account the spectral richness of hyperspectral images, to define the edge between two objects like a change in the spectral composition of the pixels rather than a simple variation of pixels intensity .

4.1   Discrimination of Two Objects

Starting from the linear mixing model (2), it is possible to define each pixel vector of an object A like :

$$\mathbf{z}_A = \mathbf{A}_A \mathbf{s}_A + \mathbf{n}_A \tag{14}$$

where $\mathbf{z}_A \in \mathbb{R}^{I_3}$ is a pixel of the object A, I_3 being the spectral band number, $\mathbf{A}_A \in \mathbb{R}^{I_3 \times k_A}$ is the matrix containing k_A endmembers associated to the object A. $\mathbf{s}_A \in \mathbb{R}^{k_A}$ is the mixing vector, and $\mathbf{n}_A \in \mathbb{R}^{I_3}$ is the noise vector.

For all the pixel of object A, it is possible to give a matricial linear mixing model like:

$$\mathbf{Z}_A = \mathbf{A}_A \mathbf{S}_A + \mathbf{N}_A \tag{15}$$

With $\mathbf{Z}_A$ the matrix containing the entire vector pixels of the object A, $\mathbf{S}_A$ the mixing matrix for all pixels of the object A and $\mathbf{N}_A$ the noise matrix.

Matrix $\mathbf{A}_A$ remains invariant for all pixels of the object A, only spectral mixtures in $\mathbf{S}_A$ vary.

In the same way, for object B, we have: $\mathbf{Z}_B = \mathbf{A}_B \mathbf{S}_B + \mathbf{N}_B$, where $\mathbf{A}_B \in \mathbb{R}^{I_3 \times k_B}$ remains invariant for all pixels of the object B.

Thanks to the linear mixture model, it becomes possible to discriminate the object A to object B, not by simply the classic study of vectors $\mathbf{z}_A$ et $\mathbf{z}_B$, but by the way of matrices $\mathbf{A}_A$ and $\mathbf{A}_B$ representing the spectral composition of objects A and B.

Indeed, to determine whether a pixel $\mathbf{z} = \mathbf{x} + \mathbf{n}$ belongs to the object A or to the object B, it simply needs to evaluate the projection of $\mathbf{x}$ on the subspaces generated by matrices $\mathbf{A}_A$ and $\mathbf{A}_B$ such that: $d_A = \|\mathbf{P}_A^{\perp} \mathbf{x}\|^2$ and $d_B = \|\mathbf{P}_B^{\perp} \mathbf{x}\|^2$, with $\mathbf{P}_A^{\perp}$ (respectively $\mathbf{P}_B^{\perp}$) the orthogonal projector on the signal subspace $\mathcal{E}_A$ related to object A(respectively $\mathcal{E}_B$ related to object B). The maximum value between d_A and d_B is then used to identify whether the pixel $\mathbf{x}$ is a part of the object A or of the object B. Indeed, all the pixels associated with an object generates a signal subspace related to this object. The norm of the projection of a pixel vector is maximum when the pixel belongs to the object described by the given subspace.

However, in practice, only $\mathbf{z}$ is known, $\mathbf{x}$ remains unknown, further more, there is no a priori knowledge about the objects in the scene and thus no more knowledge about the endmember matrices of each of the objects ($\mathbf{A}_A$ and $\mathbf{A}_B$) and about the subspaces generated by these matrices ($\mathcal{E}_A$ and $\mathcal{E}_B$), so it is impossible to determine the projectors $\mathbf{P}_A^{\perp} \mathbf{x}$ and $\mathbf{P}_B^{\perp} \mathbf{x}$ and to evaluate the values of d_A and d_B.

4.2   Signal Subspace Local Variation Between Two Objects

We only know that objects belong to the overall image, and then that all the signal subspaces $\{\mathcal{E}_{O_i}\}_{i=1...n}$ related to different objects, are included in the signal subspace $\mathcal{E}_k$ of the entire hyperspectral image, such as : $\forall i, \mathcal{E}_{O_i} \subset \mathcal{E}_k$. Thus, rates from the pixels of an object, one can estimate its signal subspace $\mathcal{E}_{O_i}$ from $\mathcal{E}_k$. If $\mathbf{Z}_{O_i}$ is the matrix containing all the pixels of an object, the signal subspace generated by $\mathbf{Z}_{O_i}$ could be estimated from $\mathcal{E}_k = \{\mathbf{u}_i\}_{i=1,...,k}$ and is obtained by minimizing:

$$\hat{\mathcal{E}}_{O_i} = \arg \min_{\mathcal{L}_{O_i}} \|\mathbf{Z}_{O_i} - \mathbf{P}_{\mathcal{L}_{O_i}} \mathbf{Z}\|_2^2 \tag{16}$$

where $\mathbf{P}_{\mathcal{L}_{O_i}}$ is the projector obtained with the minimal number of vectors $\mathbf{u}_i$ of the orthonormal basis of $\mathcal{E}_k$ minimizing (16).

So, to identify the border separating to objects A and B, we only have to identify a local signal subspace variation, and it is then possible to detect edges without knowledge about the objects and the nature of their pixels.

This assumption is confirmed by images shown Fig. 2. They were obtained by studying, with the proposed method in section 2.3, the local variation of signal subspace rank for subtensors of 5×5 pixels on 143 bands centered on each pixel of the image. Figure 2 (a) show a real-world HSI containing an almost uniform background and 4 rows of different size panels. Figure 2 (b) shows the evolution of the local rank of subtensors centered on each pixel of the Fig. 2 (a).

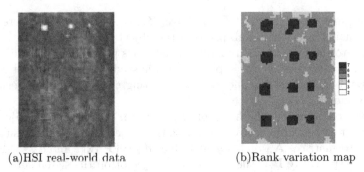

(a)HSI real-world data   (b)Rank variation map

Fig. 2. Local variation of the signal subspace rank for HSI containing small targets.

Results of Fig. 2 (b), show that it is possible to observe a link between the local rank of the signal subspace and the panels of the scene.

4.3   HSI Segmentation Proposed Method

We can now propose an algorithm for edge detection based on local rank variations.

Let an HSI be represented by the tensor $\mathcal{Z} \in \mathbb{R}^{I_1 \times I_2 \times I_3}$. Consider the known signal subspace $\mathcal{E}_k = \{\mathbf{u}_i\}_{i=1,\ldots,k}$ associated to the flattening matrix $\mathbf{Z}$ in the spectral mode. Consider a subtensor $\mathcal{Z}_i \in \mathbb{R}^{n \times n \times I_3}$ centered on a pixel i of $\mathcal{Z}$ and his flattening matrix $\mathbf{Z}_i$ in the spectral mode. According to (16), it is possible to evaluate the local signal subspace $\mathcal{E}_i$ generated by the row vectors of $\mathbf{Z}_i$ from the signal subspace $\mathcal{E}_k$ of the entire image as:

$$\hat{\mathcal{E}}_i = \arg \min_{\mathcal{L}} \|\mathbf{Z}_i - \mathbf{P}_{\mathcal{L}} \mathbf{Z}_i\|_2^2 \tag{17}$$

with $\mathbf{P}_{\mathcal{L}}$ generated from the vectors $\{\mathbf{u}_i\}_{i=1,\ldots,k}$ of $\mathcal{E}_k$ which minimize the norm. The subtensor centered on the neighboring pixel $i+1$, has an associate flattening matrix $\mathbf{Z}_{i+1} \in \mathbb{R}^{n \times n \times I_3}$. We can evaluate if all the pixel vectors of $\mathbf{Z}_{i+1}$ are included in the same signal subspace than $\mathbf{Z}_i$, by an analysis of the residual matrix $\mathbf{R}_{i+1}$ which is the difference between $\mathbf{Z}_{i+1}$ and his projection on the signal subspace $\hat{\mathcal{E}}_i$:

$$\mathbf{R}_{i+1} = \mathbf{Z}_{i+1} - \mathbf{P}_{\hat{\mathcal{E}}_i} \mathbf{Z}_{i+1} \tag{18}$$

where $\mathbf{P}_{\hat{\mathcal{E}}_i}$ is the projector on the signal subspace $\hat{\mathcal{E}}_i$ estimated by (17). Residual $\mathbf{R}_{i+1}$ is then significant of the local variation of the signal subspace around pixel vectors i et $i+1$. If the two subtensors $\mathbf{Z}_i$ et $\mathbf{Z}_{i+1}$ are associated to the same object (and have the same signal subspace $\hat{\mathcal{E}}_i = \hat{\mathcal{E}}_{i+1}$) then $\mathbf{R}_{i+1} = \mathbf{N}_{i+1}$. If not, then $\mathbf{R}_{i+1} \neq \mathbf{N}_{i+1}$ which contains the noise and the residual signal through (18). $\mathbf{R}_{i+1}$ is analysed and the result is saved in the edge detection image at the localization of the corresponding pixel i. The subspace $\hat{\mathcal{E}}_{i+1}$ generated by $\mathbf{Z}_{i+1}$ is then calculated, and this procedure is applied on all the subtensors centered on each pixel of the tensor $\mathcal{Z}$. Considering a white Gaussian noise, analysis of the residual $\mathbf{R}_{i+1}$ is based on the calculation of the criterion Dc in (13) which value is decreasing when $\mathbf{R}_i$ tends to $\mathbf{N}_i$ this permits the identification of a signal subspace from an object to an other. Algorithm 2 briefly summarizes the entire method

---

Algorithm 2 Edge detection based on local rank estimation

- **Initialisation**
  - signal subspace $\mathcal{E}_k = \mathbf{u}_1, \ldots, \mathbf{u}_k$ de $\mathbf{Z}$ estimation
  - C : edge mapping.
- **For :** i **from 1 to** m
  - $\mathbf{Z}_i \leftarrow$ calculate the flattening matrix of $\mathcal{Z}_i$ in the spectral mode.
  - $\mathcal{E}_i \leftarrow argmin_{\mathcal{L}} \|\mathbf{Z}_i - \mathbf{P}_{\mathcal{L}}\mathbf{Z}_i\|^2$: estimate the signal subspace of $\mathbf{Z}_i$ from $\mathcal{E}_k = \mathbf{u}_1, \ldots, \mathbf{u}_k$.
  - $\mathbf{Z}_{i+1} \leftarrow$ calculate the flattening matrix of $\mathcal{Z}_{i+1}$ in the spectral mode.
  - $\mathbf{R}_{i+1} \leftarrow \mathbf{Z}_{i+1} - \mathbf{P}_{\mathcal{E}_i}\mathbf{Z}_{i+1}$: residual between Z_{i+1} and his projection on the subspace $\mathcal{E}_i$ generated by $\mathbf{Z}_i$
  - $C(i+1) \leftarrow Cd(\mathbf{R}_{i+1})$. saving the residual criterion Dc .
- **EndFor**
- **Output :** C : contour map.

The analysis of pixels of a block tensor $i + 1$ requires knowledge of the signal subspace of the tensor i, that is, previous block. So, due to this memory effect, depending on the way and the direction of travel of the algorithm, the results are not necessarily the same. Then, the algorithm needs to be performed vertically, horizontally and in both way to take into account all the cases for an optimum edge detection of objects. This practice leads to the production of 4 results, the fusion of these results is then done considering the maximum of the 4 pixel by pixel detections.

5   Experimental Results

Simulated Data. In this experiment, eight real-world spectra basis of 75 bands from the USGS data bank, shown in Fig. 3, are used to generate simulated images. The subtensor size is fixed at $3 \times 3 \times 75$. Pixels $\mathbf{x}_i$ of simulated images are obtained by the linear mixing model:

$$\mathbf{x}_i = \mathbf{A}_{O_i}(\mathbf{s}_{mean} + \mathbf{s}_i) + \mathbf{n}_i \tag{19}$$

where $\mathbf{A}_{O_i}$ is the endmember matrix associated to the object O_i, $\mathbf{s}_{mean}$ is the mean vector of the object abundance, $\mathbf{s}_i$ is a zero mean Gaussian random vector with variance $\sigma_{\mathbf{S}}^2 = 0.01$ representing abundance variations around $\mathbf{s}_{mean}$, and $\mathbf{n}_i$ is a white Gaussian noise with variance $\sigma^2 = 0.01$.

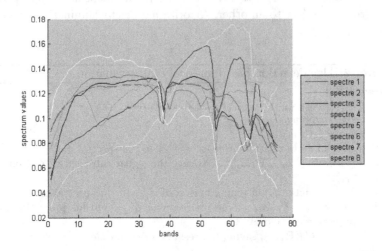

Fig. 3. The 8 spectra used for simulated data. (USGS data bank)

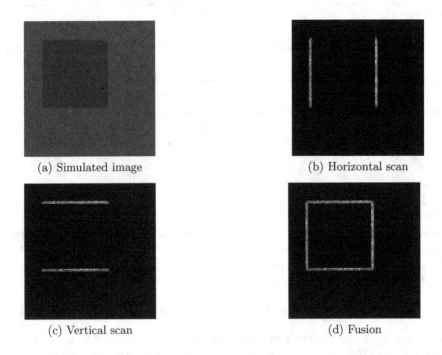

(a) Simulated image

(b) Horizontal scan

(c) Vertical scan

(d) Fusion

Fig. 4. Scan direction influence.

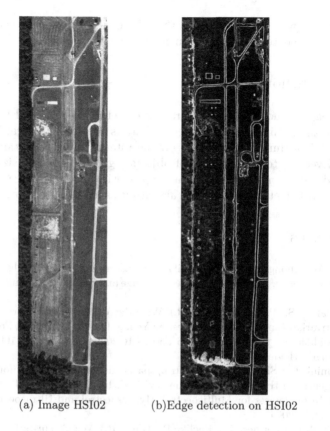

(a) Image HSI02   (b)Edge detection on HSI02

Fig. 5. Edge detection on an HYDICE image

First, to highlight the benefits of a double scan as explained in section 4.3. We use simulated image 100×100 pixels and containing an object 50×50 pixels. The background is generated from spectra (1, 2, 3) given in Fig. 3, and the object is generated using the spectra (4, 5, 6). The simulated image (shown in false color on three bands) and the results of edge detection are shown in Fig. 4 for vertical, horizontal scanning and merger of the two sweeps maintaining the maximum pixel.

The results show the good detection of object contours, and confirm the need of vertical and horizontal scanning to detect all object edges.

Real-World Data. We have also applied our edge detection algorithm to several large real-world images and objects containing small spatial dimensions. The local variation of the signal subspace is studied using subtensor with spatial dimensions of 3×3 pixels. An example is given in Fig. 5 (a): an HSI image composed with 308×1280 pixels of 148 bands from HYDICE sensor. We can see several vehicles and panels. The panels are characterized by a spectral signature in the visible wavelengths, close to the color of the soil, making them difficult to identify. Edge detection for this image is shown in Fig. 5 (b).

6   Conclusion

In this paper a novel linear algebra-based method is proposed to estimate the signal subspace dimension. The tensor data is divided in several blocks and an iterative algorithm is proposed to evaluate iteratively the relationship between spectral vectors to detect edges of objects regardless of their size in HSI. The obtained results on real-world data are promising and encourage us to integrate this approach in classical detection algorithms, such that ACE or AMF detectors.

References

1. Luo, W., Zhong, L.: Spectral similarity measure edge detection algorithm in hyperspectral image. In: Second Congres on Image and Signal Processing (CISP), pp. 1–4 (2009)
2. Verzakov, S., Paclík, P., Duin, R.P.W.: Edge detection in hyperspectral imaging: multivariate statistical approaches. In: Yeung, D.-Y., Kwok, J.T., Fred, A., Roli, F., de Ridder, D. (eds.) SSPR 2006 and SPR 2006. LNCS, vol. 4109, pp. 551–559. Springer, Heidelberg (2006)
3. Resmini, G.: Simultaneous spectral/spatial detection of edges for hyperspectral imagery: the HySPADE algorithm revisited. In: SPIE Procceeding of Algorithms and Technologiess for Multispectral, Hyperspectral and Ultraspectral imagery X, vol. 5429 (2004)
4. Dinh, V.C., Leitner, R., Paclik, P., Duin, R.P.W.: A clustering based method for edge detection in hyperspectral images. In: Salberg, A.-B., Hardeberg, J.Y., Jenssen, R. (eds.) SCIA 2009. LNCS, vol. 5575, pp. 580–587. Springer, Heidelberg (2009)
5. Zhou, Y., Wu, B., Li, D., Li, R.: Edge detection on hyperspectral imagery via manifold techniques. In: Hyperspectral Image and Signal Processing Evolution in Remote Sensing : WHISPERS, pp. 1–4 (2009)
6. Lee, M., Bruce, L.: Appliyng cellular automata to hyperspectral edge detection. In: IEEE International Geoscience and Remote Sensing Symposium (IGARSS), pp. 2202–2205 (2010)
7. Donoho, D. : High-dimensionnal data analysis: the curse and blessing of dimentionality. Math challenges of the 21th century, American Mathematical Society ed. (2000)
8. Bourennane, S., Fossati, C., Cailly, A.: Improvement of Target-Detection Algorithms Based on Adaptive Three-Dimensional Filtering. IEEE Trans. on Geosci. and Remote Sens. **49**(4), 1383–1395 (2011)
9. Liu, X., Bourennane, S., Fossati, C.: Reduction of signal-dependent noise from hyperspectral images for target detection. IEEE Trans. Geoscience and Remote Sensing **52**(9), 5396–5411 (2014)
10. Chang, D., Du, Q.: Estimation of number of spectrally distinct signal sources in hyperspectral imagery. IEEE Trans. on Geosci. and Remote Sens. **42**(3), 608–619 (2004)

11. Rao, A., Jones, D.: A denoising approach to multichannel signal estimation. IEEE Trans. on Signal Process. **48**(5), 1225–1234 (2000)
12. Bourennane, S., Fossati, C., Cailly, A.: Improvement of classification for hyperspectral images based on tensor modeling. IEEE Geosci. Remote Sens. Lett. **7**, 801–805 (2010)
13. Bioucas-Dias, J., Nascimento, J.: Hyperspectral subspace identification. IEEE Trans. Geosci. Remote Sensing **46**(8), 2435–2445 (2008)
14. Chang, C.-I., Du, Q.: Noise subspace projection approaches to determination of intrinsic dimensionality of hyperspectral imagery. In: Proc. Image and Signal Processing for Remote Sensing, SPIE, vol. 3871, pp. 34–44 (1999)
15. Bourennane, S., Fossati, C.: Dimensionality reduction and colored noise removal from hyperspectral images. Remote Sensing Lett. **6**(10), 765–774 (2015)
16. Acito, N., Diani, M., Corsini, G.: A new algorithm for robust estimation of the signal subspace in hyperspectral images in presence of rare signal components. IEEE Trans. Geosci. Remote Sensing **47**(11), 3844–3856 (2009)

Dictionary-Based Compact Data Representation for Very High Resolution Earth Observation Image Classification

Corina Văduva[1](✉), Florin-Andrei Georgescu[1,2], and Mihai Datcu[1,3]

[1] University Politehnica of Bucharest, UPB, Bucharest, Romania
{corina.vaduva,florin.andreig}@gmail.com
[2] Military Technical Academy, MTA, Bucharest, Romania
[3] German Aerospace Center, DLR, Oberpfaffenhofen, Germany
mihai.datcu@dlr.de

Abstract. In the context of fast growing data archives, with continuous changes in volume and diversity, information mining has proven to be a difficult, yet highly recommended task. The first and perhaps the most important part of the process is data representation for efficient and reliable image classification. This paper is presenting a new approach for describing the content of Earth Observation Very High Resolution images, by comparison with traditional representations based on specific features. The benefit of data compression is exploited in order to express the scene content in terms of dictionaries. The image is represented as a distribution of recurrent patterns, removing redundant information, but keeping all the explicit features, like spectral, texture and context. Further, a data domain analysis is performed using Support Vector Machine aiming to compare the influence of data representation to semantic scene annotation. WorldView2 data and a reference map are used for algorithm evaluation.

Keywords: Information mining · Feature extraction · Dictionary · Data representation · Semantic classification

1   Introduction

Nowadays, the huge amount of available information and knowledge is supported, among others, by the technological development, as well as the increasing interest towards the Earth Observation (EO) domain and its large applicability. Worldwide EO advanced equipment is continuously generating image data characterized by specific attributes, according to the acquisition sensor capabilities.

The high fidelity of such image data emphasize the value of exploring and properly exploiting the information encoded. The scene is presented as a series of correlated patterns linked to one another based on precise relationships. These patterns are usually described as features defining the physical properties of the scene. The key for a good scene representation consists of a proper feature selection. Their extraction, together with accurate adjustments during the process lead to an optimum depiction of the image content. However, the information mining process may become extremely laborious due to the defining characteristics of current EO imagery: sparse, uncertain,

© Springer International Publishing Switzerland 2015
S. Battiato et al. (Eds.): ACIVS 2015, LNCS 9386, pp. 816–825, 2015.
DOI: 10.1007/978-3-319-25903-1_70

and incomplete. This is preventing the existing data mining algorithms to be directly applied [1]. Specific workflows are normally required for each type of data.

To this aim, image representation and information extraction techniques were closely studied and improved with the EO sensors enhancements. The first representations were pixels based, and the scene classifications were considering only spectral [8] and texture properties [4]. Segmentation and object detection algorithms [9] were introduced, along with shape and spatial descriptors. Moreover, spatial interaction between objects was included, in an attempt to define high-level descriptors for the scene [7]. Patch-based classification was proven to obtain good performances, integrating a series of local features. Pixel-based analysis become less relevant due to the increased amount of observable details and the need to consider neighborhood in order to define a meaning. Recently, so-called "bag of words" approaches became widely used in the computer vision community [2], [3].

An important drawback for most of the methods for data representation lies in the fact that the analysis requires the setting of many input parameters, focusing only on certain scene charac teristic, disregarding the general understanding. In order to cope with these issues, data compression algorithms come as a tradeoff solution to assess an area based on all its aspects and features, expressing the same amount of information using fewer bits. Information theory has successfully proven that data compression algorithms are able to encode the similarities between two images [10, 11]. Therefore, we exploit this idea and focus on eliminating redundant information, keeping only individual patterns and indexing their position inside an image. We consider that this is the minimum information required to reconstruct the image and its meaning and we compare the individual patterns to a set of dictionaries.

The first attempt to exploit the advantages of data compression envisaged pattern recognition [12]; then the efforts were centered on computing similarities by using the information in the first object to encode the content of the second object [10]. In order to overcome the computational effort, dictionaries-based compressors were introduced to characterize the content of an image in terms of repetitive sequences and to identify similarities by measuring a distance between computed dictionaries [11]. The employment of compression algorithms may also highlight the possibility of considering dictionaries as features for content based image retrieval. To this respect, an experiment was presented by the authors of [14] on hyperspectral EO images. A short review of the literature illustrates that compression algorithms provide good results on various types of data. This comes to confirm that the compression-based techniques do not depend on the nature of the input data: text, biological genomes, multimedia images, videos, EO imagery [13].

In this frame, we define a patch-based approach for Very High Resolution (VHR) EO images analysis, using baseline descriptors for spectral and texture information. The novelty of this paper consists of a new approach that represents the image content focusing on data compression and dictionary extraction. The influence of these three features on the information mining performances is assessed in a segmentation process for the data domain. Support Vector Machine is used in order to obtain scene semantic classification.

2   Data Representation

The main goal for data representation techniques is to shape the fundamental characteristics of the content, reducing at the same time the dimensionality of the data without losing significant information. The diminution will reduce the storage issues and
ease the searching process in large databases. However, it should not decrease the
ability to discriminate classes of information. Further, there are presented two modalities to describe the content of an image: by extracting spectral and texture features
and a dictionary-based:

2.1   Features Extraction: Emphasizing Spectral and Texture Characteristics

Spectral and texture information are perhaps the features most used to describe one
image. Easy to compute, the offer basic and yet significant measurements about the
image, consistent to a certain extent with the human perception. We consider the histogram of color [8] to express spectral information and Webber Local Descriptor
(WLD) [4] to quantify the perceived texture in the image.

Given a multispectral image, the histogram of color is computed for each band by
discretizing the image and count the number of occurrences for each gray level. At the
end, we the histograms of color computed for each band of the image and obtain a
content descriptor focusing on the color distribution.

A different perspective on the scene is given by the arrangement and frequency of
tonal variation in particular areas of an image. This particularity of the scene is known
as texture and one of its common representations follows the Weber's law which
states that the barely perceptible disparity between two stimuli is proportional with
their amplitude. The stimulus change and its intensity is described by the differential
excitation and orientation, contributing to the definition of WLD [4].

Feature extraction techniques are intended to extract relevant information from the
image content. However, they express singular aspects, highlighting only particular
characteristics of the scene.

2.2   Dictionary Based Data Representation

Data compression procedures are known for their ability to encode information using
fewer resources than the original data. Lossless data compression usually exploit statistical redundancy to represent data without any loss of information. This paper focus on
this idea and proposes a new "bag of words" approach for data representation (Figure 1).

The authors have introduced a new descriptor aiming to encapsulate as many features as possible for image content description. First, the image is transformed into a
string S, band by band. Then the Lempel Ziv Welch (LZW) [5] compressing algorithms is used to identify recurrent patterns and stored into a repository. These patterns represent sub-strings of S and they are considered to be visual words defining a
dictionary. They are indexed into a repository. Further, we are using this index to
replace the pattern inside the string for all its recurrences. The image is therefore reduce to a shorter string, where the pixels intensities are replaced with dictionaries

describing patterns (substrings) recurrent in the scene. The distribution of the dictionaries inside the new string give us the final representation of the data. We consider the distribution a new type of content descriptor and we shall compare its performances against the traditional methods for feature extraction.

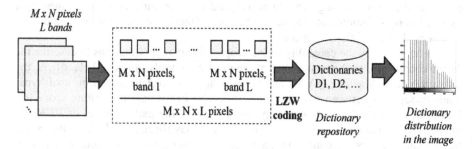

Fig. 1. Dictionary based data representation: methodology

3   Data Domain Analysis for Semantic Classification

The problem of data representation is a continuous challenge, particularly for the EO domain, due to the constant technological progress and the improvement of sensors characteristics. Moreover, the data is not always visual, and the results of automatic processing become difficult to understand due to lack of coincidence between the information that one can extract by observing the data and the statistical computations. Each feature extraction algorithm will focus on a different characteristic of the scene, highlighting a different aspect. The feature space will provide a new distribution each time a new descriptor is computed.

By modelling the data domain, the categories of objects will be delineated. As the semantic of the image content is limited and well known by a user, the classes defined should not be totally distinctive. The purpose of this paper is to study the behavior of 3 different data representation methods (histogram of color, WLD descriptor and the distribution of dictionaries) and to compare their performances through a classification procedure with a reference map of the analyzed data.

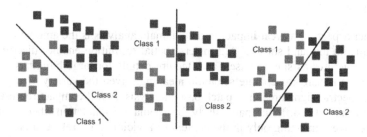

Fig. 2. Class separability according to different data representation model.

Given a certain EO scene, we divided it into small patches. We represent each patch considering the spectral and texture features and dictionary distribution. For each of these cases, we consider the result for one patch as a point in a space characterized by that particular feature selected (Figure 2).

Considering the data space as continuum, a classifier should segment the space, such that the identified segments to correspond to a semantic class, as defined by a user. It has been demonstrated to be a robust and effective method for image indexing in several data collections over the years.

In order to verify the capability of the proposed data representations to describe the image content, we will consider one of the most commonly employed classifiers, the Support Vector Machine (SVM) and we will apply it to generate an optimal hyper plane to separate between two semantic categories in the selected feature space [6]. However, the size, the content variety and especially the particularities of VHR EO images are a great challenge to overcome for any classification task. Increased spectral resolution offers more information about land structures composition and a plus in the process of class separability. At the same time, there will be a major boost in the size and complexity of the data to be analyzed. Multiple recordings of radiance reflectance can lead to different object characteristics, as presented in Figure 3.

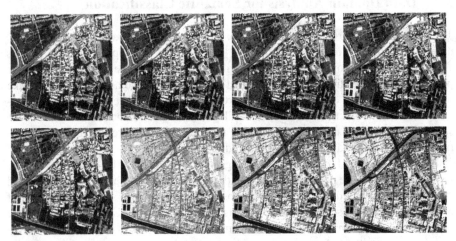

Fig. 3. Example of scene spectral distinctiveness according to the sensor ability to define wavelength intervals.

Another aspect with great impact in data domain analysis is the amount of observable details on the land surface. A 2 meters spatial resolution enables discrimination between structures as small houses, architecture details for large buildings, cars and even trees. It is hard to separate semantic meaning, given the variety of objects and available spectral signatures, in a patch based analysis. A full compact representation of the information is difficult, particularly for a semantic annotation where standalone objects receive a meaning only in the context of a vicinity. Therefore, a patch can be labeled by weighting its content and defining a relationship to the rest of the scene. Figure 4 illustrates how small patches (of 10x10 pixels) receive a meaning only when positioned inside a larger area.

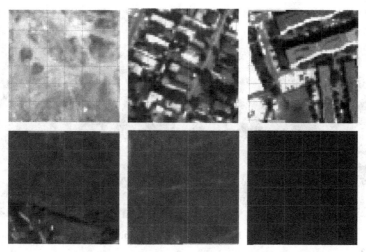

Fig. 4. Land cover semantic categories. From left to right: arid area, urban-colored, urban-grey (first line), vegetation-dense, vegetation-low, water (second line).

Consequently, the increased volume of various and inconsistent data, with irregular distribution of features inside a patch, represents an important impediment for precise separation in the data domain. In order to overcome this problem, the proposed data representation approach, the dictionary distribution considers the full arrangement and relationships inside the image for content description.

4   Experimental Results

For verification, we propose a WorldView2 image, acquired over the area of Bucharest, Romania (Figure 5). The scene covers roughly 25 square kilometers. The image is characterized by 2 m spatial resolution, 8 spectral bands and 8 bits radiometric resolution.

Stating that an image with such characteristics is better described using a patch-based approach capable to capture relevant meaning, the scene was manually annotated through a careful visual interpretation. The obtained map (Figure 7) will be considered as reference for further results verification.

The size of 10x10 pixels for the patch was selected as a compromise between the computational time, the accuracy of the classification and the spatial resolution of the image. Despite the need to consider neighborhoods as large as possible in order to provide a meaningful label, we chose a smaller patch size to limit the diversity of information inside and to better delineate categories of land cover, providing a smoother classification. We considered 6 semantic categories, as illustrated in Figure 4 and labeled using the legend in Figure 6. We have chosen the same color representation in all three classification maps. From each class, we selected a number a 20 patches to form the training set for the Support Vector Machine classifier. For each of the three data representation, we used the same training set.

Fig. 5. WorldView2 image, Bucharest, Romania.

Fig. 6. Reference annotation map.

	Arid area	C1
	Urban-Colored	C2
	Urban-Grey	C3
	Vegetation-Dense	C4
	Vegetation-Low	C5
	Water	C6

Fig. 7. Legend for classification representation.

Fig. 8. Scene classification (color histogram).   **Fig. 9.** Scene classification (WLD descriptor).

Fig. 10. Scene classification (dictionaries distribution)

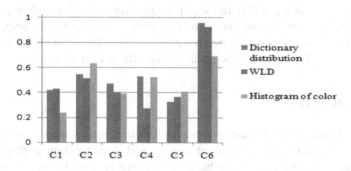

Fig. 11. F-measure chart

Table 1. Confusion matrix (scene classification using histogram of color).

	C1	C2	C3	C4	C5	C6
C1	**17.4%**	7.2%	3.7%	0.5%	0.3%	0.0%
C2	25.9%	**59.3%**	30.5%	5.0%	11.5%	0.2%
C3	54.9%	20.6%	49.3%	11.9%	3.8%	0.8%
C4	0.1%	4.9%	9.7%	**67.9%**	41.4%	31.7%
C5	1.6%	7.9%	5.8%	8.8%	**35.4%**	6.3%
C6	0.0%	0.2%	1.0%	6.0%	7.6%	**61.0%**

Table 2. Confusion matrix (scene classification using WLD)

	C1	C2	C3	C4	C5	C6
C1	**44.3%**	1.8%	1.1%	3.4%	7.6%	0.0%
C2	21.0%	**45.7%**	40.5%	25.2%	5.7%	0.1%
C3	19.7%	27.6%	**43.5%**	18.5%	3.4%	0.2%
C4	5.7%	15.1%	8.6%	45.1%	**54.7%**	5.1%
C5	8.4%	9.2%	3.8%	7.1%	**28.2%**	1.0%
C6	0.9%	0.7%	2.4%	0.8%	0.4%	**93.6%**

Table 3. Confusion matrix (scene classification using dictionary distribution).

	C1	C2	C3	C4	C5	C6
C1	**41.6%**	1.4%	0.3%	2.9%	13.6%	0.1%
C2	7.1%	**55.0%**	20.4%	27.8%	10.5%	0.1%
C3	1.8%	32.0%	**58.3%**	10.3%	5.1%	0.7%
C4	21.9%	6.3%	15.5%	**45.6%**	36.0%	1.9%
C5	27.6%	5.1%	3.6%	13.0%	**34.8%**	1.2%
C6	0.0%	0.2%	1.8%	0.4%	0.1%	**96.0%**

The results for the classifications, as well as the confusion matrixes are presented above. The complexity and variety of the data inferred with the representation performances for the three features selected to represent the image content. In the feature space defined using the histogram of color the urban colored class is best retrieved, however, there is a large percentage of arid area mistaken with the urban colored. WLD representation has difficulties in separating between the two urban classes and respectively, between the two classes of vegetation. The dictionary distribution provides increased percentage in correctly retrieving areas like urban-grey, vegetation-dense and water. The precision and recall for the latter is over 95%.

5   Conclusions

This paper introduces an innovative approach for data representation based on lossless data compression. Extracting recurrent patterns and indexing them as dictionaries, a new feature is computed as a distribution of dictionaries over the image, jointly exploiting the spectral and texture information. In order to assess its performances, we consider two standard and simple descriptors disjointedly defining spectral and texture information and compare their capability to separate precise semantic classes defined in a training process. We use SVM classifier to perform the categories separation inside the data feature space. Taking into consideration the same settings (such as size of the patches and training set), the validation measurement show that the dictionary distribution brings improvements in the classification of the scene. Due to the lack of standard EO reference datasets, the comparison was performed against a map, manually annotated by a user, according to its understanding and needs.

Acknowledgement. This work was supported by a grant of the Romanian Ministry of Education, CNCS – UEFISCDI, project number PN-II-RU-PD-2012-3 - 0477. The paper has also been financially supported within the project entitled "Horizon 2020 - Doctoral and Postdoctoral Studies: Promoting the National Interest through Excellence, Competitiveness and Responsibility in the Field of Romanian Fundamental and Applied Scientific Research", contract number POSDRU/159/1.5/S/140106. This project is co-financed by European Social Fund through Sectoral Operational Programme for Human Resources Development 2007- 2013. Investing in people!

References

1. Wu, X., Zhu, X., Wu, G.-Q., Ding, W.: Data mining with big data. IEEE Transactions on Knowledge and Data Engineering **26**(1), 97–107 (2014)
2. Sivic, J., Zisserman, A.: Video google: a text retrieval approach to object matching in videos. In: Proc. IEEE Int. Conf. Computer Vision, vol. 2, pp. 1470–1477 (2003)
3. Jegou, H., Douze, M., Schmid, C.: Improving bag-of-features for large scale image search. Int. Journal of Computer Visual **87**(3), 316–336 (2010)
4. Jie, C., Shiguang, S., Chu, H., Guoying, Z., Matti, P., Xilin, C., Wen, G.: WLD: A robust Local Image Descriptor. IEEE Transactions on Pattern Analysis and Machine Intelligence **32**(9), 1705–1720 (2009)
5. Welch, T.A.: A technique for high-performance data compression. Computer **17**(6), 8–19 (1984)
6. Camps-Valls, G., Bruzzone, L.: Kernel Methods for Remote Sensing Data Analysis. Wiley, Chichester (2009)
7. Shyu, C.R., Klaric, M., Scott, G.J., Barb, A.S., Davis, C.H., Palaniappan, K.: GeoIRIS: Geospatial Information Retrieval and Indexing System—Content Mining, Semantics Modelling, and Complex Queries. IEEE Transactions and Remote Sensing **45**(4), 839–852 (2007)
8. Swain, M., Ballard, D.: Color indexing. International Journal of Computer Vision **7**(1), 11–32 (1991)
9. Shi, J., Malik, J.: Normalized cuts and image segmentation. IEEE Transactions on Pattern Analysis and Machine Intelligence **22**(8), 888–905 (2000)
10. Li, M., Chen, X., Li, X., Ma, B., Vitanyi, P.M.: The Similarity Metric. IEEE Transactions of Information Theory **50**(12), 3250–3264 (2004)
11. Cerra, D., Datcu, M.: A fast compression-based similarity measure with applications to content-based image retrieval. Journal of Visual Communication and Image Representation **23**, 293–302 (2012)
12. Watanabe, T., Sugawara, K., Sugihara, H.: A new pattern representation scheme using data compression. IEEE Transactions on Pattern Analysis and Machine Intelligence **24**(5), 579–590 (2002)
13. Cilibrasi, R., Vitanyi, P.M.: Clustering by compression. IEEE Transaction on Information Theory **51**(4), 1523–1545 (2005)
14. Veganzones, M.A., Datcu, M., Grana, M.: Dictionary based hyperspectral image retrieval. In: Proceedings of the 1st International Conference on Pattern Recognition Applications and Methods, Vilamoura, Algarve, Portugal, pp. 426–432 (2012)

Sphere-Tree Semi-regular Remesher

Mejda Chihaoui[✉], Akram Elkefi, Wajdi Bellil, and Chokri Ben Amar

Research Laboratory in Intelligent Machines,
National Engineering School of Sfax (ENIS), University of Sfax, Sfax, Tunisia
{mejda.chihaoui,wajdi.bellil,chokri.benamar}@ieee.org,
elkefi@gmail.com

Abstract. Surface meshes have become widely used since they are frequently adopted in many computer graphic applications. These meshes are often generated by isosurface representations or scanning devices. Unfortunately, these meshes are often dense and full of redundant vertices and irregular sampling. These defects make meshes not capable to support multiple applications; such as display, compression and transmission. To solve these problems and reduce the complexity, the mesh quality (connectivity regularity) must be ameliorated. Its improvement is called re-meshing. This paper presents a novel re-meshing approach based on Sphere-Tree construction. First, we approximate the original object with a dictionary of multi-dimensional geometric shapes (spheres) called Sphere-Tree which is, then, re-meshed. Finally, we use a refinement step to avoid artifacts and produce a new semi-regular mesh.

Keywords: Surface mesh · Re-meshing · Semi-regular mesh · Approximation · Sphere-Tree · Triangulation · Refinement

1 Introduction

Surface meshes have, nowadays, been a very rich research field, since they are frequently used in many computer graphics applications; such as display, modeling [1], compression or transmission. Unfortunately, these meshes, often generated by isosurface representations and scanning devices, are complicated and irregular, i.e., there is no consistency in the way of connecting their vertices. Therefore, all the vertices have different valences or number of vertex incidents.

Due to their inconsistency, the obtained meshes are complicated and unable to support multiple applications.

Indeed, in an application like compression, the saving of information depends on the type of mesh. If it is regular or semi-regular, we can save base mesh's information and deduce other base mesh triangles from them. But when it is irregular, we are obliged to save all the object triangles' information.

The solution is then to convert an irregular mesh to the most possible regular one (semi-regular or regular mesh), which presents an approximation of the input with better quality (regularity of vertices, shape of cells and mesh). This described process is called re-meshing. It can be done by generating a new mesh from scratch [2] or by altering the input [3].

© Springer International Publishing Switzerland 2015
S. Battiato et al. (Eds.): ACIVS 2015, LNCS 9386, pp. 826–837, 2015.
DOI: 10.1007/978-3-319-25903-1_71

This surface remeshing field has rapidly increased and has created an accomplishment of many techniques [4], [5]. They consist in producing hierarchical structure (with subdivision connectivity), adapted not only to multi-resolution analysis [6], but also to many applications like compression [7], transmission, etc.

In this paper, we propose a novel approach to re-mesh an arbitrary surface onto a semi-regular mesh using a geometric shapes dictionary called Sphere-Tree. First, we begin with approximating 3D object surface using a set of spheres and/or sphere parts called Sphere-Tree. Then, this approximant Sphere-Tree is regularly triangulated, i.e., we triangulate each sphere or sphere part used to approximate 3D object surface.

Finally, we use a refinement process in order to ameliorate the connectivity of our re-meshed object surface and fill the gaps produced by the second step.

2   Related Works

Re-meshing techniques can be divided into five categories depending on the re-meshing objectives [4].

The first method is called structured re-meshing. It can be "regular", "semi-regular" or "extremely regular". A regular re-meshing approach aims to get a completely regular mesh; that's why [8] made re-meshing of irregular triangles using a regular grid. The initial irregular mesh is cut and reduced to one topologic disk. Then, it is parameterized in a 2D square in order to get a "geometric" image which preserves the geometry and modulation map used for visualization.

The second subtype is a piecewise "extremely regular mesh" in which the number of regular vertices is dominant. In this context, [9] divides 3D surface into three "reliefs" (flat regions with smooth boundaries) using Voronoi diagram. Then, the surface is regularly re-sampled into each relief to obtain a piecewise extremely regular mesh with regular connectivity in big regions. Finally, a refinement step is done to improve mesh regularity.

The third subtype is the semi-regular mesh. The regular subdivision [10] is an efficient mean to obtain a semi-regular mesh and a multi-resolution one.

Since this mesh type is based on parameterization, i.e. the correspondence between the original mesh and a parametric domain (circle, square...), this category has, also, been divided depending on parameterization into two categories: mesh with planar parameterization and that with non-planar parameterization.

Planar parameterization is done in a planar 2D domain which is, then, re-sampled in a 3D model. It is simple when original models are homeomorphic to a disk or a sphere but difficult when models are complicated. For complicated objects parameterization, [11] proposed to divide original mesh into a set of simple surfaces homeomorphic to a disk and parameterize them in a 2D plan to form atlas.

After that, to avoid the artifacts appearing between these surfaces, we bank on non-planar parameterization which makes the correspondence between the original and the base mesh vertices as they have the same topology [12]. The base mesh can be constructed using either initial surface partitioning and patches simplification [13] or progressive decimation [14]. [15] combined these three types in the so-called "mesh obtained with parameterization".

The second technique is called compatible re-meshing. Given a number of 3D meshes with partial correspondence, this method aims at generating different modified meshes which represent re-meshes of inputs and have common connectivity. The essential research area of these re-meshing techniques is "morphing". It uses "joint parameterization" to calculate parameterization of different models in a common base domain. The sphere is the most usable domain [16] especially when the original models are closed and genus 0 because it does not need to be cut into disks.

The third type, called high quality remeshing, seeks to optimize the mesh quality and the vertices distribution. A mesh is of high quality if its elements are well shaped. Its sampling is uniform or isotropic with smooth gradation [17]. It is used in many applications like rendering, compression, smoothing, etc.

Given a triangular mesh, the fourth category, i.e., the feature remeshing aims to generate a new mesh which preserves the original mesh features.

Finally, the Error-driven Re-meshing minimizes the distance between the original and the re-meshed surfaces. An efficient re-mesher optimizes the trend-off between complexity and precision calculated in function of a pre-defined distortion error. [18] treated this problem as an optimization with functional energy which calculates the deviation between final and original meshes where [19] minimized the volume between the simplified and the input meshes using an optimization algorithm based on gradient and a model of finite element interpolation defined on meshes.

3   Sphere-Tree Semi-regular Remesher

In this section, we present our novel re-meshing approach divided into three steps:

1. Sphere-Tree construction: As its name suggests, a Sphere-Tree is a set of spheres and/or spheres parts which approximates the initial 3D model.
2. Regular triangulation: Since our objective is to transform an irregular mesh to the most possible regular triangular mesh, these spheres and/or parts of spheres must be regularly triangulated.

- Refinement: this step must be used to avoid artifacts produced by the triangulation step and to ameliorate the re-meshed object connectivity.

3.1   Sphere-Tree Construction

Sphere-Trees were used particularly in collision detection [20], [21], [22]. In our approach, the Sphere-Tree construction allows us to approximate surface 3D irregular meshes. Mathematically, a Sphere-Tree is a set of spheres and/or sphere parts which approximates different parts of original mesh defined by:

$$S_{tree} = \{ \cup_{i=1..n} S_i(\Omega_i, r_i) \mid E(S_{tree}, M) < \varepsilon \tag{1}$$

S_{tree} is the Sphere-Tree. It consists of a union of n approximant spheres S_i or sphere parts. Each one is defined by a center $\Omega_i(x,y,z)$ and a radium r_i.

A Sphere-Tree is satisfying if the approximation error E between Stree and the original mesh M is lower than a parameter ε fixed by the user depending on the object complexity. The error E is the sum of the sphere's errors e_i defined by the largest distance between the sphere surface Si and the object region covered by this sphere.

Our approximation algorithm is resumed in Fig. 1.

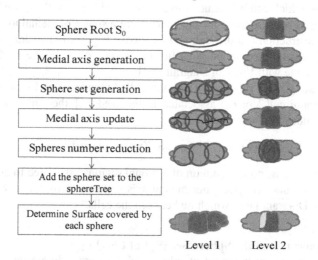

Level 1   Level 2

Fig. 1. Sphere-Tree approximation flowchart.

We start with the Sphere-Tree root S_0. It is the little sphere which includes our object. Then, for each level L_i of our Sphere-Tree, we apply the medial axis approximation using the Voronoi Diagram. After that, and from this medial axis, we generate the sphere set $\{S_i\}$ of level L_i. Then, in order to minimize the spheres number used to cover each region $R_{i,j}$ of the level L_i to a fixed number called "Branch factor Bf", used to cover each region, we respectively update the medial axis and reduce the sphere set number using the "Burst" algorithm. After that, we determine each region $R_{i,j}$ covered by a sphere $S_{i,j}$. Obviously, for the sphere root S_0, we have only one region covered by this sphere, which is all the object surface. In the next level, we get Bf regions. Finally, we add this set to the sphere-tree. This process is reapplied for all regions $R_{i,j}$ and for each level L_i until we get a good approximation of our object.

3.1.1   Sphere-Tree Root Construction

Sphere-Tree root S_0 is the smallest spherical bounding volume which includes the original mesh. It is the sphere with the smaller center for which all the object vertices are included in this sphere. The difficulty of this work depends on the complexity of the object to be covered.

To construct our Sphere-Tree root, we find the center by averaging the coordinates. Then, we fix the sphere radius as the maximum distance to the center.

3.1.2   Medial Axis Approximation

Our Sphere-Tree is composed of n levels, depending on the object size and accuracy (for example four or five). The level 0 is the Sphere-Tree root S_0. To generate a sphere set $\{S_i\}$ of level i, we rely on the medial axis approximation.

In fact, the medial Axis algorithm of a polyhedral object is defined as the set of the biggest spheres which can be included in an object. This set is, then, used to approximate a 3D object because these medial spheres are a subset of medial axis. However, Medial axis construction is a difficult and expensive task for polyhedral object; that's why a medial axis approximation is sufficient. In our approach, the medial axis approximation is done with Voronoi Diagram [23].

Given $S = \{s_1, s_2, .. s_n\}$ a finite set of n points called "seeds" in an Euclidian Space E, we call a Voronoi cell Vor (s_i) associated to the seed $\{s_i\}$ the points set which are closest to $\{s_i\}$ more than any other seed.

$$\text{Vor}(s_i) = \{x \in E | \forall q \in S \ d(x, s_i) < d(x, q)\} \qquad (2)$$

A Voronoi Diagram is, now, the union of Voronoi regions associated to all seeds $\{s_i\}$. After forming Voronoi Diagram, our medial axis can be approximated with a subset of the Voronoi Diagram faces which lie between the cells.

3.1.3   Generation of the Sphere Set $\{S_{i,j}\}$ of Level L_i

The generated sphere set is the set of spheres $\{S_{i,j}\}$ where radii are the distances between Voronoi vertices and seeds. We, iteratively, augment the number of spheres and we stop the increase when a higher number does not affect the results, i.e., the approximation error.

3.1.4   Voronoi Diagram Update

In order to minimize sphere number used to cover each region, we use an adaptive medial axis [20]. The latter ensures that the medial spheres cover the object and allows updating medial axis in order to get a Sphere-Tree which tightly fits the object. This is composed of two sub-steps. The first one, called "completing coverage", is followed to ensure that medial spheres cover the entire object. The second sub-step named "iterative improvement". It is used to ameliorate approximation by adding sample points and replacing the worst sphere in the approximation by a tighter one.

- Completing Coverage: As a large sphere can cover more points than a tight one, a sphere is replaced with a larger one when gaps exist in surface points in order to ensure that the object is entirely covered. This will require less number of medial spheres.
- Iterative improvement: When replacing a tight sphere with a larger one to cover more surface points, we affect the tight fitting. So, this process minimizes the approximation error by replacing the sphere with the worst fit. At each iteration, a new point is inserted into the Voronoi diagram and will be used to construct a sphere with a radius equal to the distance from the added vertex to its forming points.

3.1.5   Sphere Number Reduction

In order to cover a region with a predefined number of spheres called « Branch Factor », we use « Burst» method [20] which eliminates a sphere and uses two bounding ones to fill the gap produced by the sphere suppression.

This method calculates the optimum radius of the bounding sphere in order to minimize the distance between the object surface and the approximating sphere.

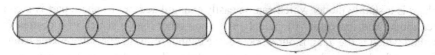

Fig. 2. Reduction of sphere number with "Burst".

3.1.6   Add of the Resulting Spheres to the Sphere-Tree

After minimizing the children spheres set constructed in level L_i, these spheres $\{S_{i,j}\}$ are added to our Sphere-Tree as children of $\{S_{i-1,j}\}$.

3.1.7   Determination of the Region Covered by Each Sphere $S_{i,j}$ of Level L_i

After generating a set of mother spheres of level L_i, and for each sphere $S_{i,j}$, we must precise the region covered by this sphere, which means determining the object surface included in the surface of the $S_{i,j}$. When an area is covered by more than one sphere, we must decide to which sphere this area belongs. Therefore, we divide overlapping vertices according to their positions with respect to a dividing plane. These regions will be the inputs of the level L_{i+1}. For each region we are asked to do the medial approximation.

3.2   Sphere-Tree Regular Triangulation

3.2.1   Triangulation and Triangulation Applied to Spheres

After approximating our mesh with a Sphere-Tree, the regular re-meshing step will be just a regular triangulation of the spheres and/or spheres parts composing our Sphere-Tree. As its name suggests, a triangulation of surface mesh consists in transforming any mesh in a triangular mesh where all vertices form triangles.

Many researches have been done like Delaunay Triangulation. In our work, we focus on regular triangulation of spheres methods. [24] presented a survey triangulation methods and two new techniques for regular triangulation of spheres based on Delaunay triangulation of vertices situated on or near a sphere. The first method consists in calculating Delaunay triangulation exactly on the sphere by construction; whereas the second one computes the convex bounding of the input set and gives some guaranties for output.

3.2.2   Sphere-Tree Triangulation

Our Sphere-Tree regulation is done using regular subdivision applied iteratively to a regular icosahedron having 12 vertices, 30 edges and 20 triangles. The principle is to subdivide the triangles of our icosahedron using midpoints of vertices and form more new triangles [25]. On the one hand, this method is efficient as it allow us to get a better distribution of triangles around the sphere poles. On the other hand, it represents a major weakness. Since the Sphere-Tree is a set of spheres and sphere parties, we must triangulate a number of spheres and spheres parts. However, the regular triangulation of a whole sphere is simple but the regular triangulation of a sphere party is remarkably more expensive in terms of complexity and time. Indeed, a sphere is a simple model which can be easily triangulated but a sphere part is a complex model and its regular triangulation is none other than a search of a re-meshing method which is the goal of our work. So, we cannot re-mesh our Sphere-Tree using a number of spheres and sphere parts triangulations. To resolve this, we propose this solution:

1. Given R, a region covered by a part of a sphere $S(r,\Omega)$, the triangulation must be done for all spheres even if their other parties are not used in the Sphere-Tree.
2. The unused sphere parts' elimination must be done after the regular triangulation step. In fact, when we do the triangulation of all the Sphere-Tree spheres even, if an object surface is approximated with a sphere party. This gives a blur effect. This is clearer in Fig. 3 when we increase mesh resolution.

Fig. 3. Re-meshed object without unused surfaces elimination

The elimination of spheres parts which are not used in approximation is done by eliminating each vertex of a sphere surface S_i which exists inside another sphere S_j. Otherwise, for each vertex v_i of S_i, if the distance between this vertex and a center c_j of a sphere S_j is shorter than the radium r_j, v_i is included in S_j and must be eliminated.

3.3   Refinement Step

As we have shown in Fig. 3, the triangulation of the entire spheres makes a blur effect to the object. Our proposed solution was to eliminate intersections. However, the elimination of some vertices especially those situated near the intersection parts produces discontinuities at the surfaces boundaries because vertex elimination produces elimination of neighbours and triangles containing this vertex (Fig. 4.a). Nevertheless, the same object presented with point cloud has no discontinuities (Fig. 4.b).

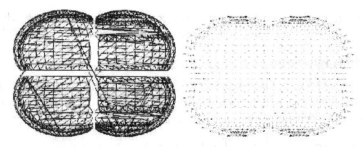

Fig. 4. Artefacts made with intersections elimination

To resolve this problem, we propose a refinement step applied in the intersected approximant surfaces boundaries. This algorithm is called Ball Pivoting Algorithm [26]. It aims at constructing triangular mesh from a cloud of points. It is a easy solution since the cloud of points that we get in the last step is already regular and triangular.

The principle is too simple: Three vertices form a triangle if a sphere of radium r specified by user touches them without containing any other vertex. From a "Triangle seed", this sphere pivots around an edge and keeps contact with edge extremities until touching another vertex in order to form another triangle. This process continues until all accessible edges are tested and it begins with another seed until all vertices are covered. The BPA has been tested with objects of millions of vertices and has been shown efficient in terms of memory cost and results quality.

4   Experimental results

We present, in this section, the results of re-meshing of the "Bunny" objects with 5k faces and "Elk" with 10k faces.

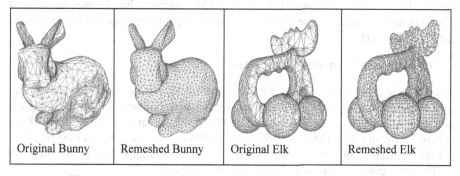

| Original Bunny | Remeshed Bunny | Original Elk | Remeshed Elk |

Fig. 5. Sphere-Tree semi-regular re-mesher of objects Bunny and Elk

For the Bunny, the medial axis approximation is initialized with 1000 spheres and, at each level, we update it so that each region has ½ of the parent sphere error   and it is covered by 250 spheres from which 8 (BF) spheres are chosen. Accordingly, for our Bunny object, we use 3 levels of approximation. For each level, each region is approximated with 8 spheres. So, it is divided into 8 sub regions. We obtain, thus, a

Sphere-Tree re-mesher with 512 spheres. Generally, a Sphere-Tree of l levels has 8^l approximant sphere. Then, these spheres are regularly triangulated and refined.

- **Quality Measurements**

We use the RMSE (Root Mean Squared Error) to measure the re-meshing quality of a semi-regular mesh Msr rebuilt from the original mesh M. RMSE calculates the geometric error d(X,Y) between two surfaces X and Y :

$$d(X, Y) = (\frac{1}{area(X)} \int_{x \in X} \left[d(x, Y)^2 dx \right])^{\frac{1}{2}} \qquad (3)$$

Where d(x,y) represents the Euclidean distance between a point x of the surface X and its nearest point to Y. It is the Hausdorff distance considering the maximum between d (X, Y) and (Y, X), because these measures are not symmetrical.

Table 1. Comparison of re-meshing approaches divided by the diagonal bounding.

Model	Mean(%bb)	RMS(%bb)
Elk [27]	0.0034	0.049
Elk [28]	0.002	0.005
Elk [29]	0.0021	0.03
Elk [30]	0.0006	0.012
Sphere-Tree (ours)	**0.0018**	**0.0024**
Homer [31]	0.0181	0.099
Homer [30].	0.029	0.035
Sphere-Tree(ours)	**0.00154**	**0.0021**

As shown in table 1, our Sphere-Tree re-meshing approach is challenging for different models. Elk is represented with 10k faces and 5k vertices, while Homer model with 12k faces and 6k vertices. These results are increasingly good when the inputs contain spherical shapes (Fig. 5).

- **Comparison in Term of Compression.**

Since the compression field gains big benefits from SR remeshers, we present a brief performance comparison of our approach with other techniques in terms of compression. Fig. 6 presents a comparison based on PSNR (Peak Signal to Noise Ratio) of our Sphere-Tree re-mesher with other approaches. PSNR is another criteria used to calculate the re-meshing quality of a semi-regular mesh M_{sr} rebuilt from the original mesh M. The more compression error there is, the lower PSNR is.

The PSNR is given by:

$$PSNR=20. \log_{10}(BB_{diag}/d) \qquad (4)$$

Where BB_{diag} is the bounding box diagonal of original mesh and d is the Hausdorff distance between M, the original surface, and M_{sr}, the re-meshed one.

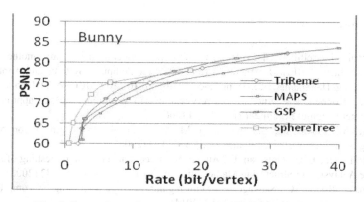

Fig. 6. Comparison of re-meshing results of the "Bunny" object

The horizontal axis is the bit rate (bits/vertex) of the decompressed file and the vertical axis shows the PSNR calculated with METRO [32] between M and the compressed semi-regular mesh MSR.

Compared with MAPS [33], GSP [34] and TriReme [35], our method is robust to irregular meshes at low and medium values of bit rate; whereas it loses its advantage for big horizontal values because objects need to be approximated with a huge number of spheres, what is now difficult if not impossible to do with our algorithm. Indeed, since our Sphere-Tree is a set of spheres, a re-meshed object file can be represented with a number of centers and radii. Indeed, good results can be obtained with small values of bit rate. The results presented in the curve were got from [12].

5   Conclusions

In this paper, we presented a survey of surface re-meshing techniques which we divided into five classes. Then, we describe the outlines of our approach. Our re-mesher begins with the approximation of the original mesh using Sphere-Tree. Then, each sphere or sphere part is regularly triangulated using regular subdivision. Finally, we refined our re-meshed object with Pivoting Ball algorithm. Our proposed technique is efficient thanks to its ability to re-mesh massive meshes that cannot be fully charged in memory. In fact, the approximation of an object with a set of spheres does not oblige us to charge a memory-massive object but to charge partially a subset of the Sphere-Tree, i.e., a number of spheres. Therefore, this segmentation makes all treatments applied to meshes faster and simpler.

We have, also, approved the efficiency of our approach in terms of compression since a mesh represented by a huge number of vertices can be represented only by a file containing a set of centres and radii of approximant spheres composing Sphere Tree, which remarkably ameliorates execution time cost.

Some results were shown to validate our approach utility, especially with low bit rate. For future work, we propose doing the approximation step not only with spheres but also with complex shapes able to produce more faithful objects to original mesh.

References

1. Othmani, M., Bellil, W., Ben Amar, C.:3D object modeling using multi-mother wavelet network. In: ACS/IEEE International Conference on Computer Systems and Applications Proceeding, Hammamet Tunisia, pp. 1–5 (2010). doi:10.1109/AICCSA.2010.5586961
2. Wu, J., Kobbelt, L.: Structure recovery via hybrid variational surface approximation. Computer Graphics Forum 24(3), 277–284 (2005)
3. Attene, M., Falcidieno, B., Spagnuolo, M.: Hierarchical mesh segmentation based on fitting primitives. Visual Computer 22(3), 181–193 (2006)
4. Alliez, P., Ucelli, G., Gotsman, C., Attene, M.: Recent advances in remeshing of surfaces. Shape Analysis and Structuring Mathematics and Visualization, pp. 53–82 (2008)
5. Payan, F., Roudet, C., Sauvage, B.: Semi-regular Triangle remeshing: A comprehensive study. Computer Graphics forum, 1–17 (2014)
6. Elkefi, A., Abbadi, S., Antonini, M., Ben Amar, C.: Compression de maillages 3D de grande résolution par transformée en ondelettes au fil de l'eau. In: GRETSI, Belgique, pp. 1013–1016 (2005)
7. Elkefi, A., Antonini, M., Ben Amar, C.: 3D scan-based wavelet transform for multiresolution meshes. In: 12th European Conference Eurasip EUSIPCO, Vienna-Austria (2004)
8. Gu, X., Gortler, S.J., Hoppe, H.: Geometry images. In: ACM SIGGRAPH 2002, vol. 21, pp. 355–361 (2002)
9. Szymczak, A., Rossignac, J., King, D.: Piecewise regular meshes: Construction and compression. Graphical Models 64(3–4), 183–198 (2003)
10. Zorin, D., Schröder, P.: Subdivision for Modeling and Animation. SIGGRAPH Course Notes (2000)
11. Lévy, B., Petitjean, S., Ray, N., Maillot, J.: Least squares conformal maps for automatic texture atlas generation. In: SIGGRAPH, pp. 362–371 (2002)
12. Roudet, C., Payan, F.: Remaillage semi-régulier pour les maillages surfaciques triangulaires: un état de l'art. In : REFIG 2011, vol. 1(1), pp. 1–14 (2011)
13. Eck, M., Derose, T., Duchamp, T., Hoppe, H., Lounsbery, M., Stuetzle, W.: Multiresolution analysis of arbitrary meshes. In: ACM SIGGRAPH 1995, pp. 173–182 (1995)
14. Lee, A.W.F., Sweldens, W., Schroder, P., Cowsar, L., Dobkin D.: MAPS: multiresolution adaptive parameterization of surfaces. In: ACM SIGGRAPH 1998, vol. 32, pp. 95–104 (1998)
15. Vincent, V.: Développement de modèles graphiques probabilistes pour analyser et remailler les maillages triangulaires 2 variétés. Ph.D. thesis, Doctoral School in Computer Sciences and Mathematics, National Institute of Applied Science. Lyon (2011)
16. Alexa, M.: Recent advances in mesh morphing. Computer Graphics Forum 21(2), 173–198 (2002)
17. Borouchaki, H., Hecht, F., Pascal, J.F.: Mesh gradation control. In: Proceedings of 6th International Meshing Roundtable, pp. 131–141(1997)
18. Hoppe, H., De Rose, T. Duchamp, T., McDonald, J., Stuetzle, W.: Mesh optimization. In: SIGGRAP, pp. 19–26 (1993)
19. Alliez, P., Laurent, N., Sanson, H., Schmitt, F.: Mesh approximation using a volume-based metric. In: Proceedings of 7th Pacific Conference on Computer Graphics and Applications, pp. 292–301 (1999)
20. Bradshaw, G., O'Sullivan, C.: Adaptive Medial Axis Approximation for Sphere-Tree Construction. ACM Transactions on Graphics, 1–26 (2004)
21. Weller, R., Zachmann, G.: Inner Sphere Trees for Proximity and Penetration Queries. Robotics: Science and Systems (2009)

22. Wang, D.: Sphere-tree based collision detection for constraint-based 6-DOF haptic rendering. In: IEEE World Haptics Conference (2013)
23. Mount, D.M.: Voronoi diagrams on the surface of a polyhedron. CAR-TR-121, CS-TR-1496. University of Maryland (1985)
24. Pedro, M.: Méthodes pour Accélérer les Triangulations de Delaunay (2010)
25. Havey, D.: Tutorial #3, The icosahedron-based geodesic sphere (2008). http://www.donhavey.com/blog/tutorials/tutorial-3-the-icosahedron-sphere
26. Bernardini, F., Mittleman, J., Rushmeier, H.E., Silva, C.T., Taubin, G.: The Ball-Pivoting Algorithm for Surface Reconstruction. IEEE Trans. Comput. Graph. 5(4), 349–359 (1999)
27. Surazhsky, V., Alliez, P., Gotsman, C.: Isotropic remeshing of surfaces: a local parameterization approach. In: 12th Intl. Meshing Roundtable, pp. 204–231 (2003)
28. Valette, S., Chassery, J.-M., Prost, R.: Generic remeshing of 3D triangular meshes with metric-dependent discrete Voronoi diagrams. IEEE Transactions on Visualization and Computer Graphics 14, 369–381 (2008)
29. Bossen, F.J., Heckbert, P.S.: A pliant method for anisotropic mesh generation. In: 5th Intl. Meshing Roundtable, pp. 63–74 (1996)
30. Cheng, S.-W., Dey, T.K., Levine, J.A.: A practical Delaunay meshing algorithm for a large class of domains. In: 16th Intl. Meshing Roundtable, pp. 477–494 (2007)
31. Dong-Ming, Y., Bruno, L., Yang, L., Feng, S., Wenping, W.: Isotropic Remeshing with Fast and Exact Computation of Restricted Voronoi Diagram. Comput. Graph. Forum 28(5), 1445–1454 (2009)
32. Cignoni, P., Rocchini, C., Scopigno, R.: Metro: measuring error on simplified surfaces. Computer Graphics Forum 17(2), 167–174 (1998)
33. Lee, A., Sweldens, W., Cowsar, P., Dobkin, D., Schroder, P.: Maps multiresolution adaptive parametrization of surfaces. In: SIGGRAPH (1998)
34. Khodakovsky, A., Litke, N., Schroder. P.: Globally smooth parameterizations with low distortion. In: ACM SIGGRAPH 2003, pp. 350–357 (2003)
35. Guskov, I.: Manifold-based approach to semiregular remeshing. Graphical Models 69, 1 (2007)

Multimedia Compression. Retrieval and Navigation

Exploring Protected Nature Through Multimodal Navigation of Multimedia Contents

Giovanni Signorello[1]([⊠]), Giovanni Maria Farinella[2], Giovanni Gallo[1,2],
Luciano Santo[3], Antonino Lopes[3], and Emanuele Scuderi[3]

[1] Centre for the Conservation and Management of Nature and Agroecosystems,
CUTGANA, University of Catania, Catania, Italy
`g.signorello@unict.it`
[2] Dipartimento di Matematica e Informatica, University of Catania, Catania, Italy
`{gfarinella,gallo}@dmi.unict.it`
[3] Xenia Progetti, Catania, Italy
`{luciano.santo,escuderi}@xeniaprogetti.it, antonino.lopes@xeniaspace.eu`

Abstract. We present a framework useful to explore naturalistic environments in a multimodal way. The multimedia information related to the different natural scenarios can be explored by the user in his home desktop through virtual tours from a web based interface, as well as from a dedicated mobile app during an on site tour of the considered natural reserves. A wearable station useful to a guide to broadcast multimedia content to the users' smartphones and tablet to better explain the naturalistic places has been developed as part of the framework. As pilot study, the framework has been employed in three different naturalistic reserves covering epigeal, hypogeum, and marine ecosystems.

Keywords: Virtual tours · Augmented reality · Multimodal fruition · Multimedia · Natural environments

1 Introduction

Current technologies enable users visiting a site of interest to enrich their experience thanks to an interactive access to different type of contents (text, audio, images, videos, 3D models, etc.). Recent computer vision based technologies enable generation, reconstruction and navigation of areas of interest, enabling also an augmented fruition experience. These technologies can be exploited to build virtual tours of sites which may be not physically accessible to the users (e.g. because remote, difficult to be accessed such as caves, or not accessible due to physical disabilities of the user).

Despite the multimodal fruition is already employed for cultural environments [1–7], it is not yet fully exploited for the navigation of naturalistic sites.

In this paper we propose a framework for the navigation of multimedia information related to a naturalistic environment which is composed by three main multimodal fruition components:

© Springer International Publishing Switzerland 2015
S. Battiato et al. (Eds.): ACIVS 2015, LNCS 9386, pp. 841–852, 2015.
DOI: 10.1007/978-3-319-25903-1_72

- an application for smartphones and tablets to allow the users of getting additional information about the natural environment.
- a web based navigation interface to allow users in retrieving multimedia information (e.g., text, audio, images, video) related to a naturalistic environment.
- a portable wearable station to allow a guide to broadcast multimedia contents to the users smartphones and tablets during a guided tour.

The overall framework gives the user the possibility to know about historical, naturalistic and cultural information of the natural sites to be explored. It allows persons with disabilities to have access to visual information related to the naturalistic places (e.g., a person with limited mobility can explore a cave with the web based virtual tour), as well as to multimedia enhanced contents (e.g., through subtitles for hearing impaired, or audio for visually impaired).

We selected three ecosystems with different peculiarities related to protected areas in Sicily (Fig. 1) as case studies for the exploitation of the proposed framework:

Terrestrial: the land of nature reserve "Complesso speleologico Villasmundo - S. Alfio" [8] has been considered (Fig. 1(a));

Cave: we chosen the nature reserve "Grotta Monello" [9] as hypogeum site (Fig. 1(b));

Marine: for this ecosystem we selected the marine protected area "Isole Ciclopi" [10] (Fig. 1(c)).

The paper is organised as following. In Section 2 the proposed framework is detailed. Section 3 concludes the paper providing hints for future works.

2   Proposed Fruition Framework

In this section we describe the proposed framework for the multimodal fruition of multimedia information related to natural sites. As previously mentioned, the framework is composed by three main components: a mobile app, a web based navigation system, and a wearable station. These three components allow a user to explore autonomously the site of interest from home (through virtual tour navigation) or onsite (with the help of the mobile app). The framework also allows to a guide to broadcast multimedia information directly on the smartphones or tablets of the user during a walking tour (through the wearable station) to better highlight peculiarity of the naturalistic site under exploration (e.g., broadcasting a thermal videos to better explain stalactite and stalagmite formation in a cave).

(a) *Complesso speleologico Villasmundo - S. Alfio*

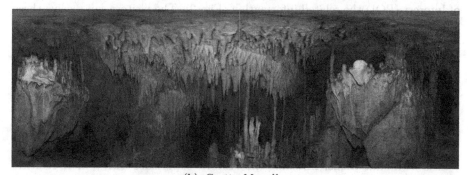

(b) *Grotta Monello*

(c) *Area Marina Protetta Isole Ciclopi*

Fig. 1. Panoramas related to the considered ecosystems: (a) terrestrial, (b) cave and (c) marine.

2.1 Fruition Through Mobile Application

The mobile application is a key element of the fruition Kit associated to each ecosystem considered in this project. It has been designed in such a way that it can be easily pre-installed into a mobile device (i.e., smartphones and tablets) that will be provided to visitors at the naturalistic site entrance. It can also be downloaded and installed on personal visitors' devices. To this aim, specific

Fig. 2. Info discovery at each POI through Mobile App.

instructions will be provided to visitors at the entrance. Thanks to this application, the visitors can follow the naturalistic itinerary, by getting in each Point of Interest (POI) the related information (Fig. 2). The visitors can receive three kinds of downloadable contents in each POI:

- Historical and cultural information included inside the application as built-in information (as text, pictures and, where available, a short video).
- Extra contents. Typically videos recorded during previous visits, downloadable through a Site Information Totem located at the naturalistic site entrance.
- Additional Info provided through the Augmented Reality (AR) technology. This will include textual contents, multimedia (audio, pictures), 3D models with animations, enriching the visitors' experience with a more realistic representation of particular elements/landscape related to the current POI.

In order to get access to AR info, visitor must be close to the POI panel, since AR activation requires the identification of a specific marker to start and show the related content. Vice-versa, simple multi-media and video contents will be built-in the application so to be available for the visitors also while walking from a POI to another. Access to AR info will be available again when they will be in front of the next Tag.

Since, nowadays, the most popular and used Operating Systems (OS) are Android and iOS, the mobile application targets these OS. In addition, because part of the naturalistic information is shown through the AR feature, all the technologies, able to support the AR on both these OS, have been properly investigated. As shown in Fig. 3, the AR plugin has to work on a game engine, which provides the needed development libraries in order to create the 3D environments. The game engine market offers several solutions, which could be used for the project. After a wide investigation, Unity 3D has been chosen since it is the most popular in creating 3D games, and it ensures continuous evolution and updates [11]. Unity 3D is a multi-platform Framework, which can adapt to both Android and iOS devices, thus allowing a strong reuse of 3D objects and animations. Furthermore, regarding the scripts to be created, Unity 3D supports an open-source implementation of .NET Framework called Mono Develop, which allows usage of C# language, thus allowing to easily adapt to the target OS.

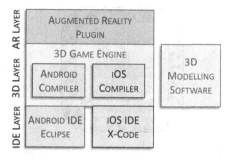

Fig. 3. Stack and relations of the development software.

This feature provides a remarkable reuse of code as well. A further strong point of Unity 3D is its full support of the physical simulation libraries (PhysX from Nvidia), which are needed to reproduce physical and mechanical events within the 3D environments (gravity, forces, collisions, and so on).

In the proposed fruition framework we have considered different 3D modeling software. The criteria used to select the most suitable one have been:

- support of 3D Rendering system, because it allows to create higher quality models.
- solutions with freeware license, because it often means a wide community of users, which suggest a continuous improvement of the solution itself.

According to those criteria, the number of possible software is reduced to eleven. Among these remaining solutions, Blender, Cinema 4D and ZModeler stand out because of their large diffusion; finally, Blender [14] has been selected because Unity 3D is capable to directly import the Blender's models from its native format, which is a strong feature because it avoids any possible compatibility issue.

In the mobile application we have considered different AR plugin. Criteria applied for selection have been:

- full compatibility of AR plugin with the chosen 3D game engine, Unity 3D;
- OS support from both Android and iOS for the AR plugin.

Based on these criteria, the final choice has been Vuforia (from Qualcomm) [15] since it is the most used by a larger community and, thanks to this, continuously updated with new features.

The implementation of the AR features requires marker creation since AR is activated by marker recognition. Attention must be paid to marker creation since the quality of the produced marker can strongly affect stability of the virtual 3D environment. The marker is an image, which contains a visual reference to the associated information which will be visualized when a mobile camera frames it. The mechanism is the following: when a mobile device detects a specific image through the applications computer-vision algorithm, it reacts by visualizing the

Fig. 4. An example of AR marker used in CET Project.

content associated to the image itself. So, in order to show the correct content, and to maintain a stable simulation of the 3D environment (avoiding lagging and blinking/unstable animations), the following criteria have to be applied while designing Tags related to the POIs:

- Univocal patterns. The target image must contain chromatic variations and not symmetrical shapes, thus avoiding any mis-recognition of the picture.
- High contrast. In order to improve recognition performances, high chromatic variations are the best practice to be applied; for this reason, Anti-Aliasing algorithms have to be reduced at most.
- High resolution. This means clearly-defined objects outlines to further improve reliable identification of the target picture.

Furthermore, in order to provide the project with homogeneous and coherent layout, marker has been designed as a "frame" target. This methodology uses the external border of the image to encrypt the information about the content to be shown. In addition, by using this approach, the central part of the image is available and even a static picture (e.g. the project Logo) can be positioned in this space, thus allowing representation of the project logo in each single Tag. This results into a homogeneous pretty graphical look for the overall solution. An example of the markers created for the CET project is shown in Fig. 4. It can be recognized the project logo in the central section and the characteristics of the external frame containing the encrypted ID information. In the example, the Frame is composed by few missing sections (blank spaces) and by many sections with different colors: both these characteristics allow a correct identification of the Tag, strongly reducing the mismatching probability.

Fig. 5 shows some screen shots of the mobile app interface for the Main Menu, the Circuits Selection Menu and POI Information. After selecting the ecosystem to visit, full list of possible associated POIs is shown on the left side of the screen, whilst cultural information are presented on the right. Further contents can be visualized thanks to three buttons at the end of the POI description:

- Play the video, to start a short video describing the POI;
- Augmented reality, to launch the AR;

Fig. 5. Mobile Application: Main menu (left), Circuit Selection menu (middle) and POI information (right).

- Start streaming, to activate the video-streaming coming from the handheld camera operated by the visit guide.

The AR feature can also be started by selecting a proper option into the Circuit Selection menu. Thanks to Vuforia AR enhanced libraries, the mobile application gives the possibility to touch and even to move 3D objects. Thus, allowing the visitors to easily interact with the simulated environment, the result is that the visitor can access a 3D menu, where options' selection is performed by touching the associated objects, behaving like 3D buttons.

This menu offers four different options to the visitors to get info about the POI:

- Text: this option opens a pop-up including all text information regarding the POI.
- 3D: in case of POI where a specific 3D model has been created, this option shows a 3D model and its animation.
- Pictures: this 3D button makes visible all the pictures related to the POI.
- Video: this option allows the visitor to watch a recorded video about the POI.

Thanks to this 3D menu, visitor can easily customize the visit experience according to his/her preference. Adults may be interested mainly in reading the information, or in seeing an audio-commented video. Young visitors might be interested in using the interaction offered by AR. In all these different fruition modalities, the developed mobile application supports the visitor by providing an interactive naturalistic experience.

2.2   Web Based Fruition

A classic and key fruition modality to promote protected natural sites is to make related information about their existence and peculiarities available on request. Almost all national parks worldwide have their own navigable website where images and videos are becoming more and more important to better capture the interests of the potential visitors. Despite the navigation of a website can be optimized to allow the users a better discovering of the multimedia information (e.g., thanks to the design of the web based user interface and considering advanced techniques for data search), this kind of remote fruition of natural places results very different from the experience that can been done by visitors during a walking tour in the protected natural site of interested.

To fill the gap between the web visit and the natural fruition experience we have included virtual tours as fruition modality. For each POI of the a certain ecosystem we have built a spherical panorama using Autopano [12] which have been then connected in a virtual tour through the use of Panotour [13]. Three examples of spherical panoramas obtained from the acquisition campaign of the terrestrial ecosystem are shown in Fig. 6. The navigable virtual tours have been enhanced by including a description and other multimedia information (images, videos, 3D Models) related to important details to be emphasised in the panoramas (e.g, images of important flowers' species which grow during the year in the terrestrial site have been included in the panoramas by considering their usual positions in the environment, images of protected fishes have been included for the underwater virtual tour of the protected marine area, videos have been included in panoramas of the hypogeum virtual tour reflecting where the fauna, e.g., bats, usually live). To open a multimedia content during the virtual tour, a web visitor can click on an icon which pops up when a specific detail is present in a certain view of the spherical panorama under exploration. Aerial videos of the terrestrial and marine ecosystems acquired with drones (i.e., quadricopters) have been also included as contents in the virtual tours.

The built virtual tours can been explored by simply opening a web browser. We have included them as contents of the mobile application discussed in Section 2.1. Because the panorama are georeferenced and associated to the predefined POIs available into the mobile app, the user can also use the panoramas during an onsite visit to explore a specific point of interest. In particular, considering that the built panoramas have been created taking into account of the gyroscope information, during a walking tour the users can activate the gyroscope fruition modality by pointing the mobile and associate a particular detail shown in the virtual panorama with the real visited environment.

The aforementioned virtual tours are embedded in the websites of the projects where the selected protected areas are available for the exploration. The developed web fruition modality allows also the advanced search among all the multimedia contents (images, videos, texts) related to the specific ecosystems by exploiting their metadata (e.g, acquisition time, geolocalization of images, data of videos related to recorded tours), tags and descriptions.

(a) *POI - Laghetto (Panorama 1)*

(b) *POI - Laghetto (Panorama 2)*

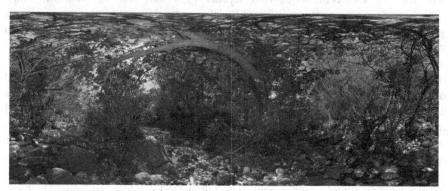

(c) *POI - Torrente Belluzza*

Fig. 6. Spherical panoramas (360° horizontal and 180° vertical field of view), of three different POIs related to the virtual tour of the terrestrial ecosystem Complesso speleologico Villasmundo - S. Alfio. The panoramas are navigable in the web based fruition modality.

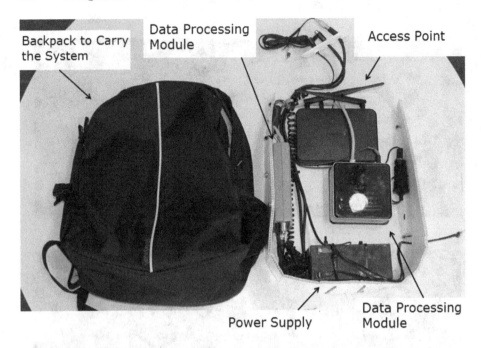

Fig. 7. The wearable system.

2.3   Wearable Station for on Site Walking Tours Fruition

A wearable station has been developed as support for the guide of a naturalistic tour (Fig. 7). Different acquisition sensors (Thermal camera, wearable video camera, underwater camera, microphones) can be connected to the developed system. A tablet is used by the guide to interact with the wearable system in order to activate the different fruition modalities and the contents broadcast. The information acquired during a guided tour can be stored for later usage (e.g., can be included as contents for the web based fruition system) or broadcasted to the mobile's users to provide additional information on specific peculiarities of a site (e.g., an underwater realtime video of the marine scenario broadcasted to the tourists' mobile during the boat tour, a thermal view of a cave scenario to observe bats behaviours, etc.). The wearable station is also able to broadcast the guided tour directly to the mobile app described in Section 2.1, on the web based fruition system as well as to a totem at the entrance of the naturalistic site. This allows remote user as well as people with disabilities to "join" the tour.

The wearable system is composed of three main modules:

Module 1: Portable acquisition system (below, backpack system), to be used by a guide. It can be connected to a thermal camera, a video camera and a microphone.

Module 2: A tablet which allows the interaction to the system in order to share the data collected on site and to acquire additional naturalistic contents during the tour. The tablet can be connected to a local network managed by the system in the backpack.

Module 3: A totem located at the entrance of the naturalistic site. The aim of the totem is to assure that people with disabilities (e.g., wheelchair's visitors) staying next to it, can activate the mobile app and enjoy the tour broadcasted by the guide through the wearable system.

3   Conclusions and Future Works

This paper presented a framework for the multimodal fruition of multimedia contents related to naturalistic sites. The proposed framework is composed by three main component: a mobile app, a web based fruition interface and a wearable station. Three different natural ecosystems in Sicily have been considered as scenarios. Computer vision technologies have been exploited to include augmented reality into the mobile app as well as to build virtual tours of the considered ecosystems. Thermal technology has been considered for the wearable station to allow a guide to better enhance hypogeum peculiarities. The framework is able to effectively present historical, natural and cultural information to the visitor allowing also a simple interaction with contents. Future works can be devoted to extend the framework to include new wearable devices (e.g., smart glasses) to better involve the visitors into the naturalistic experience. Finally, the plan is to extend the framwork to include other protected areas and reserves to allow people of enjoying more nature sites.

Acknowledgments. This work has been performed in the project CUP: G25C13000580007 with title "CET Fruizione Sostenibile Di circuiti Eco Turistici", co-funded by the European Union, Italy and Sicily, (CE) 1083/2006 (art. 69), (CE) 1828/2006 - 4.1.1 ATP PO FESR 2007-2013. The partners of the project are: CUT-GANA - University of Catania, Xenia Progetti, IMC Service and Giuseppe Maimone Editore. The authors would like to thank E. Amore, S. Costanzo, E. Mollica, L. Maimone and G. Distefano for their invaluable help.

References

1. Andolina, S., Santangelo, A., Cannella, M., Gentile, A., Agnello, F., Villa, B.: Multimodal virtual navigation of a cultural heritage site: the medieval ceiling of Steri in Palermo. In: Conference on Human System Interactions, pp. 562–567 (2009)
2. Del Bimbo, A., Ferracani, A., Lepera, V., Serra, G.: Da Cavalcaselle ad Argan: un' applicazione web per la fruizione di testimonianze di cultura artistica e letteraria. Studi di Memofonte (2011)
3. Schindler, G., Dellaert, F.: 4D Cities: Analyzing, Visualizing, and Interacting with Historical Urban Photo Collections. Journal of Multimedia **7**(2), 124–131 (2012)

4. Stanco, F., Tanasi, D., Gallo, G., Buffa, M., Basile, B.: Augmented Perception of the Past. The Case of Hellenistic Syracuse. Journal of Multimedia **7**(2), 211–216 (2012)
5. EXplora MUseum. http://www.explora-museum.com/
6. Second Canvas. http://www.secondcanvas.net/
7. Mannion, S.: Digital Learning Programmes Manager, British Museum - Augmented Reality: Beyond the Hype. The British Museum (2014)
8. Complesso speleologico Villasmundo - S. Alfio. http://www.cutgana.unict.it/aree-protette/riserva-naturale-integrale-complesso-speleologico-villasmundo-s-alfio
9. Monello, G.: http://www.cutgana.unict.it/aree-protette/riserva-naturale-integrale-grotta-monello
10. Area Marina Protetta Isole Ciclopi. http://www.cutgana.unict.it/aree-protette/area-marina-protetta-isole-ciclopi
11. Unity 3d. https://unity3d.com/
12. Autopano, Kolor. http://www.kolor.com/panorama-software-autopano-pro.html
13. Panotour, Kolor. http://www.kolor.com/ptp2
14. Blender. http://www.blender.org
15. Vuforia, Qualcom. https://www.qualcomm.com/products/vuforia

An H.264 Sensor Aided Encoder for Aerial Video Sequences with In-the-Loop Metadata Enhancement

Luca Cicala[1](✉), Cesario Vincenzo Angelino[1],
Nadir Raimondo[2], Enrico Baccaglini[2], and Marco Gavelli[2]

[1] CIRA, the Italian Aerospace Research Centre, 81043 Capua, Italy
{c.angelino,l.cicala}@cira.it
[2] Istituto Superiore Mario Boella, Torino, Italy
{raimondo,baccaglini,gavelli}@ismb.it

Abstract. Unmanned Aerial Vehicles (UAVs) are often employed to capture high resolution images in order to perform image mosaicking and/or 3D reconstruction. Images are usually stored on-board or sent to the ground using still image or video data compression. Still image encoders are preferred when low frame rates are involved, because video coding systems are based on motion estimation and compensation algorithms which fail when the motion vectors are significantly long. The latter is the case of low frame rate videos, in which the overlapping between subsequent frames is very small.

In this scenario, UAVs attitude and position metadata from the Inertial Navigation System (INS) can be employed to estimate global motion parameters without video analysis. However, a low complexity analysis can refine the motion field estimated using only the metadata.

In this work, we propose to use this refinement step in order to improve the position and attitude estimation produced by the navigation system with the aim of maximizing the encoder performance. Experiments on both simulated and real world video sequences confirm the effectiveness of the proposed approach.

1 Introduction

Unmanned Aerial Vehicles (UAV) are mainly employed in order to collect data [4]. Often this task is achieved using a set of on-board digital video cameras. Typical constraints of UAV missions are related to limited bandwidth, *e.g.*, when they operate Behind Line of Sight (BLOS), as well as battey life. In the first case, is unlikely to achieve a high frame rate acquisition especially because additional data gathered by the other payload sensors share the same data link and further reduce the bandwidth available to the video stream. On the other hand, when UAVs are used in order to acquire high resolution images for mosaicing and/or 3D reconstruction, there is no need to transmit the video stream and data are stored on-board. In this situation, the main mission contraint is the duration of the battery that supplies the vehicle.

© Springer International Publishing Switzerland 2015
S. Battiato et al. (Eds.): ACIVS 2015, LNCS 9386, pp. 853–863, 2015.
DOI: 10.1007/978-3-319-25903-1_73

It can be desirable to optimize the available resources (bandwidth, power supply) in order to improve the mission performance (more data, more flight time). When high frame rate videos are not a desiderata of the mission, one solution can be the reduction of the acquisition frame rate. In such a scenario, the video sequences are sent/stored at few frames per second (fps) and hence the overlap between two consecutive frames is lower than standard video streams. Usually at low frame rates the commercial video encorders fail in performing a good motion estimation/compensation, due to the length of the motion vectors (MVs) and to the prospective changes among frames that make hard the MV prediction. In such situations a still image encoder can be more or equally performing.

However, the motion of the UAV camera can be derived by the position and orientation data delivered by the on-board navigation systems. Moreover, the geometry of the overflight scene is approximately known and can be estimated using, for example, a laser altimeter, or the GPS (Global Positioning System) position and a Digital Terrain Model (DTM). With such an information, a global motion in the image plane can be inferred without video analysis. In [3], the authors investigate a low complexity encoder with GM based frame prediction and no block Motion Estimation (ME). For fly-over videos, it is shown that the encoder can achieve a 40% bit rate savings over a H.264 encoder with ME block size restricted to 8x8 and at lower complexity. In [10] and [12], global motion parameters are used to compensate frames that are used as reference for block ME using GM within standard MPEG-4 and H.264 codecs. In [5], the authors propose a framework tailored for UAV applications that uses the GM information and a homography model to code the stream using JPEG2000. In [11] and [2], the authors present modifications of the H.264/AVC encoder to initialize the MVs using the camera motion information from UAV sensors. These latter approaches perform block ME at a lower complexity, and transmit the derived block MVs. Both approaches guarantee the generation of a standard-compliant H.264/AVC bitstream thus no changes at the decoder side are required.

In this paper, we propose a sensor aided video encoder to be used at high resolution and low frame rates on aerial video sequences, following the studies reported in [2] and [1]. The encoder is obtained by modifying the open source implementation of H.264/AVC video coding standard (ISO/IEC, 2006) x264 [9] and fully compliant with H.264. As opposed to the previous works, here the problems of video coding and of the metadata correction are tackled in the same integrated design. This paper is focused on the improvements in terms of rate-distortion performance. Moreover, further aspects about a sensor aided encoder design, unpublished results and consideration, are reported.

The paper is organized as follows. Section 2 introduces the proposed sensor aided coding scheme with in-the-loop metadata correction. Section 3 describes how to improve the navigation data using the optical flow calculated by the proposed video encoder.In Section 4 experimental results are presented and in Section 5 conclusions and future work are discussed.

2   Sensor Aided Motion Imagery Coding

The structure of the proposed encoder is shown in Figure 1. A common H.264 encoding scheme is modified in order to take account of metadata (position and orientation) coming from the navigation system of the UAV. The camera is supposed to be internally and externally calibrated with respect to the navigation system. A Global ME (GME) is performed using metadata and a rough planar representation of the overflight scene (*i.e.*, assuming the ground to be an horizontal plane and using an altimeter to determine the distance of the aerial platform from the ground). A further MV refinement is performed by block matching, as proposed in the original version of x264, but starting from a more accurate initial estimate of the MVs, as provided by the GME module. Further, in addition to the scheme presented in the cited work, the proposed solution uses the estimated motion field as optical flow estimation for a state-of-the-art camera egomotion algorithm based on RANSAC homography model estimation and algebraic motion data extraction. The camera egomotion is used in loop with an unscented Kalman filter in order to refine the position and orientation data provided by the navigation system. Such use of the motion field will be discussed in the Subsection 3.

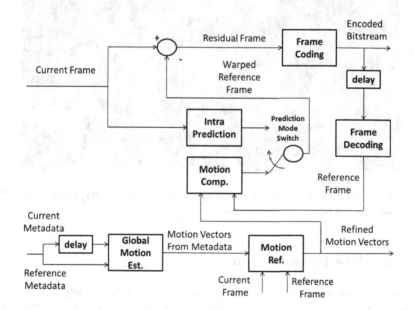

Fig. 1. Sensor aided video encoder scheme.

Figure 2 show a situation in which the ME algorithm of x264 fails while the proposed ME process, initialized with the sensor based GME, performs with success. The vectors in overlay represent the MVs found by the ME process. When an appropriate MV cannot be estimated, Intra prediction is performed instead.

Fig. 2. Top) x264 ME algorithm at low frame rates (0.5 fps). Down) Sensor aided ME. Motion vectors are represented with red arrows.

3   Metadata Enhancement

The overall data fusion architecture is sketched in Figure 3, where the sensor fusion block implements the Kalman filtering of the data provided by the Navigation System and the camera egomotion data from the video processing system. The camera egomotion module is based on the homography matrix, which relates homologous points in two different views of the same scene. In this work the correspondences are given by the refined MV provided by the encoder. Obtained a set of correspondences of points for a couple of successive frames, the homography matrix is estimated and then decomposed into his motion and structure parameters. The estimation and decomposition procedure is behind the scope of this work and will be omitted. The interested reader may refer to [6] and the reference therein.

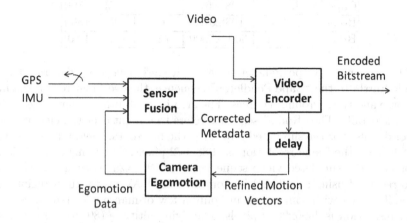

Fig. 3. Metadata improvement by sensor fusion.

The final purpose of the proposed sensor fusion algorithm is the estimation of the position and attitude of the camera, supposed internally and externally calibrated. The data fusion algorithm is based on the Unscented Kalman Filter (UKF) [13],[8], because dynamic and observation equations are non-linear in their original form. Like all the Kalman Filters, an UKF consists of two steps: model forecast and data assimilation. Sigma points are used to represent the current state distribution and to propagate the distribution to the next state and to the output. Mean and covariance of the transformed sigma points can be used to calculate the Kalman gain and to update the state prediction. Often such a filter has been used to estimate the pose of an UAV . In particular, in this work, we adopt the same solution proposed in [1]. Angular velocities and linear accelerations provided by the Inertial Measurement Unit (IMU) are used in the Kalman prediction step. GPS position and speed as well as camera egomotion parameters are used in the Kalman update step, in order to correct the position and the orientation drift due to the integration of the IMU data. A magnetometer is used also in order to correct the heading.

4   Experimental Results

4.1   Test Data

Three different aerial sequences [7] have been encoded and then their motion data have been processed. We considered low frame rate sequences (0.5 - 1 fps) and relative long MVs as this is often the case for UAV acquired high resolution video sequences. The characteristics of the three sequences are reported in Table 1.

Table 1. Aerial video sequences characteristics.

Video Seq.	FR [fps]	Res [pix x pix]	h-FOV [deg]	Speed [km/h]	Alt [m]
Cape Pend.	1	1088x672	60	250	800
Rome	0.5	1088x672	60	250	800
Brezza	1	3000x2000	73.7	2	80

The sequences "Cape Pendleton" and "Rome" have been generated using Google Earth. In the "Cape Pendleton" sequence, the overflight region is a military base and the surrounding areas. The area is substantially homogeneous and with few details. The "Rome" sequence refers to a flight over the city of Rome, rich of details. For the simulated sequences the horizontal Field Of View (FOV) is 60 degrees, the frame resolution is 1088x672 pixels. The flying altitude is 800 m for both the simulated video sequences. The "Brezza" sequence is part of a video recorded using a real multi-rotorcraft mini-UAV over a rural region poor of details (grass with some trees and only a few of man-made structures). The frame resolution is 3000x2000 pixels. The flying altitude (80 m) is much lower than the simulated video sequences. The horizontal FOV is 73.7 degrees.

Ground truth metadata are provided by the image generator for the synthetic video sequences, while for the "Brezza" sequence, they are estimated from multiple views by a bundle adjustment technique. However, in the experiments a noisy version of these metadata has been generated according to the sensor model described in [1]. The parameters of the sensor model, as reported in the cited paper, are extracted by the datasheet of a well known commercial GPS aided Attitude and Heading Reference System commonly employed in aeronautical applications.

4.2   Encoder Settings

The x264 library offers several presets. Each preset is a collection of parameters which are set in order to get a good trade-off between quality and coding time for different application scenarios. The "medium" preset is general purpose, and is compatible with low computationally demanding scenarios. Because in this scenario the video frame rate is very low (i.e. 0.5 fps), a time demanding preset, i.e. the "slower", can be also considered, in order to reach better encoding quality. These preset options for the proposed modified x264 encoder are labeled in the figures as "medium" and "slower", instead the same configurations in the original x264 encoder are labeled with the prefix "x264", and are respectively "x264_medium" and "x264_slower".

The sensor aided encoder often uses only one reference frame in the GOP, because the low overlap among the frames. For this reason, the comparison with the reference x264 encoder with only one reference frame in the GOP is presented. In this case only the "medium" preset is reported. The corresponding label is "x264_medium_ref1".

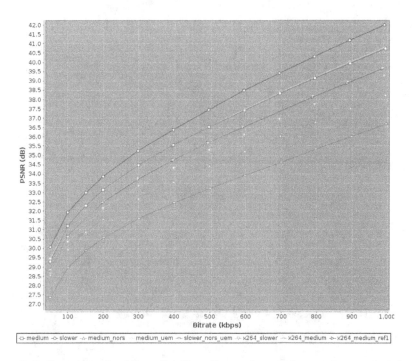

Fig. 4. R-D Curves for the "Cape Pendleton" sequence, with a resolution of 1088x672 pixels and a frame rate of 1 fps.

Two other coding option are specifically presented for the proposed sensor aided encoder. A first option excludes the refinement step of the ME through video analysis. This option is labeled as "medium_nors", where the word "medium" indicates the used preset and the acronym "nors" is for NO Refinement Search.

A further option is added in order to force the sensor aided encoder to perform the ME also when Intra coding is possible. This processing step can be useful in order to produce more accurate motion field that can be used by the sensor fusion module. These experiments, reported for the preset "medium", are labeled as "medium_uem" or "medium_nors_uem", where the latter acronym is for Use Estimated MVs.

4.3 R-D Performance

In the following experiments the Rate-Distortion (R-D) performance of the proposed sensor aided encoder, using corrected metadata, is compared to that of the x264 implementation of H.264. Eight rate-distortion curves are plotted in Figures 4-6 for each tested video sequence. On the x-label the encoding bitrate is reported, while on the y-label the PSNR (Peak Signal to Noise Ratio), that is a commonly used objective video quality measure.

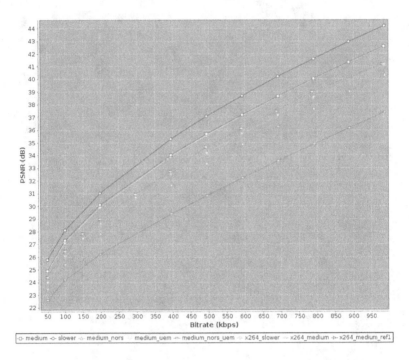

Fig. 5. R-D curves for the "Rome" sequence, with a resolution of 1088x672 pixels and a frame rate of 0.5 fps.

A first observation is that the proposed sensor aided encoder performs better than the reference x264 encoder both with the medium and the slower preset. For example, for the "Cape Pendleton" video sequence, at 400 kbps, the PSNR of the proposed encoder is 35.41 dB versus 34.76 dB of the reference with the medium preset, and 36.24 dB versus 34.31 dB, with the slower preset. For the sequence "Rome", at the same bitrate of 400 kbps, the PSNR of the sensor aided encoder is 33.93 dB versus 32.74 dB of the reference with the medium preset, and is 35.18 dB versus 32.50 dB for the slower preset.

The proposed sensor aided encoder has a similar behaviour on real video sequences also. On the sequence "Brezza", for example, at 3250 kbps, the PSNR is 35.12 dB versus 34.48 dB of x264.

It is worth to notice that the reference x264 encoder uses a complex GOP analysis in order to optimize the use of the I, P and B frames. The proposed sensor aided implementation instead, at the current stage of development, uses a more simple strategy based on only one I frame per GOP and all P frames (this strategy is reasonable, due to the continuity of the camera motion). For this reason it is more correct to compare the "medium" curve with the "x264_medium_1Ref" curve, instead of the "x264_medium" curve. Comparing these couples of curves, the proposed solution can be further appreciated.

From the figures it is also possible to note that the "slower" preset has lower quality than "medium" preset for the reference x264 encoder. This is due to

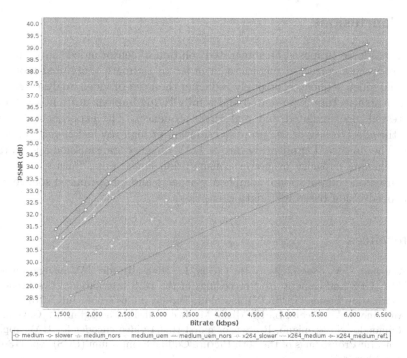

Fig. 6. R-D curves for the "Brezza" sequence, with a resolution of 3000x2000 pixels and a frame rate of 1 fps.

the large number of B-frames selected by the x264 GOP decision algorithm. In the considered scenarios, in which there is low overlap among successive frames, the use of B frames has bad effects on the output quality. The proposed sensor aided implementation, instead, uses the same GOP structure for the two different presets, that is similar to the best option selected by x264.

Analyzing only the sensor aided implementations, other considerations can be made. Comparing the "medium" and "medium_nors" curves, it is clear that the motion search refinement step, based on video analysis, is essential to reach high rate distortion performance. Instead, comparing the "medium_nors" and "medium_nors_uem" curves, it is possible to conclude that a ME pure approach cannot be preferred to a combined strategy approach, based both on Intra and Inter block prediction, at least in the case in which video analysis is not used to refine the MVs. The comparison between the "medium" and the "medium_uem" curves, however show that, using the video analysis for MVs refinement, also don't considering the Intra option, it is possible to reach a performance near to the combined approach (both Intra and Inter blocks). In the case of Cape Pendleton and Rome, the gap is negligible.

In general, the metadata correction performance is generally very good (the standard deviation of the orientation estimation error results less than 0.2 degrees for all the video sequences), so that the obtained encoding results are very similar to that obtained using the ground truth (difference in PSNR less than 0.15 dB).

5 Conclusions

In this work we proposed an integrated solution of sensor aided video encoder, able to process corrected metadata in order to estimate the global motion in an aerial video sequences, strongly reducing the need of video analysis. A novel encoder architecture is presented and a fully H.264 implementation is proposed and tested, on simulated and real video sequences. The experimental results show the effectiveness of the proposed solution at high resolution and low frame rates. The suggested applications are to UAV imagery transmission and storage, under channel capacity or power consumption constraints. Future works will be focused on computational complexity aspects and on optimized solutions for high speed vision based metadata corrections.

References

1. Angelino, C.V., Baraniello, V.R., Cicala, L.: High altitude UAV navigation using IMU, GPS and camera. In: Proceedings of the 16th International Conference on Information Fusion (FUSION), Istanbul, Turkey, pp. 647–654, July 2013
2. Angelino, C.V., Cicala, L., De Mizio, M., Leoncini, P., Baccaglini, E., Gavelli, M., Raimondo, N., Scopigno, R.: Sensor aided H.264 video encoder for UAV applications. In: Proceedings of the 30th Picture Coding Symposium (PCS), pp. 173–176, December 2013
3. Bhaskaranand, M., Gibson, J.: Global motion assisted low complexity video encoding for uav applications. IEEE Journal of Selected Topics in Signal Processing **9**(1), 139–150 (2015)
4. Chen, X.l., Zhang, S.C., Liu, J.: Design of UAV video compression system based on H.264 encoding algorithm. In: Proceedings of the 1st International Conference on Electronic and Mechanical Engineering and Information Technology (EMEIT), Harbin, China, vol. 5, pp. 2619–2622, August 2011
5. Gong, J., Zheng, C., Tian, J., Wu, D.: An image-sequence compressing algorithm based on homography transformation for unmanned aerial vehicle. In: Proceedings of the 1st International Symposium on Intelligence Information Processing and Trusted Computing (IPTC), Huanggang, China, pp. 37–40, October 2010
6. Hartley, R.I., Zisserman, A.: Multiple View Geometry in Computer Vision, 2nd edn. Cambridge University Press (2004). ISBN 0521540518
7. ISMB/CIRA: Test sequences (2013). http://www.ismb.it/mise_cira
8. Julier, S.J., Uhlmann, J.K.: Unscented filtering and nonlinear estimation. Proceedings of the IEEE **92**(3), 401–422 (2004)
9. Merritt, L., Rahul, V.: X264: A high performance h.264/avc encoder (2006). http://neuron2.net/library/avc/overview_x264_v8_5.pdf
10. Morimoto, C., Burlina, P., Chellappa, R.: Video coding using hybrid motion compensation. In: Proceedings of the 4th International Conference on Image Processing (ICIP), Santa Barbara, California, USA, vol. 1, pp. 89–92, October 1997
11. Soares, P.H.F.T., Pinho, M.D.S.: Video compression for UAV applications using a global motion estimation in the H.264 standard. In: Proceedings of the 6th International Workshop on Telecommunications, Santa Rita do Sapucaì, Brazil, vol. 1, May 2013

12. Steinbach, E., Wiegand, T., Girod, B.: Using multiple global motion models for improved block-based video coding. In: Proceedings of the 6th International Conference on Image Processing (ICIP), Kobe, Japan, vol. 2, pp. 56–60, October 1999
13. Van Der Merwe, R., Wan, E.: Sigma-point Kalman filters for probabilistic inference in dynamic state-space models. In: Proceedings of the Workshop on Advances in Machine Learning, Montreal, Canada, June 2003

Buffering Hierarchical Representation of Color Video Streams for Interactive Object Selection

François Merciol and Sébastien Lefèvre$^{(\boxtimes)}$

Université Bretagne Sud, UMR 6074 IRISA, 56000 Vannes, France
{francois.merciol,sebastien.lefevre}@irisa.fr

Abstract. Interactive video editing and analysis has a broad impact but it is still a very challenging task. Real-time video segmentation requires carefully defining how to represent the image content, and hierarchical models have shown their ability to provide efficient ways to access color image data. Furthermore, algorithms allowing fast construction of such representations have been introduced recently. Nevertheless, these methods are most often unable to address (potentially endless) video streams, due to memory limitations. In this paper, we propose a buffering strategy to build a hierarchical representation combining color, spatial, and temporal information from a color video stream. We illustrate its relevance in the context of interactive object selection.

Keywords: Hierarchical representation · α-tree · Interactive segmentation · Color video processing

1 Introduction

Proliferation of high-resolution low-cost digital video recorders results in vast amounts of video data that need to be further processed for personal or professional use. Efficient video processing solutions are required to allow popular management of video files and librairies on standard computers as well as mobile terminals (e.g., tablets, smartphones). Indeed, real-time processing allowing interactivity with the user greatly eases the subsequent user acceptability of the proposed solutions. We focus in this paper on object selection (or segmentation), that is one of the most desired tools for video editing and analysis.

Video segmentation gathers a strong research interest for more than a decade [2–4,8,14,17,22]. To illustrate, one of the most recent techniques [23] dedicated to fast segmentation allows a processing frame rate of 1.3-1.5 fps, far below current video broadcast standards. Such an example is representative of the state-of-the-art where accuracy is sought at the cost of computational complexity. Interactive object selection from color video streams is thus hardly achievable with existing techniques.

We address here this issue and propose a new interactive object selection technique. Efficiency is achieved through the design of a hierarchical representation that replaces the raw (pixel) dataset in the different steps of the process.

© Springer International Publishing Switzerland 2015
S. Battiato et al. (Eds.): ACIVS 2015, LNCS 9386, pp. 864–875, 2015.
DOI: 10.1007/978-3-319-25903-1_74

While such an approach has already shown promising results [12], it requires storing in memory the representation of the whole video sequence. We build upon this previous work and propose here a way to deal with (potentially endless) video streams without facing memory limitations, inspired from recent works on streaming or causal segmentation [5,7,13,18,25]. Furthermore, we introduce an improved object selection scheme based on bounding box input provided by the user. We also increase robustness to occlusions and motion w.r.t. our previous work [12].

The rest of the paper is organized as follows. In Sec. 2, we recall the existing work our method builds upon, namely the α-tree and its use in image/video segmentation. Our contribution is described in Sec. 3, while Sec. 4 presents its experimental evaluation on a standard dataset. We end the paper with concluding remarks and future directions.

2 Background

Our method builds upon a previous work [12] based on a hierarchical structure called the α-tree. Both are recalled in this section.

2.1 The α-Tree Model

An α-tree is a multiscale representation of an image through its α-connected components (or α-CCs). While it finds roots in early work in computer vision, it has been revisited only recently by Soille and Ouzounis [15,19]. This paradigm is very related to the single linkage procedure used in data clustering. It provides a compact representation of the image that allows its real-time processing. Furthermore, efficient algorithms have been recently introduced to ensure fast computation of this representation from complex images [9].

The concept of α-CC is an extension of the connected component (or CC). We recall that the latter is defined as a set of adjacent pixels that share the same value (either scalar for panchromatic images, or vectorial for multi- or hyperspectral ones). Representing an image by its CCs allows for higher-level analysis (similarly to computer vision techniques relying on superpixels). However, the possibly great number of CCs in an image prevents their practical use. Indeed, adjacent pixels may belong to the same structure but have slightly different values, thus belonging to different CCs. The concept of α-CC has been introduced to allow such slight variations, leading to the following definition: an α-CC is a set of adjacent pixels that share similar values i.e., values with a difference lower or equal to a threshold α. The α-CC of a pixel p will thus contain all pixels q that can be reached with a path over neighboring pixels p_i $\langle p_1 = p, \ldots, p_n = q \rangle$ from p to q such that $d(p_i, p_{i+1}) \leq \alpha$ (d being a predefined dissimilarity measure). The complexity and number of α-CCs are directly related to α. It allows building a hierarchical representation of an image, and performing subsequent multiscale analysis (e.g., in an object-oriented strategy). This representation is called an α-tree. Each level of the tree is indexed by an α value, and its nodes are the corresponding α-CCs. A leaf in the tree is a 0-CC i.e., a standard CC in the image. Increasing α leads to the connection of α-CCs, resulting in the creation of higher nodes in the tree, until the root that contains the whole image.

2.2   Video Segmentation Based on α-Tree

In a previous work [12], we have already proposed to use the α-tree to perform video segmentation. However, the tree was computed on the complete video sequence assuming space-time connectivity and representing the video as a spatio-temporal volume. More precisely, each pixel was defined by a triplet (x, y, t) with two spatial and one temporal coordinates, and the neighborhood was using the 6-connectivity (i.e., two pixels (x, y, t) and (x', y', t') are neighbors if $|x - x'| + |y - y'| + |t - t'| = 1$). The dissimilarity measure d used to build the α-CC is the Chebyshev distance computed between the colors $\mathbf{c} = (r, g, b)$ and $\mathbf{c}' = (r', g', b')$ of adjacent pixels p and p', i.e. $d(p, p') = \max(|r - r'|, |g - g'|, |b - b'|)$. This allows keeping the number of possible dissimilarity values as low as the input range of each color component (e.g. 256 levels), conversely to Euclidean distance. The height of the resulting α-tree is then bounded by this range. RGB color channels were used directly in order to avoid the additional cost of a color space transformation.

Once the α-tree representation of the full video sequence is computed, it is enriched by associating some features (size, average brightness and hue) to each node of the tree. Such features are computed incrementally, starting from the leaves of the tree up to the root, thus limiting the computational complexity. Averaging hue information is done in a specific manner to ensure the reliability of this feature (see [12] for a complete description of the method). The video representation is then ready to be analyzed for interactive segmentation. To do so, the user picks one pixel from a video frame, i.e. a leaf in the α-tree. Object selection is then achieved through a traversal of the tree in order to find the most relevant node in the path from the selected leaf to the tree root. More precisely, the size (number of pixels) of each traversed node is analyzed, and if this measure is stable for a significant number of levels in the tree, the node is used to define the object selection. Let us note that this process shares some similarity with the extraction of Maximally Stable Extremal Regions (MSER) [11].

While our previous method [12] showed promising results, it came with several limitations: (i) the α-tree has to be computed on the full video sequence before any further processing (such as interactive object selection); long video sequences, as well as (potentially endless) video streams cannot be addressed; (ii) to perform interactive object selection, user input consists of a single pixel only (i.e., a leaf in the tree); such an initialization is very error prone, and hardly provides an accurate description of complex objects (with heterogeneous content); (iii) the selection process ends with a single node from the tree, while the object might be better represented by several nodes with no heritage relations; (iv) the α-tree is computed on the spatio-temporal volume, assuming spatio-temporal continuity of the objects; this is not the case in the presence of object motion and occlusions, that could result in disconnected components that might have only the root as common ancestor in the tree. These different issues are addressed in the new method proposed in this paper.

3   Proposed Method

The method we are proposing in this paper starts with a first input from the user to define the initial contour of the object. It then propagates the selection in the following frames in an online setting. An additional step is added to deal with spatio-temporal discontinuities. We describe here these different steps.

3.1   User-Driven Object Selection

The video object selection scheme is interactive. In a frame of the video sequence (generally the second frame, see discussion below), we ask the user to delineate the object of interest through a bounding box (A in Fig. 1). We assume the object to be completely included in this box. We also compute two α-trees, one for the frame where user selection occurs (Fig. 2(b)) and one for its immediate preceding frame (Fig. 2(a)). Both α-trees are merged into a single tree (Fig. 2(c)). The goal is then to identify, among the nodes of this merged α-tree, the ones corresponding to the selected object. To do so, we first remove all nodes of the tree that overlap the background, or in other words that are not completely included in the box provided by the user (an example of such discarded node is C in Fig. 1). This can be efficiently achieved starting from the leaves corresponding to the pixels included in the box, and scanning their ancestors until the latter span over the initial bounding box. The last (i.e., closest to the root) ancestors that fit in the bounding box are kept. The selection thus results in one or several nodes. When a node is selected, all its children are too. In other words, one or several subtrees (i.e., a forest) are extracted from the α-tree to denote the selected object. However, we have observed that this strategy was prone to foreground and background mixing, since it might select nodes that are located on the interior edges of the user box. We thus add an additional constraint, relying on a reduced user selection (D in Fig. 1) built automatically using a given reducing ratio (here 50%). Nodes whose centers do not belong to this reduced zone are also discarded from the object selection (an example is E in Fig. 1). To ease understanding, only the user input and the selected objects are shown in the left image of Fig. 1. Figure 2(d) also provide some tree illustration.

3.2   Selection Propagation in the Video Stream

After having refined a selection from a user input, the next step is to propagate it in the following frames of the video sequence. Figure 2 illustrates the propagation process. This step is required since, as already stated, we do not compute an α-tree for the full video sequence but we rather process the video on a frame-by-frame basis. This allows for processing very long video sequences as well as video streams (i.e. potentially endless). The selection process described

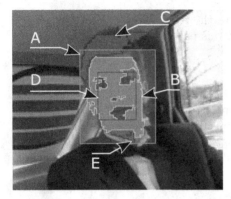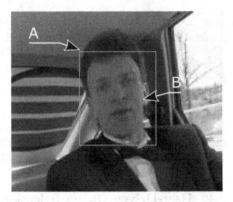

Fig. 1. Illustration of the selection process: user input (A, light green), nodes corresponding to selected object (B, yellow), discarded nodes due to background overlapping (C, orange/red), reduced user selection (D, dark green), and discarded nodes due to non strong overlapping with reduced user selection (E, orange/red).

previously and applied on an initial frame leads to two α-trees respectively built from this frame (a) and its preceding frame (b), that are subsequently merged into a single unified tree (c). To do so, temporal connectivity is considered in computing the α-CCs, possibly leading to merging two nodes at lower α values than if considering the individual trees (useless tree edges are shown dashed). Once a selection has been defined by the user (d), we keep only leaves corresponding to the current frame. Selection propagation in the next frame requires first computing the tree in this new frame (e), and then to merge both trees (f) while keeping the labels for selected nodes. The temporal connectivity allows merging spatially disconnected nodes. Again, the merged tree is filtered to keep only leaves corresponding to current pixels (g). Furthermore, in order to limit the memory footprint, we also prune the tree and remove the intermediary nodes that are not on the selection branch, thus forgetting outdated information. But storing the connectivity information (spatial from the previous frame as well as temporal for the last couple of frames) results in a tree that could not have been built from a single frame only, e.g. see (e) and (g). The process is repeated all along the video sequence, with each successive frame leading to a new individual tree (h), merged tree (i), and filtered one (j) where selection is propagated. In this last example (g)-(i), we can observe that the selection can extend to some new objects if their color similarity to the selection becomes higher. Duplicate nodes (shown in grey) along the path from the selection to the root are temporarily buffered to allow reconnection/disconnection operations.

3.3 Dealing with Spatio-Temporal Discontinuities

Extracting the object of interest in the frame where user input has been provided is much easier than in the following frames. Indeed, the selection is propagated from one frame to the next using the scheme described previously, and the selection accuracy might decrease along time. Model updating is required and

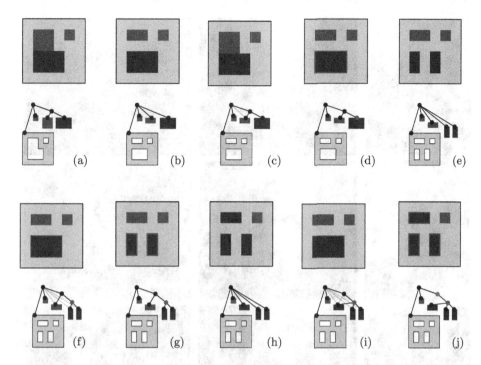

Fig. 2. Illustration of the buffering process: individual trees (a,b,e,h), after merging (c,f,i) and filtering (d,g,j). Selected nodes, useless relations, and residual nodes are shown in red, dashed, and in grey respectively.

several strategies are available. We have explored several automatic strategies but their performances were not satisfying, so we rather chose here to rely on a manual strategy. It needs to identify the frames for which an updated input is required from the user, and we use here a size criterion. More precisely, once a selection has been propagated in an incoming frame, we compare the size of the updated selection with the size of the last user input. If both sizes differ from a ratio higher than T (here $T = 2$), we consider the selection to be inaccurate since it corresponds to either a too small or too large component. This occurs in the presence of spatio-temporal discontinuities, especially observed with object motion and occlusion.

4   Experiments

We evaluate the proposed approach on a standard dataset and compare our results with the state-of-the-art. More precisely, we use the SegTrack dataset [20] that contains 6 video sequences, with length of 20–70 images of rather small size (from 320×240 pixels to 414×352 pixels), together with a reference segmentation (ground truth).

For the sake of illustration, we compare our method with some recent techniques based on selection propagation that have reported results on this dataset

Fig. 3. Sample frames for the 3 video sequences from SegTrack used for quantitative evaluation: Birdfall, Parachute, and Girl (Tab. 1).

[10,21]. Both methods rely on probabilistic modeling with Markov Random Fields (MRF), but while the former operates on pixels, the latter imposes a space-time graph structure on the data. The 3 video sequences used in this paper, BIRDFALL, PARACHUTE, and GIRL, are illustrated in Fig. 3. An illustration of the results obtained with our method is given in Fig. 4, with the error rate per frame plotted in Fig. 5. On this PARACHUTE sequence, user selection has been required 4 times. This is due to the complexity of the video sequence, with some important changes in both object illumination and pose. While these user inputs allow preventing a severe increase of the error rate, they were not sufficient enough to keep it as low as on the first frames of the video sequence (for which the tracking was less challenging).

Comparative results are provided in Tab. 1. We can see that the proposed method performs slightly better than [21], but worse than [10]. Let us recall that we are not using any motion information conversely to the state-of-the-art. Furthermore, the proposed approach is still deterministic while probabilistic

Table 1. Comparative results for interactive object selection. Accuracy is expressed as the average number (and ratio) of mis-segmented pixels (false positive plus false negative) per frame. Runtime is provided in seconds. Results are reported from [10].

	Ours	[21]	[10]
birdfall	313 (0.003)	405 (0.005)	189 (0.002)
parachute	1337 (0.009)	1042 (0.007)	228 (0.002)
girl	6632 (0.052)	8575 (0.067)	2883 (0.023)
time	11–27	480–600	120–180

Fig. 4. Sample results for the Parachute video sequence (frames 2, 12, 30, 31, 34, 35, 39, 40, 51): manual selection is shown in green, selected regions in blue, ground truth pixels are brighter.

models have achieved great successes in computer vision for decades. Besides, the α-tree model considered here leads to some spatio-temporal chaining effects that cannot be overcome without any post-processing or constraint imposed on the connectivity between pixels. These different limitations are directions for future work.

More interestingly, we can observe from Tab. 1 that the proposed solution based on tree structures brings a significant gain in terms of performance. The reported runtime of our method is 6 – 11 times less than [10], and 22 – 43

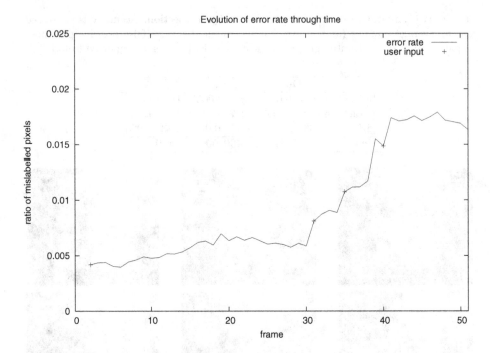

Fig. 5. Evolution of the error rate (ratio of mislabelled pixels per frame). Crosses denote frames where user input was required.

times less than [21] (let us note however that the implementation and runtime details, e.g. coding langage, CPU speed, etc. are not provided in [10,21]). Our method has been benchmarked on a Java implementation and a standard laptop configuration, thus allowing fair comparison with recent works from the state-of-the-art. We have observed CPU time wastes due to the Java Garbage Collector that call for further optimization.

We believe that it is possible to build upon the proposed technique to introduce more complex (but still tree-based) video analysis strategies, to ensure both high accuracy and efficiency. To illustrate, let us recall that many video segmentation methods rely on a first segmentation into superpixels, that might be easily produced by cutting the tree. But while extracting superpixels from a SegTrack video requires at least 500 seconds with the most efficient techniques from the state-of-the-art [24] (measured with a Dual Quad-core Intel Xeon CPU E5620 2.4 GHz, 16GB RAM running Linux), our algorithm is able to provide a set of superpixels in less than 50 seconds with a Java implementation and a standard laptop configuration (Dual-core Intel Core CPU i5-3320M 2.60GHz, 6GB RAM running Linux).

5 Conclusion

In this paper, we have explored a new way to represent video pixels through a hierarchical representation. Such a representation has been used to derive an efficient solution allowing interactive object selection from a color video stream. Results obtained on the SegTrack standard dataset are promising, with accuracies similar to the state-of-the-art but computation times much lower. Nevertheless, experimental evaluation and comparison with state-of-the-art has to be pursued, especially considering other streaming strategies recently introduced in the literature [5,7,13,18,25].

While efficiency is definitely a strength of the proposed solution, segmentation accuracy could be further improved to meet user requirements. This can be achieved following several directions. Chaining effects, a known drawback of single-linkage representations such as the α-tree, can be alleviated using more complex tree models, e.g. binary partition tree [6,16]. Improving the way the selection is propagated between two successive frames can be ensured by exploiting the object motion that is not taken into account yet. Furthermore, the introduction of probabilistic models would strengthen the robustness of the method and could also lead to better accuracy (as demonstrated recently with binary partition tree-based image segmentation [1].

More generally, we also consider applying the hierarchical representations to other computer vision problems that are facing computational and memory issues. Indeed, the proposed framework is particularly adapted to online settings. As such, a fully automatic solution that will not require manual initialization will be also appealing for addressing big video data.

References

1. Al-Dujaili, A., Merciol, F., Lefèvre, S.: GraphBPT: an efficient hierarchical data structure for image representation and probabilistic inference. In: Benediktsson, J.A., Chanussot, J., Najman, L., Talbot, H. (eds.) Mathematical Morphology and Its Applications to Signal and Image Processing. LNCS, vol. 9082, pp. 301–312. Springer, Heidelberg (2015)
2. Bai, X., Wang, J., Simons, D., Sapiro, G.: Video snapcut: robust video object cutout using localized classifiers. In: Proceedings of the SIGGRAPH, pp. 1–11 (2009)
3. Boykov, Y., Funka-Lea, G.: Graph cuts and efficient n-d image segmentation. International Journal of Computer Vision 70(2), 109–131 (2006)
4. Boykov, Y., Jolly, M.: Interactive graph cuts for optimal boundary and region segmentation of objects in n-d images. In: Proceedings of the ICCV, pp. 105–112 (2001)
5. Couprie, C., Farabet, C., LeCun, Y., Najman, L.: Causal graph-based video segmentation. In: IEEE International Conference on Image Processing, pp. 4249–4253 (2013)
6. Dorea, C., Pardas, M., Marques, F.: A motion-based binary partition tree approach to video object segmentation. IEEE International Conference on Image Processing 2, 430–433 (2005)

7. Gangapure, V.N., Nanda, S., Chowdhury, A.S., Jiang, X.: Causal video segmentation using superseeds and graph matching. In: Liu, C.-L., Luo, B., Kropatsch, W.G., Cheng, J. (eds.) GbRPR 2015. LNCS, vol. 9069, pp. 282–291. Springer, Heidelberg (2015)

8. Grundmann, M., Kwatra, V., Han, M., Essa, I.: Efficient hierarchical graph based video segmentation. IEEE CVPR (2010)

9. Havel, J., Merciol, F., Lefèvre, S.: Efficient schemes for computing α-tree representations. In: Hendriks, C.L.L., Borgefors, G., Strand, R. (eds.) ISMM 2013. LNCS, vol. 7883, pp. 111–122. Springer, Heidelberg (2013)

10. Jain, S.D., Grauman, K.: Supervoxel consistent foreground propagation in video. In: Fleet, D., Pajdla, T., Schiele, B., Tuytelaars, T. (eds.) ECCV 2014, Part IV. LNCS, vol. 8692, pp. 656–671. Springer, Heidelberg (2014)

11. Matas, J., Chum, O., Urban, M., Pajdla, T.: Robust wide-baseline stereo from maximally stable extremal regions. Image and vision computing $22(10)$, 761–767 (2004)

12. Merciol, F., Lefèvre, S.: Fast image and video segmentation based on α-tree multiscale representation. In: International Conference on Signal Image Technology Internet Systems, Naples, Italy, November 2012

13. Mukherjee, D., Wu, Q.: Streaming spatio-temporal video segmentation using gaussian mixture model. In: IEEE International Conference on Image Processing, pp. 4388–4392 (2014)

14. Interactive image segmentation by matching attributed relational graphs: Noma, A., Graciano, A., Jr, R.C., Consularo, L., I. Bloch. Pattern Recognition 45, 1159–1179 (2012)

15. Ouzounis, G.K., Soille, P.: Pattern spectra from partition pyramids and hierarchies. In: Soille, P., Pesaresi, M., Ouzounis, G.K. (eds.) ISMM 2011. LNCS, vol. 6671, pp. 108–119. Springer, Heidelberg (2011)

16. Palou, G., Salembier, P.: Hierarchical video representation with trajectory binary partition tree. In: IEEE Conference on Computer Vision and Pattern Recognition, pp. 2099–2106 (2013)

17. Price, B., Morse, B., Cohen, S.: Livecut: learning-based interactive video segmentation by evaluation of multiple propagated cues. In: IEEE International Conference on Computer Vision (2009)

18. Pu, S., Zha, H.: Streaming video object segmentation with the adaptive coherence factor. In: IEEE International Conference on Image Processing, pp. 4235–4238 (2013)

19. Soille, P.: Constrained connectivity for hierarchical image partitioning and simplification. IEEE Transactions on Pattern Analysis and Machine Intelligence $30(7)$, 1132–1145 (2008)

20. Tsai, D., Flagg, M., Rehg, J.: Motion coherent tracking with multi-label MRF optimization. British Machine Vision Conference (2010)

21. Vijayanarasimhan, S., Grauman, K.: Active frame selection for label propagation in videos. In: Fitzgibbon, A., Lazebnik, S., Perona, P., Sato, Y., Schmid, C. (eds.) ECCV 2012, Part V. LNCS, vol. 7576, pp. 496–509. Springer, Heidelberg (2012)

22. Wang, J., Bhat, P., Colburn, R., Agrawala, M., Cohen, M.: Interactive video cutout. ACM Transactions on Graphics $24(3)$, 585–594 (2005)

23. Wang, T., Han, B., Collomosse, J.: Touchcut: Fast image and video segmentation using single-touch interaction. Computer Vision and Image Understanding **120**, 14–30 (2014)
24. Xu, C., Corso, J.J.: Evaluation of super-voxel methods for early video processing. In: Proceedings of IEEE Conference on Computer Vision and Pattern Recognition (2012)
25. Xu, C., Xiong, C., Corso, J.J.: Streaming hierarchical video segmentation. In: Fitzgibbon, A., Lazebnik, S., Perona, P., Sato, Y., Schmid, C. (eds.) ECCV 2012, Part VI. LNCS, vol. 7577, pp. 626–639. Springer, Heidelberg (2012)

Multiple Description Coding
for Multi-view Video

Jing Chen[1], Canhui Cai[1(✉)], Xiaolan Wang[1], Huanqiang Zeng[1],
and Kai-Kuang Ma[2]

[1] School of Information Science and Engineering,
Huaqiao University, Xiamen 361021, China
jingzi@hqu.edu.cn, chcai@hqu.edu.cn, 413260175@qq.com,
zeng0043@hqu.edu.cn
[2] School of Electrical and Electronic Engineering,
Nanyang Technological University, Singapore 639798, Singapore
ekkma@ntu.edu.sg

Abstract. In this paper, a novel multiple description coding (MDC) scheme for multi-view video coding (MVC) is proposed that can deliver higher coding efficiency. This is achieved by separating one description into two subsequences and directly using the modes and prediction vectors computed during the encoding of one subsequence to the encoding process of the other subsequence from the same description. Such reuse strategy is made possible due to high correlation existing between the two subsequences that were generated from the input multi-view video sequence through the spatial polyphase subsampling and 'cross-interleaved' sample grouping. Due to the data reuse, the required representation bits for storage and transmission are greatly saved. Extensive simulation results experimented on the JMVC codec platform have shown that the performance of the proposed MDC scheme outperforms several state-of-the-art MDC methods for stereoscopic video and multi-view video.

Keywords: Multi-view video coding · Multiple description coding · JMVC · Mode reuse · Prediction vector reuse

1 Introduction

With the rapid development of communications network and multimedia technology, traditional two-dimensional video can no longer meet the ever-growing demand on visual computing and applications. As a new type of multimedia, multi-view video provides a brand-new visual experience for viewers, such as vivid scene, augmented reality, selectable viewing angles. It can be applied to many emerging multimedia services, such as 3DTV, free-viewpoint TV, immersive videoconferencing, remote medical diagnosis and treatment, entertainment, art exhibition, virtual reality, video surveillance systems, and so on. Therefore, multi-view video have received more and more attentions [1]-[2] and become a very active research topic in digital video processing [3]-[5].

© Springer International Publishing Switzerland 2015
S. Battiato et al. (Eds.): ACIVS 2015, LNCS 9386, pp. 876–882, 2015.
DOI: 10.1007/978-3-319-25903-1_75

As 4G mobile broadband era arrived, the internet and wireless network are serving as the main transmission channel of the multi-view video. Therefore, data error, packet loss, and excessive time delay caused by channel error, network congestion, and routing delay are completely inevitable. Since most multi-view video coding (MVC) frameworks exploit both inter-view and intra-view correlations to improve their coding efficiency, error resilience and error concealment are extremely important. Several error recovery frameworks for stereoscopic video coding have been proposed [6]-[9]. Most of them are based on error concealment approach, such as binocular stereoscopic video error concealment [7]. Generally speaking, little research has been conducted on error resilience for MVC.

Hewage et al. [7] proposed a frame concealment method for stereoscopic video by utilizing the motion correlation of image sequences. Chung et al. [8] designed a frame loss concealment algorithm for stereoscopic video based on the inter-view similarity, measured in terms of motion vectors and the pixel-intensity differences between the two views. These methods are able to conceal transmission error up to a certain extent, and they are applicable to those frames incurred with small amount of damages. When the errors become large, a more robust multi-view video coding (MVC) with strong error-resilient capability is required. For that, multiple description coding (MDC) is taken into consideration in this work, as it provides a very effective solution to overcome the video quality degradation due to channel failure, packet loss, data error, and/or transmission delay. The MDC has been extensively investigated in single-view video communications. In this paper, we extend the MDC for multi-view video.

The remaining sections of this paper are organized as follows. Section 2 provides a review of the MDC for MVC. Section 3 presents the proposed MDC algorithm that incorporates data reuse strategy. Section 4 presents extensive experimental results to demonstrate the efficiency and efficacy of the proposed algorithm. Section 5 concludes the paper.

2   Review of Multiple Description Coding for Multi-view Video

The basic idea of the MDC lies at the generation of the input source into two or more input sources, called descriptions, and they are subject to be encoded and represented in bitstreams for storage and/or transmission through different channels separately. At the receiver, if only one description is received, the decoder is still able to reconstruct the source signal with an acceptable quality. On the other hand, with more or all descriptions are received, a much improved quality of the reconstructed source video will be produced.

Existing MDC schemes developed for two-dimensional video is difficult to be directly used for MVC. This is because most of MDC greatly increase the computational load and few of them can well cooperated with hierarchical B frame coding structure of MVC. Norkin et al. [10] introduced the MDC into the stereoscopic video coding and proposed two MDC approaches, called scaling stereoscopic MDC (SS-MDC) and multi-state stereoscopic MDC (MS-MDC).

In the SS-MDC, two descriptions are formed with each description consisting of a full spatial resolution image sequence from one view and a reduced resolution (horizontally and vertically subsampled by a factor of 2 each) image sequence from the other view. If both descriptions are received, the left- and right-view sequences will be reconstructed in full resolution, respectively. If only one description is available, one full resolution view and one reduced resolution view are used to reconstruct the stereoscopic video.

In the MS-MDC, two descriptions are formed by conducting temporal sub-sampling: the odd frames from both the left- and right-view sequences form one description, while the even frames from both sequences form the other description. When both descriptions are received at the decoder, the stereoscopic video sequence will be reconstructed with the original frame rate. When only one description is available, the sequence will be reconstructed with the original frame rate restored by conducting interpolation along the temporal dimension. However, these two MDC schemes are designed for the stereoscopic video coding, which are difficult to be extended to the multi-view (more than two views) video coding.

An MDC scheme for MVC called tree-structured MDC (T-MDC) was proposed in [11]. In this approach, each view image is down-sampled to form several pixel streams. The corresponding pixel streams in different views are combined to form a description, and each description is separately encoded and transmitted. T-MDC scheme can freely change the number of descriptions. However, T-MDC changes the intrinsic structure of the MVC, which spoils the spatial correlation of multi-views and declines the coding efficiency.

The main concern of exploiting the MDC for multi-view video is: when a multi-view video is split into several descriptions, its intra-view and inter-view correlation are inevitably reduced; consequently, its coding efficiency is also degraded (e.g., the tree-structured MDC [11]). Besides, the computational complexity of the MDC schemes is increased. To address the above-mentioned two issues while increasing coding efficiency, a novel MDC algorithm is proposed for the multi-view video and described in the next section.

3   Proposed Multi-view Multiple Description Video Coding

The framework of the proposed multi-view multiple description video coding is depicted in Fig. 1. Four sub-sequences, X_{1p}, X_{1d}, X_{2d}, and X_{2p}, are generated from the original source video through the spatial polyphase subsampling [12]. The downsampled four sub-sequences are grouped into two equal-sized descriptions, X_1 (containing X_{1p} and X_{1d} and X_2 (containing X_{2p} and X_{2d}), respectively. This grouping process is accomplished by cross-interleaving samples from two sub-sequences to form one description as shown in Fig. 1. Consequently, a strong correlation is assured between the two sub-sequences in each description.

For the encoding of these two descriptions, sub-sequence X_{1p} (of description X_1) and X_{2p} (of description X_2) are separately encoded by using the

JMVC encoder. Owing to the high correlation between the two sub-sequences of each description, two macroblocks (MBs) situated at the same location from the two sub-sequences should have very similar motion contents and activities. This means that the data computed by the JMVC (in our case, the data information regarding modes and prediction vectors) during the encoding of one sub-sequence could be reused in another sub-sequence of the same description without going through the same time-consuming computation to generate its modes and prediction vectors, nor consuming bits to represent these data in the encoded bitstream. In other words, only one sub-sequence per description needs to go through the computation of mode decision, motion estimation and disparity estimation. As a result, the computational complexity is greatly reduced. It turns out that such 'data resuse' strategy is highly effective on increasing coding efficiency and reducing computational load. The bitstreams from the JMVC encoder 1 and the simplified JMVC encoder 1 are grouped to form the bitstream of the encoded description X_1; likewise, the bitstreams from the JMVC encoder 2 and the simplified JMVC encoder 2 are grouped to form the bitstream of the encoded description X_2. These two descriptions are transmitted through different channels, respectively.

At the decoder side, if a JMVC-encoded sequence, (e.g., the bitstream of X_{1p}) is received, it will be subjected to a JMVC decoder to reconstruct the subsequence $\widetilde{X}_{1p}$. Furthermore, the data information regarding the modes and prediction vectors from $\widetilde{X}_{1p}$, along with D_{1d} are sent to another JMVC decoder to rebuild the subsequence $\widetilde{X}_{1d}$. If both descriptions are available, four sub-sequences, $\widetilde{X}_{1p}$, $\widetilde{X}_{1d}$, $\widetilde{X}_{2p}$, and $\widetilde{X}_{2d}$ will be reconstructed and combined to form the original multi-view video with highest quality. If only one description is available, interpolation is conducted to reconstruct the original signal (e.g., if only description 1 is available, $\widetilde{X}_{2p}$ and $\widetilde{X}_{2d}$ will be reconstructed via interpolation from $\widetilde{X}_{1p}$ and $\widetilde{X}_{1d}$).

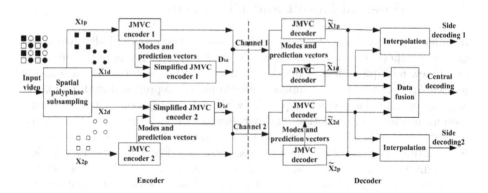

Fig. 1. Framework of the proposed multi-view multiple description video coding algorithm

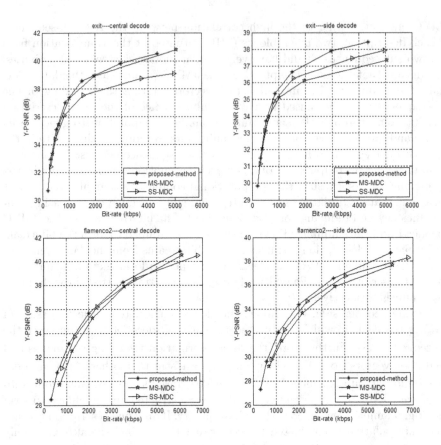

Fig. 2. Reconstruction effect of sequence video of three algorithms

4   Experimental Result and Discussion

In order to demonstrate the good performance of the proposed algorithm, two groups of experiments are performed. The first one is to compare the proposed multi-view multiple description video coding algorithm with two classical multiple description coding algorithm for stereoscopic video proposed in [10] by using a group of multi-view video sequences with different motion states (i.e., slow motion, medium speed motion, and fast motion). Fig. 2 illustrates the experimental results on sequences "Exit" and "Flamenco2". The frame size is 640×480, frame rate is set to 25, 200 frames per sequence per view are coded, and the left and right view are used. From Fig. 2, one can see that the qualities of the reconstructed signal by our central decoder and side decoder steadily outperform those by the MS-MDC and SS-MDC, and the advantage of the proposed algorithm becomes more clearly as the bitrate increases.

In the second group of experiments, T-MDC [11] is serving as the bench mark, and the test condition is set as [11]. The left eight viewpoints of sequence

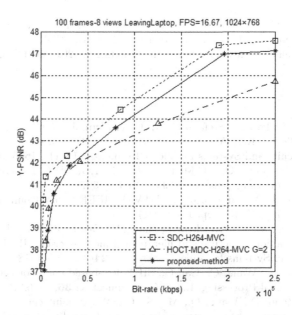

Fig. 3. Reconstruction effect of sequence video of two algorithms

"LeavingLaptop" are used as the test sequence, the frame size is 1024×768, the frame rate is 16.67, and GOP is set to 15, and 100 frames are coded. Fig. 3 shows the experimental results, which shown that the coding efficiency of the proposed algorithm is increasingly better than that of T-MDC as the bitrate increases.

5   Conclusion

An effective MDC algorithm is proposed in this paper for the encoding of multi-view video sequence. The input multi-view video sequence is first down-sampled along the horizontal direction and the vertical direction, respectively, to produce four sub-sequences. These four sub-sequences are then cross-interleaved to form two descriptions. In each description, one subsequence is directly encoded by applying the JMVC encoder, from which the determined modes and the computed prediction vectors will be unconditionally resued during the encoding of the other subsequence. Obviously, both computational complexity and bitrate can be greatly reduced through such data reuse strategy. This approach is fairly robust due to the fact that the two subsequences from each description are highly correlated, and this has been clearly justified by extensive simulation results experimented on the JMVC codec platform. All these have clearly shown the advantages and effectiveness delivered by the proposed algorithm.

Acknowledgments. This work was supported in part by the National Natural Science Foundation of China under the Grants 61372107 and 61401167, in part by the Xiamen Key Science and Technology Project Foundation under the Grant 3502Z20133024, in part by the Opening Project of State Key Laboratory of Digital Publishing Technology under the grant FZDP2015-B-001, and in part by the High-Level Talent Project Foundation of Huaqiao University under the Grants 14BS201 and 14BS204.

References

1. Smolic, A., Mueller, K., Stefanoski, N., Ostermann, J., Gotchev, A., Akar, G.B., Triantafyllidis, G., Koz, A.: Coding algorithms for 3DTV-a survey. IEEE Transactions on Circuits and Systems for Video Technology **17**(11), 1606–1620 (2007)
2. Joint Video Team of ISO/IEC MPEG ITU-T VCEG,: MVC: Experiments on coding of multi-view video plus depth. JVT-X604 (2007)
3. Tanimoto, M.: FTV and all-around 3DTV. In: IEEE Visual Communications and Image Processing (VCIP), pp. 1–4 (2011)
4. Zeng, H., Wang, X., Cai, C., Chen, J., Zhang, Y.: Fast multiview video coding using adaptive prediction structure and hierarchical mode decision. IEEE Transactions on Circuits and Systems for Video Technology **24**(9), 1566–1578 (2014)
5. Zeng, H., Ma, K., Wang, C., Cai, C.: SIFT-flow-based color correction for multiview video. Signal Processing: Image Communication **36**, 53–62 (2015)
6. Xiang, X., Zhao, D., Wang, Q., Ma, S., Ga, W.: A joint encoder-decoder error control framework for stereoscopic video coding. Journal of Visual Communication Image Representation **21**, 975–985 (2010)
7. Hewage, C., Worrall, S., Dogan, S., Kondoz, A.: Frame concealment algorithm for stereoscopic video using motion vector sharing. In: IEEE International Conference on Multimedia and Expo., pp. 485–488 (2008)
8. Chung, T.Y., Sull, S., Kim, C.S.: Frame loss concealment for stereoscopic video based on inter-view similarity of motion and intensity difference. In: IEEE International Conference on Image Processing, pp. 441–444 (2010)
9. Bilen, C., Aksay, A., Akar, G.B.: Motion and parallax aided stereoscopic full frame loss concealment method. In: IEEE Signal Processing and Communications Applications, pp. 1–4 (2007)
10. Norkin, A., Aksay, A., Bilen, C., Akar, G.B., Gotchev, A., Astola, J.: Schemes for multiple description coding of stereoscopic video. In: Gunsel, B., Jain, A.K., Tekalp, A.M., Sankur, B. (eds.) MRCS 2006. LNCS, vol. 4105, pp. 730–737. Springer, Heidelberg (2006)
11. Huo, Y., Hanzo, L.: Tree-structured multiple description coding for multiview mobile tv and camera-phone networks. In: IEEE Vehicular Technology Conference, pp. 1–5 (2011)
12. Wei, Z., Cai, C., Ma, K.K.: A novel h.264-based multiple description video coding via polyphase transform and partial prediction. In: IEEE International Symposium on Intel ligent Signal Processing and Communication System, pp. 151–154 (2006)

A Game Engine as a Generic Platform for Real-Time Previz-on-Set in Cinema Visual Effects

Timothée de Goussencourt[1,2], Jean Dellac[2], and Pascal Bertolino[1(✉)]

[1] GIPSA-lab, Grenoble Alpes University, Grenoble, France
{timothee.de-goussencourt,pascal.bertolino}@gipsa-lab.fr
[2] Solidanim, Paris, France
{tim,jdellac}@solidanim.com

Abstract. We present a complete framework designed for film production requiring live (pre) visualization. This framework is based on a famous game engine, *Unity*®. Actually, game engines possess many advantages that can be directly exploited in real-time pre-vizualization, where real and virtual worlds have to be mixed. In the work presented here, all the steps are performed in *Unity*: from acquisition to rendering. To perform real-time compositing that takes into account occlusions that occur between real and virtual elements as well as to manage physical interactions of real characters towards virtual elements, we use a low resolution depth map sensor coupled to a high resolution film camera. The goal of our system is to give the film director's creativity a flexible and powerful tool on stage, long before post-production.

Keywords: Depth map · Real-time · Compositing · Virtual production · Previz on-set · Real-virtual interaction · Unity

1 Introduction

Since the beginning of film industry, movie makers like to compose a final scene by taking parts from different sources. With the coming of computer graphics in 90's it became possible to generate virtual graphics (assets) such as virtual backgrounds or virtual characters and to mix them with real images. This action is commonly called compositing. It must deliver a final image in accordance to the storyboard and the film director's wishes. At the moment, this is most of the time a post-production process taking a lot of time and money. Previz on-set is an emerging discipline in film production to achieve live previzualisation. It fills the gap between the storyboard or the full 3D preview sequence (a.k.a. animatik) and the final image (figure 1). The main objectives of previz on-set is to improve film's director creativity during filming and also to speed-up the post-production step.

The solution that we present is a novel and distorted usage of a well-know tool of the game designers, namely the video game engine. With it, the output

© Springer International Publishing Switzerland 2015
S. Battiato et al. (Eds.): ACIVS 2015, LNCS 9386, pp. 883–894, 2015.
DOI: 10.1007/978-3-319-25903-1_76

real-time previz provided to the film's director is built from several inputs: the HD images from the film camera, the virtual assets from 3D libraries, the depth map of the scene provided by a depth sensor and the interaction between the real world and the virtual assets. The software we chose, that permits this real-time mixing is the powerful and widely-used video game engine *Unity*® [26]. Not only *Unity* is able to handle and merge the above elements in real-time but it also provides a built-in interface that allows an operator to edit in real time the content of the resulting scene without any extra complex coding. However, *Unity* is quite open and it is rather simple to implement specific real time processing with shaders as it is mandatory in the kind of application we tackle. Apart from a first use of *Unity*® in previz [18] but only for the visualisation of special effects, to our best knowledge our work is the first one to use a game engine in the particular field of previz and more generally in the mix of virtual and real worlds. In [5], we presented a preliminary version of this work. The novelty and originality of the proposed work is that we show that using a game engine is also efficient for the following aspects: (1) managing physical interactions between real and virtual worlds, (2) coupling our previous system with a camera tracking system, (3) re-using all the information captured in real-time in post-production, (4) improving the realism of the virtual assets with the real scene lighting. At last, the results presented here are also more numerous than in [5].

Fig. 1. Film building process. From left to right: first row: storyboard and animatik. Second row: previz on-set and post-production final compositing. (*all images from the PREVIZ project*)

This paper is outlined as follows: in section 2 we present some technical background features that are the bases of our solution and we compare them with relative works on this field. Section 3 describes the main points of our approach and how they are technically implemented into the game engine. The paper will be concluded with some results in section 4.

2   Technical Background

The depth information of the real scene is mandatory in previz applications and it must provided by a fast hardware system. Among them, the first generation of Kinect is based on an active stereo techniques using structured light [23]. The use of an infrared pattern has the advantage not to disturb the visible spectral domain of the scene. Another technique using infrared is the time of flight (ToF) technology in which the time that it takes for an infrared ray to hit an object of the scene and go back to the sensor is measured, providing the corresponding depth [10]. The second version of the Kinect we are using in this work uses this technology and is a good compromise in terms of price and quality. The system we present is designed for indoor small scale scenes, in a controlled environment which may correspond to an important part of virtual production needs.

Some techniques to mix high definition color frames with depth sensors have already been developed. For instance [3] uses a trifocal rig to generate high precision depth maps: the authors combine a stereo system with a monocular depth sensor, similar to [8,12,25,29]. Then, a complex global optimization workflow is needed to merge data. [21] uses a graph-cut optimization whereas [7] formulates a convex optimization problem to make depth image upsampling. All of these methods use custom rigs. The *Arri* company develops a prototype coupling professional video sensor with a ToF depth sensor [11]. Conversely, the method we propose can deal with every film camera.

Our fusion method is implemented into the popular game engine *Unity* [26]. This platform was chosen because of its great versatility and huge developers community. The graphics engine incorporated into *Unity* is built on top of most modern graphics API, achieving real-time rendering performance, which was an important prerequisite for our project. In our case, the *Unity* software is not used to build a game but to perform and display real-time image processing.

An important step of our method is compositing. Traditional compositing techniques are using a layer scheme, where all objects of the scene are precisely ordered from the closest to the furthest layer. This kind of representation is static and does not permit all the occlusion cases. In our case the final preview image is generated by composing the virtual frame with the real one regarding the depth values of their content. This technique is called depth based compositing. The registered depth maps of virtual and real scenes are compared on the GPU to generate a per pixel matting mask [2]. One of the big challenges of compositing is to ensure seamless integration of virtual layers with the camera footage [14]. In our method we focus particularly on automatic lighting and grading.

In order to add automatic interaction between real world and virtual contents, we also use body segmentation functionalities provided by the Kinect SDK [22]. Some related works dealing with real/virtual mixing can be found in [1,13].

3 Exploiting the Game Engine

This section lists the main contributions of the game engine as a natural and powerful platform for previz on-set 2. We show that the main following steps of previz are successfully addressed through *Unity*: acquiring and registering the data flows, controlling the scene, compositing the scene by mixing real images and virtual workflow, lighting the virtual assets, managing physical interactions between an actor and virtual objects, creating data backup of the whole for post-production.

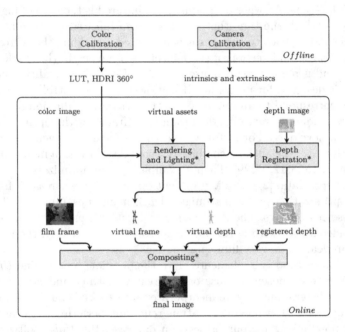

Fig. 2. Overall system workflow. Offline process is executed once at the beginning. Online process is executed in real-time for each frame into the game engine. Blocks marked by a * use shaders in their process.

3.1 Image Acquisition

A key point of our approach is to use the depth of the real scene. To that purpose, a Kinect 2 depth sensor is rigidly fixed to a high resolution film camera as shown in figure 3. The sensors baseline is minimized in order to avoid shadow problems.

The calibration of the two cameras is classical and is performed offline: the intrinsic parameters of each camera are retrieved. Then an extrinsic calibration is done to compute the relative position of the depth sensor to the film camera. A well-known technique for calibrating a camera is based on chessboard pattern recognition [27,28]. This calibration is computed only once at the beginning, all calibration parameters are saved, then loaded to the game engine at run time.

Fig. 3. Our system using different film cameras coupled with the Kinect 2. Left: Black-magic Studio HD with 14mm lens. Right: Panasonic AG-AF100A with a 18mm lens

The HD color video stream is transferred from the film camera to the computer with an SDI to USB3 acquisition card. The HD color frame (1920 × 1080 pixels) is stored in a 2D texture, a specific structure that the GPU can handle. About the depth, the sensor delivers a 512 × 424 pixels resolution, 16 bits per pixel, real-time depth map. The color sensor available on the Kinect 2 is not used. This buffer is also stored into a 2D texture structure, for a GPU use. As there is no trigger input in the Kinect to synchronize it with an external clock, we set up a circular frame buffer where each depth frame is stored with its corresponding timestamp. When a film frame arrives, the closest (in time) depth frame is selected and associated to the HD color frame. This is a way to compensate the small delay that can occur between depth and color streams.

3.2 Depth and Color Image Registration

The acquired HD color images and depth images do not fit at all: the pixel density of the color image is much higher than the one of the depth image: in our context, 1 depth pixel correspond to about 30 color pixels. Furthermore, the field of view of the depth sensor is fix and may largely differ from the one of the HD camera that depends on the used lens. The dense registration of the depth image with the color image is performed in *Unity* with a shader. Shaders are small scripts that are executed by the GPU. In this particular case, the shader is used to back-project the 3D information from the depth sensor into the main camera screen space, for each frame. The current depth texture and a grid mesh with the dimension of the depth map (512 × 424 vertices) are sent to the GPU. Each vertex is displaced in regards to the depth map value and the depth sensor intrinsic parameters. This way a 3D representation of the scene is computed in real-time using GPU capabilities. This 3D mesh is now observed according to the film camera point of view using the calibration settings. Re-projection of the low resolution depth map becomes a dense interpolation, fitting the resolution of the film camera. More details are presented in [5]. Note that shaders may also be used for many kernel-based image filtering.

3.3   Editing and Controlling

A game engine is commonly used to render in realtime a virtual scene. This is an optimised framework to deal with a lot of 3D assets, lighting and physical interactions. In our context we consider the game engine as a powerful video mixer. Several inputs are mixed together to produce the preview image, using all the great features a game engine can offer. You can program the game engine behaviour by scripting functions placed in a main loop scheme. Each time a new film frame is rendered, this main loop is called and executed.

Unity also provides a live editor mode to control in realtime each parameter of each element of the virtual scene, with a graphic user interface (GUI). That means you can modify or tune many things online: lighting parameters, add 3D assets, displace virtual contents, trig animation ... The main control settings are already included in the game engine framework, and it is also easy to add custom controls relative to your scripts into the editor interface. This point is important because the user is thus able to change online the layout of the scene in order to answer the film director's wishes. Is is also possible to build your scene as a standalone executable to achieve better performances. In this case you should construct a GUI control panel to allow online editing of the 3D scene.

3.4   Depth Based Compositing

The final step of our pipeline is the compositing of all the virtual assets with the real scene with the handling of occlusions. The point of view of the virtual scene render is either defined by hand for a static camera shot or possibly triggered by a camera tracking system for a moving shot. This render point of view, defined by a virtual camera, matches the pose and lens configuration of the real film camera. This way the virtual frame perfectly overlaps the film frame.

To handle occlusions we ask the game engine to grab the depth map of the virtual content. Then it is possible to compare the real scene depth map with the virtual scene depth map to generate a binary mask coding whether a pixel of the final rendering comes from the virtual asset frame or from the film camera frame. This mask is smoothed using a blur filter to attenuate hard discontinuities between background and foreground. The final compositing is then computed using the classic *over* operator [2], see Figure 4.

3.5   Automatic Lighting and Grading

In order to blend seamlessly the virtual assets with the real world we need to replicate the lighting [6] and color response [15] of the real scene. To achieve that, a unique high dynamic range image (HDRI) of the scene using a 360° camera (figure 5, top) is captured offline. Then the *Greta MacBeth ColorChecker* is used to calculate two transfer functions A and B stored into look up tables (LUT) (figure 5, bottom). A transfers a neutral colorspace (sRGB) to the colorspace of the film camera. B transfers the colorspace of the 360° camera to a neutral colorspace. The HDRI is transformed to the neutral colorspace using B.

Fig. 4. Example of compositing. Left: first row: film frame and registered depth map, second row: virtual character frame and depth map. Middle: binary mask. Right: final compositing

Then the result is used to light the virtual assets in neutral space using image based lighting (IBL). Finally A is applied to the rendered virtual elements, so they match the color response. *Unity* natively supports a real-time optimised IBL system, again with the use of a shader.

Fig. 5. Top: sample of a 360° high dynamic range image used to light the virtual assets. The color checker can be seen on each side of the picture. Bottom: LUT that maps the HDRI colorspace to a neutral colorspace stored into a 2D texture

3.6   Interaction Between Real and Virtual Elements

Game engines include interesting features like physics engine. That means each virtual element could physically behave like real objects. It is possible to set-up a gravity, a mass for each object and a collision detection. In our case we focus on interaction between real actors and virtual objects. Even if is technically possible to compute collision with the detailed mesh from the depth map, this will affect real-time performances. We solve this problem by using a 3D schematic representation of the human skeleton of the actors. Human pose recognition is computed with a method described in [22] and included in the Kinect SDK. When a 3D skeleton collides with a virtual object, the game engine trigs an event. This event can be bound to a script where any physical action can be planned. An example of brick wall destruction is showed in figure 6.

Fig. 6. Interaction example. Left: skeleton detection in the depth map. Right: 3D representation of the skeleton in the game engine editor. Collision detection between the skeleton of the real actor and the virtual brick wall

3.7   Data Backup and Post Processing

Previz on-set is a precious help during shooting but this is not the end of the film building process. The second main role of previz is to facilitate and improve post-production. To do this, each data stream (depth, camera tracking) is backuped independently during the shooting. This way it is possible to virtually replay the scene, but this time without any realtime constraint. But even is it possible to slow down a game engine to achieve a better rendering or give more time to computation, it is optimised for real time. So, some professional software are dedicated to compositing, such as Nuke [19] or Natron [17], and very popular in post-production studios. This is why we choose to convert the data into an openEXR [20] image sequence. This format was originally developed by Illuminated Light and Magic and it is now a standard in film industry. It supports multi-channels and until 32bits precision per channel. It is also possible to add custom information in headers, like 3D pose of the camera. This way previz data are stored into a well known formalism that professionals are used to work with.

4   Experiments

The computer used for our experiment is a laptop with an Intel i7 2.8GHz processor, 16Go RAM and a Nvidia Quadro K4100M. The Unity version 4 and 5 were also used. Our system was tested with two different film cameras used traditionally for broadcast applications (see Figure 3). Their setup includes a 18*mm* lens mounted on a Panasonic AG-AF100A and also a 14*mm* lens mounted on a Blackmagic Studio HD camera.

Our compositing results are presented in figure 7. In this sequence we coupled our method with the camera tracking system SolidTrack [24]. This allows us to move the camera freely, conserving the right virtual point of view to render 3D assets. Examples of interaction between an actor and virtual objects are shown in figures 8 and 9. The depth information is used to compute compositing, while a 3D schematic skeleton trigs in background the collision events. The first example shows a brick wall destruction whereas the second one shows hit weightless objects. Figure 10 shows the effect of color transfer to improve the rendering coherence between virtual and real contents. The overall method described here reaches real-time performance to deliver preview image synchronized with the film camera framerate. Some live video samples captured on the laptop screen are available at https://sites.google.com/site/pascalbertolino/previz2.

Fig. 7. Camera tracking and occlusions. Filmed with the Panasonic AG-AF100A camera with a 18mm lens coupled with the SolidTrack camera tracking system

Fig. 8. Example of interaction: breaking a virtual wall (from the top left to the bottom right). The character goes back a few seconds, then he hits the wall with his right fist. Filmed with the blackmagic HD studio camera with a 14mm lens

As one can see, the results are not perfect, due to the low quality of the depth map. The depth frame is noisy, and it is quite noticeable at edge. Moreover, the baseline between the film camera and the depth sensor introduces some holes in the registered depth map. But keep in mind that we are looking for previz images: in film industry, the final image is post-processed manually to get the best possible results. However, we plan to perform some guided filtering in order to improve the depth map quality by injecting the film image inside the kernel filter computation. Our method is based on an extension of the joint bilateral filter [16] described in [9].

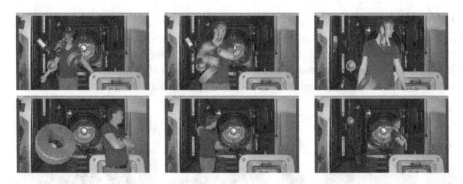

Fig. 9. Example of interaction: shooting weightless object (from the top left to the bottom right). The 3D elements are lighted using an HDRI map. Filmed with the blackmagic HD studio camera with a 14mm lens

Fig. 10. Automated scene color grading. Left: No color grading is applied. Right: Color grading applied to the virtual scene.

5   Conclusion

In this article we argue why to use a game engine as a platform for previz on-set. A game engine offers nice features: optimised for realtime, rendering and physical engine capabilities. This platform is well adapted on stage and it is adaptive and generic in regards to cameras and specific image processing. The current framework we described here is used in the context of the PREVIZ project [4] dedicated to virtual production, especially previz on-set. All data are recorded online to be re-used in post-production. This way previz on-set is also used as a guide for final compositing. In the future, using this framework, we will propose a database coupling film camera footage with registered depth maps and possibly camera tracking data. This database will be made to better understand how the data produced in previz can be used in post-production.

References

1. Bartczak, B., Schiller, I., Beder, C., Koch, R.: Integration of a time-of-flight camera into a mixed reality system for handling dynamic scenes, moving viewpoints and occlusions in real-time. In: Proceedings of the 3DPVT Workshop, Atlanta, GA, USA, June 2008

2. Blinn, J.F.: Compositing. 1. theory. IEEE Computer Graphics and Applications **14**(5), 83–87 (1994)

3. Boisson, G., Kerbiriou, P., Drazic, V., Bureller, O., Sabater, N., Schubert, A.: Fusion of kinect depth data with trifocal disparity estimation for near real-time high quality depth maps generation. In: IS&T/SPIE Electronic Imaging, pp. 90110–90110. International Society for Optics and Photonics (2014)

4. Briand, G., Bidgolirad, F., Zlapka, J.F., Lavalou, J.M., Lanouiller, M., Christie, M., Lvoff, J., Bertolino, P., Guillou, E.: On-set previsualization for vfx film production. In: International Broadcasting Convention (IBC). Netherland, Amsterdam (2014)

5. de Goussencourt, T., Bertolino, P.: Using the unity game engine as a platform for advanced real time cinema image processing. In: ICIP, Québec, Canada, September 2015

6. Debevec, P.E., Malik, J.: Recovering high dynamic range radiance maps from photographs. In: ACM SIGGRAPH 2008 classes, p. 31. ACM (2008)

7. Ferstl, D., Reinbacher, C., Ranftl, R., Rüther, M., Bischof, H.: Image guided depth upsampling using anisotropic total generalized variation. In: 2013 IEEE International Conference on Computer Vision (ICCV), pp. 993–1000. IEEE (2013)

8. Gandhi, V., Cech, J., Horaud, R.: High-resolution depth maps based on TOF-stereo fusion. In: 2012 IEEE International Conference on Robotics and Automation (ICRA), pp. 4742–4749. IEEE (2012)

9. Garcia, F., Mirbach, B., Ottersten, B., Grandidier, F., Cuesta, Á.: Pixel weighted average strategy for depth sensor data fusion. In: Proceedings - International Conference on Image Processing, ICIP, pp. 2805–2808 (2010)

10. Gokturk, S.B., Yalcin, H., Bamji, C.: A time-of-flight depth sensor-system description, issues and solutions. In: CVPRW 2004 Conference on Computer Vision and Pattern Recognition Workshop, pp. 35–35. IEEE (2004)

11. Hach, T., Steurer, J.: A novel RGB-Z camera for high-quality motion picture applications. In: Proceedings of the 10th European Conference on Visual Media Production, CVMP 2013, pp. 1–10. ACM, New York (2013)

12. Hahne, U., Alexa, M.: Combining time-of-flight depth and stereo images without accurate extrinsic calibration. International Journal of Intelligent Systems Technologies and Applications **5**(3), 325–333 (2008)

13. Izadi, S., Kim, D., Hilliges, O., Molyneaux, D., Newcombe, R., Kohli, P., Shotton, J., Hodges, S., Freeman, D., Davison, A., et al.: Kinectfusion: real-time 3d reconstruction and interaction using a moving depth camera. In: Proceedings of the 24th annual ACM symposium on User interface software and technology, pp 559–568. ACM (2011)

14. Klein, G., Murray, D.: Compositing for small cameras. In: Proceedings of the 7th IEEE/ACM International Symposium on Mixed and Augmented Reality, pp 57–60. IEEE Computer Society (2008)

15. Knecht, M., Traxler, C., Purgathofer, W., Wimmer, M.: Adaptive camera-based color mapping for mixed-reality applications. In: 2011 10th IEEE International Symposium on Mixed and Augmented Reality (ISMAR), pp 165–168. IEEE (2011)

16. Kopf, J., Cohen, M.F., Lischinski, D., Uyttendaele, M.: Joint bilateral upsampling. ACM Transactions on Graphics **26**(3), 96 (2007)
17. Natron, INRIA (2015). https://natron.inria.fr/ (Accessed May 14, 2015)
18. Northam, L., Istead, J., Kaplan, C.S.: A collaborative real time previsualization tool for video games and film. In SIGGRAPH Posters, p. 121. ACM (2012)
19. Nuke, the Foundry (2015). https://www.thefoundry.co.uk/products/nuke/ (Accessed May 14, 2015)
20. OpenEXR (2015). http://www.openexr.com/ (Accessed May 14, 2015)
21. Patra, S., Bhowmick, B., Banerjee, S., Kalra, P.: High resolution point cloud generation from kinect and hd cameras using graph cut. VISAPP (2), 311–316 (2012)
22. Shotton, J., Sharp, T., Kipman, A., Fitzgibbon, A., Finocchio, M., Blake, A., Cook, M., Moore, R.: Real-time human pose recognition in parts from single depth images. Communications of the ACM **56**(1), 116–124 (2013)
23. Shpunt, A., Zalevsky, Z.: Three-dimensional sensing using speckle patterns, US Patent 8,390,821, March 5, 2013
24. Solidanim SolidTrack system (2015). http://www.solid-track.com/ (Accessed May 14, 2015)
25. Song, Y., Glasbey, C.A., van der Heijden, G.W.A.M., Polder, G., Dieleman, J.A.: Combining stereo and time-of-flight images with application to automatic plant phenotyping. In: Heyden, A., Kahl, F. (eds.) SCIA 2011. LNCS, vol. 6688, pp. 467–478. Springer, Heidelberg (2011)
26. Unity Game Engine (2015). https://unity3d.com/ (Accessed May 14, 2015)
27. Zhang, Z.: Flexible camera calibration by viewing a plane from unknown orientations. In: Proceedings of the Seventh IEEE International Conference on Computer Vision, 1999, vol. 1, pp. 666–673. IEEE (1999)
28. Zhang, Z.: A flexible new technique for camera calibration. Pattern Analysis and Machine Intelligence, IEEE Transactions on **22**(11), 1330–1334 (2000)
29. Zhu, J., Wang, L., Yang, R., Davis, J.: Fusion of time-of-flight depth and stereo for high accuracy depth maps. In: IEEE Conference on Computer Vision and Pattern Recognition CVPR 2008, pp. 1–8. IEEE (2008)

Author Index

Printed in the United States
By Bookmasters